INTRODUCING: THE DIGITAL TOOL

A Digital Tool. Why?

The professional role of accountants is changing. Advances in technology have relegated the mechanical aspects of accounting to the computer. The "new accountants" are concerned about the implications of these numbers. What do they actually mean and what are their effects on the decision-making process, both from a company and individual investor perspective? To address this issue, the Tenth Edition of INTERMEDIATE ACCOUNTING features a new Digital Tool that develops the financial analysis and reporting skills students need for the new roles they will play in the workforce.

What Is It?

The DIGITAL TOOL is an electronic gateway, either through the CD-ROM or the Internet, to a comprehensive set of materials that uniquely prepares students to enter the profession as communicators, consultants, and decision-makers. It is comprised of three main components: Analyst's Toolkit, Professional Toolkit, and Student Helper Toolkit.

Contents of the Digital Tool

1. The Analyst's Toolkit
   - A Financial Statement Analysis primer that provides the theoretical background students need to develop skills
   - An annual report database of more than 30 real companies where students can develop their financial analysis and reporting skills
   - Company Web links with industry codes
   - Pre-formatted Excel worksheets for performing ratio analysis
   - Spreadsheet Tools (present value templates)
   - Additional Web links
   - Assignment material

2. The Professional Toolkit
   - Accountant's Writing Handbook that helps students effectively communicate results
   - Group activity model for instructors and students
   - Expanded discussion of ethics
   - Career and professional spotlights including salary information, a résumé builder, and related Web links

3. Student Helper Toolkit
   - 15 Web-based self-study questions for each chapter
   - Expanded discussion of International Accounting
   - Additional topics of interest and illustrations not covered in text

Checklist of key figures

PowerPoint slides for study and review for each chapter

Learning Styles Survey

Intermediate Accounting

TENTH EDITION

INTERMEDIATE ACCOUNTING

Volume 2

Donald E. Kieso Ph.D., C.P.A.
KPMG Peat Marwick Emeritus Professor of Accounting
Northern Illinois University
DeKalb, Illinois

Jerry J. Weygandt Ph.D., C.P.A.
Arthur Andersen Alumni Professor of Accounting
University of Wisconsin
Madison, Wisconsin

Terry D. Warfield Ph.D.
PricewaterhouseCoopers Research Scholar
University of Wisconsin
Madison, Wisconsin

John Wiley & Sons, Inc.

New York • Chichester • Weinheim
Brisbane • Singapore • Toronto

PUBLISHER:	Susan Elbe
ACQUISITIONS EDITOR:	Mark Bonadeo
DEVELOPMENTAL EDITOR:	Ellen Ford
MEDIA EDITOR:	David B. Kear
SUPPLEMENTS EDITOR:	Julie Kerr
MARKETING MANAGER:	Clancy Marshall
PRODUCTION SERVICES MANAGER:	Jeanine Furino
PHOTO EDITOR:	Nicole Horlacher
ILLUSTRATION EDITOR:	Anna Melhorn
TEXT DESIGNER:	Lee Goldstein
COVER DESIGNER:	Carol C. Grobe
PROJECT MANAGEMENT:	Elm Street Publishing Services, Inc.
COVER PHOTOS:	©James Rudnick/The Stock Market

Perspective background collage photo credits: Palm Pilot courtesy A&R Partners. Pencils ©EyeWire, Inc. Electronic Organizer and Adding Machine Tape ©CORBIS.

All "Perspectives On" and "From Classroom to Career" photographs provided courtesy of featured individuals.

This book was set in Palatino by York Graphic Services and printed and bound by Von Hoffmann Press. The cover was printed by Lehigh Press.

This book is printed on acid-free paper. ∞

Material from the Uniform CPA Examinations and Unofficial Answers, copyright © 1965, 1966, 1967, 1968, 1969, 1970, 1971, 1972, 1973, 1974, 1975, 1976, 1977, 1978, 1979, 1980, 1981, 1982, 1983, 1984, 1985, 1986, 1987, 1988, 1990, 1991, 1992, and 1993 by the American Institute of Certified Public Accountants, Inc., is adapted with permission.

This book contains quotations from *Accounting Research Bulletins, Accounting Principles Board Opinions, Accounting Principles Board Statements, Accounting Interpretations,* and *Accounting Terminology Bulletins,* copyright © 1953, 1956, 1966, 1968, 1969, 1970, 1971, 1972, 1973, 1974, 1975, 1976, 1977, 1978, 1979, 1980, 1981, 1982 by the American Institute of Certified Public Accountants, Inc., 1211 Avenue of the Americas, New York, NY 10036.

This book contains citations from various FASB pronouncements. Copyright © by Financial Accounting Standards Board, 401 Merritt 7, P.O. Box 5116, Norwalk, CT 06856 U.S.A. Reprinted with permission. Copies of complete documents are available from Financial Accounting Standards Board.

Material from the Certificate in Management Accounting Examinations, copyright © 1975, 1976, 1977, 1978, 1979, 1980, 1981, 1982, 1983, 1984, 1985, 1986, 1987, 1988, 1989, 1990, 1991, 1992, and 1993 by the Institute of Certified Management Accountants, 10 Paragon Drive, Montvale, NJ 07645, is adapted with permission.

Material from the Certified Internal Auditor Examinations, copyright © May 1984, November 1984, May 1986 by The Institute of Internal Auditors, 249 Maitland Ave., Altemonte Springs, FL 32701, is adapted with permission.

The financial statements and accompanying notes reprinted from the 1998 Annual Report of Intel Corporation are courtesy of Intel Corporation, copyright © 1999, all rights reserved.

Dedicated to our wives,

> *Donna, Enid, and Mary,*
> *and to our children,*
> *Douglas and Debra,*
> *Matt, Erin, and Lia,*
> *Andrew, Lauren, and Katie,*
> *for their*
> *Love, Support, and Encouragement*

About the Authors

Donald E. Kieso, Ph.D., C.P.A., received his bachelor's degree from Aurora University and his doctorate in accounting from the University of Illinois. He has served as chairman of the Department of Accountancy and is currently the KPMG Peat Marwick Emeritus Professor of Accountancy at Northern Illinois University. He has public accounting experience with Price Waterhouse & Co. (San Francisco and Chicago) and Arthur Andersen & Co. (Chicago) and research experience with the Research Division of the American Institute of Certified Public Accountants (New York). He has done postdoctorate work as a Visiting Scholar at the University of California at Berkeley and is a recipient of NIU's Teaching Excellence Award and four Golden Apple Teaching Awards. Professor Kieso is the author of other accounting and business books and is a member of the American Accounting Association, the American Institute of Certified Public Accountants, and the Illinois CPA Society. He has served as a member of the Board of Directors of the Illinois CPA Society, the AACSB's Accounting Accreditation Committees, the State of Illinois Comptroller's Commission, as Secretary-Treasurer of the Federation of Schools of Accountancy, and as Secretary-Treasurer of the American Accounting Association. Professor Kieso is currently serving as Chairman of the Board of Trustees and Executive Committee of Aurora University, as a member of the Boards of Directors of Castle BancGroup Inc. and the Sandwich State Bank, and as Treasurer and Director of Valley West Community Hospital. From 1989 to 1993 he served as a charter member of the national Accounting Education Change Commission. In 1988 he received the Outstanding Accounting Educator Award from the Illinois CPA Society, in 1992 he received the FSA's Joseph A. Silvoso Award of Merit and the NIU Foundation's Humanitarian Award for Service to Higher Education, and in 1995 he received a Distinguished Service Award from the Illinois CPA Society.

Jerry J. Weygandt, Ph.D., C.P.A., is Arthur Andersen Alumni Professor of Accounting at the University of Wisconsin—Madison. He holds a Ph.D. in accounting from the University of Illinois. Articles by Professor Weygandt have appeared in the *Accounting Review, Journal of Accounting Research, Accounting Horizons, Journal of Accountancy,* and other academic and professional journals. These articles have examined such financial reporting issues as accounting for price-level adjustments, pensions, convertible securities, stock option contracts, and interim reports. Professor Weygandt is author of other accounting and financial reporting books and is a member of the American Accounting Association, the American Institute of Certified Public Accountants, and the Wisconsin Society of Certified Public Accountants. He has served on numerous committees of the American Accounting Association and as a member of the editorial board of the *Accounting Review;* he also has served as President and Secretary-Treasurer of the American Accounting Association. In addition, he has been actively involved with the American Institute of Certified Public Accountants and has been a member of the Accounting Standards Executive Committee (AcSEC) of that organization. He has served on the FASB task force that examined the reporting issues related to accounting for income taxes and is presently a trustee of the Financial Accounting Foundation. Professor Weygandt has received the Chancellor's Award for Excellence in Teaching and the Beta Gamma Sigma Dean's Teaching Award. He is on the board of directors of M & I Bank of Southern Wisconsin and the Dean Foundation. Recently he received the Wisconsin Institute of CPA's Outstanding Educator's Award and the Lifetime Achievement Award.

Terry D. Warfield, Ph.D., is PricewaterhouseCoopers Research Scholar at the University of Wisconsin—Madison. He received a B.S. and M.B.A. from Indiana University and a Ph.D. in accounting from the University of Iowa. Professor Warfield's area of expertise is financial reporting, and prior to his academic career, he worked for five years in the banking industry. He served as the Academic Accounting Fellow in the Office of the Chief Accountant at the U.S. Securities and Exchange Commission in Washington, D.C., from 1995–1996. While on the staff, he worked on projects related to financial instruments and financial institutions, and he helped coordinate a symposium on intangible asset financial reporting. Professor Warfield's primary research interests concern financial accounting standards and disclosure policies. He has published scholarly articles in *The Accounting Review, Journal of Accounting and Economics, Research in Accounting Regulation,* and *Accounting Horizons,* and he has served on the editorial boards of *The Accounting Review* and *Accounting Horizons.* He has served on the Financial Accounting Standards Committee of the American Accounting Association (past Chair 1995–1996) and on the Association Council, the Nominations Committee, and the AAA-FASB Research Conference Committee. Professor Warfield has taught accounting courses at the introductory, intermediate, and graduate levels. He has received teaching awards at both the University of Iowa and the University of Wisconsin, and he was named to the Teaching Academy at the University of Wisconsin in 1995. Professor Warfield has developed and published several case studies based on his research for use in accounting classes. These cases have been selected for the AICPA Professor-Practitioner Case Development Program, and a case on hybrid securities has been published in *Issues in Accounting Education.* Professor Warfield also has developed materials on cooperative learning in accounting that have been presented at teaching workshops at the University of Wisconsin and included in instructor materials for accounting textbooks.

Preface

This edition of *Intermediate Accounting* represents an important milestone in the evolution of this textbook—the tenth edition of a text that has been a "Gateway to the Profession" for over a million students who have used its prior editions. As with the prior editions, in planning this edition we conducted extensive market research, including instructor focus groups, student focus groups, direct mail and electronic mail surveys, and one-on-one discussions with practitioners to help us focus on how the text should evolve into the next millennium.

Two themes emerged from this research. These themes confirmed development decisions made in recent editions of *Intermediate Accounting* and suggested ways that we could further enhance the usefulness of the text to students and instructors. The first theme is the continuing rapid pace of information technology and, in particular, the growth of the Internet. This continuing trend confirmed our decision to feature Intel for the specimen financial statements in the ninth edition and to continue their use in the tenth edition. Similar to *Intermediate Accounting*, Intel continues to lead its industry—one characterized by rapid-fire change and increasing diversified needs. Further support for this information technology trend is reflected in the introduction in this edition of the *Gateway to the Profession* Digital Tool.

The Digital Tool is an electronic gateway, either via the Internet or CD-ROM, to a comprehensive set of materials that supplement the already-comprehensive coverage of accounting topics in the textbook. Included are "professional tools" related to written communication, working in groups, and ethics. A financial analyst's toolkit contains a comprehensive primer on financial statement analysis and a collection of over 30 real-company financial statements that students can access for financial statement and other research. Also included are expanded discussions and illustrations for topics such as international accounting and the accounting for securitizations, and additional real-company disclosures for topics introduced in the text. We believe the *Gateway to the Profession* Digital Tool will be an invaluable resource to students that will help them get the most out of their *Intermediate Accounting* investment.

The second theme that emerged from our research is the continuing evolution of the accounting profession and accounting education away from knowledge of accounting facts to the development of skills in how to *use* accounting facts and procedures in various business contexts. This trend is reflected in the recent framework introduced by the AICPA that recommends a skill-based as opposed to a fact-based accounting curriculum and confirms the recommendations of the Accounting Education Change Commission. Accountants must act as well as think, and we believe that it is important for students to understand the how as well as the why of accounting. The content and focus of many of the elements of the *Gateway to the Profession* Digital Tool (writing, working in teams, analyst's toolkit) respond to this trend by providing an expanded set of materials that can be used to extend and apply the concepts and methods introduced within the text.

We continue to strive for a balanced discussion of conceptual and procedural presentation so that these elements are mutually reinforcing. In addition, discussions focus on explaining the rationale behind business transactions before addressing the accounting and reporting for those transactions. As in prior editions, we have thoroughly revised and updated the text to include all the latest developments in the accounting profession and practice. Benefiting from the comments and recommendations of adopters of the ninth edition, we have made significant revisions. Explanations have been expanded where necessary; complicated discussions and illustrations have been simplified; realism has been integrated to heighten interest and relevancy; and new topics and coverage have been added to maintain currency. We have deleted some ninth edition coverage from the text. To provide the instructor with no loss in material coverage and flexibility in use, discussions of less commonly used methods, more complex, or specialized topics have been moved to the Digital Tool.

NEW FEATURES

Based on extensive reviews, focus groups, and interactions with other intermediate accounting instructors and students, we have developed a number of new pedagogical features and content changes designed both to help students learn more effectively and to answer the changing needs of the course.

Digital Tool

As mentioned above, a major new resource developed for this edition is the *Gateway to the Profession* Digital Tool. The Digital Tool is an electronic gateway, either via the Internet or CD-ROM, to a comprehensive set of materials that supplement the already-comprehensive coverage of accounting topics in the textbook. When the Digital Tool icon (shown in the margin) appears in the textbook, the student is directed to expanded materials as described below. Major elements of the Digital Tool are:

Analyst's Toolkit

The Analyst's Toolkit contains the following items.

Database of Real Companies. Over 20 annual reports of well-known companies, including several international companies, are provided on the Digital Tool. These annual reports can be used in a variety of ways. For example, they can be used as illustrations of different presentations of financial information or for comparing note disclosures across companies. In addition, these reports can be used to analyze a company's financial condition and compare its prospects with other companies in the same industry. Assignment material provides some examples of different types of analysis that can be performed.

Company Web Links. Each of the companies in the database of real companies is identified by a Web address to facilitate the gathering of additional information, if desired.

Preformatted Excel Worksheets. Worksheets formatted in Excel are available for some assignments on the Digital Tool. For example, students may be asked to compute key ratios for a certain company (with a digital calculator provided), and to compare the computed ratios against those of another company. The other company's ratios are provided on a worksheet to expedite the analysis phase of the assignment.

Additional Enrichment Material. A chapter on Financial Statement Analysis is provided, with related assignment material. This chapter can also be used with the database of annual reports of real companies.

Spreadsheet Tools. Present value templates are provided which can be used to solve time value of money problems.

Additional Internet Links. A number of useful links related to financial analysis are provided to expand expertise in this area.

Professional Toolkit

Consistent with expanding beyond technical accounting knowledge, the *Gateway to the Profession* Digital Tool emphasizes certain skills necessary to become a successful accountant and financial manager.

Writing Materials. A primer on professional communications is provided that will give students a framework for writing professional materials. This primer discusses issues such as the top ten writing problems, strategies for prewriting, how to do revisions, and tips on clarity. This primer has been class tested and is effective in helping students enhance their writing skills.

Group Work Materials. Recent evaluation of accounting education has identified the need to develop more skills in group problem solving. The Digital Tool provides a second primer dealing with the role that groups play in organizations. Information on what makes a successful group, and how students can participate effectively in the group, is included.

Ethics. Expanded materials on the role of ethics in the profession are part of the Digital Tool, including references to:

- Speeches and articles on ethics in accounting.
- Codes of ethics for major professional bodies.
- Examples and additional case studies on ethics.

Career Professional Spotlights. Every student should have a good understanding of the profession that he or she is entering. Various vignettes in the Digital Tool indicate the types of work that accountants do. These vignettes are interviews with professional accountants, some well known and some only a few years out of college. Some of these interviews are included in the book but are also included, along with others that are not in the book, on the Digital Tool.

Other aspects of the spotlight on careers are also included. As part of the *Gateway to the Profession* Digital Tool, the following information is provided to help students make successful career choices:

- Salary information by region of the country.
- A résumé builder, to help students prepare a professional-looking résumé.
- Professional Web-links—important links to Web sites that can provide useful career information.

Student Helper Toolkit

Expanded Discussions and Illustrations. This section provides additional topics that are not covered in depth in the textbook. The *Gateway to the Profession* Digital Tool gives the flexibility to discuss these topics of interest in more detail.

Additional topics are as follows (with appropriate chapter linkage identified):

Chapter 3

- Presentation of worksheet using the periodic method.
- Specialized journals and methods of processing accounting data.

Chapter 6

- Present-value based measurements.

Chapter 7

- Discussion of how a four-column bank reconciliation (often referred to as the proof of cash) can be used for control purposes.
- Expanded example of transfers of receivables without recourse, with accounting entries.

Chapter 11

- Discussion of lesser-used depreciation methods, such as the retirement and replacement methods.

Chapter 17

- Comprehensive earnings per share illustration.

Chapter 18

- Illustration of accounting entries for transfers of investment securities.

Chapter 20

- Discussion of the conceptual aspects of interperiod tax allocation, including the deferred and net of tax methods.
- Discussion of accounting for intraperiod tax allocation, with examples.

Chapter 22

- Real estate leases and leveraged leases.

Chapter 24

- Discussion of the T-account method for preparing a statement of cash flows. A detailed example is provided.

Chapter 25

- Discussion of accounting for changing prices both for general and specific price level changes.
- In addition to these materials, illustrative disclosures of financial reporting practices are provided.

International Accounting. An expanded discussion of international accounting institutions, the evolution of international accounting standards, and a framework for understanding differences in accounting practice is provided. This discussion is designed to complement the international reporting problems in the textbook.

Learning Style Survey. Research on left brain/right brain differences and also on learning and personality differences suggests that each person has preferred ways to receive and communicate information. After completing this survey, students will be able to pinpoint the study aids in the text that will help them learn the material based on their particular learning styles.

In summary, the *Gateway to the Profession* Digital Tool is a comprehensive complement to the tenth edition of *Intermediate Accounting,* providing new materials as well as a new way to communicate that material. The contents of the Digital Tool will be accessible to students either on a CD-ROM or online at the Wiley Web site. In addition, the following items are provided on the Kieso web site (www.wiley.com/college/kieso).

Self-Study Multiple Choice Questions. For each chapter, 15 multiple-choice questions are provided in the Digital Tool for review purposes. In addition to the correct answer, reasons are provided as to why the answer is correct. These multiple-choice questions can be used to assess the student's understanding of the subject material covered in the course and also as a quick review of the chapter.

Checklist of Key Figures. A checklist of key figures by chapter is included.

PowerPoint Presentations. A PowerPoint presentation by chapter is provided for study and review purposes.

Calculator Solutions

Financial calculator solutions (marked with the icon shown here in the margin) are included for certain time value of money problems throughout the textbook. These solutions will help enhance student skills in using a financial calculator.

International Reporting Cases

We have extended the international coverage in the text by introducing a number of international reporting cases that are based on real companies and designed to illustrate international accounting differences. These cases illustrate the importance of adjusting international financial statements to make them comparable across countries. This emphasis reinforces the user orientation of the "Using Your Judgement" element.

ENHANCED FEATURES

We have continued and enhanced many of the features that were introduced in the ninth edition of *Intermediate Accounting,* including:

Chapter-opening Vignettes

We have updated and introduced new chapter-opening vignettes to provide an even better real-world context that helps motivate student interest in the chapter topic.

Using Your Judgment

The "Using Your Judgment" elements (Financial Reporting Problems, Financial Statement Analysis, Comparative Analysis, and Research Cases) at the end of each chapter have been revised and updated. In addition, explicit writing and group assignments have been integrated into the exercises, problems, and cases. Exercises, problems, and cases that are especially suited for group or writing assignments are identified with special icons, as shown here in the margin.

Real-World Emphasis

We believe that one of the goals of the intermediate accounting course is to orient students to the application of accounting principles and techniques in practice. Accordingly, we have continued our practice of using numerous examples from real corporations, highlighted in red, throughout the text. Illustrations and exhibits marked by the icon shown here are excerpts from actual financial statements of existing firms. In addition, the 1998 annual report of Intel Corporation, is included in Appendix 5B, and many real-company financial reports appear in the database on the Digital Tool.

Perspectives

We have retained the interviews with prominent accounting and business personalities on relevant accounting topics. These interviews give a real-world emphasis that is important for students in the intermediate accounting course who are considering choosing accounting as a career. In the tenth edition, we have updated a number of interviews from the ninth edition and added new interviews with accounting professionals as well as with young accountants who describe their transitions from school into the business world in interviews entitled "From Classroom to Career."

International Insights

International Insight paragraphs that describe or compare the accounting practices in other countries are provided in the margin. We have continued this feature to help students understand that other countries sometimes use different recognition and measurement principles to report financial information.

INTERNATIONAL INSIGHT

Streamlined Presentation

We have continued our efforts to keep the topical coverage of *Intermediate Accounting* in line with the way instructors are currently teaching the course. Accordingly, we have moved some optional topics into appendices and have omitted altogether some topics that formerly were covered in appendices, moving them to the Digital Tool. Details are noted in the list of specific content changes below.

Currency and Accuracy

Accounting continually changes as its environment changes; an up-to-date book is therefore a necessity. As in past editions, we have strived to make this edition the most up-to-date and accurate text available.

CONTENT CHANGES

The following list outlines the revisions and improvements made in chapters of the tenth edition.

Chapter 1

- New vignette.
- Updated international discussion.

Chapter 2

- Increased emphasis on fair-value accounting.
- Increased emphasis on revenue recognition.
- Revised section on materiality.

Chapter 3

- Revised discussion of inventory methods with emphasis on the perpetual inventory method.
- Simplified work sheet based on the perpetual method.
- Moved material on reversing entries to appendix.
- Discussion of subsidiary ledgers and special journals moved to the Digital Tool.
- Revised and simplified section on conversion from cash to accrual basis.
- The accounting equation has been inserted in the margin next to key journal entries in this chapter. This new feature reinforces the students' understanding of the impact of an accounting transaction on the financial statements.

Chapter 4

- New discussion and infographic that simplify the discussion related to the advantages and disadvantages of the income statement.
- New section on earnings management.
- Revised section on irregular items, emphasizing restructuring charges and reporting within the income statement.

Chapter 5

- New infographic that simplifies the discussion related to the advantages and disadvantages of the balance sheet.
- Moved discussion of subsequent events to the disclosure materials in Chapter 25.
- Introduced discussion of financial instruments.

Chapter 6

- New appendix on using a financial calculator called "Technology Tools for Time Value Problems." It illustrates how to use a financial calculator or computer spreadsheet to solve time value of money problems.
- Introduced calculator solutions for selected problems.

Chapter 7

- New vignette on sale of loans by sub-prime lenders.
- Updated discussion on control of cash and electronic commerce.
- Introduced calculator solutions.
- Additional real-company disclosures of cash and receivables.
- New graphic on impact of credit cards on bad debts.
- New discussion of allowance for loan losses used for earnings management.

Chapter 8

- New infographic on items included in inventory.
- Introduced real companies to illustrate merchandising and manufacturing inventories.

Chapter 9

- New opening vignette on inventory valuation.

Chapter 10

- New infographic on interest capitalization.
- Introduced real-company disclosure on interest capitalization.
- New infographic to summarize the accounting for exchanges.

Chapter 11

- New vignette on impairment, including discussion of international standards.
- New disclosure on impairments and property, plant, and equipment.

Chapter 12

- Revised discussion of characteristics of intangible assets.
- Expanded discussion of goodwill.
- New infographic on identifying research and development costs.
- Revised and updated discussion of start-up costs, advertising costs, and initial operating losses.
- Updated disclosures related to intangibles and research and development costs.
- Appendix updated for software costs developed or obtained for internal use.

Chapter 13

- New vignette on unearned revenues.
- New illustration summarizing payroll liabilities.
- Updated disclosures of current liabilities.

Chapter 14

- New vignette on weather bonds.
- Introduced calculator solutions.
- Updated real-company disclosure on debt extinguishment.
- Simplified discussion on the presentation and analysis of long-term debt.
- Updated real-company disclosure of long-term debt.

Chapter 15

- Updated vignette.
- New discussion on use of dividends versus treasury stock purchases.
- Revised discussion of issue costs.
- Revised discussion of debt-like preferred stock.

Chapter 16

- Updated vignette on stock splits
- Updated disclosure of the statement of stockholders' equity, including comprehensive income

Chapter 17

- Streamlined discussion of accounting for convertible debt.
- Updated discussion of preferred stock.
- Streamlined and updated discussion of political debate on stock option accounting.
- Updated real-company disclosure on stock compensation plans.
- Updated discussion in appendix on additional complications related to stock options.

Chapter 18

- New vignette on equity accounting.
- Enhanced discussion of portfolio effects of debt and equity investments.
- Moved Appendix 18A on transfers between categories to the Digital Tool.
- Moved Appendix 18B on changing from and to the equity method to Chapter 23 (*Accounting Changes*) to better illustrate these changes.
- Streamlined discussion in Appendix 18C on special issues related to investments.
- New appendix on accounting for derivatives.

Chapter 19

- New vignette on revenue recognition for Internet companies.
- Revised discussion on revenue recognition.

Chapter 20

- New vignette on management of tax costs.
- New discussion on differences between tax return and GAAP reporting.
- New real-company income tax disclosure.
- Deletion of alternative minimum tax.
- Moved discussion of intra-period tax allocation to the Digital Tool.
- Moved Appendix 20B on the conceptual aspects of inter-period tax allocation to the Digital Tool.

Chapter 21

- New vignette on wealth creation in retirement plans.
- New graphic on size of pension funds.
- Expanded discussion of trends in pensions.
- Streamlined discussion on capitalization versus non-capitalization.
- Updated discussion for new pension disclosure standard.
- Revised discussion on the Pension Reform Act and related issues.

Chapter 22

- Updated vignette on leasing.
- Streamlined discussion related to the advantages of leasing.
- Updated real-company disclosures of leases by lessees and lessors.
- Expanded discussion of rationale for sale-leaseback.

Chapter 23

- Updated discussion of motivations for changes.
- Appendix on changing from and to the equity method added.

Chapter 24

- Relocated "Usefulness of Statement of Cash Flows" section to the front of the chapter.
- Real-company disclosures used throughout the chapter.

Chapter 25

- Updated and simplified discussion of reporting for diversified companies.
- New section on subsequent events added.
- New discussion on Internet reporting.
- Updated discussion on reporting of future events.
- Updated discussion on fraudulent financial reporting and the profession's response.
- Moved the appendix "Accounting for Changing Prices" to the Digital Tool.

END-OF-CHAPTER ASSIGNMENT MATERIAL

At the end of each chapter we have provided a comprehensive set of review and homework material consisting of questions, exercises, problems, and short cases. For this edition, many of the exercises and problems have been revised or updated. In addition, the Using Your Judgment sections, which include financial reporting problems, ethics cases, financial statement analysis cases, comparative analysis cases, and research cases have all been updated. A number of international reporting cases that are based on real companies are introduced throughout the textbook. All of the assignment materials have been class tested and/or double checked for accuracy and clarity.

The questions are designed for review, self-testing, and classroom discussion purposes as well as homework assignments. Typically, a brief exercise covers one topic, an exercise one or two topics. Exercises require less time and effort to solve than problems and cases. The problems are designed to develop a professional level of achievement and are more challenging and time-consuming to solve than the exercises. Those exercises and problems that are contained in the *Excel Problems* supplements are identified by a blue computer disk icon in the margin. The cases generally require essay as opposed to quantitative solutions; they are intended to confront the student with situations calling for conceptual analysis and the exercise of judgment in identifying problems and evaluating alternatives. The Using Your Judgment assignments are designed to develop students' critical thinking, analytical, interpersonal, and communication skills.

Probably no more than one-fourth of the total exercise, problem, and case material must be used to cover the subject matter adequately; consequently, problem assignments may be varied from year to year.

COLOR DESIGN

The color coding in the design not only enlivens the textbook's appearance but, through planned and consistent usage, eases learning. Note that the financial statements are presented in beige screens with blue headers. Trial balances, work sheets, and large schedules are presented in blue screens with beige headers.

All end-of-chapter summaries and assignments (including appendices) are tabbed with a red color bar, while the five interest and annuity tables in Chapter 6 are tabbed with a blue color bar to make it easy to locate and identify them.

The color design is summarized as follows:

- The names of real-world companies in the text and illustrations are shown in red.
- Excerpts from the financial statements of real world companies are indicated by this icon .

- Other external statements have a blue heading with beige background for text.
- Internal statements show a beige heading and blue background for text.

SUPPLEMENTARY MATERIALS

Accompanying this textbook is an improved and expanded package of student learning aids and instructor teaching aids.

The *Intermediate Accounting,* 10/e, Digital Tool (CD-ROM and Web site) described in detail on pages ix–xii provides additional tools for students and instructors. Key features include:

- Analyst's Toolkit
- Professional Toolkit
- Student Helper Toolkit

Instructor Teaching Aids

Instructor's Resource System on CD-ROM

- Resource manager with friendly interface for course development and presentation.
- Includes all instructor supplements, text art, and transparencies.

Instructor's Manual: Vol. 1 Chs. 1–14
Instructor's Manual: Vol. 2 Chs. 15–25

- Lecture outlines keyed to text learning objectives
- Updated Bibliography.
- Teaching Transparency Masters.
- Section on "How to assign and evaluate ethical issues in the course."
- Sections on "How to incorporate writing" and "How to incorporate group (collaborative) work."

Solutions Manual, Vol. 1: Chs. 1–14
Solutions Manual, Vol. 2: Chs. 15–25

- Answers to all questions, brief exercises, exercises, problems, and case material provided.
- Classification Tables categorize the end-of-chapter material by topic to assist in assigning homework.
- Assignment Tables (characteristics) describe the end-of-chapter material, its difficulty level, and estimated completion time.
- All solutions triple-checked to ensure accuracy.

Test Bank, Vol. 1: Chs. 1–14
Test Bank, Vol. 2: Chs. 15–25

- Essay questions with solutions help you test students' communication skills.
- Estimated completion times facilitate test planning.
- Computations for multiple-choice problems assist you in giving partial credit.

Computerized Test Bank IBM 3.5"

- A large collection of objective questions and exercises with answers for each chapter in the text.

- Generate questions randomly or manually, and modify/customize tests with your own material.
- Create multiple versions of the same test by scrambling by type, character, number, or learning objective.

Test Preparation Service

- Simply call Wiley's Accounting Hotline (800) 541-5602 with the questions you have selected for an exam. Wiley will provide a master exam within 24 hours.

Solution Transparencies, Vol. 1: Chs. 1–14
Solution Transparencies, Vol. 2: Chs. 15–25

- Provided in organizer box with chapter file folders.
- Large, bold type size for easier class presentation.
- Provided for all exercises, problems, and cases.

PowerPoint Presentations

- Designed to enhance presentation of chapter topics and examples.
- Separate presentation for each chapter available on the Kieso Web site (www. wiley.com/college/kieso).

Teaching Transparencies

- Over 100 color figure illustrations and exhibits.
- 90% from outside the text.

Checklist of Key Figures

- Available at the Kieso Web site to both students and instructors.

Expanded Special Journal Discussion

Available under Instructor Resources at the Kieso Web site (www.wiley.com/college/kieso), this discussion includes

- Subsidiary ledgers and special journals for periodic inventory.
- Subsidiary ledgers and special journals for perpetual inventory.
- Periodic inventory method work sheet.
- Alternative treatment of prepaid expenses and unearned revenues.
- Addition problem material.

Student Learning Aids

Student Study Guide, Vol. 1: Chs. 1–14
Student Study Guide, Vol. 2: Chs. 15–25

- Chapter Learning Objectives.
- Chapter Outline—a broad overview of general chapter content with space for note-taking in class.
- Chapter Review with summary of key concepts.
- Glossary of key terms.
- Review Questions and Exercises—self-test items with supporting computations.

Workpapers, Vol. 1: Chs. 1–14
Workpapers, Vol. 2: Chs. 15–25
Electronic Working Papers. Vol. 1 Chs 1–14
Electronic Working Papers. Vol. 2 Chs 15–25

Problem Solving Survival Guide Vol. 1, Chs. 1–14
Problem Solving Survival Guide Vol. 2, Chs. 15–25

- Provides additional questions and problems to develop students' problem-solving skills.
- Explanations assist in the approach, set-up, and completion of problems.
- Tips alert students to common pitfalls and misconceptions.

Excel Problems

- Spreadsheet requirements range in difficulty (from data entry to developing spreadsheets).
- Review of intermediate accounting and Excel concepts.
- Each chapter consists of a basic tutorial, a more advanced tutorial, and two or three problems from the text.
- Each problem followed by "what-if" questions to build students' analytical skills.

Rockford Corporation: An Accounting Practice Set
Rockford Corporation: A Computerized Accounting Practice Set

- This practice set has been designed as a students' review and update of the accounting cycle and the preparation of financial statements. It is available in a print version and in a computerized version updated to a Windows platform.

ACKNOWLEDGMENTS

We thank the many users of our ninth edition who contributed to the revision through their comments and instructive criticism. Special thanks are extended to the primary reviewers of, and contributors to, our tenth edition manuscript.

Edwin Cohen *DePaul University*	Eric Sussman *University of California, Los Angeles*
Judith Doing *University of Arizona*	Diane L. Tanner *University of North Florida*
Susan Gill *Washington State University*	Paula B. Thomas *Middle Tennessee State University*
M. Zafar Iqbal *California Polytechnic State University*	James D. Waddington, Jr. *Hawaii Pacific University*
Timothy Lindquist *University of Northern Iowa*	Michael Willenborg *University of Connecticut*
Mostafa Maksy *Northeastern Illinois University*	Joni Young *University of New Mexico*
Carlton D. Stolle *Texas A&M University*	Paul Zarowin *New York University*

Other colleagues who have provided helpful criticisms and made valuable suggestions as members of focus groups, or as adopters and reviewers of previous editions include:

Charlene Abendroth *California State University—Hayward*	Kathleen Bauer *Midwestern State University*
Diana Adcox *University of North Florida*	Jon A. Booker *Tennessee Technical University*
Noel Addy *Mississippi State University*	John C. Borke *University of Wisconsin—Platteville*
James Bannister *University of Hartford*	Suzanne M. Busch *California State University—Hayward*

Eric Carlsen
Kean College of New Jersey

Patrick Delaney
Northern Illinois University

Dean S. Eiteman
Indiana University—Pennsylvania

Larry R. Falcetto
Emporia State University

Richard Fern
Eastern Kentucky University

Richard Fleischman
John Carroll University

Stephen L. Fogg
Temple University

Clyde Galbraith
West Chester University

Lynford E. Graham
Rutgers University

Jim Green
Arthur Andersen & Co.

Donald J. Griffin
Cayuga Community College

Marcia I. Halvorsen
University of Cincinnati

Gary Heesacker
Central Washington University

Wayne M. Higley
Buena Vista University

Geoffrey R. Horlick
St. Francis College

Cynthia Jeffrey
Iowa State University

Douglas W. Kieso
University of California—Irvine

Paul D. Kimmel
University of Wisconsin—Milwaukee

Martha King
Emporia State University

Florence Kirk
State University of New York at Oswego

Lisa Koonce
University of Texas—Austin

David B. Law
Youngstown State University

Henry Le Clerc
Suffolk Community College—Selden Campus

Barbara Leonard
Loyola University—Chicago

Tom Linsmeier
Michigan State University

Daphne Main
University of New Orleans

Danny Matthews
Midwestern State University

Robert J. Matthews
New Jersey City University

Robert Milbrath
University of Houston

John Mills
University of Nevada, Reno

Suzanne Morsfield
CUNY-Baruch College

Mohamed E. Moustafa
California State University—Long Beach

Kermit Natho
Georgia State University

Obeau S. Persons
Rider University

Robert Rambo
University of New Orleans

Jeffrey D. Ritter
St. Norbert College

James Sander
Butler University

Douglas Sharp
Wichita State University

John R. Simon
Northern Illinois University

Keith Smith
George Washington University

Pam Smith
Northern Illinois University

Billy S. Soo
Boston College

Dick Wasson
Southwestern College

Frank F. Weinberg
Golden Gate University

Shari H. Wescott
Houston Baptist University

William H. Wilson
Oregon Health University

Kenneth Wooling
Hampton University

Stephen A. Zeff
Rice University

We would also like to thank those colleagues who contributed to several of the unique features of this edition:

International Notes

Judith Ramaglia, *Pacific Lutheran University*

Ethics Cases

Bill N. Schwartz, *Virginia Commonwealth University*

Underlying Concepts

John Cheever, *California State Polytechnic University—Pomona*

Writing Assignments

Susan Smith, *Northern Illinois University*
Katherene P. Terrell and Robert L. Terrell, *University of Central Oklahoma*

Group Cases/Assignments

Katherene P. Terrell and Robert L. Terrell, *University of Central Oklahoma*

Perspectives and "From Classroom to Career" Interviews

Stuart Weiss, *Stuart Weiss Business Writing, Inc.*

Financial Analysis Cases and Problems

Martha King, *Emporia State University*
Carol M. Fischer, *University of Wisconsin—Waukesha*

Research Cases

Mark Bauman, *University of Illinois—Chicago*

Digital Tool Development

Paul Rifelj, *University of Wisconsin—Madison*
Craig Schedler, *Tucker, Anthony, Cleary, and Gull*

"Working in Teams" Materials

Edward Wertheim, *Northeastern University*

The Writing Handbook

Michelle Ephraim, *Worcester Polytechnic Institute*

Self-Test Materials

Larry Falcetto, *Emporia State University*

Practicing Accountants and Business Executives

From the field of corporate and public accounting, we owe thanks to the following practitioners for their technical advice and for consenting to interviews:

Tracy Barber
Deloitte & Touche

Ron Bernard
NFL Enterprises

Penelope Flugger
J.P. Morgan & Co.

John Gribble
PricewaterhouseCoopers

Darien Griffin
S.C. Johnson & Son Wax

Ed Jenkins
Financial Accounting Standards Board

Michael Lehman
Sun Microsystems, Inc.

Michelle Lippert
evoke.com

Sue McGrath
Vision Capital Management

David Miniken
Sweeney Conrad

Robert Sack
University of Virginia

Claire Schulte
Deloitte & Touche

Willie Sutton
Mutual Community Savings Bank—
Durham, NC

Gary Valenzuela
Yahoo!

Rachel Woods
PricewaterhouseCoopers

Arthur Wyatt
Arthur Andersen & Co. and the University
of Illinois—Urbana

We appreciate the exemplary support and professional commitment given us by the development, marketing, production, and editorial staffs of John Wiley & Sons, including Susan Elbe, Mark Bonadeo, Ellen Ford, Julie Kerr, Dana Bigelow, Jeanine Furino, Nicole Horlacher, Karen Kincheloe, David Kear, Hilary Newman, Anna Melhorn, and the management and staff at York Graphic Services, Inc. A special note of thanks also to Ann Torbert (editorial and content assistance) and Elm Street Publishing Services (Martha Beyerlein and Barb Lange) for facilitating the production of the manuscript. We also wish to thank Dick Wasson of Southwestern College for coordinating the efforts of the supplements authors and checkers. Finally, thanks to Lenox Softworks of Lenox, Massachusetts, for developing the format of the Digital Tool.

We appreciate the cooperation of the American Institute of Certified Public Accountants and the Financial Accounting Standards Board in permitting us to quote from their pronouncements. We thank Intel Corporation for permitting us to use its 1998 Annual Report for our specimen financial statements. We also acknowledge permission from the American Institute of Certified Public Accountants, the Institute of Management Accountants, and the Institute of Internal Auditors to adapt and use material from the Uniform CPA Examinations, the CMA Examinations, and the CIA Examinations, respectively.

If this book helps teachers instill in their students an appreciation for the challenges, worth, and limitations of accounting, if it encourages students to evaluate critically and understand financial accounting theory and practice, and if it prepares students for advanced study, professional examinations, and the successful and ethical pursuit of their careers in accounting or business, then we will have attained our objective.

Suggestions and comments from users of this book will be appreciated.

Somonauk, Illinois
Madison, Wisconsin
Madison, Wisconsin

Donald E. Kieso
Jerry J. Weygandt
Terry D. Warfield

Brief Contents

Contents

CHAPTER 22
Accounting for Leases, 1189

CHAPTER 25

Full Disclosure in Financial Reporting,   1381

CHAPTER 15

Stockholders' Equity: Contributed Capital

Stocking Up

Quick, how did the market do yesterday? If asked this question, you probably responded that the market increased or decreased, based on the change in the Dow Jones Industrial Average. And just what is the Dow Jones Industrial Average (DJIA)? It is the average of 30 U.S. "blue-chip" (high-quality) stocks which represent the various sectors of the U.S. economy and have broad public ownership. **AT&T**, **American Express**, **Coca-Cola**, **Exxon Mobil**, **General Electric**, **Merck**, and **McDonald's** are examples of the type of companies found in this index.

The DJIA and other stock market indexes are becoming of increasing importance to most Americans. The reason: More and more of the country's wealth is tied up in the stock market. For example, the following chart shows the increase of stock as a percentage of U.S. household net worth over time.

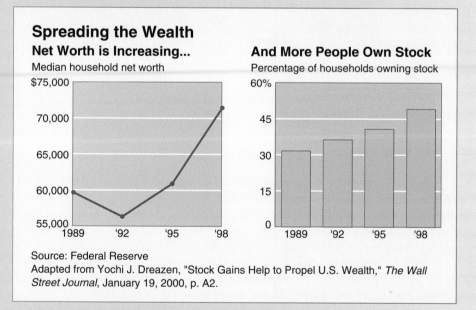

Spreading the Wealth
Net Worth is Increasing...
Median household net worth

And More People Own Stock
Percentage of households owning stock

Source: Federal Reserve
Adapted from Yochi J. Dreazen, "Stock Gains Help to Propel U.S. Wealth," *The Wall Street Journal*, January 19, 2000, p. A2.

Fueled by stock-market gains, America's wealth grew at a strong pace in the latter half of the 1990s. At the same time, a record number of Americans at all income levels now own stock, intertwining their financial well-being with the stock market like never before. The percentage of Americans owning stock surged to 48.8% in 1998, up sharply from 40.4% in 1995. And for the first time in the history of the Federal Reserve Report, stock holdings now account for more than half of Americans' financial assets, up from 40% in 1995.

LEARNING OBJECTIVES

After studying this chapter, you should be able to:

1. Discuss the characteristics of the corporate form of organization.
2. Identify the rights of stockholders.
3. Explain the key components of stockholders' equity.
4. Explain the accounting procedures for issuing shares of stock.
5. Identify the major reasons for purchasing treasury stock.
6. Explain the accounting for treasury stock.
7. Describe the major features of preferred stock.
8. Distinguish between debt and preferred stock.
9. Identify items reported as additional paid-in capital.

As indicated from the opening story, more and more people are investing in the stock market. A public debate even has begun about whether some portion of Social Security funds should be invested in stocks. The stock market is of substantial importance in any economy that functions on private ownership. It provides a market where prices are established to serve as signals and incentives to guide the allocation of the economy's financial resources. The purpose of this chapter is to explain the various accounting issues related to the different types of stock that corporations issue. The content and organization of this chapter are as follows:

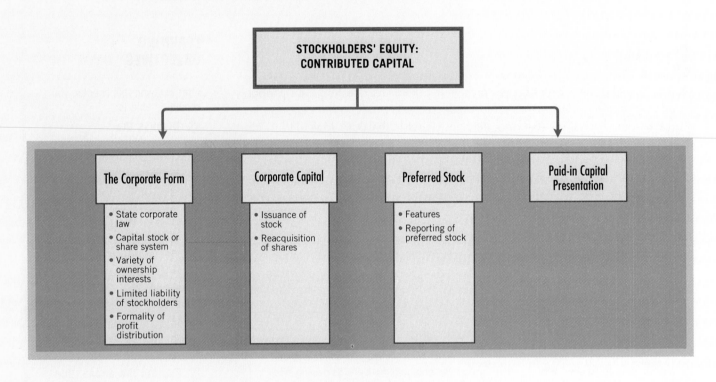

THE CORPORATE FORM

OBJECTIVE ❶
Discuss the characteristics of the corporate form of organization.

Of the three **primary forms of business organization—the proprietorship**, **the partnership, and the corporation**—the dominant form of business is the corporate form. In terms of the aggregate amount of resources controlled, goods and services produced, and people employed, the corporation is by far the leader. All of the "Fortune 500" largest industrial firms are corporations. Although the corporate form has a number of advantages (as well as disadvantages) over the other two forms, its principal advantage is its facility for attracting and accumulating large amounts of capital.

Corporations may be classified by the nature of ownership as follows:

❶ **Public sector corporations:** governmental units or business operations owned by governmental units (such as the Federal Deposit Insurance Corporation).

❷ **Private sector corporations:**
   a. **Nonstock:** nonprofit in nature and no stock issued (such as churches, charities, and colleges).
   b. **Stock:** companies that operate for profit and issue stock.
      (i) **Closed corporations (nonpublic or private enterprises):** stock held by a few stockholders (perhaps a family) and not available for public purchase.

(ii) **Open corporations (public companies):** stock widely held and available for purchase by the public.

    (a) **Listed corporation:** stock traded on an organized stock exchange.

    (b) **Unlisted or over-the-counter corporation:** stock traded in a market in which securities dealers buy from and sell to the public.

Among the special characteristics of the corporate form that affect accounting are:

❶ Influence of state corporate law.

❷ Use of the capital stock or share system.

❸ Development of a variety of ownership interests.

❹ Limited liability of stockholders.

❺ Formality of profit distribution.

State Corporate Law

Anyone who wishes to establish a corporation must submit **articles of incorporation** to the state in which incorporation is desired. Assuming the requirements are properly fulfilled, the corporation charter is issued, and the corporation is recognized as a legal entity subject to state law. Regardless of the number of states in which a corporation has operating divisions, it is incorporated in only one state.

It is to the company's advantage to incorporate in a state whose laws are favorable to the corporate form of business organization. General Motors, for example, is incorporated in Delaware; USX Corp. is a New Jersey corporation. Some corporations have increasingly been incorporating in states with laws favorable to existing management. For example, to thwart possible unfriendly takeovers, Gulf Oil changed its state of incorporation to Delaware. There, certain tactics against takeovers can be approved by the board of directors alone, without a vote of the shareholders.

Each state has its own business incorporation act, and the accounting for stockholders' equity follows the provisions of this act. In many cases states have adopted the principles contained in the Model Business Corporate Act prepared by the American Bar Association. State laws are complex and vary both in their provisions and in their definitions of certain terms. Some laws fail to define technical terms, and so terms often mean one thing in one state and another thing in a different state. These problems may be further compounded because legal authorities often interpret the effects and restrictions of the laws differently.[1]

Capital Stock or Share System

Stockholders' equity in a corporation is generally made up of a large number of units or shares. Within a given class of stock each share is exactly equal to every other share. Each owners's interest is determined by the number of shares possessed. If a company has but one class of stock divided into 1,000 shares, a person owning 500 shares controls one-half of the ownership interest of the corporation; one holding 10 shares has a one-hundredth interest.

Each share of stock has certain rights and privileges that can be restricted only by special contract at the time the shares are issued. One must examine the articles of incorporation, stock certificates, and the provisions of the state law to ascertain such restrictions on or variations from the standard rights and privileges. In the absence of restrictive provisions, each share carries the following rights:

❶ To share proportionately in profits and losses.

❷ To share proportionately in management (the right to vote for directors).

❸ To share proportionately in corporate assets upon liquidation.

INTERNATIONAL INSIGHT

In the United States, stockholders are treated equally as far as access to financial information. That is not always the case in other countries. For example, in Mexico foreign investors as well as minority investors often have difficulty obtaining financial data. These restrictions are rooted in the habits of companies that for many years have been tightly controlled by a few stockholders and managers.

OBJECTIVE ❷
Identify the rights of stockholders.

---

[1]Beatrice Melcher, "Stockholders' Equity," *Accounting Research Study No. 15* (New York: AICPA, 1973), p. 8.

④ To share proportionately in any new issues of stock of the same class—called the preemptive right.

The first three rights are to be expected in the ownership of any business; the last may be used in a corporation to protect each stockholder's proportional interest in the enterprise. **The preemptive right protects an existing stockholder from involuntary dilution of ownership interest.** Without this right, stockholders with a given percentage interest might find their interest reduced by the issuance of additional stock without their knowledge and at prices that were not favorable to them. Because the preemptive right that attaches to existing shares makes it inconvenient for corporations to make large issuances of additional stock, as they frequently do in acquiring other companies, it has been eliminated by many corporations.

The great advantage of the share system is the ease with which an interest in the business may be transferred from one individual to another. **Individuals owning shares in a corporation may sell them to others at any time and at any price without obtaining the consent of the company or other stockholders.** Each share is personal property of the owner and may be disposed of at will. All that is required of the corporation is that it maintain a list or subsidiary ledger of stockholders as a guide to dividend payments, issuance of stock rights, voting proxies, and the like. Because shares are freely and frequently transferred, it is necessary for the corporation to revise the subsidiary ledger of stockholders periodically, generally in advance of every dividend payment or stockholders' meeting. Also, the major stock exchanges require controls that the typical corporation finds uneconomic to provide. Thus **registrars and transfer agents** who specialize in providing services for recording and transferring stock are usually used. The negotiability of stock certificates is governed by the Uniform Stock Transfer Act and the Uniform Commercial Code.

INTERNATIONAL INSIGHT

The American and British systems of corporate governance and finance depend to a large extent on equity financing and the widely dispersed ownership of shares traded in highly liquid markets. The German and Japanese systems have relied more on debt financing, interlocking stock ownership, banker/directors, and worker/shareholder rights.

Variety of Ownership Interests

In every corporation one class of stock must represent the basic ownership interest. That class is called common stock. Common stock is the residual corporate interest that bears the ultimate risks of loss and receives the benefits of success. It is guaranteed neither dividends nor assets upon dissolution. But common stockholders generally control the management of the corporation and tend to profit most if the company is successful. In the event that a corporation has only one authorized issue of capital stock, that issue is by definition common stock, whether so designated in the charter or not.

In an effort to appeal to all types of investors, corporations may offer two or more classes of stock each with different rights or privileges. In the preceding section it was pointed out that each share of stock of a given issue has the same rights as other shares of the same issue and that there are four rights inherent in every share. By special stock contracts between the corporation and its stockholders, certain of these rights may be sacrificed by the stockholder in return for other special rights or privileges. Thus special classes of stock are created. Because they have certain preferential rights, they are usually called preferred stock. In return for any special preference, the preferred stockholder is always called on to sacrifice some of the inherent rights of capital stock interests.

A common type of preference is to give the preferred stockholders a prior claim on earnings. They are assured a dividend, usually at a stated rate, before any amount may be distributed to the common stockholders. In return for this preference the preferred stock may sacrifice its right to a voice in management or its right to share in profits beyond the stated rate.

A company may accomplish much the same thing by issuing two classes of common stock, Class A stock and Class B stock. In this case one of the issues is the common stock and the other issue has some preference or restriction of basic rights. For example, at one time **DeKalb Genetics Corporation** was organized with two classes of common stock, Class A and Class B. Both Class A and Class B participate equally (per share) in all dividend payments and have the same claim on assets in dissolution. The differences are that Class A is voting and Class B is not; Class B is traded publicly over the counter while Class A, which is "family owned," must be sold privately (Class A shares are convertible, one for one, into Class B shares but not vice versa). By issuing two classes of common stock, the Class A owners of DeKalb Genetics have obtained a ready market for the company's stock and yet provided an effective shield against outside takeover.[2]

Limited Liability of Stockholders

Those who "own" a corporation, the stockholders, contribute either property or services to the enterprise in return for ownership shares. **The property or service invested in the enterprise is the extent of a stockholder's possible loss.** That is, if the corporation sustains losses to such an extent that remaining assets are insufficient to pay creditors, no recourse can be had by the creditors against personal assets of the individual stockholders. In a partnership or proprietorship, personal assets of the owners can be attached to satisfy unpaid claims against the enterprise. Ownership interests in a corporation are legally protected against such a contingency. **The stockholders have limited liability—they may lose their investment but they cannot lose more than their investment.**

Stock that has a fixed per-share amount printed on each stock certificate is called par value stock. Par value has but one real significance: it establishes the maximum responsibility of a stockholder in the event of insolvency or other involuntary dissolution. Par value is thus not "value" in the ordinary sense of the word. It is merely an amount per share determined by the incorporators of the company and stated in the corporation charter or certificate of incorporation. Par value establishes the nominal value per share and is the minimum amount that must be paid in by each stockholder if the stock is to be fully paid when issued. A corporation may, however, issue its capital stock either above or below par, in which case the stock is said to be issued at a **premium or a discount**, respectively.[3]

If par value stock is issued at par or at a price above par and the corporation subsequently suffers losses so that assets to repay stockholders upon dissolution are insufficient, stockholders may lose their entire investment. If, however, the stock is issued at a price below par and the losses prove to be of such magnitude as to consume not only the stockholders' investments but also a portion of the assets required to repay creditors, the creditors can force the stockholders to pay in to the corporation the amount of the discount on their capital shares. Thus the original purchasers of stock issued at a price below par are **contingently liable** to creditors of the corporation. In other words, stockholders may lose their entire investment in a corporation if the investments are equal to or in excess of the par value of the shares they own, or, if the investments are less than their par value, they may lose the amount of their investment plus an additional amount equal to the discount at which they purchased the stock. The limited liability feature of corporate capital stock prevents them from losing any more than the par value of their stock plus any premium paid upon purchase.

It should be emphasized that **the contingent liability of a stockholder for stock purchased at a price below par**:

1 Is an obligation to the corporation's creditors, not to the corporation itself.

2 Becomes a real liability only if the amount below par must be collected in order to pay the creditors upon dissolution of the company.

3 Is the responsibility of the original certificate holder at the time of dissolution unless by contract such responsibility is transferred to a subsequent holder.

---

[2]Ironically, the voting class (which would necessarily be concerned about an unfriendly takeover) often gains the most if an acquisition does take place. That is, the acquirer is willing to pay a substantial premium for the voting shares, but not for the nonvoting ones.

[3]In most states capital stock may not be issued below par.

While the corporate form of organization grants the protective feature of limited liability to the stockholders, the corporation must guarantee not to distribute the amount of stockholders' investment unless all prior claims on corporate assets have been paid. **The corporation must maintain the corporate legal capital (generally par value of all capital stock issued) until dissolution**, and upon dissolution it must satisfy all prior claims before distributing any amounts to the stockholders.

In a proprietorship or partnership the owners can withdraw amounts at will because all their personal assets may be called on to protect creditors from loss. In a corporation, however, the owners cannot withdraw any amounts paid in because the only protection creditors have against loss is the amount paid in plus any discount below par.

Formality of Profit Distribution

The owners of an enterprise determine what is to be done with profits realized through operations. Profits may be left in the business to permit expansion or merely to provide a margin of safety, or they may be withdrawn and divided among the owners. In a proprietorship or partnership this decision is made by the owner or owners informally and requires no specific action. In a corporation, however, profit distribution is controlled by certain legal restrictions.

First, **distributions to owners must be in compliance with the state laws governing corporations**. Currently, the 50 states may be classified into one of three groups for purposes of comparing restrictions on distributions to owners.[4] Generally, in the largest group, distribution of dividends has to come from retained earnings or from current earnings. Chapter 16 covers this topic in more detail.

Second, **distributions to stockholders must be formally approved by the board of directors** and recorded in the minutes of their meetings. As the top executive body in the corporation, the board of directors must make certain that no distributions are made to stockholders that are not justified by profits, and directors are generally held personally liable to creditors if liabilities cannot be paid because company assets have been illegally paid out to stockholders.

Third, **dividends must be in full agreement with the capital stock contracts as to preferences, participation, and the like**. Once the corporation has entered into contracts with various classes of stockholders, the stipulations of such contracts must be observed.

CORPORATE CAPITAL

Owner's equity in a corporation is defined as stockholders' equity, shareholders' equity, or corporate capital. The following three categories normally appear as part of stockholders' equity:

1. Capital stock
2. Additional paid-in capital
3. Retained earnings

OBJECTIVE 3
Explain the key components of stockholders' equity.

The first two categories, capital stock and additional paid-in capital, constitute contributed (paid-in) capital; retained earnings represents the earned capital of the enterprise. Contributed capital (paid-in capital) is the total amount paid in on capital stock—the amount provided by stockholders to the corporation for use in the business. Contributed capital includes items such as the par value of all outstanding stock and premiums less discounts on issuance. Earned capital is the capital that develops if the

---

[4]See Michael L. Roberts, William D. Samson, and Michael T. Dugan, "The Stockholders' Equity Section: Form Without Substance," *Accounting Horizons*, December 1990, pp. 35–46.

business operates profitably; it consists of all undistributed income that remains invested in the enterprise.

The distinction between paid-in capital and retained earnings is important from both legal and economic points of view. Legally, dividends can be declared out of retained earnings in all states, but in many states dividends cannot be declared out of paid-in capital. Economically, management, shareholders, and others look to earnings for the continued existence and growth of the corporation.

Stockholders' equity is the difference between the assets and the liabilities of the enterprise. **Therefore, the owners' or stockholders' interest in a business enterprise is a** residual interest.[5] Stockholders' (owners') equity represents the cumulative net contributions by stockholders plus earnings that have been retained. As a residual interest, stockholders' equity has no existence apart from the assets and liabilities of the enterprise—stockholders' equity equals net assets. Stockholders' equity is not a claim to specific assets but a claim against a portion of the total assets. Its amount is not specified or fixed; it depends on the enterprise's profitability. Stockholders' equity grows if the enterprise is profitable, and it shrinks or may disappear entirely if the enterprise is unprofitable.

A final comment: Many different meanings are attached to the word **capital**, because the word often is construed differently by various user groups. **In corporation finance**, for example, capital commonly represents the total assets of the enterprise. **In law**, capital is considered that portion of stockholders' equity that is required by statute to be retained in the business for the protection of creditors. Generally, legal capital **(stated capital)** is the par value of all capital stock issued, but when shares without par value are issued, it may be:

❶ Total consideration paid in for the shares.

❷ A minimum amount stated in the applicable state incorporation law.

❸ An arbitrary amount established by the board of directors at its discretion.

Accountants for the most part define capital more narrowly than total assets but more broadly than legal capital. **When accountants refer to capital they mean stockholders' equity or owners' equity.**

Issuance of Stock

In issuing stock, the following procedures are followed: First, the stock must be authorized by the state, generally in a certificate of incorporation or charter; next, shares are offered for sale and contracts to sell stock are entered into; then, amounts to be received for the stock are collected and the shares issued.

> **OBJECTIVE ❹**
> Explain the accounting procedures for issuing shares of stock.

The accounting problems involved in the issuance of stock are discussed under the following topics:

❶ Accounting for par value stock.

❷ Accounting for no-par stock.

❸ Accounting for stock sold on a subscription basis.

❹ Accounting for stock issued in combination with other securities (lump sum sales).

❺ Accounting for stock issued in noncash transactions.

❻ Accounting for assessments on stock.

❼ Accounting for costs of issuing stock.

Par Value Stock

As indicated earlier, the par value of a stock has no relationship to its fair market value. At present, the par value associated with most capital stock issuances is very low ($1,

---

[5]"Elements of Financial Statements," *Statement of Financial Accounting Concepts No. 6* (Stamford, Conn.: FASB, 1985), par. 60.

$5, $10), which contrasts dramatically with the situation in the early 1900s when practically all stock issued had a par value of $100. The reason for this change is to permit the original sale of stock at low amounts per share and to avoid the contingent liability associated with stock sold below par. Stock with a low par value is rarely, if ever, sold below par value. In addition, in states that charge a transfer tax based on the par value of the stock, a low par value may result in lower taxes.

To show the required information for issuance of par value stock, accounts must be kept for each class of stock as follows:

① *Preferred Stock or Common Stock.* Reflects the par value of the corporation's issued shares. These accounts are credited when the shares are originally issued. No additional entries are made in these accounts unless additional shares are issued or shares are retired.

② *Paid-in Capital in Excess of Par or Additional Paid-in Capital.* Indicates any excess over par value paid in by stockholders in return for the shares issued to them. Once paid in, the excess over par becomes a part of the corporation's additional paid-in capital, and the individual stockholder has no greater claim on the excess paid in than all other holders of the same class of shares.

③ *Discount on Stock.* Indicates that the stock has been issued at less than par. The original purchaser or the current holder of shares issued below par may be called on to pay in the amount of the discount if necessary to prevent creditors from sustaining loss upon liquidation of the corporation.

To illustrate how these accounts are used, assume that Colonial Corporation sold, for $1,100, one hundred shares of stock with a par value of $5 per share. The entry to record the issuance is:

Cash	1,100	
Common Stock		500
Paid-in Capital in Excess of Par (Premium on Common Stock)		600

If the stock had been issued in return for $300, the entry would have been recorded as follows:

Cash	300	
Paid-in Capital in Excess of Par (Discount on Common Stock)	200	
Common Stock		500

No entry is generally made in the general ledger accounts at the time the corporation receives its stock authorization from the state of incorporation.

No-Par Stock

Many states permit the issuance of capital stock without par value. No-par stock is shares issued with no per-share amount printed on the stock certificate. The reasons for issuance of no-par stock are twofold. First, issuance of no-par stock **avoids the contingent liability** that might occur if par value stock were issued at a discount. Second, some confusion exists over the relationship (or rather the absence of a relationship) between the par value and fair market value. If shares have no par value, **the questionable treatment of using par value as a basis for fair value never arises**. This circumstance is particularly advantageous whenever stock is issued for property items such as tangible or intangible fixed assets. The major disadvantages of no-par stock are that some states levy a high tax on these issues, and the total may be considered legal capital.

No-par shares, like par value shares, are sold for what they will bring, but unlike par value shares, they are issued without a premium or a discount. Therefore, no contingent liability accrues to the stockholders. The exact amount received represents the credit to common or preferred stock. For example, Video Electronics Corporation is organized with authorized common stock of 10,000 shares without par value. No entry, other than a memorandum entry, need be made for the authorization inasmuch as no amount is involved. If 500 shares are then issued for cash at $10 per share, the entry should be:

Cash	5,000	
Common Stock—No-Par Value		5,000

If another 500 shares are issued for $11 per share, the entry should be:

Cash	5,500	
Common Stock—No-Par Value		5,500

True no-par stock should be carried in the accounts at issue price without any complications due to additional paid-in capital or discount. But some states permit the issuance of no-par stock and then proceed either to require or, in some cases, to permit such stock to have a stated value; that is, a minimum value below which it cannot be issued. Thus, instead of becoming no-par stock it becomes, in effect, stock with a very low par value, open to all the criticism and abuses that first encouraged the development of no-par stock.[6]

If no-par stock is required to have a minimum issue price of $5 per share and no provision is made as to how amounts in excess of $5 per share are to be handled, the board of directors usually declares all such amounts to be additional paid-in capital, which in many states is fully or partially available for dividends. Thus, no-par value stock with either a minimum stated value or a stated value assigned by the board of directors permits a new corporation to commence its operations with additional paid-in capital that may be in excess of its stated capital. For example, if 1,000 of the shares with a $5 stated value were issued at $15 per share for cash, the entry could be either

Cash	15,000	
Common Stock		15,000

or

Cash	15,000	
Common Stock		5,000
Paid-in Capital in Excess of Stated Value		10,000

In most instances the obvious advantages to the corporation of setting up an initial Additional Paid-in Capital account will influence the board of directors to require the latter entry. Whether for this or for other reasons, the prevailing tendency is to account for no-par stock with stated value as if it were par value stock with par equal to the stated value.

Stock Sold on a Subscription Basis

The preceding discussion assumed that the stock was sold for cash, but stock may also be sold on a subscription basis. Sale of subscribed stock generally occurs when new, small companies "go public" or when corporations offer stock to employees to obtain employee participation in the ownership of the business. When stock is sold on a subscription basis, the full price of the stock is not received initially. Normally only a partial payment is made, and the stock is not issued until the full subscription price is received.

Accounting for Subscribed Stock. Two new accounts are used when stock is sold on a subscription basis. The first, **Common or Preferred Stock Subscribed**, indicates the corporation's obligation to issue shares of its stock upon payment of final subscription balances by those who have subscribed for stock. This account thus signifies a commitment against the unissued capital stock. Once the subscription price is fully paid, the Common or Preferred Stock Subscribed account is debited and the Common or Preferred Stock account is credited. Common or Preferred Stock Subscribed should be presented in the stockholders' equity section below Common or Preferred Stock.

---

[6]*Accounting Trends and Techniques—1999* indicates that its 600 surveyed companies reported 654 issues of outstanding common stock, 571 par value issues, and 59 no-par issues; 13 of the no-par issues were shown at their stated (assigned) values.

UNDERLYING CONCEPTS

Subscriptions Receivable would appear to fulfill all the requirements for an *asset*. As a result of a past transaction the company expects to receive a future economic benefit. An Allowance for Doubtful Accounts would disclose the collection risk in the same manner as for Accounts Receivable.

The second account, **Subscriptions Receivable**, indicates the amount yet to be collected before subscribed stock will be issued. Controversy exists concerning the presentation of Subscriptions Receivable on the balance sheet. Some argue that Subscriptions Receivable should be reported in the current assets section (assuming, of course, that payment on the receivable will be received within the operating cycle or one year, whichever is longer). They note that it is similar to trade accounts receivable. Trade accounts receivable grow out of sales transactions in the ordinary course of business; subscriptions receivable relate to the issuance of a concern's own stock and in a sense represent funds (capital contributions) not yet paid the corporation.

Others argue that Subscriptions Receivable should be reported as **a deduction from stockholders' equity** (similar to treasury stock recorded at cost). Their reasoning is that in most states no deficiency judgment can be sought for failure of a subscriber to pay the unpaid balance of a subscription receivable. Given the risk of collectibility, the SEC requires companies to use the **contra equity approach.**[7] For example, in the prospectus of **Morlan International, Inc.**, its subscriptions receivable was reported as a contra equity in the following manner (common stock subscribed is included in Common Stock rather than shown separately):

ILLUSTRATION 15-1
Treatment of Subscriptions Receivable

MORLAN INTERNATIONAL, INC.

Stockholders' equity	
Common stock, par value $.01 a share:	
Authorized 9,000,000 shares	
Issued 3,547,638 shares	$ 35,500
Additional capital	2,146,700
Retained earnings	3,878,600
Less: Subscriptions receivable	(148,500)
Total stockholders' equity	$5,912,300

Practice now generally follows the contra equity approach. Therefore, unless stated otherwise, this practice should be followed in working homework problems.

Most states consider common or preferred stock subscribed to be similar to outstanding common or preferred stock, which means that **individuals who have signed a valid subscription contract normally have the same rights and privileges as a stockholder who holds outstanding shares of stock.**

The journal entries for handling stock sold on a subscription basis are illustrated by the following example. Lubradite Corp. offers stock on a subscription basis to selected individuals, giving them the right to purchase 10 shares of stock (par value $5) at a price of $20 per share. Fifty individuals accept the company's offer and agree to pay 50% down and to pay the remaining 50% at the end of 6 months.

At date of issuance

Subscriptions Receivable (10 × $20 × 50)	10,000	
Common Stock Subscribed (10 × $5 × 50)		2,500
Paid-in Capital in Excess of Par		7,500
(To record receipt of subscriptions for 500 shares)		
Cash	5,000	
Subscriptions Receivable		5,000
(To record receipt of first installment representing		
50% of total due on subscribed stock)		

---

[7]The SEC has specified that subscriptions receivable may be shown as an asset only if collected prior to the publication of the financial statements.

When the final payment is received and the stock is issued, the entries are:

Six months later

Cash	5,000	
Subscriptions Receivable		5,000
(To record receipt of final installment on		
subscribed stock)		
Common Stock Subscribed	2,500	
Common Stock		2,500
(To record issuance of 500 shares upon receipt of		
final installment from subscribers)		

Defaulted Subscription Accounts. Sometimes a subscriber is unable to pay all installments and defaults on the agreement. The question is what to do with the balance of the subscription account as well as the amount already paid in. The answer is a function of applicable state law. Some states permit the corporation to retain any amounts paid in on defaulted subscription accounts; other states require that any amount realized on the resale in excess of the amount due from the original subscriber be returned.

Stock Issued with Other Securities (Lump Sum Sales)

Generally, corporations sell classes of stock separately from one another so that the proceeds relative to each class, and ordinarily even relative to each lot, are known. Occasionally, two or more classes of securities are issued for a single payment or lump sum. It is not uncommon, for example, for more than one type or class of security to be issued in the acquisition of another company. The accounting problem in such **lump sum sales** is the allocation of the proceeds among the several classes of securities. The two methods of allocation available are (1) the proportional method and (2) the incremental method.

Proportional Method. If the fair market value or other sound basis for determining relative value is available for each class of security, **the lump sum received is allocated among the classes of securities on a proportional basis**, that is, the ratio that each is to the total. For instance, if 1,000 shares of $10 stated value common stock having a market value of $20 a share and 1,000 shares of $10 par value preferred stock having a market value of $12 a share are issued for a lump sum of $30,000, the allocation of the $30,000 to the two classes would be as shown below.

ILLUSTRATION 15-2
Allocation in Lump Sum
Securities Issuance—
Proportional Method

Fair market value of common (1,000 × $20) = $20,000
Fair market value of preferred (1,000 × $12) = 12,000
Aggregate fair market value $32,000

Allocated to common: $\dfrac{\$20,000}{\$32,000} \times \$30,000 = \$18,750$

Allocated to preferred: $\dfrac{\$12,000}{\$32,000} \times \$30,000 = 11,250$

Total allocation $30,000

Incremental Method. In instances where the fair market value of all classes of securities is not determinable, the incremental method may be used. The market value of the securities is used as a basis for those classes that are known and the remainder of the lump sum is allocated to the class for which the market value is not known. For instance, if 1,000 shares of $10 stated value common stock having a market value of $20 and 1,000 shares of $10 par value preferred stock having no established market value are issued for a lump sum of $30,000, the allocation of the $30,000 to the two classes would be as follows:

ILLUSTRATION 15-3
Allocation in Lump Sum
Securities Issuance—
Incremental Method

Lump sum receipt	$30,000
Allocated to common (1,000 × $20)	20,000
Balance allocated to preferred	$10,000

If no fair market value is determinable for any of the classes of stock involved in a lump sum exchange, the allocation may have to be arbitrary. An expert's appraisal may be used. Or, if it is known that one or more of the classes of securities issued will have a determinable market value in the near future, the arbitrary basis may be used with the intent to make an adjustment when the future market value is established.

Stock Issued in Noncash Transactions

Accounting for the issuance of shares of stock for property or services involves an issue of valuation. **The general rule is: Stock issued for services or property other than cash should be recorded at either the fair market value of the stock issued or the fair market value of the noncash consideration received, whichever is more clearly determinable.**

If both are readily determinable and the transaction is the result of an arm's-length exchange, there will probably be little difference in their fair market values. In such cases it should not matter which value is regarded as the basis for valuing the exchange.

If the fair market value of the stock being issued and the property or services being received are not readily determinable, the value to be assigned is generally established by the board of directors or management at an amount that they consider fair and that is not controverted by available evidence. Independent appraisals usually serve as dependable bases. The use of the book, par, or stated values as a basis of valuation for these transactions should be avoided.

Unissued stock or treasury stock (issued shares that have been reacquired but not retired) may be exchanged for the property or services. If treasury shares are used, their cost should not be regarded as the decisive factor in establishing the fair market value of the property or services. Instead, the fair market value of the treasury stock, if known, should be used to value the property or services. If the fair market value of the treasury stock is not known, the fair market value of the property or services should be used, if determinable.

The following series of transactions illustrates the procedure for recording the issuance of 10,000 shares of $10 par value common stock for a patent, in various circumstances:

1 The fair market value of the patent is not readily determinable but the fair market value of the stock is known to be $140,000.

Patent	140,000	
Common Stock (10,000 shares × $10 per share)		100,000
Paid-in Capital in Excess of Par		40,000

2 The fair market value of the stock is not readily determinable, but the fair market value of the patent is determined to be $150,000.

Patent	150,000	
Common Stock (10,000 shares × $10 per share)		100,000
Paid-in Capital in Excess of Par		50,000

3 Neither the fair market value of the stock nor the fair market value of the patent is readily determinable. An independent consultant values the patent at $125,000, and the board of directors agrees with that valuation.

Patent	125,000	
Common Stock (10,000 shares × $10 share)		100,000
Paid-in Capital in Excess of Par		25,000

In corporate law, the board of directors is granted the power to set the value of noncash transactions. This power has been abused. The issuance of stock for property or services has resulted in cases of overstated corporate capital through intentional overvaluation of the property or services received. The overvaluation of the stockholders' equity resulting from inflated asset values creates what is referred to as **watered stock**. The "water" can be eliminated from the corporate structure by simply writing down the overvalued assets.

If as a result of the issuance of stock for property or services the recorded assets are undervalued, **secret reserves** are created. An understated corporate structure or secret reserve may also be achieved by other methods: excessive depreciation or amortization charges, expensing capital expenditures, excessive write-downs of inventories or receivables, or any other understatement of assets or overstatement of liabilities. An example of a liability overstatement is an excessive provision for estimated product warranties that ultimately results in an understatement of owners' equity, thereby creating a secret reserve.

Assessments on Stock

The laws of some states provide that a corporation may assess stockholders an additional amount above their original contribution. Although this situation occurs infrequently, when stockholders are assessed, they must either pay or possibly forfeit their existing shares. Upon receiving the assessments from the stockholders, the corporation should determine whether the original stock was sold at a discount or a premium. If the stock was originally sold at a discount, the additional proceeds are credited to the discount account. If the stock was originally issued at a premium, the account Additional Paid-in Capital Arising from Assessments is credited.

Costs of Issuing Stock

Direct costs incurred to sell stock, such as underwriting costs, accounting and legal fees, printing costs, and taxes, should be reported as a reduction of the amounts paid in. Issue costs are therefore debited to Additional Paid-in Capital because they are unrelated to corporate operations. In effect, **issue costs are a cost of financing** and should reduce the proceeds received from the sale of the stock.

Management salaries and other indirect costs related to the stock issue should be expensed as incurred because it is difficult to establish a relationship between these costs and the proceeds received upon sale. In addition, corporations annually incur costs for maintaining the stockholders' records and handling ownership transfers. These recurring costs, primarily registrar and transfer agents' fees, are normally charged to expense in the period in which incurred.

Reacquisition of Shares

It is not unusual for companies to buy back their own shares. In fact, share buybacks now exceed dividends as a form of distribution to stockholders.[8] **Merrill Lynch & Co.** estimated that in a recent year more than 1,400 corporations announced buyback programs totaling over $80 billion and 2.4 billion shares. Two of the biggest stock buyback programs were **General Motors'** purchase of 20% (64 million shares) of its stock for $4.8 billion and **Santa Fe Southern Pacific's** buyback of 38% (60 million shares) of its stock for $3.4 billion in the mid-1990s. Data on recent corporate buybacks indicate that companies are continuing to spend millions of dollars to repurchase shares, as shown in the following table:

---

[8]At the beginning of the 1990s the situation was just the opposite; that is, share buybacks were less than half the level of dividends. Companies are extremely reluctant to reduce or eliminate their dividends, because they believe that this action would be viewed negatively by the market. On the other hand, many companies are no longer raising their dividends per share at the same percentage rate as increases in earnings per share, thus effectively reducing the dividend payout over time.

ILLUSTRATION 15-4
Recent Corporate
Buybacks

Company	Year	Amount of Buyback (millions)	Percent of Shares
BankAmerica	1997	$2,025	4.6%
Coca-Cola	1998	445	3.5%
Eli Lilly & Co.	1998	2,000	2.6%
Gillette	1998	1,119	1.9%
Hewlett-Packard	1998	1,292	2.0%
Torchmark	1998	126	2.6%
XL Capital LTD	1998	255	2.5%

The reasons corporations purchase their outstanding stock are varied. Some major reasons are:

OBJECTIVE 5
Identify the major reasons for purchasing treasury stock.

❶ *To provide tax efficient distributions of excess cash to shareholders.* Capital gain rates on sales of stock to the company by the stockholders are approximately half of what ordinary tax rates are. As a result, most stockholders will pay less tax if they receive cash in a buyback versus receiving a cash dividend.

❷ *To increase earnings per share and return on equity.* By reducing shares outstanding and by reducing stockholders' equity, certain performance ratios often are enhanced.

❸ *To provide stock for employee stock compensation contracts or to meet potential merger needs.* Honeywell Inc. reported that part of its purchase of one million common shares was to be used for employee stock option contracts. Other companies acquire shares to have them available for business acquisitions.

❹ *To thwart takeover attempts or to reduce the number of stockholders.* By reducing the number of shares held by the public, existing owners and managements can keep "outsiders" from gaining control or significant influence. When Ted Turner attempted to acquire CBS, CBS started a substantial buyback of its stock. Stock purchases may also be used to eliminate dissident stockholders.

❺ *To make a market in the stock.* As one company executive noted, "Our company is trying to establish a floor for the stock." By purchasing stock in the marketplace, a demand is created which may stabilize the stock price or, in fact, increase it.

Some publicly held corporations have chosen to "go private," that is, to eliminate public (outside) ownership entirely by purchasing all of their outstanding stock. Such a procedure is often accomplished through a leveraged buyout (LBO), in which management or another employee group purchases the stock of the company and finances the purchase by using the assets of the company as collateral.

Once shares are reacquired, they may either be retired or held in the treasury for reissue. If not retired, such shares are referred to as **treasury shares** or treasury stock. Technically treasury stock is a corporation's own stock that has been reacquired after having been issued and fully paid.

Treasury stock is not an asset. When treasury stock is purchased, a reduction occurs in both assets and stockholders' equity. It is inappropriate to imply that a corporation can own a part of itself. Treasury stock may be sold to obtain funds, but that possibility does not make treasury stock a balance sheet asset. When a corporation buys back some of its own outstanding stock, it has reduced its capitalization but has not acquired an asset. The possession of treasury stock does not give the corporation the right to vote, to exercise preemptive rights as a stockholder, to receive cash dividends,

UNDERLYING CONCEPTS

As indicated in Chapter 2, an asset should have probable future economic benefits. Treasury stock simply reduces common stock outstanding.

or to receive assets upon corporate liquidation. **Treasury stock is essentially the same as unissued capital stock,** and no one advocates classifying unissued capital stock as an asset in the balance sheet.[9]

Purchase of Treasury Stock

Two general methods of handling treasury stock in the accounts are the cost method and the par value method. Both methods are generally acceptable. The cost method enjoys more widespread use[10] and results in debiting the Treasury Stock account for the reacquisition cost and in reporting this account as a deduction from the total paid-in capital **and** retained earnings on the balance sheet. The par or stated value method records all transactions in treasury shares at their par value and reports the treasury stock as a deduction from capital stock only. No matter which method is used, the cost of the treasury shares acquired is considered a restriction on retained earnings in most states. Because the par or stated value method is little used, the accounting for this approach is discussed in the appendix to this chapter.

The cost method is generally used in accounting for treasury stock. This method derives its name from the fact that the Treasury Stock account is maintained at the cost of the shares purchased.[11] Under the cost method, the Treasury Stock account is debited for the cost of the shares acquired and upon reissuance of the shares is credited for this same cost. The price received for the stock when it was originally issued does not affect the entries to record the acquisition and reissuance of the treasury stock.

To illustrate, assume that Ho Company has issued 100,000 shares of $1 par value common stock at a price of $10 per share. In addition, it has retained earnings of $300,000. The stockholders' equity section on December 31, 2001, before purchase of treasury stock is as follows:

<table>
<tr><td colspan="2">Stockholders' equity</td></tr>
<tr><td colspan="2">Paid-in capital</td></tr>
<tr><td>Common stock, $1 par value, 100,000 shares issued and outstanding</td><td>$ 100,000</td></tr>
<tr><td>Additional paid-in capital</td><td>900,000</td></tr>
<tr><td>Total paid-in capital</td><td>1,000,000</td></tr>
<tr><td>Retained earnings</td><td>300,000</td></tr>
<tr><td>Total stockholders' equity</td><td>$1,300,000</td></tr>
</table>

ILLUSTRATION 15-5
Stockholders' Equity with No Treasury Stock

On January 20, 2002, Ho Company acquires 10,000 shares of its stock at $11 per share. The entry to record the reacquisition is:

January 20, 2002

Treasury Stock	110,000	
Cash		110,000

---

[9]When treasury stock is held to meet a specific short-term obligation, such as treasury shares held for issuance under a deferred compensation plan, treasury stock can be reported as an asset in the balance sheet. For example, **General Motors Corporation** at one time reported treasury stock as a separate asset item entitled "Common Stocks Held for the Incentive Program." The justification for classifying these shares as assets is that they will be used to liquidate a specific liability that appears on the balance sheet. *Accounting Trends and Techniques—1999* reported that out of 600 companies surveyed, 392 disclosed treasury stock but none classified it as an asset.

[10]*Accounting Trends and Techniques—1999* indicates that of its selected list of 600 companies, 367 carried common stock in treasury at cost and only 23 at par or stated value; 2 companies carried preferred stock in treasury at cost and 1 at par or stated value.

[11]If numerous acquisitions of blocks of treasury shares are made at different prices, inventory costing methods—such as specific identification, average, or FIFO—may be used to identify the cost at date of reissuance.

Note that Treasury Stock is debited for the cost of the shares purchased. The original paid-in capital account, Common Stock, is not affected because the number of issued shares does not change. The same is true for the additional paid-in capital account. Treasury stock is deducted from total paid-in capital and retained earnings in the stockholders' equity section.

The stockholders' equity section for Ho Company after purchase of the treasury stock is as follows:

ILLUSTRATION 15-6
Stockholders' Equity with
Treasury Stock

Stockholders' equity	
Paid-in capital	
Common stock, $1 par value, 100,000 shares issued and 90,000 outstanding	$ 100,000
Additional paid-in capital	900,000
Total paid-in capital	1,000,000
Retained earnings (see note)	300,000
Total paid-in capital and retained earnings	1,300,000
Less: Cost of treasury stock (10,000 shares)	110,000
Total stockholders' equity	$1,190,000

The cost of the treasury stock is subtracted from the total of common stock, additional paid-in capital, and retained earnings and therefore reduces stockholders' equity. Many states require a corporation to restrict retained earnings for the cost of treasury stock purchased. The restriction serves to keep intact the corporation's legal capital that is temporarily being held as treasury stock. When treasury stock is sold, the restriction is lifted.

Both the number of shares issued (100,000) and the number in the treasury (10,000) are disclosed. The difference is the number of shares of stock outstanding (90,000). The term **outstanding stock** means the number of shares of issued stock that are being held by stockholders.

Sale of Treasury Stock

Treasury stock is usually sold or retired. When treasury shares are sold, the accounting for the sale depends on the price. If the selling price of the treasury stock is equal to cost, the sale of the shares is recorded by a debit to Cash and a credit to Treasury Stock. In cases where the selling price of the treasury stock is not equal to cost, then accounting for treasury stock sold **above cost** differs from the accounting for treasury stock sold **below cost**. However, the sale of treasury stock either above or below cost increases both total assets and stockholders' equity.

Sale of Treasury Stock above Cost. When the selling price of shares of treasury stock is greater than cost, the difference is credited to Paid-in Capital from Treasury Stock. To illustrate, assume that 1,000 shares of treasury stock of Ho Company previously acquired at $11 per share are sold at $15 per share on March 10. The entry is as follows:

March 10, 2002

Cash	15,000	
Treasury Stock		11,000
Paid-in Capital from Treasury Stock		4,000

There are two reasons why the $4,000 credit in the entry would not be made to Gain on Sale of Treasury Stock: (1) Gains on sales occur when **assets** are sold, and treasury stock is not an asset. (2) A corporation does not realize a gain or suffer a loss from stock transactions with its own stockholders. Thus, paid-in capital arising from the sale of treasury stock should not be included in the measurement of net income. Paid-in capital from treasury stock is listed separately on the balance sheet as a part of paid-in capital.

Sale of Treasury Stock below Cost. When treasury stock is sold below its cost, the excess of the cost over selling price is usually debited to Paid-in Capital from Treasury Stock. Thus, if Ho Company sells an additional 1,000 shares of treasury stock on March 21 at $8 per share, the entry is as follows:

March 21, 2002

Cash	8,000	
Paid-in Capital from Treasury Stock	3,000	
Treasury Stock		11,000

Observe from the two sale entries (sale above cost and sale below cost) that (1) Treasury Stock is credited at cost in each entry, (2) Paid-in Capital from Treasury Stock is used for the difference between the cost and the resale price of the shares, and (3) the original paid-in capital account, Common Stock, is not affected.

When the credit balance in Paid-in Capital from Treasury Stock is eliminated, any additional excess of cost over selling price is debited to Retained Earnings. To illustrate, assume that Ho Company sells an additional 1,000 shares at $8 per share on April 10. The balance in the Paid-in Capital from Treasury Stock account is:

Paid-in Capital from Treasury Stock				
Mar. 21	3,000	Mar. 10	4,000
		Balance	1,000

ILLUSTRATION 15-7
Treasury Stock
Transactions in Paid-in
Capital Account

In this case, $1,000 of the excess is debited to Paid-in Capital from Treasury Stock, and the remainder is debited to Retained Earnings. The entry is:

April 10, 2002

Cash	8,000	
Paid-in Capital from Treasury Stock	1,000	
Retained Earnings	2,000	
Treasury Stock		11,000

Retiring Treasury Stock

The board of directors may approve the retirement of treasury shares. This decision results in cancellation of the treasury stock and a reduction in the number of shares of issued stock. Retired treasury shares have the status of authorized and unissued shares. The accounting effects are similar to the sale of treasury stock except that debits are made to the **paid-in capital accounts applicable to the retired shares** instead of to cash. For example, if the shares are originally sold at par, Common Stock is debited for the par value per share. If the shares are originally sold at $3 above par value, a debit to Paid-in Capital in Excess of Par Value for $3 per share is also required. To illustrate, assume that Ho Company retires 5,000 shares of its treasury stock. The entry to record this retirement is as follows:

Common Stock	5,000	
Paid-in Capital in Excess of Par	45,000	
Retained Earnings	5,000	
Treasury Stock		55,000

If the cost of treasury stock is less than the original issuance price, the difference should be credited to Paid-in Capital from Retirement of Treasury Stock. To illustrate, assume that Ho Company purchased treasury stock at $6 per share instead of $11 per share. Assuming that Ho Company retires 5,000 shares of its treasury stock, the entry to record the retirement is as follows:

Common Stock	5,000	
Paid-in Capital in Excess of Par	45,000	
Treasury Stock		30,000
Paid-in Capital from Retirement of Treasury Stock		20,000

There are two types of treasury stock retirements—actual and constructive. Cancellation of treasury shares through formal application to the secretary of state's office is an **actual retirement**. **Constructive retirement** effects the retirement on the financial statements by board authorization without formal cancellation through the secretary of state. The accounting is the same for actual and constructive retirements.

Other Methods of Accounting for Treasury Stock

INTERNATIONAL INSIGHT

Some countries which allow treasury stock purchases show such stock as an asset.

In some states treasury stock must be reported differently. For example, the applicable state law may require a permanent reduction of retained earnings, in which case the cost of the shares purchased in excess of the stated or par value would be charged to retained earnings. Many companies use the balance in Additional Paid-in Capital, regardless of its source, to absorb all charges resulting from treasury stock transactions or use a pro-rata allocation based on original issue price.[12]

Care should always be exercised in recording treasury stock transactions because of the considerable variety of possible requirements. The advice of an attorney is frequently desirable in this connection.

PREFERRED STOCK

OBJECTIVE 7
Describe the major features of preferred stock.

Preferred stock is a special class of shares that is designated "preferred" because it possesses certain preferences or features not possessed by the common stock.[13] The following features are those most often associated with preferred stock issues:

1. Preference as to dividends.
2. Preference as to assets in the event of liquidation.
3. Convertible into common stock.
4. Callable at the option of the corporation.
5. Nonvoting.

The features that distinguish preferred from common stock may be of a more restrictive and negative nature than preferences; for example, the preferred stock may be nonvoting, noncumulative, and nonparticipating.

Preferred stock is usually issued with a par value, and the dividend preference is expressed as a **percentage of the par value**. Thus, holders of 8% preferred stock with a $100 par value are entitled to an annual dividend of $8 per share. This stock is commonly referred to as 8% preferred stock. In the case of no-par preferred stock, a dividend preference is expressed as a **specific dollar amount** per share, for example, $7 per share. This stock is commonly referred to as $7 preferred stock. A preference as to dividends is not assurance that dividends will be paid; it is merely assurance that the stated dividend rate or amount applicable to the preferred stock must be paid before any dividends can be paid on the common stock.

Features of Preferred Stock

A corporation may attach whatever preferences or restrictions in whatever combination it desires to a preferred stock issue so long as it does not specifically violate its state incorporation law, and it may issue more than one class of preferred stock. The most common features attributed to preferred stock are discussed below.

---

[12]For example, the excess of cost over the reissuance price might be charged to Paid-in Capital in Excess of Par for a pro rata amount per share of any premium on the original sale of the stock, and any remaining excess is charged to Paid-in Capital from Treasury Stock and then to Retained Earnings.

[13]*Accounting Trends and Techniques—1999* reports that of its 600 surveyed companies, 99 had preferred stock outstanding; 84 had one class of preferred, and 15 had two classes.

❶ *Cumulative Preferred Stock.* Dividends not paid in any year must be made up in a later year before any profits can be distributed to common stockholders. If the directors fail to declare a dividend at the normal date for dividend action, the dividend is said to have been "passed." Any passed dividend on cumulative preferred stock constitutes a **dividend in arrears**. Because no liability exists until the board of directors declares a dividend, a dividend in arrears is not recorded as a liability but is disclosed in a note to the financial statements. (At common law, if the corporate charter is silent about the cumulative feature, the preferred stock is considered to be cumulative.) Noncumulative preferred stock is seldom issued because a passed dividend is lost forever to the preferred stockholder and so this stock issue would be less marketable.

❷ *Participating Preferred Stock.* Holders of participating preferred stock share ratably with the common stockholders in any profit distributions beyond the prescribed rate. That is 5% preferred stock, if fully participating, will receive not only its 5% return, but also dividends at the same rates as those paid to common stockholders if amounts in excess of 5% of par or stated value are paid to common stockholders. Also, participating preferred stock may not always be fully participating as described, but partially participating. For example, provision may be made that 5% preferred stock will be participating up to a maximum total rate of 10%, after which it ceases to participate in additional profit distributions; or 5% preferred stock may participate only in additional profit distributions that are in excess of a 9% dividend rate on the common stock. Although participating preferreds are not used extensively (unlike the cumulative provision), examples of companies that have used participating preferreds are **LTV Corporation**, **Southern California Edison**, and **Allied Products Corporation**.

❸ *Convertible Preferred Stock.* The stockholders may at their option exchange preferred shares for common stock at a predetermined ratio. The convertible preferred stockholder not only enjoys a preferred claim on dividends but also has the option of converting into a common stockholder with unlimited participation in earnings.

❹ *Callable Preferred Stock.* The issuing corporation can call or redeem at its option the outstanding preferred shares at specified future dates and at stipulated prices. Many preferred issues are callable. The call or redemption price is ordinarily set slightly above the original issuance price and is commonly stated in terms related to the par value. The callable feature permits the corporation to use the capital obtained through the issuance of such stock until the need has passed or it is no longer advantageous. The existence of a call price or prices tends to set a ceiling on the market value of the preferred shares unless they are convertible into common stock. When a preferred stock is called for redemption, any dividends in arrears must be paid.

Preferred stock is often issued instead of debt because a company's debt-to-equity ratio has become too high. In other instances, issuances are made through private placements with other corporations at a lower than market dividend rate because the acquiring corporation receives dividends that are largely tax free (owing to the IRS's 70% or 80% dividends received deduction).

Reporting of Preferred Stock

Preferred stock is generally reported at par value as the first item in the stockholders' equity section of a company's balance sheet. Any excess over par value is reported as part of additional paid-in capital. Dividends on preferred stock are considered a distribution of income and not an expense of the corporation. Companies must disclose the pertinent rights of the preferred stock outstanding.[14] For example, dividend and liquidation preferences, participation rights, call prices and dates, conversion or exercise prices and pertinent dates, sinking fund requirements, unusual voting rights, and significant terms of contracts to issue additional shares must be disclosed. The disclosure related to liquidation preferences should be made in the equity section of the balance sheet rather than in the notes to the financial statements to emphasize the possible effect of this restriction on future cash flows. Presented below is the stockholders' equity section of **Sequa Corporation** and related disclosures:

ILLUSTRATION 15-8
Stockholders' Equity
Section

SEQUA CORPORATION

Stockholders' equity

Preferred stock—$1 par value, 1,825,000 shares authorized; 797,000 shares of $5 cumulative convertible stock issued at December 31, 1998 (involuntary liquidation value—$17,181 at December 31, 1998)	$ 797,000
Class A common stock—no par value, 25,000,000 shares authorized; 7,273,000 shares issued at December 31, 1998	7,273,000
Class B common stock—no par value, 5,000,000 shares authorized; 3,727,000 shares issued at December 31, 1998	3,727,000
Capital in excess of par value	288,379,000
Accumulated other comprehensive loss	(1,016,000)
Retained earnings	444,669,000
	743,829,000
Less: Cost of treasury stock	78,377,000
Total shareholders' equity	$665,452,000

Note: Each share of $5.00 cumulative convertible preferred stock is convertible into 1.322 shares of Class A common stock. The preferred stock is redeemable, at the option of Sequa, at $100 per share.

OBJECTIVE 8
Distinguish between debt and preferred stock.

Preferred stock generally has no maturity date, and therefore no legal obligation exists to pay the preferred stockholder. As a result, preferred stock is classified as part of stockholders' equity. Recently more and more issuances of preferred stock have features that make the security more like debt (legal obligation to pay) than an equity instrument. For example, redeemable preferred stock is preferred stock that has a mandatory redemption period or a redemption feature that is outside the control of the issuer.[15]

---

[14]"Disclosure of Information about Capital Structure," *Statement of Financial Accounting Standards No. 129* (Norwalk, Conn.: FASB, 1997).

[15]It includes preferred stock that (1) has a fixed or determinable redemption date; (2) is redeemable at the option of the holder; or (3) has conditions for redemption that are not solely within the control of the issuer. Nonredeemable preferred stock is not redeemable or is redeemable solely at the option of the issuer. *Securities and Exchange Commission Release 33-6097* (Washington, D.C.: July 27, 1979). Note that the FASB has issued a discussion memorandum "Distinguishing between Liability and Equity Instruments and Accounting for Instruments with Characteristics of Both" that examines the conditions under which preferred stock would be reported as debt rather than as equity.

In these cases, the company has given to the holder a right to receive future cash flows of the company, and many believe this obligation should be reported as debt rather than equity. The FASB response to date has been to require disclosure in the notes of any redemption features of a preferred stock issued and a schedule of redemptions required within the next five years.

Because of the increasing use of these types of securities, the SEC prohibits companies from combining preferred stock with common stock in financial statements. Amounts must be presented separately for redeemable preferred stock,[16] nonredeemable preferred stock, and common stock. The amounts applicable to these three categories cannot be totaled or combined for SEC reporting purposes. The general heading, **stockholders' equity, should not include redeemable preferred stock.**

To illustrate, assume that Perez Inc. has redeemable preferred stock in addition to common stock, additional paid-in capital, and retained earnings.[17] Perez Inc. presents this information as follows (all amounts assumed):

> **INTERNATIONAL INSIGHT**
>
> In Switzerland, there are no specific disclosure requirements for shareholders' equity. However, companies typically disclose separate categories of capital on the balance sheet.

PEREZ INC.	
Redeemable preferred stock	$ 63,000,000
Stockholders' equity	
Common stock @ $5 par value	
Authorized 100,000,000 shares, issued 40,000,000 shares	200,000,000
Additional paid-in capital	310,000,000
Total paid-in capital	510,000,000
Retained earnings	400,000,000
Total stockholders' equity	$910,000,000

> **ILLUSTRATION 15-9**
> Balance Sheet Presentation of Redeemable Preferred Stock

Recent studies have noted that the attributes of preferred stock issuances have changed, with new issues more likely to be redeemable, callable, and exchangeable for debt, but less likely to be convertible into common stock. These changes appear to be in direct response to financial reporting standards, tax laws, and other regulations. Redeemable securities (often called trust preferred securities because of the legal form that is used) have been referred to as the Holy Grail of financial instruments. The reason: Trust preferred securities are treated as debt for tax purposes (dividends are therefore deductible for tax purposes) but not for financial reporting or debt-rating purposes. It is no wonder that the use of these types of securities is increasing dramatically.[18]

> **UNDERLYING CONCEPTS**
>
> Even though present GAAP does not dictate (or prohibit) separate classification, application of the FASB's qualitative characteristic of representational faithfulness would require that economic substance rather than the legal form or description of such securities dictate their financial statement classification.

---

[16]*SEC Release No. 33-6097*, op. cit.

[17]The initial carrying amount of redeemable preferred stock should be its fair market value at the date of issuance. If the fair value is less than the mandatory redemption amount, **periodic amortizations** using the interest method should be recorded so that the carrying value will equal the redemption amount on the mandatory redemption date. The initial carrying value should also be **periodically increased by dividends** that are not currently declared or paid but that will be due under the redemption agreement. In practice, the corresponding debit has been made to retained earnings (or to additional paid-in capital in the absence of retained earnings). This accounting treatment also applies when the redeemable preferred stock may be voluntarily redeemed by the issuer before the mandatory redemption date and when such preferred stock may be converted into another class of securities by the holder.

[18]See Ellen Engel, Merle Erickson, and Ed Maydew, "Debt-Equity Hybrid Securities," *Journal of Accounting Research*, Autumn, 1999; and Peter J. Frischmann, Paul D. Kimmel, and Terry D. Warfield, "Innovation in Preferred Stock: Current Developments and Implications for Financial Reporting," *Accounting Horizons*, September 1999.

OBJECTIVE ❾
Identify items reported as additional paid-in capital.

PRESENTATION OF PAID-IN CAPITAL

As indicated throughout this chapter, additional paid-in capital arises from the issuance of capital stock. In addition, a number of other types of transactions affect additional paid-in capital. The basic transactions affecting additional paid-in capital are expressed in account form in Illustration 15-10.

ILLUSTRATION 15-10
Transactions that Affect Paid-in Capital

Additional Paid-in Capital	
1. Discounts on capital stock issued.	1. Premiums on capital stock issued.
2. Sale of treasury stock below cost.	2. Sale of treasury stock above cost.
3. Absorption of a deficit in a recapitalization (quasi-reorganization).*	3. Additional capital arising in recapitalizations or revisions in the capital structure (quasi-reorganizations).*
4. Declaration of a liquidating dividend.*	4. Additional assessments on stockholders.
	5. Conversion of convertible bonds or preferred stock.
	6. Declaration of a "small" (ordinary) stock dividend.*

*Discussed in Chapter 16.

In balance sheet presentation, **only one amount need appear**, Additional Paid-in Capital, to summarize all of these possible transactions.[19] A subsidiary ledger or separate general ledger accounts may be kept of the different sources of additional paid-in capital because certain state laws permit dividend distributions out of designated additional paid-in capital.

No operating gains or losses or extraordinary gains and losses may be debited or credited to Additional Paid-in Capital. The profession has long discouraged bypassing net income and retained earnings through the direct write-off of losses (e.g., write-offs of bond discount, goodwill, or obsolete plant and equipment) to additional paid-in capital accounts or other capital accounts.

KEY TERMS

additional paid-in capital, *776*

callable preferred stock, *787*

common stock, *772*

contra equity approach, *778*

contributed (paid-in) capital, *774*

convertible preferred stock, *787*

cost method, *783*

cumulative preferred stock, *787*

earned capital, *774*

legal capital, *775*

leveraged buyout, *782*

limited liability, *773*

lump sum sales, *779*

no-par stock, *776*

par (stated) value method, *783*

par value stock, *773*

participating preferred stock, *787*

preemptive right, *772*

preferred stock, *772*

redeemable preferred stock, *788*

residual interest, *775*

retained earnings, *774*

stated value, *777*

stockholders' (owners') equity, *775*

subscribed stock, *777*

treasury stock, *782*

SUMMARY OF LEARNING OBJECTIVES

❶ **Discuss the characteristics of the corporate form of organization.** Among the specific characteristics of the corporate form that affect accounting are: (1) influence of state corporate law; (2) use of the capital stock or share system; (3) development of a variety of ownership interests; (4) limited liability of stockholders; (5) formality of profit distribution.

❷ **Identify the rights of stockholders.** In the absence of restrictive provisions, each share of stock carries the following rights: (1) to share proportionately in profits and losses; (2) to share proportionately in management (the right to vote for directors); (3) to share proportionately in corporate assets upon liquidation; (4) to share proportionately in any new issues of stock of the same class (called the preemptive right).

❸ **Explain the key components of stockholders' equity.** Stockholders' or owners' equity is classified into two categories: contributed capital and earned capital. Contributed capital (paid-in capital) is the term used to describe the total amount paid in on capital stock; put another way, it is the amount advanced by stockholders to the

---

[19]*Accounting Trends and Techniques—1999* reports that of its 600 surveyed companies, 527 had additional paid-in capital; 264 used the caption "Additional paid-in capital"; 139 used "Capital in excess of par or stated value" as the caption; 78 used "Paid-in capital" or "Additional capital"; and 46 used other captions.

corporation for use in the business. Contributed capital includes items such as the par value of all outstanding capital stock and premiums less any discounts on issuance. Earned capital is the capital that develops if the business operates profitably; it consists of all undistributed income that remains invested in the enterprise.

4 Explain the accounting procedures for issuing shares of stock. Accounts required to be kept for different types of stock are: (1) *Par value stock:* (a) preferred stock or common stock; (b) paid-in capital in excess of par or additional paid-in capital; and (c) discount on stock. (2) *No-par stock:* common stock or common stock and additional paid-in capital, if stated value used. (3) *Stock sold on a subscription basis:* (a) common or preferred stock subscribed; and (b) subscriptions receivable. *Stock issued in combination with other securities (lump sum sales).* The two methods of allocation available are (a) the proportional method; and (b) the incremental method. *Stock issued in noncash transactions:* When stock is issued for services or property other than cash, the property or services should be recorded at either the fair market value of the stock issued or the fair market value of the noncash consideration received, whichever is more clearly determinable.

5 Identify the major reasons for purchasing treasury stock. The reasons corporations purchase their outstanding stock are varied. Some major reasons are: (1) to provide tax-efficient distributions of excess cash to shareholders; (2) to increase earnings per share and return on equity; (3) to provide stock for employee stock compensation contracts or to meet potential merger needs; (4) to thwart takeover attempts or to reduce the number of stockholders; (5) to make a market in the stock.

6 Explain the accounting for treasury stock. The cost method is generally used in accounting for treasury stock. This method derives its name from the fact that the Treasury Stock account is maintained at the cost of the shares purchased. Under the cost method, the Treasury Stock account is debited for the cost of the shares acquired and is credited for this same cost upon reissuance. The price received for the stock when originally issued does not affect the entries to record the acquisition and reissuance of the treasury stock.

7 Describe the major features of preferred stock. Preferred stock is a special class of shares that possesses certain preferences or features not possessed by the common stock. The features that are most often associated with preferred stock issues are: (1) preference as to dividends; (2) preference as to assets in the event of liquidation; (3) convertible into common stock; (4) callable at the option of the corporation; (5) nonvoting.

8 Distinguish between debt and preferred stock. With the right combination of features (i.e., fixed return, no vote, redeemable), a preferred stockholder may possess more of the characteristics of a creditor than those of an owner. Preferred shares generally have no maturity date, but the preferred stockholder's relationship with the company may be terminated if the corporation exercises its call privilege. Many issuances of preferred stock have features that make the security more like debt than equity. As a result, companies must report separately redeemable preferred stock, nonredeemable preferred stock, and common stock. The amounts applicable to these three categories cannot be totaled or combined for financial reporting purposes.

9 Identify items reported as additional paid-in capital. Items reported as additional paid-in capital are: (1) discounts (premiums) on capital stock issued; (2) sale of treasury stock below (above) cost; (3) absorption of a deficit in a recapitalization or additional capital arising in recapitalizations or revisions in the capital structure (quasi-reorganization); (4) declaration of a liquidating dividend; (5) additional assessments on stockholders; (6) conversion of convertible bonds or preferred stock; (7) declaration of a "small" (ordinary) stock dividend.

Par Value Method

OBJECTIVE ⑩
After studying Appendix 15A, you should be able to: Explain the par value method of accounting for treasury stock.

Those who advocate accounting for treasury shares at par (or stated) value adhere to the theory that **the purchase or other acquisition of treasury shares is, in effect, a constructive retirement of those shares**. Inasmuch as the shares cannot be an asset, they must represent a retirement or at least a reduction of outstanding stock. Because outstanding shares are shown at par, they reason, **the reacquired shares must be carried at par** to indicate the proper reduction in stock outstanding.

PURCHASE OF TREASURY STOCK

To illustrate the accounting for treasury stock using the par value method, assume that Ho Company has issued 100,000 shares of $1 par value common stock at a price of $10 per share. In addition, it has retained earnings of $300,000. The stockholders' equity section on December 31, 2001, before purchase of treasury stock is as follows:

ILLUSTRATION 15A-1
Stockholders' Equity with No Treasury Stock

Stockholders' equity	
Paid-in capital	
Common stock, $1 par value 100,000 shares issued and outstanding	$ 100,000
Additional paid-in capital	900,000
Total paid-in capital	1,000,000
Retained earnings	300,000
Total stockholders' equity	$1,300,000

On January 20, 2002, Ho Company acquires 10,000 shares of its stock at $11 per share. The entry to record the reacquisition is:

January 20, 2002

Treasury Stock	10,000	
Paid-in Capital in Excess of Par	90,000[1]	
Retained Earnings	10,000	
Cash		110,000

Under the par value method, **the acquisition cost of treasury shares is compared with the amount received at the time of their original issue**. The Treasury Stock account is debited for the par value (or stated value) of the shares, and a pro rata amount of any excess over par (or stated value) on original issuance is charged to the related Paid-in Capital account. **Any excess of the acquisition cost over the original issue price is charged to Retained Earnings** and may be viewed as a dividend to the retiring stockholder. **If, however, the original issue price exceeds the acquisition price of the treasury stock, this difference is credited to Paid-in Capital from Treasury Stock** and may be viewed as a **capital contribution** from the retiring stockholders.

---

[1]This amount could be charged to Paid-in Capital from Treasury Stock if a balance existed in that account from previous transactions.

In the Ho Company example, because there was only one previous issuance of common stock (at $10 per share), the average price received is the same as the original issue price. Therefore, the $9 original excess over par per share is used to determine the total reduction in Paid-in Capital in Excess of Par. More typically, the average excess over par originally received per share is computed by dividing the total paid-in capital in excess of par from all original issuances of common stock by the number of common shares issued.

The stockholders' equity section for Ho Company after purchase of the treasury stock is as follows:

Stockholders' equity		
Paid-in capital		
Common stock, $1 par value, 100,000 shares issued		$ 100,000
Less: Treasury stock (10,000 shares at par)		10,000
Common stock outstanding		90,000
Additional paid-in capital		810,000
Total paid-in capital		900,000
Retained earnings		290,000
Total stockholders' equity		$1,190,000

ILLUSTRATION 15A-2
Stockholders' Equity with Treasury Stock

Under the par value method, treasury stock is reported in the balance sheet as a **deduction**—at par value of $10,000—from issued shares of the same class. Note also that additional paid-in capital is $90,000 less and retained earnings is $10,000 less than before the treasury stock transaction.

SALE OR RETIREMENT OF TREASURY STOCK

Treasury stock is usually sold or retired. If the treasury shares are sold or retired, the accounting treatment is similar to that accorded any original issuance of stock.

When the selling price of the shares is greater than par, the difference is credited to Paid-in Capital in Excess of Par. To illustrate, assume that 1,000 shares of treasury stock of Ho Company previously acquired at $11 per share are sold at $15 per share on March 10. The entry is as follows:

March 10, 2002

Cash	15,000	
Treasury Stock		1,000
Paid-in Capital in Excess of Par		14,000

If the treasury stock is sold at less than par, Paid-in Capital from Treasury Stock is debited. A Discount on Capital Stock is not debited because no contingent liability exists on the part of the stockholders of the reissued shares.

If stock is retired, the par value of the treasury stock and related common stock is reduced. To illustrate, assume that Ho Company retires 5,000 shares of its treasury stock. The entry to record this retirement is as follows:

Common Stock	5,000	
Treasury Stock		5,000

The par value method maintains the integrity of the various sources of capital. The cost method avoids identifying and accounting for the premiums, discounts, and other amounts related to the original issue of the specific shares acquired. For that reason, it is the simpler and more popular method.

SUMMARY OF LEARNING OBJECTIVE FOR APPENDIX 15A

⑩ Explain the par value method of accounting for treasury stock. Under the par value method, the purchase of treasury shares is viewed as a constructive retirement of those shares. Inasmuch as the shares cannot be an asset, they must represent a retirement or at least a reduction of the outstanding stock. Because shares outstanding are shown at par, the reacquired shares must be carried at par to indicate the proper reduction in stock outstanding.

Note: All **asterisked** Questions, Brief Exercises, Exercises, Problems, and Conceptual Cases relate to material contained in the appendix to the chapter.

QUESTIONS

1 Distinguish between the following types of corporations:

(a) Public sector vs. private sector.

(b) Nonstock vs. stock.

(c) Closed vs. open.

(d) Listed vs. unlisted.

2 Differentiate between capital in a legal sense, capital in a corporate finance sense, and capital in an accounting sense.

3 Discuss the special characteristics of the corporate form of business that have a direct effect on owners' equity accounting.

4 In the absence of restrictive provisions, what are the basic rights of stockholders of a corporation?

5 Distinguish between common and preferred stock.

6 Why is the distinction between paid-in capital and retained earnings important?

7 Explain each of the following terms: authorized capital stock, unissued capital stock, issued capital stock, outstanding capital stock, subscribed stock, and treasury stock.

8 Distinguish between paid-in capital and stated capital.

9 What is meant by par value, and what is its significance to stockholders?

10 Describe the accounting for the issuance for cash of no-par value common stock at a price in excess of the stated value of the common stock.

11 When might the Stock Subscription Receivable account be classified as a current asset? As a deduction in the stockholders' equity section?

12 Describe the accounting for the subscription of common stock at a price in excess of the par value of the common stock.

13 Explain the difference between the proportional method and the incremental method of allocating the proceeds of lump sum sales of capital stock.

14 What are the different bases for stock valuation when assets other than cash are received for issued shares of stock?

15 Explain how underwriting costs and accounting and legal fees associated with the issuance of stock should be recorded.

16 For what reasons might a corporation purchase its own stock?

*17 Distinguish between the cost method and the par value method of accounting for treasury stock.

18 Discuss the propriety of showing:

(a) Treasury stock as an asset.

(b) "Gain" or "loss" on sale of treasury stock as additions to or deductions from income.

(c) Dividends received on treasury stock as income.

19 What features or rights may alter the character of preferred stock?

20 Little Texas Inc. recently noted that its 4% preferred stock and 4% participating second preferred stock, which are both cumulative, have priority as to dividends up to 4% of their par value; its participating preferred stock participates equally with the common stock in any dividends in excess of 4%. What is meant by the term participating? Cumulative?

21 Where in the financial statements is preferred stock normally reported?

22 How should preferred stock redeemable by the holder be classified in the financial statements?

23 List possible sources of additional paid-in capital.

24 Goo Goo Dolls Inc. purchases 10,000 shares of its own previously issued $10 par common stock for $290,000. Assuming the shares are held in the treasury with intent to reissue, what effect does this transaction have on (a) net income, (b) total assets, (c) total paid-in capital, and (d) total stockholders' equity?

25 Indicate how each of the following accounts should be classified in the stockholders' equity section.

(a) Common Stock

(b) Retained Earnings

(c) Paid-in Capital in Excess of Par Value

(d) Treasury Stock

(e) Paid-in Capital from Treasury Stock

(f) Paid-in Capital in Excess of Stated Value

(g) Preferred Stock

*26 How is stockholders' equity affected differently by using the par value method instead of the cost method for treasury stock purchases?

BRIEF EXERCISES

BE15-1 Lost Vikings Corporation issued 300 shares of $10 par value common stock for $4,100. Prepare Lost Vikings' journal entry.

BE15-2 Lotus Turbo Inc. issued 200 shares of $5 par value common stock for $850. Prepare Lotus Turbo's journal entry.

BE15-3 Shinobi Corporation issued 600 shares of no-par common stock for $10,200. Prepare Shinobi's journal entry if (a) the stock has no stated value, and (b) the stock has a stated value of $2 per share.

BE15-4 Rambo Inc. sells 300 shares of its $10 par value common stock on a subscription basis at $45 per share. On June 1, Rambo accepts a 40% down payment. On December 1, Rambo collects the remaining 60% and issues the shares. Prepare Rambo's journal entries.

BE15-5 Lufia Corporation has the following account balances at December 31, 2001:

Common stock, $5 par value	$ 210,000
Subscriptions receivable	90,000
Retained earnings	2,340,000
Paid-in capital in excess of par	1,320,000

Prepare Lufia's December 31, 2001, stockholders' equity section.

BE15-6 Primal Rage Corporation issued 300 shares of $10 par value common stock and 100 shares of $50 par value preferred stock for a lump sum of $14,200. The common stock has a market value of $20 per share, and the preferred stock has a market value of $90 per share. Prepare the journal entry to record the issuance.

BE15-7 On February 1, 2001, Mario Andretti Corporation issued 2,000 shares of its $5 par value common stock for land worth $31,000. Prepare the February 1, 2001, journal entry.

BE15-8 Powerdrive Corporation issued 2,000 shares of its $10 par value common stock for $70,000. Powerdrive also incurred $1,500 of costs associated with issuing the stock. Prepare Powerdrive's journal entry to record the issuance of the company's stock.

BE15-9 Maverick Inc. has outstanding 10,000 shares of $10 par value common stock. On July 1, 2001, Maverick reacquired 100 shares at $85 per share. On September 1, Maverick reissued 60 shares at $90 per share. On November 1, Maverick reissued 40 shares at $83 per share. Prepare Maverick's journal entries to record these transactions using the cost method.

BE15-10 Power Rangers Corporation has outstanding 20,000 shares of $5 par value common stock. On August 1, 2001, Power Rangers reacquired 200 shares at $75 per share. On November 1, Power Rangers reissued the 200 shares at $70 per share. Power Rangers had no previous treasury stock transactions. Prepare Power Rangers' journal entries to record these transactions using the cost method.

BE15-11 Mickey Mouse Inc. is holding 500 shares of its own $5 par value common stock as treasury stock. The stock was originally issued at $13 per share and was reacquired at $14 per share. Mickey Mouse uses the cost method of accounting for treasury stock. Prepare the necessary journal entry if Mickey Mouse formally retires the treasury stock.

BE15-12 Popeye Corporation issued 450 shares of $100 par value preferred stock for $61,500. Prepare Popeye's journal entry.

*BE15-13 Mega Man Corporation has outstanding 100,000 shares of $10 par value common stock which was originally issued at an average price of $24 per share. Mega Man reacquires 300 shares at $33 per share and later reissues the shares at $37 per share. Mega Man uses the par value method of accounting for treasury stock. Prepare the journal entries to record the two transactions.

*BE15-14   Use the information from BE15-13, except assume the treasury stock was reacquired at $21 per share and later reissued at $23 per share. Prepare Mega Man's journal entries to record the two transactions.

*BE15-15   Use the information from BE15-11, except assume that Mickey Mouse uses the par value method of accounting for treasury stock. Prepare the necessary journal entry if Mickey Mouse formally retires the treasury stock.

EXERCISES

E15-1   (Recording the Issuances of Common Stock)   During its first year of operations, Collin Raye Corporation had the following transactions pertaining to its common stock.

Jan. 10   Issued 80,000 shares for cash at $6 per share.
Mar. 1   Issued 5,000 shares to attorneys in payment of a bill for $35,000 for services rendered in helping the company to incorporate.
July 1   Issued 30,000 shares for cash at $8 per share.
Sept. 1   Issued 60,000 shares for cash at $10 per share.

Instructions
(a)   Prepare the journal entries for these transactions, assuming that the common stock has a par value of $5 per share.
(b)   Prepare the journal entries for these transactions, assuming that the common stock is no par with a stated value of $3 per share.

E15-2   (Recording the Issuance of Common and Preferred Stock)   Kathleen Battle Corporation was organized on January 1, 2001. It is authorized to issue 10,000 shares of 8%, $100 par value preferred stock, and 500,000 shares of no par common stock with a stated value of $1 per share. The following stock transactions were completed during the first year.

Jan. 10   Issued 80,000 shares of common stock for cash at $5 per share.
Mar. 1   Issued 5,000 shares of preferred stock for cash at $108 per share.
Apr. 1   Issued 24,000 shares of common stock for land. The asking price of the land was $90,000; the fair market value of the land was $80,000.
May   1   Issued 80,000 shares of common stock for cash at $7 per share.
Aug. 1   Issued 10,000 shares of common stock to attorneys in payment of their bill of $50,000 for services rendered in helping the company organize.
Sept. 1   Issued 10,000 shares of common stock for cash at $9 per share.
Nov. 1   Issued 1,000 shares of preferred stock for cash at $112 per share.

Instructions
Prepare the journal entries to record the above transactions.

E15-3   (Subscribed Stock)   James Galway Inc. intends to sell capital stock to raise additional capital to allow for expansion in the rapidly growing service industry. The corporation decides to sell this stock through a subscription basis and publicly notifies the investment world. The stock is a $5 par value issue and 30,000 shares are offered at $25 a share. The terms of the subscription are 40% down and the balance at the end of six months. All shares are subscribed for during the offering period.

Instructions
Give the journal entry for the original subscription, the collection of the down payments, the collection of the balance of the subscription price, and the issuance of the common stock.

E15-4   (Stock Issued for Nonmonetary Assets)   Faith Hill Products, Inc., was formed to operate a manufacturing plant in Warnersville. The events for the formation of the corporation include the following:

1.   5,000 shares of no-par common stock were issued to investors at $22 per share.
2.   8,000 shares were issued to acquire used equipment that has a depreciated book value to the seller of $140,000.

Instructions
Prepare journal entries for the transactions above.

E15-5   (Stock Issued for Land)   Twenty-five thousand shares reacquired by Elixir Corporation for $53 per share were exchanged for undeveloped land that has an appraised value of $1,700,000. At the time of the exchange the common stock was trading at $62 per share on an organized exchange.

Instructions

    (a) Prepare the journal entry to record the acquisition of land assuming the stock was originally recorded on the cost method.

    (b) Briefly identify the possible alternatives (including those that are totally unacceptable) for quantifying the cost of the land and briefly support your choice.

E15-6 (Lump Sum Sale of Stock with Bonds) Faith Evans Corporation is a regional company which is an SEC registrant. The corporation's securities are thinly traded through the NASDAQ (National Association of Securities Dealers Quotes). Faith Evans Corp. has issued 10,000 units. Each unit consists of a $500 par, 12% subordinated debenture and 10 shares of $5 par common stock. The investment banker has retained 400 units as the underwriting fee. The other 9,600 units were sold to outside investors for cash at $880 per unit. Prior to this sale the two-week ask price of common stock was $40 per share. Twelve percent is a reasonable market yield for the debentures.

Instructions

    (a) Prepare the journal entry to record the transaction above:

        (1) Employing the incremental method assuming the interest rate on the debentures is the best market measure.

        (2) Employing the proportional method using the recent price quotes on the common stock.

    (b) Briefly explain which method is, in your opinion, the better method.

E15-7 (Lump Sum Sales of Stock with Preferred Stock) Dave Matthew Inc. issues 500 shares of $10 par value common stock and 100 shares of $100 par value preferred stock for a lump sum of $100,000.

Instructions

    (a) Prepare the journal entry for the issuance when the market value of the common shares is $165 each and market value of the preferred is $230 each.

    (b) Prepare the journal entry for the issuance when only the market value of the common stock is known and it is $170 per share.

E15-8 (Lump Sum Sale of Stock with Preferred) Cyndi Lauper Company was organized with 50,000 shares of $100 par value, 9% preferred stock and 100,000 shares of common stock without par value. During the first year, 1,000 shares of preferred and 1,000 shares of common were issued for a lump sum price of $180,000.

Instructions

What entry should be made to record this transaction under each of the following independent conditions:

    (a) Shortly after the transaction described above, 500 shares of preferred stock were sold at $116.

    (b) The directors have established a stated value of $75 a share for the common stock.

    (c) At the date of issuance, the preferred stock had a market price of $140 per share and the common stock had a market price of $40 per share.

E15-9 (Stock Issuances and Repurchase) Lindsey Hunter Corporation is authorized to issue 50,000 shares of $5 par value common stock. During 2001, Lindsey Hunter took part in the following selected transactions:

    1. Issued 5,000 shares of stock at $45 per share, less costs related to the issuance of the stock totaling $7,000.

    2. Issued 1,000 shares of stock for land appraised at $50,000. The stock was actively traded on a national stock exchange at approximately $46 per share on the date of issuance.

    3. Purchased 500 shares of treasury stock at $43 per share. The treasury shares purchased were issued in 2000 at $40 per share.

Instructions

    (a) Prepare a journal entry to record item 1.

    (b) Prepare a journal entry to record item 2.

    (c) Prepare a journal entry to record item 3 using the cost method.

E15-10 (Effect of Treasury Stock Transactions on Financials) Joe Dumars Company has outstanding 40,000 shares of $5 par common stock which had been issued at $30 per share. Joe Dumars then entered into the following transactions:

    1. Purchased 5,000 treasury shares at $45 per share.

    2. Resold 2,000 of the treasury shares at $49 per share.

    3. Resold 500 of the treasury shares at $40 per share.

    4. Retired the remaining treasury shares.

Instructions

Use the following code to indicate the effect each of the four transactions has on the financial statement categories listed in the table below, assuming Joe Dumars Company uses the cost method: (I = Increase; D = Decrease; NE = No effect).

#	Assets	Liabilities	Stockholders' Equity	Paid-in Capital	Retained Earnings	Net Income
1						
2						
3						
4						

E15-11 (Preferred Stock Entries and Dividends) Otis Thorpe Corporation has 10,000 shares of $100 par value, 8%, preferred stock and 50,000 shares of $10 par value common stock outstanding at December 31, 2001.

Instructions

Answer the questions in each of the following independent situations:

(a) If the preferred stock is cumulative and dividends were last paid on the preferred stock on December 31, 1998, what are the dividends in arrears that should be reported on the December 31, 2001, balance sheet? How should these dividends be reported?

(b) If the preferred stock is convertible into seven shares of $10 par value common stock and 4,000 shares are converted, what entry is required for the conversion assuming the preferred stock was issued at par value?

(c) If the preferred stock was issued at $107 per share, how should the preferred stock be reported in the stockholders' equity section?

E15-12 (Stockholders' Equity Section) Doug Collins Corporation's charter authorized 100,000 shares of $10 par value common stock, and 30,000 shares of 6% cumulative and nonparticipating preferred stock, par value $100 per share. The corporation engaged in the following stock transactions through December 31, 2001: 30,000 shares of common stock were issued for $350,000 and 12,000 shares of preferred stock for machinery valued at $1,475,000. Subscriptions for 4,500 shares of common have been taken, and 40% of the subscription price of $16 per share has been collected. The stock will be issued upon collection of the subscription price in full. Treasury stock of 1,000 shares of common has been purchased for $15 and accounted for under the cost method. The Retained Earnings balance is $180,000.

Instructions

Prepare the stockholders' equity section of the balance sheet in good form. Assume that state law requires that the amount of retained earnings available for dividends be restricted by an amount equal to the cost of treasury shares acquired.

E15-13 (Correcting Entries for Equity Transactions) Pistons Inc. recently hired a new accountant with extensive experience in accounting for partnerships. Because of the pressure of the new job, the accountant was unable to review what he had learned earlier about corporation accounting. During the first month, he made the following entries for the corporation's capital stock.

May 2	Cash	192,000	
	Capital Stock		192,000
	(Issued 12,000 shares of $5 par value common stock at $16 per share)		
10	Cash	600,000	
	Capital Stock		600,000
	(Issued 10,000 shares of $30 par value preferred stock at $60 per share)		
15	Capital Stock	15,000	
	Cash		15,000
	(Purchased 1,000 shares of common stock for the treasury at $15 per share)		
31	Cash	8,500	
	Capital Stock		5,000
	Gain on Sale of Stock		3,500
	(Sold 500 shares of treasury stock at $17 per share)		

Instructions

On the basis of the explanation for each entry, prepare the entries that should have been made for the capital stock transactions.

E15-14 (Analysis of Equity Data and Equity Section Preparation) For a recent 2-year period, the balance sheet of Santana Dotson Company showed the following stockholders' equity data in millions.

	2002	2001
Additional paid-in capital	$ 931	$ 817
Common stock—par	545	540
Retained earnings	7,167	5,226
Treasury stock	1,564	918
Total stockholders' equity	$7,079	$5,665
Common stock shares issued	218	216
Common stock shares authorized	500	500
Treasury stock shares	34	27

Instructions
- **(a)** Answer the following questions.
  - **(1)** What is the par value of the common stock?
  - **(2)** Was the cost per share of acquiring treasury stock higher in 2002 or in 2001?
- **(b)** Prepare the stockholders' equity section for 2002.

*E15-15 (Treasury Stock—Par Value and Cost Methods) Carver Smith Corporation reacquired 40,000 of its common shares in the market at $53 per share. The per share par value is $1; the average issue price was $30 per share.

Instructions
- **(a)** Record the purchase assuming:
  - **(1)** The par value method.
  - **(2)** The cost method.
- **(b)** Which of the methods will provide the financial statement reader with more useful information? Briefly explain.

*E15-16 (Treasury Stock—Par Value and Cost Methods) Grant Hill Inc. has outstanding 35,000 shares of $10 par common stock which has been issued at $25 per share. On July 5, 2001, Grant Hill repurchased 1,000 of these shares at $41 per share. The company then retired the treasury shares.

Instructions

Give the appropriate journal entries for the acquisition and retirement of the treasury stock under:
- **(a)** The cost method.
- **(b)** The par value method.

*E15-17 (Effect of Treasury Stock Transactions on Financials—Par Value Method) Joe Dumars Company has outstanding 40,000 shares of $5 par common stock which had been issued at $30 per share. Joe Dumars then entered into the following transactions:
1. Purchased 5,000 treasury shares at $45 per share.
2. Resold 2,000 of the treasury shares at $49 per share.
3. Resold 500 of the treasury shares at $40 per share.
4. Retired the remaining treasury shares.

Instructions

Use the following code to indicate the effect each of the four transactions has on the financial statement categories listed in the table below, assuming Joe Dumars Company uses the par value method: (I = Increase; D = Decrease; NE = No effect).

#	Assets	Liabilities	Stockholders' Equity	Paid-in Capital	Retained Earnings	Net Income
1						
2						
3						
4						

PROBLEMS

P15-1 (Subscriptions, Treasury Stock, and Lump Sum Issuances) The Nells Company had the following stockholders' equity on January 1, 2002.

Preferred stock, $100 par value, 8% cumulative, 10,000 shares authorized, no shares issued	$ —
Common stock, 200,000 shares authorized, 100,000 shares issued and outstanding, $2 par	200,000
Paid-in capital in excess of par (original issue)	2,300,000
Retained earnings, unappropriated	1,800,000
Total stockholders' equity	$4,300,000

The following transactions occurred, in the order given, during 2002:
1. Subscriptions were sold for 10,000 shares of common stock at $28 per share. The first payment was for $13 per share.
2. The second payment was for $15 per share. All payments were received on the second payment except for 1,000 shares.
3. Per the subscription contract, which requires that defaulting subscribers have all their payments refunded, Nells sends a refund check to the defaulting subscribers. At this point, common stock is issued to subscribers that have fully paid on the contract.
4. 10,000 shares of treasury stock were purchased at $20 per share. Nells uses the cost method of accounting for treasury shares.
5. All 10,000 shares of treasury stock were sold for $24 per share.
6. 2,000 shares of preferred stock and 3,000 shares of common stock were sold together for $290,000. The common stock had a market value of $27 per share.

Instructions
Prepare the journal entries to record the transactions for Nells Company for 2002.

P15-2 (Treasury Stock Transactions and Presentation) Jodz Company had the following stockholders' equity as of January 1, 2002.

Common stock, $5 par value, 20,000 shares issued	$100,000
Paid-in capital in excess of par	300,000
Retained earnings	320,000
Total stockholders' equity	$720,000

During 2002, the following transactions occurred:

Feb.	1	Jodz repurchased 2,000 shares of treasury stock at a price of $18 per share.
Mar.	1	800 shares of treasury stock repurchased above were reissued at $17 per share.
Mar.	18	500 shares of treasury stock repurchased above were reissued at $14 per share.
Apr.	22	600 shares of treasury stock repurchased above were reissued at $20 per share.

Instructions
(a) Prepare the journal entries to record the treasury stock transactions in 2002, assuming Jodz uses the cost method.
(b) Prepare the stockholders' equity section as of April 30, 2002. Net income for the first 4 months of 2002 was $110,000.

P15-3 (Equity Transactions and Statement Preparation) On January 5, 2001, Drabek Corporation received a charter granting the right to issue 5,000 shares of $100 par value, 8% cumulative and nonparticipating preferred stock and 50,000 shares of $5 par value common stock. It then completed these transactions:

Jan.	11	Accepted subscriptions to 20,000 shares of common stock at $16 per share; 40% down payments accompanied the subscription.
Feb.	1	Issued Robb Nen Corp. 4,000 shares of preferred stock for the following assets: machinery with a fair market value of $50,000; a factory building with a fair market value of $110,000; and land with an appraised value of $270,000.
Apr.	15	Collected the balance of the subscription price on the common shares and issued the stock.
July	29	Purchased 1,800 shares of common stock at $19 per share (use cost method).
Aug.	10	Sold the 1,800 treasury shares at $14 per share.
Dec.	31	Declared a $0.25 per share cash dividend on the common stock and declared the preferred dividend.
Dec.	31	Closed the Income Summary account. There was a $175,700 net income.

Instructions

(a) Record the journal entries for the transactions listed above.

(b) Prepare the stockholders' equity section of Drabek Corporation's balance sheet as of December 31, 2001.

P15-4 (Equity Transactions and Statement Preparation) Amado Company has two classes of capital stock outstanding: 8%, $20 par preferred and $5 par common. At December 31, 2000, the following accounts were included in stockholders' equity:

Preferred Stock, 150,000 shares	$ 3,000,000
Common Stock, 2,000,000 shares	10,000,000
Paid-in Capital in Excess of Par—Preferred	200,000
Paid-in Capital in Excess of Par—Common	27,000,000
Retained Earnings	4,500,000

The following transactions affected stockholders' equity during 2001:

Jan.	1	25,000 shares of preferred stock issued at $22 per share.
Feb.	1	40,000 shares of common stock issued at $20 per share.
June	1	2-for-1 stock split (par value reduced to $2.50).
July	1	30,000 shares of common treasury stock purchased at $9 per share. Amado uses the cost method.
Sept. 15		10,000 shares of treasury stock reissued at $11 per share.
Dec. 31		Net income is $2,100,000.
Dec. 31		The preferred dividend is declared, and a common dividend of 50¢ per share is declared.

Instructions

Prepare the stockholders' equity section for Amado Company at December 31, 2001. Show all supporting computations.

P15-5 (Stock Transactions—Assessment and Lump Sum) Shikai Corporation's charter authorized issuance of 100,000 shares of $10 par value common stock and 50,000 shares of $50 preferred stock. The following transactions involving the issuance of shares of stock were completed. Each transaction is independent of the others.

1. Issued a $10,000, 9% bond payable at par and gave as a bonus one share of preferred stock, which at that time was selling for $106 a share.
2. Issued 500 shares of common stock for machinery. The machinery had been appraised at $7,100; the seller's book value was $6,200. The most recent market price of the common stock is $15 a share.
3. Voted a 10% assessment on both the 10,000 shares of outstanding common and the 1,000 shares of outstanding preferred. The assessment was paid in full.
4. Issued 375 shares of common and 100 shares of preferred for a lump sum amounting to $11,300. The common had been selling at $14 and the preferred at $65.
5. Issued 200 shares of common and 50 shares of preferred for furniture and fixtures. The common had a fair market value of $16 per share and the furniture and fixtures were appraised at $6,200.

Instructions

Record the transactions listed above in journal entry form.

P15-6 (Treasury Stock—Cost Method) Before Polska Corporation engages in the treasury stock transactions listed below, its general ledger reflects, among others, the following account balances (par value of its stock is $30 per share).

Paid-in Capital in Excess of Par	Common Stock	Retained Earnings
Balance $99,000	Balance $270,000	Balance $80,000

Instructions

Record the treasury stock transactions (given below) under the cost method of handling treasury stock; use the FIFO method for purchase-sale purposes.

(a) Bought 380 shares of treasury stock at $39 per share.
(b) Bought 300 shares of treasury stock at $43 per share.
(c) Sold 350 shares of treasury stock at $42 per share.
(d) Sold 120 shares of treasury stock at $38 per share.
(e) Retired the remaining shares in the treasury.

P15-7 (Reacquisition of Stock—FIFO and Weighted Average) Indiana Inc. is a closely held toy manufacturer in the Midwest. You have been engaged as the independent public accountant to perform the first audit of Indiana. It is agreed that only current-year (2002) financial statements will be audited.

The following stockholder's equity information has been developed from Indiana records on December 31, 2001:

Common stock, no par value; no stated value; authorized 30,000 shares; issued 9,000 shares	$405,000
Retained earnings	180,000

The following stock transactions took place during 2002:

1. On March 15, Indiana issued 7,000 shares of common stock to Derrick McKey for $63 per share.
2. On March 31, Indiana reacquired 4,000 shares of common stock from Reggie Miller (Indiana's founder) for $74 per share. These shares were canceled and retired upon receipt.

For the year 2002, Indiana reported net income of $125,000.

Instructions

(a) How should the stockholders' equity information be reported in the Indiana financial statements for the year ended December 31, 2002 (1) assuming specific identification of the shares is impossible and (2) assuming application of the FIFO method? The company uses the cost method of accounting for treasury stock transactions.

(b) How would your answer in part (a) have been altered if Indiana had treated the reacquired shares as treasury stock carried at cost rather than retired?

(c) On December 30, 2003, Indiana's board of directors changed the common stock from no par, no stated value to no par with a $10 stated value per share. How will the stockholders' equity section be affected if comparative financial statements are prepared at December 31, 2003? (Apply the method used in (a)(1).)

P15-8 (Prepare Stockholders' Equity Section) Heinrich Corporation had the following stockholders' equity at January 1, 2002:

Preferred stock, 8%, $100 par value, 10,000 shares authorized, 4,000 shares issued	$ 400,000
Common stock, $2 par value, 200,000 shares authorized, 80,000 shares issued	160,000
Common stock subscribed, 10,000 shares	20,000
Additional paid-in capital—preferred	20,000
Additional paid-in capital—common	940,000
Retained earnings	780,000
	2,320,000
Less: Common stock subscriptions receivable	40,000
Total stockholders' equity	$2,280,000

During 2002 the following transactions occurred:

1. 100 shares of common stock were exchanged for equipment. The market value of the stock on the exchange date was $12 per share.
2. 1,000 shares of common stock and 100 shares of preferred stock were sold for the lump sum price of $24,500. The common stock had a market price of $14 at the time of the sale.
3. 2,000 shares of preferred stock were sold for cash at $102 per share.
4. All of the subscribers paid their subscription prices into the firm.
5. The shares of common stock were issued.
6. 1,000 shares of common stock were repurchased by the corporation at $15 per share.
7. 800 of these shares were resold at $18 per share by year-end. Heinrich uses the cost method of accounting for treasury stock.
8. Income for 2002 was $246,000.

Instructions

Prepare the stockholder's equity section of Heinrich Corporation as of December 31, 2002. (The use of T-accounts may help you organize the material.)

P15-9 (Treasury Stock—Cost Method—Equity Section Preparation) Constantine Company has the following owners' equity accounts at December 31, 2000:

Common Stock—$100 par value, authorized 8,000 shares	$480,000
Retained Earnings	294,000

Instructions

(a) Prepare entries in journal form to record the following transactions, which took place during 2001. (*Hint:* Debit retained earnings in transaction 6.)

    (1) 240 shares of outstanding stock were purchased at 97. (These are to be accounted for using the cost method.)

    (2) A $20 per share cash dividend was declared.

    (3) The dividend declared in No. 2 above was paid.

    (4) The treasury shares purchased in No. 1 above were resold at 102.

    (5) 500 shares of outstanding stock were purchased at 103.

    (6) 120 shares of outstanding stock were purchased at 106 and retired.

    (7) 330 of the shares purchased in No. 5 above were resold at 96.

(b) Prepare the stockholders' equity section of Constantine Company's balance sheet after giving effect to these transactions, assuming that the net income for 2001 was $94,000.

P15-10 (Redeemable Preferred Stock) The following information relates to Altoona Industries, Inc.:

Altoona Industries, Inc.

	2002	2001
($000)		
Series A first preferred stock—subject to mandatory redemption ($4,062,000 liquidation value in 2002 and 2001); $1.00 par value; authorized 100,000 shares; issued 40,625 shares in 2002 and 2001 (note 6)	$ 4,062	$ 4,062
Common stockholders' equity:		
Common stock, $.10 par value; authorized 20,000,000 shares; issued 5,522,602 shares in 2002 and 5,280,602 in 2001	552	528
Additional paid-in capital	10,463	6,014
Retained earnings	25,286	17,110
Common stockholders' equity	36,301	23,652

Notes to Consolidated Financial Statements Note 6: Redeemable Preferred Stock. The Company's preferred stock consists of 250,000 authorized shares of $1.00 par value First Preferred Stock of which 40,620 shares of Series A First Preferred Stock were outstanding at December 31, 2002. The Series A First Preferred Stock, which is not convertible, has a carrying value of $80.00 per share representing fair value at date of issuance based upon an independent appraisal and sales to third parties, plus accumulated accretion. The shares are entitled to cumulative dividends of $12.70 annually ($3.175 per quarter) per share and must be redeemed at 10% per year commencing on December 31, 2005, at $100.00 per share plus accrued and unpaid dividends. The Company, at its option, may redeem at that price in each year in which mandatory redemption is required an additional number of shares not exceeding the mandatory redemption and may redeem all or any part of the shares at that price plus a premium amounting to $3.55 in 2003 and declining proportionately thereafter through 2011 after which there will be no premium.

Altoona had total debt of $85,979 in 2002. A restrictive covenant on some of the debt prohibits Altoona from additional borrowing if the debt/equity ratio exceeds 2.5 or if retained earnings falls below $17,000.

Instructions

Prepare responses to the following questions based on the above information.

(a) Does the Series A preferred stock have characteristics more like common stock or like debt? Explain.

(b) What are the present GAAP requirements for redeemable preferred stock?

(c) Is Altoona in violation of its debt covenants in 2002, based upon the reported numbers above? Would your answer change if Altoona classifies the redeemable stock as debt?

(d) How should redeemable preferred stock be reported?

*P15-11 (Treasury Stock Analysis) The stockholders' equity section of Georges Bizet Company's balance sheet at December 31, 2002, was as follows:

Common stock—$100 par (authorized 50,000 shares, issued and outstanding 15,000 shares)	$1,500,000
Paid-in capital in excess of par	150,000
Retained earnings	210,000
Total stockholders' equity	$1,860,000

On January 2, 2003, having idle cash, the company repurchased 800 shares of its stock for $91,200. During the year it sold 150 of the reacquired shares at $117 per share, another 150 at $110 per share, and legally retired the remaining 500 shares.

Instructions

(a) Discuss the possible alternatives in handling these transactions.

(b) Prepare journal entries for each transaction in accordance with the method that you believe should be applied.

*P15-12 (Stock Transaction and Equity Section Preparation) Transactions of Kalila Company are as follows:

1. The company is granted a charter that authorizes issuance of 15,000 shares of $100 par value preferred stock and 15,000 shares of common stock without par value.
2. 8,000 shares of common stock are issued to founders of the corporation for land valued by the Board of Directors at $210,000. The Board establishes a par value of $5 a share for the common stock.
3. 4,200 shares of preferred stock are sold for cash at 110.
4. 600 shares of common stock are sold to an officer of the corporation for $42 a share.
5. 300 shares of outstanding preferred stock are purchased for cash at par.
6. 400 shares of outstanding preferred stock are purchased for cash at 98.
7. 500 shares of the outstanding common stock issued in No. 2 above are purchased at $49 a share.
8. 200 shares of repurchased preferred stock are reissued at 102.
9. 2,100 shares of preferred stock are issued at 99.
10. 400 shares of reacquired common stock are reissued for $39 a share.
11. 200 shares of the common stock sold in No. 10 above are repurchased for $30 a share.

Instructions

(a) Prepare entries in journal form to record the transactions listed above. No other transactions affecting the capital stock accounts have occurred. Treasury stock is to be entered in the Treasury Stock accounts at par.

(b) Assuming that the company has retained earnings from operations of $132,000, prepare the stockholders' equity section of its balance sheet after considering all the transactions given.

*P15-13 (Treasury Stock—Par Value Method) Before Polska Corporation engages in the treasury stock transactions listed below, its general ledger reflects, among others, the following account balances (par value of its stock is $30 per share).

Paid-in Capital in Excess of Par	Common Stock	Retained Earnings
Balance $99,000	Balance $270,000	Balance $80,000

Instructions

Record the treasury stock transactions (given below) under the par value method of handling treasury stock.

(a) Bought 380 shares of treasury stock at $39 per share.

(b) Bought 300 shares of treasury stock at $43 per share.

(c) Sold 350 shares of treasury stock at $42 per share.

(d) Sold 120 shares of treasury stock at $38 per share.

(e) Retired the remaining shares in the treasury.

*P15-14 (Cost and Par Value Methods) John Uteg International, a relatively new corporation, has just become liquid enough to reacquire some of its own $1 par common stock in the market for $45 per share. It decided to repurchase 40,000 shares. The company has 200,000 shares of common stock authorized and 100,000 outstanding. All shares were originally issued at $30 per share. Retained Earnings amounts to $2,420,000. Since John Uteg is only beginning to reacquire its own stock, it has not yet decided how to account for this treasury stock.

As the company's independent auditor, you have been asked by the president, Larry Falcetto, to compare the cost and par value methods, indicating which would provide more valuable, theoretically sound financial information to financial statement users.

Instructions

Using the foregoing data, draft a memo to the president comparing the two methods. Include separate appendixes illustrating the journal entries under each method and the stockholders' equity portion of the balance sheet, referring to these in your memo whenever necessary. Include the balance sheet effect of each method in your discussion. Which would you recommend as the more useful method? Might other considerations enter into your choice?

CONCEPTUAL CASES

C15-1 (Preemptive Rights and Dilution of Ownership)   Alvarado Computer Company is a small, closely held corporation. Eighty percent of the stock is held by Eduardo Alvarado, President; of the remainder, 10% is held by members of his family and 10% by Shaunda Jones, a former officer who is now retired. The balance sheet of the company at June 30, 2001, was substantially as shown below:

Assets		Liabilities and Stockholders' Equity	
Cash	$ 22,000	Current liabilities	$ 50,000
Other	450,000	Capital stock	250,000
	$472,000	Retained earnings	172,000
			$472,000

Additional authorized capital stock of $300,000 par value had never been issued. To strengthen the cash position of the company, Eduardo Alvarado issued capital stock with a par value of $100,000 to himself at par for cash. At the next stockholders' meeting, Jones objected and claimed that her interests had been injured.

Instructions
- **(a)** Which stockholder's right was ignored in the issue of shares to Eduardo Alvarado?
- **(b)** How may the damage to Jones' interests be repaired most simply?
- **(c)** If Eduardo Alvarado offered Jones a personal cash settlement and they agreed to employ you as an impartial arbitrator to determine the amount, what settlement would you propose? Present your calculations with sufficient explanation to satisfy both parties.

C15-2 (Subscribed Stock and Subscription Receivable)   Apache Corporation sold 50,000 shares of its $10 par value common stock on a subscription basis for $40 per share. By December 31, 2001, collections on these subscriptions totaled $1,300,000. No subscriptions have yet been paid in full.

Instructions
- **(a)** Discuss the meaning of the account Common Stock Subscribed and indicate how it is reported in the financial statements.
- **(b)** Discuss the arguments in favor of reporting Subscriptions Receivable as a current asset.
- **(c)** Discuss the arguments in favor of reporting Subscriptions Receivable as a contra equity account.
- **(d)** Indicate how these 50,000 shares would be presented on Apache's December 31, 2001, balance sheet under the method discussed in (c) above.

C15-3 (Issuance of Stock for Land)   Hopee Corporation is planning to issue 3,000 shares of its own $10 par value common stock for 2 acres of land to be used as a building site.

Instructions
- **(a)** What general rule should be applied to determine the amount at which the land should be recorded?
- **(b)** Under what circumstances should this transaction be recorded at the fair market value of the land?
- **(c)** Under what circumstances should this transaction be recorded at the fair market value of the stock issued?
- **(d)** Assume Hopee intentionally records this transaction at an amount greater than the fair market value of the land and the stock. Discuss this situation.

C15-4 (Equipment Purchase with Treasury Stock)   Iroquois Corporation purchased $175,000 worth of equipment in 2002 for $100,000 cash and a promise to deliver an indeterminate number of treasury shares of its $5 par common stock, with a market value of $25,000 on January 1 of each year for the next 4 years. Hence $100,000 in "market value" of treasury shares will be required to discharge the $75,000 balance due on the equipment.

The corporation then acquired 5,000 shares of its own stock in the expectation that the market value of the stock would increase substantially before the delivery dates.

Instructions
- **(a)** Discuss the propriety of recording the equipment at
    - **(1)** $100,000 (the cash payment).
    - **(2)** $175,000 (the cash price of the equipment).
    - **(3)** $200,000 (the $100,000 cash payment plus the $100,000 market value of treasury stock that must be transferred to the vendor in order to settle the obligation according to the terms of the agreement).

    (b) Discuss the arguments for treating the balance due as
        (1) A liability.
        (2) Treasury stock subscribed.
    (c) Assuming that legal requirements do not affect the decision, discuss the arguments for treating the corporation's treasury shares as
        (1) An asset awaiting ultimate disposition.
        (2) A capital element awaiting ultimate disposition.

(AICPA adapted)

C15-5 **(Secret Reserves and Watered Stock)**   It has been said that (1) the use of the LIFO inventory method during an extended period of rising prices and (2) the expensing of all human-resource costs are among the accepted accounting practices that help create "secret reserves."

Instructions
    (a) What is a "secret reserve"? How can "secret reserves" be created or enlarged?
    (b) What is the basis for saying that the two specific practices cited above tend to create "secret reserves"?
    (c) Is it possible to create a "secret reserve" in connection with accounting for a liability? If so, explain or give an example.
    (d) What are the objections to the creation of "secret reserves"?
    (e) It has also been said that "watered stock" is the opposite of a "secret reserve." What is "watered stock"?
    (f) Describe the general circumstances in which "watered stock" can arise.
    (g) What steps can be taken to eliminate "water" from a capital structure?

(AICPA adapted)

USING YOUR JUDGMENT

FINANCIAL REPORTING PROBLEM: INTEL CORPORATION

Instructions

Refer to the financial statements and accompanying notes and discussion of Intel Corporation presented in Appendix 5B and answer the following questions.

(a) What is the par or stated value of Intel's preferred stock?

(b) What percentage of Intel's authorized preferred stock was issued at December 26, 1998?

(c) What is the par or stated value of Intel's common stock? Why is the par value so small?

(d) What percentage of Intel's authorized common stock was issued at December 26, 1998?

(e) How many shares of common stock were outstanding at December 26, 1998, and December 27, 1997?

(f) What is the nature and the extent of Intel's common stock repurchase plan? How many shares did Intel repurchase and retire in 1998? What was the effect on stockholders' equity of these stock repurchase and retirements in 1998?

(g) How many shares of common stock were issued in 1998 and for what purposes?

FINANCIAL STATEMENT ANALYSIS CASE

Kellogg Corporation

Kellogg Corporation is the world's leading producer of ready-to-eat cereal products. In recent years the company has taken numerous steps aimed at improving its profitability and earnings per share. Presented below are some basic facts for the Kellogg Corporation.

(all dollars in millions)	1998	1997
Net sales	$6,762	$6,830
Net income	503	546
Total assets	5,052	4,877
Total liabilities	4,162	3,880
Common stock, $.25 par value	104	104
Capital in excess of par value	105	93
Retained earnings	1,368	1,241
Treasury stock, at cost	394	157
Preferred stock	0	0
Number of shares outstanding (in millions)	408	414

Instructions

(a) What are some of the reasons that management purchases its own stock?

(b) Explain how earnings per share might be affected by treasury stock transactions.

(c) Calculate the ratio of debt to total assets for 1997 and 1998 and discuss the implications of the change.

COMPARATIVE ANALYSIS CASE
The Coca-Cola Company versus PepsiCo, Inc.

Instructions

Go to the Digital Tool and, using The Coca-Cola Company and PepsiCo, Inc. Annual Report information, answer the following questions.

(a) What is the par or stated value of Coca-Cola's and PepsiCo's common or capital stock?

(b) What percentage of authorized shares was issued by Coca-Cola at December 31, 1998, and by PepsiCo at December 26, 1998?

(c) How many shares are held as treasury stock by Coca-Cola at December 31, 1998, and by PepsiCo at December 26, 1998?

(d) How many Coca-Cola common shares are outstanding at December 31, 1998? How many PepsiCo shares of capital stock are outstanding at December 26, 1998?

(e) How do Coca-Cola and PepsiCo describe in their balance sheet the amount paid for shares of their common or capital stock in excess of the par value and what are these amounts as of December 31, 1998, and December 26, 1998, for Coca-Cola and PepsiCo respectively?

RESEARCH CASES

Case 1
Instructions

Use EDGAR or some other source to obtain the most recent proxy statement for the company of your choice. Be aware that EDGAR denotes final proxy materials by "DEF 14A," except for election contests ("DEFC14A") and mergers/acquisitions ("DEFM14A"). Examine the proxy statement and answer the following questions. (See bottom of page 263, Research Case 1, for access of EDGAR.)

(a) On what matters are the shareholders being asked to vote?

(b) Where is the annual meeting being held? Must a shareholder attend the annual meeting in order to vote?

(c) For each of the matters up for vote, what information is included in the proxy statement to aid shareholders in making their decisions?

(d) The proxy statement is generally the best source for identifying how company management is compensated. Examine the executive compensation section of the proxy statement and list the types of compensation received.

Case 2

The September 4, 1995, issue of *Fortune* includes an article by Richard D. Hylton entitled "Stock Buybacks Are Hot—Here's How You Can Cash In."

Instructions

Read the article and answer the following questions.

(a) What was the total amount of announced intentions to repurchase shares of stock in 1994? What was this figure during the first six months of 1995?

(b) The goal of many of these repurchase programs was to increase the price of the remaining outstanding shares. Identify the three factors that will determine the impact of repurchases on share price.

(c) What did Microsoft do with the shares it repurchased? Why might they use repurchased shares for this purpose rather than issuing new shares?

ETHICS CASES

Case 1

Morris Lester is the accounting manager of LBC, which is a closely held and rapidly growing retail sporting equipment concern with 60 stores located throughout New York and New England. Morris has been asked by the CFO, Kathy Morgan, to review two agreed-upon alternatives for the purchase of a newly constructed warehouse facility located in Pittsfield, Massachusetts (defined as follows):

	Option 1	
New Building	$1,500,000	
LBC Common Stock ($100 Par Value)		$1,000,000
Paid-in Capital in Excess of Par		500,000

	Option 2	
New Building	$1,350,000	
Notes Payable (with Contractor)		$1,200,000
Cash		150,000

In addition to the above facts and figures, Morris knows that LBC would probably prefer the first option because Kathy Morgan told him earlier that, " . . . the company is experiencing tough working capital problems due to its rapid expansion in recent years."

Instructions

(a) Assuming that the value of the new warehouse was independently appraised by a real estate consulting firm at $1.5 million, what are the ethical implications that should be considered by Morris when considering both options?

(b) Assuming that the value of the new warehouse was independently appraised by a real estate consulting firm at $1.35 million, what are the ethical implications that should be considered by Morris when considering both options?

(c) Who could be harmed if LBC chose to inflate its asset values in a "watered stock" transaction?

(d) Explain how your answers to the above questions would change if LBC were a publicly traded corporation.

Case 2

Jean Loptien, president of Sycamore Corporation, is concerned about several large stockholders who have been very vocal lately in their criticisms of her leadership. She thinks they might mount a campaign to have her removed as the corporation's CEO. She decides that buying them out by purchasing their shares could eliminate them as opponents, and she is confident they would accept a "good" offer. Loptien knows the corporation's cash position is decent, so it has the cash to complete the transaction. She also knows the purchase of these shares will increase earnings per share, which should make other investors quite happy.*

Instructions

Answer the following questions:

(a) Who are the stakeholders in this situation?

(b) What are the ethical issues involved?

(c) Should Loptien authorize the transaction?

---

*Earnings per share is calculated by dividing net income available for the common shareholders by the weighted average number of shares outstanding. Therefore, if the number of shares outstanding is decreased by purchasing treasury shares, earnings per share increases.

CHAPTER 16

Stockholders' Equity: Retained Earnings

Splitsville, Where More May Be More

A recent survey of New York Stock Exchange companies shows the increase in the use of stock splits by major companies:[1]

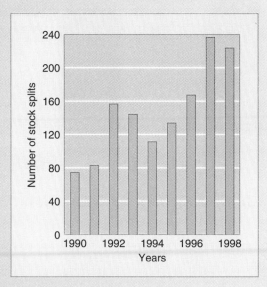

Companies recognize that stock splits may be cosmetic, but investors like them. Although a potential stock division is not sufficient reason to buy a stock, studies have shown that shares that split usually outperform those that don't, as well as the market as a whole, for several years after the split.

A stock split does not boost one's proportionate ownership of a company, yet many investors get a psychological lift from owning more shares. Nor does a stock dividend bolster a corporation's earning prospects, but a dividend boost typically accompanies a split, and this possibility attracts more investors. Also, the lower share price after the stock has split (typically down to the $60–$80 range) invites further buying by small investors. In all, as a Standard & Poor's investment newsletter states, "Companies that declare splits usually are doing well, and management is confident that earnings will continue to trend higher." Investors have seen the results of stock splits and have read them as positive signals.[2]

---

[1]Data from the New York Stock Exchange.

[2]Adapted from Shirley A. Lazo, "Splitsville, Where More May Be More," *Barron's,* June 3, 1996, p. 60.

LEARNING OBJECTIVES

After studying this chapter, you should be able to:

1. Describe the policies used in distributing dividends.
2. Identify the various forms of dividend distributions.
3. Explain the accounting for small and large stock dividends.
4. Distinguish between stock dividends and stock splits.
5. Explain the effect of different types of preferred stock dividends.
6. Identify the reasons for appropriating retained earnings.
7. Explain accounting and reporting for appropriated retained earnings.
8. Indicate how stockholders' equity is presented and analyzed.

As indicated in the opening story, companies use stock splits and stock dividends to send positive signals to their shareholders. In addition, many companies provide other types of dividend distributions. The purpose of this chapter is to discuss these and other transactions that affect retained earnings. The content and organization of the chapter are as follows:

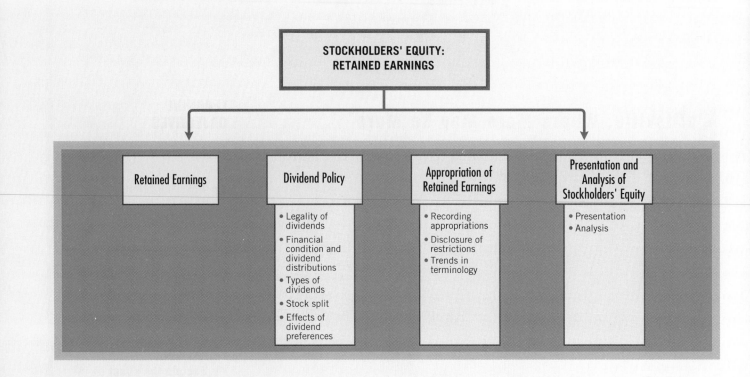

RETAINED EARNINGS

The basic source of **retained earnings**—earnings retained for use in the business—is income from operations. Stockholders assume the greatest risk in enterprise operations and stand any losses or share in any profits resulting from enterprise activities. Any income not distributed among the stockholders thus becomes additional stockholders' equity. Net income includes a considerable variety of income sources. These include the main operation of the enterprise (such as manufacturing and selling a given product), plus any ancillary activities (such as disposing of scrap or renting out unused space), plus the results of extraordinary and unusual items. All give rise to net income that increases retained earnings. The more common items that either increase or decrease retained earnings are expressed in account form below.

ILLUSTRATION 16-1
Transactions that Affect
Retained Earnings

Retained Earnings	
1. Net loss	1. Net income
2. Prior period adjustments (error corrections) and certain changes in accounting principle	2. Prior period adjustments (error corrections) and certain changes in accounting principle
3. Cash or scrip dividends	3. Adjustments due to quasi-reorganization
4. Stock dividends	
5. Property dividends	
6. Some treasury stock transactions	

Chapter 4 pointed out that the results of irregular transactions should be reported in the income statement, not the retained earnings statement. However, prior period adjustments (error corrections) should be reported as adjustments to beginning retained earnings, bypassing completely the current income statement.

DIVIDEND POLICY

Determining the proper amount of dividends to pay is a difficult financial management decision. Companies that are paying dividends are extremely reluctant to reduce or eliminate their dividend, because they believe that this action could be viewed negatively by the securities market. As a consequence, companies that have been paying cash dividends will make every effort to continue to do so. In addition, the type of shareholder the company has (taxable or nontaxable, retail investor or institutional investor) plays a large role in determining dividend policy. For example, a nontaxable entity will probably prefer cash dividends rather than a share buyback because tax considerations are not as important. As indicated in Chapter 15, more companies are becoming involved in share buyback programs and are either not starting or not increasing their present dividend program significantly.

Very few companies pay dividends in amounts equal to their legally available retained earnings. The major reasons are as follows:

❶ Agreements (bond covenants) with specific creditors to retain all or a portion of the earnings, in the form of assets, to build up additional protection against possible loss.

❷ Some state corporation laws require that earnings equivalent to the cost of treasury shares purchased be restricted against dividend declarations.

❸ Desire to retain assets that would otherwise be paid out as dividends, to finance growth or expansion. This is sometimes called internal financing, reinvesting earnings, or "plowing" the profits back into the business.

❹ Desire to smooth out dividend payments from year to year by accumulating earnings in good years and using such accumulated earnings as a basis for dividends in bad years.

❺ Desire to build up a cushion or buffer against possible losses or errors in the calculation of profits.

The reasons above are probably self-explanatory except for the second. The laws of some states require that the corporation's legal capital be restricted from distribution to stockholders so that it may serve as a protection against loss for creditors.[3]

If a company is considering declaring a dividend, two preliminary questions must be asked:

❶ Is the condition of the corporation such that a dividend is **legally permissible**?

❷ Is the condition of the corporation such that a dividend is **economically sound**?

Legality of Dividends

The legality of a dividend can be determined only by reviewing the applicable state law. Currently, the 50 states may be classified into one of three groups for purposes of comparing restrictions on dividends and other distributions to owners.[4] The largest

> **OBJECTIVE ❶**
> Describe the policies used in distributing dividends.

---

[3]If the corporation buys its own outstanding stock, it has reduced its legal capital and distributed assets to stockholders. If this were permitted, the corporation could, by purchasing treasury stock at any price desired, return to the stockholders their investments and leave creditors with little or no protection against loss.

[4]Michael L. Roberts, William D. Samson, and Michael T. Dugan, "The Stockholders' Equity Section: Form Without Substance," *Accounting Horizons*, December 1990, pp. 35–46.

group permits distributions to stockholders as long as the corporation is not insolvent. Insolvency is defined as the inability to pay debts as they come due in the normal course of business. Generally, in these states distribution in the form of dividends has to come from retained earnings or from current earnings.

A second group either follows the 1984 Revised Model Business Corporation Act or has distribution restrictions similar to it. That is, (1) the corporation must be solvent, and (2) distributions must not exceed the fair value of net assets. Under the latter criterion, distributions are not limited to retained earnings or GAAP determined current earnings. Instead of being tied to the book value of the assets, distributions are linked to the fair (appraised) value of the assets—a notable new criterion.

The remaining states use a variety of hybrid restrictions that consist of solvency and balance sheet tests of liquidity and risk. To avoid illegal distribution of corporate assets to stockholders, the relevant state corporation act should be examined and legal advice obtained.

Unfortunately, current financial statement disclosures do not include basic information such as: whether a corporation is in compliance with state legal requirements; the corporation's capacity to make distributions; or, occasionally, what legal restrictions exist regarding distributions to stockholders.

An example of the inadequacies of such disclosures is the 1987–88 stockholders' equity balance sheet sections of **Holiday Corporation** (former owner of Holiday Inns of America). Its 1987 balance sheet reported total stockholders' equity of $639 million. The 1988 balance sheet, however, revealed a **$770 million deficit** in Holiday's total stockholders' equity. How did this deficit develop? During the year, Holiday distributed a $65 per share dividend to prevent a hostile takeover. This $1.55 billion dividend to stockholders, financed with borrowed money, not only exceeded Holiday's retained earnings (then about $400 million), but exceeded total stockholders' equity as well by $770 million.

Holiday was allowed to distribute the $1.55 billion dividend (legally, under Delaware law) because the fair value of its assets exceeded its liabilities after the distribution; that is, on a fair value basis it had positive equity. Yet, the traditional balance sheet disclosures in the equity section or the accompanying notes do not contain any information (either before or after the dividend distribution), enabling financial statement readers to assess Holiday's capacity for making such distributions.

Because the traditional equivalency of minimum legal capital and par value no longer holds in many states, the stockholders' equity accounting presentation of par value, additional paid-in capital, and retained earnings is being eroded. It implies that some amount, represented by a portion of stockholders' equity, exists to protect creditors, when in many instances, it may not.

UNDERLYING CONCEPTS

Here is where substance over form is demonstrated. The limitations of the historical cost principle are highlighted by an inability to address the situation.

Financial Condition and Dividend Distributions

Good management of a business requires attention to more than the legality of dividend distributions. Consideration must be given to economic conditions, most importantly, liquidity. Assume an extreme situation as follows:

ILLUSTRATION 16-2
Balance Sheet, Showing a Lack of Liquidity

Balance Sheet			
Plant assets	$500,000	Capital stock	$400,000
		Retained earnings	100,000
	$500,000		$500,000

The depicted company has a retained earnings credit balance and generally, unless it is restricted, can declare a dividend of $100,000. But because all its assets are plant assets and used in operations, payment of a cash dividend of $100,000 would require the sale of plant assets or borrowing.

Even if we assume a balance sheet showing current assets, the question remains as to whether those cash assets are needed for other purposes.

Balance Sheet				
Cash	$100,000	Current liabilities		$ 60,000
Plant assets	460,000	Capital stock	$400,000	
		Retained earnings	100,000	500,000
	$560,000			$560,000

ILLUSTRATION 16-3
Balance Sheet, Showing Cash but Minimal Working Capital

The existence of current liabilities implies very strongly that some of the cash is needed to meet current debts as they mature. In addition, day-by-day cash requirements for payrolls and other expenditures not included in current liabilities also require cash.

Thus, before a dividend is declared, management must consider **availability of funds to pay the dividend**. Other demands for cash should perhaps be investigated by preparing a cash forecast. A dividend should not be paid unless both the present and future financial position appear to warrant the distribution.

Directors must also consider the effect of inflation and replacement costs before making a dividend commitment. During a period of significant inflation, some costs charged to expense under historical cost accounting are understated in terms of comparative purchasing power. Income is thereby overstated because certain costs have not been adjusted for inflation. For example, St. Regis Paper Company reported historical cost net income of $179 million, but when it was adjusted for general inflation, net income was only $68 million. Yet St. Regis paid cash dividends of $72 million. Were cash dividends excessive?

The SEC encourages companies to disclose their dividend policy in their annual report. Those that (1) have earnings but fail to pay dividends or (2) do not expect to pay dividends in the forseeable future are encouraged to report this information. In addition, companies that have had a consistent pattern of paying dividends are encouraged to indicate whether they intend to continue this practice in the future.

Two disclosures relative to the policy of payment or nonpayment of dividends are those of Kellogg Company and Atmel Corporation presented below.

KELLOGG COMPANY

Dividend News.   We are pleased to report that the Kellogg Company dividend rose in 1998 for the 42nd consecutive year, with an increase of 5 cents per share to $.92.

ILLUSTRATION 16-4
Disclosures about Dividend Payment Policy

ATMEL CORPORATION

Dividend Policy.   The Company has not paid any dividends on its capital stock. The Company presently intends to retain any earnings for use in business and therefore does not anticipate paying cash dividends on its outstanding shares in the foreseeable future. In addition, the Company's bank credit agreement restricts the Company's ability to pay cash dividends without the bank's consent.

Types of Dividends

Dividend distributions generally are based either on accumulated profits, that is, retained earnings, or on some other capital item such as additional paid-in capital. The natural expectation of any stockholder who receives a dividend is that the corporation

OBJECTIVE ②
Identify the various forms of dividend distributions.

has operated successfully and that he or she is receiving a share of its profits. A **liquidating dividend**—that is, a dividend not based on retained earnings—should be adequately described in the accompanying message to the stockholders so that there will be no misunderstanding about its source. Dividends are of the following types:

1. Cash dividends.
2. Property dividends.
3. Scrip dividends.
4. Liquidating dividends.
5. Stock dividends.

Dividends are commonly paid in cash but occasionally are paid in stock, scrip, or some other asset.[5] **All dividends, except for stock dividends, reduce the total stockholders' equity in the corporation,** because the equity is reduced either through an immediate or promised future distribution of assets. When a stock dividend is declared, the corporation does not pay out assets or incur a liability. It issues additional shares of stock to each stockholder and nothing more.

Cash Dividends

The board of directors votes on the declaration of cash dividends, and if the resolution is properly approved, the dividend is declared. Before it is paid, a current list of stockholders must be prepared. For this reason there is usually a time lag between declaration and payment. A resolution approved at the January 10 (**date of declaration**) meeting of the board of directors might be declared payable February 5 (**date of payment**) to all stockholders of record January 25 (**date of record**).[6]

The period from January 10 to January 25 gives time for any transfers in process to be completed and registered with the transfer agent. The time from January 25 to February 5 provides an opportunity for the transfer agent or accounting department, depending on who does this work, to prepare a list of stockholders as of January 25 and to prepare and mail dividend checks.

A declared cash dividend is a liability and, because payment is generally required very soon, is usually a current liability. The following entries are required to record the declaration and payment of an ordinary dividend payable in cash. For example, Roadway Freight Corp. on June 10 declared a cash dividend of 50 cents a share on 1.8 million shares payable July 16 to all stockholders of record June 24.

At date of declaration (June 10)

Retained Earnings (Cash Dividends Declared)	900,000	
Dividends Payable		900,000

At date of record (June 24)

No entry

At date of payment (July 16)

Dividends Payable	900,000	
Cash		900,000

To set up a ledger account that shows the amount of dividends declared during the year, Cash Dividends Declared might be debited instead of Retained Earnings at the time of declaration. This account is then closed to Retained Earnings at year-end.

---

[5]*Accounting Trends and Techniques—1999* reported that of its 600 surveyed companies, 435 paid a cash dividend on common stock, 83 paid a cash dividend on preferred stock, 9 issued stock dividends, and 10 issued or paid dividends in kind. Some companies declare more than one type of dividend in a given year.

[6]Theoretically, the ex-dividend date is the day after the date of record. However, to allow time for transfer of the shares, the stock exchanges generally advance the ex-dividend date 2 to 4 days. Therefore, the party who owns the stock on the day prior to the expressed ex-dividend date receives the dividends, and the party who buys the stock on and after the ex-dividend date does not receive the dividend. Between the declaration date and the ex-dividend date, the market price of the stock includes the dividend.

Dividends may be declared either as a certain percent of par, such as a 6% dividend on preferred stock, or as an amount per share, such as 60 cents per share on no-par common stock. In the first case, the rate is multiplied by the par value of outstanding shares to get the total dividend; in the second, the amount per share is multiplied by the number of shares outstanding. **Cash dividends are not declared and paid on treasury stock.**

Dividend policies vary among corporations. Some older, well-established firms take pride in a long, unbroken string of quarterly dividend payments. They would lower or pass the dividend only if forced to do so by a sustained decline in earnings or a critical shortage of cash.

"Growth" companies, on the other hand, pay little or no cash dividends because their policy is to expand as rapidly as internal and external financing permit. Neither Quest Medical, Inc., a small growth company, nor Federal Express Corporation, a large growth company, has ever paid cash dividends to their common stockholders. These investors hope that the price of their shares will appreciate in value and that they will realize a profit when they sell their shares. As indicated earlier, many companies are less concerned with dividend payout, and more focused on increasing share price, stock repurchase programs, and corporate earnings.

INTERNATIONAL INSIGHT
As a less preferred but still allowable treatment, international accounting standards permit firms to reduce equity by the amount of proposed dividends prior to their legal declaration.

Property Dividends

Dividends payable in assets of the corporation other than cash are called property dividends or **dividends in kind**. Property dividends may be merchandise, real estate, or investments, or whatever form the board of directors designates. Ranchers Exploration and Development Corp. reported one year that it would pay a fourth-quarter dividend in gold bars instead of cash. Because of the obvious difficulties of divisibility of units and delivery to stockholders, the usual property dividend is in the form of securities of other companies that the distributing corporation holds as an investment.

For example, when DuPont's 23% stock interest in General Motors was held by the Supreme Court to be in violation of antitrust laws, DuPont was ordered to divest itself of the GM stock within 10 years. The stock represented 63 million shares of GM's 281 million shares then outstanding. DuPont couldn't sell the shares in one block of 63 million, nor could it sell 6 million shares annually for the next 10 years without severely depressing the value of the GM stock. At that time the entire yearly trading volume in GM stock did not exceed 6 million shares. DuPont solved its problem by declaring a property dividend and distributing the GM shares as a dividend to its own stockholders.

Dresser Industries, Inc. distributed a dividend in kind and reported its accounting for the distribution as follows:

DRESSER INDUSTRIES, INC.

Notes to Consolidated Financial Statements

Note B: Dividend in Kind. The Company divested its industrial products and equipment businesses. The divestiture/spin-off was accomplished by a distribution of one INDRESCO share for every five shares of the Company's common stock. The distribution is included as charges totaling $413.9 million to retained earnings and accumulated translation adjustment in the statement of shareholders' investment.

ILLUSTRATION 16-5
Disclosure of a
Dividend in Kind

A property dividend is a nonreciprocal transfer[7] of nonmonetary assets between an enterprise and its owners. Prior to the issuance of *APB Opinion No. 29*, the accounting for such transfers was based on the carrying amount (book value) of the non-

---

[7]A nonreciprocal transfer of assets or services is in one direction, either from or to an enterprise.

monetary assets transferred. This practice was based on the rationale that there is no sale or arm's-length transaction on which to base a gain or loss and that only this method is consistent with the historical cost basis of accounting. However, the profession's current position is quite clear on this matter:

> A transfer of a nonmonetary asset to a stockholder or to another entity in a nonreciprocal transfer should be recorded at the fair value of the asset transferred, and a gain or loss should be recognized on the disposition of the asset.[8]

The **fair value** of the nonmonetary asset distributed is measured by the amount that would be realizable in an outright sale at or near the time of the distribution. Such an amount should be determined by referring to estimated realizable values in cash transactions of the same or similar assets, quoted market prices, independent appraisals, and other available evidence.[9]

The failure to recognize the fair value of nonmonetary assets transferred may both misstate the dividend and fail to recognize gains and losses on nonmonetary assets that have already been earned or incurred by the enterprise. Recording the dividend at fair value permits future comparisons of dividend rates. If cash must be distributed to stockholders in place of the nonmonetary asset, determination of the amount to be distributed is simplified.

When the property dividend is declared, the corporation should **restate at fair value the property to be distributed**, **recognizing any gain or loss** as the difference between the property's fair value and carrying value at date of declaration. The declared dividend may then be recorded as a debit to Retained Earnings (or Property Dividends Declared) and a credit to Property Dividends Payable at an amount equal to the fair value of the property to be distributed. Upon distribution of the dividend, Property Dividends Payable is debited, and the account containing the distributed asset (restated at fair value) is credited.

For example, Trendler, Inc., transferred to stockholders some of its investments in marketable securities costing $1,250,000 by declaring a property dividend on December 28, 2000, to be distributed on January 30, 2001, to stockholders of record on January 15, 2001. At the date of declaration the securities have a market value of $2,000,000. The entries are as follows:

At date of declaration (December 28, 2000)

Investments in Securities	750,000	
Gain on Appreciation of Securities		750,000
Retained Earnings (Property Dividends Declared)	2,000,000	
Property Dividends Payable		2,000,000

At date of distribution (January 30, 2001)

Property Dividends Payable	2,000,000	
Investments in Securities		2,000,000

Scrip Dividends

A scrip dividend—dividend payable in scrip—means that instead of paying the dividend now, the corporation has elected to pay it at some later date. **The scrip issued to stockholders as a dividend is merely a special form of note payable.** For example, at one time the Bank of Puerto Rico issued a $9 million note as a dividend that matured ten years later, at which time each holder of the corporation's 3 million common shares

---

[8] "Accounting for Nonmonetary Transactions," *Opinions of the Accounting Principles Board No. 29* (New York: AICPA, 1973), par. 18.

[9] According to *APB Opinion No. 29,* accounting for the distribution of nonmonetary assets to owners of an enterprise in a spin-off or other form of reorganization or liquidation should be based on the **book value** (after reduction, if appropriate, for an indicated impairment of value) of the nonmonetary assets distributed. This is an exception to the fair value treatment prescribed for nonmonetary distributions.

received $3 a share. Scrip dividends may be declared when the corporation has a sufficient retained earnings balance but is short of cash. The recipient of the scrip dividend may hold it until the due date, if one is specified, and collect the dividend or may sell it to obtain immediate cash.

When a scrip dividend is declared, the corporation debits Retained Earnings (or Scrip Dividend Declared) and credits Scrip Dividend Payable or Notes Payable to Stockholders, **reporting the payable as a liability** on the balance sheet. Upon payment, Scrip Dividend Payable is debited and Cash credited. If the scrip bears interest, the interest portion of the cash payment should be debited to Interest Expense and not treated as part of the dividend. For example, Berg Canning Company avoided missing its 84th consecutive quarterly dividend by declaring on May 27 a scrip dividend in the form of two-month promissory notes amounting to 80 cents a share on 2,545,000 shares outstanding and payable at the date of record, June 5. The notes paid interest of 10% per annum and matured on July 27. The entries are as follows:

At date of declaration (May 27)

Retained Earnings (Scrip Dividend Declared)	2,036,000	
Notes Payable to Stockholders ($.80 $\times$ 2,545,000)		2,036,000

At date of payment (July 27)

Notes Payable to Stockholders	2,036,000	
Interest Expense ($2,036,000 $\times$ 2/12 $\times$ .10)[a]	33,933	
Cash		2,069,933

[a]The interest runs from the date of declaration to the date of payment.

Liquidating Dividends

Some corporations use paid-in capital as a basis for dividends. Without proper disclosure of this fact, stockholders may erroneously believe the corporation has been operating at a profit. A further result could be subsequent sale of additional shares at a higher price than is warranted. This type of deception, intentional or unintentional, can be avoided by requiring that a clear statement of the source of every dividend accompany the dividend check.

Dividends based on other than retained earnings are sometimes described as liquidating dividends, thus implying that they are a return of the stockholder's investment rather than of profits. In other words, **any dividend not based on earnings is a reduction of corporate paid-in capital and, to that extent, it is a liquidating dividend**. We noted in Chapter 11 that companies in the extractive industries may pay dividends equal to the total of accumulated income and depletion. The portion of these dividends in excess of accumulated income represents a return of part of the stockholder's investment.

For example, McChesney Mines Inc. issued a "dividend" to its common stockholders of $1,200,000. The cash dividend announcement noted that $900,000 should be considered income and the remainder a return of capital. The entries are:

At date of declaration

Retained Earnings	900,000	
Additional Paid-in Capital	300,000	
Dividends Payable		1,200,000

At date of payment

Dividends Payable	1,200,000	
Cash		1,200,000

In some cases, management may simply decide to cease business and declare a liquidating dividend. In these cases, liquidation may take place over a number of years to ensure an orderly and fair sale of assets. For example, when **Overseas National Airways** was dissolved, it agreed to pay a liquidating dividend to its stockholders over a period of years equivalent to $8.60 per share. Each liquidating dividend payment in such cases reduces paid-in capital.

Stock Dividends

If the management wishes to "capitalize" part of the earnings (i.e., reclassify amounts from earned to contributed capital), and thus retain earnings in the business on a permanent basis, it may issue a stock dividend. In this case, **no assets are distributed**, and each stockholder has exactly the same proportionate interest in the corporation and the same total book value after the stock dividend was issued as before it was declared. Of course, the book value per share is lower because an increased number of shares is held.

While accountants agree that a stock dividend is the nonreciprocal issuance by a corporation of its own stock to its stockholders on a pro rata basis, they do not agree on the proper entries to be made at the time of a stock dividend. Some believe that the **par value** of the stock issued as a dividend should be transferred from retained earnings to capital stock. Others believe that the **fair value** of the stock issued—its market value at the declaration date—should be transferred from retained earnings to capital stock and additional paid-in capital.

The fair value position was originally adopted in this country, at least in part, in order to influence the stock dividend policies of corporations. Evidently in 1941 both the New York Stock Exchange and a majority of the Committee on Accounting Procedure (CAP) regarded periodic stock dividends as objectionable. The CAP therefore acted to make it more difficult for corporations to sustain a series of such stock dividends out of their accumulated earnings by requiring the use of fair market value when it was substantially in excess of book value.[10]

When the stock dividend is less than 20–25% of the common shares outstanding at the time of the dividend declaration, the accounting profession requires that the **fair market value** of the stock issued be transferred from retained earnings.[11] Stock dividends of less than 20–25% are often referred to as small (ordinary) stock dividends. This method of handling stock dividends is justified on the grounds that "many recipients of stock dividends look upon them as distributions of corporate earnings and usually in an amount equivalent to the fair value of the additional shares received."[12] We do not consider this a convincing argument. It is generally agreed that stock dividends are not income to the recipients, and, therefore, sound accounting should not recommend procedures simply because some recipients think they are income.[13]

To illustrate a small stock dividend, assume that a corporation has outstanding 1,000 shares of $100 par value capital stock and retained earnings of $50,000. If the cor-

UNDERLYING CONCEPTS

If the intent of the CAP was to punish companies that used stock dividends by requiring fair value, it violated the neutrality concept; that is, that standard-setting should be even-handed.

OBJECTIVE ❸
Explain the accounting for small and large stock dividends.

---

[10]This represented perhaps the earliest instance of an accounting pronouncement being affected by "economic consequences," because the Committee on Accounting Procedure described its action as being required by "proper accounting and corporate policy." See Stephen A. Zeff, "The Rise of 'Economic Consequences,'" *The Journal of Accountancy*, December 1978, pp. 53–66.

[11]American Institute of Certified Public Accountants, *Accounting Research and Terminology Bulletins*, No. 43 (New York: AICPA, 1961), Ch. 7, par. 10. A minor exception is that if the stock dividend is used to increase the marketability of the shares, par value may be used.

[12]Ibid., par. 10. One study concluded that *small* stock dividends do not always produce significant amounts of extra value on the date after issuance (ex date) and that *large* stock dividends almost always fail to generate extra value on the ex-dividend date. Taylor W. Foster III and Don Vickrey, "The Information Content of Stock Dividend Announcements," *The Accounting Review*, Vol. LIII, No. 2, April 1978, pp. 360–370.

[13]The case against treating an ordinary stock dividend as income is supported under either an **entity** or **proprietary assumption** regarding the business enterprise. If the corporation is considered an entity separate from the stockholders, the income of the corporation is corporate income and not income to the stockholders, although the equity of the stockholders in the corporation increases. This position argues that a dividend is not income to the recipients until it is realized by them as a result of a division or severance of corporate assets. The stock dividend merely distributes the "recipients'" equity over a larger number of shares. Under this interpretation, selling the stock received as a dividend has the effect of reducing the recipients' proportionate share of the corporation's equity. Under the proprietary assumption, income of the corporation is considered income to the owners, and, hence, a stock dividend represents only a reclassification of equity, inasmuch as there is no change in total proprietorship.

poration declares a 10% stock dividend, it issues 100 additional shares to current stockholders. If it is assumed that the fair value of the stock at the time of the stock dividend is $130 per share, the entry is:

At date of declaration

Retained Earnings (Stock Dividend Declared)	13,000	
Common Stock Dividend Distributable		10,000
Paid-in Capital in Excess of Par		3,000

Note that no asset or liability has been affected. The entry merely reflects a reclassification of stockholders' equity. If a balance sheet is prepared between the dates of declaration and distribution, the common stock dividend distributable should be shown in the stockholders' equity section as an addition to capital stock (whereas cash or property dividends payable are shown as current liabilities).

When the stock is issued, the entry is

At date of distribution

Common Stock Dividend Distributable	10,000	
Common Stock		10,000

No matter what the fair value is at the time of the stock dividend, each stockholder retains the same proportionate interest in the corporation.

Some state statutes specifically prohibit the issuance of stock dividends on treasury stock. In those states that permit treasury shares to participate in the distribution accompanying a stock dividend or stock split, practice is influenced by the planned use of the treasury shares. For example, if the treasury shares are intended for issuance in connection with employee stock options, the treasury shares may participate in the distribution because the number of shares under option is usually adjusted for any stock dividends or splits. But unless there are specific uses for the treasury stock, no useful purpose is served by issuing additional shares to the treasury stock since they are essentially equivalent to authorized but unissued shares.

INTERNATIONAL INSIGHT

Revaluation of assets is likely to result in revaluation capital. Such capital is available as the basis for stock dividends in some countries and for cash dividends in others. Some countries require the accumulation of such capital but do not permit it to be used as the basis for either form of dividend.

Before dividend:	
Capital stock, 1,000 shares of $100 par	$100,000
Retained earnings	50,000
Total stockholders' equity	$150,000
Stockholders' interests:	
A. 400 shares, 40% interest, book value	$ 60,000
B. 500 shares, 50% interest, book value	75,000
C. 100 shares, 10% interest, book value	15,000
	$150,000
After declaration but before distribution of 10% stock dividend:	
If fair value ($130) is used as basis for entry	
Capital stock, 1,000 shares at $100 par	$100,000
Common stock distributable, 100 shares at $100 par	10,000
Paid-in capital in excess of par	3,000
Retained earnings ($50,000 − $13,000)	37,000
Total stockholders' equity	$150,000
After declaration and distribution of 10% stock dividend:	
If fair value ($130) is used as basis for entry	
Capital stock, 1,100 shares at $100 par	$110,000
Paid-in capital in excess of par	3,000
Retained earnings ($50,000 − $13,000)	37,000
Total stockholders' equity	$150,000
Stockholders' interest:	
A. 440 shares, 40% interest, book value	$ 60,000
B. 550 shares, 50% interest, book value	75,000
C. 110 shares, 10% interest, book value	15,000
	$150,000

ILLUSTRATION 16-6
Effects of a Small (10%) Stock Dividend

To continue with our example of the effect of the small stock dividend, note in Illustration 16-6 on page 821 that the total stockholders' equity has not changed as a result of the stock dividend. Also note that the proportion of the total shares outstanding held by each stockholder is unchanged.

Stock Split

If a company has undistributed earnings over several years and a sizable balance in retained earnings has accumulated, the market value of its outstanding shares is likely to increase. Stock that was issued at prices less than $50 a share can easily attain a market value in excess of $200 a share. The higher the market price of a stock, the less readily it can be purchased by some investors. The managements of many corporations believe that for better public relations, wider ownership of the corporation stock is desirable. They wish, therefore, to have a market price sufficiently low to be within range of the majority of potential investors. To reduce the market value of shares, the common device of a stock split is employed.[14] For example, after its stock price increased by 25-fold during 1999, **Qualcomm Inc.** split its stock 4-for-1. Qualcomm's stock had risen above $500 per share, raising concerns that Qualcomm could not meet an analyst target of $1,000 per share. The split reduced the analysts' target to $250, which could better be met with wider distribution of shares at lower trading prices.[15]

From an accounting standpoint, **no entry is recorded for a stock split**; a memorandum note, however, is made to indicate that the par value of the shares has changed, and that the number of shares has increased. The lack of change in stockholders' equity is portrayed in Illustration 16-7 of a 2-for-1 stock split on 1,000 shares of $100 par value stock with the par being halved upon issuance of the additional shares:

ILLUSTRATION 16-7
Effects of a Stock Split

Stockholders' Equity before 2-for-1 Split		Stockholders' Equity after 2-for-1 Split	
Common stock, 1,000 shares at $100 par	$100,000	Common stock, 2,000 shares at $50 par	$100,000
Retained earnings	50,000	Retained earnings	50,000
	$150,000		$150,000

Stock Split and Stock Dividend Differentiated

OBJECTIVE 4
Distinguish between stock dividends and stock splits.

From a legal standpoint a stock split is distinguished from a stock dividend, because a stock split results in an increase in the number of shares outstanding and a corresponding decrease in the par or stated value per share. **A stock dividend, although it results in an increase in the number of shares outstanding, does not decrease the par value; thus it increases the total par value of outstanding shares.**

The reasons for issuing a stock dividend are numerous and varied. Stock dividends can be more of a publicity gesture, because they are considered by many as dividends

---

[14]The *DH&S Review*, May 12, 1986, page 7, listed the following as reasons behind a stock split:
1. To adjust the market price of the company's shares to a level where more individuals can afford to invest in the stock.
2. To spread the stockholder base by increasing the number of shares outstanding and making them more marketable.
3. To benefit existing stockholders by allowing them to take advantage of an imperfect market adjustment following the split.

[15]Some companies use reverse stock splits. A **reverse stock split** reduces the number of shares outstanding and increases the per share price. This technique is used when the stock price is unusually low or when management wishes to take control of the company. For example, two officers of **Metropolitan Maintenance Co.** took their company private by forcing a 1-for-3,000 reverse stock split on their stockholders. For every 3,000 old shares, one new share was issued. But anyone who had fewer than 3,000 shares received only cash for his or her stock. Only the two officers owned more than 3,000 shares, so they now own all the stock. A nice squeeze play! *Forbes,* November 19, 1984, p. 54.

and, consequently, the corporation is not criticized for retention of profits. Some corporations even lead their stockholders to believe that a stock dividend is equivalent to a cash dividend. For instance, the Board of Directors of **Wickes Companies Inc.** declared a 2½% stock dividend "in lieu of the quarterly cash dividend, which had been 26¢ per share." E. L. McNeely, chairman of Wickes, said, "This dividend continues Wickes' 88-year record of uninterrupted dividend payments." More defensible perhaps, the corporation may simply wish to retain profits in the business by capitalizing a part of retained earnings. In such a situation, a transfer is made on declaration of a stock dividend from earned capital to contributed or permanent capital.

A stock dividend, like a stock split, also may be used to increase the marketability of the stock, although marketability is often a secondary consideration. If the stock dividend is large, it has the same effect on market price as a stock split. The profession has taken the position that **whenever additional shares are issued for the purpose of reducing the unit market price, then the distribution more closely resembles a stock split than a stock dividend. This effect usually results only if the number of shares issued is more than 20–25% of the number of shares previously outstanding.**[16] A stock dividend of more than 20–25% of the number of shares previously outstanding is called a **large stock dividend.**[17] The profession also recommends that such a distribution not be called a stock dividend, but it might properly be called "a split-up effected in the form of a dividend" or "stock split." Also, since the par value of the outstanding shares is not altered, the transfer from retained earnings is only in the amount required by statute. Ordinarily this means a transfer from retained earnings to capital stock **for the par value of the stock issued** as opposed to a transfer of the market value of the shares issued as in the case of a small stock dividend.[18] For example, **Brown Group, Inc.** at one time authorized a 2-for-1 split, effected in the form of a stock dividend. As a result of this authorization, approximately 10.5 million shares were distributed and more than $39 million representing the par value of the shares issued was transferred from Retained Earnings to the Common Stock account.

To illustrate a large stock dividend (stock split-up effected in the form of a dividend), Rockland Steel, Inc. declared a 30% stock dividend on November 20, payable December 29 to stockholders of record December 12. At the date of declaration, 1,000,000 shares, par value $10, are outstanding and with a fair market value of $200 per share. The entries are:

At date of declaration (November 20)

Retained Earnings	3,000,000	
Common Stock Dividend Distributable		3,000,000

Computation: 1,000,000 shares	300,000 Additional shares
× 30%	× $10 Par value
300,000	$3,000,000

At date of distribution (December 29)

Common Stock Dividend Distributable	3,000,000	
Common Stock		3,000,000

Illustration 16-8 summarizes and compares the effects of various types of dividends and stock splits on various elements of the financial statements:

---

[16]*Accounting Research and Terminology Bulletin No. 43*, par. 13.

[17]The SEC has added more precision to the 20–25% rule. Specifically, the SEC indicates that distributions of 25% or more should be considered a "split-up effected in the form of a dividend." Distributions of less than 25% should be accounted for as a stock dividend. The SEC more precisely defined GAAP here, and as a result the SEC rule is followed by public companies.

[18]Often, a split-up effected in the form of a dividend is debited to paid-in capital instead of retained earnings to indicate that this transaction should affect only paid-in capital accounts. No reduction of retained earnings is required except as indicated by legal requirements. For homework purposes, assume that the debit is to Retained Earnings. See, for example, Taylor W. Foster III and Edmund Scribner, "Accounting for Stock Dividends and Stock Splits: Corrections to Textbook Coverage," *Issues in Accounting Education*, February 1998.

ILLUSTRATION 16-8
Effects of Dividends and
Stock Splits on Financial
Statement Elements

Effect on:	Declaration of Cash Dividend	Payment of Cash Dividend	Declaration and Distribution of		
			Small Stock Dividend	Large Stock Dividend	Stock Split
Retained earnings	Decrease	–0–	Decrease[a]	Decrease[b]	–0–
Capital stock	–0–	–0–	Increase[b]	Increase[b]	–0–
Additional paid-in capital	–0–	–0–	Increase[c]	–0–	–0–
Total stockholders' equity	Decrease	–0–	–0–	–0–	–0–
Working capital	Decrease	–0–	–0–	–0–	–0–
Total assets	–0–	Decrease	–0–	–0–	–0–
Number of shares outstanding	–0–	–0–	Increase	Increase	Increase

[a]Market value of shares.   [b]Par or stated value of shares.   [c]Excess of market value over par.

OBJECTIVE 5
Explain the effect of
different types of
preferred stock
dividends.

Effects of Dividend Preferences

The examples given below illustrate the **effects of** various **dividend preferences** on dividend distributions to common and preferred stockholders. Assume that in a given year, $50,000 is to be distributed as cash dividends, outstanding common stock has a par value of $400,000, and 6% preferred stock has a par value of $100,000. Dividends would be distributed to each class as shown below, employing the assumptions given.

1 If the preferred stock is noncumulative and nonparticipating:

ILLUSTRATION 16-9
Dividend Distribution,
Noncumulative and
Nonparticipating
Preferred

	Preferred	Common	Total
6% of $100,000	$6,000		$ 6,000
The remainder to common		$44,000	44,000
Totals	$6,000	$44,000	$50,000

2 If the preferred stock is cumulative and nonparticipating, and dividends were not paid on the preferred stock in the preceding 2 years:

ILLUSTRATION 16-10
Dividend Distribution,
Cumulative and
Nonparticipating
Preferred, with Dividends
in Arrears

	Preferred	Common	Total
Dividends in arrears, 6% of $100,000 for 2 years	$12,000		$12,000
Current year's dividend, 6% of $100,000	6,000		6,000
The remainder to common		$32,000	32,000
Totals	$18,000	$32,000	$50,000

3 If the preferred stock is noncumulative and is fully participating:[19]

---

[19]When preferred stock is participating, there may be different agreements as to how the participation feature is to be executed. However, in the absence of any specific agreement the following procedure is recommended:

   a. After the preferred stock is assigned its current year's dividend, the common stock will receive a "like" percentage of par value outstanding. In example (3), this amounts to 6% of $400,000.

   b. If there is a remainder of declared dividends for participation by the preferred and common stock, this remainder will be shared in proportion to the par value dollars outstanding in each class of stock. In example (3) this proportion is:

$$\text{Preferred} \quad \frac{\$100,000}{\$500,000} \times \$20,000 = \$4,000$$

$$\text{Common} \quad \frac{\$400,000}{\$500,000} \times \$20,000 = \$16,000$$

	Preferred	Common	Total
Current year's dividend, 6%	$ 6,000	$24,000	$30,000
Participating dividend of 4%	4,000	16,000	20,000
Totals	$10,000	$40,000	$50,000

ILLUSTRATION 16-11
Dividend Distribution, Noncumulative and Fully Participating Preferred

The participating dividend was determined as follows:
Current year's dividend:

Preferred, 6% of $100,000 = $ 6,000		
Common, 6% of $400,000 = 24,000		$ 30,000
Amount available for participation ($50,000 − $30,000)		$ 20,000
Par value of stock that is to participate ($100,000 + $400,000)		$500,000
Rate of participation ($20,000 ÷ $500,000)		4%
Participating dividend:		
Preferred, 4% of $100,000		$ 4,000
Common, 4% of $400,000		16,000
		$ 20,000

④ If the preferred stock is cumulative and is fully participating, and if dividends were not paid on the preferred stock in the preceding 2 years (the same procedure as described in example (3) is used in this example to effect the participation feature):

	Preferred	Common	Total
Dividends in arrears, 6% of $100,000 for 2 years	$12,000		$12,000
Current year's dividend, 6%	6,000	$24,000	30,000
Participating dividend, 1.6% ($8,000 ÷ $500,000)	1,600	6,400	8,000
Totals	$19,600	$30,400	$50,000

ILLUSTRATION 16-12
Dividend Distribution, Cumulative and Fully Participating Preferred, with Dividends in Arrears

APPROPRIATION OF RETAINED EARNINGS

The act of appropriating retained earnings is a policy matter requiring approval by the board of directors. According to *FASB Statement No. 5*, the appropriation of retained earnings is acceptable practice, "provided that it is shown within the stockholders' equity section of the balance sheet and is clearly identified as an appropriation of retained earnings."[20]

OBJECTIVE ⑥
Identify the reasons for appropriating retained earnings.

Appropriation of retained earnings is **nothing more than reclassification of retained earnings for a specific purpose.** An appropriation does not set aside cash: It discloses that management does not intend to distribute assets as a dividend up to the amount of the appropriation because these assets are needed by the corporation for a specified purpose. The unappropriated retained earnings is debited (reduced) by the amount of the appropriation, and a new account for the specific purpose is established and credited for the transferred amount. When the appropriation is no longer necessary, either because the specific purpose has been accomplished or the loss has occurred or because it no longer appears as a possibility, the appropriation should be returned to unappropriated retained earnings. In accordance with *FASB Statement No. 5*, **"costs or losses shall not be charged to an appropriation of retained earnings, and no part of the appropriation shall be transferred to income."**[21]

---

[20]"Accounting for Contingencies," *Statement of Financial Accounting Standards No. 5* (Stamford, Conn.: FASB, March 1975), par. 15.

[21]Ibid., par. 15.

Various reasons are advanced for appropriations of retained earnings. These include:

❶ **Legal restrictions.** As indicated earlier, some state laws prohibit the purchase of treasury stock by the corporation unless earnings available for dividends are present. Retained earnings in an amount equal to the cost of any treasury stock acquired are restricted. Earnings must be retained to substitute for capital stock temporarily acquired as treasury stock.

❷ **Contractual restrictions.** Bond indentures frequently contain a requirement that retained earnings in specified amounts be appropriated each year during the life of the bonds. The appropriation created under such a provision is commonly called Appropriation for Sinking Fund or Appropriation for Bonded Indebtedness.

❸ **Existence of possible or expected loss.** Appropriations might be established for estimated losses due to lawsuits, unfavorable contractual obligations, and other contingencies.

❹ **Protection of working capital position.** The board of directors may authorize the creation of an "Appropriation for Working Capital" out of retained earnings in order to indicate that the amount specified is not available for dividends because it is desirable to maintain a strong current position. Another example involves a decision made to finance a building program by internal financing. An "Appropriation for Plant Expansion" is created to indicate that retained earnings in the amount appropriated will not be considered by the directors as available for dividends.

Some corporations establish appropriations for general contingencies, or appropriate retained earnings for unspecified purposes. In some cases this is justified by statutory or contractual restrictions. In other cases no adequate explanation for such actions is available. The FASB does not encourage the establishment of general or unspecified appropriations.

Recording Appropriation of Retained Earnings

OBJECTIVE ❼
Explain accounting and reporting for appropriated retained earnings.

When a company records an appropriation in the accounts, the unappropriated retained earnings must be reduced by the amount of the appropriation and a new account must be established to receive the amount transferred. The new account Appropriated Retained Earnings is simply a subclassification of total retained earnings. If the appropriation merely augments a previously established amount, the account already in use should receive the credit. The appropriation is recorded as a debit to Retained Earnings and a credit to an appropriately named account that itself is just a subdivision of retained earnings. For example:

(a) An Appropriation for Plant Expansion is to be created by transfer from Retained Earnings of $400,000 a year for 5 years. The entry for each year would be:

Retained Earnings	400,000	
Retained Earnings Appropriated for		
Plant Expansion		400,000

(b) At the end of 5 years the appropriation would have a balance of $2,000,000. If we assume that the expansion plan has been completed, the appropriation is no longer required and can be returned to retained earnings.

Retained Earnings Appropriated for		
Plant Expansion	2,000,000	
Retained Earnings		2,000,000

Return of such an appropriation to retained earnings has the effect of increasing unappropriated retained earnings considerably without affecting the assets or current position. In effect, over the 5 years the company has expanded by reinvesting assets acquired through the earnings process.

Disclosure of Restrictions on Retained Earnings

In many corporations restrictions on retained earnings or dividends exist, but no formal journal entries are made. Such restrictions are **best disclosed by note**. Parenthetical notations are sometimes used, but restrictions imposed by bond indentures and loan agreements commonly require an extended explanation; notes provide a medium for more complete explanations and free the financial statements from abbreviated notations. The note disclosure should reveal the source of the restriction, pertinent provisions, and the amount of retained earnings subject to restriction, or the amount not restricted.

Restrictions may be based on the retention of a certain retained earnings balance, the corporation's ability to observe certain working capital requirements, additional borrowing, and on other considerations. The following example from the annual report of Alberto-Culver Company illustrates a note disclosing potential restrictions on retained earnings and dividends.

INTERNATIONAL INSIGHT

In Switzerland, companies are allowed to create income reserves. That is, they reduce income in years with good profits by allocating it to reserves on the balance sheet. In less profitable years, they are able to reallocate from the reserves to improve income. This "smoothes" income across years.

ALBERTO-CULVER COMPANY

Note 3 (in part): The $200 million revolving credit facility, the term note due September 2000, and the receivables agreement impose restrictions on such items as total debt, working capital, dividend payments, treasury stock purchases, and interest expense. At September 30, 1998, the company was in compliance with these arrangements, and $220 million of consolidated retained earnings was not restricted as to the payment of dividends.

ILLUSTRATION 16-13
Disclosure of Restrictions on Retained Earnings and Dividends

Trends in Terminology

As discussed in Chapter 5, the profession's recommendations relating to changes in terminology have been directed primarily to the balance sheet presentation of stockholders' equity so that words or phrases used will more accurately describe the nature of the amounts shown.

The accounting profession has suggested the term "surplus" not be used in financial statements. Substitute terminology is recommended because the term "surplus" connotes a residual or "something not needed." The use of the term is gradually decreasing. **"Retained earnings"** or some similar phrase has generally replaced "earned surplus." Apparently, consensus regarding the terminology to replace "capital surplus" and "paid-in surplus" has not yet been reached, inasmuch as these two terms still appear in some financial statements. **"Capital in excess of par (or stated value)"** or **"additional paid-in capital"** are gaining favor over the term "paid-in surplus."[22] The persistent use of "surplus" terms by some leading corporations can perhaps be attributed to the numerous state incorporation acts that still contain antiquated terminology in their provisions regulating the issuance of stock and other equity transactions.

Formerly, the term "reserve" was used in accounting to describe such diverse items as accumulated depreciation, allowances for doubtful accounts, current liabilities, and segregations of retained earnings. **The profession recommends that use of the word "reserve" be confined to appropriations of retained earnings if it is to be used at all.** The general adoption of this recommendation could help to clear up one of the most troublesome terminology areas in accounting.[23]

---

[22]*Accounting Trends and Techniques—1999* reports that the use of the term "surplus" is gradually declining. In its survey of 600 companies, 30 out of 527 companies reporting additional paid-in capital used either "capital surplus" or "paid-in surplus" for the caption. Only 1 company used the term "earned surplus."

[23]*Accounting Trends and Techniques—1999* reports that of its list of 600 selected companies, 147 continued incorrectly to use the term "reserve" in the assets or liabilities section of the balance sheet.

PRESENTATION AND ANALYSIS OF STOCKHOLDERS' EQUITY

Presentation

OBJECTIVE 8
Indicate how stockholders' equity is presented and analyzed.

The following three categories normally appear as part of stockholders' equity:

1. Capital stock (legal capital).
2. Additional paid-in capital (capital in excess of par or stated value).
3. Retained earnings or deficit.

The first two categories, capital stock and additional paid-in capital, constitute contributed (or paid-in) capital; retained earnings represents the earned capital of the enterprise. These three categories are reported in summarized form in all enterprises' balance sheets. More detail of additions and deductions to specific stockholders' equity accounts are frequently reported in a separate statement of stockholders' equity.

Balance Sheet

The presentation below is an example of a comprehensive stockholders' equity section taken from a balance sheet that includes most of the equity items discussed in Chapters 15 and 16.

ILLUSTRATION 16-14
Comprehensive
Stockholders' Equity
Presentation

FROST CORPORATION Stockholders' Equity December 31, 2000		
Capital stock		
Preferred stock, $100 par value, 7% cumulative, 100,000 shares authorized, 30,000 shares issued and outstanding		$ 3,000,000
Common stock, no par, stated value $10 per share, 500,000 shares authorized, 400,000 shares issued		4,000,000
Common stock dividend distributable, 20,000 shares		200,000
Total capital stock		7,200,000
Additional paid-in capital		
Excess over par—preferred	$ 150,000	
Excess over stated value—common	840,000	990,000
Total paid-in capital		8,190,000
Retained earnings		
Appropriated for plant expansion	2,200,000	
Unappropriated	2,160,000	4,360,000
Total paid-in capital and retained earnings		12,550,000
Less: Cost of treasury stock (2,000 shares, common)		(190,000)
Accumulated other comprehensive loss[24]		(360,000)
Total stockholders' equity		$12,000,000

---

[24] A number of items may be included in the accumulated other comprehensive loss. Among these items are "foreign currency translation adjustments" (covered in advanced accounting), "unrealized holding gains and losses for available-for-sale securities" (covered in Chapter 18), "excess of additional pension liability over unrecognized prior service cost" (covered in Chapter 21), "guarantees of employee stock option plan (ESOP) debt," "unearned or deferred compensation related to employee stock award plans," and others. *Accounting Trends and Techniques—1999* reports that of its 600 surveyed companies reporting other items in the equity section, 442 reported cumulative translation adjustments, 186 reported minimum pension liability adjustments, 148 reported unrealized losses/gains on certain investments, 119 reported unearned compensation, and 46 reported guarantees of ESOP debt. A number of companies had more than one item.

A company should disclose the pertinent rights and privileges of the various securities outstanding.[25]

Statement of Stockholders' Equity

Statements of stockholders' equity are frequently presented in the following basic format:

❶ Balance at the beginning of the period.
❷ Additions.
❸ Deductions.
❹ Balance at the end of the period.

The disclosure of changes in the separate accounts comprising stockholders' equity is required to make the financial statements sufficiently informative.[26] Disclosure of such changes may take the form of separate statements or may be made in the basic financial statements or notes thereto.[27]

A **columnar format** for the presentation of changes in stockholders' equity items in published annual reports is gaining in popularity; an example is Goodyear Tire Company's statement of stockholders' equity shown in Illustration 16-15.

ILLUSTRATION 16-15
Columnar Format for Statement of Stockholders' Equity

GOODYEAR TIRE COMPANY

Statement of Stockholders' Equity

(Dollars in millions, except per share)	Common Stock		Additional Paid-in Capital	Retained Earnings	Accumulated Other Comprehensive Income		Total Shareholders' Equity
	Shares	Amount			Foreign Currency Translation	Minimum Pension Liability	
Balance at December 31, 1997 (after deducting 39,089,885 treasury shares)	156,588,783	$156.6	$1,061.6	$2,983.4	$(778.0)	$(28.1)	$3,395.5
Comprehensive income							
Net income				682.3			
Foreign currency translation					(99.6)		
Minimum pension liability (net of tax of $.2)						1.9	
Total comprehensive income							584.6
Cash dividends—$1.20 per share				(187.9)			(187.9)
Common stock acquired	(1,500,000)	(1.5)	(83.7)				(85.2)
Common stock issued from treasury:							
Stock compensation plans	854,752	.8	38.0				38.8
Balance at December 31, 1998 (after deducting 39,735,133 treasury shares)	155,943,535	$155.9	$1,015.9	$3,477.8	$(877.6)	$(26.2)	$3,745.8

---

[25]"Disclosure of Information about Capital Structure," *Statement of Financial Accounting Standards No. 129* (Norwalk, Conn.: FASB, February 1997), par. 4.

[26]If a company has other comprehensive income, and total comprehensive income is computed only in the statement of stockholders' equity, the statement of stockholders' equity must be displayed with the same prominence as other financial statements. "Reporting Comprehensive Income," *Statement of Financial Accounting Standards No. 130* (Norwalk, Conn.: FASB, June 1997).

[27]*Accounting Trends and Techniques—1999* reports that of the 600 companies surveyed, 562 presented statements of stockholders' equity, 15 presented separate statements of retained earnings only, 7 presented combined statements of income and retained earnings, and 16 presented changes in equity items in the notes only.

The annual report of Intel in the Appendix to Chapter 5, page 224, includes a 3-year comprehensive illustration of the various items that commonly appear as either additions or deductions in a "Statement of Shareholders' Equity."

Analysis

Several ratios use stockholders' equity related amounts to evaluate a company's profitability and long-term solvency. The following four ratios are discussed and illustrated below: (1) rate of return on common stock equity, (2) payout ratio, (3) price earnings ratio, and (4) book value per share.

Rate of Return on Common Stock Equity

A widely used ratio that measures profitability from the common stockholders' viewpoint is **rate of return on common stock equity**. This ratio shows how many dollars of net income were earned for each dollar invested by the owners. It is computed by dividing net income less preferred dividends by average common stockholders' equity. For example, assume that Gerber's Inc. had net income of $360,000, declared and paid preferred dividends of $54,000, and average common stockholders' equity of $2,550,000. Gerber's ratio is computed in this manner:

ILLUSTRATION 16-16
Computation of Rate of Return on Common Stock Equity

$$\text{Rate of Return on Common Stock Equity} = \frac{\text{Net income} - \text{Preferred dividends}}{\text{Average common stockholders' equity}}$$

$$= \frac{\$360,000 - \$54,000}{\$2,550,000}$$

$$= 12\%$$

As evidenced above, because preferred stock is present, preferred dividends are deducted from net income to compute income available to common stockholders. Similarly the par value of preferred stock is deducted from total stockholders' equity to arrive at the amount of common stock equity used in this ratio.

When the rate of return on total assets is lower than the rate of return on the common stockholders investment, the company is said to be trading on the equity at a gain. **Trading on the equity** describes the practice of using borrowed money at fixed interest rates or issuing preferred stock with constant dividend rates in hopes of obtaining a higher rate of return on the money used. These issues must be given a prior claim on some or all of the corporate assets. Thus, the advantage to common stockholders of trading on the equity must come from borrowing at a lower rate of interest than the rate of return obtained on the assets borrowed. If this can be done, the capital obtained from bondholders or preferred stockholders earns enough to pay the interest or preferred dividends and to leave a margin for the common stockholders. When this condition exists, trading on the equity is profitable.

Payout Ratio

Another measure of profitability is the **payout ratio**, which is the ratio of cash dividends to net income. If preferred stock is outstanding, this ratio is computed for common stockholders by dividing cash dividends paid to common stockholders by net income available to common stockholders. Assuming that Troy Co. has cash dividends of $100,000 and net income of $500,000, and no preferred stock outstanding, the payout ratio is computed in the following manner:

$$\text{Payout Ratio} = \frac{\text{Cash dividends}}{\text{Net income} - \text{Preferred dividends}}$$

$$= \frac{\$100,000}{\$500,000}$$

$$= 20\%$$

ILLUSTRATION 16-17
Computation of Payout Ratio

It is important to some investors that the payout be sufficiently high to provide a good yield on the stock.[28] However, payout ratios have declined for many companies because many investors view appreciation in the value of the stock as more important than the amount of the dividend.

Price Earnings Ratio

The **price earnings (P/E) ratio** is an oft-quoted statistic used by analysts in discussing the investment possibility of a given enterprise. It is computed by dividing the market price of the stock by its earnings per share. For example, Soreson Co. has a market price of $50 and earnings per share of $4. Its price earnings ratio is computed as follows:

$$\text{Price Earnings Ratio} = \frac{\text{Market price of stock}}{\text{Earnings per share}}$$

$$= \frac{\$50}{\$4}$$

$$= 12.5$$

ILLUSTRATION 16-18
Computation of Price Earnings Ratio

The average price earnings ratio for the 30 stocks that constitute the Dow Jones Industrial Average in January 2000 was 31.7. A steady drop in a company's price earnings ratio indicates that investors are wary of the firm's growth potential. Some companies have high P/E ratios (also called "multiples"), while others have low multiples. For instance, **Home Depot** in 2000 enjoyed a P/E ratio of 53, while **Ford Motor** had a low P/E ratio of 7.3. The reason for this difference is linked to several factors: relative risk, stability of earnings, trends in earnings, and the market's perception of the company's growth potential.

Book Value Per Share

A much-used basis for evaluating net worth is found in the **book value** or **equity value per share** of stock. Book value per share of stock is the amount each share would receive if the company were liquidated **on the basis of amounts reported on the balance sheet**. However, the figure loses much of its relevance if the valuations on the balance sheet do not approximate fair market value of the assets. **Book value per share** is computed by dividing common stockholders' equity by outstanding common shares. Assuming that Chen Corporation's common stockholders' equity is $1,000,000 and it has 100,000 shares of common stock outstanding, its book value per share is computed as follows:

$$\text{Book Value Per Share} = \frac{\text{Common stockholders' equity}}{\text{Outstanding shares}}$$

$$= \frac{\$1,000,000}{100,000}$$

$$= \$10 \text{ per share}$$

ILLUSTRATION 16-19
Computation of Book Value Per Share

---

[28]Another closely watched ratio is the dividend yield—the cash dividend per share divided by the market price of the stock. This ratio affords investors some idea of the rate of return that will be received in cash dividends from their investment.

When preferred stock is present, an analysis of the covenants involving the preferred shares should be studied. If preferred dividends are in arrears, the preferred stock is participating, or if preferred stock has a redemption or liquidating value higher than its carrying amount, retained earnings must be allocated between the preferred and common stockholders in computing book value.

To illustrate, assume that the following situation exists:

ILLUSTRATION 16-20
Computation of Book Value Per Share—No Dividends in Arrears

Stockholders' equity	Preferred	Common
Preferred stock, 5%	$300,000	
Common stock		$400,000
Excess of issue price over par of common stock		37,500
Retained earnings		162,582
Totals	$300,000	$600,082
Shares outstanding		4,000
Book value per share		$150.02

In the preceding computation it is assumed that no preferred dividends are in arrears and that the preferred is not participating. Now assume that the same facts exist except that the 5% preferred is cumulative, participating up to 8%, and that dividends for three years before the current year are in arrears. The book value of the common stock is then computed as follows, assuming that no action has yet been taken concerning dividends for the current year.

ILLUSTRATION 16-21
Computation of Book Value Per Share—With Dividends in Arrears

Stockholders' equity	Preferred	Common
Preferred stock, 5%	$300,000	
Common stock		$400,000
Excess of issue price over par of common stock		37,500
Retained earnings:		
Dividends in arrears (3 years at 5% a year)	45,000	
Current year requirement at 5%	15,000	20,000
Participating—additional 3%	9,000	12,000
Remainder to common		61,582
Totals	$369,000	$531,082
Shares outstanding		4,000
Book value per share		$132.77

In connection with the book value computation, the analyst must know how to handle the following items: the number of authorized and unissued shares; the number of treasury shares on hand; any commitments with respect to the issuance of unissued shares or the reissuance of treasury shares; and the relative rights and privileges of the various types of stock authorized.

SUMMARY OF LEARNING OBJECTIVES

❶ Describe the policies used in distributing dividends. The state incorporation laws normally provide information concerning the legal restrictions related to the payment of dividends. Corporations rarely pay dividends in an amount equal to the legal limit. This is due, in part, to the fact that assets represented by undistributed earnings are used to finance future operations of the business. If a company is considering declaring a dividend, two preliminary questions must be asked: (1) Is the condition of the corporation such that the dividend is **legally permissible**? (2) Is the condition of the corporation such that a dividend is **economically sound**?

❷ Identify the various forms of dividend distributions. Dividends are of the following types: (1) cash dividends, (2) property dividends, (3) scrip dividends (instead of paying a dividend now, the corporation has elected to pay it at some later date; the scrip issued to stockholders as a dividend is merely a special form of note payable), (4) liquidating dividends (dividends based on other than retained earnings are sometimes described as liquidating dividends), (5) stock dividends (the nonreciprocal issuance by a corporation of its own stock to its stockholders on a pro rata basis).

❸ Explain the accounting for small and large stock dividends. Generally accepted accounting principles require that the accounting for small stock dividends (less than 20 or 25%) be based on the fair market value of the stock issued. When a stock dividend is declared, Retained Earnings is debited at the fair market value of the stock to be distributed. The entry includes a credit to Common Stock Dividend Distributable at par value times the number of shares, with any excess credited to Paid-in Capital in Excess of Par. Common stock dividend distributable is reported in the stockholders' equity section between the declaration date and the date of issuance. If the number of shares issued exceeds 20 or 25% of the shares outstanding (large stock dividend), Retained Earnings is debited at par value, and there is no additional paid-in capital.

❹ Distinguish between stock dividends and stock splits. A stock dividend is a capitalization of retained earnings that results in a reduction in retained earnings and a corresponding increase in certain contributed capital accounts. The par value and total stockholders' equity remain unchanged with a stock dividend. Also, all stockholders retain their same proportionate share of ownership in the corporation. A stock split results in an increase or decrease in the number of shares outstanding, with a corresponding decrease or increase in the par or stated value per share. No accounting entry is required for a stock split. Similar to a stock dividend, the total dollar amount of all stockholders' equity accounts remains unchanged. A stock split is usually intended to improve the marketability of the shares by reducing the market price of the stock being split.

❺ Explain the effect of different types of preferred stock dividends. Dividends paid to shareholders are affected by the dividend preferences of the preferred stock. Preferred stock can be: (1) cumulative or noncumulative, and (2) fully participating, partially participating, or nonparticipating.

❻ Identify the reasons for appropriating retained earnings. An appropriation of retained earnings serves to restrict for a specific purpose the payout of retained earnings. In general, the reason for retained earnings appropriations is the corporation's desire to reduce the basis upon which dividends are declared (unappropriated credit balance in retained earnings).

❼ Explain accounting and reporting for appropriated retained earnings. To establish an appropriation of retained earnings, a corporation prepares a journal entry, debiting unappropriated retained earnings and crediting a specific appropriations account (for example, Retained Earnings Appropriated for Sinking Fund). The entry is confined to stockholders' equity accounts and does not directly affect corporate assets or liabilities. The only way to dispose of an appropriation of retained earnings is to reverse the entry that created the appropriation. Appropriations of retained earnings are frequently disclosed in the notes to the financial statements as an alternative to making a formal entry against retained earnings.

❽ Indicate how stockholders' equity is presented and analyzed. The stockholders equity section of a balance sheet includes capital stock, additional paid-in capital, and retained earnings. Additional items that might also be presented are treasury stock and accumulated other comprehensive income. A statement of stockholders' equity is often provided. Common ratios used in this area are: rate of return on common stock equity, payout ratio, price earnings ratio, and book value per share.

KEY TERMS

appropriation of retained earnings, *825*

book value per share, *831*

cash dividends, *816*

large stock dividend, *823*

liquidating dividends, *819*

payout ratio, *830*

price earnings ratio, *831*

property dividends, *817*

rate of return on common stock equity, *830*

retained earnings, *812*

scrip dividends, *818*

small (ordinary) stock dividends, *820*

statement of stockholders' equity, *829*

stock dividends, *820*

stock split, *822*

trading on the equity, *830*

Quasi-Reorganization

OBJECTIVE 9
After studying Appendix 16A, you should be able to: Describe the accounting for a quasi-reorganization.

A corporation that consistently suffers net losses accumulates negative retained earnings, or a deficit. The laws of many states provide that no dividends may be declared and paid so long as a corporation's paid-in capital has been reduced by a deficit. In these states, a corporation with a debit balance of retained earnings must accumulate sufficient profits to offset the deficit before dividends may be paid.

This situation may be a real hardship on a corporation and its stockholders. A company that has operated unsuccessfully for several years and accumulated a deficit may have finally "turned the corner." Development of new products and new markets, a new management group, or improved economic conditions may point to much improved operating results. But, if the state law prohibits dividends until the deficit has been replaced by earnings, the stockholders must wait until such profits have been earned, which may take a considerable period of time. Furthermore, future success may depend on obtaining additional funds through the sale of stock. If no dividends can be paid for some time, the market price of any new stock issue is likely to be low, if such stock can be marketed at all.

Thus, a company with excellent prospects may be prevented from accomplishing its plans because of a deficit, although present management may have had nothing whatever to do with the years over which the deficit was accumulated. To permit the corporation to proceed with its plans might well be to the advantage of all interests in the enterprise; to require it to eliminate the deficit through profits might actually force it to liquidate.

A procedure provided for in some state laws eliminates an accumulated deficit and permits the company to proceed on much the same basis as if it had been legally reorganized, without the difficulty and expenses generally connected with a legal reorganization. This procedure, known as a **quasi-reorganization**, is justified under the concept of an accounting "fresh start."

ACCOUNTING APPROACHES

UNDERLYING CONCEPTS

No net asset writeup is permitted in a quasi-reorganization. The reason: Conservatism, as indicated in Chapter 2.

A quasi-reorganization may be accomplished under two accounting procedures. The simpler procedure, referred to as a **deficit reclassification**, results solely in eliminating a deficit in retained earnings without restating assets or liabilities. The accounting procedure is limited to a reclassification of a deficit in reported retained earnings as a reduction of paid-in capital.

The more complex accounting procedure, referred to as an **accounting reorganization** type of quasi-reorganization, involves restating the assets of the enterprise to their fair values and the liabilities to their present values with the net amount of these adjustments added to or deducted from the deficit.[1] The balance in the retained earnings ac-

---

[1]The SEC states in *SAB 78, Quasi-Reorganization* (Topic 5.S), dated August 25, 1988, that write-ups of assets or reductions of liabilities to fair and present values in a quasi-reorganization are limited to an amount sufficient to offset decreases in other assets or increases in other liabilities in their fair and present values. Therefore, there should be **no net asset writeup** in a quasi-reorganization.

Also, the SEC does not allow the "deficit reclassification" type quasi-reorganization (the simpler form) to be used by publicly held companies; thus, it may be used only by privately held companies. Both public and private companies may use the accounting reorganization type (i.e., restating assets and liabilities and eliminating the deficit).

count (debit or credit) is then closed to other capital accounts, usually Additional Paid-in Capital, so that the company has a "fresh start" with a zero balance in retained earnings.

Entries Illustrated

The series of entries shown below illustrates the accounting procedures applied in an "accounting reorganization" type of quasi-reorganization. Assume New Horizons Inc. shows a deficit of $1,000,000 before a quasi-reorganization is effected on June 30, 2001.

1 Restatement of assets and liabilities to recognize unrecorded gains and losses

Plant Assets (gain on writeup)	400,000	
Long-term Liabilities (gain on writedown)	150,000	
Retained Earnings (net adjustment)	200,000	
Intangible Assets (loss on writedown)		525,000
Inventories (loss on writedown)		225,000

2 Reduction in par value of 60,000 shares of common stock outstanding from $100 per share to $75 per share (This procedure creates sufficient additional paid-in capital to absorb the deficit)

Common Stock	1,500,000	
Additional Paid-in Capital		1,500,000

3 Elimination of deficit against additional paid-in capital

Additional Paid-in Capital	1,200,000	
Retained Earnings ($1,000,000 + $200,000)		1,200,000

Disclosure

In connection with the foregoing accounting procedures, the following requirements must be fulfilled:

1 The proposed quasi-reorganization procedure should be submitted to and receive the approval of the corporation's stockholders before it is put into effect.

2 The new asset and liability valuations should be fair and not deliberately understate or overstate assets, liabilities, and earnings.

3 After the quasi-reorganization the corporation must have a zero balance of retained earnings, although it may have additional paid-in capital arising from the quasi-reorganization.

4 In subsequent reports the retained earnings must be "dated" (1) for a period of approximately 10 years to show the fact and the date of the quasi-reorganization, and (2) for a period of at least 3 years from the quasi-reorganization date, the amount of accumulated deficit eliminated should be disclosed as illustrated in the following excerpt from the 2003 balance sheet of New Horizons, Inc.[2]

New Horizons, Inc.	
Stockholders' equity	
Common stock, $75 par value, 60,000 shares authorized and issued	$4,500,000
Additional paid-in capital arising from reduction in par value of common stock	300,000
Retained earnings since June 30, 2001, when a deficit of $1,000,000 was eliminated through a quasi-reorganization	593,640
	$5,393,640

ILLUSTRATION 16A-1
Disclosure of Quasi-Reorganization in the Balance Sheet

In times of general economic or specific industry recession or depression, the use of the quasi-reorganization procedure becomes more common as companies attempt to turn around and get a fresh start. For example, **First Wisconsin Mortgage Trust,**

---

[2]*Regulation S-X*, Securities and Exchange Commission, Rule 5-02(31)6.

because of severe real estate losses, effected a quasi-reorganization. Similarly, **Lockheed Corporation**, given its large losses on the L-1011 Tri Star program, decided to use the quasi-reorganization approach to offset a large deficit balance in retained earnings. And **Astrotech International Corporation** eliminated a $28 million deficit in Retained Earnings as it changed from an investment company to an operating company through the quasi-reorganization approach.

An example of a quasi-reorganization disclosure, shown in Illustration 16A-2, is excerpted from the Annual Report of **Midway Airlines Corporation**.

ILLUSTRATION 16A-2
Disclosure of Quasi-Reorganization in the Notes

MIDWAY AIRLINES CORPORATION

Statement of Stockholders' Equity

(000 omitted)	Preferred Stock Amount	Common Stock Amount	Additional Paid-in Capital	Retained Earnings (Accumulated Deficit)	Total
Balance at December 31, 1996	$ 11	$100	$30,989	$(70,342)	$(39,242)
Cancellation of prior stock in connection with recapitalization	(11)	(100)	111	—	—
Issuance of preferred stock	37	—	14,963	—	15,000
Issuance of common stock	—	21	8,551	—	8,572
Issuance of common stock warrants in connection with debt restructuring	—	—	1,571	—	1,571
Contributed capital	—	—	1,314	—	1,314
Reclassification of accumulated deficit pursuant to quasi-reorganization	—	—	(49,812)	49,812	—
Conversion of preferred stock	(37)	37	—	—	—
Issuance of common stock in connection with initial public offering	—	27	37,677	—	37,704
Net income	—	—	—	24,894	24,894
Balance at December 31, 1997	$ —	$ 85	$45,364	$ 4,364	$ 49,813

Quasi-Reorganization. As a result of the February 11, 1997 recapitalization, debt restructurings and retention of a new chief executive officer, the Company's Board of Directors approved a corporate readjustment of the Company's accounts in the form of a quasi-reorganization which was effected on June 30, 1997.

A quasi-reorganization is an accounting procedure which results in eliminating the accumulated deficit in retained earnings. This accounting procedure is limited to a reclassification of accumulated deficit as a reduction of paid-in capital. The Company believes the quasi-reorganization was appropriate because on completion of the recapitalization, the debt restructurings, and the installation of a new chief executive officer, the Company had substantially reduced its outstanding indebtedness, had formulated revised operating plans and as a result thereof would be able to devote its resources to its continuing operations. Because assets had been stated at approximate fair values, the quasi-reorganization had no effect on recorded assets.

The authoritative literature and accounting standards on quasi-reorganizations are generally antiquated and are permissive rather than mandatory. Moreover, "there are financial accounting and reporting issues concerning quasi-reorganizations for which the authoritative accounting literature provides no guidance or for which the guidance provided is unclear or conflicting."[3] As a result, accounting for quasi-reorganizations is in need of study and clarification.

---

[3]"Quasi-Reorganization," *Issues Paper 88-1* (New York: AICPA, September 22, 1988), 75 pp. This issues paper prepared by an AICPA Accounting Standards Division task force identified 46 issues that need to be resolved relative to accounting and reporting for quasi-reorganizations.

SUMMARY OF LEARNING OBJECTIVE FOR APPENDIX 16A

KEY TERMS

accounting
   reorganization, *834*
deficit reclassification, *834*
quasi-reorganization, *834*

❾ Describe the accounting for a quasi-reorganization. A corporation that has accumulated a large debit balance (deficit) in retained earnings may, under the laws of certain states, enter into a process known as a quasi-reorganization. This procedure consists of the following steps: (1) All assets are revalued at appropriate current values so the company will not be burdened with excessive inventory or fixed asset valuations in following years. Any loss on revaluation increases the deficit. (2) Paid-in or other types of capital must be available or must be created, at least equal in amount to the deficit. If no such capital exists, it is created through donation of outstanding stock, or by some similar means. (3) The deficit is then eliminated by a charge against paid-in capital. In addition to the steps above, a quasi-reorganization requires: (1) approval by stockholders, (2) fair and unbiased valuation of assets, (3) a zero balance in retained earnings at the conclusion of the reorganization, (4) the date of the quasi-reorganization shown with retained earnings for the succeeding 10 years, and (5) balance sheet disclosure of the amount of the deficit eliminated, for 3 years.

Note: All **asterisked** Questions, Brief Exercises, Exercises, Problems, and Conceptual Cases relate to material contained in the appendix to the chapter.

QUESTIONS

1 Distinguish among the following: contributed capital, earned capital, and equity capital.

2 What are some of the common items that increase or decrease retained earnings?

3 What factors influence the dividend policy of a company?

4 What are the characteristics of state incorporation laws relative to the legality of dividend payments?

5 Very few companies pay dividends in amounts equal to their retained earnings legally available for dividends. Why?

6 What are the principal considerations of a board of directors in making decisions involving dividend declarations? Discuss briefly.

7 In a report from the FASB, it was noted that on a price-level basis (adjusted for specific prices), dividends exceeded profits. As a result, some industries, such as primary and fabricated metals, are in effect undergoing gradual liquidation. Explain what this statement means.

8 Dividends are sometimes said to have been paid "out of retained earnings." What is the error in that statement?

9 Distinguish among: cash dividends, property dividends, scrip dividends, liquidating dividends, and stock dividends.

10 Describe the accounting entry for a stock dividend. Describe the accounting entry for a stock split.

11 Stock splits and stock dividends may be used by a corporation to change the number of shares of its stock outstanding.

(a) What is meant by a stock split effected in the form of a dividend?

(b) From an accounting viewpoint, explain how the stock split effected in the form of a dividend differs from an ordinary stock dividend.

(c) How should a stock dividend that has been declared but not yet issued be classified in a statement of financial position? Why?

12 The following comment appeared in the notes of Belinda Alvarado Corporation's annual report: "Such distributions, representing proceeds from the sale of James Buchanan, Inc. were paid in the form of partial liquidating dividends and were in lieu of a portion of the Company's ordinary cash dividends." How would a partial liquidating dividend be accounted for in the financial records?

13 This comment appeared in the annual report of Rodriguez Lopez Inc.: "The Company could pay cash or property dividends on the Class A common stock without paying cash or property dividends on the Class B common stock, but if the Company pays any cash or property dividends on the Class B common stock, it would be required to pay at least the same dividend on the Class A common stock." How is a property dividend accounted for in the financial records?

14 Thomas Dewey Corporation has consistently reported a significant amount of income and has accumulated a large balance of retained earnings. At a recent stockholders' meeting, the company's policy of declaring little or no dividends caused some controversy.

(a) Why might Thomas Dewey Corporation establish such a conservative dividend policy?

(b) What steps might Thomas Dewey take to reduce the amount of retained earnings available for dividends?

15 Aaron Burr Corp. had $100,000 of 10%, $20 par value preferred stock and 12,000 shares of $25 par value common stock outstanding throughout 2001.

(a) Assuming that total dividends declared in 2001 were $88,000, and that the preferred stock is not cumulative but is fully participating, each common share should receive 2001 dividends of what amount?

(b) Assuming that total dividends declared in 2001 were $88,000, and that the preferred stock is fully participating and cumulative with preferred dividends in arrears for 2000, preferred stockholders should receive 2001 dividends totaling what amount?

(c) Assuming that total dividends declared in 2001 were $30,000, that cumulative nonparticipating preferred stock was issued on January 1, 2000, and that $5,000 of preferred dividends were declared and paid in 2000, the common stockholders should receive 2001 dividends totaling what amount?

16 For what reasons might a company appropriate a portion of its retained earnings?

17 How should appropriations of retained earnings be created and written off?

18 Comment on the propriety of William Byrd Company reporting "paid-in surplus" and "earned surplus" in the equity section of its balance sheet.

19 Indicate the misuse and the proper use of the term "reserve."

20 What are some of the ways in which retained earnings may be restricted?

21 Is there a duplication of charges to current year's costs or expenses where a sinking fund appropriation is created for the retirement of bonds, as well as accumulated depreciation with respect to the capital assets by which such bonds are secured? Discuss briefly the point raised by this question.

*22 Outline the accounting steps involved in accomplishing a quasi-reorganization.

*23 Under what circumstances would a corporation consider submitting itself to a quasi-reorganization?

*24 What disclosures are required in the balance sheet for years subsequent to a quasi-reorganization?

BRIEF EXERCISES

BE16-1 Micro Machines Inc. declared a cash dividend of $1.50 per share on its 2 million outstanding shares. The dividend was declared on August 1, payable on September 9 to all stockholders of record on August 15. Prepare all journal entries necessary on those three dates.

BE16-2 Ren Inc. owns shares of Stimpy Corporation stock classified as available-for-sale securities. At December 31, 2001, the available-for-sale securities were carried in Ren's accounting records at their cost of $875,000 which equals their market value. On September 21, 2002, when the market value of the securities was $1,400,000, Ren declared a property dividend whereby the Stimpy securities are to be distributed on October 23, 2002, to stockholders of record on October 8, 2002. Prepare all journal entries necessary on those three dates.

BE16-3 Might and Magic Inc. declared a scrip dividend of $3.00 per share on its 100,000 outstanding shares. The dividend was declared on January 30, and is payable with interest, at a 12% annual rate, on October 31. Prepare all journal entries necessary on those two dates.

BE16-4 Radical Rex Mining Company declared, on April 20, a dividend of $700,000 payable on June 1. Of this amount, $125,000 is a return of capital. Prepare the April 20 and June 1 entries for Radical Rex.

BE16-5 Mike Holmgren Football Corporation has outstanding 200,000 shares of $10 par value common stock. The corporation declares a 5% stock dividend when the fair value of the stock is $65 per share. Prepare the journal entries for Mike Holmgren Football Corporation for both the date of declaration and the date of distribution.

BE16-6 Use the information from BE16-5, but assume Mike Holmgren Football Corporation declared a 100% stock dividend rather than a 5% stock dividend. Prepare the journal entries for both the date of declaration and the date of distribution.

BE16-7 Power Piggs Corporation has outstanding 300,000 shares of $15 par value common stock. Power Piggs declares a 3-for-1 stock split. (a) How many shares are outstanding after the split? (b) What is the par value per share after the split? (c) What is the total par value after the split? (d) What journal entry is necessary to record the split?

BE16-8 Minnesota Fats Corporation has outstanding 10,000 shares of $100 par value, 8% preferred stock and 60,000 shares of $10 par value common stock. The preferred stock was issued in January 1999, and no dividends were declared in 1999 or 2000. In 2001, Minnesota Fats declares a cash dividend of $300,000. How will the dividend be shared by common and preferred if the preferred is (a) noncumulative and (b) cumulative?

BE16-9 Pocahontas Inc. has retained earnings of $2,100,000 at December 31, 2001. On that date the board of directors decides to appropriate $800,000 of retained earnings for a legal contingency. (a) Prepare the entry to record the appropriation. (b) Indicate the amount reported as total retained earnings after the appropriation.

*****BE16-10** Monster Truck Corporation went through a quasi-reorganization by writing down plant assets by $125,000, reducing par value on its 40,000 outstanding shares from $15 to $5, and eliminating its deficit, which was $250,000 prior to the quasi-reorganization. Prepare Monster Truck's entries to record the quasi-reorganization.

EXERCISES

E16-1 (Equity Items on the Balance Sheet) The following are selected transactions that may affect stockholders' equity.

1. Recorded accrued interest earned on a note receivable.
2. Declared a cash dividend.
3. Declared and distributed a stock split.
4. Recorded a retained earnings appropriation.
5. Recorded the expiration of insurance coverage that was previously recorded as prepaid insurance.
6. Paid the cash dividend declared in item 2 above.
7. Recorded accrued interest expense on a note payable.
8. Recorded an increase in value of an investment that will be distributed as a property dividend.
9. Declared a property dividend (see item 8 above).
10. Distributed the investment to stockholders (see items 8 and 9 above).
11. Declared a stock dividend.
12. Distributed the stock dividend declared in item 11.

Instructions

In the table below, indicate the effect each of the twelve transactions has on the financial statement elements listed. Use the following code:

I = Increase   D = Decrease   NE = No effect

Item	Assets	Liabilities	Stockholders' Equity	Paid-in Capital	Retained Earnings	Net Income

E16-2   (Classification of Equity Items)   Stockholders' equity on the balance sheet of Cherese Thomas Corp. is composed of three major sections. They are: A. Capital stock; B. Additional paid-in capital; and C. Retained earnings.

Instructions
Classify each of the following items as affecting one of the three sections above or as D, an item not to be included in stockholders' equity.

(a)   Net income
(b)   Dividends Payable
(c)   Stock split
(d)   Property dividends declared
(e)   Preferred stock
(f)   Common stock subscribed
(g)   Retained earnings appropriated
(h)   Sinking fund
(i)   Paid-in capital in excess of par—common

E16-3   (Cash Dividend and Liquidating Dividend)   Lotoya Davis Corporation has ten million shares of common stock issued and outstanding. On June 1 the board of directors voted an 80 cents per share cash dividend to stockholders of record as of June 14, payable June 30.

Instructions
(a)   Prepare the journal entry for each of the dates above assuming the dividend represents a distribution of earnings.
(b)   How would the entry differ if the dividend were a liquidating dividend?
(c)   Assume Lotoya Davis Corporation holds 300,000 common shares in the treasury and as a matter of administrative convenience dividends are paid on treasury shares. How should this cash receipt be recorded?

E16-4   (Preferred Dividends)   The outstanding capital stock of Edna Millay Corporation consists of 2,000 shares of $100 par value, 8% preferred, and 5,000 shares of $50 par value common.

Instructions
Assuming that the company has retained earnings of $90,000, all of which is to be paid out in dividends, and that preferred dividends were not paid during the two years preceding the current year, state how much each class of stock should receive under each of the following conditions:

(a)   The preferred stock is noncumulative and nonparticipating.
(b)   The preferred stock is cumulative and nonparticipating.
(c)   The preferred stock is cumulative and participating.

E16-5   (Preferred Dividends)   Archibald MacLeish Company's ledger shows the following balances on December 31, 2002:

7% Preferred stock — $10 par value, outstanding 20,000 shares	$ 200,000
Common stock—$100 par value, outstanding 30,000 shares	3,000,000
Retained earnings	630,000

Instructions
Assuming that the directors decide to declare total dividends in the amount of $366,000, determine how much each class of stock should receive under each of the conditions stated below. One year's dividends are in arrears on the preferred stock.

(a)   The preferred stock is cumulative and fully participating.
(b)   The preferred stock is noncumulative and nonparticipating.
(c)   The preferred stock is noncumulative and is participating in distributions in excess of a 10% dividend rate on the common stock.

E16-6   (Stock Split and Stock Dividend)   The common stock of Alexander Hamilton Inc. is currently selling at $120 per share. The directors wish to reduce the share price and increase share volume prior to a new issue. The per share par value is $10; book value is $70 per share. Nine million shares are issued and outstanding.

Instructions
Prepare the necessary journal entries assuming:

(a)   The board votes a 2-for-1 stock split.
(b)   The board votes a 100% stock dividend.
(c)   Briefly discuss the accounting and securities market differences between these two methods of increasing the number of shares outstanding.

E16-7   (Stock Dividends)   Henry Hudson Inc. has 5 million shares issued and outstanding. The per share par value is $1, book value is $32 per share, and market value is $40 per share.

Instructions

Prepare the necessary journal entry for the date of declaration and date of issue assuming:

  (a) A 10% stock dividend is declared.
  (b) A 50% stock dividend is declared.
  (c) If Hudson has 500,000 shares of treasury stock, should the stock dividend be applied to the treasury shares? Explain.
  (d) What is the amount of the corporation's liability for the period from the declaration date to the distribution date?

E16-8 (Entries for Stock Dividends and Stock Splits) The stockholders' equity accounts of G.K. Chesterton Company have the following balances on December 31, 2002:

Common stock, $10 par, 300,000 shares issued and outstanding	$3,000,000
Paid-in capital in excess of par	1,200,000
Retained earnings	5,600,000

Shares of G.K. Chesterton Company stock are currently selling on the Midwest Stock Exchange at $37.

Instructions

Prepare the appropriate journal entries for each of the following cases:

  (a) A stock dividend of 5% is declared and issued.
  (b) A stock dividend of 100% is declared and issued.
  (c) A 2-for-1 stock split is declared and issued.

E16-9 (Dividend Entries) The following data were taken from the balance sheet accounts of John Masefield Corporation on December 31, 2001:

Current assets	$540,000
Investments	624,000
Common stock (par value $10)	500,000
Paid-in capital in excess of par	150,000
Retained earnings	840,000

Instructions

Prepare the required journal entries for the following unrelated items:

  (a) A 5% stock dividend is declared and distributed at a time when the market value of the shares is $39 per share.
  (b) A scrip dividend of $80,000 is declared.
  (c) The par value of the capital stock is reduced to $2 with a 5-for-1 stock split.
  (d) A dividend is declared January 5, 2002, and paid January 25, 2002, in bonds held as an investment; the bonds have a book value of $100,000 and a fair market value of $135,000.

E16-10 (Computation of Retained Earnings) The following information has been taken from the ledger accounts of Isaac Stern Corporation:

Total income since incorporation	$317,000
Total cash dividends paid	60,000
Proceeds from sale of donated stock	40,000
Total value of stock dividends distributed	30,000
Gains on treasury stock transactions	18,000
Unamortized discount on bonds payable	32,000
Appropriated for plant expansion	70,000

Instructions

Determine the current balance of unappropriated retained earnings.

E16-11 (Retained Earnings Appropriations and Disclosures) At December 31, 2000, the retained earnings account of Duke Ellington Inc. had a balance of $320,000. There was no appropriation at this time. During 2001, net income was $235,000. Cash dividends declared during the year were $50,000 on preferred stock and $70,000 on common stock. A stock dividend on common stock resulted in an $88,000 charge to retained earnings. At December 31, 2001, the board of directors decided to create an appropriation for contingencies of $125,000 because of an outstanding lawsuit that does not meet the criteria for accrual.

Instructions

  (a) Prepare the journal entry to record the appropriation at December 31, 2001.
  (b) Prepare a statement of unappropriated retained earnings for 2001.

(c) Prepare the retained earnings section of the December 31, 2001, balance sheet.

(d) Assume that in May 2002, the lawsuit is settled and Duke Ellington agrees to pay $113,000. At this time, the board of directors also decides to eliminate the appropriation. Prepare all necessary entries.

(e) Return to part (a), but assume that Duke Ellington decided to disclose the appropriation through a footnote at December 31, 2001, instead of preparing a formal journal entry. Prepare the necessary footnote.

E16-12 (Stockholders' Equity Section) Bruno Corporation's post-closing trial balance at December 31, 2001, was as follows:

BRUNO CORPORATION
Post-Closing Trial Balance
December 31, 2001

	Dr.	Cr.
Accounts payable		$ 310,000
Accounts receivable	$ 480,000	
Accumulated depreciation—building and equipment		185,000
Additional paid-in capital—common		
In excess of par value		1,300,000
From sale of treasury stock		160,000
Allowance for doubtful accounts		30,000
Bonds payable		300,000
Building and equipment	1,450,000	
Cash	190,000	
Common stock ($1 par value)		200,000
Dividends payable on preferred stock—cash		4,000
Inventories	560,000	
Land	400,000	
Preferred stock ($50 par value)		500,000
Prepaid expenses	40,000	
Retained earnings		301,000
Treasury stock—common at cost	170,000	
Totals	$3,290,000	$3,290,000

At December 31, 2001, Bruno had the following number of common and preferred shares:

	Common	Preferred
Authorized	600,000	60,000
Issued	200,000	10,000
Outstanding	190,000	10,000

The dividends on preferred stock are $4 cumulative. In addition, the preferred stock has a preference in liquidation of $50 per share.

Instructions

Prepare the stockholders' equity section of Bruno's balance sheet at December 31, 2001.

(AICPA adapted)

E16-13 (Participating Preferred, Stock Dividend, and Treasury Stock Retirement) The following is the stockholders' equity section of Jane Seymour Corp. at December 31, 2001:

Common stock, $20 par; authorized 200,000 shares;	
issued 90,000 shares	$ 1,800,000
Preferred stock,* $50 par; authorized 100,000 shares;	
issued 15,000 shares	750,000
Additional paid-in capital	3,150,000
Total paid-in capital	5,700,000
Retained earnings	5,213,000
Total paid-in capital and retained earnings	10,913,000
Less: Cost of treasury stock (7,500 common shares)	(742,500)
Total stockholders' equity	$10,170,500

*The preferred stock has a 12% dividend rate, is cumulative, and is participating in distributions in excess of a 15% dividend rate on the common stock.

Instructions

(a) No dividends have been paid in 1999 or 2000. On December 31, 2001, Seymour wants to pay a cash dividend of $4.00 a share to common stockholders. How much cash would be needed for the **total amount paid** to preferred and common stockholders?

(b) Instead, Jane Seymour will declare a 15% stock dividend on the outstanding common stock. The market value of the stock is $103 per share. Prepare the entry on the date of declaration.

(c) Instead, Jane Seymour will retire the treasury stock. It was originally issued at $55 a share. The current market value is $103 per share. Prepare the entry to record the retirement.

E16-14 (Dividends and Stockholders' Equity Section) Anne Cleves Company reported the following amounts in the stockholders' equity section of its December 31, 2000, balance sheet:

Preferred stock, 10%, $100 par (10,000 shares authorized, 2,000 shares issued)	$200,000
Common stock, $5 par (100,000 shares authorized, 20,000 shares issued)	100,000
Additional paid-in capital	125,000
Retained earnings	450,000
Total	$875,000

During 2001, Cleves took part in the following transactions concerning stockholders' equity.

1. Paid the annual 2000 $10 per share dividend on preferred stock and a $2 per share dividend on common stock. These dividends had been declared on December 31, 2000.
2. Purchased 1,700 shares of its own outstanding common stock for $40 per share. Cleves uses the cost method.
3. Reissued 700 treasury shares for land valued at $30,000.
4. Issued 500 shares of preferred stock at $105 per share.
5. Declared a 10% stock dividend on the outstanding common stock when the stock is selling for $45 per share.
6. Issued the stock dividend.
7. Declared the annual 2001 $10 per share dividend on preferred stock and the $2 par share dividend on common stock. These dividends are payable in 2002.
8. Appropriated retained earnings for plant expansion, $200,000.

Instructions

(a) Prepare journal entries to record the transactions described above.

(b) Prepare the December 31, 2001, stockholders' equity section. Assume 2001 net income was $330,000.

E16-15 (Comparison of Alternative Forms of Financing) Shown below is the liabilities and stockholders' equity section of the balance sheet for Jana Kingston Company and Mary Ann Benson Company. Each has assets totaling $4,200,000.

Jana Kingston Co.		Mary Ann Benson Co.	
Current liabilities	$ 300,000	Current liabilities	$ 600,000
Long-term debt, 10%	1,200,000	Common stock ($20 par)	2,900,000
Common stock ($20 par)	2,000,000	Retained earnings (Cash	
Retained earnings (Cash		dividends, $328,000)	700,000
dividends, $220,000)	700,000		
	$4,200,000		$4,200,000

For the year each company has earned the same income before interest and taxes.

	Jana Kingston Co.	Mary Ann Benson Co.
Income before interest and taxes	$1,200,000	$1,200,000
Interest expense	120,000	–0–
	1,080,000	1,200,000
Income taxes (45%)	486,000	540,000
Net income	$ 594,000	$ 660,000

At year end, the market price of Kingston's stock was $101 per share and Benson's was $63.50.

Instructions

(a) Which company is more profitable in terms of return on total assets?

(b) Which company is more profitable in terms of return on stockholders' equity?

(c) Which company has the greater net income per share of stock? Neither company issued or reacquired shares during the year.

(d) From the point of view of income, is it advantageous to the stockholders of Jana Kingston Co. to have the long-term debt outstanding? Why?

(e) What is each company's price earnings ratio?

(f) What is the book value per share for each company?

E16-16 **(Trading on the Equity Analysis)** Presented below is information from the annual report of Emporia Plastics, Inc.

Operating income	$ 532,150
Bond interest expense	135,000
	397,150
Income taxes	183,432
Net income	$ 213,718
Bonds payable	$1,000,000
Common stock	875,000
Appropriation for contingencies	75,000
Retained earnings, unappropriated	300,000

Instructions

Is Emporia Plastics Inc. trading on the equity successfully? Explain.

E16-17 **(Computation of Book Value per Share)** Morgan Sondgeroth Inc. began operations in January 1999 and reported the following results for each of its 3 years of operations:

1999 $260,000 net loss   2000 $40,000 net loss   2001 $800,000 net income

At December 31, 2001, Morgan Sondgeroth Inc. capital accounts were as follows:

8% cumulative preferred stock, par value $100; authorized, issued, and outstanding 5,000 shares	$500,000
Common stock, par value $1.00; authorized 1,000,000 shares; issued and outstanding 750,000 shares	$750,000

Morgan Sondgeroth Inc. has never paid a cash or stock dividend. There has been no change in the capital accounts since Sondgeroth began operations. The state law permits dividends only from retained earnings.

Instructions

(a) Compute the book value of the common stock at December 31, 2001.

(b) Compute the book value of the common stock at December 31, 2001, assuming that the preferred stock has a liquidating value of $106 per share.

*E16-18 **(Quasi-Reorganization)** The following account balances are available from the ledger of Glamorgan Corporation on December 31, 2000:

Common Stock—$50 par value, 20,000 shares authorized and outstanding	$1,000,000
Retained Earnings (deficit)	(190,000)

As of January 2, 2001, the corporation gave effect to a stockholder-approved quasi-reorganization by reducing the par value of the stock to $35 a share, writing down plant assets by $85,600, and eliminating the deficit.

Instructions

Prepare the required journal entries for the quasi-reorganization of Glamorgan Corporation.

*E16-19 **(Quasi-Reorganization)** The condensed balance sheets of John Ross Company immediately before and one year after it had completed a quasi-reorganization appear below:

	Before Quasi	One Year After		Before Quasi	One Year After
Current assets	$ 300,000	$ 420,000	Common stock	$2,400,000	$1,550,000
Plant assets (net)	1,700,000	1,290,000	Premium on common	220,000	
			Retained earnings	(620,000)	160,000
	$2,000,000	$1,710,000		$2,000,000	$1,710,000

For the year following the quasi-reorganization, John Ross Company reported net income of $190,000, depreciation expense of $80,000, and paid a cash dividend of $30,000. As part of the quasi-reorganization, the company wrote down inventories by $120,000. No purchases or sales of plant assets and no stock transactions occurred in the year following the quasi-reorganization.

Instructions
Prepare all the journal entries made at the time of the quasi-reorganization.

*E16-20 **(Quasi-Reorganization)** Trudy Borke Corporation is under protection of the bankruptcy court and has the following account balances at June 30, 2000.

Cash	$ (5,000)	Accounts payable	$ 450,000
Accounts receivable	320,000	Notes payable	605,000
Inventory	450,000	Taxes and wages	60,000
Equipment	860,000	Mortgage payable	150,000
Accumulated depreciation	(525,000)	Common stock	50,000
Intangibles	80,000	Retained earnings	(135,000)
Total	$1,180,000	Total	$1,180,000

The court has accepted the following proposed settlement of the company's affairs. Write down the assets by the following amounts:

Accounts receivable	$ 40,000
Inventory	$160,000
Intangibles	$ 80,000

The trade creditors (accounts payable) will reduce their claim by 30%, will accept one-year notes for 50% of their claim, and retain their current claim for the remaining 20%. The tax, wage, and mortgage claims will remain unchanged. The current common stock will be surrendered to the corporation and cancelled. In consideration thereof, the current stockholders shall be held harmless from any possible personal liability. The current holder of the note payable shall receive 1,000 shares of no par common stock in full satisfaction of the note payable. After these adjustments have been made the retained earnings shall be raised to zero by a charge against invested capital.

Instructions
(a) Prepare a balance sheet at June 30, 2000, that reflects the events listed above.
(b) Briefly discuss the nature of a quasi-reorganization.

PROBLEMS

P16-1 (Correction of Equity Items) As the newly appointed controller for Aretha Franklin Company, you are interested in analyzing the "Additional Capital" account of the company in order to present an accurate balance sheet. Your assistant, Diana Ross, who has analyzed the account from the inception of the company, submits the following summary:

	Debits	Credits
Cash dividends—preferred	$ 114,000	
Cash dividends—common	340,000	
Excess of amount paid in over par value of common stock		430,000
Discount on preferred stock	60,000	
Net income		780,000
Contra to appraisal increase of land		400,000
Additional assessments of prior years' income taxes	91,000	
Extraordinary gain		22,500
Treasury stock, preferred; issued and reacquired, at par	250,000	
Extraordinary loss	118,500	
Correction of a prior period error	55,000	
	1,028,500	1,632,500
Credit balance of additional capital account	604,000	
	$1,632,500	$1,632,500

Instructions
(a) Prepare a journal entry to close the single "Additional Capital" account now used and to establish appropriately classified accounts. Indicate how you derive the balance of each new account.

(b) If generally accepted accounting principles had been followed, what amount should have been shown as total net income?

P16-2 (Equity Shortage and Treasury Stock Settlement) The balance sheet of Bajor Inc. shows $400,000 capital stock consisting of 4,000 shares of $100 par, and retained earnings of $144,000. As controller of the company, you find that Ro Laren, the assistant treasurer, is $83,000 short in her accounts and had concealed this shortage by adding the amount to the inventory. She owns 750 shares of the company's stock and, in settlement of the shortage, offers this stock at its book value. The offer is accepted; the company pays her the excess value and distributes the 750 shares thus acquired to the other stockholders.

Instructions
- **(a)** What amount should Bajor Inc. pay the assistant treasurer?
- **(b)** By what journal entries should the foregoing transactions be recorded? (Treasury stock is recorded using the cost method.)
- **(c)** What is the total stockholders' equity after the distribution noted above?
- **(d)** What would have been done if Bajor Inc. had had a deficit of $85,000 and the 750 shares had been accepted at par?

P16-3 (Preferred Stock Dividends) Monie Love Inc. began operations in January 1998 and had the following reported net income or loss for each of its 5 years of operations:

1998	$ 225,000 loss
1999	140,000 loss
2000	180,000 loss
2001	422,500 income
2002	1,535,000 income

At December 31, 2002, Monie Love capital accounts were as follows:

Common stock, par value $15 per share; authorized 200,000 shares; issued and outstanding 50,000 shares	$ 750,000
8% nonparticipating noncumulative preferred stock, par value $100 per share; authorized, issued and outstanding 5,000 shares	500,000
5% fully participating cumulative preferred stock, par value $150 per share; authorized, issued and outstanding 10,000 shares	1,500,000

Monie Love has never paid a cash or stock dividend. There has been no change in the capital accounts since Monie Love began operations. The appropriate state law permits dividends only from retained earnings.

Instructions
Prepare a work sheet showing the maximum amount available for cash dividends on December 31, 2002, and how it would be distributable to the holders of the common shares and each of the preferred shares. Show supporting computations in good form.

(AICPA adapted)

P16-4 (Stock Dividend Involving Exchangeable Shares and Cash in Lieu of Fractional Shares) The board of directors of Edna Ferber Corporation on December 1, 2002, declared a 4% stock dividend on the common stock of the corporation, payable on December 28, 2002, only to the holders of record at the close of business December 15, 2002. They stipulated that cash dividends were to be paid in lieu of issuing any fractional shares. They also directed that the amount to be charged against retained earnings should be an amount equal to the market value of the stock on the record date multiplied by the total of (a) the number of shares issued as a stock dividend, and (b) the number of shares on which cash is paid in place of the issuance of fractional shares. The following facts are given:

1. At the dividend record date:
   - **(a)** Shares of Ferber common issued — 3,048,750
   - **(b)** Shares of Ferber common held in treasury — 1,100
   - **(c)** Shares of Ferber common included in (a) above held by persons who will receive cash in lieu of fractional shares — 222,750
2. Values of Ferber common were:
   - Par value — $ 5
   - Market value at December 1st and 15th — $21
   - Book value at December 1st and 15th — $14

Instructions
Prepare entries and explanations to record the payment of the dividend.

(AICPA adapted)

P16-5   (Cash Dividend Entries)   The books of John Dos Passos Corporation carried the following account balances as of December 31, 2001:

Cash	$ 195,000
Preferred stock, 6% cumulative, nonparticipating, $50 par	750,000
Common stock, no par value, 300,000 shares issued	1,500,000
Paid-in capital in excess of par (preferred)	150,000
Treasury stock (common 4,200 shares at cost)	33,600
Retained earnings	105,000

The preferred stock has dividends in arrears for the past year (2001)—to be settled by issuance of preferred stock.

The board of directors, at their annual meeting on December 21, 2002, declared the following: "The current year dividends shall be 6% on the preferred and $.30 per share on the common; the dividends in arrears shall be paid by issuing one share of treasury stock for each ten shares of preferred held."

The preferred is currently selling at $80 per share and the common at $8 per share. Net income for 2002 is estimated at $77,000.

Instructions
(a)   Prepare the journal entries required for the dividend declaration and payment, assuming that they occur simultaneously.
(b)   Could John Dos Passos Corporation give the preferred stockholders 2 years' dividends and common stockholders a 30 cents per share dividend, all in cash?

P16-6   (Preferred Stock Dividends)   Cajun Company has outstanding 2,500 shares of $100 par, 6% preferred stock and 15,000 shares of $10 par value common. The schedule below shows the amount of dividends paid out over the last 4 years.

Instructions
Allocate the dividends to each type of stock under assumptions (a) and (b). Express your answers in per-share amounts using the following format.

		Assumptions			
		(a) Preferred, noncumulative, and nonparticipating		(b) Preferred, cumulative, and fully participating	
Year	Paid-out	Preferred	Common	Preferred	Common
1999	$13,000				
2000	$26,000				
2001	$57,000				
2002	$76,000				

P16-7   (Dividends and splits)   Gutsy Company provides you with the following condensed balance sheet information.

Assets		Liabilities and Stockholders' Equity		
Current assets	$ 40,000	Current and long-term liabilities		$100,000
Investments in ABC stock		Stockholders' equity		
(10,000 shares at cost)	60,000	Common stock ($2 par)	$ 20,000	
Equipment (net)	250,000	Paid-in capital in excess of par	110,000	
Intangibles	60,000	Retained earnings	180,000	310,000
Total assets	$410,000	Total liabilities and		
		stockholders' equity		$410,000

Instructions
For each transaction below, indicate the dollar impact (if any) on the following five items: (1) total assets, (2) common stock, (3) paid-in capital in excess of par, (4) retained earnings, and (5) stockholders' equity. (Each situation is independent.)
(a)   Gutsy declares and pays a $.50 per share dividend.
(b)   Gutsy declares and issues a 10% stock dividend when the market price of the stock is $14 per share.

(c) Gutsy declares and issues a 40% stock dividend when the market price of the stock is $15 per share.

(d) Gutsy declares and distributes a property dividend. Gutsy gives one share of ABC stock for every two shares of Gutsy Company stock held. ABC is selling for $10 per share on the date the property dividend is declared.

(e) Gutsy declares a 2-for-1 stock split and issues new shares.

P16-8 (Entries for Stockholders' Equity Transactions) Some of the account balances of Mali Vai Company at December 31, 2001, are shown below.

6% Preferred Stock ($100 par, 2,000 shares authorized)	$ 20,000
Paid-in Capital in Excess of Par—Preferred Stock	3,000
Common Stock ($10 par, 100,000 shares authorized)	500,000
Paid-in Capital in Excess of Par—Common Stock	100,000
Unappropriated Retained Earnings	304,000
Treasury Stock—Preferred (50 shares at cost)	5,500
Treasury Stock—Common (1,000 shares at cost)	16,000
Retained Earnings Appropriated for Contingencies	75,000
Retained Earnings Appropriated for Fire Insurance	95,000

The price of the company's common stock has been increasing steadily on the market; it was $21 on January 1, 2002, advanced to $24 by July 1, and to $27 at the end of the year 2002. The preferred stock is not openly traded but was appraised at $120 per share during 2002.

Instructions

Give the proper journal entries for each of the following:

(a) The company incurred a fire loss of $71,000 to its warehouse.

(b) The company declared a property dividend on April 1. Each common stockholder was to receive one share of Washington for every 10 shares outstanding. Mali Vai had 8,000 shares of Washington (2% of total outstanding stock) which was purchased in 1999 for $68,400. The market value of Washington stock was $16 per share on April 1. Record appreciation only on the shares distributed.

(c) The company resold the 50 shares of preferred stock held in the treasury for $116 per share.

(d) On July 1, the company declared a 5% stock dividend to the common (outstanding) stockholders.

(e) The city of Wimble, in an effort to persuade the company to expand into that city, donated to Mali Vai Company a plot of land with an appraised value of $42,000 (credit to Revenue from Contribution).

(f) At the annual board of directors meeting, the board decided to "Set up an appropriation in retained earnings for the future construction of a new plant. Such appropriation to be for $125,000 per year. Also, to increase the appropriation for contingencies by $25,000 and to eliminate the appropriation for fire insurance and begin purchasing such insurance from London Insurance Company."

P16-9 (Equity Entries and Retained Earnings Statement) The stockholders' equity section of Girod Company balance sheet on January 1 of the current year is as follows:

Paid-in capital		
Common stock, par $100, 20,000 shares authorized,		
10,000 shares issued	$1,000,000	
Paid-in capital in excess of par	400,000	
Total paid-in capital		$1,400,000
Retained earnings		
Unappropriated	328,800	
Appropriated for plant expansion	120,000	
Appropriated for treasury stock	61,200	
Total retained earnings		510,000
		1,910,000
Less: Cost of treasury stock (600 shares)		61,200
Total stockholders' equity		$1,848,800

The following selected transactions occurred during the year:

1. Paid cash dividends of $1.25 per share on the common stock. The dividend had been properly recorded when declared last year. (State law prohibits cash or stock dividends on treasury shares.)

2. Declared a 10% stock dividend on the common stock when the shares were selling at $113 each in the market.
3. Made a prior period adjustment to correct an error of $70,000 which overstated net income in the previous year. The error was the result of an overstatement of ending inventory.
4. Sold all of the treasury shares for $70,200.
5. Issued the certificates for the stock dividend.
6. The board appropriated $40,000 of retained earnings for plant expansion, eliminated the appropriation for treasury stock, and declared a cash dividend of $1.65 per share on the common stock.
7. The company reported net income of $235,000 for the year.

Instructions

(a) Prepare journal entries for the selected transactions above (ignore income taxes).
(b) Compute the unappropriated retained earnings balance at December 31.

P16-10   (Equity Entries and Balance Sheet Presentation)   On December 15, 2001, the directors of Geordi Laforge Corporation voted to appropriate $90,000 of retained earnings and to retain in the business assets equal to the appropriation for use in expanding the corporation's factory building. This was the fourth of such appropriations; after it was recorded, the stockholders' equity section of Laforge's balance sheet appeared as follows:

Stockholders' equity		
Common stock, $10 par value, 300,000 shares		
authorized, 200,000 shares issued and outstanding		$2,000,000
Paid-in capital in excess of par		3,600,000
Total paid-in capital		5,600,000
Retained earnings		
Unappropriated	$1,800,000	
Appropriated for plant expansion	360,000	
Total retained earnings		2,160,000
Total stockholders' equity		$7,760,000

On January 9, 2002, the corporation entered into a contract for the construction of the factory addition for which the retained earnings were appropriated. On November 1, 2002, the addition was completed and the contractor was paid the contract price of $330,000.

On December 14, 2002, the board of directors voted to return the balance of the Retained Earnings Appropriated for Plant Expansion account to Unappropriated Retained Earnings. They also voted a 25,000 share stock dividend distributable on January 23, 2003, to the January 15, 2003, stockholders of record. The stock dividend was paid per the board's resolution. The corporation's stock was selling at $47 in the market on December 14, 2002. Laforge reported net income of $530,000 for 2001 and $600,000 for 2002.

Instructions

(a) Prepare the appropriate journal entries for Laforge Corporation for the information above (December 15, 2001, to January 23, 2003, inclusive).
(b) Prepare the stockholders' equity section of the balance sheet for Laforge at December 31, 2002, in proper accounting form.

P16-11   (Stockholders' Equity Section of Balance Sheet)   The following is a summary of all relevant transactions of Jadzia Dax Corporation since it was organized in 1999:

In 1999, 15,000 shares were authorized and 7,000 shares of common stock ($50 par value) were issued at a price of $57. In 2000, 1,000 shares were issued as a stock dividend when the stock was selling for $62. Three hundred shares of common stock were bought in 2001 at a cost of $66 per share. These 300 shares are still in the company treasury. (State law requires an appropriation of retained earnings equal to cost of treasury stock.)

In 2000, 10,000 preferred shares were authorized and the company issued 4,000 of them ($100 par value) at $113. Some of the preferred stock was reacquired by the company and later reissued for $4,700 more than it cost the company.

The corporation has earned a total of $610,000 in net income after income taxes and paid out a total of $312,600 in cash dividends since incorporation. An appropriation was made in 2001 by the board of directors from retained earnings in the amount of $75,000 for Fixed Asset Replacements.

Instructions

Prepare the stockholders' equity section of the balance sheet in proper form for Jadzia Dax Corporation as of December 31, 2001. Account for treasury stock using the cost method.

P16-12 **(Stock and Cash Dividends)** Gul Ducat Corporation has outstanding 2,000,000 shares of common stock of a par value of $10 each. The balance in its retained earnings account at January 1, 2001, was $24,000,000, and it then had Additional Paid-in Capital of $5,000,000. During 2001, the company's net income was $5,700,000. A cash dividend of 60¢ a share was paid June 30, 2001, and a 6% stock dividend was distributed to stockholders of record at the close of business on December 31, 2001. You have been asked to advise on the proper accounting treatment of the stock dividend.

The existing stock of the company is quoted on a national stock exchange. The market price of the stock has been as follows:

October 31, 2001	$31
November 30, 2001	33
December 31, 2001	38
Average price over the two-month period	35

Instructions

(a) Prepare a journal entry to record the cash dividend.

(b) Prepare a journal entry to record the stock dividend.

(c) Prepare the stockholders' equity section (including schedules of retained earnings and additional paid-in capital) of the balance sheet of Gul Ducat Corporation for the year 2001 on the basis of the foregoing information. Draft a note to the financial statements setting forth the basis of the accounting for the stock dividend and add separately appropriate comments or explanations regarding the basis chosen.

P16-13 **(Analysis and Classification of Equity Transactions)** Ohio Company was formed on July 1, 1998. It was authorized to issue 300,000 shares of $10 par value common stock and 100,000 shares of 8% $25 par value, cumulative and nonparticipating preferred stock. Ohio Company has a July 1–June 30 fiscal year.

The following information relates to the stockholders' equity accounts of Ohio Company:

Common Stock

Prior to the 2000–01 fiscal year, Ohio Company had 110,000 shares of outstanding common stock issued as follows:

1. 95,000 shares were issued for cash on July 1, 1998, at $31 per share.

2. On July 24, 1998, 5,000 shares were exchanged for a plot of land which cost the seller $70,000 in 1992 and had an estimated market value of $220,000 on July 24, 1998.

3. 10,000 shares were issued on March 1, 2000; the shares had been subscribed for $42 per share on October 31, 1999.

During the 2000–01 fiscal year, the following transactions regarding common stock took place:

October 1, 2000	Subscriptions were received for 10,000 shares at $46 per share. Cash of $92,000 was received in full payment for 2,000 shares and stock certificates were issued. The remaining subscription for 8,000 shares were to be paid in full by September 30, 2001, at which time the certificates were to be issued.
November 30, 2000	Ohio purchased 2,000 shares of its own stock on the open market at $39 per share. Ohio uses the cost method for treasury stock.
December 15, 2000	Ohio declared a 5% stock dividend for stockholders of record on January 15, 2001, to be issued on January 31, 2001. Ohio was having a liquidity problem and could not afford a cash dividend at the time. Ohio's common stock was selling at $52 per share on December 15, 2000.
June 20, 2001	Ohio sold 500 shares of its own common stock that it had purchased on November 30, 2000, for $21,000.

Preferred Stock

Ohio issued 50,000 shares of preferred stock at $44 per share on July 1, 1999.

Cash Dividends

Ohio has followed a schedule of declaring cash dividends in December and June with payment being made to stockholders of record in the following month. The cash dividends which have been declared since inception of the company through June 30, 2001, are shown below:

Declaration Date	Common Stock	Preferred Stock
12/15/99	$.30 per share	$1.00 per share
6/15/00	$.30 per share	$1.00 per share
12/15/00	—	$1.00 per share

No cash dividends were declared during June 2001 due to the company's liquidity problems.

Retained Earnings

As of June 30, 2000, Ohio's retained earnings account had a balance of $690,000. For the fiscal year ending June 30, 2001, Ohio reported net income of $40,000.

In March of 2000, Ohio received a term loan from Columbus National Bank. The bank requires Ohio to establish a sinking fund and restrict retained earnings for an amount equal to the sinking fund deposit. The annual sinking fund payment of $50,000 is due on April 30 each year; the first payment was made on schedule on April 30, 2001.

Instructions

Prepare the stockholders' equity section of the Balance Sheet, including appropriate notes, for Ohio Company as of June 30, 2001, as it should appear in its annual report to the shareholders.

(CMA adapted)

P16-14 (Stock Dividends and Stock Split) Jenny Durdil Inc. is selling its $10 par common stock for $120 per share. Five million shares are currently issued and outstanding. The board of directors wishes to stimulate interest in Jenny Durdil common stock before a forthcoming stock issue but does not wish to distribute capital at this time. The board also believes that too many adjustments to the Stockholders' Equity section, especially Retained Earnings, might discourage potential investors.

The board has considered three options for stimulating interest in the stock:

1. A 20% stock dividend
2. A 100% stock dividend
3. A 2-for-1 stock split.

Acting as financial advisor to the board, you have been asked to report briefly on each option and, considering the board's wishes, make a recommendation. Discuss the effects of each of the foregoing options.

CONCEPTUAL CASES

C16-1 (Conceptual Issues—Equity) Statements of Financial Accounting Concepts set forth financial accounting and reporting objectives and fundamentals that will be used by the Financial Accounting Standards Board in developing standards. *Concepts Statement No. 6* was issued to replace *Concepts Statement No. 3*, and it defines various elements of financial statements.

Instructions

Answer the following questions based on *SFAC No. 6.*

(a) Define and discuss the term "equity."
(b) What transactions or events change owners' equity?
(c) Define "investments by owners" and provide examples of this type of transaction. What financial statement element other than equity is typically affected by owner investments?
(d) Define "distributions to owners" and provide examples of this type of transaction. What financial statement element other than equity is typically affected by distributions?
(e) What are examples of changes within owners' equity that do not change the total amount of owners' equity?

C16-2 (Stock Dividends and Splits) The directors of Amman Corporation are considering the issuance of a stock dividend. They have asked you to discuss the proposed action by answering the following questions.

Instructions

(a) What is a stock dividend? How is a stock dividend distinguished from a stock split (1) From a legal standpoint? (2) From an accounting standpoint?
(b) For what reasons does a corporation usually declare a stock dividend? A stock split?
(c) Discuss the amount, if any, of retained earnings to be capitalized in connection with a stock dividend.

(AICPA adapted)

C16-3 (Stock Dividends) Kitakyushu Inc., a client, is considering the authorization of a 10% common stock dividend to common stockholders. The financial vice president of Kitakyushu wishes to discuss the accounting implications of such an authorization with you before the next meeting of the board of directors.

Instructions

(a) The first topic the vice president wishes to discuss is the nature of the stock dividend to the recipient. Discuss the case against considering the stock dividend as income to the recipient.

(b) The other topic for discussion is the propriety of issuing the stock dividend to all "stockholders of record" or to "stockholders of record exclusive of shares held in the name of the corporation as treasury stock." Discuss the case against issuing stock dividends on treasury shares.

(AICPA adapted)

C16-4 (Stock Dividend, Cash Dividend, and Treasury Stock) Hsuchou Company has 30,000 shares of $10 par value common stock authorized and 20,000 shares issued and outstanding. On August 15, 2001, Hsuchou purchased 1,000 shares of treasury stock for $16 per share. Hsuchou uses the cost method to account for treasury stock. On September 14, 2001, Hsuchou sold 500 shares of the treasury stock for $20 per share.

In October 2001, Hsuchou declared and distributed 1,950 shares as a stock dividend from unissued shares when the market value of the common stock was $21 per share.

On December 20, 2001, Hsuchou declared a $1 per share cash dividend, payable on January 10, 2002, to shareholders of record on December 31, 2001.

Instructions

(a) How should Hsuchou account for the purchase and sale of the treasury stock, and how should the treasury stock be presented in the balance sheet at December 31, 2001?

(b) How should Hsuchou account for the stock dividend, and how would it affect the stockholders' equity at December 31, 2001? Why?

(c) How should Hsuchou account for the cash dividend, and how would it affect the balance sheet at December 31, 2001? Why?

(AICPA adapted)

*C16-5 (Quasi-Reorganization) Jackie Henning Company, a medium-sized manufacturer, has been experiencing losses for the 5 years that it has been doing business. Although the operations for the year just ended resulted in a loss, several important changes resulted in a profitable fourth quarter, and the future operations of the company are expected to be profitable. The treasurer, Peter Henning, suggests that there be a quasi-reorganization to eliminate the accumulated deficit of $650,000.

Instructions

(a) What are the characteristics of a quasi-reorganization? In other words, of what does it consist?

(b) List the conditions under which a quasi-reorganization generally is justified.

(c) Discuss the propriety of the treasurer's proposals to eliminate the deficit of $650,000.

(AICPA adapted)

*C16-6 (Quasi-Reorganization) After operating several years, Char Lewis Corporation showed a net worth of $1,500,000, of which $300,000 was represented by 3,000 shares of $100 each, and $1,200,000 was retained earnings. Subsequently, three additional shares were issued for each share held, which made the capital stock $1,200,000 and retained earnings $300,000. The operations of later years showed an aggregate loss of $840,000, leaving a deficit of $540,000.

The corporation then reduced the par value of each share of stock to 25% of its former value, thus restoring the capital to the original amount of $300,000. The deficit was absorbed and the retained earnings shown as $360,000. It is argued that this amount represents the net operating results since organization and is, therefore, retained earnings.

Instructions

Write a memorandum, giving your opinion of these transactions; disregard their legal aspects.

USING YOUR JUDGMENT

FINANCIAL REPORTING PROBLEM: INTEL CORPORATION

Instructions

Refer to the financial statements and accompanying notes and discussion of Intel Corporation presented in Appendix 5B and answer the following questions.

(a) What amount of cash dividends per share was declared by Intel in 1998? What was the dollar amount effect of the cash dividends on Intel's stockholders' equity?

(b) What is Intel's rate of return on common stock equity for 1998 and 1997?

(c) What is Intel's payout ratio for 1998 and 1997?

(d) What is Intel's book value per share at December 26, 1998, and December 27, 1997?

(e) What was the market price range (high/low) of Intel's common stock during the quarter ended December 26, 1998?

(f) Using the high price per share in the fourth quarter of 1998, what was the price earnings ratio for Intel?

FINANCIAL STATEMENT ANALYSIS CASES

Case 1: Wiebold, Incorporated

The following note related to stockholders' equity was reported in Wiebold's annual report:

> On February 1, 1998, the Board of Directors declared a 3-for-2 stock split, distributed on February 22, 1998, to shareholders of record on February 10, 1998. Accordingly, all numbers of common shares, except unissued shares and treasury shares, and all per share data have been restated to reflect this stock split in addition to the 3-for-2 stock split declared on January 27, 1997, distributed on February 26, 1997, to shareholders of record on February 10, 1997.
>
> On the basis of amounts declared and paid, the annualized quarterly dividends per share were $0.80 in 1997, $0.75 in 1996, and $0.71 in 1995.

Instructions

(a) What is the significance of the date of record and the date of distribution?

(b) Why might Weibold have declared a 3-for-2 for stock split?

(c) What impact does Wiebold's stock split have on (1) total stockholders' equity; (2) total par value; (3) outstanding shares, and (4) book value per share?

Case 2: Garrister Information Systems Corp.

Garrister Information Systems has two classes of preferred stock—A and C—in addition to its common stock. The 1,300 shares of Series A preferred stock are nonvoting, have a 12% cumulative dividend, have liquidation preference rights over the Series C preferred stock and the common stock, and are callable by the company at any time for $1,000 per share plus cumulative unpaid dividends. Each share of Series A preferred stock is convertible into 500 shares of common stock. As of March 31, 1998, the cumulative unpaid dividends on the Series A preferred stock totaled $254,000.

Instructions

(a) Should the $254,000 in dividends not paid be reported as a liability on the balance sheet?

(b) If the par value of the Class A preferred stock is $100 per share, what dollar amount in dividends can the shareholders expect annually on the Class A preferred stock?

www.wiley.com/college/kieso

COMPARATIVE ANALYSIS CASE

The Coca-Cola Company versus PepsiCo, Inc.

Instructions

Go to the Digital Tool and, using The Coca-Cola Company and PepsiCo, Inc. Annual Report information, answer the following questions.

(a) What amounts of cash dividends per share were declared by Coca-Cola and PepsiCo in 1998? What were the dollar amount effects of the cash dividends on each company's stockholders' equity?

(b) What are Coca-Cola's and PepsiCo's rate of return on common/capital stock equity for 1998 and 1997? Which company gets the higher return on the equity of its shareholders?

(c) What are Coca-Cola's and PepsiCo's payout ratios for 1998?

(d) What was the market price range (high/low) for Coca-Cola's common stock and PepsiCo's capital stock during the fourth quarter of 1998? Which company's (Coca-Cola's or PepsiCo's) stock price increased more (%) during 1998?

(e) What was Coca-Cola's price-earnings ratio at December 31, 1998? What was PepsiCo's price-earnings ratio at December 26, 1998?

RESEARCH CASES

Case 1

As indicated in the chapter, companies are required to disclose changes in the separate accounts comprising stockholders' equity.

Instructions

Examine the financial statements of two companies of your choice and answer the following questions with regard to each company.

(a) Are the changes in the stockholders' equity accounts presented in a separate statement or in the notes to the financial statements?

(b) Is a separate statement of retained earnings presented?

(c) Which of the stockholders' equity account balances changed during the period covered? Identify the reason(s) for these changes.

Case 2

The October 3, 1994, issue of *Barron's* includes an article by Shirley A. Lazo entitled "Split Decision: One Way To Lift Shares."

Instructions

Read the article and answer the following questions.

(a) Why might a stock dividend/split have a positive effect on shareholder wealth?

(b) Why might a stock dividend/split have a negative effect on shareholder wealth?

(c) According to the study described in the article, what happens to the stock prices of banks during the month following a stock dividend/split?

(d) What conclusion was drawn from the study?

ETHICS CASES

*Case 1

"You can't writeup assets," said Nick Toby, internal audit director of Paula Nofftz International Inc., to his boss, Jim Coffin, vice president and chief financial officer. "Nonsense," said Jim, "I can do this as part of a quasi-reorganization of our company." For the last 3 years, Paula Nofftz International, a farm equipment manufacturing firm, has experienced a downturn in its profits resulting from stiff competition with overseas firms and increasing direct labor costs. Though the prospects are still gloomy, the company is hoping to turn a profit by modernizing its property, plant, and equipment (PP&E). This will require Paula Nofftz International to raise a lot of money.

Over the past few months, Jim tried to raise funds from various financial institutions. They are unwilling to consider lending capital, however, because the company's net book value of fixed assets on the balance sheet, based on historic cost, was not ample to sustain major funding. Jim attempted to explain to bankers and investors that these assets were more valuable than their recorded amounts, given that the company used accelerated depreciation methods and tended to underestimate the useful lives of assets. Jim also believes that the company's land and buildings are substantially undervalued because of rising real estate prices over the past several years.

Jim's idea is a simple one: First, declare a large dividend to shareholders of the company, such that Retained Earnings would have a large debit balance. Then, writeup the fixed assets of Paula Nofftz International to an amount equal to the deficit in the Retained Earnings account.

Instructions

(a) What are the ethical implications of Jim Coffin's creative accounting scheme?

(b) Who could be harmed if the accounting reorganization were implemented and Paula Nofftz International Inc. received additional funding?

(c) Why can't a company writeup assets when the fair value of these assets exceed their original cost?

Case 2

Donald Young, comptroller for Center Company, wants to discuss with the company president, Rhonda Santo, the possibility of paying a stock dividend. Young knows the company does not have an abundance of cash, yet he is certain Santo would like to give the stockholders something of value this year since it has been a few years since the company has paid any dividends. Young also is concerned that their cash position will not improve significantly in the near future. He feels that stockholders look to retained earnings and, if they see a large balance, believe (erroneously, of course) that the company can pay a cash dividend.

Young wants to propose that the company pay a 100% stock dividend as opposed to a cash dividend or a 2-for-1 stock split. He reasons (1) that the stockholders will receive something of value, other than cash, and (2) that retained earnings will be reduced by the stock dividend (as opposed to a split which does not affect retained earnings) so stockholders will be less likely to expect cash dividends in the near future.

Instructions

Answer the following questions:

(a) What are the ethical issues involved?

(b) Do you agree with Young's reasoning?

CHAPTER 17

Dilutive Securities and Earnings per Share

Mergers Dilute Earnings per Share

The "urge to merge" that dominated the business scene in the 1960s developed into merger mania in the 1980s. The 1990s saw fewer mergers than the 1980s, but those that did take place were some of the largest ever. Typical mergers in the 1990s were combinations of information, entertainment, or financial (banking) companies. For example, Bell Atlantic Corp. and Nynex Corp. combined in a $22.7 billion deal, Time acquired Warner Communications for $10.1 billion, Walt Disney Co. purchased Capital Cities/ABC, Inc., Chemical Bank joined with Chase Manhattan Corp., and Boeing bought McDonnell Douglas Corp. Even larger were the mergers of Nations Bank and BankAmerica ($62 billion), and Bell Atlantic and GTE ($71 billion) in 1998. Sweeping deregulation triggered many of the deals in telecommunications, banking, and utilities; cuts in military spending changed the landscape for aerospace firms.[1]

One consequence of heavy merger activity is an increase in the use of securities such as convertible bonds, convertible preferred stocks, stock warrants, and contingent shares to structure these deals. Although not common stock in form, these securities enable their holders to obtain common stock upon exercise or conversion. They are called dilutive securities or potential common stock because a reduction—dilution—in earnings per share often results when these securities become common stock.

During the 1960s, corporate officers recognized that the issuance of dilutive securities in a merger did not have the same immediate adverse effect on earnings per share as the issuance of common stock. In addition, many companies found that issuance of convertible securities did not seem to upset common stockholders, even though the common stockholders' interests were substantially diluted when these securities were later converted or exercised.

As a consequence of the massive mergers in the 1990s, the presence of dilutive securities on corporate balance sheets is now very prevalent. The usage of stock option plans, which also are dilutive in nature, is increasing. These option plans are used mainly to attract and retain executive talent and to provide tax relief for executives in high tax brackets.

LEARNING OBJECTIVES

After studying this chapter, you should be able to:

1. Describe the accounting for the issuance, conversion, and retirement of convertible securities.

2. Explain the accounting for convertible preferred stock.

3. Contrast the accounting for stock warrants and stock warrants issued with other securities.

4. Describe the accounting for stock compensation plans under generally accepted accounting principles.

5. Explain the controversy involving stock compensation plans.

6. Compute earnings per share in a simple capital structure.

7. Compute earnings per share in a complex capital structure.

[1]Farrell Kramer, "Mergers Have Been in Fashion in 1996, With Seven Big Ones," *St. Louis Post-Dispatch,* December 16, 1996, p. A7; and Geoffrey Colvin, "The Year of the Mega Merger," *Fortune,* January 11, 1999, p. 62.

The widespread use of dilutive securities has led the accounting profession to examine the area closely. Specifically, the profession has directed its attention to accounting for these securities at date of issuance and to the presentation of earnings per share figures that recognize their effect. The first section of this chapter discusses convertible securities, warrants, stock options, and contingent shares. The second section indicates how these securities are used in earnings per share computations. The content and organization of the chapter are as follows:

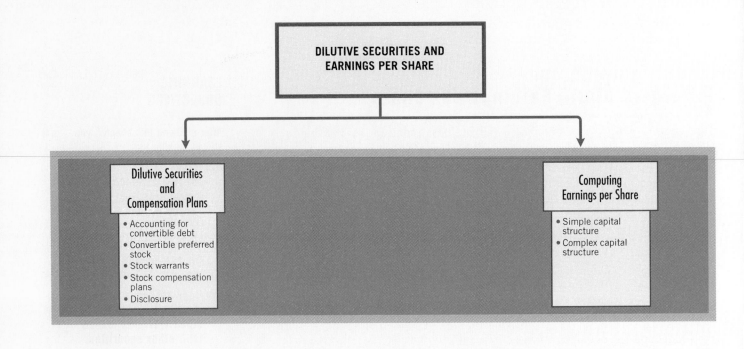

ACCOUNTING FOR CONVERTIBLE DEBT

OBJECTIVE 1
Describe the accounting for the issuance, conversion, and retirement of convertible securities.

If bonds can be converted into other corporate securities during some specified period of time after issuance, they are called **convertible bonds**. **A convertible bond combines the benefits of a bond with the privilege of exchanging it for stock at the holder's option.** It is purchased by investors who desire the security of a bond holding—guaranteed interest—plus the added option of conversion if the value of the stock appreciates significantly.

Corporations issue convertibles for two main reasons. One is the desire to raise equity capital without giving up more ownership control than necessary. To illustrate, assume that a company wants to raise $1,000,000 at a time when its common stock is selling at $45 per share. Such an issue would require sale of 22,222 shares (ignoring issue costs). By selling 1,000 bonds at $1,000 par, each convertible into 20 shares of common stock, the enterprise may raise $1,000,000 by committing only 20,000 shares of its common stock.

A second reason why companies issue convertible securities is to obtain common stock financing at cheaper rates. Many enterprises could issue debt only at high interest rates unless a convertible covenant were attached. The conversion privilege entices the investor to accept a lower interest rate than would normally be the case on a straight debt issue. For example, Amazon.com recently issued convertible bonds that pay interest at an effective yield of 4.75%, which is much lower than Amazon.com would have to pay if it issued straight debt. For this lower interest rate, the investor receives the right to buy Amazon.com's common stock at a fixed price until maturity.[2]

Accounting for convertible debt involves reporting issues at the time of (1) issuance, (2) conversion, and (3) retirement.

At Time of Issuance

The method for recording convertible bonds **at the date of issue follows the method used to record straight debt issues** (with none of the proceeds recorded as equity). Any discount or premium that results from the issuance of convertible bonds is amortized to its maturity date because it is difficult to predict when, if at all, conversion will occur. However, the accounting for convertible debt as a straight debt issue is controversial; we discuss it more fully later in this chapter.

At Time of Conversion

If bonds are converted into other securities, the principal accounting problem is to determine the amount at which to record the securities exchanged for the bond. Assume Hilton, Inc. issued at a premium of $60 a $1,000 bond convertible into 10 shares of common stock (par value $10). At the time of conversion the unamortized premium is $50, the market value of the bond is $1,200, and the stock is quoted on the market at $120. **The book value method of recording the conversion of the bonds is the method most commonly used in practice and is considered GAAP.** To illustrate the specifics of this approach, the entry for the conversion of the Hilton, Inc. bonds would be:

Bonds Payable	1,000	
Premium on Bonds Payable	50	
Common Stock		100
Paid-in Capital in Excess of Par		950

Support for the book value approach is based on the argument that an agreement was established at the date of the issuance either to pay a stated amount of cash at maturity or to issue a stated number of shares of equity securities. Therefore, when the debt is converted to equity in accordance with the preexisting contract terms, no gain or loss should be recognized upon conversion.[3]

---

[2]As with any investment, a buyer has to be careful. For example, Wherehouse Entertainment Inc., which had 6¼% convertibles outstanding, was taken private in a leveraged buyout. As a result, the convertible was suddenly as risky as a junk bond of a highly leveraged company with a coupon of only 6¼%. As one holder of the convertibles noted, "What's even worse is that the company will be so loaded down with debt that it probably won't have enough cash flow to make its interest payments. And the convertible debt we hold is subordinated to the rest of Wherehouse's debt." These types of situations have made convertibles less attractive and have led to the introduction of takeover protection covenants in some convertible bond offerings. Or, sometimes convertibles are permitted to be called at par and therefore the conversion premium may be lost.

[3]An alternative approach that has some conceptual merit uses the market value to record the conversion. The entry under the **market value approach** (market price = $1,200) would be:

Bonds Payable	1,000	
Premium on Bonds Payable	50	
Loss on Redemption of Bonds Payable	150	
Common Stock		100
Paid-in Capital in Excess of Par		1,100

Because the conversion described above is initiated by the holder of the debt instrument (rather than the issuer), it is not an "early extinguishment of debt." As a result, the gain or loss would not be classified as an extraordinary item.

Induced Conversions

Sometimes the issuer wishes to induce prompt conversion of its convertible debt to equity securities in order to reduce interest costs or to improve its debt to equity ratio. As a result, the issuer may offer some form of additional consideration (such as cash or common stock), called a "sweetener," to **induce conversion**. The sweetener should be reported as an expense of the current period at an amount equal to the fair value of the additional securities or other consideration given.

Assume that Helloid, Inc. has outstanding $1,000,000 par value convertible debentures convertible into 100,000 shares of $1 par value common stock. Helloid wishes to reduce its annual interest cost. To do so, Helloid agrees to pay the holders of its convertible debentures an additional $80,000 if they will convert. Assuming conversion occurs, the following entry is made:

Debt Conversion Expense	80,000	
Bonds Payable	1,000,000	
Common Stock		100,000
Additional Paid-in Capital		900,000
Cash		80,000

The additional $80,000 is recorded as **an expense of the current period** and not as a reduction of equity. Some argue that the cost of a conversion inducement is a cost of obtaining equity capital. As a result, they contend, it should be recognized as a cost of— a reduction of—the equity capital acquired and not as an expense. However, the FASB indicated that when an additional payment is needed to make bondholders convert, the payment is for a service (bondholders converting at a given time) and should be reported as an expense. This expense is not reported as an extraordinary item.[4]

Retirement of Convertible Debt

Should the retirement of convertible debt be considered a debt transaction or an equity transaction? In theory, it could be either. If it is treated as a debt transaction, the difference between the carrying amount of the retired convertible debt and the cash paid should result in a charge or credit to income. If it is an equity transaction, the difference should go to additional paid-in capital.

To answer the question, we need to remember that the method for recording the **issuance** of convertible bonds follows that used in recording straight debt issues. Specifically this means that no portion of the proceeds should be attributable to the conversion feature and credited to Additional Paid-in Capital. Although theoretical objections to this approach can be raised, to be consistent, a gain or loss on **retiring convertible debt needs to be recognized in the same way as a gain or loss on retiring debt** that is not convertible. For this reason, differences between the cash acquisition price of debt and its carrying amount should be reported **currently in income as a gain or loss**.[5] As indicated in Chapter 14, material gains or losses on extinguishment of debt are considered extraordinary items.

Nevertheless, failure to recognize the equity feature of convertible debt when issued creates problems upon early extinguishment. Assume that the **Amazon.com** convertible debt discussed earlier was issued at a time when the investment community attaches value to the conversion feature. Subsequently the price of Amazon.com stock decreases so sharply that the conversion feature has little or no value. If Amazon.com extinguishes its convertible debt early, a large gain develops because the book value of the debt will exceed the retirement price. Many consider this treatment incorrect, because the reduction in value of the convertible debt relates to its equity features, not

---

[4]"Induced Conversions of Convertible Debt," *Statement of Financial Accounting Standards No. 84* (Stamford, Conn.: FASB, 1985).

[5]"Early Extinguishment of Debt," *Opinions of the Accounting Principles Board No. 26* (New York: AICPA, 1972).

its debt features. Therefore, they argue, an adjustment to Additional Paid-in Capital should be made. However, present practice requires that an extraordinary gain or loss be recognized at the time of early extinguishment.

CONVERTIBLE PREFERRED STOCK

The major difference in accounting for a convertible bond and a convertible preferred stock at the date of issue is that convertible bonds are considered liabilities, whereas convertible preferreds (unless mandatory redemption exists) are considered a part of stockholders' equity.

OBJECTIVE 2
Explain the accounting for convertible preferred stock.

In addition, when convertible preferred stocks are exercised, there is no theoretical justification for recognition of a gain or loss. No gain or loss is recognized when the entity deals with stockholders in their capacity as business owners. The **book value method is employed**: Preferred Stock, along with any related Additional Paid-in Capital, is debited; Common Stock and Additional Paid-in Capital (if an excess exists) are credited.

A different treatment develops when the par value of the common stock issued exceeds the book value of the preferred stock. In that case, Retained Earnings is usually debited for the difference.

Assume Host Enterprises issued 1,000 shares of common stock (par value $2) upon conversion of 1,000 shares of preferred stock (par value $1) that was originally issued for a $200 premium. The entry would be:

Convertible Preferred Stock	1,000	
Paid-in Capital in Excess of Par (Premium on Preferred Stock)	200	
Retained Earnings	800	
Common Stock		2,000

The rationale for the debit to Retained Earnings is that the preferred stockholders are offered an additional return to facilitate their conversion to common stock. In this example, the additional return is charged to retained earnings. Many states, however, require that this charge simply reduce additional paid-in capital from other sources.

STOCK WARRANTS

Warrants are certificates entitling the holder to acquire shares of stock at a certain price within a stated period. This option is similar to the conversion privilege because warrants, if exercised, become common stock and usually have a dilutive effect (reduce earnings per share) similar to that of the conversion of convertible securities. However, a substantial difference between convertible securities and stock warrants is that upon exercise of the warrants, the holder has to pay a certain amount of money to obtain the shares.

OBJECTIVE 3
Contrast the accounting for stock warrants and stock warrants issued with other securities.

The issuance of warrants or options to buy additional shares normally arises under three situations:

❶ When issuing different types of securities, such as bonds or preferred stock, warrants are often included to make the **security more attractive**—to provide an "equity kicker."

❷ Upon the issuance of additional common stock, existing stockholders have a **preemptive right to purchase common stock** first. Warrants may be issued to evidence that right.

❸ Warrants, often referred to as stock options, are given as **compensation to executives and employees**.

The problems in accounting for stock warrants are complex and present many difficulties—some of which remain unresolved.

Stock Warrants Issued with Other Securities

Warrants issued with other securities are basically long-term options to buy common stock at a fixed price. Although some perpetual warrants are traded, generally their life is 5 years, occasionally 10.

A warrant works like this: Tenneco, Inc. offered a unit comprising one share of stock and one detachable warrant exercisable at $24.25 per share and good for 5 years. The unit sold for 22¾ ($22.75) and since the price of the common the day before the sale was 19⅞ ($19.88), the difference suggests a price of 2⅞ ($2.87) for the warrants.

In this situation, the warrants had an apparent value of 2⅞ ($2.87), even though it would not be profitable at present for the purchaser to exercise the warrant and buy the stock, because the price of the stock is much below the exercise price of $24.25.[6] The investor pays for the warrant to receive a possible future call on the stock at a fixed price when the price has risen significantly. For example, if the price of the stock rises to $30, the investor has gained $2.88 ($30 minus $24.25 minus $2.87) on an investment of $2.87, a 100% increase! But, if the price never rises, the investor loses the full $2.87.[7]

The proceeds from the sale of debt with **detachable stock warrants** should be allocated between the two securities.[8] The profession takes the position that two separable instruments are involved, that is, (1) a bond and (2) a warrant giving the holder the right to purchase common stock at a certain price. Warrants that are detachable can be traded separately from the debt and, therefore, a market value can be determined. The two methods of allocation available are:

❶ The proportional method.
❷ The incremental method.

Proportional Method

AT&T's offering of detachable 5-year warrants to buy one share of common stock (par value $5) at $25 (at a time when a share was selling for approximately $50) enabled it to price its offering of bonds at par with a moderate 8¾% yield. To place a value on the two securities one would determine (1) the value of the bonds without the warrants and (2) the value of the warrants. For example, assume that AT&T's bonds (par $1,000) sold for 99 without the warrants soon after they were issued. The market value of the warrants at that time was $30. Prior to sale the warrants will not have a market value. The allocation is based on an estimate of market value, generally as established by an investment banker, or on the relative market value of the bonds and the warrants soon after they are issued and traded. The price paid for 10,000, $1,000 bonds with the warrants attached was par, or $10,000,000. The allocation between the bonds and warrants would be made in this manner:

ILLUSTRATION 17-1
Proportional Allocation of Proceeds between Bonds and Warrants

Fair market value of bonds (without warrants) ($10,000,000 × .99)	= $ 9,900,000
Fair market value of warrants (10,000 × $30)	= 300,000
Aggregate fair market value	$10,200,000
Allocated to bonds: $\frac{\$9,900,000}{\$10,200,000}$ × $10,000,000 =	$ 9,705,882
Allocated to warrants: $\frac{\$300,000}{\$10,200,000}$ × $10,000,000 =	294,118
Total allocation	$10,000,000

[6]Later in this discussion it will be shown that the value of the warrant is normally determined on the basis of a relative market value approach because of the difficulty of imputing a warrant value in any other manner.

[7]From the illustration, it is apparent that buying warrants can be an "all or nothing" proposition.

[8]A detachable warrant means that the warrant can sell separately from the bond. *APB Opinion No. 14* makes a distinction between detachable and nondetachable warrants because nondetachable warrants must be sold with the security as a complete package; thus, no allocation is permitted.

In this situation the bonds sell at a discount and are recorded as follows:

Cash	9,705,882	
Discount on Bonds Payable	294,118	
Bonds Payable		10,000,000

In addition, the company sells warrants that are credited to paid-in capital. The entry is as follows:

Cash	294,118	
Paid-in Capital—Stock Warrants		294,118

The entries may be combined if desired; they are shown separately here to indicate that the purchaser of the bond is buying not only a bond, but also a possible future claim on common stock.

Assuming that all 10,000 warrants are exercised (one warrant per one share of stock), the following entry would be made:

Cash (10,000 × $25)	250,000	
Paid-in Capital—Stock Warrants	294,118	
Common Stock (10,000 × $5)		50,000
Paid-in Capital in Excess of Par		494,118

What if the warrants are not exercised? In that case, Paid-in Capital—Stock Warrants is debited for $294,118 and Paid-in Capital from Expired Warrants is credited for a like amount. The additional paid-in capital reverts to the former stockholders.

Incremental Method

In instances where the fair value of either the warrants or the bonds is not determinable, the incremental method used in lump sum security purchases (explained in Chapter 15, page 779) may be used. That is, the security for which the market value is determinable is used and the remainder of the purchase price is allocated to the security for which the market value is not known. Assume that the market price of the AT&T warrants was known to be $300,000, but the market price of the bonds without the warrants could not be determined. In this case, the amount allocated to the warrants and the stock would be as follows:

Lump sum receipt	$10,000,000
Allocated to the warrants	300,000
Balance allocated to bonds	$ 9,700,000

ILLUSTRATION 17-2
Incremental Allocation of Proceeds between Bonds and Warrants

Conceptual Questions

The question arises whether the allocation of value to the warrants is consistent with the handling accorded convertible debt, in which no value is allocated to the conversion privilege. The Board stated that the features of a convertible security are **inseparable** in the sense that choices are mutually exclusive: the holder either converts or redeems the bonds for cash, but cannot do both. No basis, therefore, exists for recognizing the conversion value in the accounts. The Board, however, indicated that the issuance of bonds with **detachable warrants** involves two securities, one a debt security, which will remain outstanding until maturity, and the other a warrant to purchase common stock. At the time of issuance, separable instruments exist, and therefore separate treatment is justified. **Nondetachable warrants**, however, **do not require an allocation of the proceeds between the bonds and the warrants**. The entire proceeds are recorded as debt.

Many argue that the conversion feature is not significantly different in nature from the call represented by a warrant. The question is whether, although the legal forms are different, sufficient similarities of substance exist to support the same accounting treatment. Some contend that inseparability per se is not a sufficient basis for restrict-

UNDERLYING CONCEPTS

Reporting a convertible bond solely as debt is not representationally faithful. However, the cost-benefit constraint is used to justify the failure to allocate between debt and equity.

ing allocation between identifiable components of a transaction. Examples of allocation between assets of value in a single transaction are not uncommon, such as allocation of values in basket purchases and separation of principal and interest in capitalizing long-term leases. Critics of the current accounting for convertibles say that to deny recognition of value to the conversion feature merely looks to the form of the instrument and does not deal with the substance of the transaction.

The authors disagree with the FASB as well. In both situations (convertible debt and debt issued with warrants), the investor has made a payment to the firm for an equity feature—the right to acquire an equity instrument in the future. The only real distinction between them is that the additional payment made when the equity instrument is formally acquired takes different forms. The warrant holder pays additional cash to the issuing firm; the convertible debt holder pays for stock by forgoing the receipt of interest from conversion date until maturity date and by forgoing the receipt of the maturity value itself. Thus, it is argued that the difference is one of method or form of payment only, rather than one of substance. **Until the profession officially reverses its stand in regard to accounting for convertible debt, however, only bonds issued with detachable stock warrants will result in accounting recognition of the equity feature.**[9]

INTERNATIONAL INSIGHT

International accounting standards require that the issuer of convertible debt record the liability and equity components separately.

Rights to Subscribe to Additional Shares

If the directors of a corporation decide to issue new shares of stock, the old stockholders generally have the right (preemptive privilege) to purchase newly issued shares in proportion to their holdings. The privilege, referred to as a **stock right**, saves existing stockholders from suffering a dilution of voting rights without their consent, and it may allow them to purchase stock somewhat below its market value. The warrants issued in these situations are of short duration, unlike the warrants issued with other securities.

The certificate representing the stock right states the number of shares the holder of the right may purchase, as well as the price at which the new shares may be purchased. Each share owned ordinarily gives the owner one stock right. The price is normally less than the current market value of such shares, which gives the rights a value in themselves. From the time they are issued until they expire, they may be purchased and sold like any other security.

No entry is required when rights are issued to existing stockholders. Only a memorandum entry is needed to indicate the number of rights issued to existing stockholders and to ensure that the company has additional unissued stock registered for issuance in case the rights are exercised. No formal entry is made at this time because no stock has been issued and no cash has been received.

If the rights are exercised, usually a cash payment of some type is involved. If the cash received is equal to the par value, an entry crediting Common Stock at par value is made. If it is in excess of par value, a credit to Paid-in Capital in Excess of Par develops; if it is less than par value, a charge to Paid-in Capital is appropriate.

STOCK COMPENSATION PLANS

Another form of warrant arises in stock compensation plans used to pay and motivate employees. This warrant is a **stock option**, which gives selected employees the option to purchase common stock at a given price over an extended period of time. Stock op-

---

[9]Recent research indicates that estimates of the debt and equity components of convertible bonds are subject to considerable measurement error. (Mary Barth, Wayne Landsman, and Richard Rendleman, Jr. "Option Pricing–Based Bond Value Estimates and a Fundamental Components Approach to Account for Corporate Debt," *The Accounting Review*, January 1998.) The FASB is currently working on a project that will address the accounting for securities with both debt and equity features, such as convertible bonds. A proposed standard is expected to be issued for comment in 2000.

tions are very popular because they meet the objectives of an effective compensation program.

Effective compensation has been a subject of considerable interest lately. A consensus of opinion is that effective compensation programs are ones that (1) motivate employees to high levels of performance, (2) help retain executives and allow for recruitment of new talent, (3) base compensation on employee and company performance, (4) maximize the employee's after-tax benefit and minimize the employee's after-tax cost, and (5) use performance criteria over which the employee has control. Although straight cash compensation plans (salary and, perhaps, bonus) are an important part of any compensation program, they are oriented to the short run. Many companies recognize that a more long-run compensation plan is often needed in addition to a cash component.

Long-term compensation plans attempt to develop in the executive a strong loyalty toward the company. An effective way to accomplish this goal is to give the employees "a piece of the action"—that is, an equity interest based on changes in long-term measures such as increases in earnings per share, revenues, stock price, or market share. These plans, generally referred to as **stock option plans**, come in many different forms. Essentially, they provide the executive with the opportunity to receive stock or cash in the future if the performance of the company (however measured) is satisfactory.

Stock options are the fastest-growing segment of executive pay. Executives want stock option contracts because options can make them instant millionaires if the company is successful. For example, for 365 of the largest U.S. companies, long-term compensation was mostly from exercised stock options. Here is an example of some of the higher awards and average compensation for all companies surveyed in 1998.

ILLUSTRATION 17-3
Executive Option Compensation

($000)	1998 Salary and Bonus	Long-Term Compensation (Options)	Total Pay
Top-Paid CEOs			
1. Michael Eisner Walt Disney	$5,764	$569,828	$575,592
2. Mel Karmazin CBS	4,000	197,934	201,934
3. Sanford Weill Citigroup	7,430	159,663	167,093
4. Stephen Case America Online	1,177	158,057	159,233
5. Craig Barrett Intel	2,280	114,232	116,511
6. John Welch General Electric	10,105	73,559	83,664
7. Henry Schacht Lucent Technologies	2,020	65,016	67,037
8. L. Dennis Kozlowski Tyco International	3,750	61,514	65,264
9. Henry Silverman Cendant	2,818	61,063	63,882
10. M. Douglas Ivester Coca-Cola	2,750	54,572	57,322

Source: Based on Jennifer Rheingold and Ronald Grover, "Special Report: Executive Pay," *Business Week*, April 19, 1999.

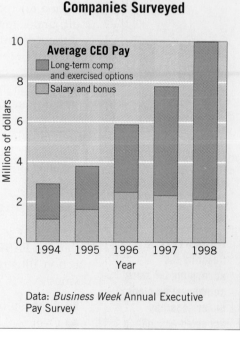

Data: *Business Week* Annual Executive Pay Survey

The Major Accounting Issue

To illustrate the most contentious accounting issue related to stock option plans, suppose that you are an employee for Hurdle Inc. and you are granted options to purchase 10,000 shares of the firm's common stock as part of your compensation. The date you receive the options is referred to as the **grant date**. The options are good for 10 years;

the market price and the exercise price for the stock are both $20 at the grant date. What is the value of the compensation you just received?

Some believe you have not received anything; that is, the difference between the market price and the exercise price is zero and therefore no compensation results. Others argue these options have value: if the stock price goes above $20 any time over the next 10 years and you exercise these options, substantial compensation results. For example, if at the end of the fourth year, the market price of the stock is $30 and you exercise your options, you will have earned $100,000 [10,000 options × ($30 − $20)], ignoring income taxes.

How should the granting of these options be reported by Hurdle Inc.? In the past, GAAP required that compensation cost be measured by the excess of the market price of the stock over its exercise price at the grant date. This approach is referred to as the **intrinsic value method** because the computation is not dependent on external circumstances: **it is the difference between the market price of the stock and the exercise price of the options at the grant date**. Hurdle would therefore not recognize any compensation expense related to your options because at the grant date the market price and exercise price were the same.

Recently the FASB issued *Statement of Financial Accounting Standards No. 123 "Accounting for Stock-Based Compensation"* which **encourages but does not require recognition of compensation cost for the fair value of stock-based compensation paid to employees for their services**.[10] The FASB position is that the accounting for the cost of employee services should be based on the value of compensation paid, which is presumed to be a measure of the value of the services received. Accordingly, the compensation cost arising from employee stock options should be measured based on the fair value of the stock options granted.[11] To determine this value, acceptable option pricing models are used to value options at the date of grant. This approach is referred to as the **fair value method** because the option value is estimated based on the many factors which determine its underlying value.[12]

The FASB met considerable resistance when it proposed requiring the fair value method for recognizing the costs of stock options in the financial statements. As a result, under the final standard, a company **can choose** to use either the intrinsic value method or fair value method when accounting for compensation cost on the income statement. However, if a company uses the intrinsic value method to recognize compensation costs for employee stock options, it must provide expanded disclosures in the notes on these costs. Specifically, companies that choose the intrinsic value method are required to disclose in a note to the financial statements pro-forma net income and earnings per share (if presented by the company), as if it had used the fair value method. The following sections discuss the accounting for stock options under both the intrinsic and fair value methods as well as the political debate surrounding stock compensation accounting.

Accounting for Stock Compensation

OBJECTIVE 4
Describe the accounting for stock compensation plans under generally accepted accounting principles.

A company is given a choice in the recognition method for stock compensation; however, **the FASB encourages adoption of the fair value method**. Our discussion in this section illustrates both methods. Stock option plans involve two main accounting issues:

❶ How should compensation expense be determined?

❷ Over what periods should compensation expense be allocated?

---

[10]"Accounting for Stock-Based Compensation," *Statement of Financial Accounting Standards No. 123* (Norwalk, Conn.: FASB, 1995).

[11]Stock options issued to non-employees in exchange for other goods or services must be recognized according to the fair value method in *SFAS 123*.

[12]These factors include the volatility of the underlying stock, the expected life of the options, the risk-free rate during the option life, and expected dividends during the option life.

Determining Expense

Using the fair value method, total compensation expense is computed based on the fair value of the options expected to vest[13] on the date the options are granted to the employee(s) (i.e., the **grant date**). Fair value for public companies is to be estimated using an option pricing model, with some adjustments for the unique factors of employee stock options. No adjustments are made after the grant date, in response to subsequent changes in the stock price—either up or down.[14]

Under the intrinsic value method (*APB Opinion No. 25*), total compensation cost is computed as the excess of the market price of the stock over the option price on the date when both the number of shares to which employees are entitled and the option or purchase price for those shares are known (the **measurement date**). For many plans, this measurement date is the **grant date**. However, the measurement date may be later for plans with variable terms (either number of shares and/or option price are not known) that depend on events after the date of grant. For such variable plans, compensation expense may have to be estimated on the basis of assumptions as to the final number of shares and the option price (usually at the exercise date).

Allocating Compensation Expense

In general, under both the fair and intrinsic value methods, compensation expense is recognized in the periods in which the employee performs the service—the **service period**. Unless otherwise specified, the service period is the vesting period—the time between the grant date and the vesting date. Thus, total compensation cost is determined at the grant date and allocated to the periods benefited by the employees' services.

Illustration

To illustrate the accounting for a stock option plan, assume that on November 1, 2000, the stockholders of Chen Company approve a plan that grants the company's five executives options to purchase 2,000 shares each of the company's $1 par value common stock. The options are granted on January 1, 2001, and may be exercised at any time within the next ten years. The option price per share is $60, and the market price of the stock at the date of grant is $70 per share. Using the intrinsic value method, the total compensation expense is computed below.

Market value of 10,000 shares at date of grant ($70 per share)	$700,000
Option price of 10,000 shares at date of grant ($60 per share)	600,000
Total compensation expense (intrinsic value)	$100,000

Using the fair value method, total compensation expense is computed by applying an acceptable fair value option pricing model (such as the Black-Scholes option pricing model). To keep this illustration simple, we will assume that the fair value option pricing model determines total compensation expense to be $220,000.

Basic Entries. The value of the options under either method is recognized as an expense in the periods in which the employee performs services. In the case of Chen Company, assume that the documents associated with issuance of the options indicate that the expected period of benefit is 2 years, starting with the grant date. The journal entries to record the transactions related to this option contract using both the intrinsic value and fair value method are shown on the following page:

[13]Vested means "to earn the rights to." An employee's award becomes vested at the date that the employee's right to receive or retain shares of stock or cash under the award is no longer contingent on remaining in the service of the employer.

[14]Nonpublic companies are permitted to use a minimum value method to estimate the value of the options. The minimum value method does not consider the volatility of the stock price when estimating option value. Nonpublic companies frequently do not have data with which to estimate this element of option value.

ILLUSTRATION 17-4
Comparison of Entries
for Option Contract—
Intrinsic Value and Fair
Value Methods

Intrinsic Value		Fair Value	
At date of grant (January 1, 2001):			
No entry		No entry	
To record compensation expense for 2001 (December 31, 2001):			
Compensation Expense	50,000	Compensation Expense	110,000
Paid-in Capital—Stock Options	50,000	Paid-in Capital—Stock Options	110,000
($100,000 ÷ 2)		($220,000 ÷ 2)	
To record compensation expense for 2002 (December 31, 2002):			
Compensation Expense	50,000	Compensation Expense	110,000
Paid-in Capital—Stock Options	50,000	Paid-in Capital—Stock Options	110,000

Under both methods, compensation expense is allocated evenly over the 2-year service period. The only difference between the two methods is the amount of compensation recognized.

Exercise. If 20% or 2,000 of the 10,000 options were exercised on June 1, 2004 (3 years and 5 months after date of grant), the following journal entry would be recorded using the **intrinsic value method**.

	June 1, 2004		
Cash (2,000 × $60)		120,000	
Paid-in Capital—Stock Options (20% × $100,000)		20,000	
Common Stock (2,000 × $1.00)			2,000
Paid-in Capital in Excess of Par			138,000

Using the **fair value approach**, the entry would be:

	June 1, 2004		
Cash (2,000 × $60)		120,000	
Paid-in Capital—Stock Options (20% × $220,000)		44,000	
Common Stock (2,000 × $1.00)			2,000
Paid-in Capital in Excess of Par			162,000

Expiration. If the remaining stock options are not exercised before their expiration date, the balance in the Paid-in Capital—Stock Options account should be transferred to a more properly titled paid-in capital account, such as Paid-in Capital from Expired Stock Options. The entry to record this transaction at the date of expiration would be as follows:

ILLUSTRATION 17-5
Comparison of Entries
for Stock Option
Expiration—Intrinsic
Value and Fair Value
Methods

Intrinsic Value		Fair Value	
January 1, 2011 (Expiration date):			
Paid-in Capital—Stock Options	80,000	Paid-in Capital—Stock Options	176,000
Paid-in Capital from Expired Stock		Paid-in Capital from Expired Stock	
Options (80% × $100,000)	80,000	Options (80% × $220,000)	176,000

Adjustment. The fact that a stock option is not exercised does not nullify the propriety of recording the costs of services received from executives and attributable to the stock option plan. Under GAAP, compensation expense is, therefore, not adjusted upon expiration of the options. However, if a stock option is forfeited because **an employee fails to satisfy a service requirement** (e.g., leaves employment), the estimate of compensation expense recorded in the current period should be adjusted (as a change in estimate). This change in estimate would be recorded by debiting Paid-in Capital—Stock Options and crediting Compensation Expense, thereby decreasing compensation expense in the period of forfeiture.

Types of Plans

Many different types of plans are used to compensate key executives. In all these plans the amount of the reward depends upon future events. Consequently, continued employment is a necessary element in almost all types of plans. The popularity of a given plan usually depends on prospects in the stock market and tax considerations. For example, if it appears that appreciation will occur in a company's stock, a plan that offers the option to purchase stock is attractive to an executive. Conversely, if it appears that price appreciation is unlikely, then compensation might be tied to some performance measure such as an increase in book value or earnings per share.

Three common compensation plans that illustrate different objectives are:

1 Stock option plans (incentive or nonqualified).
2 Stock appreciation rights plans.
3 Performance-type plans.

Most plans follow the general guideline for reporting established in the previous sections. A more detailed discussion of these plans is presented in Appendix 17A.

Noncompensatory Plans

In some companies, stock purchase plans permit all employees to purchase stock at a discounted price for a short period of time. These plans are usually classified as noncompensatory. Noncompensatory means that the primary purpose of the plan is not to compensate the employees but, rather, to enable the employer to secure equity capital or to induce widespread ownership of an enterprise's common stock among employees. Thus, compensation expense is not reported for these plans. Noncompensatory plans have three characteristics:

1 Substantially all full-time employees may participate on an equitable basis.
2 The discount from market price is small; that is, it does not exceed the greater of a per share discount reasonably offered to stockholders or the per share amount of costs avoided by not having to raise cash in a public offering.
3 The plan offers no substantive option feature.

For example, Masthead Company had a stock purchase plan under which employees who meet minimal employment qualifications are entitled to purchase Masthead stock at a 5% reduction from market price for a short period of time. The reduction from market price is not considered compensatory because the per share amount of the costs avoided by not having to raise the cash in a public offering is equal to 5%. **Plans that do not possess all of the above mentioned three characteristics are classified as compensatory.**

DISCLOSURE OF COMPENSATION PLANS

To comply with *SFAS No. 123*, companies offering stock-based compensation plans must determine the fair value of the options. Companies must then decide whether to use the fair value method and recognize expense in the income statement, or to use the intrinsic value approach and disclose in the notes the pro forma impact on net income and earnings per share (if presented), as if the fair value method had been used.

Regardless of whether the intrinsic value or fair value method is used, full disclosure should be made about the status of these plans at the end of the periods presented, including the number of shares under option, options exercised and forfeited, the weighted average option prices for these categories, the weighted average fair value of options granted during the year, and the average remaining contractual life of the options outstanding.[15] In addition to information about the status of the stock option plans, companies must also disclose the method and significant assumptions used to estimate the fair values of the stock options.

---

[15]These data should be reported separately for each different type of plan offered to employees.

Illustration 17-6 provides the disclosure by Gateway 2000, Inc. which accounts for its stock options using the intrinsic value method:

ILLUSTRATION 17-6
Disclosure of Stock
Option Plans by
Gateway 2000, Inc.

Go to the Digital Tool for additional examples of stock option disclosures.

GATEWAY 2000, INC.

Note 6: Stock Option Plans. The Company maintains various stock option plans for its employees. Employee options are generally granted at the fair market value of the related common stock at the date of grant. These options generally vest over a four-year period from the date of grant or the employee's initial date of employment. In addition, these options expire, if not exercised, ten years from the date of grant. The Company also maintains option plans for non-employee directors. Option grants to non-employee directors generally have an exercise price equal to the fair market value of the related common stock on the date of grant. These options generally vest over one to three-year periods and expire, if not exercised, ten years from the date of grant.

For all of the Company's stock option plans, options for 1,283,000, 2,582,000 and 2,728,000 shares of common stock were exercisable at December 31, 1996, 1997 and 1998 with a weighted average exercise price of $4.28, $9.86 and $17.42, respectively. In addition, options for 672,000, 556,000 and 280,000 shares of Class A common stock were exercisable at December 31, 1996, 1997 and 1998 with a weighted average exercise price of $2.06, $2.01 and $1.93, respectively. Class A common stock may be converted into an equal number of shares of common stock at any time. There were 12,309,000, 8,328,000 and 11,265,000 shares of common stock available for grant under the plans at December 31, 1996, 1997 and 1998, respectively.

The following table summarizes activity under the stock option plans for 1996, 1997 and 1998 (in thousands, except per share amounts):

	Common Stock	Weighted-Average Price	Class A Common Stock	Weighted-Average Price
Outstanding, December 31, 1995	8,739	$ 3.16	962	$2.14
Granted	3,260	15.75	—	—
Exercised	(6,305)	1.43	(241)	2.13
Forfeited	(254)	14.15	(8)	3.25
Outstanding, December 31, 1996	5,440	12.20	713	2.12
Granted	5,253	36.08	—	—
Exercised	(463)	11.56	(153)	2.50
Forfeited	(775)	23.69	—	—
Outstanding, December 31, 1997	9,455	22.98	560	2.02
Granted	6,118	45.17	—	—
Exercised	(2,143)	16.59	(280)	2.10
Forfeited	(1,103)	32.76	—	—
Outstanding, December 31, 1998	12,327	$34.19	280	$1.93

The following table summarizes information about the Company's Common Stock options outstanding at December 31, 1998 (in thousands, except per share amounts):

	Options Outstanding			Options Exercisable	
Range of Exercise Prices	Number Outstanding at 12/31/98	Weighted-Average Remaining Contractual Life	Weighted-Average Price	Number Exercisable at 12/31/98	Weighted-Average Price
$ 1.19–13.38	1,928	5.57	$ 9.01	1,259	$ 6.76
13.44–29.07	2,287	7.65	22.93	939	20.01
29.31–33.75	2,405	8.87	33.06	267	32.35
34.00–44.75	2,811	8.94	39.55	262	43.88
45.06–62.50	2,896	9.68	55.56	1	61.75

The weighted average fair value per share of options granted during 1996, 1997 and 1998 was $9.65, $21.61 and $27.33, respectively. The fair value of these options was estimated on the date of grant using the Black-Scholes option pricing model with the following weighted-average assumptions used for all grants in 1996, 1997 and 1998: dividend yield of zero percent; expected volatility of 60 percent; risk-free interest rates ranging from 4.7 to 7.2 percent; and expected lives of the options of three and one-half years from the date of vesting.

If *APB Opinion No. 25* is used in the financial statements, companies must still disclose the pro-forma net income and pro-forma earnings per share (if presented), as if the fair value method had been used to account for the stock-based compensation cost. Illustration 17-7 illustrates this disclosure, as provided by Gateway 2000, Inc.

ILLUSTRATION 17-7
Disclosure of Pro-Forma Effect of Stock Option Plans

GATEWAY 2000, INC.

Since all stock options have been granted with exercise prices equal to the fair market value of the related common stock at the date of grant, no compensation expense has been recognized under the Company's stock option plans. Had compensation cost under the plans been determined based on the estimated fair value of the stock options granted in 1996, 1997 and 1998, net income and net income per share would have been reduced to the pro forma amounts indicated below:

	1996	1997	1998
	(in thousands, except per share amounts)		
Net income—as reported	$250,679	$109,797	$346,399
Net income—pro forma	$241,729	$ 85,804	$297,470
Net income per share—as reported			
Basic	$ 1.64	$ .71	$ 2.23
Diluted	$ 1.60	$ .70	$ 2.18
Net income per share—pro forma			
Basic	$ 1.58	$ .56	$ 1.91
Diluted	$ 1.55	$ .55	$ 1.87

   The pro forma effect on net income for 1996, 1997 and 1998 is not fully representative of the pro forma effect on net income in future years because it does not take into consideration pro forma compensation expense related to the vesting of grants made prior to 1995.

Debate over Stock Option Accounting

OBJECTIVE 5
Explain the controversy involving stock compensation plans.

In general, use of the fair value approach results in greater compensation costs relative to the intrinsic value model reflected in *APB Opinion No. 25*. For example, a recent study of the companies in the Standard & Poor's 500 stock index documented that on average earnings in 1998 were overstated by 5% through the use of the intrinsic value method. And some companies, such as Guidant, 3Com, and Cendant, reported earnings under the intrinsic value model that were up to three times higher than earnings using the fair value method.

It is an understatement to say that corporate America was unhappy with the initial requirement to record compensation expense for these plans. Many small high-technology companies were particularly vocal in their opposition, arguing that only through offering stock options can they attract top professional management. They contend that if they are forced to recognize large amounts of compensation expense under these plans, they will be at a competitive disadvantage with larger companies that can withstand higher compensation charges. As one high-tech executive stated: "If your goal is to attack fat-cat executive compensation in multi-billion dollar firms, then please do so! But not at the expense of the people who are 'running lean and mean,' trying to build businesses and creating jobs in the process."

A chronology of events related to this standard demonstrates the difficulty in standard-setting when various stakeholders believe they are adversely affected.

UNDERLYING CONCEPTS
The stock option controversy involves economic consequence issues. The FASB believes the neutrality concept should be followed; others disagree, noting that factors other than accounting theory should be considered.

❶ *In June 1993 the FASB issued an exposure draft on stock options.* The recommendations were that the value of stock options issued to employees is compensation which should be recognized in the financial statements. Nonrecognition of these costs results in financial statements that are neither credible nor representationally faithful. The draft recommended that option pricing models be used to estimate the value of stock options. In addition, disclosures related to these plans would be enhanced.

② *The exposure draft met a blizzard of opposition from the business community.* Some argued stock option plans were not compensation expense; some contended that it was impossible to develop appropriate option pricing models; others said that these standards would be disastrous to American business. The economic consequences argument was used extensively. In mid-1993 Congresswoman Anna Eshoo (California) submitted a congressional resolution calling for the FASB *not* to change its current accounting rules. Eshoo stated that the FASB proposal "poses a threat to economic recovery and entrepreneurship in the United States. . . . (it) hurts low- and mid-level employees and stunts the growth of new-growth sectors, such as high technology which relies heavily on entrepreneurship."

③ *On June 30, 1993, the Equity Expansion Act of 1993 was introduced by Senator Joseph Lieberman (Connecticut).* The bill mandates that the SEC require that no compensation expense be reported on the income statement for stock option plans. Senator Lieberman's bill could have forced the FASB to bend to political pressure and thereby set a precedent for interfering in the operations of the Board.

④ *During the latter part of 1993, the FASB looked for political support but found few supporters.* The SEC commissioners all expressed reservations about the FASB's proposed ruling. However, the chief accountant of the SEC spoke in opposition to much of the lobbying effort directed against the FASB.

⑤ *In early 1994 a group of senators wrote to the SEC.* They expressed concern "that the credibility of the financial reporting process may be harmed significantly if Congress, in order to further economic or political goals, either discourages the FASB from revising what the FASB believes to be a deficient standard or overrules the FASB by writing an accounting standard directly into the Federal securities laws."

⑥ *In late 1994, the FASB decided to encourage, rather than require, recognition of compensation cost based on the fair value method and require expanded disclosures.* The FASB adopted the disclosure approach because they were concerned that the "divisiveness of the debate" could threaten the future of accounting standard-setting in the private sector. The final standard was issued in October 1995.

The stock option saga is a classic example of the difficulty the FASB faces in issuing an accounting standard. Many powerful interests aligned against the Board; even some who initially appeared to support the Board's actions later reversed themselves. The whole incident is troubling because the debate for the most part is not about the **proper accounting** but more about the **economic consequences** of the standards. If we continue to write standards so that some social, economic, or public policy goal is achieved, it will not be too long before financial reporting will lose its credibility.

SECTION 2	*COMPUTING EARNINGS PER SHARE*

INTERNATIONAL INSIGHT

In many nations (e.g., Switzerland, Sweden, Spain, and Mexico) there is no legal requirement to disclose earnings per share.

Earnings per share data are frequently reported in the financial press and are widely used by stockholders and potential investors in evaluating the profitability of a company. **Earnings per share** indicates the income earned by each share of common stock. Thus, **earnings per share is reported only for common stock**. For example, if Oscar Co. has net income of $300,000 and a weighted average of 100,000 shares of common stock outstanding for the year, earnings per share is $3 ($300,000 ÷ 100,000).

Because of the importance of earnings per share information, most companies are required to report this information on the face of the income statement.[16] The excep-

---

[16]"Earnings per Share," *Statement of Financial Accounting Standards No. 128* (Norwalk, Conn.: FASB, 1997). For an article on the usefulness of EPS reported data and the application of the qualitative characteristics of accounting information to EPS data, see Lola W. Dudley, "A Critical Look at EPS," *Journal of Accountancy,* August 1985, pp. 102–11.

tion is nonpublic companies; because of cost-benefit considerations they do not have to report this information.[17] Generally, earnings per share information is reported below net income in the income statement. For Oscar Co. the presentation would be as follows:

Net income	$300,000
Earnings per share	$3.00

ILLUSTRATION 17-8
Income Statement
Presentation of EPS

When the income statement contains intermediate components of income, earnings per share should be disclosed for each component. The following is representative:

Earnings per share:	
Income from continuing operations	$4.00
Loss from discontinued operations, net of tax	.60
Income before extraordinary item and	
cumulative effect of change in accounting principle	3.40
Extraordinary gain, net of tax	1.00
Cumulative effect of change in accounting principle, net of tax	.50
Net income	$4.90

ILLUSTRATION 17-9
Income Statement
Presentation of EPS
Components

These disclosures enable the user of the financial statements to recognize the effects of income from continuing operations on EPS, as distinguished from income or loss from irregular items.[18]

EARNINGS PER SHARE—SIMPLE CAPITAL STRUCTURE

A corporation's capital structure is **simple** if it consists only of common stock or includes no **potential common stock** that upon conversion or exercise could dilute earnings per common share. (A capital structure is **complex** if it includes securities that could have a dilutive effect on earnings per common share.) The computation of earnings per share for a simple capital structure involves two items (other than net income)—preferred stock dividends and weighted average number of shares outstanding.

OBJECTIVE 6
Compute earnings per share in a simple capital structure.

Preferred Stock Dividends

As indicated earlier, earnings per share relates to earnings per common share. When a company has both common and preferred stock outstanding, **the current year preferred stock dividend is subtracted from net income to arrive at** income available to common stockholders. The formula for computing earnings per share is then as follows:

$$\frac{\text{Net Income} - \text{Preferred Dividends}}{\text{Weighted Average Number of Shares Outstanding}} = \textbf{Earnings Per Share}$$

ILLUSTRATION 17-10
Formula for Computing
Earnings per Share

---

[17]A nonpublic enterprise is an enterprise other than (1) whose debt or equity securities are traded in a public market on a foreign or domestic stock exchange or in the over-the-counter market (including securities quoted locally or regionally) or (2) that is required to file financial statements with the SEC. An enterprise is no longer considered a nonpublic enterprise when its financial statements are issued in preparation for the sale of any class of securities in a public market.

[18]Per share amounts for discontinued operations, an extraordinary item, or the cumulative effect of an accounting change in a period should be presented either on the face of the income statement or in the notes to the financial statements.

In reporting earnings per share information, dividends on preferred stock should be subtracted from each of the intermediate components of income (income from continuing operations and income before extraordinary items) and finally from net income to arrive at income available to common stockholders. If dividends on preferred stock are declared and a net loss occurs, **the preferred dividend is added to the loss** for purposes of computing the loss per share. If the preferred stock is cumulative and the dividend is not declared in the current year, **an amount equal to the dividend that should have been declared for the current year only** should be subtracted from net income or added to the net loss. Dividends in arrears for previous years should have been included in the previous years' computations.

INTERNATIONAL INSIGHT

Where EPS disclosure is prevalent, it is usually based on the weighted average of shares outstanding. Some countries such as Australia, France, Japan, and Mexico use the number of shares outstanding at year-end.

Weighted Average Number of Shares Outstanding

In all computations of earnings per share, the weighted average number of shares outstanding during the period constitutes the basis for the per share amounts reported. Shares issued or purchased during the period affect the amount outstanding and must be **weighted by the fraction of the period they are outstanding**. The rationale for this approach is to find the equivalent number of whole shares outstanding for the year. To illustrate, assume that Stallone Inc. has the following changes in its common stock shares outstanding for the period.

ILLUSTRATION 17-11
Shares Outstanding, Ending Balance— Stallone Inc.

Date	Share Changes	Shares Outstanding
January 1	Beginning balance	90,000
April 1	Issued 30,000 shares for cash	30,000
		120,000
July 1	Purchased 39,000 shares	39,000
		81,000
November 1	Issued 60,000 shares for cash	60,000
December 31	Ending balance	141,000

To compute the weighted average number of shares outstanding, the following computation is made.

ILLUSTRATION 17-12
Weighted Average Number of Shares Outstanding

Dates Outstanding	(A) Shares Outstanding	(B) Fraction of Year	(C) Weighted Shares (A × B)
Jan. 1—Apr. 1	90,000	3/12	22,500
Apr. 1—July 1	120,000	3/12	30,000
July 1—Nov. 1	81,000	4/12	27,000
Nov. 1—Dec. 31	141,000	2/12	23,500
Weighted average number of shares outstanding			103,000

As illustrated, 90,000 shares were outstanding for 3 months, which translates to 22,500 whole shares for the entire year. Because additional shares were issued on April 1, the shares outstanding change and these shares must be weighted for the time outstanding. When 39,000 shares were purchased on July 1, the shares outstanding were reduced and again a new computation must be made to determine the proper weighted shares outstanding.

Stock Dividends and Stock Splits

When **stock dividends** or **stock splits** occur, computation of the weighted average number of shares requires restatement of the shares outstanding before the stock dividend or split. For example, assume that a corporation had 100,000 shares outstanding on January 1 and issued a 25% stock dividend on June 30. For purposes of computing a weighted average for the current year, the additional 25,000 shares outstanding as a result of the stock dividend are assumed to have been **outstanding since the beginning of the year**. Thus the weighted average for the year would be 125,000 shares.

The issuance of a stock dividend or stock split is restated, but the issuance or repurchase of stock for cash is not. Why? The reason is that stock splits and stock dividends do not increase or decrease the net assets of the enterprise; only additional shares of stock are issued and, therefore, the weighted average shares must be restated. By restating, valid comparisons of earnings per share can be made between periods before and after the stock split or stock dividend. Conversely, the issuance or purchase of stock for cash changes the amount of net assets. As a result, the company either earns more or less in the future as a result of this change in net assets. Stated another way, **a stock dividend or split does not change the shareholders' total investment**—it only increases (unless it is a reverse stock split) the number of common shares representing this investment.

To illustrate how a stock dividend affects the computation of the weighted average number of shares outstanding, assume that Rambo Company has the following changes in its common stock shares during the year.

Date	Share Changes	Shares Outstanding
January 1	Beginning balance	100,000
March 1	Issued 20,000 shares for cash	20,000
		120,000
June 1	60,000 additional shares (50% stock dividend)	60,000
		180,000
November 1	Issued 30,000 shares for cash	30,000
December 31	Ending balance	210,000

ILLUSTRATION 17-13
Shares Outstanding, Ending Balance—Rambo Company

The computation of the weighted average number of shares outstanding would be as follows:

Dates Outstanding	(A) Shares Outstanding	(B) Restatement	(C) Fraction of Year	(D) Weighted Shares (A × B × C)
Jan. 1—Mar. 1	100,000	1.50	2/12	25,000
Mar. 1—June 1	120,000	1.50	3/12	45,000
June 1—Nov. 1	180,000		5/12	75,000
Nov. 1—Dec. 31	210,000		2/12	35,000
Weighted average number of shares outstanding				180,000

ILLUSTRATION 17-14
Weighted Average Number of Shares Outstanding—Stock Issue and Stock Dividend

The shares outstanding prior to the stock dividend must be restated. The shares outstanding from January 1 to June 1 are adjusted for the stock dividend, so that these shares are stated on the same basis as shares issued subsequent to the stock dividend. Shares issued after the stock dividend do not have to be restated because they are on the new basis. The stock dividend simply restates existing shares. The same type of treatment occurs for a stock split.

If a stock dividend or stock split occurs after the end of the year, but before the financial statements are issued, the weighted average number of shares outstanding for the year (and any other years presented in comparative form) must be restated. For example, assume that Hendricks Company computes its weighted average number of shares to be 100,000 for the year ended December 31, 2001. On January 15, 2002, before the financial statements are issued, the company splits its stock 3 for 1. In this case, the weighted average number of shares used in computing earnings per share for 2001 would be 300,000 shares. If earnings per share information for 2000 is provided as comparative information, it also must be adjusted for the stock split.

Comprehensive Illustration

Sylvester Corporation has income before extraordinary item of $580,000 and an extraordinary gain, net of tax of $240,000. In addition, it has declared preferred dividends of $1 per share on 100,000 shares of preferred stock outstanding. Sylvester Corporation also has the following changes in its common stock shares outstanding during 2001.

ILLUSTRATION 17-15
Shares Outstanding,
Ending Balance—
Sylvester Corp.

Dates	Share Changes	Shares Outstanding
January 1	Beginning balance	180,000
May 1	Purchased 30,000 treasury shares	30,000
		150,000
July 1	300,000 additional shares (3 for 1 stock split)	300,000
		450,000
December 31	Issued 50,000 shares for cash	50,000
December 31	Ending balance	500,000

To compute the earnings per share information, the weighted average number of shares outstanding is determined as follows:

ILLUSTRATION 17-16
Weighted Average
Number of Shares
Outstanding

Dates Outstanding	(A) Shares Outstanding	(B) Restatement	(C) Fraction of Year	(D) Weighted Shares (A × B × C)
Jan. 1—May 1	180,000	3	4/12	180,000
May 1—Dec. 31	150,000	3	8/12	300,000
Weighted average number of shares outstanding				480,000

In computing the weighted average number of shares, the shares sold on December 31, 2001, are ignored because they have not been outstanding during the year. The weighted average number of shares is then divided into income before extraordinary item and net income to determine earnings per share. Sylvester Corporation's preferred dividends of $100,000 are subtracted from income before extraordinary item ($580,000) to arrive at income before extraordinary item available to common stockholders of $480,000 ($580,000 − $100,000). Deducting the preferred dividends from the income before extraordinary item has the effect of also reducing net income without affecting the amount of the extraordinary item. The final amount is referred to as **income available to common stockholders**.

ILLUSTRATION 17-17
Computation of Income
Available to Common
Stockholders

	(a) Income Information	(b) Weighted Shares	(c) Earnings per Share (A ÷ B)
Income before extraordinary item available to common stockholders	$480,000*	480,000	$1.00
Extraordinary gain (net of tax)	240,000	480,000	.50
Income available to common stockholders	$720,000	480,000	$1.50
*$580,000 − $100,000			

Disclosure of the per share amount for the extraordinary item (net of tax) must be reported either on the face of the income statement or in the notes to the financial statements. Income and per share information reported on the face of the income statement would be as follows:

Income before extraordinary item	$580,000
Extraordinary gain, net of tax	240,000
Net income	$820,000
Earnings per share:	
Income before extraordinary item	$1.00
Extraordinary item, net of tax	.50
Net income	$1.50

ILLUSTRATION 17-18
Earnings per Share, with
Extraordinary Item

EARNINGS PER SHARE—COMPLEX CAPITAL STRUCTURE

One problem with a **basic EPS** computation is that it fails to recognize the potentially dilutive impact on outstanding stock when a corporation has dilutive securities in its capital structure. Dilutive securities present a serious problem because conversion or exercise often has an adverse effect on earnings per share. This adverse effect can be significant and, more important, unexpected unless financial statements call attention to the potential dilutive effect in some manner.[19]

A complex capital structure exists when a corporation has convertible securities, options, warrants or other rights that upon conversion or exercise could dilute earnings per share. Therefore when a company has a complex capital structure, both a basic and diluted earnings per share are generally reported.

The computation of **diluted EPS** is similar to the computation of basic EPS. The difference is that diluted EPS includes the effect of all dilutive potential common shares that were outstanding during the period. The formula in Illustration 17-19 shows the relationship between basic EPS and diluted EPS.

OBJECTIVE 7
Compute earnings per
share in a complex
capital structure.

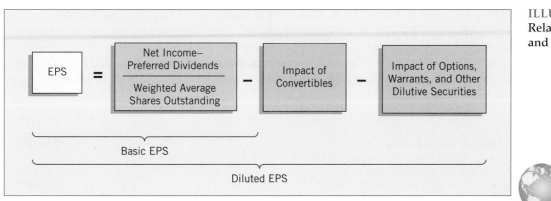

ILLUSTRATION 17-19
Relation between Basic
and Diluted EPS

Note that companies with complex capital structures will not report diluted EPS if the securities in their capital structure are antidilutive. **Antidilutive securities** are securities which upon conversion or exercise increase earnings per share (or reduce the loss per share). The purpose of the dual presentation is to inform financial statement users of situations that will likely occur and to provide "worst case" dilutive situations. If the securities are antidilutive, the likelihood of conversion or exercise is considered remote. Thus, companies that have only antidilutive securities are not permitted to increase earnings per share and are required to report only the basic EPS number.

---

[19]As noted in the opening story, issuance of these types of securities in mergers and compensation plans is more and more prevalent.

The computation of basic EPS was illustrated in the prior section. The discussion in the following sections addresses the effects of convertible and other dilutive securities on EPS calculations.

Diluted EPS—Convertible Securities

At conversion, convertible securities are exchanged for common stock. The method used to measure the dilutive effects of potential conversion on EPS is called the **if-converted method**. The if-converted method for a convertible bond assumes (1) the conversion of the convertible securities at the beginning of the period (or at the time of issuance of the security, if issued during the period), and (2) the elimination of related interest, net of tax. Thus the **denominator**—the weighted average number of shares outstanding—is increased by the additional shares assumed issued. The **numerator**—net income—is increased by the amount of interest expense, net of tax associated with those potential common shares.

Comprehensive Illustration—If-Converted Method

As an example, Marshy Field Corporation has net income for the year of $210,000 and a weighted average number of common shares outstanding during the period of 100,000 shares. The basic earnings per share is, therefore, $2.10 ($210,000 ÷ 100,000). The company has two convertible debenture bond issues outstanding. One is a 6% issue sold at 100 (total $1,000,000) in a prior year and convertible into 20,000 common shares. The other is a 10% issue sold at 100 (total $1,000,000) on April 1 of the current year and convertible into 32,000 common shares. The tax rate is 40%.

As shown in Illustration 17-20, to determine the numerator, we add back the interest on the if-converted securities less the related tax effect. Because the if-converted method assumes conversion as of the beginning of the year, no interest on the convertibles is assumed to be paid during the year. The interest on the 6% convertibles is $60,000 for the year ($1,000,000 × 6%). The increased tax expense is $24,000 ($60,000 × .40), and the interest added back net of taxes is $36,000 [$60,000 − $24,000 or simply $60,000 × (1 − .40)].

Because 10% convertibles are issued subsequent to the beginning of the year, the shares assumed to have been issued on that date, April 1, are weighted as outstanding from April 1 to the end of the year. In addition, the interest adjustment to the numerator for these bonds would only reflect the interest for nine months. Thus the interest added back on the 10% convertible would be $45,000 [$1,000,000 × 10% × 9/12 year × (1 − .4)]. The computation of earnings (the numerator) for diluted earnings per share is shown in Illustration 17-20.

ILLUSTRATION 17-20
Computation of Adjusted Net Income

Net income for the year	$210,000
Add: Adjustment for interest (net of tax)	
6% debentures ($60,000 × [1 − .40])	36,000
10% debentures ($100,000 × 9/12 × [1 − .40])	45,000
Adjusted net income	$291,000

The computation for shares adjusted for dilutive securities (the denominator) for diluted earnings per share is shown in Illustration 17-21:

ILLUSTRATION 17-21
Computation of Weighted Average Number of Shares

Weighted average number of shares outstanding	100,000
Add: Shares assumed to be issued:	
6% debentures (as of beginning of year)	20,000
10% debentures (as of date of issue, April 1; 9/12 × 32,000)	24,000
Weighted average number of shares adjusted for dilutive securities	144,000

Marshy Field would then report earnings per share based on a dual presentation on the face of the income statement; basic and diluted earnings per share are reported.[20] The presentation is shown in Illustration 17-22.

Net income for the year		$210,000
Earnings per Share (Note X)		
Basic earnings per share ($210,000 ÷ 100,000)		$2.10
Diluted earnings per share ($291,000 ÷ 144,000)		$2.02

ILLUSTRATION 17-22
Earnings per Share Disclosure

Other Factors

The example above assumed that Marshy Field's bonds were sold at the face amount. If the bonds are sold at a premium or discount, interest expense must be adjusted each period to account for this occurrence. Therefore, the amount of interest expense added back, net of tax, to net income is the interest expense reported on the income statement, not the interest paid in cash during the period.

In addition, the conversion rate on a dilutive security may change over the period the dilutive security is outstanding. In this situation, for the diluted EPS computation, the **most advantageous conversion rate available to the holder is used**. For example, assume that a convertible bond was issued January 1, 2000, with a conversion rate of 10 common shares for each bond starting January 1, 2002; beginning January 1, 2005, the conversion rate is 12 common shares for each bond; and beginning January 1, 2009, it is 15 common shares for each bond. In computing diluted EPS in 2000, the conversion rate of 15 shares to one bond is used.

Finally, if the 6% convertible debentures were instead 6% convertible preferred stock, the convertible preferred would be considered potential common shares and included in shares outstanding in diluted EPS calculations. Preferred dividends are not subtracted from net income in computing the numerator because it is assumed that the convertible preferreds are converted and are outstanding as common stock for purposes of computing EPS. Net income is used as the numerator—**no tax effect** is computed because preferred dividends generally are not deductible for tax purposes.

Diluted EPS—Options and Warrants

Stock options and warrants outstanding (whether or not presently exercisable) are included in diluted earnings per share unless they are antidilutive. Options and warrants and their equivalents are included in earnings per share computations through the **treasury stock method**.

The treasury stock method assumes that the options or warrants are exercised at the beginning of the year (or date of issue if later) and the proceeds from the exercise of options and warrants are used to purchase common stock for the treasury. If the exercise price is lower than the market price of the stock, then the proceeds from exercise are not sufficient to buy back all the shares. The incremental shares remaining are added to the weighted average number of shares outstanding for purposes of computing diluted earnings per share.

For example, if the exercise price of a warrant is $5 and the fair market value of the stock is $15, the treasury stock method would increase the shares outstanding. Exercise of the warrant would result in one additional share outstanding, but the $5 received for the one share issued is not sufficient to purchase one share in the market at $15. Three warrants would have to be exercised (and three additional shares issued) to produce enough money ($15) to acquire one share in the market. Thus, a net increase of two shares outstanding would result.

---

[20]Conversion of bonds is dilutive because EPS with conversion ($2.02) is less than basic EPS ($2.10).

In terms of larger numbers, assume 1,500 options outstanding at an exercise price of $30 for a common share and a common stock market price per share of $50. Through application of the treasury stock method there would be 600 **incremental shares** outstanding, computed as follows:[21]

ILLUSTRATION 17-23
Computation of
Incremental Shares

Proceeds from exercise of 1,500 options (1,500 × $30)	$45,000
Shares issued upon exercise of options	1,500
Treasury shares purchasable with proceeds ($45,000 ÷ $50)	900
Incremental shares outstanding (potential common shares)	600

Thus, if the exercise price of the option or warrant is **lower** than the market price of the stock, dilution occurs. If the exercise price of the option or warrant is **higher** than the market price of the stock, common shares are reduced. In this case, the options or warrants are **antidilutive** because their assumed exercise leads to an increase in earnings per share.

For both options and warrants, exercise is not assumed unless the average market price of the stock is above the exercise price during the period being reported.[22] As a practical matter, a simple average of the weekly or monthly prices is adequate, so long as the prices do not fluctuate significantly.

Comprehensive Illustration—Treasury Stock Method

To illustrate application of the treasury stock method, assume that Kubitz Industries, Inc. has net income for the period of $220,000. The average number of shares outstanding for the period was 100,000 shares. Hence, basic EPS—ignoring all dilutive securities—is $2.20. The average number of shares under outstanding options (although not exercisable at this time), at an option price of $20 per share, is 5,000 shares. The average market price of the common stock during the year was $28. The computation is shown below.

ILLUSTRATION 17-24
Computation of Earnings
per Share–Treasury Stock
Method

	Basic Earnings per Share	Diluted Earnings per Share
Average number of shares under option outstanding:		5000
Option price per share		× $20
Proceeds upon exercise of options		$100,000
Average market price of common stock		$28
Treasury shares that could be repurchased with proceeds ($100,000 ÷ $28)		3,571
Excess of shares under option over the treasury shares that could be repurchased (5,000 − 3,571)—Potential common incremental shares		1,429
Average number of common shares outstanding	100,000	100,000
Total average number of common shares outstanding and potential common shares	100,000 (A)	101,429 (C)
Net income for the year	$220,000 (B)	$220,000 (D)
Earnings per share	$2.20 (B ÷ A)	$2.17 (D ÷ C)

---

[21]The incremental number of shares may be more simply computed:

$$\frac{\text{Market Price} - \text{Option Price}}{\text{Market Price}} \times \text{Number of Options} = \text{Number of Shares}$$

$$\frac{\$50 - \$30}{\$50} \times 1,500 \text{ options} = 600 \text{ shares}$$

[22]It might be noted that options and warrants have essentially the same assumptions and computational problems, although the warrants may allow or require the tendering of some other security such as debt in lieu of cash upon exercise. In such situations, the accounting becomes quite complex, and the reader should refer to the standard for its proper disposition.

Contingent Issue Agreement

In business combinations, the acquirer may promise to issue additional shares—referred to as contingent shares—if certain conditions are met. If these shares are issuable upon the **mere passage of time or upon the attainment of a certain earnings or market price level, and this level is met at the end of the year**, they should be considered as outstanding for the computation of diluted earnings per share.[23]

For example, assume that Walz Corporation purchased Cardella Company and agreed to give the stockholders of Cardella Company 20,000 additional shares in 2004 if Cardella's net income in 2003 is $90,000; in 2002 Cardella Company's net income is $100,000. Because the 2003 stipulated earnings of $90,000 are already being attained, diluted earnings per share of Walz for 2002 would include the 20,000 contingent shares in the shares outstanding computation.

Antidilution Revisited

In computing diluted EPS, the aggregate of all dilutive securities must be considered. But first we must determine which potentially dilutive securities are in fact individually dilutive and which are antidilutive. Any security that is antidilutive should be excluded and cannot be used to offset dilutive securities.

Recall that antidilutive securities are securities whose inclusion in earnings per share computations would increase earnings per share (or reduce net loss per share). Convertible debt is antidilutive if the addition to income of the interest (net of tax) causes a greater percentage increase in income (numerator) than conversion of the bonds causes a percentage increase in common and potentially dilutive shares (denominator). In other words, convertible debt is antidilutive if conversion of the security causes common stock earnings to increase by a greater amount per additional common share than earnings per share was before the conversion.

To illustrate, assume that Kohl Corporation has a 6%, $1,000,000 debt issue that is convertible into 10,000 common shares. Net income for the year is $210,000, the weighted average number of common shares outstanding is 100,000 shares, and the tax rate is 40%. In this case assumed conversion of the debt into common stock at the beginning of the year requires the following adjustments of net income and the weighted average number of shares outstanding:

				ILLUSTRATION 17-25
Net income for the year	$210,000	Average number of shares		**Test for Antidilution**
Add: Adjustment for interest		outstanding	100,000	
(net of tax) on 6%		Add: Shares issued upon assumed		
debentures		conversion of debt	10,000	
$60,000 × (1 − .40)	36,000	Average number of common and		
Adjusted net income	$246,000	potential common shares	110,000	

Basic EPS = $210,000 ÷ 100,000 = $2.10
Diluted EPS = $246,000 ÷ 110,000 = $2.24 = **Antidilutive**

As a shortcut, the convertible debt also can be identified as antidilutive by comparing the EPS resulting from conversion, $3.60 ($36,000 additional earnings ÷ 10,000 additional shares), with EPS before inclusion of the convertible debt, $2.10.

With options or warrants, whenever the exercise price is higher than the market price, the security is antidilutive. **Antidilutive securities should be ignored in all calculations and should not be considered in computing diluted earnings per share.** This approach is reasonable because the profession's intent was to inform the investor of the **possible dilution** that might occur in reported earnings per share and not to be

---

[23]In addition to contingent issuances of stock, other types of situations that might lead to dilution are the issuance of participating securities and two-class common shares. The reporting of these types of securities in EPS computations is beyond the scope of this textbook.

concerned with securities that, if converted or exercised, would result in an increase in earnings per share. Appendix 17B to this chapter provides an extended example of how antidilution is considered in a complex situation with multiple securities.

EPS Presentation and Disclosure

If a corporation's capital structure is complex, the earnings per share presentation would be as follows:

ILLUSTRATION 17-26
EPS Presentation—
Complex Capital
Structure

Earnings per common share	
Basic earnings per share	$3.30
Diluted earnings per share	$2.70

When the earnings of a period include irregular items, per share amounts (where applicable) should be shown for income from continuing operations, income before extraordinary items, income before accounting change, and net income. Companies that report a discontinued operation, an extraordinary item, or the cumulative effect of an accounting change should present per share amounts for those line items either on the face of the income statement or in the notes to the financial statements. A presentation reporting extraordinary items only is presented in Illustration 17-27.

ILLUSTRATION 17-27
EPS Presentation, with
Extraordinary Item

Basic earnings per share	
Income before extraordinary item	$3.80
Extraordinary item	.80
Net income	$3.00
Diluted earnings per share	
Income before extraordinary item	$3.35
Extraordinary item	.65
Net income	$2.70

Earnings per share amounts must be shown for all periods presented and all prior period earnings per share amounts presented should be restated for stock dividends and stock splits. If diluted EPS data are reported for at least one period, it should be reported for all periods presented, even if it is the same as basic EPS. When results of operations of a prior period have been restated as a result of a prior period adjustment, the earnings per share data shown for the prior periods should also be restated. The effect of the restatement should be disclosed in the year of the restatement.

Complex capital structures and dual presentation of earnings require the following additional disclosures in note form:

❶ Description of pertinent rights and privileges of the various securities outstanding.

❷ A reconciliation of the numerators and denominators of the basic and diluted per share computations, including individual income and share amount effects of all securities that affect EPS.

❸ The effect given preferred dividends in determining income available to common stockholders in computing basic EPS.

❹ Securities that could potentially dilute basic EPS in the future that were not included in the computation because they would be antidilutive.

❺ Effect of conversions subsequent to year-end, but before statements have been issued.

Illustration 17-28 presents the reconciliation and the related disclosure that is needed to meet disclosure requirements of this standard.

ILLUSTRATION 17-28
Reconciliation for Basic
and Diluted EPS

	For the Year Ended 2002		
	Income (Numerator)	Shares (Denominator)	Per-Share Amount
Income before extraordinary item and accounting change	$7,500,000		
Less: Preferred stock dividends	(45,000)		
Basic EPS			
Income available to common stockholders	7,455,000	3,991,666	$1.87
Warrants		30,768	
Convertible preferred stock	45,000	308,333	
4% convertible bonds (net of tax)	60,000	50,000	
Diluted EPS			
Income available to common stockholders + assumed conversions	$7,560,000	4,380,767	$1.73

Stock options to purchase 1,000,000 shares of common stock at $85 per share were outstanding during the second half of 2002 but were not included in the computation of diluted EPS because the options' exercise price was greater than the average market price of the common shares. The options were still outstanding at the end of year 2002 and expire on June 30, 2012.[24]

Summary

As you can see, computation of earnings per share is a complex issue. It is a controversial area because many securities, although technically not common stock, have many of its basic characteristics. Some companies have issued these types of securities rather than common stock in order to avoid an adverse dilutive effect on earnings per share.

Illustration 17-29 displays graphically the elementary points of calculating earnings per share in a simple capital structure.

ILLUSTRATION 17-29
Calculating EPS, Simple
Capital Structure

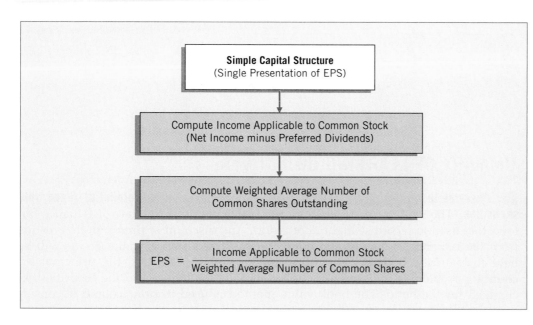

---

[24]Note that *Statement No. 123* has specific disclosure requirements as well regarding stock option plans and earnings per share disclosures.

Illustration 17-30 shows the calculation of earnings per share for a complex capital structure.

ILLUSTRATION 17-30
Calculating EPS,
Complex Capital
Structure

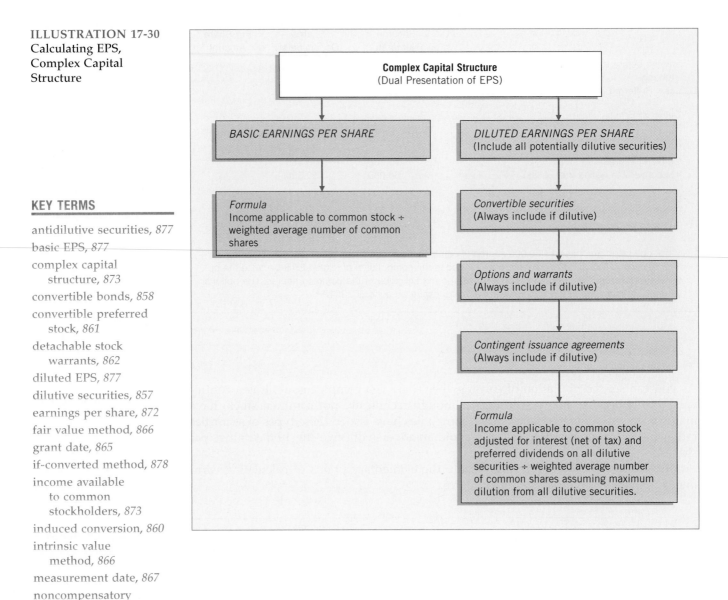

SUMMARY OF LEARNING OBJECTIVES

❶ Describe the accounting for the issuance, conversion, and retirement of convertible securities. The method for recording convertible bonds at the date of issuance follows that used to record straight debt issues. Any discount or premium that results from the issuance of convertible bonds is amortized assuming the bonds will be held to maturity. If bonds are converted into other securities, the principal accounting problem is to determine the amount at which to record the securities exchanged for the bond. The book value method is used in practice and is considered GAAP. The retirement of convertible debt is considered a debt retirement, and the difference between the carrying amount of the retired convertible debt and the cash paid should result in an extraordinary charge or credit to income.

❷ **Explain the accounting for convertible preferred stock.** When convertible preferred stock is converted, the book value method is employed; Preferred Stock, along with any related Additional Paid-in Capital, is debited, and Common Stock and Additional Paid-in Capital (if an excess exists) are credited.

❸ **Contrast the accounting for stock warrants and stock warrants issued with other securities.** *Stock rights:* No entry is required when rights are issued to existing stockholders. Only a memorandum entry is needed to indicate the number of rights issued to existing stockholders and to ensure that the company has additional unissued stock registered for issuance in case the rights are exercised. *Stock warrants:* The proceeds from the sale of debt with detachable stock warrants should be allocated between the two securities. Warrants that are detachable can be traded separately from the debt, and therefore, a market value can be determined. The two methods of allocation available are the proportional method and the incremental method. Nondetachable warrants do not require an allocation of the proceeds between the bonds and the warrants. The entire proceeds are recorded as debt.

❹ **Describe the accounting for stock compensation plans under GAAP.** Companies are given a choice in the recognition approach to stock compensation; however, the FASB encourages adoption of the fair value method. Using the fair value approach, total compensation expense is computed based on the fair value of the options that are expected to vest on the grant date. Under the intrinsic value approach, total compensation cost is computed as the excess of the market price of the stock over the option price on the date when both the number of shares to which employees are entitled and the option or purchase price for those shares are known. Under both the fair and intrinsic value methods, compensation expense is recognized in the periods in which the employee performs the services.

❺ **Explain the controversy involving stock compensation plans.** When first proposed, there was considerable opposition to the recognition provisions contained in the fair value approach, because that approach could result in substantial compensation expense that was not previously recognized. Corporate America, particularly the small, high technology sector, was quite vocal in its opposition to the proposed standard. They believed that they would be placed at a competitive disadvantage with larger companies that can withstand higher compensation charges. In response to this opposition, which was based primarily on economic consequences arguments, the FASB decided to encourage, rather than require, recognition of compensation cost based on the fair value method and require expanded disclosures.

❻ **Compute earnings per share in a simple capital structure.** When a company has both common and preferred stock outstanding, the current year preferred stock dividend is subtracted from net income to arrive at income available to common stockholders. The formula for computing earnings per share is net income less preferred stock dividends divided by the weighted average of shares outstanding.

❼ **Compute earnings per share in a complex capital structure.** A complex capital structure requires a dual presentation of earnings per share, each with equal prominence on the face of the income statement. These two presentations are referred to as basic earnings per share and diluted earnings per share. Basic earnings per share is based on the number of weighted average common shares outstanding (i.e., equivalent to EPS for a simple capital structure). Diluted earnings per share indicates the dilution of earnings per share that would have occurred if all potential issuances of common stock that would have reduced earnings per share had taken place.

Stock Options— Additional Complications

Before 1995, accounting for stock options was governed by the provisions in *APB Opinion No. 25*. This appendix discusses the provisions of *APB Opinion No. 25* because many companies do not adopt the recognition guidelines provided in *SFAS No. 123*. In addition, an expanded discussion of the types of plans used to compensate key executives is provided.

DETERMINING COMPENSATION EXPENSE

Under *APB Opinion No. 25*, total compensation expense is computed as the excess of the market price of the stock **over the option price on the measurement date**.[1] The measurement date is the first date on which are known both (1) the number of shares that an individual employee is entitled to receive and (2) the option or purchase price. The measurement date for many plans is the date an **option is granted to an employee** (i.e., the grant date). The measurement date may be later than the grant date in plans with variable terms (either number of shares or option price or both not known) that depend on events after date of grant. Usually the measurement date for plans with variable terms is the date of exercise.

If the number of shares or the option price, or both, are unknown, compensation expense may have to be estimated on the basis of assumptions about the final number of shares and the option price.

Three common plans that illustrate different accounting issues are:

❶ Stock option plans (incentive or nonqualified).
❷ Stock appreciation rights plans.
❸ Performance-type plans.

Stock Option Plans

A stock option plan can be either an incentive stock option plan or a nonqualified (or nonstatutory) stock option plan. The distinction between an incentive and a nonqualified stock option plan is based on the IRS Code and relates to the tax treatment afforded the plan.

From the perspective of the executive, the incentive stock option provides a greater tax advantage. In these plans, an executive pays no tax on the difference between the market price of the stock and the option price when the stock is purchased. Subsequently, when the shares are sold, the executive pays tax on that difference at either capital gains rates (20%) or ordinary income tax rates (usually higher than capital gains

---

[1]"Accounting for Stock Issued to Employees," *Opinions of the Accounting Principles Board No. 25* (New York: AICPA, 1972).

rates), depending upon the executive's holding period.[2] Conversely, an executive who receives a nonqualified stock option must pay taxes, at ordinary income tax rates, on the difference between the market price of the stock and the option price at the time the stock is purchased. Thus, under an incentive stock option, the payment of the tax is deferred and may be less.

From the perspective of the company, the **nonqualified option plan** provides greater tax advantages. No tax deduction is received in an incentive stock option plan, whereas in a nonqualified stock option plan the company receives a tax deduction equal to the difference between the market price and option price at the date the employee purchases the stock. To illustrate, assume that Hubbard, Inc. grants options to purchase 10,000 shares at an option price of $10 when the current market price of the stock is $10; the shares are purchased at a time when the market price is $20; and the executive sells the shares one year later at $20. A comparison of the effect of both plans on the executive and on the company is shown in Illustration 17A-1.

	Incentive Stock Option[3]	Nonqualified Stock Option
Effect on Executive:		
(assuming 36% tax bracket)		
Profit on exercise [10,000 × ($20 − $10)]	$100,000	$100,000
Tax on exercise ($100,000 × 36%)	–0–	$ 36,000
Tax on sale ($100,000 × 20%)	$ 20,000	–0–
After-tax benefit	$ 80,000	$ 64,000
Effect on Company:		
(assuming 34% corporate rate)	Zero tax deduction resulting in no tax benefit.	$100,000 tax deduction resulting in a $34,000 tax benefit.

ILLUSTRATION 17A-1
Comparison of Incentive and Nonqualified Stock Option Plans

In effect, the executive in Hubbard, Inc.'s case would incur an $80,000 benefit under the incentive stock option plan and a $64,000 benefit under the nonqualified stock option plan. The tax is also deferred until the stock is sold under the incentive stock option plan. The company receives no benefit from an incentive stock option but a $100,000 tax deduction (which becomes a $34,000 tax benefit) for the nonqualified stock option.

Incentive Stock Option Plan

Why would companies want to issue incentive stock options? The major reason is to attract high-quality personnel, and many companies believe that incentive stock options are a greater attraction than nonqualified plans. Incentive stock options are particularly helpful to smaller higher-technology enterprises that have little cash and perhaps so little taxable income that the tax deduction is not important. Granting such options helps them attract and retain key personnel for whom they must compete against larger, established companies.

In an incentive stock option plan the tax laws require that the market price of the stock and the option price at the date of grant be equal. The tax laws do not require this equality in nonqualified plans. **No compensation expense is, therefore, recorded**

---

[2]After the year 2000, capital gains will be taxed at rates not to exceed 18%, as long as the stock is held for more than 5 years.

[3]For an ISO, the executive has an alternative minimum tax (AMT) preference upon exercise, which may lead to tax payments under AMT rules. The illustration also assumes that the executive receiving an ISO receives favorable capital gains treatment.

for an incentive stock option because no excess of market price over the option price exists at the date of grant (the measurement date in this case).[4]

Nonqualified Stock Option Plans

Nonqualified stock option plans usually involve compensation expense because the market price exceeds the option price **at the date of grant** (the measurement date). Total compensation cost is measured by this difference and then allocated to the periods benefited. The option price is set by the terms of the grant and generally remains the same throughout the option period. The market price of the shares under option, however, may vary materially in the extended period during which the option is outstanding.

The options in the Chen Company illustration on pages 867–868 were nonqualified stock options. Recall that under the fair value approach (*SFAS No. 123*), the total compensation expense is measured at the grant date based on the fair value of the options that are expected to vest. Under the intrinsic value approach, compensation expense is recorded for the excess of the market price over the exercise price at the grant date.

Stock Appreciation Rights

One of the main advantages of a **nonqualified stock option** plan is that an executive may acquire shares of stock having a market price substantially above the option price. A major disadvantage is that an executive must pay income tax on the difference between the market price of the stock and the option price at the **date of exercise**. This can be a financial hardship for an executive who wishes to keep the stock (rather than sell it immediately) because he or she would have to pay not only income tax but the option price as well. Note that for **incentive stock options**, much the same problem exists; that is, the executive may have to borrow to finance the exercise price, which leads to related interest costs.

One solution to this problem was the creation of **stock appreciation rights (SARs)**. In this type of plan, the executive is given the right to receive compensation equal to the share appreciation, which is defined as the excess of the market price of the stock at the date of exercise over a pre-established price. This share appreciation may be paid in cash, shares, or a combination of both. The major advantage of SARs is that the executive often does not have to make a cash outlay at the date of exercise, but receives a payment for the share appreciation. Unlike shares acquired under a stock option plan, the shares that constitute the basis for computing the appreciation in a SARs plan are not issued. The executive is awarded only cash or stock having a market value equivalent to the appreciation.

As indicated earlier, the usual date for measuring compensation related to stock compensation plans is the date of grant. However, with SARs, the final amount of cash or shares (or a combination of the two) to be distributed is not known until the date of exercise—the measurement date. Therefore total compensation cannot be measured until this date.

How then should compensation expense be recorded during the interim periods from the date of grant to the date of exercise? Such a determination is not easy because it is impossible to know what total compensation cost will be until the date of exercise,

---

[4]Recently, the FASB has proposed rules under which expense may be recorded on incentive stock options that are re-priced after the original grant (FASB, "Proposed Interpretation: Accounting for Certain Transactions Involving Stock Compensation," March 31, 1999). Re-pricing occurs when, following a decline in the stock price, a company resets the option price to a lower level, thereby making it more likely that the option will be "in the money" and valuable to the executive. Many companies are upset with this proposed accounting because they argue that re-pricing is appropriate to protect executives from market downturns outside of their control. See John Byrne, "How to Reward Failure: Reprice Stock Options," *Business Week*, October 12, 1998.

and the service period will probably not coincide with the exercise date. The best estimate of total compensation cost for the plan at any interim period is the difference between the **current market price** of the stock and the **option price** multiplied by the number of stock appreciation rights outstanding. This total estimated compensation cost is then allocated over the service period, to record an expense (or a decrease in expense if market price falls) in each period.[5] At the end of each interim period, total compensation expense reported to date should equal the percentage of the total service period that has elapsed multiplied by the estimated compensation cost.

For example, if at the end of an interim period the service period is 40% complete and total estimated compensation is $100,000, then cumulative compensation expense reported to date should equal $40,000 ($100,000 x .40). As another illustration, in the first year of a 4-year plan, the company charges one-fourth of the appreciation to date. In the second year, it charges off two-fourths or 50% of the appreciation to date less the amount already recognized in the first year. In the third year, it charges off three-fourths of the appreciation to date less the amount recognized previously, and in the fourth year it charges off the remaining compensation expense. We will refer to this method as the **percentage approach** for allocating compensation expense.

A special problem arises when the exercise date is later than the service period. In the previous example, if the SARs were not exercised at the end of 4 years it would be necessary to account for the difference in the market price and the option price in the fifth year. In this case, compensation expense is adjusted whenever a change in the market price of the stock **occurs in subsequent reporting periods until the rights expire or are exercised, whichever comes first.**

Increases or decreases in the market value of those shares between the date of grant and the exercise date, therefore, result in a change in the measure of compensation. Some periods will have credits to compensation expense if the quoted market price of the stock falls from one period to the next; the credit to compensation expense, however, cannot exceed previously recognized compensation expense. In other words, **cumulative compensation expense cannot be negative.**

To illustrate, assume that American Hotels, Inc. establishes a SARs program on January 1, 2001, which entitles executives to receive cash at the date of exercise (anytime in the next 5 years) for the difference between the market price of the stock and the preestablished price of $10 on 10,000 SARs; the market price of the stock on December 31, 2001, is $13, and the service period runs for 2 years (2001–2002). Illustration 17A-2 indicates the amount of compensation expense to be recorded each period, assuming that the executives hold the SARs for 3 years, at which time the rights are exercised.

ILLUSTRATION 17A-2
Compensation Expense, Stock Appreciation Rights

			Stock Appreciation Rights **Schedule of Compensation Expense**					
(1)	(2)	(3)	(4)	(5)	(6)			
Date	Market Price	Pre-established Price (10,000 SARs)	Cumulative Compensation Recognizable[a]	Percentage Accrued[b]	Cumulative Compensation Accrued to Date	Expense 2001	Expense 2002	Expense 2003
12/31/01	$13	$10	$30,000	50%	$ 15,000	$15,000		
					55,000		$55,000	
12/31/02	17	10	70,000	100%	70,000			
					(20,000)			$(20,000)
12/31/03	15	10	50,000	100%	$ 50,000			

[a]Cumulative compensation for unexercised SARs to be allocated to periods of service.
[b]The percentage accrued is based upon a 2-year service period (2001–2002).

---

[5]"Accounting for Stock Appreciation Rights and Other Variable Stock Option or Award Plans," *FASB Interpretation No. 28* (Stamford, Conn.: FASB, 1978), par. 2.

In 2001 American Hotels would record compensation expense of $15,000 because 50% of the $30,000 total of compensation cost estimated at December 31, 2001, is allocable to 2001.

In 2002 the market price increased to $17 per share; therefore, the additional compensation expense of $55,000 ($70,000 minus $15,000) was recorded. The SARs were held through 2003, during which time the stock decreased to $15. The decrease is recognized by recording a $20,000 credit to compensation expense and a debit to Liability under Stock Appreciation Plan. Note that after the service period ends, since the rights are still outstanding, the rights are adjusted to market at December 31, 2003. Any such credit to compensation expense cannot exceed previous charges to expense attributable to that plan.

As the compensation expense is recorded each period, the corresponding credit should be to a liability account if the stock appreciation is to be paid in cash. If stock is to be issued, then a more appropriate credit would be to Paid-in Capital. The entry to record compensation expense in the first year, assuming that the SARs ultimately will be paid in cash, is as follows:

Compensation Expense	15,000	
Liability under Stock Appreciation Plan		15,000

The liability account would be credited again in 2002 for $55,000 and debited for $20,000 in 2003 when the negative compensation expense is recorded. The entry to record the negative compensation expense is as follows:

Liability under Stock Appreciation Plan	20,000	
Compensation Expense		20,000

At December 31, 2003, the executives receive $50,000; the entry removing the liability is as follows:

Liability under Stock Appreciation Plan	50,000	
Cash		50,000

Because compensation expense is measured by the difference between market prices of the stock from period to period, multiplied by the number of SARs, compensation expense can increase or decrease substantially from one period to the next.

For this reason, companies with substantial stock appreciation rights plans may choose to use *SFAS No. 123* guidelines because the total compensation expense is determined at the date of grant. Subsequent changes in market price are therefore ignored; total compensation expense may be lower under *SFAS No. 123*.

SARs are often issued in combination with compensatory stock options (referred to as **tandem** or **combination plans**) and the executive must then select which of the two sets of terms to exercise, thereby canceling the other. The existence of alternative plans running concurrently poses additional problems. You must determine, on the basis of the facts available each period, which of the two plans has the higher probability of exercise and then account for this plan and ignore the other.

Performance-Type Plans

Some executives have become disenchanted with stock compensation plans whose ultimate payment depends on an increase in the market price of the common stock. They do not like having their compensation and judgment of performance at the mercy of the stock market's erratic behavior. As a result, there has been a substantial increase in the use of plans whereby executives receive common stock (or cash) if specified performance criteria are attained during the performance period (generally 3 to 5 years). Most of the 200 largest companies now have some type of plan that does not rely on stock price appreciation.

The **performance criteria** employed usually are increases in return on assets or equity, growth in sales, growth in earnings per share (EPS), or a combination of these factors. A good illustration of this type of plan is that of Atlantic Richfield, which at one time offered performance units valued in excess of $700,000 to the chairman of the board. These performance units are payable in 5 years, contingent upon the company's meeting certain levels of return on stockholders' equity and cash dividends.

As another example, Honeywell uses growth in EPS as its performance criterion. When certain levels of EPS are achieved, executives receive shares of stock. If the company achieves an average annual EPS growth of 13%, the executive will earn 100% of the shares. The maximum allowable is 130%, which would require a 17% growth rate; below 9% the executives receive nothing.

A performance-type plan's measurement date is the date of exercise because the number of shares that will be issued or the cash that will be paid out when performance is achieved are not known at the date of grant. The compensation cost is allocated to the periods involved in the same manner as with stock appreciation rights; that is, the percentage approach is used.

Tandem or combination awards are popular with these plans. The executive has the choice of selecting between a performance or stock option award. Companies such as General Electric and Xerox have adopted plans of this nature. In these cases the executive has the best of both worlds: if either the stock price increases or the performance goal is achieved, the executive gains. Sometimes, the executive receives both types of plans, so that the monies received from the performance plan can finance the exercise price on the stock option plan.

Summary of Compensation Plans

A summary of compensation plans and their major characteristics is provided in Illustration 17A-3.

Type of Plan	Measurement Date	Measurement of Compensation	Allocation Period	Allocation Method
Incentive stock option				
APB Opinion No. 25	Grant	Market price less exercise price	N/A (no compensation expense)	N/A (no compensation expense)
SFAS No. 123	Grant	Option pricing model	Service	Straight-line
Nonqualified stock option				
APB Opinion No. 25	Grant	Market price less exercise price	Service	Straight-line
SFAS No. 123	Grant	Option pricing model	Service	Straight-line
Stock appreciation rights				
APB Opinion No. 25	Exercise	Market price less exercise price	Service	Percentage approach for service period, then mark to market
SFAS No. 123	Grant	Option pricing model	Service	Straight-line
Performance-type plan				
APB Opinion No. 25	Exercise	Market value of shares issued	Service	Percentage approach for service period, then mark to market
SFAS No. 123	Exercise	Market value of shares issued	Service	Percentage approach for service period, then mark to market

ILLUSTRATION 17A-3
Summary of Compensation Plans

SUMMARY OF LEARNING OBJECTIVE FOR APPENDIX 17A

⑧ Explain the accounting for various stock option plans under APB Opinion No. 25. (1) *Incentive stock option plans:* The market price and exercise price on the grant date must be equal. Because there is no compensation expense, there is no allocation problem. (2) *Nonqualified stock option plans:* Compensation is the difference between the market price and exercise price on the grant date. Compensation expense is allocated by the straight-line method during the service period. (3) *Stock appreciation rights:* The compensation is measured by the difference between market price and exercise price on the exercise date. The compensation expense is allocated by the percentage approach over the service period, then marked to market. (4) *Performance-type plan:* Compensation is measured by the market value of shares issued on the exercise date. Compensation expense is allocated by the percentage approach over the service period, then marked to market. See also Illustration 17A-3.

APPENDIX 17B

Comprehensive Earnings per Share Illustration

The purpose of this appendix is to illustrate the method of computing dilution when many securities are involved. The following section of the balance sheet of Webster Corporation is presented for analysis; assumptions related to the capital structure follow:

ILLUSTRATION 17B-1
Balance Sheet for
Comprehensive
Illustration

WEBSTER CORPORATION Selected Balance Sheet Information At December 31, 2001	
Long-term debt:	
Notes payable, 14%	$ 1,000,000
8% convertible bonds payable	2,500,000
10% convertible bonds payable	2,500,000
Total long-term debt	$ 6,000,000
Stockholders' equity:	
10% cumulative, convertible preferred stock, par value $100;	
100,000 shares authorized, 25,000 shares issued and outstanding	$ 2,500,000
Common stock, par value $1, 5,000,000 shares authorized,	
500,000 shares issued and outstanding	500,000
Additional paid-in capital	2,000,000
Retained earnings	9,000,000
Total stockholders' equity	$14,000,000

OBJECTIVE ⑨
After studying Appendix 17B, you should be able to: Compute earnings per share in a complex situation.

① Options were granted in July 1999 to purchase 50,000 shares of common stock at $20 per share. The average market price of Webster's common stock during 2001 was $30 per share. No options were exercised during 2001.

② Both the 8% and 10% convertible bonds were issued in 2000 at face value. Each convertible bond is convertible into 40 shares of common stock (each bond has a face value of $1,000).

③ The 10% cumulative, convertible preferred stock was issued at the beginning of 2001 at par. Each share of preferred is convertible into four shares of common stock.

④ The average income tax rate is 40%.

⑤ The 500,000 shares of common stock were outstanding during the entire year.

⑥ Preferred dividends were not declared in 2001.

⑦ Net income was $1,750,000 in 2001.

⑧ No bonds or preferred stock were converted during 2001.

The computation of basic earnings per share for 2001 starts with the amount based upon the weighted average of common shares outstanding, as shown in Illustration 17B-2.

Net income	$1,750,000
Less: 10% cumulative, convertible preferred stock dividend requirements	250,000
Income applicable to common stockholders	$1,500,000
Weighted average number of common shares outstanding	500,000
Earnings per common share	$3.00

ILLUSTRATION 17B-2
Computation of Earnings per Share—Simple Capital Structure

Note the following points concerning the calculation above.

① When preferred stock is cumulative, the preferred dividend is subtracted to arrive at income applicable to common stock whether the dividend is declared or not.

② The earnings per share of $3 must be computed as a starting point, because it is the per share amount that is subject to reduction due to the existence of convertible securities and options.

DILUTED EARNINGS PER SHARE

The steps for computing diluted earnings per share are:

① Determine, for each dilutive security, the per share effect assuming exercise/conversion.

② Rank the results from step 1 from smallest to largest earnings effect per share; that is, rank the results from most dilutive to least dilutive.

③ Beginning with the earnings per share based upon the weighted average of common shares outstanding ($3), recalculate earnings per share by adding the smallest per share effects from step 2. If the results from this recalculation are less than $3, proceed to the next smallest per share effect and recalculate earnings per share. This process is continued so long as each recalculated earnings per share is smaller than the previous amount. The process will end either because there are no more securities to test or a particular security maintains or increases earnings per share (is antidilutive).

We'll now apply the three steps to Webster Corporation. (Note that net income and income available to common stockholders are not the same if preferred dividends are declared or cumulative.) Webster Corporation has four securities (options, 8% and 10% convertible bonds, and the convertible preferred stock) that could reduce EPS.

The first step in the computation of diluted earnings per share is to determine a per share effect for each potentially dilutive security. Illustrations 17B-3 through 17B-6 illustrate these computations.

ILLUSTRATION 17B-3
Per Share Effect of Options (Treasury Stock Method), Diluted Earnings per Share

Number of shares under option	50,000
Option price per share	× $20
Proceeds upon assumed exercise of options	$1,000,000
Average 2001 market price of common	$30
Treasury shares that could be acquired with proceeds ($1,000,000 ÷ $30)	33,333
Excess of shares under option over treasury shares that could be repurchased (50,000 − 33,333)	16,667

Per share effect:

$$\frac{\text{Incremental Numerator Effect:} \quad \text{None}}{\text{Incremental Denominator Effect:} \quad 16{,}667 \text{ shares}} = \$0$$

ILLUSTRATION 17B-4
Per Share Effect of 8% Bonds (If-Converted Method), Diluted Earnings per Share

Interest expense for year (8% × $2,500,000)	$200,000
Income tax reduction due to interest (40% × $200,000)	80,000
Interest expense avoided (net of tax)	$120,000
Number of common shares issued assuming conversion of bonds (2,500 bonds × 40 shares)	100,000

Per share effect:

$$\frac{\text{Incremental Numerator Effect:} \quad \$120{,}000}{\text{Incremental Denominator Effect:} \quad 100{,}000 \text{ shares}} = \$1.20$$

ILLUSTRATION 17B-5
Per Share Effect of 10% Bonds (If-Converted Method), Diluted Earnings per Share

Interest expense for year (10% × $2,500,000)	$250,000
Income tax reduction due to interest (40% × $250,000)	100,000
Interest expense avoided (net of tax)	$150,000
Number of common shares issued assuming conversion of bonds (2,500 bonds × 40 shares)	100,000

Per share effect:

$$\frac{\text{Incremental Numerator Effect:} \quad \$150{,}000}{\text{Incremental Denominator Effect:} \quad 100{,}000 \text{ shares}} = \$1.50$$

ILLUSTRATION 17B-6
Per Share Effect of 10% Convertible Preferred (If-Converted Method), Diluted Earnings per Share

Dividend requirement on cumulative preferred (25,000 shares × $10)	$250,000
Income tax effect (dividends not a tax deduction)	none
Dividend requirement avoided	$250,000
Number of common shares issued assuming conversion of preferred (4 × 25,000 shares)	100,000

Per share effect:

$$\frac{\text{Incremental Numerator Effect:} \quad \$250{,}000}{\text{Incremental Denominator Effect:} \quad 100{,}000 \text{ shares}} = \$2.50$$

Illustration 17B-7 shows the ranking of all four potentially dilutive securities.

	Effect per Share
1. Options	$ 0
2. 8% convertible bonds	1.20
3. 10% convertible bonds	1.50
4. 10% convertible preferred	2.50

ILLUSTRATION 17B-7
Ranking of per Share Effects (Smallest to Largest), Diluted Earnings per Share

The next step is to determine earnings per share giving effect to the ranking in Illustration 17B-7. Starting with the earnings per share of $3 computed previously, add the incremental effects of the options to the original calculation, as follows:

Options	
Income applicable to common stockholders	$1,500,000
Add: Incremental numerator effect of options	none
Total	$1,500,000
Weighted average number of common shares outstanding	500,000
Add: Incremental denominator effect of options (Illustration 17B-3)	16,667
Total	516,667
Recomputed earnings per share ($1,500,000 ÷ 516,667 shares)	$2.90

ILLUSTRATION 17B-8
Recomputation of EPS Using Incremental Effect of Options

Since the recomputed earnings per share is reduced (from $3 to $2.90), the effect of the options is dilutive. Again, this effect could have been anticipated because the average market price ($30) exceeded the option price ($20).

Recomputed earnings per share, assuming the 8% bonds are converted, is as follows:

8% Convertible Bonds	
Numerator from previous calculation	$1,500,000
Add: Interest expense avoided (net of tax)	120,000
Total	$1,620,000
Denominator from previous calculation (shares)	516,667
Add: Number of common shares assumed issued upon conversion of bonds	100,000
Total	616,667
Recomputed earnings per share ($1,620,000 ÷ 616,667 shares)	$2.63

ILLUSTRATION 17B-9
Recomputation of EPS Using Incremental Effect of 8% Convertible Bonds

Since the recomputed earnings per share is reduced (from $2.90 to $2.63), the effect of the 8% bonds is dilutive.

Next, earnings per share is recomputed assuming the conversion of the 10% bonds. This is shown below:

10% Convertible Bonds	
Numerator from previous calculation	$1,620,000
Add: Interest expense avoided (net of tax)	150,000
Total	$1,770,000
Denominator from previous calculation (shares)	616,667
Add: Number of common shares assumed issued upon conversion of bonds	100,000
Total	716,667
Recomputed earnings per share ($1,770,000 ÷ 716,667 shares)	$2.47

ILLUSTRATION 17B-10
Recomputation of EPS Using Incremental Effect of 10% Convertible Bonds

Since the recomputed earnings per share is reduced (from $2.63 to $2.47), the effect of the 10% convertible bonds is dilutive.

The final step is the recomputation that includes the 10% preferred stock. This is shown below.

ILLUSTRATION 17B-11
Recomputation of EPS Using Incremental Effect of 10% Convertible Preferred

10% Convertible Preferred	
Numerator from previous calculation	$1,770,000
Add: Dividend requirement avoided	250,000
Total	$2,020,000
Denominator from previous calculation (shares)	716,667
Add: Number of common shares assumed issued upon conversion of preferred	100,000
Total	816,667
Recomputed earnings per share ($2,020,000 ÷ 816,667 shares)	$2.47

Since the recomputed earnings per share is not reduced, the effect of the 10% convertible preferred is not dilutive. Diluted earnings per share is $2.47, and the per share effects of the preferred are not used in the computation.

Finally, the disclosure of earnings per share on the income statement for Webster Corporation is shown below.

ILLUSTRATION 17B-12
Income Statement Presentation, EPS

Net income	$1,750,000
Basic earnings per common share (Note X)	$3.00
Diluted earnings per common share	$2.47

A company uses **income from continuing operations (adjusted for preferred dividends) to determine whether potential common stock is dilutive or antidilutive.** (Some refer to this measure as the **control number.**) To illustrate, assume that Barton Company provides the following information:

ILLUSTRATION 17B-13
Barton Company Data

Income from continuing operations	$2,400,000
Loss from discontinued operations	3,600,000
Net loss	$1,200,000
Weighted average shares of common stock outstanding	1,000,000
Potential common stock	200,000

The computation of basic and dilutive earnings per share is as follows:

ILLUSTRATION 17B-14
Basic and Diluted EPS

Basic earnings per share	
Income from continuing operations	$2.40
Loss from discontinued operations	3.60
Net loss	$1.20
Diluted earnings per share	
Income from continuing operations	$2.00
Loss from discontinued operations	3.00
Net loss	$1.00

As shown in Illustration 17B-14, basic earnings per share from continuing operations is higher than the diluted earnings per share from continuing operations. The reason:

The diluted earnings per share from continuing operations includes an additional 200,000 shares of potential common stock in its denominator.[1]

Income from continuing operations is used as the control number because many companies will show income from continuing operations (or a similar line item above net income if it appears on the income statement), but report a final net loss due to a loss on discontinued operations. If the final net loss is used as the control number, basic and diluted earnings per share would be the same because the potential common shares are antidilutive.[2]

Go to the Digital Tool for another EPS illustration with multiple dilutive securities.

SUMMARY OF LEARNING OBJECTIVE FOR APPENDIX 17B

KEY TERMS

⑨ Compute earnings per share in a complex situation. For diluted EPS, (1) determine, for each potentially dilutive security, the per share effect assuming exercise/conversion; (2) rank from most dilutive to least dilutive; (3) recalculate EPS starting with the most dilutive, and continue adding securities until EPS increases (is antidilutive).

control number, *896*

Note: All **asterisked** Questions, Brief Exercises, Exercises Problems, and Conceptual Cases relate to material contained in the appendix to the chapter.

QUESTIONS

1 Why might increased merger activity lead to the issuance of dilutive securities?

2 Briefly explain why corporations issue convertible securities.

3 Discuss the similarities and the differences between convertible debt and debt issued with stock warrants.

4 Plantagenet Corp. offered holders of its 1,000 convertible bonds a premium of $160 per bond to induce conversion into shares of its common stock. Upon conversion of all the bonds, Plantagenet Corp. recorded the $160,000 premium as a reduction of paid-in capital. Comment on Plantagenet's treatment of the $160,000 "sweetener."

5 Explain how the conversion feature of convertible debt has a value (a) to the issuer and (b) to the purchaser.

6 What are the arguments for giving separate accounting recognition to the conversion feature of debentures?

7 Four years after issue, debentures with a face value of $1,000,000 and book value of $960,000 are tendered for conversion into 80,000 shares of common stock immediately after an interest payment date when the market price of the debentures is 104 and the common stock is

selling at $14 per share (par value $10). The company records the conversion as follows:

Bonds Payable	1,000,000	
Discount on Bonds Payable		40,000
Common Stock		800,000
Paid-in Capital in Excess of Par		160,000

Discuss the propriety of this accounting treatment.

8 On July 1, 2001, Roberts Corporation issued $3,000,000 of 9% bonds payable in 20 years. The bonds include detachable warrants giving the bondholder the right to purchase for $30 one share of $1 par value common stock at any time during the next 10 years. The bonds were sold for $3,000,000. The value of the warrants at the time of issuance was $200,000. Prepare the journal entry to record this transaction.

9 What are stock rights? How does the issuing company account for them?

10 Briefly explain the accounting requirements for stock compensation plans under *Statement of Financial Accounting Standards No. 123.*

11 Weiland Corporation has an employee stock purchase plan which permits all full-time employees to purchase

---

[1]A company that does not report a discontinued operation but reports an extraordinary item or the cumulative effect of a change in accounting principle should use that line item (for example, income before extraordinary items) as the control number.

[2]If a loss from continuing operations is reported, basic and diluted earnings per share will be the same because potential common stock will be antidilutive, even if the company reports final net income. The Board believes that comparability of EPS information will be improved by using income from continuing operations as the control number.

10 shares of common stock on the third anniversary of their employment and an additional 15 shares on each subsequent anniversary date. The purchase price is set at the market price on the date purchased and no commission is charged. Discuss whether this plan would be considered compensatory.

12 What date or event does the profession believe should be used in determining the value of a stock option? What arguments support this position?

13 Over what period of time should compensation cost be allocated?

14 How is compensation expense computed using the fair value approach?

15 At December 31, 2001, Amad Company had 600,000 shares of common stock issued and outstanding, 400,000 of which had been issued and outstanding throughout the year, and 200,000 of which were issued on October 1, 2001. Net income for 2001 was $3,000,000 and dividends declared on preferred stock were $400,000. Compute Amad's earnings per common share (round to the nearest penny).

16 What effect do stock dividends or stock splits have on the computation of the weighted average number of shares outstanding?

17 Define the following terms.

(a) Basic earnings per share.

(b) Potentially dilutive security.

(c) Diluted earnings per share.

(d) Complex capital structure.

(e) Potential common stock.

18 What are the computational guidelines for determining whether a convertible security is to be reported as part of diluted earnings per share?

19 Discuss why options and warrants may be considered potentially dilutive common shares for the computation of diluted earnings per share.

20 Explain how convertible securities are determined to be potentially dilutive common shares and how those convertible senior securities that are not considered to be potentially dilutive common shares enter into the determination of earnings per share data.

21 Explain the treasury stock method as it applies to options and warrants in computing dilutive earnings per share data.

22 Earnings per share can affect market prices of common stock. Can market prices affect earnings per share? Explain.

23 What is meant by the term antidilution? Give an example.

24 What type of earnings per share presentation is required in a complex capital structure?

*25 How is antidilution determined when multiple securities are involved?

BRIEF EXERCISES

BE17-1 Sasha Verbitsky Corporation has outstanding 1,000 $1,000 bonds, each convertible into 50 shares of $10 par value common stock. The bonds are converted on December 31, 2002, when the unamortized discount is $30,000, and the market price of the stock is $21 per share. Record the conversion using the market value approach.

BE17-2 Use the information for Sasha Verbitsky Corporation given in BE17-1. Record the conversion using the book value approach.

BE17-3 Malik Sealy Corporation issued 2,000 shares of $10 par value common stock upon conversion of 1,000 shares of $50 par value preferred stock. The preferred stock was originally issued at $55 per share. The common stock is trading at $26 per share at the time of conversion. Record the conversion of the preferred stock.

BE17-4 Divac Corporation issued 1,000 $1,000 bonds at 101. Each bond was issued with one detachable stock warrant. After issuance, the bonds were selling in the market at 98, and the warrants had a market value of $40. Use the proportional method to record the issuance of the bonds and warrants.

BE17-5 Ceballos Corporation issued 1,000 $1,000 bonds at 101. Each bond was issued with one detachable stock warrant. After issuance, the bonds were selling separately at 98. The market price of the warrants without the bonds cannot be determined. Use the incremental method to record the issuance of the bonds and warrants.

BE17-6 On January 1, 2002, Johnson Corporation granted 5,000 options to executives. Each option entitles the holder to purchase one share of Johnson's $5 par value common stock at $50 per share at any time during the next 5 years. The market price of the stock is $65 per share on the date of grant. The period of benefit is two years. Prepare Johnson's journal entries for January 1, 2002, and December 31, 2002 and 2003, using the intrinsic value method.

BE17-7 Use the information given for Johnson Corporation in BE17-6. Assume the fair value option pricing model determines that total compensation expense is $140,000. Prepare Johnson's journal entries for January 1, 2002, and December 31, 2002 and 2003, using the fair value method.

BE17-8 Haley Corporation had 2002 net income of $1,200,000. During 2002, Haley paid a dividend of $2 per share on 100,000 shares of preferred stock. During 2002, Haley had outstanding 250,000 shares of common stock. Compute Haley's 2002 earnings per share.

BE17-9 Barkley Corporation had 120,000 shares of stock outstanding on January 1, 2002. On May 1, 2002, Barkley issued 45,000 shares. On July 1, Barkley purchased 10,000 treasury shares, which were reissued on October 1. Compute Barkley's weighted average number of shares outstanding for 2002.

BE17-10 Green Corporation had 200,000 shares of common stock outstanding on January 1, 2002. On May 1, Green issued 30,000 shares. **(a)** Compute the weighted average number of shares outstanding if the 30,000 shares were issued for cash. **(b)** Compute the weighted average number of shares outstanding if the 30,000 shares were issued in a stock dividend.

BE17-11 Strickland Corporation earned net income of $300,000 in 2002 and had 100,000 shares of common stock outstanding throughout the year. Also outstanding all year was $400,000 of 10% bonds, which are convertible into 16,000 shares of common. Strickland's tax rate is 40%. Compute Strickland's 2002 diluted earnings per share.

BE17-12 Sabonis Corporation reported net income of $400,000 in 2002 and had 50,000 shares of common stock outstanding throughout the year. Also outstanding all year were 5,000 shares of cumulative preferred stock, each convertible into 2 shares of common. The preferred stock pays an annual dividend of $5 per share. Sabonis' tax rate is 40%. Compute Sabonis' 2002 diluted earnings per share.

BE17-13 Sarunas Corporation reported net income of $300,000 in 2002 and had 200,000 shares of common stock outstanding throughout the year. Also outstanding all year were 30,000 options to purchase common stock at $10 per share. The average market price of the stock during the year was $15. Compute diluted earnings per share.

BE17-14 The 2002 income statement of Schrempf Corporation showed net income of $480,000 and an extraordinary loss of $120,000. Schrempf had 50,000 shares of common stock outstanding all year. Prepare Schrempf's income statement presentation of earnings per share.

BE17-15 Sam Perkins, Inc. established a stock appreciation rights (SAR) program on January 1, 2001, which entitles executives to receive cash at the date of exercise for the difference between the market price of the stock and the preestablished price of $20 on 5,000 SARs. The required service period is two years. The market price of the stock is $22 on December 31, 2001, and $29 on December 31, 2002. The SARs are exercised on January 1, 2003. Compute Perkins' compensation expense for 2001 and 2002.

EXERCISES

E17-1 (Issuance and Conversion of Bonds) For each of the unrelated transactions described below, present the entry(ies) required to record each transaction.

1. Grand Corp. issued $20,000,000 par value 10% convertible bonds at 99. If the bonds had not been convertible, the company's investment banker estimates they would have been sold at 95. Expenses of issuing the bonds were $70,000.
2. Hoosier Company issued $20,000,000 par value 10% bonds at 98. One detachable stock purchase warrant was issued with each $100 par value bond. At the time of issuance, the warrants were selling for $4.
3. On July 1, 2001, Trady Company called its 11% convertible debentures for conversion. The $10,000,000 par value bonds were converted into 1,000,000 shares of $1 par value common stock. On July 1, there was $55,000 of unamortized discount applicable to the bonds, and the company paid an additional $75,000 to the bondholders to induce conversion of all the bonds. The company records the conversion using the book value method.

E17-2 (Conversion of Bonds) Aubrey Inc. issued $4,000,000 of 10%, 10-year convertible bonds on June 1, 2001, at 98 plus accrued interest. The bonds were dated April 1, 2001, with interest payable April 1 and October 1. Bond discount is amortized semiannually on a straight-line basis.

On April 1, 2002, $1,500,000 of these bonds were converted into 30,000 shares of $20 par value common stock. Accrued interest was paid in cash at the time of conversion.

Instructions

(a) Prepare the entry to record the interest expense at October 1, 2001. Assume that accrued interest payable was credited when the bonds were issued. (Round to nearest dollar.)

(b) Prepare the entry(ies) to record the conversion on April 1, 2002. (Book value method is used.) Assume that the entry to record amortization of the bond discount and interest payment has been made.

E17-3 (Conversion of Bonds) Vargo Company has bonds payable outstanding in the amount of $500,000 and the Premium on Bonds Payable account has a balance of $7,500. Each $1,000 bond is convertible into 20 shares of preferred stock of par value of $50 per share. All bonds are converted into preferred stock.

Instructions

(a) Assuming that the book value method was used, what entry would be made?

(b) Assuming that the bonds are quoted on the market at 102 and that the preferred stock may be sold on the market at $50⅞, make the entry to record the conversion of the bonds to preferred stock. (Use the market value approach.)

E17-4 (Conversion of Bonds) On January 1, 2000, when its $30 par value common stock was selling for $80 per share, Plato Corp. issued $10,000,000 of 8% convertible debentures due in 20 years. The conversion option allowed the holder of each $1,000 bond to convert the bond into five shares of the corporation's common stock. The debentures were issued for $10,800,000. The present value of the bond payments at the time of issuance was $8,500,000 and the corporation believes the difference between the present value and the amount paid is attributable to the conversion feature. On January 1, 2001, the corporation's $30 par value common stock was split 2 for 1, and the conversion rate for the bonds was adjusted accordingly. On January 1, 2002, when the corporation's $15 par value common stock was selling for $135 per share, holders of 30% of the convertible debentures exercised their conversion options. The corporation uses the straight-line method for amortizing any bond discounts or premiums.

Instructions

(a) Prepare in general journal form the entry to record the original issuance of the convertible debentures.

(b) Prepare in general journal form the entry to record the exercise of the conversion option, using the book value method. Show supporting computations in good form.

E17-5 (Conversion of Bonds) The December 31, 2001, balance sheet of Kepler Corp. is as follows:

10% Callable, Convertible Bonds Payable (semiannual interest dates April 30 and October 31; convertible into 6 shares of $25 par value common stock per $1,000 of bond principal; maturity date April 30, 2007)	$500,000	
Discount on Bonds Payable	10,240	$489,760

On March 5, 2002, Kepler Corp. called all of the bonds as of April 30 for the principal plus interest through April 30. By April 30 all bondholders had exercised their conversion to common stock as of the interest payment date. Consequently, on April 30, Kepler Corp. paid the semiannual interest and issued shares of common stock for the bonds. The discount is amortized on a straight-line basis. Kepler uses the book value method.

Instructions

Prepare the entry(ies) to record the interest expense and conversion on April 30, 2002. Reversing entries were made on January 1, 2002. (Round to the nearest dollar.)

E17-6 (Conversion of Bonds) On January 1, 2001, Gottlieb Corporation issued $4,000,000 of 10-year, 8% convertible debentures at 102. Interest is to be paid semiannually on June 30 and December 31. Each $1,000 debenture can be converted into eight shares of Gottlieb Corporation $100 par value common stock after December 31, 2002.

On January 1, 2003, $400,000 of debentures are converted into common stock, which is then selling at $110. An additional $400,000 of debentures are converted on March 31, 2003. The market price of the common stock is then $115. Accrued interest at March 31 will be paid on the next interest date.

Bond premium is amortized on a straight-line basis.

Instructions

Make the necessary journal entries for:

(a) December 31, 2002.   (c) March 31, 2003.

(b) January 1, 2003.   (d) June 30, 2003.

Record the conversions using the book value method.

E17-7 (Issuance of Bonds with Warrants) Illiad Inc. has decided to raise additional capital by issuing $170,000 face value of bonds with a coupon rate of 10%. In discussions with their investment bankers, it was determined that to help the sale of the bonds, detachable stock warrants should be issued at the rate of one warrant for each $100 bond sold. The value of the bonds without the warrants is considered to be $136,000, and the value of the warrants in the market is $24,000. The bonds sold in the market at issuance for $152,000.

Instructions
  (a) What entry should be made at the time of the issuance of the bonds and warrants?
  (b) If the warrants were nondetachable, would the entries be different? Discuss.

E17-8 (Issuance of Bonds with Detachable Warrants) On September 1, 2001, Sands Company sold at 104 (plus accrued interest) 4,000 of its 9%, 10-year, $1,000 face value, nonconvertible bonds with detachable stock warrants. Each bond carried two detachable warrants; each warrant was for one share of common stock at a specified option price of $15 per share. Shortly after issuance, the warrants were quoted on the market for $3 each. No market value can be determined for the bonds above. Interest is payable on December 1 and June 1. Bond issue costs of $30,000 were incurred.

Instructions
Prepare in general journal format the entry to record the issuance of the bonds.

(AICPA adapted)

E17-9 (Issuance of Bonds with Stock Warrants) On May 1, 2001, Friendly Company issued 2,000 $1,000 bonds at 102. Each bond was issued with one detachable stock warrant. Shortly after issuance, the bonds were selling at 98, but the market value of the warrants cannot be determined.

Instructions
  (a) Prepare the entry to record the issuance of the bonds and warrants.
  (b) Assume the same facts as part (a), except that the warrants had a fair value of $30. Prepare the entry to record the issuance of the bonds and warrants.

E17-10 (Issuance and Exercise of Stock Options) On November 1, 2001, Columbo Company adopted a stock option plan that granted options to key executives to purchase 30,000 shares of the company's $10 par value common stock. The options were granted on January 2, 2002, and were exercisable 2 years after the date of grant if the grantee was still an employee of the company; the options expired 6 years from date of grant. The option price was set at $40 and the fair value option pricing model determines the total compensation expense to be $450,000.

  All of the options were exercised during the year 2004; 20,000 on January 3 when the market price was $67, and 10,000 on May 1 when the market price was $77 a share.

Instructions
Prepare journal entries relating to the stock option plan for the years 2002, 2003, and 2004 under the fair value method. Assume that the employee performs services equally in 2002 and 2003.

E17-11 (Issuance, Exercise, and Termination of Stock Options) On January 1, 2002, Titania Inc. granted stock options to officers and key employees for the purchase of 20,000 shares of the company's $10 par common stock at $25 per share. The options were exercisable within a 5-year period beginning January 1, 2004, by grantees still in the employ of the company, and expiring December 31, 2008. The service period for this award is 2 years. Assume that the fair value option pricing model determines total compensation expense to be $350,000.

  On April 1, 2003, 2,000 option shares were terminated when the employees resigned from the company. The market value of the common stock was $35 per share on this date.

  On March 31, 2004, 12,000 option shares were exercised when the market value of the common stock was $40 per share.

Instructions
Prepare journal entries using the fair value method to record issuance of the stock options, termination of the stock options, exercise of the stock options, and charges to compensation expense, for the years ended December 31, 2002, 2003, and 2004.

E17-12 (Issuance, Exercise, and Termination of Stock Options) On January 1, 2000, Nichols Corporation granted 10,000 options to key executives. Each option allows the executive to purchase one share of Nichols' $5 par value common stock at a price of $20 per share. The options were exercisable within a 2-year period beginning January 1, 2002, if the grantee is still employed by the company at the time of the exercise. On the grant date, Nichols' stock was trading at $25 per share, and a fair value option-pricing model determines total compensation to be $400,000.

On May 1, 2002, 8,000 options were exercised when the market price of Nichols' stock was $30 per share. The remaining options lapsed in 2004 because executives decided not to exercise their options.

Instructions

Prepare the necessary journal entries related to the stock option plan for the years 2000 through 2004. Nichols uses the fair value approach to account for stock options.

*E17-13 (Stock Appreciation Rights) On December 31, 1997, Beckford Company issues 150,000 stock appreciation rights to its officers entitling them to receive cash for the difference between the market price of its stock and a preestablished price of $10. The market price fluctuates as follows: 12/31/98—$14; 12/31/99—$8; 12/31/00—$20; 12/31/01—$19. The service period is 4 years and the exercise period is 7 years. The company elects to use *APB Opinion No. 25* accounting for this transaction.

Instructions

(a) Prepare a schedule that shows the amount of compensation expense allocable to each year affected by the stock appreciation rights plan.

(b) Prepare the entry at December 31, 2001, to record compensation expense, if any, in 2001.

(c) Prepare the entry on December 31, 2001, assuming that all 150,000 SARs are exercised.

*E17-14 (Stock Appreciation Rights) Capulet Company establishes a stock appreciation rights program that entitles its new president Ben Davis to receive cash for the difference between the market price of the stock and a preestablished price of $30 (also market price) on December 31, 1998, on 30,000 SARs. The date of grant is December 31, 1998 and the required employment (service) period is 4 years. President Davis exercises all of the SARs in 2004. The market value of the stock fluctuates as follows: 12/31/99—$36; 12/31/00—$39; 12/31/01—$45; 12/31/02—$36; 12/31/03—$48. The company elects to use *APB Opinion No. 25* accounting for this transaction.

Instructions

(a) Prepare a 5-year (1999–2003) schedule of compensation expense pertaining to the 30,000 SARs granted President Davis.

(b) Prepare the journal entry for compensation expense in 1999, 2002, and 2003 relative to the 30,000 SARs.

E17-15 (Weighted Average Number of Shares) Newton Inc. uses a calendar year for financial reporting. The company is authorized to issue 9,000,000 shares of $10 par common stock. At no time has Newton issued any potentially dilutive securities. Listed below is a summary of Newton's common stock activities.

1. Number of common shares issued and outstanding at December 31, 1999	2,000,000
2. Shares issued as a result of a 10% stock dividend on September 30, 2000	200,000
3. Shares issued for cash on March 31, 2001	2,000,000
Number of common shares issued and outstanding at December 31, 2001	4,200,000

4. A 2-for-1 stock split of Newton's common stock took place on March 31, 2002.

Instructions

(a) Compute the weighted average number of common shares used in computing earnings per common share for 2000 on the 2001 comparative income statement.

(b) Compute the weighted average number of common shares used in computing earnings per common share for 2001 on the 2001 comparative income statement.

(c) Compute the weighted average number of common shares to be used in computing earnings per common share for 2001 on the 2002 comparative income statement.

(d) Compute the weighted average number of common shares to be used in computing earnings per common share for 2002 on the 2002 comparative income statement.

(CMA adapted)

E17-16 (EPS: Simple Capital Structure) On January 1, 2002, Wilke Corp. had 480,000 shares of common stock outstanding. During 2002, it had the following transactions that affected the common stock account.

February 1	Issued 120,000 shares
March 1	Issued a 10% stock dividend
May 1	Acquired 100,000 shares of treasury stock
June 1	Issued a 3-for-1 stock split
October 1	Reissued 60,000 shares of treasury stock

Instructions

(a) Determine the weighted average number of shares outstanding as of December 31, 2002.

(b) Assume that Wilke Corp. earned net income of $3,456,000 during 2002. In addition, it had 100,000 shares of 9%, $100 par nonconvertible, noncumulative preferred stock outstanding for the entire year. Because of liquidity considerations, however, the company did not declare and pay a preferred dividend in 2002. Compute earnings per share for 2002, using the weighted average number of shares determined in part (a).

(c) Assume the same facts as in part (b), except that the preferred stock was cumulative. Compute earnings per share for 2002.

(d) Assume the same facts as in part (b), except that net income included an extraordinary gain of $864,000 and a loss from discontinued operations of $432,000. Both items are net of applicable income taxes. Compute earnings per share for 2002.

E17-17 (EPS: Simple Capital Structure) Ace Company had 200,000 shares of common stock outstanding on December 31, 2002. During the year 2003 the company issued 8,000 shares on May 1 and retired 14,000 shares on October 31. For the year 2003 Ace Company reported net income of $249,690 after a casualty loss of $40,600 (net of tax).

Instructions

What earnings per share data should be reported at the bottom of its income statement, assuming that the casualty loss is extraordinary?

E17-18 (EPS: Simple Capital Structure) Flagstad Inc. presented the following data:

Net income	$2,500,000
Preferred stock: 50,000 shares outstanding,	
$100 par, 8% cumulative, not convertible	5,000,000
Common stock: Shares outstanding 1/1	750,000
Issued for cash, 5/1	300,000
Acquired treasury stock for cash, 8/1	150,000
2-for-1 stock split, 10/1	

Instructions

Compute earnings per share.

E17-19 (EPS: Simple Capital Structure) A portion of the combined statement of income and retained earnings of Seminole Inc. for the current year follows:

Income before extraordinary item		$15,000,000
Extraordinary loss, net of applicable		
income tax (Note 1)		1,340,000
Net income		13,660,000
Retained earnings at the beginning of the year		83,250,000
		96,910,000
Dividends declared:		
On preferred stock—$6.00 per share	$ 300,000	
On common stock—$1.75 per share	14,875,000	15,175,000
Retained earnings at the end of the year		$81,735,000

Note 1. During the year, Seminole Inc. suffered a major casualty loss of $1,340,000 after applicable income tax reduction of $1,200,000.

At the end of the current year, Seminole Inc. has outstanding 8,500,000 shares of $10 par common stock and 50,000 shares of 6% preferred.

On April 1 of the current year, Seminole Inc. issued 1,000,000 shares of common stock for $32 per share to help finance the casualty.

Instructions

Compute the earnings per share on common stock for the current year as it should be reported to stockholders.

E17-20 (EPS: Simple Capital Structure) On January 1, 2002, Lennon Industries had stock outstanding as follows:

6% Cumulative preferred stock, $100 par value,	
issued and outstanding 10,000 shares	$1,000,000
Common stock, $10 par value, issued and	
outstanding 200,000 shares	2,000,000

To acquire the net assets of three smaller companies, Lennon authorized the issuance of an additional 160,000 common shares. The acquisitions took place as follows:

Date of Acquisition		Shares Issued
Company A	April 1, 2002	50,000
Company B	July 1, 2002	80,000
Company C	October 1, 2002	30,000

On May 14, 2002, Lennon realized a $90,000 (before taxes) insurance gain on the expropriation of investments originally purchased in 1991.

On December 31, 2002, Lennon recorded net income of $300,000 before tax and exclusive of the gain.

Instructions

Assuming a 50% tax rate, compute the earnings per share data that should appear on the financial statements of Lennon Industries as of December 31, 2002. Assume that the expropriation is extraordinary.

E17-21 (EPS: Simple Capital Structure) At January 1, 2002, Langley Company's outstanding shares included:

> 280,000 shares of $50 par value, 7% cumulative preferred stock
> 900,000 shares of $1 par value common stock

Net income for 2002 was $2,530,000. No cash dividends were declared or paid during 2002. On February 15, 2003, however, all preferred dividends in arrears were paid, together with a 5% stock dividend on common shares. There were no dividends in arrears prior to 2002.

On April 1, 2002, 450,000 shares of common stock were sold for $10 per share and on October 1, 2002, 110,000 shares of common stock were purchased for $20 per share and held as treasury stock.

Instructions

Compute earnings per share for 2002. Assume that financial statements for 2002 were issued in March 2003.

E17-22 (EPS with Convertible Bonds, Various Situations) In 2000 Bonaparte Enterprises issued, at par, 60 $1,000, 8% bonds, each convertible into 100 shares of common stock. Bonaparte had revenues of $17,500 and expenses other than interest and taxes of $8,400 for 2001 (assume that the tax rate is 40%). Throughout 2001, 2,000 shares of common stock were outstanding; none of the bonds was converted or redeemed.

Instructions

- **(a)** Compute diluted earnings per share for 2001.
- **(b)** Assume the same facts as those assumed for part (a), except that the 60 bonds were issued on September 1, 2001 (rather than in 2000), and none have been converted or redeemed.
- **(c)** Assume the same facts as assumed for part (a), except that 20 of the 60 bonds were actually converted on July 1, 2001.

E17-23 (EPS with Convertible Bonds) On June 1, 1999, Mowbray Company and Surrey Company merged to form Lancaster Inc. A total of 800,000 shares were issued to complete the merger. The new corporation reports on a calendar-year basis.

On April 1, 2001, the company issued an additional 400,000 shares of stock for cash. All 1,200,000 shares were outstanding on December 31, 2001.

Lancaster Inc. also issued $600,000 of 20-year, 8% convertible bonds at par on July 1, 2001. Each $1,000 bond converts to 40 shares of common at any interest date. None of the bonds have been converted to date.

Lancaster Inc. is preparing its annual report for the fiscal year ending December 31, 2001. The annual report will show earnings per share figures based upon a reported after-tax net income of $1,540,000 (the tax rate is 40%).

Instructions

Determine for 2001:

- **(a)** The number of shares to be used for calculating:
  - **(1)** Basic earnings per share.
  - **(2)** Diluted earnings per share.
- **(b)** The earnings figures to be used for calculating:
  - **(1)** Basic earnings per share.
  - **(2)** Diluted earnings per share.

(CMA adapted)

E17-24 (EPS with Convertible Bonds and Preferred Stock) The Simon Corporation issued 10-year, $5,000,000 par, 7% callable convertible subordinated debentures on January 2, 2001. The bonds have a par value of $1,000, with interest payable annually. The current conversion ratio is 14:1, and in 2 years it will increase to 18:1. At the date of issue, the bonds were sold at 98. Bond discount is amortized on a straight-line basis. Simon's effective tax was 35%. Net income in 2001 was $9,500,000, and the company had 2,000,000 shares outstanding during the entire year.

Instructions

(a) Prepare a schedule to compute both basic and diluted earnings per share.

(b) Discuss how the schedule would differ if the security was convertible preferred stock.

E17-25 (EPS with Convertible Bonds and Preferred Stock) On January 1, 2001, Crocker Company issued 10-year, $2,000,000 face value, 6% bonds, at par. Each $1,000 bond is convertible into 15 shares of Crocker common stock. Crocker's net income in 2001 was $300,000, and its tax rate was 40%. The company had 100,000 common stock outstanding throughout 2001. None of the bonds were exercised in 2001.

Instructions

(a) Compute diluted earnings per share for 2001.

(b) Compute diluted earnings per share for 2001, assuming the same facts as above, except that $1,000,000 of 6% convertible preferred stock was issued instead of the bonds. Each $100 preferred share is convertible into 5 shares of Crocker common stock.

E17-26 (EPS with Options, Various Situations) Venzuela Company's net income for 2001 is $50,000. The only potentially dilutive securities outstanding were 1,000 options issued during 2000, each exercisable for one share at $6. None has been exercised, and 10,000 shares of common were outstanding during 2001. The average market price of Venzuela's stock during 2001 was $20.

Instructions

(a) Compute diluted earnings per share (round to nearest cent).

(b) Assume the same facts as those assumed for part (a), except that the 1,000 options were issued on October 1, 2001 (rather than in 2000). The average market price during the last 3 months of 2001 was $20.

E17-27 (EPS with Contingent Issuance Agreement) Winsor Inc. recently purchased Holiday Corp., a large midwestern home painting corporation. One of the terms of the merger was that if Holiday's income for 2001 was $110,000 or more, 10,000 additional shares would be issued to Holiday's stockholders in 2002. Holiday's income for 2000 was $120,000.

Instructions

(a) Would the contingent shares have to be considered in Winsor's 2000 earnings per share computations?

(b) Assume the same facts, except that the 10,000 shares are contingent on Holiday's achieving a net income of $130,000 in 2001. Would the contingent shares have to be considered in Winsor's earnings per share computations for 2000?

E17-28 (EPS with Warrants) Howat Corporation earned $360,000 during a period when it had an average of 100,000 shares of common stock outstanding. The common stock sold at an average market price of $15 per share during the period. Also outstanding were 15,000 warrants that could be exercised to purchase one share of common stock for $10 for each warrant exercised.

Instructions

(a) Are the warrants dilutive?

(b) Compute basic earnings per share.

(c) Compute diluted earnings per share.

PROBLEMS

P17-1 (Entries for Various Dilutive Securities) The stockholders' equity section of McLean Inc. at the beginning of the current year appears below:

Common stock, $10 par value, authorized 1,000,000 shares, 300,000 shares issued and outstanding	$3,000,000
Paid-in capital in excess of par	600,000
Retained earnings	570,000

During the current year the following transactions occurred:

1. The company issued to the stockholders 100,000 rights. Ten rights are needed to buy one share of stock at $32. The rights were void after 30 days. The market price of the stock at this time was $34 per share.
2. The company sold to the public a $200,000, 10% bond issue at par. The company also issued with each $100 bond one detachable stock purchase warrant, which provided for the purchase of common stock at $30 per share. Shortly after issuance, similar bonds without warrants were selling at 96 and the warrants at $8.
3. All but 10,000 of the rights issued in (1) were exercised in 30 days.
4. At the end of the year, 80% of the warrants in (2) had been exercised, and the remaining were outstanding and in good standing.
5. During the current year, the company granted stock options for 5,000 shares of common stock to company executives. The company using a fair value option pricing model determines that each option is worth $10. The option price is $30. The options were to expire at year-end and were considered compensation for the current year.
6. All but 1,000 shares related to the stock option plan were exercised by year-end. The expiration resulted because one of the executives failed to fulfill an obligation related to the employment contract.

Instructions

(a) Prepare general journal entries for the current year to record the transactions listed above.
(b) Prepare the stockholders' equity section of the balance sheet at the end of the current year. Assume that retained earnings at the end of the current year is $750,000.

P17-2 (Entries for Conversion, Amortization, and Interest of Bonds) Counter Inc. issued $1,500,000 of convertible 10-year bonds on July 1, 2001. The bonds provide for 12% interest payable semiannually on January 1 and July 1. The discount in connection with the issue was $34,000, which is being amortized monthly on a straight-line basis.

The bonds are convertible after one year into 8 shares of Counter Inc.'s $100 par value common stock for each $1,000 of bonds.

On August 1, 2002, $150,000 of bonds were turned in for conversion into common. Interest has been accrued monthly and paid as due. At the time of conversion any accrued interest on bonds being converted is paid in cash.

Instructions (Round to nearest dollar)

Prepare the journal entries to record the conversion, amortization, and interest in connection with the bonds as of:

(a) August 1, 2002 (assume the book value method is used).
(b) August 31, 2002.
(c) December 31, 2002, including closing entries for end-of-year.

(AICPA adapted)

P17-3 (Stock Option Plan) ISU Company adopted a stock option plan on November 30, 1999, that provided that 70,000 shares of $5 par value stock be designated as available for the granting of options to officers of the corporation at a price of $8 a share. The market value was $12 a share on November 30, 1999.

On January 2, 2000, options to purchase 28,000 shares were granted to president Don Pedro—15,000 for services to be rendered in 2000 and 13,000 for services to be rendered in 2001. Also on that date, options to purchase 14,000 shares were granted to vice president Beatrice Leonato—7,000 for services to be rendered in 2000 and 7,000 for services to be rendered in 2001. The market value of the stock was $14 a share on January 2, 2000. The options were exercisable for a period of one year following the year in which the services were rendered.

In 2001 neither the president nor the vice president exercised their options because the market price of the stock was below the exercise price. The market value of the stock was $7 a share on December 31, 2001, when the options for 2000 services lapsed.

On December 31, 2002, both president Pedro and vice president Leonato exercised their options for 13,000 and 7,000 shares, respectively, when the market price was $16 a share.

Instructions

Prepare the necessary journal entries in 1999 when the stock option plan was adopted, in 2000 when options were granted, in 2001 when options lapsed and in 2002 when options were exercised. The company elects to use the intrinsic value method following *APB Opinion No. 25*.

P17-4 (EPS with Complex Capital Structure) Diane Leto, controller at Dewey Yaeger Pharmaceutical Industries, a public company, is currently preparing the calculation for basic and diluted earnings per share and the related disclosure for Yaeger's external financial statements. Below is selected financial information for the fiscal year ended June 30, 2002.

DEWEY YAEGER PHARMACEUTICAL INDUSTRIES
Selected Statement of
Financial Position Information
June 30, 2002

Long-term debt	
Notes payable, 10%	$ 1,000,000
7% convertible bonds payable	5,000,000
10% bonds payable	6,000,000
Total long-term debt	$12,000,000
Shareholders' equity	
Preferred stock, 8.5% cumulative, $50 par value,	
100,000 shares authorized, 25,000 shares issued	
and outstanding	$ 1,250,000
Common stock, $1 par, 10,000,000 shares authorized,	
1,000,000 shares issued and outstanding	1,000,000
Additional paid-in capital	4,000,000
Retained earnings	6,000,000
Total shareholders' equity	$12,250,000

The following transactions have also occurred at Yaeger.

1. Options were granted in 2000 to purchase 100,000 shares at $15 per share. Although no options were exercised during 2002, the average price per common share during fiscal year 2002 was $20 per share.
2. Each bond was issued at face value. The 7% convertible debenture will convert into common stock at 50 shares per $1,000 bond. It is exercisable after 5 years and was issued in 2001.
3. The 8.5% preferred stock was issued in 2000.
4. There are no preferred dividends in arrears; however, preferred dividends were not declared in fiscal year 2002.
5. The 1,000,000 shares of common stock were outstanding for the entire 2002 fiscal year.
6. Net income for fiscal year 2002 was $1,500,000, and the average income tax rate is 40%.

Instructions

For the fiscal year ended June 30, 2002, calculate Dewey Yaeger Pharmaceutical Industries':

(a) Basic earnings per share.
(b) Diluted earnings per share.

P17-5 (Simple EPS and EPS with Stock Options) As auditor for Banquo & Associates, you have been assigned to check Duncan Corporation's computation of earnings per share for the current year. The controller, Mac Beth, has supplied you with the following computations:

Net income	$3,374,960
Common shares issued and outstanding:	
Beginning of year	1,285,000
End of year	1,200,000
Average	1,242,500
Earnings per share	

$$\frac{\$3,374,960}{1,242,500} = \$2.72 \text{ per share}$$

You have developed the following additional information:

1. There are no other equity securities in addition to the common shares.
2. There are no options or warrants outstanding to purchase common shares.
3. There are no convertible debt securities.
4. Activity in common shares during the year was as follows:

Outstanding, Jan. 1	1,285,000
Treasury shares acquired, Oct. 1	(250,000)
	1,035,000
Shares reissued, Dec. 1	165,000
Outstanding, Dec. 31	1,200,000

Instructions

(a) On the basis of the information above, do you agree with the controller's computation of earnings per share for the year? If you disagree, prepare a revised computation of earnings per share.

(b) Assume the same facts as those in (a), except that options had been issued to purchase 140,000 shares of common stock at $10 per share. These options were outstanding at the beginning of the year and none had been exercised or canceled during the year. The average market price of the common shares during the year was $25 and the ending market price was $35. Prepare a computation of earnings per share.

P17-6 (Basic EPS: Two-Year Presentation) Hillel Corporation is preparing the comparative financial statements for the annual report to its shareholders for fiscal years ended May 31, 2000, and May 31, 2001. The income from operations for each year was $1,800,000 and $2,500,000, respectively. In both years, the company incurred a 10% interest expense on $2,400,000 of debt, an obligation that requires interest-only payments for 5 years. The company experienced a loss of $500,000 from a fire in its Scotsland facility in February 2001, which was determined to be an extraordinary loss. The company uses a 40% effective tax rate for income taxes.

The capital structure of Hillel Corporation on June 1, 1999, consisted of 2 million shares of common stock outstanding and 20,000 shares of $50 par value, 8%, cumulative preferred stock. There were no preferred dividends in arrears, and the company had not issued any convertible securities, options, or warrants.

On October 1, 1999, Hillel sold an additional 500,000 shares of the common stock at $20 per share. Hillel distributed a 20% stock dividend on the common shares outstanding on January 1, 2000. On December 1, 2000, Hillel was able to sell an additional 800,000 shares of the common stock at $22 per share. These were the only common stock transactions that occurred during the two fiscal years.

Instructions

(a) Identify whether the capital structure at Hillel Corporation is a simple or complex capital structure, and explain why.

(b) Determine the weighted average number of shares that Hillel Corporation would use in calculating earnings per share for the fiscal year ended
   (1) May 31, 2000.
   (2) May 31, 2001.

(c) Prepare, in good form, a comparative income statement, beginning with income from operations, for Hillel Corporation for the fiscal years ended May 31, 2000, and May 31, 2001. This statement will be included in Hillel's annual report and should display the appropriate earnings per share presentations.

(CMA adapted)

P17-7 (EPS Computation of Basic and Diluted EPS) Edmund Halvor of the controller's office of East Aurora Corporation was given the assignment of determining the basic and diluted earnings per share values for the year ending December 31, 2001. Halvor has compiled the information listed below.

1. The company is authorized to issue 8,000,000 shares of $10 par value common stock. As of December 31, 2000, 3,000,000 shares had been issued and were outstanding.
2. The per share market prices of the common stock on selected dates were as follows:

	Price per Share
July 1, 2000	$20.00
January 1, 2001	21.00
April 1, 2001	25.00
July 1, 2001	11.00
August 1, 2001	10.50
November 1, 2001	9.00
December 31, 2001	10.00

3. A total of 700,000 shares of an authorized 1,200,000 shares of convertible preferred stock had been issued on July 1, 2000. The stock was issued at its par value of $25, and it has a cumulative dividend of $3 per share. The stock is convertible into common stock at the rate of one share of convertible preferred for one share of common. The rate of conversion is to be automatically adjusted

for stock splits and stock dividends. Dividends are paid quarterly on September 30, December 31, March 31, and June 30.

4. East Aurora Corporation is subject to a 40% income tax rate.
5. The after-tax net income for the year ended December 31, 2001 was $13,550,000.

The following specific activities took place during 2001.

1. January 1—A 5% common stock dividend was issued. The dividend had been declared on December 1, 2000, to all stockholders of record on December 29, 2000.
2. April 1—A total of 200,000 shares of the $3 convertible preferred stock was converted into common stock. The company issued new common stock and retired the preferred stock. This was the only conversion of the preferred stock during 2001.
3. July 1—A 2-for-1 split of the common stock became effective on this date. The Board of Directors had authorized the split on June 1.
4. August 1—A total of 300,000 shares of common stock were issued to acquire a factory building.
5. November 1—A total of 24,000 shares of common stock were purchased on the open market at $9 per share. These shares were to be held as treasury stock and were still in the treasury as of December 31, 2001.
6. Common stock cash dividends—Cash dividends to common stockholders were declared and paid as follows:
   April 15—$.30 per share
   October 15—$.20 per share
7. Preferred stock cash dividends—Cash dividends to preferred stockholders were declared and paid as scheduled.

Instructions
(a) Determine the number of shares used to compute basic earnings per share for the year ended December 31, 2001.
(b) Determine the number of shares used to compute diluted earnings per share for the year ended December 31, 2001.
(c) Compute the adjusted net income to be used as the numerator in the basic earnings per share calculation for the year ended December 31, 2001.

P17-8 **(Computation of Basic and Diluted EPS)** The following information pertains to Prancer Company for 2001:

Net income for the year	$1,200,000
8% convertible bonds issued at par ($1,000 per bond). Each bond is convertible into 40 shares of common stock.	2,000,000
6% convertible, cumulative preferred stock, $100 par value. Each share is convertible into 3 shares of common stock.	3,000,000
Common stock, $10 par value	6,000,000
Common stock options (granted in a prior year) to purchase 50,000 of common stock at $20 per share	500,000
Tax rate for 2001	40%
Average market price of common stock	$25 per share

There were no changes during 2001 in the number of common shares, preferred shares, or convertible bonds outstanding. There is no treasury stock.

Instructions
(a) Compute basic earnings per share for 2001.
(b) Compute diluted earnings per share for 2001.

P17-9 **(EPS with Stock Dividend and Extraordinary Items)** Cordelia Corporation is preparing the comparative financial statements to be included in the annual report to stockholders. Cordelia employs a fiscal year ending May 31.

Income from operations before income taxes for Cordelia was $1,400,000 and $660,000, respectively, for fiscal years ended May 31, 2001 and 2000. Cordelia experienced an extraordinary loss of $500,000 because of an earthquake on March 3, 2001. A 40% combined income tax rate pertains to any and all of Cordelia Corporation's profits, gains, and losses.

Cordelia's capital structure consists of preferred stock and common stock. The company has not issued any convertible securities or warrants and there are no outstanding stock options.

Cordelia issued 50,000 shares of $100 par value, 6% cumulative preferred stock in 1997. All of this stock is outstanding, and no preferred dividends are in arrears.

There were 1,500,000 shares of $1 par common stock outstanding on June 1, 1999. On September 1, 1999, Cordelia sold an additional 400,000 shares of the common stock at $17 per share. Cordelia distributed a 20% stock dividend on the common shares outstanding on December 1, 2000. These were the only common stock transactions during the past 2 fiscal years.

Instructions

(a) Determine the weighted average number of common shares that would be used in computing earnings per share on the current comparative income statement for:
   (1) The year ended May 31, 2000.
   (2) The year ended May 31, 2001.

(b) Starting with income from operations before income taxes, prepare a comparative income statement for the years ended May 31, 2001 and 2000. The statement will be part of Cordelia Corporation's annual report to stockholders and should include appropriate earnings per share presentation.

(c) The capital structure of a corporation is the result of its past financing decisions. Furthermore, the earnings per share data presented on a corporation's financial statements is dependent upon the capital structure.
   (1) Explain why Cordelia Corporation is considered to have a simple capital structure.
   (2) Describe how earnings per share data would be presented for a corporation that has a complex capital structure.

(CMA adapted)

CONCEPTUAL CASES

C17-1 (Warrants Issued with Bonds and Convertible Bonds) Incurring long-term debt with an arrangement whereby lenders receive an option to buy common stock during all or a portion of the time the debt is outstanding is a frequent corporate financing practice. In some situations the result is achieved through the issuance of convertible bonds; in others the debt instruments and the warrants to buy stock are separate.

Instructions

(a) (1) Describe the differences that exist in current accounting for original proceeds of the issuance of convertible bonds and of debt instruments with separate warrants to purchase common stock.
   (2) Discuss the underlying rationale for the differences described in (a)1 above.
   (3) Summarize the arguments that have been presented in favor of accounting for convertible bonds in the same manner as accounting for debt with separate warrants.

(b) At the start of the year Biron Company issued $18,000,000 of 12% notes along with warrants to buy 1,200,000 shares of its $10 par value common stock at $18 per share. The notes mature over the next 10 years starting one year from date of issuance with annual maturities of $1,800,000. At the time, Biron had 9,600,000 shares of common stock outstanding and the market price was $23 per share. The company received $20,040,000 for the notes and the warrants. For Biron Company, 12% was a relatively low borrowing rate. If offered alone, at this time, the notes would have been issued at a 22% discount. Prepare the journal entry (or entries) for the issuance of the notes and warrants for the cash consideration received.

(AICPA adapted)

C17-2 (Convertible Bonds) On February 1, 1998, Parsons Company sold its 5-year, $1,000 par value, 8% bonds, which were convertible at the option of the investor into Parsons Company common stock at a ratio of 10 shares of common stock for each bond. The convertible bonds were sold by Parsons Company at a discount. Interest is payable annually each February 1. On February 1, 2001, Wong Company, an investor in the Parsons Company convertible bonds, tendered 1,000 bonds for conversion into 10,000 shares of Parsons Company common stock that had a market value of $120 per share at the date of the conversion.

Instructions

How should Parsons Company account for the conversion of the convertible bonds into common stock under both the book value and market value methods? Discuss the rationale for each method.

(AICPA adapted)

C17-3 (Stock Warrants—Various Types) For various reasons a corporation may issue warrants to purchase shares of its common stock at specified prices that, depending on the circumstances, may be less than, equal to, or greater than the current market price. For example, warrants may be issued:

1. To existing stockholders on a pro rata basis.
2. To certain key employees under an incentive stock option plan.
3. To purchasers of the corporation's bonds.

Instructions

For each of the three examples of how stock warrants are used:

(a) Explain why they are used.
(b) Discuss the significance of the price (or prices) at which the warrants are issued (or granted) in relation to (1) the current market price of the company's stock, and (2) the length of time over which they can be exercised.
(c) Describe the information that should be disclosed in financial statements, or notes thereto, that are prepared when stock warrants are outstanding in the hands of the three groups listed above.

(AICPA adapted)

*C17-4 (Stock Options and Stock Appreciation Rights—Intrinsic Value Model) In 1999 Sanford Co. adopted a plan to give additional incentive compensation to its dealers to sell its principal product, fire extinguishers. Under the plan Sanford transferred 9,000 shares of its $1 par value stock to a trust with the provision that Sanford would have to forfeit interest in the trust and no part of the trust fund could ever revert to Sanford. Shares were to be distributed to dealers on the basis of their shares of fire extinguisher purchases from Sanford (above certain minimum levels) over the 3-year period ending June 30, 2002.

In 1999 the stock was closely held. The book value of the stock was $7.90 per share as of June 30, 1999, and in 1999 additional shares were sold to existing stockholders for $8 per share. On the basis of this information, market value of the stock was determined to be $8 per share.

In 1999 when the shares were transferred to the trust, Sanford charged prepaid expenses for $72,000 ($8 per share market value) and credited capital stock for $9,000 and additional paid-in capital for $63,000. The prepaid expense was charged to operations over a 3-year period ended June 30, 2002.

Sanford sold a substantial number of shares of its stock to the public in 2001 at $60 per share.

In July 2002 all shares of the stock in the trust were distributed to the dealers. The market value of the shares at date of distribution of the stock from the trust had risen to $110 per share. Sanford obtained a tax deduction equal to that market value for the tax year ended June 30, 2003.

Instructions

(Note: Use *APB Opinion No. 25* to solve this problem.)

(a) How much should be reported as selling expense in each of the years noted above assuming that the company uses the intrinsic value model?
(b) Sanford is also considering other types of option plans. One such plan is a stock appreciation right (SAR) plan. What is a stock appreciation right plan? What is a potential disadvantage of a SAR plan from the viewpoint of the company?

C17-5 (Stock Compensation Plans) Presented below is an excerpt from a speech given by SEC Commissioner J. Carter Beese, Jr.

. . . I believe investors will be far better off if the value of stock options is reported in a footnote rather than on the face of the income statement. By allowing footnote disclosures, we will protect shareholders' current and future investments by not raising the cost of capital for the innovative, growth companies that depend on stock options to attract and retain key employees. I've said it before and I'll say it again: the stock option accounting debate essentially boils down to one thing—the cost of capital. And as long as we can adequately protect investors without raising the cost of capital to such a vital segment of our economy, why would we want to do it any other way?

The FASB has made the assertion that when it comes to public policy, they lack the competence to weigh various national goals. I also agree with the sentiment that, as a general matter, Congress should not be in the business of writing accounting standards.

But the SEC has the experience and the capability to determine exactly where to draw the regulatory lines to best serve investors and our capital markets. That is our mandate, and that is what we do, day in and day out.

But we may have to act sooner rather than later. As we speak, the FASB's proposals are raising the cost of venture capital. That's because venture capitalists are pricing deals based on their exit strategies, which usually include cashing out in public offerings. The FASB's proposals, however, provide incentives for companies to stay private longer—they are able to use options more freely to attract and retain key employees, and they avoid the earnings hit that going public would entail. Even worse, as venture capital deals become less profitable because of the FASB's proposed actions, venture capitalists are starting to look overseas for alternative investment opportunities that lack the investment drag now associated with certain American ventures.

I acknowledge that the FASB deserves some degree of freedom to determine what they believe is the best accounting approach. At the same time, however, I cannot stand by idly for long and watch venture capital increase in price or even flee this country because of a myopic search for an accounting holy grail. At some point, I believe that the SEC must inject itself into this debate, and help the FASB determine what accounting approach is ultimately in the best interests of investors as a whole.

We owe it to shareholders, issuers and all market participants, and indeed our country, to make the best decision in accordance with the public good, not just technical accounting theory.

Instructions

(a) What are the major recommendations of *SFAS No. 123* on "Accounting for Stock-Based Compensation Plans"?

(b) Write a response to Commissioner Beese, defending the use of the concept of neutrality in financial accounting and reporting.

C17-6 (EPS: Preferred Dividends, Options, and Convertible Debt) "Earnings per share" (EPS) is the most featured single financial statistic about modern corporations. Daily published quotations of stock prices have recently been expanded to include for many securities a "times earnings" figure that is based on EPS. Stock analysts often focus their discussions on the EPS of the corporations they study.

Instructions

(a) Explain how dividends or dividend requirements on any class of preferred stock that may be outstanding affect the computation of EPS.

(b) One of the technical procedures applicable in EPS computations is the "treasury stock method." Briefly describe the circumstances under which it might be appropriate to apply the treasury stock method.

(c) Convertible debentures are considered potentially dilutive common shares. Explain how convertible debentures are handled for purposes of EPS computations.

(AICPA adapted)

C17-7 (EPS Concepts and Effect of Transactions on EPS) Fernandez Corporation, a new audit client of yours, has not reported earnings per share data in its annual reports to stockholders in the past. The treasurer, Angelo Balthazar, requested that you furnish information about the reporting of earnings per share data in the current year's annual report in accordance with generally accepted accounting principles.

Instructions

(a) Define the term "earnings per share" as it applies to a corporation with a capitalization structure composed of only one class of common stock and explain how earnings per share should be computed and how the information should be disclosed in the corporation's financial statements.

(b) Discuss the treatment, if any, that should be given to each of the following items in computing earnings per share of common stock for financial statement reporting.

(1) Outstanding preferred stock issued at a premium with a par value liquidation right.

(2) The exercise at a price below market value but above book value of a common stock option issued during the current fiscal year to officers of the corporation.

(3) The replacement of a machine immediately prior to the close of the current fiscal year at a cost 20% above the original cost of the replaced machine. The new machine will perform the same function as the old machine that was sold for its book value.

(4) The declaration of current dividends on cumulative preferred stock.

(5) The acquisition of some of the corporation's outstanding common stock during the current fiscal year. The stock was classified as treasury stock.

(6) A 2-for-1 stock split of common stock during the current fiscal year.

(7) A provision created out of retained earnings for a contingent liability from a possible lawsuit.

C17-8 (EPS, Anti-dilution) Matt Kacskos, a stockholder of Howat Corporation, has asked you, the firm's accountant, to explain why his stock warrants were not included in diluted EPS. In order to explain this situation, you must briefly explain what dilutive securities are, why they are included in the EPS calculation, and why some securities are antidilutive and thus not included in this calculation.

Instructions

Write Mr. Kacskos a 1–1.5 page letter explaining why the warrants are not included in the calculation. Use the following data to help you explain this situation.

Howat Corporation earned $228,000 during the period, when it had an average of 100,000 shares of common stock outstanding. The common stock sold at an average market price of $25 per share during the period. Also outstanding were 15,000 warrants that could be exercised to purchase one share of common stock at $30 per warrant.

USING YOUR JUDGMENT

FINANCIAL REPORTING PROBLEM: INTEL CORPORATION

Instructions

Refer to the financial statements and accompanying notes and discussion of Intel Corporation presented in Appendix 5B and answer the following questions.

(a) Under Intel's stock participation plan, eligible employees may purchase shares of Intel's common stock at 85% of fair market value. (1) How many shares are authorized to be issued under the plan? (2) How many were available for issuance at December 26, 1998? (3) How many shares were purchased by employees in 1998 under the plan and how much was paid for those shares?

(b) Intel has a stock option plan (referred to as the EOP plan) under which officers, key employees, and directors may be granted options to purchase Intel common stock. (1) What is the range of exercise prices for options outstanding under the EOP plan at December 26, 1998? (2) How many years from the grant date do these EOP plan options expire? (3) To what accounts are the proceeds from these option exercises credited? (4) What is the number of shares of outstanding options at December 26, 1998 under the EOP plan and at what weighted average exercise price? (5) How many options are exercisable under the EOP plan at December 26, 1998, and at what price?

(c) What number of weighted average common shares outstanding was used by Intel in computing earnings per share for 1998, 1997, and 1996? What was Intel's diluted earnings per share in 1998, 1997, and 1996?

FINANCIAL STATEMENT ANALYSIS CASE

Kellogg Company

Kellogg Company in its 1998 Annual Report in Note 1—Accounting Policies made the following comment about its accounting for employee stock options and other stock-based compensation:

> **Stock compensation.** The Company follows Accounting Principles Board Opinion (APB) #25, "Accounting for Stock Issued to Employees," in accounting for its employee stock options and other stock-based compensation. Under APB #25, because the exercise price of the Company's employee stock options equals the market price of the underlying stock on the date of the grant, no compensation expense is recognized. As permitted, the Company has elected to adopt only the disclosure provisions of Statement of Financial Accounting Standards (SFAS) #123, "Accounting for Stock-Based Compensation."

Instructions

In electing to adopt only the disclosure provisions of *FASB Statement No. 123*, what minimum disclosures was Kellogg Company required to make in its notes to the financial statement about its employee stock options and other stock-based compensation?

COMPARATIVE ANALYSIS CASE

The Coca-Cola Company versus PepsiCo, Inc.

Instructions

Go to the Digital Tool and using The Coca-Cola Company and PepsiCo, Inc. Annual Report information, answer the following questions.

(a) What employee stock option compensation plans are offered by Coca-Cola and PepsiCo?

(b) How many options are outstanding at year-end 1998 for both Coca-Cola and PepsiCo?

(c) How many options were granted by Coca-Cola and PepsiCo to officers and employees during 1998?

(d) How many options were exercised during 1998?

(e) What was the range of option prices exercised by Coca-Cola and PepsiCo employees during 1998?

(f) What are the weighted average number of shares used by Coca-Cola and PepsiCo in 1998, 1997, and 1996 to compute diluted earnings per share?

(g) What was the diluted net income per share for Coca-Cola and PepsiCo for 1998, 1997, and 1996?

RESEARCH CASES

Case 1

Instructions

Examine a copy of *Statement of Financial Accounting Standards No. 123*, "Accounting for Stock-Based Compensation," and answer the following questions.

(a) As indicated in Chapter 1, the passage of a new Financial Accounting Standards Board statement requires the support of five of the seven members of the Board. What was the vote with regard to SFAS 123? Which members of the Board dissented?

(b) What was the major objection cited by the dissenters? What reasoning was used to support this objection?

(c) The dissenters expressed a preference for measuring the fair value of stock options at the vesting date instead of the grant date. Under what circumstances would they have accepted the modified grant method? Why?

Case 2

The November 1995 issue the *The CPA Journal* includes an article by Anthony Cocco and Daniel Ivancevich entitled "Recognition of Footnote Disclosure of Compensatory Fixed Stock Options?"

Instructions

Read the article and answer the following questions.

(a) Identify two financial statement ratios that will be affected by recognition of fixed stock options. How will they be affected?

(b) Under what condition does the impact of expensing stock compensation take on less importance?

(c) What "signal" might be sent to investors if a company chooses to recognize stock compensation expense despite the negative impact on the financial statements?

(d) Do you feel that the example provided by the authors makes a strong case for recognition over disclosure?

INTERNATIONAL REPORTING CASE

Clearly Canadian Beverage is a Canadian company engaged in the manufacturing and distribution of its Clearly Canadian line of carbonated mineral water and natural fruit-flavored sparkling beverages, noncarbonated beverages, and bottled water. Its shares are traded on the NASDAQ exchange. Because its shares trade on a U.S. exchange, Clearly Canadian Beverage must either prepare its financial statements in accordance with U.S. GAAP or prepare a reconciliation of its financial statements (based on Canadian standards) to how they would be reported under U.S. GAAP. As a result of this requirement, Clearly Canadian presented the following information in its financial statements to meet the U.S. GAAP reconciliation requirement.

This is an international reporting case.

CLEARLY CANADIAN BEVERAGE

Reconciliation to Accounting Principles Generally Accepted in the United States of America

Differences in generally accepted accounting principles (GAAP) between Canada and the United States as they pertain to these consolidated financial statements are as follows:

	1998	1997
	$	$
Net earnings (loss) under Canadian GAAP	310	(12,266)
Foreign currency adjustments—see note A	—	(408)
Earnings (loss) under U.S. GAAP	310	(12,674)
Unrealized holding gains (losses)—see note B	(1,044)	1,742
Foreign currency translation adjustments	(1,983)	—
Comprehensive loss—see note C	(2,717)	(10,932)
Basic earnings (loss) per post-consolidated share before comprehensive income (loss) adjustments (expressed in dollars)	0.05	(2.26)

Note A: Change in reporting currency. Under U.S. GAAP, a change in reporting currency would require a restatement of prior years' financial statements using a weighted average exchange rate for each year in the statement of operations, and current and historical rates for monetary and non-monetary assets and liabilities on the balance sheet.

Note B: Unrealized holding gains (losses). Under U.S. GAAP, the long-term investments in publicly traded companies would be shown at fair market value.

Note C: Comprehensive income (loss). U.S. GAAP requires disclosure of comprehensive income (loss), which is intended to reflect all changes in equity except those resulting from contributions to owners.

In addition, Clearly Canadian provided the following disclosure related to its stock compensation plans: Under a stock option plan, as amended and restated June 27, 1997, the Company may grant options to eligible employees of the Company, provided that the number of shares issuable does not exceed 941,176 post-consolidated common shares of the Company. Options may be issued under the stock option plan as determined at the sole discretion of the Company's board of directors. Options may be issued for a term of up to 10 years at an exercise price to be determined by the Company's board of directors, provided that the exercise price is not less than the average closing price of the Company's shares traded through the facilities of The Toronto Stock Exchange for the 10 trading days preceding the date on which the options are granted.

The Company applies APB Opinion 25, "Accounting for Stock Issued to Employees", and related Interpretations in accounting for the plan. Under APB Opinion 25, because the exercise price of the Company's employee stock options equals the market price of the underlying stock on the date of grant, no compensation cost is recognized.

Statement of Financial Accounting Standards No. 123, "Accounting for Stock-Based Compensation" (SFAS 123), requires the Company to provide pro forma information regarding net income and earnings per share as if compensation cost for the Company's stock option plans had been determined in accordance with the fair value based method prescribed in SFAS 123. The Company estimates the fair value of each stock option at the grant date by using the Black-Scholes option-pricing model with the following weighted-average assumptions used for grants in 1998: dividend yield of $nil (1997—$nil); expected volatility of 70% (1997—70%); risk-free interest rate of 4.7% (1997—4.54%); and expected life to nine years (1997—nine years).

Under the accounting provisions of SFAS 123, the Company's U.S. GAAP profit of $310,000 would have been decreased to a loss of $288,000.

Instructions

Use the information in the Clearly Canadian disclosure to respond to the following questions.

(a) What are the major differences between earnings reported by Clearly Canadian Beverage and earnings under U.S. GAAP?

(b) What are the major differences between earnings reported by Clearly Canadian Beverage and comprehensive income under U.S. GAAP?

(c) What do you think are some reasons why Clearly Canadian Beverage might not want to prepare its financial statements in accordance with U.S. GAAP?

(d) What is the impact of *SFAS 123* accounting on Clearly Canadian's profit? Why isn't this adjustment reflected in the reconciliation schedule?

ETHICS CASE

The executive officers of Coach Corporation have a performance-based compensation plan. The performance criteria of this plan is linked to growth in earnings per share. When annual EPS growth is 12%, the Coach executives earn 100% of the shares; if growth is 16%, they earn 125%. If EPS growth is lower than 8%, the executives receive no additional compensation.

In 2000, Joanna Becker, the controller of Coach, reviews year-end estimates of bad debt expense and warranty expense. She calculates the EPS growth at 15%. Peter Reiser, a member of the executive group, remarks over lunch one day that the estimate of bad debt expense might be decreased, increasing EPS growth to 16.1%. Becker is not sure she should do this because she believes that the current estimate of bad debts is sound. On the other hand, she recognizes that a great deal of subjectivity is involved in the computation.

Instructions

Answer the following questions:

(a) What, if any, is the ethical dilemma for Becker?

(b) Should Becker's knowledge of the compensation plan be a factor that influences her estimate?

(c) How should Becker respond to Reiser's request?

CHAPTER 18

Investments

Is Coke in Control Here?

The Coca-Cola Company (Coke) owns 42% of the shares of **Coca-Cola Enterprises** (a U.S. bottling business) and 43% of **Coca-Cola Amatil** (a European and Asian bottling business). These bottling businesses are very important to The Coca-Cola Company, because they are the primary distributors of Coca-Cola products. Furthermore, these companies are very dependent on Coca-Cola, which provides significant marketing and distribution development support. Indeed, an argument can be made that the bottling companies are controlled by Coca-Cola, because they would not exist without its support.

However, because The Coca-Cola Company does not own more than 50% of the shares in these companies, it does not prepare consolidated financial statements. Instead, Coca-Cola accounts for these investments using the equity method. Under the equity method, Coca-Cola reports a single income item for its profits from the bottlers, and only the net amount of its investment is reported in the balance sheet.

Equity method accounting gives Coca-Cola a pristine balance sheet and income statement, by keeping the assets and liabilities and the profit margins of these bottlers separate from its beverage-making business. What's more, as summarized in the following table, many countries allow proportional consolidation, an accounting method that includes part of the assets, liabilities, and income of investees in the financial statements of the investor company.

International Reporting of Less than 50% Equity Investments

Countries/Standards	Method(s) Allowed
U.S. GAAP: United Kingdom, Brazil, Mexico	Equity
IASC: France, Germany, Netherlands, Italy, Japan	Proportional consolidation or equity

This variation in practice makes it difficult to compare Coca-Cola to other international beverage companies and is part of the reason why U.S. and international accounting standards-setters are studying the accounting rules for equity investments like Coca-Cola's.[1]

LEARNING OBJECTIVES

After studying this chapter, you should be able to:

❶ Identify the three categories of debt securities and describe the accounting and reporting treatment for each category.

❷ Identify the categories of equity securities and describe the accounting and reporting treatment for each category.

❸ Explain the equity method of accounting and compare it to the fair value method for equity securities.

❹ Describe the disclosure requirements for investments in debt and equity securities.

❺ Discuss the accounting for impairments of debt and equity investments.

❻ Describe the accounting for transfer of investment securities between categories.

---

[1]Based on Morgan Stanley Dean Witter, "Apples to Apples, Global Beverage: Thirst for Knowledge," May 25, 1999.

As indicated in the opening story, the measurement, recognition, and disclosure for certain investments are under study by U.S. and international standards-setters. This chapter addresses the accounting for debt and equity investments. Appendices to this chapter cover special issues related to investments and accounting for derivative instruments. The content and organization of this chapter are as follows:

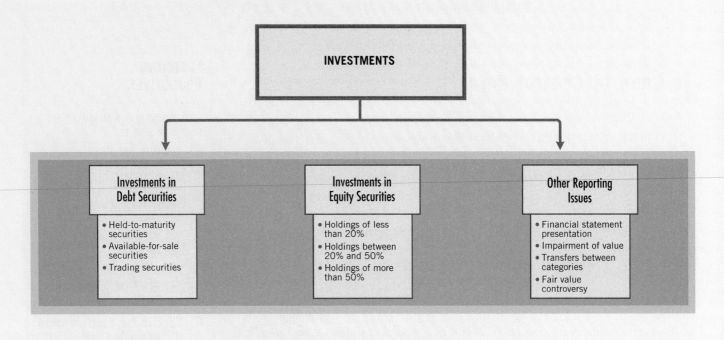

Companies have different motivations for investing in securities issued by other companies.[2] One motivation is to earn a high rate of return. A company can receive interest revenue from a debt investment or dividend revenue from an equity investment. In addition, capital gains on both types of securities can be realized. Another motivation for investing (in equity securities) is to secure certain operating or financing arrangements with another company. As in the opening story, Coca-Cola is able to exercise some control over bottler companies based on its significant (but not controlling) equity investment.

To provide useful information, the accounting for investments is based on the type of security (debt or equity) and management's intent with respect to the investment. As indicated in Illustration 18-1, our study of investments is organized by type of security. Within each section, we explain how the accounting for investments in debt and equity securities varies according to management intent.

---

[2]A security is a share, participation, or other interest in property or in an enterprise of the issuer or an obligation of the issuer that: (a) either is represented by an instrument issued in bearer or registered form or, if not represented by an instrument, is registered in books maintained to record transfers by or on behalf of the issuer; (b) is of a type commonly dealt in on securities exchanges or markets or, when represented by an instrument, is commonly recognized in any area in which it is issued or dealt in as a medium for investment; and (c) either is one of a class or series or by its terms is divisible into a class or series of shares, participations, interests, or obligations. From "Accounting for Certain Investments in Debt and Equity Securities," *Statement of Financial Accounting Standards No. 115* (Norwalk, Conn.: FASB, 1993), p. 48, par. 137.

Types of Security	Management Intent	Valuation Approach	Authoritative Literature
Debt (Section 1)	No plans to sell	Amortized cost	"Accounting for Certain Investments in Debt and Equity Securities," *SFAS No. 115*
	Plan to sell	Fair value	
Equity (Section 2)	Plan to sell	Fair value	
	Exercise some control	Equity method	"The Equity Method of Accounting for Investments in Common Stock," *APB Opinion No. 18*

ILLUSTRATION 18-1
Summary of Investment Accounting Approaches

INVESTMENTS IN DEBT SECURITIES   SECTION 1

Debt securities are instruments representing a creditor relationship with an enterprise. Debt securities include U.S. government securities, municipal securities, corporate bonds, convertible debt, commercial paper, and all securitized debt instruments. Trade accounts receivable and loans receivable are not debt securities because they do not meet the definition of a security.

Investments in debt securities are grouped into three separate categories for accounting and reporting purposes. These categories are as follows:

Held-to-maturity: Debt securities that the enterprise has the positive intent and ability to hold to maturity.

Trading: Debt securities bought and held primarily for sale in the near term to generate income on short-term price differences.

Available-for-sale: Debt securities not classified as held-to-maturity or trading securities.

Illustration 18-2 identifies these categories, along with the accounting and reporting treatments required for each.

OBJECTIVE 1
Identify the three categories of debt securities and describe the accounting and reporting treatment for each category.

Category	Valuation	Unrealized Holding Gains or Losses	Other Income Effects
Held-to-maturity	Amortized cost	Not recognized	Interest when earned; gains and losses from sale.
Trading securities	Fair value	Recognized in net income	Interest when earned; gains and losses from sale.
Available-for-sale	Fair value	Recognized as other comprehensive income and as separate component of stockholders' equity	Interest when earned; gains and losses from sale.

ILLUSTRATION 18-2
Accounting for Debt Securities by Category

UNDERLYING CONCEPTS

Debt securities are reported at fair value not only because the information is relevant but also because it is reliable.

Amortized cost is the acquisition cost adjusted for the amortization of discount or premium, if appropriate. **Fair value** is the amount at which a financial instrument could be exchanged in a current transaction between willing parties, other than in a forced or liquidation sale.[3]

HELD-TO-MATURITY SECURITIES

Only debt securities can be classified as held-to-maturity because, by definition, equity securities have no maturity date. A debt security should be classified as **held-to-maturity** only if the reporting entity has **both (1) the positive intent** and **(2) the ability to hold those securities to maturity**. A company should not classify a debt security as held-to-maturity if the company intends to hold the security for an indefinite period of time. Likewise, if the enterprise anticipates that a sale may be necessary due to changes in interest rates, foreign currency risk, liquidity needs, or other asset-liability management reasons, the security should not be classified as held-to-maturity.[4]

Held-to-maturity securities are accounted for at amortized cost, not fair value. If management intends to hold certain investment securities to maturity and has no plans to sell them, fair values (selling prices) are not relevant for measuring and evaluating the cash flows associated with these securities. Finally, because held-to-maturity securities are not adjusted to fair value, they do not increase the volatility of either reported earnings or reported capital as do trading securities and available-for-sale securities.

To illustrate the accounting for held-to-maturity debt securities, assume that Robinson Company purchased $100,000 of 8% bonds of Evermaster Corporation on January 1, 2001, paying $92,278. The bonds mature January 1, 2006; interest is payable each July 1 and January 1. The discount of $7,722 ($100,000 − $92,278) provided an effective interest yield of 10%. The entry to record the investment is:[5]

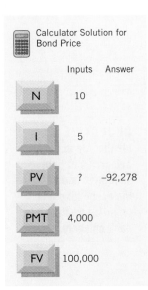

Calculator Solution for Bond Price

	Inputs	Answer
N	10	
I	5	
PV	?	−92,278
PMT	4,000	
FV	100,000	

January 1, 2001

Held-to-Maturity Securities	92,278	
Cash		92,278

A Held-to-Maturity Securities account is used to indicate the type of debt security purchased. Discounts and premiums on long-term investments in bonds are amortized in a manner similar to discounts and premiums on bonds payable, discussed in Chapter 14. Illustration 18-3 shows the effect of the discount amortization on the interest revenue recorded each period for the investment in Evermaster Corporation bonds.

---

[3]Ibid., pp. 47–48. The fair value is **readily determinable** if its sale price or other quotations are available on SEC registered exchanges, or, for over-the-counter securities, are published by recognized national publication systems. Foreign shares have readily determinable fair values if they trade in markets comparable in breadth and scope to the described U.S. markets.

[4]The FASB defines situations where, even though a security is sold before maturity, it has constructively been held to maturity, and thus does not represent a violation of the held-to-maturity requirement. These include selling a security close enough to maturity (such as three months) so that interest rate risk is no longer an important pricing factor. Additionally, if the enterprise has already collected a substantial portion of the principal of the security (at least 85%) it is considered to have been held to its maturity date.

[5]Investments acquired at par, at a discount, or at a premium are generally recorded in the accounts at cost, including brokerage and other fees but excluding the accrued interest; generally they are not recorded at maturity value. The use of a separate discount or premium account as a valuation account is acceptable procedure for investments, but in practice it has not been widely used. This traditional exclusion of a separate discount or premium account has not yet changed even though *APB Opinion No. 21* recommends the disclosure of unamortized discount or premium on notes and bonds receivable.

	8% Bonds Purchased to Yield 10%			
Date	Cash Received	Interest Revenue	Bond Discount Amortization	Carrying Amount of Bonds
1/1/01				$ 92,278
7/1/01	$ 4,000ᵃ	$ 4,614ᵇ	$ 614ᶜ	92,892ᵈ
1/1/02	4,000	4,645	645	93,537
7/1/02	4,000	4,677	677	94,214
1/1/03	4,000	4,711	711	94,925
7/1/03	4,000	4,746	746	95,671
1/1/04	4,000	4,783	783	96,454
7/1/04	4,000	4,823	823	97,277
1/1/05	4,000	4,864	864	98,141
7/1/05	4,000	4,907	907	99,048
1/1/06	4,000	4,952	952	100,000
	$40,000	$47,722	$7,722	

ᵃ$4,000 = $100,000 × .08 × 6/12
ᵇ$4,614 = $92,278 × .10 × 6/12
ᶜ$614 = $4,614 − $4,000
ᵈ$92,892 = $92,278 + $614

As indicated in Chapter 14, the **effective interest method** is required unless some other method—such as the straight-line method—yields a similar result. The effective interest method is applied to bond investments in a fashion similar to that described for bonds payable. The effective interest rate or yield is computed at the time of investment and is applied to its beginning carrying amount (book value) for each interest period to compute interest revenue. The investment carrying amount is increased by the amortized discount or decreased by the amortized premium in each period.

The journal entry to record the receipt of the first semiannual interest payment on July 1, 2001 (using the data in Illustration 18-3), is:

UNDERLYING CONCEPTS

The use of some simpler method which yields results similar to the effective interest method is an application of the materiality concept.

July 1, 2001

Cash	4,000	
Held-to-Maturity Securities	614	
Interest Revenue		4,614

Because Robinson Company is on a calendar-year basis, it accrues interest and amortizes the discount at December 31, 2001, as follows:

December 31, 2001

Interest Receivable	4,000	
Held-to-Maturity Securities	645	
Interest Revenue		4,645

Again, the interest and amortization amounts are provided in Illustration 18-3.

Robinson Company would report the following items related to its investment in Evermaster bonds in its December 31, 2001, financial statements:

ILLUSTRATION 18-4
Reporting of Held-to-Maturity Securities

Balance Sheet	
Current assets	
Interest receivable	$ 4,000
Long-term investments	
Held-to-maturity securities, at amortized cost	$93,537
Income Statement	
Other revenues and gains	
Interest revenue	$ 9,259

The sale of a held-to-maturity debt security close enough to its maturity date that a change in the market interest rates would not significantly affect the security's fair value may be considered a sale at maturity. If Robinson Company sells its investment in Evermaster bonds on November 1, 2005, for example, at 99¾ plus accrued interest, the following computations and entries would be made. The discount amortization from July 1, 2005, to November 1, 2005, is $635 (⁴⁄₆ × $952). The entry to record this discount amortization is as follows:

November 1, 2005

Held-to-Maturity Securities	635	
Interest Revenue		635

The computation of the realized gain on the sale is shown in Illustration 18-5.

ILLUSTRATION 18-5
Computation of Gain on Sale of Bonds

Selling price of bonds (exclusive of accrued interest)		$99,750
Less: Book value of bonds on November 1, 2005:		
Amortized cost, July 1, 2005	$99,048	
Add: Discount amortized for the period July 1, 2005, to November 1, 2005	635	
		99,683
Gain on sale of bonds		$ 67

The entry to record the sale of the bonds is:

November 1, 2005

Cash	102,417	
Interest Revenue (⁴⁄₆ × $4,000)		2,667
Held-to-Maturity Securities		99,683
Gain on Sale of Securities		67

The credit to Interest Revenue represents accrued interest for 4 months, for which the purchaser pays cash. The debit to Cash represents the selling price of the bonds, $99,750, plus accrued interest of $2,667. The credit to the Held-to-Maturity Securities account represents the book value of the bonds on the date of sale, and the credit to Gain on Sale of Securities represents the excess of the selling price over the book value of the bonds.

AVAILABLE-FOR-SALE SECURITIES

UNDERLYING CONCEPTS

Recognizing unrealized gains and losses is an application of the concept of comprehensive income.

Investments in debt securities that are in the **available-for-sale** category are reported at fair value. The unrealized gains and losses related to changes in the fair value of available-for-sale debt securities are recorded in an unrealized holding gain or loss account. This account is reported as other comprehensive income and as a separate component of stockholders' equity until realized. Thus, **changes in fair value are not reported as part of net income until the security is sold**. This approach reduces the volatility of net income.

Illustration: Single Security

To illustrate the accounting for available-for-sale securities, assume that Graff Corporation purchases $100,000, 10%, 5-year bonds on January 1, 2001, with interest payable on July 1 and January 1. The bonds sell for $108,111 which results in a bond premium of $8,111 and an effective interest rate of 8%.

The entry to record the purchase of the bonds is as follows:

January 1, 2001

Available-for-Sale Securities	108,111	
Cash		108,111

Illustration 18-6 discloses the effect of the premium amortization on the interest revenue recorded each period using the effective interest method.

ILLUSTRATION 18-6
Schedule of Interest
Revenue and Bond
Premium Amortization—
Effective Interest Method

10% Bonds Purchased to Yield 8%			
Date	Cash Received	Interest Revenue	Bond Premium Amortization	Carrying Amount of Bonds
1/1/01				$108,111
7/1/01	$ 5,000ᵃ	$ 4,324ᵇ	$ 676ᶜ	107,435ᵈ
1/1/02	5,000	4,297	703	106,732
7/1/02	5,000	4,269	731	106,001
1/1/03	5,000	4,240	760	105,241
7/1/03	5,000	4,210	790	104,451
1/1/04	5,000	4,178	822	103,629
7/1/04	5,000	4,145	855	102,774
1/1/05	5,000	4,111	889	101,885
7/1/05	5,000	4,075	925	100,960
1/1/06	5,000	4,040	960	100,000
	$50,000	$41,889	$8,111	

ᵃ$5,000 = $100,000 × .10 × 6/12
ᵇ$4,324 = $108,111 × .08 × 6/12
ᶜ$676 = $5,000 − $4,324
ᵈ$107,435 = $108,111 − $676

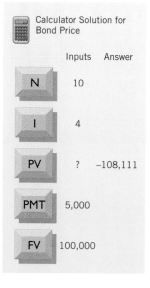

Calculator Solution for Bond Price

	Inputs	Answer
N	10	
I	4	
PV	?	−108,111
PMT	5,000	
FV	100,000	

The entry to record interest revenue on July 1, 2001, would be as follows:

July 1, 2001

Cash	5,000	
Available-for-Sale Securities		676
Interest Revenue		4,324

At December 31, 2001, Graff would make the following entry to recognize interest revenue:

December 31, 2001

Interest Receivable	5,000	
Available-for-Sale Securities		703
Interest Revenue		4,297

As a result, Graff would report interest revenue for 2001 of $8,621 ($4,324 + $4,297).

To apply the fair value method to these debt securities, assume that at year-end the fair value of the bonds is $105,000. Comparing this fair value with the carrying amount (amortized cost) of the bonds at December 31, 2001, as shown in Illustration 18-6, Graff recognizes an unrealized holding loss of $1,732 ($106,732 − $105,000). This loss is reported as other comprehensive income and as a separate component of stockholders' equity. The entry is as follows:

December 31, 2001

Unrealized Holding Gain or Loss—Equity	1,732	
Securities Fair Value Adjustment (Available-for-Sale)		1,732

A valuation account is used instead of crediting the Available-for-Sale Securities account. The use of the Securities Fair Value Adjustment (Available-for-Sale) account enables the company to maintain a record of its amortized cost. Because the adjustment account has a credit balance in this case, it is subtracted from the balance of the Available-for-Sale Securities account to arrive at fair value. The fair value is the amount reported on the balance sheet. At each reporting date, the bonds would be reported at fair value with an adjustment to the Unrealized Holding Gain or Loss—Equity account.

Illustration: Portfolio of Securities

To illustrate the accounting for a portfolio of securities, assume that Webb Corporation has two debt securities that are classified as available-for-sale. Illustration 18-7 provides information on amortized cost, fair value, and the amount of the unrealized gain or loss.

ILLUSTRATION 18-7
Computation of
Securities Fair Value
Adjustment—Available-
for-Sale Securities (2002)

Available-for-Sale Debt Security Portfolio December 31, 2002			
Investments	Amortized Cost	Fair Value	Unrealized Gain (Loss)
Watson Corporation 8% bonds	$ 93,537	$103,600	$ 10,063
Anacomp Corporation 10% bonds	200,000	180,400	(19,600)
Total of portfolio	$293,537	$284,000	(9,537)
Previous securities fair value adjustment balance			0
Securities fair value adjustment—Cr.			$ (9,537)

The total fair value of Webb's available-for-sale portfolio is $284,000. The gross unrealized gains are $10,063 and the gross unrealized losses are $19,600 resulting in a net unrealized loss of $9,537. That is, the fair value of available-for-sale securities is $9,537 lower than its amortized cost. An adjusting entry is made to a valuation allowance to record the decrease in value and to record the loss as follows:

December 31, 2002

Unrealized Holding Gain or Loss—Equity	9,537	
Securities Fair Value Adjustment (Available-for-Sale)		9,537

The unrealized holding loss of $9,537 is reported as other comprehensive income and a reduction of stockholders' equity. As indicated earlier, unrealized holding gains and losses related to investments that are classified in the available-for-sale category are not included in net income.

Sale of Available-for-Sale Securities

If bonds carried as investments in available-for-sale securities are sold before the maturity date, entries must be made to amortize the discount or premium to the date of sale and to remove from the Available-for-Sale Securities account the amortized cost of bonds sold. To illustrate, assume that the Webb Corporation sold the Watson bonds (from Illustration 18-7) on July 1, 2003, for $90,000. Assume that the entry to recognize the discount amortization and the receipt of interest through July 1, 2003, has been recorded and the amortized cost is $94,214. The computation of the realized loss is as follows:

ILLUSTRATION 18-8
Computation of Loss on
Sale of Bonds

Amortized cost (Watson bonds)	$94,214
Less: Selling price of bonds	90,000
Loss on sale of bonds	$ 4,214

The entry to record the sale of the Watson bonds is as follows:

July 1, 2003

Cash	90,000	
Loss on Sale of Securities	4,214	
Available-for-Sale Securities		94,214

This realized loss is reported in the Other Expenses and Losses section of the income statement. Assuming no other purchases and sales of bonds in 2003, Webb Corporation prepares the following information on December 31, 2003:

Available-for-Sale Debt Security Portfolio December 31, 2003			
Investments	Amortized Cost	Fair Value	Unrealized Gain (Loss)
Anacomp Corporation 10% bonds (total portfolio)	$200,000	$195,000	$(5,000)
Previous securities fair value adjustment balance—Cr.			(9,537)
Securities fair value adjustment—Dr.			$ 4,537

As shown in Illustration 18-9, Webb Corporation has an unrealized holding loss of $5,000. However, the Securities Fair Value Adjustment account already has a credit balance of $9,537. To reduce the adjustment account balance to $5,000, it is debited for $4,537, as follows:

December 31, 2003

Securities Fair Value Adjustment (Available-for-Sale)	4,537	
Unrealized Holding Gain or Loss—Equity		4,537

Financial Statement Presentation

Webb Corporation's December 31, 2003, balance sheet and the 2003 income statement would contain the following items and amounts (the Anacomp bonds are long-term investments but are not intended to be held to maturity):

ILLUSTRATION 18-10
Reporting of Available-
for-Sale Securities

Balance Sheet	
Current assets	
Interest receivable	$ xxx
Investments	
Available-for-sale securities, at fair value	$195,000
Stockholders' equity	
Accumulated other comprehensive loss	$ 5,000
Income Statement	
Other revenues and gains	
Interest revenue	$ xxx
Other expenses and losses	
Loss on sale of securities	$ 4,214

Some favor including the unrealized holding gain or loss in net income rather than showing it as other comprehensive income.[6] However, some companies, particularly financial institutions, noted that recognizing gains and losses on assets, but not liabilities, would introduce substantial volatility in net income. They argued that often hedges exist between assets and liabilities so that gains in assets are offset by losses in liabilities, and vice versa. In short, to recognize gains and losses only on the asset side is unfair and not representative of the economic activities of the company.

This argument was convincing to the FASB. As a result, these unrealized gains and losses are **not included in net income**. However, even this approach does not solve some of the problems, because volatility of capital still results. This is of concern to financial institutions because regulators restrict financial institutions' operations based

---

[6]In Chapter 4, we discussed the reporting of other comprehensive income and the concept of comprehensive income. "Reporting Comprehensive Income," *Statement of Financial Accounting Standards No. 130* (Norwalk, Conn.: FASB, 1997).

upon their level of capital. In addition, companies can still manage their net income by engaging in gains trading (i.e., selling the winners and holding the losers).

TRADING SECURITIES

Trading securities are held with the intention of selling them in a short period of time. Trading in this context means frequent buying and selling, and trading securities are used to generate profits from short-term differences in price. The holding period for these securities is generally less than 3 months and more probably is measured in days or hours. **These securities are reported at fair value, with unrealized holding gains and losses reported as part of net income. Any discount or premium is not amortized.** A holding gain or loss is the net change in the fair value of a security from one period to another, exclusive of dividend or interest revenue recognized but not received. In short, the FASB says to adjust the trading securities to fair value, at each reporting date. In addition, the change in value is reported as part of net income, not other comprehensive income.

To illustrate, assume that on December 31, 2002, Western Publishing Corporation determined its trading securities portfolio to be as shown in Illustration 18-11 (assume that 2002 is the first year that Western Publishing held trading securities). At the date of acquisition, these trading securities were recorded at cost, including brokerage commissions and taxes, in the account entitled Trading Securities. This is the first valuation of this recently purchased portfolio.

ILLUSTRATION 18-11
Computation of
Securities Fair Value
Adjustment—Trading
Securities Portfolio (2002)

Trading Debt Security Portfolio December 31, 2002			
Investments	Cost	Fair Value	Unrealized Gain (Loss)
Burlington Northern 10% bonds	$ 43,860	$ 51,500	$7,640
Chrysler Corporation 11% bonds	184,230	175,200	(9,030)
Time Warner 8% bonds	86,360	91,500	5,140
Total of portfolio	$314,450	$318,200	3,750
Previous securities fair value adjustment balance			0
Securities fair value adjustment—Dr.			$3,750

The total cost of Western's trading portfolio is $314,450. The gross unrealized gains are $12,780 ($7,640 + $5,140) and the gross unrealized losses are $9,030, resulting in a net unrealized gain of $3,750. The fair value of trading securities is $3,750 greater than its cost.

At December 31, an adjusting entry is made to a valuation allowance, referred to as Securities Fair Value Adjustment (Trading), to record the increase in value and to record the unrealized holding gain:

December 31, 2002

Securities Fair Value Adjustment (Trading)	3,750	
Unrealized Holding Gain or Loss—Income		3,750

Because the Securities Fair Value Adjustment account balance is a debit, it is added to the cost of the Trading Securities account to arrive at a fair value for the trading securities. The fair value of the securities is the amount reported on the balance sheet.

When securities are actively traded, the FASB believes that financial reporting is improved when the economic events affecting the company (changes in fair value) and related unrealized gains and losses are reported in the same period. Including changes in fair value in income provides more relevant information to current stockholders whose composition may be different next period.

INVESTMENTS IN EQUITY SECURITIES   SECTION 2

Equity securities are described as securities representing ownership interests such as common, preferred, or other capital stock. They also include rights to acquire or dispose of ownership interests at an agreed-upon or determinable price such as warrants, rights, and call options or put options. Convertible debt securities and redeemable preferred stocks are not treated as equity securities. When equity securities are purchased, their cost includes the purchase price of the security plus broker's commissions and other fees incidental to the purchase.

> **OBJECTIVE 2**
> Identify the categories of equity securities and describe the accounting and reporting treatment for each category.

The degree to which one corporation (investor) acquires an interest in the common stock of another corporation (investee) generally determines the accounting treatment for the investment subsequent to acquisition. Investments by one corporation in the common stock of another can be classified according to the percentage of the voting stock of the investee held by the investor:

> **INTERNATIONAL INSIGHT**
> Historically, consolidation practices in Europe differ in terms of how the group of companies is determined. The U.K. approach focuses on ownership and the legal right to control; in contrast, the German approach focuses on management control.

1. Holdings of less than 20% (fair value method)—investor has passive interest.
2. Holdings between 20% and 50% (equity method)—investor has significant influence.
3. Holdings of more than 50% (consolidated statements)—investor has controlling interest.

These levels of interest or influence and the corresponding valuation and reporting method that must be applied to the investment are graphically displayed in Illustration 18-12.

Percentage of Ownership	0% ⟶	⟶ 20% ⟵	⟶ 50% ⟵	⟶ 100%
Level of Influence	Little or None	Significant	Control	
Valuation Method	Fair Value Method	Equity Method	Consolidation	

ILLUSTRATION 18-12
Levels of Influence Determine Accounting Methods

The accounting and reporting for equity securities therefore depends upon the level of influence and the type of security involved, as shown in Illustration 18-13.

Category	Valuation	Unrealized Holding Gains or Losses	Other Income Effects
Holdings less than 20%			
1. Available-for-sale	Fair value	Recognized in other comprehensive income and as separate component of stockholders' equity	Dividends declared; gains and losses from sale.
2. Trading	Fair value	Recognized in net income	Dividends declared; gains and losses from sale.
Holdings between 20% and 50%	Equity	Not recognized	Proportionate shares of investee's net income (adjusted for appropriate amortization).
Holdings more than 50%	Consolidation	Not recognized	Not applicable

ILLUSTRATION 18-13
Accounting and Reporting for Equity Securities by Category

HOLDINGS OF LESS THAN 20%

As mentioned earlier, equity securities are recorded at cost. In some cases, cost is difficult to determine. For example, equity securities acquired in **exchange for noncash consideration** (property or services) should be recorded at (1) the fair value of the consideration given or (2) the fair value of the security received, whichever is more clearly determinable. The absence of clearly determinable values for the property or services or a market price for the security acquired may require the use of appraisals or estimates to arrive at a cost.

The purchase of two or more classes of securities for a lump sum price calls for the allocation of the cost to the different classes in some equitable manner. If fair values (market prices) are available for each class of security, the lump sum cost may be apportioned on the basis of the **relative fair values**. If the market price is available for one security but not for the other, the **incremental method** may be used and the market price assigned to the one and the cost excess to the other. If market prices are not available at the date of acquisition of several securities, it may be necessary to defer cost apportionment until evidence of at least one value becomes available. In some instances cost apportionment may have to wait until one of the securities is sold. In such cases, the proceeds from the sale of the one security may be subtracted from the lump sum cost, leaving the residual cost to be assigned as the cost of the other.[7]

When an investor has an interest of less than 20%, it is presumed that the investor has little or no influence over the investee. In such cases, if market prices are available, the investment is valued and reported subsequent to acquisition using the **fair value method**.[8] The fair value method requires that companies classify equity securities at acquisition as **available-for-sale securities** or **trading securities**. Because equity securities have no maturity date, they cannot be classified as held-to-maturity.

Available-for-Sale Securities

Available-for-sale securities when acquired are recorded at cost. To illustrate, assume that on November 3, 2002, Republic Corporation purchased common stock of three companies, each investment representing less than a 20% interest:

	Cost
Northwest Industries, Inc.	$259,700
Campbell Soup Co.	317,500
St. Regis Pulp Co.	141,350
Total cost	$718,550

These investments would be recorded as follows:

November 3, 2002

Available-for-Sale Securities	718,550	
Cash		718,550

---

[7]Accounting for numerous purchases of securities requires that information regarding the cost of individual purchases be preserved, as well as the dates of purchases and sales. If **specific identification** is not possible, the use of an **average cost** may be used for multiple purchases of the same class of security. The **first-in, first-out method** of assigning costs to investments at the time of sale is also acceptable and is normally employed.

[8]When market prices are not available, the investment is valued and reported at cost in periods subsequent to acquisition. This approach is often referred to as the **cost method**. Dividends are recognized as dividend revenue when received, and the portfolio is valued and reported at acquisition cost. No gains or losses are recognized until the securities are sold.

On December 6, 2002, Republic receives a cash dividend of $4,200 on its investment in the common stock of Campbell Soup Co. The cash dividend is recorded as follows:

December 6, 2002

Cash	4,200	
Dividend Revenue		4,200

All three of the investee companies reported net income for the year but only Campbell Soup declared and paid a dividend to Republic. But, as indicated before, when an investor owns less than 20% of the common stock of another corporation, it is presumed that the investor has relatively little influence on the investee. As a result, **net income earned by the investee is not considered a proper basis for recognizing income from the investment by the investor**. The reason is that the investee may choose to retain for use in the business increased net assets resulting from profitable operations. Therefore, **net income is not considered earned by the investor until cash dividends are declared by the investee**.

At December 31, 2002, Republic's available-for-sale equity security portfolio has the following cost and fair value:

Available-for-Sale Equity Security Portfolio
December 31, 2002

Investments	Cost	Fair Value	Unrealized Gain (Loss)
Northwest Industries, Inc.	$259,700	$275,000	$ 15,300
Campbell Soup Co.	317,500	304,000	(13,500)
St. Regis Pulp Co.	141,350	104,000	(37,350)
Total of portfolio	$718,550	$683,000	(35,550)
Previous securities fair value adjustment balance			0
Securities fair value adjustment—Cr.			$(35,550)

ILLUSTRATION 18-14
Computation of Securities Fair Value Adjustment—Available-for-Sale Equity Security Portfolio (2002)

For Republic's available-for-sale equity securities portfolio the gross unrealized gains are $15,300 and the gross unrealized losses are $50,850 ($13,500 + $37,350), resulting in a net unrealized loss of $35,550. The fair value of the available-for-sale securities portfolio is $35,550 less than its cost. As with available-for-sale **debt** securities, the net unrealized gains and losses related to changes in the fair value of available-for-sale **equity** securities are recorded in an Unrealized Holding Gain or Loss—Equity account that is reported as a **part of other comprehensive income and as a component of stockholders' equity until realized**. In this case, Republic prepares an adjusting entry debiting the Unrealized Holding Gain or Loss—Equity account and crediting the Securities Fair Value Adjustment account to record the decrease in fair value and to record the loss as follows:

December 31, 2002

Unrealized Holding Gain or Loss—Equity	35,550	
Securities Fair Value Adjustment (Available-for-Sale)		35,550

On January 23, 2003, Republic sold all of its Northwest Industries, Inc. common stock receiving net proceeds of $287,220. The realized gain on the sale is computed as follows:

Net proceeds from sale	$287,220
Cost of Northwest shares	259,700
Gain on sale of stock	$ 27,520

ILLUSTRATION 18-15
Computation of Gain on Sale of Stock

The sale is recorded as follows:

January 23, 2003

Cash	287,220	
Available-for-Sale Securities		259,700
Gain on Sale of Stock		27,520

In addition, assume that on February 10, 2003, Republic purchased 20,000 shares of Continental Trucking at a market price of $12.75 per share plus brokerage commissions of $1,850 (total cost, $256,850).

On December 31, 2003, Republic's portfolio of available-for-sale securities is as follows:

ILLUSTRATION 18-16
Computation of Securities Fair Value Adjustment—Available-for-Sale Equity Security Portfolio (2003)

Available-for-Sale Equity Security Portfolio December 31, 2003			
Investments	Cost	Fair Value	Unrealized Gain (Loss)
Continental Trucking	$256,850	$278,350	$21,500
Campbell Soup Co.	317,500	362,550	45,050
St. Regis Pulp Co.	141,350	139,050	(2,300)
Total of portfolio	$715,700	$779,950	64,250
Previous securities fair value adjustment balance—Cr.			(35,550)
Securities fair value adjustment—Dr.			$99,800

At December 31, 2003, the fair value of Republic's available-for-sale equity securities portfolio exceeds cost by $64,250 (unrealized gain). The Securities Fair Value Adjustment account had a credit balance of $35,550 at December 31, 2002. To adjust Republic's December 31, 2003, available-for-sale portfolio to fair value requires that the Securities Fair Value Adjustment account be debited for $99,800 ($35,550 + $64,250). The entry to record this adjustment is as follows:

December 31, 2003

Securities Fair Value Adjustment (Available-for-Sale)	99,800	
Unrealized Holding Gain or Loss—Equity		99,800

Trading Securities

The accounting entries to record trading equity securities are the same as for available-for-sale equity securities except for recording the unrealized holding gain or loss. For trading equity securities, the unrealized holding gain or loss is **reported as part of net income**. Thus, the account title Unrealized Holding Gain or Loss—Income is used. When a sale is made, the remainder of the gain or loss is recognized in income.

HOLDINGS BETWEEN 20% AND 50%

An investor corporation may hold an interest of less than 50% in an investee corporation and thus not possess legal control. However, as shown in the opening story about Coca-Cola, an investment in voting stock of less than 50% can still give Coke (the investor) the ability to exercise significant influence over the operating and financial policies of its bottlers.[9] To provide a guide for accounting for investors when 50% or less of the common voting stock is held and to develop an operational definition of "sig-

---

[9]"The Equity Method of Accounting for Investments in Common Stock," *Opinions of the Accounting Principles Board No. 18* (New York: AICPA, 1971), par. 17.

nificant influence," the APB in *Opinion No. 18* noted that ability to exercise influence may be indicated in several ways. Examples would be: representation on the board of directors, participation in policy-making processes, material intercompany transactions, interchange of managerial personnel, or technological dependency. Another important consideration is the extent of ownership by an investor in relation to the concentration of other shareholdings. However, substantial or majority ownership of the voting stock of an investee by another investor does not necessarily preclude the ability to exercise significant influence by the investor.[10]

Judgment is frequently required in determining whether an investment of 20% or more results in "significant influence" over the policies of an investee. In the late 1970s and early 1980s an increased number of "hostile" merger and takeover attempts created situations where "significant influence" over investees was difficult to determine. The FASB therefore provided examples of cases in which an investment of 20% or more might not enable an investor to exercise significant influence:

(a) The investee opposes the investor's acquisition of its stock. For example, the investee files suit against the investor, or files a complaint with a governmental regulatory agency.

(b) The investor and investee sign an agreement under which the investor surrenders significant shareholder rights. This commonly occurs when an investee is resisting a takeover attempt by the investor, and the investor agrees to limit its shareholding in the investee.

(c) The investor's ownership share does not result in "significant influence" because majority ownership of the investee is concentrated among a small group of shareholders who operate the investee without regard to the views of the investor.

(d) The investor needs or wants more financial information than that which is publicly issued by the investee, tries to obtain it from the investee, and fails.

(e) The investor tries and fails to obtain representation on the investee's board of directors.[11]

The FASB says this list of examples is not all-inclusive. It is meant to provide examples of the types of evidence requiring further analysis when determining whether or not an investor is able to exert "significant influence" over an investee.

To achieve a reasonable degree of uniformity in application of the "significant influence" criterion, the profession concluded that an investment (direct or indirect) of 20% or more of the voting stock of an investee should lead to a presumption that in the absence of evidence to the contrary, an investor has the ability to exercise significant influence over an investee.

In instances of "significant influence" (generally an investment of 20% or more), the investor is required to account for the investment using the **equity method**.

Equity Method

Under the equity method a substantive economic relationship is acknowledged between the investor and the investee. The investment is originally recorded at the cost of the shares acquired but is subsequently adjusted each period for changes in the net assets of the investee. That is, the **investment's carrying amount is periodically increased (decreased) by the investor's proportionate share of the earnings (losses) of the investee and decreased by all dividends received by the investor from the investee**. The equity method recognizes that investee's earnings increase investee's net assets, and that investee's losses and dividends decrease these net assets.

> **OBJECTIVE ③**
> Explain the equity method of accounting and compare it to the fair value method for equity securities.

---

[10]Ibid.

[11]"Criteria for Applying the Equity Method of Accounting for Investments in Common Stock," *Interpretations of the Financial Accounting Standards Board No. 35* (Stamford, Conn.: FASB, 1981).

To illustrate the equity method and compare it with the fair value method, assume that Maxi Company purchases a 20% interest in Mini Company. To apply the fair value method in this example, assume that Maxi does not have the ability to exercise significant influence and the securities are classified as available-for-sale. Where the equity method is applied in this example, assume that the 20% interest permits Maxi to exercise significant influence. The entries are shown in Illustration 18-17.

ILLUSTRATION 18-17
Comparison of Fair Value Method and Equity Method

Entries by Maxi Company

Fair Value Method		Equity Method	

On January 2, 2002, Maxi Company acquired 48,000 shares (20% of Mini Company common stock) at a cost of $10 a share.

Available-for-Sale Securities	480,000		Investment in Mini Stock	480,000	
Cash		480,000	Cash		480,000

For the year 2002, Mini Company reported net income of $200,000; Maxi Company's share is 20% or $40,000.

No entry			Investment in Mini Stock	40,000	
			Revenue from Investment		40,000

At December 31, 2002, the 48,000 shares of Mini Company have a fair value (market price) of $12 a share, or $576,000.

Securities Fair Value Adjustment			No entry
(Available-for-Sale)	96,000		
Unrealized Holding Gain			
or Loss—Equity		96,000	

On January 28, 2003, Mini Company announced and paid a cash dividend of $100,000; Maxi Company received 20% or $20,000.

Cash	20,000		Cash	20,000	
Dividend Revenue		20,000	Investment in Mini Stock		20,000

For the year 2003, Mini reported a net loss of $50,000; Maxi Company's share is 20% or $10,000.

No entry			Loss on Investment	10,000	
			Investment in Mini Stock		10,000

At December 31, 2003, the Mini Company 48,000 shares have a fair value (market price) of $11 a share, or $528,000.

Unrealized Holding Gain			No entry
or Loss—Equity	48,000		
Securities Fair Value Adjustment			
(Available-for-Sale)		48,000	

INTERNATIONAL INSIGHT

In the European Community, the Seventh Directive requires the use of the equity method of accounting for investments in affiliates. However, there is still strong disagreement internationally concerning accounting for such investments. Currently, some nations (U.S., U.K., Japan) require the use of the equity method; others (Sweden, Switzerland) do not.

UNDERLYING CONCEPTS

Revenue to be recognized should be earned and realized or realizable. A low level of ownership indicates that the income from an investee should be deferred until cash is received.

Note that under the fair value method only the cash dividends received from Mini Company are reported as revenue by Maxi Company. **The earning of net income by the investee is not considered a proper basis for recognition of income from the investment by the investor.** The reason is that increased net assets resulting from the investee's profitable operation may be permanently retained in the business by the investee. Therefore, revenue is not considered earned by the investor until dividends are received from the investee.

Under the equity method, Maxi Company reports as revenue its share of the net income reported by Mini Company; the cash dividends received from Mini Company are recorded as a decrease in the investment carrying value. As a result, the investor records its share of the net income of the investee in the year when it is earned. In this case, the investor can ensure that any net asset increases of the investee resulting from net income will be paid in dividends if desired. To wait until a dividend is received ignores the fact that the investor is better off if the investee has earned income.

Using dividends as a basis for recognizing income poses an additional problem. For example, assume that the investee reports a net loss, but the investor exerts influence to force a dividend payment from the investee. In this case, the investor reports income, even though the investee is experiencing a loss. **In other words, if dividends are used as a basis for recognizing income, the economics of the situation are not properly reported.**

Expanded Illustration of the Equity Method

Under the equity method, periodic investor revenue consists of the investor's proportionate share of investee earnings (adjusted to eliminate intercompany gains and losses) and **amortization of the difference between the investor's initial cost and the investor's proportionate share of the underlying book value of the investee at date of acquisition**. And, if the investee's net income includes extraordinary items, the investor treats a proportionate share of the extraordinary items as an extraordinary item, rather than as ordinary investment revenue before extraordinary items.

Assume that on January 1, 2002, Investor Company purchased 250,000 shares of Investee Company's 1,000,000 shares of outstanding common stock for $8,500,000. Investee Company's total net worth or book value was $30,000,000 at the date of Investor Company's 25% investment. Investor Company thereby paid $1,000,000 [$8,500,000 − .25($30,000,000)] in excess of book value. It was determined that $600,000 of this is attributable to its share of **undervalued depreciable assets** of Investee Company and $400,000 to **unrecorded goodwill**. Investor Company estimated the average remaining life of the undervalued assets to be 10 years and decided upon a 40-year amortization period for goodwill (the maximum length of time allowed). For the year 2002, Investee Company reported net income of $2,800,000 including an extraordinary loss of $400,000, and paid dividends at June 30, 2002 of $500,000 and at December 31, 2002 of $900,000. The following entries would be recorded on the books of Investor Company to report its long-term investment using the equity method.

January 1, 2002

Investment in Investee Stock	8,500,000	
Cash		8,500,000
(To record the acquisition of 250,000 shares of Investee Company common stock)		

June 30, 2002

Cash	125,000	
Investment in Investee Stock		125,000
[To record dividend received ($500,000 × .25) from Investee Company]		

The entries on December 31, however, are more complex. In addition to the dividend received, Investor Company must recognize its share of Investee Company's income. **Both an ordinary and extraordinary component must be recorded** by Investor Company, because Investee Company's income includes both. Furthermore, Investor Company paid more than the book value for an interest in Investee Company's net assets. As a result, this additional cost must be allocated to the proper accounting periods.

December 31, 2002

Investment in Investee Stock	700,000	
Loss from Investment (extraordinary)	100,000	
Revenue from Investment (ordinary)		800,000
[To record share of Investee Company ordinary income ($3,200,000 × .25) and extraordinary loss ($400,000 × .25)]		

December 31, 2002

Cash	225,000	
Investment in Investee Stock		225,000
[To record dividend received ($900,000 × .25) from Investee Company]		

December 31, 2002

Revenue from Investment (ordinary)	70,000	
Investment in Investee Stock		70,000

(To record amortization of investment cost in excess
of book value represented by:

Undervalued depreciable assets—$600,000 ÷ 10 = $60,000
Unrecorded goodwill—$400,000 ÷ 40 = 10,000
Total $70,000)

The investment in Investee Company is presented in the balance sheet of Investor Company at a carrying amount of $8,780,000 computed as shown below.

ILLUSTRATION 18-18
Computation of
Investment Carrying
Amount

Investment in Investee Company		
Acquisition cost, 1/1/02	$8,500,000	
Plus: Share of 2002 income before extraordinary item	800,000	$9,300,000
Less: Share of extraordinary loss	100,000	
Dividends received 6/30 and 12/31	350,000	
Amortization of undervalued depreciable assets	60,000	
Amortization of unrecorded goodwill	10,000	520,000
Carrying amount, 12/31/02		$8,780,000

In the preceding illustration the investment cost exceeded the underlying book value. In some cases, an investor may acquire an investment at a **cost less than the underlying book value**. In such cases specific assets are assumed to be **overvalued** and, if depreciable, the excess of the investee's book value over the investor's acquisition cost is amortized into investment revenue over the remaining lives of the assets. Investment revenue is increased under the presumption that the investee's net income as reported is actually understated because the investee is charging depreciation on overstated asset values.

Investee Losses Exceed Carrying Amount

If an investor's share of the investee's losses exceeds the carrying amount of the investment, should the investor recognize additional losses? Ordinarily the investor should discontinue applying the equity method and not recognize additional losses.

If the investor's potential loss is not limited to the amount of its original investment (by guarantee of the investee's obligations or other commitment to provide further financial support), however, or if imminent return to profitable operations by the investee appears to be assured, it is appropriate for the investor to recognize additional losses.[12]

Changing from and to the Equity Method

If the investor level of influence of ownership falls below that necessary for continued use of the equity method, a change must be made to the fair value method. And an investment in common stock of an investee that has been accounted for by other than the equity method may become qualified for use of the equity method by an increase in the level of ownership. Both of these situations are discussed and illustrated in Chapter 23.

Disclosures Required Under the Equity Method

The significance of an investment to the investor's financial position and operating results should determine the extent of disclosures. The following disclosures in the investor's financial statements generally apply to the equity method:

Go to the Digital Tool for
disclosures related to equity
investments.

---

[12]"The Equity Method of Accounting for Investments in Common Stock," op. cit., par. 19(i).

❶ The name of each investee and the percentage of ownership of common stock.

❷ The accounting policies of the investor with respect to investments in common stock.

❸ The difference, if any, between the amount in the investment account and the amount of underlying equity in the net assets of the investee.

❹ The aggregate value of each identified investment based on quoted market price (if available).

❺ When investments of 20% or more interest are in the aggregate material in relation to the financial position and operating results of an investor, it may be necessary to present summarized information concerning assets, liabilities, and results of operations of the investees, either individually or in groups, as appropriate.

In addition, the investor is expected to disclose the reasons for **not** using the equity method in cases of 20% or more ownership interest and *for* using the equity method in cases of less than 20% ownership interest.

HOLDINGS OF MORE THAN 50%

When one corporation acquires a voting interest of more than 50%—**controlling interest**—in another corporation, the investor corporation is referred to as the **parent** and the investee corporation as the **subsidiary**. The investment in the common stock of the subsidiary is presented as a long-term investment on the separate financial statements of the parent.

When the parent treats the subsidiary as an investment, **consolidated financial statements** are generally prepared instead of separate financial statements for the parent and the subsidiary. Consolidated financial statements disregard the distinction between separate legal entities and treat the parent and subsidiary corporations as a single economic entity. The subject of when and how to prepare consolidated financial statements is discussed extensively in advanced accounting. Whether or not consolidated financial statements are prepared, the investment in the subsidiary is generally accounted for on the parent's books **using the equity method** as explained in this chapter.

UNDERLYING CONCEPTS

The consolidation of financial results of different companies follows the economic entity assumption and disregards legal entities. The key objective is to provide useful information to financial statement users.

INTERNATIONAL INSIGHT

In contrast to U.S. firms, financial statements of non-U.S. companies often include both consolidated (group) statements and parent company financial statements.

OTHER REPORTING ISSUES   SECTION 3

We have identified the basic issues involved in accounting for investments in debt and equity securities. In addition, the following issues relate to both of these types of securities.

❶ Financial statement presentation
❷ Impairment of value
❸ Transfers between categories
❹ Fair value controversy

FINANCIAL STATEMENT PRESENTATION OF INVESTMENTS

Reclassification Adjustments

As indicated in Chapter 4, changes in unrealized holding gains and losses related to available-for-sale securities are reported as part of other comprehensive income. Companies have the option to display the components of other comprehensive income (1) in a combined statement of income and comprehensive income, (2) in a separate statement of comprehensive income that begins with net income, or (3) in a statement of stockholders' equity.

The reporting of changes in unrealized gains or losses in comprehensive income is straightforward unless securities are sold during the year. In this situation, double counting results when realized gains or losses are reported as part of net income but also are shown as part of other comprehensive income in the current period or in previous periods.

To ensure that gains and losses are not counted twice when a sale occurs, a **reclassification adjustment** is necessary. To illustrate, assume that Open Company has the following two available-for-sale securities in its portfolio at the end of 2001 (its first year of operations):

ILLUSTRATION 18-19
Available-for-Sale
Security Portfolio (2001)

Investments	Cost	Fair Value	Unrealized Holding Gain (Loss)
Lehman Inc. common stocks	$ 80,000	$105,000	$25,000
Woods Co. common stocks	120,000	135,000	15,000
Total of portfolio	$200,000	$240,000	40,000
Previous securities fair value adjustment balance			–0–
Securities fair value adjustment—Dr.			$40,000

If Open Company reports net income in 2001 of $350,000, a statement of comprehensive income would be reported as follows:

ILLUSTRATION 18-20
Statement of
Comprehensive Income
(2001)

OPEN CO. Statement of Comprehensive Income For the Year Ended 12/31/01	
Net income	$350,000
Other comprehensive income	
Holding gains arising during period	40,000
Comprehensive income	$390,000

During 2002, Open Company sold the Lehman Inc. common stock for $105,000 and realized a gain on the sale of $25,000 ($105,000 − $80,000). At the end of 2002, the fair value of the Woods Co. common stock increased an additional $20,000 to $155,000. The computation of the change in the securities fair value adjustment account is computed as follows:

ILLUSTRATION 18-21
Available-for-Sale
Security Portfolio (2002)

Investments	Cost	Fair Value	Unrealized Holding Gain (Loss)
Woods Co. common stocks	$120,000	$155,000	$35,000
Previous securities fair value adjustment balance—Dr.			(40,000)
Securities fair value adjustment—Cr.			$ (5,000)

Illustration 18-21 indicates that an unrealized holding loss of $5,000 should be reported in comprehensive income in 2002. In addition, Open Company realized a gain of $25,000 on the sale of the Lehman common stock. Comprehensive income includes both realized and unrealized components, and therefore the total holding gain (loss) recognized in 2002 is $20,000, computed as follows:

Unrealized holding gain (loss)	$ (5,000)
Realized holding gain	25,000
Total holding gain recognized	**$ 20,000**

ILLUSTRATION 18-22
Computation of Total
Holding Gain (Loss)

Open Company reports net income of $720,000 in 2002, which includes the realized gain on sale of the Lehman securities. A statement of comprehensive income for 2002 is shown in Illustration 18-23, indicating how the components of holding gains (losses) are reported.

OPEN COMPANY
Statement of Comprehensive Income
For the Year Ended 12/31/02

Net income (includes $25,000 realized gain on Lehman shares)		$720,000
Other comprehensive income		
Holding gains arising during period ($155,000 − $135,000)	$20,000	
Less: Reclassification adjustment for gains included in net income	(25,000)	(5,000)
Comprehensive income		$715,000

ILLUSTRATION 18-23
Statement of
Comprehensive Income
(2002)

In 2001, the unrealized gain on the Lehman Co. common stock was included in comprehensive income. In 2002, it was sold and the realized gain reported in net income which increases comprehensive income again. To avoid double counting this gain, a reclassification adjustment is made to eliminate the realized gain from the computation of comprehensive income.

A company has the option to display reclassification adjustments on the face of the financial statement in which comprehensive income is reported or it may disclose these reclassification adjustments in the notes to the financial statements.

Comprehensive Illustration

To illustrate the reporting of investment securities and related gain or loss on available-for-sale securities, assume that on January 1, 2001, Hinges Co. had cash and common stock of $50,000.[13] At that date the company had no other asset, liability, or equity balance. On January 2, Hinges Co. purchased for cash $50,000 of equity securities that are classified as available-for-sale. On June 30, Hinges Co. sold part of the available-for-sale security portfolio, realizing a gain as follows:

Fair value of securities sold	$22,000
Less: Cost of securities sold	20,000
Realized gain	$ 2,000

ILLUSTRATION 18-24
Computation of Realized
Gain

Hinges Co. did not purchase or sell any other securities during 2001. It received $3,000 in dividends during the year. At December 31, 2001, the remaining portfolio is:

Fair value of portfolio	$34,000
Less: Cost of portfolio	30,000
Unrealized gain	$ 4,000

ILLUSTRATION 18-25
Computation of
Unrealized Gain

The company's income statement for 2001 is shown in Illustration 18-26.

---

[13]This example adapted from Dennis R. Beresford, L. Todd Johnson and Cheri L. Reither "Is a Second Income Statement Needed?" *Journal of Accountancy*, April 1996, p. 71.

ILLUSTRATION 18-26
Income Statement

HINGES CO. Income Statement For the Year Ended December 31, 2001	
Dividend revenue	$3,000
Realized gains on investment in securities	2,000
Net income	$5,000

The company decides to report its change in the unrealized holding gain in a statement of comprehensive income as follows:

ILLUSTRATION 18-27
Statement of
Comprehensive Income

HINGES CO. Statement of Comprehensive Income For the Year Ended December 31, 2001		
Net income		$5,000
Other comprehensive income:		
Holding gains arising during the period	$6,000	
Less: Reclassification adjustment for gains included in net income	2,000	4,000
Comprehensive income		$9,000

Its statement of stockholders' equity would show the following:

ILLUSTRATION 18-28
Statement of
Stockholders' Equity

HINGES CO. Statement of Stockholders' Equity For the Year Ended December 31, 2001				
	Common Stock	Retained Earnings	Accumulated Other Comprehensive Income	Total
Beginning balance	$50,000	$–0–	$–0–	$50,000
Add: Net income		5,000		5,000
Other comprehensive income			4,000	4,000
Ending balance	$50,000	$5,000	$4,000	$59,000

A comparative balance sheet is shown below:

ILLUSTRATION 18-29
Comparative Balance
Sheet

HINGES CO. Comparative Balance Sheet		
	1/1/01	12/31/01
Assets		
Cash	$50,000	$25,000
Available-for-sale securities		34,000
Total assets	$50,000	$59,000
Stockholders' equity		
Common stock	$50,000	$50,000
Retained earnings		5,000
Accumulated other comprehensive income		4,000
Total stockholders' equity	$50,000	$59,000

This example indicates how an unrealized gain or loss on available-for-sale securities affects all the financial statements. It should be noted that the components that comprise accumulated comprehensive income must be disclosed.

Companies are required to present individual amounts for the three categories of investments either on the balance sheet or in the related notes. Trading securities should be reported at aggregate fair value as current assets. Individual held-to-maturity and available-for-sale securities are classified as current or noncurrent depending upon the circumstances.

Held-to-maturity securities should be classified as current or noncurrent, based on the maturity date of the individual securities. Debt securities identified as available-for-sale should be classified as current or noncurrent, based on maturities and expectations as to sales and redemptions in the following year. Equity securities identified as available-for-sale should be classified as current if these securities are available for use in current operations. Thus, if the invested cash used to purchase the equity securities is considered a contingency fund to be used whenever a need arises, then the securities should be classified as current.

For securities classified as available-for-sale and separately for securities classified as held-to-maturity, a company should describe:

(a) Aggregate fair value, gross unrealized holding gains, gross unrealized losses, and amortized cost basis by major security type (debt and equity).
(b) Information about the contractual maturities of debt securities. Maturity information may be combined in appropriate groupings such as (1) within 1 year, (2) after 1 year through 5 years, (3) after 5 years through 10 years, and (4) after 10 years.

In classifying investments, management's expressed intent should be supported by evidence, such as the history of the company's investment activities, events subsequent to the balance sheet date, and the nature and purpose of the investment.

Companies have to be extremely careful with debt securities held to maturity. If a debt security in this category is sold prematurely, the sale may "taint" the entire held-to-maturity portfolio. That is, a management's statement regarding "intent" is no longer as credible and, therefore, the securities might have to be reclassified; this could lead to unfortunate consequences. An interesting by-product of this situation is that companies that wish to retire their debt securities early are finding it difficult to do so; the holder will not sell because the securities are classified as held-to-maturity.

OBJECTIVE 4
Describe the disclosure requirements for investments in debt and equity securities.

Go to the Digital Tool for actual company disclosures related to investments and comprehensive income.

IMPAIRMENT OF VALUE

Every investment should be evaluated at each reporting date to determine if it has suffered a loss in value that is other than temporary (**impairment**). A bankruptcy or a significant liquidity crisis being experienced by an investee are examples of situations in which a loss in value to the investor may be permanent. **If the decline is judged to be other than temporary, the cost basis of the individual security is written down to a new cost basis.** The amount of the write-down is accounted for as a realized loss and, therefore, included in net income.

For debt securities, the impairment test is to determine whether "it is probable that the investor will be unable to collect all amounts due according to the contractual terms." **For equity securities**, the guideline is less precise. Any time realizable value is lower than the carrying amount of the investment, an impairment must be considered. Factors involved are the length of time and the extent to which the fair value has been less than cost, the financial condition and near-term prospects of the issuer, and the intent and ability of the investor company to retain its investment to allow for any anticipated recovery in fair value.

To illustrate an impairment, assume that Strickler Company holds available-for-sale bond securities with a par value and amortized cost of $1 million. The fair value of these securities is $800,000. Strickler has previously reported an unrealized loss on these securities of $200,000 as part of other comprehensive income. In evaluating the securities, Strickler now determines it probable that it will not be able to collect all amounts due. In this case, the unrealized loss of $200,000 will be reported as a loss on

OBJECTIVE 5
Discuss the accounting for impairments of debt and equity investments.

impairment of $200,000 and included in income, with the bonds stated at their new cost basis. The journal entry to record this impairment would be as follows:

Loss on Impairment	200,000	
Securities Fair Value Adjustment (Available-for-Sale)	200,000	
Unrealized Holding Gain or Loss—Equity		200,000
Available-for-Sale Securities		200,000

The new cost basis of the investment in debt securities is $800,000. Subsequent increases and decreases in the fair value of impaired available-for-sale securities are included as other comprehensive income.[14]

The impairment test used for debt and equity securities is based on a fair value test. This test is slightly different from the impairment test for loans discussed in Appendix 14A, which was based on discounted cash flows using the historical effective interest rate. The FASB rejected the discounted cash flow alternative for securities because of the availability of market price information.

TRANSFERS BETWEEN CATEGORIES

OBJECTIVE 6
Describe the accounting for transfer of investment securities between categories.

Transfers between any of the categories are accounted for at fair value. Thus, if available-for-sale securities are transferred to held-to-maturity investments, the new investment (held-to-maturity) is recorded at the date of transfer at **fair value** in the new category. Similarly, if held-to-maturity investments are transferred to available-for-sale investments, the new investments (available-for-sale) are recorded at **fair value**. This **fair value** rule assures that a company cannot escape recognition of fair value simply by transferring securities to the held-to-maturity category. Illustration 18-30 summarizes the accounting treatment for transfers. **This illustration assumes that adjusting entries to report changes in fair value for the current period are not yet recorded.**

FAIR VALUE CONTROVERSY

FASB Statement No. 115 leaves many issues unresolved. Many parties are dissatisfied with its results: some think it goes too far, others think it does not go far enough. In this section we look at some of the major unresolved issues.

Measurement Based on Intent

Debt securities can be classified as held-to-maturity, available-for-sale, or trading. As a result, three identical debt securities could be reported in three different ways in the financial statements. Some argue such treatment is confusing. Furthermore, the held-to-maturity category is based solely on intent, which is a subjective evaluation. What is not subjective is the market price of the debt instrument, which is observable in the marketplace. In other words, the three classifications are subjective, and therefore arbitrary classifications will result.

Gains Trading

Certain debt securities can be classified as held-to-maturity and therefore reported at amortized cost; other debt and equity securities can be classified as available-for-sale and reported at fair value with the unrealized gain or loss reported as other comprehensive income. In either case, a company can become involved in "gains trading" (also referred to as "cherry picking"). In gains trading, companies sell their "winners," reporting the gains in income, and hold on to the losers.

---

[14]Amortization of any discount related to the debt securities is not permitted after recording the impairment. The new cost basis of impaired held-to-maturity securities would not change unless additional impairment occurred.

ILLUSTRATION 18-30
Accounting for Transfers

Type of Transfer	Measurement Basis	Impact of Transfer on Stockholders' Equity	Impact of Transfer on Net Income
Transfer from Trading to Available-for-Sale	Security transferred at fair value at the date of transfer, which is the new cost basis of the security.	The unrealized gain or loss at the date of transfer increases or decreases stockholders' equity.	The unrealized gain or loss at the date of transfer is recognized in income.
Transfer from Available-for-Sale to Trading	Security transferred at fair value at the date of transfer, which is the new cost basis of the security.	The unrealized gain or loss at the date of transfer increases or decreases stockholders' equity.	The unrealized gain or loss at the date of transfer is recognized in income.
Transfer from Held-to-Maturity to Available-for-Sale*	Security transferred at fair value at the date of transfer.	The separate component of stockholders' equity is increased or decreased by the unrealized gain or loss at the date of transfer.	None
Transfer from Available-for-Sale to Held-to-Maturity	Security transferred at fair value at the date of transfer.	The unrealized gain or loss at the date of transfer carried as a separate component of stockholders' equity is amortized over the remaining life of the security.	None

Statement No. 115 states that these types of transfers should be rare.

Go to the Digital Tool for examples of the entries for recording transfers between categories.

Liabilities Not Fairly Valued

Many argue that if investment securities are going to be reported at fair value, so also should liabilities. They note that by recognizing changes in value on only one side (the asset side), a high degree of volatility can occur in the income and stockholders' equity amounts. It is further argued that financial institutions are involved in asset and liability management (not just asset management) and that viewing only one side may lead managers to make uneconomic decisions as a result of the accounting. Although the Board was sympathetic with this view, it noted that certain debt securities were still reported at amortized cost and that other types of securities were excluded from the scope of this standard. In addition, serious valuation issues arose in relation to some types of liabilities. As a result, liabilities were excluded from consideration.[15]

Subjectivity of Fair Values

Some people question the relevance of fair value measures for investments in securities, arguing in favor of reporting based on amortized cost. They believe that amortized cost provides relevant information because it focuses on the decision to acquire the asset, the earning effects of that decision that will be realized over time, and the ultimate recoverable value of the asset. They argue that fair value ignores those concepts and focuses instead on the effects of transactions and events that do not involve the

---

[15]In a recent preliminary report concerning valuation of financial instruments, the FASB indicated its support for valuing liabilities at fair value. "Reporting Financial Instruments and Certain Related Assets and Liabilities at Fair Value," *FASB Preliminary Views* (Norwalk, Conn.: FASB, 1999).

enterprise, reflecting opportunity gains and losses whose recognition in the financial statement is, in their view, not appropriate until they are realized.

SUMMARY

The major debt and equity securities and their reporting treatment are summarized below.

ILLUSTRATION 18-31
Summary of Treatment of Major Debt and Equity Securities

Category	Balance Sheet	Income Statement
Trading (debt and equity securities)	Investments shown at fair value. Current assets.	Interest and dividends are recognized as revenue. Unrealized holding gains and losses are included in net income.
Available-for-sale (debt and equity securities)	Investments shown at fair value. Current or long-term assets. Unrealized holding gains and losses are a separate component of stockholders' equity.	Interest and dividends are recognized as revenue. Unrealized holding gains and losses are **not** included in net income but in other comprehensive income.
Held-to-maturity (debt securities)	Investments shown at amortized cost. Current or long-term assets.	Interest is recognized as revenue.
Equity method and/or consolidation (equity securities)	Investments originally are carried at cost, are periodically adjusted by the investor's share of the investee's earnings or losses, and are decreased by all dividends received from the investee. Classified long term.	Revenue is recognized to the extent of the investee's earnings or losses reported subsequent to the date of investment (adjusted by amortization of the difference between cost and underlying book value).

KEY TERMS

amortized cost, *919*

available-for-sale securities, *922*

consolidated financial statements, *935*

controlling interest, *935*

debt securities, *919*

effective interest method, *921*

equity method, *931*

equity securities, *927*

exchange for noncash consideration, *928*

fair value, *919*

fair value method, *928*

gains trading, *941*

held-to-maturity securities, *920*

holding gain or loss, *926*

impairment, *939*

incremental method, *928*

investee, *927*

investor, *927*

parent, *935*

reclassification adjustments, *936*

relative fair values, *928*

Securities Fair Value Adjustment account, *923*

security, *918*

significant influence, *931*

subsidiary, *935*

trading securities, *926*

SUMMARY OF LEARNING OBJECTIVES

❶ Identify the three categories of debt securities and describe the accounting and reporting treatment for each category. (1) *Held-to-maturity debt securities* are carried and reported at amortized cost. (2) *Trading debt securities* are valued for reporting purposes at fair value, with unrealized holding gains or losses included in net income. (3) *Available-for-sale debt securities* are valued for reporting purposes at fair value, with unrealized holding gains or losses reported as other comprehensive income and as a separate component of stockholders' equity.

❷ Identify the categories of equity securities and describe the accounting and reporting treatment for each category. The degree to which one corporation (investor) acquires an interest in the common stock of another corporation (investee) generally determines the accounting treatment for the investment. Long-term investments by one corporation in the common stock of another can be classified according to the percentage of the voting stock of the investee held by the investor.

❸ Explain the equity method of accounting and compare it to the fair value method for equity securities. Under the equity method a substantive economic relationship is acknowledged between the investor and the investee. The investment is originally recorded at cost but is subsequently adjusted each period for changes in the net assets of the investee. That is, the investment's carrying amount is periodically increased (decreased) by the investor's proportionate share of the earnings (losses) of the investee and decreased by all dividends received by the investor from the investee. Under the fair value method the equity investment is reported by the investor at fair value each reporting period irrespective of the investee's earnings or dividends paid to the investor. The equity method is applied to investment holdings between 20% and 50% of ownership, whereas the fair value method is applied to holdings below 20%.

④ Describe the disclosure requirements for investments in debt and equity securities. A reclassification adjustment is necessary when realized gains or losses are reported as part of net income but also are shown as part of other comprehensive income in the current or in previous periods. Unrealized holding gains or losses related to available-for-sale securities should be reported in other comprehensive income and the aggregate balance as accumulated comprehensive income on the balance sheet. Trading securities should be reported at aggregate fair value as current assets. Individual held-to-maturity and available-for-sale securities are classified as current or noncurrent depending upon the circumstances. For available-for-sale and held-to-maturity securities, a company should describe: aggregate fair value, gross unrealized holding gains, gross unrealized losses, amortized cost basis by type (debt and equity), and information about the contractual maturity of debt securities.

⑤ Discuss the accounting for impairments of debt and equity investments. Impairments of debt and equity securities are losses in value that are determined to be other than temporary, are based on a fair value test, and are charged to income.

⑥ Describe the accounting for transfer of investment securities between categories. Transfers of securities between categories of investments are accounted for at fair value, with unrealized holding gains or losses treated in accordance with the nature of the transfer.

APPENDIX 18A

Special Issues Related to Investments

Special issues relate to accounting for investments: (1) revenue from investments in equity securities; (2) dividends received in stock; (3) stock rights; (4) cash surrender value of life insurance; and (5) accounting for funds.

REVENUE FROM INVESTMENTS IN EQUITY SECURITIES

Revenue recognized from investments—whether under the equity or the fair value method—should be included in the income statement of the investor. Under the fair value method, the dividends received (or receivable if declared but unpaid) are reported as dividend revenue.

OBJECTIVE ⑦
After studying Appendix 18A, you should be able to: Discuss the special issues that relate to accounting for investments.

The gains or losses on sales of investments also are factors in determining the net income for the period. The gain or loss resulting from the sale of long-term investments, unless it is the result of a major casualty, an expropriation, or the introduction of a new law prohibiting its ownership (which may be viewed as unusual and nonrecurring), is reported as **part of current income from operations** and is not an extraordinary item.

Dividends that are paid in some form of assets other than cash are called **property dividends**. In such instances, the fair market value of the property received becomes the basis for debiting an appropriate asset account and crediting Dividend Revenue.

Occasionally an investor receives a dividend that is in part, or entirely, a **liquidating dividend**.[1] The investor should reduce the investment account for the amount of the liquidating portion of the dividend and credit Dividend Revenue for the balance. To illustrate, assume that Donley Inc. purchases a 1% investment in Rodriguez Co. for $60,000 on December 31, 2001. In 2002, Rodriguez has no income but declares and pays a dividend of $3,000 to Donley. The entry by Donley to record this transaction is as follows:

Cash	3,000	
Available-for-Sale Securities		3,000

DIVIDENDS RECEIVED IN STOCK

If the investee corporation declares a dividend distributable in its own stock of the same class, instead of in cash, each stockholder owns a larger number of shares but retains the same proportionate interest in the firm as before. The issuing corporation has distributed no assets; it has merely transferred a specified amount of retained earnings to paid-in capital, thus indicating that this amount will not provide a basis in the future for cash dividends.

Therefore, shares received as a result of a stock dividend or stock split do not constitute revenue to the recipients. The reason they do not is that the recipients' interest in the issuing corporation is unchanged and the issuing corporation has not distributed any of its assets. The **recipient of such additional shares would make no formal entry**, but should make a memorandum entry and record a notation in the investments account to show that additional shares have been received.

Although no dollar amount is entered at the time of the receipt of stock dividends, the fact that additional shares have been received must be considered in computing the carrying amount of any shares sold. The cost of the original shares purchased (plus the effect of any adjustments under the equity method) now constitutes the total carrying amount of both those shares plus the additional shares received, because no price was paid for the additional shares. The carrying amount per share is computed by dividing the total shares into the carrying amount of the original shares purchased.

To illustrate, assume that 100 shares of Flemal Company common stock are purchased for $9,600, and that 2 years later the company issues to stockholders one additional share for every two shares held; 150 shares of stock that cost a total of $9,600 are then held. Therefore, if 60 shares are sold for $4,300, the carrying amount of the 60 shares would be computed as shown below, assuming that the investment has been accounted for under the fair value method.

ILLUSTRATION 18A-1
Computation of the Carrying Amount of Shares Received in a Stock Dividend

Cost of 100 shares originally purchased	$9,600
Cost of 50 shares received as stock dividend	0
Carrying amount of 150 shares held	$9,600

Carrying amount per share is $9,600/150, or $64.
Carrying amount of 60 shares sold is 60 × $64, or $3,840.

---

[1]A company can receive a dividend from preacquisition retained earnings of the investee, which the investor should treat as a liquidating dividend. From the investee's point of view, however, it is not a liquidating dividend.

The entry to record the sale is:

Cash	4,300	
Available-for-Sale Securities		3,840
Gain on Sale of Stock		460

A total of 90 shares is still retained, and they are carried in the Available-for-Sale Securities account at $9,600 − $3,840, or $5,760. Thus the carrying amount for those shares remaining is also $64 per share, or a total of $5,760 for the 90 shares.

STOCK RIGHTS

When a corporation is about to offer for sale additional shares of an issue already outstanding, it may forward to present holders of that issue certificates permitting them to purchase **additional shares in proportion to their present holdings**. These certificates represent rights to purchase additional shares and are called **stock rights**. In rights offerings, rights generally are issued on the basis of one right per share, but it may take many rights to purchase one new share.

The certificate representing the stock rights, called a **warrant**, states the number of shares that the holder of the right may purchase and also the price at which they may be purchased. If this price is less than the current market value of such shares, the rights have an intrinsic value, and from the time they are issued until they expire they may be purchased and sold like any other security.

Stock rights have three important dates:

1. The date the rights offering is announced.
2. The date as of which the certificates or rights are issued.
3. The date the rights expire.

From the date the right is announced until it is issued, the share of stock and the right are not separable, and the share is described as **rights-on**. After the certificate or right is received and up to the time it expires, the share and right can be sold separately. A share sold separately from an effective stock right is sold **ex-rights**.

When a right is received, the stockholders have actually received nothing that they did not have before, because the shares already owned brought them the right; they have received no distribution of the corporation assets. The carrying amount of the original shares held is now the carrying amount of those shares plus the rights, and it should be allocated between the two on the basis of their total market values at the time the rights are received. If the value allocated to the rights is maintained in a separate account, an entry would be made debiting Available-for-Sale Securities (Stock Rights) and crediting Available-for-Sale Securities.

Disposition of Rights

The investor who receives rights to purchase additional shares has three alternatives:

1. To exercise the rights by purchasing additional stock.
2. To sell the rights.
3. To permit them to expire without selling or using them.

If the investor buys additional stock, the carrying amount of the original shares allocated to the rights becomes a part of the carrying amount of the new shares purchased. If the investor sells the rights, the allocated carrying amount compared with the selling price determines the gain or loss on sale. If the investor permits the rights to expire, a loss is suffered, and the investment should be reduced accordingly. The following example illustrates the problem involved.

Shares owned before issuance of rights—100.
Cost of shares owned—$50 a share for a total cost of $5,000.
Rights received—one right for every share owned, or 100 rights; two
  rights are required to purchase one new share at $50.
Market value at date rights issued: Shares $60 a share
                                  Rights $3 a right

Total market value of shares (100 × $60)	$6,000
Total market value of rights (100 × $3)	300
Combined market value	$6,300

Cost allocated to stock: $\dfrac{\$6,000}{\$6,300} \times \$5,000 = \$4,761.90$

Cost allocated to rights: $\dfrac{\$300}{\$6,300} \times \$5,000 = \underline{\quad 238.10}$

                                          $\$5,000.00$

Cost allocated to each share of stock: $\dfrac{\$4,761.90}{100} = \$47.619$

Cost allocated to each right: $\dfrac{\$238.10}{100} = \$2.381$

The reduction in the carrying amount of the stock from $5,000 to $4,761.90 and the acquisition of the rights with an allocated cost of $238.10 would be recorded as follows:

Available-for-Sale Securities (Stock Rights)	238.10	
Available-for-Sale Securities		238.10

If some of the original shares are later sold, their cost for purposes of determining gain or loss on sale is $47.619 per share, as computed above. If 10 of the original shares are sold at $58 per share, the entry would be:

Cash	580.00	
Available-for-Sale Securities		476.19
Gain on Sale of Stock		103.81

Entries for Stock Rights

Rights may be sold or used to purchase additional stock or permitted to expire. If 40 rights to purchase 20 shares of stock are sold at $3.00 each, the entry is:

Cash	120.00	
Available-for-Sale Securities (Stock Rights)		95.24
Gain on Sale of Stock Rights		24.76

The amount removed from the stock rights account is the amount allocated to 40 rights, 40 × $2.381.

If rights to purchase 20 shares of stock are exercised and 20 additional shares are purchased at the offer price of $50, the entry is:

Available-for-Sale Securities	1,095.24	
Cash		1,000.00
Available-for-Sale Securities (Stock Rights)		95.24

If these shares are sold in the future, their cost should be considered to be $1,095.24, or $54.762 per share—the price paid of $50 per share plus the amount allocated to two rights of $4.762.

If the remaining 20 rights are permitted to expire, the amount allocated to these rights should be removed from the general ledger account by this entry:

Loss on Expiration of Stock Rights	47.62	
Available-for-Sale Securities (Stock Rights)		47.62

The balances of the general ledger investment accounts are shown in Illustration 18A-3.

Available-for-Sale Securities (Stock)			
Purchase of original 100 shares @ $50 per share	5,000.00	Cost allocated to 100 rights received	238.10
Purchase of 20 shares by exercise of rights	1,095.24	Sale of 10 shares of original purchase	476.19
		Balance	5,380.95
	6,095.24		6,095.24
Balance	5,380.95*		

*Analysis of Balance:

90 shares of original purchase, at allocated cost of $47.619 per share	$4,285.71
20 shares purchased through exercise of rights, carried at $54.762 per share (cash paid of $50.00, plus $4.762 for allocated cost of two rights)	1,095.24
Balance of account, as above	$5,380.95

Available-for-Sale Securities (Stock Rights)			
Cost allocated to 100 rights received	283.10	Sale of 40 rights	95.24
		Exercise of 40 rights	95.24
		Expiration of 20 rights	47.62
	238.10		238.10
Balance	–0–		

ILLUSTRATION 18A-3
Balances of General
Ledger Investment
Accounts

CASH SURRENDER VALUE OF LIFE INSURANCE

There are many different kinds of insurance. The kinds usually carried by businesses include (1) casualty insurance, (2) liability insurance, and (3) life insurance. Certain types of **life insurance** constitute an investment, whereas casualty insurance and liability insurance do not. The three common types of life insurance policies that companies often carry on the lives of their principal officers are (a) **ordinary life**, (b) **limited payment**, and (c) **term insurance**. During the period that ordinary life and limited payment policies are in force, there is a cash surrender value and a loan value. Term insurance ordinarily has no cash surrender value or loan value.

If the insured officers or their heirs are the beneficiaries of the policy, the premiums paid by the company represent expense to the company and, for income tax purposes, income (excluding the first $50,000 of coverage) to the officer insured. In this case the cash surrender value of the policy does not represent an asset to the company.

If the company, however, is the beneficiary and has the right to cancel the policy at its own option, the cash surrender value of the policy or policies is an asset of the company. Accordingly, part of the premiums paid is not an expense, because the cash surrender value increases each year. Only the difference between the premium paid and the increase in cash surrender value represents expense to the company.

For example, if Zima Corporation pays an insurance premium of $2,300 on a $100,000 policy covering its president and, as a result, the cash surrender value of the policy increases from $15,000 to $16,400 during the period, the entry to record the premium payment is:

Life Insurance Expense	900	
Cash Surrender Value of Life Insurance	1,400	
Cash		2,300

If the insured officer were to die halfway through the most recent period of coverage for which the $2,300 premium payment was made, the following entry would be made (assuming cash surrender value of $15,700 and refund of a pro rata share of the premium paid):

Cash [$100,000 + (1/2 of $2,300)]	101,150	
Cash Surrender Value of Life Insurance		16,400
Life Insurance Expense (1/2 × $900)		450
Gain on Life Insurance Coverage ($100,000 − $15,700)		84,300

The gain on life insurance coverage is not generally reported as an extraordinary item because it is considered to be a "normal" business transaction.

The cash surrender value of such life insurance policies should be reported in the balance sheet as a **long-term investment**, inasmuch as it is unlikely that the policies will be surrendered and canceled in the immediate future. The premium is not deductible for tax purposes, however, and the proceeds of such policies are not taxable as income.

To illustrate such a disclosure, Alico Inc. reported information related to its cash surrender value as follows:

ILLUSTRATION 18A-4
Disclosure of Cash
Surrender Value

ALICO INC.

Other investments (Note 4)	
Cash surrender value of life insurance	$448,000

Note 4. The company purchased as owner and beneficiary, individual life insurance policies on the lives of certain officers and employees as a means of funding substantially all of such additional benefits. The company's accounting policy with respect to such insurance coverage is to charge operations with the annual premium cost, net of increase in cash surrender value.

FUNDS

Assets may be set aside in special funds for specific purposes and, therefore, become unavailable for ordinary operations of the business. Assets segregated in the special funds are then available when needed for the intended purposes.

There are two general types of funds: (1) those in which cash is set aside to meet specific current obligations, and (2) those that are not directly related to current operations and are therefore in the nature of long-term investments.

Several funds of the first type, discussed in preceding chapters, include the following:

Fund	Purpose
Petty Cash Fund	Payment of small expenditures, in currency
Payroll Cash Account	Payment of salaries and wages
Dividend Cash Account	Payment of dividends
Interest Fund	Payment of interest on long-term debt

In general, these funds are used to handle more expeditiously the payments of certain current obligations, to maintain better control over such expenditures, and to divide adequately the responsibility for cash disbursements. They are ordinarily shown as current assets (as part of Cash if immaterial), because the obligations to which they relate are ordinarily current liabilities.

Funds of the second type are similar to long-term investments, as they do not relate directly to current operations. They are ordinarily shown in the long-term investments section of the balance sheet or in a separate section if relatively large in amount. The more common funds of this type and the purpose of each are listed below:

Fund	Purpose
Sinking Fund	Payment of long-term debt
Plant Expansion Fund	Purchase or construction of additional plant
Stock Redemption Fund	Retirement of capital stock (usually preferred stock)
Contingency Fund	Payment of unforeseen obligations

Because the cash set aside will not be needed until some time in the future, it is usually invested in securities so that revenue may be earned on the fund assets. The assets of a fund may or may not be placed in the hands of a trustee. If appointed, the trustee becomes the custodian of the assets, accounts to the company for them, and reports fund revenues and expenses.

Entries for Funds

To keep track of the assets, revenues, and expenses of funds, it is desirable to maintain separate accounts. For example, if a fund is kept for the redemption of a preferred stock issue that was issued with a redemption provision at par after a certain date, the following accounts relating to that fund might be kept:

Stock Redemption Fund Cash

Stock Redemption Fund Investments

Stock Redemption Fund Revenue

Stock Redemption Fund Expenses

Gain on Sale of Stock Redemption Fund Investments

Loss on Sale of Stock Redemption Fund Investments

When cash is transferred from the regular cash account, perhaps periodically, the entry is:

Stock Redemption Fund Cash	30,000	
Cash		30,000

Securities purchased by the fund are recorded at cost:

Stock Redemption Fund Investments	27,000	
Stock Redemption Fund Cash		27,000

If securities purchased for the fund are to be held temporarily, they would be treated in the accounts in the same manner as short-term investments, described earlier in this chapter. If they are to be held for a long period of time, they are treated in accordance with the entries described for long-term investments. In both cases the securities purchased are recorded at cost when acquired, but if bonds are purchased as long-term investments for the fund, premium or discount should be amortized.

If we assume that the entry above records the purchase at a premium of 10-year bonds of a par value of $25,000 on April 1, the issue date, and that the bonds bear interest at 8%, the entry for the receipt of semiannual interest on October 1 is:

Stock Redemption Fund Cash	1,000	
Stock Redemption Fund Revenue		1,000

At December 31, entries are made to record amortization of premium for 9 months and to accrue interest on the bonds for 3 months:

Stock Redemption Fund Revenue	150	
Stock Redemption Fund Investments		150
(To record amortization of premium for 9 months, 9/12 of 1/10 of $2,000)		
Interest Receivable on Stock Redemption Fund Investments	500	
Stock Redemption Fund Revenue		500
(To record accrued interest for 3 months, 3/12 of 8% of $25,000)		

Expenses of the fund paid are recorded by debiting Stock Redemption Fund Expenses and crediting Stock Redemption Fund Cash.

When the investments held by the fund are disposed of, the entries to record the sale are similar to regular stock sales. Any revenue and expense accounts set up to record fund transactions should be closed to Income Summary at the end of the accounting period and reflected in earnings of the current period.

The entry for retirement of the preferred stock is:

Preferred Stock	500,000	
Stock Redemption Fund Cash		500,000

Any balance remaining in the Stock Redemption Fund Cash account is transferred back to a general cash account.

In some cases, a company purchases its own stock or bonds when it is using a stock redemption fund or sinking fund. In these situations, the treasury stock should be deducted from common stock (or the Stockholders' Equity section), and treasury bonds should be deducted from bonds payable. Dividend revenue or interest revenue should not be recorded for these securities.

Distinction between Funds and Reserves

Although funds and reserves (appropriations) are not similar, they are sometimes confused because they may be related and often have similar titles. A simple distinction may be drawn: **A fund is always an asset and always has a debit balance; a reserve (if used only in the limited sense recommended) is an appropriation of retained earnings, always has a credit balance, and is never an asset.**

This distinction is illustrated by reconsidering the entries made in connection with a stock redemption fund discussed earlier. The fund was originally established by the entry:

Stock Redemption Fund Cash	30,000	
Cash		30,000

Some of this cash was used to purchase investments; the assets of the fund were then cash and investments. Ultimately the investments were sold, and the stock redemption fund cash was used to retire the preferred stock.

If the company chose to do so, it could establish an appropriation for stock redemption at the same time to reduce the retained earnings apparently available for dividends. Appropriated retained earnings is established by periodic transfers from retained earnings, as follows:

Retained Earnings	30,000	
Appropriation for Stock Redemption		30,000

It will have a credit balance and will be shown in the stockholders' equity section of the balance sheet. When the stock is retired by payment of cash from the stock redemption fund, the appropriation is transferred back to retained earnings:

Appropriation for Stock Redemption	500,000	
Retained Earnings		500,000

The fund was an asset accumulated to retire stock and had a debit balance; the appropriation was a subdivision of retained earnings and had a credit balance. The fund was used to redeem the stock; the appropriation was transferred back to retained earnings.

SUMMARY OF LEARNING OBJECTIVE FOR APPENDIX 18A

7 **Discuss the special issues that relate to accounting for investments.** The special issues that relate to investments are: recognizing revenue from investments in equity securities; recognizing dividends received in shares of stock (stock dividends and stock splits); allocating cost between stocks and stock rights; accounting for changes in the cash surrender value of life insurance; and accounting for assets set aside in special funds.

Accounting for Derivative Instruments

It has been said that until the early 1970s most financial managers worked in a cozy, if unthrilling world. Since then, however, constant change caused by volatile markets, new technology, and deregulation has increased the risks to businesses. For example, in 1971 currencies were allowed to float freely. After that came oil price shocks, high inflation, and wide swings in interest rates. The response from the financial community was to develop products to manage the risks due to changes in market prices.

These products—often referred to as derivatives—are useful for risk management because the fair values or cash flows of these instruments can be used to offset the changes in fair values or cash flows of the assets that are at risk. The growth in use of derivatives has been aided by the development of powerful computing and communication technology, which provides new ways to analyze information about markets as well as the power to process high volumes of payments.

UNDERSTANDING DERIVATIVES

In order to understand derivatives, consider the following examples.

Illustration—Forward Contract

Let's assume that you believe that the price of Microsoft's stock will increase substantially in the next three months. Unfortunately, you do not have the cash resources to purchase the stock today. You therefore enter into a contract with your broker for delivery of 100 shares of Microsoft stock in three months at the price of $110 per share. As a result of the contract, you **have received the right** to receive 100 shares of Microsoft stock in three months and you **have an obligation** to pay $110 per share at that time. In this situation you have entered into a **forward contract**, a type of derivative. The benefit of this derivative contract to you is that you are able to buy Microsoft stock today and take delivery in three months. If the price goes up, as you expect, you win. If the price goes down, you lose.

Illustration—Option Contract

Let's suppose that instead of entering into the forward contract for delivery of the stock in three months, you tell your broker that you are undecided about whether to purchase Microsoft stock and need two weeks to decide. You enter into a different type of contract with your broker, one that gives you the right to purchase Microsoft stock at its current price any time within the next two weeks. As part of the contract the broker charges you $300 for holding the contract open for two weeks at a set price. In this situation, you have entered into an **option contract**, another type of derivative. As a result of this contract, **you have received the right**, **but not the obligation** to purchase this stock. The benefit of this contract to you is that if the price of the Microsoft stock increases in the next two weeks, you exercise your option. In this case, the cost of the stock to you is the price of the stock stated in the contract plus the cost of the option contract. If the price does not increase, you do not exercise the contract but you incur a cost for the option.

For both the forward contract and the option contract, the delivery of the stock was for a future date and the value of the contract was based on the underlying asset—the Microsoft stock. These financial instruments are referred to as **derivatives** because their value is *derived from* values of other assets (for example, stocks, bonds, or commodities) or is related to a market-determined indicator (for example, interest rates or the Standard and Poor's 500 stock composite index).

In this chapter, we will discuss the accounting for three different types of derivatives:

❶ Financial forwards or financial futures.
❷ Options.
❸ Swaps.

WHO USES DERIVATIVES?

OBJECTIVE ⑧
After studying Appendix 18B, you should be able to: Explain who uses derivatives and why they are used.

Whether it is protection for changes in interest rates, the weather, stock prices, oil prices, or foreign currencies, derivative contracts can be used to smooth the fluctuations caused by various types of risks. In other words, any individual or company that wants to ensure against different types of business risks often can use derivative contracts to achieve this objective.

Producers and Consumers

To illustrate who might use derivatives, assume that Heartland Ag is a large producer of potatoes for the consumer market. Heartland believes the present price for potatoes is excellent, but unfortunately it will take two months to harvest its potatoes and deliver them to the market. Because Heartland Ag is concerned that the price of potatoes will drop, it signs a contract in which it agrees to sell its potatoes today at the current market price for delivery in two months.

Who would buy this contract? Suppose on the other side of the contract is McDonald's Corporation who wants to have potatoes (for French fries) in two months and is worried that prices will increase. McDonald's is therefore agreeable to delivery in two months at current prices because it knows that it will need potatoes in two months and that it can make an acceptable profit at this price level.

In this situation, if the price of potatoes increases before delivery, you might conclude that Heartland loses and McDonald's wins. Conversely, if prices decrease, Heartland wins and McDonald's loses. However the objective is not to gamble on the outcome. In other words, regardless of which way the price moves, both Heartland and McDonald's should be pleased because both have received a price at which an acceptable profit is obtained. In this case, Heartland is a **producer** and McDonald's is a **consumer**. Both companies are often referred to as **hedgers** because they are hedging their positions to ensure an acceptable financial result.

Commodity prices are volatile and depend on weather, crop disasters, and general economic conditions. For the producer and the consumer to plan effectively, it makes good sense to lock in specific future revenues or costs in order to run their businesses successfully.

Speculators and Arbitrageurs

In some cases, instead of McDonald's taking a position in the forward contract, a speculator may purchase the contract from Heartland. The **speculator** is betting that the price of potatoes will increase and therefore the value of the forward contract will increase. The speculator, who may be in the market for only a few hours, will then sell the forward contract to another speculator or to a company like McDonald's.

Another user of derivatives is **arbitrageurs**. These market players attempt to exploit inefficiencies in various derivative markets. They seek to lock in profits by simultaneously entering into transactions in two or more markets. For example, an arbitrageur might trade in a futures contract and at the same time in the commodity underlying the futures contract, hoping to achieve small price gains on the difference between the two. Speculators and arbitrageurs are very important to markets because they keep the market liquid on a daily basis.

WHY USE DERIVATIVES?

In the previous illustrations, we explained why Heartland Ag (the producer) and McDonald's (the consumer) would become involved in a derivative contract. Consider other types of situations that companies face.

❶ Airlines, like Delta, Southwest, and United, are affected by changes in the price of jet fuel.

❷ Financial institutions, such as Citigroup, Bankers Trust, and M&I Bank, are involved in borrowing and lending funds which are affected by changes in interest rates.

❸ Multinational corporations, like Cisco Systems, Coca-Cola, and General Electric, are subject to changes in foreign exchange rates.

It is not surprising therefore that you find most corporations involved in some form of derivatives transactions. Here are some reasons given by companies in their annual reports as to why they use derivatives:

❶ Exxon Mobil uses derivative instruments primarily for purposes of hedging its exposure to fluctuations in interest rates, foreign currency exchange rates, and hydrocarbon prices.

❷ Caterpillar's risk management policy includes the use of derivative financial instruments to manage foreign currency exchange rates, interest rates, and commodity price exposure.

❸ Johnson & Johnson uses derivative financial instruments to manage the impact of interest rate and foreign exchange rate changes on earnings and cash flows.

Many corporations therefore use derivatives extensively and successfully. However, derivatives can be dangerous, and it is critical that all parties involved understand the risks and rewards associated with these contracts.[1]

BASIC PRINCIPLES IN ACCOUNTING FOR DERIVATIVES

> **OBJECTIVE ❾**
> Understand the basic guidelines for accounting for derivatives.

In *SFAS No. 133*, the FASB concluded that derivatives such as forwards and options are assets and liabilities and should be reported in the balance sheet at **fair value**.[2] The Board believes that fair value will provide statement users the best information

---

[1]There are some well-publicized examples of companies that have suffered considerable losses using derivatives. For example, companies such as Showa Shell Sekiyu (Japan), Metallgesellschaft (Germany), Procter & Gamble (U.S.), and Air Products & Chemicals (U.S.) have incurred significant losses from investments in derivative instruments.

[2]Accounting for Derivative Instruments and Hedging Activities," *Statement of Financial Accounting Standards No. 133* (Stamford, Conn.: FASB, 1998). All derivative instruments, whether financial or not, are covered under this standard. Our discussion in this chapter focuses on derivative financial instruments because of their widespread use in practice.

about derivative financial instruments.[3] Relying on some other basis of valuation for derivatives, such as historical cost, does not make sense because many derivatives have a historical cost of zero. Furthermore, given the well-developed markets for derivatives and for the assets from which derivatives derive their value, the Board believed that reliable fair value amounts could be determined for derivative instruments.

On the income statement, any unrealized gain or loss should be recognized in income if the derivative is used for speculation purposes. If the derivative is used for hedging purposes, the accounting for any gain or loss depends on the type of hedge used. The accounting for hedged transactions is discussed later in the appendix.

In summary, the following guidelines are used in accounting for derivatives.

❶ Derivatives should be recognized in the financial statements as assets and liabilities.

❷ Derivatives should be reported at fair value.

❸ Gains and losses resulting from speculation in derivatives should be recognized immediately in income.

❹ Gains and losses resulting from hedge transactions are reported in different ways, depending upon the type of hedge.

ILLUSTRATION OF DERIVATIVE FINANCIAL INSTRUMENT — SPECULATION

OBJECTIVE ❿
Describe the accounting for derivative financial instruments.

To illustrate the measurement and reporting of a derivative financial instrument for speculative purposes, we examine a derivative whose value is related to the market price of Laredo Inc. common stock. As in the previous Microsoft example, you could realize a gain from the increase in the value of the Laredo shares with the use of a derivative financial instrument, such as a call option.[4] A **call option** gives the holder the right, but not the obligation to buy shares at a preset price (often referred to as the **strike price** or the **exercise price**).

For example, assume you enter into a call option contract with Baird Investment Co., which gives you the option to purchase Laredo stock at $100 per share.[5] If the price of Laredo stock increases above $100, you can exercise this option and purchase the shares for $100 per share. If Laredo's stock never increases above $100 per share, the call option is worthless and you recognize a loss.

Accounting Entries

To illustrate the accounting for a call option, assume that you purchased a call option contract on January 2, 2000, when Laredo shares are trading at $100 per share. The terms of the contract give you the option to purchase 1,000 shares (referred to as the

---

[3]*Fair value* is defined as the amount at which an asset (or liability) could be bought (incurred) or sold (settled) between two willing parties (i.e., not forced or in liquidation). Quoted market prices in active markets are the best evidence of fair value and should be used if available. In the absence of market prices, the prices of similar assets or liabilities or accepted present value techniques can be used. "Disclosures About Fair Value of Financial Instruments," *Statement of Financial Accounting Standards No. 107* (Stamford, Conn.: FASB, 1991) paras. 5–6, 11. The Board's long-term objective is to require fair value measurement and recognition for all financial instruments (*SFAS No. 133*, para. 216).

[4]You could use a different type of option contract—a **put option**—to realize a gain if you speculate that the Laredo stock will decline in value. A put option gives the holder the option to sell shares at a preset price. Thus, a put option **increases** in value when the underlying asset **decreases** in value.

[5]Baird Investment Company is referred to as the **counterparty**. Counterparties frequently are investment bankers or other entities that hold inventories of financial instruments.

notional amount) of Laredo stock at an option price of $100 per share; the option expires on April 30, 2000. You purchase the call option for $400 and make the following entry:

January 2, 2000

Call Option	400	
Cash		400

This payment (referred to as the **option premium**) is generally much less than the cost of purchasing the shares directly. The option premium is comprised of two amounts: (1) intrinsic value and (2) time value. The formula to compute the option premium is as follows:

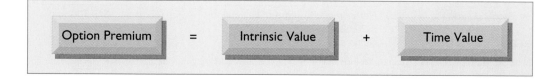

ILLUSTRATION 18B-1
Option Price Formula

Intrinsic value is the difference between the market price and the preset strike price at any point in time. It represents the amount realized by the option holder if the option were exercised immediately. On January 2, 2000, the intrinsic value is zero because the market price is equal to the preset strike price.

Time value refers to the option's value over and above its intrinsic value. Time value reflects the possibility that the option has a fair value greater than zero because there is some expectation that the price of Laredo shares will increase above the strike price during the option term. As indicated, the time value for the option is $400.[6]

On March 31, 2000, the price of Laredo shares has increased to $120 per share and the intrinsic value of the call option contract is now $20,000. That is, you could exercise the call option and purchase 1,000 shares from Baird Co. for $100 per share and then sell the shares in the market for $120 per share. This gives you a gain of $20,000 ($120,000 − $100,000) on the option contract.[7] The entry to record the increase in the intrinsic value of the option is as follows:

March 31, 2000

Call Option	20,000	
Unrealized Holding Gain or Loss—Income		20,000

A market appraisal indicates that the time value of the option at March 31, 2000, is $100.[8] The entry to record this change in value of the option is as follows:

March 31, 2000

Unrealized Holding Gain or Loss—Income	300	
Call Option ($400 − $100)		300

At March 31, 2000, the call option is reported in your balance sheet at fair value of $20,100.[9] The unrealized holding gain increases net income for the period, while the loss on the time value of the option decreases net income.

---

[6]This cost is estimated using option-pricing models, such as the Black-Scholes model. The fair value estimate is affected by the volatility of the underlying stock, the expected life of the option, the risk-free rate of interest, and expected dividends on the underlying stock during the option term.

[7]In practice, you generally do not have to actually buy and sell the Laredo shares to settle the option and realize the gain. This is referred to as the **net settlement** feature of option contracts.

[8]The decline in value reflects both the decreased likelihood that the Laredo shares will continue to increase in value over the option period and the shorter time to maturity of the option contract.

[9]As indicated earlier, the total value of the option at any point in time is equal to the intrinsic value plus the time value.

On April 1, 2000, the entry to record the settlement of the call option contract with Baird Investment Co. is as follows:

April 1, 2000

Cash	20,000	
Loss on Settlement of Call Option	100	
Call Option		20,100

Illustration 18B-2 summarizes the effects of the call option contract on your net income.

ILLUSTRATION 18B-2
Effect on Income—
Derivative Financial
Instrument

Date	Transaction	Income (Loss) Effect
March 31, 2000	Net increase in value of call option ($20,000 − $300)	$19,700
April 1, 2000	Settle call option	(100)
	Total net income	$19,600

The accounting summarized in Illustration 18B-2 is in accord with *SFAS No. 133*. That is, because the call option meets the definition of an asset, it is recorded in the balance sheet on March 31, 2000. Furthermore, the call option is reported at fair value with any gains or losses reported in income.

Differences between Traditional and Derivative Financial Instruments

What is the difference between a traditional and derivative financial instrument? A derivative financial instrument has three basic characteristics:[10]

1 **The instrument has (1) one or more underlyings and (2) an identified payment provision.** An underlying is a specified interest rate, security price, commodity price, index of prices or rates, or other market-related variable. Payment is determined by the interaction of the underlying with the face amount or the number of shares, or other units specified in the derivative contract (referred to as notional amounts). For example, the value of the call option increased in value when the value of the Laredo stock increased. In this case, the underlying was the stock price. The change in the stock price is multiplied by the number of shares (notional amount) to arrive at the payment provision.

2 **The instrument requires little or no investment at the inception of the contract.** To illustrate, you paid a small premium to purchase the call option—an amount much less than if the Laredo shares were purchased as a direct investment.

3 **The instrument requires or permits net settlement.** As indicated in the call option example, you could realize a profit on the call option without taking possession of the shares. This **net settlement** feature serves to reduce the transaction costs associated with derivatives.

Illustration 18B-3 summarizes the differences between traditional and derivative financial instruments. We use a trading security for the traditional financial instrument and a call option as an example of a derivative financial instrument.

---

[10]In *SFAS No. 133*, the FASB identifies these same features as the key characteristics of derivatives. The FASB used these broad characteristics so that the definitions and hence the standard could be applied to yet-to-be-developed derivatives (para 249).

Feature	Traditional Financial Instrument (Trading Security)	Derivative Financial Instrument (Call Option)
Payment provision	Stock price times the number of shares.	Change in stock price (underlying) times number of shares (notional amount).
Initial investment	Investor pays full cost.	Initial investment is much less than full cost.
Settlement	Deliver stock to receive cash.	Receive cash equivalent, based on changes in stock price times the number of shares.

ILLUSTRATION 18B-3
Features of Traditional and Derivative Financial Instruments

As indicated, to make the initial investment in Laredo stock (traditional financial instrument), you would have to pay the full cost of this stock. If you purchase the Laredo stock and the price increases, you could profit. But you also are at risk for a loss if the Laredo shares decline in value. In contrast, derivatives require little initial investment and most derivatives are not exposed to all risks associated with ownership in the underlying. For example, the call option contract can only increase in value. That is, if the price of Laredo stock falls below $100 per share, you will not exercise the option, because the call option is worthless.

Finally, unlike the situation with a traditional financial instrument, you could realize a profit on the call option (related to the price of the Laredo stock) without ever having to take possession of the shares. These distinctions between traditional and derivative financial instruments explain in part the popularity of derivatives but also suggest that the accounting might be different.

DERIVATIVES USED FOR HEDGING

Flexibility in use and the low-cost features of derivatives relative to traditional financial instruments explain why derivatives have become so popular in recent years. An additional use for derivatives is in risk management. For example, companies such as **Coca-Cola**, **Exxon**, and **General Electric**, which borrow and lend substantial amounts in credit markets are exposed to significant **interest rate risk**. That is, they face substantial risk that the fair values or cash flows of interest-sensitive assets or liabilities will change if interest rates increase or decrease. These same companies also have significant international operations and are exposed to **exchange rate risk**—the risk that changes in foreign currency exchange rates will negatively impact the profitability of their international businesses.

Because the value and/or cash flows of derivative financial instruments can vary according to changes in interest rates or foreign currency exchange rates, derivatives can be used to offset the risks that a firm's fair values or cash flows will be negatively impacted by these market forces. This use of derivatives is referred to as hedging.

SFAS No. 133 established accounting and reporting standards for derivative financial instruments used in hedging activities.[11] Special accounting is allowed for two types of hedges—fair value and cash flow hedges.[12]

---

[11]The hedge accounting provisions of *SFAS No. 133* are the major new elements in the standard and contain some of the more difficult accounting issues. The provisions were needed because of growth in the quantity and variety of derivative financial instruments used for hedging and due to the lack of, and inconsistency in, existing accounting standards for derivatives used in hedging transactions.

[12]*SFAS No. 133* also addresses the accounting for certain foreign currency hedging transactions. In general, these transactions are special cases of the two hedges discussed here. Understanding of foreign currency hedging transactions requires knowledge of consolidation of multinational entities, which is beyond the scope of this textbook.

OBJECTIVE ⓫
Explain how to account
for a fair value hedge.

Fair Value Hedge

In a *fair value hedge*, a derivative is used to hedge or offset the exposure to changes in the fair value of a recognized asset or liability or of an unrecognized firm commitment. In a perfectly hedged position, the gain or loss on the fair value of the derivative and that of the hedged asset or liability should be equal and offsetting. A common type of fair value hedge is the use of interest rate swaps (discussed below) to hedge the risk that changes in interest rates will impact the fair value of debt obligations. Another typical fair value hedge is the use of put options to hedge the risk that an equity investment will decline in value.

Interest Rate Swap—A Fair Value Hedge

Options and futures have certain disadvantages. First because they are traded on organized securities exchanges, options and futures have standardized terms and lack the flexibility needed to tailor contracts to specific circumstances. In addition, most types of derivatives have relatively short time horizons and therefore cannot be used to reduce any type of long-term risk exposure.

As a result, a very popular type of derivative used by many corporations is a swap. A **swap** is a transaction between two parties in which the first party promises to make a payment to the second party. Similarly the second party promises to make a simultaneous payment to the first party. The most common type of swap is the **interest rate swap**, in which one party makes payments based on a fixed or floating rate and the second party does just the opposite. In most cases, large money-center banks find the two parties and handle the flow of payments between the two parties, as shown below:

ILLUSTRATION 18B-4
Swap Transaction

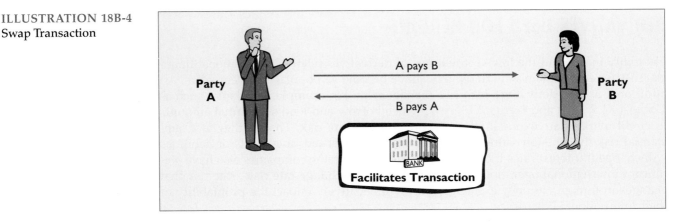

Accounting Entries

To illustrate the accounting for a fair value hedge, assume that Jones Company issues $1,000,000 of 5-year, 8% fixed-rate bonds on January 2, 2001. The entry to record this transaction is as follows:

January 2, 2001

Cash	1,000,000	
Bonds Payable		1,000,000

A fixed interest rate was offered to appeal to investors, but Jones is concerned that if market interest rates decline, the fair value of the liability will increase and the company will suffer an economic loss.[13] To protect against the risk of loss, Jones decides to hedge the risk of a decline in interest rates by entering into a 5-year **interest rate swap** contract. The terms of the swap contract to Jones are:

---

[13]This economic loss arises because Jones is locked into the 8% interest payments even if rates decline.

❶ Jones will receive fixed payments at 8% (based on the $1,000,000 amount).

❷ Jones will pay variable rates, based on the market rate in effect throughout the life of the swap contract. The variable rate at the inception of the contract is 6.8%.

As depicted in Illustration 18B-5, by using this swap Jones can change the interest on the bonds payable from a fixed rate to a variable rate.

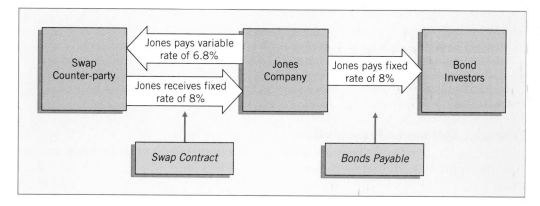

ILLUSTRATION 18B-5
Interest Rate Swap

The settlement dates for the swap correspond to the interest payment dates on the debt (December 31). On each interest payment (settlement date), Jones and the counterparty will compute the difference between current market interest rates and the fixed rate of 8% and determine the value of the swap.[14] As a result, if interest rates decline, the value of the swap contract to Jones increases (Jones has a gain), while at the same time Jones's fixed-rate debt obligation increases (Jones has an economic loss). The swap is an effective risk-management tool in this setting because its value is related to the same underlying (interest rates) that will affect the value of the fixed-rate bond payable. Thus, if the value of the swap goes up, it offsets the loss related to the debt obligation.

Assuming that the swap was entered into on January 2, 2001 (the same date as the issuance of the debt), the swap at this time has no value; therefore no entry is necessary:

January 2, 2001

No entry required. Memorandum to indicate that the swap contract is signed.

At the end of 2001, the interest payment on the bonds is made. The journal entry to record this transaction is as follows:

December 31, 2001

Interest Expense	80,000	
Cash (8% × $1,000,000)		80,000

At the end of 2001, market interest rates have declined substantially and therefore the value of the swap contract has increased. Recall (see Illustration 18B-5) that in the swap, Jones is to receive a fixed rate of 8%, or $80,000 ($1,000,000 × 8%), and pay a variable rate (which in this case is 6.8%), or $68,000. Jones therefore receives $12,000 ($80,000 − $68,000) as a settlement payment on the swap contract on the first interest payment date. The entry to record this transaction is as follows:

December 31, 2001

Cash	12,000	
Interest Expense		12,000

---

[14]The underlying for an interest rate swap is some index of market interest rates. The most commonly used index is the London Interbank Offer Rate, or LIBOR. In this example, we assumed the LIBOR is 6.8%.

In addition, a market appraisal indicates that the value of the interest rate swap has increased $40,000. This increase in value is recorded as follows:[15]

December 31, 2001

Swap Contract	40,000	
Unrealized Holding Gain or Loss—Income		40,000

This swap contract is reported in the balance sheet, and the gain on the hedging transaction is reported in the income statement. Because interest rates have declined, the company records a loss and a related increase in its liability as follows:

December 31, 2001

Unrealized Holding Gain or Loss—Income	40,000	
Bonds Payable		40,000

The loss on the hedging activity is reported in net income, and bonds payable in the balance sheet is adjusted to fair value.

Financial Statement Presentation

Illustration 18B-6 indicates how the asset and liability related to this hedging transaction are reported on the balance sheet.

ILLUSTRATION 18B-6
Balance Sheet
Presentation of Fair Value
Hedge

JONES COMPANY Balance Sheet (partial) December 31, 2001	
Current assets	
Swap contract	$40,000
Long-term liabilities	
Bonds payable	$1,040,000

The effect on the Jones Company balance sheet is the addition of the swap asset and an increase in the carrying value of the bonds payable. Illustration 18B-7 indicates how the effects of this swap transaction are reported in the income statement.

ILLUSTRATION 18B-7
Income Statement
Presentation of Fair Value
Hedge

JONES COMPANY Income Statement (partial) For the Year Ended December 31, 2001		
Interest expense ($80,000 − $12,000)		$68,000
Other income		
Unrealized holding gain—swap contract	$40,000	
Unrealized holding loss—bonds payable	(40,000)	
Net gain (loss)		$0

On the income statement, interest expense of $68,000 is reported. Jones has effectively changed the debt's interest rate from fixed to variable. That is, by receiving a fixed rate and paying a variable rate on the swap, the fixed rate on the bond payable is converted to variable, which results in an effective interest rate of 6.8% in 2001.[16] Also, the gain on the swap offsets the loss related to the debt obligation, and therefore the net gain or loss on the hedging activity is zero.

---

[15]Theoretically, this fair value change reflects the present value of expected future differences in variable and fixed interest rates.

[16]Similar accounting and measurement will be applied at future interest payment dates. Thus, if interest rates increase, Jones will continue to receive 8% on the swap (records a loss) but will also be locked into the fixed payments to the bondholders at an 8% rate (records a gain).

The overall impact of the swap transaction on the financial statements is shown in Illustration 18B-8.

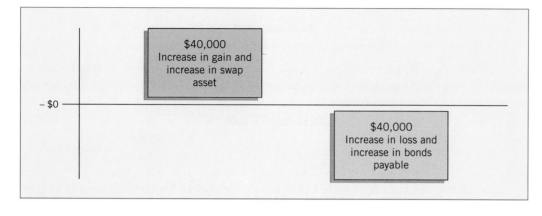

ILLUSTRATION 18B-8
Impact on Financial Statements of Fair Value Hedge

In summary, the accounting for fair value hedges (as illustrated in the Jones example) **records the derivative at its fair value in the balance sheet with any gains and losses recorded in income**. Thus, the gain on the swap offsets or hedges the loss on the bond payable due to the decline in interest rates. By adjusting the hedged item (the bond payable in the Jones case) to fair value, with the gain or loss recorded in earnings, the accounting for the Jones bond payable deviates from amortized cost. This special accounting is justified in order to report accurately the nature of the hedging relationship between the swap and the bond payable in the balance sheet (both the swap and the debt obligation are recorded at fair value) and in the income statement (offsetting gains and losses are reported in the same period).

Cash Flow Hedge

Cash flow hedges are used to hedge exposures to **cash flow risk**, which is exposure to the variability in cash flows. Special accounting is allowed for cash flow hedges. Generally, derivatives are measured and reported at fair value on the balance sheet, and gains and losses are reported directly in net income. However, derivatives used in cash flow hedges are accounted for at fair value on the balance sheet, but **gains or losses are recorded in equity as part of other comprehensive income**.

To illustrate the accounting for cash flow hedges, assume that in September 2000 Allied Can Co. anticipates purchasing 1,000 metric tons of aluminum in January 2001. Allied is concerned that prices for aluminum will increase in the next few months. To control its costs in producing cans, Allied wants to protect against possible price increases for aluminum inventory. To hedge the risk that it might have to pay higher prices for inventory in January 2001, Allied enters into an aluminum futures contract.

A **futures contract** gives the holder the right and the obligation to purchase an asset at a preset price for a specified period of time.[17] In this case, the aluminum futures contract gives Allied the right and the obligation to purchase 1,000 metric tons of aluminum for $1,550 per ton. This contract price is good until the contract expires in January 2001. The underlying for this derivative is the price of aluminum. If the price of aluminum rises above $1,550, the value of the futures contract to Allied increases, because Allied will be able to purchase the aluminum at the lower price of $1,550 per ton.[18]

OBJECTIVE 12
Explain how to account for a cash flow hedge.

INTERNATIONAL INSIGHT
Under IASC rules, unrealized holding gains or losses on cash flow hedges are recorded as adjustments to the value of the hedged item, not in other comprehensive income.

---

[17]A **futures contract** is a firm contractual agreement between a buyer and seller for a specified asset on a fixed date in the future. The contract also has a standard specification so both parties know exactly what is being traded. A **forward** is similar but is not traded on an exchange and does not have standardized conditions.

[18]As with the earlier call option example, the actual aluminum does not have to be exchanged. Rather, the parties to the futures contract settle by paying the cash difference between the futures price and the price of aluminum on each settlement date.

Assuming that the futures contract was entered into on September 1, 2000, and that the price to be paid today for inventory to be delivered in January—the **spot price**—was equal to the contract price, the futures contract has no value. Therefore no entry is necessary:

September 2000

No entry required. Memorandum to indicate that the futures contract is signed.

At December 31, 2000, the price for January delivery of aluminum has increased to $1,575 per metric ton. Allied would make the following entry to record the increase in the value of the futures contract:

December 31, 2000

Futures Contract	25,000	
Unrealized Holding Gain or Loss—Equity		25,000
([$1,575 − $1,550] × 1,000 tons)		

The futures contract is reported in the balance sheet as a current asset. The gain on the futures contract is reported as part of other comprehensive income. Since Allied has not yet purchased and sold the inventory, this is an **anticipated transaction**. In this type of transaction, gains or losses on the futures contract are accumulated in equity as part of other comprehensive income until the period in which the inventory is sold and earnings is affected.

In January 2001, Allied purchases 1,000 metric tons of aluminum for $1,575 and makes the following entry.[19]

January 2001

Aluminum Inventory	1,575,000	
Cash ($1,575 × 1,000 tons)		1,575,000

At the same time, Allied makes final settlement on the futures contract and makes the following entry:

January 2001

Cash	25,000	
Futures Contract ($1,575,000 − $1,550,000)		25,000

Through use of the futures contract derivative, Allied has been able to fix the cost of its inventory. The $25,000 futures contract settlement offsets the amount paid to purchase the inventory at the prevailing market price of $1,575,000, so that the net cash outflow is at $1,550 per metric ton, as desired. In this way, Allied has hedged the cash flow for the purchase of inventory, as depicted in Illustration 18B-9.

ILLUSTRATION 18B-9
Effect of Hedge on Cash Flows

Anticipated Cash Flows		Actual Cash Flows
Wish to fix cash paid for inventory at $1,550,000	=	Actual cash paid $1,575,000 Less: Cash received on futures contract (25,000) Final cash paid $1,550,000

There are no income effects at this point. The gain on the futures contract is accumulated in equity as part of other comprehensive income until the period when the inventory is sold and earnings is affected through cost of goods sold.

---

[19]In practice, futures contracts are settled on a daily basis; for our purposes we show only one settlement for the entire amount.

For example, assume that the aluminum is processed into finished goods (cans). The total cost of the cans (including the aluminum purchases in January 2001) is $1,700,000. Allied sells the cans in July 2001 for $2,000,000. The entry to record this sale is as follows:

July 2001

Cash	2,000,000	
Sales Revenue		2,000,000
Cost of Goods Sold	1,700,000	
Inventory (Cans)		1,700,000

Since the effect of the anticipated transaction has now affected earnings, Allied makes the following entry related to the hedging transaction:

July 2001

Unrealized Holding Gain or Loss—Equity	25,000	
Cost of Goods Sold		25,000

The gain on the futures contract, which was reported as part of other comprehensive income, now reduces cost of goods sold. As a result, the cost of aluminum included in the overall cost of goods sold is $1,550,000. The futures contract has worked as planned to manage the cash paid for aluminum inventory and the amount of cost of goods sold.

OTHER REPORTING ISSUES

The examples above illustrate the basic reporting issues related to the accounting for derivatives. Additional issues of importance are as follows:

1 The accounting for embedded derivatives.
2 Qualifying hedge criteria.
3 Disclosures about financial instruments and derivatives.

> **OBJECTIVE 13**
> Identify special reporting issues related to derivative financial instruments that cause unique accounting problems.

Embedded Derivatives

As indicated at the beginning of this appendix, a major impetus for unifying and improving the accounting standards for derivatives was the rapid innovation in the development of complex financial instruments. In recent years, this innovation has led to the development of **hybrid securities**, which have characteristics of both debt and equity and often are a combination of traditional and derivative financial instruments. For example, a convertible bond (as discussed in Chapter 17) is a hybrid instrument because it is comprised of a debt security, referred to as the **host security**, combined with an option to convert the bond to shares of common stock, the **embedded derivative**.

To provide consistency in accounting for similar derivative instruments, embedded derivatives are required to be accounted for similarly to other derivative instruments. Therefore, a derivative that is embedded in a hybrid security should be separated from the host security and accounted for using the accounting for derivatives. This separation process is referred to as **bifurcation**.[20] Thus, an investor in a convertible bond is required to separate the stock option component of the instrument and account for the derivative (the stock option) at fair value and the host instrument (the debt) according to GAAP, as if there were no embedded derivative.[21]

---

[20]Such a derivative can also be designated as a hedging instrument, and the hedge accounting provisions outlined earlier in the chapter would be applied.

[21]The **issuer** of the convertible bonds would not bifurcate the option component of the convertible bonds payable. *SFAS No. 133* explicitly precludes embedded derivative accounting for an embedded derivative that is indexed to an entity's own common stock. If the conversion feature was tied to **another company's** stock, this derivative would be bifurcated.

INTERNATIONAL INSIGHT

IASC qualifying hedge criteria are similar to those used in *SFAS No. 133.*

Qualifying Hedge Criteria

The FASB identified certain criteria that hedging transactions must meet before the special accounting for hedges is required; these criteria are designed to ensure that hedge accounting is used in a consistent manner across different hedge transactions. The general criteria relate to the following areas:

❶ Designation, documentation, and risk management. At inception of the hedge, there must be formal documentation of the hedging relationship, the entity's risk management objective, and the **strategy** for undertaking the hedge. Designation refers to identifying the hedging instrument, the hedged item or transaction, the nature of the risk being hedged, and how the hedging instrument will offset changes in the fair value or cash flows attributable to the hedged risk. The FASB decided that designation and documentation is critical to the implementation of the special hedge accounting model. Without these requirements, there was concern that companies would try to apply the hedge accounting provisions retroactively only in response to negative changes in market conditions, in order to offset the negative impact of a transaction on the financial statements. Allowing special hedge accounting in such a setting could mask the speculative nature of the original transaction.

❷ Effectiveness of the hedging relationship. At inception and on an ongoing basis, the hedging relationship is expected to be highly effective in achieving offsetting changes in fair value or cash flows. Assessment of effectiveness is required whenever financial statements are prepared. The general guideline for effectiveness is that the fair values or cash flows of the hedging instrument (the derivative) and the hedged item exhibit a high degree of correlation. In practice, high effectiveness is assumed when the correlation is close to one (for example, within plus or minus .10). In our earlier hedging examples (interest rate swap and the futures contract on aluminum inventory), the fair values and cash flows were exactly correlated. That is, when the cash payment for the inventory purchase increased, it was offset dollar for dollar by the cash received on the futures contract. If the effectiveness criterion is not met, either at inception or because of changes following inception of the hedging relationship, special hedge accounting is no longer allowed, and the derivative should be accounted for as a free-standing derivative.[22]

❸ Effect on reported earnings of changes in fair values or cash flows. A change in the fair value of a hedged item or variation in the cash flow of a hedged forecasted transaction must have the potential to change the amount recognized in reported earnings. There is no need for special hedge accounting, if both the hedging instrument and the hedged item are accounted for at fair value under existing GAAP. In this case, the offsetting gains and losses will be properly reflected in earnings. For example, special accounting is not needed for a fair value hedge of a trading security, because both the investment and the derivative are accounted for at fair value on the balance sheet with gains or losses reported in earnings. Thus, "special" hedge accounting is necessary only when there is a mismatch of the accounting effects for the hedging instrument and the hedged item under GAAP.[23]

---

[22]The accounting for the part of a derivative that is not effective in a hedge is at fair value with gains and losses recorded in income.

[23]An important criterion specific to cash flow hedges is that the forecasted transaction in a cash flow hedge "is likely to occur." This probability (defined as significantly greater than the term "more likely than not") should be supported by observable facts such as frequency of similar past transactions and the firm's financial and operational ability to carry out the transaction.

Disclosure Provisions

Because *SFAS No. 133* provides comprehensive accounting guidance for derivatives, this standard replaces the disclosure provisions in *SFAS No. 105* and *SFAS No. 119* and amends the disclosure rules in *SFAS No. 107*.[24] Thus, *SFAS No. 107* provides general guidance for traditional financial instrument disclosures, and *SFAS No. 133* addresses the disclosures for derivative financial instruments.

> **OBJECTIVE** 🔟
> Describe the disclosure requirements for traditional and derivative financial instruments.

As a consequence of these two pronouncements, the primary requirements for disclosures related to financial instruments are as follows:

❶ A company should disclose the fair value and related carrying value of its financial instruments in the body of the financial statements, in a note, or in a summary table form that makes it clear whether the amounts represent assets or liabilities.

❷ The fair value disclosures should distinguish between financial instruments held or issued for purposes other than trading. For derivative financial instruments, the firm should disclose its objectives for holding or issuing those instruments (speculation or hedging), the hedging context (fair value or cash flow), and its strategies for achieving risk management objectives.

❸ In disclosing fair values of financial instruments, a company should not combine, aggregate, or net the fair value of separate financial instruments, even if those instruments are considered to be related.

❹ A company should display as a separate classification of other comprehensive income the net gain or loss on derivative instruments designated in cash flow hedges.

❺ Companies are encouraged, but not required, to provide quantitative information about market risks of derivative financial instruments, and also of its other assets and liabilities, that is consistent with the way the company manages and adjusts risks and that is useful for comparing the results of its use of derivative financial instruments.

While these additional disclosures of fair value provide useful information to financial statement users, they are generally provided as supplemental information only. The balance sheet continues to rely primarily on historical cost. Exceptions to this general rule are the fair value requirements for certain investment securities and derivative financial instruments, as illustrated earlier. Illustration 18B-10 on page 966 provides a fair value disclosure for **Intel Corporation**.

The fair values of cash and cash equivalents, short-term investments, and short-term debt approximate cost because of the immediate and short-term maturities of these financial instruments. The fair value of marketable securities (and some derivatives) is based on quoted market prices at the reporting date. The fair value of long-term debt and some derivatives is based on market prices for similar instruments or by discounting expected cash flows at rates currently available to the company for instruments with similar risks and maturities.

UNDERLYING CONCEPTS

Providing supplemental information on the fair values of financial instruments illustrates application of the full disclosure principle.

If a company is unable to arrive at an estimate of fair value, it must disclose information relevant to the estimate of fair value (such as the terms of the instrument) and the reason why it is unable to arrive at an estimate of fair value.[25]

---

[24]*SFAS No. 105* refers to "Disclosure of Information about Financial Instruments with Off-Balance Sheet Risk and Financial Instruments with Concentrations of Credit Risk," *Statement of Financial Accounting Standards No. 105* (Stamford, Conn.: FASB, 1990). *SFAS No. 119* refers to "Disclosure about Derivative Financial Instruments and Fair Value of Financial Instruments," *Statement of Financial Accounting Standards No. 119* (Stamford, Conn.: FASB, 1994).

[25]*SFAS No. 107* lists a number of exceptions to this requirement; most of these exceptions are covered in other standards. The exception list includes such items as: pension and postretirement benefits; employee stock options; insurance contracts; lease contracts; warranties, rights, and obligations; purchase obligations; equity method investments; minority interests; and instruments classified as stockholders' equity in the entity's balance sheet.

ILLUSTRATION 18B-10
Intel Corporation Fair
Value Disclosure

INTEL CORPORATION

Fair values of financial instruments
The estimated fair values of financial instruments outstanding at fiscal year-ends were as follows:

(in millions)	1998		1997	
	Carrying Amount	Estimated Fair Value	Carrying Amount	Estimated Fair Value
Cash and cash equivalents	$2,038	$2,038	$4,102	$4,102
Short-term investments	4,821	4,821	5,561	5,561
Trading assets	316	316	195	195
Long-term investments	5,375	5,375	1,821	1,821
Non-marketable instruments	571	716	387	497
Options creating synthetic money market instruments	474	474	—	—
Swaps hedging investments in debt securities	(33)	(33)	64	64
Swaps hedging investments in equity securities	2	2	8	8
Short-term debt	(159)	(159)	(212)	(212)
Long-term debt redeemable within one year	—	—	(110)	(109)
Long-term debt	(702)	(696)	(448)	(448)
Swaps hedging debt	—	1	—	(1)
Currency forward contracts	(1)	(1)	26	28
Currency options	—	—	1	1

Summary of *SFAS No. 133*

Illustration 18B-11 provides a summary of the accounting provisions for derivatives and hedging transactions.

ILLUSTRATION 18B-11
Summary of Derivative
Accounting Under *SFAS
133*

Derivative Use	Accounting for Derivative	Accounting for Hedged Item	Common Example
Speculation	At fair value with unrealized holding gains and losses recorded in income.	Not applicable	Call or put option on an equity security.
Hedging			
Fair value	At fair value with holding gains and losses recorded in income.	At fair value with gains and losses recorded in income.	Interest rate swap hedge of a fixed-rate debt obligation.
Cash flow	At fair value with unrealized holding gains and losses from the hedge recorded in other comprehensive income and reclassified in income when the hedged transaction's cash flows affect earnings.	Use other generally accepted accounting principles for the hedged item.	Use of a futures contract to hedge a forecasted purchase of inventory.

As indicated in Illustration 18B-11, the general accounting for derivatives is based on fair values. *SFAS No. 133* also establishes **special accounting guidance** when derivatives are used **for hedging purposes**. For example, when an interest rate swap was used to hedge the bonds payable in a fair value hedge (see Jones Co. earlier), unrealized losses on the bonds payable were recorded in earnings, which is not GAAP for bonds issued without such a hedge. This special accounting is justified in order to accurately report the nature of the hedging relationship in the balance sheet (both the swap and the liability are recorded at fair value) and in the income statement (offsetting gains and losses are reported in the same period).

Special accounting also is used for cash flow hedges. Derivatives used in qualifying cash flow hedges are accounted for at fair value on the balance sheet, but unrealized holding gains or losses are recorded in other comprehensive income until the hedged item is sold or settled. In a cash flow hedge, the hedged item continues to be recorded at its historical cost.

COMPREHENSIVE HEDGE ACCOUNTING EXAMPLE

To demonstrate a comprehensive example of the hedge accounting provisions, using a fair value hedge, let's assume that on April 1, 2000, Hayward Co. purchased 100 shares of Sonoma stock at a market price of $100 per share. Hayward does not intend to actively trade this investment and consequently classifies the Sonoma investment as "available-for-sale." Hayward makes the following entry to record this available-for-sale investment:

April 1, 2000

Available-for-Sale Securities	10,000	
Cash		10,000

Available-for-sale securities are recorded at fair value on the balance sheet, and unrealized gains and losses are reported in equity as part of other comprehensive income.[26] Fortunately for Hayward, the value of the Sonoma shares increases to $125 per share during 2000. Hayward makes the following entry to record the gain on this investment:

December 31, 2000

Security Fair Value Adjustment (Available-for-Sale)	2,500	
Unrealized Holding Gain or Loss—Equity		2,500

Illustration 18B-12 indicates how the Sonoma investment is reported in Hayward's balance sheet:

HAYWARD CO. Balance Sheet (partial) December 31, 2000	
Assets	
Available-for-sale securities (at fair value)	$12,500
Stockholders' Equity	
Accumulated other comprehensive income	
Unrealized holding gain	$2,500

ILLUSTRATION 18B-12
Balance Sheet Presentation of Available-for-Sale Securities

While Hayward has benefited from an increase in the price of Sonoma shares, it is exposed to the risk that the price of the Sonoma stock will decline. To hedge this risk, Hayward locks in its gain on the Sonoma investment by purchasing a put option on 100 shares of Sonoma stock.

Hayward enters into the put option contract on January 2, 2001, and designates the option as a fair value hedge of the Sonoma investment. This put option (which expires in two years) gives Hayward the option to sell Sonoma shares at a price of $125. Since the exercise price is equal to the current market price, no entry is necessary at inception of the put option:[27]

---

[26]The distinction between trading and available-for-sale investments is discussed in Chapter 18.

[27]To simplify the example, we assume no premium is paid for the option.

January 2, 2001

No entry required. Memorandum to indicate that put option contract is signed and is designated as a fair value hedge for the Sonoma investment.

At December 31, 2001, the price of the Sonoma shares has declined to $120 per share. Hayward records the following entry for the Sonoma investment:

December 31, 2001

Unrealized Holding Gain or Loss—Income	500	
Security Fair Value Adjustment (Available-for-Sale)		500

Note that upon designation of the hedge, the accounting for the available-for-sale security changes from regular GAAP in that the unrealized holding loss is recorded in income, not in equity. If Hayward had not followed this accounting, a mismatch of gains and losses in the income statement would result. Thus, special accounting for the available-for-sale security is necessary in a fair value hedge.

The following journal entry records the increase in value of the put option on Sonoma shares:

December 31, 2001

Put Option	500	
Unrealized Holding Gain or Loss—Income		500

The decline in the price of Sonoma shares results in an increase in the fair value of the put option. That is, Hayward could realize a gain on the put option by purchasing 100 shares in the open market for $120 and then exercise the put option, selling the shares for $125. This results in a gain to Hayward of $500 (100 shares × [$125 − $120]).[28]

Illustration 18B-13 indicates how the amounts related to the Sonoma investment and the put option are reported.

ILLUSTRATION 18B-13
Balance Sheet
Presentation of Fair Value
Hedge

HAYWARD CO. Balance Sheet (partial) December 31, 2001	
Assets	
Available-for-sale securities (at fair value)	$12,000
Put option	$500

The increase in fair value on the option offsets or hedges the decline in value on Hayward's available-for-sale security. By using fair value accounting for both financial instruments, the financial statements reflect the underlying substance of Hayward's net exposure to the risks of holding Sonoma stock. By using fair value accounting for both these financial instruments, the balance sheet reports the amount that Hayward would receive on the investment and the put option contract if they were sold and settled respectively.

Illustration 18B-14 illustrates the reporting of the effects of the hedging transaction on income for the year ended December 31, 2001.

ILLUSTRATION 18B-14
Income Statement
Presentation of Fair Value
Hedge

HAYWARD CO. Income Statement (partial) For the Year Ended December 31, 2001	
Other Income	
Unrealized holding gain—put option	$500
Unrealized holding loss—available-for-sale securities	(500)

[28]In practice, Hayward generally does not have to actually buy and sell the Sonoma shares to realize this gain. Rather, unless the counterparty wants to hold Hayward shares, the contract can be "closed out" by having the counterparty pay Hayward $500 in cash. This is an example of the net settlement feature of derivatives.

The income statement indicates that the gain on the put option offsets the loss on the available-for-sale securities.[29] The reporting for these financial instruments, even when they reflect a hedging relationship, illustrates why the FASB argued that fair value accounting provides the most relevant information about financial instruments, including derivatives.

CONTROVERSY AND CONCLUDING REMARKS

SFAS No. 133 represents FASB's effort to develop accounting guidance for derivatives. Many believe that these new rules are needed to properly measure and report derivatives in financial statements. Others argue that reporting derivatives at fair value results in unrealized gains and losses that are difficult to interpret. Concerns also were raised concerning the complexity and cost of implementing the standard, since prior to *SFAS No. 133,* many derivatives were not recognized in financial statements.

The FASB, as part of its due process, worked to respond to these concerns. For example, from the beginning of the project in 1992, the FASB held over 100 meetings and received comments from over 400 constitutents or constituent groups. In response to these comments, the FASB revised the original proposal to make the provisions easier to apply. And recently, the FASB delayed the effective date for *SFAS No. 133* to give preparers more time to understand the standard and to develop the information systems necessary to implement the standard. More than 120 companies requested the delay, arguing that the rule could complicate companies' efforts to deal with the year 2000 (Y2K) problem. These Y2K problems arise when computers confuse the years 1900 and 2000 when making calculations.[30]

The authors believe that the long-term benefits of this standard will far outweigh any short-term implementation costs. As the volume and complexity of derivatives and hedging transactions continues to grow, the risk that investors and creditors will be exposed to unexpected losses arising from derivative transactions also increases. Without this standard, statement readers do not have comprehensive information in financial statements concerning many derivative financial instruments and the effects of hedging transactions using derivatives.

SUMMARY OF LEARNING OBJECTIVES FOR APPENDIX 18B

(8) Explain who uses derivatives and why they are used. Any company or individual that wants to ensure against different types of business risks often uses derivative contracts to achieve this objective. In general, these transactions involve some type of hedge. Speculators also are in the market, attempting to find an enhanced return. Speculators are very important to the market because they keep the market liquid on a daily basis. Arbitrageurs also are in the market and attempt to exploit inefficiencies in various derivative contracts. Derivatives are used primarily for purposes of hedging a company's exposure to fluctuations in interest rates, foreign currency exchange rates, and commodity prices.

KEY TERMS

anticipated transaction, *962*
bifurcation, *963*
call option, *954*
cash flow hedge, *961*
derivative financial instrument, derivative, *952*
designation, *964*
documentation, *964*
embedded derivative, *963*
fair value, *953*
fair value hedge, *958*
futures contract, *961*
hedging, *957*
highly effective, *964*
host security, *963*
hybrid security, *963*
interest rate swap, *958*
intrinsic value, *955*
net settlement, *955*
notional amount, *955*
option premium, *955*
put option, *954*
risk management, *964*
spot price, *962*
strike (exercise) price, *954*
swap, *958*
time value, *955*
underlying, *956*

---

[29]Note that the fair value changes in the option contract will not offset **increases** in the value of the Hayward investment. Should the price of Sonoma stock increase above $125 per share, Hayward would have no incentive to exercise the put option.

[30]The original implementation date was set for June 15, 1999; the proposal will delay this until June 15, 2000. Interestingly, some companies have adopted the standard early because the rules provide better accounting for some derivatives relative to the rules in place before *SFAS No. 133.* "U.S. Companies Find New Accounting Rule Costly, Inefficient," by Paula Froelich, Dow Jones News Service (March 2, 1999). It is likely that this standard will be amended to address various implementation issues in the near future.

⑨ Understand the basic guidelines for accounting for derivatives. Derivatives should be recognized in the financial statements as assets and liabilities and reported at fair value. Gains and losses resulting from speculation should be recognized immediately in income. Gains and losses resulting from hedge transactions are reported in different ways, depending upon the type of hedge.

⑩ Describe the accounting for derivative financial instruments. Derivative financial instruments are reported in the balance sheet and recorded at fair value. Except for derivatives used in hedging, realized and unrealized gains and losses on derivative financial instruments are recorded in income.

⑪ Explain how to account for a fair value hedge. The derivative used in a qualifying fair value hedge is recorded at its fair value in the balance sheet with any gains and losses recorded in income. In addition, the item being hedged with the derivative is also accounted for at fair value. By adjusting the hedged item to fair value, with the gain or loss recorded in earnings, the accounting for the hedged item may deviate from GAAP in the absence of a hedge relationship. This special accounting is justified in order to report accurately the nature of the hedging relationship between the derivative hedging instruments and the hedged item (both are reported in the balance sheet, with offsetting gains and losses reported in income in the same period).

⑫ Explain how to account for a cash flow hedge. Derivatives used in qualifying cash flow hedges are accounted for at fair value on the balance sheet, but gains or losses are recorded in equity as part of other comprehensive income. These gains or losses are accumulated and reclassified in income when the hedged transaction's cash flows affect earnings. Accounting is according to GAAP for the hedged item.

⑬ Identify special reporting issues related to derivative financial instruments that cause unique accounting problems. A derivative that is embedded in a hybrid security should be separated from the host security and accounted for using the accounting for derivatives. This separation process is referred to as bifurcation. Special hedge accounting is allowed only for hedging relationships that meet certain criteria. The main criteria are that (1) there is formal documentation of the hedging relationship, the entity's risk management objective, and the strategy for undertaking the hedge, and that the derivative is designated as either a cash flow or fair value hedge; (2) the hedging relationship is expected to be highly effective in achieving offsetting changes in fair value or cash flows; and (3) "special" hedge accounting is necessary only when there is a mismatch of the accounting effects for the hedging instrument and the hedged item under GAAP.

⑭ Describe the disclosure requirements for traditional and derivative financial instruments. Companies must disclose the fair value and related carrying value of its financial instruments, and these disclosures should distinguish between amounts that represent assets or liabilities. The disclosures should distinguish between financial instruments held or issued for purposes other than trading. For derivative financial instruments, the firm should disclose whether the instruments are used for speculation or hedging. In disclosing fair values of financial instruments, a company should not combine, aggregate, or net the fair value of separate financial instruments, even if those instruments are considered to be related. A company should display as a separate classification of other comprehensive income the net gain or loss on derivative instruments designated in cash flow hedges. Companies are encouraged, but not required, to provide quantitative information about market risks of derivative financial instruments.

A visit with
Penelope Flugger

PENELOPE FLUGGER is a Managing Director of J.P. Morgan & Co. She joined the company in 1975 as an assistant comptroller, assuming responsibility for the audit department in 1982. In 1994, she assumed responsibility for control and quality initiatives in Morgan's technology and operations group. Before joining Morgan, she was an audit manager with Price Waterhouse. She holds a bachelor's degree in accounting from the University of Illinois and an MBA from Baruch College, CUNY.

Investment Banking Accounting

There weren't very many women in the accounting profession when you started, were there? When I was a student at the University of Illinois in the early 1960s, there were very few women students. But I had some great professors who were very encouraging and gave me the confidence to go into public accounting. When I graduated, there were only two "Big Eight" firms in Chicago who would hire women. I went to work for Price Waterhouse in New York in 1964 on the audit staff. That summer, 225 people started at Price Waterhouse in New York. There was only one other woman.

Why did you leave public accounting? I had some very good clients, some of the top clients of the firm, so I was lucky in that respect. After a few years, I started to specialize in the brokerage industry, which I found very interesting. I was PW's banking industry specialist and was involved in the AICPA banking committee. But I decided that I wasn't cut out for public accounting, particularly the salesmanship aspect, and decided that I wanted to work for one of the three big banks in New York City—Citicorp, Morgan, or Chase. Luckily, I got job offers from all three, and took the one from Morgan.

Describe some highlights of your career at J.P. Morgan. Initially, I was in charge of the bank's accounting policy and procedures department as well as being in charge of SEC reporting. After a few years, I moved into areas such as international banking and consolidations. From there, I got involved in systems development, because I was very interested in how to make financial reporting easier. After about seven years, the firm asked if I would take over the internal audit department, where I spent about ten years, changing the approach to internal auditing and developing a training program so that we could use it as an entry-level recruiting tool.

What suggestions have you had in the teaching of accounting and auditing? I met the authors of your book when I was a member of the Accounting Education Change Commission. Part of my interest was that changes in accounting education weren't keeping up with what we needed. When I was in auditing, I was complaining that I was hiring from colleges but had to completely retrain these new graduates because they just didn't understand the business. Because internal auditing was so hard to recruit for, I spent time with professors at the schools where we were recruiting. The students were taught discrete things about accounting, marketing, etc. without any idea about how to put it together. They couldn't figure out how things would flow through an organization. I would see people who would pass the CPA exam but couldn't relate it to business.

What has been your role as chairman of the Financial Executives Institute? The FEI is an organization of 14,000 financial executives of major corporations. We represent our members with regulatory bodies such as the FASB, AICPA, etc. In financial accounting, the major issue is how to make sure that accounting reflects business reality. For instance, we'll mark an asset to market, but in a hedge transaction we don't mark the liability to market, so there often seems to be a disconnect between accounting principles and the business reality. You try to keep a balance so that you don't fix one side and create a bigger problem. We also have committees dealing with taxation, pension fund investment, employee benefits, etc. We try to get our voice heard on issues such as the balanced budget, tax reduction, and other initiatives that we think are important.

What are some major issues currently facing you at J.P. Morgan? With the current focus on business process re-engineering and quality, we're spending a lot of time trying to identify our fixed and variable costs. In an investment banking firm you've got to adjust your costs quickly as the markets go up and down. If you don't have a handle on what's fixed and what's variable, your profits get adversely affected, and the market doesn't wait to give you time to fix that. If you build a fixed-cost system that accommodates 20,000 trades a day, and all of a sudden you're trading only 5,000 transactions in that particular instrument, then you have quadrupled the cost to process those transactions.

What are some advantages of industry vs. public accounting for new graduates? If you know what industry you want to go into, then I think you have a leg up in industry. Industry has changed the way it treats entry-level people. Training is much better now than it used to be. And there are more options. If you like consulting work like you would get in public accounting, then we also have a track that allows you to do consulting work. My advice to students is that when they take a job, they should be having fun. If you don't enjoy the job but you have to do it for 40 more years, then that can be a horrible life sentence. Most students take their first job based on who they interview with and where they think the glamour is. That's unfortunate, because the person they interview with is probably not who they're going to work with.

Note: All **asterisked** Questions, Exercises, Problems, and Conceptual Cases relate to material contained in the appendixes to the chapter.

QUESTIONS

1 Distinguish between a debt security and an equity security.

2 What purpose does the variety in bond features (types and characteristics) serve?

3 What is the cost of a long-term investment in bonds?

4 What are the problems of accounting for bond investments between interest dates?

5 Identify and explain the three types of classifications for investments in debt securities.

6 When should a debt security be classified as held-to-maturity?

7 Explain how trading securities are accounted for and reported.

8 At what amount should trading, available-for-sale, and held-to-maturity securities be reported on the balance sheet?

9 Indicate how unrealized holding gains and losses should be reported for investment securities classified as trading, available-for-sale, and held-to-maturity.

10 (a) Assuming no Securities Fair Value Adjustment (Available-for-Sale) account balance at the beginning of the year, prepare the adjusting entry at the end of the year if Laura Company has an unrealized holding loss of $70,000 on its available-for-sale securities. (b) Assume the same information as part (a), except that Laura Company has a debit balance in its Securities Fair Value Adjustment (Available-for-Sale) account of $10,000 at the beginning of the year. Prepare the adjusting entry at year-end.

11 On July 1, 2002, Ingalls Company purchased $2,000,000 of Wilder Company's 8% bonds, due on July 1, 2009. The bonds, which pay interest semiannually on January 1 and July 1, were purchased for $1,750,000 to yield 10%. Determine the amount of interest revenue Ingalls should report on its income statement for year ended December 31, 2002.

12 If the bonds in question 11 are classified as available-for-sale and they have a fair value at December 31, 2002, of $1,802,000, prepare the journal entry (if any) at December 31, 2002, to record this transaction.

13 How is the premium or discount handled relative to a trading debt security?

14 On what basis should stock acquired or exchanged for noncash consideration be recorded?

15 Identify and explain the different types of classifications for investment in equity securities.

16 Why are held-to-maturity investments applicable only to debt securities?

17 Emily Company sold 10,000 shares of Dickinson Co. common stock for $27.50 per share, incurring $1,770 in brokerage commissions. These securities were classified as trading and originally cost $250,000. Prepare the entry to record the sale of these securities.

18 Distinguish between the accounting treatment for available-for-sale equity securities and trading equity securities.

19 What constitutes "significant influence" when an investor's financial interest is below the 50% level?

20 Explain how the investment account is affected by investee activities under the equity method.

21 When the equity method is applied, what disclosures should be made in the investor's financial statements?

22 Molly Pitcher Co. uses the equity method to account for investments in common stock. What accounting should be made for dividends received in excess of Pitcher's share of investee's earnings subsequent to the date of investment?

23 Louisa Inc. uses the equity method to account for investments in Alcott common stock. The purchase price paid by Louisa implies a fair value of Alcott's depreciable assets in excess of Alcott's net asset carrying values. How should Louisa account for this excess?

24 In applying the equity method, what recognition, if any, does the investor give to the excess of its investment cost over its proportionate share of the investee book value at the date of acquisition? What recognition, if any, is given if the investment cost is less than the underlying book value?

25 Elizabeth Corp. has an investment carrying value (equity method) on its books of $170,000 representing a 40% interest in Dole Company, which suffered a $620,000 loss this year. How should Elizabeth Corp. handle its proportionate share of Dole's loss?

26 Where on the asset side of the balance sheet are trading securities, available-for-sale securities, and held-to-maturity securities reported? Explain.

27 Explain why reclassification adjustments are necessary.

28 Briefly discuss how a transfer of securities from the available-for-sale category to the trading category affects stockholders' equity and income.

29 When is a debt security considered impaired? Explain how to account for the impairment of an available-for-sale debt security.

*30 How is a stock dividend accounted for by the recipient? How is a stock split accounted for by the recipient?

*31 What three dates are significant in relation to stock rights? What are the alternatives available to the recipient of stock rights?

*32 Rosie Jones Co. owns 300 shares of Barb Mucha Corporation common stock acquired on June 10, 2002, at a total cost of $12,000. On December 2, 2003, Rosie Jones received 300 stock rights from Barb Mucha. Each right entitles the holder to acquire one share of stock for $45. The market price of Barb Mucha's stock on this date, ex-rights, was $50, and the market price of each right was $5. Rosie Jones sold its rights the same date for $5 a right less a $90 commission. Determine the gain on sale of the rights by Rosie Jones.

*33 Distinguish between a fund and a reserve.

*34 What are the two general types of funds? Give three examples of each type of fund.

*35 What is meant by the term underlying as it relates to derivative financial instruments?

*36 What are the main distinctions between a traditional financial instrument and a derivative financial instrument?

*37 What is the purpose of a fair value hedge?

*38 In what situation will bonds payable carrying amounts not be reported at cost or amortized cost?

*39 Why might a company become involved in an interest rate swap contract to receive fixed interest payments and pay variable?

*40 What is the purpose of a cash flow hedge?

*41 Where are gains and losses related to cash flow hedges involving anticipated transactions reported?

*42 What are hybrid securities? Give an example of a hybrid security.

BRIEF EXERCISES

BE18-1 Moonwalker Company purchased, as a held-to-maturity investment, $50,000 of the 9%, 5-year bonds of Prime Time Corporation for $46,304, which provides an 11% return. Prepare Moonwalker's journal entries for (a) the purchase of the investment, and (b) the receipt of annual interest and discount amortization. Assume effective interest amortization is used.

BE18-2 Mask Corporation purchased, as a held-to-maturity investment, $40,000 of the 8%, 5-year bonds of Phantasy Star, Inc. for $43,412, which provides a 6% return. The bonds pay interest semiannually. Prepare Masks' journal entries for (a) the purchase of the investment, and (b) the receipt of semiannual interest and premium amortization. Assume effective interest amortization is used.

BE18-3 Use the information from BE18-1, but assume the bonds are purchased as an available-for-sale security. Prepare Moonwalker's journal entries for (a) the purchase of the investment, (b) the receipt of annual interest and discount amortization, and (c) the year-end fair value adjustment. The bonds have a year-end fair value of $47,200.

BE18-4 Use the information from BE18-2, but assume the bonds are purchased as an available-for-sale security. Prepare Mask's journal entries for (a) the purchase of the investment, (b) the receipt of semiannual interest and premium amortization, and (c) the year-end fair value adjustment. Assume the first interest payment is received on December 31, when the fair value of the bonds is $42,900.

BE18-5 Pete Sampras Corporation purchased for $22,500 as a trading investment bonds with a face value of $20,000. At December 31, Sampras received annual interest of $2,000, and the fair value of the bonds was $20,900. Prepare Sampras' journal entries for (a) the purchase of the investment, (b) the interest received, and (c) the fair value adjustment.

BE18-6 Pacman Corporation purchased 300 shares of Galaga Inc. common stock as an available-for-sale investment for $9,900. During the year, Galaga paid a cash dividend of $3.25 per share. At year-end, Galaga stock was selling for $34.50 per share. Prepare Pacman's journal entries to record (a) the purchase of the investment, (b) the dividends received, and (c) the fair value adjustment.

BE18-7 Use the information from BE18-6, but assume the stock was purchased as a trading security. Prepare Pacman's journal entries to record (a) the purchase of the investment, (b) the dividends received, and (c) the fair value adjustment.

BE18-8 Penn Corporation purchased for $300,000 a 25% interest in Teller, Inc. This investment enables Penn to exert significant influence over Teller. During the year Teller earned net income of $180,000 and paid dividends of $60,000. Prepare Penn's journal entries related to this investment.

BE18-9 Muhammad Corporation purchased for $630,000 a 30% interest in Ali Corporation on January 2, 2002. At that time, the book value of Ali's net assets was $1,900,000. Any excess of cost over book value is attributable to unrecorded goodwill with a useful life of 20 years. Prepare Muhammad's December 31, 2002, entry to amortize the excess of cost over book value.

BE18-10   The following information relates to Cargill Co. for 2001: net income, $800,000; unrealized holding gain of $20,000 related to available-for-sale securities during the year; accumulated other comprehensive income of $60,000 on January 1, 2001. Determine (a) other comprehensive income for 2001, (b) comprehensive income for 2001, and (c) accumulated other comprehensive income at December 31, 2001.

*BE18-11   Rocky Corporation owns 200 shares of Bullwinkle, Inc. which cost $11,000 and are held as an available-for-sale investment. Rocky receives 20 shares of Bullwinkle as a stock dividend and later sells 60 shares for $3,340. Prepare Rocky's entry to record receipt of the stock dividend and the sale of 60 shares.

*BE18-12   In 2001, Rolling Thunder Corporation purchased 200 shares of Twin Cobra common stock for $8,000. In July, Rolling Thunder received rights to purchase 50 shares of stock (1 right received for every 4 shares held) for $35 each. When the rights are received, the fair values are $42 per share of stock and $12 per right. In August, the rights are sold for $625. Prepare Rolling Thunder's journal entries to record the receipt of the rights and the sale of the rights.

*BE18-13   Three Kingdoms Corporation paid an insurance premium of $3,150 on a life insurance policy covering its president. As a result, the cash surrender value of the policy increased from $20,550 to $22,468. Prepare Three Kingdoms' journal entry to record the premium payment.

*BE18-14   Seaquest Corporation established a sinking fund by transferring $100,000 from the regular cash account. At the same time, the corporation established a $100,000 retained earnings appropriation for bond retirement. Prepare Seaquest's journal entries to record these transactions.

EXERCISES

E18-1   (Entries for Debt Securities)   On July 1, 2001, Barone Corporation purchased $200,000 of the 9%, 10-year bonds of Wayne Company for $185,216. This investment will provide Barone an effective yield of 11%. Interest is received semiannually on June 30 and December 31. The bonds have a fair value of $188,500 on December 31, 2001.

Instructions
Prepare journal entries for Barone to record (1) the purchase of these securities and (2) any entries required at December 31, 2001, assuming:

   (a)   Barone intends, and has the ability, to hold these securities to maturity.
   (b)   Barone does not intend to hold these securities to maturity.

E18-2   (Entries for Held-to-Maturity Securities)   On January 1, 2001, Hi and Lois Company purchased 12% bonds, having a maturity value of $300,000, for $322,744.44. The bonds provide the bondholders with a 10% yield. They are dated January 1, 2001, and mature January 1, 2006, with interest receivable December 31 of each year. Hi and Lois Company uses the effective interest method to allocate unamortized discount or premium. The bonds are classified in the held-to-maturity category.

Instructions
   (a)   Prepare the journal entry at the date of the bond purchase.
   (b)   Prepare a bond amortization schedule.
   (c)   Prepare the journal entry to record the interest received and the amortization for 2001.
   (d)   Prepare the journal entry to record the interest received and the amortization for 2002.

E18-3   (Entries for Available-for-Sale Securities)   Assume the same information as in E18-2 except that the securities are classified as available-for-sale. The fair value of the bonds at December 31 of each year-end is as follows:

2001	$320,500	2004	$310,000
2002	$309,000	2005	$300,000
2003	$308,000		

Instructions
   (a)   Prepare the journal entry at the date of the bond purchase.
   (b)   Prepare the journal entries to record the interest received and recognition of fair value for 2001.
   (c)   Prepare the journal entry to record the recognition of fair value for 2002.

E18-4   (Effective Interest versus Straight-Line Bond Amortization)   On January 1, 2001, Phantom Company acquires $200,000 of Spiderman Products, Inc., 9% bonds at a price of $185,589. The interest is payable each December 31, and the bonds mature December 31, 2003. The investment will provide Phantom Company a 12% yield. The bonds are classified as held-to-maturity.

Instructions

(a) Prepare a 3-year schedule of interest revenue and bond discount amortization, applying the straight-line method.

(b) Prepare a 3-year schedule of interest revenue and bond discount amortization, applying the effective interest method.

(c) Prepare the journal entry for the interest receipt of December 31, 2002, and the discount amortization under the straight-line method.

(d) Prepare the journal entry for the interest receipt of December 31, 2002, and the discount amortization under the effective interest method.

E18-5 (Entries for Available-for-Sale and Trading Securities) The following information is available for Barkley Company at December 31, 2001, regarding its investments:

Securities	Cost	Fair Value
3,000 shares of Myers Corporation Common Stock	$40,000	$48,000
1,000 shares of Cole Incorporated Preferred Stock	25,000	22,000
	$65,000	$70,000

Instructions

(a) Prepare the adjusting entry (if any) for 2001, assuming the securities are classified as trading.

(b) Prepare the adjusting entry (if any) for 2001, assuming the securities are classified as available-for-sale.

(c) Discuss how the amounts reported in the financial statements are affected by the entries in (a) and (b).

E18-6 (Trading Securities Entries) On December 21, 2001, Tiger Company provided you with the following information regarding its trading securities.

December 31, 2001

Investments (Trading)	Cost	Fair Value	Unrealized Gain (Loss)
Clemson Corp. stock	$20,000	$19,000	$(1,000)
Colorado Co. stock	10,000	9,000	(1,000)
Buffaloes Co. stock	20,000	20,600	600
Total of portfolio	$50,000	$48,600	(1,400)
Previous securities fair value adjustment balance			–0–
Securities fair value adjustment—Cr.			$(1,400)

During 2002, Colorado Company stock was sold for $9,400. The fair value of the stock on December 31, 2002, was: Clemson Corp. stock—$19,100; Buffaloes Co. stock—$20,500.

Instructions

(a) Prepare the adjusting journal entry needed on December 31, 2001.

(b) Prepare the journal entry to record the sale of the Colorado Company stock during 2002.

(c) Prepare the adjusting journal entry needed on December 31, 2002.

E18-7 (Available-for-Sale Securities Entries and Reporting) Rams Corporation purchases equity securities costing $73,000 and classifies them as available-for-sale securities. At December 31, the fair value of the portfolio is $65,000.

Instructions

Prepare the adjusting entry to report the securities properly. Indicate the statement presentation of the accounts in your entry.

E18-8 (Available-for-Sale Securities Entries and Financial Statement Presentation) At December 31, 2000, the available-for-sale equity portfolio for Steffi Graf, Inc., is as follows:

Security	Cost	Fair Value	Unrealized Gain (Loss)
A	$17,500	$15,000	($2,500)
B	12,500	14,000	1,500
C	23,000	25,500	2,500
Total	$53,000	$54,500	1,500
Previous securities fair value adjustment balance—Dr.			400
Securities fair value adjustment—Dr.			$1,100

On January 20, 2001, Steffi Graf, Inc. sold security A for $15,100. The sale proceeds are net of brokerage fees.

Instructions
(a) Prepare the adjusting entry at December 31, 2000, to report the portfolio at fair value.
(b) Show the balance sheet presentation of the investment related accounts at December 31, 2000. (Ignore notes presentation.)
(c) Prepare the journal entry for the 2001 sale of security A.

E18-9 (Comprehensive Income Disclosure) Assume the same information as E18-8 and that Steffi Graf Inc. reports net income in 2000 of $120,000 and in 2001 of $140,000. Total unrealized holding gains (including any realized holding gain or loss) arising during 2001 totals $40,000.

Instructions
(a) Prepare a statement of comprehensive income for 2000 starting with net income.
(b) Prepare a statement of comprehensive income for 2001 starting with net income.

E18-10 (Equity Securities Entries) Arantxa Corporation made the following cash purchases of securities during 2001, which is the first year in which Arantxa invested in securities:

1. On January 15, purchased 10,000 shares of Sanchez Company's common stock at $33.50 per share plus commission $1,980.
2. On April 1, purchased 5,000 shares of Vicario Co.'s common stock at $52.00 per share plus commission $3,370.
3. On September 10, purchased 7,000 shares of WTA Co.'s preferred stock at $26.50 per share plus commission $4,910.

On May 20, 2001, Arantxa sold 4,000 shares of Sanchez Company's common stock at a market price of $35 per share less brokerage commissions, taxes, and fees of $3,850. The year-end fair values per share were: Sanchez $30, Vicario $55, and WTA $28. In addition, the chief accountant of Arantxa told you that Arantxa Corporation holds these securities with the intention of selling them in order to earn profits from appreciation in prices.

Instructions
(a) Prepare the journal entries to record the above three security purchases.
(b) Prepare the journal entry for the security sale on May 20.
(c) Compute the unrealized gains or losses and prepare the adjusting entries for Arantxa on December 31, 2001.

E18-11 (Journal Entries for Fair Value and Equity Methods) Presented below are two independent situations:

Situation 1
Conchita Cosmetics acquired 10% of the 200,000 shares of common stock of Martinez Fashion at a total cost of $13 per share on March 18, 2001. On June 30, Martinez declared and paid a $75,000 cash dividend. On December 31, Martinez reported net income of $122,000 for the year. At December 31, the market price of Martinez Fashion was $15 per share. The securities are classified as available-for-sale.

Situation 2
Monica, Inc., obtained significant influence over Seles Corporation by buying 30% of Seles' 30,000 outstanding shares of common stock at a total cost of $9 per share on January 1, 2001. On June 15, Seles declared and paid a cash dividend of $36,000. On December 31, Seles reported a net income of $85,000 for the year.

Instructions
Prepare all necessary journal entries in 2001 for both situations.

E18-12 (Equity Method with Revalued Assets) On January 1, 2002, Jana Company purchased 2,500 shares (25%) of the common stock of Novotna Co. for $355,000. Additional information related to the identifiable assets and liabilities of Novotna Co. at the date of acquisition is as follows:

	Cost	Fair Value
Assets not subject to depreciation	$ 500,000	$ 500,000
Assets subject to depreciation (10 years remaining)	800,000	860,000
Total identifiable assets	$1,300,000	$1,360,000
Liabilities	$ 100,000	$ 100,000

During 2002, Novotna Co. reported the following information on its income statement:

Income before extraordinary item	$200,000
Extraordinary gain (net of tax)	70,000
Net income	$270,000
Dividends declared and paid by Novotna Co. during 2002 were	$120,000

Instructions

(a) Prepare the journal entry to record the purchase by Jana Company of Novotna Co. on January 1, 2002.

(b) Prepare the journal entries to record Jana's equity in the net income and dividends of Novotna Co. for 2002. Depreciable assets are depreciated on a straight-line basis, and goodwill is amortized over 20 years.

E18-13 (Securities Entries—Buy and Sell) Buddy Lazier Company has the following securities in its trading portfolio of securities on December 31, 2001.

Investments (Trading)	Cost	Fair Value
1,500 shares of Davy Jones, Inc., Common	$ 73,500	$ 69,000
5,000 shares of Richie Hearn Corp., Common	180,000	175,000
400 shares of Alessandro Zampedri, Inc., Preferred	60,000	61,600
	$313,500	$305,600

All of the securities were purchased in 2001.

In 2002, Lazier completed the following securities transactions:

March 1 Sold the 1,500 shares of Davy Jones, Inc., Common, @ $45 less fees of $1,200.
April 1 Bought 700 shares of Roberto Guerrero Corp., Common, @ $75 plus fees of $1,300.

Lazier Company's portfolio of trading securities appeared as follows on December 31, 2002.

Investments (Trading)	Cost	Fair Value
5,000 shares of Richie Hearn Corp., Common	$180,000	$175,000
700 shares of Guerrero Corp., Common	53,800	50,400
400 shares of Zampedri Preferred	60,000	58,000
	$293,800	$283,400

Instructions

Prepare the general journal entries for Lazier Company for:

(a) The 2001 adjusting entry.
(b) The sale of the Davy Jones stock.
(c) The purchase of the Roberto Guerrero stock.
(d) The 2002 adjusting entry for the trading portfolio (including the Zampedri preferred).

E18-14 (Fair Value and Equity Method Compared) Jaycie Phelps Inc. acquired 20% of the outstanding common stock of Theresa Kulikowski Inc. on December 31, 2000. The purchase price was $1,200,000 for 50,000 shares. Kulikowski Inc. declared and paid an $0.85 per share cash dividend on June 30 and on December 31, 2001. Kulikowski reported net income of $730,000 for 2001. The fair value of Kulikowski's stock was $27 per share at December 31, 2001.

Instructions

(a) Prepare the journal entries for Jaycie Phelps Inc. for 2001, assuming that Phelps cannot exercise significant influence over Kulikowski. The securities should be classified as available-for-sale.

(b) Prepare the journal entries for Jaycie Phelps Inc. for 2001, assuming that Phelps can exercise significant influence over Kulikowski.

(c) At what amount is the investment in securities reported on the balance sheet under each of these methods at December 31, 2001? What is the total net income reported in 2001 under each of these methods?

E18-15 (Equity Method with Revalued Assets) On January 1, 2002, Kerri Strug Inc. purchased 40% of the common stock of Amy Chow Company for $400,000. The balance sheet reported the following information related to Chow Company at the date of acquisition.

Assets not subject to depreciation	$200,000
Assets subjects to depreciation (8-year life remaining)	600,000
Liabilities	100,000

Additional information:

1. Both book value and fair value are the same for assets not subject to depreciation and the liabilities.

2. The fair market value of the assets subject to depreciation is $680,000.
3. The company depreciates its assets on a straight-line basis; intangible assets are amortized over 10 years.
4. Amy Chow Company reports net income of $160,000 and declares and pays dividends of $125,000 in 2002.

Instructions
(a) Prepare the journal entry to record Strug's purchase of Chow Company.
(b) Prepare the journal entries to record Strug's equity in the net income and dividends of Chow Company for 2002.
(c) Assume the same facts as above, except that Chow's net income included an extraordinary loss (net of tax) of $30,000. Prepare the journal entries to record Strug's equity in the net income of Chow Company for 2002.

E18-16 (Equity Method with Revalued Assets) On January 1, 2001, Warner Corporation purchased 30% of the common shares of Vermeil Company for $180,000. The book value of Vermeil's net assets was $500,000 on that date. During the year, Vermeil earned net income of $80,000 and paid dividends of $20,000. Any excess of cost over book value is attributable to unrecorded goodwill and is amortized over 20 years.

Instructions
(a) Prepare the entries for Warner to record the purchase and any additional entries related to this investment in Vermeil Company in 2001.
(b) Repeat the requirements in part (a), assuming the same facts as above, except that Vermeil's net income included an extraordinary loss (net of tax) of $10,000.

E18-17 (Impairment of Debt Securities) Dominique Moceanu Corporation has municipal bonds classified as available-for-sale at December 31, 2001. These bonds have a par value of $800,000, an amortized cost of $800,000, and a fair value of $720,000. The unrealized loss of $80,000 previously recognized as other comprehensive income and as a separate component of stockholders' equity is now determined to be other than temporary; that is, the company believes that impairment accounting is now appropriate for these bonds.

Instructions
(a) Prepare the journal entry to recognize the impairment.
(b) What is the new cost basis of the municipal bonds? Given that the maturity value of the bonds is $800,000, should Moceanu Corporation accrete the difference between the carrying amount and the maturity value over the life of the bonds?
(c) At December 31, 2002, the fair value of the municipal bonds is $760,000. Prepare the entry (if any) to record this information.

*E18-18 (Determine Proper Income Reporting) Presented below are three independent situations that you are to solve:

1. Lauren Bacall Inc. received dividends from its common stock investments during the year ended December 31, 2002, as follows:
   (a) A cash dividend of $12,000 is received from Big Sleep Corporation. (Bacall owns a 2% interest in Big Sleep.)
   (b) A cash dividend of $60,000 is received from Key Largo Corporation. (Bacall owns a 30% interest in Key Largo.) A majority of Bacall's directors are also directors of Key Largo Corporation.
   (c) A stock dividend of 300 shares from Orient Express Inc. was received on December 10, 2002, on which date the quoted market value of Orient's shares was $10 per share. Becall owns less than 1% of Orient's common stock.
   Determine how much dividend income Bacall should report in its 2002 income statement.
2. On January 3, 2002, Barbara Bach Co. purchased as a long-term investment 5,000 shares of Ringo Starr Co. common stock for $79 per share, which represents a 2% interest. On December 31, 2002, the market price of the stock was $83 per share. On March 3, 2003, it sold all 5,000 shares of Starr stock for $102 per share. The company regularly sells securities of this type. The income tax rate is 35%. Determine the amount of gain or loss on disposal that should be reported on the income statement in 2003.
3. Nastassia Kinski Co. owns a 5% interest in Magdalene Corporation, which declared a cash dividend of $620,000 on November 27, 2002, to shareholders of record on December 16, 2002, payable on January 6, 2003. In addition, on October 15, 2002, Kinski received a liquidating dividend of $10,200 from Terminal Velocity Company. Kinski owns 6% of Terminal Velocity Co. Determine the amount of dividend income Kinski should report in its financial statements for 2002.

*E18-19 **(Entries for Stock Rights)**   On January 10, 2001, Kevin Bacon Company purchased 240 shares, $50 par value (a 3% interest), of common stock of Diner Corporation for $24,000 as a long-term investment. On July 12, 2001, Diner Corporation announced that one right would be issued for every two shares of stock held.

July 30, 2001	Rights to purchase 120 shares of stock at $100 per share are received. The market value of the stock is $120 per share and the market value of the rights is $30 per right.
Aug. 10	The rights to purchase 50 shares of stock are sold at $29 per right.
Aug. 11	The additional 70 rights are exercised, and 70 shares of stock are purchased at $100 per share.
Nov. 15	50 shares of those purchased on January 10, 2001, are sold at $128 per share.

Instructions
Prepare general journal entries on the books of Bacon Company for each of the foregoing transactions.

*E18-20 **(Entries for Stock Rights)**   Pearl Bailey Company purchases 240 shares of common stock of Carmen Jones Inc. on February 17. The $100 par stock, costing $27,300, is to be a long-term investment for Bailey Company.

1. On June 30, Jones Inc. announces that rights are to be issued. One right will be received for every two shares owned.
2. The rights mentioned in (1) are received on July 15; 120 shares of $100 par stock may be purchased with these rights at par. The stock is currently selling for $120 per share. Market value of the stock rights is $20 per right.
3. On August 5, 70 rights are exercised, and 70 shares of stock are purchased at par.
4. On August 12, the remaining stock rights are sold at $23 per right.
5. On September 28, Bailey Company sells 50 shares of those purchased February 17, at $124 a share.

Instructions
Prepare necessary journal entries for the five numbered items above.

*E18-21 **(Investment in Life Insurance Policy)**   Bain Company pays the premiums on two insurance policies on the life of its president, Barbara Bain. Information concerning premiums paid in 2002 is given below.

			Dividends	Net	Cash Surrender Value	
Beneficiary	Face	Prem.	Cr. to Prem.	Prem.	1/1/02	12/31/02
1. Bain Co.	$250,000	$8,500	$2,940	$5,560	$35,000	$37,900
2. President's spouse	75,000	3,000		3,000	9,000	9,750

Instructions
(a) Prepare entries in journal form to record the payment of premiums in 2002.
(b) If the president died in January 2003, and the beneficiaries are paid the face amounts of the policies, what entry would the Bain Company make?

*E18-22 **(Entries and Disclosure for Bond Sinking Fund)**   The general ledger of Joe Don Baker Company shows an account for Bonds Payable with a balance of $2,000,000. Interest is payable on these bonds semiannually. Of the $2,000,000, bonds in the amount of $400,000 were recently purchased at par by the sinking fund trustee and are held in the sinking fund as an investment of the fund. The annual rate of interest is 10%.

Instructions
(a) What entry or entries should be made by Baker Company to record payment of the semiannual interest? (The company makes interest payments directly to bondholders.)
(b) Illustrate how the bonds payable and the sinking fund accounts should be shown in the balance sheet. Assume that the sinking fund investments other than Baker Company's bonds amount to $511,000, and that the sinking fund cash amounts to $16,000.

*E18-23 **(Entries for Plant Expansion Fund, Numbers Omitted)**   The transactions given below relate to a fund being accumulated by Mel Brooks Electrical Company over a period of 20 years for the construction of additional buildings.

1. Cash is transferred from the general cash account to the fund.
2. Preferred stock of Rick Moranis Company is purchased as an investment of the fund.
3. Bonds of John Candy Corporation are purchased between interest dates at a discount as an investment of the fund.
4. Expenses of the fund are paid from the fund cash.
5. Interest is collected on John Candy Corporation bonds.

6. Bonds held in the fund are sold at a gain between interest dates.
7. Dividends are received on Rick Moranis Company preferred stock.
8. Common stocks held in the fund are sold at a loss.
9. Cash is paid from the fund for building construction.
10. The cash balance remaining in the fund is transferred to general cash.

Instructions
Prepare journal entries to record the miscellaneous transactions listed above with amounts omitted.

*E18-24 (Derivative Transaction)   On January 2, 2000, Jones Company purchases a call option for $300 on Merchant common stock. The call option gives Jones the option to buy 1,000 shares of Merchant at a strike price of $50 per share. The market price of a Merchant share is $50 on January 2, 2000 (the intrinsic value is therefore $0). On March 31, 2000, the market price for Merchant stock is $53 per share, and the time value of the option is $200.

Instructions
(a) Prepare the journal entry to record the purchase of the call option on January 2, 2000.
(b) Prepare the journal entry(ies) to recognize the change in the fair value of the call option as of March 31, 2000.
(c) What was the effect on net income of entering into the derivative transaction for the period January 2 to March 31, 2000?

*E18-25 (Fair Value Hedge)   On January 2, 2001, MacCloud Co. issued a 4-year, $100,000 note at 6% fixed interest, interest payable semiannually. MacCloud now wants to change the note to a variable rate note.
As a result, on January 2, 2001, MacCloud Co. enters into an interest rate swap where it agrees to receive 6% fixed and pay LIBOR of 5.7% for the first 6 months on $100,000. At each 6-month period, the variable rate will be reset. The variable rate is reset to 6.7% on June 30, 2001.

Instructions
(a) Compute the net interest expense to be reported for this note and related swap transaction as of June 30, 2001.
(b) Compute the net interest expense to be reported for this note and related swap transaction as of December 31, 2001.

*E18-26 (Cash Flow Hedge)   On January 2, 2000, Parton Company issues a 5-year, $10,000,000 note at LIBOR, with interest paid annually. The variable rate is reset at the end of each year. The LIBOR rate for the first year is 5.8%.
Parton Company decides it prefers fixed-rate financing and wants to lock in a rate of 6%. As a result, Parton enters into an interest rate swap to pay 6% fixed and receive LIBOR based on $10 million. The variable rate is reset to 6.6% on January 2, 2001.

Instructions
(a) Compute the net interest expense to be reported for this note and related swap transactions as of December 31, 2000.
(b) Compute the net interest expense to be reported for this note and related swap transactions as of December 31, 2001.

*E18-27 (Fair Value Hedge)   Sarazan Company issues a 4-year, 7.5% fixed-rate interest only, nonprepayable $1,000,000 note payable on December 31, 2000. It decides to change the interest rate from a fixed rate to variable rate and enters into a swap agreement with M&S Corp. The swap agreement specifies that Sarazan will receive a fixed rate at 7.5% and pay variable with settlement dates that match the interest payments on the debt. Assume that interest rates have declined during 2001 and that Sarazan received $13,000 as an adjustment to interest expense for the settlement at December 31, 2001. The loss related to the debt (due to interest rate changes) was $48,000. The value of the swap contract increased $48,000.

Instructions
(a) Prepare the journal entry to record the payment of interest expense on December 31, 2001.
(b) Prepare the journal entry to record the receipt of the swap settlement on December 31, 2001.
(c) Prepare the journal entry to record the change in the fair value of the swap contract on December 31, 2001.
(d) Prepare the journal entry to record the change in the fair value of the debt on December 31, 2001.

*E18-28 (Fair Value Hedge)   Using the same information from E18-27, consider the effects of the swap on M&S Corp. The $1,000,000 nonprepayable note is classified as an available-for-sale security by M&S Corp.

Instructions

(a) Prepare the journal entry to record the receipt of interest revenue on December 31, 2001.

(b) Prepare the journal entry to record the payment of the swap settlement on December 31, 2001.

(c) Prepare the journal entry to record the change in the fair value of the swap contract on December 31, 2001.

(d) Prepare the journal entry to record the change in the fair value of the available-for-sale debt security on December 31, 2001.

PROBLEMS

P18-1 (Debt Securities) Presented below is an amortization schedule related to Kathy Baker Company's 5-year, $100,000 bond with a 7% interest rate and a 5% yield, purchased on December 31, 1999, for $108,660.

Date	Cash Received	Interest Revenue	Bond Premium Amortization	Carry Amount of Bonds
12/31/99				$108,660
12/31/00	$7,000	$5,433	$1,567	107,093
12/31/01	7,000	5,354	1,646	105,447
12/31/02	7,000	5,272	1,728	103,719
12/31/03	7,000	5,186	1,814	101,905
12/31/04	7,000	5,095	1,905	100,000

The following schedule presents a comparison of the amortized cost and fair value of the bonds at year-end:

	12/31/00	12/31/01	12/31/02	12/31/03	12/31/04
Amortized cost	$107,093	$105,447	$103,719	$101,905	$100,000
Fair value	$106,500	$107,500	$105,650	$103,000	$100,000

Instructions

(a) Prepare the journal entry to record the purchase of these bonds on December 31, 1999, assuming the bonds are classified as held-to-maturity securities.

(b) Prepare the journal entry(ies) related to the held-to-maturity bonds for 2000.

(c) Prepare the journal entry(ies) related to the held-to-maturity bonds for 2002.

(d) Prepare the journal entry(ies) to record the purchase of these bonds, assuming they are classified as available-for-sale.

(e) Prepare the journal entry(ies) related to the available-for-sale bonds for 2000.

(f) Prepare the journal entry(ies) related to the available-for-sale bonds for 2002.

P18-2 (Debt Securities Available-for-Sale) On January 1, 2002, Bon Jovi Company purchased $200,000, 8% bonds of Mercury Co. for $184,557. The bonds were purchased to yield 10% interest. Interest is payable semiannually on July 1 and January 1. The bonds mature on January 1, 2007. Bon Jovi Company uses the effective interest method to amortize discount or premium. On January 1, 2004, Bon Jovi Company sold the bonds for $185,363 after receiving interest to meet its liquidity needs.

Instructions

(a) Prepare the journal entry to record the purchase of bonds on January 1. Assume that the bonds are classified as available-for-sale.

(b) Prepare the amortization schedule for the bonds.

(c) Prepare the journal entries to record the semiannual interest on July 1, 2002, and December 31, 2002.

(d) If the fair value of Mercury bonds is $186,363 on December 31, 2003, prepare the necessary adjusting entry. (Assume the securities fair value adjustment balance on January 1, 2003, is a debit of $3,375.)

(e) Prepare the journal entry to record the sale of the bonds on January 1, 2004.

P18-3 (Available-for-Sale Debt Securities) Presented below is information taken from a bond investment amortization schedule with related fair values provided. These bonds are classified as available-for-sale.

	12/31/01	12/31/02	12/31/03
Amortized cost	$491,150	$519,442	$550,000
Fair value	$499,000	$506,000	$550,000

Instructions

(a) Indicate whether the bonds were purchased at a discount or at a premium.

(b) Indicate whether the amortization schedule is based on the effective interest method and how you can determine which method is used.

(c) Prepare the adjusting entry to record the bonds at fair value at December 31, 2001. The Securities Fair Value Adjustment account has a debit balance of $1,000 prior to adjustment.

(d) Prepare the adjusting entry to record the bonds at fair value at December 31, 2002.

P18-4 **(Equity Securities Entries and Disclosures)** Incognito Company has the following securities in its investment portfolio on December 31, 2001 (all securities were purchased in 2001): (1) 3,000 shares of Bush Co. common stock which cost $58,500, (2) 10,000 shares of David Sanborn Ltd. common stock which cost $580,000, and (3) 6,000 shares of Abba Company preferred stock which cost $255,000. The Securities Fair Value Adjustment account shows a credit of $10,100 at the end of 2001.

In 2002, Incognito completed the following securities transactions:

1. On January 15, sold 3,000 shares of Bush's common stock at $23 per share less fees of $2,150.

2. On April 17, purchased 1,000 shares of Tractors' common stock at $31.50 per share plus fees of $1,980.

On December 31, 2002, the market values per share of these securities were: Bush $20, Sanborn $62, Abba $40, and Tractors $29. In addition, the accounting supervisor of Incognito told you that, even though all these securities have readily determinable fair values, Incognito will not actively trade these securities because the top management intends to hold them for more than one year.

Instructions

(a) Prepare the entry for the security sale on January 15, 2002.

(b) Prepare the journal entry to record the security purchase on April 17, 2002.

(c) Compute the unrealized gains or losses and prepare the adjusting entry for Incognito on December 31, 2002.

(d) How should the unrealized gains or losses be reported on Incognito's balance sheet?

P18-5 **(Trading and Available-for-Sale Securities Entries)** Gypsy Kings Company has the following portfolio of investment securities at September 30, 2001, its last reporting date.

Trading Securities	Cost	Fair Value
Dan Fogelberg, Inc. common (5,000 shares)	$225,000	$200,000
Petra, Inc. preferred (3,500 shares)	133,000	140,000
Tim Weisberg Corp. common (1,000 shares)	180,000	179,000

On October 10, 2001, the Fogelberg shares were sold at a price of $54 per share. In addition, 3,000 shares of Los Tigres common stock were acquired at $59.50 per share on November 2, 2001. The December 31, 2001 fair values were: Petra $96,000, Los Tigres $132,000, and the Weisberg common $193,000. All the securities are classified as trading.

Instructions

(a) Prepare the journal entries to record the sale, purchase, and adjusting entries related to the trading securities in the last quarter of 2001.

(b) How would the entries in part (a) change if the securities were classified as available-for-sale?

P18-6 **(Available-for-Sale and Held-to-Maturity Debt Securities Entries)** The following information relates to the debt securities investments of the Yellowjackets Company.

1. On February 1, the company purchased 12% bonds of Vanessa Williams Co. having a par value of $500,000 at 100 plus accrued interest. Interest is payable April 1 and October 1.

2. On April 1, semiannual interest is received.

3. On July 1, 9% bonds of Chieftains, Inc. were purchased. These bonds with a par value of $200,000 were purchased at 100 plus accrued interest. Interest dates are June 1 and December 1.

4. On September 1, bonds of a par value of $100,000, purchased on February 1, are sold at 99 plus accrued interest.

5. On October 1, semiannual interest is received.

6. On December 1, semiannual interest is received.

7. On December 31, the fair value of the bonds purchased February 1 and July 1 are 95 and 93, respectively.

Instructions

(a) Prepare any journal entries you consider necessary, including year-end entries (December 31), assuming these are available-for-sale securities.

(b) If Yellowjackets classified these as held-to-maturity securities, explain how the journal entries would differ from those in part (a).

P18-7 (Applying Fair Value Method) Pacers Corp. is a medium-sized corporation specializing in quarrying stone for building construction. The company has long dominated the market, at one time achieving a 70% market penetration. During prosperous years, the company's profits, coupled with a conservative dividend policy, resulted in funds available for outside investment. Over the years, Pacers has had a policy of investing idle cash in equity securities. In particular, Pacers has made periodic investments in the company's principal supplier, Ricky Pierce Industries. Although the firm currently owns 12 percent of the outstanding common stock of Pierce Industries, Pacers does not have significant influence over the operations of Pierce Industries.

Cheryl Miller has recently joined Pacers as Assistant Controller, and her first assignment is to prepare the 2000 year-end adjusting entries for the accounts that are valued by the "fair value" rule for financial reporting purposes. Miller has gathered the following information about Pacers' pertinent accounts.

1. Pacers has trading securities related to Dale Davis Motors and Rik Smits Electric. During this fiscal year, Pacers purchased 100,000 shares of Davis Motors for $1,400,000; these shares currently have a market value of $1,600,000. Pacers' investment in Smits Electric has not been a profitable; the company acquired 50,000 shares of Smits in April 2000 at $20 per share, a purchase that currently has a value of $620,000.

2. Prior to 2000, Pacers invested $22,500,000 in Ricky Pierce Industries and has not changed its holdings this year. This investment in Ricky Pierce Industries was valued at $21,500,000 on December 31, 1999. Pacers' 12% ownership of Ricky Pierce Industries has a current market value of $22,275,000.

Instructions

(a) Prepare the appropriate adjusting entries for Pacers as of December 31, 2000, to reflect the application of the "fair value" rule for both classes of securities described above.

(b) For both classes of securities presented above, describe how the results of the valuation adjustments made in Instruction (a) would be reflected in the body of and/or notes to Pacers' 2000 financial statements.

P18-8 (Financial Statement Presentation of Available-for-Sale Investments) Woolford Company has the following portfolio of available-for-sale securities at December 31, 2001.

Security	Quantity	Percent Interest	Per Share Cost	Per Share Market
Favre, Inc.	2,000 shares	8%	$11	$16
Walsh Corp.	5,000 shares	14%	23	17
Dilfer Company	4,000 shares	2%	31	24

Instructions

(a) What should be reported on Woolford's December 31, 2001, balance sheet relative to these long-term available-for-sale securities?

On December 31, 2002, Woolford's portfolio of available-for-sale securities consisted of the following common stocks.

Security	Quantity	Percent Interest	Per Share Cost	Per Share Market
Walsh Corp.	5,000 shares	14%	$23	$30
Dilfer Company	4,000 shares	2%	31	23
Dilfer Company	2,000 shares	1%	25	23

At the end of year 2002, Woolford Company changed its intent relative to its investment in Favre, Inc. and reclassified the shares to trading securities status when the shares were selling for $9 per share.

(b) What should be reported on the face of Woolford's December 31, 2002, balance sheet relative to available-for-sale securities investments? What should be reported to reflect the transactions above in Woolford's 2002 income statement?

(c) Assuming that comparative financial statements for 2001 and 2002 are presented, draft the footnote necessary for full disclosure of Woolford's transactions and position in equity securities.

P18-9 (Gain on Sale of Securities and Comprehensive Income) On January 1, 2001, Enid Inc. had the following balance sheet:

ENID INC.
Balance Sheet
as of January 1, 2001

Assets		Equity	
Cash	$ 50,000	Common stock	$250,000
Available-for-sale securities	240,000	Accumulated other comprehensive income	40,000
Total	$290,000	Total	$290,000

The accumulated other comprehensive income related to unrealized holding gains on available-for-sale securities. The fair value of Enid Inc.'s available-for-sale securities at December 31, 2001, was $190,000; its cost was $120,000. No securities were purchased during the year. Enid Inc.'s income statement for 2001 was as follows (Ignore income taxes):

ENID INC.
Income Statement
For the Year Ended December 31, 2001

Dividend revenue	$15,000
Gain on sale of available-for-sale securities	20,000
Net income	$35,000

Instructions

(Assume all transactions during the year were for cash.)

(a) Prepare the journal entry to record the sale of the available-for-sale securities in 2001.

(b) Prepare a statement of comprehensive income for 2001.

(c) Prepare a balance sheet as of December 31, 2001.

P18-10 (Entries for Long-Term Investments) Octavio Paz Corp. carries an account in its general ledger called "Investments," which contained the following debits for investment purchases, and no credits.

Feb. 1, 2001	Chiang Kai-Shek Company common stock, $100 par, 200 shares	$ 37,400
April 1	U.S. Government bonds, 11%, due April 1, 2011, interest payable April 1 and October 1, 100 bonds of $1,000 par each	100,000
July 1	Claude Monet Company 12% bonds, par $50,000, dated March 1, 2001 purchased at 104 plus accrued interest, interest payable annually on March 1, due March 1, 2021	54,000

Instructions

(a) Prepare entries necessary to classify the amounts into proper accounts, assuming that all the securities are classified as available-for-sale.

(b) Prepare the entry to record the accrued interest and amortization of premium on December 31, 2001, using the straight-line method.

(c) The fair values of the securities on December 31, 2001, were:

Chiang Kai-shek Company common stock	$ 33,800 (1% interest)
U.S. Government bonds	124,700
Claude Monet Company bonds	58,600

What entry or entries, if any, would you recommend be made?

(d) The U.S. Government bonds were sold on July 1, 2002, for $119,200 plus accrued interest. Give the proper entry.

P18-11 (Available-for-Sale and Equity Method) Carlos Fuentes Incorporated is a publicly traded company that manufactures products to clean and demagnetize video and audio tape recorders and players. The company grew rapidly during its first 10 years and made three public offerings during this period. During its rapid growth period, Carlos Fuentes acquired common stock in Yukasato Inc. and Dimna Importers. In 1991 Fuentes acquired 25% of Yukasato's common stock for $588,000 and properly accounts for this investment using the equity method. For its fiscal year ended November 30, 1999, Yukasato Inc. reported net income of $250,000 and paid dividends of $100,000. In 1993 Fuentes acquired 10% of Dimna Importers' common stock for $204,000, and properly accounts for this investment using the fair value method. Fuentes has a policy of investing idle cash in equity securities. The following data pertain to the securities in Fuentes' investment portfolio.

Available-for-Sale Securities at November 30, 2001

Security	Cost	Fair Value
Bettino Craxi Electric	$326,000	$314,000
Pierre Renoir Inc.	184,000	181,000
George Seferis Company	95,000	98,500
	$605,000	593,500
Dimna Importers	204,000	198,000
	$809,000	$791,500

Available-for-Sale Securities at November 30, 2002

Security	Cost	Fair Value
Bettino Craxi Electric	$326,000	$323,000
Pierre Renoir Inc.	184,000	180,000
Golda Meir Limited	105,000	108,000
	$615,000	611,000
Dimna Importers	204,000	205,000
	$819,000	$816,000

On November 14, 2002, Tasha Yar was hired by Funetes as assistant controller. Her first assignment was to propose the entries to record the November activity and the November 30, 2002, year-end adjusting entries for the investments in available-for-sale securities and the long-term investment in common stock. Using Fuentes' ledger of investment transactions and the data given above, Yar proposed the following entries and submitted them to Miles O'Brien, controller, for review.

Entry 1 (November 8, 2002)

Cash	99,500	
Available-for-Sale Securities		98,500
Gain on Sale of Securities		1,000

To record the sale of George Seferis Company stock for $99,500.

Entry 2 (November 26, 2002)

Available-for-Sale Securities	105,000	
Cash		105,000

To record the purchase of Golda Meir common stock for $102,200 plus brokerage fees of $2,800.

Entry 3 (November 30, 2002)

Unrealized Holding Gain or Loss—Equity	3,000	
Securities Fair Value Adjustment (Available-for-Sale)		3,000

To recognize a loss equal to the excess of cost over market value of equity securities.

Entry 4 (November 30, 2002)

Cash	38,500	
Dividend Revenue		38,500

To record dividends received from securities.
Yukasato Inc. $25,000
Dimna Importers   9,000
Bettino Craxi Electric 4,500

Entry 5 (November 30, 2002)

Investment in Yukasato Inc.	62,500	
Revenue from Investment		62,500

To record share of Yukasato Inc. income under the equity method, $250,000 × .25

Instructions

(a) Distinguish between the characteristics of available-for-sale investments and held-to-maturity investments.

(b) The journal entries proposed by Tasha Yar will establish the value of Fuentes Incorporated's equity investments to be reported on the company's external financial statements. Review each of the journal entries proposed by Yar and indicate whether or not it is in accordance with the applicable reporting standards. If an entry is incorrect, prepare the correct entry or entries that should have been made.

(c) Because Fuentes Incorporated owns more than 20% of Yukasato Inc., Miles O'Brien has adopted the equity method to account for the investment in Yukasato Inc. Under what circumstances would it be inappropriate to use the equity method to account for a 25% interest in the common stock of Yukasato Inc.?

P18-12   (Fair Value and Equity Methods)   On January 1, 2001, Howard Corporation acquired 10,000 of the 50,000 outstanding shares of common stock of Kline Company for $25 per share. The balance sheet of Kline Company reported the following information at the date of the acquisition:

Assets not subject to depreciation	$290,000
Assets subject to depreciation	860,000
Liabilities	150,000

Additional information:
1. Kline reported net income of $100,000 and paid dividends of $30,000 in 2001.
2. On the date of the acquisition, the fair value is the same as the book value for both the assets not subject to depreciation and the liabilities.
3. On the date of the acquisition, the fair value of the assets subject to depreciation is $960,000.
4. Kline's stock had a fair value of $24 per share on December 31, 2001.
5. Intangibles are amortized over 20 years and assets subject to depreciation have a remaining useful life of 8 years.

Instructions
   (a)   Prepare the journal entries for Howard Corporation for 2001, assuming that Howard *cannot* exercise significant influence over Kline Company.
   (b)   Prepare the journal entries for Howard Corporation for 2001, assuming that Howard can exercise significant influence over Kline Company.

P18-13   (Available-for-Sale Securities—Statement Presentation)   Maryam Alvarez Corp. invested its excess cash in available-for-sale securities during 2000. As of December 31, 2000, the portfolio of available-for-sale securities consisted of the following common stocks:

Security	Quantity	Cost	Fair Value
Keesha Jones, Inc.	1,000 shares	$15,000	$21,000
Eola Corp.	2,000 shares	50,000	42,000
Yevette Aircraft	2,000 shares	72,000	60,000
Totals		$137,000	$123,000

Instructions
   (a)   What should be reported on Alvarez' December 31, 2000, balance sheet relative to these securities? What should be reported on Alvarez' 2000 income statement?
        On December 31, 2001, Alvarez' portfolio of available-for-sale securities consisted of the following common stocks:

Security	Quantity	Cost	Fair Value
Keesha Jones, Inc.	1,000 shares	$15,000	$20,000
Keesha Jones, Inc.	2,000 shares	38,000	40,000
King Company	1,000 shares	16,000	12,000
Yevette Aircraft	2,000 shares	72,000	22,000
Totals		$141,000	$94,000

        During the year 2001, Alvarez Corp. sold 2,000 shares of Eola Corp. for $38,200 and purchased 2,000 more shares of Keesha Jones, Inc. and 1,000 shares of King Company.
   (b)   What should be reported on Alvarez' December 31, 2001, balance sheet? What should be reported on Alvarez' 2001 income statement?
        On December 31, 2002, Alvarez' portfolio of available-for-sale securities consisted of the following common stocks:

Security	Quantity	Cost	Fair Value
Yevette Aircraft	2,000 shares	$72,000	$82,000
King Company	500 shares	8,000	6,000
Totals		$80,000	$88,000

        During the year 2002, Alvarez Corp. sold 3,000 shares of Keesha Jones, Inc. for $39,900 and 500 shares of King Company at a loss of $2,700.
   (c)   What should be reported on the face of Alvarez' December 31, 2002, balance sheet? What should be reported on Alvarez' 2002 income statement?
   (d)   What would be reported in a statement of comprehensive income at (1) December 31, 2000; and (2) December 31, 2001?

*P18-14 (Stock Rights—Comprehensive) Millard Company holds 300 shares of common stock of Fillmore's Decorating Inc. that it purchased for $31,629 as a long-term investment. On January 15, 2002, it is announced that one right will be issued for every 4 shares of Fillmore's Decorating Inc. stock held.

Instructions
(a) Prepare entries on Millard Company's books for the transactions below that occurred after the date of this announcement. Show all computations in good form.
(1) 100 shares of stock are sold rights-on for $11,500.
(2) Rights to purchase 50 additional shares of stock at par value of $100 per share are received. The market value of the stock on this date is $105 per share and the market value of the rights is $6 per right.
(3) The rights are exercised, and 50 additional shares are purchased at $100 per share.
(4) 100 shares of the stock originally held are sold at $106 per share.
(b) If the rights had not been exercised but instead had been sold at $6 per right, what would have been the amount of the gain or loss on the sale of the rights?
(c) If the stock purchased through the exercise of the rights is later sold at $107 per share, what is the amount of the gain or loss on the sale?
(d) If the rights had not been exercised, but had been allowed to expire, what would be the proper entry?

*P18-15 (Entries for Sinking Fund) The transactions given below relate to a sinking fund for retirement of long-term bonds of John Fremont Roofing:

1. In accordance with the terms of the bond indenture, cash in the amount of $150,000 is transferred at the end of the first year, from the regular cash account to the sinking fund.
2. Cordell Hull Siding Company 10% bonds of a par value of $50,000, maturing in 5 years, are purchased for $47,000.
3. 500 shares of Robert Lee Company 8% preferred stock ($50 par value) are purchased at $54 per share.
4. Annual interest of $5,000 is received on Cordell Hull Siding Company bonds. (Amortize a full year of discount using straight-line amortization.)
5. Sinking fund expenses of $480 are paid from sinking fund cash.
6. Anne Hutchinson Glass Company 9% bonds with interest payable February 1 and August 1 are purchased on April 15 at par value of $60,000 plus accrued interest.
7. Dividends of $2,000 are received on Robert Lee Company preferred stock.
8. All the Hutchinson Glass Company bonds are sold on September 1 at 101 plus accrued interest. Assume interest collected August 1 was properly recorded.
9. Investments carried in the fund at $1,583,000 are sold for $1,538,000.
10. The fund contains cash of $1,627,000 after disposing of all investments and paying all expenses. $1,600,000 of this amount is used to retire the bonds payable at maturity date.
11. The remaining cash balance is returned to the general account.

Instructions
Prepare the journal entries required by John Fremont Roofing for the transactions above.

*P18-16 (Derivative Financial Instrument) The treasurer of Miller Co. has read on the Internet that the stock price of Ewing Inc. is about to take off. In order to profit from this potential development, Miller Co. purchased a call option on Ewing common shares on July 7, 2000, for $240. The call option is for 200 shares (notional value), and the strike price is $70. The option expires on January 31, 2001. The following data are available with respect to the call option:

Date	Market Price of Ewing Shares	Time Value of Call Option
September 30, 2000	$77 per share	$180
December 31, 2000	$75 per share	65
January 4, 2001	$76 per share	30

Instructions
Prepare the journal entries for Miller Co. for the following dates:
(a) July 7, 2000—Investment in call option on Ewing shares.
(b) September 30, 2000—Miller prepared financial statements.
(c) December 31, 2000—Miller prepares financial statements.
(d) January 4, 2001—Miller settles the call option on the Ewing shares.

*P18-17 (Derivative Financial Instrument) Johnstone Co. purchased a put option on Ewing common shares on July 7, 2000, for $240. The put option is for 200 shares, and the strike price is $70. The option expires on January 31, 2001. The following data are available with respect to the put option:

Date	Market Price of Ewing Shares	Time Value of Put Option
September 30, 2000	$77 per share	$125
December 31, 2000	$75 per share	50
January 31, 2001	$78 per share	0

Instructions

Prepare the journal entries for Johnstone Co. for the following dates:

(a) January 7, 2000—Investment in put option on Ewing shares.
(b) September 30, 2000—Johnstone prepares financial statements.
(c) December 31, 2000—Johnstone prepares financial statements.
(d) January 31, 2001—Put option expires.

P18-18 (Free-standing Derivative) Warren Co. purchased a put option on Echo common shares on January 7, 2001, for $360. The put option is for 400 shares, and the strike price is $85. The option expires on July 31, 2001. The following data are available with respect to the put option:

Date	Market Price of Echo Shares	Time Value of Put Option
March 31, 2001	$80 per share	$200
June 30, 2001	$82 per share	90
July 6, 2001	$77 per share	25

Instructions

Prepare the journal entries for Warren Co. for the following dates:

(a) January 7, 2001—Investment in put option on Echo shares.
(b) March 31, 2001—Warren prepares financial statements.
(c) June 30, 2001—Warren prepares financial statements.
(d) July 6, 2001—Warren settles the call option on the Echo shares.

*P18-19 (Fair Value Hedge Interest Rate Swap) On December 31, 2000, Mercantile Corp. had a $10,000,000 8% fixed rate note outstanding, payable in 2 years. It decides to enter into a 2-year swap with Chicago First Bank to convert the fixed-rate debt to variable-rate debt. The terms of the swap indicate that Mercantile will receive interest at a fixed rate of 8.0% and will pay a variable rate equal to the 6-month LIBOR rate, based on the $10,000,000 amount. The LIBOR rate on December 31, 2000, is 7%. The LIBOR rate will be reset every 6 months and will be used to determine the variable rate to be paid for the following 6-month period.

Mercantile Corp. designates the swap as a fair value hedge. Assume that the hedging relationship meets all the conditions necessary for hedge accounting. The 6-month LIBOR rate and the swap and debt fair values are as follows:

Date	6-Month LIBOR Rate	Swap Fair Value	Debt Fair Value
December 31, 2000	7.0%	—	$10,000,000
June 30, 2001	7.5%	(200,000)	9,800,000
December 31, 2001	6.0%	60,000	10,060,000

Instructions

(a) Present the journal entries to record the following transactions:
  (1) The entry, if any, to record the swap on December 31, 2000.
  (2) The entry to record the semiannual debt interest payment on June 30, 2001.
  (3) The entry to record the settlement of the semiannual swap amount receivables at 8%, less amount payable at LIBOR, 7%.
  (4) The entry to record the change in the fair value of the debt on June 30, 2001.
  (5) The entry to record the change in the fair value of the swap at June 30, 2001.
(b) Indicate the amount(s) reported on the balance sheet and income statement related to the debt and swap on December 31, 2000.
(c) Indicate the amount(s) reported on the balance sheet and income statement related to the debt and swap on June 30, 2001.
(d) Indicate the amount(s) reported on the balance sheet and income statement related to the debt and swap on December 31, 2001.

*P18-20 (Cash Flow Hedge) LEW Jewelry Co. uses gold in the manufacture of its products. LEW anticipates that it will need to purchase 500 ounces of gold in October 2000, for jewelry that will be shipped for the holiday shopping season. However, if the price of gold increases, LEW's cost to produce its jewelry will increase, which could reduce its profit margins.

To hedge the risk of increased gold prices, on April 1, 2000, LEW enters into a gold futures contract and designates this futures contract as a cash flow hedge of the anticipated gold purchase. The notional amount of the contract is 500 ounces, and the terms of the contract give LEW the option to purchase gold at a price of $300 per ounce. The price will be good until the contract expires on October 31, 2000.

Assume the following data with respect to the price of the call options and the gold inventory purchase:

Date	Spot Price for October Delivery
April 1, 2000	$300 per ounce
June 30, 2000	$310 per ounce
September 30, 2000	$315 per ounce

Instructions
Prepare the journal entries for the following transactions:

(a) April 1, 2000—Inception of the futures contract, no premium paid.
(b) June 30, 2000—LEW Co. prepares financial statements.
(c) September 30, 2000—LEW Co. prepares financial statements.
(d) October 10, 2000—LEW Co. purchases 500 ounces of gold at $315 per ounce and settles the futures contract.
(e) December 20, 2000—LEW sells jewelry containing gold purchased in October 2000 for $350,000. The cost of the finished goods inventory is $200,000.
(f) Indicate the amount(s) reported on the balance sheet and income statement related to the futures contract on June 30, 2000.
(g) Indicate the amount(s) reported in the income statement related to the futures contract and the inventory transactions on December 31, 2000.

*P18-21 (Fair Value Hedge)   On November 3, 2001, Sprinkle Co. invested $200,000 in 4,000 shares of the common stock of Johnstone Co. Sprinkle classified this investment as available-for-sale. Sprinkle Co. is considering making a more significant investment in Johnstone Co. at some point in the future but has decided to wait and see how the stock does over the next several quarters.

To hedge against potential declines in the value of Johnstone stock during this period, Sprinkle also purchased a put option on the Johnstone stock. Sprinkle paid an option premium of $600 for the put option, which gives Sprinkle the option to sell 4,000 Johnstone shares at a strike price of $50 per share; the option expires on July 31, 2002. The following data are available with respect to the values of the Johnstone stock and the put option:

Date	Market Price of Johnstone Shares	Time Value of Put Option
December 31, 2001	$50 per share	$375
March 31, 2002	$45 per share	175
June 30, 2002	$43 per share	40

Instructions
(a) Prepare the journal entries for Sprinkle Co. for the following dates:

(1) November 3, 2001—Investment in Johnstone stock and the put option on Johnstone shares.
(2) December 31, 2001—Sprinkle Co. prepares financial statements.
(3) March 31, 2002—Sprinkle prepares financial statements.
(4) June 30, 2002—Sprinkle prepares financial statements.
(5) July 1, 2002—Sprinkle settles the put option and sells the Johnstone shares for $43 per share.

(b) Indicate the amount(s) reported on the balance sheet and income statement related to the Johnstone investment and the put option on December 31, 2001.
(c) Indicate the amount(s) reported on the balance sheet and income statement related to the Johnstone investment and the put option on June 30, 2002.

CONCEPTUAL CASES

C18-1 (Issues Raised about Investment Securities)   You have just started work for Andre Love Co. as part of the controller's group involved in current financial reporting problems. Jackie Franklin, controller for Love, is interested in your accounting background because the company has experienced a series of financial reporting surprises over the last few years. Recently, the controller has learned from the company's auditors that an FASB *Statement* may apply to its investment in securities. She assumes that you are familiar with this pronouncement and asks how the following situations should be reported in the financial statements.

Situation 1

Trading securities in the current asset section have a fair value of $4,200 lower than cost.

Situation 2

A trading security whose fair value is currently less than cost is transferred to the available-for-sale category.

Situation 3

An available-for-sale security, whose fair value is currently less than cost, is classified as noncurrent but is to be reclassified as current.

Situation 4

A company's portfolio of available-for-sale securities consists of the common stock of one company. At the end of the prior year the fair value of the security was 50% of original cost, and this reduction in market value was reported as an other than temporary impairment. However, at the end of the current year the fair value of the security had appreciated to twice the original cost.

Situation 5

The company has purchased some convertible debentures that it plans to hold for less than a year. The fair value of the convertible debenture is $7,700 below its cost.

Instructions

What is the effect upon carrying value and earnings for each of the situations above? Assume that these situations are unrelated.

C18-2   (Equity Securities)   James Joyce Co. has the following available-for-sale securities outstanding on December 31, 2000 (its first year of operations):

	Cost	Fair Value
Anna Wickham Corp. Stock	$20,000	$19,000
D H Lawrence Company Stock	10,000	8,800
Edith Sitwell Company Stock	20,000	20,600
	$50,000	$48,400

During 2001 D H Lawrence Company stock was sold for $9,200, the difference between the $9,200 and the "fair value" of $8,800 being recorded as a "Gain on Sale of Securities." The market price of the stock on December 31, 2001, was: Anna Wickham Corp. stock—$19,900; Edith Sitwell Company stock—$20,500.

Instructions

   (a)   What justification is there for valuing available-for-sale securities at fair value and reporting the unrealized gain or loss as part of stockholders' equity?

   (b)   How should James Joyce Company apply this rule on December 31, 2000? Explain.

   (c)   Did James Joyce Company properly account for the sale of the D H Lawrence Company stock? Explain.

   (d)   Are there any additional entries necessary for James Joyce Company at December 31, 2001, to reflect the facts on the financial statements in accordance with generally accepted accounting principles? Explain.

(AICPA adapted)

C18-3   (Financial Statement Effect of Equity Securities)   Presented below are three unrelated situations involving equity securities:

Situation 1

An equity security, whose market value is currently less than cost, is classified as available-for-sale but is to be reclassified as trading.

Situation 2

A noncurrent portfolio with an aggregate market value in excess of cost includes one particular security whose market value has declined to less than one-half of the original cost. The decline in value is considered to be other than temporary.

Situation 3

The portfolio of trading securities has a cost in excess of fair value of $13,500. The available-for-sale portfolio has a fair value in excess of cost of $28,600.

Instructions

What is the effect upon carrying value and earnings for each of the situations above? Complete your response to each situation before proceeding to the next situation.

C18-4 **(Equity Securities, Current and Noncurrent)** The Financial Accounting Standards Board issued its *Statement No. 115* to clarify accounting methods and procedures with respect to certain debt and all equity securities. An important part of the statement concerns the distinction between held-to-maturity, available-for-sale, and trading securities.

Instructions
- **(a)** Why does a company maintain an investment portfolio of held-to-maturity, available-for-sale, and trading securities?
- **(b)** What factors should be considered in determining whether investments in securities should be classified as held-to-maturity, available-for-sale, and trading, and how do these factors affect the accounting treatment for unrealized losses?

C18-5 **(Investment Accounted for under the Equity Method)** On July 1, 2002, Sylvia Warner Company purchased for cash 40% of the outstanding capital stock of Robert Graves Company. Both Sylvia Warner Company and Robert Graves Company have a December 31 year-end. Graves Company, whose common stock is actively traded in the over-the-counter market, reported its total net income for the year to Warner Company and also paid cash dividends on November 15, 2002, to Warner Company and its other stockholders.

Instructions
How should Warner Company report the above facts in its December 31, 2002, balance sheet and its income statement for the year then ended? Discuss the rationale for your answer.

(AICPA adapted)

C18-6 **(Equity Investment)** On July 1, 2001, Cheryl Munns Company purchased for cash 40% of the outstanding capital stock of Huber Corporation. Both Munns and Huber have a December 31 year-end. Huber Corporation, whose common stock is actively traded on the American Stock Exchange, paid a cash dividend on November 15, 2001, to Munns Company and its other stockholders. It also reported its total net income for the year of $920,000 to Munns Company.

Instructions
Prepare a one-page memorandum of instructions on how Cheryl Munns Company should report the above facts in its December 31, 2001, balance sheet and its 2001 income statement. In your memo, identify and describe the method of valuation you recommend. Provide rationale where you can. Address your memo to the chief accountant at Cheryl Munns Company.

*C18-7 **(Investment in Life Insurance Policy)** In the course of your examination of the financial statements of Emanual Ax Corporation as of December 31, 2002, the following entry came to your attention.

January 4, 2002		
Receivable from Insurance Company	1,000,000	
Cash Surrender Value of Life Insurance Policies		132,000
Retained Earnings		163,000
Donated Capital from Life Insurance Proceeds		705,000
(Disposition of the proceeds of the life insurance policy on Mr. Cliburn's life. Mr. Cliburn died on January 1, 2002.)		

You are aware that Mr. Van Cliburn, an officer-stockholder in the small manufacturing firm, insisted that the corporation's board of directors authorize the purchase of an insurance policy to compensate for any loss of earning potential upon his death. The corporation paid $295,000 in premiums prior to Mr. Cliburn's death, and was the sole beneficiary of the policy. At the date of death there had been no premium prepayment and no rebate was due. In prior years cash surrender value in the amount of $132,000 had been recorded in the accounts.

Instructions
- **(a)** What is the cash surrender value of a life insurance policy?
- **(b)** How should the cash surrender value of a life insurance policy be classified in the financial statements while the policy is in force? Why?
- **(c)** Comment on the propriety of the entry recording the insurance receivable.

*C18-8 **(Basic Investment Concepts and Classification of Sinking Fund)**

Part A
To manufacture and sell its products, a company must invest in inventories, plant and equipment, and other operating assets. In addition, a manufacturing company often finds it desirable or necessary to invest a portion of its available resources, either directly or through the operation of special funds, in stocks, bonds, and other securities.

Instructions

(a) List the reasons why a manufacturing company might invest funds in stocks, bonds, and other securities.

(b) What are the criteria for classifying investments as current or noncurrent assets?

Part B

Because of favorable market prices, the trustee of George Washington Company's bond sinking fund invested the current year's contribution to the fund in the company's own bonds. The bonds are being held in the fund without cancellation. The fund also includes cash and securities of other companies.

Instructions

Describe three methods of classifying the bond sinking fund on the balance sheet of George Washington Company. Include a discussion of the propriety of using each method.

*C18-9 (Classification of Sinking Fund) Clara Barton Inc. administers the sinking fund applicable to its own outstanding long-term bonds. The following four proposals relate to the accounting treatment of sinking fund cash and securities.

1. To mingle sinking fund cash with general cash and sinking fund securities with other securities, and to show both as current assets on the balance sheet.

2. To keep sinking fund cash in a separate bank account and sinking fund securities separate from other securities, but on the balance sheet to treat cash as a part of the general cash and the securities as part of general investments, both being shown as current assets.

3. To keep sinking fund cash in a separate bank account and sinking fund securities separate from other securities, but to combine the two accounts on the balance sheet under one caption, such as "Sinking Fund Cash and Investments," to be listed as a noncurrent asset.

4. To keep sinking fund cash in a separate bank account and sinking fund securities separate from other securities, and to identify each separately on the balance sheet among the current assets.

Instructions

Identify the proposal that is most appropriate. Give the reasons for your selection.

USING YOUR JUDGMENT

FINANCIAL REPORTING PROBLEM: INTEL CORPORATION

Instructions

Refer to the financial statements and accompanying notes and discussion of Intel Corporation presented in Appendix 5B and answer the following questions:

(a) What investments are reported by Intel in its balance sheet (description, classification, and amount) of December 26, 1998?

(b) What does Intel disclose in notes to the financial statements as its policy relative to its investments? How does Intel classify its marketable investments? What method of assigning cost to securities sold does Intel apply? How are Intel's investments in non-marketable instruments recorded and where are they reported in the balance sheet?

(c) Intel states in its notes that **all** of its marketable investments are reported at **fair value**. How is fair value determined by Intel?

(d) How does Intel use derivative financial instruments? What are Intel's accounting policies for its derivative instruments?

FINANCIAL STATEMENT ANALYSIS CASE

Union Planters

Union Planters is a Tennessee bank holding company (that is, it is a corporation that owns banks). It manages $32 billion in assets, the largest of which is its loan portfolio of $19 billion. In addition to its loan portfolio, however, like other banks it has significant debt and stock investments. The nature of these investments varies from short-term in nature to long-term in nature, and as a consequence, consistent with the requirements of accounting rules, Union Planters reports its investments in two different categories—trading and available-for-sale. The following facts were found in Union Planters' 1998 Annual Report:

(all dollars in millions)	Amortized Cost	Gross Unrealized Gains	Gross Unrealized Losses	Fair Value
Trading account assets	$ 275	—	—	$ 275
Securities available for sale	8,209	$108	$15	8,302
Net income				224
Net securities gains (losses)				(9)

Instructions

(a) Why do you suppose Union Planters purchases investments, rather than simply making loans? Why does it purchase investments that vary in nature both in terms of their maturities and in type (debt versus stock)?

(b) How must Union Planters account for its investments in each of the two categories?

(c) In what ways does classifying investments into two different categories assist investors in evaluating the profitability of a company like Union Planters?

(d) Suppose that the management of Union Planters was not happy with its 1998 net income. What step could it have taken with its investment portfolio that would have definitely increased 1998 reported profit? How much could it have increased reported profit? Why do you suppose it chose not to do this?

COMPARATIVE ANALYSIS CASE

The Coca-Cola Company versus PepsiCo, Inc.

Instructions

Go to the Digital Tool and, using The Coca-Cola Company and PepsiCo, Inc. Annual Report information, answer the following questions.

(a) Based on the information contained in these financial statements, determine each of the following for each company:

  (1) Cash used in (for) investing activities during 1998 (from the Statement of Cash Flows).

  (2) Cash used for acquisitions and investments in unconsolidated affiliates (or principally bottling companies) during 1998.

  (3) Total investment in unconsolidated affiliates (or investments and other assets) at December 31, 1998.

  (4) What conclusions concerning the management of investments can be drawn from these data?

(b) (1) Briefly identify from Coca-Cola's December 31, 1998, balance sheet the investments it reported as being accounted for under the equity method. (2) What is the amount of investments Coca-Cola reported in its 1998 balance sheet as "cost method investments," and what is the nature of these investments?

(c) In its note number 8 on Financial Instruments, what total amounts did Coca-Cola report at December 31, 1998, as: (1) trading securities; (2) available-for-sale securities; and (3) held-to-maturity securities?

(d) (1) Briefly, according to its note, what is PepsiCo's policy relative to the use of derivative instruments? (2) Briefly, what is Coca-Cola's policy relative to the use of derivative instruments?

RESEARCH CASES

Case 1

You have heard that G. D. Searle & Co. is developing a drug that will cure the common cold. Given the potentially enormous impact on the company's earnings and cash flow, you are interested in investing in Searle and want to do a background investigation.

Instructions

Use *Moody's Industrial Manual* to answer the following questions.

(a) What is the parent company of Searle? What portion of Searle does the parent own?

(b) When did the parent acquire Searle? What was the acquisition price?

(c) How would the financial results of Searle be reflected in the parent company's financial statements?

Case 2

The July 6, 1995, edition of *The Wall Street Journal* includes an article by Jim Carlton and David P. Hamilton entitled "Packard Bell Sells 20% Stake to NEC for $170 Million; Deal Gives Japanese Firm Unprecedented Access to the U.S. PC Market."

Instructions

Read the article and answer the following questions.

(a) Why did Packard Bell sell shares to NEC?

(b) Identify a similar transaction between two other computer companies.

(c) Under U.S. GAAP, how would NEC account for its investment in Packard Bell?

(d) Packard Bell was considering a sale of common shares to the general public. Why didn't it select this option?

ETHICS CASE

Addison Manufacturing holds a large portfolio of debt and equity securities as an investment. The fair value of the portfolio is greater than its original cost, even though some securities have decreased in value.

Ted Abernathy, the financial vice president, and Donna Nottebart, the controller, are near year-end in the process of classifying for the first time this securities portfolio in accordance with *FASB Statement No. 115.* Abernathy wants to classify those securities that have increased in value during the period as trading securities in order to increase net income this year. He wants to classify all the securities that have decreased in value as available-for-sale (the equity securities) and as held-to-maturity (the debt securities).

Nottebart disagrees and wants to classify those securities that have decreased in value as trading securities and those that have increased in value as available-for-sale (equity) and held-to-maturity (debt). She contends that the company is having a good earnings year and that recognizing the losses will help to smooth the income this year. As a result, the company will have built-in gains for future periods when the company may not be as profitable.

Instructions

Answer the following questions:

(a) Will classifying the portfolio as each proposes actually have the effect on earnings that each says it will?

(b) Is there anything unethical in what each of them proposes? Who are the stakeholders affected by their proposals?

(c) Assume that Abernathy and Nottebart properly classify the entire portfolio into trading, available-for-sale, and held-to-maturity categories, but then each proposes to sell just before year-end the securities with gains or with losses, as the case may be, to accomplish their effect on earnings. Is this unethical?

A visit with
Ed Jenkins

Edmund L. Jenkins, who holds an M.B.A. from the University of Michigan and a B.A from Albion College, is chairman of the Financial Accounting Standards Board in Norwalk, Connecticut. Prior to assuming this five-year term in 1997, Mr. Jenkins was a partner with Arthur Andersen & Co. Over a 38-year career at this Big Five accounting firm, Mr. Jenkins was directly involved in setting professional standards for Arthur Andersen's worldwide audit staff and partners. He was a founding member of the FASB's Emerging Issues Task Force and was Chairman of the AICPA Special Committee on Financial Reporting, which issued a path-breaking report in 1994. The report called for disclosure of a broader array of information such as business strategy, which was resisted by some business executives who were reluctant to disclose confidential information that would help competitors.

Standard Setting

How has the accounting profession changed over the past 30 years? The accounting profession has certainly expanded its scope of practice. When I entered the profession, services included traditional accounting and auditing, tax, and a narrow approach to consulting, usually related to the development and installation of information systems. But the demands of clients and the ability of CPAs to understand a company's business through their role as auditors created a demand for broader consulting services such as strategic planning and financing techniques. Today, we have a very broad, exciting scope of practice. Some might even say it's too exciting, that it has gone beyond where it should in terms of protecting the auditor's ability to be independent and objective.

What are your responsibilities as chairman of the FASB? I'm responsible for carrying out our mission, which is to see that financial reporting does the best possible job of meeting the information needs of investors as they go about carrying out their decision-making activities with respect to the allocation of capital. That means that we need to keep abreast of new types of transactions where standards may need to be developed, or to revamp standards that may need to be improved based on our research, which includes observing what goes on in the marketplace and listening to our constituents in the business community.

Accounting for stock options is particularly timely with so many Internet companies going public. But this has been a contentious issue for the Board. Why? The Board tried to change the standard about four or five years ago, but was unable to do so because of pressure from Congress. So, we're faced with having a standard in place, *APB Opinion 25*, which is more than 25 years old and was appropriate only when options were granted to half a dozen executives in the company. In recent years, the use of options has exploded in popularity, particularly in high technology, where it may represent the majority of the total compensation package for all employees. As a result, the impact on a company is much greater than was contemplated by the framers of *APB Opinion 25*. Today, we have ways of valuing options that weren't available 25 years ago. But current accounting says that you don't attribute any value to the option if it meets certain tests. Or, if you do value the option, you base it on the change in the underlying stock value, which may overstate the value of the option itself. So current accounting is an all-or-nothing approach to stock options, which creates an unrealistic recognition or lack of recognition of the cost involved in issuing options.

The FASB was originally established as an independent private-sector standards-setter not subject to the political process. Our goal has always been to develop information for investors and other users that is objective, that's neutral from a public policy standpoint, and that reflects the economics of the transaction. But on this issue, the FASB found itself in a position where going forward would have jeopardized its ability to remain in existence. The Board backed away, which in retrospect was unfortunate because it has served to encourage people to put pressure on us when they don't like the direction that a particular standard is going. For instance, our project on derivatives generated a lot of pressure from industry and in Congress, but we resisted it, and we were able to issue a new standard. Prior to our action, derivatives weren't accounted for at all, and the risk associated with their usage wasn't being communicated. Yet the implications of derivatives became very apparent when Orange County faced bankruptcy after its investment officers pursued there risky hedging strategies without adequate disclosure.

Are you receiving similar pressure with the new rules on business combinations? Yes. There are many companies that object to eliminating pooling-of-interest accounting, although we also have some companies that support its elimination. Today, companies have explicit strategies to grow through acquisition, often using highly valued stock as opposed to internal growth. The impact of the decision to use purchase versus pooling-of-interest accounting is much greater, especially with the very high stock multiples that we have today. That's because purchase accounting results in an annual goodwill charge-off that reflects the excess purchase price over the fair market value of assets. There has been a very significant trend outside of the U.S. to either eliminate or reduce the use of pooling. So all of those reasons entered into the Board's decision to move forward on this project.

How would you write off goodwill? There have been a number of suggestions on the topic. One is that you would write it off immediately upon acquisition, perhaps because you don't believe it meets the test of being an asset. Another approach is to recognize it, but

not write it off at all, because unless a company is getting into trouble, goodwill doesn't have a finite life. It exists forever and might even grow if the company is successful enough. However, the approach that we've adopted is that goodwill should be amortized like any other asset, that sustaining goodwill arises from subsequent investment activity through advertising, high-quality products, good customer relations, and so on. Since it arises from efforts that take place subsequent to the business combination, it has a finite life, because without maintenance it would go away very fast.

What new issues are you tackling? There's a big question about whether the so-called "new economy," of technology and Internet companies requires an entirely different kind of financial reporting. In these companies, the intangible assets, e.g. software engineering talent or research and development, are often much more valuable than traditional fixed assets such as plant and equipment. At present, we do not have a good way to account for the cost or the benefit of these intangibles, whether purchased or generated internally. We're doing some basic research into that area now, and certainly it will be on our agenda as we look forward a few years.

Can new college graduates go to work for the FASB? Yes, we have a program which we call a Postgraduate Internship, where we take individuals, usually with bachelor's degrees, right off the campus, bring them to the FASB for a year in a paid position, and they work directly on projects. Frankly, it's amazing what they can do and the contributions they make. Every intern gets an opportunity to do research, develop positions, and make presentations to the Board on specific technical issues. The research might involve examining the accounting of various business transactions or looking at issues that have been raised in practice by accounting firms or the Securities and Exchange Commission. The accounting departments or business schools nominate candidates, and we accept about six or seven every year, although there are many more applicants. So it's quite competitive.

Can mid-career professionals go to work for you? Yes. We have a program which we call a Fellow Program, which takes experienced individuals, mostly from accounting firms but sometimes from industry or academia, who have been with their companies or firms for quite a long time, maybe ten years or so. They come in for two-year periods and then go back to their organizations, usually with a promotion, we hope.

Revenue Recognition

Cyberspace Trading for Revenues

Since the time when early man traded tools for animal skins and frontier farmers traded cows for horses, barter has been an accepted form of commerce. Today, the practice of trading for goods and services appears to be catching on in a big way on the Internet. Consider **Sportsline, USA**. Its sports-related Internet advertising address is constantly being promoted on **CBS** telecasts of sporting events. This is not surprising, since CBS is part owner of this dot-com venture. How does Sportsline make money? Looking at the cash flow, it is not clear. For example, in the first half of 1999, none of Sportsline's revenue of $24 million was received in cash. Instead Sportsline sells advertising on its site in exchange for advertising and other services on its customers' Internet sites.

A lot of commerce is being transacted on such virtual trading posts, and much of the reported revenue comes from barter. For example, in a recent quarter, barter revenue comprised greater than 10 percent of the revenues at Internet companies such as **Ivillage**, **Salon.com**, **Earthweb**, **Verticalnet**, and **Edgar Online**. However, the growth in these types of exchanges is raising concerns that the financial picture for the Internet industry is being distorted. Because these companies rarely report positive net incomes, reported revenues (without deducting expenses) have become a key valuation indicator, with strong revenue growth leading to higher stock prices. As one expert noted, "Valuations for these companies are being driven by revenues, and barter creates the potential for distortion in a company's revenues."

This potential distortion has caught the attention of accounting regulators. Lynn Turner, the Securities and Exchange Commission's Chief Accountant, says he too is concerned about the proportion of dot-com revenues coming from barter and that his staff is monitoring these practices. According to Mr. Turner, "We want to make sure that the information being reported gives investors a true notion of what is really going on with revenues and that they are reliable numbers. . . . We're always concerned that someone will push the envelope too far." Some bartering dot-coms may be pushing the financial reporting envelope too far by trading relevant and reliable numbers for higher reported revenues.[1]

LEARNING OBJECTIVES

After studying this chapter, you should be able to:

1. Apply the revenue recognition principle.

2. Describe accounting issues involved with revenue recognition at point of sale.

3. Apply the percentage-of-completion method for long-term contracts.

4. Apply the completed-contract method for long-term contracts.

5. Identify the proper accounting for losses on long-term contracts.

6. Describe the installment sales method of accounting.

7. Explain the cost recovery method of accounting.

---

[1]Based on Edward Wyatt, "A Whole Other Type of E-Trade," *The New York Times*, October 20, 1999.

As indicated in the opening story about barter transactions on the Internet, "When should revenue be recognized?" is a complex question. In some cases, the many methods of marketing products and services make it difficult to develop guidelines that will apply to all situations. The purpose of this chapter is to provide you with general guidelines used in most business transactions. The content and organization of the chapter are as follows:

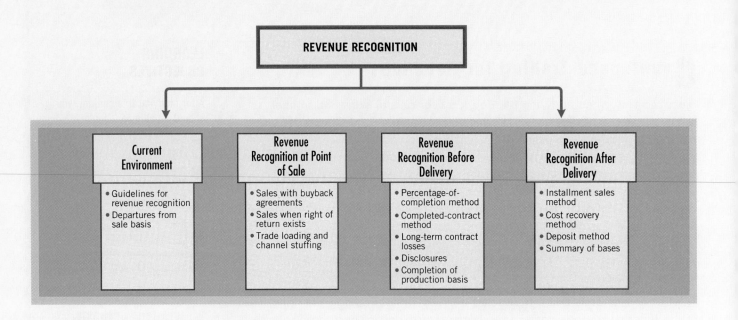

THE CURRENT ENVIRONMENT

The issue of the proper time to recognize revenue has received considerable attention over the last few years. A series of highly publicized cases of companies recognizing revenue prematurely has caused the SEC to increase its enforcement actions in this area. In some of these cases significant adjustments to previously issued financial statements were made. As indicated by Lynn Turner, chief accountant of the SEC, "When people cross over the boundaries of legitimate reporting, the Commission will take appropriate action to ensure the fairness and integrity that investors need and depend on every day."[2]

Inappropriate recognition of revenue can occur in any industry. Products that are sold to distributors for resale pose different risks than products or services that are sold directly to customers. Sales in high-technology industries where rapid product obsolescence is a significant issue pose different risks than sale of inventory with a longer life, such as farm or construction equipment, automobiles, trucks, and appliances.[3]

The opening story indicates the difficulties often associated with revenue recognition in new industries. As indicated, a number of dot-com companies have turned themselves into virtual trading posts, swapping ad space with one another. In these situa-

---

[2]The SEC has made it clear that it will not tolerate abuses of the financial reporting process and that those who fail to adhere to "certain standards" will be prosecuted.

[3]Adapted from American Institute of Certified Public Accountants, Inc., *Audit Issues in Revenue Recognition* (New York: AICPA, 1999).

tions, an equal amount of revenue and expense is reported, so there is no effect on cash flows and net income. But, Internet stocks often trade on revenue multiples, not earnings multiples, and therefore reporting of higher revenue amounts may affect stock valuations. In addition, the SEC has expressed concern that dot-com companies are increasing their revenue by including product sales in their revenue even though they are acting only as the distributor (middle-person) on behalf of other companies. In other words, dot-com companies should be reporting only a distribution (brokerage) fee for selling another company's products.[4]

Guidelines for Revenue Recognition

In general, the guidelines for revenue recognition are quite broad. In addition, certain industries have very specific guidelines that provide additional insight into when revenue should be recognized. The revenue recognition principle provides that revenue is recognized[5] when (1) it is realized or realizable and (2) it is earned.[6] Revenues are realized when goods and services are exchanged for cash or claims to cash (receivables). Revenues are realizable when assets received in exchange are readily convertible to known amounts of cash or claims to cash. Revenues are earned when the entity has substantially accomplished what it must do to be entitled to the benefits represented by the revenues, that is, when the earnings process is complete or virtually complete.[7]

Four revenue transactions are recognized in accordance with this principle.

> **OBJECTIVE 1**
> Apply the revenue recognition principle.

1. Revenue from selling products is recognized at the date of sale, usually interpreted to mean the date of delivery to customers.

2. Revenue from services rendered is recognized when services have been performed and are billable.

3. Revenue from permitting others to use enterprise assets, such as interest, rent, and royalties, is recognized as time passes or as the assets are used.

4. Revenue from disposing of assets other than products is recognized at the date of sale.

These revenue transactions are diagrammed in Illustration 19-1.

> **UNDERLYING CONCEPTS**
> Revenues are inflows of assets and/or settlements of liabilities from delivering or producing goods, rendering services, or other earning activities that constitute an enterprise's ongoing major or central operations during a period.

---

[4]Recently the SEC noted that if a company performs as an agent or broker without assuming the risks and rewards of ownership of the goods, sales should be reported on a net (fee) basis ("Revenue Recognition in Financial Statements," *SEC Staff Accounting Bulletin No. 101,* December 3, 1999).

[5]Recognition is "the process of formally recording or incorporating an item in the accounts and financial statements of an entity" (*SFAC No. 3,* par. 83). "Recognition includes depiction of an item in both words and numbers, with the amount included in the totals of the financial statements" (*SFAC No. 5,* par. 6). For an asset or liability, recognition involves recording not only acquisition or incurrence of the item but also later changes in it, including removal from the financial statements previously recognized.

Recognition is not the same as realization, although the two are sometimes used interchangeably in accounting literature and practice. *Realization* is "the process of converting non-cash resources and rights into money and is most precisely used in accounting and financial reporting to refer to sales of assets for cash or claims to cash" (*SFAC No. 3,* par. 83).

[6]"Recognition and Measurement in Financial Statements of Business Enterprises," *Statement of Financial Accounting Concepts No. 5* (Stamford, Conn.: FASB, 1984), par. 83.

[7]Gains (as contrasted to revenues) commonly result from transactions and other events that do not involve an "earning process." For gain recognition, being earned is generally less significant than being realized or realizable. Gains are commonly recognized at the time of sale of an asset, disposition of a liability, or when prices of certain assets change.

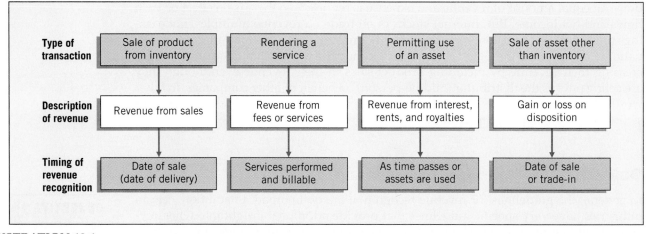

ILLUSTRATION 19-1
Revenue Recognition
Classified by Nature of
Transaction

The preceding statements describe the conceptual nature of revenue and are the basis of accounting for revenue transactions. Yet, in practice, there are departures from the revenue recognition principle (the full accrual method). Revenue is sometimes recognized at other points in the earning process, owing in great measure to the considerable variety of revenue transactions.

Departures from the Sale Basis

An FASB study found some common **reasons for departures from the sale basis**.[8] One reason is a desire to **recognize earlier** in the earning process than the time of sale the effect of earning activities (revenue) if there is a high degree of certainty about the amount of revenue earned. A second reason is a desire to **delay recognition** of revenue beyond the time of sale if the degree of uncertainty concerning the amount of either revenue or costs is sufficiently high or if the sale does not represent substantial completion of the earnings process.

This chapter is devoted exclusively to the discussion and illustration of two of the four general types of revenue transactions described earlier, namely, (1) selling products and (2) rendering services—both of which are **sales transactions**. The other two types of revenue transactions—(3) revenue from permitting others to use enterprise assets and (4) revenue from disposing of assets other than products—are discussed in several other sections of the textbook. Our discussion of product sales transactions is organized around the following topics:

Go to the Digital Tool for examples of revenue recognition policies.

❶ Revenue recognition at point of sale (delivery).

❷ Revenue recognition before delivery.

❸ Revenue recognition after delivery.

❹ Revenue recognition for special sales transactions—franchises and consignments.

This organization of revenue recognition topics is depicted graphically below.

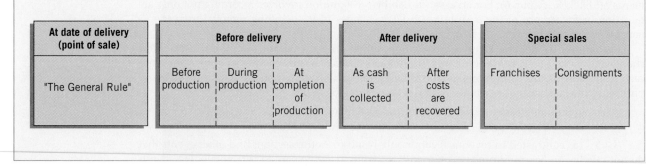

ILLUSTRATION 19-2
Revenue Recognition
Alternatives

_____
[8]Henry R. Jaenicke, *Survey of Present Practices in Recognizing Revenues, Expenses, Gains, and Losses*, A Research Report (Stamford, Conn.: FASB, 1981), p. 11.

REVENUE RECOGNITION AT POINT OF SALE (DELIVERY)

OBJECTIVE ②
Describe accounting
issues involved with
revenue recognition at
point of sale.

According to the FASB in *Concepts Statement No. 5,* the two conditions for recognizing revenue (being realized or realizable and being earned) are usually met by the time product or merchandise is delivered or services are rendered to customers.[9] Revenues from manufacturing and selling activities are commonly recognized at **point of sale** (usually meaning delivery).[10] Problems of implementation, however, can arise; three such situations are discussed below: (1) sales with buyback agreements, (2) sales when right of return exists, and (3) trade loading and channel stuffing.

Sales with Buyback Agreements

If a company sells a product in one period and agrees to buy it back in the next accounting period, has the company sold the product? As indicated in Chapter 8, legal title has transferred in this situation, but the economic substance of the transaction is that retention of risks of ownership are retained by the seller. The profession has taken steps to curtail the recognition of revenue from this practice. When a repurchase agreement exists at a set price and this price covers all costs of the inventory plus related holding costs, the inventory and related liability remain on the seller's books.[11] In other words, no sale.

Sales When Right of Return Exists

Whether cash or credit sales are involved, a special problem arises with claims for returns and allowances. In Chapter 7, the accounting treatment for normal returns and allowances was presented. However, certain companies experience such a **high rate of returns**—a high ratio of returned merchandise to sales—that they find it necessary to postpone reporting sales until the return privilege has substantially expired. For example, in the publishing industry the rate of return approaches 25% for hardcover books and 65% for some magazines. Other types of companies that experience high return rates are perishable food dealers, rack jobbers or distributors who sell to retail outlets, record and tape companies, and some toy and sporting goods manufacturers. Returns in these industries are frequently made either through a right of contract or as a matter of practice involving "guaranteed sales" agreements or consignments.

UNDERLYING CONCEPTS

This is an example of *realized* but *unearned revenue.* When high rates of return exist and cannot be reasonably estimated, a question arises as to whether the earnings process has been substantially completed.

Three alternative revenue recognition methods are available when the seller is exposed to continued risks of ownership through return of the product. These are: (1) not recording a sale until all return privileges have expired; (2) recording the sale, but reducing sales by an estimate of future returns; and (3) recording the sale and accounting for the returns as they occur. The FASB concluded that if a company sells its product but gives the buyer the right to return it, then revenue from the sales transaction shall be recognized at the time of sale only if **all** of the following six conditions have been met.[12]

---

[9]It should be noted that the SEC believes that revenue is realized or realizable and earned when all of the following criteria are met: (1) Persuasive evidence of an arrangement exists; (2) delivery has occurred or services have been rendered; (3) the seller's price to the buyer is fixed or determinable; and (4) collectability is reasonably assured. See "Revenue Recognition in Financial Statements," *SEC Staff Accounting Bulletin No. 101,* December 3, 1999. The SEC provided more specific guidance because the general criteria were sometimes difficult to interpret.

[10]*Statement of Financial Accounting Concepts No. 5,* op. cit., par. 84.

[11]"Accounting for Product Financing Arrangements," *Statement of Financial Accounting Standards No. 49* (Stamford, Conn.: FASB, 1981).

[12]"Revenue Recognition When Right of Return Exists," *Statement of Financial Accounting Standards No. 48* (Stamford, Conn.: FASB, 1981), par. 6.

❶ The seller's price to the buyer is substantially fixed or determinable at the date of sale.

❷ The buyer has paid the seller, or the buyer is obligated to pay the seller and the obligation is not contingent on resale of the product.

❸ The buyer's obligation to the seller would not be changed in the event of theft or physical destruction or damage of the product.

❹ The buyer acquiring the product for resale has economic substance apart from that provided by the seller.

❺ The seller does not have significant obligations for future performance to directly bring about resale of the product by the buyer.

❻ The amount of future returns can be reasonably estimated.

What if revenue cannot be recognized at the time of sale because the six conditions are not met? In that case sales revenue and cost of sales that are not recognized at the time of sale because the six conditions above are not met should be recognized either when the return privilege has substantially expired or when those six conditions subsequently are met (whichever occurs first). Sales revenue and cost of sales reported in the income statement should be reduced to report estimated returns.

Trade Loading and Channel Stuffing

Some companies record revenues at date of delivery with neither buyback nor unlimited return provisions. Although they appear to be following acceptable point of sale revenue recognition practices, they are recognizing revenues and earnings prematurely. The domestic cigarette industry at one time engaged in a distribution practice known as **trade loading**. "Trade loading is a crazy, uneconomic, insidious practice through which manufacturers—trying to show sales, profits, and market share they don't actually have—induce their wholesale customers, known as the trade, to buy more product than they can promptly resell."[13] In total, the cigarette industry appears to have exaggerated a couple years' operating profits by as much as $600 million by taking the profits from future years.

In the computer software industry this same practice is referred to as **channel stuffing**. When a software maker needed to make its financial results look good, it offered deep discounts to its distributors to overbuy and recorded revenue when the software left the loading dock.[14] Of course, the distributors' inventories become bloated and the marketing channel gets stuffed but the software maker's financials are improved—but only to the detriment of future periods' results, unless the process is repeated.

Trade loading and channel stuffing hype sales, distort operating results, and window dress financial statements. If used without an appropriate allowance for sales returns, channel stuffing is a classic example of booking tomorrow's revenue today. **The practices of trade loading and channel stuffing need to be discouraged.** Business managers need to be aware of the ethical dangers of misleading the financial community by engaging in such practices to improve their financial statements.

REVENUE RECOGNITION BEFORE DELIVERY

For the most part, recognition at the point of sale (delivery) is used because most of the uncertainties concerning the earning process are removed and the exchange price is known. Under certain circumstances, however, revenue is recognized prior to completion and delivery. The most notable example is long-term construction contract accounting where the percentage-of-completion method is applicable.

---

[13]"The $600 Million Cigarette Scam," *Fortune*, December 4, 1989, p. 89.

[14]"Software's Dirty Little Secret," *Forbes*, May 15, 1989, p. 128.

Long-term contracts such as construction-type contracts, development of military and commercial aircraft, weapons delivery systems, and space exploration hardware frequently provide that the seller (builder) may bill the purchaser at intervals, as various points in the project are reached. When the project consists of separable units such as a group of buildings or miles of roadway, passage of title and billing may take place at stated stages of completion, such as the completion of each building unit or every 10 miles of road. Such contract provisions provide for delivery in installments, and the accounting records should report this by recording sales when installments are "delivered."[15]

Two distinctly different methods of accounting for long-term construction contracts are recognized.[16] They are:

1. **Percentage-of-Completion Method.** Revenues and gross profit are recognized each period based upon the progress of the construction, that is, the percentage of completion. Construction costs **plus gross profit earned to date** are accumulated in an inventory account (Construction in Process), and progress billings are accumulated in a contra inventory account (Billings on Construction in Process).

2. **Completed-Contract Method.** Revenues and gross profit are recognized only when the contract is completed. Construction costs are accumulated in an inventory account (Construction in Process), and progress billings are accumulated in a contra inventory account (Billings on Construction in Process).

INTERNATIONAL INSIGHT

International accounting standards are congruent with U.S. GAAP on long-term contract requirements.

The rationale for using percentage-of-completion accounting is that under most of these contracts the buyer and seller have obtained enforceable rights. The buyer has the legal right to require specific performance on the contract; the seller has the right to require progress payments that provide evidence of the buyer's ownership interest. As a result, a continuous sale occurs as the work progresses, and revenue should be recognized accordingly.

The profession requires that the percentage-of-completion method be used when estimates of progress toward completion, revenues, and costs are reasonably dependable and **all** the following conditions exist:[17]

1. The contract clearly specifies the enforceable rights regarding goods or services to be provided and received by the parties, the consideration to be exchanged, and the manner and terms of settlement.
2. The buyer can be expected to satisfy all obligations under the contract.
3. The contractor can be expected to perform the contractual obligations.

UNDERLYING CONCEPTS

The percentage-of-completion method recognizes revenue from long-term contracts in the periods that the revenue is earned. The firm contract fixes the selling price. And, if costs are estimable and collection reasonably assured, the revenue recognition concept is not violated.

The completed-contract method should be used only (1) when an entity has primarily short-term contracts, or (2) when the conditions for using the percentage-of-completion method cannot be met, or (3) when there are inherent hazards in the contract beyond the normal, recurring business risks. The presumption is that **percentage-of-completion is the better method and that the completed-contract method should be used only when the percentage-of-completion method is inappropriate**.

Percentage-of-Completion Method

The **percentage-of-completion method** recognizes revenues, costs, and gross profit as progress is made toward completion on a long-term contract. To defer recognition of these items until completion of the entire contract is to misrepresent the efforts (costs)

OBJECTIVE 3
Apply the percentage-of-completion method for long-term contracts.

---

[15]*Statement of Financial Accounting Concepts No. 5,* par. 84, item c.

[16]*Accounting Trends and Techniques—1999* reports that, of the 91 of its 600 sample companies that referred to long-term construction contracts, 88 used the percentage-of-completion method and 1 used the completed-contract method (2 were not determinable).

[17]"Accounting for Performance of Construction-Type and Certain Production-Type Contracts," *Statement of Position 81-1* (New York: AICPA, 1981), par. 23.

and accomplishments (revenues) of the interim accounting periods. In order to apply the percentage-of-completion method, one must have some basis or standard for measuring the progress toward completion at particular interim dates.

Measuring the Progress toward Completion

As one practicing accountant wrote, "The big problem in applying the percentage-of-completion method that cannot be demonstrated in an example has to do with the ability to make reasonably accurate estimates of completion and the final gross profit."[18] Various methods are used in practice to determine the **extent of progress toward completion**; the most common are "cost-to-cost method," "efforts expended methods," and "units of work performed method."

The objective of all the methods is to measure the extent of progress in terms of costs, units, or value added. The various measures (costs incurred, labor hours worked, tons produced, stories completed, etc.) are identified and classified as input and output measures. Input measures (costs incurred, labor hours worked) are made in terms of efforts devoted to a contract. Output measures (tons produced, stories of a building completed, miles of a highway completed) are made in terms of results. Neither are universally applicable to all long-term projects; their use requires careful tailoring to the circumstances and the exercise of judgment.

Both input and output measures have certain disadvantages. The input measure is based on an established relationship between a unit of input and productivity. If inefficiencies cause the productivity relationship to change, inaccurate measurements result. Another potential problem, called "front-end loading," produces higher estimates of completion by virtue of incurring significant costs up front. Some early-stage construction costs should be disregarded if they do not relate to contract performance, for example, costs of uninstalled materials or costs of subcontracts not yet performed.

Output measures can result in inaccurate measures if the units used are not comparable in time, effort, or cost to complete. For example, using stories completed can be deceiving; completing the first story of an eight-story building may require more than one-eighth the total cost because of the substructure and foundation construction.

One of the more popular input measures used to determine the progress toward completion is the cost-to-cost basis. Under the cost-to-cost basis, the percentage of completion is measured by comparing costs incurred to date with the most recent estimate of the total costs to complete the contract, as shown in the following formula:

ILLUSTRATION 19-3
Formula for Percentage of Completion, Cost-to-Cost Basis

$$\frac{\text{Costs incurred to date}}{\text{Most recent estimate of total costs}} = \text{Percent complete}$$

The percentage that costs incurred bear to total estimated costs is applied to the total revenue or the estimated total gross profit on the contract in arriving at the revenue or the gross profit amounts to be recognized to date.

ILLUSTRATION 19-4
Formula for Total Revenue to Be Recognized to Date

$$\text{Percent complete} \times \begin{array}{c}\text{Estimated total}\\ \text{revenue (or gross}\\ \text{profit)}\end{array} = \begin{array}{c}\text{Revenue (or gross}\\ \text{profit) to be}\\ \text{recognized to date}\end{array}$$

To find the amounts of revenue and gross profit recognized each period, we would need to subtract total revenue or gross profit recognized in prior periods, as shown in the following formula:

---

[18]Richard S. Hickok, "New Guidance for Construction Contractors: 'A Credit Plus,'" *The Journal of Accountancy*, March 1982, p. 46.

Revenue (or gross profit) to be recognized to date	− Revenue (or gross profit) recognized in prior periods	= Current period revenue (or gross profit)

ILLUSTRATION 19-5
Formula for Amount of Current Period Revenue, Cost-to-Cost Basis

Because **the profession specifically recommends the cost-to-cost method** (without excluding other bases for measuring progress toward completion), we have adopted it for use in our illustrations.[19]

Illustration of Percentage-of-Completion Method—Cost-to-Cost Basis

To illustrate the percentage-of-completion method, assume that the Hardhat Construction Company has a contract starting July 2001, to construct a $4,500,000 bridge that is expected to be completed in October 2003, at an estimated cost of $4,000,000. The following data pertain to the construction period (note that by the end of 2002 the estimated total cost has increased from $4,000,000 to $4,050,000):

	2001	2002	2003
Costs to date	$1,000,000	$2,916,000	$4,050,000
Estimated costs to complete	3,000,000	1,134,000	—
Progress billings during the year	900,000	2,400,000	1,200,000
Cash collected during the year	750,000	1,750,000	2,000,000

The percent complete would be computed as follows:

ILLUSTRATION 19-6
Application of Percentage-of-Completion Method, Cost-to-Cost Basis

	2001	2002	2003
Contract price	$4,500,000	$4,500,000	$4,500,000
Less estimated cost:			
Costs to date	1,000,000	2,916,000	4,050,000
Estimated costs to complete	3,000,000	1,134,000	—
Estimated total costs	4,000,000	4,050,000	4,050,000
Estimated total gross profit	$ 500,000	$ 450,000	$ 450,000
Percent complete:	25%	72%	100%
	$\left(\dfrac{\$1,000,000}{\$4,000,000}\right)$	$\left(\dfrac{\$2,916,000}{\$4,050,000}\right)$	$\left(\dfrac{\$4,050,000}{\$4,050,000}\right)$

On the basis of the data above, the following entries would be prepared to record (1) the costs of construction, (2) progress billings, and (3) collections. These entries appear as summaries of the many transactions that would be entered individually as they occur during the year:

ILLUSTRATION 19-7
Journal Entries— Percentage-of-Completion Method, Cost-to-Cost Basis

	2001		2002		2003	
To record cost of construction:						
Construction in Process	1,000,000		1,916,000		1,134,000	
Materials, Cash, Payables, etc.		1,000,000		1,916,000		1,134,000
To record progress billings:						
Accounts Receivable	900,000		2,400,000		1,200,000	
Billings on Construction in Process		900,000		2,400,000		1,200,000
To record collections:						
Cash	750,000		1,750,000		2,000,000	
Accounts Receivable		750,000		1,750,000		2,000,000

---

[19]Committee on Accounting Procedure, "Long-Term Construction-Type Contracts," *Accounting Research Bulletin No. 45* (New York: AICPA, 1955), p. 7.

In this illustration, the costs incurred to date as a proportion of the estimated total costs to be incurred on the project are a measure of the extent of progress toward completion. The estimated revenue and gross profit to be recognized for each year are calculated as follows:

ILLUSTRATION 19-8
Percentage-of-Completion, Revenue and Gross Profit, by Year

		2001	2002	2003
Revenue recognized in:				
2001	$4,500,000 × 25%	$1,125,000		
2002	$4,500,000 × 72%		$3,240,000	
	Less: Revenue recognized in 2001		1,125,000	
	Revenue in 2002		$2,115,000	
2003	$4,500,000 × 100%			$4,500,000
	Less: Revenue recognized in 2001 and 2002			3,240,000
	Revenue in 2003			$1,260,000
Gross profit recognized in:				
2001	$500,000 × 25%	$ 125,000		
2002	$450,000 × 72%		$ 324,000	
	Less: Gross profit recognized in 2001		125,000	
	Gross profit in 2002		$ 199,000	
2003	$450,000 × 100%			$ 450,000
	Less: Gross profit recognized in 2001 and 2002			324,000
	Gross profit in 2003			$ 126,000

The entries to recognize revenue and gross profit each year and to record completion and final approval of the contract are shown below.

ILLUSTRATION 19-9
Journal Entries to Recognize Revenue and Gross Profit and to Record Contract Completion—Percentage-of-Completion Method, Cost-to-Cost Basis

	2001		2002		2003	
To recognize revenue and gross profit:						
Construction in Process (gross profit)	125,000		199,000		126,000	
Construction Expenses	1,000,000		1,916,000		1,134,000	
Revenue from Long-Term Contract		1,125,000		2,115,000		1,260,000
To record completion of the contract:						
Billings on Construction in Process					4,500,000	
Construction in Process						4,500,000

Note that gross profit as computed above is debited to Construction in Process, while Revenue from Long-Term Contract is credited for the amounts as computed above. The difference between the amounts recognized each year for revenue and gross profit is debited to a nominal account, Construction Expenses (similar to cost of goods sold in a manufacturing enterprise), which is reported in the income statement. That amount is the actual cost of construction incurred in that period. For example, in the Hardhat Construction Company cost-to-cost illustration the actual costs of $1,000,000 in 2001 are used to compute both the gross profit of $125,000 and the percent complete (25%).

Costs must continue to be accumulated in the Construction in Process account to maintain a record of total costs incurred (plus recognized profit) to date. Although theoretically a series of "sales" takes place using the percentage-of-completion method, the inventory cost cannot be removed until the construction is completed and transferred to the new owner. The Construction in Process account would include the following summarized entries over the term of the construction project.

Construction in Process				
2001 construction costs	$1,000,000	12/31/03	to close	
2001 recognized gross profit	125,000		completed	
2002 construction costs	1,916,000		project	$4,500,000
2002 recognized gross profit	199,000			
2003 construction costs	1,134,000			
2003 recognized gross profit	126,000			
Total	$4,500,000	Total		$4,500,000

ILLUSTRATION 19-10
Content of Construction in Process Account—Percentage-of-Completion Method

The Hardhat Construction Company illustration contained a **change in estimate** in the second year, 2002, when the estimated total costs increased from $4,000,000 to $4,050,000. By adjusting the percent completed to the new estimate of total costs and then deducting the amount of revenues and gross profit recognized in prior periods from revenues and gross profit computed for progress to date, the change in estimate is accounted for in a **cumulative catch-up manner**. That is, the change in estimate is accounted for **in the period of change** so that the balance sheet at the end of the period of change and the accounting in subsequent periods are as they would have been if the revised estimate had been the original estimate.

Financial Statement Presentation—Percentage of Completion

Generally when a receivable from a sale is recorded, the Inventory account is reduced. In this case, however, both the receivable and the inventory continue to be carried. Subtracting the balance in the Billings account from Construction in Process avoids double-counting the inventory. During the life of the contract, the difference between the Construction in Process and the Billings on Construction in Process accounts is reported in the balance sheet **as a current asset if a debit, and as a current liability if a credit**.

When the costs incurred plus the gross profit recognized to date (the balance in Construction in Process) exceed the billings, this excess is reported as a current asset entitled "Cost and Recognized Profit in Excess of Billings." The unbilled portion of revenue recognized to date can be calculated at any time by subtracting the billings to date from the revenue recognized to date as illustrated below for 2001 for Hardhat Construction:

Contract revenue recognized to date: $4,500,000 $\times \dfrac{\$1,000,000}{\$4,000,000} =$	$1,125,000
Billings to date	900,000
Unbilled revenue	$ 225,000

ILLUSTRATION 19-11
Computation of Unbilled Contract Price at 12/31/01

When the billings exceed costs incurred and gross profit to date, this excess is reported as a current liability entitled "Billings in Excess of Costs and Recognized Profit."

When a company has a number of projects, and costs exceed billings on some contracts and billings exceed costs on others, the contracts should be segregated. The asset side should include only those contracts on which costs and recognized profit exceed billings, and the liability side includes only those on which billings exceed costs and recognized profit. Separate disclosures of the dollar volume of billings and costs are preferable to a summary presentation of the net difference.

Using data from the previous illustration, the Hardhat Construction Company would report the status and results of its long-term construction activities under the percentage-of-completion method as follows:

ILLUSTRATION 19-12
Financial Statement
Presentation—
Percentage-of-
Completion Method

HARDHAT CONSTRUCTION COMPANY

	2001	2002	2003
Income Statement			
Revenue from long-term contracts	$1,125,000	$2,115,000	$1,260,000
Costs of construction	1,000,000	1,916,000	1,134,000
Gross profit	$ 125,000	$ 199,000	$ 126,000

Balance Sheet (12/31)

Current assets			
Accounts receivable		$ 150,000	$ 800,000
Inventories			
Construction in process	$1,125,000		
Less: Billings	900,000		
Costs and recognized profit			
in excess of billings		$ 225,000	
Current liabilities			
Billings ($3,300,000) in excess of costs and			
recognized profit ($3,240,000)			$ 60,000

Note 1. Summary of significant accounting policies.
Long-Term Construction Contracts. The company recognizes revenues and reports profits from long-term construction contracts, its principal business, under the percentage-of-completion method of accounting. These contracts generally extend for periods in excess of one year. The amounts of revenues and profits recognized each year are based on the ratio of costs incurred to the total estimated costs. Costs included in construction in process include direct materials, direct labor, and project-related overhead. Corporate general and administrative expenses are charged to the periods as incurred and are not allocated to construction contracts.

OBJECTIVE ④
Apply the completed-contract method for long-term contracts.

Completed-Contract Method

Under the **completed-contract method**, revenue and gross profit are recognized only at point of sale, that is, when the contract is completed. Costs of long-term contracts in process and current billings are accumulated, but there are **no interim charges or credits to income statement accounts for revenues, costs, and gross profit**.

UNDERLYING CONCEPTS

The completed-contract method does not violate the *matching concept* because the costs are also deferred until the completion of the contract.

The principal advantage of the completed-contract method is that reported revenue is based on final results rather than on estimates of unperformed work. Its major disadvantage is that it does not reflect current performance when the period of a contract extends into more than one accounting period. Although operations may be fairly uniform during the period of the contract, revenue is not reported until the year of completion, creating a distortion of earnings.

The **annual entries** to record costs of construction, progress billings, and collections from customers would be identical to those illustrated under the percentage-of-completion method with the significant exclusion of the recognition of revenue and gross profit. For the bridge project of Hardhat Construction Company illustrated on the preceding pages, the following entries are made in 2003 under the completed-contract method to recognize revenue and costs and to close out the inventory and billing accounts:

Billings on Construction in Process	4,500,000	
Revenue from Long-Term Contracts		4,500,000
Costs of Construction	4,050,000	
Construction in Process		4,050,000

Comparing the two methods in relation to the same bridge project, the Hardhat Construction Company would have recognized gross profit as follows:

ILLUSTRATION 19-13
Comparison of Gross
Profit Recognized under
Different Methods

	Percentage-of-Completion	Completed-Contract
2001	$125,000	$ 0
2002	199,000	0
2003	126,000	450,000

Hardhat Construction would report its long-term construction activities as follows:

ILLUSTRATION 19-14
Financial Statement
Presentation—
Completed-Contract
Method

HARDHAT CONSTRUCTION COMPANY

	2001	2002	2003
Income Statement			
Revenue from long-term contracts	—	—	$4,500,000
Costs of construction	—	—	4,050,000
Gross profit	—	—	$ 450,000

Balance Sheet (12/31)			
Current assets			
Accounts receivable		$150,000	$800,000
Inventories			
Construction in process	$1,000,000		
Less: Billings	900,000		
Unbilled contract costs		$100,000	
Current liabilities			
Billings ($3,300,000) in excess of contract			
costs ($2,916,000)			$384,000

Note 1. Summary of significant accounting policies.
Long-Term Construction Contracts. The company recognizes revenues and reports profits from long-term construction contracts, its principal business, under the completed-contract method. These contracts generally extend for periods in excess of one year. Contract costs and billings are accumulated during the periods of construction, but no revenues or profits are recognized until completion of the contract. Costs included in construction in process include direct material, direct labor, and project-related overhead. Corporate general and administrative expenses are charged to the periods as incurred.

Long-Term Contract Losses

Two types of losses can become evident under long-term contracts:[20]

OBJECTIVE 5
Identify the proper accounting for losses on long-term contracts.

❶ *Loss in Current Period on a Profitable Contract.* This condition arises when, during construction, there is a significant increase in the estimated total contract costs but the increase does not eliminate all profit on the contract. Under the percentage-of-completion method only, the estimated cost increase requires a current period adjustment of excess gross profit recognized on the project in prior periods. This adjustment is recorded as a loss in the current period because it is a **change in accounting estimate** (discussed in Chapter 23).

❷ *Loss on an Unprofitable Contract.* Cost estimates at the end of the current period may indicate that a loss will result on completion of the entire contract. Under both the percentage-of-completion and the completed-contract methods, the entire expected contract loss must be recognized in the current period.

The treatment described for unprofitable contracts is consistent with the accounting custom of anticipating foreseeable losses to avoid overstatement of current and future income (conservatism).

UNDERLYING CONCEPTS
Conservatism justifies recognizing the losses immediately. Loss recognition does not require *realization;* it only requires evidence that an impairment of asset value has occurred.

Loss in Current Period

To illustrate a loss in the current period on a contract expected to be profitable upon completion, assume that on December 31, 2002, Hardhat Construction Company estimates the costs to complete the bridge contract at $1,468,962 instead of $1,134,000 (refer to page 1007). Assuming all other data are the same as before, Hardhat would compute the percent complete and recognize the loss as shown in Illustration 19-15.

---

[20]Sak Bhamornsiri, "Losses from Construction Contracts," *The Journal of Accountancy,* April 1982, p. 26.

Compare these computations with those for 2002 in Illustration 19-6. The "percent complete" has dropped from 72% to 66½% due to the increase in estimated future costs to complete the contract.

The 2002 loss of $48,500 is a cumulative adjustment of the "excessive" gross profit recognized on the contract in 2001. **Instead of restating the prior period, the prior period misstatement is absorbed entirely in the current period.** In this illustration, the adjustment was large enough to result in recognition of a loss.

ILLUSTRATION 19-15
Computation of
Recognizable Loss,
2002—Loss in Current
Period

Cost to date (12/31/02)	$2,916,000
Estimated costs to complete (revised)	1,468,962
Estimated total costs	$4,384,962
Percent complete ($2,916,000 ÷ $4,384,962)	66½%
Revenue recognized in 2002	
($4,500,000 × 66½%) − $1,125,000	$1,867,500
Costs incurred in 2002	1,916,000
Loss recognized in 2002	$ 48,500

Hardhat Construction would record the loss in 2002 as follows:

Construction Expenses	1,916,000	
Construction in Process (loss)		48,500
Revenue from Long-Term Contract		1,867,500

The loss of $48,500 will be reported on the 2002 income statement as the difference between the reported revenues of $1,867,500 and the costs of $1,916,000.[21] **Under the completed-contract method, no loss is recognized in 2002 because the contract is still expected to result in a profit** to be recognized in the year of completion.

Loss on an Unprofitable Contract

To illustrate the accounting for an overall loss on a long-term contract, assume that at December 31, 2002, Hardhat Construction Company estimates the costs to complete the bridge contract at $1,640,250 instead of $1,134,000. Revised estimates relative to the bridge contract appear as follows:

	2001 Original Estimates	2002 Revised Estimates
Contract price	$4,500,000	$4,500,000
Estimated total cost	4,000,000	4,556,250*
Estimated gross profit	$ 500,000	
Estimated loss		$ (56,250)
*($2,916,000 + $1,640,250)		

Under the percentage-of-completion method, $125,000 of gross profit was recognized in 2001 (see Illustration 19-8). This $125,000 must be offset in 2002 because it is no longer expected to be realized. In addition, the total estimated loss of $56,250 must be recognized in 2002 since losses must be recognized as soon as estimable. Therefore, a total loss of $181,250 ($125,000 + $56,250) must be recognized in 2002.

---

[21]In 2003 Hardhat Construction will recognize the remaining 33½% of the revenue, $1,507,500, with costs of $1,468,962 as expected, and report a gross profit of $38,538. The total gross profit over the 3 years of the contract would be $115,038 [$125,000 (2001) − $48,500 (2002) + $38,538 (2003)], which is the difference between the total contract revenue of $4,500,000 and the total contract costs of $4,384,962.

The revenue recognized in 2002 is computed as follows:

Revenue recognized in 2002:		
Contract price		$4,500,000
Percent complete		× 64%*
Revenue recognizable to date		2,880,000
Less: Revenue recognized prior to 2002		1,125,000
Revenue recognized in 2002		$1,755,000
*Cost to date (12/31/02)	$2,916,000	
Estimated cost to complete	1,640,250	
Estimated total costs	$4,556,250	
Percent complete: $2,916,000 ÷ $4,556,250 = 64%		

ILLUSTRATION 19-16
Computation of Revenue Recognizable, 2002—Unprofitable Contract

To compute the construction costs to be expensed in 2002 we add the total loss to be recognized in 2002 ($125,000 + $56,250) to the revenue to be recognized in 2002. This computation is shown below:

Revenue recognized in 2002 (computed above)		$1,755,000
Total loss recognized in 2002:		
Reversal of 2001 gross profit	$125,000	
Total estimated loss on the contract	56,250	181,250
Construction cost expensed in 2002		$1,936,250

ILLUSTRATION 19-17
Computation of Construction Expense, 2002—Unprofitable Contract

Hardhat Construction would record the long-term contract revenues, expenses, and loss in 2002 as follows:

Construction Expenses	1,936,250	
Construction in Process (Loss)		181,250
Revenue from Long-Term Contracts		1,755,000

At the end of 2002, Construction in Process has a balance of $2,859,750 as shown below:[22]

Construction in Process			
2001 Construction costs	1,000,000		
2001 Recognized gross profit	125,000		
2002 Construction costs	1,916,000	2002 Recognized loss	181,250
Balance 2,859,750			

ILLUSTRATION 19-18
Content of Construction in Process Account at End of 2002—Unprofitable Contract

Under the completed-contract method, the contract loss of $56,250 is also recognized in the year in which it first became evident through the following entry in 2002:

Loss from Long-Term Contracts	56,250	
Construction in Process (Loss)		56,250

---

[22]If the costs in 2003 are $1,640,250 as projected, at the end of 2003 the Construction in Process account will have a balance of $1,640,250 + $2,859,790, or $4,500,000, equal to the contract price. When the revenue remaining to be recognized in 2003 of $1,620,000 [$4,500,000 (total contract price) − $1,125,000 (2001) − $1,755,000 (2002)] is matched with the construction expense to be recognized in 2003 of $1,620,000 [total costs of $4,556,250 less the total costs recognized in prior years of $2,936,250 (2001, $1,000,000; 2002, $1,936,250)], a zero profit results. Thus the total loss has been recognized in 2002, the year in which it first became evident.

Just as the Billings account balance cannot exceed the contract price, neither can the balance in Construction in Process exceed the contract price. In circumstances where the Construction in Process balance exceeds the billings, the recognized loss may be deducted on the balance sheet from such accumulated costs. That is, under both the percentage-of-completion and the completed-contract methods, the provision for the loss (the credit) may be combined with Construction in Process, thereby reducing the inventory balance. In those circumstances, however (as in the 2002 illustration above), where the billings exceed the accumulated costs, the amount of the estimated loss must be reported separately on the balance sheet as a current liability. That is, under both the percentage-of-completion and the completed-contract methods, the amount of the loss of $56,250, as estimated in 2002, would be taken from the Construction in Process account and reported separately as a current liability entitled Estimated Liability from Long-Term Contracts.[23]

Disclosures in Financial Statements

In addition to making the financial statement disclosures required of all businesses, construction contractors usually make some unique disclosures. Generally these additional disclosures are made in the notes to the financial statements. For example, a construction contractor should disclose the method of recognizing revenue,[24] the basis used to classify assets and liabilities as current (the nature and length of the operating cycle), the basis for recording inventory, the effects of any revision of estimates, the amount of backlog on uncompleted contracts, and the details about receivables (billed and unbilled, maturity, interest rates, retainage provisions, and significant individual or group concentrations of credit risk).

Completion of Production Basis

UNDERLYING CONCEPTS

This is not an exception to the revenue recognition principle. At the completion of production, realization is virtually assured and the earning process is substantially completed.

In certain cases revenue is recognized at the completion of production even though no sale has been made. Examples of such situations involve precious metals or agricultural products with assured prices. Under the completion of production basis, revenue is recognized when these metals are mined or agricultural crops harvested because the sales price is reasonably assured, the units are interchangeable, and no significant costs are involved in distributing the product (see discussion in Chapter 9, page 457, "Valuation at Net Realizable Value").[25] When sale or cash receipt precedes production and delivery, as in the case of magazine subscriptions, revenues may be recognized as earned by production and delivery.[26]

REVENUE RECOGNITION AFTER DELIVERY

In some cases, the collection of the sales price is not reasonably assured and revenue recognition is deferred. One of two methods is generally employed to defer revenue recognition until the cash is received, that is, **the installment sales method** or **the cost recovery method**. In some situations cash is received prior to delivery or transfer of the property and is recorded as a deposit because the sale transaction is incomplete. This is referred to as the **deposit method**.

---

[23]*Construction Contractors,* Audit and Accounting Guide (New York: AICPA, 1981), pp. 148–149.

[24]Ibid., p. 30.

[25]Such revenue satisfies the criteria of *Concepts Statement No. 5* since the assets are readily realizable and the earning process is virtually complete (see par. 84, item c).

[26]*Statement of Financial Accounting Concepts No. 5,* par. 84, item b.

Installment Sales Accounting Method

The installment sales method **emphasizes collection rather than sale. It recognizes income in the periods of collection rather than in the period of sale.** This method is justified on the basis that when there is no reasonable approach for estimating the degree of collectibility, revenue should not be recognized until cash is collected.

OBJECTIVE 6
Describe the installment sales method of accounting.

The expression "installment sales" is generally used to describe any type of sale for which payment is required in periodic installments over an extended period of time. It is used in retailing where all types of farm and home equipment and furnishings are sold on an installment basis. It is also sometimes used in the heavy equipment industry in which machine installations are paid for over a long period. A more recent application of the method is in land development sales.

Because payment for the product or property sold is spread over a relatively long period, the risk of loss resulting from uncollectible accounts is greater in installment sales transactions than in ordinary sales. Consequently, various devices are used to protect the seller. In merchandising, the two most common are (1) the use of a conditional sales contract that provides that title to the item sold does not pass to the purchaser until all payments have been made, and (2) use of notes secured by a chattel (personal property) mortgage on the article sold. Either of these permits the seller to "repossess" the goods sold if the purchaser defaults on one or more payments. The repossessed merchandise is then resold at whatever price it will bring to compensate the seller for the uncollected installments and the expense of repossession.

UNDERLYING CONCEPTS

Realization is a critical part of revenue recognition. Thus, if a high degree of uncertainty exists about collectibility, revenue recognition must be deferred.

Under the installment sales method of accounting, income recognition is deferred until the period of cash collection. Both revenues and costs of sales are recognized in the period of sale but the related gross profit is deferred to those periods in which cash is collected. Thus, **instead of the sale being deferred to the future periods of anticipated collection and then related costs and expenses being deferred, only the proportional gross profit is deferred,** which is equivalent to deferring both sales and cost of sales. Other expenses, that is, selling expense, administrative expense, and so on, are not deferred.

Thus, the theory that cost and expenses should be matched against sales is applied in installment sales transactions through the gross profit figure but no further. Companies using the installment sales method of accounting generally record operating expenses without regard to the fact that some portion of the year's gross profit is to be deferred. This practice is often justified on the basis that (1) these expenses do not follow sales as closely as does the cost of goods sold, and (2) accurate apportionment among periods would be so difficult that it could not be justified by the benefits gained.[27]

INTERNATIONAL INSIGHT

In Japan installment method accounting is frequently used whenever the collection period exceeds two years whether or not there is any uncertainty with regard to the collectibility of cash.

Acceptability of the Installment Sales Method

The use of the installment sales method for revenue recognition has fluctuated widely. Until the early 1960s it was widely used and accepted for installment sales transactions. As installment sales transactions increased during the sixties, somewhat paradoxically, acceptance and application of the installment sales method for financial accounting purposes decreased. In 1966 the APB concluded that except in special circumstances, "the installment method of recognizing revenue is not acceptable."[28]

The rationale for this position is that because the installment sales method of accounting recognizes no income until cash is collected, it is not in accordance with the accrual accounting concept. On the other hand, the installment sales method is

---

[27]In addition, other theoretical deficiencies of the installment sales method could be cited. For example, see Richard A. Scott and Rita K. Scott, "Installment Accounting: Is It Inconsistent?" *The Journal of Accountancy*, November 1979.

[28]"Omnibus Opinion," *Opinions of the Accounting Principles Board No. 10* (New York: AICPA, 1966), par. 12.

frequently justified on the grounds that the risk of not collecting an account receivable may be so great that the sale itself is not sufficient evidence that recognition should occur. In some cases, this reasoning may be valid but not in a majority of cases. The general approach is that if a sale has been completed, it should be recognized; if bad debts are expected, they should be recorded as separate estimates of uncollectibles. Although collection expenses, repossession expenses, and bad debts are an unavoidable part of installment sales activities, the incurrence of these costs and the collectibility of the receivables are reasonably predictable.

We study this topic in financial accounting because the method is acceptable in cases where a reasonable basis of estimating the degree of collectibility is deemed not to exist. In addition, weaknesses in the sales method of revenue recognition became very apparent when the franchise and land development booms of the 1960s and 1970s produced many failures and disillusioned investors. Application of the installment sales method to **franchise and license operations** resulted in the abuse described earlier as "front-end loading" (recognizing revenue prematurely, such as when the franchise is granted or the license issued rather than as it is earned or as the cash is received). Many **land development** ventures were susceptible to the same abuses. As a result, the FASB prescribes application of the installment sales method of accounting for sales of real estate under certain circumstances.[29]

Procedure for Deferring Revenue and Cost of Sales of Merchandise

One could easily work out a procedure that deferred both the uncollected portion of the sales price and the proportionate part of the cost of the goods sold. Instead of apportioning both sales price and cost over the period of collection, however, **only the gross profit is deferred**. This procedure has exactly the same effect as deferring both sales and cost of sales but requires only one deferred account rather than two.

The steps to be used are as follows:

For the sales in any one year:

❶ During the year, record both sales and cost of sales in the regular way, using the special accounts described later, and compute the rate of gross profit on installment sales transactions.

❷ At the end of the year, apply the rate of gross profit to the cash collections of the current year's installment sales to arrive at the realized gross profit.

❸ The gross profit not realized should be deferred to future years.

For sales made in prior years:

❶ The gross profit rate of each year's sales must be applied against cash collections of accounts receivable resulting from that year's sales to arrive at the realized gross profit.

From the preceding discussion of the general practice followed in taking up income from installment sales, it is apparent that special accounts must be used. These accounts provide certain special information required to determine the realized and unrealized gross profit in each year of operations. The requirements for special accounts are as follows:

---

[29]"Accounting for Sales of Real Estate," *Statement of Financial Accounting Standards No. 66* (Norwalk, Conn.: FASB, 1982), pars. 45–47. The installment sales method of accounting must be applied to a retail land sale that meets **all** of the following criteria: (1) the period of cancellation of the sale with refund of the down payment and any subsequent payments has expired; (2) cumulative cash payments equal or exceed 10% of the sales value; and (3) the seller is financially capable of providing all promised contract representations (e.g., land improvements, off-site facilities).

❶ Installment sales transactions must be kept separate in the accounts from all other sales.

❷ Gross profit on sales sold on installment must be determinable.

❸ The amount of cash collected on installment sales accounts receivable must be known, and, further, the total collected on the current year's and on each preceding year's sales must be determinable.

❹ Provision must be made for carrying forward each year's deferred gross profit.

In each year, ordinary operating expenses are charged to expense accounts and are closed to the Income Summary account as under customary accounting procedure. Thus, the only peculiarity in computing net income under the installment sales method as generally applied is **the deferral of gross profit until realized by accounts receivable collection**.

To illustrate the installment sales method in accounting for the sales of merchandise, assume the following data:

	2001	2002	2003
Installment sales	$200,000	$250,000	$240,000
Cost of installment sales	150,000	190,000	168,000
Gross profit	$ 50,000	$ 60,000	$ 72,000
Rate of gross profit on sales	25%ᵃ	24%ᵇ	30%ᶜ
Cash receipts			
2001 sales	$ 60,000	$100,000	$ 40,000
2002 sales		100,000	125,000
2003 sales			80,000

$$^a \frac{\$50,000}{\$200,000} \qquad ^b \frac{\$60,000}{\$250,000} \qquad ^c \frac{\$72,000}{\$240,000}$$

To simplify the illustration, interest charges have been excluded. Summary entries in general journal form for year 2001 are shown below.

2001

Installment Accounts Receivable, 2001	200,000	
Installment Sales		200,000
(To record sales made on installment in 2001)		
Cash	60,000	
Installment Accounts Receivable, 2001		60,000
(To record cash collected on installment receivables)		
Cost of Installment Sales	150,000	
Inventory (or Purchases)		150,000
(To record cost of goods sold on installment in 2001 on either a perpetual or a periodic inventory basis)		
Installment Sales	200,000	
Cost of Installment Sales		150,000
Deferred Gross Profit, 2001		50,000
(To close installment sales and cost of installment sales for the year)		
Deferred Gross Profit, 2001	15,000	
Realized Gross Profit on Installment Sales		15,000
(To remove from deferred gross profit the profit realized through cash collections; $60,000 × 25%)		
Realized Gross Profit on Installment Sales	15,000	
Income Summary		15,000
(To close profits realized by collections)		

The realized and deferred gross profit is computed for the year 2001 as follows:

ILLUSTRATION 19-19
Computation of Realized
and Deferred Gross
Profit, Year 1

2001	
Rate of gross profit current year	25%
Cash collected on current year's sales	$60,000
Realized gross profit (25% of $60,000)	15,000
Gross profit to be deferred ($50,000 − $15,000)	35,000

Summary entries in journal form for year 2 (2002) are shown below.

2002		
Installment Accounts Receivable, 2002	250,000	
Installment Sales		250,000
(To record sales made on installment in 2002)		
Cash	200,000	
Installment Accounts Receivable, 2001		100,000
Installment Accounts Receivable, 2002		100,000
(To record cash collected on installment receivables)		
Cost of Installment Sales	190,000	
Inventory (or Purchases)		190,000
(To record cost of goods sold on installment in 2002)		
Installment Sales	250,000	
Cost of Installment Sales		190,000
Deferred Gross Profit, 2002		60,000
(To close installment sales and cost of installment sales for the year)		
Deferred Gross Profit, 2001 ($100,000 × 25%)	25,000	
Deferred Gross Profit, 2002 ($100,000 × 24%)	24,000	
Realized Gross Profit on Installment Sales		49,000
(To remove from deferred gross profit the profit realized through collections)		
Realized Gross Profit on Installment Sales	49,000	
Income Summary		49,000
(To close profits realized by collections)		

The realized and deferred gross profit is computed for the year 2002 as follows:

ILLUSTRATION 19-20
Computation of Realized
and Deferred Gross
Profit, Year 2

2002	
Current year's sales	
Rate of gross profit	24%
Cash collected on current year's sales	$100,000
Realized gross profit (24% of $100,000)	24,000
Gross profit to be deferred ($60,000 − $24,000)	36,000
Prior year's sales	
Rate of gross profit—2001	25%
Cash collected on 2001 sales	$100,000
Gross profit realized in 2002 on 2001 sales (25% of $100,000)	25,000
Total gross profit realized in 2002	
Realized on collections of 2001 sales	$ 25,000
Realized on collections of 2002 sales	24,000
Total	$ 49,000

The entries in 2003 would be similar to those of 2002, and the total gross profit taken up or realized would be $64,000, as shown by the following computations:

ILLUSTRATION 19-21
Computation of Realized
and Deferred Gross
Profit, Year 3

2003	
Current year's sales	
Rate of gross profit	30%
Cash collected on current year's sales	$ 80,000
Gross profit realized on 2003 sales (30% of $80,000)	24,000
Gross profit to be deferred ($72,000 − $24,000)	48,000
Prior years' sales	
2001 sales	
Rate of gross profit	25%
Cash collected	$ 40,000
Gross profit realized in 2003 on 2001 sales (25% of $40,000)	10,000
2002 sales	
Rate of gross profit	24%
Cash collected	$125,000
Gross profit realized in 2003 on 2002 sales (24% of $125,000)	30,000
Total gross profit realized in 2003	
Realized on collections of 2001 sales	$ 10,000
Realized on collections of 2002 sales	30,000
Realized on collections of 2003 sales	24,000
Total	$ 64,000

Additional Problems of Installment Sales Accounting

In addition to computing realized and deferred gross profit currently, other problems are involved in accounting for installment sales transactions. These problems are related to:

1. Interest on installment contracts.
2. Uncollectible accounts.
3. Defaults and repossessions.

Interest on Installment Contracts. Because the collection of installment receivables is spread over a long period, it is customary to charge the buyer interest on the unpaid balance. A schedule of equal payments consisting of interest and principal is set up. Each successive payment is attributable to a smaller amount of interest and a correspondingly larger amount attributable to principal, as shown in Illustration 19-22. This illustration assumes that an asset costing $2,400 is sold for $3,000 with interest of 8% included in the three installments of $1,164.10.

ILLUSTRATION 19-22
Installment Payment
Schedule

Date	Cash (Debit)	Interest Earned (Credit)	Installment Receivables (Credit)	Installment Unpaid Balance	Realized Gross Profit (20%)
1/2/01	—	—	—	$3,000.00	—
1/2/02	$1,164.10[a]	$240.00[b]	$ 924.10[c]	2,075.90[d]	$184.82[e]
1/2/03	1,164.10	166.07	998.03	1,077.87	199.61
1/2/04	1,164.10	86.23	1,077.87	−0−	215.57
					$600.00

[a]Periodic payment = Original unpaid balance ÷ PV of an annuity of $1.00 for three periods at 8%; $1,164.10 = $3,000 ÷ 2.57710.
[b]$3,000.00 × .08 = $240.
[c]$1,164.10 − $240.00 = $924.10.
[d]$3,000.00 − $924.10 = $2,075.90.
[e]$924.10 × .20 = $184.82.

Interest should be accounted for separately from the gross profit recognized on the installment sales collections during the period. It is recognized as interest revenue at the time of the cash receipt.

Uncollectible Accounts. The problem of bad debts or uncollectible accounts receivable is somewhat different for concerns selling on an installment basis because of a repossession feature commonly incorporated in the sales agreement. This feature gives the selling company an opportunity to recoup any uncollectible accounts through repossession and resale of repossessed merchandise. If the experience of the company indicates that repossessions do not, as a rule, compensate for uncollectible balances, it may be advisable to provide for such losses through charges to a special bad debt expense account just as is done for other credit sales.

Defaults and Repossessions. Depending on the terms of the sales contract and the policy of the credit department, the seller can repossess merchandise sold under an installment arrangement if the purchaser fails to meet payment requirements. Repossessed merchandise may be reconditioned before being offered for sale. It may be resold for cash or installment payments.

The accounting for **repossessions** recognizes that the related installment receivable account is not collectible and that it should be written off. Along with the account receivable, the applicable deferred gross profit must be removed from the ledger using the following entry:

Repossessed Merchandise (an inventory account)	xx	
Deferred Gross Profit	xx	
Installment Accounts Receivable		xx

The entry above assumes that the repossessed merchandise is to be recorded on the books at exactly the amount of the uncollected account less the deferred gross profit applicable. This assumption may or may not be proper. The condition of the merchandise repossessed, the cost of reconditioning, and the market for second-hand merchandise of that particular type must all be considered. **The objective should be to put any asset acquired on the books at its fair value or, when fair value is not ascertainable, at the best possible approximation of fair value.** If the fair value of the merchandise repossessed is less than the uncollected balance less the deferred gross profit, a "loss on repossession" should be recorded at the date of repossession.

Some contend that repossessed merchandise should be entered at a valuation that will permit the company to make its regular rate of gross profit on resale. If it is entered at its approximated cost to purchase, the regular rate of gross profit could be provided for upon its ultimate sale, but that is completely a secondary consideration. It is more important that the asset acquired by repossession be recorded at fair value in accordance with the general practice of carrying assets at acquisition price as represented by the fair market value at the date of acquisition.

To illustrate the required entry, assume that a refrigerator was sold to Marilyn Hunt for $500 on September 1, 2001. Terms require a down payment of $200 and $20 on the first of every month for 15 months, starting October 1, 2001. It is further assumed that the refrigerator cost $300 and that it is sold to provide a 40% rate of gross profit on selling price. At the year-end, December 31, 2001, a total of $60 should have been collected in addition to the original down payment.

If Hunt makes her January and February payments in 2002 and then defaults, the account balances applicable to Hunt at time of default would be:

Installment Account Receivable ($500 − $200 − $20 − $20 − $20 − $20 − $20)	200 (dr.)
Deferred Gross Profit [40% × ($500 − $200 − $20 − $20 − $20)]	96 (cr.)

The deferred gross profit applicable to the Hunt account still has the December 31, 2001, balance because no entry has yet been made to take up gross profit realized by 2002 cash collections. The regular entry at the end of 2002, however, will take up the gross profit realized by all cash collections including amounts received from Hunt. Hence, the balance of deferred gross profit applicable to Hunt's account may be computed by applying the gross profit rate for the year of sale to the 2002 balance of Hunt's account receivable, 40% of $200, or $80. The account balances should therefore be considered as:

Installment Account Receivable (Hunt)	200 (dr.)
Deferred Gross Profit (applicable to Hunt after	
recognition of $8 of profit in both January and February)	80 (cr.)

If the estimated fair value of the article repossessed is set at $70, the following entry would be required to record the repossession:

Deferred Gross Profit	80	
Repossessed Merchandise	70	
Loss on Repossession	50	
Installment Account Receivable (Hunt)		200

The amount of the loss is determined by (1) subtracting the deferred gross profit from the amount of the account receivable, to determine the unrecovered cost (or book value) of the merchandise repossessed, and (2) subtracting the estimated fair value of the merchandise repossessed from the unrecovered cost to get the amount of the loss on repossession. The loss on the refrigerator in our example is computed as shown in Illustration 19-23.

Balance of account receivable (representing uncollected selling price)	$200
Less: Deferred gross profit	80
Unrecovered cost	120
Less: Estimated fair value of merchandise repossessed	70
Loss (Gain) on repossession	$ 50

ILLUSTRATION 19-23
Computation of Loss on Repossession

As pointed out earlier, the loss on repossession may be charged to Allowance for Doubtful Accounts if such an account is carried.

Financial Statement Presentation of Installment Sales Transactions

If installment sales transactions represent a significant part of total sales, full disclosure of installment sales, the cost of installment sales, and any expenses allocable to installment sales is desirable. If, however, installment sales transactions constitute an insignificant part of total sales, it may be satisfactory to include only the realized gross profit in the income statement as a special item following the gross profit on sales, as shown below.

HEALTH MACHINE COMPANY Statement of Income For the Year Ended December 31, 2002	
Sales	$620,000
Cost of goods sold	490,000
Gross profit on sales	130,000
Gross profit realized on installment sales	51,000
Total gross profit on sales	$181,000

ILLUSTRATION 19-24
Disclosure of Installment Sales Transactions— Insignificant Amount

If more complete disclosure of installment sales transactions is desired, a presentation similar to the following may be used:

ILLUSTRATION 19-25
Disclosure of Installment
Sales Transactions—
Significant Amount

	Installment Sales	Other Sales	Total
HEALTH MACHINE COMPANY			
Statement of Income			
For the Year Ended December 31, 2002			
Sales	$248,000	$620,000	$868,000
Cost of goods sold	182,000	490,000	672,000
Gross profit on sales	66,000	130,000	196,000
Less: Deferred gross profit on installment sales of this year	47,000		47,000
Realized gross profit on this year's sales	19,000	130,000	149,000
Add: Gross profit realized on installment sales of prior years	32,000		32,000
Gross profit realized this year	$ 51,000	$130,000	$181,000

The apparent awkwardness of this method of presentation is difficult to avoid if full disclosure of installment sales transactions is to be provided in the income statement. One solution, of course, is to prepare a separate schedule showing installment sales transactions with only the final figure carried into the income statement.

In the balance sheet it is generally considered desirable to classify installment accounts receivable by year of collectibility. There is some question as to whether installment accounts that are not collectible for two or more years should be included in current assets. If installment sales are part of normal operations, they may be considered as current assets because they are collectible within the operating cycle of the business. Little confusion should result from this practice if maturity dates are fully disclosed, as illustrated in the following example:

ILLUSTRATION 19-26
Disclosure of Installment
Accounts Receivable,
by Year

Current assets		
Notes and accounts receivable		
Trade Customers	$78,800	
Less: Allowance for doubtful accounts	3,700	
	75,100	
Installment accounts collectible in 2002	22,600	
Installment accounts collectible in 2003	47,200	$144,900

On the other hand, receivables from an installment contract, or contracts, resulting from a transaction **not** related to normal operations should be reported in the Other Assets section if due beyond one year.

Repossessed merchandise is a part of inventory and should be included as such in the Current Asset section of the balance sheet. Any gain or loss on repossessions should be included in the income statement in the Other Revenues and Gains or Other Expenses and Losses section.

Deferred gross profit on installment sales is generally treated as unearned revenue and is classified as a current liability. Theoretically, deferred gross profit consists of three elements: (1) income tax liability to be paid when the sales are reported as realized revenue (current liability); (2) allowance for collection expense, bad debts, and repossession losses (deduction from installment accounts receivable); and (3) net income (retained earnings, restricted as to dividend availability). Because of the difficulty in allocating deferred gross profit among these three elements, however, the whole amount is frequently reported as unearned revenue.

In contrast, the FASB in *SFAC No. 3* states that "no matter how it is displayed in financial statements, deferred gross profit on installment sales is conceptually an asset valuation—that is, a reduction of an asset."[30] We support the FASB position but we

---

[30]See *Statement of Financial Accounting Concepts No. 3*, pars. 156–158.

recognize that until an official standard on this topic is issued, financial statements will probably continue to report such deferred gross profit as a current liability.

Cost Recovery Method

Under the cost recovery method, no profit is recognized until cash payments by the buyer exceed the seller's cost of the merchandise sold. After all costs have been recovered, any additional cash collections are included in income. The income statement for the period of sale reports sales revenue, the cost of goods sold, and the gross profit—both the amount (if any) that is recognized during the period and the amount that is deferred. The deferred gross profit is offset against the related receivable—reduced by collections—on the balance sheet. Subsequent income statements report the gross profit as a separate item of revenue when it is recognized as earned.

APB Opinion No. 10 allows a seller to use the cost recovery method to account for sales in which "there is no reasonable basis for estimating collectibility." This method is required under *FASB Statements No. 45* (franchises) and *No. 66* (real estate) where a high degree of uncertainty exists related to the collection of receivables.[31]

To illustrate the cost recovery method, assume that early in 2001, Fesmire Manufacturing sells inventory with a cost of $25,000 to Higley Company for $36,000 with payments receivable of $18,000 in 2001, $12,000 in 2002, and $6,000 in 2003. If the cost recovery method applies to this sale transaction and the cash is collected on schedule, cash collections, revenue, cost, and gross profit are recognized as follows:[32]

> **OBJECTIVE 7**
> Explain the cost recovery method of accounting.

	2001	2002	2003
Cash collected	$18,000	$12,000	$6,000
Revenue	$36,000	–0–	–0–
Cost of goods sold	25,000	–0–	–0–
Deferred gross profit	11,000	$11,000	$6,000
Recognized gross profit	–0–	5,000*	6,000
Deferred gross profit balance (end of period)	$11,000	$ 6,000	$ –0–

*$25,000 − $18,000 = $7,000 of unrecovered cost at the end of 2001; $12,000 − $7,000 = $5,000, the excess of cash received in 2002 over unrecovered cost.

ILLUSTRATION 19-27
Computation of Gross Profit—Cost Recovery Method

Under the cost recovery method, total revenue and cost of goods sold are reported in the period of sale similar to the installment sales method. However, unlike the installment sales method, which recognizes income as cash is collected, the cost recovery method recognizes profit only when cash collections exceed the total cost of the goods sold.

The journal entry to record the deferred gross profit on this transaction (after the sale and the cost of sale were recorded in the normal manner) at the end of 2001 is as follows:

---

[31]"Omnibus Opinion—1966," *Opinions of the Accounting Principles Board No. 10* (New York: AICPA, 1969), footnote 8, page 149; "Accounting for Franchise Fee Revenue," *Statement of Financial Accounting Standards No. 45* (Stamford, Conn.: FASB, 1981), par. 6; "Accounting for Sales of Real Estate," *Statement of Financial Accounting Standards No. 66,* pars. 62 and 63.

[32]An alternative format for computing the amount of gross profit recognized annually is shown below:

Year	Cash Received	Original Cost Recovered	Balance of Unrecovered Cost	Gross Profit Realized
Beginning balance	—	—	$25,000	—
12/31/01	$18,000	$18,000	7,000	$ –0–
12/31/02	12,000	7,000	–0–	5,000
12/31/03	6,000	–0–	–0–	6,000

2001

Sales	36,000	
Cost of Sales		25,000
Deferred Gross Profit		11,000
(To close sales and cost of sales and to record deferred gross profit on sales accounted for under the cost recovery method)		

In 2002 and 2003, the deferred gross profit becomes realized gross profit as the cumulative cash collections exceed the total costs by recording the following entries:

2002

Deferred Gross Profit	5,000	
Realized Gross Profit		5,000
(To recognize gross profit to the extent that cash collections in 2002 exceed costs)		

2003

Deferred Gross Profit	6,000	
Realized Gross Profit		6,000
(To recognize gross profit to the extent that cash collections in 2003 exceed costs)		

Deposit Method

In some cases, cash is received from the buyer before transfer of the goods or property. There is not sufficient transfer of the risks and rewards of ownership for a sale to be recorded. In such cases the seller has not performed under the contract and has no claim against the purchaser. The method of accounting for these incomplete transactions is the **deposit method**. Under the deposit method the seller reports the cash received from the buyer as a deposit on the contract and classifies it as a liability (refundable deposit or customer advance) on the balance sheet. The seller continues to report the property as an asset on its balance sheet, along with any related existing debt. Also, the seller continues to charge depreciation expense as a period cost for the property. **No revenue or income should be recognized until the sale is complete.**[33] At that time, the deposit account is closed and one of the revenue recognition methods discussed in this chapter is applied to the sale.

The **major difference between the installment and cost recovery methods and the deposit method** is that in the installment and cost recovery methods it is assumed that the seller has performed on the contract, but cash collection is highly uncertain. In the deposit method, the seller has not performed and no legitimate claim exists. The **deposit method** postpones recognizing a sale until a determination can be made as to whether a sale has occurred for accounting purposes. Revenue recognition is delayed until a future event occurs. If there has not been sufficient transfer of risks and rewards of ownership, even if a deposit has been received, recognition of the sale should be postponed until sufficient transfer has occurred. In that sense, the deposit method is not a revenue recognition method as are the installment and cost recovery methods.

Summary of Product Revenue Recognition Bases

The revenue recognition bases or methods, the criteria for their use, and the reasons for departing from the sale basis are summarized in Illustration 19-28.

---

[33]*Statement of Financial Accounting Standards No. 66,* par. 65.

Recognition Basis (or Method of Applying a Basis)	Criteria for Use	Reason(s) for Departing from Sale Basis
Percentage-of-completion method	Long-term construction of property; dependable estimates of extent of progress and cost to complete; reasonable assurance of collectibility of contract price; expectation that both contractor and buyer can meet obligations; and absence of inherent hazards that make estimates doubtful.	Availability of evidence of ultimate proceeds; better measure of periodic income; avoidance of fluctuations in revenues, expenses, and income; performance is a "continuous sale" and therefore not a departure from the sale basis.
Completed-contract method	Use on short-term contracts, and whenever percentage-of-completion cannot be used on long-term contracts.	Existence of inherent hazards in the contract beyond the normal, recurring business risks; conditions for using the percentage-of-completion method are absent.
Completion-of-production basis	Immediate marketability at quoted prices; unit interchangeability; difficulty of determining costs; and no significant distribution costs.	Known or determinable revenues; inability to determine costs and thereby defer expense recognition until sale.
Installment sales method and cost recovery method	Absence of reasonable basis for estimating degree of collectibility and costs of collection.	Collectibility of the receivable is so uncertain that gross profit (or income) is not recognized until cash is actually received.
Deposit method	Cash received before the sales transaction is completed.	No recognition of revenue and income because there is not sufficient transfer of the risks and rewards of ownership.

ILLUSTRATION 19-28
Revenue Recognition
Bases Other Than the
Sale Basis for Products[34]

CONCLUDING REMARKS

As indicated, revenue recognition principles are sometimes difficult to apply and often vary by industry. Recently the SEC has attempted to provide more guidance in this area because of the concern that the revenue recognition principle is sometimes being incorrectly applied. In some cases there has even been intentional misstatement of revenue to achieve better financial results. The latter practice is fraudulent financial reporting, and the SEC is vigorously prosecuting these situations.

For our capital markets to be efficient, investors must have confidence that the financial information provided is both relevant and reliable. As a result, it is imperative that aggressive revenue recognition practices be eliminated. It is our hope that recent efforts by the SEC and the accounting profession will lead to higher quality reporting in this area.

SUMMARY OF LEARNING OBJECTIVES

❶ Apply the revenue recognition principle. The revenue recognition principle provides that revenue is recognized (1) when it is realized or realizable and (2) when it is earned. Revenues are realized when goods and services are exchanged for cash or claims to cash. Revenues are realizable when assets received in exchanges are readily convertible to known amounts of cash or claims to cash. Revenues are earned when the

---

[34]Adapted from *Survey of Present Practices in Recognizing Revenues, Expenses, Gains, and Losses,* op. cit., pp. 12 and 13.

entity has substantially accomplished what it must do to be entitled to the benefits represented by the revenues, that is, when the earnings process is complete or virtually complete.

2 **Describe accounting issues involved with revenue recognition at point of sale.** The two conditions for recognizing revenue are usually met by the time product or merchandise is delivered or services are rendered to customers. Revenues from manufacturing and selling activities are commonly recognized at time of sale. Problems of implementation can arise because of (1) sales with buyback agreements, (2) revenue recognition when right of return exists, and (3) trade loading and channel stuffing.

3 **Apply the percentage-of-completion method for long-term contracts.** To apply the percentage-of-completion method to long-term contracts, one must have some basis for measuring the progress toward completion at particular interim dates. One of the most popular input measures used to determine the progress toward completion is the cost-to-cost basis. Using this basis, the percentage of completion is measured by comparing costs incurred to date with the most recent estimate of the total costs to complete the contract. The percentage that costs incurred bear to total estimated costs is applied to the total revenue or the estimated total gross profit on the contract in arriving at the revenue or the gross profit amounts to be recognized to date.

4 **Apply the completed-contract method for long-term contracts.** Under this method, revenue and gross profit are recognized only at point of sale, that is, when the contract is completed. Costs of long-term contracts in process and current billings are accumulated, but there are no interim charges or credits to income statement accounts for revenues, costs, and gross profit. The annual entries to record costs of construction, progress billings, and collections from customers would be identical to those for the percentage-of-completion method with the significant exclusion of the recognition of revenue and gross profit.

5 **Identify the proper accounting for losses on long-term contracts.** Two types of losses can become evident under long-term contracts: (1) *Loss in current period on a profitable contract:* Under the percentage-of-completion method only, the estimated cost increase requires a current period adjustment of excess gross profit recognized on the project in prior periods. This adjustment is recorded as a loss in the current period because it is a change in accounting estimate. (2) *Loss on an unprofitable contract:* Under both the percentage-of-completion and the completed-contract methods, the entire expected contract loss must be recognized in the current period.

6 **Describe the installment sales method of accounting.** The installment sales method recognizes income in the periods of collection rather than in the period of sale. The installment method of accounting is justified on the basis that when there is no reasonable approach for estimating the degree of collectibility, revenue should not be recognized until cash is collected.

7 **Explain the cost recovery method of accounting.** Under the cost recovery method, no profit is recognized until cash payments by the buyer exceed the seller's cost of the merchandise sold. After all costs have been recovered, any additional cash collections are included in income. The income statement for the period of sale reports sales revenue, the cost of goods sold, and the gross profit—both the amount that is recognized during the period and the amount that is deferred. The deferred gross profit is offset against the related receivable on the balance sheet. Subsequent income statements report the gross profit as a separate item of revenue when it is recognized as earned.

APPENDIX **19A**

Revenue Recognition for Special Sales Transactions

To supplement our presentation of revenue recognition, we have chosen to cover two common yet unique types of business transactions—**franchises** and **consignments**.

FRANCHISES

Accounting for franchise sales was chosen because of its popularity, complexity, and applicability to many of the previously discussed revenue recognition bases. In accounting for franchise sales, the accountant must analyze the transaction and, considering all the circumstances, must use judgment in selecting and applying one or more of the revenue recognition bases and then, possibly, monitor the situation over a long period of time.

> **OBJECTIVE ❽**
> After studying Appendix 19A, you should be able to: Explain revenue recognition for franchises and consignment sales.

As indicated throughout this chapter, revenue is recognized on the basis of two criteria: (1) when it is realized or realizable (occurrence of an exchange for cash or claims to cash), and (2) when it is earned (completion or virtual completion of the earnings process). These criteria are appropriate for most business activities, but for some sales transactions they simply do not adequately define when revenue should be recognized. The fast-growing franchise industry has given accountants special concern and challenge.

Four types of franchising arrangements have evolved: (1) manufacturer-retailer, (2) manufacturer-wholesaler, (3) service sponsor-retailer, and (4) wholesaler-retailer. The fastest growing category of franchising, and the one that caused a reexamination of appropriate accounting, has been the third category, **service sponsor-retailer**. Included in this category are such industries and businesses as:

Soft ice cream/frozen yogurt stores (Tastee Freeze, TCBY, Dairy Queen)

Food drive-ins (McDonald's, KFC, Burger King)

Restaurants (TGI Friday's, Pizza Hut, Denny's)

Motels (Holiday Inn, Marriott, Best Western)

Auto rentals (Avis, Hertz, National)

Part-time help (Manpower, Kelly Girl)

Others (H & R Block, Meineke Mufflers, 7-Eleven Stores)

Franchise companies derive their revenue from one or both of two sources: (1) from the sale of initial franchises and related assets or services, and (2) from continuing fees based on the operations of franchises. The franchisor (the party who grants business rights under the franchise) normally provides the franchisee (the party who operates the franchised business) with the following services:

❶ Assistance in site selection.
   (a) Analyzing location.
   (b) Negotiating lease.

② Evaluation of potential income.

③ Supervision of construction activity.
   (a) Obtaining financing.
   (b) Designing building.
   (c) Supervising contractor while building.

④ Assistance in the acquisition of signs, fixtures, and equipment.

⑤ Bookkeeping and advisory services.
   (a) Setting up franchisee's records.
   (b) Advising on income, real estate, and other taxes.
   (c) Advising on local regulations of the franchisee's business.

⑥ Employee and management training.

⑦ Quality control.

⑧ Advertising and promotion.[1]

During the 1960s and early 1970s it was standard practice for franchisors to recognize the entire franchise fee at the date of sale whether the fee was received then or was collectible over a long period of time. Frequently, franchisors recorded the entire amount as revenue in the year of sale even though many of the services were yet to be performed and uncertainty existed regarding the collection of the entire fee.[2] In effect the franchisors were counting their fried chickens before they were hatched.

However, a **franchise agreement** may provide for refunds to the franchisee if certain conditions are not met, and franchise fee profit can be reduced sharply by future costs of obligations and services to be rendered by the franchisor. To curb the abuses in revenue recognition that existed and to standardize the accounting and reporting practices in the franchise industry, the FASB issued *Statement No. 45*.

Initial Franchise Fees

The **initial franchise fee** is consideration for establishing the franchise relationship and providing some initial services. Initial franchise fees are to be recorded as revenue only when and as the franchisor makes "substantial performance" of the services it is obligated to perform and collection of the fee is reasonably assured. **Substantial performance** occurs when the franchisor has no remaining obligation to refund any cash received or excuse any nonpayment of a note and has performed all the initial services required under the contract. According to *FASB No. 45* "commencement of operations by the franchisee shall be presumed to be the earliest point at which substantial performance has occurred, unless it can be demonstrated that substantial performance of all obligations, including services rendered voluntarily, has occurred before that time."[3]

Illustration of Entries for Initial Franchise Fee

To illustrate, assume that Tum's Pizza Inc. charges an initial franchise fee of $50,000 for the right to operate as a franchisee of Tum's Pizza. Of this amount, $10,000 is payable when the agreement is signed and the balance is payable in five annual payments of $8,000 each. In return for the initial franchise fee, the franchisor will help locate the site, negotiate the lease or purchase of the site, supervise the construction activity, and provide the bookkeeping services. The credit rating of the franchisee indicates that money

---

[1]Archibald E. MacKay, "Accounting for Initial Franchise Fee Revenue," *The Journal of Accountancy,* January 1970, pp. 66–67.

[2]In 1987 and 1988 the SEC ordered a half-dozen fast-growing startup franchisors, including Jiffy Lube International, Moto Photo, Inc., Swensen's, Inc., and LePeep Restaurants, Inc., to defer their initial franchise fee recognition until earned. See "Claiming Tomorrow's Profits Today," *Forbes,* October 17, 1988, p. 78.

[3]"Accounting for Franchise Fee Revenue," *Statement of Financial Accounting Standards No. 45* (Stamford, Conn.: FASB, 1981), par. 5.

can be borrowed at 8%. The present value of an ordinary annuity of five annual receipts of $8,000 each discounted at 8% is $31,941.68. The discount of $8,058.32 represents the interest revenue to be accrued by the franchisor over the payment period.

❶ If there is reasonable expectation that the down payment may be refunded and if substantial future services remain to be performed by Tum's Pizza Inc., the entry should be:

Cash	10,000.00	
Notes Receivable	40,000.00	
Discount on Notes Receivable		8,058.32
Unearned Franchise Fees		41,941.68

❷ If the probability of refunding the initial franchise fee is extremely low, the amount of future services to be provided to the franchisee is minimal, collectibility of the note is reasonably assured, and substantial performance has occurred, the entry should be:

Cash	10,000.00	
Notes Receivable	40,000.00	
Discount on Notes Receivable		8,058.32
Revenue from Franchise Fees		41,941.68

❸ If the initial down payment is not refundable, represents a fair measure of the services already provided, with a significant amount of services still to be performed by the franchisor in future periods, and collectibility of the note is reasonably assured, the entry should be:

Cash	10,000.00	
Notes Receivable	40,000.00	
Discount on Notes Receivable		8,058.32
Revenue from Franchise Fees		10,000.00
Unearned Franchise Fees		31,941.68

❹ If the initial down payment is not refundable and no future services are required by the franchisor, but collection of the note is so uncertain that recognition of the note as an asset is unwarranted, the entry should be:

Cash	10,000	
Revenue from Franchise Fees		10,000

❺ Under the same conditions as those listed under 4 except that the down payment is refundable or substantial services are yet to be performed, the entry should be:

Cash	10,000	
Unearned Franchise Fees		10,000

In cases 4 and 5—where collection of the note is extremely uncertain—cash collections may be recognized using the installment method or the cost recovery method.[4]

Continuing Franchise Fees

Continuing franchise fees are received in return for the continuing rights granted by the franchise agreement and for providing such services as management training, advertising and promotion, legal assistance, and other support. Continuing fees should be reported as revenue when they are earned and receivable from the franchisee, unless a portion of them has been designated for a particular purpose, such as providing a specified amount for building maintenance or local advertising. In that case, the

---

[4]A study that compared four revenue recognition procedures—installment sales basis, spreading recognition over the contract life, percentage-of-completion basis, and substantial performance—for franchise sales concluded that the percentage-of-completion method is the most acceptable revenue recognition method; the substantial performance method was found sometimes to yield ultra-conservative results. See Charles H. Calhoun III, "Accounting for Initial Franchise Fees: Is It a Dead Issue?" *The Journal of Accountancy,* February 1975, pp. 60–67.

portion deferred shall be an amount sufficient to cover the estimated cost in excess of continuing franchise fees and provide a reasonable profit on the continuing services.

Bargain Purchases

In addition to paying continuing franchise fees, franchisees frequently purchase some or all of their equipment and supplies from the franchisor. The franchisor would account for these sales as it would for any other product sales. Sometimes, however, the franchise agreement grants the franchisee the right to make **bargain purchases** of equipment or supplies after the initial franchise fee is paid. If the bargain price is lower than the normal selling price of the same product, or if it does not provide the franchisor a reasonable profit, then a portion of the initial franchise fee should be deferred. The deferred portion would be accounted for as an adjustment of the selling price when the franchisee subsequently purchases the equipment or supplies.

Options to Purchase

A franchise agreement may give the franchisor an **option to purchase** the franchisee's business. As a matter of management policy, the franchisor may reserve the right to purchase a profitable franchised outlet, or to purchase one that is in financial difficulty. If it is probable at the time the option is given that the franchisor will ultimately purchase the outlet, then the initial franchise fee should not be recognized as revenue but should be recorded as a liability. When the option is exercised, the liability would reduce the franchisor's investment in the outlet.

Franchisor's Cost

Franchise accounting also involves proper accounting for the **franchisor's cost**. The objective is to match related costs and revenues by reporting them as components of income in the same accounting period. Franchisors should ordinarily defer **direct costs** (usually incremental costs) relating to specific franchise sales for which revenue has not yet been recognized. Costs should not be deferred, however, without reference to anticipated revenue and its realizability.[5] **Indirect costs** of a regular and recurring nature such as selling and administrative expenses that are incurred irrespective of the level of franchise sales should be expensed as incurred.

Disclosures of Franchisors

Disclosure of all significant commitments and obligations resulting from franchise agreements, including a description of services that have not yet been substantially performed, is required. Any resolution of uncertainties regarding the collectibility of franchise fees should be disclosed. Initial franchise fees should be segregated from other franchise fee revenue if they are significant. Where possible, revenues and costs related to franchisor-owned outlets should be distinguished from those related to franchised outlets.

CONSIGNMENTS

In some arrangements the delivery of the goods by the manufacturer (or wholesaler) to the dealer (or retailer) is not considered to be full performance and a sale because the manufacturer retains title to the goods. This specialized method of marketing certain types of products makes use of a device known as a consignment. Under this arrangement, the consignor (manufacturer) ships merchandise to the consignee

---

[5]"Accounting for Franchise Fee Revenue," p. 17.

(dealer), who is to act as an agent for the consignor in selling the merchandise. Both consignor and consignee are interested in selling—the former to make a profit or develop a market, the latter to make a commission on the sales.

The consignee accepts the merchandise and agrees to exercise due diligence in caring for and selling it. Cash received from customers is remitted to the consignor by the consignee, after deducting a sales commission and any chargeable expenses.

A modified version of the sale basis of revenue recognition is used by the consignor. That is, revenue is recognized only after the consignor receives notification of sale and the cash remittance from the consignee. The merchandise is carried throughout the consignment as the inventory of the consignor, separately classified as Merchandise on Consignment. It is not recorded as an asset on the consignee's books. Upon sale of the merchandise, the consignee has a liability for the net amount due the consignor. The consignor periodically receives from the consignee a report called **account sales** that shows the merchandise received, merchandise sold, expenses chargeable to the consignment, and the cash remitted. Revenue is then recognized by the consignor.

To illustrate consignment accounting entries, assume that Nelba Manufacturing Co. ships merchandise costing $36,000 on consignment to Best Value Stores. Nelba pays $3,750 of freight costs and Best Value pays $2,250 for local advertising costs that are reimbursable from Nelba. By the end of the period, two-thirds of the consigned merchandise has been sold for $40,000 cash. Best Value notifies Nelba of the sales, retains a 10% commission, and remits the cash due Nelba. The following journal entries would be made by the consignor (Nelba) and the consignee (Best Value):

NELBA MFG. CO. (Consignor)			BEST VALUE STORES (Consignee)		
Shipment of consigned merchandise					
Inventory on Consignment	36,000		No entry (record memo of merchandise		
Finished Goods Inventory		36,000	received).		
Payment of freight costs by consignor					
Inventory on Consignment	3,750		No entry.		
Cash		3,750			
Payment of advertising by consignee					
No entry until notified.			Receivable from Consignor	2,250	
			Cash		2,250
Sales of consigned merchandise					
No entry until notified.			Cash	40,000	
			Payable to Consignor		40,000
Notification of sales and expenses and remittance of amount due					
Cash	33,750		Payable to Consignor	40,000	
Advertising Expense	2,250		Receivable from		
Commission Expense	4,000		Consignor		2,250
Revenue from			Commission Revenue		4,000
Consignment Sales		40,000	Cash		33,750
Adjustment of inventory on consignment for cost of sales					
Cost of Goods Sold	26,500		No entry.		
Inventory on Consignment		26,500			
[2/3 ($36,000 + $3,750) = $26,500]					

ILLUSTRATION 19A-1
Entries for Consignment
Sales

Under the consignment arrangement, the manufacturer (consignor) accepts the risk that the merchandise might not sell and relieves the dealer (consignee) of the need to commit part of its working capital to inventory. A variety of different systems and account titles are used to record consignments, but they all share the common goal of postponing the recognition of revenue until it is known that a sale to a third party has occurred.

(b) Given the nature of Chou Foods Inc.'s agreement with its franchisees, when should revenue be recognized? Discuss the question of revenue recognition for both the initial franchise fee and the additional monthly fee of 2% of sales and give illustrative entries for both types of revenue.

(c) Assuming that Chow Foods Inc. sells some franchises for $100,000, which includes a charge of $20,000 for the rental of equipment for its useful life of 10 years, that $50,000 of the fee is payable immediately and the balance on non-interest-bearing notes at $10,000 per year, that no portion of the $20,000 rental payment is refundable in case the franchisee goes out of business, and that title to the equipment remains with the franchisor, what would be the preferable method of accounting for the rental portion of the initial franchise fee? Explain.

(AICPA adapted)

1 Explain the curren
recognition.

2 When is revenue co
ditions should exis
all or part of the
transaction?

3 When is revenue re
(a) Revenue from
services rendered?
to use enterprise as
assets other than p

4 Identify several typ
the types of busine
is common.

5 What are the three a
able to a seller that i
ership through retu

6 Under what condit
continued risks of
sold recognize sale

7 What are the two b
term construction c
that determine whe
should be used.

8 F. Scott Fitzgerald
contract to construc
The total estimated
Costs incurred in th
lion. F. Scott Fitzge
uses the percentage
revenue and gross
ognize in the first y

9 For what reasons s
method be used o
whenever possible?

10 What methods are
tent of progress tow
put measures" and
be used to determi

11 What are the two t
dent in accounting
nature of each type
for?

12 Under the percenta
the Construction in
struction in Proces
sheet?

USING YOUR JUDGMENT

FINANCIAL REPORTING PROBLEM: INTEL CORPORATION

Instructions

Refer to the financial statements and accompanying notes and discussion of Intel Corporation presented in Appendix 5B and answer the following questions.

(a) What were Intel's net revenues for 1998? Where did those revenues rank among Fortune's 500 largest industrial companies in 1998?

(b) What was the percentage of increase in Intel's revenues from 1997 to 1998? From 1996 to 1998? From 1993 to 1998?

(c) In its notes Intel states that it defers recognition of sales and income on shipments to distributors until the merchandise is sold by the distributors. What is the justification for deferring this recognition?

(d) In which foreign countries (geographic areas) did Intel experience significant revenues in 1998?

FINANCIAL STATEMENT ANALYSIS CASE

Westinghouse Electric Corporation

The following note appears in the "Summary of Significant Accounting Policies" section of the Annual Report of Westinghouse Electric Corporation.

> **Note 1 (in Part): Revenue Recognition.** Sales are primarily recorded as products are shipped and services are rendered. The percentage-of-completion method of accounting is used for nuclear steam supply system orders with delivery schedules generally in excess of five years and for certain construction projects where this method of accounting is consistent with industry practice.
>
> WFSI revenues are generally recognized on the accrual method. When accounts become delinquent for more than two payment periods, usually 60 days, income is recognized only as payments are received. Such delinquent accounts for which no payments are received in the current month, and other accounts on which income is not being recognized because the receipt of either principal or interest is questionable, are classified as nonearning receivables.

Instructions

(a) Identify the revenue recognition methods used by Westinghouse Electric as discussed in its note on significant accounting policies.

(b) Under what conditions are the revenue recognition methods identified in the first paragraph of Westinghouse's note above acceptable?

(c) From the information provided in the second paragraph of Westinghouse's note, identify the type of operation being described and defend the acceptability of the revenue recognition method.

COMPARATIVE ANALYSIS CASE

The Coca-Cola Company versus PepsiCo, Inc.

Instructions

Go to the Digital Tool site and, using The Coca-Cola Company and PepsiCo, Inc. Annual Report information, answer the following questions.

(a) What were Coca-Cola's and PepsiCo's net revenues (sales) for the year 1998? Which company increased its revenues the most (dollars and percentage) from 1997 to 1998?

(b) In which foreign countries (geographic areas) did Coca-Cola and PepsiCo experience significant revenues in 1998? Compare the amounts of foreign revenues to U.S. revenues for both Coca-Cola and PepsiCo.

RESEARCH CASES

Case 1

Companies registered with the Securities and Exchange Commission are required to file a current report on Form 8-K upon the occurrence of certain events.

Instructions

Use EDGAR or some other source to identify 8-Ks recently filed by two companies of your choice. Examine the 8-Ks and answer the following questions with regard to each.

(a) What corporate event or transaction triggered the filing of the Form 8-K?

(b) Identify any financial statements or exhibits included in the filing. How might these items help investors in evaluating the event/transaction?

Case 2

The December 19, 1994, issue of *Business Week* includes an article by Mark Maremont entitled "Numbers Game at Bausch & Lomb."

Instructions

Read the article and answer the following questions.

(a) What effect did the change in the contact lens division's sales strategy have on its 1993 sales and net income?

(b) According to the accounting experts referenced in the article, why was Bausch & Lomb not correct in recognizing revenue?

(c) How did Bausch & Lomb defend its accounting treatment?

(d) How was the problem resolved in October 1994?

ETHICS CASES

Case 1

Nimble Health and Racquet Club (NHRC), which operates eight clubs in the Chicago metropolitan area, offers one-year memberships. The members may use any of the eight facilities but must reserve racquetball court time and pay a separate fee before using the court. As an incentive to new customers, NHRC advertised that any customers not satisfied for any reason could receive a refund of the remaining portion of unused membership fees. Membership fees are due at the beginning of the individual membership period; however, customers are given the option of financing the membership fee over the membership period at a 15 percent interest rate.

Some customers have expressed a desire to take only the regularly scheduled aerobic classes without paying for a full membership. During the current fiscal year, NHRC began selling coupon books for aerobic classes only to accommodate these customers. Each book is dated and contains 50 coupons that may be redeemed for any regularly scheduled aerobic class over a one-year period. After the one-year period, unused coupons are no longer valid.

During 1995, NHRC expanded into the health equipment market by purchasing a local company that manufactures rowing machines and cross-country ski machines. These machines are used in NHRC's facilities and are sold through the clubs and mail order catalogs. Customers must make a 20 percent down payment when placing an equipment order; delivery is 60–90 days after order placement. The machines are sold with a 2-year unconditional guarantee. Based on past experience, NHRC expects the costs to repair machines under guarantee to be 4 percent of sales.

NHRC is in the process of preparing financial statements as of May 31, 2001, the end of its fiscal year. James Hogan, corporate controller, expressed concern over the company's performance for the year and decided to review the preliminary financial statements prepared by Barbara Hardy, NHRC's assistant controller. After reviewing the statements, Hogan proposed that the following changes be reflected in the May 31, 2001, published financial statements.

1 Membership revenue should be recognized when the membership fee is collected.

2 Revenue from the coupon books should be recognized when the books are sold.

3 Down payments on equipment purchases and expenses associated with the guarantee on the rowing and cross-country machines should be recognized when paid.

Hardy indicated to Hogan that the proposed changes are not in accordance with generally accepted accounting principles, but Hogan insisted that the changes be made. Hardy believes that Hogan wants to manipulate income to forestall any potential financial problems and increase his year-end bonus. At this point, Hardy is unsure what action to take.

Instructions

(a) (1) Describe when Nimble Health and Racquet Club (NHRC) should recognize revenue from membership fees, court rentals, and coupon book sales.

(2) Describe how NHRC should account for the down payments on equipment sales, explaining when this revenue should be recognized.

(3) Indicate when NHRC should recognize the expense associated with the guarantee of the rowing and cross-country machines.

(b) Discuss why James Hogan's proposed changes and his insistence that the financial statement changes be made is unethical. Structure your answer around or to include the following aspects of ethical conduct: competence, confidentiality, integrity, and/or objectivity.

(c) Identify some specific actions Barbara Hardy could take to resolve this situation.

(CMA adapted)

Case 2

Midwest Health Club offers one-year memberships. Membership fees are due in full at the beginning of the individual membership period. As an incentive to new customers, MHC advertised that any customers not satisfied for any reason could receive a refund of the remaining portion of unused membership fees. As a result of this policy, Stanley Hack, corporate controller, recognized revenue ratably over the life of the membership.

MHC is in the process of preparing its year-end financial statements. Phyllis Cavaretta, MHC's treasurer, is concerned about the company's lackluster performance this year. She reviews the financial statements Hack prepared and tells Hack to recognize membership revenue when the fees are received.

Instructions

Answer the following questions:

(a) What are the ethical issues involved?

(b) What should Hack do?

CHAPTER 20

Accounting for Income Taxes

Use It, but Don't Abuse It

As part of prudent management, companies are expected to manage all costs in order to maximize shareholder value. For example, good managers look for the best prices for raw materials and supplies that go into making their products, and are expected to be savvy bargainers in negotiating labor and other service contracts to minimize the overall cost of doing business.

Another set of costs that companies manage are those related to taxes. For example, by using accelerated depreciation methods for fixed assets, companies reduce their tax bills. With faster tax write-offs on fixed assets, companies report lower taxable income and pay lower taxes in the early years of the assets' lives, thereby managing tax costs.

What happens when companies cross the line from prudent tax management to abusive tax avoidance? Recently more companies appear to be crossing that line. As indicated in the following chart, corporate taxes as a share of profits have dropped from 26.6% in 1994 to just 21.8% in 1999.

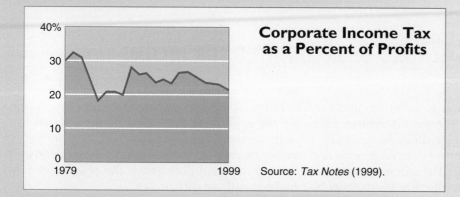

However, the IRS has been increasing its scrutiny of transactions that are done only to avoid taxes and that do not serve any legitimate business purpose. For example, in one recent case a company purchased and sold the same securities within an hour's time, simply to benefit from a multi-million dollar foreign tax credit. The tax judge in this case not only denied the credit but also imposed a 20% penalty. Thus, companies can manage their tax costs as long as they do not abuse the tax code.[1]

___

[1]Based on Howard Gleckman and Lorraine Woellert, "Kiss the Tax Shelter Goodbye? The Courts Crack Down on Egregious Corporate Tax Avoidance," *Business Week,* November 15, 1999, p. 50.

LEARNING OBJECTIVES

After studying this chapter, you should be able to:

1. Identify differences between pretax financial income and taxable income.
2. Describe a temporary difference that results in future taxable amounts.
3. Describe a temporary difference that results in future deductible amounts.
4. Explain the purpose of a deferred tax asset valuation allowance.
5. Describe the presentation of income tax expense in the income statement.
6. Describe various temporary and permanent differences.
7. Explain the effect of various tax rates and tax rate changes on deferred income taxes.
8. Apply accounting procedures for a loss carryback and a loss carryforward.
9. Describe the presentation of deferred income taxes in financial statements.
10. Identify special issues related to deferred income taxes.
11. Indicate the basic principles of the asset-liability method.

As the opening story indicates, income taxes are a major cost of business to most corporations. As a result, companies spend a considerable amount of time and effort to minimize their tax payments. The purpose of this chapter is to discuss the basic guidelines that companies must follow in reporting income taxes. The content and organization of the chapter are as follows:

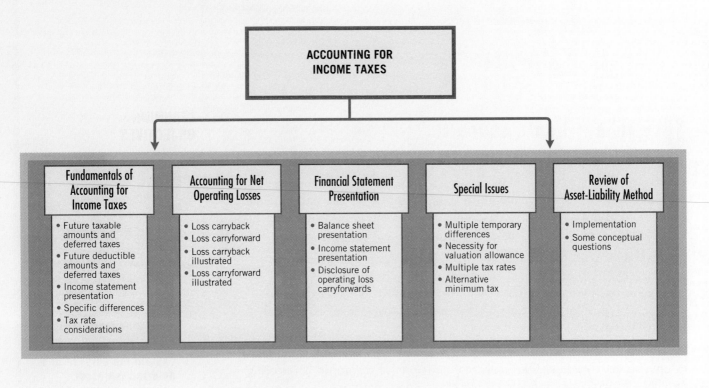

FUNDAMENTALS OF ACCOUNTING FOR INCOME TAXES

OBJECTIVE ❶
Identify differences between pretax financial income and taxable income.

INTERNATIONAL INSIGHT

In some countries, taxable income and pretax financial income are the same. As a consequence, accounting for differences between tax and book income is not significant.

Up to this point, you have learned the basic guidelines that corporations use to report information to investors and creditors. You should recognize that corporations also must file income tax returns following the guidelines developed by the Internal Revenue Service (IRS). Because GAAP and tax regulations are different in a number of ways, pretax financial income and taxable income frequently differ. Consequently, the amount that a company reports as tax expense will differ from the amount of taxes payable to the IRS. Illustration 20-1 highlights these differences.

Pretax financial income is a financial reporting term often referred to as income before taxes, income for financial reporting purposes, or income for book purposes. Pretax financial income is determined according to GAAP and is measured with the objective of providing useful information to investors and creditors. **Taxable income** (income for tax purposes) is a tax accounting term used to indicate the amount upon which income tax payable is computed. Taxable income is determined according to the Internal Revenue Code (the tax code), which is designed to raise money to support government operations.

To illustrate how differences in GAAP and IRS rules affect financial reporting and taxable income, assume that Chelsea Inc. reported revenues of $130,000 and expenses of $60,000 in each of its first three years of operations. Illustration 20-2 shows the (partial) income statement over these three years.

ILLUSTRATION 20-1
Fundamental Differences
between Financial and
Tax Reporting

ILLUSTRATION 20-2
Financial Reporting
Income

CHELSEA INC. GAAP Reporting			
	2002	2003	2004	Total
Revenues	$130,000	$130,000	$130,000	
Expenses	60,000	60,000	60,000	
Pretax financial income	**$ 70,000**	**$ 70,000**	**$ 70,000**	**$210,000**
Income tax expense (40%)	$ 28,000	$ 28,000	$ 28,000	$ 84,000

For tax purposes (following the tax code), Chelsea reported the same expenses to the IRS in each of the years, but taxable revenues were $100,000 in 2002, $150,000 in 2003, and $140,000 in 2004 as shown in Illustration 20-3.

ILLUSTRATION 20-3
Tax Reporting Income

CHELSEA INC. Tax Reporting			
	2002	2003	2004	Total
Revenues	$100,000	$150,000	$140,000	
Expenses	60,000	60,000	60,000	
Taxable income	**$ 40,000**	**$ 90,000**	**$ 80,000**	**$210,000**
Income tax payable (40%)	$ 16,000	$ 36,000	$ 32,000	$ 84,000

Income tax expense and income tax payable differ over the three years but in total are the same, as shown in Illustration 20-4.

ILLUSTRATION 20-4
Comparison of Income
Tax Expense to Income
Tax Payable

CHELSEA INC. Income Tax Expense and Income Tax Payable				
	2002	2003	2004	Total
Income tax expense	$28,000	$28,000	$28,000	$84,000
Income tax payable	16,000	36,000	32,000	84,000
Difference	$12,000	($ 8,000)	($ 4,000)	$ 0

The differences between income tax expense and income tax payable arise because for financial reporting, the full accrual method is used to report revenues, whereas for tax purposes a modified cash basis is used. As a result, Chelsea reports pretax financial income of $70,000 and income tax expense of $28,000 for each of the three years. However, taxable income fluctuates. For example, in 2002 taxable income is only $40,000, which means that just $16,000 is owed to the IRS that year. The income tax payable is classified as a current liability on the balance sheet.

As indicated in Illustration 20-4, for Chelsea the $12,000 ($28,000 − $16,000) difference between income tax expense and income tax payable in 2002 reflects taxes that will be paid in future periods. This $12,000 difference is often referred to as a **deferred tax amount**. In this case it is a **deferred tax liability**; in cases where taxes will be lower in the future, Chelsea would record a **deferred tax asset**. We explain the measurement and accounting for deferred tax liabilities and assets in the following two sections.

Future Taxable Amounts and Deferred Taxes

OBJECTIVE 2
Describe a temporary difference that results in future taxable amounts.

The example summarized in Illustration 20-4 shows how income tax payable can be different from income tax expense. One way that this can happen is when there are temporary differences between the amounts reported for tax purposes and those reported for book purposes. A temporary difference is the difference between the tax basis of an asset or liability and its reported (carrying or book) amount in the financial statements that will result in taxable amounts or deductible amounts in future years. Taxable amounts increase taxable income in future years, and deductible amounts decrease taxable income in future years.

In Chelsea Inc.'s situation, the only difference between the book basis and tax basis of the assets and liabilities relates to accounts receivable that arose from revenue recognized for book purposes. Illustration 20-5 indicates that accounts receivable are reported at $30,000 in the December 31, 2002, GAAP-basis balance sheet, but the receivables have a zero tax basis.

ILLUSTRATION 20-5
Temporary Difference,
Sales Revenue

Per Books	12/31/02	Per Tax Return	12/31/02
Accounts receivable	$30,000	Accounts receivable	$–0–

What will happen to this $30,000 temporary difference that originated in 2002 for Chelsea Inc.? Assuming that Chelsea expects to collect $20,000 of the receivables in 2003 and $10,000 in 2004, this collection will result in future taxable amounts of $20,000 in 2003 and $10,000 in 2004. These future taxable amounts will cause taxable income to exceed pretax financial income in both 2003 and 2004.

In the FASB's view, an assumption inherent in a company's GAAP balance sheet is that the assets and liabilities will be recovered and settled at their reported amounts (carrying amounts). The FASB believes that this assumption creates a requirement under accrual accounting to recognize currently the deferred tax consequences of temporary differences, that is, the amount of income taxes that would be payable (or refundable) when the reported amounts of the assets are recovered and the liabilities are settled, respectively. The following diagram illustrates the reversal or turn around of the temporary difference described in Illustration 20-5 and the resulting taxable amounts in future periods.

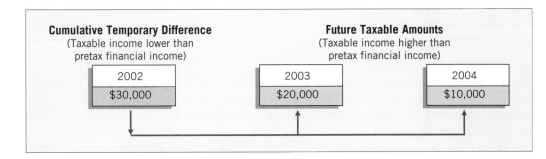

ILLUSTRATION 20-6
Reversal of Temporary
Difference, Chelsea Inc.

We have assumed that Chelsea will collect the accounts receivable and report the $30,000 collection as taxable revenues in future tax returns. A payment of income tax in both 2003 and 2004 will therefore occur. We therefore should record in Chelsea's books in 2002 the deferred tax consequences of the revenue and related receivables reflected in the 2002 financial statements. This necessitates the recording of a deferred tax liability.

Deferred Tax Liability

A **deferred tax liability** is the deferred tax consequences attributable to taxable temporary differences. In other words, **a deferred tax liability represents the increase in taxes payable in future years as a result of taxable temporary differences existing at the end of the current year**. Recall from the Chelsea example that income tax payable is $16,000 ($40,000 × 40%) in 2002 (Illustration 20-4). In addition, a temporary difference exists at year-end because the revenue and related accounts receivable are reported differently for book and tax purposes. The book basis of accounts receivable is $30,000 and the tax basis is zero. Thus, the total deferred tax liability at the end of 2002 is $12,000, computed as follows:

Book basis of accounts receivable	$30,000
Tax basis of accounts receivable	–0–
Cumulative temporary difference at the end of 2002	30,000
Tax rate	40%
Deferred tax liability at the end of 2002	$12,000

ILLUSTRATION 20-7
Computation of Deferred
Tax Liability, End of 2002

Another way to compute the deferred tax liability is to prepare a schedule that indicates the taxable amounts scheduled for the future as a result of existing temporary differences. Such a schedule is particularly useful when the computations become more complex.

	Future Years		
	2003	2004	Total
Future taxable amounts	$20,000	$10,000	$30,000
Tax rate	40%	40%	
Deferred tax liability at the end of 2002	$ 8,000	$ 4,000	$12,000

ILLUSTRATION 20-8
Schedule of Future
Taxable Amounts

Because it is the first year of operations for Chelsea, there is no deferred tax liability at the beginning of the year. The income tax expense for 2002 is computed as follows:

ILLUSTRATION 20-9
Computation of Income
Tax Expense, 2002

Deferred tax liability at end of 2002	$12,000
Deferred tax liability at beginning of 2002	–0–
Deferred tax expense for 2002	12,000
Current tax expense for 2002 (Income tax payable)	16,000
Income tax expense (total) for 2002	$28,000

This computation indicates that income tax expense has two components—current tax expense (which is the amount of income tax payable for the period) and deferred tax expense. Deferred tax expense is the increase in the deferred tax liability balance from the beginning to the end of the accounting period.

Taxes due and payable are credited to Income Tax Payable; the increase in deferred taxes is credited to Deferred Tax Liability; and the sum of those two items is debited to Income Tax Expense. For Chelsea Inc. the following entry is made at the end of 2002:

Income Tax Expense	28,000	
Income Tax Payable		16,000
Deferred Tax Liability		12,000

At the end of 2003 (the second year) the difference between the book basis and the tax basis of the accounts receivable is $10,000. This difference is multiplied by the applicable tax rate to arrive at the deferred tax liability of $4,000 ($10,000 × 40%) to be reported at the end of 2003. Income tax payable for 2003 is $36,000 (Illustration 20-3), the income tax expense for 2003 is as follows:

ILLUSTRATION 20-10
Computation of Income
Tax Expense, 2003

Deferred tax liability at end of 2003	$ 4,000
Deferred tax liability at beginning of 2003	12,000
Deferred tax expense (benefit) for 2003	(8,000)
Current tax expense for 2003 (Income tax payable)	36,000
Income tax expense (total) for 2003	$28,000

The journal entry to record income tax expense, the change in the deferred tax liability, and income tax payable for 2003 is as follows:

Income Tax Expense	28,000	
Deferred Tax Liability	8,000	
Income Tax Payable		36,000

In the entry to record income taxes at the end of 2004, the Deferred Tax Liability is reduced by $4,000. The Deferred Tax Liability account appears as follows at the end of 2004:

ILLUSTRATION 20-11
Deferred Tax Liability
Account after Reversals

Deferred Tax Liability			
2003	8,000	2002	12,000
2004	4,000		

The Deferred Tax Liability account has a zero balance at the end of 2004.

Some analysts dismiss deferred tax liabilities when assessing the financial strength of a company.[2] But the FASB indicates that the deferred tax liability meets the definition of a liability established in *Statement of Financial Accounting Concepts No. 6,* "Elements of Financial Statements" because:

❶ It results from a past transaction. In the Chelsea example, services were performed for customers and revenue was recognized in 2002 for financial reporting purposes but was deferred for tax purposes.

❷ It is a present obligation. Taxable income in future periods will be higher than pretax financial income as a result of this temporary difference. Thus, a present obligation exists.

❸ It represents a future sacrifice. Taxable income and taxes due in future periods will result from events that have already occurred. The payment of these taxes when they come due is the future sacrifice.

Summary of Income Tax Accounting Objectives

One objective of accounting for income taxes is to recognize the amount of taxes payable or refundable for the current year. In Chelsea's case, income tax payable is $16,000 for 2002.

A **second objective** is to recognize deferred tax liabilities and assets for the future tax consequences of events that have already been recognized in the financial statements or tax returns. Chelsea sold services to customers that resulted in accounts receivable of $30,000 in 2002; the $30,000 was reported on the 2002 income statement—it was not reported on the tax return as income. It will appear on future tax returns as income when it is collected. As a result, a $30,000 temporary difference exists at the end of 2002 which will cause future taxable amounts. A deferred tax liability of $12,000 is reported on the balance sheet at the end of 2002, which represents the increase in taxes payable in future years ($8,000 in 2003 and $4,000 in 2004) as a result of a temporary difference existing at the end of the current year. The related deferred tax liability is reduced by $8,000 at the end of 2003 and by another $4,000 at the end of 2004.

In addition to affecting the balance sheet, deferred taxes have an impact on income tax expense in each of the three years affected. In 2002, taxable income ($40,000) is less than pretax financial income ($70,000). Income tax payable for 2002 is therefore $16,000 (based on taxable income). Deferred tax expense of $12,000 is caused by the increase in the Deferred Tax Liability account on the balance sheet. Income tax expense is then $28,000 for 2002.

In 2003 and 2004, however, taxable income will be more than pretax financial income due to the reversal of the temporary difference ($20,000 in 2003 and $10,000 in 2004). Income tax payable will therefore be higher than income tax expense in 2003 and 2004. The Deferred Tax Liability account will be debited for $8,000 in 2003 and $4,000 in 2004. Credits for these amounts are recorded in Income Tax Expense (often referred to as a deferred tax benefit).

INTERNATIONAL INSIGHT

In Japan and Korea, deferred taxes are not recognized; in Sweden, they are generally recognized only through consolidation.

Future Deductible Amounts and Deferred Taxes

Assume that during 2002, Cunningham Inc. estimated its warranty costs related to the sale of microwave ovens to be $500,000 paid evenly over the next 2 years. For book purposes, in 2002 Cunningham reported warranty expense and a related estimated liability for warranties of $500,000 in its financial statements. For tax purposes, **the war-**

OBJECTIVE ❸
Describe a temporary difference that results in future deductible amounts.

---

[2]A study by D. Givoly and C. Hayn, "The Valuation of the Deferred Tax Liability: Evidence from the Stock Market," *The Accounting Review,* April 1992, provides evidence that the stock market views deferred tax liabilities arising from temporary differences as similar to other liabilities. More recently, a study by B. Ayers, "Deferred Tax Accounting Under *SFAS No. 109:* An Empirical Investigation of Its Incremental Value-Relevance Relative to *APB No. 11,*" *The Accounting Review,* April 1998, indicates that *SFAS No. 109* increased the usefulness of deferred tax amounts in financial statements.

ranty tax deduction is not allowed until paid; therefore, no warranty liability is recognized on a tax basis balance sheet. Thus, the balance sheet difference at the end of 2002 is as follows:

ILLUSTRATION 20-12
Temporary Difference,
Warranty Liability

Per Books	12/31/02	Per Tax Return	12/31/02
Estimated liability for warranties	$500,000	Estimated liability for warranties	$–0–

When the warranty liability is paid, an expense (deductible amount) will be reported for tax purposes. Because of this temporary difference, Cunningham Inc. should recognize in 2002 the tax benefits (positive tax consequences) for the tax deductions that will result from the future settlement of the liability. This future tax benefit is reported in the December 31, 2002, balance sheet as a **deferred tax asset**.

Another way to think about this situation is as follows: Deductible amounts will occur in future tax returns. These **future deductible amounts** will cause taxable income to be less than pretax financial income in the future as a result of an existing temporary difference. Cunningham's temporary difference originates (arises) in one period (2002) and reverses over two periods (2003 and 2004). This situation is diagramed as follows:

ILLUSTRATION 20-13
Reversal of Temporary
Difference,
Cunningham Inc.

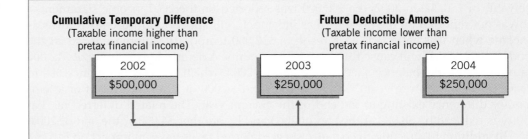

Deferred Tax Asset

A **deferred tax asset** is the deferred tax consequence attributable to deductible temporary differences. In other words, a **deferred tax asset represents the increase in taxes refundable (or saved) in future years as a result of deductible temporary differences existing at the end of the current year**.

To illustrate, assume that Hunt Co. accrues a loss and a related liability of $50,000 in 2002 for financial reporting purposes because of pending litigation. This amount is not deductible for tax purposes until the period the liability is paid, which is expected to be 2003. As a result, a deductible amount will occur in 2003 when the liability (Estimated Litigation Liability) is settled, causing taxable income to be lower than pretax financial income. The computation of the deferred tax asset at the end of 2002 (assuming a 40% tax rate) is as follows:

ILLUSTRATION 20-14
Computation of Deferred
Tax Asset, End of 2002

Book basis of litigation liability	$50,000
Tax basis of litigation liability	–0–
Cumulative temporary difference at the end of 2002	50,000
Tax rate	40%
Deferred tax asset at the end of 2002	$20,000

Another way to compute the deferred tax asset is to prepare a schedule that indicates the deductible amounts scheduled for the future as a result of deductible temporary differences. This schedule is shown in Illustration 20-15.

	Future Years
Future deductible amounts	$50,000
Tax rate	40%
Deferred tax asset at the end of 2002	$20,000

ILLUSTRATION 20-15
Schedule of Future
Deductible Amounts

Assuming that 2002 is Hunt's first year of operations, and income tax payable is $100,000, the income tax expense is computed as follows:

Deferred tax asset at end of 2002	$ 20,000
Deferred tax asset at beginning of 2002	–0–
Deferred tax expense (benefit) for 2002	(20,000)
Current tax expense for 2002 (Income tax payable)	100,000
Income tax expense (total) for 2002	$ 80,000

ILLUSTRATION 20-16
Computation of Income
Tax Expense, 2002

The **deferred tax benefit** results from the increase in the deferred tax asset from the beginning to the end of the accounting period. The deferred tax benefit is a negative component of income tax expense. The total income tax expense of $80,000 on the income statement for 2002 is then comprised of two elements—current tax expense of $100,000 and deferred tax benefit of $20,000. For Hunt Co. the following journal entry is made at the end of 2002 to record income tax expense, deferred income taxes, and income tax payable.

Income Tax Expense	80,000	
Deferred Tax Asset	20,000	
Income Tax Payable		100,000

At the end of 2003 (the second year) the difference between the book value and the tax basis of the litigation liability is zero. Therefore, there is no deferred tax asset at this date. Assuming that income tax payable for 2003 is $140,000, the computation of income tax expense for 2003 is as follows:

Deferred tax asset at the end of 2003	$ –0–
Deferred tax asset at the beginning of 2003	20,000
Deferred tax expense (benefit) for 2003	20,000
Current tax expense for 2003 (Income tax payable)	140,000
Income tax expense (total) for 2003	$160,000

ILLUSTRATION 20-17
Computation of Income
Tax Expense, 2003

The journal entry to record income taxes for 2003 is as follows:

Income Tax Expense	160,000	
Deferred Tax Asset		20,000
Income Tax Payable		140,000

The total income tax expense of $160,000 on the income statement for 2003 is then comprised of two elements—current tax expense of $140,000 and deferred tax expense of $20,000.

The Deferred Tax Asset account would appear as follows at the end of 2003:

Deferred Tax Asset			
2002	20,000	2003	20,000

ILLUSTRATION 20-18
Deferred Tax Asset
Account after Reversals

A key issue in accounting for income taxes is whether a deferred tax asset should be recognized in the financial records. We believe that a deferred tax asset meets the three main conditions for an item to be recognized as an asset:

❶ *It results from a past transaction.* In the Hunt Co. example, the accrual of the loss contingency is the past event that gives rise to a future deductible temporary difference.

❷ *It gives rise to a probable benefit in the future.* Taxable income is higher than pretax financial income in the current year (2002). However, in the next year the exact opposite occurs; that is, taxable income is lower than pretax financial income. Because this deductible temporary difference reduces taxes payable in the future, a probable future benefit exists at the end of the current period.

❸ *The entity controls access to the benefits.* Hunt Co. has the ability to obtain the benefit of existing deductible temporary differences by reducing its taxes payable in the future. Hunt Co. has the exclusive right to that benefit and can control others' access to it.

Deferred Tax Asset—Valuation Allowance

OBJECTIVE ❹
Explain the purpose of a deferred tax asset valuation allowance.

A deferred tax asset is recognized for all deductible temporary differences. However, a deferred tax asset should be reduced by a valuation allowance if, based on all available evidence, **it is** more likely than not that some portion or all of the deferred tax asset **will not be realized**. More likely than not means a level of likelihood that is at least slightly more than 50%.

Assume that Jensen Co. has a deductible temporary difference of $1,000,000 at the end of its first year of operations. Its tax rate is 40%, which means a deferred tax asset of $400,000 ($1,000,000 × 40%) is recorded. Assuming that income taxes payable are $900,000, the journal entry to record income tax expense, the deferred tax asset, and income tax payable is as follows:

Income Tax Expense	500,000	
Deferred Tax Asset	400,000	
Income Tax Payable		900,000

After careful review of all available evidence, it is determined that it is more likely than not that $100,000 of this deferred tax asset will not be realized. The journal entry to record this reduction in asset value is as follows:

Income Tax Expense	100,000	
Allowance to Reduce Deferred Tax Asset		
to Expected Realizable Value		100,000

In this journal entry, income tax expense is increased in the current period because a favorable tax benefit is not expected to be realized for a portion of the deductible temporary difference. **A valuation allowance is simultaneously established to recognize the reduction in the carrying amount of the deferred tax asset.** This valuation account is a contra account and may be reported on the financial statements in the following manner:

ILLUSTRATION 20-19
Balance Sheet Presentation of Valuation Allowance Account

Deferred tax asset	$400,000
Less: Allowance to reduce deferred tax	
asset to expected realizable value	100,000
Deferred tax asset (net)	$300,000

This allowance account is evaluated at the end of each accounting period. If, at the end of the next period, the deferred tax asset is still $400,000, but now $350,000 of this asset is expected to be realized, then the following entry is made to adjust the valuation account:

Allowance to Reduce Deferred Tax Asset		
to Expected Realizable Value	50,000	
Income Tax Expense		50,000

All available evidence, both positive and negative, should be carefully considered to determine whether, based on the weight of available evidence, a valuation allowance is needed. For example, if the company has been experiencing a series of loss years, a reasonable assumption is that these losses will continue and the benefit of the future deductible amounts will be lost. The use of a valuation account under other conditions will be discussed later in the chapter.

Income Statement Presentation

OBJECTIVE 5
Describe the presentation of income tax expense in the income statement.

Whether the change in deferred income taxes should be added to or subtracted from income tax payable in computing income tax expense depends on the circumstances. For example, an increase in a deferred tax liability would be added to income tax payable. On the other hand, an increase in a deferred tax asset would be subtracted from income tax payable. The formula to compute income tax expense (benefit) is as follows:

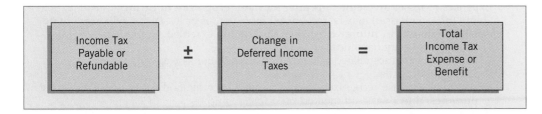

ILLUSTRATION 20-20
Formula to Compute Income Tax Expense

In the income statement or in the notes to the financial statements, the significant components of income tax expense attributable to continuing operations should be disclosed. Given the information related to Chelsea Inc. on page 1062, Chelsea's income statement might be reported as follows:

ILLUSTRATION 20-21
Income Statement Presentation of Income Tax Expense

CHELSEA INC. Income Statement For the Year Ending December 31, 2002		
Revenues		$130,000
Expenses		60,000
Income before income taxes		70,000
Income tax expense		
Current	$16,000	
Deferred	12,000	28,000
Net income		$ 42,000

As illustrated, both the current portion (amount of income tax payable for the period) and the deferred portion of income tax expense are reported. Another option is to simply report the total income tax expense on the income statement, and then in the notes to the financial statements indicate the current and deferred portions. Income tax expense is often referred to as "Provision for Income Taxes." Using this terminology, the current provision is $16,000 and the provision for deferred taxes is $12,000.

Specific Differences

OBJECTIVE 6
Describe various temporary and permanent differences.

Numerous items create differences between pretax financial income and taxable income. For purposes of accounting recognition, these differences are of two types: (1) temporary differences, and (2) permanent differences.

Temporary Differences

Temporary differences that will result in taxable amounts in future years when the related assets are recovered are often called taxable temporary differences; temporary differences that will result in deductible amounts in future years when the related book liabilities are settled are often called deductible temporary differences. Taxable temporary differences give rise to recording deferred tax liabilities; deductible temporary differences give rise to recording deferred tax assets. Examples of temporary differences are provided in Illustration 20-22.[3]

ILLUSTRATION 20-22
Examples of Temporary Differences

A. **Revenues or gains are taxable after they are recognized in financial income.** An asset (e.g., accounts receivable or investment) may be recognized for revenues or gains that will result in **taxable amounts in future years** when the asset is recovered. Examples:
   1. Installment sale accounted for on the accrual basis for financial reporting purposes and on the installment (cash) basis for tax purposes.
   2. Contracts accounted for under the percentage-of-completion method for financial reporting purposes and a portion of related gross profit deferred for tax purposes.
   3. Investments accounted for under the equity method for financial reporting purposes and under the cost method for tax purposes.
   4. Gain on involuntary conversion of nonmonetary asset which is recognized for financial reporting purposes but deferred for tax purposes.

B. **Expenses or losses are deductible after they are recognized in financial income.** A liability (or contra asset) may be recognized for expenses or losses that will result in **deductible amounts in future years** when the liability is settled. Examples:
   1. Product warranty liabilities.
   2. Estimated liabilities related to discontinued operations or restructurings.
   3. Litigation accruals.
   4. Bad debt expense recognized using the allowance method for financial reporting purposes; direct write-off method used for tax purposes.

C. **Revenues or gains are taxable before they are recognized in financial income.** A liability may be recognized for an advance payment for goods or services to be provided in future years. For tax purposes, the advance payment is included in taxable income upon the receipt of cash. Future sacrifices to provide goods or services (or future refunds to those who cancel their orders) that settle the liability will result in **deductible amounts in future years**. Examples:
   1. Subscriptions received in advance.
   2. Advance rental receipts.
   3. Sales and leasebacks for financial reporting purposes (income deferral) and reported as sales for tax purposes.
   4. Prepaid contracts and royalties received in advance.

D. **Expenses or losses are deductible before they are recognized in financial income.** The cost of an asset may have been deducted for tax purposes faster than it was expensed for financial reporting purposes. Amounts received upon future recovery of the amount of the asset for financial reporting (through use or sale) will exceed the remaining tax basis of the asset and thereby result in **taxable amounts in future years**. Examples:
   1. Depreciable property, depletable resources, and intangibles.
   2. Deductible pension funding exceeding expense.
   3. Prepaid expenses that are deducted on the tax return in the period paid.

Determining a company's temporary differences may prove difficult. A company should prepare a balance sheet for tax purposes that can be compared with its GAAP balance sheet; many of the differences between the two balance sheets would be temporary differences.

Originating and Reversing Aspects of Temporary Differences. An originating temporary difference is the initial difference between the book basis and the tax basis of an asset or liability, regardless of whether the tax basis of the asset or liability exceeds or is exceeded by the book basis of the asset or liability. A reversing difference, on the

---

[3]*SFAS No. 109* gives more examples of temporary differences. We have presented the most common types.

other hand, occurs when a temporary difference that originated in prior periods is eliminated and the related tax effect is removed from the deferred tax account.

For example, assume that Sharp Co. has tax depreciation in excess of book depreciation of $2,000 in 1998, 1999, and 2000, and that it has an excess of book depreciation over tax depreciation of $3,000 in 2001 and 2002 for the same asset. Assuming a tax rate of 30% for all years involved, the Deferred Tax Liability account would reflect the following:

ILLUSTRATION 20-23
Tax Effects of Originating and Reversing Differences

	Deferred Tax Liability				
Tax Effects	2001	900	1998	600	Tax Effects
of	2002	900	1999	600	of
Reversing Differences			2000	600	Originating Differences

The originating differences for Sharp in each of the first three years would be $2,000, and the related tax effect of each originating difference would be $600. The reversing differences in 2001 and 2002 would each be $3,000, and the related tax effect of each would be $900.

Permanent Differences

Some differences between taxable income and pretax financial income are permanent. Permanent differences are caused by items that (1) enter into pretax financial income but **never** into taxable income or (2) enter into taxable income but **never** into pretax financial income.

Congress has enacted a variety of tax law provisions in an effort to attain certain political, economic, and social objectives. Some of these provisions exclude certain revenues from taxation, limit the deductibility of certain expenses, and permit the deduction of certain other expenses in excess of costs incurred. A corporation that has tax-free income, nondeductible expenses, or allowable deductions in excess of cost has an effective tax rate that is different from the statutory (regular) tax rate.

Since permanent differences affect only the period in which they occur, they do not give rise to future taxable or deductible amounts. As a result, **there are no deferred tax consequences to be recognized**. Examples of permanent differences are shown in Illustration 20-24.

ILLUSTRATION 20-24
Examples of Permanent Differences

A. **Items are recognized for financial reporting purposes but not for tax purposes.**
Examples:
1. Interest received on state and municipal obligations.
2. Expenses incurred in obtaining tax-exempt income.
3. Proceeds from life insurance carried by the company on key officers or employees.
4. Premiums paid for life insurance carried by the company on key officers or employees (company is beneficiary).
5. Fines and expenses resulting from a violation of law.
6. Compensation expense associated with certain employee stock options.

B. **Items are recognized for tax purposes but not for financial reporting purposes.**
Examples:
1. "Percentage depletion" of natural resources in excess of their cost.
2. The deduction for dividends received from U.S. corporations, generally 70% or 80%.

Temporary and Permanent Differences Illustrated

To illustrate the computations used when both temporary and permanent differences exist, assume that the Bio-Tech Company reports pretax financial income of $200,000 in each of the years 2000, 2001, and 2002. The company is subject to a 30% tax rate, and has the following differences between pretax financial income and taxable income:

❶ An installment sale of $18,000 in 2000 is reported for tax purposes over an 18-month period at a constant amount per month beginning January 1, 2001. The entire sale is recognized for book purposes in 2000.

❷ Premium paid for life insurance carried by the company on key officers is $5,000 in 2001 and 2002. This is not deductible for tax purposes, but is expensed for book purposes.

The first item is a temporary difference and the second is a permanent difference. The reconciliation of Bio-Tech Company's pretax financial income to taxable income and the computation of income tax payable is shown in Illustration 20-25.

ILLUSTRATION 20-25
Reconciliation and
Computation of Income
Taxes Payable

	2000	2001	2002
Pretax financial income	$200,000	$200,000	$200,000
Permanent difference			
Nondeductible expense		5,000	5,000
Temporary difference			
Installment sale	(18,000)	12,000	6,000
Taxable income	182,000	217,000	211,000
Tax rate	30%	30%	30%
Income tax payable	$ 54,600	$ 65,100	$ 63,300

Note that differences causing pretax financial income to exceed taxable income are deducted from pretax financial income when determining taxable income. Conversely, differences causing pretax financial income to be less than taxable income are added to pretax financial income in determining taxable income.

Both permanent and temporary differences are considered in reconciling pretax financial income to taxable income. Since the permanent difference (nondeductible expense) does not result in future taxable or deductible amounts, deferred income taxes are not recorded for this difference.

The journal entries to record income taxes for Bio-Tech for 2000, 2001, and 2002 are as follows:

December 31, 2000

Income Tax Expense ($54,600 + $5,400)	60,000	
Deferred Tax Liability ($18,000 × 30%)		5,400
Income Tax Payable ($182,000 × 30%)		54,600

December 31, 2001

Income Tax Expense ($65,100 − $3,600)	61,500	
Deferred Tax Liability ($12,000 × 30%)	3,600	
Income Tax Payable ($217,000 × 30%)		65,100

December 31, 2002

Income Tax Expense ($63,300 − $1,800)	61,500	
Deferred Tax Liability ($6,000 × 30%)	1,800	
Income Tax Payable ($211,000 × 30%)		63,300

Bio-Tech has one temporary difference which originates in 2000 and reverses in 2001 and 2002. A deferred tax liability is recognized at the end of 2000 because the temporary difference causes future taxable amounts. As the temporary difference reverses, the deferred tax liability is reduced. There is no deferred tax amount associated with the difference caused by the nondeductible insurance expense because it is a permanent difference.

Although a statutory (enacted) tax rate of 30% applies for all three years, the effective rate is different. The **effective tax rate** is computed by dividing total income tax expense for the period by pretax financial income. The effective rate is 30% for 2000 ($60,000 ÷ $200,000 = 30%) and 30.75% for 2001 and 2002 ($61,500 ÷ $200,000 = 30.75%).

Tax Rate Considerations

In our previous illustrations, the enacted tax rate did not change from one year to the next. Thus, to compute the deferred income tax amount to be reported on the balance sheet, the cumulative temporary difference is simply multiplied by the current tax rate. Using Bio-Tech as an example, the cumulative temporary difference of $18,000 is multiplied by the enacted tax rate, 30% in this case, to arrive at a deferred tax liability of $5,400 ($18,000 × 30%) at the end of 2000.

OBJECTIVE 7
Explain the effect of various tax rates and tax rate changes on deferred income taxes.

Future Tax Rates

What happens if tax rates are different for future years? In this case, the **enacted tax rate** expected to apply should be used. Therefore, presently enacted changes in the tax rate that become effective for a particular future year(s) must be considered when determining the tax rate to apply to existing temporary differences. For example, assume that Warlen Co. at the end of 1999 has the following cumulative temporary difference of $300,000 computed as follows:

Book basis of depreciable assets	$1,000,000
Tax basis of depreciable assets	700,000
Cumulative temporary difference	$ 300,000

ILLUSTRATION 20-26
Computation of Cumulative Temporary Difference

Furthermore, assume that the $300,000 will reverse and result in taxable amounts in the following years when the enacted tax rates are as follows:

	2000	2001	2002	2003	2004	Total
Future taxable amounts	$80,000	$70,000	$60,000	$50,000	$40,000	$300,000
Tax rate	40%	40%	35%	30%	30%	
Deferred tax liability	$32,000	$28,000	$21,000	$15,000	$12,000	$108,000

ILLUSTRATION 20-27
Deferred Tax Liability Based on Future Rates

The total deferred tax liability at the end of 1999 is $108,000. Tax rates other than the current rate may be used only when the future tax rates have been enacted into law, as is apparently the case in this example. **If new rates are not yet enacted into law for future years, the current rate should be used.**

In determining the appropriate enacted tax rate for a given year, companies are required to use the **average tax rate**. The Internal Revenue Service and other taxing jurisdictions tax income on a graduated tax basis. For a U.S. corporation, the first $50,000 of taxable income is taxed at 15%, the next $25,000 at 25%, with higher incremental levels of income being taxed at rates as high as 39%. In computing deferred income taxes, companies for which graduated tax rates are a significant factor are therefore required to **determine the average tax rate and use that rate**.

Revision of Future Tax Rates

When a change in the tax rate is enacted into law, its effect on the existing deferred income tax accounts should be recorded immediately. **The effect is reported as an adjustment to income tax expense in the period of the change.**

Assume that on December 10, 1999, a new income tax act is signed into law that lowers the corporate tax rate from 40% to 35%, effective January 1, 2001. If Hostel Co. has one temporary difference at the beginning of 1999 related to $3 million of excess tax depreciation, then it has a Deferred Tax Liability account with a balance of $1,200,000 ($3,000,000 × 40%) at January 1, 1999. If taxable amounts related to this difference are scheduled to occur equally in 2000, 2001, and 2002, the deferred tax liability at the end of 1999 should be $1,100,000 computed as follows:

ILLUSTRATION 20-28
Schedule of Future
Taxable Amounts and
Related Tax Rates

	2000	2001	2002	Total
Future taxable amounts	$1,000,000	$1,000,000	$1,000,000	$3,000,000
Tax rate	40%	35%	35%	
Deferred tax liability	$ 400,000	$ 350,000	$ 350,000	$1,100,000

An entry, therefore, would be made at the end of 1999 to recognize the decrease of $100,000 ($1,200,000 − $1,100,000) in the deferred tax liability as follows:

Deferred Tax Liability	100,000	
Income Tax Expense		100,000

Corporate tax rates do not change often and, therefore, the current rate will usually be employed. However, state and foreign tax rates change more frequently and they require adjustments in deferred income taxes accordingly.[4]

ACCOUNTING FOR NET OPERATING LOSSES

OBJECTIVE 8
Apply accounting procedures for a loss carryback and a loss carryforward.

A **net operating loss (NOL)** occurs for tax purposes in a year when tax-deductible expenses exceed taxable revenues. An inequitable tax burden would result if companies were taxed during profitable periods without receiving any tax relief during periods of net operating losses. Under certain circumstances, therefore, the federal tax laws permit taxpayers to use the losses of one year to offset the profits of other years. This income-averaging provision is accomplished through the **carryback and carryforward of net operating losses**. Under this provision, a company pays no income taxes for a year in which it incurs a net operating loss. In addition, it may select one of the two options discussed below.

Loss Carryback

Through use of a **loss carryback**, a company may carry the net operating loss back 2 years and receive refunds for income taxes paid in those years. The loss must be applied to the earlier year first and then to the second year. Any loss remaining after the 2-year carryback may be **carried forward** up to 20 years to offset future taxable income. The following diagram illustrates the loss carryback procedure, assuming a loss in 2002.

ILLUSTRATION 20-29
Loss Carryback
Procedure

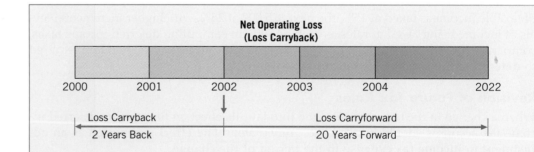

_____

[4]Tax rate changes nearly always will have a substantial impact on income numbers and the reporting of deferred income taxes on the balance sheet. As a result, you can expect to hear an economic consequences argument every time that Congress decides to change the tax rates. For example, when Congress raised the corporate rate from 34% to 35% in 1993, companies took an additional "hit" to earnings if they were in a deferred tax liability position.

Loss Carryforward

A company may elect to forgo the loss carryback and use only the loss carryforward option, offsetting future taxable income for up to 20 years.[5] Illustration 20-30 shows this approach.

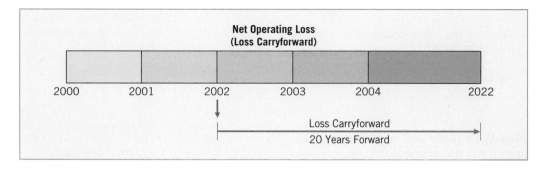

ILLUSTRATION 20-30
Loss Carryforward
Procedure

Operating losses can be substantial. IBM Corporation's total losses exceeded $15 billion dollars for the years 1992 and 1993, representing billions of dollars in potential tax savings. Companies that have suffered substantial losses are often attractive merger candidates because in certain cases the acquirer may use these losses to reduce its own income taxes.

Loss Carryback Illustrated

To illustrate the accounting procedures for a net operating loss carryback, assume that Groh Inc. has no temporary or permanent differences. Groh experiences the following:

Year	Taxable Income or Loss	Tax Rate	Tax Paid
1998	$ 50,000	35%	$17,500
1999	100,000	30%	30,000
2000	200,000	40%	80,000
2001	(500,000)	—	–0–

In 2001, Groh Inc. incurs a net operating loss that it decides to carry back. Under the law, the carryback must be applied first to the **second year preceding the loss year**. Therefore, the loss would be carried back first to 1999. Any unused loss would then be carried back to 2000. Accordingly, Groh would file amended tax returns for 1999 and 2000, receiving refunds for the $110,000 ($30,000 + $80,000) of taxes paid in those years.

For accounting as well as tax purposes, the $110,000 represents the tax effect (tax benefit) **of the loss carryback**. This tax effect should be recognized in 2001, the loss year. Since the tax loss gives rise to a refund that is both measurable and currently realizable, the associated tax benefit should be recognized in this loss period.

The following journal entry is appropriate for 2001:

Income Tax Refund Receivable	110,000	
Benefit Due to Loss Carryback (Income Tax Expense)		110,000

---

[5]The election to forgo the 2-year carryback period might be advantageous when a taxpayer had tax credit carryovers that might be wiped out and lost because of the carryback of the net operating loss. However, use of the carryback option provides an immediate inflow of cash at a time when alternate sources of cash may not be available. For this reason many companies with net operating losses, including companies that do not expect to return to profitable operations for a period of time, choose to carry their losses back.

The account debited, **Income Tax Refund Receivable**, is reported on the balance sheet as a current asset at December 31, 2001. The account credited is reported on the income statement for 2001 as follows:

GROH INC. Income Statement (partial) for 2001	
Operating loss before income taxes	$(500,000)
Income tax benefit	
Benefit due to loss carryback	110,000
Net loss	$(390,000)

Since the $500,000 net operating loss for 2001 exceeds the $300,000 total taxable income from the 2 preceding years, the remaining $200,000 loss is to be carried forward.

Loss Carryforward Illustrated

If a net operating loss is not fully absorbed through a carryback or if the company decides not to carry the loss back, then it can be carried forward for up to 20 years.[6] Because carryforwards are used to offset future taxable income, the **tax effect of a loss carryforward** represents **future tax savings**. Realization of the future tax benefit is dependent upon future earnings, the prospect of which may be highly uncertain.

The key accounting issue is whether there should be different requirements for recognition of a deferred tax asset for (a) deductible temporary differences and (b) operating loss carryforwards. The FASB's position is that in substance these items are the same—both are amounts that are deductible on tax returns in future years. As a result, the Board concluded that there should not be different requirements for recognition of a deferred tax asset from deductible temporary differences and operating loss carryforwards.[7]

Carryforward without Valuation Allowance

To illustrate the accounting for an operating loss carryforward, return to the Groh Inc. example from the preceding section. In 2001 the company would record the tax effect of the $200,000 loss carryforward as a deferred tax asset of $80,000 ($200,000 × 40%) assuming that the enacted future tax rate is 40%. The journal entries to record the benefits of the carryback and the carryforward in 2001 would be as follows:

To recognize benefit of loss carryback

Income Tax Refund Receivable	110,000	
Benefit Due to Loss Carryback (Income Tax Expense)		110,000

To recognize benefit of loss carryforward

Deferred Tax Asset	80,000	
Benefit Due to Loss Carryforward (Income Tax Expense)		80,000

The income tax refund receivable of $110,000 will be realized immediately as a refund of taxes paid in the past. A Deferred Tax Asset is established for the benefits of future tax savings. The two accounts credited are contra income tax expense items, which would be presented on the 2001 income statement as follows:

---

[6]The length of the carryforward period has varied. It has increased from 7 years to 20 years over a period of time.

[7]This requirement is controversial because many do not believe it is appropriate to recognize deferred tax assets except when they are assured beyond a reasonable doubt. Others argue that deferred tax assets for loss carryforwards should never be recognized until income is realized in the future.

ILLUSTRATION 20-32
Recognition of the Benefit of the Loss Carryback and Carryforward in the Loss Year

GROH INC. Income Statement (partial) for 2001		
Operating loss before income taxes		$(500,000)
Income tax benefit		
Benefit due to loss carryback	$110,000	
Benefit due to loss carryforward	80,000	190,000
Net loss		$(310,000)

The $110,000 **current tax benefit** is the income tax refundable for the year, which is determined by applying the carryback provisions of the tax law to the taxable loss for 2001. The $80,000 is the **deferred tax benefit** for the year, which results from an increase in the deferred tax asset.

For 2002, assume that Groh Inc. returns to profitable operations and has taxable income of $250,000 (prior to adjustment for the NOL carryforward) subject to a 40% tax rate. Groh Inc. would then realize the benefits of the carryforward for tax purposes in 2002 which were recognized for accounting purposes in 2001. The income tax payable for 2002 is computed as follows:

Taxable income prior to loss carryforward	$250,000
Loss carryforward deduction	(200,000)
Taxable income for 2002	50,000
Tax rate	40%
Income tax payable for 2002	$ 20,000

ILLUSTRATION 20-33
Computation of Income Tax Payable with Realized Loss Carryforward

The journal entry to record income taxes in 2002 would be as follows:

Income Tax Expense	100,000	
Deferred Tax Asset		80,000
Income Tax Payable		20,000

The Deferred Tax Asset account is reduced because the benefits of the NOL carryforward are realized in 2002.

The 2002 income statement that appears below would **not report** the tax effects of either the loss carryback or the loss carryforward, because both had been reported previously.

GROH INC. Income Statement (partial) for 2002		
Income before income taxes		$250,000
Income tax expense		
Current	$20,000	
Deferred	80,000	100,000
Net income		$150,000

ILLUSTRATION 20-34
Presentation of the Benefit of Loss Carryforward Realized in 2002, Recognized in 2001

Carryforward with Valuation Allowance

Return to the Groh Inc. example. Assume that it is more likely than not that the entire NOL carryforward will not be realized in future years. In this situation, Groh Inc. records the tax benefits of $110,000 associated with the $300,000 NOL carryback, as previously described. In addition, it records a Deferred Tax Asset of $80,000 ($200,000 ×

40%) for the potential benefits related to the loss carryforward and an allowance to reduce the deferred tax asset by the same amount. The journal entries in 2001 are as follows:

To recognize benefit of loss carryback

Income Tax Refund Receivable	110,000	
Benefit Due to Loss Carryback (Income Tax Expense)		110,000

To recognize benefit of loss carryforward

Deferred Tax Asset	80,000	
Benefit Due to Loss Carryforward (Income Tax Expense)		80,000

To record allowance amount

Benefit Due to Loss Carryforward (Income Tax Expense)	80,000	
Allowance to Reduce Deferred Tax Asset to		
Expected Realizable Value		80,000

The latter entry indicates that because positive evidence of sufficient quality and quantity is not available to counteract the negative evidence, a valuation allowance is needed. The presentation in the 2001 income statement would be as follows:

ILLUSTRATION 20-35
Recognition of Benefit of
Loss Carryback Only

GROH INC.	
Income Statement (partial) for 2001	
Operating loss before income taxes	$(500,000)
Income tax benefit	
Benefit due to loss carryback	110,000
Net loss	$(390,000)

In 2002, assuming that the company has taxable income of $250,000 (before considering the carryforward) subject to a tax rate of 40%, the deferred tax asset is realized and the allowance is no longer needed. The following entries would be made:

To record current and deferred income taxes

Income Tax Expense	100,000	
Deferred Tax Asset		80,000
Income Tax Payable		20,000

To eliminate allowance and recognize loss carryforward

Allowance to Reduce Deferred Tax Asset to		
Expected Realizable Value	80,000	
Benefit Due to Loss Carryforward (Income Tax Expense)		80,000

The $80,000 Benefit Due to the Loss Carryforward is computed by multiplying the $200,000 loss carryforward by the 40% tax rate. This amount is reported on the 2002 income statement because it was not recognized in 2001. Assuming that the income for 2002 is derived from continuing operations, the income statement would be presented as follows:

ILLUSTRATION 20-36
Recognition of Benefit of
Loss Carryforward When
Realized

GROH INC.		
Income Statement (partial) for 2002		
Income before income taxes		$250,000
Income tax expense		
Current	$20,000	
Deferred	80,000	
Benefit due to loss carryforward	(80,000)	20,000
Net income		$230,000

Another method is to report only one line for total income tax expense of $20,000 on the face of the income statement and disclose the components of income tax expense in the notes to the financial statements.

FINANCIAL STATEMENT PRESENTATION

The proper presentation of income taxes in the financial statements is illustrated below.

Balance Sheet Presentation

Deferred tax accounts are reported on the balance sheet as assets and liabilities. They should be classified as a net current amount and a net noncurrent amount. **An individual deferred tax liability or asset is classified as current or noncurrent based on the classification of the related asset or liability for financial reporting purposes.** A deferred tax asset or liability is considered to be related to an asset or liability if reduction of the asset or liability will cause the temporary difference to reverse or turn around. A deferred tax liability or asset that is not related to an asset or liability for financial reporting, including a deferred tax asset related to a loss carryforward, shall be classified according to the expected reversal date of the temporary difference.

> **OBJECTIVE ⑨**
> Describe the presentation of deferred income taxes in financial statements.

To illustrate, assume that Morgan Inc. records bad debt expense using the allowance method for accounting purposes and the direct write-off method for tax purposes. The company currently has Accounts Receivable and Allowance for Doubtful Accounts balances of $2 million and $100,000, respectively. In addition, given a 40% tax rate, it has a debit balance in the Deferred Tax Asset account of $40,000 (40% × $100,000). The $40,000 debit balance in the Deferred Tax Asset account is considered to be related to the Accounts Receivable and the Allowance for Doubtful Accounts balances because collection or write-off of the receivables will cause the temporary difference to reverse. Therefore, the Deferred Tax Asset account is classified as current, the same as the Accounts Receivable and Allowance for Doubtful Accounts balances.

In practice, most companies engage in a large number of transactions that give rise to deferred taxes. The balances in the deferred tax accounts should be analyzed and classified on the balance sheet in two categories: one for the net current amount and one for the net noncurrent amount. This procedure is summarized as indicated below.

❶ *Classify the amounts as current or noncurrent.* If they are related to a specific asset or liability, they should be classified in the same manner as the related asset or liability. If not so related, they should be classified on the basis of the expected reversal date of the temporary difference.

❷ *Determine the net current amount* by summing the various deferred tax assets and liabilities classified as current. If the net result is an asset, report on the balance sheet as a current asset; if a liability, report as a current liability.

❸ *Determine the net noncurrent amount* by summing the various deferred tax assets and liabilities classified as noncurrent. If the net result is an asset, report on the balance sheet as a noncurrent asset; if a liability, report as a long-term liability.

To illustrate, assume that K. Scott Company has four deferred tax items at December 31, 2002. An analysis reveals the following:

ILLUSTRATION 20-37
Classification of
Temporary Differences as
Current or Noncurrent

Temporary Difference	Resulting Deferred Tax (Asset)	Liability	Related Balance Sheet Account	Classification
1. Rent collected in advance: recognized when earned for accounting purposes and when received for tax purposes.	$(42,000)		Unearned Rent	Current
2. Use of straight-line depreciation for accounting purposes and accelerated depreciation for tax purposes.		$214,000	Equipment	Noncurrent
3. Recognition of profits on installment sales during period of sale for accounting purposes and during period of collection for tax purposes.		45,000	Installment Accounts Receivable	Current
4. Warranty liabilities: recognized for accounting purposes at time of sale; for tax purposes at time paid.	(12,000)		Estimated Liability under Warranties	Current
Totals	$(54,000)	$259,000		

The deferred taxes to be classified as current net to a $9,000 asset ($42,000 + $12,000 − $45,000), and the deferred taxes to be classified as noncurrent net to a $214,000 liability. Consequently, deferred income taxes would appear as follows on K. Scott's December 31, 2002, balance sheet:

ILLUSTRATION 20-38
Balance Sheet
Presentation of Deferred
Income Taxes

Current assets	
Deferred tax asset	$ 9,000
Long-term liabilities	
Deferred tax liability	$214,000

As indicated earlier, a deferred tax asset or liability **may not be related** to an asset or liability for financial reporting purposes. One example is an operating loss carryforward. In this case, a deferred tax asset is recorded, but there is no related, identifiable asset or liability for financial reporting purposes. In these limited situations, deferred income taxes should be classified according to the **expected reversal date** of the temporary difference. That is, the tax effect of any temporary difference reversing next year should be reported as current and the remainder should be reported as noncurrent. If a deferred tax asset is noncurrent, it should be classified in the "Other assets" section.

The total of all deferred tax liabilities, the total of all deferred tax assets, and the total valuation allowance should be disclosed. In addition, (1) any net change during the year in the total valuation allowance and (2) the types of temporary differences, carryforwards, or carrybacks that give rise to significant portions of deferred tax liabilities and assets should be disclosed.

Income tax payable is shown as a current liability on the balance sheet. Corporations are required to make estimated tax payments to the Internal Revenue Service quarterly. These estimated payments are recorded by a debit to Prepaid Income Taxes. As a result, the balance of the Income Tax Payable is offset by the balance of the Prepaid Income Taxes account when reporting income taxes on the balance sheet.

Income Statement Presentation

Income tax expense (or benefit) should be allocated to continuing operations, discontinued operations, extraordinary items, the cumulative effect of accounting changes, and prior period adjustments. This approach is referred to as intraperiod tax allocation and is illustrated later in the chapter.

In addition, the significant components of income tax expense attributable to continuing operations should be disclosed:

❶ Current tax expense or benefit.

❷ Deferred tax expense or benefit, exclusive of other components listed below.

❸ Investment tax credits.

❹ Government grants (to the extent they are recognized as a reduction of income tax expense).

❺ The benefits of operating loss carryforwards (resulting in a reduction of income tax expense).

❻ Tax expense that results from allocating certain tax benefits either directly to paid-in capital or to reduce goodwill or other noncurrent intangible assets of an acquired entity.

❼ Adjustments of a deferred tax liability or asset for enacted changes in tax laws or rates or a change in the tax status of an enterprise.

❽ Adjustments of the beginning-of-the-year balance of a valuation allowance because of a change in circumstances that causes a change in judgment about the realizability of the related deferred tax asset in future years.

In the notes, companies are also required to reconcile (using percentages or dollar amounts) income tax expense attributable to continuing operations with the amount that results from applying domestic federal statutory tax rates to pretax income from continuing operations. The estimated amount and the nature of each significant reconciling item should be disclosed. An example from the 1998 Annual Report of **PepsiCo, Inc.** is presented in Illustration 20-39. For another example, refer to **Intel Corporation**'s Annual Report at the end of Chapter 5. (See Note on page 231).

These income tax disclosures are required for several reasons. Some of the reasons are:

Go to the Digital Tool for additional examples of deferred tax disclosures.

❶ *Assessment of Quality of Earnings.* Many investors seeking to assess the quality of a company's earnings are interested in the reconciliation of pretax financial income to taxable income. Earnings that are enhanced by a favorable tax effect should be examined carefully, particularly if the tax effect is nonrecurring. For example, one year **Wang Laboratories** reported net income of $3.3 million, or 82 cents a share, versus $3.1 million, or 77 cents a share, in the preceding period. The entire increase in net income and then some resulted form a lower effective tax rate.

❷ *Better Predictions of Future Cash Flows.* Examination of the deferred portion of income tax expense provides information as to whether taxes payable are likely to be higher or lower in the future. A close examination may disclose the company's policy regarding capitalization of costs, recognition of revenue, and other policies giving rise to a difference between pretax financial income and taxable income. As a result, it may be possible to predict future reductions in deferred tax liabilities leading to a loss of liquidity because actual tax payments will be higher than the tax expense reported on the income statement.[8]

❸ *Helpful in Setting Governmental Policy.* Understanding the amount companies currently pay and the effective tax rate is helpful to government policymakers. In the early 1970s, when the oil companies were believed to have earned excess profits, many politicians and other interested parties attempted to determine their effective tax rates. Unfortunately, at that time such information was not available in published annual reports.

---

[8]An article by R. P. Weber and J. E. Wheeler, "Using Income Tax Disclosures to Explore Significant Economic Transactions," *Accounting Horizons*, September 1992, discusses how deferred tax disclosures can be used to assess the quality of earnings and to predict future cash flows.

ILLUSTRATION 20-39
Disclosure of Income
Taxes—PepsiCo, Inc.

PEPSICO, INC.

Note 12: Income Taxes

U.S. and foreign income from continuing operations before income taxes:

	1998	1997	1996
U.S.	$1,629	$1,731	$1,630
Foreign	634	578	(64)
	$2,263	$2,309	$1,566

Provision for income taxes on income from continuing operations:

	1998	1997	1996
Current: Federal	$ (193)	$ 598	$ 254
Foreign	267	110	138
State	46	59	72
	120	767	464
Deferred: Federal	136	23	204
Foreign	4	15	(41)
State	10	13	(3)
	150	51	160
	$ 270	$ 818	$ 624

Reconciliation of the U.S. Federal statutory tax rate to our effective tax rate on continuing operations:

	1998	1997	1996
U.S. Federal statutory tax rate	35.0%	35.0%	35.0%
State income tax, net of Federal tax benefit	1.6	2.0	2.9
Effect of lower taxes on foreign results	(3.0)	(5.5)	(4.4)
Settlement of prior years' audit issues	(5.7)	(1.7)	(2.9)
Puerto Rico settlement	(21.8)	—	—
Effect of unusual impairment and other items	3.4	2.2	9.7
Other, net	2.4	3.4	(0.5)
Effective tax rate on continuing operations	11.9%	35.4%	39.8%

Deferred taxes are recorded to give recognition to temporary differences between the tax bases of assets or liabilities and their reported amounts in the financial statements. We record the tax effect of the temporary differences as deferred tax assets or deferred tax liabilities. Deferred tax assets generally represent items that can be used as a tax deduction or credit in future years. Deferred tax liabilities generally represent items that we have taken a tax deduction for, but have not yet recorded in the income statement.

Deferred tax liabilities (assets):

	1998	1997
Intangible assets other than nondeductible goodwill	$1,444	$1,363
Property, plant and equipment	665	500
Safe harbor leases	109	115
Zero coupon notes	79	84
Other	473	335
Gross deferred tax liabilities	2,770	2,397
Net operating loss carryforwards	(562)	(520)
Postretirement benefits	(246)	(247)
Various current liabilities and other	(702)	(510)
Gross deferred tax assets	(1,510)	(1,277)
Deferred tax assets valuation allowance	571	458
Net deferred tax assets	(939)	(819)
Net deferred tax liabilities	$1,831	$1,578
Included in:		
Prepaid expenses, deferred income taxes and other current assets	$ (172)	$ (119)
Deferred income taxes	2,003	1,697
	$1,831	$1,578

Deferred tax liabilities are not recognized for temporary differences related to investments in foreign subsidiaries and in unconsolidated foreign affiliates that are essentially permanent in duration. It would not be practicable to determine the amount of any such deferred tax liabilities.

Net operating losses of $2.7 billion at year-end 1998 were carried forward and are available to reduce future taxable income of certain subsidiaries in a number of foreign and state jurisdictions. These net operating losses will expire as follows: $96 million in 1999, $2.4 billion between 2000 and 2012, while $201 million may be carried forward indefinitely.

Disclosure of Operating Loss Carryforwards

The amounts and expiration dates of any operating loss carryforwards for tax purposes should be disclosed. From this disclosure, the reader can determine the amount of income that may be recognized in the future on which no income tax will be paid. For example, the PepsiCo disclosure in Illustration 20-39 indicates that PepsiCo has $2.7 billion in net operating loss carryforwards that can be used to reduce future taxes up to the year 2012.

Loss carryforwards can be extremely valuable to a potential acquirer. At one time, Dalfort Company received nearly $360 million in operating loss carryforwards and other credits as a result of its ownership of Braniff Airlines. Many speculate that Dalfort bought Levitz Furniture Corp. (a large discounter of quality furniture) so that it could offset its carryforward losses from Braniff against Levitz's earnings. Companies that have suffered substantial losses may find themselves worth more "dead" than alive because their tax losses have little value to themselves but great value to other enterprises. In short, substantial tax carryforwards can have real economic value.[9]

SPECIAL ISSUES

A number of issues merit special attention when accounting for deferred income taxes. These are as follows:

OBJECTIVE 10
Identify special issues related to deferred income taxes.

1. Multiple temporary differences.
2. Necessity for a valuation allowance.
3. Multiple tax rates.
4. Alternative minimum tax.

Multiple Temporary Differences

To simplify the accounting when multiple temporary differences are involved, the following schedules should prove useful. Assume that Griggs Co. has two temporary differences in its first year of operations, one involving an installment sale and the other involving warranty costs. Other assumptions made should be apparent from the presentation of the scheduled material.

	Future Years		
	2003	2004	Total
Future taxable (deductible) amounts:			
Installment sale	$100,000	$100,000	$200,000
Warranty costs	(40,000)	(50,000)	(90,000)

ILLUSTRATION 20-40
Schedule of Future Taxable and Deductible Amounts

The deferred income taxes to be reported at the end of 2002 are computed as follows:

Temporary Differences	Future Taxable (Deductible) Amounts	Tax Rate	Deferred Tax (Asset)	Liability
Installment sale	$200,000	40%		$80,000
Warranty costs	(90,000)	40%	$(36,000)	
	$110,000		$(36,000)	$80,000

Because of a flat rate, these totals can be reconciled: $110,000 × 40% = ($36,000) + $80,000

ILLUSTRATION 20-41
Computation of Deferred Income Taxes

---

[9]The IRS frowns on acquisitions done solely to obtain operating loss carryforwards. If the merger is determined to be solely tax motivated, then the deductions will be disallowed. But because it is very difficult to determine whether a merger is or is not tax motivated, the "purchase of operating loss carryforwards" continues.

The journal entry to record income tax expense for 2002, assuming income tax payable is $500,000 is as follows:

Income Tax Expense	544,000	
Deferred Tax Asset	36,000	
Income Tax Payable		500,000
Deferred Tax Liability		80,000

Necessity for Valuation Allowance

All positive and negative information should be considered in determining whether a valuation allowance is needed. Whether a deferred tax asset will be realized depends on whether sufficient taxable income exists or will exist within the carryback or carryforward period available under tax law. The following possible sources of taxable income may be available under the tax law to realize a tax benefit for deductible temporary differences and carryforwards:

ILLUSTRATION 20-42
Possible Sources of
Taxable Income

Taxable Income Sources
a. Future reversals of existing taxable temporary differences
b. Future taxable income exclusive of reversing temporary differences and carryforwards
c. Taxable income in prior carryback year(s) if carryback is permitted under the tax law
d. Tax-planning strategies that would, if necessary, be implemented to: (1) Accelerate taxable amounts to utilize expiring carryforwards (2) Change the character of taxable or deductible amounts from ordinary income or loss to capital gain or loss (3) Switch from tax-exempt to taxable investments.[10]

If any one of these sources is sufficient to support a conclusion that a valuation allowance is not necessary, other sources need not be considered.

Forming a conclusion that a valuation allowance is not needed is difficult when there is negative evidence such as cumulative losses in recent years. Other examples of negative evidence include (but are not limited to) the following:

ILLUSTRATION 20-43
Negative Evidence to
Support Need for
Valuation Account

Negative Evidence
a. A history of operating loss or tax credit carryforwards expiring unused
b. Losses expected in early future years (by a presently profitable entity)
c. Unsettled circumstances that, if unfavorably resolved, would adversely affect future operations and profit levels on a continuing basis in future years
d. A carryback, carryforward period that is so brief that it would limit realization of tax benefits if (1) a significant deductible temporary difference is expected to reverse in a single year or (2) the enterprise operates in a traditionally cyclical business.

Examples (not prerequisites) of positive evidence that might support a conclusion that a valuation allowance is not needed when there is negative evidence include the following:

---

[10]"Accounting for Income Taxes," *Statement of Financial Accounting Standards No. 109* (Norwalk, Conn.: FASB, 1992). A tax planning strategy is an action that would be implemented to realize a tax benefit for an operating loss or tax credit carryforward before it expires. Tax planning strategies are considered when assessing the need for and amount of a valuation allowance for deferred tax assets.

ILLUSTRATION 20-44
Positive Evidence against
Need for Valuation
Account

Positive Evidence

a. Existing contracts or firm sales backlog that will produce more than enough taxable income to realize the deferred tax asset based on existing sale prices and cost structures

b. An excess of appreciated asset value over the tax basis of the entity's net assets in an amount sufficient to realize the deferred tax asset

c. A strong earnings history exclusive of the loss that created the future deductible amount (tax loss carryforward or deductible temporary difference) coupled with evidence indicating that the loss (for example, an unusual, infrequent, or extraordinary item) is an aberration rather than a continuing condition.[11]

The use of this valuation account provides management with an opportunity to manage its earnings. As one accounting expert notes: "The 'more likely than not' provision is perhaps the most judgmental clause in accounting." What some companies might do is set up valuation accounts and then use the valuation account to increase income as needed. Others could take the income immediately to increase capital or to offset large negative charges to income.[12]

Multiple Tax Rates

As indicated previously, the **enacted future tax rate** should be used to measure deferred taxes. This rate is applied to future taxable and deductible amounts arising from temporary differences. If there is a phased-in change in tax rates, selection of the future tax rate used to apply to a particular temporary difference requires some knowledge of when related taxable or deductible amounts will occur.

Deferred Tax Liability

Assume that Crandall Inc. at the end of 2002 (its third year of operations) has $2,400,000 of taxable temporary differences that are expected to result in taxable amounts of $800,000 in each of the following 3 years, 2003–2005. Enacted tax rates are 35% for 2001–2002, 40% for 2003–2005, and 45% for 2006 and thereafter. Assuming that taxable income is expected in 2003–2005, the deferred tax liability at December 31, 2002, is $960,000, which is computed as follows:

ILLUSTRATION 20-45
Computation of Deferred
Tax Liability

	Future Years			
	2003	2004	2005	Total
Future taxable amounts	$800,000	$800,000	$800,000	$2,400,000
Enacted future tax rate	40%	40%	40%	
Deferred tax liability at 12/31/02	$320,000	$320,000	$320,000	$ 960,000

Now assume that Crandall Inc. is expected to incur **losses** for tax purposes in 2003–2005. The tax rate to use to compute the deferred tax liability is 35% if realization of the tax benefit for those losses in years 2003–2005 will be by loss carryback to 2001–2002. The deferred tax liability at December 31, 2002, under this assumption is $840,000 ($2,400,000 × 35%).

If, on the other hand, realization of the tax benefit for those tax losses in 2003–2005 will be by loss carryforward to 2006 and thereafter, the tax rate to be used is 45%. In

---

[11]Ibid., par. 23 and 24.

[12]A recent study of the valuation allowances recorded by companies since *SFAS No. 109* was issued indicates that valuation allowance balances are related to the factors identified as positive and negative evidence. There is little evidence that the valuation is used for earnings management. See G. S. Miller and D. J. Skinner, "Determinants of the Valuation Allowance for Deferred Tax Assets under *SFAS No. 109*," *The Accounting Review*, April 1998.

this situation, the deferred tax liability is $1,080,000 ($2,400,000 × 45%) at December 31, 2002.

Deferred Tax Asset

To illustrate the measurement of a deferred tax asset, assume that Miller Co. has a $9,000,000 deductible temporary difference at the end of 2002 (its second year of operations). The $9,000,000 is expected to result in tax deductions of $3,000,000 in each of the next three years (2003–2005). Enacted tax rates are 30% for 2001 and 2002 and 40% for 2003 and thereafter. The tax rate to be used to measure the deferred tax asset is 40% if Miller expects to realize a tax benefit for the deductible temporary differences by offsetting taxable income earned in future years. Under this assumption, the amount of the deferred tax asset at December 31, 2002, is $3,600,000 ($9,000,000 × 40%).

Alternatively, the tax rate to be used is 30% if Miller expects to realize a tax benefit for the deductible temporary differences by loss carryback refund (that is, if Miller expects tax losses rather than taxable income in the future). In this case, the deferred tax asset at December 31, 2002, is $2,700,000 ($9,000,000 x 30%).

Valuation Allowance

Assume that Miller reports a $3,600,000 ($9,000,000 × 40%) deferred tax asset at December 31, 2002, which is expected to be realized by offsetting taxable income in future years. Also assume that taxable income and taxes payable in both 2001 and 2002 were $4,500,000 and $1,350,000, respectively. Realization of a tax benefit of, at least, $2,700,000 is assured because carryback refunds totalling $2,700,000 ($9,000,000 × 30%) can be used even if no taxable income is earned in future years. Recognition of a valuation allowance for the other $900,000 ($3,600,000 − $2,700,000) of the deferred tax asset depends on management's assessment of whether, based on the weight of available evidence, a portion or all of the tax benefit of the deductible temporary differences will be realized in future years.

Alternative Minimum Tax

The current tax law requires a corporation to compute its potential tax liability using the regular tax system and an alternative minimum tax (AMT) system.[13] The **alternative minimum tax system** is used to ensure that corporations do not avoid paying a fair share of income taxes through various tax avoidance approaches.[14]

For any given year, a corporation's annual income tax liability is the greater of the regular tax or the alternative minimum tax. Any deferred income taxes are computed using the regular tax rate(s), without regard to whether the company is subject to the alternative minimum tax now or is expected to be affected by it in the future. A company that pays the alternative minimum tax is entitled to a credit against its regular tax liability in subsequent years. Thus, paying the AMT gives the entity a tax credit carryforward.

A **tax credit carryforward** is similar to a future deductible amount with one major difference. A future deductible amount will offset **future taxable income** and a tax credit carryforward will offset **income taxes payable** in the future. If a tax rate of 40% applies, a tax credit of $1,000 is more valuable than a deduction of $1,000. The former will save $1,000 in tax and the latter will save only $400 in tax.

---

[13]Companies most likely to be affected by the AMT are capital-intensive companies subject to significant depreciation deductions. Also companies that significantly reduce regular tax liabilities by using the completed-contract method, or by using the installment method for reporting sales of certain real property often pay taxes at AMT rates.

[14]The reason for the alternative minimum tax is quite simple: During the 1981–1984 period many of the nation's largest corporations paid little if any income tax, and few paid at the full statutory rate. The alternative minimum tax now ensures that most corporations will pay a certain minimum amount of tax.

A deferred tax asset is recognized for an AMT credit carryforward. The need for a related valuation allowance must then be assessed. The AMT computations and considerations are extremely complex and require a background in income tax accounting. We will generalize here to say that unless there is a significant amount of tax preference items (determined by a set of complex income tax rules), total taxes paid over the entire life of a company will be based on the regular tax system, not the AMT system; **thus, an AMT credit carryforward will usually be judged to be realized in the future and a related valuation account will not be necessary**.

REVIEW OF THE ASSET-LIABILITY METHOD

The FASB believes that the asset-liability method (sometime referred to as the liability approach) is the most consistent method for accounting for income taxes. One objective of this approach is to recognize the amount of taxes payable or refundable for the current year. A second objective is to recognize **deferred tax liabilities and assets** for the **future tax consequences** of events that have been recognized in the financial statements or tax returns.

To implement the objectives, the following basic principles are applied in accounting for income taxes at the date of the financial statements:

a. A current tax liability or asset is recognized for the estimated taxes payable or refundable on the tax return for the current year.

b. A deferred tax liability or asset is recognized for the estimated future tax effects attributable to temporary differences and carryforwards.

c. The measurement of current and deferred tax liabilities and assets is based on provisions of the enacted tax law; the effects of future changes in tax laws or rates are not anticipated.

d. The measurement of deferred tax assets is reduced, if necessary, by the amount of any tax benefits that, based on available evidence, are not expected to be realized.[15]

Implementation of the Asset-Liability Method

The procedures for the computation of deferred income taxes are as follows:

Annual Procedures

a. Identify (1) the types and amounts of existing temporary differences and (2) the nature and amount of each type of operating loss and tax credit carryforward and the remaining length of the carryforward period.

b. Measure the total deferred tax liability for taxable temporary differences using the applicable tax rate.

c. Measure the total deferred tax asset for deductible temporary differences and operating loss carryforwards using the applicable tax rate.

d. Measure deferred tax assets for each type of tax credit carryforward.

e. Reduce deferred tax assets by a **valuation allowance** if, based on the weight of available evidence, it is *more likely than not* that some portion or all of the deferred tax assets will not be realized. The valuation allowance should be sufficient to reduce the deferred tax assets to the amount that is more likely than not to be realized.[16]

These procedures are illustrated graphically in Illustration 20-47.

OBJECTIVE ⑪
Indicate the basic principles of the asset-liability method.

INTERNATIONAL INSIGHT

Nations that recognize deferred taxes using the liability method include, among others, Australia, Germany, the United Kingdom, and Spain. IASC standards for taxes also use the liability method. The European Directives do not specify the accounting for deferred taxes.

ILLUSTRATION 20-46
Procedures for Computation of Deferred Income Taxes

---

[15]"Accounting for Income Taxes," par. 6 and 8, 1992.

[16]"Accounting for Income Taxes," par. 17.

ILLUSTRATION 20-47
Procedures for
Computing and
Reporting Deferred
Income Taxes

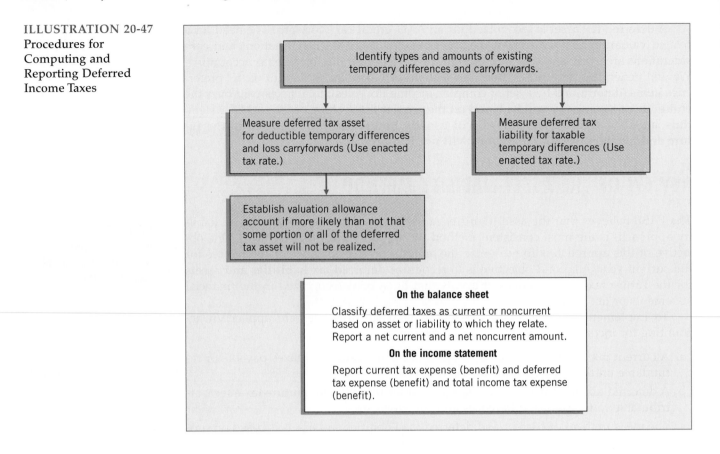

Some Conceptual Questions

The asset-liability method is the approach that the Board deemed most appropriate to record deferred income taxes. However, some conceptual questions remain. Presented below are three important issues.

❶ *Failure to Discount.* Without discounting the asset or liability (that is, failing to consider its present value), financial statements do not indicate the appropriate benefit of tax deferral or the burden of tax prepayment. Thus, comparability of the financial statements is impaired because a dollar related to short-term deferral appears to be of the same value as a dollar of longer-term deferral.

❷ *Classification Issue.* Consistent with the asset-liability approach, deferred tax assets and liabilities should be classified on the balance sheet based on when they will be realized or settled. Previously, the Board took the position that deferred taxes related to temporary differences reversing next period should be reported as current. Many believe this approach is correct and therefore disagree with the present requirements.

❸ *Dual Criteria for Recognition of Deferred Tax Asset.* Many believe that future deductible amounts arising from net operating loss carryforwards are different from future deductible amounts arising from normal operations. One rationale provided is that a deferred tax asset arising from normal operations results in a tax prepayment—a prepaid tax asset. In the case of loss carryforwards, no tax prepayment has been made.

Others argue that realization of a loss carryforward is less likely—and thus should require a more severe test—than for a net deductible amount arising from normal operations. Some have suggested that the test be changed from "more likely than not" to "probable" realization. Still others have indicated that because of the nature of net operating losses, deferred tax assets should never be established for these items.

The above controversies assume that the asset-liability approach is used. Others argue that completely different types of approaches should be used to report deferred income taxes.

As an aid to understanding deferred income taxes, the following glossary[17] is provided:

Go to the Digital Tool for a discussion of conceptual approaches to interperiod tax allocation.

KEY DEFERRED INCOME TAX TERMS

CARRYBACKS. Deductions or credits that cannot be utilized on the tax return during a year and that may be carried back to reduce taxable income or taxes paid in a prior year. An **operating loss carryback** is an excess of tax deductions over gross income in a year; a **tax credit carryback** is the amount by which tax credits available for utilization exceed statutory limitations.

CARRYFORWARDS. Deductions or credits that cannot be utilized on the tax return during a year and that may be carried forward to reduce taxable income or taxes payable in a future year. An **operating loss carryforward** is an excess of tax deductions over gross income in a year; a **tax credit carryforward** is the amount by which tax credits available for utilization exceed statutory limitations.

CURRENT TAX EXPENSE (BENEFIT). The amount of income taxes paid or payable (or refundable) for a year as determined by applying the provisions of the enacted tax law to the taxable income or excess of deductions over revenues for that year.

DEDUCTIBLE TEMPORARY DIFFERENCE. Temporary differences that result in deductible amounts in future years when the related asset or liability is recovered or settled, respectively.

DEFERRED TAX ASSET. The deferred tax consequences attributable to deductible temporary differences and carryforwards.

DEFERRED TAX CONSEQUENCES. The future effects on income taxes as measured by the enacted tax rate and provisions of the enacted tax law resulting from temporary differences and carryforwards at the end of the current year.

DEFERRED TAX EXPENSE (BENEFIT). The change during the year in an enterprise's deferred tax liabilities and assets.

DEFERRED TAX LIABILITY. The deferred tax consequences attributable to taxable temporary differences.

INCOME TAXES. Domestic and foreign federal (national), state, and local (including franchise) taxes based on income.

INCOME TAXES CURRENTLY PAYABLE (REFUNDABLE). Refer to current tax expense (benefit).

INCOME TAX EXPENSE (BENEFIT). The sum of current tax expense (benefit) and deferred tax expense (benefit).

TAXABLE INCOME. The excess of taxable revenues over tax deductible expenses and exemptions for the year as defined by the governmental taxing authority.

TAXABLE TEMPORARY DIFFERENCE. Temporary differences that result in taxable amounts in future years when the related asset or liability is recovered or settled, respectively.

TAX-PLANNING STRATEGY. An action that meets certain criteria and that would be implemented to realize a tax benefit for an operating loss or tax credit carryforward before it expires. Tax-planning strategies are considered when

---

[17]Ibid., Appendix E.

assessing the need for and amount of a valuation allowance for deferred tax assets.

TEMPORARY DIFFERENCE. A difference between the tax basis of an asset or liability and its reported amount in the financial statements that will result in taxable or deductible amounts in future years when the reported amount of the asset or liability is recovered or settled, respectively.

VALUATION ALLOWANCE. The portion of a deferred tax asset for which it is more likely than not that a tax benefit will not be realized.

SUMMARY OF LEARNING OBJECTIVES

❶ Identify differences between pretax financial income and taxable income. Pretax financial income (or income for book purposes) is computed in accordance with generally accepted accounting principles. Taxable income (or income for tax purposes) is computed in accordance with prescribed tax regulations. Because tax regulations and GAAP are different in many ways, pretax financial income and taxable income frequently differ. Differences may exist, for example, in the timing of revenue recognition and the timing of expense recognition.

❷ Describe a temporary difference that results in future taxable amounts. A credit sale that is recognized as revenue for book purposes in the period it is earned but is deferred and reported as revenue for tax purposes in the period it is collected will result in future taxable amounts. The future taxable amounts will occur in the periods the receivable is recovered and the collections are reported as revenue for tax purposes. This results in a deferred tax liability.

❸ Describe a temporary difference that results in future deductible amounts. An accrued warranty expense that is paid for and is deductible for tax purposes in a period later than the period in which it is incurred and recognized for book purposes will result in future deductible amounts. The future deductible amounts will occur in the periods during which the related liability for book purposes is settled. This results in a deferred tax asset.

❹ Explain the purpose of a deferred tax asset valuation allowance. A deferred tax asset should be reduced by a valuation allowance if, based on all available evidence, it is more likely than not (a level of likelihood that is at least slightly more than 50%) that some portion or all of the deferred tax asset will not be realized. All available evidence, both positive and negative, should be carefully considered to determine whether, based on the weight of available evidence, a valuation allowance is needed.

❺ Describe the presentation of income tax expense in the income statement. The significant components of income tax expense should be disclosed in the income statement or in the notes to the financial statements. The most commonly encountered components are the current expense (or benefit) and the deferred expense (or benefit).

❻ Describe various temporary and permanent differences. Examples of temporary differences are: (1) revenue or gains that are taxable after they are recognized in financial income; (2) expenses or losses that are deductible after they are recognized in financial income; (3) revenues or gains that are taxable before they are recognized in financial income; (4) expenses or losses that are deductible before they are recognized in financial income. Examples of permanent differences are: (1) items recognized for financial reporting purposes but not for tax purposes; and (2) items recognized for tax purposes but not for financial reporting purposes.

7 Explain the effect of various tax rates and tax rate changes on deferred income taxes. Tax rates other than the current rate may be used only when the future tax rates have been enacted into law. When a change in the tax rate is enacted into law, its effect on the deferred income tax accounts should be recognized immediately. The effects are reported as an adjustment to income tax expense in the period of the change.

8 Apply accounting procedures for a loss carryback and a loss carryforward. A company may carry a net operating loss back 2 years and receive refunds for income taxes paid in those years. The loss must be applied to the earlier year first and then to the second year. Any loss remaining after the 2-year carryback may be carried forward up to 20 years to offset future taxable income. A company may forgo the loss carryback and use the loss carryforward, offsetting future taxable income for up to 20 years.

9 Describe the presentation of deferred income taxes in financial statements. Deferred tax accounts are reported on the balance sheet as assets and liabilities. They should be classified as a net current and a net noncurrent amount. An individual deferred tax liability or asset is classified as current or noncurrent based on the classification of the related asset or liability for financial reporting. A deferred tax liability or asset that is not related to an asset or liability for financial reporting, including a deferred tax asset related to a loss carryforward, shall be classified according to the expected reversal date of the temporary difference.

10 Identify special issues related to deferred income taxes. A number of issues related to deferred income taxes are special: (1) multiple temporary differences; (2) necessity for a valuation allowance; (3) multiple tax rates; (4) alternative minimum tax.

11 Indicate the basic principles of the asset-liability method. The following basic principles are applied in accounting for income taxes at the date of the financial statements: (1) a current tax liability or asset is recognized for the estimated taxes payable or refundable on the tax return for the current year; (2) a deferred tax liability or asset is recognized for the estimated future tax effects attributable to temporary differences and carryforwards using the enacted tax rate; (3) the measurement of current and deferred tax liabilities and assets is based on provisions of the enacted tax law; (4) the measurement of deferred tax assets is reduced, if necessary, by the amount of any tax benefits that, based on available evidence, are not expected to be realized.

APPENDIX 20A

Comprehensive Illustration of Interperiod Tax Allocation

> **OBJECTIVE 12**
> After studying Appendix 20A, you should be able to: Understand and apply the concepts and procedures of interperiod tax allocation.

This appendix presents a comprehensive illustration of a deferred income tax problem with several temporary and permanent differences. The illustration follows one company through two complete years (2001 and 2002). **Study it carefully.** It should help you understand the concepts and procedures presented in the chapter.

FIRST YEAR — 2001

Allman Company, which began operations at the beginning of 2001, produces various products on a contract basis. Each contract generates a gross profit of $80,000. Some of Allman's contracts provide for the customer to pay on an installment basis whereby one-fifth of the contract revenue is collected in each of the following four years. Gross profit is recognized in the year of completion for financial reporting purposes (accrual basis) and in the year cash is collected for tax purposes (installment basis).

Presented below is information related to Allman's operations for 2001:

1 In 2001, the company completed seven contracts that allow for the customer to pay on an installment basis. The related gross profit amount of $560,000 was recognized for financial reporting purposes, whereas only $112,000 of gross profit on installment sales was reported on the 2001 tax return. The future collections on the related installment receivables are expected to result in taxable amounts of $112,000 in each of the next four years.

2 At the beginning of 2001, Allman Company purchased depreciable assets with a cost of $540,000. For financial reporting purposes, Allman depreciates these assets using the straight-line method over a 6-year service life. For tax purposes, the assets fall in the 5-year recovery class and Allman uses the MACRS system. The depreciation schedules for both financial reporting and tax purposes follow:

Year	Depreciation for Financial Reporting Purposes	Depreciation for Tax Purposes	Difference
2001	$ 90,000	$108,000	$(18,000)
2002	90,000	172,800	(82,800)
2003	90,000	103,680	(13,680)
2004	90,000	62,208	27,792
2005	90,000	62,208	27,792
2006	90,000	31,104	58,896
	$540,000	$540,000	$ –0–

3 The company warrants their product for 2 years from the date of completion of a contract. During 2001 product warranty liability accrued for financial reporting purposes was $200,000, and the amount paid for the satisfaction of warranty liability was $44,000. The remaining $156,000 is expected to be settled by expenditures of $56,000 in 2002 and $100,000 in 2003.

4 In 2001 nontaxable municipal bond interest revenue was $28,000.

5 During 2001 nondeductible fines and penalties of $26,000 were paid.

6 Pretax financial income for 2001 amounts to $412,000.

7 Tax rates enacted before the end of 2001:

2001	50%
2002 and later years	40%

8 The accounting period is the calendar year.

9 The company is expected to have taxable income in all future years.

Taxable Income and Income Tax Payable—2001

The first step is to determine Allman Company's income tax payable for 2001 by calculating its taxable income. This computation is as follows:

Pretax financial income for 2001	$412,000
Permanent differences:	
Nontaxable revenue—municipal bond interest	(28,000)
Nondeductible expenses—fines and penalties	26,000
Temporary differences:	
Excess gross profit per books ($560,000 − $112,000)	(448,000)
Excess depreciation per tax ($108,000 − $90,000)	(18,000)
Excess warranty expense per books ($200,000 − $44,000)	156,000
Taxable income for 2001	$100,000

ILLUSTRATION 20A-1
Computation of Taxable Income, 2001

Income tax payable is computed on taxable income for $100,000 as follows:

Taxable income for 2001	$100,000
Tax rate	50%
Income tax payable (current tax expense) for 2001	$ 50,000

ILLUSTRATION 20A-2
Computation of Income Tax Payable, End of 2001

Computing Deferred Income Taxes—End of 2001

The following schedule is helpful in summarizing the temporary differences and the resulting future taxable and deductible amounts:

	Future Years					
	2002	2003	2004	2005	2006	Total
Future taxable (deductible) amounts:						
Installment sales	$112,000	$112,000	$112,000	$112,000		$448,000
Depreciation	(82,800)	(13,680)	27,792	27,792	$58,896	18,000
Warranty costs	(56,000)	(100,000)				(156,000)

ILLUSTRATION 20A-3
Schedule of Future Taxable and Deductible Amounts, End of 2001

The amounts of deferred income taxes to be reported at the end of 2001 are computed as follows:

Temporary Difference	Future Taxable (Deductible) Amounts	Tax Rate	Deferred Tax (Asset)	Liability
Installment sales	$448,000	40%		$179,200
Depreciation	18,000	40%		7,200
Warranty costs	(156,000)	40%	$(62,400)	
Totals	$310,000		$(62,400)	$186,400*

*Because only a single tax rate is involved in all relevant years, these totals can be reconciled: $310,000 × 40% = ($62,400) + $186,400.

ILLUSTRATION 20A-4
Computation of Deferred Income Taxes, End of 2001

The temporary difference caused by the use of the accrual basis for financial reporting purposes and the installment method for tax purposes will result in future taxable amounts; hence, a deferred tax liability will arise. Because of the installment contracts completed in 2001, a temporary difference of $448,000 originates that will reverse in equal amounts over the next 4 years. The company is expected to have taxable income in all future years, and there is only one enacted tax rate applicable to all future years. Therefore, that rate (40%) is used to compute the entire deferred tax liability resulting from this temporary difference.

The temporary difference caused by different depreciation policies for books and for tax purposes originates over 3 years and then reverses over 3 years. This difference will cause deductible amounts in 2002 and 2003 and taxable amounts in 2004, 2005, and 2006, which sum to a net future taxable amount of $18,000 (which is the cumulative temporary difference at the end of 2001). Because the company is expected to have taxable income in all future years and because there is only one tax rate enacted for all of the relevant future years, that rate is applied to the net future taxable amount to determine the related net deferred tax liability.

The third temporary difference, caused by different methods of accounting for warranties, will result in deductible amounts in each of the 2 future years it takes to reverse. Because the company expects to report a positive income on all future tax returns and because there is only one tax rate enacted for each of the relevant future years, that 40% rate is used to calculate the resulting deferred tax asset.

Deferred Tax Expense (Benefit) and the Journal Entry to Record Income Taxes—2001

To determine the deferred tax expense (benefit), the beginning and ending balances of the deferred income tax accounts must be compared.

ILLUSTRATION 20A-5
Computation of Deferred
Tax Expense (Benefit),
2001

Deferred tax asset at the end of 2001	$ 62,400
Deferred tax asset at the beginning of 2001	–0–
Deferred tax expense (benefit)	$ (62,400)
Deferred tax liability at the end of 2001	$186,400
Deferred tax liability at the beginning of 2001	–0–
Deferred tax expense (benefit)	$186,400

The $62,400 increase in the deferred tax asset causes a deferred tax benefit to be reflected in the income statement. The $186,400 increase in the deferred tax liability during 2001 results in a deferred tax expense. These two amounts **net** to a deferred tax expense of $124,000 for 2001.

ILLUSTRATION 20A-6
Computation of Net
Deferred Tax Expense,
2001

Deferred tax expense (benefit)	$ (62,400)
Deferred tax expense (benefit)	186,400
Net deferred tax expense for 2001	$124,000

The total income tax expense is then computed as follows:

ILLUSTRATION 20A-7
Computation of Total
Income Tax Expense, 2001

Current tax expense for 2001	$ 50,000
Deferred tax expense for 2001	124,000
Income tax expense (total) for 2001	$174,000

The journal entry to record income tax payable, deferred income taxes, and income tax expense is as follows:

Income Tax Expense	174,000	
Deferred Tax Asset	62,400	
Income Tax Payable		50,000
Deferred Tax Liability		186,400

Financial Statement Presentation—2001

Deferred tax assets and liabilities are to be classified as current and noncurrent on the balance sheet based on the classifications of related assets and liabilities. When there is more than one category of deferred taxes, they are classified into a net current amount and a net noncurrent amount. The classification of Allman's deferred tax accounts at the end of 2001 is as follows:

Temporary Difference	Resulting Deferred Tax (Asset)	Liability	Related Balance Sheet Account	Classification
Installment sales		$179,200	Installment Receivable	Current
Depreciation		7,200	Plant Assets	Noncurrent
Warranty costs	$(62,400)		Warranty Obligation	Current
Totals	$(62,400)	$186,400		

ILLUSTRATION 20A-8
Classification of Deferred Tax Accounts, End of 2001

For the first temporary difference, there is a related asset on the balance sheet, installment accounts receivable. That asset is classified as a current asset because the company has a trade practice of selling to customers on an installment basis; hence, the resulting deferred tax liability is classified as a current liability. There are assets on the balance sheet that are related to the depreciation difference—the property, plant, and equipment being depreciated. The plant assets are classified as noncurrent; therefore, the resulting deferred tax liability is to be classified as noncurrent. Since Allman's operating cycle is at least 4 years in length, the entire $156,000 warranty obligation is classified as a current liability. Thus, the related deferred tax asset of $62,400 is classified as current.[1]

The balance sheet at the end of 2001 reports the following amounts:

Current liabilities	
Income tax payable	$ 50,000
Deferred tax liability ($179,200 − $62,400)	116,800
Long-term liabilities	
Deferred tax liability	$ 7,200

ILLUSTRATION 20A-9
Balance Sheet Presentation of Deferred Taxes, 2001

The income statement for 2001 reports the following:

Income before income taxes		$412,000
Income tax expense		
Current	$ 50,000	
Deferred	124,000	174,000
Net income		$238,000

ILLUSTRATION 20A-10
Income Statement Presentation of Income Tax Expense, 2001

---

[1]If Allman's operating cycle was less than one year in length, $56,000 of the warranty obligation would be expected to be settled within one year of the December 31, 2001, balance sheet and would require the use of current assets to settle it; thus $56,000 of the warranty obligation would be a current liability and the remaining $100,000 warranty obligation would be classified as a long-term (noncurrent) liability. This would mean $22,400 ($56,000 × 40%) of the related deferred tax asset would be classified as a current asset and $40,000 ($100,000 × 40%) of the deferred tax asset would be classified as a noncurrent asset. In doing homework problems, unless it is evident otherwise, assume a company's operating cycle is not longer than a year.

SECOND YEAR — 2002

❶ During 2002 the company collected $112,000 from customers for the receivables arising from contracts completed in 2001. Recovery of the remaining receivables is expected to result in taxable amounts of $112,000 in each of the following 3 years.

❷ In 2002 the company completed four new contracts that allow for the customer to pay on an installment basis. These installment sales created new installment receivables. Future collections of these receivables will result in reporting gross profit of $64,000 for tax purposes in each of the next four years.

❸ During 2002 Allman continued to depreciate the assets acquired in 2001 according to the depreciation schedules appearing on page 1090. Thus, depreciation amounted to $90,000 for financial reporting purposes and $172,800 for tax purposes.

❹ An analysis at the end of 2002 of the product warranty liability account showed the following details:

Balance of liability at beginning of 2002	$156,000
Expense for 2002 income statement purposes	180,000
Amount paid for contracts completed in 2001	(56,000)
Amount paid for contracts completed in 2002	(50,000)
Balance of liability at end of 2002	$230,000

The balance of the liability is expected to require expenditures in the future as follows:

$100,000 in 2003 due to 2001 contracts	
$ 50,000 in 2003 due to 2002 contracts	
$ 80,000 in 2004 due to 2002 contracts	
$230,000	

❺ During 2002 nontaxable municipal bond interest revenue was $24,000.

❻ A loss of $172,000 was accrued for financial reporting purposes because of pending litigation. This amount is not tax deductible until the period the loss is realized, which is estimated to be 2010.

❼ Pretax financial income for 2002 amounts to $504,800.

❽ The enacted tax rates still in effect are:

2001	50%
2002 and later years	40%

Taxable Income and Income Tax Payable—2002

The computation of taxable income for 2002 is as follows:

ILLUSTRATION 20A-11
Computation of Taxable Income, 2002

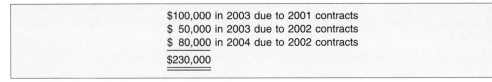

Pretax financial income for 2002	$504,800
Permanent difference:	
Nontaxable revenue—municipal bond interest	(24,000)
Reversing temporary differences:	
Collection on 2001 installment sales	112,000
Payments on warranties from 2001 contracts	(56,000)
Originating temporary differences:	
Excess gross profit per books—2002 contracts	(256,000)
Excess depreciation per tax	(82,800)
Excess warranty expense per books—2002 contracts	130,000
Loss accrual per books	172,000
Taxable income for 2002	$500,000

Income tax payable for 2002 is computed as follows:

Taxable income for 2002	$500,000
Tax rate	40%
Income tax payable (current tax expense) for 2002	$200,000

ILLUSTRATION 20A-12
Computation of Income
Tax Payable, End of 2002

Computing Deferred Income Taxes—End of 2002

The following schedule is helpful in summarizing the temporary differences existing at the end of 2002 and the resulting future taxable and deductible amounts.

ILLUSTRATION 20A-13
Schedule of Future
Taxable and Deductible
Amounts, End of 2002

	Future Years					
	2003	2004	2005	2006	2010	Total
Future taxable (deductible) amounts:						
Installment sales—2001	$112,000	$112,000	$112,000			$336,000
Installment sales—2002	64,000	64,000	64,000	$64,000		256,000
Depreciation	(13,680)	27,792	27,792	58,896		100,800
Warranty costs	(150,000)	(80,000)				(230,000)
Loss accrual					$(172,000)	(172,000)

The amounts of deferred income taxes to be reported at the end of 2002 are computed as follows:

ILLUSTRATION 20A-14
Computation of Deferred
Income Taxes, End of
2002

Temporary Difference	Future Taxable (Deductible) Amounts	Tax Rate	Deferred Tax (Asset)	Liability
Installment sales	$592,000*	40%		$236,800
Depreciation	100,800	40%		40,320
Warranty costs	(230,000)	40%	$ (92,000)	
Loss accrual	(172,000)	40%	(68,800)	
Totals	$290,800		$(160,800)	$277,120**

*Cumulative temporary difference = $336,000 + $256,000
**Because of a flat tax rate, these totals can be reconciled: $290,800 × 40% = $(160,800) + $277,120

Deferred Tax Expense (Benefit) and the Journal Entry to Record Income Taxes—2002

To determine the deferred tax expense (benefit), the beginning and ending balances of the deferred income tax accounts must be compared.

ILLUSTRATION 20A-15
Computation of Deferred
Tax Expense (Benefit),
2002

Deferred tax asset at the end of 2002	$160,800
Deferred tax asset at the beginning of 2002	62,400
Deferred tax expense (benefit)	$ (98,400)
Deferred tax liability at the end of 2002	$277,120
Deferred tax liability at the beginning of 2002	186,400
Deferred tax expense (benefit)	$ 90,720

The deferred tax expense (benefit) and the total income tax expense for 2002 are, therefore, as follows:

Deferred tax expense (benefit)	$ (98,400)
Deferred tax expense (benefit)	90,720
Deferred tax benefit for 2002	(7,680)
Current tax expense for 2002	200,000
Income tax expense (total) for 2002	$192,320

The deferred tax expense of $90,720 and the deferred tax benefit of $98,400 net to a deferred tax benefit of $7,680 for 2002.

The journal entry to record income taxes for 2002 is as follows:

Income Tax Expense	192,320	
Deferred Tax Asset	98,400	
Income Tax Payable		200,000
Deferred Tax Liability		90,720

Financial Statement Presentation — 2002

The classification of Allman's deferred tax accounts at the end of 2002 is as follows:

Temporary Difference	Resulting Deferred Tax (Asset)	Liability	Related Balance Sheet Account	Classification
Installment sales		$236,800	Installment Receivables	Current
Depreciation		40,320	Plant Assets	Noncurrent
Warranty costs	$ (92,000)		Warranty Obligation	Current
Loss accrual	(68,800)		Litigation Obligation	Noncurrent
Totals	$(160,800)	$277,120		

The new temporary difference introduced in 2002 (due to the litigation loss accrual) results in a litigation obligation that is classified as a long-term liability. Thus, the related deferred tax asset is noncurrent.

The balance sheet at the end of 2002 reports the following amounts:

Other assets (noncurrent)	
Deferred tax asset ($68,800 − $40,320)	$ 28,480
Current liabilities	
Income tax payable	$200,000
Deferred tax liability ($236,800 − $92,000)	144,800

The income statement for 2002 reports the following:

Income before income taxes		$504,800
Income tax expense		
Current	$200,000	
Deferred	(7,680)	192,320
Net income		$312,480

SUMMARY OF LEARNING OBJECTIVE FOR APPENDIX 20A

⑫ Understand and apply the concepts and procedures of interperiod tax allocation. Accounting for deferred taxes includes calculating taxable income and income tax payable for the year, computing deferred income taxes at the end of the year, determining deferred tax expense (benefit) and making the journal entry to record income taxes, and classifying deferred tax assets and liabilities as current and noncurrent in the financial statements.

QUESTIONS

1 Explain the difference between pretax financial income and taxable income.

2 What are the two objectives of accounting for income taxes?

3 Interest on municipal bonds is referred to as a permanent difference when determining the proper amount to report for deferred taxes. Explain the meaning of permanent differences and give two other examples.

4 Explain the meaning of a temporary difference as it relates to deferred tax computations and give three examples.

5 Differentiate between an originating temporary difference and a reversing difference.

6 The book basis of depreciable assets for Guinan Co. is $900,000, and the tax basis is $700,000 at the end of 2002. The enacted tax rate is 34% for all periods. Determine the amount of deferred taxes to be reported on the balance sheet at the end of 2002.

7 Borg Inc. has a deferred tax liability of $68,000 at the beginning of 2002. At the end of 2002, it reports accounts receivable on the books at $80,000 and the tax basis at zero (its only temporary difference). If the enacted tax rate is 34% for all periods, and income tax payable for the period is $230,000, determine the amount of total income tax expense to report for 2002.

8 What is the difference between a future taxable amount and a future deductible amount? When is it appropriate to record a valuation account for a deferred tax asset?

9 Pretax financial income for Mott Inc. is $300,000, and its taxable income is $100,000 for 2002. Its only temporary difference at the end of the period relates to a $90,000 difference due to excess depreciation for tax purposes. If the tax rate is 40% for all periods, compute the amount of income tax expense to report in 2002. No deferred income taxes existed at the beginning of the year.

10 How are deferred tax assets and deferred tax liabilities reported on the balance sheet?

11 Describe the procedures involved in segregating various deferred tax amounts into current and noncurrent categories.

12 How is it determined whether deferred tax amounts are considered to be "related" to specific assets or liability amounts?

13 At the end of the year, North Carolina Co. has pretax financial income of $550,000. Included in the $550,000 is $70,000 interest income on municipal bonds, $30,000 fine for dumping hazardous waste, and depreciation of $60,000. Depreciation for tax purposes is $45,000. Compute income taxes payable, assuming the tax rate is 30% for all periods.

14 Raleigh Co. has one temporary difference at the beginning of 2002 of $500,000. The deferred tax liability established for this amount is $150,000, based on a tax rate of 30%. The temporary difference will provide the following taxable amounts: $100,000 in 2003; $200,000 in 2004, and $200,000 in 2005. If a new tax rate for 2005 of 25% is enacted into law at the end of 2002, what is the journal entry necessary in 2002 (if any) to adjust deferred taxes?

15 What are some of the reasons that the components of income tax expense should be disclosed and a reconciliation between the effective tax rate and the statutory tax rate be provided?

16 Differentiate between "carryback" and "carryforward." Which can be accounted for with the greater certainty when it arises? Why?

17 What are the possible treatments for tax purposes of a net operating loss? What are the circumstances that determine the option to be applied? What is the proper treatment of a net operating loss for financial reporting purposes?

18 What is the alternative minimum tax and how does it affect the computation of deferred income taxes?

19 What controversy relates to the accounting for net operating loss carryforwards?

BRIEF EXERCISES

BE20-1 In 2002, Speedy Gonzalez Corporation had pretax financial income of $168,000 and taxable income of $110,000. The difference is due to the use of different depreciation methods for tax and accounting purposes. The effective tax rate is 40%. Compute the amount to be reported as income taxes payable at December 31, 2002.

BE20-2 At December 31, 2002, Thunderforce Inc. owned equipment that had a book value of $80,000 and a tax basis of $48,000 due to the use of different depreciation methods for accounting and tax purposes. The effective tax rate is 35%. Compute the amount Thunderforce should report as a deferred tax liability at December 31, 2002.

BE20-3 At December 31, 2001, Yserbius Corporation had a deferred tax liability of $25,000. At December 31, 2002, the deferred tax liability is $42,000. The corporation's 2002 current tax expense is $43,000. What amount should Yserbius report as total 2002 tax expense?

BE20-4 At December 31, 2002, Deep Space Nine Corporation had an estimated warranty liability of $125,000 for accounting purposes and $0 for tax purposes. (The warranty costs are not deductible until paid.) The effective tax rate is 40%. Compute the amount Deep Space Nine should report as a deferred tax asset at December 31, 2002.

BE20-5 At December 31, 2001, Next Generation Inc. had a deferred tax asset of $35,000. At December 31, 2002, the deferred tax asset is $59,000. The corporation's 2002 current tax expense is $61,000. What amount should Next Generation report as total 2002 tax expense?

BE20-6 At December 31, 2002, Stargate Corporation has a deferred tax asset of $200,000. After a careful review of all available evidence, it is determined that it is more likely than not that $80,000 of this deferred tax asset will not be realized. Prepare the necessary journal entry.

BE20-7 Steven Seagal Corporation had income before income taxes of $175,000 in 2002. Seagal's current income tax expense is $40,000, and deferred income tax expense is $30,000. Prepare Seagal's 2002 income statement, beginning with income before income taxes.

BE20-8 Tazmania Inc. had pretax financial income of $154,000 in 2002. Included in the computation of that amount is insurance expense of $4,000 which is not deductible for tax purposes. In addition, depreciation for tax purposes exceeds accounting depreciation by $14,000. Prepare Tazmania's journal entry to record 2002 taxes, assuming a tax rate of 45%.

BE20-9 Terminator Corporation has a cumulative temporary difference related to depreciation of $630,000 at December 31, 2002. This difference will reverse as follows: 2003, $42,000; 2004, $294,000; and 2005, $294,000. Enacted tax rates are 34% for 2003 and 2004, and 40% for 2005. Compute the amount Terminator should report as a deferred tax liability at December 31, 2002.

BE20-10 At December 31, 2001, Tick Corporation had a deferred tax liability of $680,000, resulting from future taxable amounts of $2,000,000 and an enacted tax rate of 34%. In May 2002, a new income tax act is signed into law that raises the tax rate to 38% for 2002 and future years. Prepare the journal entry for Tick to adjust the deferred tax liability.

BE20-11 Valis Corporation had the following tax information:

Year	Taxable Income	Tax Rate	Taxes Paid
1999	$300,000	35%	$105,000
2000	$325,000	30%	$ 97,500
2001	$400,000	30%	$120,000

In 2002 Valis suffered a net operating loss of $450,000, which it elected to carry back. The 2002 enacted tax rate is 29%. Prepare Valis's entry to record the effect of the loss carryback.

BE20-12 Zoop Inc. incurred a net operating loss of $500,000 in 2002. Combined income for 2000 and 2001 was $400,000. The tax rate for all years is 40%. Prepare the journal entries to record the benefits of the carryback and the carryforward.

BE20-13 Use the information for Zoop Inc. given in BE20-12. Assume that it is more likely than not that the entire net operating loss carryforward will not be realized in future years. Prepare all the journal entries necessary at the end of 2002.

BE20-14 Vectorman Corporation has temporary differences at 12/31/02 that result in the following deferred taxes:

Deferred tax liability—current	$38,000
Deferred tax asset—current	($52,000)
Deferred tax liability—noncurrent	$96,000
Deferred tax asset—noncurrent	($27,000)

Indicate how these balances would be presented in Vectorman's 12/31/02 balance sheet.

EXERCISES

E20-1 (One Temporary Difference, Future Taxable Amounts, One Rate, No Beginning Deferred Taxes)
South Carolina Corporation has one temporary difference at the end of 2002 that will reverse and cause taxable amounts of $55,000 in 2003, $60,000 in 2004, and $65,000 in 2005. South Carolina's pretax financial income for 2002 is $300,000 and the tax rate is 30% for all years. There are no deferred taxes at the beginning of 2002.

Instructions
- **(a)** Compute taxable income and income taxes payable for 2002.
- **(b)** Prepare the journal entry to record income tax expense, deferred income taxes, and income taxes payable for 2002.
- **(c)** Prepare the income tax expense section of the income statement for 2002, beginning with the line "Income before income taxes."

E20-2 (Two Differences, No Beginning Deferred Taxes, Tracked through 2 Years) The following information is available for Wenger Corporation for 2001:

1. Excess of tax depreciation over book depreciation, $40,000. This $40,000 difference will reverse equally over the years 2002–2005.
2. Deferral, for book purposes, of $20,000 of rent received in advance. The rent will be earned in 2002.
3. Pretax financial income, $300,000.
4. Tax rate for all years, 40%.

Instructions
- **(a)** Compute taxable income for 2001.
- **(b)** Prepare the journal entry to record income tax expense, deferred income taxes, and income taxes payable for 2001.
- **(c)** Prepare the journal entry to record income tax expense, deferred income taxes, and income taxes payable for 2002, assuming taxable income of $325,000.

E20-3 (One Temporary Difference, Future Taxable Amounts, One Rate, Beginning Deferred Taxes)
Bandung Corporation began 2002 with a $92,000 balance in the Deferred Tax Liability account. At the end of 2002, the related cumulative temporary difference amounts to $350,000, and it will reverse evenly over the next 2 years. Pretax accounting income for 2002 is $525,000, the tax rate for all years is 40%, and taxable income for 2002 is $405,000.

Instructions
- **(a)** Compute income taxes payable for 2002.
- **(b)** Prepare the journal entry to record income tax expense, deferred income taxes, and income taxes payable for 2002.
- **(c)** Prepare the income tax expense section of the income statement for 2002 beginning with the line "Income before income taxes."

E20-4 (Three Differences, Compute Taxable Income, Entry for Taxes) Zurich Company reports pretax financial income of $70,000 for 2002. The following items cause taxable income to be different than pretax financial income:

1. Depreciation on the tax return is greater than depreciation on the income statement by $16,000.
2. Rent collected on the tax return is greater than rent earned on the income statement by $22,000.
3. Fines for pollution appear as an expense of $11,000 on the income statement.

Zurich's tax rate is 30% for all years and the company expects to report taxable income in all future years. There are no deferred taxes at the beginning of 2002.

Instructions
- **(a)** Compute taxable income and income taxes payable for 2002.
- **(b)** Prepare the journal entry to record income tax expense, deferred income taxes, and income taxes payable for 2002.

E20-23 (Depreciation, Temporary Difference Tracked over 5 Years) Patricia Ford Co. purchased depreciable assets costing $600,000 on January 2, 2000. For tax purposes, the company uses the elective straight-line depreciation method over the recovery period of 3 years. (*Hint:* The half-year convention must be used on these assets.) For financial reporting purposes, the company uses straight-line depreciation over 5 years. The enacted tax rate is 34% for all years. This depreciation difference is the only temporary difference the company has. Assume that Ford has taxable income of $240,000 in each of the years 2000–2004.

Instructions

Determine the amount of deferred income taxes and indicate where it should be reported in the balance sheet for each year from 2000 to 2004.

E20-24 (Two Temporary Differences, Multiple Rates, Future Taxable Income) Svetlana Boginskaya Inc. has two temporary differences at the end of 2001. The first difference stems from installment sales and the second one results from the accrual of a loss contingency. Boginskaya's accounting department has developed a schedule of future taxable and deductible amounts related to these temporary differences as follows:

	2002	2003	2004	2005
Taxable amounts	$40,000	$50,000	$60,000	$80,000
Deductible amounts		(15,000)	(19,000)	
	$40,000	$35,000	$41,000	$80,000

As of the beginning of 2001, the enacted tax rate is 34% for 2001 and 2002 and 38% for 2003–2006. At the beginning of 2001, the company had no deferred income taxes on its balance sheet. Taxable income for 2001 is $500,000. Taxable income is expected in all future years.

Instructions

(a) Prepare the journal entry to record income tax expense, deferred income taxes, and income taxes payable for 2001.

(b) Indicate how deferred income taxes would be classified on the balance sheet at the end of 2001.

E20-25 (Two Differences, One Rate, First Year) The differences between the book basis and tax basis of the assets and liabilities of JoAnn Castle Corporation at the end of 2001 are presented below:

	Book Basis	Tax Basis
Accounts receivable	$50,000	$–0–
Litigation liability	30,000	–0–

It is estimated that the litigation liability will be settled in 2002. The difference in accounts receivable will result in taxable amounts of $30,000 in 2002 and $20,000 in 2003. The company has taxable income of $350,000 in 2001 and is expected to have taxable income in each of the following 2 years. Its enacted tax rate is 34% for all years. This is the company's first year of operations. The operating cycle of the business is 2 years.

Instructions

(a) Prepare the journal entry to record income tax expense, deferred income taxes, and income tax payable for 2001.

(b) Indicate how deferred income taxes will be reported on the balance sheet at the end of 2001.

E20-26 (NOL Carryback and Carryforward, Valuation Account versus No Valuation Account) Spamela Hamderson Inc. reports the following pretax income (loss) for both financial reporting purposes and tax purposes (assume the carryback provision is used for a net operating loss):

Year	Pretax Income (Loss)	Tax Rate
2000	$120,000	34%
2001	90,000	34%
2002	(280,000)	38%
2003	220,000	38%

The tax rates listed were all enacted by the beginning of 2000.

Instructions

(a) Prepare the journal entries for the years 2000–2003 to record income tax expense (benefit) and income tax payable (refundable) and the tax effects of the loss carryback and carryforward, assuming that at the end of 2002 the benefits of the loss carryforward are judged more likely than not to be realized in the future.

(b) Using the assumption in (a), prepare the income tax section of the 2002 income statement beginning with the line "Operating loss before income taxes."

(c) Prepare the journal entries for 2002 and 2003, assuming that based on the weight of available evidence, it is more likely than not that one-fourth of the benefits of the carryforward will not be realized.

(d) Using the assumption in (c), prepare the income tax section of the 2002 income statement beginning with the line "Operating loss before income taxes."

E20-27 (NOL Carryback and Carryforward, Valuation Account Needed) Denise Beilman Inc. reports the following pretax income (loss) for both book and tax purposes (assume the carryback provision is used where possible for a net operating loss):

Year	Pretax Income (Loss)	Tax Rate
2000	$120,000	40%
2001	90,000	40%
2002	(280,000)	45%
2003	120,000	45%

The tax rates listed were all enacted by the beginning of 2000.

Instructions

(a) Prepare the journal entries for years 2000–2003 to record income tax expense (benefit) and income tax payable (refundable) and the tax effects of the loss carryback and carryforward, assuming that based on the weight of available evidence, it is more likely than not that one-half of the benefits of the carryforward will not be realized.

(b) Prepare the income tax section of the 2002 income statement beginning with the line "Operating loss before income taxes."

(c) Prepare the income tax section of the 2003 income statement beginning with the line "Income before income taxes."

E20-28 (NOL Carryback and Carryforward, Valuation Account Needed) Meyer reported the following pretax financial income (loss) for the years 2000–2004:

2000	$240,000
2001	350,000
2002	120,000
2003	(570,000)
2004	180,000

Pretax financial income (loss) and taxable income (loss) were the same for all years involved. The enacted tax rate was 34% for 2000 and 2001, and 40% for 2002–2004. Assume the carryback provision is used first for net operating losses.

Instructions

(a) Prepare the journal entries for the years 2002–2004 to record income tax expense, income tax payable (refundable), and the tax effects of the loss carryback and carryforward, assuming that based on the weight of available evidence, it is more likely than not that one-fifth of the benefits of the carryforward will not be realized.

(b) Prepare the income tax section of the 2003 income statement beginning with the line "Income (loss) before income taxes."

PROBLEMS

P20-1 (Three Differences, No Beginning Deferred Taxes, Multiple Rates) The following information is available for Swanson Corporation for 2001:

1. Depreciation reported on the tax return exceeded depreciation reported on the income statement by $100,000. This difference will reverse in equal amounts of $25,000 over the years 2002–2005.
2. Interest received on municipal bonds was $10,000.
3. Rent collected in advance on January 1, 2001, totaled $60,000 for a 3-year period. Of this amount, $40,000 was reported as unearned at December 31, for book purposes.
4. The tax rates are 40% for 2001 and 35% for 2002 and subsequent years.
5. Income taxes of $360,000 are due per the tax return for 2001.
6. No deferred taxes existed at the beginning of 2001.

Instructions

(a) Compute taxable income for 2001.

(b) Compute pretax financial income for 2001.

(c) Prepare the journal entries to record income tax expense, deferred income taxes, and income taxes payable for 2001 and 2002. Assume taxable income was $980,000 in 2002.

(d) Prepare the income tax expense section of the income statement for 2001, beginning with "Income before income taxes."

P20-2 (One Temporary Difference, Tracked for 4 Years, One Permanent Difference, Change in Rate)
The pretax financial income of Kristal Parker-Gregory Company differs from its taxable income throughout each of 4 years as follows:

Year	Pretax Financial Income	Taxable Income	Tax Rate
2002	$280,000	$180,000	35%
2003	320,000	225,000	40%
2004	350,000	270,000	40%
2005	420,000	580,000	40%

Pretax financial income for each year includes a nondeductible expense of $30,000 (never deductible for tax purposes). The remainder of the difference between pretax financial income and taxable income in each period is due to one depreciation temporary difference. No deferred income taxes existed at the beginning of 2002.

Instructions

(a) Prepare journal entries to record income taxes in all 4 years. Assume that the change in the tax rate to 40% was not enacted until the beginning of 2003.

(b) Draft the income tax section of the income statement for 2003.

P20-3 (Second Year of Depreciation Difference, Two Differences, Single Rate, Extraordinary Item)
The following information has been obtained for the Tracy Kerdyk Corporation.

1. Prior to 2001, taxable income and pretax financial income were identical.
2. Pretax financial income is $1,700,000 in 2001 and $1,400,000 in 2002.
3. On January 1, 2001, equipment costing $1,000,000 is purchased. It is to be depreciated on a straight-line basis over 5 years for tax purposes and over 8 years for financial reporting purposes. (*Hint:* Use the half-year convention for tax purposes.)
4. Interest of $60,000 was earned on tax-exempt municipal obligations in 2002.
5. Included in 2002 pretax financial income is an extraordinary gain of $200,000, which is fully taxable.
6. The tax rate is 35% for all periods.
7. Taxable income is expected in all future years.

Instructions

(a) Compute taxable income and income tax payable for 2002.

(b) Prepare the journal entry to record 2002 income tax expense, income tax payable, and deferred taxes.

(c) Prepare the bottom portion of Kerdyk's 2002 income statement, beginning with "Income before income taxes and extraordinary item."

(d) Indicate how deferred income taxes should be presented on the December 31, 2002, balance sheet.

P20-4 (Multiple Rates, Future Losses versus Future Income) Vijay Singh Co. started operations in 2001. A reconciliation of its pretax financial income to its taxable income for 2001 is as follows:

Pretax financial income	$24,000,000
Litigation accrual for book purposes	8,000,000
Excess depreciation for tax purposes	(3,000,000)
Taxable income	$29,000,000

As of the beginning of 2001, enacted tax rates are 35% for 2001 and 2002, and 40% for all subsequent years. It is estimated that the litigation accrual will be settled in 2006 and that the temporary difference due to the excess depreciation of tax purposes will reverse equally over the 3-year period from 2002 to 2004.

Instructions

(a) Determine the income tax payable, deferred income taxes, and income tax expense to be reported for 2001 assuming that taxable income is expected in all future years.

(b) Classify the deferred income taxes computed in (a) into current and noncurrent components. Explain where the deferred taxes should appear on the balance sheet.

(c) Determine the income tax payable, deferred income taxes, and income tax expense for 2001 assuming that net operating losses are expected to appear on tax returns for 2002 through 2006 and taxable income is very likely for 2007 and later years.

(d) Classify the deferred income taxes computed in (c) into current and noncurrent components. Explain where the deferred taxes should appear on the balance sheet.

P20-5 (Actual NOL without Valuation Account) Mark O'Meara Inc. reported the following pretax income (loss) and related tax rates during the years 1997–2003:

	Pretax Income (loss)	Tax Rate
1997	$ 40,000	30%
1998	25,000	30%
1999	60,000	30%
2000	80,000	40%
2001	(200,000)	45%
2002	70,000	40%
2003	90,000	35%

Pretax financial income (loss) and taxable income (loss) were the same for all years since O'Meara began business. The tax rates from 2000 to 2003 were enacted in 2000.

Instructions

(a) Prepare the journal entries for the years 2001–2003 to record income tax payable (refundable), income tax expense (benefit), and the tax effects of the loss carryback and carryforward. Assume that O'Meara elects the carryback provision where possible and expects to realize the benefits of any loss carryforward in the year that immediately follows the loss year.

(b) Indicate the effect the 2001 entry(ies) has on the December 31, 2001, balance sheet.

(c) Indicate how the bottom portion of the income statement, starting with "Operating loss before income taxes," would be reported in 2001.

(d) Indicate how the bottom portion of the income statement, starting with "Income before income taxes," would be reported in 2002.

P20-6 (Two Differences, Two Rates, Future Income Expected) Presented below are two independent situations related to future taxable and deductible amounts resulting from temporary differences existing at December 31, 2001.

1. Pirates Co. has developed the following schedule of future taxable and deductible amounts:

	2002	2003	2004	2005	2006
Taxable amounts	$300	$300	$300	$ 300	$300
Deductible amount	—	—	—	(1,400)	—

2. Eagles Co. has the following schedule of future taxable and deductible amounts:

	2002	2003	2004	2005
Taxable amounts	$300	$300	$ 300	$300
Deductible amount	—	—	(2,000)	—

Both Pirates Co. and Eagles Co. have taxable income of $3,000 in 2001 and expect to have taxable income in all future years. The tax rates enacted as of the beginning of 2001 are 30% for 2001–2004 and 35% for years thereafter. All of the underlying temporary differences relate to noncurrent assets and liabilities.

Instructions

For each of these two situations, compute the net amount of deferred income taxes to be reported at the end of 2001 and indicate how it should be classified on the balance sheet.

P20-7 (One Temporary Difference, Tracked 3 Years, Change in Rates, Income Statement Presentation) Gators Corp. sold an investment on an installment basis. The total gain of $60,000 was reported for financial reporting purposes in the period of sale. The company qualifies to use installment method for tax purposes. The installment period is 3 years; one-third of the sale price is collected in the period of sale. The tax rate was 35% in 2001 and 30% in 2002 and 2003. The 30% tax rate was not enacted in law until 2002. The accounting and tax data for the 3 years is shown below.

	Financial Accounting	Tax Return
2001 (35% tax rate)		
Income before temporary difference	$ 70,000	$70,000
Temporary difference	60,000	20,000
Income	$130,000	$90,000
2002 (30% tax rate)		
Income before temporary difference	$ 70,000	$70,000
Temporary difference	–0–	20,000
Income	$ 70,000	$90,000
2003 (30% tax rate)		
Income before temporary difference	$70,000	$70,000
Temporary difference	–0–	20,000
Income	$70,000	$90,000

Instructions

(a) Prepare the journal entries to record the income tax expense, deferred income taxes, and the income tax payable at the end of each year. No deferred income taxes existed at the beginning of 2001.

(b) Explain how the deferred taxes will appear on the balance sheet at the end of each year. (Assume the Installment Accounts Receivable is classified as a current asset.)

(c) Draft the income tax expense section of the income statement for each year, beginning with "Income before income taxes."

P20-8 (Two Differences, 2 Years, Compute Taxable Income and Pretax Financial Income) The following information was disclosed during the audit of Thomas Muster Inc.

1.

Year	Amount Due per Tax Return
2001	$140,000
2002	112,000

2. On January 1, 2001, equipment costing $400,000 is purchased. For financial reporting purposes, the company uses straight-line depreciation over a 5-year life. For tax purposes, the company uses the elective straight-line method over a 5-year life. (*Hint:* For tax purposes, the half-year convention must be used.)

3. In January 2002, $225,000 is collected in advance rental of a building for a 3-year period. The entire $225,000 is reported as taxable income in 2002, but $150,000 of the $225,000 is reported as unearned revenue in 2002 for financial reporting purposes. The remaining amount of unearned revenue is to be earned equally in 2003 and 2004.

4. The tax rate is 40% in 2001 and all subsequent periods. (*Hint:* To find taxable income in 2001 and 2002 the related income tax payable amounts will have to be grossed up.)

5. No temporary differences existed at the end of 2000. Muster expects to report taxable income in each of the next 5 years.

Instructions

(a) Determine the amount to report for deferred income taxes at the end of 2001 and indicate how it should be classified on the balance sheet.

(b) Prepare the journal entry to record income taxes for 2001.

(c) Draft the income tax section of the income statement for 2001 beginning with "Income before income taxes." (*Hint:* You must compute taxable income and then combine that with changes in cumulative temporary differences to arrive at pretax financial income.)

(d) Determine the deferred income taxes at the end of 2002 and indicate how they should be classified on the balance sheet.

(e) Prepare the journal entry to record income taxes for 2002.

(f) Draft the income tax section of the income statement for 2002 beginning with "Income before income taxes."

P20-9 (Five Differences, Compute Taxable Income and Deferred Taxes, Draft Income Statement) Martha King Company began operations at the beginning of 2000. The following information pertains to this company.

1. Pretax financial income for 2000 is $100,000.
2. The tax rate enacted for 2000 and future years is 40%
3. Differences between the 2000 income statement and tax return are listed below:
   (a) Warranty expense accrued for financial reporting purposes amounts to $5,000. Warranty deductions per the tax return amount to $2,000.
   (b) Gross profit on construction contracts using the percentage-of-completion method for books amounts to $92,000. Gross profit on construction contracts for tax purposes amounts to $62,000.
   (c) Depreciation of property, plant, and equipment for financial reporting purposes amounts to $60,000. Depreciation of these assets amounts to $80,000 for the tax return.
   (d) A $3,500 fine paid for violation of pollution laws was deducted in computing pretax financial income.
   (e) Interest revenue earned on an investment in tax-exempt municipal bonds amounts to $1,400. (Assume (a) is short-term in nature; assume (b) and(c) are long-term in nature.)
4. Taxable income is expected for the next few years.

Instructions

(a) Compute taxable income for 2000.
(b) Compute the deferred taxes at December 31, 2000, that relate to the temporary differences described above. Clearly label them as deferred tax asset or liability.
(c) Prepare the journal entry to record income tax expense, deferred taxes, and income taxes payable for 2000.
(d) Draft the income tax expense section of the income statement begining with "Income before income taxes."

CONCEPTUAL CASES

C20-1 (Objectives and Principles for Accounting for Income Taxes) The amount of income taxes due to the government for a period of time is rarely the amount reported on the income statement for that period as income tax expense.

Instructions

(a) Explain the objectives of accounting for income taxes in general purpose financial statements.
(b) Explain the basic principles that are applied in accounting for income taxes at the date of the financial statements to meet the objectives discussed in (a).
(c) List the steps in the annual computation of deferred tax liabilities and assets.

C20-2 (Basic Accounting for Temporary Differences) The Iva Majoli Company appropriately uses the asset-liability method to record deferred income taxes. Iva Majoli reports depreciation expense for certain machinery purchased this year using the modified accelerated cost recovery system (MACRS) for income tax purposes and the straight-line basis for financial reporting purposes. The tax deduction is the larger amount this year.

Iva Majoli received rent revenues in advance this year. These revenues are included in this year's taxable income. However, for financial reporting purposes, these revenues are reported as unearned revenues, a current liability.

Instructions

(a) What are the principles of the asset-liability approach?
(b) How would Majoli account for the temporary differences?
(c) How should Majoli classify the deferred tax consequences of the temporary differences on its balance sheet?

C20-3 (Identify Temporary Differences and Classification Criteria) The asset-liability approach for recording deferred income taxes is an integral part of generally accepted accounting principles.

Instructions

(a) Indicate whether each of the following independent situations should be treated as a temporary difference or a permanent difference and explain why.
   (1) Estimated warranty costs (covering a 3-year warranty) are expensed for financial reporting purposes at the time of sale but deducted for income tax purposes when paid.
   (2) Depreciation for book and income tax purposes differs because of different bases of carrying the related property, which was acquired in a trade-in. The different bases are a result of different rules used for book and tax purposes to compute the basis of property acquired in a trade-in.

(3) A company properly uses the equity method to account for its 30% investment in another company. The investee pays dividends that are about 10% of its annual earnings.

(4) A company reports a gain on an involuntary conversion of a nonmonetary asset to a monetary asset. The company elects to replace the property within the statutory period using the total proceeds so the gain is not reported on the current year's tax return.

(b) Discuss the nature of the deferred income tax accounts and possible classifications in a company's balance sheet. Indicate the manner in which these accounts are to be reported.

C20-4 (Identify Permanent or Temporary Differences, Future Taxable or Deductible Amounts, Deferred Tax Asset or Liability) Listed below are 16 of the more common items that are treated differently for financial reporting purposes than they are for tax purposes.

1. Excess of charge to accounting records (allowance method) over charge to tax return (direct write-off method) for uncollectible receivables.
2. Excess of accrued pension expense over amount paid.
3. The 80% deduction for dividends received from U.S. corporations.
4. Installment sales of investments are accounted for on the accrual basis for financial reporting purposes and on the installment (cash) basis for tax purposes.
5. Expenses incurred in obtaining tax-exempt income.
6. A trademark acquired directly from the government is capitalized and amortized over subsequent periods for accounting purposes and expensed for tax purposes.
7. Prepaid advertising expense deferred for accounting purposes and deducted as an expense for tax purposes.
8. Premiums paid on life insurance of officers (corporation is the beneficiary).
9. Penalty for filing a late tax return.
10. Proceeds of life insurance policies on lives of officers.
11. Estimated future warranty costs.
12. Fine for polluting.
13. Excess of tax depreciation over accounting depreciation.
14. Tax-exempt interest revenue.
15. Excess of percentage depletion for tax purposes over cost depletion.
16. Estimated gross profit on long-term construction contract is reported in the income statement; some of this gross profit is deferred for tax purposes.

Instructions

For each item above:

(a) Indicate if it is:
  (1) A permanent difference, or
  (2) A temporary difference.

(b) Indicate if it will:
  (1) Create future taxable amounts, or
  (2) Create future deductible amounts, or
  (3) Not affect any future tax returns.

(c) Indicate if it usually will:
  (1) Result in reporting a deferred tax liability, or
  (2) Result in reporting a deferred tax asset, or
  (3) Not result in reporting any deferred taxes.

C20-5 (Accounting and Classification of Deferred Income Taxes)

Part A

This year Lindsay Davenport Company has each of the following items in its income statement:

1. Gross profits on installment sales.
2. Revenues on long-term construction contracts.
3. Estimated costs of product warranty contracts.
4. Premiums on officers' life insurance with Davenport as beneficiary.

Instructions

(a) Under what conditions would deferred income taxes need to be reported in the financial statements?

(b) Specify when deferred income taxes would need to be recognized for each of the items above, and indicate the rationale for such recognition.

Part B

Davenport Company's president has heard that deferred income taxes can be classified in different ways in the balance sheet.

Instructions
Identify the conditions under which deferred income taxes would be classified as a noncurrent item in the balance sheet. What justification exists for such classification?

(AICPA adapted)

C20-6 (Explain Computation of Deferred Tax Liability for Multiple Tax Rates) At December 31, 2002, Martina Hingis Corporation has one temporary difference which will reverse and cause taxable amounts in 2003. In 2002 a new tax act set taxes equal to 45% for 2002, 40% for 2003, and 34% for 2004 and years thereafter.

Instructions
Explain what circumstances would call for Martina Hingis to compute its deferred tax liability at the end of 2002 by multiplying the cumulative temporary difference by:

(a) 45%.
(b) 40%.
(c) 34%.

C20-7 (Explain Future Taxable and Deductible Amounts, How Carryback and Carryforward Affects Deferred Taxes) Mary Joe Fernandez and Meredith McGrath are discussing accounting for income taxes. They are currently studying a schedule of taxable and deductible amounts that will arise in the future as a result of existing temporary differences. The schedule is as follows:

	Current Year	Future Years			
	2002	2003	2004	2005	2006
Taxable income	$850,000				
Taxable amounts		$375,000	$375,000	$ 375,000	$375,000
Deductible amounts				(2,400,000)	
Enacted tax rate	50%	45%	40%	35%	30%

Instructions
(a) Explain the concept of future taxable amounts and future deductible amounts as illustrated in the schedule.
(b) How do the carryback and carryforward provisions affect the reporting of deferred tax assets and deferred tax liabilities?

USING YOUR JUDGMENT

FINANCIAL REPORTING PROBLEM: INTEL CORPORATION

Instructions

Refer to the financial statements and accompanying notes and discussion of Intel Corporation presented in Appendix 5B and answer the following questions.

(a) What amounts relative to income taxes does Intel report in its:

    (1) 1998 income statement?

    (2) December 26, 1998 balance sheet?

    (3) 1998 statement of cash flows?

(b) Intel's provision for income taxes in 1996, 1997, and 1998 was computed at what effective tax rates (see notes to the financial statements)?

(c) How much of Intel's 1998 total provision for income taxes was current tax expense and how much was deferred tax expense?

(d) What did Intel report as the significant components (the details) of its December 26, 1998 deferred tax assets and liabilities?

(e) Briefly, what does Intel disclose about the Internal Revenue Services's (IRS) examinations of its U.S. income tax returns?

FINANCIAL STATEMENT ANALYSIS CASE

Homestake Mining Company

Homestake Mining Company is a 120-year-old international gold mining company with substantial gold mining operations and exploration in the United States, Canada, and Australia. At December 31, 1998, Homestake reported the following items related to income taxes (thousands of dollars):

Total current taxes	$ 26,349
Total deferred taxes	(39,436)
Total income and mining taxes (the provision for taxes per its income statement)	(13,087)
Deferred tax liabilities	$303,050
Deferred tax assets, net of valuation allowance of $207,175	95,275
Net deferred tax liability	$207,775

Note 6: The classification of deferred tax assets and liabilities is based on the related asset or liability creating the deferred tax. Deferred taxes not related to a specific asset or liability are classified based on the estimated period of reversal.

Tax loss carryforwards (U.S., Canada, Australia, and Chile)	$71,151
Tax credit carryforwards	$12,007

Instructions

(a) What is the significance of Homestake's 1998 disclosure of "Current taxes" of $26,349 and "Deferred taxes" of $(39,436)?

(b) Explain the concept behind Homestake's disclosure of gross deferred tax liabilities (future taxable amounts) and gross deferred tax assets (future deductible amounts).

(c) Homestake reported tax loss carryforwards of $71,151 and tax credit carryforwards of $12,007. How do the carryback and carryforward provisions affect the reporting of deferred tax assets and deferred tax liabilities?

COMPARATIVE ANALYSIS CASE

The Coca-Cola Company versus PepsiCo, Inc.

Instruction

Go to the Digital Tool and, using The Coca-Cola Company and PepsiCo, Inc. Annual Report information, answer the following questions.

(a) What are the amounts of Coca-Cola's and PepsiCo's provision for income taxes for the year 1998? Of each company's 1998 provision for income taxes, what portion is current expense and what portion is deferred expense?

(b) What amount of cash was paid in 1998 for income taxes by Coca-Cola and by PepsiCo?

(c) What was the U.S. federal statutory tax rate in 1998? What was the effective tax rate in 1998 for Coca-Cola and PepsiCo? Why might their effective tax rates differ?

(d) For the year-end 1998 what amounts were reported by Coca-Cola and PepsiCo as (a) gross deferred tax assets and (b) gross deferred tax liabilities?

(e) Do either Coca-Cola or PepsiCo disclose any net operating loss carrybacks and/or carryforwards at year-end 1998? What are the amounts and when do the carryforwards expire?

RESEARCH CASES

Case 1

As discussed in the chapter, companies must consider all positive and negative information in determining whether a deferred tax asset valuation allowance is needed.

Instructions

Examine the balance sheets and income tax footnotes for two companies that have recorded deferred tax assets, and answer the following questions with regard to each company.

(a) What is the gross amount of the deferred tax asset recorded by the company? Express this amount as a percentage of total assets.

(b) Did the company record a valuation allowance? How large was the allowance?

(c) What evidence, if any, did the company cite with regard to the need for a valuation allowance? Do you consider the company's disclosure to be adequate?

Case 2

The deferred tax liability requires special considerations for financial statement readers.

Instructions

Obtain a recent edition of a financial statement analysis textbook, read the section related to the deferred tax liability, and answer the following questions.

(a) What are the major analytical issues associated with deferred tax liabilities?

(b) What type of adjustments to deferred tax liabilities do analysts make when examining financial statements?

INTERNATIONAL REPORTING CASE

Tomkins PLC is a British company that operates in four business sectors: industrial and automotive engineering; construction components; food manufacturing; and professional, garden, and leisure products. Tomkins prepares its accounts in accordance with United Kingdom (U.K.) accounting standards. Like U.S. reporting, U.K. financial reporting is investor-oriented. As a result, British companies report different income amounts for tax and financial reporting purposes. British companies receive different tax treatment for such items as depreciation (capital allowances), and they receive tax credits for operating losses. Tomkins reported income of £305 million in 1999 and reported total shareholders' funds of £2,221 million at May 31, 1999. Tomkins provided the following disclosures related to taxes in its May 31, 1999, annual report.

Principal Accounting Policies—Tax

The tax charge is based on the profit for the year and takes into account tax deferred due to timing differences between the treatment of certain items for tax and accounting purposes. Deferred tax is calculated under the liability method and it is considered probable that all liabilities will crystallise. Deferred tax assets are not recognised in respect of provisions for post-retirement benefits.

Note 5: Tax on Profit on Ordinary Activities

	1999 £ million	1998 £ million
Corporation tax at 31%	56.6	69.6
Overseas tax	85.5	95.8
Deferred tax–UK (see note 16)	5.1	(7.1)
–Overseas (see note 16)	7.3	9.2
Associated undertakings' tax	0.7	3.0
	155.2	170.5

The tax charge on exceptional items in 1999 and 1998 is £nil.

Note 16: Provisions for Liabilities and Charges

	1999 £ million	1998 £ million
The deferred tax provision comprises:	98.5	102.9
Excess of capital allowances over depreciation charged	40.8	25.5
Other timing differences	—	(30.3)
Advance corporation tax recoverable	139.3	98.1

Results under U.S. Accounting Principles

The consolidated financial statements are prepared in conformity with accounting principles generally accepted in the UK (UK GAAP) which differ in certain respects from those generally accepted in the United States (US GAAP). The significant areas of difference affecting the Tomkins consolidated financial statements are described below:

Deferred Income Tax. In Tomkins consolidated financial statements, deferred tax is calculated under the liability method and it is considered probable that all liabilities will crystallise. Deferred tax assets are not recognised in respect of provision for post-retirement benefits. Under US GAAP, deferred taxes are provided for all temporary differences on a full liability basis. Deferred tax assets are also recognized to the extent that their realisation is more likely than not.

If Tomkins had used U.S. GAAP for deferred taxes, its income would have been lower by £8.2 million in 1999. Stockholders' equity at May 31, 1999, would have been £87.5 million higher if Tompkins had applied U.S. GAAP.

Instructions

Use the information in the Tomkins disclosure to answer the following.

(a) Prepare the journal entry that would be required to reconcile Tomkins' income to U.S. GAAP for the differences in deferred taxes under U.S. and U.K. accounting standards.

(b) Prepare the journal entry that would be required to reconcile Tomkins' shareholders' equity to U.S. GAAP for the differences in deferred taxes under U.S. and U.K. accounting standards at the end of 1999.

(c) In light of the information disclosed under "Principal Accounting Policies—Tax," explain why you think Tomkins' equity under U.S. GAAP would be higher at May 31, 1999.

(d) Tomkins indicates that "Deferred tax is calculated under the liability method and it is considered probable that all (deferred tax) liabilities will crystallise [be realized]." Does this approach cause any problems in comparing the financial statements of U.S. and U.K. companies? Explain.

ETHICS CASE

Henrietta Aguirre, CPA, is the newly hired director of corporate taxation for Mesa Incorporated, which is a publicly traded corporation. Ms. Aguirre's first job with Mesa was the review of the company's accounting practices on deferred income taxes. In doing her review, she noted differences between tax and book depreciation methods that permitted Mesa to realize a sizable deferred tax liability on its balance sheet. As a result, Mesa did not have to report current income tax expenses. Aguirre also discovered that Mesa has an explicit policy of selling off fixed assets before they reversed in the deferred tax liability account. This policy, coupled with the rapid expansion of its fixed asset base, allowed Mesa to "defer" all income taxes payable for several years, even though it always has reported positive earnings and an increasing EPS. Aguirre checked with the legal department and found the policy to be legal, but she's uncomfortable with the ethics of it.

Instructions

Answer the following questions.

(a) Why would Mesa have an explicit policy of selling assets before they reversed in the deferred tax liability account?

(b) What are the ethical implications of Mesa's "deferral" of income taxes?

(c) Who could be harmed by Mesa's ability to "defer" income taxes payable for several years, despite positive earnings?

(d) In a situation such as this, what are Ms. Aguirre's professional responsibilities as a CPA?

CHAPTER 21

Accounting for Pensions and Postretirement Benefits

Who Wants to Be a Millionaire?

Many people dream of becoming millionaires. Increasingly, however, more and more of these people are finding that you do not have to win on a game show to have this dream come true. In the past decade, tax-favored retirement plans, in which employees receive tax incentives to save for retirement, have produced a growing number of "401K millionaires."

401K is the section number of the tax code that allows employees to contribute a part of their earnings to an investment fund that grows on a tax-deferred basis until the funds are withdrawn at retirement. In many cases, employers also contribute to the employee's retirement fund as part of the benefit package. In some cases these contributions are made in addition to the company-sponsored retirement plans, as a way to attract and retain good workers. Many employees like 401Ks because the employee can control the investment fund. In many company-sponsored plans, employees may not retain their retirement benefits if they do not stay at the company a long time.

Tax incentives combined with employee concerns that Social Security will not provide an adequate retirement income safety net have provided the impetus for employees to set up 401K-type plans. For example, the amounts contributed to these accounts more than tripled in the 1990s, with more than 44 million people owning accounts and a total of more than $1.5 trillion invested. Of these retirement investors, an increasing number are becoming millionaires by virtue of their contributions to these accounts and the strong stock market performance, since many of these funds are invested in common stocks. In 1995 there were 120 millionaires out of 700,000 401K accounts at T. Rowe Price. Within two years, T. Rowe Price reported 308 millionaires out of 870,000 401Ks.

The popularity of these plans, including their flexibility and the incentives they provide for individual savings, has even caught the eye of Congress as it debates ways to shore up the Social Security system. Recent estimates indicate that Social Security will be bankrupt by the year 2032. One proposal for dealing with the retirement shortfall is to allow workers to allocate part of their Social Security taxes to private investment funds, similar to a 401K.[1] So "who wants to be a millionaire?" More and more people are saying "I do," and many will be able to realize that dream by taking advantage of tax incentives and by taking control of their own retirement income planning.

---

[1]E. Schuerenberg, "Will Privatizing Fix Social Security?" *Fortune*, May 1, 1999, p. 129.

LEARNING OBJECTIVES

After studying this chapter, you should be able to:

1. Distinguish between accounting for the employer's pension plan and accounting for the pension fund.
2. Identify types of pension plans and their characteristics.
3. Explain alternative measures for valuing the pension obligation.
4. Identify the components of pension expense.
5. Utilize a work sheet for employer's pension plan entries.
6. Describe the amortization of unrecognized prior service costs.
7. Explain the accounting procedure for recognizing unexpected gains and losses.
8. Explain the corridor approach to amortizing unrecognized gains and losses.
9. Explain the recognition of a minimum liability.
10. Describe the reporting requirements for pension plans in financial statements.

As the opening story indicates, many employees are increasingly concerned about retirement planning. To attract and reward high-quality employees, most companies have established pension plans to help employees meet their retirement savings goals. These companies offer investment programs for employee contributions, and some also contribute to employees' retirement funds as part of the overall compensation package. The substantial growth of these plans, both in number of employees covered and the dollar amounts of retirement benefits, has increased the significance of pension costs in relation to a company's financial position.[2] The purpose of this chapter is to discuss the accounting issues related to pension plans. The content and organization of the chapter are as follows:

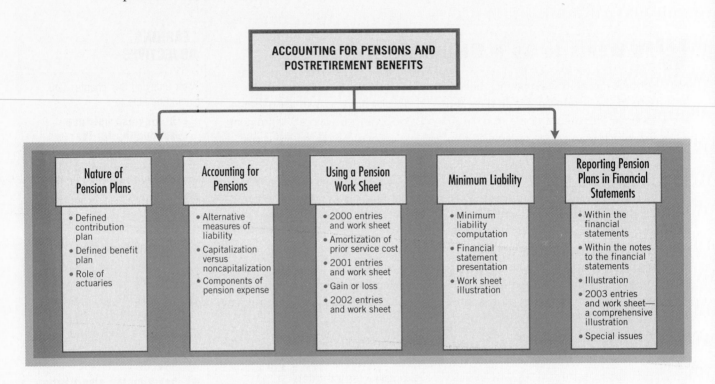

NATURE OF PENSION PLANS

OBJECTIVE ❶
Distinguish between accounting for the employer's pension plan and accounting for the pension fund.

A **pension plan** is an arrangement whereby an employer provides benefits (payments) to employees after they retire for services they provided while they were working. Pension accounting may be divided and separately treated as **accounting for the employer** and **accounting for the pension fund.** The company or employer is the organization sponsoring the pension plan. It incurs the cost and makes contributions to the pension fund. The fund or plan is the entity that receives the contributions from the employer, administers the pension assets, and makes the benefit payments to the pension recipients (retired employees). Illustration 21-1 shows the three entities involved in a pension plan and indicates the flow of cash between them.

---

[2]For example, in 1980, private pension plans had assets of $671.3 billion. By 1997, pension plan assets totaled nearly $5 trillion.

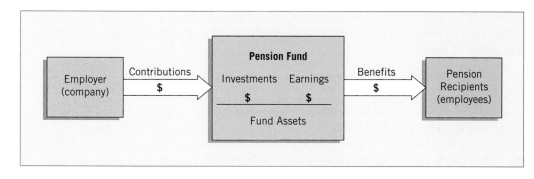

ILLUSTRATION 21-1
Flow of Cash among
Pension Plan Participants

The pension plan above is being **funded**:[3] that is, the employer (company) sets funds aside for future pension benefits by making payments to a funding agency that is responsible for accumulating the assets of the pension fund and for making payments to the recipients as the benefits become due. In an insured plan, the funding agency is an insurance company; in a trust fund plan, the funding agency is a trustee.

Some plans are **contributory**; in these, the employees bear part of the cost of the stated benefits or voluntarily make payments to increase their benefits. Other plans are **noncontributory**, in which the employer bears the entire cost. Companies generally design **qualified pension plans** in accord with federal income tax requirements that permit **deductibility of the employer's contributions to the pension fund and tax-free status of earnings from pension fund assets**.

The need for proper administration of and sound accounting for pension funds becomes apparent when one appreciates the size of these funds. Listed below are the pension fund assets and pension expenses of seven major companies as of December 31, 1998.

ILLUSTRATION 21-2
Pension Fund Assets and
Expense

Company ($ in millions)	Size of Pension Fund	1998 Pension Expense	Pension Expense as % of Operating Profit
Ford	$52,377	$1,071	16.0%
General Motors	80,983	1,642	35.6
Kellogg's	1,318	46	5.1
John Deere	5,661	100	6.4
Caterpillar	8,756	4	0.2
Coca-Cola	1,516	68	1.4
Pepsi	2,045	83	3.2

As indicated, pension expense is a substantial percentage of total profit for many companies.[4]

The fund should be a separate legal and accounting entity for which a set of books is maintained and financial statements are prepared. Maintaining books and records and preparing financial statements for the fund, known as "accounting for employee benefit plans," is not the subject of this chapter.[5] Instead this chapter is devoted to the

---

[3]When used as a verb, **fund** means to pay to a funding agency (as to fund future pension benefits or to fund pension cost). Used as a noun, it refers to assets accumulated in the hands of a funding agency (trustee) for the purpose of meeting pension benefits when they become due.

[4]Some have suggested that pension funds are the new owners of America's giant corporations. A recent study indicates that during the 1990s, pension funds (private and public) held or owned approximately 25% of the market value of corporate stock outstanding and accounted for 32% of the daily trading volume on the New York Stock Exchange. The enormous size (and the social significance) of these funds is staggering.

[5]The FASB issued a separate standard covering the accounting and reporting for employee benefit plans. "Accounting and Reporting by Defined Benefit Pension Plans," *Statement of Financial Accounting Standards No. 35* (Stamford, Conn.: FASB, 1979).

pension accounting and reporting problems of the employer as the sponsor of a pension plan. The two most common types of pension plans are **defined contribution plans** and **defined benefit plans**.

Defined Contribution Plan

OBJECTIVE ②
Identify types of pension plans and their characteristics.

In a defined contribution plan, the employer agrees to contribute to a pension trust a certain sum each period based on a formula. This formula may consider such factors as age, length of employee service, employer's profits, and compensation level. **Only the employer's contribution is defined**; no promise is made regarding the ultimate benefits paid out to the employees.

The size of the pension benefits that the employee finally collects under the plan depends on the amounts originally contributed to the pension trust, the income accumulated in the trust, and the treatment of forfeitures of funds caused by early terminations of other employees. The amounts originally contributed are usually turned over to an **independent third-party trustee** who acts on behalf of the beneficiaries—the participating employees. The trustee assumes ownership of the pension assets and is accountable for their investment and distribution. The trust is separate and distinct from the employer.

The accounting for a defined contribution plan is straightforward. The employee gets the benefit of gain or the risk of loss from the assets contributed to the pension plan. The employer's responsibility is simply to make a contribution each year based on the formula established in the plan. As a result, the employer's annual cost (pension expense) is just the amount that it is obligated to contribute to the pension trust. A liability is reported on the employer's balance sheet only if the contribution has not been made in full, and an asset is reported only if more than the required amount has been contributed.

Go to the Digital Tool to examine disclosures for defined contribution plans.

In addition to pension expense, the only disclosures required by the employer under a defined contribution plan are a plan description, including employee groups covered, the basis for determining contributions, and the nature and effect of significant matters affecting comparability from period to period.[6]

Defined Benefit Plan

A defined benefit plan defines the benefits that the employee will receive at the time of retirement. The formula that is typically used provides for the benefits to be a function of the employee's years of service and the employee's compensation level when he or she nears retirement. It is necessary to determine what the contribution should be today to meet the pension benefit commitments that will arise at retirement. Many different contribution approaches could be used. Whatever funding method is employed, it should provide enough money at retirement to meet the benefits defined by the plan.

The employees are the beneficiaries of a defined contribution trust, but the employer is the beneficiary of a defined benefit trust. The trust's primary purpose under a defined benefit plan is to safeguard assets and to invest them so that there will be enough to pay the employer's obligation to the employees when they retire. **In form**, the trust is a separate entity; **in substance**, the trust assets and liabilities belong to the employer. That is, **as long as the plan continues, the employer is responsible for the payment of the defined benefits (without regard to what happens in the trust)**. Any shortfall in the accumulated assets held by the trust must be made up by the employer. Any excess accumulated in the trust can be recaptured by the employer, either through reduced future funding or through a reversion of funds.

The accounting for a defined benefit plan is complex. Because the benefits are defined in terms of uncertain future variables, an appropriate funding pattern must be

INTERNATIONAL INSIGHT

Outside the U.S., private pension plans are less common because many other nations tend to rely on government-sponsored pension plans. Consequently, accounting for defined benefit pension plans is typically a less important issue elsewhere.

---

[6]"Employers' Accounting for Pension Plans," *Statement of Financial Accounting Standards No. 87* (Stamford, Conn.: FASB, 1985), pars. 63–66.

established to assure that enough funds will be available at retirement to provide the benefits promised. This funding level depends on a number of factors such as turnover, mortality, length of employee service, compensation levels, and interest earnings.

Employers are at risk with defined benefit plans because they must be sure to make enough contributions to meet the cost of benefits that are defined in the plan. The expense recognized each period is not necessarily equal to the cash contribution. Similarly, the liability is controversial because its measurement and recognition relate to unknown future variables. Unfortunately, the accounting issues related to this type of plan are complex. **Our discussion in the following sections primarily deals with defined benefit plans.**[7]

The Role of Actuaries in Pension Accounting

Because the problems associated with pension plans involve complicated actuarial considerations, actuaries are engaged to ensure that the plan is appropriate for the employee group covered.[8] Actuaries are individuals who are trained through a long and rigorous certification program to assign probabilities to future events and their financial effects. The insurance industry employs actuaries to assess risks and to advise on the setting of premiums and other aspects of insurance policies. Employers rely heavily on actuaries for assistance in developing, implementing, and funding pension plans.

It is actuaries who make predictions (called actuarial assumptions) of mortality rates, employee turnover, interest and earnings rates, early retirement frequency, future salaries, and any other factors necessary to operate a pension plan. They assist by computing the various pension measures that affect the financial statements, such as the pension obligation, the annual cost of servicing the plan, and the cost of amendments to the plan. In summary, accounting for defined benefit pension plans is highly reliant upon information and measurements provided by actuaries.

ACCOUNTING FOR PENSIONS

In accounting for pension plans, two questions arise: (1) What amounts of employer's liability and of pension obligation should be reported in the financial statements? (2) What is the pension expense for the period? Attempting to answer the first question has produced much controversy.

---

[7]As discussed in the opening story, although defined benefit plans continue to be used, recent trends indicate growing participation in defined contribution plans. For example, a recent survey of over 45 million employees indicates that defined benefit plan participation was at 50% of full-time employees in 1997 (down from 59% in 1991). Participation in defined contribution plans grew from 48% of full-time employees in 1991 to 57% of full-time employees in 1997 (U.S. Department of Labor, Bureau of Labor Statistics, News Release, "Employee Benefits in Medium and Large Private Establishments, 1997," January 7, 1999). The recordkeeping requirements for the defined benefit plans are onerous and, therefore, companies have become more reluctant to use these plans. Also, the benefits in a defined contribution plan are easier for the employee to understand; they tend to prefer them over the defined benefit plan. In terms of total assets, recent Federal Reserve statistics indicate that assets in private defined benefit and contribution plans were about equal in 1998 (more than $2 trillion in each). In some cases, a defined contribution plan is offered in combination with a defined benefit plan.

[8]An actuary's primary purpose is to ensure that the company has established an appropriate funding pattern to meet its pension obligations. This computation entails the development of a set of assumptions and continued monitoring of these assumptions to assure their realism. That the general public has little understanding of what an actuary does is illustrated by the following excerpt from *The Wall Street Journal*: "A polling organization once asked the general public what an actuary was and received among its more coherent responses the opinion that it was a place where you put dead actors."

Alternative Measures of the Liability

Most agree that an employer's **pension obligation** is the deferred compensation obligation it has to its employees for their service under the terms of the pension plan, but there are alternative ways of measuring it.[9] One measure of the obligation is to base it only on the benefits vested to the employees. Vested benefits are those that the employee is entitled to receive even if the employee renders no additional services under the plan. Under most pension plans, a certain minimum number of years of service to the employer is required before an employee achieves vested benefits status. The vested benefit obligation is computed using current salary levels and includes only vested benefits.

Another measure of the obligation is to base the computation of the deferred compensation amount on all years of service performed by employees under the plan—both vested and nonvested—using **current salary levels**. This measurement of the pension obligation is called the accumulated benefit obligation.

A third measure bases the computation of the deferred compensation amount on both vested and nonvested service **using future salaries.** This measurement of the pension obligation is called the projected benefit obligation. Because future salaries are expected to be higher than current salaries, this approach results in the largest measurement of the pension obligation.

The choice between these measures is critical because it affects the amount of the pension liability and the annual pension expense reported. The diagram in Illustration 21-3 presents the differences in these three measurements. Regardless of the approach used, the estimated future benefits to be paid are discounted to present value.

ILLUSTRATION 21-3
Different Measures of the Pension Obligation

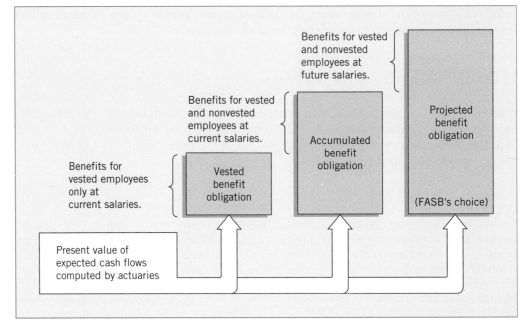

Minor changes in the interest rate used to discount pension benefits can dramatically affect the measurement of the employer's obligation. For example, a 1% decrease in the discount rate can increase pension liabilities 15%. Discount rates used to measure the pension liability are required to be changed at each measurement date to reflect current interest rates.

---

[9]One measure of the pension obligation is to determine the amount that the Pension Benefit Guaranty Corporation would require the employer to pay if it defaulted (this amount is limited to 30% of the employer's net worth). The accounting profession rejected this approach for financial reporting because it is too hypothetical and ignores the going concern concept.

Which of these approaches did the profession adopt? **In general, the profession adopted the projected benefit obligation, which is the present value of vested and nonvested benefits accrued to date based on employees' future salary levels.**[10] As you will learn later, however, the profession uses the accumulated benefit obligation in certain situations.

Those critical of the projected benefit obligation argue that using future salary levels is tantamount to adding future obligations to existing ones. Those in favor of the projected benefit obligation contend that a promise by an employer to pay benefits based on a percentage of the employees' future salary is far different from a promise to pay a percentage of their current salary, and such a difference should be reflected in the pension liability and pension expense.

INTERNATIONAL INSIGHT

Whereas the U.S. requires companies to base pension expense on estimated future compensation levels, Germany and Japan do not.

Capitalization versus Noncapitalization

Prior to issuance of *FASB Statement No. 87*, accounting for pension plans followed a **noncapitalization approach**. Noncapitalization, often referred to as **off-balance-sheet financing**, was achieved because the balance sheet reported an asset or liability for the pension plan arrangement only if the amount actually funded during the year by the employer was different from the amount reported by the employer as pension expense for the year. As the employees worked during each year, the employer incurred pension cost and became obligated to fund that amount by making cash payments to the pension fund (viewed as a third-party trust). When the trust paid benefits to retirees, the employer recorded no entries because its own assets or liabilities were not reduced.

The accounting profession has been tending toward a **capitalization approach**, supporting the **economic substance** of the pension plan arrangement over its legal form. Under this view, the employer has a liability for pension benefits that it has promised to pay for employee services already performed. As pension expense is incurred—as the employees work—the employer's liability increases. Funding the plan has no effect on the amount of the liability; only the employer's promises and the employee's services affect the liability. The pension liability is reduced through the payment of benefits to retired employees.

Under a defined benefit plan, if additional funds are necessary to meet the pension obligation, the source is the employer. From the capitalization point of view, underfunding does not increase the liability, and funding more than the amount expensed does not create a prepaid expense. Capitalization means measuring and reporting in the financial statements a fair representation of the employers' pension assets and liabilities.

The FASB in *Statement No. 87* adopted an approach that leans toward capitalization. But, proposals to adopt a full capitalization (total accrual) approach, requiring the recognition of balance sheet items where none existed before, were strongly opposed. *FASB Statement No. 87* **represents a compromise that combines some of the features of capitalization with some of the features of noncapitalization.** As we will learn in more detail later in this chapter, some elements of the pension plan are not recognized in the accounts and the financial statements (that is, not capitalized).

Because of this, the accounting for pensions, outlined in *Statement No. 87* and demonstrated in the balance of this chapter, is not perfectly logical, totally complete, or conceptually sound. The FASB is not entirely at fault. Because of the financial complexity of defined benefit pensions, many well-intentioned, competent people could not agree on the economic substance of such plans. As a result, they did not agree on how to account for them. Because of the difficulties in gaining a consensus among

---

[10]When the term "present value of benefits" is used throughout this chapter, it really means the actuarial present value of benefits. Actuarial present value is the amount payable adjusted to reflect the time value of money **and** the probability of payment (by means of decrements for events such as death, disability, withdrawals, or retirement) between the present date and the expected date of payment. For simplicity, we will use the term "present value" instead of "actuarial present value" in our discussion.

the Board members and support from preparers as well as users of financial statements, *Statement No. 87* involves several compromises that make it less than an ideal application of the capitalization method. In its defense, however, *Statement No. 87* is a great improvement over previous accounting pronouncements and represents a first step toward a conceptually sound approach to employers' accounting for pension plans.

Components of Pension Expense

OBJECTIVE ④
Identify the components of pension expense.

There is broad agreement that pension cost should be accounted for on the **accrual basis.**[11] The profession recognizes that **accounting for pension plans requires measurement of the cost and its identification with the appropriate time periods.** The determination of pension cost, however, is extremely complicated because it is a function of the following components:

UNDERLYING CONCEPTS

The matching concept and the definition of a liability justify accounting for pension cost on the accrual basis. This requires recording an expense when the future benefits are earned by the employees and recognizing an existing obligation to pay pensions later based on current services received.

❶ **Service Cost.** Service cost is the expense caused by the increase in pension benefits payable (the projected benefit obligation) to employees because of their services rendered during the current year. Actuaries compute **service cost** as the present value of the new benefits earned by employees during the year.

❷ **Interest on the Liability.** Because a pension is a deferred compensation arrangement, there is a time value of money factor. As a result, it is recorded on a discounted basis. **Interest expense accrues each year on the projected benefit obligation just as it does on any discounted debt.** The accountant receives help from the actuary in selecting the interest rate, referred to as the **settlement rate**.

❸ **Actual Return on Plan Assets.** The return earned by the accumulated pension fund assets in a particular year is relevant in measuring the net cost to the employer of sponsoring an employee pension plan. Therefore, **annual pension expense should be adjusted for interest and dividends that accumulate within the fund as well as increases and decreases in the market value of the fund assets.**

❹ **Amortization of Unrecognized Prior Service Cost.** Pension plan amendments (including initiation of a pension plan) often include provisions to increase benefits (in rare situations to decrease benefits) for employee service provided in prior years. Because plan amendments are granted with the expectation that the employer will realize economic benefits in future periods, **the cost (prior service cost) of providing these retroactive benefits is allocated to pension expense in the future, specifically to the remaining service-years of the affected employees.**

❺ **Gain or Loss.** Volatility in pension expense can be caused by sudden and large changes in the market value of plan assets and by changes in the projected benefit obligation (which changes when actuarial assumptions are modified or when actual experience differs from expected experience). Two items comprise this gain or loss: (1) the difference between the actual return and the expected return on plan assets and (2) amortization of the unrecognized net gain or loss from previous periods. This computation is complex and will be discussed later in the chapter.

The **components of pension expense** and their effect on total pension expense (increase or decrease) are shown in Illustration 21-4.

---

[11]Until the mid-1960s, with few exceptions, companies applied the **cash basis** of accounting to pension plans by recognizing the amount paid in a particular accounting period as the pension expense for the period. The problem was that the amount paid or funded in a fiscal period depended on financial management and was too often discretionary. For example, funding could be based on the availability of cash, the level of earnings, or other factors unrelated to the requirements of the plan. Application of the cash basis made it possible to manipulate the amount of pension expense appearing in the income statement simply by varying the cash paid to the pension fund.

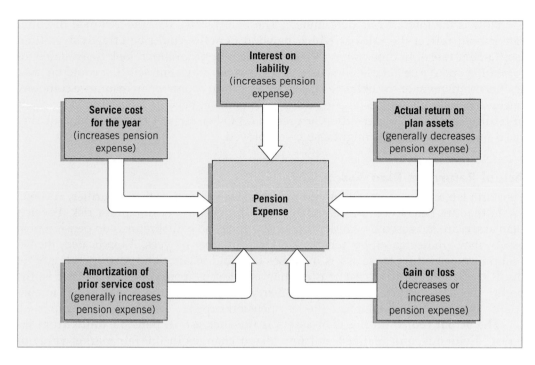

ILLUSTRATION 21-4
Components of Annual
Pension Expense

Service Cost

In *FASB Statement No. 87*, the Board states that the service cost component recognized in a period **should be determined as the** actuarial present value **of benefits attributed by the pension benefit formula to employee service during the period**. That is, the actuary predicts the additional benefits that must be paid under the plan's benefit formula as a result of the employees' current year's service and then discounts the cost of those future benefits back to their present value.

The Board concluded that **future compensation levels had to be considered in measuring the present obligation and periodic pension expense if the plan benefit formula incorporated them**. In other words, the present obligation resulting from a promise to pay a benefit of 1% of an employee's **final pay** is different from an employer's promise to pay 1% of **current pay**. To ignore this fact would be to ignore an important aspect of pension expense. Thus, the **benefits/years-of-service actuarial method** is the approach adopted by the FASB.

Some object to this determination, arguing that a company should have more freedom to select an expense recognition pattern. Others believe that incorporating future salary increases into current pension expense is accounting for events that have not happened yet. They argue that if the plan were terminated today, only liabilities for accumulated benefits would have to be paid. **Nevertheless the Board indicates that the projected benefit obligation provides a more realistic measure on a going concern basis of the employer's obligation under the plan and, therefore, should be used as the basis for determining service cost.**

Interest on the Liability

The second component of pension expense is interest on the liability, or interest expense. As indicated earlier, a pension is a deferred compensation arrangement under which this element of wages is deferred and a liability is created. Because the liability is not paid until maturity, it is recorded on a discounted basis and accrues interest over the life of the employee. **The interest component is the interest for the period on the projected benefit obligation outstanding during the period.** The FASB did not address the question of how often to compound the interest cost. To simplify our illustrations and problem materials, we use a simple interest computation, applying it to the beginning-of-the-year balance of the projected benefit liability.

How is the interest rate determined? The Board states that the assumed discount rate should **reflect the rates at which pension benefits could be effectively settled (settlement rates)**. In determining these rates, it is appropriate to look to available information about rates implicit in current prices of annuity contracts that could be used to effect settlement of the obligation. (Under an annuity contract an insurance company unconditionally guarantees to provide specific pension benefits to specific individuals in return for a fixed consideration or premium.) Other rates of return on high-quality fixed-income investments might also be employed.

Actual Return on Plan Assets

Pension plan assets are usually investments in stocks, bonds, other securities, and real estate that are held to earn a reasonable return, generally at minimum risk. Pension plan assets are increased by employer contributions and actual returns on pension plan assets; they are decreased by benefits paid to retired employees. As indicated, the actual return earned on these assets increases the fund balance and correspondingly reduces the employer's net cost of providing employees' pension benefits. That is, the higher the actual return on the pension plan assets, the less the employer has to contribute eventually and, therefore the less pension expense that needs to be reported.

The actual return on the plan assets **is the increase in pension funds from interest, dividends, and realized and unrealized changes in the fair market value of the plan assets.** The actual return is computed by adjusting the change in the plan assets for the effects of contributions during the year and benefits paid out during the year. The following equation, or a variation thereof, can be used to compute the actual return:

ILLUSTRATION 21-5
Equation for Computing
Actual Return

$$
\text{Actual Return} = \left(\begin{array}{l} \text{Plan} \\ \text{Assets} \\ \text{Ending} \\ \text{Balance} \end{array} - \begin{array}{l} \text{Plan} \\ \text{Assets} \\ \text{Beginning} \\ \text{Balance} \end{array} \right) - \text{Contributions} - \text{Benefits Paid}
$$

Stated another way, the actual return on plan assets is the difference between the **fair value of the plan assets** at the beginning of the period and the end of the period, adjusted for contributions and benefit payments. Computation of the actual return on the basis of the equation above is illustrated below using some assumed amounts:

ILLUSTRATION 21-6
Computation of Actual
Return on Plan Assets

Fair value of plan assets at end of period		$5,000,000
Deduct: Fair value of plan assets at beginning of period		4,200,000
Increase in fair value of plan assets		800,000
Deduct: Contributions to plan during period	$500,000	
Less benefits paid during period	300,000	200,000
Actual return on plan assets		$ 600,000

If the actual return on the plan assets is positive (gain) during the period, it is subtracted in the computation of pension expense. If the actual return is negative (loss) during the period, it is added in the computation of pension expense.[12]

---

[12]At this point, we are using the actual rate of return. As shown later, for purposes of computing pension expense, the expected rate of return is used.

USING A PENSION WORK SHEET

Before covering in detail the other pension expense components (amortization of un-recognized prior service cost and gains and losses) which seem to get progressively more complex, we will illustrate the basic accounting entries for the first three components: (1) service cost, (2) interest on the liability, and (3) actual return on plan assets.

Important to accounting for pensions under *Statement No. 87* is the fact that **several significant items of the pension plan are unrecognized in the accounts and in the financial statements**. Among the compromises the FASB made in issuing *Statement No. 87* was the nonrecognition (noncapitalization) of the following pension items:

❶ Projected benefit obligation.
❷ Pension plan assets.
❸ Unrecognized prior service costs.
❹ Unrecognized net gain or loss.

As discussed later, the employer is required to **disclose in notes** to the financial statements all of these four noncapitalized items, but they are not recognized in the body of the financial statements. In addition, the exact amount of these items must be known at all times because they are used in the computation of annual pension expense. Therefore, **in order to track these off-balance-sheet pension items, memo entries and accounts have to be maintained outside the formal general ledger accounting system**. A work sheet unique to pension accounting will be utilized to record both the formal entries and the memo entries to keep track of all the employer's relevant pension plan items and components.[13]

The format of the **pension work sheet** is shown below:

> **OBJECTIVE ❺**
> Utilize a work sheet for employer's pension plan entries.

ILLUSTRATION 21-7
Basic Format of Pension Work Sheet

	General Journal Entries			Memo Record	
Items	Annual Pension Expense	Cash	Prepaid/ Accrued Cost	Projected Benefit Obligation	Plan Assets

The left-hand "General Journal Entries" columns of the work sheet record entries in the formal general ledger accounts. The right-hand "Memo Record" columns maintain balances on the unrecognized (noncapitalized) pension items. On the first line of the work sheet, the beginning balances (if any) are recorded. Subsequently, transactions and events related to the pension plan are recorded, using debits and credits and using both sets of records as if they were one for recording the entries. For each transaction or event, the debits must equal the credits. The balance in the Prepaid/Accrued Cost column should equal the net balance in the memo record.

2000 Entries and Work Sheet

To illustrate the use of a work sheet and how it helps in accounting for a pension plan, assume that on January 1, 2000, Zarle Company adopts *FASB Statement No. 87* to account for its defined benefit pension plan. The following facts apply to the pension plan for the year 2000:

---

[13]The use of this pension entry work sheet is recommended and illustrated by Paul B. W. Miller, "The New Pension Accounting (Part 2)," *Journal of Accountancy*, February 1987, pp. 86–94.

Plan assets, January 1, 2000, are $100,000.

Projected benefit obligation, January 1, 2000, is $100,000.

Annual service cost is $9,000.

Settlement rate is 10%.

Actual return on plan assets is $10,000.

Contributions (funding) are $8,000.

Benefits paid to retirees during the year are $7,000.

Using the data presented above, the work sheet in Illustration 21-8 presents the beginning balances and all of the pension entries recorded by Zarle Company in 2000. The beginning balances for the projected benefit obligation and the pension plan assets are recorded on the first line of the work sheet in the memo record. They are not recorded in the formal general journal and, therefore, are not reported as a liability and an asset in the financial statements of Zarle Company. These two significant pension items are off-balance-sheet amounts that affect pension expense but are not recorded as assets and liabilities in the employer's books.

ILLUSTRATION 21-8
Pension Work Sheet—
2000

	General Journal Entries			Memo Record	
Items	Annual Pension Expense	Cash	Prepaid/ Accrued Cost	Projected Benefit Obligation	Plan Assets
Balance, Jan. 1, 2000			—	100,000 Cr.	100,000 Dr.
(a) Service cost	9,000 Dr.			9,000 Cr.	
(b) Interest cost	10,000 Dr.			10,000 Cr.	
(c) Actual return	10,000 Cr.				10,000 Dr.
(d) Contributions		8,000 Cr.			8,000 Dr.
(e) Benefits				7,000 Dr.	7,000 Cr.
Journal entry for 2000	9,000 Dr.	8,000 Cr.	1,000 Cr.*		
Balance, Dec. 31, 2000			1,000 Cr.**	112,000 Cr.	111,000 Dr.

*$9,000 − $8,000 = $1,000.
**$112,000 − $111,000 = $1,000.

Entry (a) records the service cost component, which increases pension expense $9,000 and increases the liability (projected benefit obligation) $9,000. Entry (b) accrues the interest expense component, which increases both the liability and the pension expense by $10,000 (the beginning projected benefit obligation multiplied by the settlement rate of 10%). Entry (c) records the actual return on the plan assets, which increases the plan assets and decreases the pension expense. Entry (d) records Zarle Company's contribution (funding) of assets to the pension fund; cash is decreased $8,000 and plan assets are increased $8,000. Entry (e) records the benefit payments made to retirees, which results in equal $7,000 decreases to the plan assets and the projected benefit obligation.

The "formal journal entry" on December 31, which is the entry made to formally record the pension expense in 2000, is as follows:

2000

Pension Expense	9,000	
Cash		8,000
Prepaid/Accrued Pension Cost		1,000

The credit to Prepaid/Accrued Pension Cost for $1,000 represents the difference between the 2000 pension expense of $9,000 and the amount funded of $8,000. Prepaid/Accrued Pension Cost (credit) is a liability because the plan is underfunded by $1,000. The Prepaid/Accrued Pension Cost account balance of $1,000 also equals the net of the balances in the memo accounts. This reconciliation of the off-balance-sheet items with the prepaid/accrued pension cost reported in the balance sheet is shown in Illustration 21-9.

Projected benefit obligation (Credit)	$(112,000)
Plan assets at fair value (Debit)	111,000
Prepaid/accrued pension cost (Credit)	(1,000)

ILLUSTRATION 21-9
Pension Reconciliation
Schedule—December 31,
2000

If the net of the memo record balances is a credit, the reconciling amount in the prepaid/accrued cost column will be a credit equal in amount. If the net of the memo record balances is a debit, the prepaid/accrued cost amount will be a debit equal in amount. The work sheet is designed to produce this reconciling feature which will be useful later in the preparation of the required notes related to pension disclosures.

In this illustration, the debit to Pension Expense exceeds the credit to Cash, resulting in a credit to Prepaid/Accrued Pension Cost—the recognition of a liability. If the credit to Cash exceeded the debit to Pension Expense, Prepaid/Accrued Pension Cost would be debited—the recognition of an asset.

Amortization of Unrecognized Prior Service Cost (PSC)

When a defined benefit plan is either initiated (adopted) or amended, credit is often given to employees for years of service provided before the date of initiation or amendment. As a result of prior service credits, the projected benefit obligation is usually greater than it was before. In many cases, the increase in the projected benefit obligation is substantial. One question that arises is whether an expense and related liability for these prior service costs (PSC) should be fully reported at the time a plan is initiated or amended. The FASB has taken the position that no expense for these costs and in some cases no liability should be recognized at the time of the plan's adoption or amendment. The Board's rationale is that the employer would not provide credit for past years of service unless it expected to receive benefits in the future. As a result, **the retroactive benefits should not be recognized as pension expense entirely in the year of amendment but should be recognized during the service periods of those employees who are expected to receive benefits under the plan (the remaining service life of the covered active employees)**.

The cost of the retroactive benefits (including benefits that are granted to existing retirees) is the increase in the projected benefit obligation at the date of the amendment. The amount of the prior service cost is computed by an actuary. Amortization of the unrecognized prior service cost is an accounting function performed with the assistance of an actuary.

The Board prefers a **years-of-service** amortization method that is similar to a units-of-production computation. First, the total number of service-years to be worked by all of the participating employees is computed. Second, the unrecognized prior service cost is divided by the total number of service-years, to obtain a cost per service-year (the unit cost). Third, the number of service-years consumed each year is multiplied by the cost per service-year, to obtain the annual amortization charge.

To illustrate the amortization of the unrecognized prior service cost under the years-of-service method, assume that Zarle Company's defined benefit pension plan covers 170 employees. In its negotiations with its employees, Zarle Company amends its pension plan on January 1, 2001, and grants $80,000 of prior service costs to its employees. The employees are grouped as follows according to expected years of retirement:

OBJECTIVE 6
Describe the
amortization of
unrecognized prior
service costs.

**INTERNATIONAL
INSIGHT**

In the U.S., prior service cost is generally amortized over the average remaining service life of employees. In Germany, prior service cost is recognized immediately. In the Netherlands, prior service cost may either be recognized immediately or directly charged to shareholders' equity.

Group	Number of Employees	Expected Retirement on Dec. 31
A	40	2001
B	20	2002
C	40	2003
D	50	2004
E	20	2005
	170	

The computation of the service-years per year and the total service-years is shown in Illustration 21-10.

ILLUSTRATION 21-10
Computation of Service-Years

	Service-Years					
Year	A	B	C	D	E	Total
2001	40	20	40	50	20	170
2002		20	40	50	20	130
2003			40	50	20	110
2004				50	20	70
2005					20	20
	40	40	120	200	100	500

Computed on the basis of a prior service cost of $80,000 and a total of 500 service-years for all years, the cost per service-year is $160 ($80,000 ÷ 500). The annual amount of amortization based on a $160 cost per service-year is computed as follows:

ILLUSTRATION 21-11
Computation of Annual Prior Service Cost Amortization

Year	Total Service-Years	×	Cost per Service-Year	=	Annual Amortization
2001	170		$160		$27,200
2002	130		160		20,800
2003	110		160		17,600
2004	70		160		11,200
2005	20		160		3,200
	500				$80,000

FASB Statement No. 87 allows an alternative method of computing amortization of unrecognized prior service cost; **employers may use straight-line amortization over the average remaining service life of the employees.** In this case, with 500 service years and 170 employees, the average would be 2.94 years (500 ÷ 170). Using this method, the $80,000 cost would be charged to expense at $27,211 ($80,000 ÷ 2.94) in 2001, $27,211 in 2002, and $25,578 ($27,211 × .94) in 2003.

If the Board had adopted full capitalization of all elements of the pension plan, the prior service cost would have been capitalized as an intangible asset—pension goodwill—and amortized over its useful life. The intangible asset (goodwill) comes from the assumption that the cost of additional pension benefits increases loyalty and productivity (and reduces turnover) among the affected employees. However, prior service cost is accounted for off-balance-sheet and is called **unrecognized prior service cost**. Although not recognized on the balance sheet, prior service cost is a factor in computing pension expense.

2001 Entries and Work Sheet

Continuing the Zarle Company illustration into 2001, we note that a January 1, 2001, amendment to the pension plan grants to employees prior service benefits having a present value of $80,000. The annual amortization amounts, as computed in the previous section using the years-of-service approach ($27,200 for 2001), are employed in this illustration. The following facts apply to the pension plan for the year 2001.

On January 1, 2001, Zarle Company grants prior service benefits having a present value of $80,000.

Annual service cost is $9,500.

Settlement rate is 10%.

Actual return on plan assets is $11,100.

Annual contributions (funding) are $20,000.

Benefits paid to retirees during the year are $8,000.

Amortization of prior service cost (PSC) using the years-of-service method is $27,200.

The following work sheet presents all of the pension entries and information recorded by Zarle Company in 2001:

ILLUSTRATION 21-12
Pension Work Sheet—
2001

	General Journal Entries			Memo Record		
Items	Annual Pension Expense	Cash	Prepaid/ Accrued Cost	Projected Benefit Obligation	Plan Assets	Unrecognized Prior Service Cost
Balance, Dec. 31, 2000			1,000 Cr.	112,000 Cr.	111,000 Dr.	
(f) Prior service cost				80,000 Cr.		80,000 Dr.
Balance, Jan. 1, 2001			1,000 Cr.	192,000 Cr.	111,000 Dr.	80,000 Dr.
(g) Service cost	9,500 Dr.			9,500 Cr.		
(h) Interest cost	19,200 Dr.[a]			19,200 Cr.		
(i) Actual return	11,100 Cr.				11,100 Dr.	
(j) Amortization of PSC	27,200 Dr.					27,200 Cr.
(k) Contributions		20,000 Cr.			20,000 Dr.	
(l) Benefits				8,000 Dr.	8,000 Cr.	
Journal entry for 2001	44,800 Dr.	20,000 Cr.	24,800 Cr.			
Balance, Dec. 31, 2001			25,800 Cr.	212,700 Cr.	134,100 Dr.	52,800 Dr.

[a]$19,200 = $192,000 × 10%.

The first line of the work sheet shows the beginning balances of the Prepaid/Accrued Pension Cost account and the memo accounts. Entry (f) records Zarle Company's granting of prior service cost by adding $80,000 to the projected benefit obligation and to the unrecognized (noncapitalized) prior service cost. Entries (g), (h), (i), (k), and (l) are similar to the corresponding entries in 2000. Entry (j) records the 2001 amortization of unrecognized prior service cost by debiting Pension Expense by $27,200 and crediting the new Unrecognized Prior Service Cost account by the same amount.

The journal entry on December 31 to formally record the pension expense—the sum of the annual pension expense column—for 2001 is as follows:

2001

Pension Expense	44,800	
Cash		20,000
Prepaid/Accrued Pension Cost		24,800

Because the expense exceeds the funding, the Prepaid/Accrued Pension Cost account is credited for the $24,800 difference and is a liability. In 2001, as in 2000, the balance of the Prepaid/Accrued Pension Cost account ($25,800) is equal to the net of the balances in the memo accounts as shown in Illustration 21-13.

ILLUSTRATION 21-13
Pension Reconciliation
Schedule—December 31,
2001

Projected benefit obligation (Credit)	$(212,700)
Plan assets at fair value (Debit)	134,100
Funded status	(78,600)
Unrecognized prior service cost (Debit)	52,800
Prepaid/accrued pension cost (Credit)	$ (25,800)

The reconciliation is the formula that makes the work sheet work. It relates the components of pension accounting, recorded and unrecorded, to one another.

Gain or Loss

Of great concern to companies that have pension plans are the uncontrollable and unexpected swings in pension expense that could be caused by (1) sudden and large changes in the market value of plan assets and (2) changes in actuarial assumptions that affect the amount of the projected benefit obligation. If these gains or losses were to impact fully the financial statements in the period of realization or incurrence, substantial fluctuations in pension expense would result. Therefore, the profession decided to reduce the volatility associated with pension expense by using **smoothing techniques** that dampen and in some cases fully eliminate the fluctuations.

Smoothing Unexpected Gains and Losses on Plan Assets

One component of pension expense, actual return on plan assets, reduces pension expense (assuming the actual return is positive). A large change in the actual return can substantially affect pension expense for a year. Assume a company has a 40% return in the stock market for the year. Should this substantial, and perhaps one-time, event affect current pension expense?

Actuaries ignore current fluctuations when they develop a funding pattern to pay expected benefits in the future. They develop an expected rate of return and multiply it by an asset value weighted over a reasonable period of time to arrive at an expected return on plan assets. This return is then used to determine its funding pattern.

The Board adopted the actuary's approach to dampen wide swings that might occur in the actual return. That is, the expected return on the plan assets is to be included as a component of pension expense, not the actual return in a given year. To achieve this goal, the expected rate of return (the actuary's rate) is multiplied by the fair value of the plan assets or a market-related asset value of the plan assets (throughout our Zarle Company illustrations, market-related value and fair value of plan assets are assumed equal). The **market-related asset value is a calculated value that recognizes changes in fair value in a systematic and rational manner over not more than 5 years.**[14]

What happens to the difference between the expected return and the actual return, often referred to as the unexpected gain or loss—also called asset gains and losses by the FASB? Asset gains (occurring when actual return is greater than expected return) and asset losses (occurring when actual return is less than expected return) are recorded in an Unrecognized Net Gain or Loss account and combined with unrecognized gains and losses accumulated in prior years.

To illustrate the computation of an unexpected asset gain or loss and its related accounting, assume that Shierer Company in 2002 has an actual return on plan assets of $16,000 when the expected return is $13,410 (the expected rate of return of 10% times the beginning-of-the-year plan assets). The unexpected asset gain of $2,590 ($16,000 − $13,410) is credited to Unrecognized Net Gain or Loss and debited to Pension Expense.

Smoothing Unexpected Gains and Losses on the Pension Liability

In estimating, the projected benefit obligation (the liability), actuaries make assumptions about such items as mortality rate, retirement rate, turnover rate, disability rate, and salary amounts. Any change in these actuarial assumptions changes the amount of the projected benefit obligation. Seldom does actual experience coincide exactly with the actuarial predictions. These unexpected gains or losses from changes in the projected benefit obligation are called liability gains and losses.

Liability gains (resulting from unexpected decreases in the liability balance) and liability losses (resulting from unexpected increases) are deferred (unrecognized). The liability gains and losses are combined in the same Unrecognized Net Gain or Loss

---

[14]Different ways of calculating market-related value may be used for different classes of assets (for example, an employer might use fair value for bonds and a 5-year-moving-average for equities), but the manner of determining market-related value should be applied consistently from year to year for each asset class.

account used for asset gains and losses. They are accumulated from year to year, off-balance-sheet, in a memo record account.

Corridor Amortization

Because the asset gains and losses and the liability gains and losses can be offsetting, the accumulated total unrecognized net gain or loss may not grow very large. But, it is possible that no offsetting will occur and that the balance in the Unrecognized Net Gain or Loss account will continue to grow. To limit its growth, the FASB invented the corridor approach for amortizing the accumulated balance in the Unrecognized Gain or Loss account when it gets too large. **The** unrecognized net gain or loss **balance is considered too large and must be amortized when it exceeds the arbitrarily selected FASB criterion of 10% of the larger of the beginning balances of the projected benefit obligation or the market-related value of the plan assets.**

To illustrate the corridor approach, assume data on the projected benefit obligation and the plan assets over a period of 6 years as shown in Illustration 21-14.

Beginning-of-the-Year Balances	Projected Benefit Obligation	Market-Related Asset Value	Corridor* +/− 10%
1999	$1,000,000	$ 900,000	$100,000
2000	1,200,000	1,100,000	120,000
2001	1,300,000	1,700,000	170,000
2002	1,500,000	2,250,000	225,000
2003	1,700,000	1,750,000	175,000
2004	1,800,000	1,700,000	180,000

*The corridor becomes 10% of the larger (in boldface) of the projected benefit obligation or the market-related plan asset value.

ILLUSTRATION 21-14
Computation of the Corridor

How the corridor works becomes apparent when the data above are portrayed graphically as in the diagram in Illustration 21-15.

ILLUSTRATION 21-15
Graphic Illustration of the Corridor

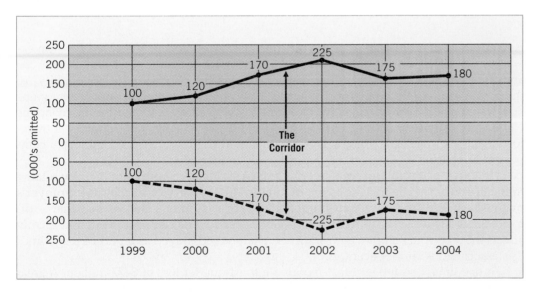

If the balance of the Unrecognized Net Gain or Loss account stays within the upper and lower limits of the corridor, no amortization is required—the unrecognized net gain or loss balance is carried forward unchanged.

If amortization is required, the minimum amortization shall be the excess divided by the average remaining service period of active employees expected to receive benefits under the plan. Any systematic method of amortization of unrecognized gains and losses may be used in lieu of the minimum, provided it is greater than the minimum, is used consistently for both gains and losses, and is disclosed.

Illustration of Unrecognized Gains/Losses

In applying the corridor, the Board decided that amortization of the excess unrecognized net gain or loss should be included as a component of pension expense only if, at the **beginning of the year**, the unrecognized net gain or loss exceeded the corridor. That is, if no unrecognized net gain or loss exists at the beginning of the period, no recognition of gains or losses can result in that period.

To illustrate the amortization of unrecognized net gains and losses, assume the following information for Soft-White, Inc.:

	2000	2001	2002
		(beginning of the year)	
Projected benefit obligation	$2,100,000	$2,600,000	$2,900,000
Market-related asset value	2,600,000	2,800,000	2,700,000
Unrecognized net loss	–0–	400,000	300,000

If the average remaining service life of all active employees is 5.5 years, the schedule to amortize the unrecognized net loss is as follows:

ILLUSTRATION 21-16
Corridor Test and
Gain/Loss Amortization
Schedule

Year	Projected Benefit Obligation[a]	Plan Assets[a]	Corridor[b]	Cumulative Unrecognized Net Loss[a]	Minimum Amortization of Loss (For Current Year)
2000	$2,100,000	$2,600,000	$260,000	$ –0–	$ –0–
2001	2,600,000	2,800,000	280,000	400,000	21,818[c]
2002	2,900,000	2,700,000	290,000	678,182[d]	70,579[d]

[a]All as of the beginning of the period.
[b]10% of the greater of projected benefit obligation or plan assets market-related value.
[c]$400,000 − $280,000 = $120,000; $120,000 ÷ 5.5 = $21,818
[d]$400,000 − $21,818 + $300,000 = $678,182; $678,182 − $290,000 = $388,182; $388,182 ÷ 5.5 = $70,579.

As indicated from Illustration 21-16, the loss recognized in 2001 increased pension expense by $21,818. This amount is small in comparison with the total loss of $400,000 and indicates that the corridor approach dampens the effects (reduces volatility) of these gains and losses on pension expense. The rationale for the corridor is that gains and losses result from refinements in estimates as well as real changes in economic value and that over time some of these gains and losses will offset one another. It therefore seems reasonable that gains and losses should not be recognized fully as a component of pension expense in the period in which they arise.

However, **gains and losses that arise from a single occurrence not directly related to the operation of the pension plan and not in the ordinary course of the employer's business should be recognized immediately.** For example, a gain or loss that is directly related to a plant closing, a disposal of a segment, or a similar event that greatly affects the size of the employee work force, shall be recognized as a part of the gain or loss associated with that event.

At one time, **Bethlehem Steel** reported a third-quarter loss of $477 million. A great deal of this loss was attributable to future estimated benefits payable to workers who were permanently laid off. In this situation, the loss should be treated as an adjustment to the gain or loss on the plant closing and should not affect pension cost for the current or future periods.

Summary of Calculations for Asset Gain or Loss

The difference between the actual return on plan assets and the expected return on plan assets is the unexpected (deferred) asset gain or loss component. This component defers the difference between the actual return and expected return on plan assets in computing current year pension expense. Thus, after considering this component, **it is really the expected return on plan assets (not the actual return) that determines current pension expense**.

The amortized net gain or loss is determined by amortizing the unrecognized gain or loss at the beginning of the year subject to the corridor limitation. In other words, **if the unrecognized gain or loss is greater than the corridor, these net gains and losses are subject to amortization**. This minimum amortization is computed by dividing the net gains or losses subject to amortization by the average remaining service period. When the unexpected gain or loss is combined with the amortization of prior years' actuarial gains and losses, the net amortized and unexpected gains and losses is determined (often referred to simply as gain or loss). This summary is illustrated graphically below:

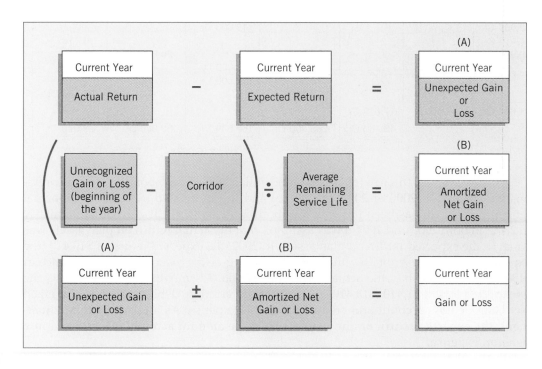

ILLUSTRATION 21-17
Graphic Summary of Gain or Loss Computation

In essence, these gains and losses are subject to triple smoothing. That is, the asset gain or loss is smoothed by using the expected return. Then the unrecognized gain or loss at the beginning of the year is not amortized unless it is greater than the corridor. Finally, the excess is spread over the remaining service life of existing employees.

2002 Entries and Work Sheet

Continuing the Zarle Company illustration, the following facts apply to the pension plan for 2002:

Annual service cost is $13,000.

Settlement rate is 10%; expected earnings rate is 10%.

Actual return on plan assets is $12,000.

Amortization of prior service cost (PSC) is $20,800.

Annual contributions (funding) are $24,000.

Benefits paid to retirees during the year are $10,500.

Changes in actuarial assumptions establish the end-of-year projected benefit obligation at $265,000.

The work sheet shown in Illustration 21-18 presents all of the pension entries and information recorded by Zarle Company in 2002. On the first line of the work sheet are recorded the beginning balances that relate to the pension plan. In this case, the beginning balances for Zarle Company are the ending balances from the 2001 Zarle Company pension work sheet in Illustration 21-12.

ILLUSTRATION 21-18
Pension Work Sheet—
2002

	General Journal Entries			Memo Record			
Items	Annual Pension Expense	Cash	Prepaid/ Accrued Cost	Projected Benefit Obligation	Plan Assets	Unrecognized Prior Service Cost	Unrecognized Net Gain or Loss
Bal., December 31, 2001			25,800 Cr.	212,700 Cr.	134,100 Dr.	52,800 Dr.	
(m) Service cost	13,000 Dr.			13,000 Cr.			
(n) Interest cost	21,270 Dr.			21,270 Cr.			
(o) Actual return	12,000 Cr.				12,000 Dr.		
(p) Unexpected loss	1,410 Cr.						1,410 Dr.
(q) Amortization of PSC	20,800 Dr.					20,800 Cr.	
(r) Contributions		24,000 Cr.			24,000 Dr.		
(s) Benefits				10,500 Dr.	10,500 Cr.		
(t) Liability increase				28,530 Cr.			28,530 Dr.
Journal entry for 2002	41,660 Dr.	24,000 Cr.	17,660 Cr.				
Bal., December 31, 2002			43,460 Cr.	265,000 Cr.	159,600 Dr.	32,000 Dr.	29,940 Dr.

Entries (m), (n), (o), (q), (r), and (s) are similar to the corresponding entries previously explained in 2000 or 2001. Entries (o) and (p) are related. Recording the actual return in entry (o) has been illustrated in both 2000 and 2001; it is recorded similarly in 2002. In both 2000 and 2001 it was assumed that the actual return on plan assets was equal to the expected return on plan assets. In 2002, the expected return of $13,410 (the expected rate of return of 10% times the beginning-of-the-year plan assets balance of $134,100) is higher than the actual return of $12,000. To smooth pension expense, the unexpected loss of $1,410 ($13,410 − $12,000) is deferred by debiting the Unrecognized Net Gain or Loss account and crediting Pension Expense. **As a result of this adjustment, the expected return on the plan assets is the amount actually used to compute pension expense.**

Entry (t) records the change in the projected benefit obligation resulting from a change in actuarial assumptions. As indicated, the actuary has now computed the ending balance to be $265,000. Given that the memo record balance at December 31 is $236,470 ($212,700 + $13,000 + $21,270 − $10,500), a difference of $28,530 ($265,000 − $236,470) is indicated. This $28,530 increase in the employer's liability is an unexpected loss that is deferred by debiting it to the Unrecognized Net Gain or Loss account.

The journal entry on December 31 to formally record pension expense for 2002 is as follows:

2002

Pension Expense	41,660	
Cash		24,000
Prepaid/Accrued Pension Cost		17,660

As illustrated in the work sheets of 2000 and 2001, the balance of the Prepaid/ Accrued Pension Cost account at December 31, 2002, of $43,460 is equal to the net of the balances in the memo accounts as shown below:

ILLUSTRATION 21-19
Pension Reconciliation
Schedule—December 31,
2002

Projected benefit obligation (Credit)	$(265,000)
Plan assets at fair value (Debit)	159,600
Funded status	(105,400)
Unrecognized prior service cost (Debit)	32,000
Unrecognized net loss (Debit)	29,940
Prepaid/accrued pension cost (Credit)	$ (43,460)

MINIMUM LIABILITY

If the FASB had decided to capitalize pension plan assets and liabilities, Zarle Company in our previous illustration would have reported on December 31, 2002, a liability of $265,000, plan assets of $159,600, and unrecognized prior service cost (goodwill) of $32,000 plus an unrecognized net loss of $29,940. Instead it reports only accrued pension cost of $43,460 as a liability. The Board was well aware of this discrepancy. It believed that an employer with a projected benefit obligation in excess of the fair value of pension plan assets has a liability and that an employer with a fair value of plan assets in excess of projected benefit obligation has an asset. Nevertheless, when the Board was faced with the final decision on this matter, it decided that to require the reporting of these amounts in the financial statements would be too great a change in practice at that time, because up to then none of these amounts had been reported in the balance sheet.

The Board, therefore, developed a compromise approach that requires immediate recognition of a liability (referred to as the minimum liability) when the accumulated benefit obligation exceeds the fair value of plan assets. The purpose of this minimum liability requirement is to assure that if a significant plan amendment or actuarial loss occurs, a liability will be recognized at least to the extent of the unfunded portion of the accumulated benefit obligation.

Note that the plan assets are compared to the smaller **accumulated** benefit obligation instead of the larger projected benefit obligation. The rationale for using the accumulated benefit obligation is that if the liability were settled today, it would be settled on the basis of current salary rates, not future salary rates. Therefore, it is argued that the accumulated benefit obligation should be used, not the projected benefit obligation. Although the compromise approach frequently ignores a portion of the liability, it does help to report some balance sheet effects when a plan amendment or a large loss occurs. **The Board does not permit the recording of an additional asset if the fair value of the pension plan exceeds the accumulated benefit obligation.**

UNDERLYING CONCEPTS

Recognizing the smaller benefit obligation ignores the going concern concept. A going concern would not expect to settle the obligation today at current salaries and wages. A going concern would expect to settle the obligation based upon future salary levels.

Minimum Liability Computation

If a liability for accrued pension cost is already reported, only an additional liability to equal the required minimum liability (unfunded accumulated benefit) is recorded. To illustrate, assume that Largent Inc. amends its pension plan on December 31, 2000, giving retroactive benefits to its employees, as follows:

INTERNATIONAL INSIGHT

Only the U.S. requires companies to revalue their pension plan obligations each year. Other nations tend to require revaluation at approximately 3-year intervals.

Projected benefit obligation	$8,000,000
Accumulated benefit obligation	7,000,000
Plan assets (at fair value)	5,000,000
Market-related asset value	4,900,000
Unrecognized prior service cost	2,500,000
Accrued pension cost	500,000

The unfunded accumulated benefit is computed as follows:

Accumulated benefit obligation	$7,000,000
Plan assets (at fair value)	5,000,000
Unfunded accumulated benefit obligation (minimum liability)	$2,000,000

ILLUSTRATION 21-20
Computation of Unfunded Accumulated Benefit (Minimum Liability)

Note that the fair value of the plan assets is used, not the market-related asset value, to compute the unfunded accumulated benefit obligation. In this case, an additional $1,500,000 is required to be recorded as a liability and reported on the financial statements. The computation of the additional liability is as follows:

ILLUSTRATION 21-21
Computation of
Additional Liability
Required—Accrued
Pension Cost Balance

Unfunded accumulated benefit obligation (minimum liability)	$2,000,000
Accrued pension cost (balance at December 31, 2000)	500,000
Additional liability required	$1,500,000

Largent Inc. would combine the accrued pension cost and the additional liability into one amount and report it in the balance sheet as accrued pension cost or pension liability in the amount of $2,000,000.

If Largent Inc. had a prepaid pension cost of $300,000 instead of an accrued pension cost of $500,000, an additional liability of $2,300,000 would be recorded as follows:

ILLUSTRATION 21-22
Computation of
Additional Liability
Required—Prepaid
Pension Cost Balance

Unfunded accumulated benefit obligation (minimum liability)	$2,000,000
Prepaid pension cost	300,000
Additional liability required	$2,300,000

The existing balance in the prepaid pension cost (debit) is **combined** with the additional liability (credit) into one amount and reported as accrued pension cost or pension liability in the net amount of $2,000,000.

Financial Statement Presentation

INTERNATIONAL INSIGHT

IASC standards do not account for a minimum liability.

When it is necessary to adjust the accounts to recognize a minimum liability, the debit should be to an intangible asset that is called Intangible Asset—Deferred Pension Cost. The entry to record the liability and related intangible asset for Largent Inc. (first case) is:

Intangible Asset—Deferred Pension Cost	1,500,000	
Additional Pension Liability		1,500,000

One exception to the general rule of reporting an intangible asset is when the **additional liability exceeds the amount of unrecognized prior service cost**. In this case, the excess is debited to Excess of Additional Pension Liability Over Unrecognized Prior Service Cost. When the additional liability exceeds the unrecognized prior service cost, the excess must have resulted from an actuarial loss, such as an increase in the benefit obligation due to an increase in retiree longevity. The justification for recognizing an intangible asset up to the amount of the unrecognized prior service cost is that an amendment to an existing plan increases goodwill with employees and therefore benefits the company in the future. Such is not the case when the additional liability exceeds the unrecognized prior service cost.

When this excess develops, it should be reported as a reduction of other comprehensive income. In addition, its cumulative balance is reported as a component of accumulated other comprehensive income on the balance sheet. Because the excess of additional pension liability over unrecognized prior service cost reduces stockholders' equity, it is often referred to as a contra equity account. To illustrate, assume that Largent Inc. has common stock, with a total par value of $1,000,000, additional paid-in capital of $400,000, and retained earnings of $700,000. In addition, it has an additional liability that exceeds the unrecognized prior service cost by $200,000. A condensed version of Largent's stockholders' equity section is provided in Illustration 21-23.[15]

---

[15]This treatment is similar to the reporting of the unrealized holding loss on available-for-sale securities discussed in earlier chapters. Note that the components of accumulated other comprehensive income must be shown in the stockholders' equity section of the balance sheet, or the notes, or the statement of stockholders' equity.

ILLUSTRATION 21-23
Balance Sheet
Presentation of Excess of
Additional Pension
Liability

Stockholders' Equity Section	
Common stock	$1,000,000
Additional paid-in capital	400,000
Total paid-in capital	1,400,000
Retained earnings	700,000
Accumulated other comprehensive income	(200,000)
Total stockholders' equity	$1,900,000

The amount of the additional liability required should be evaluated each reporting period along with the related intangible asset or contra equity account. At each reporting date, these items may be increased, decreased, or totally eliminated. Neither the intangible asset nor the contra equity account is amortized from period to period; the balances are merely adjusted up or down.

The minimum liability approach for the Zarle Company pension plan for all three years 2000, 2001, and 2002 is illustrated in the following schedule (values are assumed for the accumulated benefit obligation):

ILLUSTRATION 21-24
Minimum Liability
Computations

	December 31		
	2000	2001	2002
Accumulated benefit obligation	$(80,000)	$(164,000)	$(240,600)
Plan assets at fair value	111,000	134,100	159,600
Unfunded accumulated benefit obligation (minimum liability)	$ –0–	(29,900)	(81,000)
Accrued pension cost	1,000	25,800	43,460
Additional liability	$ –0–	(4,100)	(37,540)
Unrecognized prior service cost*		52,800	32,000
Contra equity charge**		$ –0–	$ (5,540)

*Maximum intangible asset recognizable.
**Difference charged to Excess of Additional Pension Liability Over Unrecognized Prior Service Cost.

In 2000, the fair value of the plan assets exceeds the accumulated benefit obligation; therefore, no additional liability need be reported. **The Board does not permit the recognition of a net investment in the pension plan when the plan assets exceed the pension obligation.**

In 2001, the minimum liability amount ($29,900) exceeds the accrued pension cost liability already recorded ($25,800), so an additional liability of $4,100 ($29,900 – $25,800) is recorded as follows:

December 31, 2001

Intangible Asset—Deferred Pension Cost	4,100	
Additional Pension Liability		4,100

In 2002, the minimum liability ($81,000) exceeds the accrued pension cost liability ($43,460), so an additional liability of $37,540 must be reported at the end of 2002. Since a balance of $4,100 already exists in the Additional Pension Liability account, it is credited for $33,440 ($37,540 – $4,100). Also, since the additional liability exceeds the unrecognized prior service cost by $5,540, the excess is debited to the contra equity account, Excess of Additional Pension Liability over Unrecognized Prior Service Cost. The remaining $27,900 ($33,440 – $5,540) is debited to the Intangible Asset—Deferred Pension Cost. The entry on December 31, 2002, to adjust the minimum liability is as follows:

December 31, 2002

Intangible Asset—Deferred Pension Cost	27,900	
Excess of Additional Pension Liability over		
Unrecognized Prior Service Cost	5,540	
Additional Pension Liability		33,440

As the additional liability changes, the combined debit balance of the intangible asset and contra equity accounts fluctuates by the same amount.

Work Sheet Illustration

To illustrate how the pension work sheet is affected by the minimum liability computation, a revised version of the 2002 work sheet of Zarle Company is shown in Illustration 21-25. The boldface items [entry (u)] relate to adjustments caused by recognition of the minimum liability at the end of 2001 and 2002.

	General Journal Entries					
Items	Annual Pension Expense	Cash	Prepaid/ Accrued Cost	Additional Liability	Pension Intangible	Contra Equity
Balance, Dec. 31, 2001			25,800 Cr.	4,100 Cr.	4,100 Dr.	
(m) Service cost	13,000 Dr.					
(n) Interest cost	21,270 Dr.					
(o) Actual return	12,000 Cr.					
(p) Unexpected loss	1,410 Cr.					
(q) Amortization of PSC	20,800 Dr.					
(r) Contributions		24,000 Cr.				
(s) Benefits						
(t) Liability change (Incr.)						
(u) Minimum liab. adj.				33,440 Cr.	27,900 Dr.	5,540 Dr.
Journal entry for 2002	41,660 Dr.	24,000 Cr.	17,660 Cr.			
Balance, Dec. 31, 2002			43,460 Cr.	37,540 Cr.	32,000 Dr.	5,540 Dr.

	Memo Entries			
Items	Projected Benefit Obligation	Plan Assets	Unrecognized Prior Service Cost	Unrecognized Net Gain or Loss
Balance, Dec. 31, 2001	212,700 Cr.	134,100 Dr.	52,800 Dr.	
(m) Service cost	13,000 Cr.			
(n) Interest cost	21,270 Cr.			
(o) Actual return		12,000 Dr.		
(p) Unexpected loss				1,410 Dr.
(q) Amortization of PSC			20,800 Cr.	
(r) Contributions		24,000 Dr.		
(s) Benefits	10,500 Dr.	10,500 Cr.		
(t) Liability increase	28,530 Cr.			28,530 Dr.
(u) Minimum liab. adj.				
Journal entry for 2002				
Balance, Dec. 31, 2002	265,000 Cr.	159,600 Dr.	32,000 Dr.	29,940 Dr.

ILLUSTRATION 21-25
Revised Pension Work Sheet—2002, Revised to Include Minimum Liability Computation

As illustrated in prior work sheets, the balance in the Prepaid/Accrued Pension Cost account ($43,460) equals the net of the balances in the memo accounts ($265,000 − [$159,600 + $32,000 + $29,940]). In this case, the Additional Liability is combined with the Prepaid/Accrued Pension Cost to determine the minimum pension liability in the balance sheet. This computation is shown in Illustration 21-26.

Projected benefit obligation (Credit)	$(265,000)
Plan assets at fair value (Debit)	159,600
Funded status	(105,400)
Unrecognized prior service cost (Debit)	32,000
Unrecognized net loss (Debit)	29,940
Prepaid/accrued pension cost (Credit)	(43,460)
Additional liability (Credit)	(37,540)
Accrued pension cost liability recognized in the balance sheet (minimum liability)	$ (81,000)

ILLUSTRATION 21-26
Reconciliation
Schedule—2002, Revised
to Show Additional
Pension Liability

REPORTING PENSION PLANS IN FINANCIAL STATEMENTS

OBJECTIVE ❿
Describe the reporting
requirements for
pension plans in
financial statements.

One might suspect that a phenomenon as significant and complex as pensions would involve extensive reporting and disclosure requirements. We will cover these requirements in two categories: (1) those within the financial statements, and (2) those within the notes to the financial statements.

Within the Financial Statements

If the amount funded (credit to Cash) by the employer to the pension trust is **less than the annual expense** (debit to Pension Expense), a credit balance accrual of the difference arises in the long-term liability section. It might be described as Accrued Pension Cost, Liability for Pension Expense Not Funded, or Due to Pension Fund. A liability is classified as current when it requires the disbursement of cash within the next year.

If the amount funded to the pension trust during the period is **greater than the amount charged to expense**, an asset equal to the difference arises. This asset is reported as Prepaid Pension Cost, Deferred Pension Expense, or Prepaid Pension Expense in the current assets section if it is current in nature, and in the other assets section if it is long-term in nature.

If the **accumulated benefit obligation exceeds the fair value of pension plan assets**, an additional liability is recorded. The debit is either to an Intangible Asset—Deferred Pension Cost or to a contra account to stockholders' equity entitled Excess of Additional Pension Liability Over Unrecognized Prior Service Cost. If the debit is less than unrecognized prior service cost, it is reported as an intangible asset. If the debit is greater than unrecognized prior service cost, the excess debit is reported as part of other comprehensive income and the accumulated balance as a component of accumulated other comprehensive income.

Within the Notes to the Financial Statements

Pension plans are frequently important to an understanding of financial position, results of operations, and cash flows of a company. Therefore, the following information, if not disclosed in the body of the financial statements, should be disclosed in the notes.[16]

❶ A schedule showing all the major components of pension expense should be reported.
Rationale: Information provided about the components of pension expense helps users better understand how pension expense is determined and is useful in forecasting a company's net income.

---

[16]"Employers' Disclosure about Pensions and Other Postretirement Benefits," *Statement of Financial Accounting Standards No. 132* (Stamford, Conn.: FASB, 1998). This statement modifies the disclosure requirements of *SFAS No. 87.* In our view, these new disclosure requirements are easier to understand and more streamlined than the disclosure requirements mandated prior to *SFAS No. 132.*

❷ A **reconciliation** showing how the projected benefit obligation and the fair value of the plan assets changed from the beginning to the end of the period is required. *Rationale:* Disclosing the projected benefit obligation, the fair value of the plan assets, and changes in them should help users understand the economics underlying the obligations and resources of these plans. The Board believes that explaining the changes in the projected benefit obligation and fair value of plan assets in the form of a reconciliation provides a more complete disclosure and makes the financial statements more understandable.

❸ The **funded status** of the plan (difference between the projected benefit obligation and fair value of the plan assets) and the amounts recognized and not recognized in the financial statements must be disclosed. *Rationale:* Providing a reconciliation of the plan's funded status to the amount reported in the balance sheet highlights the difference between the funded status and the balance sheet presentation.[17]

❹ A disclosure of the rates used in measuring the benefit amounts (discount rate, expected return on plan assets, rate of compensation) should be disclosed. *Rationale:* Disclosure of these rates permits the reader to determine the reasonableness of the assumptions applied in measuring the pension liability and pension expense.

In summary, the disclosure requirements are extensive, and purposely so. One factor that has been a challenge for useful pension reporting in the past has been the lack of consistency in terminology. Furthermore, a substantial amount of offsetting is inherent in the measurement of pension expense and the pension liability. These disclosures are designed to address these concerns and take some of the mystery out of pension reporting.

Illustration of Pension Note Disclosure

In the following sections we provide illustrations and explain the key pension disclosure elements.

Components of Pension Expense

The Board requires disclosure of the individual pension expense components—(1) service cost, (2) interest cost, (3) expected return on assets, (4) other deferrals and amortization—so that more sophisticated readers can understand how pension expense is determined. Providing information on the components should also be useful in predicting future pension expense. Using the information from the Zarle Company illustration—specifically, the expense component information taken from the left hand column of the work sheet in Illustration 21-25—an example of this part of the disclosure in presented in the following schedule:

ILLUSTRATION 21-27
Summary of Expense Components—2000, 2001, 2002

ZARLE COMPANY			
Components of Net Periodic Pension Expense	2000	2001	2002
Service cost	$ 9,000	$ 9,500	$13,000
Interest cost	10,000	19,200	$21,270
Expected return on plan assets	(10,000)	(11,100)	(13,410)*
Amortization of prior service cost	–0–	27,200	20,800
Net periodic pension expense	$ 9,000	$44,800	$41,660

*Note that the expected return must be disclosed, not the actual. In 2002, the expected return is $13,410, which is the actual gain ($12,000) adjusted by the unrecognized loss ($1,410).

---

[17]The vested benefit obligation does not need to be disclosed, since it is not used in the accounting for the fund. If the accumulated benefit obligation is greater than the fair value of the plan assets, it must be disclosed to inform readers how the minimum liability was computed.

Reconciliation and Funded Status of Plan

By providing a reconciliation of the changes in the assets and liabilities from the beginning of the year to the end of the year, statement readers can better understand the underlying economics of the plan. In essence, this disclosure (reconciliation) contains the information in the pension work sheet for the projected benefit obligation and plan asset columns.

In addition, the Board also requires a disclosure of the funded status of the plan. That is, the off-balance-sheet assets, liabilities, and unrecognized gains and losses must be reconciled with the on-balance-sheet liability or asset. Many believe this is the key to understanding the accounting for pensions. Why is such a disclosure important? The FASB acknowledged that the delayed recognition of some pension elements may exclude the most current and the most relevant information about the pension plan from the financial statements. This important information, however, is provided within this disclosure.

Using the information for Zarle Company, the following schedule provides an example of the reconciliation.

UNDERLYING CONCEPTS

This represents another compromise between relevance and reliability. The disclosure of the unrecognized items attempts to balance these objectives.

ZARLE COMPANY Pension Disclosure			
	2000	2001	2002
Change in benefit obligation			
Benefit obligation at beginning of year	$100,000	$112,000	$212,700
Service cost	9,000	9,500	13,000
Interest cost	10,000	19,200	21,270
Amendments (Prior service cost)	–0–	80,000	–0–
Actuarial loss	–0–	–0–	28,530
Benefits paid	(7,000)	(8,000)	(10,500)
Benefit obligation at end of year	112,000	212,700	265,000
Change in plan assets			
Fair value of plan assets at beginning of year	100,000	111,000	134,100
Actual return on plan assets	10,000	11,100	12,000
Contributions	8,000	20,000	24,000
Benefits paid	(7,000)	(8,000)	(10,500)
Fair value of plan assets at end of year	111,000	134,100	159,600
Funded status	(1,000)	(78,600)	(105,400)
Unrecognized net actuarial loss	–0–	–0–	29,940
Unrecognized prior service cost	–0–	52,800	32,000
Prepaid (accrued) benefit cost	**(1,000)**	**(25,800)**	**(43,460)**
Minimum liability adjustment included in:			
Intangible assets	–0–	(4,100)	(32,000)
Stockholders' equity	–0–	–0–	(5,540)
Accrued pension cost liability in the balance sheet	$ (1,000)	$ (29,900)	$ (81,000)

ILLUSTRATION 21-28
Pension Disclosure for Zarle Company—2000, 2001, 2002

The 2000 column reveals that the projected benefit obligation is underfunded by $1,000. The 2001 column reveals that the underfunded liability of $78,600 is reported in the balance sheet at $29,900, due to the unrecognized prior service cost of $52,800 and the $4,100 additional liability. Finally, the 2002 column indicates that underfunded liability of $105,400 is recognized in the balance sheet at only $81,000 because of $32,000 in unrecognized prior service costs, $29,940 of unrecognized net loss, and $37,540 additional liability (with $5,540 of the minimum liability recorded in stockholders' equity).

Illustration 21-29 provides the complete postretirement benefit disclosure for Gillette Company.[18] This disclosure shows how companies are providing information on the rates used in measuring the benefit amounts.

UNDERLYING CONCEPTS

Does it make a difference to users of financial statements whether pension information is recognized in the financial statements or disclosed only in the notes? The FASB was not sure, so in accord with the full disclosure principle, it decided to provide extensive pension plan disclosures.

---

[18]Note that the Gillette disclosure combines the disclosures for pensions and other postretirement benefits in one disclosure. This is one way the new standard streamlined the reporting on benefit plans. The accounting for other postretirement benefits is discussed in Appendix 21A.

ILLUSTRATION 21-29
Gillette Company
Pension Disclosure

GILLETTE COMPANY

Pension Plans and Other Retiree Benefits. The company has various retirement programs, including defined benefit, defined contribution and other plans, that cover most employees worldwide. In 1998, the Company began funding its pension plans in Germany by contributing $252 million to a newly established pension trust. Other retiree benefits are health care and life insurance benefits provided to eligible retired employees, principally in the United States. The components of benefit expense follow.

(Millions of dollars)	Pension Benefits			Other Retiree Benefits		
	1998	1997	1996	1998	1997	1996
Components of new benefit expense						
Service cost-benefits earned	$ 67	$ 64	$ 61	$ 6	$ 5	$ 2
Interest cost on benefit obligation	123	115	109	17	17	19
Estimated return on assets	(157)	(118)	(103)	(3)	(2)	(2)
Net amortization	5	6	12	(7)	(8)	(3)
	38	67	79	13	12	16
Defined contribution plans	2	4	4	—	—	—
Foreign plans not on SFAS 87	10	8	7	—	—	—
Total benefit expense	$ 50	$ 79	$ 90	$13	$12	$16

The funded status of the Company's principal defined benefit and other retiree benefit plans and the amounts recognized in the balance sheet at December 31 follow.

(Millions of dollars)	Pension Benefits		Other Retiree Benefits	
	1998	1997	1998	1997
Change in benefit obligation:				
Balance at beginning of year	$1,790	$1,689	$ 248	$ 266
Benefit payments	(105)	(83)	(14)	(13)
Service and interest costs	190	179	23	22
Amendments	45	4	1	1
Actuarial (gains) losses	88	52	(16)	(28)
Currency translation adjustment	10	(51)	(2)	—
Balance at end of year	2,018	1,790	240	248
Change in fair value of plan assets:				
Balance at beginning of year	1,540	1,278	33	24
Actual return on plan assets	203	272	6	6
Employer contribution	299	57	(3)	3
Benefit payments	(86)	(69)	—	—
Currency translation adjustment	—	2	—	—
Balance at end of year	1,956	1,540	36	33
Plan assets less than benefit obligation	(62)	(250)	(204)	(215)
Unrecognized prior service cost and transition obligation	53	36	(1)	—
Unrecognized net loss (gain)	54	17	(100)	(87)
Minimum liability adjustment included in:				
Intangible assets	(17)	(15)	—	—
Stockholders' equity	(47)	(20)	—	—
Net accrued benefit cost included in consolidated balance sheet	$ (19)	$ (232)	$(305)	$(302)

The values at December 31 for pension plans with accumulated benefit obligations in excess of plan assets follow.

(Millions of dollars)	1998	1997
Projected benefit obligation	$570	$506
Accumulated benefit obligation	506	429
Fair value of plan assets	304	30

The weighted average assumptions used in determining related obligations of pension benefit plans are shown below.

(Percent)	1998	1997	1996
Discount rate	6.3	7.1	7.1
Long-term rate of return on assets	8.6	9.3	9.4
Rate of compensation increase	3.9	4.9	4.8

The weighted average assumptions used in determining related obligations of other retiree benefit plans are shown below.

(Percent)	1998	1997	1996
Discount rate	6.5	7.0	7.0
Long-term rate of return on assets	9.0	9.0	9.0

The assumed health care cost trend rate for 1999 is 6.5%, decreasing to 4.5% by 2001. A one percentage point increase in the trend rate would have increased the accumulated postretirement benefit obligation by 12%, and interest and service cost by 13%. A one percentage point decrease in the trend rate would have decreased the accumulated postretirement benefit obligation by 10%, and interest and service cost by 11%.

Go to the Digital Tool for additional postretirement benefit disclosures.

2003 Entries and Work Sheet—A Comprehensive Illustration

Incorporating the corridor computation, the minimum liability recognition, and the required disclosures, the Zarle Company pension plan accounting is continued based on the following facts for 2003:

Service cost is $16,000.

Settlement rate is 10%; expected rate of return 10%.

Actual return on plan assets is $22,000.

Amortization of unrecognized prior service cost is $17,600.

Annual contributions (funding) are $27,000.

Benefits paid to retirees during the year are $18,000.

Accumulated benefit obligation is $263,000 at the end of 2003.

Average service life of all covered employees is 20 years.

To facilitate accumulation and recording of the components of pension expense and maintenance of the unrecognized amounts related to the pension plan, the following work sheet is prepared from the basic data presented above. Beginning-of-the-year 2003 account balances are the December 31, 2002, balances from the revised 2002 pension work sheet of Zarle Company in Illustration 21-25.

ILLUSTRATION 21-30
Comprehensive Pension Work Sheet—2003

	General Journal Entries					
Items	Annual Pension Expense	Cash	Prepaid/ Accrued Cost	Additional Liability	Pension Intangible	Contra Equity Charge
Balance, Dec. 31, 2002			43,460 Cr.	37,540 Cr.	32,000 Dr.	5,540 Dr.
(aa) Service cost	16,000 Dr.					
(bb) Interest cost	26,500 Dr.					
(cc) Actual return	22,000 Cr.					
(dd) Unexpected gain	6,040 Dr.					
(ee) Amortization of PSC	17,600 Dr.					
(ff) Contributions		27,000 Cr.				
(gg) Benefits						
(hh) Unrecog. loss amort.	172 Dr.					
(ii) Minimum liab. adj.				25,912 Dr.	20,372 Cr.	5,540 Cr.
Journal entry for 2003	44,312 Dr.	27,000 Cr.	17,312 Cr.			
Balance Dec. 31, 2003			60,772 Cr.	11,628 Cr.	11,628 Dr.	–0–

	Memo Entries			
Items	Projected Benefit Obligation	Plan Assets	Unrecognized Prior Service Cost	Unrecognized Net Gain or Loss
Balance, Dec. 31, 2002	265,000 Cr.	159,600 Dr.	32,000 Dr.	29,940 Dr.
(aa) Service cost	16,000 Cr.			
(bb) Interest cost	26,500 Cr.			
(cc) Actual return		22,000 Dr.		
(dd) Unexpected gain				6,040 Cr.
(ee) Amortization of PSC			17,600 Cr.	
(ff) Contributions		27,000 Dr.		
(gg) Benefits	18,000 Dr.	18,000 Cr.		
(hh) Unrecog. loss amort.				172 Cr.
(ii) Minimum liab. adj.				
Journal entry for 2003				
Balance Dec. 31, 2003	289,500 Cr.	190,600 Dr.	14,400 Dr.	23,728 Dr.

Work Sheet Explanations and Entries

Entries (aa) through (gg) are similar to the corresponding entries previously explained in the prior years' work sheets with the exception of entry (dd). In 2002 the expected return on plan assets exceeded the actual return producing an unexpected loss. In 2003 the actual return of $22,000 exceeds the expected return of $15,960 ($159,600 × 10%), resulting in an unexpected gain of $6,040, entry (dd). By netting the gain of $6,040 against the actual return of $22,000, pension expense is affected only by the expected return of $15,960.

A new entry (hh) in Zarle Company's work sheet results from application of the corridor test on the accumulated balance of unrecognized net gain or loss. Zarle Company begins 2003 with a balance in the unrecognized net loss account of $29,940. The corridor criterion must be applied in 2003 to determine whether the balance is excessive and should be amortized. In 2003 the corridor is 10% of the larger of the beginning-of-the-year projected benefit obligation of $265,000 or the plan asset's market-related asset value (assumed to be fair market value) of $159,600. The corridor for 2003, thus, is $26,500 ($265,000 × 10%). Because the balance in the Unrecognized Net Loss account is $29,940, the excess (outside the corridor) is $3,440 ($29,940 − $26,500). The $3,440 excess is amortized over the average remaining service life of all employees. Using an average remaining service life of 20 years, the amortization in 2003 is $172 ($3,440 ÷ 20). In the 2003 pension work sheet, the $172 is recorded as a debit to Pension Expense and a credit to the Unrecognized Net Loss account. A schedule showing the computation of the $172 amortization charge is presented below:

ILLUSTRATION 21-31
Computation of 2003
Amortization Charge
(Corridor Test)

2003 Corridor Test	
Unrecognized net (gain) or loss at beginning of year	$29,940
10% of larger of PBO or market-related asset value of plan assets	26,500
Amortizable amount	$ 3,440
Average service life of all employees	20 years
2003 amortization ($3,440 ÷ 20 years)	$172

The journal entry to formally record pension expense for 2003 is as follows:

2003

Pension Expense	44,312	
Cash		27,000
Prepaid/Accrued Pension Cost		17,312

The minimum liability, additional liability, and the amount reported as a contra equity charge at the end of 2003 are computed as follows:

ILLUSTRATION 21-32
Minimum Liability
Computation—2003

	December 31, 2003
Accumulated benefit obligation (ABO)	$(263,000)
Plan assets at fair value	190,600
Unfunded accumulated benefit obligation (minimum liability)	(72,400)
Accrued pension cost	60,772
Additional liability	(11,628)
Unrecognized prior service cost	14,400
Contra equity charge	$ −0−

As indicated in the above computation, the additional liability balance on December 31, 2003, is $11,628. The balance of $37,540 of additional liability carried over from 2002 requires a downward adjustment of $25,912 ($37,540 − $11,628). The balance in the pension intangible account should also be $11,628; it is, therefore, credited for $20,372 to reduce the balance of $32,000 to the desired amount of $11,628. Because the unrecognized prior service cost balance exceeds the additional liability, no contra equity charge is required. The entry to adjust the minimum liability (the three accounts related thereto) at December 31, 2003, is as follows:

2003

Additional Pension Liability	25,912	
Intangible Asset—Deferred Pension Cost		20,372
Excess of Additional Pension Liability		
over Unrecognized Prior Service Cost		5,540

Financial Statement Presentation

The financial statements of Zarle Company at December 31, 2003, present the following items relative to its pension plan:

ZARLE COMPANY
Balance Sheet
As of December 31, 2003

Assets		Liabilities	
Intangible assets		Long-term liabilities	
Deferred pension cost	$11,628	Accrued pension cost	$72,400

ILLUSTRATION 21-33
Balance Sheet
Presentation of Pension
Costs—2003

The prepaid/accrued pension cost balance of $60,772 and the additional liability balance of $11,628 on the work sheet are combined and reported as one pension liability of $72,400 in the balance sheet.

ZARLE COMPANY
Income Statement
For the Year Ended December 31, 2003

Operating expenses	
Pension expense*	$44,312

*Pension expense is frequently reported as "Employee benefits."

ILLUSTRATION 21-34
Income Statement
Presentation of Pension
Expense—2003

ZARLE COMPANY
Statement of Cash Flows
For the Year Ended December 31, 2003

Cash flow from operating activities		
Net income (assumed)		$905,000
Adjustments to reconcile net income to net		
cash provided by operating activities:		
Increase in accrued pension liability	$17,312	

Note: Significant noncash investing and financing activities

Decrease of $20,372 in intangible asset and decrease of $5,540 in contra equity due to decrease of $25,912 in minimum liability.

ILLUSTRATION 21-35
Statement of Cash Flows
Presentation of Pension
Liability

Note Disclosure

The minimum note disclosure by Zarle Company of the pension plan for 2003 is shown in Illustration 21-36. Note that in the reconciliation schedule in Illustration 21-36, the adjustment required to recognize the minimum liability of $11,628 is included in order to reconcile to the $72,400 accrued pension cost reported in the balance sheet.

ILLUSTRATION 21-36
Minimum Note
Disclosure of Pension
Plan, Zarle Company,
2003

ZARLE COMPANY
Notes to the Financial Statements

Note D. The company has a pension plan covering substantially all of its employees. The plan is non-contributory and provides pension benefits that are based on the employee's compensation during the three years immediately preceding retirement. The pension plan's assets consist of cash, stocks, and bonds. The company's funding policy is consistent with the relevant government (ERISA) and tax regulations.

Net pension expense for 2003 is comprised of the following components of pension cost:

Service cost	$16,000
Interest on projected benefit obligation	26,500
Expected return on plan assets	(15,960)
Net other components of pension expense[19]	17,772
Net pension expense	$44,312

The following schedule reports changes in the benefit obligation and plan assets during the year and reconciles the funded status of the plan with amounts reported in the company's balance sheet at December 31, 2003:

Change in benefit obligation

Benefit obligation at beginning of year	$265,000
Service cost	16,000
Interest cost	26,500
Amendments (Prior service cost)	–0–
Actuarial gain	–0–
Benefits paid	(18,000)
Benefit obligation at end of year	289,500

Change in plan assets

Fair value of plan assets at beginning of year	159,600
Actual return on plan assets	22,000
Contributions	27,000
Benefits paid	(18,000)
Fair value of plan assets at end of year	190,600
Funded status	(98,900)
Unrecognized net actuarial loss	23,728
Unrecognized prior service cost	14,400
Prepaid (accrued) benefit cost	**(60,772)**
Minimum liability adjustment included in:	
Intangible assets	(11,628)
Stockholders' equity	–0–
Accrued pension cost liability in the balance sheet	$ (72,400)

The weighted-average discount rate used in determining the 2003 projected benefit obligation was 10%. The rate of increase in future compensation levels used in computing the 2003 projected benefit obligation was 4.5%. The weighted-average expected long-term rate of return on the plan's assets was 10%.

Special Issues

The Pension Reform Act of 1974

The Employee Retirement Income Security Act of 1974 **(ERISA)** affects virtually every private retirement plan in the United States. It attempts to safeguard employees' pension rights by mandating many pension plan requirements, including minimum funding, participation, and vesting.

---

[19]"Net other components of pension expense" in this example is comprised of amortization of prior service cost ($17,600) plus amortization of the unrecognized loss ($172). Amortization of prior service cost and amortization of the unrecognized net gain or loss are combined when reporting the components of pension expense.

These requirements can influence the employers' costs significantly. Under this legislation, annual funding is no longer discretionary; an employer must fund the plan in accordance with an actuarial funding method that over time will be sufficient to pay for all pension obligations. If funding is not carried out in a reasonable manner, fines may be imposed and tax deductions denied.

Plan administrators are required to publish a comprehensive description and summary of their plans and detailed annual reports accompanied by many supplementary schedules and statements. ERISA further mandates that the required reports, statements, and supplementary schedules be subjected to audit by qualified independent public accountants.

Another important provision of the Act is the creation of the Pension Benefit Guaranty Corporation (PBGC). **The PBGC's purpose is to administer terminated plans** and to impose liens on the employer's assets for certain unfunded pension liabilities. If a plan is terminated, the PBGC can effectively impose a lien against the employer's assets for the excess of the present value of guaranteed vested benefits over the pension fund assets. This lien generally has had the status of a tax lien and, therefore, takes priority over most other creditorship claims. This section of the Act gives the PBGC the power to force an involuntary termination of a pension plan whenever the risks related to nonpayment of the pension obligation seem too great. Because ERISA restricts the lien that the PBGC can impose to 30% of net worth, the PBGC must monitor all plans to ensure that net worth is sufficient to meet the pension benefit obligations.[20]

A large number of terminated plans have caused the PBGC to pay out substantial benefits. Currently the PBGC receives its funding from employers, who contribute a certain dollar amount for each employee covered under the plan.

An interesting accounting problem relates to the manner of disclosing the possible termination of a plan. When, for example, should a contingent liability be disclosed, if a company is experiencing financial difficulty and may not be able to meet its pension obligations if its plan is terminated? At present this issue is unresolved, and considerable judgment would be needed to analyze a company with these contingent liabilities.[21]

Pension Terminations

A congressman at one time noted that "employers are simply treating their employee pension plans like company piggy banks, to be raided at will." What this congressman was referring to is the practice by some companies that have pension plan assets in excess of projected benefit obligations of paying off the obligation and pocketing the difference. ERISA prevents companies from recapturing excess assets unless they pay participants what is owed to them and then terminate the plan. As a result, companies are buying annuities to pay off the pension claimants and using the excess funds for other corporate purposes.[22]

For example, pension plan terminations netted $363 million for **Occidental Petroleum Corp.**, $95 million for **Stroh's Brewery Co.**, $58 million for **Kellogg Co.**, and $29 million for **Western Airlines**. Since 1980, many large companies have terminated their

UNDERLYING CONCEPTS

Many plans are underfunded but still quite viable. For example **Loews Corp.** has a $159 million shortfall. But Loew's had earnings of $594 million and a good net worth. Thus, the going concern assumption permits us to ignore these pension underfundings in many cases because in the long run they are not significant.

---

[20]The major problems in underfunding are occurring in four labor-intensive industries—steel, autos, rubber, and airlines. **General Motors'** plan at one time was 92% funded but still had a deficit of over $6 billion.

[21]**Pan American** is a good illustration of how difficult it is to assess when to terminate. When Pan Am filed for bankruptcy in 1991, it had a pension liability of $900 million. From 1983 to 1991, the IRS gave it six waivers so it did not have to make contributions. When the plan was terminated, there was little net worth upon which a lien could be imposed.

[22]A real question exists as to whose money it is. Some argue that the excess funds belong to the employees, not the employer. In addition, given that the funds have been reverting to the employer, critics charge that cost-of-living increases and the possibility of other increased benefits are reduced, because companies will be reluctant to use those excess funds to pay for such increases.

pension plans and captured billions in surplus assets. All of this is quite legal, but is it ethical? It should be noted that federal legislation recently enacted requires the company to pay an excise tax of anywhere from 20% to 50% on the gains.

The accounting issue that arises from these terminations is whether a gain should be recognized by the corporation when these assets revert back to the company (often called **asset reversion** transactions). The issue is complex because, in some cases, a new defined benefit plan is started after the old one has been eliminated. Therefore some contend that there has been no change in substance, but merely one in form.

Up to this point the profession has required that these gains be reported if the companies switched from a defined benefit plan to a defined contribution plan. Otherwise, the gain is deferred and amortized over at least 10 years in the future. Many questioned this reporting treatment. As a result the FASB issued *FASB Statement No. 88* that requires recognition in earnings of a new gain or loss when the employer settles a pension obligation either by lump-sum cash payments to participants or by purchasing nonparticipating annuity contracts.[23]

Cash-Balance Pension Plans

Recently, some companies have adopted hybrid pension plans, which combine features of defined benefit and defined contribution plans. These cash-balance plans allow employees to transfer their pension benefits when they change employers. This portability-of-benefit feature is popular with younger workers who, unlike earlier generations of workers, expect to change employers several times during their working lives. Such plans are controversial because the change to a cash-balance plan often reduces benefits to older workers. Consequently, the introduction of these plans has drawn the attention of Congress and the IRS to ensure their fairness to all workers.[24]

From an accounting standpoint, cash-balance plans are accounted for similar to a defined benefit plan. This is because employers bear the investment risk in cash-balance plans. Interestingly, when an employer adopts a cash-balance plan, the measurement of the future benefit obligation to employees generally is lower, compared to a traditional defined benefit plan. As a result, when a defined benefit plan is converted to a cash-balance plan, the employer many times will record a negative prior service cost adjustment. The amortization of this prior service cost results in a reduction in pension expense.[25]

Concluding Observation

Hardly a day goes by without the financial press analyzing in depth some issues related to pension plans in the United States. This is hardly surprising, since U.S. pension funds now hold over $5 trillion in assets. As should be obvious by now, the accounting issues related to pension plans are complex. *FASB Statement No. 87* clarifies many of these issues and should help users understand the financial implications of a company's pension plans on its financial position, results of operations, and cash flows.

Critics still argue, however, that much remains to be done. One issue in particular relates to the delayed recognition of certain events. Changes in pension plan obliga-

---

[23]"Employers' Accounting for Settlements and Curtailments of Defined Benefit Pension Plans and for Termination Benefits," *Statement of Financial Accounting Standards No. 88* (Stamford, Conn.: FASB, 1985). Some companies have established pension poison pills as an antitakeover measure. These plans require asset reversions from termination of a plan to benefit employees and retirees rather than the acquiring company. For a discussion of pension poison pills, see Eugene E. Comiskey and Charles W. Mulford, "Interpreting Pension Disclosures: A Guide for Lending Officers," *Commercial Lending Review,* Winter 1993–94, Vol. 9, No. 1.

[24]E. Schultz, "IRS Set to Continue to Give Green Light on Pension Plan," *The Wall Street Journal,* September 2, 1999, p. A2.

[25]See A. T. Arcady and F. Mellors, "Cash-Balance Conversions," *Journal of Accountancy,* February 2000, pp. 22–28.

tions and changes in the value of plan assets are not recognized immediately but are systematically incorporated over subsequent periods.

SUMMARY OF LEARNING OBJECTIVES

❶ **Distinguish between accounting for the employer's pension plan and accounting for the pension fund.** The company or employer is the organization sponsoring the pension plan. It incurs the cost and makes contributions to the pension fund. The fund or plan is the entity that receives the contributions from the employer, administers the pension assets, and makes the benefit payments to the pension recipients (retired employees). The fund should be a separate legal and accounting entity for which a set of books is maintained and financial statements are prepared.

❷ **Identify types of pension plans and their characteristics.** The two most common types of pension arrangements are: (1) *Defined contribution plans:* the employer agrees to contribute to a pension trust a certain sum each period based on a formula. This formula may consider such factors as age, length of employee service, employer's profits, and compensation level. Only the employer's contribution is defined; no promise is made regarding the ultimate benefits paid out to the employees. (2) *Defined benefit plans:* define the benefits that the employee will receive at the time of retirement. The formula typically used provides for the benefits to be a function of the employee's years of service and the employer's compensation level when he or she nears retirement.

❸ **Explain alternative measures for valuing the pension obligation.** One measure of the pension obligation bases it only on the benefits vested to the employees. Vested benefits are those that the employee is entitled to receive even if the employee renders no additional services under the plan. The *vested benefits pension obligation* is computed using current salary levels and includes only vested benefits. Another measure of the obligation, called the *accumulated benefit obligation,* bases the computation of the deferred compensation amount on all years of service performed by employees under the plan—both vested and nonvested—using current salary levels. A third measure, called the *projected benefit obligation,* bases the computation of the deferred compensation amount on both vested and nonvested service using future salaries.

❹ **Identify the components of pension expense.** Pension expense is a function of the following components: (1) service cost; (2) interest on the liability; (3) actual return on plan assets; (4) amortization of unrecognized prior service cost; and (5) gain or loss.

❺ **Utilize a work sheet for pension plan entries.** A work sheet unique to pension accounting may be utilized to record both the formal entries and the memo entries to keep track of all the employer's relevant pension plan items and components.

❻ **Describe the amortization of unrecognized prior service costs.** The amount of the prior service cost is computed by an actuary. Amortization of the unrecognized prior service cost is an accounting function performed with the assistance of an actuary. The Board prefers a "years-of-service" amortization method that is similar to a units-of-production computation. First, the total estimated number of service-years to be worked by all of the participating employees is computed. Second, the unrecognized prior service cost is divided by the total number of service-years to obtain a cost per service-year (the unit cost). And third, the number of service-years consumed each year is multiplied by the cost per service-year to obtain the annual amortization charge.

KEY TERMS

accrued pension cost, *1140*
accumulated benefit obligation, *1124*
actual return on plan assets, *1128*
actuarial present value, *1127*
actuaries, *1123*
additional liability, *1139*
asset gains and losses, *1134*
cash-balance plans, *1152*
components of pension expense, *1126*
contributory pension plan, *1121*
corridor approach, *1135*
defined benefit plan, *1122*
defined contribution plan, *1122*
ERISA, *1150*
expected rate of return, *1134*
expected return on plan assets, *1134*
fair value of plan assets, *1128*
funded pension plan, *1121*
funded status, *1144*
interest on the liability (interest expense), *1127*
liability gains and losses, *1134*
market-related asset value, *1139*
minimum liability, *1139*
noncontributory pension plan, *1121*
pension plan, *1120*
pension work sheet, *1129*
prepaid pension cost, *1140*
prior service cost (PSC), *1131*
projected benefit obligation, *1124*
qualified pension plan, *1121*
reconciliation, *1144*
retroactive benefits, *1131*
service cost, *1127*

⑦ Explain the accounting procedure for recognizing unexpected gains and losses. In estimating the projected benefit obligation (the liability), actuaries make assumptions about such items as mortality rate, retirement rate, turnover rate, disability rate, and salary amounts. Any change in these actuarial assumptions changes the amount of the projected benefit obligation. These unexpected gains or losses from changes in the projected benefit obligation are liability gains and losses. Liability gains (resulting from unexpected decreases in the liability balance) and liability losses (resulting from unexpected increases) are deferred (unrecognized). The liability gains and losses are combined in the same Unrecognized Net Gain or Loss account used for asset gains and losses and are accumulated from year to year, off-balance-sheet, in a memo record account.

⑧ Explain the corridor approach to amortizing unrecognized gains and losses. The unrecognized net gain or loss balance is considered too large and must be amortized when it exceeds the arbitrarily selected FASB criterion of 10% of the larger of the beginning balances of the projected benefit obligation or the market-related value of the plan assets. If the balance of the unrecognized net gain or loss account stays within the upper and lower limits of the corridor, no amortization is required.

⑨ Explain the recognition of a minimum liability. Immediate recognition of a liability (referred to as the minimum liability) is required when the accumulated benefit obligation exceeds the fair value of plan assets. The purpose of this minimum liability requirement is to assure that if a significant plan amendment or actuarial loss occurs, a liability will be recognized at least to the extent of the unfunded portion of the accumulated benefit obligation.

⑩ Describe the reporting requirements for pension plans in financial statements. The current financial statement disclosure requirements for pension plans are as follows: (1) The components of net periodic pension expense for the period. (2) A schedule showing changes in the benefit obligation and plan assets during the year. (3) A schedule reconciling the funded status of the plan with amounts reported in the employer's statement of financial position. (4) The weighted-average assumed discount rate, the rate of compensation increase used to measure the projected benefit obligation, and the weighted-average expected long-term rate of return on plan assets.

MICHELE LIPPERT
is the controller for evoke.com, an Internet communications company founded in 1997. Prior to her current position, she was an assistant controller for a cycling apparel company and, before that, a tax accountant with a mid-size CPA firm and an auditor with another firm. Lippert, who holds a bachelor's degree in accounting from Truman State University in Missouri, passed the CPA examination in one sitting.

What does evoke.com do?

We offer a comprehensive suite of Web-based voice, video, and data collaboration services that allow users to get business done better and faster. As an example, we allow clients to view a business presentation over the Internet while they are participating in a conference call. Perhaps 30 people throughout the country could view the same slide presentation, while interacting over the phone. Others who do not have access to telephone and computer simultaneously could still listen to the call through their computers, and push questions or comments on the presentation via the Internet. In addition, we can take video content, such as a video from a company's annual meeting, encode it, and present it over the Internet. We do a lot of work for the sports and entertainment industries, such as using cameras in racecars or presenting music videos for distribution over the Internet. Some presentations require a password, such as an annual meeting, which a company might want to restrict to shareholders. Other events could be open to anyone.

Why did you leave public accounting?

The hours were very long, sometimes for months at a time. Even though I still work long hours occasionally, I have found the money and benefits to be better in industry. And, of course, there's the lure of stock options. High-tech companies tend to start you at a lower salary, but offer options that could be very lucrative. It's risky, because a lot of venture-capital backed companies go out of business. Still, I don't have dependents, and I'm young enough to be able to take a risk like this.

What advice would you give students who would like to follow in your footsteps?

I don't think I could have done this straight out of college. Having a public accounting background helped me a lot. It gave me a basis for everything I'm doing right now. As we speak, we have auditors here, and my CPA background makes this go a lot smoother, because I know what they're looking for.

You've worked in auditing and tax. What's the difference?

Auditing requires you to go into a company, go through their accounts, and substantiate certain numbers to make sure everything is correctly stated. Once the audit is done, the tax people come in. They'll determine what is deductible for tax purposes and advise clients on actions they could take to lower taxes in the future. In addition, the tax people have to distinguish expenses allowable for financial statement purposes from those allowed for tax purposes. For instance, depreciation is calculated differently for tax and for book purposes. There's also a calculation that deals with capitalizing certain inventory costs for tax purposes that were expenses for financial statement purposes. Other items to be reconciled include disallowed tax expenses such as penalties and the 50% limitation on meals and entertainment.

Any tips on passing the CPA exam?

Learn the material the first time around, instead of trying to cram before the test.

APPENDIX **21A**

Accounting for Postretirement Benefits

IBM Corporation's adoption of a new accounting standard on postretirement benefits in March 1991 resulted in a $2.3 billion charge and a historical curiosity—IBM's first-ever quarterly loss. **General Electric Co.** disclosed that its charge for adoption of the same new FASB standard would be $2.7 billion, and in the fourth quarter of 1993, **AT&T Co.** absorbed a $2.1 billion pretax hit for postretirement benefits. What is this standard, and how could its adoption have so grave an impact on companies' earnings?

ACCOUNTING GUIDANCE

After a decade of study, the FASB in December 1990 issued *Statement No. 106*, "Employers' Accounting for Postretirement Benefits Other Than Pensions." It alone is the cause for those large charges to income. This standard accounts for health care and other welfare benefits provided to retirees, their spouses, dependents, and beneficiaries.[1] These other welfare benefits include life insurance offered outside a pension plan, dental care as well as medical care, eye care, legal and tax services, tuition assistance, day care, and housing assistance.[2] Because health-care benefits are the largest of the other postretirement benefits, this item is used to illustrate accounting for postretirement benefits.

For many employers (about 95%) this standard required a change from the predominant practice of accounting for postretirement benefits on a pay-as-you-go (cash) basis to an accrual basis. Similar to pension accounting, the accrual basis necessitates measurement of the employer's obligation to provide future benefits and accrual of the cost during the years that the employee provides service.

One of the reasons companies have not prefunded these benefit plans is that payments to prefund health-care costs, unlike excess contributions to a pension trust, are not tax deductible. Another reason is that postretirement health-care benefits were once perceived to be a low-cost employee benefit that could be changed or eliminated at will and, therefore, not a legal liability. Now, the accounting definition of a liability goes beyond the notion of a legally enforceable claim to encompass equitable or

---

[1]*Accounting Trends and Techniques—1999* reports that of its 600 surveyed companies, 373 report benefit plans that provide postretirement health-care benefits. Surprisingly, such coverage translates into a total health-care liability estimated at more than $400 billion and perhaps as much as $2 trillion, which is largely unfunded.

[2]"OPEB" is the acronym frequently used to describe postretirement benefits covered by *FASB Statement No. 106.* This term came into being before the scope of the statement was narrowed from "other postemployment benefits" to "other postretirement benefits," thereby excluding postemployment benefits related to severance pay or wage continuation to disabled, terminated, or laid-off employees.

constructive obligations as well, making it clear that the postretirement benefit promise is a liability.[3]

DIFFERENCES BETWEEN PENSION BENEFITS AND HEALTH-CARE BENEFITS

OBJECTIVE (11)
After studying Appendix 21A, you should be able to: Identify the differences between pensions and postretirement health-care benefits.

The FASB used *Statement No. 87* on pensions as a reference for the accounting prescribed in *Statement No. 106* on health-care and other nonpension postretirement benefits.[4] Why didn't the FASB cover both types of postretirement benefits in the earlier pension accounting statement? The apparent similarities between the two benefits mask some significant differences. These differences are shown in Illustration 21A-1.[5]

Item	Pensions	Health-Care Benefits
Funding	Generally funded.	Generally *NOT* funded.
Benefit	Well-defined and level dollar amount.	Generally uncapped and great variability.
Beneficiary	Retiree (maybe some benefit to surviving spouse).	Retiree, spouse, and other dependents.
Benefit Payable	Monthly.	As needed and used.
Predictability	Variables are reasonably predictable.	Utilization difficult to predict. Level of cost varies geographically and fluctuates over time.

ILLUSTRATION 21A-1
Differences between Pensions and Postretirement Health-Care Benefits

Two of the differences presented in Illustration 21A-1 highlight why measuring the future payments for health-care benefit plans is so much more difficult than for pension plans:

❶ Many postretirement plans do not set a limit on health-care benefits. No matter how serious the illness or how long it lasts, the benefits continue to flow. (Even if the employer uses an insurance company plan, the premiums will escalate according to the increased benefits provided.)

❷ The level of health-care benefit utilization and health-care costs is difficult to predict. The increased longevity and unexpected illnesses (e.g., AIDS) along with new medical technologies (e.g., MRI scans) and cures (e.g., radiation) cause changes in health-care utilization.

Additionally, although health-care benefits are generally covered by the fiduciary and reporting standards for employee benefit funds under ERISA, the stringent minimum vesting, participation, and funding standards that apply to pensions do not apply to health-care benefits. Nevertheless, as you will learn, many of the basic concepts and much of the accounting terminology and measurement methodology applicable to

---

[3]"Elements of Financial Statements," *Statement of Financial Accounting Concepts No. 6* (Stamford, Conn.: 1985), page 13, footnote 21.

[4]In November 1992 the FASB issued *Statement of Financial Accounting Standards No. 112,* "Employers' Accounting for Postemployment Benefits," which covers postemployment benefits that are not accounted for under *SFAS No. 87* (pensions), *SFAS No. 88* (settlements, curtailments, and termination benefits), or *SFAS No. 106* (postretirement benefits other than pensions). *SFAS No. 112* requires an employer to recognize the obligation to provide postemployment benefits in accordance with *SFAS No. 43,* similar to accounting for compensated absences (see Chapter 13). These *SFAS No. 112* benefits include, but are not limited to, salary continuation, disability-related benefits, severance benefits, and continuance of health-care benefits and life insurance for inactive or former (e.g., terminated, disabled, or deceased) employees or their beneficiaries.

[5]D. Gerald Searfoss and Naomi Erickson, "The Big Unfunded Liability: Postretirement Health-Care Benefits," *Journal of Accountancy,* November 1988, pp. 28–39.

pensions are applicable to other postretirement benefits accounting. Therefore, throughout the following discussion and illustrations, we point out the similarities and differences in the accounting and reporting for these two types of postretirement benefits.

POSTRETIREMENT BENEFITS ACCOUNTING PROVISIONS

Health-care and other postretirement benefits for current and future retirees and their dependents are forms of deferred compensation earned through employee service and subject to acrrual during the years an employee is working. The period of time over which the postretirement benefit cost is accrued, called the attribution period, is the period of service during which the employee earns the benefits under the terms of the plan. This attribution period (shown in Illustration 21A-2) generally begins when an employee is hired and ends on the date the employee is eligible to receive the benefits and ceases to earn additional benefits by performing service, the vesting date.[6]

ILLUSTRATION 21A-2
Range of Possible
Attribution Periods

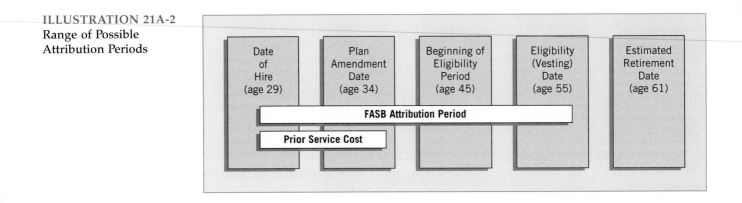

Obligations under Postretirement Benefits

In defining the obligation for postretirement benefits, many concepts similar to pension accounting are maintained, but some new and modified terms are designed specifically for postretirement benefits. Two of the most important are (a) expected postretirement benefit obligation and (b) accumulated postretirement benefit obligation.

Expected Postretirement Benefit Obligation (EPBO). The EPBO is the actuarial present value as of a particular date of **all benefits expected to be paid after retirement to employees and their dependents**. The EPBO is not recorded in the financial statements, but it is used in measuring periodic expense.

Accumulated Postretirement Benefit Obligation (APBO). The APBO is the actuarial present value of **future benefits attributed to employees' services rendered to a particular date**. The APBO is equal to the EPBO for retirees and active employees fully eligible for benefits. Before the date an employee achieves full eligibility, the APBO is only a portion of the EPBO. Or stated another way, the difference between the APBO and the EPBO is the future service costs of active employees who are not yet fully eligible.

Illustration 21A-3 contrasts the EPBO and the APBO.

---

[6]This is a benefit-years-of-service approach (the projected unit credit actuarial cost method). The FASB found no compelling reason to switch from the traditional pension accounting approach. It rejected the employee's full service period (i.e., to the estimated retirement date) because it was unable to identify any approach that would appropriately attribute benefits beyond the date full eligibility for those benefits is attained. Full eligibility is attained by meeting specified age, service, or age and service requirements of the plan.

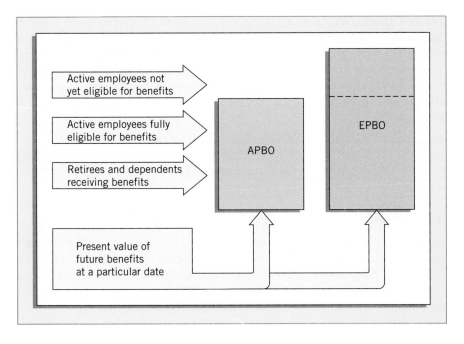

At the date an employee is fully eligible (the end of the attribution period), the APBO and the EPBO relative to that employee are equal.

Postretirement Expense

Postretirement expense, also referred to as **net periodic postretirement benefit cost**, is the employer's annual postretirement benefit expense, which consists of many of the familiar components used to compute annual pension expense. The components of net periodic postretirement benefit cost are:[7]

❶ *Service Cost.* The portion of the EPBO attributed to employee service during the period.

❷ *Interest Cost.* The increase in the APBO attributable to the passage of time. It is computed by applying the beginning-of-the-year discount rate to the beginning-of-the-year APBO, adjusted for benefit payments to be made during the period. The discount rate is based on the rates of return on high-quality, fixed-income investments that are currently available.[8]

❸ *Actual Return on Plan Assets.* The change in the fair value of the plan's assets adjusted for contributions and benefit payments made during the period. Because the postretirement expense is charged or credited for the gain or loss on plan assets (the difference between the actual and the expected return), this component is really expected return.

❹ *Amortization of Prior Service Cost.* The amortization of the cost of retroactive benefits resulting from plan amendments or a plan initiation that takes place after *Statement No. 106* takes effect. The typical amortization period, beginning at the date of the plan amendment, is the remaining service periods through the full eligibility date.

---

[7]"Employers' Accounting for Postretirement Benefits Other Than Pensions," *Statement of Financial Accounting Standards No. 106* (Norwalk, Conn.: FASB, 1990), paras. 46–66. And see, James R. Wilbert and Kenneth E. Dakdduk, "The New FASB 106: How to Account for Postretirement Benefits," *Journal of Accountancy*, August 1991, pp. 36–41.

[8]The FASB concluded that the discount rate for measuring the present value of the postretirement benefit obligation and the service cost component should be the same as that applied to pension measurements. It chose not to label it the settlement rate in order to clarify that the objective of the discount rate is to measure the time value of money.

❺ *Gains and Losses.* In general, changes in the APBO resulting from changes in assumptions or from experience different from that assumed. For funded plans, this component also includes the difference between actual return and expected return on plan assets (computed the same as for pensions—actual based on fair value and expected based on market-related value). Gains or losses can be recognized immediately or can be based on a "corridor approach" similar to that used for pension accounting.

❻ *Amortization of Transition Obligation.* The straight-line amortization of the unrecognized APBO at the time *FASB Statement No. 106* is adopted. This component of expense is not present if the transition obligation is recognized immediately.

The Transition Amount

At the beginning of the year of adoption of *FASB Statement No. 106*, a **transition amount** (obligation or asset) is computed as the difference between (1) the APBO and (2) the fair value of the plan assets, plus any accrued obligation or less any prepaid cost (asset). Because most plans are unfunded and most employers are accruing postretirement benefit costs for the first time, large transition obligations occur.

The accounting treatment of this transition amount was one of the most controversial issues in postretirement benefit standard setting. The primary concern of many was that an immediate charge to expense for unrecognized past costs, accompanied by recognition of the total unrecognized liability, would have a large negative impact on reported earnings in the year of the change. Of equal concern to others was that the alternative, deferral and amortization of the expense, accompanied by a rapidly increasing liability, would be a drain on reported earnings for many years. And providing the option of immediate write-off or deferral and amortization was also problematic because of the lack of comparability that would result. Nevertheless, the FASB decided to permit employers to choose between the immediate recognition (e.g., the $2.3 billion charge taken by **IBM** in the first quarter of 1991) and deferral and amortization:

> **Immediate recognition.** As an immediate write-off, the transition amount is recognized in the income statement as the "effect of a change in accounting principle" (net of tax)[9] and in the balance sheet as a long-term liability entitled Postretirement Benefit Obligation. Restatement of previously issued annual financial statements is not permitted.

> **Deferred recognition.** Employers choosing deferred recognition must amortize the transition amount on a straight-line basis over the average remaining service period to expected retirement of the employees in place at the time of transition and expected to receive benefits.[10] If the remaining service period is less than 20 years, the employer may elect a 20-year amortization period. But, the transition amount may not be amortized more slowly than it is paid off (referred to as the "pay-as-you-go constraint").[11]

Once chosen, the method cannot be changed. That is, after once electing to amortize the transition amount, the employer cannot record the remainder of its unamor-

---

[9]The FASB uses the term "effect" rather than "cumulative effect," and because of the unique transition provision and calculations involved, the retroactive effects on prior periods are generally not determinable and therefore pro forma disclosures are not required. The per share effects of the accounting change are required to be shown on the face of the income statement.

[10]For amortization of the transition amount (and for gains and losses as well), the Board chose the longer "retirement date" as opposed to the "full eligibility date" for pragmatic reasons—the magnitude of the transition amount argued for a longer amortization period to minimize the effect on current financial statements.

[11]In pension accounting, the transition amount must be amortized over the average remaining service life of existing employees or optionally over a 15-year period if the remaining service life is less than 15 years.

tized transition obligation in a subsequent year under the immediate recognition method.

ILLUSTRATIVE ACCOUNTING ENTRIES

Like pension accounting, several significant items of the postretirement plan are unrecognized in the accounts and in the financial statements. These off-balance-sheet items are:

❶ Expected postretirement benefit obligation (EPBO)
❷ Accumulated postretirement benefit obligation (APBO)
❸ Postretirement benefit plan assets
❹ Unrecognized transition amount
❺ Unrecognized prior service cost
❻ Unrecognized net gain or loss

The EPBO is not recognized in the financial statements or disclosed in the notes. It is recomputed each year and used by the actuary in measuring the annual service cost. Because of the numerous assumptions and actuarial complexity involved in measuring annual service cost, we have omitted these computations of the EPBO.

All five of the other off-balance-sheet items listed above must be disclosed by the employer in notes to the financial statements. In addition, as in pension accounting, the exact amount of these items must be known because they are used in the computation of postretirement expense. Therefore, in order to track these off-balance-sheet postretirement benefit items, the work sheet illustrated in pension accounting will be utilized to record both the formal general journal entries and the memo entries.

2000 Entries and Work Sheet

To illustrate the use of a work sheet in accounting for a postretirement benefits plan, assume that on January 1, 2000, Quest Company adopts *Statement No. 106* to account for its health-care benefit plan. The following facts apply to the postretirement benefits plan for the year 2000.

Plan assets at fair value on January 1, 2000, are zero.

Actual and expected returns on plan assets are zero.

APBO, January 1, 2000, is $400,000.

Service cost is $22,000.

No prior service cost exists.

Discount rate is 8%.

Contributions (funding) to plan during the year are $38,000.

Benefit payments to employees from plan are $28,000.

Average remaining service to full eligibility: 21 years.

Average remaining service to expected retirement: 25 years.

Transition amount to be amortized.

Using the preceding data, the following work sheet presents the beginning balances and all of the postretirement benefit entries recorded by Quest Company in 2000.

	General Journal Entries			Memo Record		
Items	Annual Postretirement Expense	Cash	Prepaid/ Accrued Cost	APBO	Plan Assets	Unrecognized Transition Amount
Balance, Jan. 1, 2000				400,000 Cr.		400,000 Dr.
(a) Service cost	22,000 Dr.			22,000 Cr.		
(b) Interest cost	32,000 Dr.			32,000 Cr.		
(c) Contributions		38,000 Cr.			38,000 Dr.	
(d) Benefits				28,000 Dr.	28,000 Cr.	
(e) Amortization:						
Transition	16,000 Dr.***					16,000 Cr.
Journal entry for 2000	70,000 Dr.	38,000 Cr.	32,000 Cr.*			
Balance, Dec. 31, 2000			32,000 Cr.**	426,000 Cr.	10,000 Dr.	384,000 Dr.

*$70,000 − $38,000 = $32,000.
**$426,000 − ($10,000 + $384,000) = $32,000
***$400,000 ÷ 25 = $16,000

ILLUSTRATION 21A-4
Postretirement Benefits
Work Sheet—2000

On the first line of the work sheet, the beginning balances of the APBO and the unrecognized transition amount are recorded in the memo record columns. The transition amount is the difference between the APBO and the fair value of plan assets, in this case $400,000 ($400,000 − $0).

Entry (a) records the service cost component, which increases postretirement expense $22,000 and increases the liability (APBO) $22,000. Entry (b) accrues the interest expense component, which increases both the liability (APBO) and the expense by $32,000 (the beginning APBO multiplied by the discount rate of 8%). Entry (c) records Quest Company's contribution (funding) of assets to the postretirement benefit fund; cash is decreased $38,000 and plan assets are increased $38,000. Entry (d) records the benefit payments made to retirees, which results in equal $28,000 decreases to the plan assets and the liability (APBO). Entry (e) records the amortization of the unrecognized transition amount. It is amortized over the average remaining service to expected retirement, 25 years. The amortized amount of $16,000 ($400,000 ÷ 25) increases post retirement expense and decreases the unrecognized transition amount.

The entry on December 31, which is the adjusting entry made to formally record the postretirement expense in 2000, is as follows:

December 31, 2000

Postretirement Expense	70,000	
Cash		38,000
Prepaid/Accrued Cost		32,000

The credit to Prepaid/Accrued Cost for $32,000 represents the difference between the 2000 postretirement expense of $70,000 and the amount funded of $38,000. The $32,000 credit balance is a liability because the plan is underfunded. The Prepaid/ Accrued Cost account balance of $32,000 also equals the net of the balances in the memo accounts. This reconciliation of the off-balance-sheet items with the prepaid/accrued cost reported in the balance sheet is shown below (similar to the pension reconciliation schedule).

ILLUSTRATION 21A-5
Postretirement Benefits
Reconciliation
Schedule—December 31,
2000

Accumulated postretirement benefit obligation (Credit)	$(426,000)
Plan assets at fair value (Debit)	10,000
Funded status (Credit)	(416,000)
Unrecognized transition amount (Debit)	384,000
Prepaid/accrued cost (Credit)	$ (32,000)

Preparation of this reconciliation schedule is necessary as part of the required note disclosures.

Recognition of Gains and Losses

Gains and losses represent changes in the APBO or the value of plan assets resulting either from actual experience different from that expected or from changes in actuarial assumptions. The FASB noted that "recognizing the effects of revisions in estimates in full in the period in which they occur may produce financial statements that portray more volatility than is inherent in the employer's obligation."[12] Therefore, as in pension accounting, gains and losses are not required to be recognized immediately[13] but may be deferred in the period when they occur and amortized in future years.

The Corridor Approach

Consistent with pension accounting, deferred gains and losses are amortized as a component of net periodic expense if, as of the beginning of the period, they exceed a "corridor." The corridor is defined as the greater of 10% of the APBO or 10% of the market-related value of plan assets. The corridor approach is intended to reduce postretirement expense volatility by providing a reasonable opportunity for gains and losses to offset over time without affecting net periodic expense.

Amortization Methods

If amortization is required, the minimum amortization amount is the excess (beyond the corridor) gain or loss divided by the average remaining service life to expected retirement of all active employees. Any systematic method of amortization may be used provided that (1) the amount amortized in any period is equal to or greater than the minimum amount; (2) the method is applied consistently; and (3) the method is applied similarly for both gains and losses.

The amount of unrecognized gain or loss is recomputed each year and amortized over the average remaining service life if the net amount exceeds the "corridor."

2001 Entries and Work Sheet

Continuing the Quest Company illustration into 2001 the following facts apply to the postretirement benefits plan for the year 2001:

Actual return on plan assets is $600.

Expected return on plan assets is $800.

Discount rate is 8%.

Increase in APBO due to change in actuarial assumptions is $60,000.

Service cost is $26,000.

Contributions (funding) to plan during the year are $50,000.

Benefit payments to employees during the year are $35,000.

Average remaining service to full eligibility: 21 years.

Average remaining service to expected retirement: 25 years.

The work sheet in Illustration 21A-6 presents all of the postretirement benefit entries and information recorded by Quest Company in 2001. The beginning balances entered on the first line of the Quest Company work sheet are the ending balances from the 2000 Quest Company postretirement benefits work sheet in Illustration 21A-4.

---

[12]*FASB Statement No. 106,* par. 293.

[13]If an employer adopts a consistent policy of immediately recognizing gains and losses: (1) the amount of any **net gain** in excess of net losses previously recognized in income would first offset any unamortized **transition obligation**; and (2) the amount of any **net loss** in excess of net gains previously recognized in net income would first offset any unamortized **transition asset** (existence of a transition asset, however, is unlikely).

	General Journal Entries			Memo Record			
Items	Annual Postretirement Expense	Cash	Prepaid/ Accrued Cost	APBO	Plan Assets	Unrecognized Transition Amount	Unrecognized Net Gain or Loss
Balances, Jan. 1, 2001			32,000 Cr.	426,000 Cr.	10,000 Dr.	384,000 Dr.	
(f) Service cost	26,000 Dr.			26,000 Cr.			
(g) Interest cost	34,080 Dr.			34,080 Cr.			
(h) Actual return	600 Cr.				600 Dr.		
(i) Unexpected loss	200 Cr.						200 Dr.
(j) Contributions		50,000 Cr.			50,000 Dr.		
(k) Benefits				35,000 Dr.	35,000 Cr.		
(l) Amortization:							
Transition	16,000 Dr.					16,000 Cr.	
(m) Inc. in APBO—Loss				60,000 Cr.			60,000 Dr.
Journal entry for 2001	75,280 Dr.	50,000 Cr.	25,280 Cr.*				
Balance, Dec. 31, 2001			57,280 Cr.**	511,080 Cr.	25,600 Dr.	368,000 Dr.	60,200 Dr.

*$75,280 − $50,000 = $25,280
**$511,080 − ($25,600 + $368,000 + $60,200) = $57,280

ILLUSTRATION 21A-6
Postretirement Benefits
Work Sheet—2001

Entries (f), (g), (j), (k), and (l) are similar to the corresponding entries previously explained in 2000. Entries (h) and (i) are related. The expected return of $800 is higher than the actual return of $600. To smooth postretirement expense, the unexpected loss of $200 ($800 − $600) is deferred by debiting Unrecognized Net Gain or Loss and crediting Postretirement Expense. As a result of this adjustment, the expected return on the plan assets is the amount actually used to compute postretirement expense.

Entry (m) records the change in the APBO resulting from a change in actuarial assumptions. This $60,000 increase in the employer's accumulated liability is an unexpected loss that is deferred by debiting it to Unrecognized Net Gain or Loss.

The journal entry on December 31 to formally record net periodic expense for 2001 is as follows:

December 31, 2001

Postretirement Expense	75,280	
Cash		50,000
Prepaid/Accrued Cost		25,280

The balance of the Prepaid/Accrued Cost account as December 31, 2001, of $57,280 is equal to the net of the balances in the memo accounts as shown in the following reconciliation schedule.

ILLUSTRATION 21A-7
Postretirement Benefits
Reconciliation
Schedule—December 31,
2001

Accumulated postretirement benefit obligation (Credit)	$(511,080)
Plan assets at fair value (Debit)	25,600
Funded status (Credit)	(485,480)
Unrecognized transition amount (Debit)	368,000
Unrecognized net gain or loss (Debit)	60,200
Prepaid/accrued cost (Credit)	$ (57,280)

Amortization of Unrecognized Net Gain or Loss in 2002

Because of the beginning-of-the-year balance in unrecognized net gain or loss, the corridor test for amortization of the balance must be applied at the end of 2002. Illustration 21A-8 shows the computation of the amortization charge for unrecognized net gain or loss.

2002 Corridor Test	
Unrecognized net gain or loss at beginning of year	$60,200
10% of greater of APBO or market-related value of plan assets ($511,080 × .10)	51,108
Amortizable amount	$ 9,092
Average remaining service to expected retirement	25 years
2002 amortization of loss ($9,092 ÷ 25)	$364

ILLUSTRATION 21A-8
Computation of Amortization Charge (Corridor Test)—2002

DISCLOSURES IN NOTES TO THE FINANCIAL STATEMENTS

The disclosures required for other postretirement benefit plans are similar to and just as detailed and extensive as those required for pensions. By recognizing these similarities, under the provisions of *FASB Statement No. 132*, pension and other postretirement benefit disclosures can be combined. This disclosure for **Gillette Company** was provided in Illustration 21-29. As noted there, the following disclosures are required:

❶ Postretirement expense for the period, separately identifying all components of that cost.

❷ A schedule showing changes in postretirement benefit obligations and plan assets during the year.

❸ A schedule reconciling the funded status of the plan with amounts reported in the employer's balance sheet, separately identifying the reconciling items.

❹ The assumptions and rates used in computing the EPBO and APBO, including assumed health care cost trend rates; assumed discount rates; and the effect of a one-percentage-point increase in the assumed health care cost trend rate on the measurement of the APBO, the service cost, and the interest cost.

ACTUARIAL ASSUMPTIONS AND CONCEPTUAL ISSUES

The measurement of the EPBO and the APBO and the net periodic postretirement benefit cost is involved and complex. Due to the uncertainties in forecasting health care costs, rates of utilization, changes in government health programs, and the differences employed in nonmedical assumptions (discount rate, employee turnover, rate of pre-65 retirement, spouse-age difference, etc.), estimates of postretirement benefit costs may have a large margin of error. Is the information, therefore, relevant, reliable, or verifiable? The FASB concluded "that the obligation to provide postretirement benefits meets the definition of a liability, is representationally faithful, is relevant to financial statement users, and can be measured with sufficient reliability at a justifiable cost."[14] Failure to accrue an obligation and an expense prior to payment of benefits is considered to be an unfaithful representation of what financial statements purport to represent.[15]

The FASB took a momentous step by requiring the accrual of postretirement benefits as a liability. Many opposed the requirement warning that the standard would devastate earnings. Others argued that putting "soft" numbers on the balance sheet was inappropriate and, finally, others noted that it would force companies to curtail these benefits to employees.

---

[14]*FABS Statement No. 106*, par. 163.

[15]The FASB does not require recognition of a "minimum liability" for postretirement benefit plans. The Board concluded that the postretirement transition provisions that provide for delayed recognition should not be overridden by a requirement to recognize a liability that would accelerate recognition of that obligation in the balance sheet.

The authors believe that the FASB deserves special praise for this standard. Because the Board addressed this issue, companies now recognize the magnitude of these costs. This recognition has led to efforts to control escalating health-care costs. As John Ruffle, former president of the Financial Accounting Foundation noted, "The Board has done American industry a gigantic favor. Over the long term, industry will look back and say thanks."

SUMMARY OF LEARNING OBJECTIVES FOR APPENDIX 21A

⑪ Identify the differences between pensions and postretirement health-care benefits. Pension plans are generally funded, but health-care benefit plans are not. Pension benefits are generally well-defined and level in amount, but health-care benefits are generally uncapped and variable. Pension benefits are payable monthly, but health-care benefits are paid as needed and used. Pension plan variables are reasonably predictable, whereas health-care plan variables are difficult to predict.

⑫ Contrast accounting for pensions to accounting for other postretirement benefits. Many of the basic concepts and much of the accounting terminology and measurement methodology applicable to pensions also apply to other postretirement benefit accounting. Because other postretirement benefit plans are unfunded, large transition obligations occur; these may be immediately written off or amortized over 20 years. Two significant concepts peculiar to accounting for other postretirement benefits are (a) expected postretirement benefit obligation (EPBO) and (b) accumulated postretirement benefit obligation (APBO).

Note: All **asterisked** Questions, Brief Exercises, Exercises, Problems, and Conceptual Cases relate to material covered in the appendix to the chapter.

QUESTIONS

1 What is a private pension plan? How does a contributory pension plan differ from a noncontributory plan?

2 Differentiate between a defined contribution pension plan and a defined benefit pension plan. Explain how the employer's obligation differs between the two types of plans.

3 Differentiate between "accounting for the employer" and "accounting for the pension fund."

4 The meaning of the term "fund" depends on the context in which it is used. Explain its meaning when used as a noun. Explain its meaning when it is used as a verb.

5 What is the role of an actuary relative to pension plans? What are actuarial assumptions?

6 What factors must be considered by the actuary in measuring the amount of pension benefits under a defined benefit plan?

7 Name three approaches to measuring benefits from a pension plan and explain how they differ.

8 Distinguish between the noncapitalization approach and the capitalization approach with regard to accounting for pension plans. Which approach does *FASB Statement No. 87* adopt?

9 Explain how cash basis accounting for pension plans differs from accrual basis accounting for pension plans. Why is cash basis accounting generally considered unacceptable for pension plan accounting?

10 Identify the five components that comprise pension expense. Briefly explain the nature of each component.

11 What is service cost and what is the basis of its measurement?

12 In computing the interest component of pension expense, what interest rates may be used?

13 Explain the difference between service cost and prior service cost.

14 What is meant by "prior service cost"? When is prior service cost recognized as pension expense?

15 What are "liability gains and losses," and how are they accounted for?

16 If pension expense recognized in a period exceeds the current amount funded by the employer, what kind of account arises and how should it be reported in the financial statements? If the reverse occurs—that is, current funding by the employer exceeds the amount recognized as pension expense—what kind of account arises and how should it be reported?

17 Given the following items and amounts, compute the actual return on plan assets: fair value of plan assets at the beginning of the period, $9,200,000; benefits paid during the period, $1,400,000; contributions made during the period, $1,000,000; and fair value of the plan assets at the end of the period, $10,150,000.

18 How does an "asset gain or loss" develop in pension accounting? How does a "liability gain or loss" develop in pension accounting?

19 What is the meaning of "corridor amortization"?

20 Explain when a minimum liability is recognized and how it is reported in the financial statements.

21 Explain the nature of a debit to an intangible asset account when an additional pension liability must be recorded. How does the amount of unrecognized prior service cost influence the amount recognized as an intangible asset?

22 At the end of the current period, Jacob Inc. had an accumulated benefit obligation of $400,000, pension plan assets (at fair value) of $300,000, and a balance in prepaid pension cost of $41,000. Assuming that Jacob Inc. follows *FASB Statement No. 87*, what are the accounts and amounts that will be reported on the company's balance sheet as pension assets or pension liabilities?

23 At the end of the current year, Joshua Co. has unrecognized prior service cost of $9,150,000. In addition, it recognized a minimum liability of $10,500,000 for the year.

Where should the unrecognized prior service cost be reported on the balance sheet? Where should the debit related to the establishment of the minimum liability be reported?

24 Determine the meaning of the following terms:

(a) Contributory plan.

(b) Vested benefits.

(c) Retroactive benefits.

(d) Years-of-service method.

25 Of what value to the financial statement reader is the schedule reconciling the funded status of the plan with amounts reported in the employer's balance sheet?

26 A headline in *The Wall Street Journal* stated "Firms Increasingly Tap Their Pension Funds to Use Excess Assets." What is the accounting issue related to the use of these "excess assets" by companies?

*27 What are postretirement benefits other than pensions?

*28 Why didn't the FASB cover both types of postretirement benefits—pensions and health-care—in the earlier pension accounting statement?

*29 What is the transition amount in pension accounting and the transition amount in postretirement benefit accounting? And, how does the accounting treatment for these transition amounts differ under *Statement Nos. 87* and *106*? Why is the accounting for the transition amount so controversial?

*30 What are the major differences between postretirement health-care benefits and pension benefits?

*31 What is the difference between the APBO and the EPBO? What are the components of postretirement expense?

BRIEF EXERCISES

BE21-1 The following information is available for Jack Borke Corporation for 2002:

Service	$29,000
Interest on P.B.O.	22,000
Return on plan assets	20,000
Amortization of unrecognized prior service cost	15,200
Amortization of unrecognized net loss	500

Compute Borke's 2002 pension expense.

BE21-2 For Becker Corporation, year-end plan assets were $2,000,000. At the beginning of the year, plan assets were $1,680,000. During the year, contributions to the pension fund were $120,000 while benefits paid were $200,000. Compute Becker's actual return on plan assets.

BE21-3 At January 1, 2002, Uddin Company had plan assets of $250,000 and a projected benefit obligation of the same amount. During 2002, service cost was $27,500, the settlement rate was 10%, actual and expected return on plan assets were $25,000, contributions were $20,000, and benefits paid were $17,500. Prepare a pension work sheet for Uddin Company for 2002.

BE21-4 For 2002, Potts Company had pension expense of $32,000 and contributed $25,000 to the pension fund. Prepare Potts Company's journal entry to record pension expense and funding.

BE21-5 Duesbury Corporation amended its pension plan on January 1, 2002, and granted $120,000 of unrecognized prior service costs to its employees. The employees are expected to provide 2,000 service years in the future, with 350 service years in 2002. Compute unrecognized prior service cost amortization for 2002.

BE21-6 At December 31, 2002, Conway Corporation had a projected benefit obligation of $510,000, plan assets of $322,000, unrecognized prior service cost of $127,000, and accrued pension cost of $61,000. Prepare a pension reconciliation schedule for Conway.

BE21-7 Hunt Corporation had a projected benefit obligation of $3,100,000 and plan assets of $3,300,000 at January 1, 2002. Hunt's unrecognized net pension loss was $475,000 at that time. The average remaining service period of Hunt's employees is 7.5 years. Compute Hunt's minimum amortization of pension loss.

BE21-8 Judy O'Neill Corporation provides the following information at December 31, 2001:

Accumulated benefit obligation	$2,800,000
Plan assets at fair value	2,000,000
Accrued pension cost	200,000
Unrecognized prior service cost	1,100,000

Compute the additional liability that O'Neill must record at December 31, 2001.

BE21-9 At December 31, 2002, Judy O'Neill Corporation (see BE21-8) has the following balances:

Accumulated benefit obligation	$3,400,000
Plan assets at fair value	2,420,000
Accrued pension cost	235,000
Unrecognized prior service cost	990,000

O'Neill's Additional Pension Liability was $600,000 at December 31, 2001. Prepare O'Neill's December 31, 1999, entry to adjust Additional Pension Liability.

BE21-10 At December 31, 2001, Jeremiah Corporation was not required to report any additional pension liability. At December 31, 2002, the additional liability required is $600,000, and unrecognized prior service cost was $425,000. Prepare Jeremiah's December 31, 2002, entry to adjust Additional Pension Liability.

*BE21-11 Caleb Corporation has the following information available concerning its postretirement benefit plan for 2002:

Service cost	$40,000
Interest cost	52,400
Actual return on plan assets	26,900
Amortization of unrecognized transition amount	24,600

Compute Caleb's 2002 postretirement expense.

*BE21-12 For 2002, Benjamin Inc. computed its annual postretirement expense as $240,900. Benjamin's contribution to the plan during 2002 was $160,000. Prepare Benjamin's 2002 entry to record postretirement expense.

EXERCISES

E21-1 **(Pension Expense, Journal Entries)** The following information is available for the pension plan of Kiley Company for the year 2001:

Actual and expected return on plan assets	$ 12,000
Benefits paid to retirees	40,000
Contributions (funding)	95,000
Interest/discount rate	10%
Prior service cost amortization	8,000
Projected benefit obligation, January 1, 2001	500,000
Service cost	60,000

Instructions

(a) Compute pension expense for the year 2001.

(b) Prepare the journal entry to record pension expense and the employer's contribution to the pension plan in 2001.

E21-2 (Computation of Pension Expense) Rebekah Company provides the following information about its defined benefit pension plan for the year 2002:

Service cost	$ 90,000
Contribution to the plan	105,000
Prior service cost amortization	10,000
Actual and expected return on plan assets	64,000
Benefits paid	40,000
Accrued pension cost liability at January 1, 2002	10,000
Plan assets at January 1, 2002	640,000
Projected benefit obligation at January 1, 2002	800,000
Unrecognized prior service cost balance at January 1, 2002	150,000
Interest/discount (settlement) rate	10%

Instructions
Compute the pension expense for the year 2002.

E21-3 (Preparation of Pension Work Sheet with Reconciliation) Using the information in E21-2 prepare a pension work sheet inserting January 1, 2002, balances, showing December 31, 2002, balances and the journal entry recording pension expense.

E21-4 (Basic Pension Work Sheet) The following facts apply to the pension plan of Trudy Borke Inc. for the year 2002:

Plan assets, January 1, 2002	$490,000
Projected benefit obligation, January 1, 2002	490,000
Settlement rate	8.5%
Annual pension service cost	40,000
Contributions (funding)	30,000
Actual return on plan assets	49,700
Benefits paid to retirees	33,400

Instructions
Using the preceding data, compute pension expense for the year 2002. As part of your solution, prepare a pension work sheet that shows the journal entry for pension expense for 2002 and the year-end balances in the related pension accounts.

E21-5 (Application of Years-of-Service Method) Janet Valente Company has five employees participating in its defined benefit pension plan. Expected years of future service for these employees at the beginning of 2002 are as follows:

Employee	Future Years of Service
Ed	3
Paul	4
Mary	6
Dave	6
Caroline	6

On January 1, 2002, the company amended its pension plan increasing its projected benefit obligation by $60,000.

Instructions
Compute the amount of prior service cost amortization for the years 2002 through 2007 using the years-of-service method setting up appropriate schedules.

E21-6 (Computation of Actual Return) James Paul Importers provides the following pension plan information:

Fair value of pension plan assets, January 1, 2002	$2,300,000
Fair value of pension plan assets, December 31, 2002	2,725,000
Contributions to the plan in 2002	250,000
Benefits paid retirees in 2002	350,000

Instructions
From the data above, compute the actual return on the plan assets for 2002.

E21-7 (Basic Pension Work Sheet) The following defined pension data of Doreen Corp. apply to the year 2002:

Projected benefit obligation, 1/1/02 (before amendment)	$560,000
Plan assets, 1/1/02	546,200
Prepaid/accrued pension cost (credit)	13,800
On January 1, 2002, Doreen Corp., through plan amendment,	
grants prior service benefits having a present value of	100,000
Settlement rate	9%
Annual pension service cost	58,000
Contributions (funding)	55,000
Actual return on plan assets	52,280
Benefits paid to retirees	40,000
Prior service cost amortization for 2002	17,000

Instructions

For 2002, prepare a pension work sheet for Doreen Corp. that shows the journal entry for pension expense and the year-end balances in the related pension accounts.

E21-8 (Application of the Corridor Approach)   Dougherty Corp. has beginning-of-the-year present values for its projected benefit obligation and market-related values for its pension plan assets:

	Projected Benefit Obligation	Plan Assets Value
2000	$2,000,000	$1,900,000
2001	2,400,000	2,500,000
2002	2,900,000	2,600,000
2003	3,600,000	3,000,000

The average remaining service life per employee in 2000 and 2001 is 10 years and in 2002 and 2003 is 12 years. The unrecognized net gain or loss that occurred during each year is as follows: 2000, $280,000 loss; 2001, $90,000 loss; 2002, $10,000 loss; and 2003, $25,000 gain (in working the solution the unrecognized gains and losses must be aggregated to arrive at year-end balances).

Instructions

Using the corridor approach, compute the amount of unrecognized net gain or loss amortized and charged to pension expense in each of the four years, setting up an appropriate schedule.

E21-9 (Disclosures: Pension Expense and Reconciliation Schedule)   Mildred Enterprises provides the following information relative to its defined benefit pension plan:

Balances or Values at December 31, 2002

Projected benefit obligation	$2,737,000
Accumulated benefit obligation	1,980,000
Vested benefit obligation	1,645,852
Fair value of plan assets	2,278,329
Unrecognized prior service cost	205,000
Unrecognized net loss (1/1/02 balance, –0–)	45,680
Accrued pension cost liability	207,991
Other pension plan data:	
Service cost for 2002	$ 94,000
Unrecognized prior service cost amortization for 2002	45,000
Actual return on plan assets in 2002	130,000
Expected return on plan assets in 2002	175,680
Interest on January 1, 2002, projected benefit obligation	253,000
Contributions to plan in 2002	92,329
Benefits paid	140,000

Instructions

(a) Prepare the note disclosing the components of pension expense for the year 2002.

(b) Reconcile the funded status of the plan with the amount reported in the December 31, 2002, balance sheet.

E21-10 (Pension Work Sheet with Reconciliation Schedule)   Melanie Vail Corp. sponsors a defined benefit pension plan for its employees. On January 1, 2002, the following balances relate to this plan:

Plan assets	$480,000
Projected benefit obligation	625,000
Prepaid/accrued pension cost (credit)	45,000
Unrecognized prior service cost	100,000

As a result of the operation of the plan during 2002, the following additional data are provided by the actuary:

Service cost for 2002	$90,000
Settlement rate, 9%	
Actual return on plan assets in 2002	57,000
Amortization of prior service cost	19,000
Expected return on plan assets	52,000
Unexpected loss from change in projected benefit obligation,	
due to change in actuarial predictions	76,000
Contributions in 2002	99,000
Benefits paid retirees in 2002	85,000

Instructions

(a) Using the data above, compute pension expense for Melanie Vail Corp. for the year 2002 by preparing a pension work sheet that shows the journal entry for pension expense and the year-end balances in the related pension accounts.

(b) At December 31, 2002, prepare a schedule reconciling the funded status of the plan with the pension amount reported on the balance sheet.

E21-11 (Minimum Liability Computation, Entry) The following information is available for McGwire Corporation's defined benefit pension plan for the years 2001 and 2002.

	December 31,	
	2001	**2002**
Accrued pension cost balance	$ –0–	$ 45,000
Accumulated benefit obligation	260,000	370,000
Fair value of plan assets	255,000	300,000
Prepaid pension cost balance	30,000	–0–
Projected benefit obligation	350,000	455,000
Unrecognized prior service cost	125,000	110,000

Instructions

(a) Compute the amount of additional liability, if any, that McGwire must record at the end of each year.

(b) Prepare the journal entries, if any, necessary to record a minimum liability for 2001 and 2002.

E21-12 (Pension Expense, Journal Entries, Statement Presentation, Minimum Liability) Desiree Griseta Company sponsors a defined benefit pension plan for its employees. The following data relate to the operation of the plan for the year 2001 in which no benefits were paid:

1. The actuarial present value of future benefits earned by employees for services rendered in 2001 amounted to $56,000.
2. The company's funding policy requires a contribution to the pension trustee amounting to $145,000 for 2001.
3. As of January 1, 2001, the company had a projected benefit obligation of $1,000,000, an accumulated benefit obligation of $800,000, and an unrecognized prior service cost of $400,000. The fair value of pension plan assets amounted to $600,000 at the beginning of the year. The market-related asset value was equal to $600,000. The actual and expected return on plan assets was $54,000. The settlement rate was 9%. No gains or losses occurred in 2001 and no benefits were paid.
4. Amortization of unrecognized prior service cost was $40,000 in 2001 amortization of unrecognized net gain or loss was not required in 2001.

Instructions

(a) Determine the amounts of the components of pension expense that should be recognized by the company in 2001.

(b) Prepare the journal entry or entries to record pension expense and the employer's contribution to the pension trustee in 2001.

(c) Indicate the amounts that would be reported on the income statement and the balance sheet for the year 2001. The accumulated benefit obligation on December 31, 2001, was $830,000.

E21-13 (Pension Expense, Journal Entries, Minimum Liability, Statement Presentation) Nellie Altom Company received the following selected information from its pension plan trustee concerning the operation of the company's defined benefit pension plan for the year ended December 31, 2001.

	January 1, 2001	December 31, 2001
Projected benefit obligation	$2,000,000	$2,077,000
Market-related and fair value of plan assets	800,000	1,130,000
Accumulated benefit obligation	1,600,000	1,720,000
Actuarial (gains) losses (Unrecognized net (gain) or loss)	–0–	(200,000)

The service cost component of pension expense for employee services rendered in the current year amounted to $77,000 and the amortization of unrecognized prior service cost was $115,000. The company's actual funding (contributions) of the plan in 2001 amounted to $250,000. The expected return on plan assets and the actual rate were both 10%; the interest/discount (settlement) rate was 10%. No prepaid/accrued pension cost existed on January 1, 2001. Assume no benefits paid in 2001.

Instructions
(a) Determine the amounts of the components of pension expense that should be recognized by the company in 2001.
(b) Prepare the journal entries to record pension expense and the employer's contribution to the pension plan in 2001.
(c) Indicate the pension-related amounts that would be reported on the income statement and the balance sheet for Nellie Altom Company for the year 2001. (Compute the minimum liability.)

E21-14 (Computation of Actual Return, Gains and Losses, Corridor Test, Prior Service Cost, Minimum Liability, Pension Expense, and Reconciliation) Linda Berstler Company sponsors a defined benefit pension plan. The corporation's actuary provides the following information about the plan:

	January 1, 2002	December 31, 2002
Vested benefit obligation	$1,500	$1,900
Accumulated benefit obligation	1,900	2,730
Projected benefit obligation	2,800	3,645
Plan assets (fair value)	1,700	2,620
Settlement rate and expected rate of return		10%
Prepaid/(accrued) pension cost	–0–	?
Unrecognized prior service cost	1,100	?
Service cost for the year 2002		400
Contributions (funding in 2002)		800
Benefits paid in 2002		200

The average remaining service life per employee is 20 years.

Instructions
(a) Compute the actual return on the plan assets in 2002.
(b) Compute the amount of the unrecognized net gain or loss as of December 31, 2002 (assume the January 1, 2002, balance was zero).
(c) Compute the amount of unrecognized net gain or loss amortization for 2002 (corridor approach).
(d) Compute the amount of prior service cost amortization for 2002.
(e) Compute the minimum liability to be reported at December 31, 2002.
(f) Compute pension expense for 2002.
(g) Prepare a schedule reconciling the plan's funded status with the amounts reported in the December 31, 2002, balance sheet.

E21-15 (Work Sheet for E21-14) Using the information in E21-14 about Linda Berstler Company's defined benefit pension plan, prepare a 2002 pension work sheet with supplementary schedules of computations. Prepare the journal entries at December 31, 2002, to record pension expense and any "additional liability." Also, prepare a schedule reconciling the plan's funded status with the pension amounts reported in the balance sheet.

E21-16 (Pension Expense, Minimum Liability, Journal Entries) Walker Company provides the following information related to its defined benefit pension plan for 2001:

Accrued pension cost balance (January 1)	$ 25,000
Accumulated benefit obligation (December 31)	400,000
Actual and expected return on plan assets	15,000
Additional pension liability balance (January 1)	10,000
Contributions (funding) in 2001	150,000
Fair value of plan assets (December 31)	350,000
Interest/discount rate	10%
Projected benefit obligation (January 1)	700,000
Service cost	90,000

Instructions

(a) Compute pension expense and prepare the journal entry to record pension expense and the employer's contribution to the pension plan in 2001.

(b) Prepare the journal entry to record the minimum liability for 2001.

E21-17 **(Pension Expense, Minimum Liability, Statement Presentation)** Blum Foods Company obtained the following information from the insurance company that administers the company's employee-defined benefit pension plan:

	For Year Ended December 31		
	2001	2002	2003
Plan assets (at fair value)	$280,000	$398,000	$586,000
Accumulated benefit obligation	378,000	512,000	576,000
Pension expense	95,000	128,000	130,000
Employer's funding contribution	110,000	150,000	125,000
Prior service cost not yet recognized in earnings	494,230	451,365	400,438

Prior to 2001 cumulative pension expense was equal to cumulative contributions. The company has adopted the requirements of the FASB standard on "Employers' Accounting for Pensions." Assume that the market-related asset value is equal to the fair value of plan assets for all three years.

Instructions

(a) Prepare the journal entries to record pension expense, employer's funding contribution, and the adjustment to a minimum pension liability for the years 2001, 2002, and 2003. (Preparation of a pension work sheet is not a requirement of this exercise; insufficient information is given to prepare one.)

(b) Indicate the pension related amounts that would be reported on the company's income statement and balance sheet for 2001, 2002, and 2003.

E21-18 **(Minimum Liability, Journal Entries, Balance Sheet Items)** Presented below is partial information related to the pension fund of Rose Bryhan Inc.

Funded Status (end of year)	2001	2002	2003
Assets and obligations			
Market-related asset value	$1,300,000	$1,650,000	$1,900,000
Plan assets (at fair value)	1,300,000	1,670,000	1,950,000
Accumulated benefit obligation	1,150,000	1,480,000	2,060,000
Projected benefit obligation	1,600,000	1,910,000	2,500,000
Unfunded accumulated benefits			110,000
Overfunded accumulated benefits	150,000	190,000	
Amounts to be recognized			
(Accrued)/prepaid pension cost at beginning of year	$ –0–	$ 19,000	$ 16,000
Pension expense	(250,000)	(268,000)	(300,000)
Contribution	269,000	265,000	277,000
(Accrued)/prepaid pension cost at end of year	$ 19,000	$ 16,000	$ (7,000)

The company's unrecognized prior service cost is $637,000 at the end of 2003.

Instructions

(a) What pension-related amounts are reported on the balance sheet of Rose Bryhan Inc. for 2001, 2002, and 2003?

(b) What are the journal entries made to record pension expense in 2001, 2002, and 2003?

(c) What journal entries (if any) are necessary to record a minimum liability for 2001, 2002, and 2003?

E21-19 **(Reconciliation Schedule, Minimum Liability, and Unrecognized Loss)** Presented below is partial information related to Jean Burr Company at December 31, 2001:

Market-related asset value	$700,000
Projected benefit obligation	930,000
Accumulated benefit obligation	865,000
Plan assets (at fair value)	700,000
Vested benefits	200,000
Prior service cost not yet recognized in pension expense	120,000
Gains and losses	–0–

Instructions

(a) Present the schedule reconciling the funded status with the asset/liability reported on the balance sheet. Assume no asset or liability existed at the beginning of period for pensions on Jean Burr Company's balance sheet.

(b) Assume the same facts as in (a) except that Jean Burr Company has an unrecognized loss of $16,000 during 2001.

(c) Explain the rationale for the treatment of the unrecognized loss and the prior service cost not yet recognized in pension expense.

E21-20 (Amortization of Unrecognized Net Gain or Loss [Corridor Approach], Pension Expense Computation) The actuary for the pension plan of Joyce Bush Inc. calculated the following net gains and losses:

Unrecognized Net Gain or Loss	
Incurred during the Year	(Gain) or Loss
2001	$300,000
2002	480,000
2003	(210,000)
2004	(290,000)

Other information about the company's pension obligation and plan assets is as follows:

As of January 1,	Projected Benefit Obligation	Plan Assets (market-related asset value)
2001	$4,000,000	$2,400,000
2002	4,520,000	2,200,000
2003	4,980,000	2,600,000
2004	4,250,000	3,040,000

Joyce Bush Inc. has a stable labor force of 400 employees who are expected to receive benefits under the plan. The total service-years for all participating employees is 5,600. The beginning balance of unrecognized net gain or loss is zero on January 1, 2001. The market-related value and the fair value of plan assets are the same for the four-year period. Use the average remaining service life per employee as the basis for amortization.

Instructions

(Round to the nearest dollar)

Prepare a schedule which reflects the minimum amount of unrecognized net gain or loss amortized as a component of net periodic pension expense for each of the years 2001, 2002, 2003, and 2004. Apply the "corridor" approach in determining the amount to be amortized each year.

E21-21 (Amortization of Unrecognized Net Gain or Loss [Corridor Approach]) Lowell Company sponsors a defined benefit pension plan for its 600 employees. The company's actuary provided the following information about the plan:

	January 1,	December 31,	
	2001	2001	2002
Projected benefit obligation	$2,800,000	$3,650,000	$4,400,000
Accumulated benefit obligation	1,900,000	2,430,000	2,900,000
Plan assets (fair value and market related asset value)	1,700,000	2,900,000	2,100,000
Unrecognized net (gain) or loss (for purposes of the corridor calculation)	–0–	101,000	(24,000)
Discount rate (current settlement rate)	11%	8%	
Actual and expected asset return rate	10%	10%	

The average remaining service life per employee is 10.5 years. The service cost component of net periodic pension expense for employee services rendered amounted to $400,000 in 2001 and $475,000 in 2002. The unrecognized prior service cost on January 1, 2001, was $1,155,000. No benefits have been paid.

Instructions

(Round to the nearest dollar)

(a) Compute the amount of unrecognized prior service cost to be amortized as a component of net periodic pension expense for each of the years 2001 and 2002.

(b) Prepare a schedule which reflects the amount of unrecognized gain or loss to be amortized as a component of net periodic pension expense for 2001 and 2002.

(c) Determine the total amount of net periodic pension expense to be recognized by Lowell Company in 2001 and 2002.

*E21-22 (Postretirement Benefit Expense Computation) Rose Chance Inc. provides the following information related to its postretirement benefits for the year 2003:

Accumulated postretirement benefit obligation at January 1, 2003	$810,000
Actual and expected return on plan assets	34,000
Unrecognized prior service cost amortization	21,000
Amortization of transition amount (loss)	5,000
Discount rate	10%
Service cost	88,000

Instructions
Compute postretirement benefit expense for 2003.

*E21-23 (Postretirement Benefit Expense Computation) Marvelous Marvin Co. provides the following information about its postretirement benefit plan for the year 2002:

Service cost	$ 90,000
Prior service cost amortization	3,000
Contribution to the plan	16,000
Actual and expected return on plan assets	62,000
Benefits paid	40,000
Plan assets at January 1, 2002	710,000
Accumulated postretirement benefit obligation at January 1, 2002	810,000
Unrecognized prior service cost balance at January 1, 2002	20,000
Amortization of transition amount (Loss)	5,000
Unrecognized transition amount at January 1, 2002	80,000
Discount rate	9%

Instructions
Compute the postretirement benefit expense for 2002.

*E21-24 (Postretirement Benefit Work Sheet) Using the information in *E21-23 prepare a work sheet inserting January 1, 2002, balances, showing December 31, 2002, balances, and the journal entry recording postretirement benefit expense.

*E21-25 (Postretirement Benefit Reconciliation Schedule) Presented below is partial information related to Sandra Conley Co. at December 31, 2003:

Accumulated postretirement benefit obligation	$ 950,000
Expected postretirement benefit obligation	1,000,000
Plan assets (at fair value)	650,000
Prior service cost not yet recognized in postretirement expense	60,000
Gain and losses	–0–
Unrecognized transition amount (Loss)	100,000

Instructions
(a) Present the schedule reconciling the funded status with the asset/liability reported on the balance sheet. Assume no asset or liability existed at the beginning of the period for postretirement benefits on Sandra Conley Co.'s balance sheet.
(b) Assume the same facts as in (a) except that Sandra Conley Co. has an unrecognized loss of $20,000 during 2003.

PROBLEMS

P21-1 (Two-Year Work Sheet and Reconciliation Schedule) On January 1, 2002, Diana Peter Company has the following defined benefit pension plan balances:

Projected benefit obligation	$4,200,000
Fair value of plan assets	4,200,000

The interest (settlement) rate applicable to the plan is 10%. On January 1, 2003, the company amends its pension agreement so that prior service costs of $500,000 are created. Other data related to the pension plan are:

	2002	2003
Service costs	$150,000	$180,000
Unrecognized prior service costs amortization	–0–	90,000
Contributions (funding) to the plan	140,000	185,000
Benefits paid	200,000	280,000
Actual return on plan assets	252,000	260,000
Expected rate of return on assets	6%	8%

Instructions

(a) Prepare a pension work sheet for the pension plan for 2002 and 2003.

(b) As of December 31, 2003, prepare a schedule reconciling the funded status with the reported liability (accrued pension cost).

P21-2 (Three-Year Work Sheet, Journal Entries, and Reconciliation Schedules) Katie Day Company adopts acceptable accounting for its defined benefit pension plan on January 1, 2002, with the following beginning balances: Plan assets, $200,000; projected benefit obligation, $200,000. Other data relating to 3 years' operation of the plan are as follows:

	2002	2003	2004
Annual service cost	$16,000	$ 19,000	$ 26,000
Settlement rate and expected rate of return	10%	10%	10%
Actual return on plan assets	17,000	21,900	24,000
Annual funding (contributions)	16,000	40,000	48,000
Benefits paid	14,000	16,400	21,000
Unrecognized prior service cost (plan amended, 1/1/03)		160,000	
Amortization of unrecognized prior service cost		54,400	41,600
Change in actuarial assumptions establishes a December 31, 2004, projected benefit obligation of:			520,000

Instructions

(a) Prepare a pension work sheet presenting all 3 years' pension balances and activities.

(b) Prepare the journal entries (from the work sheet) to reflect all pension plan transactions and events at December 31 of each year.

(c) At December 31 of each year prepare a schedule reconciling the funded status of the plan with the pension amounts reported in the financial statements.

P21-3 (Pension Expense, Journal Entries, Minimum Pension Liability, Amortization of Unrecognized Loss, Reconciliation Schedule) Paul Dobson Company sponsors a defined benefit plan for its 100 employees. On January 1, 2001 (date company starts following *FASB Statement No. 87*), the company's actuary provided the following information:

Unrecognized prior service cost	$150,000
Pension plan assets (fair value and market-related asset value)	200,000
Accumulated benefit obligation	260,000
Projected benefit obligation	350,000

The average remaining service period for the participating employees is 10.5 years. All employees are expected to receive benefits under the plan. On December 31, 2001, the actuary calculated that the present value of future benefits earned for employee services rendered in the current year amounted to $52,000; the projected benefit obligation was $452,000; fair value of pension assets was $276,000; the accumulated benefit obligation amounted to $365,000; and the market-related asset value is $276,000. The expected return on plan assets and the discount rate on the projected benefit obligation were both 10%. The actual return on plan assets is $11,000. The company's current year's contribution to the pension plan amounted to $65,000. No benefits were paid during the year.

Instructions

(Round to the nearest dollar)

(a) Determine the components of pension expense that the company would recognize in 2001. (With only one year involved, you need not prepare a work sheet.)

(b) Prepare the journal entries to record the pension expense and the company's funding of the pension plan in 2001.

(c) Assume Paul Dobson Company elects to recognize the minimum pension liability in its balance sheet for the year ended December 31, 2001. Prepare the journal entry to record the minimum liability.

(d) Compute the amount of the 2001 increase/decrease in unrecognized gains or losses and the amount to be amortized in 2001 and 2002.

(e) Prepare a schedule reconciling the funded status of the plan with the pension amounts reported in the financial statement as of December 31, 2001.

P21-4 (Pension Expense, Minimum Liability, Journal Entries for Two Years) Mantle Company sponsors a defined benefit pension plan. The following information related to the pension plan is available for 2001 and 2002:

	2001	2002
Plan assets (fair value), December 31	$380,000	$465,000
Projected benefit obligation, January 1	600,000	700,000
Prepaid/(accrued) pension cost balance, January 1	(40,000)	?
Unrecognized prior service cost, January 1	250,000	240,000
Service cost	60,000	90,000
Actual and expected return on plan assets	24,000	30,000
Amortization of prior service cost	10,000	12,000
Contributions (funding)	110,000	120,000
Accumulated benefit obligation, December 31	500,000	550,000
Additional pension liability balance, January 1	50,000	?
Interest/settlement rate	9%	9%

Instructions
(a) Compute pension expense for 2001 and 2002.
(b) Prepare the journal entries to record the pension expense and the company's funding of the pension plan for both years.
(c) Compute the minimum liability for 2001 and 2002.
(d) Prepare the journal entries to record the minimum liability for both years.

P21-5 (Computation of Pension Expense, Amortization of Unrecognized Net Gain or Loss (Corridor Approach), Journal Entries for Three Years, and Minimum Pension Liability Computation) Dubel Toothpaste Company initiates a defined benefit pension plan for its 50 employees on January 1, 2001. The insurance company which administers the pension plan provided the following information for the years 2001, 2002, and 2003:

	For Year Ended December 31,		
	2001	2002	2003
Plan assets (fair value)	$50,000	$ 85,000	$170,000
Accumulated benefit obligation	45,000	165,000	292,000
Projected benefit obligation	55,000	200,000	324,000
Unrecognized net (gain) loss (for purposes of corridor calculation)	–0–	(24,500)	84,500
Employer's funding contribution (made at end of year)	50,000	60,000	95,000

There were no balances as of January 1, 2001, when the plan was initiated. The actual and expected return on plan assets was 10% over the 3-year period but the settlement rate used to discount the company's pension obligation was 13% in 2001, 11% in 2002, and 8% in 2003. The service cost component of net periodic pension expense amounted to the following: 2001, $55,000; 2002, $85,000; and 2003, $119,000. The average remaining service life per employee is 12 years. No benefits were paid in 2001, $30,000 of benefits were paid in 2002, and $18,500 of benefits were paid in 2003 (all benefits paid at end of year).

Instructions
(Round to the nearest dollar)

(a) Calculate the amount of net periodic pension expense that the company would recognize in 2001, 2002, and 2003.
(b) Prepare the journal entries to record net periodic pension expense, employer's funding contribution, and the adjustment to reflect a minimum pension liability for the years 2001, 2002, and 2003.

P21-6 (Computation of Unrecognized Prior Service Cost Amortization, Pension Expense, Journal Entries, Net Gain or Loss, and Reconciliation Schedule) Ekedahl Inc. has sponsored a noncontributory-defined benefit pension plan for its employees since 1984. Prior to 2001, cumulative net pension expense recognized equaled cumulative contributions to the plan. Management has elected to recognize the minimum pension liability requirement in the balance sheet for the year ending December 31, 2001. Other relevant information about the pension plan on January 1, 2001, is as follows:

1. The company has 200 employees who are expected to receive benefits under the plan. All these employees are expected to receive benefits under the plan. The average remaining service life per employee is 13 years.

2. The projected benefit obligation amounted to $5,000,000 and the fair value of pension plan assets was $3,000,000. The market-related asset value was also $3,000,000. Unrecognized prior service cost was $2,000,000.

On December 31, 2001, the projected benefit obligation and the accumulated benefit obligation were $4,750,000 and $4,025,000, respectively. The fair value of the pension plan assets amounted to $3,900,000 at the end of the year. The market-related asset value was $3,790,000. A 10% settlement rate and a 10% expected asset return rate was used in the actuarial present value computations in the pension plan. The present value of benefits attributed by the pension benefit formula to employee service in 2001 amounted to $200,000. The employer's contribution to the plan assets amounted to $575,000 in 2001. This problem assumes no payment of pension benefits.

Instructions
(Round all amounts to the nearest dollar)

(a) Prepare a schedule, based on the average remaining life per employee, showing the unrecognized prior service cost that would be amortized as a component of pension expense for 2001, 2002, and 2003.
(b) Compute pension expense for the year 2001.
(c) Prepare the journal entries required to report the accounting for the company's pension plan for 2001.
(d) Compute the amount of the 2001 increase/decrease in unrecognized net gains or losses and the amount to be amortized in 2001 and 2002.
(e) Prepare a schedule reconciling the funded status of the plan with the pension amounts reported in the financial statements as of December 31, 2001.

P21-7 (Pension Work Sheet, Minimum Liability) Farrey Corp. sponsors a defined benefit pension plan for its employees. On January 1, 2003, the following balances related to this plan:

Plan assets (fair value)	$520,000
Projected benefit obligation	725,000
Prepaid/accrued pension cost (credit)	33,000
Unrecognized prior service cost	81,000
Unrecognized net gain or loss (debit)	91,000

As a result of the operation of the plan during 2003, the actuary provided the following additional data at December 31, 2003:

Service cost for 2003	$108,000
Settlement rate, 9%; expected return rate, 10%.	
Actual return on assets in 2003	48,000
Amortization of prior service cost	25,000
Market-related asset value at 1/1/03	550,000
Contributions in 2003	138,000
Benefits paid retirees in 2003	85,000
Average remaining service life of active employees	10 years
Accumulated benefit obligation at 12/31/03	671,000

Instructions
Using the preceding data, compute pension expense for Farrey Corp. for the year 2003 by preparing a pension work sheet that shows the journal entry for pension expense and any additional pension liability. (The minimum pension liability must be computed and the corridor approach must be applied to the unrecognized gain or loss.) Use the market related asset value to compute the expected return.

P21-8 (Comprehensive 2-Year Work Sheet) Glesen Company sponsors a defined benefit pension plan for its employees. The following data relate to the operation of the plan for the years 2002 and 2003:

	2002	2003
Projected benefit obligation, January 1	$650,000	
Plan assets (fair value and market related value), January 1	410,000	
Prepaid/accrued pension cost (credit), January 1	80,000	
Additional pension liability, January 1	12,300	
Intangible asset-deferred pension cost, January 1	12,300	
Unrecognized prior service cost, January 1	160,000	
Service cost	40,000	$ 59,000
Settlement rate	10%	10%
Expected rate of return	10%	10%
Actual return on plan assets	36,000	61,000
Amortization of prior service cost	70,000	55,000

Annual contributions	72,000	81,000
Benefits paid retirees	31,500	54,000
Increase in projected benefit obligation due to changes in actuarial assumptions	87,000	–0–
Accumulated benefit obligation at December 31	721,800	789,000
Average service life of all employees		20 years
Vested benefit obligation at December 31		464,000

Instructions

(a) Prepare a pension work sheet presenting both years 2002 and 2003 and accompanying computations including the computation of the minimum liability (2002 and 2003) and amortization of the unrecognized loss (2003) using the corridor approach.

(b) Prepare the journal entries (from the work sheet) to reflect all pension plan transactions and events at December 31 of each year.

(c) At December 31, 2003, prepare a schedule reconciling the funded status of the pension plan with the pension amounts reported in the financial statements.

P21-9 (Comprehensive Pension Work Sheet) Connie Harpin was recently promoted to assistant controller of Glomski Corporation, having previously served Glomski as a staff accountant. One of the responsibilities of her new position is to prepare the annual pension accrual. Judy Gralapp, the corporate controller, provided Harpin with last year's workpapers and information from the actuary's annual report. The pension work sheet for the prior year is presented below.

	Journal Entry			**Memo Records**		
	Pension Expense	Cash	Prepaid (Accrued) Cost	Projected Benefit Obligation	Plan Assets	Unrecognized Prior Service Cost
June 1, 2001[1]				$(20,000)	$20,000	
Service cost[1]	$1,800			(1,800)		
Interest[2]	1,200			(1,200)		
Actual return[3]	(1,600)				1,600	
Contribution[1]		$(1,000)			1,000	
Benefits paid[1]				900	(900)	
Prior service cost[4]				(2,000)		$2,000
Journal entry	$1,400	$(1,000)	$(400)			
May 31, 2002, balance			$(400)	$(24,100)	$21,700	$2,000

[1]Per actuary's report.
[2]Beginning projected benefit obligation × settlement rate of 6%.
[3]Expected return was $1,600 (beginning plan assets × expected return of 8%).
[4]A plan amendment that granted employees retroactive benefits for work performed in earlier periods took effect on May 31, 2002. The amendment increased the May 31, 2002, projected benefit obligation by $2,000. No amortization was recorded in the fiscal year ended May 31, 2002.

Pertinent information from the actuary's report for the year ended May 31, 2003, is presented below. The report indicated no actuarial gains or losses in the fiscal year ended May 31, 2003.

Contribution	$ 425	Actual return on plan assets	$ 1,736
Service cost	$ 3,000	Benefits paid	$ 500
Settlement rate	6%	Average remaining service life	10 years
Expected return	8%	Fair value plan assets 5-31-02	$21,700
Accumulated benefit obligation 5-31-02	$21,000	Fair value plan assets 5-31-03	$23,361
Accumulated benefit obligation 5-31-03	$27,000		

When briefing Harpin, Gralapp indicated that the prior service cost is to be amortized over the average remaining service life. Gralapp also informed her that, in the current year, there will be an initial adoption of minimum pension liability reporting.

Instructions

(a) Prepare the pension worksheet for Glomski Corporation for the year ended May 31, 2003.

(b) Prepare the journal entries required to reflect the accounting for Glomski Corporation's pension plan for the year ended May 31, 2003.

(c) If the additional pension liability and the unrecognized prior service cost were $3,700 and $1,800, respectively, at May 31, 2003, explain how Glomski Corporation would report the $3,700 in its financial statements.

P21-10 **(Comprehensive 2-Year Work Sheet)** Ingrid Mount Co. has the following defined benefit pension plan balances on January 1, 2000:

Projected benefit obligation	$4,500,000
Fair value of plan assets	4,500,000

The interest (settlement) rate applicable to the plan is 10%. On January 1, 2001, the company amends its pension agreement so that prior service costs of $600,000 are created. Other data related to the pension plan are:

	2000	2001
Service costs	$150,000	$170,000
Unrecognized prior service costs amortization	–0–	90,000
Contributions (funding) to the plan	150,000	184,658
Benefits paid	220,000	280,000
Actual return on plan assets	252,000	250,000
Expected rate of return on assets	6%	8%

Instructions

(a) Prepare a pension work sheet for the pension plan in 2000.

(b) Prepare any journal entries related to the pension plan that would be needed at December 31, 2000.

(c) Prepare a pension work sheet for 2001 and any journal entries related to the pension plan as of December 31, 2001.

(d) As of December 31, 2001, prepare a schedule reconciling the funded status with the reported liability (accrued pension cost).

*P21-11 **(Postretirement Benefit Work Sheet with Reconciliation)** Dusty Hass Foods Inc. sponsors a postretirement medical and dental benefit plan for its employees. The company adopts the provisions of *Statement No. 106* beginning January 1, 2002. The following balances relate to this plan on January 1, 2002.

Plan assets	$ 200,000
Expected postretirement benefit obligation	1,420,000
Accumulated postretirement benefit obligation	882,000
No prior service costs exist.	

As a result of the plan's operation during 2002, the following additional data are provided by the actuary:

Service cost for 2002 is $70,000
Discount rate is 9%
Contributions to plan in 2002 are $60,000
Expected return on plan assets is $9,000
Actual return on plan assets is $15,000
Benefits paid to employees from plan are $44,000
Average remaining service to full eligibility: 20 years
Average remaining service to expected retirement: 22 years
Transition amount to be amortized: ?

Instructions

(a) Using the preceding data, compute the net periodic postretirement benefit cost for 2002 by preparing a work sheet that shows the journal entry for postretirement expense and the year-end balances in the related postretirement benefit memo accounts. (Assume that contributions and benefits are paid at the end of the year.)

(b) At December 31, 2002, prepare a schedule reconciling the funded status of the plan with the postretirement amount reported on the balance sheet.

CONCEPTUAL CASES

C21-1 **(Pension Terminology and Theory)** Many business organizations have been concerned with providing for the retirement of employees since the late 1800s. During recent decades a marked increase in this concern has resulted in the establishment of private pension plans in most large companies and in many medium- and small-sized ones.

The substantial growth of these plans, both in numbers of employees covered and in amounts of retirement benefits, has increased the significance of pension cost in relation to the financial position, results of operations, and cash flows of many companies. In examining the costs of pension plans, a CPA encounters certain terms. The components of pension costs that the terms represent must be dealt with appropriately if generally accepted accounting principles are to be reflected in the financial statements of entities with pension plans.

Instructions

(a) Define a private pension plan. How does a contributory pension plan differ from a noncontributory plan?

(b) Differentiate between "accounting for the employer" and "accounting for the pension fund."

(c) Explain the terms "funded" and "pension liability" as they relate to:
   (1) The pension fund.
   (2) The employer.

(d) (1) Discuss the theoretical justification for accrual recognition of pension costs.
   (2) Discuss the relative objectivity of the measurement process of accrual versus cash (pay-as-you-go) accounting for annual pension costs.

(e) Distinguish among the following as they relate to pension plans:
   (1) Service cost.
   (2) Prior service costs.
   (3) Actuarial funding methods.
   (4) Vested benefits.

C21-2 (Pension Terminology) The following items appear on Hollingsworth Company's financial statements.

1. Under the caption Assets:
   Prepaid pension cost.
   Intangible asset—Deferred pension cost.
2. Under the caption Liabilities:
   Accrued pension cost.
3. Under the caption Stockholders' Equity:
   Excess of additional pension liability over unrecognized prior service cost as a component of Accumulated Other Comprehensive Income.
4. On the income statement:
   Pension expense.

Instructions

Explain the significance of each of the items above on corporate financial statements. (*Note:* All items set forth above are not necessarily to be found on the statements of a single company.)

C21-3 (Basic Terminology) In examining the costs of pension plans, Leah Hutcherson, CPA, encounters certain terms. The components of pension costs that the terms represent must be dealt with appropriately if generally accepted accounting principles are to be reflected in the financial statements of entities with pension plans.

Instructions

(a) (1) Discuss the theoretical justification for accrual recognition of pension costs.
   (2) Discuss the relative objectivity of the measurement process of accrual versus cash (pay-as-you-go) accounting for annual pension costs.

(b) Explain the following terms as they apply to accounting for pension plans:
   (1) Market-related asset value.
   (2) Actuarial funding methods.
   (3) Projected benefit obligation.
   (4) Corridor approach.

(c) What information should be disclosed about a company's pension plans in its financial statements and its notes?

(AICPA adapted)

C21-4 (Basic Concepts of Pension Reporting) Helen Kaufman, president of Express Mail Inc., is discussing the possibility of developing a pension plan for its employees with Esther Knox, controller, and Jason Nihles, assistant controller. Their conversation is as follows:

HELEN KAUFMAN: If we are going to compete with our competitors, we must have a pension plan to attract good talent.

ESTHER KNOX: I must warn you, Helen, that a pension plan will take a large bit out of our income. The only reason why we have been so profitable is the lack of a pension cost in our income statement. In some of our competitors' cases, pension expense is 30% of pretax income.

JASON NIHLES: Why do we have to worry about a pension cost now anyway? Benefits do not vest until after 10 years of service. If they do not vest, then we are not liable. We should not have to report an expense until we are legally liable to provide benefits.

HELEN KAUFMAN: But, Jason, the employees would want credit for prior service with full vesting 10 years after starting service, not 10 years after starting the plan. How would we allocate the large prior service cost?

JASON NIHLES: Well, I believe that the prior service cost is a cost of providing a pension plan for employees forever. It is an intangible asset that will not diminish in value because it will increase the morale of our present and future employees and provide us with a competitive edge in acquiring future employees.

HELEN KAUFMAN: I hate to disagree, but I believe the prior service cost is a benefit only to the present employees. This prior service is directly related to the composition of the employee group at the time the plan is initiated and is in no way related to any intangible benefit received by the company because of the plan's existence. Therefore, I propose that the prior service cost be amortized over the remaining lives of the existing employees.

ESTHER KNOX (somewhat perturbed): But what about the income statement? You two are arguing theory without consideration of our income figure.

HELEN KAUFMAN: Settle down, Esther.

ESTHER KNOX: Sorry, perhaps Jason's approach to resolving this approach is the best one. I am just not sure.

Instructions

(a) Assuming that Express Mail Inc. establishes a pension plan, how should their liability for pensions be computed in the first year?
(b) How should their liability be computed in subsequent years?
(c) How should pension expense be computed each year?
(d) Assuming that the pension fund is set up in a trusteed relationship, should the assets of the fund be reported on the books of Express Mail Inc.?
(e) What interest rate factor should be used in the present value computations?
(f) How should gains and losses be reported?

C21-5 (Major Pension Concepts) Lyons Corporation is a medium-sized manufacturer of paperboard containers and boxes. The corporation sponsors a noncontributory, defined benefit pension plan that covers its 250 employees. Spring Meissner has recently been hired as president of Lyons Corporation. While reviewing last year's financial statements with Sara Montgomery, controller, Meissner expressed confusion about several of the items in the footnote to the financial statements relating to the pension plan. In part, the footnote reads as follows.

> **Note J.** The company has a defined benefit pension plan covering substantially all of its employees. The benefits are based on years of service and the employee's compensation during the last four years of employment. The company's funding policy is to contribute annually the maximum amount allowed under the federal tax code. Contributions are intended to provide for benefits expected to be earned in the future as well as those earned to date.

Effective for the year ending December 31, 2001, Lyons Corporation adopted the provisions of *Statement of Financial Accounting Standard No. 87*—Employer's Accounting for Pensions. The net periodic pension expense on Lyons Corporation's comparative Income Statement was $72,000 in 2002 and $57,680 in 2001.

The following are selected figures from the plan's funded status and amount recognized in the Lyons Corporation's Statement of Financial Position at December 31, 2002 ($000 omitted):

Actuarial present value of benefit obligations:	
Accumulated benefit obligation	
(including vested benefits of $636)	$ (870)
Projected benefit obligation	$(1,200)
Plan assets at fair value	1,050
Projected benefit obligation in	
excess of plan assets	$ (150)

Given that Lyons Corporation's work force has been stable for the last 6 years, Meissner could not understand the increase in the net periodic pension expense. Montgomery explained that the net periodic pension expense consists of several elements, some of which may decrease of the net expense.

Instructions

(a) The determination of the net periodic pension expense is a function of five elements. List and briefly describe each of the elements.

(b) Describe the major difference and the major similarity between the accumulated benefit obligation and the projected benefit obligation.

(c) **(1)** Explain why pension gains and losses are not recognized on the income statement in the period in which they arise.

  (2) Briefly describe how pension gains and losses are recognized.

(d) Under what conditions must Lyons recognize an additional minimum liability?

(CMA adapted)

C21-6 **(Implications of *FASB Statement No. 87*)** Ruth Moore and Carl Nies have to do a class presentation on the pension pronouncement "Employers' Accounting for Pension Plans." In developing the class presentation, they decided to provide the class with a series of questions related to pensions and then discuss the answers in class. Given that the class has all read *FASB Statement No. 87,* they felt this approach would provide a lively discussion. Here are the situations:

1. In an article in *Business Week* prior to *FASB No. 87,* it was reported that the discount rates used by the largest 200 companies for pension reporting ranged from 5 to 11%. How can such a situation exist, and does the new pension pronouncement alleviate this problem?

2. An article indicated that when *FASB Statement No. 87* was issued, it caused an increase in the liability for pensions for approximately 20% of companies. Why might this situation occur?

3. A recent article noted that while "smoothing" is not necessarily an accounting virtue, pension accounting has long been recognized as an exception—an area of accounting in which at least some dampening of market swings is appropriate. This is because pension funds are managed so that their performance is insulated from the extremes of short-term market swings. A pension expense that reflects the volatility of market swings might, for that reason, convey information of little relevance. Are these statements true?

4. Companies as diverse as American Hospital Supply, Ashland Oil, Digital Equipment, GTE, Ralston Purina, and Signal Cos. held assets twice as large as they needed to fund their pension plans at one time. Are these assets reported on the balance sheet of these companies per the pension pronouncement? If not, where are they reported?

5. Understanding the impact of the changes required in pension reporting requires detailed information about its pension plan(s) and an analysis of the relationship of many factors, particularly:
   (a) the type of plan(s) and any significant amendments.
   (b) the plan participants.
   (c) the funding status.
   (d) the actuarial funding method and assumptions currently used.
   What impact does each of these items have on financial statement presentation?

6. An article noted "You also need to decide whether to amortize gains and losses using the corridor method, or to use some other systematic method. Under the corridor approach, only gains and losses in excess of 10% of the greater of the projected benefit obligation or the plan assets would have to be amortized." What is the corridor method and what is its purpose?

7. Some companies may have to establish an intangible asset-deferred pension cost if the plan assets at fair value are less than the accumulated benefit obligation. What is the nature of this intangible asset and how is it amortized each period?

8. In its exposure draft on pensions, the Board required a note that discussed the sensitivity of pension expense to changes in the interest rate and the salary progression assumption. This note might read as follows:

At December 31, 2001, the weighted-average discount rate and rate of increase in future compensation levels used in determining the actuarial present value of the projected benefit obligation were 9% and 6%, respectively. Those assumptions can have a significant effect on the amounts reported. To illustrate, increasing the discount rate assumption to 10% would have decreased the projected benefit obligation and net periodic pension expense by $340,000 and $50,000, respectively, for the year ended December 31, 2001. Increasing the rate of change of future compensation levels to 7% would have increased the projected benefit obligation and net periodic pension cost by $180,000 and $30,000, respectively, for the year ended December 31, 2001.

Why do you believe this disclosure was eliminated from the final pronouncement?

Instructions

What answers do you believe Ruth and Carl gave to each of these questions?

C21-7 **(Unrecognized Gains and Losses, Corridor Amortization)** Rachel Avery, accounting clerk in the personnel office of Clarence G. Avery Corp., has begun to compute pension expense for 2001 but is not sure whether or not she should include the amortization of unrecognized gains/losses. She is currently working with the following beginning-of-the-year present values for the projected benefit obligation and market-related values for the pension plan:

	Projected Benefit Obligation	Plan Assets Value
1998	$2,200,000	$1,900,000
1999	2,400,000	2,600,000
2000	2,900,000	2,600,000
2001	3,900,000	3,000,000

The average remaining service life per employee in 1998 and 1999 is 10 years and in 2000 and 2001 is 12 years. The unrecognized net gain or loss that occurred during each year is as follows:

1998	$280,000 loss
1999	90,000 loss
2000	12,000 loss
2001	25,000 gain

(In working the solution, you must aggregate the unrecognized gains and losses to arrive at year-end balances.)

Instructions

You are the manager in charge of accounting. Write a memo to Rachel Avery, explaining why in some years she must amortize some of the unrecognized net gains and losses and in other years she does not need to. In order to explain this situation fully, you must compute the amount of unrecognized net gain or loss that is amortized and charged to pension expense in each of the 4 years listed above. Include an appropriate amortization schedule, referring to it whenever necessary.

USING YOUR JUDGMENT

FINANCIAL REPORTING PROBLEM: INTEL CORPORATION

Instructions

Refer to the financial statements and accompanying notes and discussion of Intel Corporation presented in Appendix 5B and answer the following questions.

(a) What kind of pension plan does Intel provide its employees in the United States (and Puerto Rico)? What does the plan provide employees?

(b) What was Intel's pension expense for 1998, 1997, and 1996 for the U.S. and Puerto Rico plans?

(c) What is the impact of Intel's pension plans on its financial statements?

(d) If you were an employee at Intel, would you be happy with the benefit package? Explain.

FINANCIAL STATEMENT ANALYSIS CASE

*General Electric

A *Wall Street Journal* article discussed a $1.8 billion charge to income made by General Electric for postretirement benefit costs. It was attributed to previously unrecognized health-care and life insurance cost. As financial vice president and controller for Peake, Inc., you found this article interesting because the president recently expressed concern about the company's rising health costs. The president, Martha Beyerlein, was particularly concerned with health care cost premiums being paid for retired employees. She wondered what charge Peake, Inc. will have to take for its postretirement benefit program.

Instructions

As financial vice president and controller of Peake, Inc., explain what the charge was that General Electric made against income and what the options are for Peake, Inc. in accounting for and reporting any transition amount when it adopts *FASB Statement No. 106*.

COMPARATIVE ANALYSIS CASE

The Coca-Cola Company versus PepsiCo, Inc.

Instructions

Go to the Digital Tool and, using The Coca-Cola Company and PepsiCo, Inc. Annual Report information, answer the following questions:

(a) What kind of pension plans do Coca-Cola and PepsiCo provide their employees?

(b) What are the pension plan funding policies of Coca-Cola and PepsiCo?

(c) What net periodic pension expense (cost) did Coca-Cola and PepsiCo report in 1998?

(d) What is the year-end 1998 funded status of Coca-Cola's and PepsiCo's U.S. plans?

(e) What relevant rates were used by Coca-Cola and PepsiCo in computing their pension amounts?

RESEARCH CASES

Case 1

Instructions

Examine the pension footnotes of three companies of your choice and answer the following questions.

(a) For each company, identify the following three assumptions: (1) the weighted-average discount rate, (2) the rate of compensation increase used to measure the projected benefit obligation, and (3) the weighted-average expected long-run rate of return on plan assets.

(b) Comment on any significant differences between the assumptions used by each firm.

(c) Did any of the companies change their assumptions during the period covered by the footnote? If so, what was the effect on the financial statements?

Case 2

The December 1995 issue of *Accounting Horizons* includes an article by Alan I. Blankley and Edward P. Swanson entitled "A Longitudinal Study of *SFAS 87* Pension Rate Assumptions." The article represents an excellent example of how academic research can address controversial accounting issues.

Instructions

Read the "introduction" section of the article and answer the following questions.

(a) According to the business press, firms are manipulating estimates of expected rates of return on plan assets and discount rates. What are the effects of these alleged manipulations?

(b) What was the reaction of the Securities and Exchange Commission?

(c) What is the purpose of the article? How did the authors obtain the data used in their study?

(d) What are the authors' major conclusions?

INTERNATIONAL REPORTING CASE

Volvo, a Swedish company that operates in the automotive and transport equipment industry, prepares its financial statements in accordance with Swedish accounting standards. In 1998, Volvo had income of 8,638 million SEK (Swedish Kronor) with assets of 204,426 million SEK at December 31, 1998. Volvo sponsors a pension plan for its employees in Sweden and the U.S. and provided the following disclosure related to its pension provisions in the notes to its financial statements:

VOLVO

Note 22: Provisions for postemployment benefits

	1996	1997	1998
Provisions for pensions	1,937	1,905	1,451
Provisions for other postemployment benefits	1,213	1,391	1,485
Total	3,150	3,296	2,936

The amounts shown for Provisions for postemployment benefits correspond to the actuarially calculated value of obligations not insured with a third party or secured through transfers of funds to pension foundations. The amount of pensions falling due within one year is included. The Swedish Group companies have insured their pension obligations with third parties. Group pension costs in 1998 amounted to 3,567. The greater part of pension costs consist of continuing payments to independent organizations that administer pension plans. Assets in pension foundations at market value exceeded the corresponding pension obligations by 425.

Volvo's shares trade on the NASDAQ in the United States (and on several European stock exchanges as well). As a consequence of listing its shares in the U.S., Volvo provides additional disclosure in its notes on the differences in accounting for its pension plans under U.S. and Swedish accounting standards. If Volvo had applied U.S. GAAP to its pensions, income would have been 313 million SEK higher in 1998, and stockholders' equity would have been 1,548 higher at December 31, 1998. The following excerpt about pension accounting differences between the U.S. and Sweden was taken from Volvo's notes.

> **Significant differences between Swedish and U.S. accounting principles**
> **Note J:** *Provision for pensions and other postemployment benefits.* The greater part of the Volvo Group's pension commitments are defined contribution plans; that is, they are met through regular payments to independent authorities or organs that administer pension plans. There is no difference between U.S. and Swedish accounting principles in accounting for these pension plans.
>
> Other pension commitments are defined benefit plans; that is, the employee is entitled to receive a certain level of pension, usually related to the employee's final salary. In these cases the annual pension cost is calculated based on the current value of future pension payments. In Volvo's consolidated accounts, provisions for pensions and pension costs for the year in the individual companies are calculated based on local rules and directives. In accordance with U.S. GAAP provisions for pensions and pension costs for the year should always be calculated as specified in SFAS 87, "Employers Accounting for Pensions". The difference lies primarily in the choice of discount rates and the circumstance that U.S. calculations of capital-valuation, in contrast to the Swedish, are based on salaries calculated at time of retirement.

Instructions

Use the information on Volvo to respond to the following requirements.

(a) What are the key differences in accounting for pensions under U.S. and Swedish standards?

(b) Briefly explain how differences in U.S. and Swedish standards for pensions would affect the amounts reported in the financial statements.

(c) In light of the differences identified above, what are the likely reason(s) that Volvo's income and equity would be higher under U.S. GAAP than under Swedish accounting standards?

ETHICS CASES

Case 1

Cardinal Technology recently merged with College Electronix, a computer graphics manufacturing firm. In performing a comprehensive audit of CE's accounting system, Richard Nye, internal audit manager for Cardinal Technology, discovered that the new subsidiary did not capitalize pension assets and liabilities, subject to the requirements of *FASB Statement No. 87*.

The net present value of CE's pension assets was $15.5 million, the vested benefit obligation was $12.9 million, and the projected benefit obligation was $17.4 million. Nye reported this audit finding to Renée Selma, the newly appointed controller of CE. A few days later Selma called Nye for his advice on what to do. Selma started her conversation by asking, "Can't we eliminate the negative income effect of our pension dilemma simply by terminating the employment of nonvested employees before the end of our fiscal year?"

Instructions

Answer the following question:

How should Nye respond to Selma's remark about firing nonvested employees?

Case 2

Philip Regan, Chief Executive Officer of Relief Dynamics Inc., a large defense contracting firm, is considering ways to improve the company's financial position after several years of sharply declining profitability. One way to do this is to reduce or completely eliminate Relief's commitment to present and future retirees who have full medical and dental benefits coverage. Despite financial problems, Relief still is committed to providing excellent pension benefits.

Instructions

Answer the following questions:

(a) What factors should Regan consider before making his decision to cut postretirement health benefits?

(b) Does your answer to the above question change if Relief Dynamics was paying Phil Regan, CEO, a salary of $30 million per year?

(c) In your opinion, how did FASB's *Statement No. 106* influence the commitment of many organizations to its employees?

CHAPTER 22

Accounting for Leases

More Companies Ask "Why Buy?"

Leasing has grown tremendously in popularity and today is the fastest growing form of capital investment. Instead of borrowing money to buy an airplane, a computer, a nuclear core, or a satellite, a company leases it. Even the gambling casinos lease their slot machines. Airlines and railroads lease huge amounts of equipment; many hotel and motel chains lease their facilities; and most retail chains lease the bulk of their retail premises and warehouses. The popularity of leasing is evidenced in the fact that 541 of 600 companies surveyed by the AICPA in 1999 disclosed lease data.[1]

A classic example is the airline industry. Many travelers on airlines such as **United**, **Delta**, and **Southwest** believe the planes they are flying are owned by these airlines. But in many cases nothing could be further from the truth. Here are the lease percentages for the major U.S. airlines.

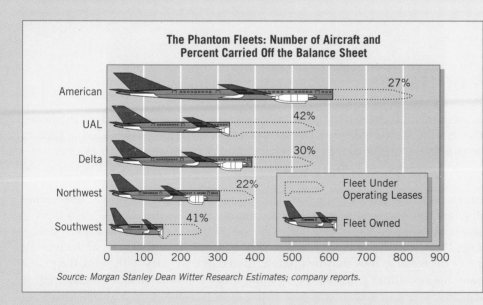

The Phantom Fleets: Number of Aircraft and Percent Carried Off the Balance Sheet

American — 27%
UAL — 42%
Delta — 30%
Northwest — 22%
Southwest — 41%

0   100   200   300   400   500   600   700   800   900

Fleet Under Operating Leases
Fleet Owned

Source: Morgan Stanley Dean Witter Research Estimates; company reports.

Why do airline companies lease many of their airplanes? One reason is the favorable accounting treatment that airlines receive if they lease rather than purchase. By not reporting the airplane and related borrowing on their balance sheets, companies lower their debt to equity ratios. In addition, companies that lease often report higher net income in the earlier years of the life of the airplane.

---

[1] AICPA, *Accounting Trends and Techniques—1999.*

LEARNING OBJECTIVES

After studying this chapter, you should be able to:

1. Explain the nature, economic substance, and advantages of lease transactions.

2. Describe the accounting criteria and procedures for capitalizing leases by the lessee.

3. Contrast the operating and capitalization methods of recording leases.

4. Identify the classifications of leases for the lessor.

5. Describe the lessor's accounting for direct financing leases.

6. Identify special features of lease arrangements that cause unique accounting problems.

7. Describe the effect of residual values, guaranteed and unguaranteed, on lease accounting.

8. Describe the lessor's accounting for sales-type leases.

9. Describe the disclosure requirements for leases.

Because of the increased significance and prevalence of lease arrangements indicated in the opening story, the need for uniform accounting and complete informative reporting of these transactions has intensified. In this chapter, we will look at the accounting issues related to leasing. The content and organization of this chapter are as follows:

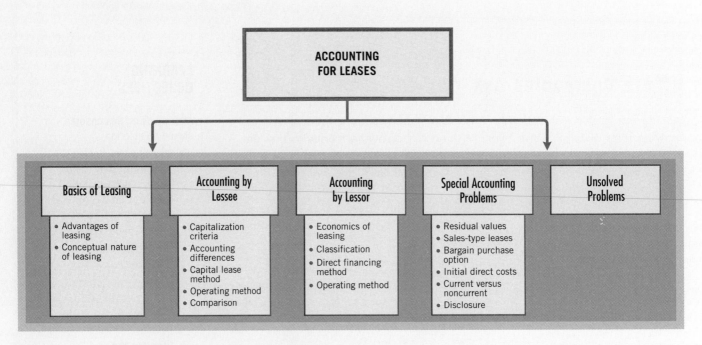

BASICS OF LEASING

OBJECTIVE 1
Explain the nature, economic substance, and advantages of lease transactions.

A **lease** is a contractual agreement between a **lessor** and a **lessee** that gives the lessee the right to use specific property, owned by the lessor, for a specified period of time in return for stipulated, and generally periodic, cash payments (rents). An essential element of the lease agreement is that the lessor conveys less than the total interest in the property.

Because a lease is a contract, the provisions agreed to by the lessor and lessee may vary widely and may be limited only by their ingenuity. The **duration**—lease term—of the lease may be anything from a short period of time to the entire expected economic life of the asset. The **rental payments** may be level from year to year, increasing in amount, or decreasing; they may be predetermined or may vary with sales, the prime interest rate, the consumer price index, or some other factor. In most cases the rent is set to enable the lessor to recover the cost of the asset plus a fair return over the life of the lease.

The **obligations for taxes, insurance, and maintenance** (executory costs) may be assumed by either the lessor or the lessee, or they may be divided. **Restrictions** comparable to bond indentures may limit the lessee's activities regarding dividend payments or the incurrence of further debt and lease obligations in order to protect the lessor from default on the rents. The lease contract may be **noncancelable** or may grant the right to **early termination** on payment of a set scale of prices plus a penalty. In case of **default**, the lessee may be liable for all future payments at once, receiving title to the property in exchange; or the lessor may have the right to sell to a third party and collect from the lessee all or a portion of the difference between the sale price and the lessor's unrecovered cost.

Alternatives for the lessee at termination of the lease may range from none to the right to purchase the leased asset at the fair market value or the right to renew or buy at a nominal price.

Advantages of Leasing

Although leasing is not without its disadvantages, the growth in its use suggests that it often has a genuine advantage over owning property. Some of the commonly discussed advantages to the lessee of leasing are:

❶ *100% Financing at Fixed Rates.* Leases are often signed without requiring any money down from the lessee, which helps to conserve scarce cash—an especially desirable feature for new and developing companies. In addition, lease payments often remain fixed, which protects the lessee against inflation and increases in the cost of money. The following comment regarding a conventional loan is typical: "Our local bank finally came up to 80% of the purchase price but wouldn't go any higher, and they wanted a floating interest rate. We just couldn't afford the down payment and we needed to lock in a final payment rate we knew we could live with."

❷ *Protection against Obsolescence.* Leasing equipment reduces risk of obsolescence to the lessee, and in many cases passes the risk of residual value to the lessor. For example, Syntex Corp. (a pharmaceutical maker) leases computers. Syntex is permitted under the lease agreement to turn in an old computer for a new model at any time, canceling the old lease and writing a new one. The cost of the new lease is added to the balance due on the old lease, less the old computer's trade-in value. As the treasurer of Syntex remarked, "Our instinct is to purchase." But if a new computer comes along in a short time "then leasing is just a heck of a lot more convenient than purchasing."

❸ *Flexibility.* Lease agreements may contain less restrictive provisions than other debt agreements. Innovative lessors can tailor a lease agreement to the lessee's special needs. For instance, rental payments can be structured to meet the timing of cash revenues generated by the equipment so that payments are made when the equipment is productive.

❹ *Less Costly Financing.* Some companies find leasing cheaper than other forms of financing. For example, start-up companies in depressed industries, or companies in low tax brackets may lease as a way of claiming tax benefits that might otherwise be lost. Depreciation deductions offer no benefit to companies that have little if any taxable income. Through leasing, these tax benefits are used by the leasing companies or financial institutions, which can pass some of these tax benefits back to the user of the asset in the form of lower rental payments.

❺ *Alternative Minimum Tax Problems.* As indicated in Chapter 20, all companies are subject to an alternative minimum tax (AMT). Under the AMT rules, a portion of accelerated depreciation deductions are considered tax preference items that are added to a company's regular taxable income to arrive at the alternative minimum taxable income (AMTI). The company must pay whichever is higher—the regular tax or the AMT. Since ownership of equipment can contribute to an increase in AMTI and, ultimately, to an alternative minimum tax liability in excess of the regular tax liability, companies often find leasing a way to avoid the onerous alternative tax provisions.

❻ *Off-Balance-Sheet Financing.* Certain leases do not add debt on a balance sheet or affect financial ratios, and they may add to borrowing capacity.[2] Such **off-balance-**

INTERNATIONAL INSIGHT

Some companies double dip. That is, the leasing rules of the lessor's and lessee's countries may be different, permitting both parties to be an owner of the asset. Thus, both lessor and lessee receive the tax benefits related to depreciation. By structuring the lease to take advantage of these international differences, both the lessee and lessor benefit.

---

[2]As demonstrated later in this chapter, certain types of lease arrangements are not capitalized on the balance sheet. The liability section is thereby relieved of large future lease commitments that, if recorded, would adversely affect the debt-to-equity ratio. The reluctance to record lease obligations as liabilities is one of the primary reasons capitalized lease accounting is resisted. For an excellent discussion on the effects of the failure to capitalize long-term lease commitments, see Eugene A. Imhoff, Jr., Robert C. Lipe, and David W. Wright, "Operating Leases: Impact of Constructive Capitalization," *Accounting Horizons,* March 1991.

sheet financing is critical to some companies. For example, as shown in our opening story, the airlines use lease arrangements extensively, which results in a great deal of off-balance-sheet financing. Illustration 22-1 indicates that debt levels are understated by a substantial amount for many airlines that lease aircraft.

ILLUSTRATION 22-1
Net Reported Debt and
Debt Adjustment of
Leases, 1997

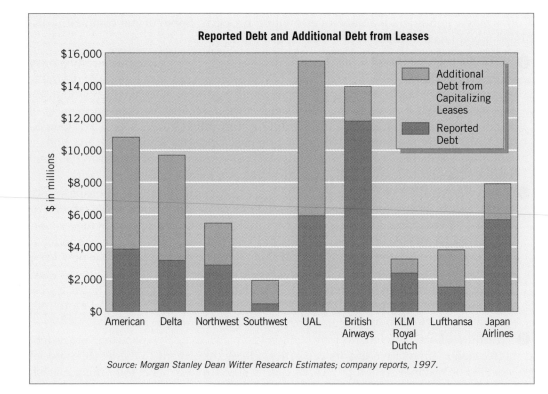

Conceptual Nature of a Lease

If United Airlines borrows $47 million on a 10-year note from National City Bank to purchase a Boeing 757 jet plane, it is clear that an asset and related liability should be reported on United's balance sheet at that amount. If United purchases the 757 for $47,000,000 directly from Boeing through an installment purchase over 10 years, it is equally clear that an asset and related liability should be reported (i.e., the installment transaction should be "capitalized"). However, if United **leases** the Boeing 757 for 10 years through a noncancelable lease transaction with payments of the same amount as the installment purchase transaction, differences of opinion start to develop over how this transaction should be reported. The various views on **capitalization of leases** are as follows:

❶ *Do Not Capitalize Any Leased Assets.* Because the lessee does not have ownership of the property, capitalization is considered inappropriate. Furthermore, a lease is an "executory" contract requiring continuing performance by both parties. Because other executory contracts (such as purchase commitments and employment contracts) are not capitalized at present, leases should not be capitalized, either.

❷ *Capitalize Leases That Are Similar to Installment Purchases.* Accountants should report transactions in accordance with their economic substance; therefore, if installment purchases are capitalized, so also should leases that have similar characteristics. For example, United Airlines is committed to the same payments over a 10-year period for either a lease or an installment purchase; lessees make rental payments, whereas owners make mortgage payments. Why shouldn't the financial statements report these transactions in the same manner?

❸ *Capitalize All Long-Term Leases.* Under this approach, the only requirement for capitalization is the long-term right to use the property. This property-rights approach capitalizes all long-term leases.[3]

❹ *Capitalize Firm Leases Where the Penalty for Nonperformance Is Substantial.* A final approach is to capitalize only "firm" (noncancelable) contractual rights and obligations. "Firm" means that it is unlikely that performance under the lease can be avoided without a severe penalty.[4]

UNDERLYING CONCEPTS
The issue of how to report leases is the classic case of substance versus form. Although technically legal title does not pass in lease transactions, the benefits from the use of the property do transfer.

In short, the various viewpoints range from no capitalization to capitalization of all leases. The FASB apparently agrees with the capitalization approach when the lease is similar to an installment purchase, noting that **a lease that transfers substantially all of the benefits and risks of property ownership should be capitalized**. Transfer of ownership can be assumed only if there is a high degree of performance to the transfer, that is, the lease is noncancelable. Noncancelable means that the lease contract is cancelable only upon the outcome of some remote contingency or that the cancellation provisions and penalties of the contract are so costly to the lessee that cancellation probably will not occur. Only noncancelable leases may be capitalized.

This viewpoint leads to three basic conclusions: (1) The characteristics that indicate that substantially all of the benefits and risks of ownership have been transferred must be identified. (2) The same characteristics should apply consistently to the lessee and the lessor. (3) Those leases that do **not** transfer substantially all the benefits and risks of ownership are operating leases. They should not be capitalized but rather accounted for as rental payments and receipts.

ACCOUNTING BY LESSEE

If a lessee **capitalizes** a lease, the **lessee** records an asset and a liability generally equal to the present value of the rental payments. **The lessor**, having transferred substantially all the benefits and risks of ownership, recognizes a sale by removing the asset from the balance sheet and replacing it with a receivable. The typical journal entries for the lessee and the lessor, assuming equipment is leased and is capitalized, appear as follows:

OBJECTIVE ❷
Describe the accounting criteria and procedures for capitalizing leases by the lessee.

Lessee			Lessor		
Leased Equipment	XXX		Lease Receivable (net)	XXX	
Lease Obligation		XXX	Equipment		XXX

ILLUSTRATION 22-2
Journal Entries for Capitalized Lease

Having capitalized the asset, the lessee records the depreciation. The lessor and lessee treat the lease rental payments as consisting of interest and principal.

If the lease is not capitalized, no asset is recorded by the lessee and no asset is removed from the lessor's books. When a lease payment is made, the lessee records rental expense and the lessor recognizes rental revenue.

For a lease to be recorded as a capital lease, the lease must be noncancelable, and meet one or more of the following four criteria:

---

[3]The property rights approach was originally recommended in a research study by the AICPA: John H. Myers, "Reporting of Leases in Financial Statements," *Accounting Research Study No. 4* (New York: AICPA, 1964), pp. 10–11. Recently, this view has received additional support. See Peter H. Knutson, "Financial Reporting in the 1990s and Beyond," Position Paper (Charlottesville, Va.: AIMR, 1993), and Warren McGregor, "Accounting for Leases: A New Approach," Special Report (Norwalk, Conn.: FASB, 1996).

[4]Yuji Ijiri, *Recognition of Contractual Rights and Obligations*, Research Report (Stamford, Conn.: FASB, 1980).

ILLUSTRATION 22-3
Capitalization Criteria
for Lessee

> **Capitalization Criteria (Lessee)**
> - The lease transfers ownership of the property to the lessee.
> - The lease contains a bargain purchase option.[5]
> - The lease term is equal to 75% or more of the estimated economic life of the leased property.
> - The present value of the minimum lease payments (excluding executory costs) equals or exceeds 90% of the fair value of the leased property.[6]

ILLUSTRATION 22-4
Diagram of Lessee's
Criteria for Lease
Classification

Leases that **do not meet any of the four criteria** are classified and accounted for by the lessee as **operating leases**. Illustration 22-4 shows that a lease meeting any one of the four criteria results in the lessee having a capital lease.

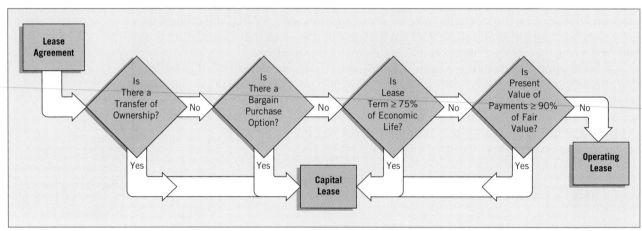

In keeping with the FASB's reasoning that a significant portion of the value of the asset is consumed in the first 75% of its life, neither the third nor the fourth criterion is to be applied when the inception of the lease occurs during the last 25% of the life of the asset.

Capitalization Criteria

The four **capitalization criteria** that apply to lessees are controversial and can be difficult to apply in practice. They are discussed in detail in the following pages.

Transfer of Ownership Test

If the lease transfers ownership of the asset to the lessee, it is a capital lease. This criterion is not controversial and is easily implemented in practice.

Bargain Purchase Option Test

**UNDERLYING
CONCEPTS**

Capitalization of leases illustrates the necessity for good definitions. The lease fits the definition of an asset, as it gives the lessee the economic benefits that flow from the possession or the use of the asset.

A **bargain purchase option** is a provision allowing the lessee to purchase the leased property for a price that is **significantly lower** than the property's expected fair value at the date the option becomes exercisable. At the inception of the lease, the difference between the option price and the expected fair market value must be large enough to make exercise of the option reasonably assured.

For example, assume that you were to lease a Honda Accord for $599 per month for 40 months with an option to purchase for $100 at the end of the 40-month period. If the estimated fair value of the Honda Accord is $3,000 at the end of the 40 months,

---

[5]A bargain purchase option is defined in the next section.

[6]"Accounting for Leases," *FASB Statement No. 13* as amended and interpreted through May 1980 (Stamford, Conn.: FASB, 1980), par. 7.

the $100 option to purchase is clearly a bargain, and therefore capitalization is required. In other cases, the criterion may not be as easy to apply, and determining now that a certain future price is a bargain can be difficult.

Economic Life Test (75% Test)

If the lease period equals or exceeds 75% of the asset's economic life, most of the risks and rewards of ownership are transferred to the lessee, and capitalization is therefore appropriate. However, determining the lease term and the economic life of the asset can be troublesome.

The lease term is generally considered to be the fixed, noncancelable term of the lease. However, this period can be extended if a bargain renewal option is provided in the lease agreement. A bargain renewal option is a provision allowing the lessee to renew the lease for a rental that is lower than the expected fair rental at the date the option becomes exercisable. At the inception of the lease, the difference between the renewal rental and the expected fair rental must be great enough to make exercise of the option to renew reasonably assured.

For example, if a Dell PC is leased for 2 years at a rental of $100 per month and subsequently can be leased for $10 per month for another 2 years, it clearly is a bargain renewal option, and the lease term is considered to be 4 years. However, with bargain renewal options, as with bargain purchase options, it is sometimes difficult to determine what is a bargain.[7]

Determining estimated economic life can also pose problems, especially if the leased item is a specialized item or has been used for a significant period of time. For example, determining the economic life of a nuclear core is extremely difficult because it is subject to much more than normal "wear and tear." The FASB takes the position that if the lease starts during the last 25% of the life of the asset, the economic life test cannot be used as a basis to classify a lease as a capital lease.

INTERNATIONAL INSIGHT

In some nations (e.g., Italy, Japan) accounting principles do not specify criteria for capitalization of leases. In others (e.g., Sweden, Switzerland) such criteria exist, but capitalization of the leases is optional.

Recovery of Investment Test (90% Test)

If the present value of the minimum lease payments equals or exceeds 90% of the fair market value of the asset, then the leased asset should be capitalized. The rationale for this test is that if the present value of the minimum lease payments is reasonably close to the market price of the asset, the asset is effectively being purchased.

In determining the present value of the minimum lease payments, three important concepts are involved: (1) minimum lease payments, (2) executory costs, and (3) discount rate.

Minimum Lease Payments. These are payments the lessee is obligated to make or can be expected to make in connection with the leased property. Minimum lease payments include the following:

1. *Minimum Rental Payments*—Minimum payments the lessee is obligated to make to the lessor under the lease agreement. In some cases, the minimum rental payments may be equal to the minimum lease payments. However, the minimum lease payments also may include a guaranteed residual value (if any), penalty for failure to renew, or a bargain purchase option (if any), as noted on the next page.

---

[7]The original lease term is also extended for leases having the following: substantial penalties for nonrenewal; periods for which the lessor has the option to renew or extend the lease; renewal periods preceding the date a bargain purchase option becomes exercisable; and renewal periods in which any lessee guarantees of the lessor's debt are expected to be in effect or in which there will be a loan outstanding from the lessee to the lessor. The lease term, however, can never extend beyond the time a bargain purchase option becomes exercisable. "Accounting for Leases: Sale-Leaseback Transactions Involving Real Estate; Sales-Type Leases of Real Estate; Definition of the Lease Term; Initial Direct Costs of Direct Financing Leases," *Statement of Financial Accounting Standards No. 98* (Stamford, Conn.: FASB, 1988).

② *Guaranteed Residual Value*—The residual value is the estimated fair (market) value of the leased property at the end of the lease term. The lessor often transfers the risk of loss to the lessee or to a third party through a guarantee of the estimated residual value. The **guaranteed residual value** is (1) the certain or determinable amount at which the lessor has the right to require the lessee to purchase the asset or (2) the amount the lessee or the third-party guarantor guarantees the lessor will realize. If it is not guaranteed in full, the **unguaranteed residual value** is the estimated residual value exclusive of any portion guaranteed.[8]

③ *Penalty for Failure to Renew or Extend the Lease*—The amount payable that is required of the lessee if the agreement specifies that the lease must be extended or renewed and the lessee fails to do so.

④ *Bargain Purchase Option*—As indicated earlier, an option given to the lessee to purchase the equipment at the end of the lease term at a price that is fixed sufficiently below the expected fair value, so that, at the inception of the lease, purchase appears to be reasonably assured.

Executory costs (defined below) are not included in the lessee's computation of the present value of the minimum lease payments.

Executory Costs. Like most assets, leased tangible assets require the incurrence of insurance, maintenance, and tax expenses—called **executory costs**—during their economic life. If the lessor retains responsibility for the payment of these "ownership-type costs," a portion of each lease payment that represents executory costs **should be excluded** in computing the present value of the minimum lease payments because it does not represent payment on or reduction of the obligation. If the portion of the minimum lease payments that represents executory costs is not determinable from the provisions of the lease, an estimate of such amount must be made. Many lease agreements, however, specify that executory costs be paid to the appropriate third parties directly by the lessee; in these cases, the rental payment can be used **without adjustment** in the present value computation.

Discount Rate. The lessee computes the present value of the minimum lease payments using the **lessee's incremental borrowing rate**, which is defined as: "The rate that, at the inception of the lease, the lessee would have incurred to borrow the funds necessary to buy the leased asset on a secured loan with repayment terms similar to the payment schedule called for in the lease."[9] Assume, for example, that Mortenson Inc. decides to lease computer equipment for a 5-year period at a cost of $10,000 a year. To determine whether the present value of these payments is less than 90% of the fair market value of the property, the lessee discounts the payments using its incremental borrowing rate. Determining that rate will often require judgment because it is based on a hypothetical purchase of the property.

However, there is one exception to this rule: If (1) the lessee knows the **implicit interest rate computed by the lessor** and (2) it is less than the lessee's incremental borrowing rate, then the **lessee must use the lessor's implicit rate**. The **interest rate implicit in the lease** is the discount rate that, when applied to the minimum lease payments and any unguaranteed residual value accruing to the lessor, causes the aggregate present value to be equal to the fair value of the leased property to the lessor.[10]

---

[8]A lease provision requiring the lessee to make up a residual value deficiency that is attributable to damage, extraordinary wear and tear, or excessive usage is not included in the minimum lease payments. Such costs are recognized as period costs when incurred. "Lessee Guarantee of the Residual Value of Leased Property," *FASB Interpretation No. 19* (Stamford, Conn.: FASB, 1977), par. 3.

[9]*FASB Statement No. 13,* op. cit., par. 5 (1).

[10]Ibid., par. 5 (k).

The purpose of this exception is twofold: First, the implicit rate of the lessor is generally a **more realistic rate** to use in determining the amount (if any) to report as the asset and related liability for the lessee. Second, the guideline is provided to ensure that the lessee **does not use an artificially high incremental borrowing rate** that would cause the present value of the minimum lease payments to be less than 90% of the fair market value of the property and thus make it possible to avoid capitalization of the asset and related liability. The lessee may argue that it cannot determine the implicit rate of the lessor and therefore the higher rate should be used. However, in many cases, the implicit rate used by the lessor can be approximated. The determination of whether or not a reasonable estimate could be made will require judgment, particularly where the result from using the incremental borrowing rate comes close to meeting the 90% test. Because **the lessee may not capitalize the leased property at more than its fair value** (as discussed later), the lessee is prevented from using an excessively low discount rate.

Asset and Liability Accounted for Differently

In a capital lease transaction, the lessee is using the lease as a source of financing. The lessor finances the transaction (provides the investment capital) through the leased asset, and the lessee makes rent payments, which actually are installment payments. Therefore, over the life of the property rented, **the rental payments to the lessor constitute a payment of principal plus interest**.

Asset and Liability Recorded

Under the capital lease method, the lessee treats the lease transaction as if an asset were being purchased in a financing transaction in which an asset is acquired and an obligation created. Therefore, the lessee records a capital lease as an asset and a liability at the lower of (1) the present value of the minimum lease payments (excluding executory costs) or (2) the fair market value of the leased asset at the inception of the lease. The rationale for this approach is that the leased asset should not be recorded for more than its fair market value.

Depreciation Period

One troublesome aspect of accounting for the depreciation of the capitalized leased asset relates to the period of depreciation. If the lease agreement transfers ownership of the asset to the lessee (criterion 1) or contains a bargain purchase option (criterion 2)— the leased asset is depreciated in a manner consistent with the lessee's normal depreciation policy for owned assets, **using the economic life of the asset**. On the other hand, if the lease does not transfer ownership or does not contain a bargain purchase option, then it is depreciated over the **term of the lease**. In this case, the leased asset reverts to the lessor after a certain period of time.

Effective Interest Method

Throughout the term of the lease, the effective interest method is used to allocate each lease payment between principal and interest. This method produces a periodic interest expense equal to a constant percentage of the carrying value of the lease obligation.

The discount rate used by the lessee to determine the present value of the minimum lease payments must be used by the lessee when applying the effective interest method to capital leases.

Depreciation Concept

Although the amounts initially capitalized as an asset and recorded as an obligation are computed at the same present value, the **depreciation of the asset and the discharge of the obligation are independent accounting processes** during the term of the lease. The lessee should depreciate the leased asset by applying conventional depreciation methods: straight-line, sum-of-the-years'-digits, declining-balance, units of production, etc.

The FASB uses the term "amortization" more frequently than "depreciation" to recognize intangible leased property rights. The authors prefer "depreciation" to describe the write-off of a tangible asset's expired services.

Capital Lease Method (Lessee)

Lessor Company and Lessee Company sign a lease agreement dated January 1, 2002, that calls for Lessor Company to lease equipment to Lessee Company beginning January 1, 2002. The terms and provisions of the lease agreement and other pertinent data are as follows:

1 The term of the lease is 5 years, and the lease agreement is noncancelable, requiring equal rental payments of $25,981.62 at the beginning of each year (annuity due basis).

2 The equipment has a fair value at the inception of the lease of $100,000, an estimated economic life of 5 years, and no residual value.

3 Lessee Company pays all of the executory costs directly to third parties except for the property taxes of $2,000 per year, which are included in the annual payments to the lessor.

4 The lease contains no renewal options, and the equipment reverts to Lessor Company at the termination of the lease.

5 Lessee Company's incremental borrowing rate is 11% per year.

6 Lessee Company depreciates on a straight-line basis similar equipment that it owns.

7 Lessor Company set the annual rental to earn a rate of return on its investment of 10% per year; this fact is known to Lessee Company.[11]

The lease meets the criteria for classification as a capital lease for the following reasons: (1) The lease term of 5 years, being equal to the equipment's estimated economic life of 5 years, satisfies the 75% test. (2) The present value of the minimum lease payments ($100,000 as computed below) exceeds 90% of the fair value of the property ($100,000).

The minimum lease payments are $119,908.10 ($23,981.62 × 5), and the amount capitalized as leased assets is computed as the present value of the minimum lease payments (excluding executory costs—property taxes of $2,000) as follows:

ILLUSTRATION 22-5
Computation of
Capitalized Lease
Payments

> Capitalized amount = ($25,981.62 − $2,000) × present value of an annuity due of 1 for 5 periods at 10% (Table 6-5)
> = $23,981.62 × 4.16986
> = $100,000

The lessor's implicit interest rate of 10% is used instead of the lessee's incremental borrowing rate of 11% because (1) it is lower and (2) the lessee has knowledge of it.

The entry to record the capital lease on Lessee Company's books on January 1, 2002, is:

Leased Equipment under Capital Leases	100,000	
Obligations under Capital Leases		100,000

Note that the preceding entry records the obligation at the net amount of $100,000 (the present value of the future rental payments) rather than at the gross amount of $119,908.10 ($23,981.62 × 5).

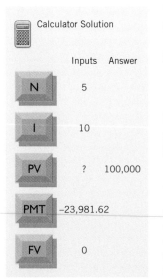

	Inputs	Answer
N	5	
I	10	
PV	?	100,000
PMT	−23,981.62	
FV	0	

Calculator Solution

---

[11]If Lessee Company had an incremental borrowing rate of, say, 9% (lower than the 10% rate used by Lessor Company) and it did not know the rate used by Lessor Company, the present value computation would have yielded a capitalized amount of $101,675.35 ($23,981.62 × 4.23972). And, because this amount exceeds the $100,000 fair value of the equipment, Lessee Company would have had to capitalize the $100,000 and use 10% as its effective rate for amortization of the lease obligation.

The journal entry to record the **first lease payment on January 1, 2002**, is:

Property Tax Expense	2,000.00	
Obligations under Capital Leases	23,981.62	
Cash		25,981.62

Each lease payment of $25,981.62 consists of three elements: (1) a reduction in the lease obligation, (2) a financing cost (interest expense), and (3) executory costs (property taxes). The total financing cost (interest expense) over the term of the lease is $19,908.10, the difference between the present value of the lease payments ($100,000) and the actual cash disbursed, net of executory costs ($119,908.10). Therefore, the annual interest expense, applying the effective interest method, is a function of the outstanding obligation, as shown in Illustration 22-6:

LESSEE COMPANY					
Lease Amortization Schedule					
(Annuity due basis)					
Date	Annual Lease Payment	Executory Costs	Interest (10%) on Unpaid Obligation	Reduction of Lease Obligation	Lease Obligation
	(a)	(b)	(c)	(d)	(e)
1/1/02					$100,000.00
1/1/02	$ 25,981.62	$ 2,000	$ –0–	$ 23,981.62	76,018.38
1/1/03	25,981.62	2,000	7,601.84	16,379.78	59,638.60
1/1/04	25,981.62	2,000	5,963.86	18,017.76	41,620.84
1/1/05	25,981.62	2,000	4,162.08	19,819.54	21,801.30
1/1/06	25,981.62	2,000	2,180.32*	21,801.30	–0–
	$129,908.10	$10,000	$19,908.10	$100,000.00	

(a) Lease payment as required by lease.
(b) Executory costs included in rental payment.
(c) Ten percent of the preceding balance of (e) except for 1/1/02; since this is an annuity due, no time has elapsed at the date of the first payment and no interest has accrued.
(d) (a) minus (b) and (c).
(e) Preceding balance minus (d).
*Rounded by 19 cents.

ILLUSTRATION 22-6
Lease Amortization Schedule for Lessee—Annuity Due Basis

At the end of Lessee Company's fiscal year, December 31, 2002, **accrued interest** is recorded as follows:

Interest Expense	7,601.84	
Interest Payable		7,601.84

Depreciation of the leased equipment over its lease term of 5 years, applying Lessee Company's normal depreciation policy (straight-line method), results in the following entry on December 31, 2002:

Depreciation Expense—Capital Leases	20,000	
Accumulated Depreciation—Capital Leases		20,000
($100,000 ÷ 5 years)		

At December 31, 2002, the assets recorded under capital leases are separately identified on the lessee's balance sheet. Similarly, the related obligations are separately identified. The portion due within one year or the operating cycle, whichever is longer, is classified with current liabilities and the rest with noncurrent liabilities. For example, the current portion of the 12/31/02 total obligation of $76,018.38 in the lessee's amortization schedule is the amount of the reduction in the obligation in 2003, or $16,379.78. The liability section as it relates to lease transactions at 12/31/02 would appear as follows:

ILLUSTRATION 22-7
Reporting Current and
Noncurrent Lease
Liabilities

Current liabilities	
Interest payable	$ 7,601.84
Obligations under capital leases	16,379.78
Noncurrent liabilities	
Obligations under capital leases	$59,638.60

The journal entry to record the lease payment of January 1, 2003, is as follows:

Property Tax Expense	2,000.00	
Interest Expense (or Interest Payable)	7,601.84	
Obligations under Capital Leases	16,379.78	
Cash		25,981.62

Entries through 2006 would follow the pattern above. Other executory costs (insurance and maintenance) assumed by Lessee Company would be recorded in a manner similar to that used to record any other operating costs incurred on assets owned by Lessee Company.

Upon expiration of the lease, the amount capitalized as leased equipment is fully amortized and the lease obligation is fully discharged. If not purchased, the equipment would be returned to the lessor, and the leased equipment and related accumulated depreciation accounts would be removed from the books.[12] If the equipment is purchased at termination of the lease at a price of $5,000 and the estimated life of the equipment is changed from 5 to 7 years, the following entry might be made:

Equipment ($100,000 + $5,000)	105,000	
Accumulated Depreciation—Capital Leases	100,000	
Leased Equipment under Capital Leases		100,000
Accumulated Depreciation—Equipment		100,000
Cash		5,000

Operating Method (Lessee)

Under the **operating method**, rent expense (and the associated liability) accrues day by day to the lessee as the property is used. **The lessee assigns rent to the periods benefiting from the use of the asset and ignores, in the accounting, any commitments to make future payments.** Appropriate accruals or deferrals are made if the accounting period ends between cash payment dates. For example, assume that the capital lease illustrated in the previous section did not qualify as a capital lease and was therefore to be accounted for as an operating lease. The first-year charge to operations would have been $25,981.62, the amount of the rental payment. The journal entry to record this payment on January 1, 2002, would be as follows:

Rent Expense	25,981.62	
Cash		25,981.62

The rented asset, as well as any long-term liability for future rental payments, is not reported on the balance sheet. Rent expense would be reported on the income statement. In addition, **note disclosure is required for all operating leases that have noncancelable lease terms in excess of one year**. An illustration of the type of note disclosure required for an operating lease (as well as other types of leases) is provided in Illustrations 22-32 to 22-35 later in this chapter.

---

[12]If the lessee purchases a leased asset **during the term of a "capital lease,"** it is accounted for like a renewal or extension of a capital lease. "Any difference between the purchase price and the carrying amount of the lease obligation shall be recorded as an adjustment of the carrying amount of the asset." See "Accounting for Purchase of a Leased Asset by the Lessee During the Term of the Lease," *FASB Interpretation No. 26* (Stamford, Conn.: FASB, 1978), par. 5.

Comparison of Capital Lease with Operating Lease

As indicated on the previous page, if the lease had been accounted for as an operating lease, the first-year charge to operations would have been $25,981.62, the amount of the rental payment. Treating the transaction as a capital lease, however, resulted in a first-year charge of $29,601.84: depreciation of $20,000 (assuming straight-line), interest expense of $7,601.84 (per Illustration 22-8), and executory costs of $2,000. Illustration 22-8 shows that **while the total charges to operations are the same over the lease term whether the lease is accounted for as a capital lease or as an operating lease, under the capital lease treatment the charges are higher in the earlier years and lower in the later years.**[13]

> **OBJECTIVE 3**
> Contrast the operating and capitalization methods of recording leases.

LESSEE COMPANY							
Schedule of Charges to Operations							
Capital Lease versus Operating Lease							
		Capital Lease			Operating Lease Charge	Difference	
Year	Depreciation	Executory Costs	Interest	Total Charge			
2002	$ 20,000	$ 2,000	$ 7,601.84	$ 29,601.84	$ 25,981.62	$ 3,620.22	
2003	20,000	2,000	5,963.86	27,963.86	25,981.62	1,982.24	
2004	20,000	2,000	4,162.08	26,162.08	25,981.62	180.46	
2005	20,000	2,000	2,180.32	24,180.32	25,981.62	(1,801.30)	
2006	20,000	2,000	—	22,000.00	25,981.62	(3,981.62)	
	$100,000	$10,000	$19,908.10	$129,908.10	$129,908.10	$ –0–	

ILLUSTRATION 22-8
Comparison of Charges to Operations—Capital vs. Operating Leases

If an accelerated method of depreciation is used, the differences between the amounts charged to operations under the two methods would be even larger in the earlier and later years.

In addition, using the capital lease approach would have resulted in an asset and related liability of $100,000 initially reported on the balance sheet; no such asset or liability would be reported under the operating method. Therefore, the following differences occur if a capital lease instead of an operating lease is employed:

❶ an increase in the amount of reported debt (both short-term and long-term),

❷ an increase in the amount of total assets (specifically long-lived assets), and

❸ a lower income early in the life of the lease and, therefore, lower retained earnings.

Thus, many companies believe that capital leases have a detrimental impact on their financial position as their debt to total equity ratio increases and their rate of return on total assets decreases. As a result, the business community resists capitalizing leases.

Whether their resistance is well founded is a matter of conjecture. From a cash flow point of view, the company is in the same position whether the lease is accounted for as an operating or a capital lease. The reason why managers often argue against capitalization is that it can more easily lead to **violation of loan covenants**; it can affect the **amount of compensation received** by owners (for example, a stock compensation plan tied to earnings); and finally, it can **lower rates of return** and **increase debt**

---

[13]The higher charges in the early years is one reason lessees are reluctant to adopt the capital lease accounting method. Lessees (especially those of real estate) claim that it is really no more costly to operate the leased asset in the early years than in the later years; thus, they advocate an even charge similar to that provided by the operating method.

to equity relationships, thus making the company less attractive to present and potential investors.[14]

ACCOUNTING BY LESSOR

Earlier in this chapter we discussed leasing's advantages to the lessee. Three important benefits are available to the lessor:

❶ *Interest Revenue.* Leasing is a form of financing; therefore, financial institutions and leasing companies find leasing attractive because it provides competitive interest margins.

❷ *Tax Incentives.* In many cases, companies that lease cannot use the tax benefit, but leasing provides them with an opportunity to transfer such tax benefits to another party (the lessor) in return for a lower rental rate on the leased asset. To illustrate, Boeing Aircraft at one time sold one of its 767 jet planes to a wealthy investor who didn't need the plane but could use the tax benefit. The investor then leased the plane to a foreign airline, for whom the tax benefit was of no use. Everyone gained. Boeing was able to sell its 767, the investor received the tax benefits, and the foreign airline found a cheaper way to acquire a 767.[15]

❸ *High Residual Value.* Another advantage to the lessor is the return of the property at the end of the lease term. Residual values can produce very large profits. Citicorp at one time assumed that the commercial aircraft it was leasing to the airline industry would have a residual value of 5% of their purchase price. It turned out that they were worth 150% of their cost—a handsome profit. However, 3 years later these same planes slumped to 80% of their cost, but still far more than 5%.

Economics of Leasing

The lessor determines the amount of the rental, basing it on the rate of return—the implicit rate—needed to justify leasing the asset. The key factors considered in establishing the rate of return are the credit standing of the lessee, the length of the lease, and the status of the residual value (guaranteed versus unguaranteed). In the Lessor Company/Lessee Company example on pages 1198–1200, the implicit rate of the lessor was 10%, the cost of the equipment to the lessor was $100,000 (also fair market value), and the estimated residual value was zero. Lessor Company determined the amount of the lease payment in the following manner:

ILLUSTRATION 22-9
Computation of
Lease Payments

Fair market value of leased equipment	$100,000.00
Less: Present value of the residual value	–0–
Amount to be recovered by lessor through lease payments	$100,000.00
Five beginning-of-the-year lease payments to yield a 10% return ($100,000 ÷ 4.16986[a])	$ 23,981.62

[a]PV of an annuity due of 1 for 5 years at 10% (Table 6-5)

---

[14]One study indicates that management's behavior did change as a result of *FASB No. 13*. For example, many companies restructure their leases to avoid capitalization; others increase their purchases of assets instead of leasing; and others, faced with capitalization, postpone their debt offerings or issue stock instead. However, it is interesting to note that the study found no significant effect on stock or bond prices as a result of capitalization of leases. A. Rashad Abdel-khalik, "The Economic Effects on Lessees of *FASB Statement No. 13*, Accounting for Leases," Research Report (Stamford, Conn.: FASB, 1981).

[15]Some would argue that there is a loser—the U.S. government. The tax benefits enable the profitable investor to reduce or eliminate taxable income.

If a residual value were involved (whether guaranteed or not), the lessor would not have to recover as much from the lease payments. Therefore, the lease payments would be less (this situation is shown in Illustration 22-17).

Classification of Leases by the Lessor

From the standpoint of the **lessor**, all leases may be classified for accounting purposes as one of the following:

(a) Operating leases.

(b) Direct financing leases.

(c) Sales-type leases.

If at the date of the lease agreement (inception) the lessor is party to a lease that meets **one or more** of the following Group I criteria (1, 2, 3, and 4) and **both** of the following Group II criteria (1 and 2), the lessor shall classify and account for the arrangement as a direct financing lease or as a sales-type lease.[16] (Note that the Group I criteria are identical to the criteria that must be met in order for a lease to be classified as a capital lease by a lessee, as shown in Illustration 22-3.)

> **Capitalization Criteria (Lessor)**
>
> Group I
> - The lease transfers ownership of the property to the lessee.
> - The lease contains a bargain purchase option.
> - The lease term is equal to 75% or more of the estimated economic life of the leased property.
> - The present value of the minimum lease payments (excluding executory costs) equals or exceeds 90% of the fair value of the leased property.
>
> Group II
> - Collectibility of the payments required from the lessee is reasonably predictable.
> - No important uncertainties surround the amount of unreimbursable costs yet to be incurred by the lessor under the lease (lessor's performance is substantially complete or future costs are reasonably predictable).

OBJECTIVE 4
Identify the classifications of leases for the lessor.

ILLUSTRATION 22-10
Capitalization Criteria for Lessor

INTERNATIONAL INSIGHT

U.S. GAAP is consistent with International Standard No. 17 (Accounting for Leases). However, the international standard is a relatively simple statement of basic principles, whereas the U.S. rules on leases are more prescriptive and detailed.

Why the Group II requirements? The answer is that the profession wants to make sure that the lessor has really transferred the risks and benefits of ownership. If collectibility of payments is not predictable or if performance by the lessor is incomplete, then the criteria for revenue recognition have not been met and it should be accounted for as an operating lease.

For example, computer leasing companies at one time used to buy **IBM** equipment, lease it, and remove the leased assets from their balance sheets. In leasing the asset, the computer lessors stated that they would be willing to substitute new IBM equipment if obsolescence occurred. However, when IBM introduced a new computer line, IBM refused to sell it to the computer leasing companies. As a result, a number of the lessors could not meet their contracts with their customers and were forced to take back the old equipment. What the computer leasing companies had taken off the books now had to be reinstated. Such a case demonstrates one reason for the Group II requirements.

The distinction for the lessor between a direct financing lease and a sales-type lease is the presence or absence of a manufacturer's or dealer's profit (or loss): A

---

[16]*FASB Statement No. 13*, op. cit., pars. 6, 7, and 8.

sales-type lease involves a manufacturer's or dealer's profit, and a direct financing lease does not. The profit (or loss) to the lessor is evidenced by the difference between the fair value of the leased property at the inception of the lease and the lessor's cost or carrying amount (book value). Normally, sales-type leases arise when manufacturers or dealers use leasing as a means of marketing their products. For example, a computer manufacturer will lease its computer equipment to businesses and institutions. Direct financing leases generally result from arrangements with lessors that are primarily engaged in financing operations, such as lease-finance companies, banks, insurance companies, and pension trusts. However, a lessor need not be a manufacturer or dealer to recognize a profit (or loss) at the inception of a lease that requires application of sales-type lease accounting.

All leases that do not qualify as direct financing or sales-type leases are classified and accounted for by the lessors as operating leases. Illustration 22-11 shows the circumstances under which a lease is classified as operating, direct financing, or sales-type for the lessor.

ILLUSTRATION 22-11
Diagram of Lessor's
Criteria for Lease
Classification

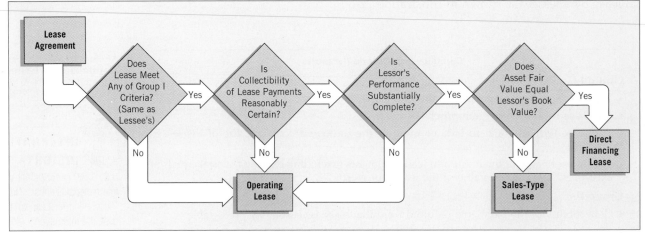

As a consequence of the additional Group II criteria for lessors, it is possible that a lessor having not met both criteria will classify a lease as an **operating** lease but the lessee will classify the same lease as a **capital** lease. In such an event, both the lessor and lessee will carry the asset on their books, and both will depreciate the capitalized asset.

For purposes of comparison with the lessee's accounting, only the operating and direct financing leases will be illustrated in the following section. The more complex sales-type lease will be discussed later in the chapter.

Direct Financing Method (Lessor)

OBJECTIVE 5
Describe the lessor's accounting for direct financing leases.

Leases that are in substance the financing of an asset purchase by a lessee require the lessor to substitute a "lease payments receivable" for the leased asset. The information necessary to record a **direct financing lease** is as shown on the next page.

The computation of the gross investment (lease payments receivable) is often confusing because of the uncertainty as to how to account for the residual values. Remember that "minimum lease payments" includes:

1. Rental payments (excluding executory costs).
2. Bargain purchase option (if any).
3. Guaranteed residual value (if any).
4. Penalty for failure to renew (if any).

DIRECT FINANCING TERMS

1 *Gross Investment ("Lease Payments Receivable").* The minimum lease payments plus the unguaranteed residual value accruing to the lessor at the end of the lease term.[17]

2 *Unearned Interest Revenue.* The difference between the gross investment (the receivable) and the fair market value of the property.[18]

3 *Net Investment.* The gross investment (the receivable) less the unearned interest revenue included therein.

When "lease payments receivable" is defined as minimum lease payments plus unguaranteed residual value, it means that residual value, both guaranteed (because it is included as part of "minimum lease payments") and unguaranteed (because it is added back in to compute the gross investment), is included as part of lease payments receivable if it is relevant to the lessor (that is, if the lessor expects to get the asset back).

In addition, if the lessor pays any executory costs, then the rental payment should be reduced by that amount for purposes of computing minimum lease payments. In other words, lease payments receivable includes:

1 Rental payments (less executory costs paid by the lessor).

2 Bargain purchase option (if any).

3 Guaranteed or unguaranteed residual value (if any).

4 Penalty for failure to renew (if any).

The **unearned interest revenue is amortized to revenue** over the lease term by applying the effective interest method. Thus, a constant rate of return is produced on the net investment in the lease.

The following presentation, utilizing the data from the preceding Lessor Company/Lessee Company illustration on pages 1198–1200, illustrates the accounting treatment accorded a direct financing lease. The information relevant to Lessor Company in accounting for this lease transaction is repeated as follows:

1 The term of the lease is 5 years beginning January 1, 2002, noncancelable, and requires equal rental payments of $25,981.62 at the beginning of each year; payments include $2,000 of executory costs (property taxes).

2 The equipment has a cost of $100,000 to Lessor Company, a fair value at the inception of the lease of $100,000, an estimated economic life of 5 years, and no residual value.

3 No initial direct costs were incurred in negotiating and closing the lease transaction.

4 The lease contains no renewable options and the equipment reverts to Lessor Company at the termination of the lease.

---

[17]Ibid., par. 17. If the lessee agrees to make up any deficiency below a stated amount that the lessor realizes in residual value at the end of the lease term, that stated amount is the guaranteed residual value.

Initially the unguaranteed residual value could be classified in a separate account. If the unguaranteed residual value is included in the Lease Payments Receivable account, it would be reclassified by the lessor at the end of the lease term if not purchased by the lessee.

[18]In a direct financing lease, the cost or carrying amount of the asset should be used instead of fair market value. In most cases, however, cost or carrying amount is equal to fair market value, so fair market value is used here. The use of fair market value will simplify subsequent discussion in this area. Significant differences between cost or carrying amount and fair market value exist for sales-type leases.

⑤ Collectibility is reasonably assured and no additional costs (with the exception of the property taxes being collected from the lessee) are to be incurred by Lessor Company.

⑥ Lessor Company set the annual lease payments to ensure a rate of return of 10% (implicit rate) on its investment as follows (as shown in Illustration 22-9):

ILLUSTRATION 22-12
Computation of
Lease Payments

Fair market value of leased equipment	$100,000.00
Less: Present value of residual value	–0–
Amount to be recovered by lessor through lease payments	$100,000.00
Five beginning-of-the-year lease payments to yield a 10% return ($100,000 ÷ 4.16986[a])	$ 23,981.62

[a]PV of an annuity due of 1 for 5 years at 10% (Table 6-5).

The lease meets the criteria for classification as a direct financing lease because (1) the lease term exceeds 75% of the equipment's estimated economic life, (2) the present value of the minimum lease payments exceeds 90% of the equipment's fair value, (3) collectibility of the payments is reasonably assured, and (4) there are no further costs to be incurred by Lessor Company. It is not a sales-type lease because there is no difference between the fair value ($100,000) of the equipment and the lessor's cost ($100,000).

The lease payments receivable (gross investment) is calculated as follows:

ILLUSTRATION 22-13
Computation of Lease
Payments Receivable

Lease payments receivable = Minimum lease payments minus executory costs paid by lessor plus unguaranteed residual value
= [($25,981.62 − $2,000) × 5] + $0
= $119,908.10

The unearned interest revenue is computed as the difference between the lease payments receivable and the lessor's fair market value of the leased asset:

ILLUSTRATION 22-14
Computation of
Unearned Interest
Revenue

Unearned interest revenue = Lease payments receivable minus asset's fair market value
= $119,908.10 − $100,000
= $19,908.10

The net investment in direct financing leases is $100,000; that is, the gross investment of $119,908.10 minus the unearned interest revenue of $19,908.10.

The lease of the asset, the resulting receivable, and the unearned interest revenue are recorded January 1, 2002 (the inception of the lease) as follows:

Lease Payments Receivable	119,908.10	
Equipment		100,000.00
Unearned Interest Revenue—Leases		19,908.10

The unearned interest revenue is classified on the balance sheet as a deduction from the lease payments receivable if the receivable is reported gross. Generally, the lease payments receivable, although **recorded** at the gross investment amount, is **reported** in the balance sheet at the "net investment" amount (gross investment less unearned interest revenue) and entitled "Net investment in capital leases." It is classified either as current or noncurrent, depending upon when the net investment is to be recovered.

The leased equipment with a cost of $100,000, which represents Lessor Company's investment, is replaced with a net lease receivable. In a manner similar to the lessee's treatment of interest, Lessor Company applies the effective interest method and recognizes interest revenue as a function of the unrecovered net investment, as shown in Illustration 22-15.

ILLUSTRATION 22-15
Lease Amortization
Schedule for Lessor—
Annuity Due Basis

LESSOR COMPANY
Lease Amortization Schedule
(Annuity due basis)

Date	Annual Lease Payment	Executory Costs	Interest (10%) on Net Investment	Net Investment Recovery	Net Investment
	(a)	(b)	(c)	(d)	(e)
1/1/02					$100,000.00
1/1/02	$ 25,981.62	$ 2,000.00	$ −0−	$ 23,981.62	76,018.38
1/1/03	25,981.62	2,000.00	7,601.84	16,379.78	59,638.60
1/1/04	25,981.62	2,000.00	5,963.86	18,017.76	41,620.84
1/1/05	25,981.62	2,000.00	4,162.08	19,819.54	21,801.30
1/1/06	25,981.62	2,000.00	2,180.32*	21,801.30	−0−
	$129,908.10	$10,000.00	$19,908.10	$100,000.00	

(a) Annual rental that provides a 10% return on net investment.
(b) Executory costs included in rental payment.
(c) Ten percent of the preceding balance of (e) except for 1/1/02.
(d) (a) minus (b) and (c).
(e) Preceding balance minus (d).
*Rounded by 19 cents.

On January 1, 2002, the journal entry to record receipt of the first year's lease payment is as follows:

Cash	25,981.62	
Lease Payments Receivable		23,981.62
Property Tax Expense/Property Taxes Payable		2,000.00

On 12/31/02 the interest revenue earned during the first year is recognized through the following entry:

Unearned Interest Revenue—Leases	7,601.84	
Interest Revenue—Leases		7,601.84

At December 31, 2002, the net investment under capital leases is reported in the lessor's balance sheet among current assets or noncurrent assets, or both. The portion due within one year or the operating cycle, whichever is longer, is classified as a current asset and the rest with noncurrent assets.

The total net investment at 12/31/02 is equal to $83,620.22 (the balance at 1/1/02, $76,018.38 plus interest receivable for 2002 of $7,601.84). The current portion is the net investment to be received in 2003, $16,379.78, plus the interest of $7,601.84. The remainder, $59,638.60 (Lease Payments Receivable of $71,944.86 [$23,981.62 × 3] minus Unearned Interest Revenue of $12,306.26 [$5,963.86 + $4,162.08 + $2,180.32]) should be reported in the noncurrent assets section.

The asset sections as it relates to lease transactions at 12/31/02 would appear as follows:

ILLUSTRATION 22-16
Reporting Lease
Transactions by Lessor

Current assets	
Net investment in capital leases	$23,981.62
Noncurrent assets (investments)	
Net investment in capital leases	$59,638.60

The following entries record receipt of the second year's lease payment and recognition of the interest earned:

January 1, 2003

Cash	25,981.62	
Lease Payments Receivable		23,981.62
Property Tax Expense/Property Taxes Payable		2,000.00

December 31, 2003

Unearned Interest Revenue—Leases	5,963.86	
Interest Revenue—Leases		5,963.86

Journal entries through 2006 would follow the same pattern except that no entry would be recorded in 2006 (the last year) for earned interest. Because the receivable is fully collected by 1/1/06, no balance (investment) is outstanding during 2006 to which Lessor Company could attribute any interest. Upon expiration of the lease (whether an ordinary annuity or an annuity due), the gross receivable and the unearned interest revenue would be fully written off. **Lessor Company recorded no depreciation.** If the equipment is sold to Lessee Company for $5,000 upon expiration of the lease, Lessor Company would recognize disposition of the equipment as follows:

Cash	5,000	
Gain on Sale of Leased Equipment		5,000

Operating Method (Lessor)

Under the **operating method** each rental receipt by the lessor is recorded as rental revenue. The **leased asset is depreciated in the normal manner**, with the depreciation expense of the period matched against the rental revenue. The amount of revenue recognized in each accounting period is a level amount (straight-line basis) regardless of the lease provisions, unless another systematic and rational basis is more representative of the time pattern in which the benefit is derived from the leased asset. In addition to the depreciation charge, maintenance costs and the cost of any other services rendered under the provisions of the lease that pertain to the current accounting period are charged to expense. Costs paid to independent third parties such as appraisal fees, finder's fees, and costs of credit checks are amortized over the life of the lease.

To illustrate the operating method, assume that the direct financing lease illustrated above did not qualify as a capital lease and was therefore to be accounted for as an operating lease. The entry to record the cash rental receipt, assuming the $2,000 was for property tax expense, would be as follows:

Cash	25,981.62	
Rental Revenue		25,981.62

Depreciation is recorded by the lessor as follows (assuming a straight-line method, a cost basis of $100,000, and a 5-year life):

Depreciation Expense—Leased Equipment	20,000	
Accumulated Depreciation—Leased Equipment		20,000

If property taxes, insurance, maintenance, and other operating costs during the year are the obligation of the lessor, they are recorded as expenses chargeable against the gross rental revenues.

If the lessor owned plant assets that it used in addition to those leased to others, **the leased equipment and accompanying accumulated depreciation would be separately classified** in an account such as Equipment Leased to Others or Investment in Leased Property. If significant in amount or in terms of activity, the rental revenues and accompanying expenses are separated in the income statement from sales revenue and cost of goods sold.

SPECIAL ACCOUNTING PROBLEMS

OBJECTIVE 6
Identify special features of lease arrangements that cause unique accounting problems.

The features of lease arrangements that cause unique accounting problems are:

❶ Residual values.
❷ Sales-type leases (lessor).
❸ Bargain purchase options.
❹ Initial direct costs.

⑤ Current versus noncurrent.

⑥ Disclosure.

Residual Values

Up to this point, we have generally ignored discussion of residual values in order that the basic accounting issues related to lessee and lessor accounting could be developed. Accounting for residual values is complex and will probably provide you with the greatest challenge in understanding lease accounting.

Meaning of Residual Value

The residual value is the **estimated fair value** of the leased asset at the end of the lease term. Frequently, a significant residual value exists at the end of the lease term, especially when the economic life of the leased asset exceeds the lease term. If title does not pass automatically to the lessee (criterion 1) and a bargain purchase option does not exist (criterion 2), the lessee returns physical custody of the asset to the lessor at the end of the lease term.[19]

Guaranteed versus Unguaranteed

The residual value may be unguaranteed or guaranteed by the lessee. If the lessee agrees to make up any deficiency below a stated amount that the lessor realizes in residual value at the end of the lease term, that stated amount is the **guaranteed residual value**.

The guaranteed residual value is employed in lease arrangements for two reasons. The first is a business reason: It protects the lessor against any loss in estimated residual value, thereby ensuring the lessor of the desired rate of return on investment. The second is an accounting benefit that you will learn from the discussion at the end of this chapter.

Lease Payments

A guaranteed residual value—by definition—has more assurance of realization than does an unguaranteed residual value. As a result, the lessor may adjust lease payments because the certainty of recovery has been increased. After this rate is established, however, it makes no difference from an accounting point of view whether the residual value is guaranteed or unguaranteed. The net investment to be recorded by the lessor (once the rate is set) will be the same.

Assume the same data as in the Lessee Company/Lessor Company illustrations except that a residual value of $5,000 is estimated at the end of the 5-year lease term. In addition, a 10% return on investment (ROI) is assumed,[20] whether the residual value is guaranteed or unguaranteed. Lessor Company would compute the amount of the lease payments as follows:

Lessor's Computation of Lease Payments (10% ROI) Guaranteed or Unguaranteed Residual Value *(Annuity due basis, including residual value)*	
Fair market value of leased asset to lessor	$100,000.00
Less: Present value of residual value ($5,000 × .62092, Table 6-2)	3,104.60
Amount to be recovered by lessor through lease payments	$ 96,895.40
Five periodic lease payments ($96,895.40 ÷ 4.16986, Table 6-5)	$ 23,237.09

ILLUSTRATION 22-17
Lessor's Computation of Lease Payments

---

[19]When the lease term and the economic life are not the same, the residual value and the salvage value of the asset will probably differ. For simplicity, we will assume that residual value and salvage value are the same, even when the economic life and lease term vary.

[20]Technically the rate of return demanded by the lessor would be different depending upon whether the residual value was guaranteed or unguaranteed. We are ignoring this difference in subsequent sections to simplify the illustrations.

Contrast the foregoing lease payment amount to the lease payments of $23,981.62 as computed in Illustration 22-9, where no residual value existed. The payments are less because the lessor's total recoverable amount of $100,000 is reduced by the present value of the residual value.

Lessee Accounting for Residual Value

Whether the estimated residual value is guaranteed or unguaranteed has both economic and accounting consequence to the lessee. The accounting difference is that the **minimum lease payments**, the basis for capitalization, includes the guaranteed residual value but excludes the unguaranteed residual value.

OBJECTIVE 7
Describe the effect of residual values, guaranteed and unguaranteed, on lease accounting.

Guaranteed Residual Value (Lessee Accounting). A guaranteed residual value affects the lessee's computation of minimum lease payments and, therefore, the amounts capitalized as a leased asset and a lease obligation. In effect, **it is an additional lease payment that will be paid in property or cash, or both, at the end of the lease term.** Using the rental payments as computed by the lessor in Illustration 22-17, the minimum lease payments are $121,185.45 ([$23,237.09 × 5] + $5,000). The capitalized present value of the minimum lease payments (excluding executory costs) is computed as follows:

ILLUSTRATION 22-18
Computation of Lessee's Capitalized Amount— Guaranteed Residual Value

Lessee's Capitalized Amount (10% Rate) (Annuity due basis; including **guaranteed** residual value)	
Present value of five annual rental payments ($23,237.09 × 4.16986, Table 6-5)	$ 96,895.40
Present value of guaranteed residual value of $5,000 due five years after date of inception: ($5,000 × .62092, Table 6-2)	3,104.60
Lessee's capitalized amount	$100,000.00

Lessee Company's schedule of interest expense and amortization of the $100,000 lease obligation that produces a $5,000 final guaranteed residual value payment at the end of five years is shown in Illustration 22-19.

ILLUSTRATION 22-19
Lease Amortization Schedule for Lessee— Guaranteed Residual Value

	LESSEE COMPANY Lease Amortization Schedule (Annuity due basis, **guaranteed** residual value—GRV)				
Date	Lease Payment Plus GRV	Executory Costs	Interest (10%) on Unpaid Obligation	Reduction of Lease Obligation	Lease Obligation
	(a)	(b)	(c)	(d)	(e)
1/1/02					$100,000.00
1/1/02	$ 25,237.09	$ 2,000	–0–	$ 23,237.09	76,762.91
1/1/03	25,237.09	2,000	$ 7,676.29	15,560.80	61,202.11
1/1/04	25,237.09	2,000	6,120.21	17,116.88	44,085.23
1/1/05	25,237.09	2,000	4,408.52	18,828.57	25,256.66
1/1/06	25,237.09	2,000	2,525.67	20,711.42	4,545.24
12/31/06	5,000.00*		454.76**	4,545.24	–0–
	$131,185.45	$10,000	$21,185.45	$100,000.00	

(a) Annual lease payment as required by lease.　　*Represents the guaranteed residual value.
(b) Executory costs included in rental payment.　　**Rounded by 24 cents.
(c) Preceding balance of (e) × 10%, except 1/1/02.
(d) (a) minus (b) and (c).
(e) Preceding balance minus (d).

The journal entries (Illustration 22-24 on page 1213) to record the leased asset and obligation, depreciation, interest, property tax, and lease payments are then made on the basis that the residual value is guaranteed. The format of these entries is the same as illustrated earlier, although the amounts are different because of the guaranteed residual value. The leased asset is recorded at $100,000 and is depreciated over 5 years. To compute depreciation, the guaranteed residual value is subtracted from the cost of the leased asset. Assuming that the straight-line method is used, the depreciation expense each year is $19,000 ([$100,000 − $5,000] ÷ 5 years).

At the end of the lease term, before the lessee transfers the asset to the lessor, the lease asset and obligation accounts have the following balances:

Leased equipment under capital leases	$100,000.00	Interest payable	$ 454.76
Less: Accumulated depreciation—		Obligations under capital leases	4,545.24
capital leases	95,000.00		
	$ 5,000.00		$5,000.00

ILLUSTRATION 22-20
Account Balances on Lessee's Books at End of Lease Term—Guaranteed Residual Value

If, at the end of the lease, the fair market value of the residual value is less than $5,000, Lessee Company will have to record a loss. Assume that Lessee Company depreciated the leased asset down to its residual value of $5,000 but that the fair market value of the residual value at 12/31/06 was $3,000. In this case, the Lessee Company would have to report a loss of $2,000. The following journal entry would be made, assuming cash was paid to make up the residual value deficiency:

Loss on Capital Lease	2,000.00	
Interest Expense (or Interest Payable)	454.76	
Obligations under Capital Leases	4,545.24	
Accumulated Depreciation—Capital Leases	95,000.00	
Leased Equipment under Capital Leases		100,000.00
Cash		2,000.00

If the fair market value exceeds $5,000, a gain may be recognized. Gains on guaranteed residual values may be apportioned to the lessor and lessee in whatever ratio the parties initially agree.

If the lessee depreciated the total cost of the asset ($100,000), a misstatement would occur; that is, the carrying amount of the asset at the end of the lease term would be zero, but the obligation under the capital lease would be stated at $5,000. Thus, if the asset was worth $5,000, the lessee would end up reporting a gain of $5,000 when it transferred the asset to the lessor. As a result, depreciation would be overstated and net income understated in 2002–2005, but in the last year (2006) net income would be overstated.

Unguaranteed Residual Value (Lessee Accounting). An unguaranteed residual value from the lessee's viewpoint is the same as no residual value in terms of its effect upon the lessee's method of computing the minimum lease payments and the capitalization of the leased asset and the lease obligation. Assume the same facts as those above except that the $5,000 residual value is **unguaranteed instead of guaranteed**. The amount of the annual lease payments would be the same, $23,237.09. Whether the residual value is guaranteed or unguaranteed, Lessor Company's amount to be recovered through lease rentals is the same, that is, $96,895.40. The minimum lease payments are $116,185.45 ($23,237.09 × 5). Lessee Company would capitalize the following amount:

Lessee's Capitalized Amount (10% Rate)	
(Annuity due basis, including **unguaranteed** residual value)	
Present value of 5 annual rental payments of $23,237.09 × 4.16986	
(Table 6-5)	$96,895.40
Unguaranteed residual value of $5,000 (not capitalized by lessee)	–0–
Lessee's capitalized amount	$96,895.40

ILLUSTRATION 22-21
Computation of Lessee's Capitalized Amount— Unguaranteed Residual Value

The Lessee Company's schedule of interest expense and amortization of the lease obligation of $96,895.40, assuming an unguaranteed residual value of $5,000 at the end of 5 years, is shown in Illustration 22-22.

ILLUSTRATION 22-22
Lease Amortization Schedule for Lessee—Unguaranteed Residual Value

LESSEE COMPANY					
Lease Amortization Schedule (10%)					
(Annuity due basis, unguaranteed residual value)					
Date	Annual Lease Payments	Executory Costs	Interest (10%) on Unpaid Obligation	Reduction of Lease Obligation	Lease Obligation
	(a)	(b)	(c)	(d)	(e)
1/1/02					$96,895.40
1/1/02	$ 25,237.09	$ 2,000	–0–	$23,237.09	73,658.31
1/1/03	25,237.09	2,000	$ 7,365.83	15,871.26	57,787.05
1/1/04	25,237.09	2,000	5,778.71	17,458.38	40,328.67
1/1/05	25,237.09	2,000	4,032.87	19,204.22	21,124.45
1/1/06	25,237.09	2,000	2,112.64*	21,124.45	–0–
	$126,185.45	$10,000	$19,290.05	$96,895.40	

(a) Annual lease payment as required by lease.
(b) Executory costs included in rental payment.
(c) Preceding balance of (e) × 10%.
(d) (a) minus (b) and (c).
(e) Preceding balance minus (d).
*Rounded by 19 cents.

The journal entries (Illustration 22-24 on page 1213) to record the leased asset and obligation, depreciation, interest, property tax, and payments on the lease obligation are then made on the basis that the residual value is unguaranteed. The format of these entries is the same as illustrated earlier. Note that the leased asset is recorded at $96,895.40 and is depreciated over 5 years. Assuming that the straight-line method is used, the depreciation expense each year is $19,379.08 ($96,895.40 ÷ 5 years). At the end of the lease term, before the lessee transfers the asset to the lessor, the following balances in the accounts result, as illustrated below.

ILLUSTRATION 22-23
Account Balances on Lessee's Books at End of Lease Term—Unguaranteed Residual Value

Leased equipment under capital leases	$96,895	Obligations under capital leases	$–0–
Less: Accumulated depreciation—capital leases	96,895		
	$ –0–		

Assuming that the asset had a fair market value of $3,000, no loss would be reported by the lessee. Assuming that the leased asset has been fully depreciated and that the lease obligation has been fully amortized, no entry is required at the end of the lease term, except to remove the asset from the books.

If the lessee depreciated the asset down to its unguaranteed residual value, a misstatement would occur. That is, the carrying amount of the leased asset would be $5,000 at the end of the lease, but the obligation under the capital lease would be stated at zero before the transfer of the asset. Thus, the lessee would end up reporting a loss of $5,000 when it transferred the asset to the lessor. Depreciation would be understated and net income is overstated in 2002–2005, but in the last year (2006) net income would be understated because of the recorded loss.

Lessee Entries Involving Residual Values. The entries by Lessee Company for both a guaranteed and an unguaranteed residual value are shown in Illustration 22-24 in comparative form.

ILLUSTRATION 22-24
Comparative Entries for
Guaranteed and
Unguaranteed Residual
Values, Lessee Company

Guaranteed Residual Value			Unguaranteed Residual Value		
Capitalization of Lease 1/1/02:					
Leased Equipment under			Leased Equipment under		
Capital Leases	100,000.00		Capital Leases	96,895.40	
Obligations under			Obligations under		
Capital Leases		100,000.00	Capital Leases		96,895.40
First Payment 1/1/02:					
Property Tax Expense	2,000.00		Property Tax Expense	2,000.00	
Obligations under			Obligations under		
Capital Leases	23,237.09		Capital Leases	23,237.09	
Cash		25,237.09	Cash		25,237.09
Adjusting Entry for Accrued Interest 12/31/02:					
Interest Expense	7,676.29		Interest Expense	7,365.83	
Interest Payable		7,676.29	Interest Payable		7,365.83
Entry to Record Depreciation 12/31/02:					
Depreciation Expense—			Depreciation Expense—		
Capital Leases	19,000.00		Capital Leases	19,379.08	
Accumulated Depreciation—			Accumulated Depreciation—		
Capital Leases		19,000.00	Capital Leases		19,379.08
([$100,000 − $5,000] ÷5 years)			($96,895.40 ÷ 5 years)		
Second Payment 1/1/03:					
Property Tax Expense	2,000.00		Property Tax Expense	2,000.00	
Obligations under			Obligations under		
Capital Leases	15,560.80		Capital Leases	15,871.26	
Interest Expense			Interest Expense		
(or Interest Payable)	7,676.29		(or Interest Payable)	7,365.83	
Cash		25,237.09	Cash		25,237.09

Lessor Accounting for Residual Value

As indicated earlier, the net investment to be recovered by the lessor is the same whether the residual value is guaranteed or unguaranteed. The lessor works on the assumption that **the residual value will be realized at the end of the lease term whether guaranteed or unguaranteed**. The lease payments required by the lessor to earn a certain return on investment are the same ($23,237.09) whether the residual value is guaranteed or unguaranteed.

Using the Lessee Company/Lessor Company data and assuming a residual value (either guaranteed or unguaranteed) of $5,000 and classification of the lease as a direct financing lease, the following necessary amounts are computed:

ILLUSTRATION 22-25
Computation of Direct
Financing Lease Amounts
by Lessor

Gross investment = ($23,237.09 × 5) + $5,000 = $121,185.45
Unearned interest revenue = $121,185.45 − $100,000 = $21,185.45
Net investment = $121,185.45 − $21,185.45 = $100,000

The schedule for amortization with guaranteed or unguaranteed residual value is the same:

ILLUSTRATION 22-26
Lease Amortization
Schedule, for Lessor—
Guaranteed or
Unguaranteed Residual
Value

LESSOR COMPANY
Lease Amortization Schedule
(Annuity due basis, **guaranteed** or **unguaranteed** residual value)

Date	Annual Lease Payment Plus Residual Value	Executory Costs	Interest (10%) on Net Investment	Net Investment Recovery	Net Investment
	(a)	(b)	(c)	(d)	(e)
1/1/02					$100,000.00
1/1/02	$ 25,237.09	$ 2,000.00	$ –0–	$ 23,237.09	76,762.91
1/1/03	25,237.09	2,000.00	7,676.29	15,560.80	61,202.11
1/1/04	25,237.09	2,000.00	6,120.21	17,116.88	44,085.23
1/1/05	25,237.09	2,000.00	4,408.52	18,828.57	25,256.66
1/1/06	25,237.09	2,000.00	2,525.67	20,711.42	4,545.24
12/31/06	5,000.00	–0–	454.76*	4,545.24	–0–
	$131,185.45	$10,000.00	$21,185.45	$100,000.00	

(a) Annual lease payment as required by lease.
(b) Executory costs included in rental payment.
(c) Preceding balance of (e) × 10%, except 1/1/02.
(d) (a) minus (b) and (c).
(e) Preceding balance minus (d).
*Rounded by 24 cents.

Using the amounts computed above, the following entries would be made by Lessor Company during the first year for this direct financing lease. Note the similarity to the lessee's entries in Illustration 22-24:

ILLUSTRATION 22-27
Entries for Either
Guaranteed or
Unguaranteed Residual
Value, Lessor Company

Inception of Lease 1/1/02:		
Lease Payments Receivable	121,185.45	
Equipment		100,000.00
Unearned Interest Revenue—Leases		21,185.45
First Payment Received 1/1/02:		
Cash	25,237.09	
Lease Payments Receivable		23,237.09
Property Tax Expense/Property Taxes Payable		2,000.00
Adjusting Entry for Accrued Interest 12/31/02:		
Unearned Interest Revenue—Leases	7,676.29	
Interest Revenue—Leases		7,676.29

Sales-Type Leases (Lessor)

As already indicated, the primary difference between a direct financing lease and a **sales-type lease** is the manufacturer's or dealer's gross profit (or loss). A diagram illustrating these relationships is shown in Illustration 22-28 below and on the next page:

ILLUSTRATION 22-28
Direct Financing versus
Sales-Type Leases

Direct Financing Lease

Equals Fair Market Value

Cost of Asset

Gross Investment

Unearned Interest Revenue

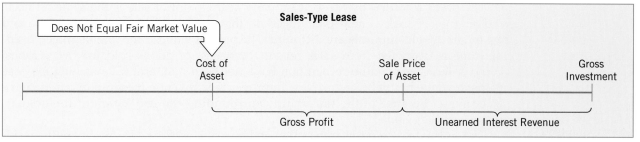

ILLUSTRATION 22-28
Continued

The information necessary to record the sales-type lease is as follows:

SALES-TYPE LEASE TERMS

❶ *Gross Investment* (also *"Lease Payments Receivable"*). The minimum lease payments plus the unguaranteed residual value accruing to the lessor at the end of the lease term.

❷ *Unearned Interest Revenue*. The gross investment less the fair market value of the asset.

❸ *Sales Price of the Asset*. The present value of the minimum lease payments.

❹ *Cost of Goods Sold*. The cost of the asset to the lessor, less the present value of any unguaranteed residual value.

The gross investment and the unearned interest revenue are the same whether a guaranteed or an unguaranteed residual value is involved.

When recording sales revenue and cost of goods sold, there is a difference in the accounting for guaranteed and unguaranteed residual values. The guaranteed residual value can be considered part of sales revenue because the lessor knows that the entire asset has been sold. There is less certainty that the unguaranteed residual portion of the asset has been "sold" (i.e., will be realized); therefore, sales and cost of goods sold are recognized only for the portion of the asset for which realization is assured. However, **the gross profit amount on the sale of the asset is the same whether a guaranteed or unguaranteed residual value is involved**.

To illustrate a sales-type lease with a guaranteed residual value and a sales-type lease with an unguaranteed residual value, assume the same facts as in the preceding direct financing lease situation (pages 1205–1208). The estimated residual value is $5,000 (the present value of which is $3,104.60), and the leased equipment has an $85,000 cost to the dealer, Lessor Company. Assume that the fair market value of the residual value is $3,000 at the end of the lease term.

The amounts relevant to a sales-type lease are computed as follows:

> **OBJECTIVE ❽**
> Describe the lessor's accounting for sales-type leases.

	Sales-Type Lease	
	Guaranteed Residual Value	Unguaranteed Residual Value
Gross investment	$121,185.45 ([$23,237.09 × 5] + $5,000)	Same
Unearned interest revenue	$21,185.45 ($121,185.45 − $100,000)	Same
Sales price of the asset	$100,000 ($96,895.40 + $3,104.60)	$96,895.40
Cost of goods sold	$85,000	$81,895.40 ($85,000 − $3,104.60)
Gross profit	$15,000 ($100,000 − $85,000)	$15,000 ($96,895.40 − $81,895.40)

ILLUSTRATION 22-29
Computation of Lease Amounts by Lessor Company—Sales-Type Lease

The profit recorded by Lessor Company at the point of sale is the same, $15,000, whether the residual value is guaranteed or unguaranteed, **but the sales revenue and cost of goods sold amounts are different**. The present value of the unguaranteed residual value is deducted from sales revenue and cost of goods sold for two reasons: (1) the criteria for revenue recognition have not been met, and (2) matching expense against revenue not yet recognized is improper. The revenue recognition criteria have not been met **because of the uncertainty surrounding the realization of the unguaranteed residual value**.

The entries to record this transaction on January 1, 2002, and the receipt of the residual value at the end of the lease term are presented below.

ILLUSTRATION 22-30
Entries for Guaranteed and Unguaranteed Residual Values, Lessor Company—Sales-Type Lease

Guaranteed Residual Value			Unguaranteed Residual Value		
To record sales-type lease at inception (January 1, 2002):					
Cost of Goods Sold	85,000.00		Cost of Goods Sold	81,895.40	
Lease Payments			Lease Payments		
Receivable	121,185.45		Receivable	121,185.45	
Sales Revenue		100,000.00	Sales Revenue		96,895.40
Unearned Interest Revenue		21,185.45	Unearned Interest Revenue		21,185.45
Inventory		85,000.00	Inventory		85,000.00
To record receipt of the first lease payment (January 1, 2002):					
Cash	25,237.09		Cash	25,237.09	
Lease Payments Receivable		23,237.09	Lease Payments Receivable		23,237.09
Prop. Tax Exp./Prop. Tax. Pay.		2,000.00	Prop. Tax Exp./Prop. Tax Pay.		2,000.00
To recognize interest revenue earned during the first year (December 31, 2002):					
Unearned Interest Revenue	7,676.29		Unearned Interest Revenue	7,676.29	
Interest Revenue		7,676.29	Interest Revenue		7,676.29
(See lease amortization schedule, Illustration 22-26 on page 1214.)					
To record receipt of the second lease payment (January 1, 2003):					
Cash	25,237.09		Cash	25,237.09	
Lease Payments Receivable		23,237.09	Lease Payments Receivable		23,237.09
Prop. Tax Exp./Prop. Tax. Pay.		2,000.00	Prop. Tax Exp./Prop. Tax Pay.		2,000.00
To recognize interest revenue earned during the second year (December 31, 2003):					
Unearned Interest Revenue	6,120.21		Unearned Interest Revenue	6,120.21	
Interest Revenue		6,120.21	Interest Revenue		6,120.21
To record receipt of residual value at end of lease term (December 31, 2006):					
Inventory	3,000		Inventory	3,000	
Cash	2,000		Loss on Capital Lease	2,000	
Lease Payments Receivable		5,000	Lease Payments Receivable		5,000

The **estimated unguaranteed residual value in a sales-type lease** (and a direct financing-type lease) **must be reviewed periodically**. If the estimate of the unguaranteed residual value declines, the accounting for the transaction must be revised using the changed estimate. The decline represents a reduction in the lessor's net investment and is recognized as a loss in the period in which the residual estimate is reduced. Upward adjustments in estimated residual value are not recognized.

Bargain Purchase Option (Lessee)

A bargain purchase option allows the lessee to purchase the leased property for a future price that is substantially lower than the property's expected future fair value. The price is so favorable at the lease's inception that the future exercise of the option appears to be reasonably assured. If a bargain purchase option exists, **the lessee must increase the present value of the minimum lease payments by the present value of the option price**.

For example, assume that Lessee Company in the illustration on page 1210 had an option to buy the leased equipment for $5,000 at the end of the 5-year lease term when the fair value is expected to be $18,000. The significant difference between the option price and the fair value creates a bargain purchase option, the exercise of which is reasonably assured. Four computations are affected by a bargain purchase option in the same manner that they are by a guaranteed residual value: (1) the amount of the five lease payments necessary for the lessor to earn a 10% return on net investment, (2) the amount of the minimum lease payments, (3) the amount capitalized as leased assets and lease obligation, and (4) the amortization of the lease obligation. Therefore, the computations, amortization schedule, and entries that would be prepared for this $5,000 bargain purchase option are identical to those shown for the $5,000 guaranteed residual value.

The only difference between the accounting treatment for a bargain purchase option and a guaranteed residual value of identical amounts and circumstances is in the **computation of the annual depreciation**. In the case of a guaranteed residual value, the lessee depreciates the asset over the lease term, whereas in the case of a bargain purchase option, the lessee uses the **economic life** of the asset.

Initial Direct Costs (Lessor)

Initial direct costs are of two types.[21] The first, **incremental direct costs**, are costs paid to independent third parties, incurred in originating a lease arrangement. Examples would include cost of independent appraisal of collateral used to secure a lease, or the cost of an outside credit check of the lessee or a broker's fee for finding the lessee.

The second type, **internal direct costs**, are the costs directly related to specified activities performed **by the lessor** on a given lease. Examples are evaluating the prospective lessee's financial condition; evaluating and recording guarantees, collateral, and other security arrangements; negotiating lease terms and preparing and processing lease documents; and closing the transaction. The costs directly related to an employee's time spent on a specific lease transaction are also considered initial direct costs.

On the other hand, initial direct costs should **not** include **internal indirect costs** related to activities performed by the lessor for advertising, servicing existing leases, and establishing and monitoring credit policies; nor should they include costs for supervision and administration. In addition, expenses such as rent and depreciation are not considered initial direct costs.

For **operating leases**, the lessor should defer initial direct costs and **allocate them over the lease term** in proportion to the recognition of rental income. In a **sales-type lease** transaction, the lessor expenses the initial direct costs in the year of incurrence; that is, they are **expensed in the period** in which the profit on the sale is recognized.

In a **direct financing lease**, however, initial direct costs are added to the net investment in the lease and **amortized over the life of the lease as a yield adjustment**. In addition, the unamortized deferred initial direct costs that are part of the lessor's investment in the direct financing lease must be disclosed. If the carrying value of the asset in the lease is $4,000,000 and the lessor incurs initial direct costs of $35,000, then the net investment in the lease would be $4,035,000. The yield would be adjusted to ensure proper amortization of this amount over the life of the lease and would be lower than the initial rate of return.

Current versus Noncurrent

The classification of the lease obligation/net investment was presented earlier in an annuity due situation. As indicated in Illustration 22-7, the lessee's current liability is the payment ($23,981.62) to be made on January 1 of the next year. Similarly, as shown in

---

[21]"Accounting for Nonrefundable Fees and Costs Associated with Originating or Acquiring Loans and Initial Direct Costs of Leases," *Statement of Financial Accounting Standards No. 91* (Stamford: Conn.: FASB, 1987).

Illustration 22-16, the lessor's current asset is the amount to be collected ($23,981.62) on January 1 of the next year. In both of these annuity due instances, the balance sheet date is December 31 and the due date of the lease payment is January 1 (less than one year), so the present value ($23,981.62) of the payment due the following January 1 is the same as the rental payment ($23,981.62).

What happens if the situation is an ordinary annuity rather than an annuity due situation? For example, assume that the rent is to be paid at the end of the year (December 31) rather than at the beginning (January 1). *FASB Statement No. 13* does not indicate how to measure the current and noncurrent amounts; it requires that for the lessee the "obligations shall be separately identified on the balance sheet as obligations under capital leases and shall be subject to the same considerations as other obligations in classifying them with current and noncurrent liabilities in classified balance sheets."[22] **The most common method of measuring the current liability portion in ordinary annuity leases is the change in the present value method.**[23]

To illustrate the change in the present value method, assume an ordinary annuity situation with the same facts as the Lessee Company/Lessor Company case, excluding the $2,000 of executory costs. Because the rents are paid at the end of the period instead of at the beginning, the five rents are set at $26,379.73 to have an effective interest rate of 10%. The ordinary annuity amortization schedule appears as follows:

ILLUSTRATION 22-31
Lease Amortization
Schedule—Ordinary
Annuity Basis

	LESSEE COMPANY/LESSOR COMPANY			
	Lease Amortization Schedule			
	(Ordinary annuity basis)			
Date	Annual Lease Payment	Interest 10%	Reduction of Principal	Balance of Lease Obligation/ Net Investment
1/1/02				$100,000.00
12/31/02	$ 26,379.73	$10,000.00	$ 16,379.73	83,620.27
12/31/03	26,379.73	8,362.03	18,017.70	65,602.57
12/31/04	26,379.73	6,560.26	19,819.47	45,783.10
12/31/05	26,379.73	4,578.31	21,801.42	23,981.68
12/31/06	26,379.73	2,398.05*	23,981.68	–0–
	$131,898.65	$31,898.65	$100,000.00	

*Rounded by 12 cents.

The current portion of the lease obligation/net investment under the **change in the present value method** as of December 31, 2002, would be $18,017.70 ($83,620.27 − $65,602.57); and as of December 31, 2003, it would be $19,819.47 ($65,602.57 − $45,783.10). The portion of the lease obligation/net investment that is not current is classified as such; that is, $65,602.57 is the noncurrent portion at December 31, 2002.

Thus, both the annuity due and the ordinary annuity situations report the reduction of principal for the next period as a current liability/current asset. In the annuity due situation, interest is accrued during the year but is not paid until the next period. As a result, **a current liability/current asset arises for both the principal reduction and the interest** that was incurred/earned in the preceding period.

In the ordinary annuity situation, the interest accrued during the period is also paid in the same period; consequently, only the principal reduction is shown as a current liability/current asset.

---

[22]"Accounting for Leases," op. cit., par. 16.

[23]For additional discussion on this approach and possible alternatives, see R. J. Swieringa, "When Current Is Noncurrent and Vice Versa!" *The Accounting Review,* January 1984, pp. 123–30, and A. W. Richardson, "The Measurement of the Current Portion of the Long-Term Lease Obligations—Some Evidence from Practice," *The Accounting Review,* October 1985, pages 744–52.

Disclosing Lease Data

Disclosures Required of the Lessee

OBJECTIVE 9
Describe the disclosure requirements for leases.

The FASB requires that the following information with respect to leases be disclosed in the **lessee's** financial statements or in the notes.[24]

(a) For capital leases:
  i. The gross amount of assets at each balance sheet date categorized by nature or function. This information may be combined with comparable information for owned assets.
  ii. Future *minimum lease payments* as of the latest balance sheet date, in the aggregate and for each of five succeeding fiscal years. Separate deductions for *executory costs* included in the *minimum lease payments* and for the amount of imputed interest necessary to reduce net *minimum lease payments* to present value.
  iii. Total noncancelable minimum sublease rentals to be received in the future, as of the latest balance sheet date.
  iv. Total *contingent rentals.*
  v. Assets recorded under capital leases and the accumulated amortization thereon shall be separately identified in the lessee's balance sheet or notes. Likewise, related obligations shall be separately identified as obligations under capital leases. Depreciation on capitalized leased assets should be separately disclosed.

(b) For operating leases having initial or remaining noncancelable *lease terms* in excess of one year:
  i. Future minimum rental payments required as of the latest balance sheet date, in the aggregate and for each of the five succeeding fiscal years.
  ii. Total minimum rentals to be received in the future under noncancelable subleases as of the latest balance sheet date.

(c) For all operating leases, rental expense for each period with separate amounts for minimum rentals, *contingent rentals,* and sublease rentals. Rental payments under leases with *terms* of a month or less that were not renewed need not be included.

(d) A general description of the lessee's arrangements including, but not limited to:
  i. The basis on which *contingent rental* payments are determined.
  ii. The existence and terms of renewal or purchase options and escalation clauses.
  iii. Restrictions imposed by lease agreements, such as those concerning dividends, additional debt, and further leasing.

ILLUSTRATION 22-32
Lessee's Disclosures

Disclosures Required of the Lessor

The FASB requires that **lessors** disclose in the financial statements or in the notes the following information when leasing "is a significant part of the lessor's business activities in terms of revenue, net income, or assets."[25]

(a) For sales-type and direct financing leases:
  i. The components of the net investment in sales-type and direct financing leases as of each balance sheet date:
    a. Future *minimum lease payments* to be received, with separate deductions for (i) *executory costs* and (ii) the accumulated allowance for uncollectible *minimum lease payments* receivable.
    b. The *unguaranteed residual values* accruing to the lessor.
    c. Unearned revenue.
  ii. Future *minimum lease payments* to be received for each of the five succeeding fiscal years.
  iii. The amount of unearned revenue included in income to offset *initial direct costs* charged against income for

each period for which an income statement is presented. (For direct financing leases only.)
  iv. Total *contingent rentals* included in income for each period for which an income statement is presented.

(b) For operating leases:
  i. The cost and carrying amount, if different, of leased property according to nature or function, and total amount of accumulated depreciation.
  ii. Minimum future rentals on noncancelable leases as of the latest balance sheet date, in aggregate and for each of five succeeding fiscal years.
  iii. Total *contingent rentals* included in income for each period for which an income statement is presented.

(c) A general description of the lessor's leasing arrangements.

ILLUSTRATION 22-33
Lessor's Disclosures

Disclosures Illustrated

The financial statement excerpts from the 1999 Annual Report of The Penn Traffic Company in Illustration 22-34 present the statement and note disclosures typical of a **lessee** having both capital leases and operating leases.

---

[24]"Accounting for Leases," *FASB Statement No. 13,* as amended and interpreted through May 1980 (Stamford, Conn.: FASB, 1980), par. 16.

[25]Ibid., par. 23.

ILLUSTRATION 22-34
Disclosure of Leases
by Lessee

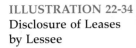

Go to the Digital Tool for
additional lease disclosures.

PENN TRAFFIC COMPANY

(Dollar amounts in thousands)

Assets—Capital Leases (Note 6)	1999	1998
Capital leases	$157,667	$190,638
Less: Accumulated amortization	(66,735)	(75,057)
	90,932	115,581

Current Liabilities		
Current portion of obligations under capital leases (Note 6)	$ 11,516	$ 13,518

Noncurrent Liabilities		
Obligations under capital leases (Note 6)	98,029	121,436

Note 6: Leases

The Company principally operates in leased store facilities with terms of up to 20 years with renewable options for additional periods. The Company follows the provisions of Statement of Financial Accounting Standards No. 13, "Accounting for Leases" ("SFAS 13"), in determining the criteria for capital leases. Leases that do not meet such criteria are classified as operating leases and related rentals are charged to expense in the year incurred.

For Fiscal 1999, 1998 and 1997, capital lease amortization expense was $11.8 million, $13.8 million and $14.5 million, respectively.

The following is a summary by year of future minimum rental payments for capitalized leases and for operating leases that have initial or remaining noncancelable terms in excess of one year as of January 30, 1999:

Fiscal Years Ending:	Total	Operating	Capital
	(in thousands of dollars)		
2000	$ 60,728	$ 37,715	$ 23,013
2001	58,308	36,908	21,400
2002	53,080	34,172	18,908
2003	47,183	30,204	16,979
2004	42,037	27,557	14,480
Later years	295,008	198,633	96,375
Total minimum lease payments	$556,344	$365,189	191,155
Less: Executory costs			(477)
Net minimum capital lease payments			190,678
Less: Estimated amount representing interest			(81,133)
Present value of net minimum capital lease payments			109,545
Less: Current portion			(11,516)
Long-term obligations under capital lease at January 30, 1999			$ 98,029

Minimum rental payments and related executory costs for operating leases were as follows:

	Fiscal Year Ended		
	January 30, 1999	January 31, 1998	February 1, 1997
	(in thousands of dollars)		
Minimum rentals and executory costs	$ 46,250	$ 44,560	$ 45,067
Contingent rentals	3,082	2,691	2,760
Less: Sublease payments	(10,865)	(9,577)	(10,086)
Net rental payments	$ 38,467	$ 37,674	$ 37,741

The following note from the 1998 Annual Report of Dana Corporation illustrates the disclosures of a **lessor**.

DANA CORPORATION

Notes to Financial Statements
(in millions)
Note 1 (In Part): Summary of Significant Accounting Policies
Lease Financing
Lease financing consists of direct financing leases, leveraged leases and equipment on operating leases. Income on direct financing leases is recognized by a method which produces a constant periodic rate of return on the outstanding investment in the lease. Income on leveraged leases is recognized by a method which produces a constant rate of return on the outstanding net investment in the lease, net of the related deferred tax liability, in the years in which the net investment is positive. Initial direct costs are deferred and amortized using the interest method over the lease period. Equipment under operating leases is recorded at cost, net of accumulated depreciation. Income from operating leases is recognized ratably over the term of the leases.

The components of the net investment in direct financing leases are as follows:

	December 31,	
	1997	1998
Total minimum lease payments	$743.7	$137.7
Residual values	89.5	34.8
Deferred initial direct costs	15.5	2.3
	848.7	174.8
Less: Unearned income	182.9	57.3
	$665.8	$117.5

The following is a schedule, by year, of total minimum lease payments receivable on direct financing leases as of December 31, 1998:

Year Ending December 31:	
1999	$ 23.9
2000	21.8
2001	18.5
2002	14.6
2003	11.5
Later years	47.4
Total minimum lease payments receivable	$137.7

ILLUSTRATION 22-35
Disclosure of Leases by Lessor

LEASE ACCOUNTING—UNSOLVED PROBLEMS

As indicated at the beginning of this chapter, lease accounting is a much abused area in which strenuous efforts are being made to circumvent *Statement No. 13.* In practice, the accounting rules for capitalizing leases have been rendered partially ineffective by the strong desires of lessees to resist capitalization. Leasing generally involves large dollar amounts that when capitalized materially increase reported liabilities and adversely affect the debt-to-equity ratio. Lease capitalization is also resisted because charges to expense made in the early years of the lease term are higher under the capital lease method than under the operating method, frequently without tax benefit. As a consequence, "let's beat *Statement No. 13*" is one of the most popular games in town.[26]

---

[26]Richard Dieter, "Is Lessee Accounting Working?" *The CPA Journal,* August 1979, pp. 13–19. This article provides interesting examples of abuses of *Statement No. 13,* discusses the circumstances that led to the current situation, and proposes a solution.

To avoid leased asset capitalization, lease agreements are designed, written, and interpreted so that none of the four capitalized lease criteria are satisfied from the lessee's viewpoint. Devising lease agreements in such a way has not been too difficult when the following specifications have been met.

❶ Make certain that the lease does not specify the transfer of title of the property to the lessee.

❷ Do not write in a bargain purchase option.

❸ Set the lease term at something less than 75% of the estimated economic life of the leased property.

❹ Arrange for the present value of the minimum lease payments to be less than 90% of the fair value of the leased property.

The real challenge lies in disqualifying the lease as a capital lease to the lessee while having the same lease qualify as a capital (sales or financing) lease to the lessor. Unlike lessees, lessors try to avoid having lease arrangements classified as operating leases.[27]

Avoiding the first three criteria is relatively simple, but it takes a little ingenuity to avoid the "90% recovery test" for the lessee while satisfying it for the lessor. Two of the factors involved in this effort are (1) the use of the incremental borrowing rate by the lessee when it is higher than the implicit interest rate of the lessor, by making information about the implicit rate unavailable to the lessee; and (2) residual value guarantees.

The lessee's use of the higher interest rate is probably the more popular subterfuge. While lessees are knowledgeable about the fair value of the leased property and, of course, the rental payments, they generally are not aware of the estimated residual value used by the lessor. Therefore the lessee who does not know exactly the lessor's implicit interest rate might use a different incremental borrowing rate.

The residual value guarantee is the other unique, yet popular, device used by lessees and lessors. In fact, a whole new industry has emerged to circumvent symmetry between the lessee and the lessor in accounting for leases. The residual value guarantee has spawned numerous companies whose principal, or even sole, function is to guarantee the residual value of leased assets. These **third-party guarantors** (insurers), for a fee, assume the risk of deficiencies in leased asset residual value.

Because the guaranteed residual value is included in the minimum lease payments for the lessor, the 90% recovery of fair market value test is satisfied. The lease is a nonoperating lease to the lessor. But because the residual value is guaranteed by a third party, the minimum lease payments of the lessee do not include the guarantee. Thus, by merely transferring some of the risk to a third party, lessees can alter substantially the accounting treatment by converting what would otherwise be capital leases to operating leases.[28]

Much of this circumvention is encouraged by the nature of the criteria, which stem from weaknesses in the basic objective of *Statement No. 13*. Accounting standard-setting bodies continue to have poor experience with arbitrary break points or other size and percentage criteria—that is, rules like "90% of," "75% of," etc. Some believe that a more workable solution would be to require capitalization of all leases that ex-

---

[27]The reason is that most lessors are financial institutions and do not want these types of assets on their balance sheets. In fact, banks and savings and loans are not permitted to report these assets on their balance sheets except for relatively short periods of time. Furthermore, the capital lease transaction from the lessor's standpoint provides higher income flows in the earlier periods of the lease.

[28]As an aside, third-party guarantors have experienced some difficulty. **Lloyd's of London**, at one time, insured the fast growing U.S. computer-leasing industry in the amount of $2 billion against revenue losses and losses in residual value if leases were canceled. Because of "overnight" technological improvements and the successive introductions of more efficient and less expensive computers by computer manufacturers, lessees in abundance canceled their leases. As the market for second-hand computers became flooded and residual values plummeted, third-party guarantor Lloyd's of London projected a loss of $400 million. Much of the third-party guarantee business was stimulated by the lessees' and lessors' desire to circumvent *FASB Statement No. 13*.

tend for some defined period (such as one year) on the basis that the lessee has acquired an asset (a property right) and a corresponding liability rather than on the basis that the lease transfers substantially all the risks and rewards of ownership.

Three years after it issued *Statement No. 13,* a majority of the FASB expressed "the tentative view that, if *Statement 13* were to be reconsidered, they would support a property right approach in which all leases are included as 'rights to use property' and as 'lease obligations' in the lessee's balance sheet."[29] Recently, the FASB and other international standard setters have issued a report on lease accounting that proposes the capitalization of more leases.[30]

ILLUSTRATIONS OF DIFFERENT LEASE ARRANGEMENTS

To illustrate concepts discussed in this chapter, assume that Morgan Bakeries is involved in four different lease situations. Each of these leases is noncancelable and in no case does Morgan receive title to the properties leased during or at the end of the lease term. All leases start on January 1, 2002, with the first rental due at the beginning of the year. The additional information is shown in Illustration 22-36.

ILLUSTRATION 22-36
Illustrative Lease Situations, Lessors

	Harmon, Inc.	Arden's Oven Co.	Mendota Truck Co.	Appleland Computer
Type of property	Cabinets	Oven	Truck	Computer
Yearly rental	$6,000	$15,000	$5,582.62	$3,557.25
Lease term	20 years	10 years	3 years	3 years
Estimated economic life	30 years	25 years	7 years	5 years
Purchase option	None	$75,000 at end of 10 years $4,000 at end of 15 years	None	$3,000 at end of 3 years, which approximates fair market value
Renewal option	None	5-year renewal option at $15,000 per year	None	1 year at $1,500; no penalty for non-renewal; standard renewal clause
Fair market value at inception of lease	$60,000	$120,000	$20,000	$10,000
Cost of asset to lessor	$60,000	$120,000	$15,000	$10,000
Residual value				
Guaranteed	–0–	–0–	$7,000	–0–
Unguaranteed	$5,000	–0–	–0–	$3,000
Incremental borrowing rate of lessee	12%	12%	12%	12%
Executory costs paid by	*Lessee* $300 per year	*Lessee* $1,000 per year	*Lessee* $500 per year	*Lessor* Estimated to be $500 per year
Present value of minimum lease payments Using incremental borrowing rate of lessee	$50,194.68	$115,153.35	$20,000	$8,224.16
Using implicit rate of lessor	Not known	Not known	Not known	Known by lessee, $8,027.48
Estimated fair market value at end of lease	$5,000	$80,000 at end of 10 years $60,000 at end of 15 years	Not available	$3,000

[29]"Is Lessee Accounting Working?" op. cit., p. 19.

[30]H. Nailor and A. Lennard, "Capital Leases: Implementation of a New Approach," *Financial Accounting Series No. 206A* (Norwalk, Conn.: FASB, 2000).

Harmon, Inc.

The following is an analysis of the Harmon, Inc. lease:

❶ Transfer of title? No.

❷ Bargain purchase option? No.

❸ Economic life test (75% test). The lease term is 20 years and the estimated economic life is 30 years. Thus it does **not** meet the 75% test.

❹ Recovery of investment test (90% test):

Fair market value	$60,000	Rental payments	$	6,000
Rate	90%	PV of annuity due for		
90% of fair market value	$54,000	20 years at 12%		× 8.36578
		PV of rental payments		$50,194.68

Because the present value of the minimum lease payments is less than 90% of the fair market value, the 90% test is not met. Both Morgan and Harmon should account for this lease as an operating lease, as indicated by the January 1, 2002, entries shown below.

ILLUSTRATION 22-37
Comparative Entries for Operating Lease

Morgan Bakeries (Lessee)			Harmon, Inc. (Lessor)		
Rent Expense	6,000		Cash	6,000	
Cash		6,000	Rental Revenue		6,000

Arden's Oven Co.

The following is an analysis of the Arden's Oven Co. lease.

❶ Transfer of title? No.

❷ Bargain purchase option? The $75,000 option at the end of 10 years does not appear to be sufficiently lower than the expected fair value of $80,000 to make it reasonably assured that it will be exercised. However, the $4,000 at the end of 15 years when the fair value is $60,000 does appear to be a bargain. From the information given, criterion 2 is therefore met. Note that both the guaranteed and the unguaranteed residual values are assigned zero values because the lessor does not expect to repossess the leased asset.

❸ Economic life test (75% test): Given that a bargain purchase option exists, the lease term is the initial lease period of 10 years plus the 5-year renewal option since it precedes a bargain purchase option. Even though the lease term is now considered to be 15 years, this test is still not met because 75% of the economic life of 25 years is 18.75 years.

❹ Recovery of investment test (90% test):

Fair market value	$120,000	Rental payments	$ 15,000.00
Rate	90%	PV of annuity due for	
90% of fair market value	$108,000	15 years at 12%	× 7.62817
		PV of rental payments	$114,422.55

PV of bargain purchase option: = $4,000(PVF$_{15,12\%}$) = $4,000(.18270) = $730.80

PV of rental payments	$114,422.55
PV of bargain purchase option	730.80
PV of minimum lease payments	$115,153.35

The present value of the minimum lease payments if greater than 90% of the fair market value; therefore, the 90% test is met. Morgan Bakeries should account for this as a capital lease because both criterion 2 and criterion 4 are met. Assuming that Arden's implicit rate is the same as Morgan's incremental borrowing rate, the following entries are made on January 1, 2002.

Morgan Bakeries (Lessee)		Arden's Oven Co. (Lessor)		
Leased Asset—Oven 115,153.35		Lease Payments		
Obligation under		Receivable	229,000*	
Capital Lease	115,153.35	Unearned Interest		
		Revenue		109,000
		Asset—Oven		120,000
		*([$15,000 × 15] + $4,000)		

ILLUSTRATION 22-38
Comparative Entries for Capital Lease—Bargain Purchase Option

Morgan Bakeries would depreciate the leased asset over its economic life of 25 years, given the bargain purchase option. Arden's does not use sales-type accounting because the fair market value and the cost of the asset are the same at the inception of the lease.

Mendota Truck Co.

The following is an analysis of the Mendota Truck Co. lease.

1. **Transfer of title?** No.
2. **Bargain purchase option?** No.
3. **Economic life test (75% test):** The lease term is three years and the estimated economic life is seven years. Thus it does **not** meet the 75% test.
4. **Recovery of investment test (90% test):**

Fair market value	$20,000	Rental payments	$ 5,582.62
Rate	90%	PV of annuity due for	
90% of fair market value	$18,000	3 years at 12%	× 2.69005
		PV of rental payments	$15,017.54

(Note: adjusted for $.01 due to rounding)

PV of guaranteed residual value: = $7,000(PVF$_{3.12\%}$) = $7,000(.71178) = $4,982.46

PV of rental payments	$15,017.54
PV of guaranteed residual value	4,982.46
PV of minimum lease payments	$20,000.00

The present value of the minimum lease payments is greater than 90% of the fair market value; therefore, the 90% test is met. Assuming that Mendota's implicit rate is the same as Morgan's incremental borrowing rate, the following entries are made on January 1, 2002.

Morgan Bakeries (Lessee)		Mendota Truck Co. (Lessor)		
Leased Asset—Truck 20,000.00		Lease Payments		
Obligation under		Receivable	23,747.86*	
Capital Lease	20,000.00	Cost of Goods Sold	15,000.00	
		Inventory—Truck		15,000.00
		Sales		20,000.00
		Unearned Interest		
		Revenue		3,747.86
		*[($5,582.62 × 3) + $7,000]		

ILLUSTRATION 22-39
Comparative Entries for Capital Lease

The leased asset is depreciated by Morgan over three years to its guaranteed residual value.

Appleland Computer

The following is an analysis of the Appleland Computer lease.

① **Transfer of title?** No.

② **Bargain purchase option?** No. The option to purchase at the end of 3 years at approximate fair market value is clearly not a bargain.

③ **Economic life test (75% test):** The lease term is 3 years and no bargain renewal period exists. Therefore the 75% test is **not** met.

④ **Recovery of investment test (90% test):**

Fair market value	$10,000	Rental payments	$3,557.25
Rate	90%	Less executory costs	500.00
90% of fair market value	$ 9,000		3,057.25
		PV of annuity due factor for 3 years at 12%	× 2.69005
		PV of minimum lease payments using incremental borrowing rate	$8,224.16

The present value of the minimum lease payments using the incremental borrowing rate is $8,224.16; using the implicit rate, it is $8,027.48 (see Illustration 22-36). The implicit rate of the lessor is, therefore, higher than the incremental borrowing rate. Given this situation, the lessee uses the $8,224.16 (lower interest rate when discounting) when comparing with the 90% of fair market value. Because the present value of the minimum lease payments is lower than 90% of the fair market value, the recovery of investment test is **not** met.

The following entries are made on January 1, 2002, indicating an operating lease.

ILLUSTRATION 22-40
Comparative Entries for Operating Lease

Morgan Bakeries (Lessee)		Appleland Computer (Lessor)	
Rent Expense 3,557.25		Cash 3,557.25	
Cash	3,557.25	Rental Revenue	3,557.25

If the lease payments had been $3,557.25 with no executory costs involved, this lease arrangement would have qualified for capital lease accounting treatment.

SUMMARY OF LEARNING OBJECTIVES

① **Explain the nature, economic substance, and advantages of lease transactions.** A lease is a contractual agreement between a lessor and a lessee that conveys to the lessee the right to use specific property (real or personal), owned by the lessor, for a specified period of time. In return for this right, the lessee agrees to make periodic cash payments (rents) to the lessor. The advantages of lease transactions are: (1) 100% financing; (2) protection against obsolescence, (3) flexibility, (4) less costly financing, (5) possible tax advantages, and (6) off-balance-sheet financing.

② **Describe the accounting criteria and procedures for capitalizing leases by the lessee.** A lease is a capital lease if one or more of the following criteria are met: (1) the lease transfers ownership of the property to the lessee; (2) the lease contains a bargain purchase option; (3) the lease term is equal to 75% or more of the estimated economic life of the leased property; (4) the present value of the minimum lease payments (excluding executory costs) equals or exceeds 90% of the fair value of the leased property. For a capital lease, the lessee records an asset and a liability at the lower of (1) the present value of the minimum lease payments or (2) the fair market value of the leased asset at the inception of the lease.

③ Contrast the operating and capitalization methods of recording leases. The total charges to operations are the same over the lease term whether the lease is accounted for as a capital lease or as an operating lease; under the capital lease treatment, the charges are higher in the earlier years and lower in the later years. If an accelerated method of depreciation is used, the differences between the amounts charged to operations under the two methods would be even larger in the earlier and later years. The following occurs if a capital lease instead of an operating lease is employed: (1) an increase in the amount of reported debt (both short-term and long-term), (2) an increase in the amount of total assets (specifically long-lived assets), and (3) a lower income early in the life of the lease and, therefore, lower retained earnings.

④ Identify the classifications of leases for the lessor. From the standpoint of the lessor, all leases may be classified for accounting purpose as follows: (1) operating leases, (2) direct financing leases, (3) sales-type leases. The lessor should classify and account for an arrangement as a direct financing lease or a sales-type lease if, at the date of the lease agreement, one or more of the Group I criteria (as shown in learning objective 2 for lessees) are met and both of the following Group II criteria are met. *Group II:* (1) Collectibility of the payments required from the lessee is reasonably predictable; and (2) no important uncertainties surround the amount of unreimbursable costs yet to be incurred by the lessor under the lease. All leases that fail to meet the criteria are classified and accounted for by the lessor as operating leases.

⑤ Describe the lessor's accounting for direct financing leases. Leases that are in substance the financing of an asset purchase by a lessee require the lessor to substitute a "lease payments receivable" for the leased asset. The information necessary to record a direct financing lease is: (1) gross investment ("lease payments receivable"), (2) unearned interest revenue, and (3) net investment. There often is uncertainty as to how to account for the residual values when computing gross investment. When "lease payments receivable" is defined as minimum lease payments plus unguaranteed residual value, it means that the residual value, whether guaranteed or unguaranteed, is included as part of lease payments receivable if it is relevant to the lessor (i.e., if the lessor expects to get the asset back).

⑥ Identify special features of lease arrangements that cause unique accounting problems. The features of lease arrangements that cause unique accounting problems are: (1) residual values; (2) sales-type leases (lessor); (3) bargain purchase options; (4) initial direct costs; (5) current versus noncurrent; and (6) disclosures.

⑦ Describe the effect of residual values, guaranteed and unguaranteed, on lease accounting. Whether the estimated residual value is guaranteed or unguaranteed is of both economic and accounting consequence to the lessee. The accounting difference is that the minimum lease payments, the basis for capitalization, includes the guaranteed residual value but excludes the unguaranteed residual value. A guaranteed residual value affects the lessee's computation of minimum lease payments and, therefore, the amounts capitalized as a leased asset and a lease obligation. In effect, it is an additional lease payment that will be paid in property or cash, or both, at the end of the lease term. An unguaranteed residual value from the lessee's viewpoint is the same as no residual value in terms of its effect upon the lessee's method of computing the minimum lease payments and the capitalization of the leased asset and the lease obligation.

⑧ Describe the lessor's accounting for sales-type leases. The information needed to record the sales-type lease is as follows: (1) gross investment (also "lease payments receivable"); (2) unearned interest revenue; (3) sales price of the asset; and (4) cost of goods sold. The gross investment and the unearned interest revenue are the same whether a guaranteed or an unguaranteed residual value is involved. When recording sales revenue and cost of goods sold, there is a difference in the accounting for guaranteed and unguaranteed residual values. The guaranteed residual value can be

KEY TERMS

bargain purchase option, *1194*

bargain renewal option, *1195*

capital lease, *1193*

capitalization criteria, *1194*

capitalization of leases, *1192*

cost of goods sold (sales-type lease), *1215*

direct financing lease, *1204*

effective interest method, *1197*

executory costs, *1196*

gross investment, *1205, 1215*

guaranteed residual value, *1196*

implicit interest rate, *1196*

incremental borrowing rate, *1196*

initial direct costs, *1217*

lease, *1190*

lease payments receivable, *1205, 1215*

lease term, *1190*

lessee, *1190*

lessor, *1190*

manufacturer's or dealer's profit, *1203*

minimum lease payments, *1195*

net investment, *1205*

noncancelable, *1193*

off-balance-sheet financing, *1191*

operating lease, *1194*

sales price (sales-type lease), *1215*

sales-type lease, *1214*

third-party guarantors, *1222*

unearned interest revenue, *1205, 1215*

unguaranteed residual value, *1211*

considered part of sales revenue because the lessor knows that the entire asset has been sold. There is less certainty that the unguaranteed residual portion of the asset has been "sold"; therefore, sales and cost of goods sold are recognized only for the portion of the asset for which realization is assured. However, the gross profit amount on the sale of the asset is the same whether a guaranteed or unguaranteed residual value is involved.

⑨ Describe the disclosure requirements for leases. The disclosure requirements for the **lessee** are classified as follows: (1) capital leases; (2) operating leases having initial or remaining noncancelable lease terms in excess of one year; (3) all operating leases; and (4) a general description of the lessee's arrangements. The disclosure requirements for the **lessor** are classified as follows: (1) sales-type and direct financing leases; (2) operating leases; and (3) a general description of the lessor's leasing arrangements.

Go to the Digital Tool for an expanded discussion of real estate leases and leveraged leases.

APPENDIX **22A**

Sale-Leasebacks

OBJECTIVE ⑩
After studying Appendix 22A, you should be able to: Describe the lessee's accounting for sale-leaseback transactions.

The term **sale-leaseback** describes a transaction in which the owner of the property (seller-lessee) sells the property to another and simultaneously leases it back from the new owner. The use of the property is generally continued without interruption.

Sale-leasebacks are common. Financial institutions (**Bank of America** and **First Chicago**) have used this technique for their administrative offices, public utilities (**Ohio Edison** and **Pinnacle West Corporation**) for their generating plants, and airlines (**Continental** and **Alaska Airlines**) for their aircraft. The advantages of a sale-leaseback from the seller's viewpoint usually involve two primary considerations.

❶ *Financing*—If the purchase of equipment has already been financed, a sale-leaseback can allow the seller to refinance at lower rates, assuming rates have dropped. In addition, a sale-leaseback can provide another source of working capital, particularly when liquidity is tight.

❷ *Taxes*—At the time a company purchased equipment, it may not have known that it would be subject to a minimum tax and that ownership might increase its minimum tax liability. By selling the property, the seller-lessee may deduct the entire lease payment, which is not subject to minimum tax considerations.

DETERMINING ASSET USE

UNDERLYING CONCEPTS

A sale-leaseback is similar in substance to the parking of inventories discussed in Chapter 8. The ultimate economic benefits remain under the control of the "seller," thus the definition of an asset is satisfied.

To the extent the **seller-lessee's use** of the asset sold continues after the sale, the sale-leaseback is really a form of financing, and therefore **no gain or loss should be recognized** on the transaction. In short, the seller-lessee is simply borrowing funds. On the other hand, if the **seller-lessee gives up the right to the use** of the asset sold, the transaction is in substance a sale, and **gain or loss recognition** is appropriate. Trying to ascertain when the lessee has given up the use of the asset is difficult, however, and complex rules have been formulated to identify this situation.[1] To understand the profession's position in this area, the basic accounting for the lessee and lessor are discussed below.

Lessee

If the lease meets one of the four criteria for treatment as a capital lease (see Illustration 22-4), the **seller-lessee accounts for the transaction as a sale and the lease as a capital lease**. Any profit or loss experienced by the seller-lessee from the sale of the assets that are leased back under a capital lease should be **deferred and amortized over the lease term** (or the economic life if either criterion 1 or 2 is satisfied) in proportion to the amortization of the leased assets. If Lessee, Inc. sells equipment having a book value of $580,000 and a fair value of $623,110 to Lessor, Inc. for $623,110 and leases the equipment back for $50,000 a year for 20 years, the profit of $43,110 should be amortized over the 20-year period at the same rate that the $623,110 is depreciated.[2] The $43,110 is credited to **"Unearned Profit on Sale-Leaseback."**

If none of the capital lease criteria are satisfied, **the seller-lessee accounts for the transaction as a sale and the lease as an operating lease**. Under an operating lease, such profit or loss should be deferred and amortized in proportion to the rental payments over the period of time the assets are expected to be used by the lessee.

There are exceptions to these two general rules. They are:

❶ *Losses Recognized*—The profession requires that, when the fair value of the asset is **less than the book value** (carrying amount), a loss must be recognized immediately up to the amount of the difference between the book value and fair value. For example, if Lessee, Inc. sells equipment having a book value of $650,000 and a fair value of $623,110, the difference of $26,890 should be charged to a loss account.[3]

❷ *Minor Leaseback*—Leasebacks in which the present value of the rental payments are 10% or less of the fair value of the asset are defined as minor leasebacks. In this case, the seller-lessee gives up most of the rights to the use of the asset sold. Therefore, the transaction is a sale, and full gain or loss recognition is appropriate. It is not a financing transaction because the risks of ownership have been transferred.[4]

Lessor

If the lease meets one of the criteria in Group I and both of the criteria in Group II (see Illustration 22-11), the **purchaser-lessor** records the transaction as a purchase and a direct financing lease. If the lease does not meet the criteria, the purchaser-lessor records the transaction as a purchase and an operating lease.

---

[1]Sales and leasebacks of real estate are often accounted for differently. A discussion of the issues related to these transactions is beyond the scope of this textbook. See *Statement of Financial Accounting Standards No. 98*, op. cit.

[2]*Statement of Financial Accounting Standards No. 28*, "Accounting for Sales with Leasebacks" (Stamford, Conn.: FASB, 1979).

[3]There can be two types of losses in sale-leaseback arrangements. One is a **real economic loss** that results when the carrying amount of the asset is higher than the fair market value of the asset. In this case, the loss should be recognized. An **artificial loss** results when the sale price is below the carrying amount of the asset but the fair market value is above the carrying amount. In this case the loss is more in the form of prepaid rent and should be deferred and amortized in the future.

[4]In some cases the seller-lessee retains more than a minor part but less than substantially all; the computations to arrive at these values are complex and beyond the scope of this textbook.

SALE-LEASEBACK ILLUSTRATION

To illustrate the accounting treatment accorded a sale-leaseback transaction, assume that Lessee Corp. on January 1, 2002, sells a used Boeing 747 having a carrying amount on its books of $75,500,000, to Lessor Corp. for $80,000,000 and immediately leases the aircraft back under the following conditions:

❶ The term of the lease is 15 years, noncancelable, and requires equal rental payments of $10,487,443 at the beginning of each year.

❷ The aircraft has a fair value of $80,000,000 on January 1, 2002, and an estimated economic life of 15 years.

❸ Lessee Corp. pays all executory costs.

❹ Lessee Corp. depreciates similar aircraft that it owns on a straight-line basis over 15 years.

❺ The annual payments assure the lessor a 12% return.

❻ The incremental borrowing rate of Lessee Corp. is 12%.

This lease is a capital lease to Lessee Corp. because the lease term exceeds 75% of the estimated life of the aircraft and because the present value of the lease payments exceeds 90% of the fair value of the aircraft to the lessor. Assuming that collectibility of the lease payments is reasonably predictable and that no important uncertainties exist in relation to unreimbursable costs yet to be incurred by the lessor, Lessor Corp. should classify this lease as a direct financing lease.

The typical journal entries to record the transactions relating to this lease for both Lessee Corp. and Lessor Corp. for the first year are presented below.

ILLUSTRATION 22A-1
Comparative Entries for
Sale-Leaseback for
Lessee and Lessor

Lessee Corp.		Lessor Corp.	
Sale of Aircraft by Lessee to Lessor Corp., January 1, 2002:			
Cash 80,000,000		Aircraft 80,000,000	
Aircraft	75,500,000	Cash	80,000,000
Unearned Profit on		Lease Payments	
Sale-Leaseback	4,500,000	Receivable 157,311,645	
Leased Aircraft under		Aircraft	80,000,000
Capital Leases 80,000,000		Unearned Interest	
Obligations under		Revenue	77,311,645
Capital Leases	80,000,000	($10,487,443 × 15 = $157,311,645)	
First Lease Payment, January 1, 2002:			
Obligations under		Cash 10,487,443	
Capital Leases 10,487,443		Lease Payments	
Cash	10,487,443	Receivable	10,487,443
Incurrence and Payment of Executory Costs by Lessee Corp. throughout 2002:			
Insurance, Maintenance,		(No entry)	
Taxes, etc. XXX			
Cash or Accounts Payable	XXX		
Depreciation Expense on the Aircraft, December 31, 2002:			
Depreciation Expense 5,333,333		(No entry)	
Accumulated Depr.—			
Capital Leases	5,333,333		
($80,000,000 ÷ 15)			
Amortization of Profit on Sale-Leaseback by Lessee Corp., December 31, 2002:			
Unearned Profit on		(No entry)	
Sale-Leaseback 300,000			
Depreciation Expense	300,000		
($4,500,000 ÷ 15)			

Note: A case might be made for crediting Revenue instead of Depreciation Expense.

	Lessee Corp.			Lessor Corp.		
Interest for 2002, December 31, 2002:						
Interest Expense	8,341,507[a]		Unearned Interest Revenue	8,341,507		
Interest Payable		8,341,507	Interest Revenue			8,341,507[a]

[a]**Partial Lease Amortization Schedule:**

Date	Annual Rental Payment	Interest 12%	Reduction of Balance	Balance
1/1/02				$80,000,000
1/1/02	$10,487,443	$ –0–	$10,487,443	69,512,557
1/1/03	10,487,443	8,341,507	2,145,936	67,366,621

SUMMARY OF LEARNING OBJECTIVE FOR APPENDIX 22A

KEY TERMS

minor leaseback, *1229*
sale-leaseback, *1228*

⑩ Describe the lessee's accounting for sale-leaseback transactions. If the lease meets one of the four criteria for treatment as a capital lease, the seller-lessee accounts for the transaction as a sale and the lease as a capital lease. Any profit experienced by the seller-lessee from the sale of the assets that are leased back under a capital lease should be deferred and amortized over the lease term (or the economic life if either criterion 1 or 2 is satisfied) in proportion to the amortization of the leased assets. If none of the capital lease criteria are satisfied, the seller-lessee accounts for the transaction as a sale and the lease as an operating lease. Under an operating lease, such profit should be deferred and amortized in proportion to the rental payments over the period of time the assets are expected to be used by the lessee.

Note: All **asterisked** Questions, Exercises, Problems, and Conceptual Cases relate to material contained in the appendix to the chapter.

QUESTIONS

1 Jackie Remmers Co. is expanding its operations and is in the process of selecting the method of financing this program. After some investigation, the company determines that it may (1) issue bonds and with the proceeds purchase the needed assets, or (2) lease the assets on a long-term basis. Without knowing the comparative costs involved, answer these questions:

(a) What might be the advantages of leasing the assets instead of owning them?

(b) What might be the disadvantages of leasing the assets instead of owning them?

(c) In what way will the balance sheet be differently affected by leasing the assets as opposed to issuing bonds and purchasing the assets?

2 Mildred Natalie Corp. is considering leasing a significant amount of assets. The president, Joan Elaine Robinson, is attending an informal meeting in the afternoon with a potential lessor. Because her legal advisor cannot be reached, she has called on you, the controller, to brief her on the general provisions of lease agreements to which she should give consideration in such preliminary discussions with a possible lessor. Identify the gen-

eral provisions of the lease agreement that the president should be told to include in her discussion with the potential lessor.

3 Identify the two recognized lease accounting methods for lessees and distinguish between them.

4 Wayne Higley Company rents a warehouse on a month-to-month basis for the storage of its excess inventory. The company periodically must rent space whenever its production greatly exceeds actual sales. For several years the company officials have discussed building their own storage facility, but this enthusiasm wavers when sales increase sufficiently to absorb the excess inventory. What is the nature of this type of lease arrangement, and what accounting treatment should be accorded it?

5 Distinguish between minimum rental payments and minimum lease payments, and indicate what is included in minimum lease payments.

6 Explain the distinction between a direct financing lease and a sales-type lease for a lessor.

7 Outline the accounting procedures involved in applying the operating method by a lessee.

8 Outline the accounting procedures involved in applying the capital lease method by a lessee.

9 Identify the lease classifications for lessors and the criteria that must be met for each classification.

10 Outline the accounting procedures involved in applying the direct financing method.

11 Outline the accounting procedures involved in applying the operating method by a lessor.

12 Joan Elbert Company is a manufacturer and lessor of computer equipment. What should be the nature of its lease arrangements with lessees if the company wishes to account for its lease transactions as sales-type leases?

13 Gordon Graham Corporation's lease arrangements qualify as sales-type leases at the time of entering into the transactions. How should the corporation recognize revenues and costs in these situations?

14 Joann Skabo, M.D. (lessee) has a noncancelable 20-year lease with Cheryl Countryman Realty, Inc. (lessor) for the use of a medical building. Taxes, insurance, and maintenance are paid by the lessee in addition to the fixed annual payments, of which the present value is equal to the fair market value of the leased property. At the end of the lease period, title becomes the lessee's at a nominal price. Considering the terms of the lease described above, comment on the nature of the lease transaction and the accounting treatment that should be accorded it by the lessee.

15 The residual value is the estimated fair value of the leased property at the end of the lease term.

(a) Of what significance is (1) an unguaranteed and (2) a guaranteed residual value in the lessee's accounting for a capitalized lease transaction?

(b) Of what significance is (1) an unguaranteed and (2) a guaranteed residual value in the lessor's accounting for a direct financing lease transaction?

16 How should changes in the estimated residual value be handled by the lessor?

17 Describe the effect of a "bargain purchase option" on accounting for a capital lease transaction by a lessee.

18 What are "initial direct costs" and how are they accounted for?

19 What disclosures should be made by a lessee if the leased assets and the related obligation are not capitalized?

*20 What is the nature of a "sale-leaseback" transaction?

BRIEF EXERCISES

BE22-1 WarpSpeed Corporation leased equipment from Photon Company. The lease term is 5 years and requires equal rental payments of $30,000 at the beginning of each year. The equipment has a fair value at the inception of the lease of $138,000, an estimated useful life of 8 years, and no residual value. WarpSpeed pays all executory costs directly to third parties. Photon set the annual rental to earn a rate of return of 10%, and this fact is known to WarpSpeed. The lease does not transfer title or contain a bargain purchase option. How should WarpSpeed classify this lease?

BE22-2 Waterworld Company leased equipment from Costner Company. The lease term is 4 years and requires equal rental payments of $37,283 at the beginning of each year. The equipment has a fair value at the inception of the lease of $130,000, an estimated useful life of 4 years, and no salvage value. Waterworld pays all executory costs directly to third parties. The appropriate interest rate is 10%. Prepare Waterworld's January 1, 2002, journal entries at the inception of the lease.

BE22-3 Rick Kleckner Corporation recorded a capital lease at $200,000 on January 1, 2002. The interest rate is 12%. Kleckner Corporation made the first lease payment of $35,947 on January 1, 2002. The lease requires eight annual payments. The equipment has a useful life of 8 years with no salvage value. Prepare Kleckner Corporation's December 31, 2002, adjusting entries.

BE22-4 Use the information for Rick Kleckner Corporation from BE22-3. Assume that at December 31, 2002, Kleckner made an adjusting entry to accrue interest expense of $19,686 on the lease. Prepare Kleckner's January 1, 2003, journal entry to record the second lease payment of $35,947.

BE22-5 Jana Kingston Corporation enters into a lease on January 1, 2002, that does not transfer ownership or contain a bargain purchase option. It covers 3 years of the equipment's 8-year useful life, and the present value of the minimum lease payments is less than 90% of the fair market value of the asset leased. Prepare Jana Kingston's journal entry to record its January 1, 2002, annual lease payment of $37,500.

BE22-6 Karen A. Henkel Corporation leased equipment that was carried at a cost of $150,000 to Sharon Swander Company. The term of the lease is 6 years beginning January 1, 2002, with equal rental payments of $30,677 at the beginning of each year. All executory costs are paid by Swander directly to third parties. The fair value of the equipment at the inception of the lease is $150,000. The equipment has a useful life of 6 years with no salvage value. The lease has an implicit interest rate of 9%, no bargain purchase option, and no transfer of title. Collectibility is reasonably assured with no additional cost to be incurred by Henkel. Prepare Karen A. Henkel Corporation's January 1, 2002, journal entries at the inception of the lease.

BE22-7   Use the information for Karen A. Henkel Corporation from BE22-6. Assume the direct financing lease was recorded at a present value of $150,000. Prepare Karen A. Henkel's December 31, 2002, entry to record interest.

BE22-8   Jennifer Brent Corporation owns equipment that cost $72,000 and has a useful life of 8 years with no salvage value. On January 1, 2002, Jennifer Brent leases the equipment to Donna Havaci Inc. for one year with one rental payment of $15,000 on January 1. Prepare Jennifer Brent Corporation's 2002 journal entries.

BE22-9   Indiana Jones Corporation enters into a 6-year lease of machinery on January 1, 2002, which requires 6 annual payments of $30,000 each, beginning January 1, 2002. In addition, Indiana Jones guarantees the lessor a residual value of $20,000 at lease-end. The machinery has a useful life of 6 years. Prepare Indiana Jones' January 1, 2002, journal entries assuming an interest rate of 10%.

BE22-10   Use the information for Indiana Jones Corporation from BE22-9. Assume that for Lost Ark Company, the lessor, collectibility is reasonably predictable, there are no important uncertainties concerning costs, and the carrying amount of the machinery is $155,013. Prepare Lost Ark's January 1, 2002, journal entries.

BE22-11   Starfleet Corporation manufactures replicators. On January 1, 2002, it leased to Ferengi Company a replicator that had cost $110,000 to manufacture. The lease agreement covers the 5-year useful life of the replicator and requires 5 equal annual rentals of $45,400 each. An interest rate of 12% is implicit in the lease agreement. Collectibility of the rentals is reasonably assured, and there are no important uncertainties concerning costs. Prepare Starfleet's January 1, 2002, journal entries.

***BE22-12**   On January 1, 2002, Acme Animation sold a truck to Coyote Finance for $35,000 and immediately leased it back. The truck was carried on Acme's books at $28,000. The term of the lease is 5 years, and title transfers to Acme at lease-end. The lease requires five equal rental payments of $9,233 at the end of each year. The appropriate rate of interest is 10%, and the truck has a useful life of 5 years with no salvage value. Prepare Acme's 2002 journal entries.

EXERCISES

E22-1   (Lessee Entries; Capital Lease with Unguaranteed Residual Value)   On January 1, 2001, Burke Corporation signed a 5-year noncancelable lease for a machine. The terms of the lease called for Burke to make annual payments of $8,668 at the beginning of each year, starting January 1, 2001. The machine has an estimated useful life of 6 years and a $5,000 unguaranteed residual value. The machine reverts back to the lessor at the end of the lease term. Burke uses the straight-line method of depreciation for all of its plant assets. Burke's incremental borrowing rate is 10%, and the Lessor's implicit rate is unknown.

Instructions
   (a)   What type of lease is this? Explain.
   (b)   Compute the present value of the minimum lease payments.
   (c)   Prepare all necessary journal entries for Burke for this lease through January 1, 2002.

E22-2   (Lessee Computations and Entries; Capital Lease with Guaranteed Residual Value)   Pat Delaney Company leases an automobile with a fair value of $8,725 from John Simon Motors, Inc., on the following terms:

   1.   Noncancelable term of 50 months.
   2.   Rental of $200 per month (at end of each month; present value at 1% per month is $7,840).
   3.   Estimated residual value after 50 months is $1,180 (the present value at 1% per month is $715). Delaney Company guarantees the residual value of $1,180.
   4.   Estimated economic life of the automobile is 60 months.
   5.   Delaney Company's incremental borrowing rate is 12% a year (1% a month). Simon's implicit rate is unknown.

Instructions
   (a)   What is the nature of this lease to Delaney Company?
   (b)   What is the present value of the minimum lease payments?
   (c)   Record the lease on Delaney Company's books at the date of inception.

(d) Record the first month's depreciation on Delaney Company's books (assume straight-line).
(e) Record the first month's lease payment.

E22-3 **(Lessee Entries; Capital Lease with Executory Costs and Unguaranteed Residual Value)** On January 1, 2002, Lahey Paper co. signs a 10-year noncancelable lease agreement to lease a storage building from Sheffield Storage Company. The following information pertains to this lease agreement:

1. The agreement requires equal rental payments of $72,000 beginning on January 1, 2002.
2. The fair value of the building on January 1, 2002 is $440,000.
3. The building has an estimated economic life of 12 years, with an unguaranteed residual value of $10,000. Lahey Paper Co. depreciates similar buildings on the straight-line method.
4. The lease is nonrenewable. At the termination of the lease, the building reverts to the lessor.
5. Lahey Paper's incremental borrowing rate is 12% per year. The lessor's implicit rate is not known by Lahey Paper Co.
6. The yearly rental payment includes $2,470.51 of executory costs related to taxes on the property.

Instructions

Prepare the journal entries on the lessee's books to reflect the signing of the lease agreement and to record the payments and expenses related to this lease for the years 2002 and 2003. Lahey Paper's corporate year end is December 31.

E22-4 **(Lessor Entries; Direct Financing Lease with Option to Purchase)** Castle Leasing Company signs a lease agreement on January 1, 2002, to lease electronic equipment to Jan Way Company. The term of the noncancelable lease is 2 years and payments are required at the end of each year. The following information relates to this agreement:

1. Jan Way Company has the option to purchase the equipment for $16,000 upon the termination of the lease.
2. The equipment has a cost and fair value of $160,000 to Castle Leasing Company; the useful economic life is 2 years, with a salvage value of $16,000.
3. Jan Way Company is required to pay $5,000 each year to the lessor for executory costs.
4. Castle Leasing Company desires to earn a return of 10% on its investment.
5. Collectibility of the payments is reasonably predictable, and there are no important uncertainties surrounding the costs yet to be incurred by the lessor.

Instructions

(a) Prepare the journal entries on the books of Castle Leasing to reflect the payments received under the lease and to recognize income for the years 2002 and 2003.
(b) Assuming that Jan Way Company exercises its option to purchase the equipment on December 31, 2003, prepare the journal entry to reflect the sale on Castle's books.

E22-5 **(Type of Lease; Amortization Schedule)** Mike Maroscia Leasing Company leases a new machine that has a cost and fair value of $95,000 to Maggie Sharrer Corporation on a 3-year noncancelable contract. Maggie Sharrer Corporation agrees to assume all risks of normal ownership including such costs as insurance, taxes, and maintenance. The machine has a 3-year useful life and no residual value. The lease was signed on January 1, 2002; Mike Maroscia Leasing Company expects to earn a 9% return on its investment. The annual rentals are payable on each December 31.

Instructions

(a) Discuss the nature of the lease arrangement and the accounting method that each party to the lease should apply.
(b) Prepare an amortization schedule that would be suitable for both the lessor and the lessee and that covers all the years involved.

E22-6 **(Lessor Entries; Sales-Type Lease)** Crosley Company, a machinery dealer, leased a machine to Dexter Corporation on January 1, 2001. The lease is for an 8-year period and requires equal annual payments of $35,013 at the beginning of each year. The first payment is received on January 1, 2001. Crosley had purchased the machine during 2000 for $160,000. Collectibility of lease payments is reasonably predictable, and no important uncertainties surround the amount of costs yet to be incurred by Crosley. Crosley set the annual rental to ensure an 11% rate of return. The machine has an economic life of 10 years with no residual value and reverts to Crosley at the termination of the lease.

Instructions

(a) Compute the amount of each of the following:
   (1) Gross investment.
   (2) Unearned interest revenue.
(b) Prepare all necessary journal entries for Crosley for 2001.

E22-7 (Lessee-Lessor Entries; Sales-Type Lease) On January 1, 2001, Bensen Company leased equipment to Flynn Corporation. The following information pertains to this lease:

1. The term of the noncancelable lease is 6 years, with no renewal option. The equipment reverts to the lessor at the termination of the lease.
2. Equal rental payments are due on January 1 of each year, beginning in 2001.
3. The fair value of the equipment on January 1, 2001, is $150,000, and its cost is $120,000.
4. The equipment has an economic life of 8 years, with an unguaranteed residual value of $10,000. Flynn depreciates all of its equipment on a straight-line basis.
5. Bensen set the annual rental to ensure an 11% rate of return. Flynn's incremental borrowing rate is 12%, and the implicit rate of the lessor is unknown.
6. Collectibility of lease payments is reasonably predictable, and no important uncertainties surround the amount of costs yet to be incurred by the lessor.

Instructions
(a) Discuss the nature of this lease to Bensen and Flynn.
(b) Calculate the amount of the annual rental payment.
(c) Prepare all the necessary journal entries for Flynn for 2001.
(d) Prepare all the necessary journal entries for Bensen for 2001.

E22-8 (Lessee Entries with Bargain Purchase Option) The following facts pertain to a noncancelable lease agreement between Mike Mooney Leasing Company and Denise Rode Company, a lessee.

Inception date:	May 1, 2001
Annual lease payment due at the beginning of each year, beginning with May 1, 2001	$21,227.65
Bargain purchase option price at end of lease term	$ 4,000.00
Lease term	5 years
Economic life of leased equipment	10 years
Lessor's cost	$65,000.00
Fair value of asset at May 1, 2001	$91,000.00
Lessor's implicit rate	10%
Lessee's incremental borrowing rate	10%

The collectibility of the lease payments is reasonably predictable, and there are no important uncertainties surrounding the costs yet to be incurred by the lessor. The lessee assumes responsibility for all executory costs.

Instructions
(Round all numbers to the nearest cent.)
(a) Discuss the nature of this lease to Rode Company.
(b) Discuss the nature of this lease to Mooney Company.
(c) Prepare a lease amortization schedule for Rode Company for the 5-year lease term.
(d) Prepare the journal entries on the lessee's books to reflect the signing of the lease agreement and to record the payments and expenses related to this lease for the years 2001 and 2002. Rode's annual accounting period ends on December 31. Reversing entries are used by Rode.

E22-9 (Lessor Entries with Bargain Purchase Option) A lease agreement between Mooney Leasing Company and Rode Company is described in E22-8.

Instructions
(Round all numbers to the nearest cent.)
Refer to the data in E22-8 and do the following for the lessor:
(a) Compute the amount of gross investment at the inception of the lease.
(b) Compute the amount of net investment at the inception of the lease.
(c) Prepare a lease amortization schedule for Mooney Leasing Company for the 5-year lease term.
(d) Prepare the journal entries to reflect the signing of the lease agreement and to record the receipts and income related to this lease for the years 2001, 2002, and 2003. The lessor's accounting period ends on December 31. Reversing entries are not used by Mooney.

E22-10 (Computation of Rental; Journal Entries for Lessor) Morgan Marie Leasing Company signs an agreement on January 1, 2001, to lease equipment to Cole William Company. The following information relates to this agreement.

1. The term of the noncancelable lease is 6 years with no renewal option. The equipment has an estimated economic life of 6 years.

2. The cost of the asset to the lessor is $245,000. The fair value of the asset at January 1, 2001, is $245,000.
3. The asset will revert to the lessor at the end of the lease term at which time the asset is expected to have a residual value of $43,622, none of which is guaranteed.
4. Cole William Company assumes direct responsibility for all executory costs.
5. The agreement requires equal annual rental payments, beginning on January 1, 2001.
6. Collectibility of the lease payments is reasonably predictable. There are no important uncertainties surrounding the amount of costs yet to be incurred by the lessor.

Instructions
(Round all numbers to the nearest cent.)
   (a) Assuming the lessor desires a 10% rate of return on its investment, calculate the amount of the annual rental payment required. Round to the nearest dollar.
   (b) Prepare an amortization schedule that would be suitable for the lessor for the lease term.
   (c) Prepare all of the journal entries for the lessor for 2001 and 2002 to record the lease agreement, the receipt of lease payments, and the recognition of income. Assume the lessor's annual accounting period ends on December 31.

E22-11 **(Amortization Schedule and Journal Entries for Lessee)** Laura Potts Leasing Company signs an agreement on January 1, 2001, to lease equipment to Janet Plote Company. The following information relates to this agreement.

1. The term of the noncancelable lease is 5 years with no renewal option. The equipment has an estimated economic life of 5 years.
2. The fair value of the asset at January 1, 2001, is $80,000.
3. The asset will revert to the lessor at the end of the lease term, at which time the asset is expected to have a residual value of $7,000, none of which is guaranteed.
4. Plote Company assumes direct responsibility for all executory costs, which include the following annual amounts: (1) $900 to Rocky Mountain Insurance Company for insurance; (2) $1,600 to Laclede County for property taxes.
5. The agreement requires equal annual rental payments of $18,142.95 to the lessor, beginning on January 1, 2001.
6. The lessee's incremental borrowing rate is 12%. The lessor's implicit rate is 10% and is known to the lessee.
7. Plote Company uses the straight-line depreciation method for all equipment.
8. Plote uses reversing entries when appropriate.

Instructions
(Round all numbers to the nearest cent.)
   (a) Prepare an amortization schedule that would be suitable for the lessee for the lease term.
   (b) Prepare all of the journal entries for the lessee for 2001 and 2002 to record the lease agreement, the lease payments, and all expenses related to this lease. Assume the lessee's annual accounting period ends on December 31.

E22-12 **(Accounting for an Operating Lease)** On January 1, 2001, Doug Nelson Co. leased a building to Patrick Wise Inc. The relevant information related to the lease is as follows:

1. The lease arrangement is for 10 years.
2. The leased building cost $4,500,000 and was purchased for cash on January 1, 2001.
3. The building is depreciated on a straight-line basis. Its estimated economic life is 50 years.
4. Lease payments are $275,000 per year and are made at the end of the year.
5. Property tax expense of $85,000 and insurance expense of $10,000 on the building were incurred by Nelson in the first year. Payment on these two items was made at the end of the year.
6. Both the lessor and the lessee are on a calendar-year basis.

Instructions
   (a) Prepare the journal entries that Nelson Co. should make in 2001.
   (b) Prepare the journal entries that Wise Inc. should make in 2001.
   (c) If Nelson paid $30,000 to a real estate broker on January 1, 2001, as a fee for finding the lessee, how much should be reported as an expense for this item in 2001 by Nelson Co.?

E22-13 **(Accounting for an Operating Lease)** On January 1, 2002, a machine was purchased for $900,000 by Tom Young Co. The machine is expected to have an 8-year life with no salvage value. It is to be depreciated on a straight-line basis. The machine was leased to St. Leger Inc. on January 1, 2002, at an annual rental of $210,000. Other relevant information is as follows:

1. The lease term is for 3 years.
2. Tom Young Co. incurred maintenance and other executory costs of $25,000 in 2002 related to this lease.
3. The machine could have been sold by Tom Young Co. for $940,000 instead of leasing it.
4. St. Leger is required to pay a rent security deposit of $35,000 and to prepay the last month's rent of $17,500.

Instructions
   (a) How much should Tom Young Co. report as income before income tax on this lease for 2002?
   (b) What amount should St. Leger Inc. report for rent expense for 2002 on this lease?

E22-14   (Operating Lease for Lessee and Lessor)   On February 20, 2001, Barbara Brent Inc., purchased a machine for $1,500,000 for the purpose of leasing it. The machine is expected to have a 10-year life, no residual value, and will be depreciated on the straight-line basis. The machine was leased to Chuck Rudy Company on March 1, 2001, for a 4-year period at a monthly rental of $19,500. There is no provision for the renewal of the lease or purchase of the machine by the lessee at the expiration of the lease term. Brent paid $30,000 of commissions associated with negotiating the lease in February 2001:

Instructions
   (a) What expense should Chuck Rudy Company record as a result of the facts above for the year ended December 31, 2001? Show supporting computations in good form.
   (b) What income or loss before income taxes should Brent record as a result of the facts above for the year ended December 31, 2001? (*Hint:* Amortize commissions over the life of the lease.)

(AICPA adapted)

*E22-15   (Sale and Leaseback)   On January 1, 2001, Hein Do Corporation sells a computer to Liquidity Finance Co. for $680,000 and immediately leases the computer back. The relevant information is as follows:

1. The computer was carried on Hein Do's books at a value of $600,000.
2. The term of the noncancelable lease is 10 years; title will transfer to Hein Do.
3. The lease agreement requires equal rental payments of $110,666.81 at the end of each year.
4. The incremental borrowing rate of Hein Do Corporation is 12%. Hein Do is aware that Liquidity Finance Co. set the annual rental to insure a rate of return of 10%.
5. The computer has a fair value of $680,000 on January 1, 2001, and an estimated economic life of 10 years.
6. Hein Do pays executory costs of $9,000 per year.

Instructions
Prepare the journal entries for both the lessee and the lessor for 2001 to reflect the sale and leaseback agreement. No uncertainties exist, and collectibility is reasonably certain.

*E22-16   (Lessee-Lessor, Sale-Leaseback)   Presented below are four independent situations:
   (a) On December 31, 2002, Nancy Zarle Inc. sold computer equipment to Erin Daniell Co. and immediately leased it back for 10 years. The sales price of the equipment was $520,000, its carrying amount $400,000, and its estimated remaining economic life 12 years. Determine the amount of deferred revenue to be reported from the sale of the computer equipment on December 31, 2002.
   (b) On December 31, 2002, Linda Wasicsko Co. sold a machine to Cross Co. and simultaneously leased it back for one year. The sale price of the machine was $480,000, the carrying amount $420,000, and it had an estimated remaining useful life of 14 years. The present value of the rental payments for the one year is $35,000. At December 31, 2002, how much should Linda Wasicsko report as deferred revenue from the sale of the machine?
   (c) On January 1, 2002, Joe McKane Corp. sold an airplane with an estimated useful life of 10 years. At the same time, Joe McKane leased back the plane for 10 years. The sales price of the airplane was $500,000, the carrying amount $379,000, and the annual rental $73,975.22. Joe McKane Corp. intends to depreciate the leased asset using the sum-of-the-years'-digits depreciation method. Discuss how the gain on the sale should be reported at the end of 2002 in the financial statements.
   (d) On January 1, 2002, Dick Sondgeroth Co. sold equipment with an estimated useful life of 5 years. At the same time, Dick Sondgeroth leased back the equipment for 2 years under a lease classified as an operating lease. The sales price (fair market value) of the equipment was $212,700, the carrying amount was $300,000, the monthly rental under the lease $6,000, and the present value of the rental payments $115,753. For the year ended December 31, 2002, determine which items would be reported on its income statement for the sale-leaseback transaction.

PROBLEMS

P22-1 (Lessee-Lessor Entries; Sales-Type Lease) Stine Leasing Company agrees to lease machinery to Potter Corporation on January 1, 2001. The following information relates to the lease agreement:

1. The term of the lease is 7 years with no renewal option, and the machinery has an estimated economic life of 9 years.
2. The cost of the machinery is $420,000, and the fair value of the asset on 1/1/01 is $560,000.
3. At the end of the lease term the asset reverts to the lessor. At the end of the lease term the asset is expected to have a guaranteed residual value of $80,000. Potter depreciates all of its equipment on a straight-line basis.
4. The lease agreement requires equal annual rental payments, beginning on January 1, 2001.
5. The collectibility of the lease payments is reasonably predictable and there are no important uncertainties surrounding the amount of costs yet to be incurred by the lessor.
6. Stine desires a 10% rate of return on its investments. Potter's incremental borrowing rate is 11%, and the lessor's implicit rate is unknown.

Instructions
(a) Discuss the nature of this lease for both the lessee and the lessor.
(b) Calculate the amount of the annual rental payment required.
(c) Compute the present value of the minimum lease payments.
(d) Prepare the journal entries Potter would make in 2001 and 2002 related to the lease arrangement.
(e) Prepare the journal entries Stine would make in 2001 and 2002.

P22-2 (Lessee-Lessor Entries; Operating Lease) Synergetics Inc. leased a new crane to M. K. Gumowski Construction under a 5-year noncancelable contract starting January 1, 2002. Terms of the lease require payments of $22,000 each January 1, starting January 1, 2002. Synergetics will pay insurance, taxes, and maintenance charges on the crane, which has an estimated life of 12 years, a fair value of $160,000, and a cost to Synergetics of $160,000. The estimated fair value of the crane is expected to be $45,000 at the end of the lease term. No bargain purchase or renewal options are included in the contract. Both Synergetics and Gumowski adjust and close books annually at December 31. Collectibility of the lease payments is reasonably certain and no uncertainties exist relative to unreimbursable lessor costs. Gumowski's incremental borrowing rate is 10% and Synergetics' implicit interest rate of 9% is known to Gumowski.

Instructions
(a) Identify the type of lease involved and give reasons for your classification. Discuss the accounting treatment that should be applied by both the lessee and the lessor.
(b) Prepare all the entries related to the lease contract and leased asset for the year 2002 for the lessee and lessor, assuming:
(1) Insurance, $500.
(2) Taxes, $2,000.
(3) Maintenance, $650.
(4) Straight-line depreciation and salvage value, $10,000.
(c) Discuss what should be presented in the balance sheet and income statement and related notes of both the lessee and the lessor at December 31, 2002.

P22-3 (Lessee-Lessor Entries, Balance Sheet Presentation; Sales-Type Lease) Cascade Industries and Barbara Hardy Inc. enter into an agreement that requires Barbara Hardy Inc. to build three diesel-electric engines to Cascade's specifications. Upon completion of the engines, Cascade has agreed to lease them for a period of 10 years and to assume all costs and risks of ownership. The lease is noncancelable, becomes effective on January 1, 2002, and requires annual rental payments of $620,956 each January 1, starting January 1, 2002.

Cascade's incremental borrowing rate is 10%, and the implicit interest rate used by Barbara Hardy Inc. and known to Cascade is 8%. The total cost of building the three engines is $3,900,000. The economic life of the engines is estimated to be 10 years with residual value set at zero. Cascade depreciates similar equipment on a straight-line basis. At the end of the lease, Cascade assumes title to the engines. Collectibility of the lease payments is reasonably certain and no uncertainties exist relative to unreimbursable lessor costs.

Instructions
(Round all numbers to the nearest dollar.)
(a) Discuss the nature of this lease transaction from the viewpoints of both lessee and lessor.
(b) Prepare the journal entry or entries to record the transaction on January 1, 2002, on the books of Cascade Industries.

(c) Prepare the journal entry or entries to record the transaction on January 1, 2002, on the books of Barbara Hardy Inc.

(d) Prepare the journal entries for both the lessee and lessor to record the first rental payment on January 1, 2002.

(e) Prepare the journal entries for both the lessee and lessor to record interest expense (revenue) at December 31, 2002. (Prepare a lease amortization schedule for 2 years.)

(f) Show the items and amounts that would be reported on the balance sheet (not notes) at December 31, 2002, for both the lessee and the lessor.

P22-4 (Balance Sheet and Income Statement Disclosure—Lessee) The following facts pertain to a noncancelable lease agreement between Ben Alschuler Leasing Company and John McKee Electronics, a lessee, for a computer system.

Inception date:	October 1, 2001
Lease term	6 years
Economic life of leased equipment	6 years
Fair value of asset at October 1, 2001	$200,255
Residual value at end of lease term	–0–
Lessor's implicit rate	10%
Lessee's incremental borrowing rate	10%
Annual lease payment due at the beginning of each year, beginning with October 1, 2001	$41,800

The collectibility of the lease payments is reasonably predictable, and there are no important uncertainties surrounding the costs yet to be incurred by the lessor. The lessee assumes responsibility for all executory costs, which amount to $5,500 per year and are to be paid each October 1, beginning October 1, 2001. (This $5,500 is not included in the rental payment of $41,800.) The asset will revert to the lessor at the end of the lease term. The straight-line depreciation method is used for all equipment.

The following amortization schedule has been prepared correctly for use by both the lessor and the lessee in accounting for this lease. The lease is to be accounted for properly as a capital lease by the lessee and as a direct financing lease by the lessor.

Date	Annual Lease Payment/ Receipt	Interest (10%) on Unpaid Obligation/ Net Investment	Reduction of Lease Obligation/ Net Investment	Balance of Lease Obligation/ Net Investment
10/01/01				$200,255
10/01/01	$ 41,800		$ 41,800	158,455
10/01/02	41,800	$15,846	25,954	132,501
10/01/03	41,800	13,250	28,550	103,951
10/01/04	41,800	10,395	31,405	72,546
10/01/05	41,800	7,255	34,545	38,001
10/01/06	41,800	3,799*	38,001	–0–
	$250,800	$50,545	$200,255	

*Rounding error is $1.

Instructions

(Round all numbers to the nearest cent.)

(a) Assuming the lessee's accounting period ends on September 30, answer the following questions with respect to this lease agreement:

(1) What items and amounts will appear on the lessee's income statement for the year ending September 30, 2002?

(2) What items and amounts will appear on the lessee's balance sheet at September 30, 2002?

(3) What items and amounts will appear on the lessee's income statement for the year ending September 30, 2003?

(4) What items and amounts will appear on the lessee's balance sheet at September 30, 2003?

(b) Assuming the lessee's accounting period ends on December 31, answer the following questions with respect to this lease agreement:

(1) What items and amounts will appear on the lessee's income statement for the year ending December 31, 2001?

(2) What items and amounts will appear on the lessee's balance sheet at December 31, 2001?

   (3) What items and amounts will appear on the lessee's income statement for the year ending December 31, 2002?
   (4) What items and amounts will appear on the lessee's balance sheet at December 31, 2002?

P22-5 **(Balance Sheet and Income Statement Disclosure—Lessor)**   Assume the same information as in P22-4.

Instructions
(Round all numbers to the nearest cent.)
   (a) Assuming the lessor's accounting period ends on September 30, answer the following questions with respect to this lease agreement:
   (1) What items and amounts will appear on the lessor's income statement for the year ending September 30, 2002?
   (2) What items and amounts will appear on the lessor's balance sheet at September 30, 2002?
   (3) What items and amounts will appear on the lessor's income statement for the year ending September 30, 2003?
   (4) What items and amounts will appear on the lessor's balance sheet at September 30, 2003?

   (b) Assuming the lessor's accounting period ends on December 31, answer the following questions with respect to this lease agreement:
   (1) What items and amounts will appear on the lessor's income statement for the year ending December 31, 2001?
   (2) What items and amounts will appear on the lessor's balance sheet at December 31, 2001?
   (3) What items and amounts will appear on the lessor's income statement for the year ending December 31, 2002?
   (4) What items and amounts will appear on the lessor's balance sheet at December 31, 2002?

P22-6   **(Lessee Entries with Residual Value)**   The following facts pertain to a noncancelable lease agreement between Frank Voris Leasing Company and Tom Zarle Company, a lessee.

Inception date:	January 1, 2001
Annual lease payment due at the beginning of each year, beginning with January 1, 2001	$81,365
Residual value of equipment at end of lease term, guaranteed by the lessee	$50,000
Lease term	6 years
Economic life of leased equipment	6 years
Fair value of asset at January 1, 2001	$400,000.00
Lessor's implicit rate	12%
Lessee's incremental borrowing rate	12%

The lessee assumes responsibility for all executory costs, which are expected to amount to $4,000 per year. The asset will revert to the lessor at the end of the lease term. The lessee has guaranteed the lessor a residual value of $50,000. The lessee uses the straight-line depreciation method for all equipment.

Instructions
(Round all numbers to the nearest cent.)
   (a) Prepare an amortization schedule that would be suitable for the lessee for the lease term.
   (b) Prepare all of the journal entries for the lessee for 2001 and 2002 to record the lease agreement, the lease payments, and all expenses related to this lease. Assume the lessee's annual accounting period ends on December 31 and reversing entries are used when appropriate.

P22-7   **(Lessee Entries and Balance Sheet Presentation; Capital Lease)**   Hilary Brennan Steel Company as lessee signed a lease agreement for equipment for 5 years, beginning December 31, 2001. Annual rental payments of $32,000 are to be made at the beginning of each lease year (December 31). The taxes, insurance, and the maintenance costs are the obligation of the lessee. The interest rate used by the lessor in setting the payment schedule is 10%; Brennan's incremental borrowing rate is 12%. Brennan is unaware of the rate being used by the lessor. At the end of the lease, Brennan has the option to buy the equipment for $1, considerably below its estimated fair value at that time. The equipment has an estimated useful life of 7 years and no salvage value has been added. Brennan uses the straight-line method of depreciation on similar owned equipment.

Instructions

(Round all numbers to the nearest dollar.)

(a) Prepare the journal entry or entries, with explanations, that should be recorded on December 31, 2001, by Brennan. (Assume no residual value.)

(b) Prepare the journal entry or entries, with explanations, that should be recorded on December 31, 2002, by Brennan. (Prepare the lease amortization schedule for all five payments.)

(c) Prepare the journal entry or entries, with explanations, that should be recorded on December 31, 2003, by Brennan.

(d) What amounts would appear on Brennan's December 31, 2003, balance sheet relative to the lease arrangement?

P22-8 (Lessee Entries and Balance Sheet Presentation; Capital Lease) On January 1, 2002, Charlie Doss Company contracts to lease equipment for 5 years, agreeing to make a payment of $94,732 (including the executory costs of $6,000) at the beginning of each year, starting January 1, 2002. The taxes, the insurance, and the maintenance, estimated at $6,000 a year, are the obligations of the lessee. The leased equipment is to be capitalized at $370,000. The asset is to be amortized on a double-declining-balance basis and the obligation is to be reduced on an effective-interest basis. Doss's incremental borrowing rate is 12%, and the implicit rate in the lease is 10%, which is known by Doss. Title to the equipment transfers to Doss when the lease expires. The asset has an estimated useful life of 5 years and no residual value.

Instructions

(Round all numbers to the nearest dollar.)

(a) Explain the probable relationship of the $370,000 amount to the lease arrangement.

(b) Prepare the journal entry or entries that should be recorded on January 1, 2002, by Charlie Doss Company.

(c) Prepare the journal entry to record depreciation of the leased asset for the year 2002.

(d) Prepare the journal entry to record the interest expense for the year 2002.

(e) Prepare the journal entry to record the lease payment of January 1, 2003, assuming reversing entries are not made.

(f) What amounts will appear on the lessee's December 31, 2002, balance sheet relative to the lease contract?

P22-9 (Lessee Entries, Capital Lease with Monthly Payments) John Roesch Inc. was incorporated in 2000 to operate as a computer software service firm with an accounting fiscal year ending August 31. Roesch's primary product is a sophisticated on-line inventory-control system; its customers pay a fixed fee plus a usage charge for using the system.

Roesch has leased a large, Alpha-3 computer system from the manufacturer. The lease calls for a monthly rental of $50,000 for the 144 months (12 years) of the lease term. The estimated useful life of the computer is 15 years.

Each scheduled monthly rental payment includes $4,000 for full-service maintenance on the computer to be performed by the manufacturer. All rentals are payable on the first day of the month beginning with August 1, 2001, the date the computer was installed and the lease agreement was signed.

The lease is noncancelable for its 12-year term, and it is secured only by the manufacturer's chattel lien on the Alpha-3 system. Roesch can purchase the Alpha-3 system from the manufacturer at the end of the 12-year lease term for 75% of the computer's fair value at that time.

This lease is to be accounted for as a capital lease by Roesch, and it will be depreciated by the straight-line method with no expected salvage value. Borrowed funds for this type of transaction would cost Roesch 12% per year (1% per month). Following is a schedule of the present value of $1 for selected periods discounted at 1% per period when payments are made at the beginning of each period.

Periods (months)	Present Value of $1 per Period Discounted at 1% per Period
1	1.000
2	1.990
3	2.970
143	76.658
144	76.899

Instructions

Prepare, in general journal form, all entries Roesch should have made in its accounting records during August 2001 relating to this lease. Give full explanations and show supporting computations for each entry. Remember, August 31, 2001, is the end of Roesch's fiscal accounting period and it will be preparing financial statements on that date. Do not prepare closing entries.

(AICPA adapted)

P22-10 **(Lessor Computations and Entries; Sales-Type Lease with Unguaranteed RV)** Thomas Hanson Company manufactures a computer with an estimated economic life of 12 years and leases it to Flypaper Airlines for a period of 10 years. The normal selling price of the equipment is $210,482, and its unguaranteed residual value at the end of the lease term is estimated to be $20,000. Flypaper will pay annual payments of $30,000 at the beginning of each year and all maintenance, insurance, and taxes. Hanson incurred costs of $135,000 in manufacturing the equipment and $4,000 in negotiating and closing the lease. Hanson has determined that the collectibility of the lease payments is reasonably predictable, that no additional costs will be incurred, and that the implicit interest rate is 10%.

Instructions
(Round all numbers to the nearest dollar.)
   (a) Discuss the nature of this lease in relation to the lessor and compute the amount of each of the following items:
      (1) Gross investment.
      (2) Unearned interest revenue.
      (3) Sales price.
      (4) Cost of sales.
   (b) Prepare a 10-year lease amortization schedule.
   (c) Prepare all of the lessor's journal entries for the first year.

P22-11 **(Lessee Computations and Entries; Capital Lease with Unguaranteed Residual Value)** Assume the same data as in P22-10 with Flypaper Airlines Co. having an incremental borrowing rate of 10%.

Instructions
(Round all numbers to the nearest dollar.)
   (a) Discuss the nature of this lease in relation to the lessee and compute the amount of the initial obligation under capital leases.
   (b) Prepare a 10-year lease amortization schedule.
   (c) Prepare all of the lessee's journal entries for the first year.

P22-12 **(Lessor Computations; Unearned Revenue Recognized Using Sum-of-Month's-Digits)** During 2002, Frank Beals Robinson Leasing Co. began leasing equipment to small manufacturers. Below is information regarding leasing arrangement.

   1. Frank Beals Robinson Leasing Co. leases equipment with terms from 3 to 5 years depending upon the useful life of the equipment. At the expiration of the lease, the equipment will be sold to the lessee at 10% of the lessor's cost, the expected salvage value of the equipment.
   2. The amount of the lessee's monthly payment is computed by multiplying the lessor's cost of the equipment by the payment factor applicable to the term of lease.

Term of Lease	Payment Factor
3 years	3.32%
4 years	2.63%
5 years	2.22%

   3. The excess of the gross contract receivable for equipment rentals over the cost (reduced by the estimated salvage value at the termination of the lease) is recognized as revenue over the term of the lease under the sum-of-the-year's-digits method computed on a monthly basis.
   4. The following leases were entered into during 2002:

Machine	Dates of Lease	Period of Lease	Machine Cost
Die	7/1/02–6/30/06	4 years	$150,000
Press	9/1/02–8/31/05	3 years	$120,000

Instructions
   (a) Prepare a schedule of gross contracts receivable for equipment rentals at the dates of the lease for the die and press machines.
   (b) Prepare a schedule of unearned lease income at December 31, 2002, for each machine lease.
   (c) Prepare a schedule computing the present dollar value of lease payments receivable (gross investment) for equipment rentals at December 31, 2002. (The present dollar value of the "lease receivables for equipment rentals" is the outstanding amount of the gross lease receivables less the unearned lease income included therein.) Without prejudice to your solution to part (b), assume that the unearned lease income at December 31, 2002, was $68,000.

(AICPA adapted)

P22-13 (Basic Lessee Accounting with Difficult PV Calculation) In 1999 Judy Yin Trucking Company negotiated and closed a long-term lease contract for newly constructed truck terminals and freight storage facilities. The buildings were erected to the company's specifications on land owned by the company. On January 1, 2000, Judy Yin Trucking Company took possession of the lease properties. On January 1, 2000 and 2001, the company made cash payments of $1,048,000 that were recorded as rental expenses.

Although the terminals have a composite useful life of 40 years, the noncancelable lease runs for 20 years from January 1, 2000, with a bargain purchase option available upon expiration of the lease.

The 20-year lease is effective for the period January 1, 2000, through December 31, 2019. Advance rental payments of $900,000 are payable to the lessor on January 1 of each of the first 10 years of the lease term. Advance rental payments of $320,000 are due on January 1 for each of the last 10 years of the lease. The company has an option to purchase all of these leased facilities for $1 on December 31, 2019. It also must make annual payments to the lessor of $125,000 for property taxes and $23,000 for insurance. The lease was negotiated to assure the lessor a 6% rate of return.

Instructions
(Round all numbers to the nearest dollar.)
(a) Prepare a schedule to compute for Judy Yin Trucking Company the discounted present value of the terminal facilities and related obligation at January 1, 2000.
(b) Assuming that the discounted present value of terminal facilities and related obligation at January 1, 2000, was $8,400,000, prepare journal entries for Judy Yin Trucking Company to record the:
   (1) Cash payment to the lessor on January 1, 2002.
   (2) Amortization of the cost of the leased properties for 2002 using the straight-line method and assuming a zero salvage value.
   (3) Accrual of interest expense at December 31, 2002.
   Selected present value factors are as follows:

Periods	For an Ordinary Annuity of $1 at 6%	For $1 at 6%
1	.943396	.943396
2	1.833393	.889996
8	6.209794	.627412
9	6.801692	.591898
10	7.360087	.558395
19	11.158117	.330513
20	11.469921	.311805

(AICPA adapted)

P22-14 (Lessor Computations and Entries; Sales-Type Lease with Guaranteed Residual Value) Laura Jennings Inc. manufactures an X-ray machine with an estimated life of 12 years and leases it to Craig Gocker Medical Center for a period of 10 years. The normal selling price of the machine is $343,734, and its guaranteed residual value at the end of the lease term is estimated to be $15,000. The hospital will pay rents of $50,000 at the beginning of each year and all maintenance, insurance, and taxes. Laura Jennings Inc. incurred costs of $210,000 in manufacturing the machine and $14,000 in negotiating and closing the lease. Laura Jennings Inc. has determined that the collectibility of the lease payments is reasonably predictable, that there will be no additional costs incurred, and that the implicit interest rate is 10%.

Instructions
(Round all numbers to the nearest dollar.)
(a) Discuss the nature of this lease in relation to the lessor and compute the amount of each of the following items:
   (1) Gross investment.   (3) Sales price.
   (2) Unearned interest revenue. (4) Cost of sales.
(b) Prepare a 10-year lease amortization schedule.
(c) Prepare all of the lessor's journal entries for the first year.

P22-15 (Lessee Computations and Entries; Capital Lease with Guaranteed Residual Value) Assume the same data as in P22-14 and that Craig Gocker Medical Center has an incremental borrowing rate of 10%.

Instructions
(Round all numbers to the nearest dollar.)
(a) Discuss the nature of this lease in relation to the lessee and compute the amount of the initial obligation under capital leases.
(b) Prepare a 10-year lease amortization schedule.
(c) Prepare all of the lessee's journal entries for the first year.

P22-16 (Operating Lease vs. Capital Lease) You are auditing the December 31, 2000, financial statements of Sarah Shamess, Inc., manufacturer of novelties and party favors. During your inspection of the company garage, you discovered that a 1999 Shirk automobile not listed in the equipment subsidiary ledger is parked in the company garage. You ask Sally Straub, plant manager, about the vehicle, and she tells you that the company did not list the automobile because the company was only leasing it. The lease agreement was entered into on January 1, 2000, with Jack Hayes New and Used Cars.

You decide to review the lease agreement to ensure that the lease should be afforded operating lease treatment, and you discover the following lease terms:

1. Noncancelable term of 50 months.
2. Rental of $180 per month (at the end of each month; present value at 1% per month is $7,055).
3. Estimated residual value after 50 months is $1,100 (the present value at 1% per month is $699). Shamess guarantees the residual value of $1,100.
4. Estimated economic life of the automobile is 60 months.
5. Shamess's incremental borrowing rate is 12% per year (1% per month).

Instructions

You are a senior auditor writing a memo to your supervisor, the audit partner in charge of this audit, to discuss the above situation. Be sure to include (a) why you inspected the lease agreement, (b) what you determined about the lease, and (c) how you advised your client to account for this lease. Explain every journal entry that you believe is necessary to record this lease properly on the client's books. (It is also necessary to include the fact that you communicated this information to your client.)

P22-17 (Lessee-Lessor Accounting for Residual Values) Jodie Lanier Dairy leases its milking equipment from Steve Zeff Finance Company under the following lease terms:

1. The lease term is 10 years, noncancelable, and requires equal rental payments of $25,250 due at the beginning of each year starting January 1, 2001.
2. The equipment has a fair value and cost at the inception of the lease (January 1, 2001) of $185,078, an estimated economic life of 10 years, and a residual value (which is guaranteed by Lanier Dairy) of $20,000.
3. The lease contains no renewable options and the equipment reverts to Steve Zeff Finance Company upon termination of the lease.
4. Lanier Dairy's incremental borrowing rate is 9% per year; the implicit rate is also 9%.
5. Lanier Dairy depreciates similar equipment that it owns on a straight-line basis.
6. Collectibility of the payments is reasonably predictable, and there are no important uncertainties surrounding the costs yet to be incurred by the lessor.

Instructions

(a) Evaluate the criteria for classification of the lease and describe the nature of the lease. In general, discuss how the lessee and lessor should account for the lease transaction.
(b) Prepare the journal entries for the lessee and lessor at January 1, 2001, and December 31, 2001 (the lessee's and lessor's year-end). Assume no reversing entries.
(c) What would have been the amount capitalized by the lessee upon the inception of the lease if:
    (1) The residual value of $20,000 had been guaranteed by a third party, not the lessee?
    (2) The residual value of $20,000 had not been guaranteed at all?
(d) On the lessor's books, what would be the amount recorded as the Net Investment at the inception of the lease, assuming:
    (1) The residual value of $20,000 had been guaranteed by a third party?
    (2) The residual value of $20,000 had not been guaranteed at all?
(e) Suppose the useful life of the milking equipment is 20 years. How large would the residual value have to be at the end of 10 years in order for the lessee to qualify for the operating method? (Assume that the residual value would be guaranteed by a third party.) (*Hint:* The lessee's annual payments will be appropriately reduced as the residual value increases.)

CONCEPTUAL CASES

C22-1 (Lessee Accounting and Reporting) On January 1, 2002, Sandy Hayes Company entered into a noncancelable lease for a machine to be used in its manufacturing operations. The lease transfers ownership of the machine to Yen Quach by the end of the lease term. The term of the lease is 8 years. The minimum lease payment made by Yen Quach on January 1, 2002, was one of eight equal annual payments. At the inception of the lease, the criteria established for classification as a capital lease by the lessee were met.

Instructions

(a) What is the theoretical basis for the accounting standard that requires certain long-term leases to be capitalized by the lessee? Do not discuss the specific criteria for classifying a specific lease as a capital lease.

(b) How should Hayes account for this lease at its inception and determine the amount to be recorded?

(c) What expenses related to this lease will Hayes incur during the first year of the lease, and how will they be determined?

(d) How should Hayes report the lease transaction on its December 31, 2002, balance sheet?

C22-2 (Lessor and Lessee Accounting and Disclosure) Laurie Gocker Inc. entered into a lease arrangement with Nathan Morgan Leasing Corporation for a certain machine. Morgan's primary business is leasing and it is not a manufacturer or dealer. Gocker will lease the machine for a period of 3 years, which is 50% of the machine's economic life. Morgan will take possession of the machine at the end of the initial 3-year lease and lease it to another, smaller company that does not need the most current version of the machine. Gocker does not guarantee any residual value for the machine and will not purchase the machine at the end of the lease term.

Gocker's incremental borrowing rate is 15%, and the implicit rate in the lease is 14%. Gocker has no way of knowing the implicit rate used by Morgan. Using either rate, the present value of the minimum lease payments is between 90% and 100% of the fair value of the machine at the date of the lease agreement.

Gocker has agreed to pay all executory costs directly and no allowance for these costs is included in the lease payments.

Morgan is reasonably certain that Gocker will pay all lease payments, and, because Gocker has agreed to pay all executory costs, there are no important uncertainties regarding costs to be incurred by Morgan. Assume that no indirect costs are involved.

Instructions

(a) With respect to Gocker (the lessee), answer the following:

(1) What type of lease has been entered into? Explain the reason for your answer.

(2) How should Gocker compute the appropriate amount to be recorded for the lease or asset acquired?

(3) What accounts will be created or affected by this transaction and how will the lease or asset and other costs related to the transaction be matched with earnings?

(4) What disclosures must Gocker make regarding this leased asset?

(b) With respect to Morgan (the lessor), answer the following:

(1) What type of leasing arrangement has been entered into? Explain the reason for your answer.

(2) How should this lease be recorded by Morgan, and how are the appropriate amounts determined?

(3) How should Morgan determine the appropriate amount of earnings to be recognized from each lease payment?

(4) What disclosures must Morgan make regarding this lease?

(AICPA adapted)

C22-3 (Lessee Capitalization Criteria) On January 1, Melanie Shinault Company, a lessee, entered into three noncancelable leases for brand-new equipment, Lease L, Lease M, and Lease N. None of the three leases transfers ownership of the equipment to Melanie Shinault at the end of the lease term. For each of the three leases, the present value at the beginning of the lease term of the minimum lease payments, excluding that portion of the payments representing executory costs such as insurance, maintenance, and taxes to be paid by the lessor, is 75% of the fair value of the equipment.

The following information is peculiar to each lease:

1. Lease L does not contain a bargain purchase option; the lease term is equal to 80% of the estimated economic life of the equipment.

2. Lease M contains a bargain purchase option; the lease term is equal to 50% of the estimated economic life of the equipment.

3. Lease N does not contain a bargain purchase option; the lease term is equal to 50% of the estimated economic life of the equipment.

Instructions

  (a) How should Melanie Shinault Company classify each of the three leases above, and why? Discuss the rationale for your answer.

  (b) What amount, if any, should Melanie Shinault record as a liability at the inception of the lease for each of the three leases above?

  (c) Assuming that the minimum lease payments are made on a straight-line basis, how should Melanie Shinault record each minimum lease payment for each of the three leases above?

(AICPA adapted)

C22-4   (Comparison of Different Types of Accounting by Lessee and Lessor)

Part 1

Capital leases and operating leases are the two classifications of leases described in FASB pronouncements from the standpoint of the **lessee.**

Instructions

  (a) Describe how a capital lease would be accounted for by the lessee both at the inception of the lease and during the first year of the lease, assuming the lease transfers ownership of the property to the lessee by the end of the lease.

  (b) Describe how an operating lease would be accounted for by the lessee both at the inception of the lease and during the first year of the lease, assuming equal monthly payments are made by the lessee at the beginning of each month of the lease. Describe the change in accounting, if any, when rental payments are not made on a straight-line basis.

  Do **not** discuss the criteria for distinguishing between capital leases and operating leases.

Part 2

Sales-type leases and direct financing leases are two of the classifications of leases described in FASB pronouncements from the standpoint of the **lessor.**

Instructions

Compare and contrast a sales-type lease with a direct financing lease as follows:

  (a) Gross investment in the lease.

  (b) Amortization of unearned interest revenue.

  (c) Manufacturer's or dealer's profit.

  Do **not** discuss the criteria for distinguishing between the leases described above and operating leases.

(AICPA adapted)

C22-5   (Lessee Capitalization of Bargain Purchase Option)   Brad Hayes Corporation is a diversified company with nationwide interests in commercial real estate developments, banking, copper mining, and metal fabrication. The company has offices and operating locations in major cities throughout the United States. Corporate headquarters for Brad Hayes Corporation is located in a metropolitan area of a midwestern state, and executives connected with various phases of company operations travel extensively. Corporate management is currently evaluating the feasibility of acquiring a business aircraft that can be used by company executives to expedite business travel to areas not adequately served by commercial airlines. Proposals for either leasing or purchasing a suitable aircraft have been analyzed, and the leasing proposal was considered to be more desirable.

The proposed lease agreement involves a twin-engine turboprop Viking that has a fair market value of $1,000,000. This plane would be leased for a period of 10 years beginning January 1, 2002. The lease agreement is cancelable only upon accidental destruction of the plane. An annual lease payment of $141,780 is due on January 1 of each year; the first payment is to be made on January 1, 2002. Maintenance operations are strictly scheduled by the lessor, and Brad Hayes Corporation will pay for these services as they are performed. Estimated annual maintenance costs are $6,900. The lessor will pay all insurance premiums and local property taxes, which amount to a combined total of $4,000 annually and are included in the annual lease payment of $141,780. Upon expiration of the 10-year lease, Brad Hayes Corporation can purchase the Viking for $44,440. The estimated useful life of the plane is 15 years, and its salvage value in the used plane market is estimated to be $100,000 after 10 years. The salvage value probably will never be less than $75,000 if the engines are overhauled and maintained as prescribed by the manufacturer. If the purchase option is not exercised, possession of the plane will revert to the lessor, and there is no provision for renewing the lease agreement beyond its termination on December 31, 2011.

Brad Hayes Corporation can borrow $1,000,000 under a 10-year term loan agreement at an annual interest rate of 12%. The lessor's implicit interest rate is not expressly stated in the lease agreement, but this rate appears to be approximately 8% based on ten net rental payments of $137,780 per year and the initial market value of $1,000,000 for the plane. On January 1, 2002, the present value of all net rental payments and the purchase option of $44,440 is $888,890 using the 12% interest rate. The present value of all net rental payments and the $44,440 purchase option on January 1, 2002, is $1,022,226 using the 8% interest rate implicit in the lease agreement. The financial vice-president of Brad Hayes Corporation has established that this lease agreement is a capital lease as defined in *Statement of Financial Accounting Standards No. 13*, "Accounting for Leases."

Instructions

(a) What is the appropriate amount that Brad Hayes Corporation should recognize for the leased aircraft on its balance sheet after the lease is signed?

(b) Without prejudice to your answer in part (a), assume that the annual lease payment is $141,780 as stated in the question, that the appropriate capitalized amount for the leased aircraft is $1,000,000 on January 1, 2002, and that the interest rate is 9%. How will the lease be reported in the December 31, 2002, balance sheet and related income statement? (Ignore any income tax implications.)

(CMA adapted)

*C22-6 (Sale-Leaseback) On January 1, 2001, Laura Dwyer Company sold equipment for cash and leased it back. As seller-lessee, Laura Dwyer retained the right to substantially all of the remaining use of the equipment.

The term of the lease is 8 years. There is a gain on the sale portion of the transaction. The lease portion of the transaction is classified appropriately as a capital lease.

Instructions

(a) What is the theoretical basis for requiring lessees to capitalize certain long-term leases? **Do not discuss the specific criteria for classifying a lease as a capital lease.**

(b) (1) How should Laura Dwyer account for the sale portion of the sale-leaseback transaction at January 1, 2001?

(2) How should Laura Dwyer account for the leaseback portion of the sale-leaseback transaction at January 1, 2001?

(c) How should Laura Dwyer account for the gain on the sale portion of the sale-leaseback transaction during the first year of the lease? Why?

(AICPA adapted)

*C22-7 (Sale-Leaseback) On December 31, 2001, Laura Truttman Co. sold 6-month old equipment at fair value and leased it back. There was a loss on the sale. Laura Truttman pays all insurance, maintenance, and taxes on the equipment. The lease provides for eight equal annual payments, beginning December 31, 2002, with a present value equal to 85% of the equipment's fair value and sales price. The lease's term is equal to 80% of the equipment's useful life. There is no provision for Laura Truttman to reacquire ownership of the equipment at the end of the lease term.

Instructions

(a) (1) Why is it important to compare an equipment's fair value to its lease payments' present value and its useful life to the lease term?

(2) Evaluate Laura Truttman's leaseback of the equipment in terms of each of the four criteria for determination of a capital lease.

(b) How should Laura Truttman account for the sale portion of the sale-leaseback transaction at December 31, 2001?

(c) How should Laura Truttman report the leaseback portion of the sale-leaseback transaction on its December 31, 2002, balance sheet?

USING YOUR JUDGMENT

FINANCIAL REPORTING PROBLEM: INTEL CORPORATION

Instructions
Refer to the financial statements and accompanying notes and discussion of Intel Corporation presented in Appendix 5B and answer the following questions.

(a) What types of leases are used for a portion of Intel's capital equipment and facilities rented?

(b) What amount of rental expense was reported by Intel in 1996, 1997, and 1998?

(c) What minimum annual rental commitments under all noncancelable leases at December 26, 1998, did Intel disclose?

FINANCIAL STATEMENT ANALYSIS CASE

Presented in Illustration 22-34 are the financial statement disclosures from the 1999 Annual Report of The Penn Traffic Company.

Instructions
Answer the following questions related to these disclosures.

(a) What are the total obligations under capital leases for the fiscal year-ended February 3, 1999, for Penn Traffic?

(b) What is the book value of the assets under capital lease at the year-ended February 3, 1999, for Penn Traffic? Explain why there is a difference between the amounts reported for assets and liabilities under capital leases.

(c) What is the total rental expense reported for leasing activity for the year-ended February 3, 1999, for Penn Traffic?

(d) Estimate the off-balance-sheet liability due to Penn Traffic's operating leases at fiscal year-end 1999.

COMPARATIVE ANALYSIS CASE

UAL, Inc., versus Southwest Airlines

Instructions
Go to the Digital Tool and using the UAL, Inc. and Southwest Airlines Annual Report Information, answer the following questions.

(a) What types of leases are used by Southwest and on what assets are these leases primarily used?

(b) How long-term are some of Southwest's leases? What are some of the characteristics or provisions of Southwest's (as lessee) leases?

(c) What did Southwest report in 1998 as its future minimum annual rental commitments under noncancelable leases?

(d) At year-end 1998, what was the present value of the minimum rental payments under Southwest's capital leases? How much imputed interest was deducted from the future minimum annual rental commitments to arrive at the present value?

(e) What were the amounts and details reported by Southwest for rental expense in 1998, 1997, and 1996?

(f) How does UAL's use of leases compare with Southwest's?

RESEARCH CASES

Case 1

The accounting for operating leases is a controversial issue. Many contend that firms employing operating leases are utilizing significantly more assets and are more highly leveraged than indicated by the balance sheet alone. As a result, analysts often use footnote disclosures to "constructively capitalize" operating lease obligations. One way to do so is to increase a firm's assets and liabilities by the present value of all future minimum rental payments.

Instructions

(a) Obtain the most recent annual report for a firm that relies heavily on operating leases (firms in the airline and retail industries are good candidates). The schedule of future minimum rental payments is usually included in the "Commitments and Contingencies" footnote. Use the schedule to determine the present value of future minimum rental payments, assuming a discount rate of 10%.

(b) Calculate the company's debt-to-total-assets ratio with and without the present value of operating lease payments. Is there a significant difference?

*Case 2

The December 1995 issue of *Management Accounting* includes an article by Renita Wolf entitled "Sale/Leasebacks of Corporate Real Estate Holdings."

Instructions

Read the article and answer the following questions.

(a) What are some advantages of a sale/leaseback?

(b) How does the cost of a lease compare to the cost of traditional long-term debt financing?

(c) What might a sale/leaseback signal to investors?

(d) Identify the types of investors engaging in sale/leasebacks.

INTERNATIONAL REPORTING CASE

As discussed in the chapter, U.S. GAAP accounting for leases allows companies to use off-balance-sheet financing for the purchase of operating assets. International accounting standards are similar to U.S. GAAP in that under these rules, companies can keep leased assets and obligations off their balance sheets. However, under *International Accounting Standard No. 17 (IAS 17)*, leases are capitalized based on the subjective evaluation of whether the risks and rewards of ownership are transferred in the lease. In Japan, virtually all leases are treated as operating leases. Furthermore, unlike U.S. and IAS standards, the Japanese rules do not require disclosure of future minimum lease payments.

Presented below are recent financial data for three major airlines that lease some part of their aircraft fleet. American Airlines prepares its financial statements under U.S. GAAP and leases approximately 27% of its fleet. KLM Royal Dutch Airlines and Japan Airlines (JAL) present their statements in accordance with their home country GAAP (Netherlands and Japan respectively). KLM leases about 22% of its aircraft, and JAL leases approximately 50% of its fleet.

Financial Statement Data	American Airlines (millions of dollars)	KLM Royal Dutch Airlines (millions of guilders)	Japan Airlines (millions of yen)
As-reported			
Assets	20,915	19,205	2,042,761
Liabilities	14,699	13,837	1,857,800
Income	985	606	4,619
Estimated impact of capitalizing operating leases on:[1]			
Assets	5,897	1,812	244,063
Liabilities	6,886	1,776	265,103
Income	(143)	24	(9,598)

[1]Based on *Apples to Apples: Global Airlines: Flight to Quality* (New York: N.Y.: Morgan Stanley Dean Witter, October 1998).

Instructions

(a) Using the as-reported data for each of the airlines, compute the rate of return on assets and the debt to assets ratio. Compare these companies on the basis of this analysis.

(b) Adjust the as-reported numbers of the three companies for the effects of non-capitalization of leases and then redo the analysis in part (a).

(c) The following statement was overheard in the library: "Non-capitalization of operating leases is not that big a deal for profitability analysis based on rate of return on assets, since the operating lease payments (under operating lease accounting) are about the same as the sum of the interest and depreciation expense under capital lease treatment." Do you agree? Explain.

(d) Since the accounting for leases worldwide is similar, does your analysis above suggest there is a need for an improved accounting standard for leases? (*Hint:* Reflect on comparability of information about these companies' leasing activities, when leasing is more prevalent in one country than in others.)

ETHICS CASE

Cuby Corporation entered into a lease agreement for 10 photocopy machines for its corporate headquarters. The lease agreement qualifies as an operating lease in all terms except there is a bargain purchase option. After the 5-year lease term, the corporation can purchase each copier for $1,000, when the anticipated market value is $2,500.

Glenn Beckert, the financial vice president, thinks the financial statements must recognize the lease agreement as a capital lease because of the bargain purchase agreement. The controller, Donna Kessinger, disagrees: "Although I don't know much about the copiers themselves, there is a way to avoid recording the lease liability." She argues that the corporation might claim that copier technology advances rapidly and that by the end of the lease term the machines will most likely not be worth the $1,000 bargain price.

Instructions

Answer the following questions:

(a) What ethical issue is at stake?

(b) Should the controller's argument be accepted if she does not really know much about copier technology? Would it make a difference if the controller were knowledgeable about the pace of change in copier technology?

(c) What should Beckert do?

A visit with
Tracey Barber

Tracey Barber is a partner in the national office of Deloitte & Touche. After graduating from Georgetown University in 1984 with a major in business administration, she began her career on the audit staff in the firm's Washington, D.C., office. After ten years with the firm, she was appointed to serve two years as a Professional Accounting Fellow at the Securities & Exchange Commission, returning to Deloitte & Touche in 1996 as a partner.

A Career in Public Accounting

Describe your early years at the firm. When you first start working, you get audit assignments in a variety of industries. Some of the companies are publicly held. Others are small businesses. But the variety is very interesting. In the first few years as a new staff accountant, you are just trying to get a wide variety of experience so that you can see what interests you. One benefit of public accounting is that you get to see a lot of different businesses. My first assignment happened to be a water utility client, which was the luck of the draw.

While I was progressing up the ranks, I determined that I would specialize in financial institutions. In addition to their accounting issues, I was very interested in the impact that financial institutions have on the economy. And so, I was assigned to work with many of the office's financial institution clients.

Although you might think that working in Washington, D.C., would mean auditing the federal government, I saw very little of that. To be sure, the type of clients you have is dependent on the office in which you work. For instance, in New York, you'll probably work with a lot of Fortune 500 companies because so many are headquartered there, whereas if you work in the San Francisco Bay area, then you'll see a lot of technology companies.

Regardless of the type of clients you serve, your career can move very rapidly if you are ambitious and enthusiastic. Within eight years, I was promoted from staff accountant to senior accountant, then manager, and then senior manager with the firm. As a senior manager, you are preparing to become a partner, and you begin to really manage the relationship with the client. This means you will take part in discussions with company executives, giving you a much better understanding of the client's business concerns that you can then use to develop additional opportunities for the firm to serve the client.

How does one make partner at an accounting firm? In addition to being able to work with clients and bring in new business, it's important to develop a niche where the firm has a particular need. As I said, early on I decided to specialize in the financial services industry including insurance companies, investment companies, and mortgage banking. So, you look at what the firm needs, and what your developmental goals are, and you put those two together. In addition to an industry specialty, I decided that I wanted to become a consultation resource to deal with technical accounting issues, which helps us better serve our clients. I've always been very goal-oriented and knew that because I was in public accounting, I could go as far as I wanted, as long as I was willing to work to do that.

How did you happen to work for the SEC? To distinguish myself within the firm, and because of the intellectual challenge, I decided to apply to become a Professional Accounting Fellow at the Securities & Exchange Commission. You must be nominated by your firm, write a research paper, and go through an interviewing process with the SEC to be selected. I chose the SEC because I believed it would help me to develop expertise that would be valuable in furthering my career upon completion of that assignment. While at the SEC, I got to be part of the accounting standard-setting process, and I expanded my network of contacts particularly because I worked with all of the Big Five accounting firms, the Emerging Issues Task Force, and the Auditing Standards Board. In the Office of the Chief Accountant, some of the most difficult and complicated accounting issues are analyzed and resolved.

At the time, derivatives were a hot topic, as Orange County, California, faced bankruptcy because of adverse consequences associated with the use of financial instruments and the lack of disclosure to bondholders. In addition, Wall Street continued to invent more complicated instruments that corporations were employing to modify risks such as currency or interest rate movements. It became clear to the SEC and others in the standard-setting process that these financial instruments were no longer used by just a few companies, but rather were widespread. The existing hedge accounting rules did not require transparency in the accounting for these transactions or they allowed for too much discretion on the part of management to achieve desired accounting results. In fact, after many years of debate over the accounting, the FASB issued *Statement 133* which requires companies to recognize derivatives at fair value.

After you left the SEC, what did you do? After working with the SEC, I rejoined Deloitte & Touche as a partner in our national office where I consult with other partners at the firm on technical issues. For instance, a practice partner with a public client will call because he or she is concerned about the accounting for a particular transaction. My group researches, discusses, and concludes with respect to the issue, similar to the approach we used at the SEC. In addition, I

might help a client communicate with the SEC about a proposed transaction.

For example, the SEC announced in late 1998 that the staff didn't like the way companies were valuing in-process research and development after a business combination. The SEC was concerned that companies were allocating too much of the purchase price to in-process research and development, which must be written off immediately rather than amortized like goodwill. A large number of companies were forced to restate their financial statements to reflect a lower allocation to in-process R & D.

In my role, I help our clients determine the appropriate response to the SEC's inquiries on topics such as this. My plan is to continue to be a technical resource for the firm, but soon I also will resume working directly with clients.

What accounting issues arise for Internet companies? We have a large number of clients that are either pure "dot-coms," or bricks and mortar companies that are entering into e-commerce in a significant way. A lot of questions that we're getting in that area have to do with revenue recognition. It's a big concern because their stock prices generally reflect revenue more than earnings. There are often no price-to-earnings multiples for investors to gauge, because many of the companies don't have earnings. One question is whether an Internet company can record gross sales or whether it should record only net commissions. For instance, let's say an Internet company sells clothes over the Internet. But it's really just an order processing facility, and never actually receives the clothes in inventory. There is diversity in that some companies record gross revenues, and some record only the fees or commissions on the sale. Another revenue recognition issue relates to barter transactions, where two companies trade advertising banners. Is this really revenue for each company? Right now, the Emerging Issues Task Force at the FASB is looking into these types of subjects and concluded at a recent meeting that barter transactions must meet certain criteria in order to be revenue.

What advice do you give college students? When I look back on college, it was very important to me to get a background that would allow me to do a variety of things after college. As a business major with a concentration in accounting, I was able to take finance, marketing, and management, and it was interesting to put all of these activities together in the financial statements. Similarly, public accounting is a great place to understand all the parts of a business and their economic impact through the financial reporting process. This broad background is why it's not surprising that many CEOs started out in public accounting.

CHAPTER 23

Accounting Changes and Error Analysis

An Art or a Science?

Is accounting an art or a science? One look at how many companies change accounting principles and estimates in a given year suggests that accounting is more art than science. For example, a recent survey of 600 large companies indicated that approximately one-third experienced some type of change in accounting in the past year.

Many of these changes are highlighted in the financial press, as indicated by the following headlines:

"Accounting Change at **Mobil** Makes First-Quarter Profit into $145 Million Loss"

"**Westvaco** Reports Three Accounting Changes"

"**Flagstar** Restates Financial Results"

"Aeronautical Company Revises Estimates of Service Lives of Boeing 747s"

"**J.P. Stevens, Inc.**, Changes to the LIFO Method of Determining Inventory Cost"

Why do such changes in accounting occur? First, the accounting profession may **mandate** that a new accounting principle is to be used. For example, you have studied new standards on such topics as investments, stock options, earnings per share, income taxes, and pensions. To illustrate, **Chrysler** (now **DaimlerChrysler**) changed its method of revenue recognition on sales of vehicles to rental companies because of a recent accounting pronouncement.

Second, **changing economic conditions** may cause a company to change its method of accounting. Significant inflation often prompts companies to switch from FIFO to LIFO. As indicated in the above headlines, **J.P. Stevens** undoubtedly changed its method of accounting for inventories to minimize the impact of inflation on earnings and taxes.

Third, **changes in technology and in operations** may require a company to revise the service lives, depreciation method, or the expected salvage value of depreciable assets. **AT&T** changed its estimates and depreciation methods as a result of changes in its competitive environment and in telecommunications technology.

So, what do you think: Is accounting an art or a science?

LEARNING OBJECTIVES

After studying this chapter, you should be able to:

1. Identify the types of accounting changes.
2. Describe the accounting for changes in accounting principles.
3. Understand how to account for cumulative-effect accounting changes.
4. Understand how to account for retroactive accounting changes.
5. Understand how to account for changes to LIFO.
6. Describe the accounting for changes in estimates.
7. Identify changes in a reporting entity.
8. Describe the accounting for correction of errors.
9. Identify economic motives for changing accounting methods.
10. Analyze the effect of errors.

As indicated in the opening story, accounting changes do occur. In addition, changes in accounting are needed when accounting errors are discovered. The purpose of this chapter is to discuss the various types of accounting changes and error corrections and how they are reported in the financial statements. The content and organization of the chapter are as follows:

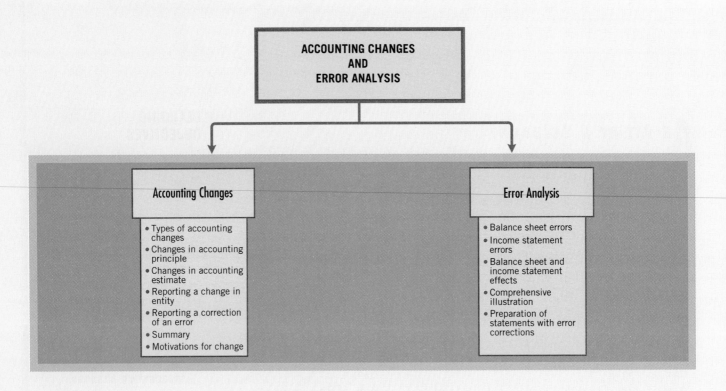

ACCOUNTING CHANGES AND ERROR ANALYSIS

Accounting Changes
- Types of accounting changes
- Changes in accounting principle
- Changes in accounting estimate
- Reporting a change in entity
- Reporting a correction of an error
- Summary
- Motivations for change

Error Analysis
- Balance sheet errors
- Income statement errors
- Balance sheet and income statement effects
- Comprehensive illustration
- Preparation of statements with error corrections

SECTION 1   *ACCOUNTING CHANGES*

Before the issuance of *APB Opinion No. 20*, "Accounting Changes," companies had considerable flexibility to use alternative accounting treatments for essentially equivalent situations. When steel companies changed their methods of depreciating plant assets from accelerated to straight-line depreciation, the effect of the change was presented in many different ways. The cumulative difference between the depreciation charges that had been recorded and what would have been recorded could have been reported in the income statement of the period of the change. Or, the change could have been ignored, and the undepreciated asset balance simply depreciated on a straight-line basis in the future. Or, companies could have restated the prior periods on the basis that the straight-line approach had always been used.

TYPES OF ACCOUNTING CHANGES

OBJECTIVE ❶
Identify the types of accounting changes.

When accounting alternatives exist, comparability of the statements between periods and between companies is diminished and useful historical trend data are obscured. The profession's first step in this area, then, was to establish categories for the different types of changes and corrections that occur in practice.[1] The three types of accounting changes are:

❶ *Change in Accounting Principle.* A change from one generally accepted accounting principle to another generally accepted accounting principle: for example, a change in the method of depreciation from double-declining to straight-line depreciation of plant assets.

❷ *Change in Accounting Estimate.* A change that occurs as the result of new information or as additional experience is acquired. An example is a change in the estimate of the useful lives of depreciable assets.

❸ *Change in Reporting Entity.* A change from reporting as one type of entity to another type of entity: for example, changing specific subsidiaries that constitute the group of companies for which consolidated financial statements are prepared.[2]

A fourth category necessitates changes in the accounting, though it is not classified as an accounting change.

❹ **Errors in Financial Statements.** Errors occur as a result of mathematical mistakes, mistakes in the application of accounting principles, or oversight or misuse of facts that existed at the time financial statements were prepared. An example is the incorrect application of the retail inventory method for determining the final inventory value.

Changes are classified in these four categories because the individual characteristics of each category necessitate different methods of recognizing these changes in the financial statements. Each of these items is discussed separately to investigate its unusual characteristics and to determine how each item should be reported in the accounts and how the information should be disclosed in comparative statements.

CHANGES IN ACCOUNTING PRINCIPLE

A change in accounting principle involves a change from one generally accepted accounting principle to another. For example, a company might change the basis of inventory pricing from average cost to LIFO. Or it might change the method of depreciation on plant assets from accelerated to straight-line, or vice versa. Yet another change might be from the completed-contract to percentage-of-completion method of accounting for construction contracts.

A careful examination must be made in each circumstance to ensure that a change in principle has actually occurred. **A change in accounting principle is not considered to result from the adoption of a new principle in recognition of events that have occurred for the first time or that were previously immaterial.** For example, when a depreciation method that is adopted for **newly** acquired plant assets is different from the method or methods used for **previously recorded** assets of a similar class, a change in accounting principle has **not occurred**. Certain marketing expenditures that were previously immaterial and expensed in the period incurred may become material and acceptably deferred and amortized without a change in accounting principle occurring.

Finally, **if the accounting principle previously followed was not acceptable, or if the principle was applied incorrectly, a change to a generally accepted accounting**

---

[1]"Accounting Changes," *Opinions of the Accounting Principles Board No. 20* (New York: AICPA, 1971).

[2]*Accounting Trends and Techniques—1999* in its survey of 600 annual reports identified the following specific types of accounting changes reported:

Software development costs	37	Software revenue recognition	4
Start-up costs	29	Impairment of long-lived assets	3
Business process reengineering costs	10	Reporting entity	2
Inventories	5	Other	13
Depreciable lives	4		

principle is considered a correction of an error. A switch from the cash or income tax basis of accounting to the accrual basis is considered a correction of an error. If the company deducted salvage value when computing double-declining depreciation on plant assets and later recomputed depreciation without deduction of estimated salvage value, an error is corrected.

Three approaches have been suggested for reporting changes in accounting principles in the accounts:

Retroactively. The cumulative effect of the use of the new method on the financial statements at the beginning of the period is computed. A **retroactive adjustment** of the financial statements is then made, recasting the financial statements of prior years on a basis consistent with the newly adopted principle. Advocates of this position argue that only by restatement of prior periods can changes in accounting principles lead to comparable financial statements. If this approach is not used, the year previous to the change will be on the old method; the year of the change will report the entire cumulative adjustment in income; and the following year will present financial statements on the new basis without the cumulative effect of the change. Consistency is considered essential in providing meaningful earnings-trend data and other financial relationships necessary to evaluate the business.

Currently. The cumulative effect of the use of the new method on the financial statements at the beginning of the period is computed. This adjustment is then reported in the current year's income statement as a **special item** between the captions "Extraordinary items" and "Net income." Advocates of this position argue that restating financial statements for prior years results in a loss of confidence by investors in financial reports. How will a present or prospective investor react when told that the earnings computed 5 years ago are now entirely different? Restatement, if permitted, also might upset many contractual and other arrangements that were based on the old figures. For example, profit-sharing arrangements computed on the old basis might have to be recomputed and completely new distributions made, which might create numerous legal problems. Many practical difficulties also exist; the cost of restatement may be excessive, or restatement may be impossible on the basis of data available.

Prospectively **(in the future)**. Previously reported results remain; no change is made. Opening balances are not adjusted, and no attempt is made to allocate charges or credits for prior events. Advocates of this position argue that once management presents financial statements based on acceptable accounting principles, they are final; management cannot change prior periods by adopting a new principle. According to this line of reasoning, the cumulative adjustment in the current year is not appropriate, because such an approach includes amounts that have little or no relationship to the current year's income or economic events.

Before the adoption of *APB Opinion No. 20*, all three of the approaches above were used. *APB Opinion No. 20*, however, settled this issue by establishing guidelines for changes depending on the type of change in accounting principle involved. We have classified these changes in accounting principle into three categories:

❶ Cumulative-effect type accounting change.
❷ Retroactive-effect type accounting change.
❸ Change to the LIFO method of inventory.

Cumulative-Effect Type Accounting Change

OBJECTIVE ❸
Understand how to account for cumulative-effect accounting changes.

The general requirement established by the profession was that the **current, or "catch-up," method should be used to account for changes in accounting principles**. The general requirements are as follows:

❶ The current or catch-up approach should be employed. The **cumulative effect** of the adjustment should be reported in the income statement between the captions "extraordinary items" and "net income."
❷ Financial statements for prior periods included for comparative purposes should not be restated.

③ Income before extraordinary items and net income, computed on a **pro-forma (as if)** basis should be shown on the face of the income statement for all periods. They are presented **as if the newly adopted principle had been applied during all periods affected**. Related earnings per share data should also be reported. The reader, then, has some understanding of how restated financial statements appear.[3]

INTERNATIONAL INSIGHT

In Canada, Hong Kong, and the United Kingdom, changes in accounting principles are accounted for retroactively. That is, the changes are accounted for as prior year adjustments.

Illustration

Assume that Lang Inc. decided at the beginning of 2002 to change from the sum-of-the-years'-digits method of depreciation to the straight-line method for financial reporting for its buildings. For tax purposes, the company has employed the straight-line method and will continue to do so. The assets originally cost $120,000 in 2000 and have an estimated useful life of 15 years. The data assumed for this illustration are:

Year	Sum-of-the-Years'- Digits Depreciation	Straight-Line Depreciation	Difference	Tax Effect 40%	Effect on Income (net of tax)
2000	$15,000[a]	$ 8,000[b]	$ 7,000	$2,800	$4,200
2001	14,000	8,000	6,000	2,400	3,600
	$29,000	$16,000	$13,000	$5,200	$7,800

[a]$120,000 \times \dfrac{15}{120} = \$15,000$ [b]$\$120,000 \div 15 = \$8,000$

ILLUSTRATION 23-1
Data for Change in Depreciation Method

Lang Inc. has income before extraordinary items and cumulative effect of changes in accounting principle of $130,000 in 2002 and $111,000 in 2001. Also, Lang Inc. has an extraordinary loss (net of tax) of $30,000 in 2002 and an extraordinary gain (net of tax) of $10,000 in 2001.

Journal Entry

Although the journal entry can be made any time during the year, it is effective **as of the beginning of the year**. The entry made to record this change to straight-line depreciation in 2002 should be:

Accumulated Depreciation	13,000	
Deferred Tax Asset		5,200
Cumulative Effect of Change in Accounting Principle—Depreciation		7,800

The debit of $13,000 to Accumulated Depreciation is the excess of the sum-of-the-years'-digits depreciation over the straight-line depreciation. The credit to the Deferred Tax Asset of $5,200 is recorded to eliminate this account from the financial statements. Prior to the change in accounting principle, sum-of-the-years'-digits was used for book but not tax purposes, which gave rise to a debit balance in the Deferred Tax Asset account of $5,200. The cumulative effect on income resulting from the difference between sum-of-the-years'-digits depreciation and straight-line depreciation is reduced by the tax effect on that difference. Now that the company intends to use the straight-line method for both tax and book purposes, no deferred income taxes related to depreciation should exist and the Deferred Tax Asset account should be eliminated.

Income Statement Presentation

The cumulative effect of the change in accounting principle should be reported on the income statement between the captions "Extraordinary items" and "Net income." The cumulative effect is not an extraordinary item but is reported on a net-of-tax basis similar to that used for extraordinary items. This information is shown in Illustration 23-2.

---

[3]Ibid., par. 21.

ILLUSTRATION 23-2
Income Statement
without Pro-Forma
Amounts

	2002	2001
Income before extraordinary item and cumulative effect of a change in accounting principles	$130,000	$111,000
Extraordinary item, net of tax	(30,000)	10,000
Cumulative effect on prior years of retroactive application of new depreciation method, net of tax	7,800	
Net income	$107,800	$121,000
Per share amounts		
Earnings per share (10,000 shares)		
Income before extraordinary item and cumulative effect of a change in accounting principle	$13.00	$11.10
Extraordinary item	(3.00)	1.00
Cumulative effect on prior years of retroactive application of new depreciation method	.78	
Net income	$10.78	$12.10

UNDERLYING CONCEPTS

The pro-forma treatment attempts to restore the comparability of the income statements.

Note that depreciation expense for 2002 is computed on the straight-line basis.

Pro-Forma Amounts

Pro-forma amounts permit financial statements users to determine the net income that would have been shown if the newly adopted principle had been in effect in earlier periods. In other words, how would Lang Inc.'s income be reported if the straight-line method had been used in 2001? To determine this amount, the prior year (2001) is re-stated, assuming that the straight-line method is used. The computation is as follows:

ILLUSTRATION 23-3
Computation of Pro-
Forma Income, 2001

Income before extraordinary item (2001) not restated	$111,000
Excess of sum-of-the-years-digits depreciation over straight-line depreciation	3,600
Pro-forma income before extraordinary item (2001)	$114,600

This and other information is shown on the face of the income statement as follows:

ILLUSTRATION 23-4
Income Statement with
Pro-Forma Amounts

Pro-forma (as if) amounts, assuming retroactive application of new depreciation method:

	2002	2001
Income before extraordinary item	$130,000	$114,600
Earnings per common share	$13.00	$11.46
Net income	$100,000[a]	$124,600[b]
Earnings per common share	$10.00	$12.46

[a]($130,000 − $30,000 = $100,000)
[b]($114,600 + $10,000 = $124,600)

The $130,000 of 2002 income before extraordinary item needs no restatement like the 2001 income because the new straight-line method of depreciation is used in 2002.

Pro-forma information is useful to individuals interested in assessing the trend of earnings over a period of time. Pro-forma information, which is only shown as supplementary information, may be reported in the income statement, in a separate schedule, or in the notes to the financial statements.

The pro-forma amounts should include both (1) the direct effects of a change and (2) nondiscretionary adjustments in items based on income before taxes or net income (such as profit-sharing expense and certain royalties) that would have been recognized if the newly adopted principle had been followed in prior periods; related income tax effects should be recognized for both (1) and (2). If an income statement is presented for the current period only, the actual and pro-forma amounts (including earnings per share) for the immediately preceding period should be disclosed.

Summary Illustration

Illustration 23-5 indicates how this information is presented on the income statement.[4] The appropriate note disclosure is also provided.

ILLUSTRATION 23-5
Cumulative-Effect Type
Accounting Change

Cumulative-Effect Type Accounting Change
Reporting the Change in 2-Year Comparative Statements

	2002	2001
Income before extraordinary item and cumulative effect of a change in accounting principles	$130,000	$111,000
Extraordinary item, net of tax	(30,000)	10,000
Cumulative effect on prior years of retroactive application of new depreciation method, net of tax (Note A)	7,800	
Net income	$107,800	$121,000
Per share amounts		
Earnings per share (10,000 shares)		
Income before extraordinary item and cumulative effect of a change in accounting principle	$13.00	$11.10
Extraordinary item	(3.00)	1.00
Cumulative effect on prior years of rectroactive application of new depreciation method	.78	
Net income	$10.78	$12.10

Pro-forma (as if) amounts, assuming retroactive application of new depreciation method:

	2002	2001
Income before extraordinary item	$130,000	$114,600
Earnings per common share	$13.00	$11.46
Net income	$100,000	$124,600
Earnings per common share	$10.00	$12.46

Note A: Change in Depreciation Method for Plant Assets. In 2002 depreciation of plant assets is computed by use of the straight-line method. In prior years, beginning in 2000, depreciation of buildings was computed by the sum-of-the-years'-digits method. The new method of depreciation was adopted in recognition of . . . (state justification for the change of depreciation method) . . . and has been applied retroactively to building acquisitions of prior years to determine the cumulative effect. The effect of the change in 2002 was to increase income before extraordinary item by approximately $3,000 (or 30 cents per share). The adjustment necessary for retroactive application of the new method, amounting to $7,800, is included in income of 2002. The pro-forma amounts shown on the income statement have been adjusted for the effect of retroactive application on depreciation, and the pro-forma effect for related income taxes.

Retroactive-Effect Type Accounting Change

OBJECTIVE 4
Understand how to account for retroactive accounting changes.

In certain circumstances, a change in accounting principle may be handled retroactively. Under the retroactive treatment the cumulative effect of the new method on the financial statements at the beginning of the period is computed. A retroactive adjustment of the financial statements presented is made by **recasting the statements of prior**

---

[4]In practice, 3-year comparative income statements are prepared. For reasons of simplicity, we have presented 2-year comparatives.

years on a basis consistent with the newly adopted principle. Any part of the cumulative effect attributable to years prior to those presented is treated as an adjustment of beginning retained earnings of the earliest year presented. In such situations, the nature of and justification for the change and the effect on net income and related per share amounts should be disclosed for each period presented. The five situations that require the restatement of all prior period financial statements are:

1. A change from the LIFO inventory valuation method to another method.
2. A change in the method of accounting for long-term construction-type contracts.
3. A change to or from the "full-cost" method of accounting in the extractive industries.
4. Issuance of financial statements by a company for the first time to obtain additional equity capital, to effect a business combination, or to register securities. (This procedure may be used only by closely held companies and then only once.)
5. A professional pronouncement recommends that a change in accounting principle be treated retroactively. For example, *FASB No. 11* requires that retroactive treatment be given for changes in "Accounting for Contingencies" and *FASB Statement No. 73* requires retroactive treatment for a change from retirement-replacement-betterment accounting to depreciation accounting.[5]

INTERNATIONAL INSIGHT

IAS 8 generally requires restatement of prior years for accounting changes. However, IAS 8 permits the cumulative effect method or prospective method if the amounts to restate prior periods are not reasonably determinable.

Why did the profession provide for these exceptions? Though the reasons are varied, the major one is that reporting the cumulative adjustment in the period of the change might have such a large effect on net income that the income figure would be misleading. A perfect illustration is the experience of **Chrysler Corporation** (now **DaimlerChrysler**) when it changed its inventory accounting from LIFO to FIFO. If the change had been handled correctly, Chrysler would have had to report a $53,500,000 adjustment to net income, which would have resulted in net income of $45,900,000 instead of a net loss of $7,600,000.

As another illustration, in the early 1980s the railroad industry switched from the retirement-replacement method of depreciating railroad equipment to a more generally used method such as straight-line depreciation. Cumulative effect treatment meant that a substantial adjustment would be made to income in the period of change. Many in the railroad industry argued that the adjustment was so large that to include the cumulative effect in the current year instead of restating prior years would distort the information and make it less useful. Such situations lend support to restatement so that comparability is not seriously affected.

Illustration

To illustrate the retroactive method, assume that Denson Construction Co. has accounted for its income from long-term construction contracts using the completed-contract method. In 2002, the company changed to the percentage-of-completion method because management believes that this approach provides a more appropriate measure of the income earned. For tax purposes (assume a 40% enacted tax rate), the company has employed the completed-contract method and plans to continue using this method in the future.

Illustration 23-6 provides the information for analysis:

---

[5]"Accounting for Contingencies—Transition Method," *Statement of the Financial Accounting Standards Board No. 11* (Stamford, Conn.: FASB, 1975); "Reporting a Change in Accounting for Railroad Track Structures," *Statement of the Financial Accounting Standards Board No. 73* (Stamford, Conn.: FASB, 1983). Note that the FASB standard on "Accounting for Income Taxes" permits the company to use either the cumulative effect approach or the retroactive method in changing from the deferred method to the asset-liability method. In addition, if the company elects the cumulative effect approach, pro-forma amounts are not required because of the cost and difficulty of developing this information.

ILLUSTRATION 23-6
Data for Change in
Accounting for Long-
Term Construction
Contracts

Year		Pretax Income from Percentage-of-Completion	Completed-Contract	Difference in Income Difference	Tax Effect 40%	Income Effect (net of tax)
Prior to	2001	$600,000	$400,000	$200,000	$80,000	$120,000
In	2001	180,000	160,000	20,000	8,000	12,000
Total at beginning of	2002	$780,000	$560,000	$220,000	$88,000	$132,000
In	2002	$200,000	$190,000	$ 10,000	$ 4,000	$ 6,000

The entry to record the change in 2002 would be:

Construction in Process	220,000	
Deferred Tax Liability		88,000
Retained Earnings		132,000

The Construction in Process account is increased by $220,000, representing the adjustment in prior years' income of $132,000 and the adjustment in prior years' tax expense of $88,000. The Deferred Tax Liability account is used to recognize a tax liability for future taxable amounts. That is, in future periods taxable income will be higher than book income as a result of current temporary differences, and, therefore, a deferred tax liability must be reported in the current year.

Income Statement Presentation

The bottom portion of the income statement for Denson Construction Co., **before giving effect to the retroactive change in accounting principle**, would be as follows:

Income Statement	2002	2001
Net income	$114,000[a]	$96,000[a]
Per Share Amounts		
Earnings per share (100,000 shares)	$1.14	$.96

[a]The net income for the two periods is computed as follows:
2002 $190,000 − .40($190,000) = $114,000
2001 $160,000 − .40($160,000) = $96,000

ILLUSTRATION 23-7
Income Statement before
Retroactive Change

The bottom portion of the income statement for Denson Construction Co., **after giving effect to the retroactive change in accounting principle**, would be as follows:

Income Statement	2002	2001
Net income	$120,000[a]	$108,000[a]
Per Share Amounts		
Earnings per share (100,000 shares)	$1.20	$1.08

[a]The net income for the two periods is computed as follows:
2002 $200,000 − .40($200,000) = $120,000
2001 $180,000 − .40($180,000) = $108,000

ILLUSTRATION 23-8
Income Statement after
Retroactive Change

Note that the 2-year comparative income statement (Illustration 23-8) has a major difference from the earlier 2-year comparative income statement (Illustration 23-5). No pro-forma information is necessary when changes in accounting principles are handled retroactively, because the income numbers for previous periods are restated.

Retained Earnings Statement

Assuming a retained earnings balance of $1,600,000 at the beginning of 2001, the retained earnings statement **before giving effect to the retroactive change in accounting principle**, would appear as follows:

ILLUSTRATION 23-9
Retained Earnings
Statement before
Retroactive Change

Retained Earnings Statement		
	2002	2001
Balance at beginning of year	$1,696,000	$1,600,000
Net income	114,000	96,000
Balance at end of year	$1,810,000	$1,696,000

A comparative retained earnings statement, **after giving effect to the retroactive change in accounting principle**, would be as follows:

ILLUSTRATION 23-10
Retained Earnings
Statement after
Retroactive Change

Retained Earnings Statement		
	2002	2001
Balance at beginning of year, as previously reported	$1,696,000	$1,600,000
Add: Adjustment for the cumulative effect on prior years of applying retroactively the new method of accounting for long-term contracts (Note A)	132,000	120,000
Balance at beginning of year, as adjusted	1,828,000	1,720,000
Net income	120,000	108,000
Balance at end of year	$1,948,000	$1,828,000

Note A: Change in Method of Accounting for Long-Term Contracts. The company has accounted for revenue and costs for long-term construction contracts by the percentage-of-completion method in 2002, whereas in all prior years revenue and costs were determined by the completed-contract method. The new method of accounting for long-term contracts was adopted to recognize . . . (state justification for change in accounting principle) . . . and financial statements of prior years have been restated to apply the new method retroactively. For income tax purposes, the completed-contract method has been continued. The effect of the accounting change on income of 2002 was an increase of $6,000 net of related taxes and on income of 2001 as previously reported was an increase of $12,000 net of related taxes. The balances of retained earnings for 2001 and 2002 have been adjusted for the effect of applying retroactively the new method of accounting.

An expanded retained earnings statement is included in this 2-year comparative presentation to indicate the type of adjustment that is needed to restate the beginning balance of retained earnings. In 2001, the beginning balance was adjusted for the excess of the percentage-of-completion income over the completed-contract income prior to 2001 ($120,000). In 2002, the beginning balance was adjusted for the $120,000 cumulative difference plus the additional $12,000 for 2001.

No such adjustments are necessary when the current or catch-up method is employed, because the cumulative effect of the change on net income is reported in the income statement of the current year and no prior period reports are restated. It is ordinarily appropriate to prepare a retained earnings or stockholders' equity statement when presenting comparative statements regardless of what type of accounting change is involved; an illustration was provided for the retroactive method only to explain the additional computations required.

Change to LIFO Method

OBJECTIVE 5
Understand how to account for changes to LIFO.

As indicated, the cumulative effect of any accounting change should be shown in the income statement between "Extraordinary items" and "Net income," except for the conditions mentioned in the preceding section. In addition, this rule does not apply when a company changes to the LIFO method of inventory valuation. In such a situation, **the**

base-year inventory for all subsequent LIFO calculations is the opening inventory in the year the method is adopted. There is no restatement of prior years' income because it is just too impractical. A restatement to LIFO would be subject to assumptions as to the different years that the layers were established, and these assumptions would ordinarily result in the computation of a number of different earnings figures. The only adjustment necessary may be to restate the beginning inventory to a cost basis from a lower of cost or market approach.

Disclosure then is limited to showing the effect of the change on the results of operations in the period of change. Also the reasons for omitting the computations of the cumulative effect and the pro-forma amounts for prior years should be explained. Finally, the company should disclose the justification for the change to LIFO. The Annual Report of the Quaker Oats Company indicates the type of disclosure necessary.

ILLUSTRATION 23-11
Disclosure of Change to LIFO

THE QUAKER OATS COMPANY

Note 1 (In Part): Summary of Significant Accounting Policies

Inventories. Inventories are valued at the lower of cost or market, using various cost methods, and include the cost of raw materials, labor and overhead. The percentage of year-end inventories valued using each of the methods is as follows:

June 30	1989	1988	1987
Average quarterly cost	21%	54%	52%
Last-in, first-out (LIFO)	65%	29%	31%
First-in, first-out (FIFO)	14%	17%	17%

Effective July 1, 1988, the Company adopted the LIFO cost flow assumption for valuing the majority of remaining U.S. Grocery Products inventories. The Company believes that the use of the LIFO method better matches current costs with current revenues. The cumulative effect of this change on retained earnings at the beginning of the year is not determinable, nor are the pro-forma effects of retroactive application of LIFO to prior years. The effect of this change on fiscal 1989 was to decrease net income by $16.0 million, or $.20 per share.

If the LIFO method of valuing certain inventories were not used, total inventories would have been $60.1 million, $24.0 million and $14.6 million higher than reported at June 30, 1989, 1988, and 1987, respectively.

In practice, many companies defer the formal adoption of LIFO until year-end. Management thus has an opportunity to assess the impact that a change to LIFO will have on the financial statements and to evaluate the desirability of a change for tax purposes. As indicated in Chapter 8, many companies use LIFO because of the advantages of this inventory valuation method in a period of inflation.

CHANGES IN ACCOUNTING ESTIMATE

The preparation of financial statements requires estimating the effects of future conditions and events. The following are examples of items that require estimates:

① Uncollectible receivables.
② Inventory obsolescence.
③ Useful lives and salvage values of assets.
④ Periods benefited by deferred costs.
⑤ Liabilities for warranty costs and income taxes.
⑥ Recoverable mineral reserves.

OBJECTIVE ⑥
Describe the accounting for changes in estimates.

Future conditions and events and their effects cannot be perceived with certainty; therefore, estimating requires the exercise of judgment. Accounting estimates will change as new events occur, as more experience is acquired, or as additional information is obtained.

Changes in estimates must be handled prospectively. That is, no changes should be made in previously reported results. Opening balances are not adjusted, and no attempt is made to "catch-up" for prior periods. Financial statements of prior periods are not restated, and pro-forma amounts for prior periods are not reported. Instead, the effects of all changes in estimate are accounted for in (1) the period of change if the change affects that period only or (2) the period of change and future periods if the change affects both. As a result, changes in estimates are viewed as **normal recurring corrections and adjustments**, the natural result of the accounting process, and retroactive treatment is prohibited.

The circumstances related to a change in estimate are different from those surrounding a change in accounting principle. If changes in estimates were handled on a retroactive basis, or on a cumulative-effect basis, continual adjustments of prior years' income would occur. It seems proper to accept the view that because new conditions or circumstances exist, the revision fits the new situation and should be handled in the current and future periods.

To illustrate, Underwriters Labs Inc. purchased a building for $300,000 which was originally estimated to have a useful life of 15 years and no salvage value. Depreciation has been recorded for 5 years on a straight-line basis. On January 1, 2002, the estimate of the useful life is revised so that the asset is considered to have a total life of 25 years. Assume that the useful life for financial reporting and tax purposes is the same. The accounts at the beginning of the sixth year are as follows:

ILLUSTRATION 23-12
Book Value after 5 Years' Depreciation

Building	$300,000
Less: Accumulated depreciation—building (5 × $20,000)	100,000
Book value of building	$200,000

The entry to record depreciation for the year 2002 is:

Depreciation Expense	10,000	
Accumulated Depreciation—Building		10,000

The $10,000 depreciation charge is computed as follows:

ILLUSTRATION 23-13
Depreciation after Change in Estimate

$$\text{Depreciation charge} = \frac{\text{Book value of asset}}{\text{Remaining service live}} = \frac{\$200,000}{25 \text{ years} - 5 \text{ years}} = \$10,000$$

The disclosure of a change in estimated useful lives appeared in the Annual Report of **Ampco–Pittsburgh Corporation**.

ILLUSTRATION 23-14
Disclosure of Change in Estimated Useful Lives

AMPCO–PITTSBURGH CORPORATION

Note 11: Change in Accounting Estimate. The Corporation revised its estimate of the useful lives of certain machinery and equipment. Previously, all machinery and equipment, whether new when placed in use or not, were in one class and depreciated over 15 years. The change principally applies to assets purchased new when placed in use. Those lives are now extended to 20 years. These changes were made to better reflect the estimated periods during which such assets will remain in service. The change had the effect of reducing depreciation expense and increasing net income by approximately $991,000 ($.10 per share).

Differentiating between a change in an estimate and a change in an accounting principle is sometimes difficult. Is it a change in principle or a change in estimate when a company changes from deferring and amortizing certain marketing costs to recording them as an expense as incurred because future benefits of these costs have become doubtful? In such a case, **whenever it is impossible to determine whether a change in principle or a change in estimate has occurred, the change should be considered a change in estimate.**

A similar problem occurs in differentiating between a change in estimate and a correction of an error, although the answer is more clear cut. How do we determine whether the information was overlooked in earlier periods (an error) or whether the information is now available for the first time (change in estimate)? Proper classification is important because corrections of errors have a different accounting treatment from that given changes in estimates. The general rule is that **careful estimates that later prove to be incorrect should be considered changes in estimate.** Only when the estimate was obviously computed incorrectly because of lack of expertise or in bad faith should the adjustment be considered an error. There is no clear demarcation line here, and good judgment must be used in light of all the circumstances.[6]

REPORTING A CHANGE IN ENTITY

An accounting change that results in financial statements that are actually the statements of a different entity should be reported by **restating the financial statements of all prior periods presented**, to show the financial information for the new reporting entity for all periods.

> **OBJECTIVE 7**
> Identify changes in a reporting entity.

Examples of a change in reporting entity are:

1. Presenting consolidated statements in place of statements of individual companies.

2. Changing specific subsidiaries that constitute the group of companies for which consolidated financial statements are presented.

3. Changing the companies included in combined financial statements.

4. Accounting for a pooling of interests.

5. A change in the cost, equity, or consolidation method of accounting for subsidiaries and investments.[7] A change in the reporting entity does not result from creation, cessation, purchase, or disposition of a subsidiary or other business unit.

The financial statements of the year in which the change in reporting entity is made should disclose the nature of the change and the reason for it. The effect of the change on income before extraordinary items, net income, and earnings per share amounts should be reported for all periods presented. These disclosures need not be repeated in subsequent periods' financial statements. The Annual Report of Hewlett-Packard Company illustrates a note disclosing a change in reporting entity.

---

[6]In evaluating reasonableness, the auditor should use one or a combination of the following approaches:

   (a) Review and test the process used by management to develop the estimate.

   (b) Develop an independent expectation of the estimate to corroborate the reasonableness of management's estimate.

   (c) Review subsequent events or transactions occurring prior to completion of fieldwork. "Auditing Accounting Estimates," *Statement on Auditing Standards No. 57* (New York: AICPA, 1988).

[7]An illustration of the accounting for a change from and to the equity method is provided in Appendix 23A.

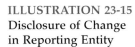

ILLUSTRATION 23-15
Disclosure of Change
in Reporting Entity

HEWLETT-PACKARD COMPANY

Note: Accounting and Reporting Changes (In Part)

Consolidation of Hewlett-Packard Finance Company. The company implemented *Statement of Financial Accounting Standards No. 94 (SFAS 94),* "Consolidation of All Majority-owned Subsidiaries." With the adoption of *SFAS 94*, the company consolidated the accounts of Hewlett-Packard Finance Company (HPFC), a wholly owned subsidiary previously accounted for under the equity method, with those of the company. The change resulted in an increase in consolidated assets and liabilities but did not have a material effect on the company's financial position. Since HPFC was previously accounted for under the equity method, the change did not affect net earnings. Prior years' consolidated financial information has been restated to reflect this change for comparative purposes.

REPORTING A CORRECTION OF AN ERROR

OBJECTIVE 8
Describe the
accounting for
correction of errors.

APB Opinion No. 20 also discussed how a correction of an error should be handled in the financial statements. (No authoritative guidelines existed previously.) The conclusions of *APB Opinion No. 20* were reaffirmed in *FASB Statement No. 16.*[8] No business, large or small, is immune from errors. The risk of material errors, however, may be reduced through the installation of good internal control and the application of sound accounting procedures.

The following are examples of accounting errors:

❶ A change from an accounting principle that is **not** generally accepted to an accounting principle that is acceptable. The rationale adopted is that the prior periods were incorrectly presented because of the application of an improper accounting principle. Example: a change from the cash or income tax basis of accounting to the accrual basis.

❷ Mathematical mistakes that result from adding, subtracting, and so on. Example: the totaling of the inventory count sheets incorrectly in computing the inventory value.

❸ Changes in estimate that occur because the estimates are not prepared in good faith. Example: the adoption of a clearly unrealistic depreciation rate.

❹ An oversight, such as the failure to accrue or defer certain expenses and revenues at the end of the period.

❺ A misuse of facts, such as the failure to use salvage value in computing the depreciation base for the straight-line approach.

❻ The incorrect classification of a cost as an expense instead of an asset and vice versa.

As soon as they are discovered, errors must be corrected by proper entries in the accounts and reported in the financial statements. **The profession requires that corrections of errors be treated as prior period adjustments**, be recorded in the year in which the error was discovered, and be reported in the financial statements as an adjustment to the beginning balance of retained earnings. If comparative statements are presented, the prior statements affected should be restated to correct for the error. The disclosures need not be repeated in the financial statements of subsequent periods.

Illustration

To illustrate, in 2002 the bookkeeper for Selectric Company discovered that in 2001 the company failed to record in the accounts $20,000 of depreciation expense on a newly constructed building. The depreciation is correctly included in the tax return. Because of numerous temporary differences, reported net income for 2001 was $150,000 and

---

[8]"Prior Period Adjustments," *Statement of Financial Accounting Standards No. 16* (Stamford, Conn.: FASB, 1977), p. 5.

taxable income was $110,000. The following entry was made for income taxes (assume a 40% effective tax rate in 2001):

Income Tax Expense	60,000	
Income Tax Payable		44,000
Deferred Tax Liability		16,000

As a result of the $20,000 omission error in 2001:

Depreciation expense (2001) **was** understated	$20,000
Accumulated depreciation **is** understated	20,000
Income tax expense (2001) **was** overstated ($20,000 × 40%)	8,000
Net income (2001) **was** overstated	12,000
Deferred tax liability **is** overstated ($20,000 × 40%)	8,000

The entry made in 2002 to correct the omission of $20,000 of depreciation in 2001 would be:

2002 Correcting Entry

Retained Earnings	12,000	
Deferred Tax Liability	8,000	
Accumulated Depreciation—Buildings		20,000

The journal entry to record the correction of the error is the same whether single-period or comparative financial statements are prepared; however, presentation on the financial statements will differ. If single-period (noncomparative) statements are presented, the error should be reported as an adjustment to the opening balance of retained earnings of the period in which the error is discovered (see Illustration 23-16).

Retained earnings, January 1, 2002		
As previously reported		$350,000
Correction of an error (depreciation)	$20,000	
Less: Applicable income tax reduction	8,000	(12,000)
Adjusted balance of retained earnings, January 1, 2002		338,000
Add: Net income 2002		400,000
Retained earnings, December 31, 2002		$738,000

ILLUSTRATION 23-16
Reporting an Error—
Single-Period Financial
Statement

Comparative Statements

If comparative financial statements are prepared, adjustments should be made to correct the amounts for all affected accounts reported in the statements for all periods reported. The data for each year being presented should be restated to the correct basis, and any **catch-up adjustment should be shown as a prior period adjustment to retained earnings for the earliest period being reported**. For example, in the case of Selectric Company, the error of omitting the depreciation of $20,000 in 2001, which was discovered in 2002, results in the restatement of the 2001 financial statements when presented in comparison with those of 2002. The following accounts in the 2001 financial statements (presented in comparison with those of 2002) would have been restated:

In the balance sheet:	
Accumulated depreciation—buildings	$20,000 increase
Deferred tax liability	$ 8,000 decrease
Retained earnings, ending balance	$12,000 decrease
In the income statement:	
Depreciation expense—buildings	$20,000 increase
Tax expense	$ 8,000 decrease
Net income	$12,000 decrease
In the retained earnings statement:	
Retained earnings, ending balance (due to lower net income for the period)	$12,000 decrease

ILLUSTRATION 23-17
Reporting an Error—
Comparative Financial
Statements

The 2002 financial statements in comparative form with those of 2001 are prepared as if the error had not occurred. At a minimum, such comparative statements in 2002 would include a note in the financial statements calling attention to restatement of the 2001 statements and disclosing the effect of the correction on income before extraordinary items, net income, and the related per share amounts.

SUMMARY OF ACCOUNTING CHANGES AND CORRECTIONS OF ERRORS

The development of guidelines in reporting accounting changes and corrections has helped resolve several significant and long-standing accounting problems. Yet, because of diversity in situations and characteristics of the items encountered in practice, the application of professional judgment is of paramount importance. In applying these guidelines, the primary objective is to serve the user of the financial statements; achieving such service requires accuracy, full disclosure,[9] and an absence of misleading inferences. The principal distinction and treatments presented in the earlier discussion are summarized in Illustration 23-18 on the next page.

Changes in accounting principle are considered appropriate only when the enterprise demonstrates that the alternative generally accepted accounting principle that is adopted is **preferable** to the existing one. In applying the profession's guidelines, preferability among accounting principles should be determined on the basis of whether the new principle constitutes an **improvement in financial reporting**, not on the basis of the income tax effect alone. But it is not always easy to determine what is an improvement in financial reporting. **How does one measure preferability or improvement?** The Quaker Oats Company, for example argues that a change in accounting principle to LIFO inventory valuation "better matches current costs with current revenues" (see Illustration 23-11, page 1263). Conversely, another enterprise might change from LIFO to FIFO because it wishes to report a more realistic ending inventory. How do you determine which is the better of these two arguments? The auditor must have some "standard" or "objective" as a basis for determining the preferable method. Because no universal standard or objective is generally accepted, the problem of determining preferability continues to be a difficult one.

Initially the SEC took the position that the auditor should indicate whether a change in accounting principle was preferable. The SEC has since modified this approach, noting that greater reliance may be placed on management's judgment in assessing preferability. Even though the criterion of preferability is difficult to apply, the general guidelines established have acted as a deterrent to capricious changes in accounting principles.[10] **If an FASB standard creates a new principle or expresses preference for or rejects a specific accounting principle, a change is considered clearly acceptable.** Similarly, other authoritative documents, such as AcSEC's statements of position and AICPA industry audit guides, are considered preferable accounting when a change in accounting principles is contemplated.

UNDERLYING CONCEPTS

This is an example of two widely accepted concepts conflicting. Which is more important, matching (emphasis on the income statement) or qualitative characteristic of representational faithfulness (emphasis on the balance sheet)?

---

[9]A change in accounting principle, a change in the reporting entity (special type of change in accounting principle), and a correction of an error involving a change in accounting principle require an explanatory paragraph in the auditor's report discussing lack of consistency from one period to the next. A change in accounting estimate does not affect the auditor's opinion relative to consistency; however, if the change in estimate has a material effect on the financial statements, disclosure may still be required. Error correction not involving a change in accounting principle does not require disclosure relative to consistency.

[10]If management has not provided reasonable justification for the change in accounting principle, the auditor should express a qualified opinion or, if the effect of the change is sufficiently material, the auditor should express an adverse opinion on the financial statements. "Reports on Audited Financial Statements," *Statement on Auditing Standards No. 58* (New York: AICPA, 1988).

- **Changes in accounting principle.**

  General Rule:

  Employ the current or catch-up approach by:

  a. Reporting current results on the new basis.

  b. Reporting the cumulative effect of the adjustment in the current income statement between the captions "Extraordinary items" and "Net income."

  c. Presenting prior period financial statements as previously reported.

  d. Presenting pro-forma data on income and earnings per share for all prior periods presented.

  Exceptions:

  Employ the retroactive approach by:

  a. Restating the financial statements of all prior periods presented.

  b. Disclosing in the year of the change the effect on net income and earnings per share for all prior periods presented.

  c. Reporting an adjustment to the beginning retained earnings balance in the statement of retained earnings.

  Employ the change to LIFO approach by:

  a. Not restating prior years' income.

  b. Using opening inventory in the year the method is adopted as the base-year inventory for all subsequent LIFO computations.

  c. Disclosing the effect of the change on the current year, and the reasons for omitting the computation of the cumulative effect and pro-forma amounts for prior years.

- **Changes in accounting estimate.**

  Employ the current and prospective approach by:

  a. Reporting current and future financial statements on the new basis.

  b. Presenting prior period financial statements as previously reported.

  c. Making no adjustments to current period opening balances for purposes of catch-up, and making no pro-forma presentations.

- **Changes in reporting entity.**

  Employ the retroactive approach by:

  a. Restating the financial statements of all prior periods presented.

  b. Disclosing in the year of change the effect on net income and earnings per share data for all prior periods presented.

- **Changes due to error.**

  Employ the retroactive approach by:

  a. Correcting all prior period statements presented.

  b. Restating the beginning balance of retained earnings for the first period presented when the error effects occur in a period prior to that one.

ILLUSTRATION 23-18
Summary of Guidelines for Accounting Changes and Errors

MOTIVATIONS FOR CHANGE

Difficult as it is to determine which accounting standards have the strongest conceptual support, other complications make the process even more complex. These complications stem from the fact that managers (and others) have a self-interest in how the financial statements make the company look. Managers naturally wish to show their financial performance in the best light. A **favorable profit picture** can influence investors, and a strong liquidity position can influence creditors. **Too favorable a profit picture**, however, can provide union negotiators and government regulators with ammunition during bargaining talks. Hence, managers might have varying profit motives depending on economic times and whom they seek to impress.

Research has provided additional insight into why companies may prefer certain accounting methods. Some of these reasons are as follows:

OBJECTIVE 9
Identify economic motives for changing accounting methods.

❶ *Political Costs.* As companies become larger and more politically visible, politicians and regulators devote more attention to them. Many suggest that these politicians and regulators can "feather their own nests" by imposing regulations on these organizations for the benefit of their own constituents. Thus the larger the firm, the more likely it is to become subject to regulation such as antitrust and the more likely it is to be required to pay higher taxes. Therefore, companies that are politically visible may attempt to report income numbers that are low, to avoid the scrutiny of regulators. Companies thus hope to reduce their exposure to the perception of monopoly power. In addition, other constituents such as labor unions may be less willing to ask for wage increases if reported income is low. Researchers have found that the larger the company, the more likely it is to adopt income decreasing approaches in selecting accounting methods.[11]

② *Capital Structure.* A number of studies have indicated that the capital structure of the company can affect the selection of accounting methods. For example, a company with a high debt-to-equity ratio is more likely to be constrained by debt covenants. That is, a company may have a debt covenant that indicates that it cannot pay any dividends if retained earnings fall below a certain level. As a result, this type of company is more likely to select accounting methods that will increase net income. For example, one group of writers indicated that a company's capital structure affected its decision whether to expense or capitalize interest.[12] Others indicated that full cost accounting was selected instead of successful efforts by companies that have high debt-to-equity ratios.[13]

③ *Bonus Payments.* If bonus payments paid to management are tied to income, it has been found that management will select accounting methods that maximize their bonus payments. Thus, in selecting accounting methods, management does concern itself with the effect of accounting income changes on their compensation plans.[14]

④ *Smooth Earnings.* Substantial increases in earnings attract the attention of politicians, regulators, and competitors. In addition, large increases in income create problems for management because the same results are difficult to achieve the following year. Executive compensation plans would use these higher numbers as a baseline and make it difficult for management to earn bonuses in subsequent years. Conversely, large decreases in earnings might be viewed as a signal that the company is in financial trouble. Furthermore, substantial decreases in income raise concerns on the part of stockholders, lenders, and other interested parties about the competency of management. Thus, companies have an incentive to "manage" or "smooth" earnings. Management therefore believes that a steady 10% growth a year is much better than a 30% growth one year and a 10% decline the next.[15] In other words, management usually prefers a gradually increasing income report (often referred to as income smoothers) and sometimes changes accounting methods to ensure such a result.

---

[11]Ross L. Watts and Jerold L. Zimmerman, "Positive Accounting Theory: A Ten-Year Perspective," *The Accounting Review,* January 1990.

[12]R. M. Bowen, E. W. Noreen, and J. M. Lacy, "Determinants of the Corporate Decision to Capitalize Interest," *Journal of Accounting and Economics,* August 1981.

[13]See, for example, Dan S. Dhaliwal, "The Effect of the Firm's Capital Structure on the Choice of Accounting Methods," *The Accounting Review,* January 1980; and W. Bruce Johnson and Ramachandran Ramanan, "Discretionary Accounting Changes from 'Successful Efforts' to 'Full Cost' Methods: 1970–1976," *The Accounting Review,* January 1988. The latter study found that firms that changed to full cost were more likely to exhibit higher levels of financial risk (leverage) than firms that retained successful efforts.

[14]See, for example, Mark Zmijewski and Robert Hagerman, "An Income Strategy Approach to the Positive Theory of Accounting Standard Setting/Choice," *Journal of Accounting and Economics,* 1985.

[15]O. Douglas Moses, "Income Smoothing and Incentives: Empirical Tests Using Accounting Changes," *The Accounting Review,* April 1987. Findings provide evidence that smoothers are associated with firm size, the existence of bonus plans, and the divergence of actual earnings from expectations.

Management pays careful attention to the accounting it follows and often changes accounting methods not for conceptual reasons, but rather for economic reasons. As indicated throughout this textbook, such arguments have come to be known as "economic consequences arguments," since they focus on the supposed impact of the accounting method on the behavior of investors, creditors, competitors, governments, or managers of the reporting companies themselves, rather than addressing the conceptual justification for accounting standards.[16]

To counter these pressures, standard setters such as the FASB have declared, as part of their conceptual framework, that they will assess the merits of proposed standards from a position of neutrality. That is, the soundness of standards should not be evaluated on the grounds of their possible impact on behavior. It is not the FASB's place to choose standards according to the kinds of behavior they wish to promote and the kinds they wish to discourage. At the same time, it must be admitted that some standards **will** often have the effect of influencing behavior. Yet their justification should be conceptual and not in terms of their impact.

ERROR ANALYSIS SECTION 2

As indicated earlier, material errors are unusual in large corporations because internal control procedures coupled with the diligence of the accounting staff are ordinarily sufficient to find any major errors in the system. Smaller businesses may face a different problem. These enterprises may not be able to afford an internal audit staff or to implement the necessary control procedures to ensure that accounting data are always recorded accurately.[17]

OBJECTIVE 10
Analyze the effect of errors.

In practice, firms do not correct for errors discovered that do not have a significant effect on the presentation of the financial statements. For example, the failure to record accrued wages of $5,000 when the total payroll for the year is $1,750,000 and net income is $940,000 is not considered significant, and no correction is made. Obviously, defining materiality is difficult, and experience and judgment must be used to determine whether adjustment is necessary for a given error. **All errors discussed in this section are assumed to be material and to require adjustment.** Also, all tax effects are ignored in this section.

Three questions must be answered in error analysis:

① What type of error is involved?
② What entries are needed to correct for the error?
③ How are financial statements to be restated once the error is discovered?

As indicated earlier, errors are **treated as prior period adjustments and reported in the current year as adjustments to the beginning balance of Retained Earnings**. If comparative statements are presented, the prior statements affected should be restated to correct for the error.

Three types of errors can occur. Because each type has its own peculiarities, it is important to differentiate among them.

---

[16]Lobbyists use economic consequences arguments—and there are many of them—to put pressure on standard setters. We have seen examples of these arguments in the oil and gas industry about successful efforts versus full cost, in the technology area with the issue of mandatory expensing of research and developmental costs, and so on.

[17]See Mark L. DeFord and James Jiambalvo, "Incidence and Circumstances of Accounting Errors," *The Accounting Review,* July 1991, for examples of different types of errors and why these errors might have occurred.

BALANCE SHEET ERRORS

These errors affect only the presentation of an asset, liability, or stockholders' equity account. Examples are the classification of a short-term receivable as part of the investment section; the classification of a note payable as an account payable; and the classification of plant assets as inventory. Reclassification of the item to its proper position is needed when the error is discovered. If comparative statements that include the error year are prepared, the balance sheet for the error year is restated correctly.

INCOME STATEMENT ERRORS

These errors affect only the presentation of the nominal accounts in the income statement. Errors involve the improper classification of revenues or expenses, such as recording interest revenue as part of sales; purchases as bad debt expense; and depreciation expense as interest expense. An income statement classification error has no effect on the balance sheet and no effect on net income. A reclassification entry is needed when the error is discovered, if it is discovered in the year it is made. If the error occurred in prior periods, no entry is needed at the date of discovery because the accounts for the current year are correctly stated. If comparative statements that include the error year are prepared, the income statement for the error year is restated correctly.

BALANCE SHEET AND INCOME STATEMENT EFFECTS

The third type of error involves both the balance sheet and income statement. For example, assume that accrued wages payable were overlooked by the bookkeeper at the end of the accounting period. The effect of this error is to understate expenses, understate liabilities, and overstate net income for that period of time. This type of error affects both the balance sheet and the income statement and is classified in one of two ways—counterbalancing or noncounterbalancing.

Counterbalancing errors are errors that will be offset or corrected over two periods. In the previous illustration, the failure to record accrued wages is considered a counterbalancing error because over a 2-year period the error will no longer be present. In other words the failure to record accrued wages in the previous period means: (1) net income for the first period is overstated; (2) accrued wages payable (a liability) is understated, and (3) wages expense is understated. In the next period, net income is understated; accrued wages payable (a liability) is correctly stated; and wages expense is overstated. For the **2 years combined**: (1) net income is correct; (2) wages expense is correct; and (3) accrued wages payable at the end of the second year is correct. Most errors in accounting that affect both the balance sheet and income statement are counterbalancing errors.

Noncounterbalancing errors are errors that are not offset in the next accounting period, for example, the failure to capitalize equipment that has a useful life of 5 years. If we expense this asset immediately, expenses will be overstated in the first period but understated in the next four periods. At the end of the second period, the effect of the error is not fully offset. Net income is correct in the aggregate only at the end of 5 years, because the asset is fully depreciated at this point. Thus, **noncounterbalancing errors are those that take longer than two periods to correct themselves**.

Only in rare instances is an error never reversed, for example, when land is initially expensed. Because land is not depreciable, theoretically the error is never offset unless the land is sold.

Counterbalancing Errors

The usual types of counterbalancing errors are illustrated on the following pages. In studying these illustrations, a number of points should be remembered. First, determine whether or not the books have been closed for the period in which the error is found:

❶ If the books have been closed:
  a. If the error is already counterbalanced, no entry is necessary.
  b. If the error is not yet counterbalanced, an entry is necessary to adjust the present balance of retained earnings.

❷ If the books have not been closed:
  a. If the error is already counterbalanced and the company is in the second year, an entry is necessary to correct the current period and to adjust the beginning balance of Retained Earnings.
  b. If the error is not yet counterbalanced, an entry is necessary to adjust the beginning balance of Retained Earnings and correct the current period.

Second, if comparative statements are presented, restatement of the amounts for comparative purposes is necessary. **Restatement is necessary even if a correcting journal entry is not required.** To illustrate, assume that Sanford's Cement Co. failed to accrue revenue in 1999 when earned, but recorded the revenue in 2000 when received. The error was discovered in 2002. No entry is necessary to correct for this error because the effects have been counterbalanced by the time the error is discovered in 2002. However, if comparative financial statements for 1999 through 2002 are presented, the accounts and related amounts for the years 1999 and 2000 should be restated correctly for financial reporting purposes.

Failure to Record Accrued Wages

On December 31, 2001, Hurley Enterprises did not accrue wages in the amount of $1,500. The entry in 2002 to correct this error, assuming that the books have not been closed for 2002, is:

Retained Earnings	1,500	
Wages Expense		1,500

The rationale for this entry is as follows: (1) When the accrued wages of 2001 are paid in 2002 an additional debit of $1,500 is made to 2002 Wages Expense. (2) Wages Expense—2002 is overstated by $1,500. (3) Because 2001 accrued wages were not recorded as Wages Expense—2001, the net income for 2001 was overstated by $1,500. (4) Because 2001 net income is overstated by $1,500, the Retained Earnings account is overstated by $1,500 because net income is closed to Retained Earnings.

If the books have been closed for 2002, no entry is made because the error is counterbalanced.

Failure to Record Prepaid Expenses

In January 2001 Hurley Enterprises purchased a 2-year insurance policy costing $1,000; Insurance Expense was debited, and Cash was credited. No adjusting entries were made at the end of 2001.

The entry on December 31, 2002, to correct this error, assuming that the books have not been closed for 2002, is:

Insurance Expense	500	
Retained Earnings		500

If the books have been closed for 2002, no entry is made because the error is counterbalanced.

Understatement of Unearned Revenue

On December 31, 2001, Hurley Enterprises received $50,000 as a prepayment for renting certain office space for the following year. The entry made at the time of receipt of the rent payment was a debit to Cash and a credit to Rent Revenue. No adjusting entry was made as of December 31, 2001. The entry on December 31, 2002, to correct for this error, assuming that the books have not been closed for 2002, is:

Retained Earnings	50,000	
Rent Revenue		50,000

If the books have been closed for 2002, no entry is made because the error is counterbalanced.

Overstatement of Accrued Revenue

On December 31, 2001, Hurley Enterprises accrued as interest revenue $8,000 that applied to 2002. The entry made on December 31, 2001, was to debit Interest Receivable and credit Interest Revenue. The entry on December 31, 2002, to correct for this error, assuming that the books have not been closed for 2002, is:

Retained Earnings	8,000	
Interest Revenue		8,000

If the books have been closed for 2002, no entry is made because the error is counterbalanced.

Overstatement of Purchases

Hurley Enterprises' accountant recorded a purchase of merchandise for $9,000 in 2001 that applied to 2002. The physical inventory for 2001 was correctly stated. The company uses the periodic inventory method. The entry on December 31, 2002, to correct for this error, assuming that the books have not been closed for 2002, is:

Purchases	9,000	
Retained Earnings		9,000

If the books have been closed for 2002, no entry is made because the error is counterbalanced.

Noncounterbalancing Errors

Because such errors do not counterbalance over a 2-year period, the entries for noncounterbalancing errors are more complex and correcting entries are needed, even if the books have been closed.

Failure to Record Depreciation

Assume that on January 1, 2001, Hurley Enterprises purchased a machine for $10,000 that had an estimated useful life of 5 years. The accountant incorrectly expensed this machine in 2001. The error was discovered in 2002. If we assume that the company desires to use straight-line depreciation on this asset, the entry on December 31, 2002, to correct for this error, given that the books have not been closed, is:

Machinery	10,000	
Depreciation Expense	2,000	
Retained Earnings		8,000[a]
Accumulated Depreciation		4,000[a]

[a]Computations:

Retained Earnings

Overstatement of expense in 2001	$10,000
Proper depreciation for 2001 (20% × $10,000)	(2,000)
Retained earnings understated as of Dec. 31, 2001	$ 8,000

Accumulated Depreciation

Accumulated depreciation (20% × $10,000 × 2)	$ 4,000

If the books have been closed for 2002, the entry is:

Machinery	10,000	
Retained Earnings		6,000[a]
Accumulated Depreciation		4,000

[a]Computations:

Retained Earnings

Retained earnings understated as of Dec. 31, 2001	$ 8,000
Proper depreciation for 2002 (20% × $10,000)	(2,000)
Retained earnings understated as of Dec. 31, 2002	$ 6,000

Failure to Adjust for Bad Debts

Companies sometimes use a specific charge-off method in accounting for bad debt expense when a percentage of sales is more appropriate. Adjustments are often made to change from the specific writeoff to some type of allowance method. For example, assume that Hurley Enterprises has recognized bad debt expense when the debts have actually become uncollectible as follows:

	2001	2002
From 2001 sales	$550	$690
From 2002 sales		700

Hurley estimates that an additional $1,400 will be charged off in 2003, of which $300 is applicable to 2001 sales and $1,100 to 2002 sales. The entry on December 31, 2002, assuming that the **books have not been closed for 2002**, is:

Bad Debt Expense	410[a]	
Retained Earnings	990[a]	
Allowance for Doubtful Accounts		1,400

[a]Computations:

Allowance for doubtful accounts—additional $300 for 2001 sales and $1,100 for 2002 sales.
Bad debts and retained earnings balance:

	2001	2002
Bad debts charged for	$1,240[b]	$ 700
Additional bad debts anticipated in 2003	300	1,100
Proper bad debt expense	1,540	1,800
Charges currently made to each period	(550)	(1,390)
Bad debt adjustment	$ 990	$ 410

[b]$550 + $690 = $1,240

If the **books have been closed for 2002**, the entry is:

Retained Earnings	1,400	
Allowance for Doubtful Accounts		1,400

COMPREHENSIVE ILLUSTRATION: NUMEROUS ERRORS

In some circumstances a combination of errors occurs. A work sheet is therefore prepared to facilitate the analysis. The following problem demonstrates the use of a work sheet. The mechanics of the work sheet preparation should be obvious from the solution format.

The income statements of the Hudson Company for the years ended December 31, 2000, 2001, and 2002 indicate the following net incomes.

2000	$17,400
2001	20,200
2002	11,300

An examination of the accounting records of the Hudson Company for these years indicates that several errors were made in arriving at the net income amounts reported. The following errors were discovered:

❶ Wages earned by workers but not paid at December 31 were consistently omitted from the records. The amounts omitted were:

December 31, 2000 $1,000
December 31, 2001 $1,400
December 31, 2002 $1,600

These amounts were recorded as expenses when paid in the year following that in which they were earned.

❷ The merchandise inventory on December 31, 2000, was overstated by $1,900 as the result of errors made in the footings and extensions on the inventory sheets.

❸ Unexpired insurance of $1,200, applicable to 2002, was expensed on December 31, 2001.

❹ Interest receivable in the amount of $240 was not recorded on December 31, 2001.

❺ On January 2, 2001, a piece of equipment costing $3,900 was sold for $1,800. At the date of sale the equipment had accumulated depreciation of $2,400. The cash received was recorded as Miscellaneous Income in 2001. In addition, depreciation was recorded for this equipment in both 2001 and 2002 at the rate of 10% of cost.

The first step in preparing the work sheet is to prepare a schedule showing the corrected net income amounts for the years ended December 31, 2000, 2001, and 2002. Each correction of the amount originally reported is clearly labeled. The next step is to indicate the balance sheet accounts affected as of December 31, 2002. The completed work sheet for Hudson Company is as follows.

ILLUSTRATION 23-19
Work Sheet to Correct Income and Balance Sheet Errors

HUDSON COMPANY
Work Sheet to Correct Income and Balance Sheet Errors

	Work Sheet Analysis of Changes in Net Income				Balance Sheet Correction at December 31, 2002		
	2000	2001	2002	Totals	Debit	Credit	Account
Net income as reported	$17,400	$20,200	$11,300	$48,900			
Wages unpaid, 12/31/00	(1,000)	1,000		–0–			
Wages unpaid, 12/31/01		(1,400)	1,400	–0–			
Wages unpaid, 12/31/02			(1,600)	(1,600)		$1,600	Wages Payable
Inventory overstatement, 12/31/00	(1,900)	1,900		–0–			
Unexpired insurance, 12/31/01		1,200	(1,200)	–0–			
Interest receivable, 12/31/01		240	(240)	–0–			
Correction for entry made upon sale of equipment, 1/2/01		(1,500)		(1,500)	$2,400	3,900	Accumulated Depreciation Machinery
Overcharge of depreciation, 2001[a]		390		390	390		Accumulated Depreciation
Overcharge of depreciation, 2002			390	390	390		Accumulated Depreciation
Corrected net income	$14,500	$22,030	$10,050	$46,580			

[a]Cost	$ 3,900
Accumulated depreciation	2,400
Book value	1,500
Proceeds from sale	1,800
Gain on sale	300
Income reported	(1,800)
Adjustment	$ (1,500)

Correcting entries **if the books have not been closed** on December 31, 2002, are:

Retained Earnings	1,400	
Wages Expense		1,400
(To correct improper charge to Wages Expense for 2002)		
Wages Expense	1,600	
Wages Payable		1,600
(To record proper wages expense for 2002)		
Insurance Expense	1,200	
Retained Earnings		1,200
(To record proper insurance expense for 2002)		
Interest Revenue	240	
Retained Earnings		240
(To correct improper credit to Interest Revenue in 2002)		
Retained Earnings	1,500	
Accumulated Depreciation	2,400	
Machinery		3,900
(To record writeoff of machinery in 2001 and adjustment		
of Retained Earnings)		
Accumulated Depreciation	780	
Depreciation Expense		390
Retained Earnings		390
(To correct improper charge for depreciation expense		
in 2001 and 2002)		

If the books have been closed for 2002, the correcting entries are:

Retained Earnings	1,600	
Wages Payable		1,600
(To record proper wage expense for 2002)		
Retained Earnings	1,500	
Accumulated Depreciation	2,400	
Machinery		3,900
(To record writeoff of machinery in 2001 and		
adjustment of Retained Earnings)		
Accumulated Depreciation	780	
Retained Earnings		780
(To correct improper charge for depreciation expense		
in 2001 and 2002)		

PREPARATION OF FINANCIAL STATEMENTS WITH ERROR CORRECTIONS

Up to now, our discussion of error analysis has been concerned with the identification of the type of error involved and the accounting for its correction in the accounting records. The correction of the error should be presented on comparative financial statements. In addition, 5- or 10-year summaries are given for the interested financial reader. The following situation illustrates how a typical year's financial statements are restated given many different errors.

Dick & Wally's Outlet is a small retail outlet in the town of Holiday. Lacking expertise in accounting, they do not keep adequate records. As a result, numerous errors occurred in recording accounting information. The errors are listed below:

❶ The bookkeeper inadvertently failed to record a cash receipt of $1,000 on the sale of merchandise in 2002.

❷ Accrued wages expense at the end of 2001 was $2,500; at the end of 2002, $3,200. The company does not accrue for wages; all wages are charged to Administrative Expenses.

❸ No allowance had been set up for estimated uncollectible receivables. Dick and Wally decided to set up such an allowance for the estimated probable losses as of

December 31, 2002 for 2001 accounts of $700, and for 2002 accounts of $1,500. It is also decided to correct the charge against each year so that it shows the losses (actual and estimated) relating to that year's sales. Accounts have been written off to bad debt expense (selling expense) as follows:

	In 2001	In 2002
2001 accounts	$400	$2,000
2002 accounts		1,600

④ Unexpired insurance not recorded at the end of 2001 was $600, and at the end of 2002, $400. All insurance is charged to Administrative Expenses.

⑤ An account payable of $6,000 should have been a note payable.

⑥ During 2001, an asset that cost $10,000 and had a book value of $4,000 was sold for $7,000. At the time of sale Cash was debited and Miscellaneous Income was credited for $7,000.

⑦ As a result of the last transaction, the company overstated depreciation expense (an administrative expense) in 2001 by $800 and in 2002 by $1,200.

ILLUSTRATION 23-20
Work Sheet to Analyze Effect of Errors in Financial Statements

A work sheet that begins with the unadjusted trial balance of Dick & Wally's Outlet is presented in Illustration 23-20. The correcting entries and their effect on the financial statements can be determined by examining the work sheet.

DICK & WALLY'S OUTLET
Work Sheet Analysis to Adjust Financial Statements for the Year 2002

	Trial Balance Unadjusted		Adjustments		Income Statement Adjusted		Balance Sheet Adjusted	
	Debit	Credit	Debit	Credit	Debit	Credit	Debit	Credit
Cash	3,100		(1) 1,000				4,100	
Accounts Receivable	17,600						17,600	
Notes Receivable	8,500						8,500	
Inventory	34,000						34,000	
Property, Plant and Equipment	112,000			(6) 10,000[a]			102,000	
Accumulated Depreciation		83,500	(6) 6,000[a]					75,500
			(7) 2,000					
Investments	24,300						24,300	
Accounts Payable		14,500	(5) 6,000					8,500
Notes Payable		10,000		(5) 6,000				16,000
Capital Stock		43,500						43,500
Retained Earnings		20,000	(3) 2,700[b]					
			(6) 4,000[a]	(4) 600				
			(2) 2,500	(7) 800				12,200
Sales		94,000		(1) 1,000		95,000		
Cost of Goods Sold	21,000				21,000			
Selling Expenses	22,000			(3) 500[b]	21,500			
Administrative Expenses	23,000		(2) 700	(4) 400	22,700			
			(4) 600	(7) 1,200				
Totals	265,500	265,500						
Wages Payable				(2) 3,200				3,200
Allowance for Doubtful Accounts				(3) 2,200[b]				2,200
Unexpired Insurance			(4) 400				400	
Net Income					29,800			29,800
Totals			25,900	25,900	95,000	95,000	190,900	190,900

Computations:

[a]Machinery

Proceeds from sale	$7,000
Book value of machinery	4,000
Gain on sale	3,000
Income credited	7,000
Retained earnings adjustment	$4,000

[b]Bad Debts

	2001	2002
Bad debts charged for	$2,400	$1,600
Additional bad debts anticipated	700	1,500
	3,100	3,100
Charges currently made to each year	(400)	(3,600)
Bad debt adjustment	$2,700	$ (500)

SUMMARY OF LEARNING OBJECTIVES

① Identify the types of accounting changes. The three different types of accounting changes are: (1) *Change in accounting principle:* a change from one generally accepted accounting principle to another generally accepted accounting principle. (2) *Change in accounting estimate:* a change that occurs as the result of new information or as additional experience is acquired. (3) *Change in reporting entity:* a change from reporting as one type of entity to another type of entity.

② Describe the accounting for changes in accounting principles. A change in accounting principle involves a change from one generally accepted accounting principle to another. A change in accounting principle is not considered to result from the adoption of a new principle in recognition of events that have occurred for the first time or that were previously immaterial. If the accounting principle previously followed was not acceptable, or if the principle was applied incorrectly, a change to a generally accepted accounting principle is considered a correction of an error.

③ Understand how to account for cumulative-effect accounting changes. The general requirement for changes in accounting principle is that the cumulative effect of the change (net of tax) be shown at the bottom of the current year's income statement and that pro-forma net income and earnings per share amounts be reported for all prior periods presented.

④ Understand how to account for retroactive accounting changes. A number of accounting principle changes are handled in a retroactive manner; that is, prior years' financial statements are recast on a basis consistent with the newly adopted principle, and any part of the effect attributable to years prior to those presented is treated as an adjustment of the earliest retained earnings presented.

⑤ Understand how to account for changes to LIFO. In changing to LIFO, the base year inventory for all subsequent LIFO calculations is the opening inventory in the year the method is adopted. There is no restatement of prior years' income because it is just too impractical to do so.

⑥ Describe the accounting for changes in estimates. Changes in estimates must be handled prospectively; that is, no changes should be made in previously reported results. Opening balances are not adjusted, and no attempt is made to "catch up" for prior periods. Financial statements of prior periods are not restated, and pro-forma amounts for prior periods are not reported.

⑦ Identify changes in a reporting entity. An accounting change that results in financial statements that are actually the statements of a different entity should be reported by restating the financial statements of all prior periods presented, to show the financial information for the new reporting entity for all periods.

⑧ Describe the accounting for correction of errors. As soon as they are discovered, errors must be corrected by proper entries in the accounts and reported in the financial statements. The profession requires that corrections of errors be treated as prior period adjustments, be recorded in the year in which the error was discovered, and be reported in the financial statements as an adjustment to the beginning balance of retained earnings. If comparative statements are presented, the prior statements affected should be restated to correct for the error. The disclosures need not be repeated in the financial statements of subsequent periods.

⑨ Identify economic motives for changing accounting methods. Managers might have varying profit motives depending on economic times and whom they seek to impress. Some of the reasons for changing accounting methods are: (1) political costs, (2) capital structure, (3) bonus payments, and (4) smooth earnings.

KEY TERMS

change in accounting estimate, *1255*
change in accounting principle, *1255*
change in reporting entity, *1255*
correction of an error, *1266*
counterbalancing errors, *1272*
cumulative effect changes, *1256*
current changes, *1256*
noncounterbalancing errors, *1272*
pro-forma, *1257*
prospective changes, *1256*
retroactive changes, *1256*

⑩ Analyze the effect of errors. Three types of errors can occur: (1) *Balance sheet errors:* affect only the presentation of an asset, liability, or stockholders' equity account. (2) *Income statement errors:* affect only the presentation of the nominal accounts in the income statement. (3) *Balance sheet and income statement effect:* involves both the balance sheet and income statement. Errors are classified into two types: (1) *Counterbalancing errors:* will be offset or corrected over two periods. (2) *Noncounterbalancing errors:* are not offset in the next accounting period and take longer than two periods to correct themselves.

APPENDIX **23A**

Changing from and to the Equity Method

As noted in the chapter, an accounting change that results in financial statements for a different entity should be reported by **restating the financial statements of all prior periods presented**. An example of a change in reporting entity is when a company's level of ownership or influence changes, such that it should change from or to the equity method. We present illustrations for these changes in entity in the following two sections.

CHANGE FROM THE EQUITY METHOD

If the investor level of influence or ownership falls below that necessary for continued use of the equity method, a change must be made to the fair value method. The earnings or losses that were previously recognized by the investor under the equity method should **remain as part of the carrying amount** of the investment with no retroactive restatement to the new method.

    When a change is made **from the equity method to the fair value method, the cost basis for accounting purposes is the carrying amount of the investment at the date of the change**. In addition, amortizing the excess of acquisition price over the proportionate share of book value acquired attributable to undervalued depreciable assets and unrecorded goodwill ceases when the change of methods occurs. In other words, the new method is applied in its entirety once the equity method is no longer appropriate. At the next reporting date, the investor should record the unrealized holding gain or loss to recognize the difference between the carrying amount and fair value.

Dividends in Excess of Earnings

To the extent that dividends received by the investor in subsequent periods exceed its share of the investee's earnings for such periods (all periods following the change in method), they should be accounted for as a **reduction of the investment carrying amount**, rather than as revenue.

OBJECTIVE ⑪
After studying Appendix 23A, you should be able to: Make the computations and prepare the entries necessary to record a change from or to the equity method of accounting.

To illustrate, assume that on January 1, 1999, Investor Company purchased 250,000 shares of Investee Company's 1,000,000 shares of outstanding stock for $8,500,000. Investor correctly accounted for this investment using the equity method. After accounting for dividends received, investee net income, and amortization of Investor's share of goodwill in 1999, Investor reported its investment in Investee Company at $8,780,000 at December 31, 1999. On January 2, 2000, Investee Company sold 1,500,000 additional shares of its own common stock to the public, thereby reducing Investor Company's ownership from 25% to 10%. The net income (or loss) and dividends of Investee Company for the years 2000 through 2002 are as shown below.

Year	Investor's Share of Investee Income (Loss)	Investee Dividends Received by Investor
2000	$600,000	$ 400,000
2001	350,000	400,000
2002	–0–	210,000
Totals	$950,000	$1,010,000

ILLUSTRATION 23A-1
Income Earned and
Dividends Received

Assuming a change from the equity method to the fair value method as of January 2, 2000, Investor Company's reported investment in Investee Company and its reported income would be as shown below.

Year	Dividend Revenue Recognized	Cumulative Excess of Share of Earnings Over Dividends Received	Investment at December 31
2000	$400,000	$200,000[a]	$8,780,000
2001	400,000	150,000[b]	8,780,000
2002	150,000	(60,000)[c]	8,780,000 – $60,000 = $8,720,000

[a]$600,000 – $400,000 = $200,000
[b]($350,000 – $400,000) + $200,000 = $150,000
[c]$150,000 – $210,000 = $(60,000)

ILLUSTRATION 23A-2
Impact on Investment
Carrying Amount

The following entries would be recorded by Investor Company to recognize the above dividends and earnings data for the 3 years subsequent to the change in methods:

2000 and 2001

Cash	400,000	
Dividend Revenue		400,000
(To record dividend received from Investee Company)		

2002

Cash	210,000	
Available-for-Sale Securities		60,000
Dividend Revenue		150,000
(To record dividend revenue from Investee Company in 2002 and to recognize cumulative excess of dividends received over share of Investee earnings in periods subsequent to change from equity method)		

CHANGE TO THE EQUITY METHOD

When converting to the equity method, a retroactive adjustment is necessary. Such a change involves **adjusting retroactively the carrying amount of the investment, results of current and prior operations, and retained earnings of the investor as if the**

equity method has been in effect during all of the previous periods in which this investment was held.[1] When changing from the fair value method to the equity method, it is also necessary to eliminate any balances in the Unrealized Holding Gain or Loss—Equity account and the Securities Fair Value Adjustment account. In addition, the available-for-sale classification for this investment is eliminated, and the investment in stock under the equity method is recorded.

For example, on January 2, 2001, Amsted Corp. purchased for $500,000 cash 10% of the outstanding shares of Cable Company common stock. On that date, the net assets of Cable Company had a book value of $3,000,000. The excess of cost over the underlying equity in net assets of Cable Company is attributed to goodwill, which is amortized over 40 years. On January 2, 2003, Amsted Corp. purchased an additional 20% of Cable Company's stock for $1,200,000 cash when the book value of Cable's net assets was $4,000,000. Now having a 30% interest, Amsted Corp. must use the equity method. From January 2, 2001, to January 2, 2003, Amsted Corp. used the fair value method and categorized these securities as available-for-sale. At January 2, 2003, Amsted has a credit balance of $92,000 in its Unrealized Holding Gain or Loss—Equity account and a debit balance in its Securities Fair Value Adjustment account of the same amount. Assume that this adjustment was made on December 31, 2001. The net income reported by Cable Company and the Cable Company dividends received by Amsted during the period 2001 through 2003 were as follows:

ILLUSTRATION 23A-3
Income Earned and
Dividends Received

Year	Cable Company Net Income	Cable Co. Dividends Paid to Amsted
2001	$ 500,000	$ 20,000
2002	1,000,000	30,000
2003	1,200,000	120,000

The journal entries recorded from January 2, 2001, through December 31, 2003, relative to Amsted Corp.'s investment in Cable Company, reflecting the data above and a change from the fair value method to the equity method, are as follows.[2]

January 2, 2001

Available-for-Sale Securities	500,000	
Cash		500,000
(To record the purchase of a 10% interest in Cable Company)		

December 31, 2001

Cash	20,000	
Dividend Revenue		20,000
(To record the receipt of cash dividends from Cable Company)		
Securities Fair Value Adjustment (Available-for-Sale)	92,000	
Unrealized Holding Gain or Loss—Equity		92,000
(To record increase in fair value of securities)		

December 31, 2002

Cash	30,000	
Dividend Revenue		30,000
(To record the receipt of cash dividends from Cable Company)		

---

[1]"The Equity Method of Accounting for Investments in Common Stock," *Opinions of the Accounting Principles Board No. 18* (New York: AICPA, 1971), par. 17.

[2]Adapted from Paul A. Pacter, "Applying APB Opinion No. 18—Equity Method," *Journal of Accountancy*, September 1971, pp. 59–60.

January 2, 2003

Investment in Cable Stock	1,290,000	
Cash		1,200,000
Retained Earnings		90,000

(To record the purchase of an additional interest in Cable Company and to reflect retroactively a change from the fair value method to the equity method of accounting for the investment. The $90,000 adjustment is computed as follows:

	2001	2002	Total
Amsted Corp. equity in earnings of Cable Company (10%)	$50,000	$100,000	$150,000
Amortization of excess of acquisition price over underlying equity [$500,000 − (10% × $3,000,000)] ÷ 40 years = $5,000 per year	(5,000)	(5,000)	(10,000)
Dividend received	(20,000)	(30,000)	(50,000)
Prior period adjustment	$25,000	$ 65,000	$ 90,000)

January 2, 2003

Investment in Cable Stock	500,000	
Available-for-Sale Securities		500,000

(To reclassify initial 10% interest to equity method)

January 2, 2003

Unrealized Holding Gain or Loss—Equity	92,000	
Securities Fair Value Adjustment (Available-for-Sale)		92,000

(To eliminate fair value accounts for change to equity method)

December 31, 2003

Investment in Cable Stock	345,000	
Revenue from Investment		345,000

[To record equity in earnings of Cable Company (30% of $1,200,000) less $15,000 amortization of goodwill[a]]

[a]Goodwill amortization includes $5,000 [$500,000 − (10% × $3,000,000) ÷ 40 years] from 2001 purchase of 10% interest plus $10,000 [$1,200,000 − (20% × $4,000,000) ÷ 40 years] from 2003 purchase of 20% interest.

Cash	120,000	
Investment in Cable Stock		120,000

(To record the receipt of cash dividends from Cable Company)

Changing to the equity method is accomplished by placing the accounts related to and affected by the investment on the same basis as if the equity method had always been the basis of accounting for that investment. Thus, the effects of this accounting change are reported using the retroactive approach.

SUMMARY OF LEARNING OBJECTIVE FOR APPENDIX 23A

⑪ **Make the computations and prepare the entries necessary to record a change from or to the equity method of accounting.** When changing from the equity method to the fair value method, the cost basis for accounting purposes is the carrying amount used for the investment at the date of change. The new method is applied in its entirety once the equity method is no longer appropriate. When changing to the equity method, a retroactive adjustment of the carrying amount, of results of current and past operations, and of retained earnings is necessary to make the accounts as if the equity method has been in effect during all of the periods in which the investment was held.

Note: All **asterisked** Brief Exercises, Exercises, and Problems relate to material contained in the appendix to the chapter.

QUESTIONS

1 In recent years, *The Wall Street Journal* has indicated that many companies have changed their accounting principles. What are the major reasons why companies change accounting methods?

2 State how each of the following items is reflected in the financial statements:

(a) Change from straight-line method of depreciation to sum-of-the-years'-digits.

(b) Change from FIFO to LIFO method for inventory valuation purposes.

(c) Charge for failure to record depreciation in a previous period.

(d) Litigation won in current year, related to prior period.

(e) Change in the realizability of certain receivables.

(f) Writeoff of receivables.

(g) Change from the percentage-of-completion to the completed-contract method for reporting net income.

3 What are the advantages of employing the current or catch-up method for handling changes in accounting principle?

4 Explain when pro-forma amounts are reported and why these amounts are useful to financial statement readers.

5 Define a change in estimate and provide an illustration. When is a change in accounting estimate affected by a change in accounting principle?

6 Sandwich State Bank has followed the practice of capitalizing certain marketing costs and amortizing these costs over their expected life. In the current year, the bank determined that the future benefits from these costs were doubtful. Consequently, the bank adopted the policy of expensing these costs as incurred. How should this accounting change be reported in the comparative financial statements?

7 Indicate how the following items are recorded in the accounting records in the current year of Tami Agler Co.:

(a) Large writeoff of goodwill.

(b) A change in depreciating plant assets from accelerated to the straight-line method.

(c) Large writeoff of inventories because of obsolescence.

(d) Change from the cash basis to accrual basis of accounting.

(e) Change from LIFO to FIFO method for inventory valuation purposes.

(f) Change in the estimate of service lives for plant assets.

8 R. M. Andrews Construction Co. had followed the practice of expensing all materials assigned to a construction job without recognizing any salvage inventory. On December 31, 2001, it was determined that salvage inventory should be valued at $62,000. Of this amount, $29,000 arose during the current year. How does this information affect the financial statements to be prepared at the end of 2001?

9 E. A. Basler Inc. wishes to change from the sum-of-the-years'-digits to the straight-line depreciation method for financial reporting purposes. The auditor indicates that a change would be permitted only if it is to a preferable method. What difficulties develop in assessing preferability?

10 Discuss how a change to the LIFO method of inventory valuation is handled.

11 How should consolidated financial statements be reported this year when statements of individual companies were presented last year?

12 Karen Beers controlled four domestic subsidiaries and one foreign subsidiary. Prior to the current year, Beers had excluded the foreign subsidiary from consolidation. During the current year, the foreign subsidiary was included in the financial statements. How should this change in accounting principle be reflected in the financial statements?

13 Clara Beverage Co., a closely held corporation, is in the process of preparing financial statements to accompany an offering of its common stock. The company at this time has decided to switch from the accelerated depreciation method to the straight-line method of depreciation to better present its financial operations. How should this change in accounting principle be reported in the financial statements?

14 Distinguish between counterbalancing and non-counterbalancing errors. Give an example of each.

15 Discuss and illustrate how a correction of an error in previously issued financial statements should be handled.

16 Prior to 2002, Mary Boudreau Inc. excluded manufacturing overhead costs from work in process and finished goods inventory. These costs have been expensed as incurred. In 2002, the company decided to change its accounting methods for manufacturing inventories to full costing by including these costs as product costs. Assuming that these costs are material, how should this change be reflected in the financial statements for 2001 and 2002?

17 Lou Brady Corp. failed to record accrued salaries for 1999, $2,000; 2000, $2,100; and 2001, $3,900. What is the amount of the overstatement or understatement of Retained Earnings at December 31, 2002?

18 In January 2001, installation costs of $8,000 on new machinery were charged to Repair Expense. Other costs of this machinery of $30,000 were correctly recorded and have been depreciated using the straight-line method with an estimated life of 10 years and no salvage value. At December 31, 2002, it is decided that the machinery has a useful life of 20 years, starting with January 1, 2002. What entry(ies) should be made in 2002 to correctly record transactions related to machinery, assuming the machinery has no salvage value? The books have not been closed for 2002 and depreciation expense has not yet been recorded for 2002.

19 On January 2, 2001, $100,000 of 11%, 20-year bonds were issued for $97,000. The $3,000 discount was charged to Interest Expense. The bookkeeper, John Castle, records interest only on the interest payment dates of January 1 and July 1. What is the effect on reported net income for 2001 of this error, assuming straight-line amortization of the discount? What entry is necessary to correct for this error, assuming that the books are not closed for 2001?

20 An account payable of $13,000 for merchandise purchased on December 23, 2001, was recorded in January 2002. This merchandise was not included in inventory at December 31, 2001. What effect does this error have on reported net income for 2001? What entry should be made to correct for this error, assuming that the books are not closed for 2001?

21 Equipment was purchased on January 2, 2001, for $18,000, but no portion of the cost has been charged to depreciation. The corporation wishes to use the straight-line method for these assets, which have been estimated to have a life of 10 years and no salvage value. What effect does this error have on net income in 2001. What entry is necessary to correct for this error, assuming that the books are not closed for 2001?

BRIEF EXERCISES

BE23-1 Larry Beaty Corporation decided at the beginning of 2002 to change from double-declining balance depreciation to straight-line depreciation for financial reporting. The company will continue to use MACRS for tax purposes. For years prior to 2002, depreciation expense under the two methods was as follows: double-declining balance $128,000, and straight-line $80,000. The tax rate is 35%. Prepare Beaty's 2002 journal entry to record the change in accounting principle.

BE23-2 Bruce Bickner Company changed depreciation methods in 2002 from straight-line to double-declining balance, resulting in a cumulative-effect adjustment of $84,000. The 2002 income before the change was $250,000. Bickner had 10,000 shares of common stock outstanding all year. Prepare Bickner's 2002 income statement beginning with income before cumulative effect.

BE23-3 Robert Boey, Inc., changed from the LIFO cost flow assumption to the FIFO cost flow assumption in 2002. The increase in the prior year's income before taxes is $1,000,000. The tax rate is 40%. Prepare Boey's 2002 journal entry to record the change in accounting principle.

BE23-4 Nancy Castle Company purchased a computer system for $60,000 on January 1, 2000. It was depreciated based on a 7-year life and an $18,000 salvage value. On January 1, 2002, Castle revised these estimates to a total useful life of 4 years and a salvage value of $10,000. Prepare Castle's entry to record 2002 depreciation expense.

BE23-5 In 2002, John Hiatt Corporation discovered that equipment purchased on January 1, 2000, for $75,000 was expensed at that time. The equipment should have been depreciated over 5 years, with no salvage value. The effective tax rate is 30%. Prepare Hiatt's 2002 journal entry to correct the error.

BE23-6 At January 1, 2002, William R. Monat Company reported retained earnings of $2,000,000. In 2002, Monat discovered that 2001 depreciation expense was understated by $500,000. In 2002, net income was $900,000 and dividends declared were $250,000. The tax rate is 40%. Prepare a 2002 retained earnings statement for William R. Monat Company.

BE23-7 Indicate the effect—**U**nderstate, **O**verstate, **N**o Effect—that each of the following errors has on 2001 net income and 2002 net income:

	2001	2002
(a) Wages payable were not recorded at 12/31/01.	_____	_____
(b) Equipment purchased in 2000 was expensed.	_____	_____
(c) Equipment purchased in 2001 was expensed.	_____	_____
(d) 2001 ending inventory was overstated.	_____	_____
(e) Goodwill amortization was not recorded in 2002.	_____	_____

***BE23-8** Robocop Corporation owns stock of Terminator, Inc. Prior to 2002, the investment was accounted for using the equity method. In early 2002, Robocop sold part of its investment in Terminator, and began using the fair value method. In 2002, Terminator earned net income of $80,000 and paid dividends of

$95,000. Prepare Robocop's entries related to Terminator's net income and dividends, assuming Robocop now owns 8% of Terminator's stock.

*BE23-9 Rocket Corporation has owned stock of Knight Corporation since 1998. At December 31, 2001, its balances related to this investment were:

Available-for-Sale Securities	$185,000
Securities Fair Value Adj (AFS)	34,000 Dr.
Unrealized Holding Gain or Loss—Equity	34,000 Cr.

On January 1, 2002, Rocket purchased additional stock of Knight Company for $445,000 and now has significant influence over Knight. If the equity method had been used in 1998–2001, income would have been $33,000 greater than dividends received. Prepare Rocket's journal entries to record the purchase of the investment and the change to the equity method.

EXERCISES

E23-1 (Error and Change in Principle—Depreciation) Joy Cunningham Co. purchased a machine on January 1, 1999, for $550,000. At that time it was estimated that the machine would have a 10-year life and no salvage value. On December 31, 2002, the firm's accountant found that the entry for depreciation expense had been omitted in 2000. In addition, management has informed the accountant that they plan to switch to straight-line depreciation, starting with the year 2002. At present, the company uses the sum-of-the-years'-digits method for depreciating equipment.

Instructions
Prepare the general journal entries the accountant should make at December 31, 2002 (ignore tax effects).

E23-2 (Change in Principle and Change in Estimate—Depreciation) Kathleen Cole Inc. acquired the following assets in January of 1999:

Equipment, estimated service life, 5 years; salvage value, $15,000	$525,000
Building, estimated service life, 30 years; no salvage value	$693,000

The equipment has been depreciated using the sum-of-the-years'-digits method for the first 3 years for financial reporting purposes. In 2002, the company decided to change the method of computing depreciation to the straight-line method for the equipment, but no change was made in the estimated service life or salvage value. It was also decided to change the total estimated service life of the building from 30 years to 40 years, with no change in the estimated salvage value. The building is depreciated on the straight-line method.

The company has 100,000 shares of capital stock outstanding. Results of operations for 2002 and 2001 are shown below:

	2002	2001
Income before cumulative effect of change in computing depreciation for 2002: depreciation for 2002 has been computed on the straight-line basis for both the equipment and building[a]	$385,000	$380,000
Income per share before cumulative effect of change in computing depreciation for 2002	$3.85	$3.80

[a]It should be noted that the computation for depreciation expense for 2002 and 2001 for the building was based on the original estimate of service life for 30 years.

Instructions
(a) Compute the cumulative effect of the change in accounting principle to be reported in the income statement for 2002, and prepare the journal entry to record the change. (Ignore tax effects.)
(b) Present comparative data for the years 2001 and 2002, starting with income before cumulative effect of accounting change. Prepare pro-forma data. Do not prepare the footnote. (Ignore tax effects.)

E23-3 (Change in Principle and Change in Estimated Depreciation) On January 1, 1998, Jackson Company purchased a building and equipment that have the following useful lives, salvage values, and costs:

Building, 40-year estimated useful life, $50,000 salvage value, $800,000 cost
Equipment, 12-year estimated useful life, $10,000 salvage value, $100,000 cost

The building has been depreciated under the double-declining balance method through 2001. In 2002, the company decided to switch to the straight-line method of depreciation. Jackson also decided to change the total useful life of the equipment to 9 years, with a salvage value of $5,000 at the end of that time. The equipment is depreciated using the straight-line method.

Instructions

    (a) Compute the cumulative effect of the change in accounting principle for 2002.

    (b) Prepare the journal entry(ies) necessary to record the changes made in 2002.

    (c) Compute depreciation expense on the equipment for 2002.

E23-4 **(Change in Estimate—Depreciation)** Peter M. Dell Co. purchased equipment for $510,000 which was estimated to have a useful life of 10 years with a salvage value of $10,000 at the end of that time. Depreciation has been entered for 7 years on a straight-line basis. In 2002, it is determined that the total estimated life should be 15 years with a salvage value of $5,000 at the end of that time.

Instructions

    (a) Prepare the entry (if any) to correct the prior years' depreciation.

    (b) Prepare the entry to record depreciation for 2002.

E23-5 **(Change in Principle—Depreciation)** Gerald Englehart Industries changed from the double-declining balance to the straight-line method in 2002 on all its plant assets. For tax purposes, assume that the amount of tax depreciation is higher than the double-declining balance depreciation for each of the 3 years. The appropriate information related to this change is as follows:

Year	Double-Declining Balance Depreciation	Straight-Line Depreciation	Difference
2000	$250,000	$125,000	$125,000
2001	225,000	125,000	100,000
2002	202,500	125,000	77,500

Net income for 2001 was reported at $270,000; net income for 2002 was reported at $300,000, excluding any adjustment for the cumulative effect of a change in depreciation methods. The straight-line method of depreciation was employed in computing net income for 2002.

Instructions

    (a) Assuming a tax rate of 34%, what is the amount of the cumulative effect adjustment in 2002?

    (b) Prepare the journal entry(ies) to record the cumulative effect adjustment in the accounting records.

    (c) Starting with income before cumulative effect of change in accounting principle, prepare the remaining portion of the income statement for 2001 and 2002. Indicate the pro-forma net income that should be reported. Ignore per share computations and note disclosures.

E23-6 **(Change in Principle—Depreciation)** At the end of fiscal 2002, management of Carol Dilbeck Manufacturing Company has decided to change its depreciation method from the double-declining balance method to the straight-line method for financial reporting purposes. For federal income taxes the company will continue to use the MACRS method. The income tax rate for all years is 30%. At the end of fiscal 2002, the company has 200,000 common shares issued and outstanding. Information regarding depreciation expense and income after income taxes is as follows:

Depreciation expense to date under:

	MACRS	Straight-Line	Double-Declining Balance
Pre-2001	$1,000,000	$400,000	$950,000
2001	300,000	150,000	260,000
2002	280,000	140,000	250,000

Reported income after income taxes:

2001	$1,200,000
2002	1,400,000

Instructions

    (a) Prepare the journal entries to record the change in accounting method in 2002 and indicate how the change in depreciation method would be reported in the income statement of 2002. Also indicate how earnings per share would be disclosed. (*Hint:* Adjust Deferred Tax Liability account.)

    (b) Show the amount of depreciation expense to be reported in 2002.

E23-7 **(Change in Principle—Long-term Contracts)** Pam Erickson Construction Company changed from the completed-contract to the percentage-of-completion method of accounting for long-term construction contracts during 2002. For tax purposes, the company employs the completed-contract method and will continue this approach in the future. (*Hint:* Adjust all tax consequences through the Deferred Tax Liability account.) The appropriate information related to this change is as follows:

	Pretax Income from:		
	Percentage-of-Completion	Completed-Contract	Difference
2001	$780,000	$590,000	$190,000
2002	700,000	480,000	220,000

Instructions
   (a) Assuming that the tax rate is 35%, what is the amount of net income that would be reported in 2002?
   (b) What entry(ies) are necessary to adjust the accounting records for the change in accounting principle?

E23-8 (Various Changes in Principle—Inventory Methods) Below is the net income of Anita Ferreri Instrument Co., a private corporation, computed under the three inventory methods using a periodic system.

	FIFO	Average Cost	LIFO
1999	$26,000	$24,000	$20,000
2000	30,000	25,000	21,000
2001	28,000	27,000	24,000
2002	34,000	30,000	26,000

Instructions (Ignore tax considerations)
   (a) Assume that in 2002 Ferreri decided to change from the FIFO method to the average cost method of pricing inventories. Prepare the journal entry necessary for the change that took place during 2002, and show all the appropriate information needed for reporting on a comparative basis.
   (b) Assume that in 2002 Ferreri, which had been using the LIFO method since incorporation in 1999, changed to the FIFO method of pricing inventories. Prepare the journal entry necessary for the change, and show all the appropriate information needed for reporting on a comparative basis.

E23-9 (Change in Principle—Inventory Methods) Garner Company began operations on January 1, 1999, and uses the average cost method of pricing inventory. Management is contemplating a change in inventory methods for 2002. The following information is available for the years 1999–2001:

	Net Income Computed Using		
	Average Cost Method	FIFO Method	LIFO Method
1999	$15,000	$20,000	$12,000
2000	18,000	24,000	14,000
2001	20,000	27,000	17,000

Instructions
   (a) Prepare the journal entry necessary to record a change from the average cost method to the FIFO method in 2002.
   (b) Show the comparative income statements for 2001 and 2002, starting with income before the cumulative effect of change in accounting principle. Assume net income for 2002 was $32,000.
   (c) Assume Garner Company used the LIFO method instead of the average cost method during the years 1999–2001. In 2002, Garner changed to the FIFO method. Prepare the journal entry necessary to record the change in principle.

E23-10 (Error Correction Entries) The first audit of the books of Bruce Gingrich Company was made for the year ended December 31, 2002. In examining the books, the auditor found that certain items had been overlooked or incorrectly handled in the last 3 years. These items are:

   1. At the beginning of 2000, the company purchased a machine for $510,000 (salvage value of $51,000) that had a useful life of 6 years. The bookkeeper used straight-line depreciation, but failed to deduct the salvage value in computing the depreciation base for the 3 years.
   2. At the end of 2001, the company failed to accrue sales salaries of $45,000.
   3. A tax lawsuit that involved the year 2000 was settled late in 2002. It was determined that the company owed an additional $85,000 in taxes related to 2000. The company did not record a liability in 2000 or 2001 because the possibility of loss was considered remote, and charged the $85,000 to a loss account in 2002.
   4. Gingrich Company purchased another company early in 2000 and recorded goodwill of $450,000. Gingrich had not amortized goodwill because its value had not diminished.

5. In 2002, the company changed its basis of inventory pricing from FIFO to LIFO. The cumulative effect of this change was to decrease net income by $71,000. The company debited this cumulative effect to Retained Earnings. LIFO was used in computing income for 2002.

6. In 2002, the company wrote off $87,000 of inventory considered to be obsolete; this loss was charged directly to Retained Earnings.

Instructions

Prepare the journal entries necessary in 2002 to correct the books, assuming that the books have not been closed. The proper amortization period for goodwill is 40 years. Disregard effects of corrections on income tax.

E23-11 (Change in Principle and Error; Financial Statements) Presented below are the comparative statements for Denise Habbe Inc.

	2002	2001
Sales	$340,000	$270,000
Cost of sales	200,000	142,000
Gross profit	140,000	128,000
Expenses	88,000	50,000
Net income	$ 52,000	$ 78,000
Retained earnings (Jan. 1)	$125,000	$ 72,000
Net income	52,000	78,000
Dividends	(30,000)	(25,000)
Retained earnings (Dec. 31)	$147,000	$125,000

The following additional information is provided:

1. In 2002, Denise Habbe Inc. decided to switch its depreciation method from sum-of-the-years'-digits to the straight-line method. The differences in the two depreciation methods for the assets involved are:

	2002	2001
Sum-of-the-years'-digits	$30,000[a]	$40,000
Straight-line	25,000	25,000

[a]The 2002 income statement contains depreciation expense of $30,000.

2. In 2002, the company discovered that the ending inventory for 2001 was overstated by $24,000; ending inventory for 2002 is correctly stated.

Instructions

(a) Prepare the revised income and retained earnings statement for 2001 and 2002, assuming comparative statements (ignore income tax effects). Do not prepare footnotes or pro-forma amounts.

(b) Prepare the revised income and retained earnings statement for 2002, assuming a noncomparative presentation (ignore income tax effects). Do not prepare footnotes or pro-forma amounts.

E23-12 (Error Analysis and Correcting Entry) You have been engaged to review the financial statements of Linette Gottschalk Corporation. In the course of your examination you conclude that the bookkeeper hired during the current year is not doing a good job. You notice a number of irregularities as follows:

1. Year-end wages payable of $3,400 were not recorded because the bookkeeper thought that "they were immaterial."

2. Accrued vacation pay for the year of $31,100 was not recorded because the bookkeeper "never heard that you had to do it."

3. Insurance for a 12-month period purchased on November 1 of this year was charged to insurance expense in the amount of $2,640 because "the amount of the check is about the same every year."

4. Reported sales revenue for the year is $2,120,000. This includes all sales taxes collected for the year. The sales tax rate is 6%. Because the sales tax is forwarded to the State Department of Revenue, the Sales Tax Expense account is debited because the bookkeeper thought that "the sales tax is a selling expense." At the end of the current year, the balance in the Sales Tax Expense account is $103,400.

Instructions

Prepare the necessary correcting entries, assuming that Gottschalk uses a calendar-year basis.

E23-13 (Error Analysis and Correcting Entry) The reported net incomes for the first 2 years of Sandra Gustafson Products, Inc., were as follows: 2001—$147,000; 2002—$185,000. Early in 2003, the following errors were discovered:

1. Depreciation of equipment for 2001 was overstated $17,000.
2. Depreciation of equipment for 2002 was understated $38,500.
3. December 31, 2001, inventory was understated $50,000.
4. December 31, 2002, inventory was overstated $16,200.

Instructions

Prepare the correcting entry necessary when these errors are discovered. Assume that the books are closed. Ignore income tax considerations.

E23-14 (Error Analysis)   Peter Henning Tool Company's December 31 year-end financial statements contained the following errors:

	December 31, 2001	December 31, 2002
Ending inventory	$9,600 understated	$8,100 overstated
Depreciation expense	$2,300 understated	—

An insurance premium of $66,000 was prepaid in 2001 covering the years 2001, 2002, and 2003. The entire amount was charged to expense in 2001. In addition, on December 31, 2002, fully depreciated machinery was sold for $15,000 cash, but the entry was not recorded until 2003. There were no other errors during 2001 or 2002, and no corrections have been made for any of the errors. Ignore income tax considerations.

Instructions

(a) Compute the total effect of the errors on 2002 net income.
(b) Compute the total effect of the errors on the amount of Henning's working capital at December 31, 2002.
(c) Compute the total effect of the errors on the balance of Henning's retained earnings at December 31, 2002.

E23-15 (Error Analysis; Correcting Entries)   A partial trial balance of Julie Hartsack Corporation is as follows on December 31, 2002:

	Dr.	Cr.
Supplies on hand	$ 2,700	
Accrued salaries and wages		$ 1,500
Interest receivable on investments	5,100	
Prepaid insurance	90,000	
Unearned rent		–0–
Accrued interest payable		15,000

Additional adjusting data:

1. A physical count of supplies on hand on December 31, 2002, totaled $1,100.
2. Through oversight, the Accrued Salaries and Wages account was not changed during 2002. Accrued salaries and wages on December 31, 2002, amounted to $4,400.
3. The Interest Receivable on Investments account was also left unchanged during 2002. Accrued interest on investments amounts to $4,350 on December 31, 2002.
4. The unexpired portions of the insurance policies totaled $65,000 as of December 31, 2002.
5. $28,000 was received on January 1, 2002 for the rent of a building for both 2002 and 2003. The entire amount was credited to rental income.
6. Depreciation for the year was erroneously recorded as $5,000 rather than the correct figure of $50,000.
7. A further review of depreciation calculations of prior years revealed that depreciation of $7,200 was not recorded. It was decided that this oversight should be corrected by a prior period adjustment.

Instructions

(a) Assuming that the books have not been closed, what are the adjusting entries necessary at December 31, 2002? Ignore income tax considerations.
(b) Assuming that the books have been closed, what are the adjusting entries necessary at December 31, 2002? Ignore income tax considerations.

E23-16 (Error Analysis)   The before-tax income for Lonnie Holdiman Co. for 2001 was $101,000 and $77,400 for 2002. However, the accountant noted that the following errors had been made:

1. Sales for 2001 included amounts of $38,200 which had been received in cash during 2001, but for which the related products were delivered in 2002. Title did not pass to the purchaser until 2002.
2. The inventory on December 31, 2001, was understated by $8,640.

3. The bookkeeper in recording interest expense for both 2001 and 2002 on bonds payable made the following entry on an annual basis:

| Interest Expense | 15,000 | |
| Cash | | 15,000 |

The bonds have a face value of $250,000 and pay a stated interest rate of 6%. They were issued at a discount of $15,000 on January 1, 2001, to yield an effective interest rate of 7%. (Assume that the effective yield method should be used.)

4. Ordinary repairs to equipment had been erroneously charged to the Equipment account during 2001 and 2002. Repairs in the amount of $8,500 in 2001 and $9,400 in 2002 were so charged. The company applies a rate of 10% to the balance in the Equipment account at the end of the year in its determination of depreciation charges.

Instructions

Prepare a schedule showing the determination of corrected income before taxes for 2001 and 2002.

E23-17 (Error Analysis) When the records of Debra Hanson Corporation were reviewed at the close of 2002, the errors listed below were discovered. For each item indicate by a check mark in the appropriate column whether the error resulted in an overstatement, an understatement, or had no effect on net income for the years 2001 and 2002.

	2001			2002		
Item	Over-statement	Under-statement	No Effect	Over-statement	Under-statement	No Effect
1. Failure to record amortization of patent in 2002.						
2. Failure to record the correct amount of ending 2001 inventory. The amount was understated because of an error in calculation.						
3. Failure to record merchandise purchased in 2001. Merchandise was also omitted from ending inventory in 2001 but was not yet sold.						
4. Failure to record accrued interest on notes payable in 2001; amount was recorded when paid in 2002.						
5. Failure to reflect supplies on hand on balance sheet at end of 2001.						

E23-18 (Accounting for Accounting Changes and Errors) Listed below are various types of accounting changes and errors.

_____ 1. Change in a plant asset's salvage value.
_____ 2. Change due to overstatement of inventory.
_____ 3. Change from sum-of-the-years'-digits to straight-line method of depreciation.
_____ 4. Change from presenting unconsolidated to consolidated financial statements.
_____ 5. Change from LIFO to FIFO inventory method.
_____ 6. Change in the rate used to compute warranty costs.
_____ 7. Change from an unacceptable accounting principle to an acceptable accounting principle.
_____ 8. Change in a patent's amortization period.
_____ 9. Change from completed-contract to percentage-of-completion method on construction contracts.
_____ 10. Change from FIFO to average-cost inventory method.

Instructions

For each change or error, indicate how it would be accounted for using the following code letters:

    a. Accounted for currently.
    b. Accounted for prospectively.
    c. Accounted for retroactively.
    d. None of the above.

*E23-19 (Change from Fair Value to Equity) On January 1, 2001, Barbra Streisand Co. purchased 25,000 shares (a 10% interest) in Elton John Corp. for $1,400,000. At the time, the book value and the fair value of John's net assets were $13,000,000.

    On July 1, 2002, Streisand paid $3,040,000 for 50,000 additional shares of John common stock, which represented a 20% investment in John. The fair value of John's identifiable assets net of liabilities was equal to their carrying amount of $14,200,000. As a result of this transaction, Streisand owns 30% of John and can exercise significant influence over John's operating and financial policies. Intangible assets are amortized over 10 years.

    John reported the following net income and declared and paid the following dividends:

	Net Income	Dividend per Share
Year ended 12/31/01	$700,000	None
Six months ended 6/30/02	500,000	None
Six months ended 12/31/02	815,000	$1.55

Instructions

Determine the ending balance that Streisand Co. should report as its investment in John Corp. at the end of 2002.

*E23-20 (Change from Equity to Fair Value) Dan Aykroyd Corp. was a 30% owner of John Belushi Company, holding 210,000 shares of Belushi's common stock on December 31, 2000. The investment account had the following entries:

Investment in Belushi

1/1/99 Cost	$3,180,000	12/6/99 Dividend received	$150,000
12/31/99 Share of income	390,000	12/31/99 Amortization of under-	
12/31/00 Share of income	510,000	valued assets	30,000
		12/5/00 Dividend received	240,000
		12/31/00 Amortization of under-	
		valued assets	30,000

On January 2, 2001, Aykroyd sold 126,000 shares of Belushi for $3,440,000, thereby losing its significant influence. During the year 2001 Belushi experienced the following results of operations and paid the following dividends to Aykroyd.

	Belushi Income (Loss)	Dividends Paid to Aykroyd
2001	$300,000	$50,400

At December 31, 2001, the fair value of Belushi shares held by Aykroyd is $1,570,000. This is the first reporting date since the January 2 sale.

Instructions

    (a) What effect does the January 2, 2001, transaction have upon Aykroyd's accounting treatment for its investment in Belushi?
    (b) Compute the carrying amount in Belushi as of December 31, 2001.
    (c) Prepare the adjusting entry on December 31, 2001, applying the fair value method to Aykroyd's long-term investment in Belushi Company securities.

PROBLEMS

P23-1 (Change in Estimate, Principle, and Error Correction) Roland Company is in the process of having its financial statements audited for the first time as of December 31, 2001. The auditor has found the following items that occurred in previous years:

    1. Roland purchased equipment on January 2, 1998, for $65,000. At that time, the equipment had an estimated useful life of 10 years with a $5,000 salvage value. The equipment is depreciated on a straight-line basis. On January 2, 2001, as a result of additional information, the company determined that the equipment had a total estimated useful life of 7 years with a $3,000 salvage value.

2. During 2001 Roland changed from the double-declining balance method for its building to the straight-line method. The auditor provided the following computations which present depreciation on both bases:

	2001	2000	1999
Straight-line	$27,000	$27,000	$27,000
Declining-balance	48,600	54,000	60,000

3. Roland purchased a machine on July 1, 1998, at a cost of $80,000. The machine has a salvage value of $8,000 and a useful life of 8 years. Roland's bookkeeper recorded straight-line depreciation during each year but failed to consider the salvage value.

Instructions

(a) Prepare the necessary journal entries to record each of the preceding changes or errors. The books for 2001 have not been closed.

(b) Compute the 2001 depreciation expense on the equipment.

(c) Show the comparative statements for 2000 and 2001, starting with income before the cumulative effect of change in accounting principle. Income before depreciation expense was $300,000 in 2001, and net income was $210,000 in 2000.

P23-2 (Comprehensive Accounting Change and Error Analysis Problem) On December 31, 2002, before the books were closed, the management and accountants of Eloise Keltner Inc. made the following determinations about three depreciable assets:

1. Depreciable asset A was purchased January 2, 1999. It originally cost $495,000 and, for depreciation purposes, the straight-line method was originally chosen. The asset was originally expected to be useful for 10 years and have a zero salvage value. In 2002, the decision was made to change the depreciation method from straight-line to sum-of-the-years'-digits, and the estimates relating to useful life and salvage value remained unchanged.

2. Depreciable asset B was purchased January 3, 1998. It originally cost $120,000 and, for depreciation purposes, the straight-line method was chosen. The asset was originally expected to be useful for 15 years and have a zero salvage value. In 2002, the decision was made to shorten the total life of this asset to 9 years and to estimate the salvage value at $3,000.

3. Depreciable asset C was purchased January 5, 1998. The asset's original cost was $140,000, and this amount was entirely expensed in 1998. This particular asset has a 10-year useful life and no salvage value. The straight-line method was chosen for depreciation purposes.

Additional data:

1. Income in 2002 before depreciation expense amount to $400,000.
2. Depreciation expense on assets other than A, B, and C totaled $55,000 in 2002.
3. Income in 2001 was reported at $370,000.
4. Ignore all income tax effects.
5. 100,000 shares of common stock were outstanding in 2001 and 2002.

Instructions

(a) Prepare all necessary entries in 2002 to record these determinations.

(b) Prepare comparative income statements for Eloise Keltner Inc. for 2001 and 2002, starting with income before the cumulative effects of any change in accounting principle.

(c) Prepare comparative retained earnings statements for Eloise Keltner Inc. for 2001 and 2002. The company had retained earnings of $200,000 at December 31, 2000.

P23-3 (Comprehensive Accounting Change and Error Analysis Problem) Larry Kingston Inc. was organized in late 1999 to manufacture and sell hosiery. At the end of its fourth year of operation, the company has been fairly successful, as indicated by the following reported net incomes.

1999	$140,000[a]	2001	$205,000
2000	160,000[b]	2002	276,000

[a]Includes a $12,000 increase because of change in bad debt experience rate.
[b]Includes extraordinary gain of $40,000.

The company has decided to expand operations and has applied for a sizable bank loan. The bank officer has indicated that the records should be audited and presented in comparative statements to facilitate analysis by the bank. Larry Kingston Inc., therefore, hired the auditing firm of Check & Doublecheck Co. and has provided the following additional information.

1. In early 2000, Larry Kingston Inc. changed its estimate from 2% to 1% on the amount of bad debt expense to be charged to operations. Bad debt expense for 1999, if a 1% rate had been used, would have been $12,000. The company, therefore, restated its net income for 1999.
2. In 2002, the auditor discovered that the company had changed its method of inventory pricing from LIFO to FIFO. The effect on the income statements for the previous years is as follows:

	1999	2000	2001	2002
Net income unadjusted—LIFO basis	$140,000	$160,000	$205,000	$276,000
Net income unadjusted—FIFO basis	155,000	165,000	215,000	260,000
	$ 15,000	$ 5,000	$ 10,000	($ 16,000)

3. In 2000, the company changed its method of depreciation from the accelerated method to the straight-line approach. The company used the straight-line method in 2000. The effect on the income statement for the previous year is as follows:

	1999
Net income unadjusted—accelerated method	$140,000
Net income unadjusted—straight-line method	147,000
	$ 7,000

4. In 2002, the auditor discovered that:
   a. The company incorrectly overstated the ending inventory by $11,000 in 2001.
   b. A dispute developed in 2000 with the Internal Revenue Service over the deductibility of entertainment expenses. In 1999, the company was not permitted these deductions, but a tax settlement was reached in 2002 that allowed these expenses. As a result of the court's finding, tax expenses in 2002 were reduced by $60,000.

Instructions

(a) Indicate how each of these changes or corrections should be handled in the accounting records. Ignore income tax considerations.

(b) Present comparative income statements for the years 1999 to 2002, starting with income before extraordinary items. Do not prepare pro-forma amounts. Ignore income tax considerations.

P23-4 (Change in Principle—LIFO to Average Cost; Income Statements—Periodic) The management of Scott Kreiter Instrument Company had concluded, with the concurrence of its independent auditors, that results of operations would be more fairly presented if Kreiter changed its method of pricing inventory from last-in, first-out (LIFO) to average cost in 2001. Given below is the 5-year summary of income and a schedule of what the inventories might have been if stated on the average cost method.

SCOTT KREITER INSTRUMENT COMPANY
Statement of Income and Retained Earnings
For the Years Ended May 31

	1997	1998	1999	2000	2001
Sales—net	$13,964	$15,506	$16,673	$18,221	$18,898
Cost of goods sold					
Beginning inventory	1,000	1,100	1,000	1,115	1,237
Purchases	13,000	13,900	15,000	15,900	17,100
Ending inventory	(1,100)	(1,000)	(1,115)	(1,237)	(1,369)
Total	12,900	14,000	14,885	15,778	16,968
Gross profit	1,064	1,506	1,788	2,443	1,930
Administrative expenses	700	763	832	907	989
Income before taxes	364	743	956	1,536	941
Income taxes (50%)	182	372	478	768	471
Net income	182	371	478	768	470
Retained earnings—beginning	1,206	1,388	1,759	2,237	3,005
Retained earnings—ending	$ 1,388	$ 1,759	$ 2,237	$ 3,005	$ 3,475
Earnings per share	$ 1.82	$ 3.71	$ 4.78	$ 7.68	$ 4.70

Schedule of Inventory Balances Using Average Cost Method
Year Ended May 31

1996	1997	1998	1999	2000	2001
$950	$1,124	$1,091	$1,270	$1,480	$1,699

Instructions

Prepare comparative statements for the 5 years, assuming that Kreiter changed its method of inventory pricing to average cost. Indicate the effects on net income and earnings per share for the years involved. (All amounts except EPS are rounded up to the nearest dollar.)

P23-5 (Financial Statement Effect of Changes in Principle and Estimate) James N. McInnes Corporation has decided that in the preparation of its 2002 financial statements two changes should be made from the methods used in prior years:

1. *Depreciation.* McInnes has always used an accelerated method for tax and financial reporting purposes but has decided to change during 2002 to the straight-line method for financial reporting only. Assume that the accelerated method for tax and reporting purposes has been the same in the past. The effect of this change is as follows:

	Excess of Accelerated Depreciation over Straight-line Depreciation
Prior to 2001	$1,365,000
2001	106,050
2002	103,950
	$1,575,000

Depreciation is charged to cost of sales and to selling, general, and administrative expenses on the basis of 75% and 25%, respectively.

2. *Bad debt expense.* In the past, McInnes has recognized bad debt expense equal to 1.5% of net sales. After careful review it has been decided that a rate of 1.75% is more appropriate for 2002. Bad debt expense is charged to selling, general, and administrative expenses.

The following information is taken from preliminary financial statements, prepared before giving effect to the two changes:

MCINNES CORPORATION
Condensed Balance Sheet
December 31, 2002
With Comparative Figures for 2001

	2002	2001
Assets		
Current assets	$43,561,000	$43,900,000
Plant assets, at cost	45,792,000	43,974,000
Less: Accumulated depreciation	23,761,000	22,946,000
	$65,592,000	$64,928,000
Liabilities and Stockholders' Equity		
Current liabilities	$21,124,000	$23,650,000
Long-term debt	15,154,000	14,097,000
Capital stock	11,620,000	11,620,000
Retained earnings	17,694,000	15,561,000
	$65,592,000	$64,928,000

MCINNES CORPORATION
Income Statement
For the Year Ended December 31, 2002
With Comparative Figures for 2001

	2002	2001
Net sales	$80,520,000	$78,920,000
Cost of goods sold	54,847,000	53,074,000
	25,673,000	25,846,000
Selling, general, and administrative expenses	19,540,000	18,411,000
	6,133,000	7,435,000
Other income (expense), net	(1,198,000)	(1,079,000)
Income before income taxes	4,935,000	6,356,000
Income taxes	2,220,750	2,860,200
Net income	$ 2,714,250	$ 3,495,800

There have been no temporary differences between any book and tax items prior to the changes above. The effective tax rate is 45%.

Instructions

For the items listed below compute the amounts that would appear on the comparative (2002 and 2001) financial statements of McInnes Corporation after adjustment for the two accounting changes. Show amounts for both 2002 and 2001, and prepare supporting schedules as necessary.

(a) Accumulated depreciation.
(b) Deferred tax liability (cumulative).
(c) Selling, general, and administrative expenses.
(d) Current portion of federal income tax expense.
(e) Deferred portion of federal income tax expense.
(f) Retained earnings.
(g) Pro-forma net income.

P23-6 **(Error Corrections)** You have been assigned to examine the financial statements of Vickie L. Lemke Company for the year ended December 31, 2002. You discover the following situations:

1. Depreciation of $3,200 for 2002 on delivery vehicles was not recorded.
2. The physical inventory count on December 31, 2001, improperly excluded merchandise costing $19,000 that had been temporarily stored in a public warehouse. Lemke uses a periodic inventory system.
3. The physical inventory count on December 31, 2002, improperly included merchandise with a cost of $8,500 that had been recorded as a sale on December 27, 2002, and held for the customer to pick up on January 4, 2003.
4. A collection of $5,600 on account from a customer received on December 31, 2002, was not recorded until January 2, 2003.
5. In 2002, the company sold for $3,700 fully depreciated equipment that originally cost $22,000. The company credited the proceeds from the sale to the Equipment account.
6. During November 2002, a competitor company filed a patent-infringement suit against Lemke claiming damages of $220,000. The company's legal counsel has indicated that an unfavorable verdict is probable and a reasonable estimate of the court's award to the competitor is $125,000. The company has not reflected or disclosed this situation in the financial statements.
7. Lemke has a portfolio of trading securities. No entry has been made to adjust to market. Information on cost and market value is as follows:

	Cost	Market
December 31, 2001	$95,000	$95,000
December 31, 2002	$84,000	$82,000

8. At December 31, 2002, an analysis of payroll information shows accrued salaries of $12,200. The Accrued Salaries Payable account had a balance of $16,000 at December 31, 2002, which was unchanged from its balance at December 31, 2001.

9. A large piece of equipment was purchased on January 3, 2002, for $32,000 and was charged to Repairs Expense. The equipment is estimated to have a service life of 8 years and no residual value. Lemke normally uses the straight-line depreciation method for this type of equipment.

10. A $15,000 insurance premium paid on July 1, 2001, for a policy that expires on June 30, 2004, was charged to insurance expense.

11. A trademark was acquired at the beginning of 2001 for $50,000. No amortization has been recorded since its acquisition. The maximum allowable amortization period is to be used.

Instructions

Assume the trial balance has been prepared but the books have not been closed for 2002. Assuming all amounts are material, prepare journal entries showing the adjustments that are required. Ignore income tax considerations.

P23-7 (Error Corrections and Changes in Principle) Patricia Voga Company is in the process of adjusting and correcting its books at the end of 2002. In reviewing its records, the following information is compiled.

1. Voga has failed to accrue sales commissions payable at the end of each of the last 2 years, as follows:

December 31, 2001	$4,000
December 31, 2002	$2,500

2. In reviewing the December 31, 2002, inventory, Voga discovered errors in its inventory-taking procedures that have caused inventories for the last 3 years to be incorrect, as follows:

December 31, 2000	Understated	$16,000
December 31, 2001	Understated	$21,000
December 31, 2002	Overstated	$ 6,700

Voga has already made an entry that established the incorrect December 31, 2002, inventory amount.

3. At December 31, 2002, Voga decided to change the depreciation method on its office equipment from double-declining balance to straight-line. Assume that tax depreciation is higher than the double-declining depreciation taken for each period. The following information is available (the tax rate is 40%):

	Double-Declining Balance	Straight-Line	Pretax Difference	Tax Effect	Difference, Net of Tax
Prior to 2002	$70,000	$40,000	$30,000	$12,000	$18,000
2002	12,000	10,000	2,000	800	1,200

Voga has already recorded the 2002 depreciation expense using the double-declining balance method.

4. Before 2002, Voga accounted for its income from long-term construction contracts on the completed contract basis. Early in 2002, Voga changed to the percentage-of-completion basis for both accounting and tax purposes. Income for 2002 has been recorded using the percentage-of-completion method. The income tax rate is 40%. The following information is available:

	Pretax Income	
	Percentage of Completion	Completed Contract
Prior to 2002	$150,000	$95,000
2002	60,000	20,000

Instructions

Prepare the journal entries necessary at December 31, 2002, to record the above corrections and changes. The books are still open for 2002. Voga has not yet recorded its 2002 income tax expense and payable amounts so current year tax effects may be ignored. Prior year tax effects must be considered in items 3 and 4.

P23-8 (Change in Principle) Plato Corporation performs year-end planning in November of each year before their calendar year ends in December. The preliminary estimated net income is $3 million. The CFO, Mary Sheets, meets with the company president, S. A. Plato, to review the projected numbers. She presents the following projected information:

PLATO CORPORATION
Projected Income Statement
For the Year Ended December 31, 2001

Sales		$29,000,000
Cost of goods sold	$14,000,000	
Depreciation	2,600,000	
Operating expenses	6,400,000	23,000,000
Income before income taxes		$ 6,000,000
Provision for income taxes		3,000,000
Net income		$ 3,000,000

PLATO CORPORATION
Selected Balance Sheet Information
at December 31, 2001

Estimated cash balance	$ 5,000,000
Available-for-sale securities (at cost)	10,000,000
Security fair value adjustment account (1/1/01)	200,000

Estimated market value at December 31, 2001:

Security	Cost	Estimated Market
A	$ 2,000,000	$ 2,200,000
B	4,000,000	3,900,000
C	3,000,000	3,000,000
D	1,000,000	2,800,000
Total	$10,000,000	$11,900,000

Equipment	$3,000,000
Accumulated depreciation (5-year SL)	1,200,000
New robotic equipment (purchased 1/1/01)	5,000,000
Accumulated depreciation (5-year DDB)	2,000,000

The corporation has never used robotic equipment before, and Sheets assumed an accelerated method because of the rapidly changing technology in robotic equipment. The company normally uses straight-line depreciation for production equipment.

Plato explains to Sheets that it is important for the corporation to show an $8,000,000 net income before taxes because Plato receives a $1,000,000 bonus if the income before taxes and bonus reaches $8,000,000. He also cautions that he will not pay more than $3,000,000 in income taxes to the government.

Instructions

   (a) What can Sheets do within GAAP to accommodate the president's wishes to achieve $8,000,000 income before taxes and bonus? Present the revised income statement based on your decision.

   (b) Are the actions ethical? Who are the stakeholders in this decision, and what effect does Sheets' actions have on their interests?

P23-9 (Comprehensive Error Analysis)   On March 5, 2002, you were hired by Gretchen Hollenbeck Inc., a closely held company, as a staff member of its newly created internal auditing department. While reviewing the company's records for 2000 and 2001, you discover that no adjustments have yet been made for the items listed below.

Items

   1. Interest income of $14,100 was not accrued at the end of 2000. It was recorded when received in February 2001.

   2. A computer costing $8,000 was expensed when purchased on July 1, 2000. It is expected to have a 4-year life with no salvage value. The company typically uses straight-line depreciation for all fixed assets.

   3. Research and development costs of $33,000 were incurred early in 2000. They were capitalized and were to be amortized over a 3-year period. Amortization of $11,000 was recorded for 2000 and $11,000 for 2001.

4. On January 2, 2000, Hollenbeck leased a building for 5 years at a monthly rental of $8,000. On that date, the company paid the following amounts, which were expensed when paid.

Security deposit	$25,000
First month's rent	8,000
Last month's rent	8,000
	$41,000

5. The company received $30,000 from a customer at the beginning of 2000 for services that it is to perform evenly over a 3-year period beginning in 2000. None of the amount received was reported as unearned revenue at the end of 2000.
6. Merchandise inventory costing $18,200 was in the warehouse at December 31, 2000, but was incorrectly omitted from the physical count at that date. The company uses the periodic inventory method.

Instructions

Indicate the effect of any errors on the net income figure reported on the income statement for the year ending December 31, 2000, and the retained earnings figure reported on the balance sheet at December 31, 2001. Assume all amounts are material and ignore income tax effects. Using the following format, enter the appropriate dollar amounts in the appropriate columns. Consider each item independent of the other items. It is not necessary to total the columns on the grid.

Item	Net Income for 2000		Retained Earnings at 12/31/01	
	Understated	Overstated	Understated	Overstated

(CIA adapted)

P23-10 (Error Analysis) Mary Keeton Corporation has used the accrual basis of accounting for several years. A review of the records, however, indicates that some expenses and revenues have been handled on a cash basis because of errors made by an inexperienced bookkeeper. Income statements prepared by the bookkeeper reported $29,000 net income for 2001 and $37,000 net income for 2002. Further examination of the records reveals that the following items were handled improperly.

1. Rent was received from a tenant in December 2001; the amount, $1,300, was recorded as income at that time even though the rental pertained to 2002.
2. Wages payable on December 31 have been consistently omitted from the records of that date and have been entered as expenses when paid in the following year. The amounts of the accruals recorded in this manner were:

December 31, 2000	$1,100
December 31, 2001	1,500
December 31, 2002	940

3. Invoices for office supplies purchased have been charged to expense accounts when received. Inventories of supplies on hand at the end of each year have been ignored, and no entry has been made for them.

December 31, 2000	$1,300
December 31, 2001	740
December 31, 2002	1,420

Instructions

Prepare a schedule that will show the corrected net income for the years 2001 and 2002. All items listed should be labeled clearly. Ignore income tax considerations.

P23-11 (Error Analysis and Correcting Entries) Sally Kolb Corporation is in the process of negotiating a loan for expansion purposes. Kolb's books and records have never been audited and the bank has requested that an audit be performed. Kolb has prepared the following comparative financial statements for the years ended December 31, 2002 and 2001:

SALLY KOLB CORPORATION
Balance Sheet
As of December 31, 2002 and 2001

	2002	2001
Assets		
Current assets		
Cash	$ 163,000	$ 82,000
Accounts receivable	392,000	296,000
Allowance for doubtful accounts	(37,000)	(18,000)
Available-for-sale securities, at cost	78,000	78,000
Merchandise inventory	207,000	202,000
Total current assets	803,000	640,000
Plant assets		
Property, plant, and equipment	167,000	169,500
Accumulated depreciation	(121,600)	(106,400)
Total fixed assets	45,400	63,100
Total assets	$ 848,400	$703,100
Liabilities and Stockholders' Equity		
Liabilities		
Accounts payable	$ 121,400	$196,100
Stockholders' equity		
Common stock, par value $10, authorized 50,000 shares, issued and outstanding 20,000 shares	260,000	260,000
Retained earnings	467,000	247,000
Total stockholders' equity	727,000	507,000
Total liabilities and stockholders' equity	$ 848,400	$703,100

SALLY KOLB CORPORATION
Statement of Income
For the Years Ended December 31, 2002 and 2001

	2002	2001
Sales	$1,000,000	$900,000
Cost of sales	430,000	395,000
Gross profit	570,000	505,000
Operating expenses	210,000	205,000
Administrative expenses	140,000	105,000
Net income	350,000	310,000
	$ 220,000	$195,000

During the course of the audit, the following additional facts were determined:

1. An analysis of collections and losses on accounts receivable during the past 2 years indicates a drop in anticipated losses due to bad debts. After consultation with management it was agreed that the loss experience rate on sales should be reduced from the recorded 2% to $1\frac{1}{2}\%$, beginning with the year ended December 31, 2002.

2. An analysis of available-for-sale securities revealed that the total market valuation for these investments as of the end of each year was as follows:

December 31, 2001	$82,000
December 31, 2002	$65,000

3. The merchandise inventory at December 31, 2001, was overstated by $8,900 and the merchandise inventory at December 31, 2002, was overstated by $13,600.

4. On January 2, 2001, equipment costing $30,000 (estimated useful life of 10 years and residual value of $5,000) was incorrectly charged to operating expenses. Kolb records depreciation on the straight-

line method. In 2002, fully depreciated equipment (with no residual value) that originally cost $17,500 was sold as scrap for $2,800. Kolb credited the proceeds of $2,800 to the equipment account.

5. An analysis of 2001 operating expenses revealed that Kolb charged to expense a 4-year insurance premium of $4,700 on January 15, 2001.

Instructions

(a) Prepare the journal entries to correct the books at December 31, 2002. The books for 2002 have not been closed. Ignore income taxes.

(b) Prepare a schedule showing the computation of corrected net income for the years ended December 31, 2002 and 2001, assuming that any adjustments are to be reported on comparative statements for the 2 years. The first items on your schedule should be the net income for each year. Ignore income taxes. (Do not prepare financial statements.)

(AICPA adapted)

P23-12 **(Error Analysis and Correcting Entries)** You have been asked by a client to review the records of Larry Landers Company, a small manufacturer of precision tools and machines. Your client is interested in buying the business, and arrangements have been made for you to review the accounting records.

Your examination reveals the following:

1. Landers Company commenced business on April 1, 1999, and has been reporting on a fiscal year ending March 31. The company has never been audited, but the annual statements prepared by the bookkeeper reflect the following income before closing and before deducting income taxes:

Year Ended March 31	Income Before Taxes
2000	$ 71,600
2001	111,400
2002	103,580

2. A relatively small number of machines have been shipped on consignment. These transactions have been recorded as ordinary sales and billed as such. On March 31 of each year, machines billed and in the hands of consignees amounted to:

2000	$6,500
2001	none
2002	5,590

Sales price was determined by adding 30% to cost. Assume that the consigned machines are sold the following year.

3. On March 30, 2001, two machines were shipped to a customer on a C.O.D. basis. The sale was not entered until April 5, 2001, when cash was received for $6,100. The machines were not included in the inventory at March 31, 2001. (Title passed on March 30, 2001.)

4. All machines are sold subject to a five-year warranty. It is estimated that the expense ultimately to be incurred in connection with the warranty will amount to $1/2$ of 1% of sales. The company has charged an expense account for warranty costs incurred.

Sales per books and warranty costs were:

Year Ended March 31	Sales	Warranty Expense for Sales Made In 2000	2001	2002	Total
2000	$ 940,000	$760			$ 760
2001	1,010,000	360	$1,310		1,670
2002	1,795,000	320	1,620	$1,910	3,850

5. A review of the corporate minutes reveals the manager is entitled to a bonus of $1/2$ of 1% of the income before deducting income taxes and the bonus. The bonuses have never been recorded or paid.

6. Bad debts have been recorded on a direct writeoff basis. Experience of similar enterprises indicates that losses will approximate $1/4$ of 1% of sales. Bad debts written off were:

	Bad Debts Incurred on Sales Made In 2000	2001	2002	Total
2000	$750			$ 750
2001	800	$ 520		1,320
2002	350	1,800	$1,700	3,850

7. The bank deducts 6% on all contracts financed. Of this amount, $\frac{1}{2}$% is placed in a reserve to the credit of Landers Company that is refunded to Landers as finance contracts are paid in full. The reserve established by the bank has not been reflected in the books of Landers. The excess of credits over debits (net increase) to the reserve account with Landers on the books of the bank for each fiscal year were as follows:

2000	$ 3,000
2001	3,900
2002	5,100
	$12,000

8. Commissions on sales have been entered when paid. Commissions payable on March 31 of each year were:

2000	$1,400
2001	800
2002	1,120

Instructions
(a) Present a schedule showing the revised income before income taxes for each of the years ended March 31, 2000, 2001, and 2002. Make computations to the nearest whole dollar.
(b) Prepare the journal entry or entries you would give the bookkeeper to correct the books. Assume the books have not yet been closed for the fiscal year ended March 31, 2001. Disregard correction of income taxes.

(AICPA adapted)

*P23-13 **(Fair Value to Equity Method with Goodwill)** On January 1, 2000, Latoya Inc. paid $700,000 for 10,000 shares of Jones Company's voting common stock, which was a 10% interest in Jones. At that date the net assets of Jones totaled $6,000,000. The fair values of all of Jones' identifiable assets and liabilities were equal to their book values. Latoya does not have the ability to exercise significant influence over the operating and financial policies of Jones. Latoya received dividends of $2.00 per share from Jones on October 1, 2000. Jones reported net income of $500,000 for the year ended December 31, 2000.

On July 1, 2001, Latoya paid $2,325,000 for 30,000 additional shares of Jones Company's voting common stock which represents a 30% investment in Jones. The fair values of all of Jones' identifiable assets net of liabilities were equal to their book values of $6,550,000. As a result of this transaction, Latoya has the ability to exercise significant influence over the operating and financial policies of Jones. Latoya received dividends of $2.00 per share from Jones on April 1, 2001, and $2.50 per share on October 1, 2001. Jones reported net income of $650,000 for the year ended December 31, 2001, and $400,000 for the 6 months ended December 31, 2001. Latoya amortizes goodwill over a 10-year period.

Instructions
(a) Prepare a schedule showing the income or loss before income taxes for the year ended December 31, 2000, that Latoya should report from its investment in Jones in its income statement issued in March 2001.
(b) During March 2002, Latoya issues comparative financial statements for 2000 and 2001. Prepare schedules showing the income or loss before income taxes for the years ended December 31, 2000 and 2001, that Latoya should report from its investment in Jones.

(AICPA adapted)

*P23-14 **(Change from Fair Value to Equity Method)** On January 3, 1999, Calvin Company purchased for $500,000 cash a 10% interest in Coolidge Corp. On that date the net assets of Coolidge had a book value of $3,750,000. The excess of cost over the underlying equity in net assets is attributable to undervalued depreciable assets having a remaining life of 10 years from the date of Calvin's purchase.

The fair value of Calvin's investment in Coolidge securities is as follows: December 31, 1999, $570,000; December 31, 2000, $515,000.

On January 2, 2001, Calvin purchased an additional 30% of Coolidge's stock for $1,545,000 cash when the book value of Coolidge's net assets was $4,150,000. The excess was attributable to depreciable assets having a remaining life of 8 years.

During 1999, 2000, and 2001 the following occurred:

	Coolidge Net Income	Dividends Paid by Coolidge to Calvin
1999	$350,000	$15,000
2000	400,000	20,000
2001	550,000	70,000

Instructions
On the books of Calvin Company prepare all journal entries in 1999, 2000, and 2001 that relate to its investment in Coolidge Corp., reflecting the data above and a change from the fair value method to the equity method.

CONCEPTUAL CASES

C23-1 (Analysis of Various Accounting Changes and Errors) Erin Kramer Inc. has recently hired a new independent auditor, Jodie Larson, who says she wants "to get everything straightened out." Consequently, she has proposed the following accounting changes in connection with Erin Kramer Inc.'s 2002 financial statements:

1. At December 31, 2001, the client had a receivable of $820,000 from Holly Michael Inc. on its balance sheet. Holly Michael Inc. has gone bankrupt, and no recovery is expected. The client proposes to write off the receivable as a prior period item.
2. The client proposes the following changes in depreciation policies:
    (a) For office furniture and fixtures it proposes to change from a 10-year useful life to an 8-year life. If this change had been made in prior years, retained earnings at December 31, 2001, would have been $250,000 less. The effect of the change on 2002 income alone is a reduction of $60,000.
    (b) For its manufacturing assets the client proposes to change from double-declining balance depreciation to straight line. If straight-line depreciation had been used for all prior periods, retained earnings would have been $380,800 greater at December 31, 2001. The effect of the change on 2002 income alone is a reduction of $48,800.
    (c) For its equipment in the leasing division the client proposes to adopt the sum-of-the-years'-digits depreciation method. The client had never used SYD before. The first year the client operated a leasing division was 2002. If straight-line depreciation were used, 2002 income would be $110,000 greater.
3. In preparing its 2001 statements, one of the client's bookkeepers overstated ending inventory by $235,000 because of a mathematical error. The client proposes to treat this item as a prior period adjustment.
4. In the past, the client has spread preproduction costs in its furniture division over 5 years. Because its latest furniture is of the "fad" type, it appears that the largest volume of sales will occur during the first 2 years after introduction. Consequently, the client proposes to amortize preproduction costs on a per-unit basis, which will result in expensing most of such costs during the first 2 years after the furniture's introduction. If the new accounting method had been used prior to 2002, retained earnings at December 31, 2001, would have been $375,000 less.
5. For the nursery division the client proposes to switch from FIFO to LIFO inventories because it believes that LIFO will provide a better matching of current costs with revenues. The effect of making this change on 2002 earnings will be an increase of $320,000. The client says that the effect of the change on December 31, 2001, retained earnings cannot be determined.
6. To achieve a better matching of revenues and expenses in its building construction division, the client proposes to switch from the completed-contract method of accounting to the percentage-of-completion method. Had the percentage-of-completion method been employed in all prior years, retained earnings at December 31, 2001, would have been $1,175,000 greater.

Instructions
(a) For each of the changes described above decide whether:
    (1) The change involves an accounting principle, accounting estimate, or correction of an error.
    (2) Restatement of opening retained earnings is required.
(b) Do any of the changes require presentation of pro-forma amounts?
(c) What would be the proper adjustment to the December 31, 2001, retained earnings? What would be the "cumulative effect" shown separately in the 2002 income statement?

C23-2 (Analysis of Various Accounting Changes and Errors) Various types of accounting changes can affect the financial statements of a business enterprise differently. Assume that the following list describes changes that have a material effect on the financial statements for the current year of your business enterprise.

As indicated in the opening story, an examination of W. T. Grant's cash flow provided by operations would have shown the significant lack of liquidity and financial inflexibility that eventually caused the company's bankruptcy. The purpose of this chapter is to explain the main components of a statement of cash flows and the types of information it provides. The content and organization of the chapter are as follows:

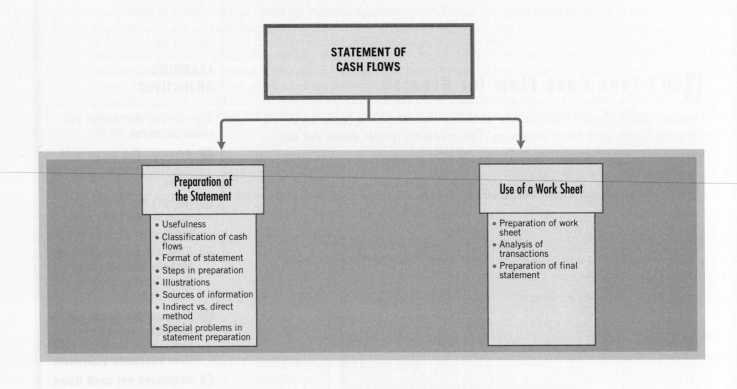

SECTION 1   *PREPARATION OF THE STATEMENT OF CASH FLOWS*

OBJECTIVE ①
Describe the purpose of the statement of cash flows.

The primary purpose of the statement of cash flows is to provide information about an entity's cash receipts and cash payments during a period. A secondary objective is to provide information on a cash basis about its operating, investing, and financing activities. **The statement of cash flows therefore reports cash receipts, cash payments, and net change in cash resulting from operating, investing, and financing activities of an enterprise during a period, in a format that reconciles the beginning and ending cash balances.**

USEFULNESS OF THE STATEMENT OF CASH FLOWS

The information in a statement of cash flows should help investors, creditors, and others assess the following:[2]

① *The entity's ability to generate future cash flows.* A primary objective of financial reporting is to provide information that makes it possible to predict the amounts,

---

[2]"The Statement of Cash Flows," *Statement of Financial Accounting Standards No. 95* (Stamford, Conn.: FASB, 1987), pars. 4 and 5.

timing, and uncertainty of future cash flows. By examining relationships between items such as sales and net cash flow from operating activities, or net cash flow from operating activities and increases or decreases in cash, it is possible to make better predictions of the amounts, timing, and uncertainty of future cash flows than is possible using accrual basis data.

❷ *The entity's ability to pay dividends and meet obligations.* Simply put, cash is essential. If a company does not have adequate cash, employees cannot be paid, debts cannot be settled, dividends cannot be paid, and equipment cannot be acquired. A statement of cash flows indicates how cash is used and where it comes from. Employees, creditors, stockholders, and customers should be particularly interested in this statement, because it alone shows the flows of cash in a business.

❸ *The reasons for the difference between net income and net cash flow from operating activities.* The net income number is important, because it provides information on the success or failure of a business enterprise from one period to another. But some people are critical of accrual basis net income because estimates must be made to arrive at it. As a result, the reliability of the number is often challenged. Such is not the case with cash. Thus, as illustrated in the opening story, readers of the financial statements benefit from knowing the reasons for the difference between net income and net cash flow from operating activities. Then they can assess for themselves the reliability of the income number.

❹ *The cash and noncash investing and financing transactions during the period.* By examining a company's investing activities (purchase and sales of assets other than its products) and its financing transactions (borrowings and repayments of borrowings, investments by owners and distributions to owners), a financial statement reader can better understand why assets and liabilities increased or decreased during the period. For example, the following questions might be answered:

> How did cash increase when there was a net loss for the period?
>
> How were the proceeds of the bond issue used?
>
> How was the expansion in plant and equipment financed?
>
> Why were dividends not increased?
>
> How was the retirement of debt accomplished?
>
> How much money was borrowed during the year?
>
> Is cash flow greater or less than net income?

CLASSIFICATION OF CASH FLOWS

The statement of cash flows classifies cash receipts and cash payments by operating, investing, and financing activities.[3] Transactions and other events characteristic of each kind of activity are as follows:

OBJECTIVE ❷
Identify the major classifications of cash flows.

❶ **Operating activities** involve the cash effects of transactions that enter into the determination of net income, such as cash receipts from sales of goods and services

---

[3]The basis recommended by the FASB for the statement of cash flows is actually "cash and cash equivalents." **Cash equivalents** are short-term, highly liquid investments that are both: (a) readily convertible to known amounts of cash, and (b) so near their maturity that they present insignificant risk of changes in interest rates. Generally, only investments with original maturities of three months or less qualify under this definition. Examples of cash equivalents are treasury bills, commercial paper, and money market funds purchased with cash that is in excess of immediate needs.

Although we use the term "cash" throughout our discussion and illustrations in this chapter, we mean cash and cash equivalents when reporting the cash flows and the net increase or decrease in cash.

and cash payments to suppliers and employees for acquisitions of inventory and expenses.

❷ **Investing activities** generally involve long-term assets and include (a) making and collecting loans, and (b) acquiring and disposing of investments and productive long-lived assets.

❸ **Financing activities** involve liability and stockholders' equity items and include (a) obtaining cash from creditors and repaying the amounts borrowed, and (b) obtaining capital from owners and providing them with a return on, and a return of, their investment.

Illustration 24-1 classifies the typical cash receipts and payments of a business enterprise that are classified according to operating, investing, and financing activities.

ILLUSTRATION 24-1
Classification of Typical
Cash Inflows and
Outflows

Operating
    Cash inflows
        From sales of goods or services.
        From returns on loans (interest) and on equity
            securities (dividends).
    Cash outflows
        To suppliers for inventory.
        To employees for services.
        To government for taxes.
        To lenders for interest.
        To others for expenses.
	Income
	Statement
	Items

Investing
    Cash inflows
        From sale of property, plant, and equipment.
        From sale of debt or equity securities of other entities.
        From collection of principal on loans to other entities.
    Cash outflows
        To purchase property, plant, and equipment.
        To purchase debt or equity securities of other entities.
        To make loans to other entities.
	Generally
	Long-Term
	Asset Items

Financing
    Cash inflows
        From sale of equity securities.
        From issuance of debt (bonds and notes).
    Cash outflows
        To stockholders as dividends.
        To redeem long-term debt or reacquire capital stock.
	Generally
	Long-Term
	Liability
	and Equity
	Items

INTERNATIONAL INSIGHT

According to International Accounting Standards, "cash and cash equivalents" can be defined as "net monetary assets," that is, "cash and demand deposits and highly liquid investments less short-term borrowings."

Some cash flows relating to investing or financing activities are classified as operating activities.[4] For example, receipts of investment income (interest and dividends) and payments of interest to lenders are classified as operating activities. Conversely, some cash flows relating to operating activities are classified as investing or financing activities. For example, the cash received from the sale of property, plant, and equipment at a gain, although reported in the income statement, is classified as an investing activity, and the effects of the related gain would not be included in net cash flow from

---

[4]For exceptions to the treatment of purchases and sales of loans and securities by banks and brokers, see *Statement of Financial Accounting Standards No. 102* (February 1989) and "Relevance Gained: FASB Modifies Cash Flow Statement Requirements for Banks," James Don Edwards and Cynthia D. Heagy, *Journal of Accountancy,* June 1991. Banks and brokers are required to classify cash flows from purchases and sales of loans and securities specifically for resale and carried at market value **as operating activities.** This requirement recognizes that for these firms these assets are similar to inventory in other businesses.

operating activities. Likewise, a gain or loss on the payment (extinguishment) of debt would generally be part of the cash outflow related to the repayment of the amount borrowed and therefore is a financing activity.

FORMAT OF THE STATEMENT OF CASH FLOWS

The three activities discussed in the preceding paragraphs constitute the general format of the statement of cash flows. The cash flows from operating activities section always appears first, followed by the investing and financing activities sections. The individual inflows and outflows from investing and financing activities are reported separately, that is, they are reported gross, not netted against one another. Thus, cash outflow from the purchase of property is reported separately from the cash inflow from the sale of property. Similarly, the cash inflow from the issuance of debt is reported separately from the cash outflow from its retirement. The net increase or decrease in cash reported during the period should reconcile the beginning and ending cash balances as reported in the comparative balance sheets.

The skeleton format of the statement of cash flows is:

COMPANY NAME Statement of Cash Flows Period Covered		
Cash flows from operating activities		
Net income		XXX
Adjustments to reconcile net income to net cash provided by operating activities:		
(List of individual items)	XX	XX
Net cash flow from operating activities		XXX
Cash flows from investing activities		
(List of individual inflows and outflows)	XX	
Net cash provided (used) by investing activities		XXX
Cash flows from financing activities		
(List of individual inflows and outflows)	XX	
Net cash provided (used) by financing activities		XXX
Net increase (decrease) in cash		XXX
Cash at beginning of period		XXX
Cash at end of period		XXX

ILLUSTRATION 24-2
Format of the Statement of Cash Flows

STEPS IN PREPARATION

Unlike the other major financial statements, the statement of cash flows is not prepared from the adjusted trial balance. The information to prepare this statement usually comes from three sources:

Comparative balance sheets provide the amount of the changes in assets, liabilities, and equities from the beginning to the end of the period.

Current income statement data help the reader determine the amount of cash provided by or used by operations during the period.

Selected transaction data from the general ledger provide additional detailed information needed to determine how cash was provided or used during the period.

Preparing the statement of cash flows from the data sources above involves three major steps:

Step 1. Determine the change in cash. This procedure is straightforward because the difference between the beginning and the ending cash balance can be easily computed from an examination of the comparative balance sheets.

Step 2. Determine the net cash flow from operating activities. This procedure is complex; it involves analyzing not only the current year's income statement but also comparative balance sheets as well as selected transaction data.

Step 3. Determine net cash flows from investing and financing activities. All other changes in the balance sheet accounts must be analyzed to determine their effects on cash.

On the following pages we work through these three steps in the process of preparing the statement of cash flows for a company over several years.

FIRST ILLUSTRATION — 2000

To illustrate a statement of cash flows, we will use the **first year of operations** for Tax Consultants Inc. The company started on January 1, 2000, when it issued 60,000 shares of $1 par value common stock for $60,000 cash. The company rented its office space and furniture and equipment and performed tax consulting services throughout the first year. The comparative balance sheets at the beginning and end of the year 2000 appear as follows:

ILLUSTRATION 24-3
Comparative Balance
Sheet, Tax Consultants
Inc., Year 1

TAX CONSULTANTS INC. Comparative Balance Sheet			
Assets	Dec. 31, 2000	Jan. 1, 2000	Change Increase/Decrease
Cash	$49,000	$–0–	$49,000 Increase
Accounts receivable	36,000	–0–	36,000 Increase
Total	$85,000	$–0–	
Liabilities and Stockholders' Equity			
Accounts payable	$ 5,000	$–0–	5,000 Increase
Common stock ($1 par)	60,000	–0–	60,000 Increase
Retained earnings	20,000	–0–	20,000 Increase
Total	$85,000	$–0–	

The income statement and additional information for Tax Consultants Inc. are as follows:

ILLUSTRATION 24-4
Income Statement, Tax
Consultants Inc., Year 1

TAX CONSULTANTS INC. Income Statement For the Year Ended December 31, 2000	
Revenues	$125,000
Operating expenses	85,000
Income before income taxes	40,000
Income tax expense	6,000
Net income	$ 34,000

Additional Information
Examination of selected data indicates that a dividend of $14,000 was paid during the year.

Step 1: Determine the Change in Cash

To prepare a statement of cash flows, the first step, **determining the change in cash**, is a simple computation. Tax Consultants Inc. had no cash on hand at the beginning of the year 2000, but $49,000 was on hand at the end of 2000; thus, the change in cash for 2000 was an increase of $49,000. The other two steps are more complex and involve additional analysis.

Step 2: Determine Net Cash Flow from Operating Activities

A useful starting point in **determining net cash flow from operating activities**[5] is to understand why net income must be converted. Under generally accepted accounting principles, most companies must use the accrual basis of accounting requiring that revenue be recorded when earned and that expenses be recorded when incurred. Net income may include credit sales that have not been collected in cash and expenses incurred that may not have been paid in cash. Thus, under the accrual basis of accounting, net income will not indicate the net cash flow from operating activities.

> **OBJECTIVE ③**
> Differentiate between net income and net cash flows from operating activities.

To arrive at net cash flow from operating activities, it is necessary to report revenues and expenses on a **cash basis. This is done by eliminating the effects of income statement transactions that did not result in a corresponding increase or decrease in cash.** The relationship between net income and net cash flow from operating activities is graphically depicted as follows:

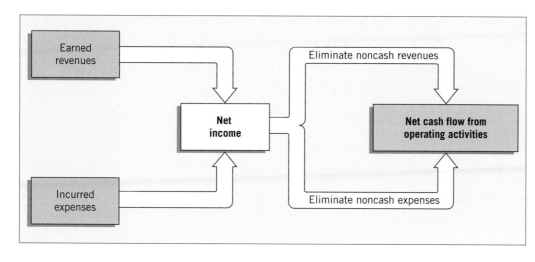

ILLUSTRATION 24-5
Net Income versus Net Cash Flow from Operating Activities

In this chapter, we use the term net income to refer to accrual-based net income. The conversion of net income to net cash flow from operating activities may be done through either a direct method or an indirect method as explained in the following discussion.

Direct Method

The **direct method** (also called the income statement method) reports cash receipts and cash disbursements from operating activities. The difference between these two amounts is the net cash flow from operating activities. In other words, the direct method deducts from operating cash receipts the operating cash disbursements. The direct method results in the presentation of a condensed cash receipts and cash disbursements statement.

> **OBJECTIVE ④**
> Contrast the direct and indirect methods of calculating net cash flow from operating activities.

As indicated from the accrual-based income statement, Tax Consultants Inc. reported revenues of $125,000. However, because the company's accounts receivable in-

---

[5]"Net cash flow from operating activities" is a generic phrase, which is replaced in the statement of cash flows with either "net cash **provided by** operating activities" if operations increase cash or "net cash **used by** operating activities" if operations decrease cash.

creased during 2000 by $36,000, only $89,000 ($125,000 − $36,000) in cash was collected on these revenues. Similarly, Tax Consultants Inc. reported operating expenses of $85,000, but accounts payable increased during the period of $5,000. Assuming that these payables related to operating expenses, cash operating expenses were $80,000 ($85,000 − $5,000). Because no taxes payable exist at the end of the year, the $6,000 income tax expense for 2000 must have been paid in cash during the year. Then the computation of net cash flow from operating activities is as follows:

ILLUSTRATION 24-6
Computation of Net Cash Flow from Operating Activities, Year 1—Direct Method

Cash collected from revenues	$89,000
Cash payments for expenses	80,000
Income before income taxes	9,000
Cash payments for income taxes	6,000
Net cash provided by operating activities	$ 3,000

"Net cash provided by operating activities" is the equivalent of cash basis net income ("net cash used by operating activities" would be equivalent to cash basis net loss).

Indirect Method

The **indirect method** (or reconciliation method) starts with net income and converts it to net cash flow from operating activities. In other words, **the indirect method adjusts net income for items that affected reported net income but did not affect cash.** To compute net cash flow from operating activities, noncash charges in the income statement are added back to net income and noncash credits are deducted. Explanations for the two adjustments to net income in this example, namely, the increases in accounts receivable and accounts payable, are as follows.

Increase in Accounts Receivable—Indirect Method. When accounts receivable increase during the year, revenues on an accrual basis are higher than revenues on a cash basis because goods sold on account are reported as revenues. In other words, operations of the period led to increased revenues, but not all of these revenues resulted in an increase in cash. Some of the increase in revenues resulted in an increase in accounts receivable. To convert net income to net cash flow from operating activities, the increase of $36,000 in accounts receivable must be deducted from net income.

Increase in Accounts Payable—Indirect Method. When accounts payable increase during the year, expenses on an accrual basis are higher than they are on a cash basis because expenses are incurred for which payment has not taken place. To convert net income to net cash flow from operating activities, the increase of $5,000 in accounts payable must be added to net income.

As a result of the accounts receivable and accounts payable adjustments, net cash provided by operating activities is determined to be $3,000 for the year 2000. This computation is shown as follows:

ILLUSTRATION 24-7
Computation of Net Cash Flow from Operating Activities, Year 1—Indirect Method

Net income		$34,000
Adjustments to reconcile net income to net cash provided by operating activities:		
Increase in accounts receivable	$(36,000)	
Increase in accounts payable	5,000	(31,000)
Net cash provided by operating activities		$ 3,000

Note that net cash provided by operating activities is the same whether the direct or the indirect method is used.

Step 3: Determine Net Cash Flows from Investing and Financing Activities

Once the net cash flow from operating activities is computed, the next step is to determine whether any other changes in balance sheet accounts caused an increase or decrease in cash. For example, an examination of the remaining balance sheet accounts shows that both common stock and retained earnings have increased. The common stock increase of $60,000 resulted from the issuance of common stock for cash. The issuance of common stock is a receipt of cash from a financing activity and is reported as such in the statement of cash flows. The retained earnings increase of $20,000 is caused by two items:

❶ Net income of $34,000 increased retained earnings.

❷ Dividends declared of $14,000 decreased retained earnings.

Net income has been converted into net cash flow from operating activities as explained earlier. The additional data indicate that the dividend was paid. Thus, the dividend payment on common stock is reported as a cash outflow, classified as a financing activity.

> **OBJECTIVE ❺**
> Determine net cash flows from investing and financing activities.

Statement of Cash Flows—2000

We are now ready to prepare the statement of cash flows. The statement starts with the operating activities section. Either the direct or indirect method may be used to report net cash flow from operating activities. The FASB **encourages** the use of the direct method over the indirect method. And, if the direct method of reporting net cash flow from operating activities is used, the FASB **requires** that the reconciliation of net income to net cash flow from operating activities be provided in a separate schedule. If the indirect method is used, the reconciliation may be either reported within the statement of cash flows or provided in a separate schedule, with the statement of cash flows reporting only the **net** cash flow from operating activities.[6] Therefore, the indirect method, which is also used more extensively in practice,[7] is used throughout this chapter. In doing homework assignments, you should follow instructions for use of either the direct or indirect method. The advantages and disadvantages of these two methods are discussed later in this chapter.

> **OBJECTIVE ❻**
> Prepare a statement of cash flows.

The statement of cash flows for Tax Consultants Inc. is as follows:

TAX CONSULTANTS INC.
Statement of Cash Flows
For the Year Ended December 31, 2000
Increase (Decrease) in Cash

Cash flows from operating activities		
Net income		$34,000
Adjustments to reconcile net income to net cash provided by operating activities:		
Increase in accounts receivable	$(36,000)	
Increase in accounts payable	5,000	(31,000)
Net cash provided by operating activities		3,000
Cash flows from financing activities		
Issuance of common stock	60,000	
Payment of cash dividends	(14,000)	
Net cash provided by financing activities		46,000
Net increase in cash		49,000
Cash, January 1, 2000		–0–
Cash, December 31, 2000		$49,000

ILLUSTRATION 24-8
Statement of Cash Flows, Tax Consultants Inc., Year 1

---

[6]"The Statement of Cash Flows," pars. 27 and 30.

[7]*Accounting Trends and Techniques—1999* reports that out of its 600 surveyed companies, 593 (approximately 99%) used the indirect method, while only 7 used the direct method.

As indicated, the $60,000 increase in common stock results in a cash inflow from a financing activity. The payment of $14,000 in cash dividends is classified as a use of cash from a financing activity. The $49,000 increase in cash reported in the statement of cash flows agrees with the increase of $49,000 shown as the change in the cash account in the comparative balance sheets.

SECOND ILLUSTRATION — 2001

Tax Consultants Inc. continued to grow and prosper during its second year of operations. Land, building, and equipment were purchased, and revenues and earnings increased substantially over the first year. Information related to the second year of operations for Tax Consultants Inc. is presented in Illustrations 24-9 and 24-10.

ILLUSTRATION 24-9
Comparative Balance Sheet, Tax Consultants Inc., Year 2

TAX CONSULTANTS INC.
Comparative Balance Sheet
December 31

Assets	2001	2000	Change Increase/Decrease
Cash	$ 37,000	$49,000	$ 12,000 Decrease
Accounts receivable	26,000	36,000	10,000 Decrease
Prepaid expenses	6,000	–0–	6,000 Increase
Land	70,000	–0–	70,000 Increase
Building	200,000	–0–	200,000 Increase
Accumulated depreciation—building	(11,000)	–0–	11,000 Increase
Equipment	68,000	–0–	68,000 Increase
Accumulated depreciation—equipment	(10,000)	–0–	10,000 Increase
Total	$386,000	$85,000	
Liabilities and Stockholders' Equity			
Accounts payable	$ 40,000	$ 5,000	35,000 Increase
Bonds payable	150,000	–0–	150,000 Increase
Common stock ($1 par)	60,000	60,000	–0–
Retained earnings	136,000	20,000	116,000 Increase
Total	$386,000	$85,000	

ILLUSTRATION 24-10
Income Statement, Tax Consultants Inc., Year 2

TAX CONSULTANTS INC.
Income Statement
For the Year Ended December 31, 2001

Revenues		$492,000
Operating expenses (excluding depreciation)	$269,000	
Depreciation expense	21,000	290,000
Income from operations		202,000
Income tax expense		68,000
Net income		$134,000

Additional Information
(a) In 2001, the company paid an $18,000 cash dividend.
(b) The company obtained $150,000 cash through the issuance of long-term bonds.
(c) Land, building, and equipment were acquired for cash.

Step 1: Determine the Change in Cash

To prepare a statement of cash flows from the available information, the first step is to determine the change in cash. As indicated from the information presented, cash decreased $12,000 ($49,000 − $37,000).

Step 2: Determine Net Cash Flow from Operating Activities—Indirect Method

Using the indirect method, we adjust net income of $134,000 on an accrual basis to arrive at net cash flow from operating activities. Explanations for the adjustments to net income are as follows.

Decrease in Accounts Receivable

When accounts receivable decrease during the period, revenues on a cash basis are higher than revenues on an accrual basis, because cash collections are higher than revenues reported on an accrual basis. To convert net income to net cash flow from operating activities, the decrease of $10,000 in accounts receivable must be added to net income.

Increase in Prepaid Expenses

When prepaid expenses (assets) increase during a period, expenses on an accrual basis income statement are lower than they are on a cash basis income statement. Expenditures (cash payments) have been made in the current period, but expenses (as charges to the income statement) have been deferred to future periods. To convert net income to net cash flow from operating activities, the increase of $6,000 in prepaid expenses must be deducted from net income. An increase in prepaid expenses results in a decrease in cash during the period.

Increase in Accounts Payable

Like the increase in 2000, the 2001 increase of $35,000 in accounts payable must be added to net income to convert to net cash flow from operating activities. A greater amount of expense was incurred than cash disbursed.

Depreciation Expense (Increase in Accumulated Depreciation)

The purchase of depreciable assets is shown as a use of cash in the investing section in the year of acquisition. The depreciation expense of $21,000 (also represented by the increase in accumulated depreciation) is a noncash charge that is added back to net income to arrive at net cash flow from operating activities. The $21,000 is the sum of the depreciation on the building of $11,000 and the depreciation on the equipment of $10,000.

Other charges to expense for a period that do not require the use of cash, such as the amortization of intangible assets and depletion expense, are treated in the same manner as depreciation. Depreciation and similar noncash charges are frequently listed in the statement as the first adjustments to net income.

As a result of the foregoing items, net cash provided by operating activities is $194,000 as shown in Illustration 24-11.

Net income		$134,000
Adjustments to reconcile net income to		
net cash provided by operating activities:		
Depreciation expense	$21,000	
Decrease in accounts receivable	10,000	
Increase in prepaid expenses	(6,000)	
Increase in accounts payable	35,000	60,000
Net cash provided by operating activities		$194,000

ILLUSTRATION 24-11
Computation of Net Cash Flow from Operating Activities, Year 2—Indirect Method

Step 3: Determine Net Cash Flows from Investing and Financing Activities

After you have determined the items affecting net cash provided by operating activities, the next step involves analyzing the remaining changes in balance sheet accounts. The following accounts were analyzed:

Increase in Land

As indicated from the change in the land account, land of $70,000 was purchased during the period. This transaction is an investing activity that is reported as a use of cash.

Increase in Building and Related Accumulated Depreciation

As indicated in the additional data, and from the change in the building account, an office building was acquired using cash of $200,000. This transaction is a cash outflow reported in the investing section. The accumulated depreciation account increase of $11,000 is fully explained by the depreciation expense entry for the period. As indicated earlier, the reported depreciation expense has no effect on the amount of cash.

Increase in Equipment and Related Accumulated Depreciation

An increase in equipment of $68,000 resulted because equipment was purchased for cash. This transaction should be reported as an outflow of cash from an investing activity. The increase in Accumulated Depreciation—Equipment was explained by the depreciation expense entry for the period.

Increase in Bonds Payable

The bonds payable account increased $150,000. Cash received from the issuance of these bonds represents an inflow of cash from a financing activity.

Increase in Retained Earnings

Retained earnings increased $116,000 during the year. This increase can be explained by two factors: (1) net income of $134,000 increased retained earnings; (2) dividends of $18,000 decreased retained earnings. Payment of the dividends is a financing activity that involves a cash outflow.

Statement of Cash Flows—2001

Combining the foregoing items, we get a statement of cash flows for 2001 for Tax Consultants Inc., using the indirect method to compute net cash flow from operating activities.

ILLUSTRATION 24-12
Statement of Cash Flows, Tax Consultants Inc., Year 2

TAX CONSULTANTS INC. Statement of Cash Flows For the Year Ended December 31, 2001 Increase (Decrease) in Cash		
Cash flows from operating activities		
Net income		$134,000
Adjustments to reconcile net income to net cash provided by operating activities:		
Depreciation expense	$ 21,000	
Decrease in accounts receivable	10,000	
Increase in prepaid expenses	(6,000)	
Increase in accounts payable	35,000	60,000
Net cash provided by operating activities		194,000
Cash flows from investing activities		
Purchase of land	(70,000)	
Purchase of building	(200,000)	
Purchase of equipment	(68,000)	
Net cash used by investing activities		(338,000)
Cash flows from financing activities		
Issuance of bonds	150,000	
Payment of cash dividends	(18,000)	
Net cash provided by financing activities		132,000
Net decrease in cash		(12,000)
Cash, January 1, 2001		49,000
Cash, December 31, 2001		$ 37,000

THIRD ILLUSTRATION — 2002

Our third illustration covering the 2002 operations of Tax Consultants Inc. is slightly more complex; it again uses the indirect method to compute and present net cash flow from operating activities.

Tax Consultants Inc. experienced continued success in 2002 and expanded its operations to include the sale of selected lines of computer software that are used in tax return preparation and tax planning. Thus, inventories is one of the new assets appearing in its December 31, 2002, balance sheet. The comparative balance sheets, income statements, and selected data for 2002 are shown in Illustrations 24-13 and 24-14.

ILLUSTRATION 24-13
Comparative Balance Sheet, Tax Consultants Inc., Year 3

TAX CONSULTANTS INC.
Comparative Balance Sheet
December 31

Assets	2002	2001	Change Increase/Decrease
Cash	$ 54,000	$ 37,000	$ 17,000 Increase
Accounts receivable	68,000	26,000	42,000 Increase
Inventories	54,000	–0–	54,000 Increase
Prepaid expenses	4,000	6,000	2,000 Decrease
Land	45,000	70,000	25,000 Decrease
Buildings	200,000	200,000	–0–
Accumulated depreciation—buildings	(21,000)	(11,000)	10,000 Increase
Equipment	193,000	68,000	125,000 Increase
Accumulated depreciation—equipment	(28,000)	(10,000)	18,000 Increase
Totals	$569,000	$386,000	
Liabilities and Stockholders' Equity			
Accounts payable	$ 33,000	$ 40,000	7,000 Decrease
Bonds payable	110,000	150,000	40,000 Decrease
Common stock ($1 par)	220,000	60,000	160,000 Increase
Retained earnings	206,000	136,000	70,000 Increase
Totals	$569,000	$386,000	

ILLUSTRATION 24-14
Income Statement, Tax Consultants Inc., Year 3

TAX CONSULTANTS INC.
Income Statement
For the Year Ended December 31, 2002

Revenues		$890,000
Cost of goods sold	$465,000	
Operating expenses	221,000	
Interest expense	12,000	
Loss on sale of equipment	2,000	700,000
Income from operations		190,000
Income tax expense		65,000
Net income		$125,000

Additional Information
(a) Operating expenses include depreciation expense of $33,000 and amortization of prepaid expenses of $2,000.
(b) Land was sold at its book value for cash.
(c) Cash dividends of $55,000 were paid in 2002.
(d) Interest expense of $12,000 was paid in cash.
(e) Equipment with a cost of $166,000 was purchased for cash. Equipment with a cost of $41,000 and a book value of $36,000 was sold for $34,000 cash.
(f) Bonds were redeemed at their book value for cash.
(g) Common stock ($1 par) was issued for cash.

Step 1: Determine the Change in Cash

The first step in the preparation of the statement of cash flows is to determine the change in cash. As is shown in the comparative balance sheet, cash increased $17,000 in 2002. The second and third steps are discussed below and on the following pages.

Step 2: Determine Net Cash Flow from Operating Activities—Indirect Method

Explanations of the adjustments to net income of $125,000 are as follows.

Increase in Accounts Receivable

The increase in accounts receivable of $42,000 represents recorded accrual basis revenues in excess of cash collections in 2002; the increase is deducted from net income to convert from the accrual basis to the cash basis.

Increase in Inventories

The increase in inventories of $54,000 represents an operating use of cash for which an expense was not incurred. This amount is therefore deducted from net income to arrive at cash flow from operations. In other words, when inventory purchased exceeds inventory sold during a period, cost of goods sold on an accrual basis is lower than on a cash basis.

Decrease in Prepaid Expenses

The decrease in prepaid expenses of $2,000 represents a charge to the income statement for which there was no cash outflow in the current period. The decrease is added back to net income to arrive at net cash flow from operating activities.

Decrease in Accounts Payable

When accounts payable decrease during the year, cost of goods sold and expenses on a cash basis are higher than they are on an accrual basis, because on a cash basis the goods and expenses are recorded as expense when paid. To convert net income to net cash flow from operating activities, the decrease of $7,000 in accounts payable must be deducted from net income.

Depreciation Expense (Increase in Accumulated Depreciation)

Accumulated Depreciation—Buildings increased $10,000 ($21,000 − $11,000). The Buildings account did not change during the period, which means that $10,000 of depreciation was recorded in 2002.

Accumulated Depreciation—Equipment increased by $18,000 ($28,000 − $10,000) during the year. But Accumulated Depreciation—Equipment was decreased by $5,000 as a result of the sale during the year. Thus, depreciation for the year was $23,000. The reconciliation of Accumulated Depreciation—Equipment is as follows:

Beginning balance	$10,000
Add: Depreciation for 2002	23,000
	33,000
Deduct: Sale of equipment	5,000
Ending balance	$28,000

The total depreciation of $33,000 ($10,000 + $23,000) charged to the income statement must be added back to net income to determine net cash flow from operating activities.

Loss on Sale of Equipment

Equipment having a cost of $41,000 and a book value of $36,000 was sold for $34,000. As a result, the company reported a loss of $2,000 on its sale. To arrive at net cash flow from operating activities, it is necessary to add back to net income the loss on the sale of the equipment. The reason is that the loss is a noncash charge to the income statement; it did not reduce cash but it did reduce net income.

From the foregoing items, the operating activities section of the statement of cash flows is prepared as shown in Illustration 24-15.

Cash flows from operating activities		
Net income		$125,000
Adjustments to reconcile net income to		
net cash provided by operating activities:		
Depreciation expense	$33,000	
Increase in accounts receivable	(42,000)	
Increase in inventories	(54,000)	
Decrease in prepaid expenses	2,000	
Decrease in accounts payable	(7,000)	
Loss on sale of equipment	2,000	(66,000)
Net cash provided by operating activities		59,000

ILLUSTRATION 24-15
Operating Activities Section of Cash Flows Statement

Step 3: Determine Net Cash Flows from Investing and Financing Activities

By analyzing the remaining changes in the balance sheet accounts, we can identify cash flows from investing and financing activities.

Land

Land decreased $25,000 during the period. As indicated from the information presented, land was sold for cash at its book value. This transaction is an investing activity reported as a $25,000 source of cash.

Equipment

An analysis of the equipment account indicates the following:

Beginning balance	$ 68,000
Purchase of equipment	166,000
	234,000
Sale of equipment	41,000
Ending balance	$193,000

Equipment with a fair value of $166,000 was purchased for cash—an investing transaction reported as a cash outflow. The sale of the equipment for $34,000 is also an investing activity, but one that generates a cash inflow.

Bonds Payable

Bonds payable decreased $40,000 during the year. As indicated from the additional information, bonds were redeemed at their book value. This financing transaction used cash of $40,000.

Common Stock

The common stock account increased $160,000 during the year. As indicated from the additional information, common stock of $160,000 was issued at par. This is a financing transaction that provided cash of $160,000.

Retained Earnings

Retained earnings changed $70,000 ($206,000 − $136,000) during the year. The $70,000 change in retained earnings is the result of net income of $125,000 from operations and the financing activity of paying cash dividends of $55,000.

Statement of Cash Flows—2002

The statement of cash flows as shown in Illustration 24-16 is prepared by combining the foregoing items.

ILLUSTRATION 24-16
Statement of Cash Flows,
Tax Consultants Inc.,
Year 3

TAX CONSULTANTS INC.
Statement of Cash Flows
For the Year Ended December 31, 2002
Increase (Decrease) in Cash

Cash flows from operating activities		
Net income		$125,000
Adjustments to reconcile net income to		
net cash provided by operating activities:		
Depreciation expense	$ 33,000	
Increase in accounts receivable	(42,000)	
Increase in inventories	(54,000)	
Decrease in prepaid expenses	2,000	
Decrease in accounts payable	(7,000)	
Loss on sale of equipment	2,000	(66,000)
Net cash provided by operating activities		59,000
Cash flows from investing activities		
Sale of land	25,000	
Sale of equipment	34,000	
Purchase of equipment	(166,000)	
Net cash used by investing activities		(107,000)
Cash flows from financing activities		
Redemption of bonds	(40,000)	
Sale of common stock	160,000	
Payment of dividends	(55,000)	
Net cash provided by financing activities		65,000
Net increase in cash		17,000
Cash, January 1, 2002		37,000
Cash, December 31, 2002		$ 54,000

SOURCES OF INFORMATION FOR THE STATEMENT OF CASH FLOWS

Important points to remember in the preparation of the statement of cash flows are as follows:

OBJECTIVE 7
Identify sources of
information for a
statement of cash
flows.

❶ Comparative balance sheets provide the basic information from which the report is prepared. Additional information obtained from analyses of specific accounts is also included.

❷ An analysis of the Retained Earnings account is necessary. The net increase or decrease in Retained Earnings without any explanation is a meaningless amount in the statement, because it might represent the effect of net income, dividends declared, appropriations of retained earnings, or prior period adjustments.

❸ The statement includes all changes that have passed through cash or have resulted in an increase or decrease in cash.

❹ Writedowns, amortization charges, and similar "book" entries, such as depreciation of plant assets, are considered as neither inflows nor outflows of cash because they have no effect on cash. To the extent that they have entered into the determination of net income, however, they must be added back to or subtracted from net income to arrive at net cash flow from operating activities.

NET CASH FLOW FROM OPERATING ACTIVITIES — INDIRECT VERSUS DIRECT METHOD

As we discussed previously, the two different methods available to adjust income from operations on an accrual basis to net cash flow from operating activities are the indirect (reconciliation) method and the direct (income statement) method.

The FASB encourages use of the direct method and permits use of the indirect method. Yet, if the direct method is used, the Board requires that a reconciliation of net income to net cash flow from operating activities be provided in a separate schedule. Therefore, under either method the indirect (reconciliation) method must be prepared and reported.

Indirect Method

For consistency and comparability and because it is the most widely used method in practice, we used the indirect method in the illustrations just presented. We determined net cash flows from operating activities by adding back to or deducting from net income those items that had no effect on cash. The following diagram presents more completely the common types of adjustments that are made to net income to arrive at net cash flow from operating activities.

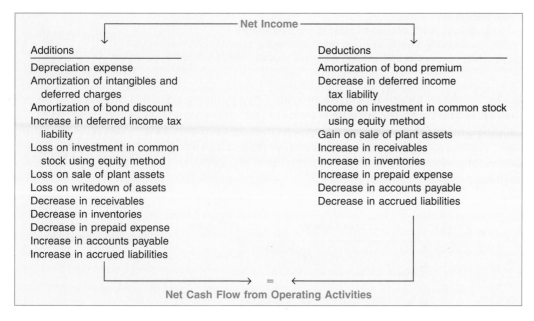

ILLUSTRATION 24-17
Adjustments Needed to Determine Net Cash Flow from Operating Activities—Indirect Method

The additions and deductions listed above reconcile net income to net cash flow from operating activities, illustrating the reason for referring to the indirect method as the reconciliation method.

Direct Method—An Illustration

Under the direct method the statement of cash flows reports net cash flow from operating activities as major classes of operating cash receipts (e.g., cash collected from customers and cash received from interest and dividends) and cash disbursements (e.g., cash paid to suppliers for goods, to employees for services, to creditors for interest, and to government authorities for taxes).

The direct method is illustrated here in more detail to help you understand the difference between accrual-based income and net cash flow from operating activities and to illustrate the data needed to apply the direct method. Emig Company, which began business on January 1, 2002, has the following selected balance sheet information:

ILLUSTRATION 24-18
Balance Sheet Accounts, Emig Co.

	December 31	
	2002	2001
Cash	$159,000	–0–
Accounts receivable	15,000	–0–
Inventory	160,000	–0–
Prepaid expenses	8,000	–0–
Property, plant, and equipment (net)	90,000	–0–
Accounts payable	60,000	–0–
Accrued expenses payable	20,000	–0–

Emig Company's December 31, 2002, income statement and additional information are:

ILLUSTRATION 24-19
Income Statement, Emig Co.

Revenues from sales		$780,000
Cost of goods sold		450,000
Gross profit		330,000
Operating expenses	$160,000	
Depreciation	10,000	170,000
Income before income taxes		160,000
Income tax expense		48,000
Net income		$112,000

Additional Information:
(a) Dividends of $70,000 were declared and paid in cash.
(b) The accounts payable increase resulted from the purchase of merchandise.
(c) Prepaid expenses and accrued expenses payable relate to operating expenses.

Under the **direct method**, net cash provided by operating activities is computed by **adjusting each item in the income statement** from the accrual basis to the cash basis. To simplify and condense the operating activities section, only major classes of operating cash receipts and cash payments are reported. The difference between these major classes of cash receipts and cash payments is the net cash provided by operating activities as shown in Illustration 24-20.

ILLUSTRATION 24-20
Major Classes of Cash Receipts and Payments

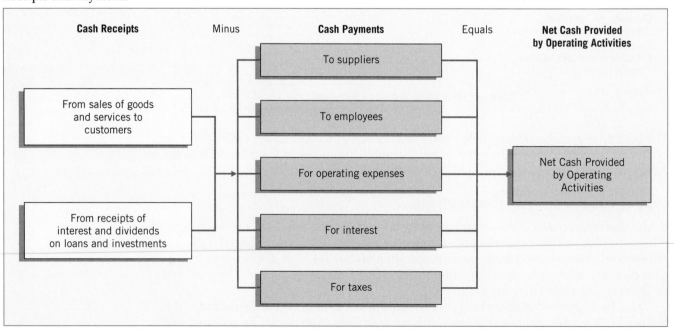

An efficient way to apply the direct method is to analyze the revenues and expenses reported in the income statement in the order in which they are listed. Cash receipts and cash payments related to these revenues and expenses should then be determined. The direct method adjustments for Emig Company in 2002 to determine net cash provided by operating activities are presented in the following sections.

Cash Receipts from Customers

The income statement for Emig Company reported revenues from customers of $780,000. To determine cash receipts from customers, it is necessary to consider the change in accounts receivable during the year. When accounts receivable increase during the year, revenues on an accrual basis are higher than cash receipts from customers. In other words, operations led to increased revenues, but not all of these revenues resulted in cash receipts. To determine the amount of increase in cash receipts, deduct the amount of the increase in accounts receivable from the total sales revenues. Conversely, a decrease in accounts receivable is added to sales revenues, because cash receipts from customers then exceed sales revenues.

For Emig Company, accounts receivable increased $15,000. Thus, cash receipts from customers were $765,000, computed as follows:

Revenues from sales	$780,000
Deduct: Increase in accounts receivable	15,000
Cash receipts from customers	$765,000

Cash receipts from customers may also be determined from an analysis of the Accounts Receivable account as shown below.

Accounts Receivable

1/1/02	Balance	–0–	Receipts from customers	765,000
	Revenue from sales	780,000		
12/31/02	Balance	15,000		

The relationships between cash receipts from customers, revenues from sales, and changes in accounts receivable are shown in Illustration 24-21.

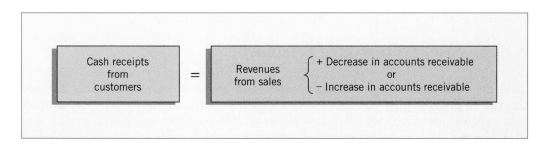

ILLUSTRATION 24-21
Formula to Compute Cash Receipts from Customers

Cash Payments to Suppliers

Emig Company reported cost of goods sold on its income statement of $450,000. To determine cash payments to suppliers, it is first necessary to find purchases for the year. To find purchases, cost of goods sold is adjusted for the change in inventory. When inventory increases during the year, it means that purchases this year exceed cost of goods sold. As a result, the increase in inventory is added to cost of goods sold to arrive at purchases.

In 2002, Emig Company's inventory increased $160,000. Purchases, therefore, are computed as follows:

Cost of goods sold	$450,000
Add: Increase in inventory	160,000
Purchases	$610,000

After purchases are computed, cash payments to suppliers are determined by adjusting purchases for the change in accounts payable. When accounts payable increase during the year, purchases on an accrual basis are higher than they are on a cash basis. As a result, an increase in accounts payable is deducted from purchases to arrive at cash payments to suppliers. Conversely, a decrease in accounts payable is added to purchases because cash payments to suppliers exceed purchases. Cash payments to suppliers were $550,000, computed as follows:

Purchases	$610,000
Deduct: Increase in accounts payable	60,000
Cash payments to suppliers	$550,000

Cash payments to suppliers may also be determined from an analysis of the Accounts Payable account as shown below.

Accounts Payable

Payments to suppliers	550,000	1/1/02	Balance	–0–
			Purchases	610,000
		12/31/02	Balance	60,000

The relationships between cash payments to customers, cost of goods sold, changes in inventory, and changes in accounts payable are shown in Illustration 24-22.

ILLUSTRATION 24-22
Formula to Compute
Cash Payments to
Suppliers

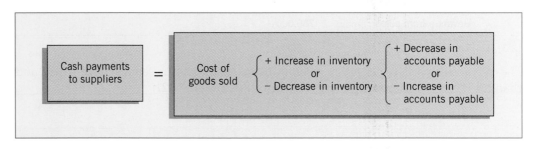

Cash Payments for Operating Expenses

Operating expenses of $160,000 were reported on Emig's income statement. To determine the cash paid for operating expenses, this amount must be adjusted for any changes in prepaid expenses and accrued expenses payable. For example, when prepaid expenses increased $8,000 during the year, cash paid for operating expenses was $8,000 higher than operating expenses reported on the income statement. To convert operating expenses to cash payments for operating expenses, the increase of $8,000 must be added to operating expenses. Conversely, if prepaid expenses decrease during the year, the decrease must be deducted from operating expenses.

Operating expenses must also be adjusted for changes in accrued expenses payable. When accrued expenses payable increase during the year, operating expenses on an accrual basis are higher than they are on a cash basis. As a result, an increase in accrued expenses payable is deducted from operating expenses to arrive at cash payments for operating expenses. Conversely, a decrease in accrued expenses payable is added to operating expenses because cash payments exceed operating expenses.

Emig Company's cash payments for operating expenses were $148,000, computed as follows:

Operating expenses	$160,000
Add: Increase in prepaid expenses	8,000
Deduct: Increase in accrued expenses payable	(20,000)
Cash payments for operating expenses	$148,000

The relationships among cash payments for operating expenses, changes in prepaid expenses, and changes in accrued expenses payable are shown in the following formula.

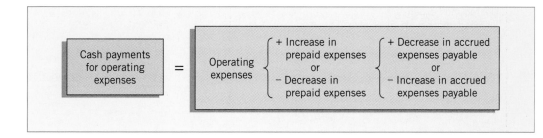

ILLUSTRATION 24-23
Formula to Compute Cash Payments for Operating Expenses

Note that depreciation expense was not considered because it is a noncash charge.

Cash Payments for Income Taxes

The income statement for Emig shows income tax expense of $48,000. This amount equals the cash paid because the comparative balance sheet indicated no income taxes payable at either the beginning or end of the year.

The computations illustrated above are summarized in the following schedule:

Accrual Basis		Adjustment	Add (Subtract)	Cash Basis
Revenues from sales	$780,000 −	Increase in accounts receivable	$(15,000)	$765,000
Cost of goods sold	450,000 +	Increase in inventory	160,000	
	−	Increase in accounts payable	(60,000)	550,000
Operating expenses	160,000 +	Increase in prepaid expenses	8,000	
	−	Increase in accrued expenses payable	(20,000)	148,000
Depreciation expense	10,000 −	Depreciation expense	(10,000)	−0−
Income tax expense	48,000			48,000
Total expense	668,000			746,000
Net income	$112,000	Net cash provided by operating activities		$ 19,000

ILLUSTRATION 24-24
Accrual Basis to Cash Basis

Presentation of the direct method for reporting net cash flow from operating activities takes the following form for the Emig Company illustration:

ILLUSTRATION 24-25
Operating Activities Section—Direct Method, 2002

EMIG COMPANY Statement of Cash Flows (partial)		
Cash flows from operating activities		
Cash received from customers		$765,000
Cash payments:		
To suppliers	$ 550,000	
For operating expenses	148,000	
For income taxes	48,000	746,000
Net cash provided by operating activities		$ 19,000

If Emig Company uses the direct method to present the net cash flows from operating activities, it must provide in a separate schedule the reconciliation of net income to net cash provided by operating activities. The reconciliation assumes the identical form and content of the indirect method of presentation as shown below:

ILLUSTRATION 24-26
Reconciliation of Net Income to Net Cash Provided by Operating Activities

Reconciliation		
Net income		$112,000
Adjustments to reconcile net income to net cash provided by operating activities:		
Depreciation expense	$ 10,000	
Increase in accounts receivable	(15,000)	
Increase in inventory	(160,000)	
Increase in prepaid expenses	(8,000)	
Increase in accounts payable	60,000	
Increase in accrued expense payable	20,000	(93,000)
Net cash provided by operating activities		$ 19,000

The reconciliation may be presented at the bottom of the statement of cash flows when the direct method is used or in a separate schedule.

Direct Versus Indirect Controversy

The most contentious decision that the FASB faced in issuing *Statement No. 95* was choosing between the direct method and the indirect method of determining net cash flow from operating activities. Companies lobbied against the direct method, urging adoption of the indirect method. Commercial lending officers expressed a strong preference to the FASB that the direct method be required.

In Favor of the Direct Method

The principal advantage of the direct method is that **it shows operating cash receipts and payments**. That is, it is more consistent with the objective of a statement of cash flows—to provide information about cash receipts and cash payments—than the indirect method, which does not report operating cash receipts and payments.

Supporters of the direct method contend that knowledge of the specific sources of operating cash receipts and the purposes for which operating cash payments were made in past periods is useful in estimating future operating cash flows. Furthermore, information about amounts of major classes of operating cash receipts and payments is more useful than information only about their arithmetic sum (the net cash flow from operating activities). Such information is more revealing of an enterprise's ability (1) to generate sufficient cash from operating activities to pay its debts, (2) to reinvest in its operations, and (3) to make distributions to its owners.[8]

Many corporate providers of financial statements say that they do not currently collect information in a manner that allows them to determine amounts such as cash received from customers or cash paid to suppliers directly from their accounting systems. But supporters of the direct method contend that the incremental cost of assimilating such operating cash receipts and payments data is not significant.

In Favor of the Indirect Method

The principal advantage of the indirect method is that **it focuses on the differences between net income and net cash flow from operating activities**. That is, it provides a useful link between the statement of cash flows and the income statement and balance sheet.

---

[8]"Statement of Cash Flows," pars. 107 and 111.

Many providers of financial statements contend that it is less costly to adjust net income to net cash flow from operating activities (indirect) than it is to report gross operating cash receipts and payments (direct). Supporters of the indirect method also state that the direct method, which effectively reports income statement information on a cash rather than an accrual basis, may erroneously suggest that net cash flow from operating activities is as good as, or better than, net income as a measure of performance.

Special Rules Applying to Direct and Indirect Methods

Companies that use the direct method are required, at a minimum, to report separately the following classes of operating cash receipts and payments:

Receipts
❶ Cash collected from customers (including lessees, licensees, etc.).
❷ Interest and dividends received.
❸ Other operating cash receipts, if any.

Payments
❶ Cash paid to employees and suppliers of goods or services (including suppliers of insurance, advertising, etc.).
❷ Interest paid.
❸ Income taxes paid.
❹ Other operating cash payments, if any.

Companies are encouraged to provide further breakdowns of operating cash receipts and payments that they consider meaningful.

Companies using the indirect method are required to disclose separately changes in inventory, receivables, and payables to reconcile net income to net cash flow from operating activities. In addition, interest paid (net of amount capitalized) and income taxes paid must be disclosed elsewhere in the financial statements or accompanying notes.[9] The FASB requires these separate and additional disclosures so that users may approximate the direct method. Also, an acceptable alternative presentation of the indirect method is to report net cash flow from operating activities as a single line item in the statement of cash flows and to present the reconciliation details elsewhere in the financial statements.

INTERNATIONAL INSIGHT

Consolidated statements of cash flows may be of limited use to analysts evaluating multinational companies. Without disaggregation, users of such statements are not able to determine "where in the world" the funds are sourced and used.

SPECIAL PROBLEMS IN STATEMENT PREPARATION

Some of the special problems related to preparing the statement of cash flows were discussed in connection with the preceding illustrations. Other problems that arise with some frequency in the preparation of this statement may be categorized as follows:

❶ Adjustments similar to depreciation.
❷ Accounts receivable (net).
❸ Other working capital changes.
❹ Net losses.
❺ Gains.
❻ Stock options.
❼ Postretirement benefit costs.

OBJECTIVE ❽
Identify special problems in preparing a statement of cash flows.

---

[9]*Accounting Trends and Techniques — 1999* reports that of the 600 companies surveyed in 1998, 323 disclosed interest paid in notes to the financial statements, 251 disclosed interest at the bottom of the statement of cash flows, 8 disclosed interest within the statement of cash flows, and 18 reported no separate amount. Income taxes paid during the year were disclosed in a manner similar to interest payments.

⑧ Extraordinary items.

⑨ Significant noncash transactions.

Adjustments Similar to Depreciation

Depreciation expense is the most common adjustment to net income that is made to arrive at net cash flow from operating activities. But there are numerous other noncash expense or revenue items. Examples of expense items that must be added back to net income are the **amortization of intangible assets** such as goodwill and patents, and the **amortization of deferred costs** such as bond issue costs. These charges to expense involve expenditures made in prior periods that are being amortized currently and reduce net income without affecting cash in the current period.

Also, **amortization of bond discount or premium** on long-term bonds payable affects the amount of interest expense, but neither changes cash. As a result, amortization of these items should be added back to (discount) or subtracted from (premium) net income to arrive at net cash flow from operating activities. In a similar manner, **changes in deferred income taxes** affect net income but have no effect on cash. For example, **Kroger Co.** at one time experienced an increase in its liability for deferred taxes of approximately $42 million. Tax expense was increased and net income was decreased by this amount, but cash was not affected; therefore, $42 million would be added back to net income on a statement of cash flows. Conversely, **General Electric Company** at one time had a decrease in its liability for deferred taxes of $171 million. Tax expense decreased and net income increased by this amount, but cash flow was unaffected. Therefore, GE subtracted this amount from net income to arrive at net cash flow from operating activities.

Another common adjustment to net income is **a change related to an investment in common stock** when income or loss is accrued under the equity method. Recall that under the equity method, the investor (1) debits the investment account and credits revenue for its share of the investee's net income and (2) credits dividends received to the investment account. Therefore, the net increase in the investment account does not affect cash flow and must be deducted from net income in arriving at net cash flow from operating activities. To illustrate, assume that Victor Co. owns 40% of Milo Inc. and during the year Milo Inc. reports net income of $100,000 and pays a cash dividend of $30,000. This information is reported in Victor Co.'s statement of cash flows as a deduction from net income in the following manner—Equity in earnings of Milo Co., net of dividends, $28,000.

If the fair value method is used, income of the investee is not recognized and any cash dividend received is recorded as revenue. In this case, no adjustment to net income in the statement of cash flows is necessary for any cash dividend received.

Accounts Receivable (Net)

Up to this point, we have assumed that no allowance for doubtful accounts—a contra account—was needed to offset accounts receivable. However, if an allowance for doubtful accounts is needed, how does it affect the determination of net cash flow from operating activities? For example, assume that Redmark Co. reports net income of $40,000 and has the following balances related to accounts receivable:

ILLUSTRATION 24-27
Accounts Receivable
Balances, Redmark Co.

	2002	2001	Change Increase/Decrease
Accounts receivable	$105,000	$90,000	$15,000 Increase
Allowance for doubtful accounts	10,000	4,000	6,000 Increase
Accounts receivable (net)	$ 95,000	$86,000	9,000 Increase

The proper reporting treatment using the indirect and direct methods is illustrated in the following sections.

Indirect Method

Because an increase in the Allowance for Doubtful Accounts is caused by a charge to bad debts expense, an increase in the Allowance for Doubtful Accounts should be added back to net income to arrive at net cash flow from operating activities. One method for presenting this information in a statement of cash flows is as follows:

REDMARK CO. Statement of Cash Flows (partial) For the Year 2002		
Cash flows from operating activities		
Net income		$40,000
Adjustments to reconcile net income to net		
cash provided by operating activities:		
Increase in accounts receivable	$(15,000)	
Increase in allowance for doubtful accounts	6,000	(9,000)
		$31,000

ILLUSTRATION 24-28
Presentation of Allowance for Doubtful Accounts—Indirect Method

As indicated, the increase in the Allowance for Doubtful Accounts balance is caused by a charge to bad debt expense for the year. Because bad debt expense is a noncash charge, it must be added back to net income in arriving at net cash flow from operating activities.

Instead of separately analyzing the allowance account, a short-cut approach is to net the allowance balance against the receivable balance and compare the change in accounts receivable on a net basis. This presentation would be as follows:

REDMARK CO. Statement of Cash Flows (partial) For the Year 2002	
Cash flows from operating activities	
Net income	$40,000
Adjustments to reconcile net income to	
net cash provided by operating activities:	
Increase in accounts receivable (net)	(9,000)
	$31,000

ILLUSTRATION 24-29
Net Approach to Allowance for Doubtful Accounts—Indirect Method

This short-cut procedure works also if the change in the allowance account was caused by a writeoff of accounts receivable. In this case, both the Accounts Receivable and the Allowance for Doubtful Accounts are reduced, and no effect on cash flows occurs. Because of its simplicity, you should use the net approach on your homework assignments.

Direct Method

If the direct method is used, the Allowance for Doubtful Accounts should **not be netted against the Accounts Receivable**. To illustrate, assume that Redmark Co.'s net income of $40,000 comprised the following items:

ILLUSTRATION 24-30
Income Statement,
Redmark Co.

REDMARK CO. Income Statement For the Year 2002		
Sales		$100,000
Expenses:		
Salaries	$46,000	
Utilities	8,000	
Bad debts	6,000	60,000
Net income		$ 40,000

If the $9,000 increase in accounts receivable (net) is deducted from sales for the year, cash sales would be reported at $91,000 ($100,000 − $9,000) and cash payments for operating expenses at $60,000. Both items are misstated because cash sales should be reported at $85,000 ($100,000 − $15,000), and total cash payments for operating expenses should be reported at $54,000 ($60,000 − $6,000). The proper presentation is as follows:

ILLUSTRATION 24-31
Bad Debts—Direct
Method

REDMARK CO. Statement of Cash Flows (partial) For the Year 2002		
Cash flows from operating activities		
Cash received from customers		$85,000
Salaries paid	$46,000	
Utilities paid	8,000	54,000
Net cash provided by operating activities		$31,000

An added complication develops when accounts receivable are written off. Simply adjusting sales for the change in accounts receivable will not provide the proper amount of cash sales. The reason is that the writeoff of the accounts receivable is not a cash collection. Thus an additional adjustment is necessary.

Other Working Capital Changes

Up to this point, all of the changes in working capital items (current asset and current liability items) have been handled as adjustments to net income in determining net cash flow from operating activities. You must be careful, however, because **some changes in working capital, although they affect cash, do not affect net income**. Generally, these are investing or financing activities of a current nature. For example, the purchase of **short-term available-for-sale securities** for $50,000 cash has no effect on net income but it does cause a $50,000 decrease in cash.[10] This transaction is reported as a cash flow from investing activities and reported gross as follows:[11]

Cash flows from investing activities	
Purchase of short-term available-for-sale securities	$(50,000)

Another example is the issuance of a $10,000 **short-term nontrade note payable** for cash. This change in a working capital item has no effect on income from operations but it increases cash $10,000. It is reported in the statement of cash flows as follows:

---

[10]If the basis of the statement of cash flows is cash **and cash equivalents** and the short-term investment is considered a cash equivalent, then nothing would be reported in the statement because the balance of cash and cash equivalents does not change as a result of this transaction.

[11]"Accounting for Certain Investments in Debt and Equity Securities," *Statement of Financial Accounting Standards No. 115* (Norwalk, CT: 1993), par. 118.

Cash flows from financing activities
Issuance of short-term note $10,000

Another change in a working capital item that has no effect on income from operations or on cash is a **cash dividend payable**. Although the cash dividends when paid will be reported as a financing activity, the declared but unpaid dividend is not reported on the statement of cash flows.

Because **trading securities** are bought and held principally for the purpose of selling them in the near term, the cash flows from purchases and sales of trading securities should be classified as cash flows from **operating activities**.[12]

Net Losses

If an enterprise reports a net loss instead of a net income, the net loss must be adjusted for those items that do not result in a cash inflow or outflow. The net loss after adjusting for the charges or credits not affecting cash may result in a negative **or** a positive cash flow from operating activities. For example, if the net loss was $50,000 and the total amount of charges to be added back was $60,000, then net cash provided by operating activities is $10,000, as shown in this computation:

Net loss		$(50,000)
Adjustments to reconcile net income to net cash provided by operating activities:		
Depreciation of plant assets	$55,000	
Amortization of patents	5,000	60,000
Net cash provided by operating activities		$ 10,000

ILLUSTRATION 24-32
Computation of Net Cash Flow from Operating Activities—Cash Inflow

If the company experiences a net loss of $80,000 and the total amount of the charges to be added back is $25,000, the presentation appears as follows:

Net loss	$(80,000)
Adjustments to reconcile net income to net cash used by operating activities:	
Depreciation of plant assets	25,000
Net cash used by operating activities	$(55,000)

ILLUSTRATION 24-33
Computation of Net Cash Flow from Operating Activities—Cash Outflow

Although it is not illustrated in this chapter, a negative cash flow may result even if the company reports a net income.

Gains

In the third illustration (2002) of Tax Consultants Inc., the company experiences a loss of $2,000 from the sale of equipment. This loss was added to net income to compute net cash flow from operating activities because **the loss is a noncash charge in the income statement**. If a gain from a sale of equipment is experienced, it too requires that net income be adjusted. Because the gain is reported in the statement of cash flows as part of the cash proceeds from the sale of equipment under investing activities, **the gain is deducted from net income to avoid double counting**—once as part of net income and again as part of the cash proceeds from the sale.

---

[12]Ibid., par. 118.

Stock Options

If a company has a stock option plan, compensation expense will be recorded during the period(s) in which the employee performs the services. Although compensation expense is debited, stockholders' equity (the paid-in capital accounts) is credited, and cash remains unaffected by the amount of the expense. **Therefore, net income has to be increased by the amount of compensation expense from stock options in computing net cash flow from operating activities.**

Postretirement Benefit Costs

If a company has postretirement costs such as an employee pension plan, chances are that the pension expense recorded during a period will either be higher than the cash funded (when there is an unfunded liability) or lower than the cash funded (when there is a deferred or prepaid pension cost). When the expense is higher or lower than the cash paid, **net income must be adjusted by the difference between cash paid and the expense reported** in computing net cash flow from operating activities.

Extraordinary Items

Cash flows from extraordinary transactions and other events whose effects are included in net income, but which are not related to operations, should be reported **either as investing activities or as financing activities**. For example, if Tax Consultants Inc. had extinguished its long-term bond debt of $40,000 by paying the bondholders $35,000 in cash, it would have recognized a $3,000 extraordinary gain ($5,000 gain less $2,000 of taxes). In the statement of cash flows (indirect method), the $5,000 gain would be deducted from net income in the operating activities section and the $35,000 cash outflow for debt extinguishment would be reported as a financing activity as follows:

Cash flows from financing activities	
Retirement of long-term bonds	$(35,000)

UNDERLYING CONCEPTS

By rejecting the requirement to allocate taxes to the various activities, the Board invoked the cost-benefit constraint. The information would be beneficial, but the cost of providing such information would exceed the benefits of providing the information.

Note that in this example the gain is handled at its gross amount ($5,000), not net of tax. The cash paid to retire the bonds is reported as a financing activity at $35,000, also exclusive of the tax effect. The FASB requires that **all income taxes paid be classified as operating cash outflows**. Some suggested that income taxes paid be allocated to investing and financing transactions. But, the Board decided that allocation of income taxes paid to operating, investing, and financing activities would be so complex and arbitrary that the benefits, if any, would not justify the costs involved. Under both the direct method and the indirect method the total amount of income taxes paid must be disclosed.[13]

Significant Noncash Transactions

Because the statement of cash flows reports only the effects of operating, investing, and financing activities in terms of cash flows, some significant noncash transactions and

---

[13]For an insightful article on some weaknesses and limitations in the statement of cash flows caused by implementation of *FASB Statement No. 95*, see Hugo Nurnberg, "Inconsistencies and Ambiguities in Cash Flow Statements Under *FASB Statement No. 95*," *Accounting Horizons*, June 1993, pp. 60–73. Nurnberg identifies the inconsistencies caused by the three-way classification of all cash receipts and cash payments, gross versus net of tax, the ambiguous disclosure requirements for noncash investing and financing transactions, and the ambiguous presentation of third-party financing transactions. See also Paul R. Bahnson, Paul B. W. Miller, and Bruce P. Budge, "Nonarticulation in Cash Flow Statements and Implications for Education, Research, and Practice," *Accounting Horizons*, December 1996, pp. 1–15.

other events that are investing or financing activities are omitted from the body of the statement. Among the more common of these noncash transactions that should be reported or disclosed in some manner are the following:

❶ Acquisition of assets by assuming liabilities (including capital lease obligations) or by issuing equity securities.

❷ Exchanges of nonmonetary assets.

❸ Refinancing of long-term debt.

❹ Conversion of debt or preferred stock to common stock.

❺ Issuance of equity securities to retire debt.

These noncash items are not to be incorporated in the statement of cash flows. If material in amount, these disclosures may be either narrative or summarized in a separate schedule at the bottom of the statement, or they may appear in a separate note or supplementary schedule to the financial statements. The presentation of these significant noncash transactions or other events in a separate schedule at the bottom of the statement of cash flows is shown as follows:

Net increase in cash	$3,717,000
Cash at beginning of year	5,208,000
Cash at end of year	$8,925,000
Noncash investing and financing activities	
Purchase of land and building through issuance of 250,000 shares of	
common stock	$1,750,000
Exchange of Steadfast, NY, land for Bedford, PA, land	$2,000,000
Conversion of 12% bonds to 50,000 shares of common stock	$ 500,000

ILLUSTRATION 24-34
Schedule Presentation of Noncash Investing and Financing Activities

These noncash transactions might be presented in a separate note as follows:

Note G: Significant noncash transactions. During the year the company engaged in the following significant noncash investing and financing transactions:	
Issued 250,000 shares of common stock to purchase land and building	$1,750,000
Exchanged land in Steadfast, NY, for land in Bedford, PA	$2,000,000
Converted 12% bonds due 2001 to 50,000 shares of common stock	$ 500,000

ILLUSTRATION 24-35
Note Presentation of Noncash Investing and Financing Activities

Certain other significant noncash transactions or other events are generally not reported in conjunction with the statement of cash flows. Examples of these types of transactions are **stock dividends, stock splits, and appropriations of retained earnings.** These items, neither financing nor investing activities, are generally reported in conjunction with the statement of stockholders' equity or schedules and notes pertaining to changes in capital accounts.

USE OF A WORK SHEET

SECTION 2

When numerous adjustments are necessary, or other complicating factors are present, **a work sheet is often used to assemble and classify the data that will appear on the statement of cash flows.** The work sheet (a **"spreadsheet"** when using computer software) is merely a device that aids in the preparation of the statement; its use is optional. The skeleton format of the work sheet for preparation of the statement of cash flows using the indirect method is shown in Illustration 24-36.

OBJECTIVE ❾
Explain the use of a work sheet in preparing a statement of cash flows.

Go to the Digital Tool for examples of cash flow statements, including disclosure of significant noncash transactions.

ILLUSTRATION 24-36
Format of Work Sheet for
Preparation of Statement
of Cash Flows

XYZ COMPANY
Statement of Cash Flows
For the Year Ended . . .

Balance Sheet Accounts	End of Prior Year Balances	Reconciling Items		End of Current Year Balances
		Debits	Credits	
Debit balance accounts	XX	XX	XX	XX
	XX	XX	XX	XX
Totals	XXX			XXX
Credit balance accounts	XX	XX	XX	XX
	XX	XX	XX	XX
Totals	XXX			XXX
Statement of Cash Flows Effects				
Operating activities				
Net income		XX		
Adjustments		XX	XX	
Investing activities				
Receipts and payments		XX	XX	
Financing activities				
Receipts and payments		XX	XX	
Totals		XXX	XXX	
Increase (decrease) in cash		(XX)	XX	
Totals		XXX	XXX	

The following guidelines are important in using a work sheet:

1 In the balance sheet accounts section, **accounts with debit balances are listed separately from those with credit balances**. This means, for example, that Accumulated Depreciation is listed under credit balances and not as a contra account under debit balances. The beginning and ending balances of each account are entered in the appropriate columns. The transactions that caused the change in the account balance during the year are entered as reconciling items in the two middle columns. After all reconciling items have been entered, each line pertaining to a balance sheet account should foot across. That is, the beginning balance plus or minus the reconciling item(s) must equal the ending balance. When this agreement exists for all balance sheet accounts, all changes in account balances have been reconciled.

2 The bottom portion of the work sheet consists of the operating, investing, and financing activities sections. Accordingly, it provides the information necessary to prepare the formal statement of cash flows. **Inflows of cash are entered as debits in the reconciling columns and outflows of cash are entered as credits in the reconciling columns.** Thus, in this section, the sale of equipment for cash at book value is entered as a debit under inflows of cash from investing activities. Similarly, the purchase of land for cash is entered as a credit under outflows of cash from investing activities.

3 **The reconciling items shown in the work sheet are not entered in any journal or posted to any account.** They do not represent either adjustments or corrections of the balance sheet accounts. They are used only to facilitate the preparation of the statement of cash flows.

PREPARATION OF THE WORK SHEET

The preparation of a work sheet involves a series of prescribed steps. The steps in this case are:

Step 1. Enter the balance sheet accounts and their beginning and ending balances in the balance sheet accounts section.

Step 2. Enter the data which explain the changes in the balance sheet accounts (other than cash) and their effects on the statement of cash flows in the reconciling columns of the work sheet.

Step 3. Enter the increase or decrease in cash on the cash line and at the bottom of the work sheet. This entry should enable the totals of the reconciling columns to be in agreement.

To illustrate the preparation and use of a work sheet and to illustrate the reporting of some of the special problems discussed in the prior section, the following comprehensive illustration is presented for Satellite Corporation. Again, the indirect method serves as the basis for the computation of net cash provided by operating activities. The financial statements and other data related to Satellite Corporation are presented with the balance sheet and the statement of income and retained earnings shown on the following pages. Additional explanations related to the preparation of the work sheet are provided throughout the discussion that follows the financial statements.

ILLUSTRATION 24-37
Comparative Balance Sheet, Satellite Corporation

SATELLITE CORPORATION
Comparative Balance Sheet
December 31, 2002 and 2001

	2002	2001	Difference Incr. or Decr.
Assets			
Cash	$ 59,000	$ 66,000	$ 7,000 Decr.
Accounts receivable (net)	104,000	51,000	53,000 Incr.
Inventories	493,000	341,000	152,000 Incr.
Prepaid expenses	16,500	17,000	500 Decr.
Investments in stock of Porter Co.			
(equity method)	18,500	15,000	3,500 Incr.
Land	131,500	82,000	49,500 Incr.
Equipment	187,000	142,000	45,000 Incr.
Accumulated depreciation—equipment	(29,000)	(31,000)	2,000 Decr.
Buildings	262,000	262,000	—
Accumulated depreciation—buildings	(74,100)	(71,000)	3,100 Incr.
Goodwill	7,600	10,000	2,400 Decr.
Total assets	$1,176,000	$884,000	
Liabilities			
Accounts payable	$ 132,000	$131,000	1,000 Incr.
Accrued liabilities	43,000	39,000	4,000 Incr.
Income tax payable	3,000	16,000	13,000 Decr.
Notes payable (long-term)	60,000	—	60,000 Incr.
Bonds payable	100,000	100,000	—
Premium on bonds payable	7,000	8,000	1,000 Decr.
Deferred tax liability (long-term)	9,000	6,000	3,000 Incr.
Total liabilities	354,000	300,000	
Stockholders' Equity			
Common stock ($1 par)	60,000	50,000	10,000 Incr.
Additional paid-in capital	187,000	38,000	149,000 Incr.
Retained earnings	592,000	496,000	96,000 Incr.
Treasury stock	(17,000)	—	17,000 Incr.
Total stockholders' equity	822,000	584,000	
Total liabilities and stockholders' equity	$1,176,000	$884,000	

ILLUSTRATION 24-38
Income and Retained
Earnings Statements,
Satellite Corporation

SATELLITE CORPORATION
Combined Statement of Income and Retained Earnings
For the Year Ended December 31, 2002

Net sales		$526,500
Other revenue		3,500
Total revenues		530,000
Expense		
Cost of goods sold		310,000
Selling and administrative expenses		47,000
Other expenses and losses		12,000
Total expenses		369,000
Income before income tax and extraordinary item		161,000
Income tax		
Current	$47,000	
Deferred	3,000	50,000
Income before extraordinary item		111,000
Gain on condemnation of land (net of $2,000 tax)		6,000
Net income		117,000
Retained earnings, January 1		496,000
Less:		
Cash dividends	6,000	
Stock dividend	15,000	21,000
Retained earnings, December 31		$592,000
Per share:		
Income before extraordinary item		$2.02
Extraordinary item		.11
Net income		$2.13

Additional Information

(a) Other income of $3,500 represents Satellite's equity share in the net income of Porter Co., an equity investee. Satellite owns 22% of Porter Co.

(b) An analysis of the equipment account and related accumulated depreciation indicates the following:

	Equipment Dr./(Cr.)	Accum. Dep. Dr./(Cr.)	Gain or (Loss)
Balance at end of 2001	$142,000	$(31,000)	
Purchases of equipment	53,000		
Sale of equipment	(8,000)	2,500	$(1,500)
Depreciation for the period		(11,500)	
Major repair charged to accumulated depreciation		11,000	
Balance at end of 2002	$187,000	$(29,000)	

(c) Land in the amount of $60,000 was purchased through the issuance of a long-term note; in addition, certain parcels of land costing $10,500 were condemned. The state government paid Satellite $18,500, resulting in an $8,000 gain which has a $2,000 tax effect.

(d) The change in the accumulated depreciation—buildings, goodwill, and premium on bonds payable accounts resulted from depreciation and amortization entries.

(e) An analysis of the paid-in capital accounts in stockholders' equity discloses the following:

	Common Stock	Additional Paid-In Capital
Balance at end of 2001	$50,000	$ 38,000
Issuance of 2% stock dividend	1,000	14,000
Sale of stock for cash	9,000	135,000
Balance at end of 2002	$60,000	$187,000

(f) Interest paid (net of amount capitalized) is $9,000; income taxes paid is $62,000.

ANALYSIS OF TRANSACTIONS

The following discussion provides an explanation of the individual adjustments that appear on the work sheet in Illustration 24-39 (page 1345). Because cash is the basis for the analysis, the cash account is reconciled last. Because income is the first item that appears on the statement of cash flows, it is handled first.

Change in Retained Earnings

Net income for the period is $117,000; the entry for it on the work sheet is as follows:

(1)

Operating—Net Income	117,000	
Retained Earnings		117,000

Net income is reported on the bottom section of the work sheet and **is the starting point for preparation of the statement of cash flows (under the indirect method).**

Retained earnings was also affected by a stock dividend and a cash dividend. The retained earnings statement reports a stock dividend of $15,000. The work sheet entry for this transaction is as follows:

(2)

Retained Earnings	15,000	
Common Stock		1,000
Additional Paid-in Capital		14,000

The issuance of stock dividends is not a cash operating, investing, or financing item; therefore, **although this transaction is entered on the work sheet for reconciling purposes, it is not reported in the statement of cash flows.**

The cash dividends paid of $6,000 represents a financing activity cash outflow. The following work sheet entry is made:

(3)

Retained Earnings	6,000	
Financing—Cash Dividends		6,000

The beginning and ending balances of retained earnings are reconciled by the entry of the three items above.

Accounts Receivable (Net)

The increase in accounts receivable (net) of $53,000 represents adjustments that did not result in cash inflows during 2002. As a result, the increase of $53,000 would be deducted from net income. The following work sheet entry is made:

(4)

Accounts Receivable (net)	53,000	
Operating—Increase in Accounts Receivable (net)		53,000

Inventories

The increase in inventories of $152,000 represents an operating use of cash. The incremental investment in inventories during the year reduces cash without increasing the cost of goods sold. The work sheet entry is made as follows:

(5)

Inventories	152,000	
Operating—Increase in Inventories		152,000

Prepaid Expense

The decrease in prepaid expenses of $500 represents a charge in the income statement for which there was no cash outflow in the current period. It should be added back to net income through the following entry:

	(6)		
Operating—Decrease in Prepaid Expenses		500	
Prepaid Expenses			500

Investment in Stock

The investment in the stock of Porter Co. increased $3,500, which reflects Satellite's share of the income earned by its equity investee during the current year. Although revenue, and therefore income per the income statement, was increased $3,500 by the accounting entry that recorded Satellite's share of Porter Co.'s net income, no cash (dividend) was provided. The following work sheet entry is made:

	(7)		
Investment in Stock of Porter Co.		3,500	
Operating—Equity in Earnings of Porter Co.			3,500

Land

Land in the amount of $60,000 was purchased through the issuance of a long-term note payable. This transaction did not affect cash; it is considered a significant noncash investing/financing transaction that would be disclosed either in a separate schedule below the statement of cash flows or in the accompanying notes. The following entry is made to reconcile the work sheet:

	(8)		
Land		60,000	
Notes Payable			60,000

In addition to the noncash transaction involving the issuance of a note to purchase land, the Land account was decreased by the condemnation proceedings. The work sheet entry to record the receipt of $18,500 for land having a book value of $10,500 is as follows:

	(9)		
Investing—Proceeds from Condemnation of Land		18,500	
Land			10,500
Operating—Gain on Condemnation of Land			8,000

The extraordinary gain of $8,000 is deducted from net income in reconciling net income to net cash flow from operating activities because the transaction that gave rise to the gain is an item whose cash effect is already classified as an investing cash inflow. The Land account is now reconciled.

Equipment and Accumulated Depreciation

An analysis of Equipment and Accumulated Depreciation shows that a number of transactions have affected these accounts. Equipment in the amount of $53,000 was purchased during the year. The entry to record this transaction on the work sheet is as follows:

	(10)		
Equipment		53,000	
Investing—Purchase of Equipment			53,000

In addition, equipment with a book value of $5,500 was sold at a loss of $1,500. The entry to record this transaction on the work sheet is as follows:

	(11)		
Investing—Sale of Equipment		4,000	
Operating—Loss on Sale of Equipment		1,500	
Accumulated Depreciation—Equipment		2,500	
Equipment			8,000

The proceeds from the sale of the equipment provided cash of $4,000. In addition, the loss on the sale of the equipment has reduced net income, but did not affect cash;

therefore, it is added back to net income to report accurately cash provided by operating activities.

Depreciation on the equipment was reported at $11,500 and is presented on the work sheet in the following manner:

(12)

Operating—Depreciation Expense—Equipment	11,500	
Accumulated Depreciation—Equipment		11,500

The depreciation expense is added back to net income because it reduced income but did not affect cash.

Finally, a major repair to the equipment in the amount of $11,000 was charged to Accumulated Depreciation—Equipment. Because this expenditure required cash, the following work sheet entry is made:

(13)

Accumulated Depreciation—Equipment	11,000	
Investing—Major Repairs of Equipment		11,000

The balances in the Equipment and related Accumulated Depreciation accounts are reconciled after adjustment for the foregoing items.

Building Depreciation and Amortization of Goodwill

Depreciation expense on the buildings of $3,100 and amortization of goodwill of $2,400 are both expenses in the income statement that reduced net income but did not require cash outflows in the current period. The following work sheet entry is made:

(14)

Operating—Depreciation Expense—Buildings	3,100	
Operating—Amortization of Goodwill	2,400	
Accumulated Depreciation—Buildings		3,100
Goodwill		2,400

Other Noncash Charges or Credits

An analysis of the remaining accounts indicates that changes in the Accounts Payable, Accrued Liabilities, Income Tax Payable, Premium on Bonds Payable, and Deferred Tax Liability balances resulted from charges or credits to net income that did not affect cash. Each of these items should be individually analyzed and entered in the work sheet. We have summarized in the following compound entry to the work sheet these noncash, income-related items:

(15)

Income Tax Payable	13,000	
Premium on Bonds Payable	1,000	
Operating—Increase in Accounts Payable	1,000	
Operating—Increase in Accrued Liabilities	4,000	
Operating—Increase in Deferred Tax Liability	3,000	
Operating—Decrease in Income Tax Payable		13,000
Operating—Amortization of Bond Premium		1,000
Accounts Payable		1,000
Accrued Liabilities		4,000
Deferred Tax Liability		3,000

Common Stock and Related Accounts

A comparison of the common stock balances and the additional paid-in capital balances shows that transactions during the year affected these accounts. First, a stock dividend of 2% was issued to stockholders. As indicated in the discussion of work sheet entry (2), no cash was provided or used by the stock dividend transaction. In addition to the shares issued via the stock dividend, Satellite sold shares of common stock at $16 per share. The work sheet entry to record this transaction is as follows:

(16)

Financing—Sale of Common Stock	144,000	
Common Stock		9,000
Additional Paid-in Capital		135,000

Also, the company purchased shares of its common stock in the amount of $17,000. The work sheet entry to record this transaction is as follows:

(17)

Treasury Stock	17,000	
Financing—Purchase of Treasury Stock		17,000

Final Reconciling Entry

The final entry to reconcile the change in cash and to balance the work sheet is shown below.

(18)

Decrease in Cash	7,000	
Cash		7,000

The $7,000 amount is the difference between the beginning and ending cash balance.

Once it has been determined that the differences between the beginning and ending balances per the work sheet columns have been accounted for, the reconciling trans-actions columns can be totaled, and they should balance. The statement of cash flows can be prepared entirely from the items and amounts that appear at the bottom of the work sheet under "Statement of Cash Flows Effects," as shown in Illustration 24-39 on the next page.

SATELLITE CORPORATION
Work Sheet for Preparation of Statement of Cash Flows
For the Year Ended December 31, 2002

	Balance 12/31/01	Reconciling Items—2002 Debits	Reconciling Items—2002 Credits	Balance 12/31/02
Debits				
Cash	$ 66,000		(18) $ 7,000	$ 59,000
Accounts receivable (net)	51,000	(4) $ 53,000		104,000
Inventories	341,000	(5) 152,000		493,000
Prepaid expenses	17,000		(6) 500	16,500
Investment (equity method)	15,000	(7) 3,500		18,500
Land	82,000	(8) 60,000	(9) 10,500	131,500
Equipment	142,000	(10) 53,000	(11) 8,000	187,000
Buildings	262,000			262,000
Goodwill	10,000		(14) 2,400	7,600
Treasury stock		(17) 17,000		17,000
Total debits	$986,000			$1,296,100
Credits			(11) 2,500	
Accum. depr.—equipment	$ 31,000	(13) 11,000	(12) 11,500	$ 29,000
Accum. depr.—buildings	71,000		(14) 3,100	74,100
Accounts payable	131,000		(15) 1,000	132,000
Accrued liabilities	39,000		(15) 4,000	43,000
Income tax payable	16,000	(15) 13,000		3,000
Notes payable	–0–		(8) 60,000	60,000
Bonds payable	100,000			100,000
Premium on bonds payable	8,000	(15) 1,000		7,000
Deferred tax liability	6,000		(15) 3,000	9,000
Common stock	50,000		(2) 1,000	
			(16) 9,000	60,000
Additional paid-in capital	38,000		(2) 14,000	
			(16) 135,000	187,000
Retained earnings	496,000	(2) 15,000	(1) 117,000	
		(3) 6,000		592,000
Total credits	$986,000			$1,296,100

Statement of Cash Flows Effects				
Operating activities				
Net income		(1) 117,000		
Increase in accounts receivable (net)			(4) 53,000	
Increase in inventories			(5) 152,000	
Decrease in prepaid expenses		(6) 500		
Equity in earnings of Porter Co.			(7) 3,500	
Gain on condemnation of land			(9) 8,000	
Loss on sale of equipment		(11) 1,500		
Depr. expense—equipment		(12) 11,500		
Depr. expense—buildings		(14) 3,100		
Amortization of goodwill		(14) 2,400		
Increase in accounts payable		(15) 1,000		
Increase in accrued liabilities		(15) 4,000		
Increase in deferred tax liability		(15) 3,000		
Decrease in income tax payable			(15) 13,000	
Amortization of bond premium			(15) 1,000	
Investing activities				
Proceeds from condemnation of land		(9) 18,500		
Purchase of equipment			(10) 53,000	
Sale of equipment		(11) 4,000		
Major repairs of equipment			(13) 11,000	
Financing activities				
Payment of cash dividend			(3) 6,000	
Issuance of common stock		(16) 144,000		
Purchase of treasury stock			(17) 17,000	
Totals		697,500	704,500	
Decrease in cash		(18) 7,000		
Totals		$704,500	$704,500	

PREPARATION OF FINAL STATEMENT

Presented below is a formal statement of cash flows prepared from the data compiled in the lower portion of the work sheet.

ILLUSTRATION 24-40
Statement of Cash Flows, Satellite Corporation

SATELLITE CORPORATION
Statement of Cash Flows
For the Year Ended December 31, 2002
Increase (Decrease) in Cash

Cash flows from operating activities		
Net income		$117,000
Adjustments to reconcile net income to net		
cash used by operating activities:		
Depreciation expense	$ 14,600	
Amortization of goodwill	2,400	
Amortization of bond premium	(1,000)	
Equity in earnings of Porter Co.	(3,500)	
Gain on condemnation of land	(8,000)	
Loss on sale of equipment	1,500	
Increase in deferred tax liability	3,000	
Increase in accounts receivable (net)	(53,000)	
Increase in inventories	(152,000)	
Decrease in prepaid expenses	500	
Increase in accounts payable	1,000	
Increase in accrued liabilities	4,000	
Decrease in income tax payable	(13,000)	(203,500)
Net cash used by operating activities		(86,500)
Cash flows from investing activities		
Proceeds from condemnation of land	18,500	
Purchase of equipment	(53,000)	
Sale of equipment	4,000	
Major repairs of equipment	(11,000)	
Net cash used by investing activities		(41,500)
Cash flows from financing activities		
Payment of cash dividend	(6,000)	
Issuance of common stock	144,000	
Purchase of treasury stock	(17,000)	
Net cash provided by financing activities		121,000
Net decrease in cash		(7,000)
Cash, January 1, 2002		66,000
Cash, December 31, 2002		$ 59,000
Supplemental Disclosures of Cash Flow Information:		
Cash paid during the year for:		
Interest (net of amount capitalized)		$ 9,000
Income taxes		$ 62,000
Supplemental Schedule of Noncash Investing and Financing Activities:		
Purchase of land for $60,000 in exchange for a $60,000 long-term note.		

Go to the Digital Tool for discussion of the T-account approach to preparation of the statement of cash flows.

www.wiley.com/college/kieso

SUMMARY OF LEARNING OBJECTIVES

❶ **Describe the purpose of the statement of cash flows.** The primary purpose of the statement of cash flows is to provide information about cash receipts and cash payments of an entity during a period. A secondary objective is to report the entity's operating, investing, and financing activities during the period.

KEY TERMS

cash equivalents, *1311*
direct method, *1315*
financing activities, *1312*
indirect method, *1316*
investing activities, *1312*
operating activities, *1311*
significant noncash
  transactions, *1336*
statement of cash
  flows, *1310*

② Identify the major classifications of cash flows. The cash flows are classified as: (1) Operating activities—transactions that result in the revenues, expenses, gains, and losses that determine net income. (2) Investing activities—lending money and collecting on those loans, and acquiring and disposing of investments, plant assets, and intangible assets. (3) Financing activities—obtaining cash from creditors and repaying loans, issuing and reacquiring capital stock, and paying cash dividends.

③ Differentiate between net income and net cash flows from operating activities. Net income on an accrual basis must be adjusted to determine net cash flow from operating activities because some expenses and losses do not cause cash outflows and some revenues and gains do not provide cash inflows.

④ Contrast the direct and indirect methods of calculating net cash flow from operating activities. Under the direct approach, major classes of operating cash receipts and cash disbursements are calculated. The computations are summarized in a schedule of changes from the accrual to the cash basis income statement. Presentation of the direct approach of reporting net cash flow from operating activities takes the form of a condensed cash basis income statement. The indirect method adds back to net income the noncash expenses and losses and subtracts the noncash revenues and gains.

⑤ Determine net cash flows from investing and financing activities. Once the net cash flow from operating activities is computed, the next step is to determine whether any other changes in balance sheet accounts caused an increase or decrease in cash. Net cash flows from investing and financing activities can be determined by examining the changes in noncurrent balance sheet accounts.

⑥ Prepare a statement of cash flows. Preparing the statement involves three major steps: (1) determine the change in cash. This is the difference between the beginning and the ending cash balance shown on the comparative balance sheets. (2) determine the net cash flow from operating activities. This procedure is complex; it involves analyzing not only the current year's income statement but also the comparative balance sheets and the selected transaction data. (3) determine cash flows from investing and financing activities. All other changes in the balance sheet accounts must be analyzed to determine the effects on cash.

⑦ Identify sources of information for a statement of cash flows. The information to prepare the statement usually comes from three sources: (1) comparative balance sheets. Information in these statements indicate the amount of the changes in assets, liabilities, and equities during the period. (2) current income statement. Information in this statement is used in determining the cash provided by operations during the period. (3) selected transaction data. These data from the general ledger provide additional detailed information needed to determine how cash was provided or used during the period.

⑧ Identify special problems in preparing a statement of cash flows. These special problems are: (1) adjustments similar to depreciation; (2) accounts receivable (net); (3) other working capital changes; (4) net losses; (5) gains; (6) stock options; (7) postretirement benefit costs; (8) extraordinary items; and (9) significant noncash transactions.

⑨ Explain the use of a work sheet in preparing a statement of cash flows. When numerous adjustments are necessary, or other complicating factors are present, a work sheet is often used to assemble and classify the data that will appear on the statement of cash flows. The work sheet is merely a device that aids in the preparation of the statement; its use is optional.

FROM CLASSROOM TO CAREER

WILLIE SUTTON

is an accountant with Mutual Community Savings Bank in Durham, North Carolina. He has held this position since graduating Summa Cum Laude from North Carolina Central University in 1994. Prior to attending college, he served for three years in the United States Army. Currently, he is working on his MBA from NCCU.

Why did you join the Army after high school?

It was the only way that I could pay my way through college. Perhaps I could have financed college some other way, but I came from a poor family and was attracted to the college scholarships that the Army offered. For the most part, I enjoyed my experience in the Army, because it taught me discipline and hard work. It was probably one of the best decisions that I ever made, because without it, I probably wouldn't have been able to go to college and be where I am right now.

Did you find it advantageous to start college at an older age?

Perhaps it was because of age, but I can remember noticing that a lot of the students weren't as focused as I was. I knew a lot of students who would stay up all night getting their work done, but I was able to manage my time better. As a teenager, I watched my parents get up every day and not miss a day of work, and I learned discipline from that as well as my Army experience. Age is less of an issue in the MBA program that I have been attending at night, where there are some students who are much older than I am.

Describe Mutual Community Savings Bank.

This is a community bank with three branches, two in Durham and one in Greensboro, North Carolina. The bank is publicly held, which means management has to worry about the stock price (ticker symbol MTUC) as well as whether the bank is profitable and providing good customer service. I have found that working for a smaller institution provides me with a lot of exposure to many different areas of the bank that I wouldn't otherwise get with a larger bank.

What topic from Intermediate Accounting relates to your current position?

As you can imagine, the management and control of cash is very important in a bank. One of the most important things that I do is to go over the tellers' work at the end of the day after all the transactions have been calculated and closed out. There are usually some differences between what the system says and what the teller actually has in cash. In addition, working with the bank's Treasurer, I compile annual and quarterly financial statements and a variety of regulatory reports that generally draw on my accounting education. But my duties have broadened beyond accounting and into the bank's computer operations, where I have management duties. Many of our customers are elderly, and they tend to visit the bank a little bit more than young people, and some of them resist the new technology. But most have become accustomed to direct deposit of payroll checks and automatic payment of certain bills. In addition, we are in the process of converting to an online banking system, which will make us more competitive with some of the larger banks in the area.

QUESTIONS

1 What is the purpose of the statement of cash flows? What information does it provide?

2 Of what use is the statement of cash flows?

3 Differentiate between investing activities, financing activities, and operating activities.

4 What are the major sources of cash (inflows) in a statement of cash flows? What are the major uses (outflows) of cash?

5 Identify and explain the major steps involved in preparing the statement of cash flows.

6 Identify the following items as (1) operating, (2) investing, or (3) financing activities: purchase of land; payment of dividends; cash sales; and purchase of treasury stock.

7 Unlike the other major financial statements, the statement of cash flows is not prepared from the adjusted trial balance. From what sources does the information to prepare this statement come and what information does each source provide?

8 Why is it necessary to convert accrual-based net income to a cash basis when preparing a statement of cash flows?

9 Differentiate between the direct method and the indirect method by discussing each method.

10 Bonnie Raitt Company reported net income of $3.5 million in 2002. Depreciation for the year was $520,000; accounts receivable increased $500,000; and accounts payable increased $350,000. Compute net cash flow from operating activities using the indirect method.

11 Sophie B. Hawkins Co. reported sales on an accrual basis of $100,000. If accounts receivable increased $30,000, and the allowance for doubtful accounts increased $9,000 after a writeoff of $4,000, compute cash sales.

12 Your roommate is puzzled. During the last year, the company in which she is a stockholder reported a net loss of $675,000, yet its cash increased $321,000 during the same period of time. Explain to your roommate how this situation could occur.

13 The board of directors of Kenny G Corp. declared cash dividends of $260,000 during the current year. If dividends payable was $85,000 at the beginning of the year and $70,000 at the end of the year, how much cash was paid in dividends during the year?

14 Explain how the amount of cash payments to suppliers is computed under the direct method.

15 The net income for Silverchair Company for 2002 was $320,000. During 2002, depreciation on plant assets was $114,000, amortization of goodwill was $40,000, and the company incurred a loss on sale of plant assets of $21,000. Compute net cash flow from operating activities.

16 Each of the following items must be considered in preparing a statement of cash flows for Frogstomp Inc. for the year ended December 31, 2002. State where each item is to be shown in the statement, if at all.

   (a) Plant assets that had cost $20,000 $6\frac{1}{2}$ years before and were being depreciated on a straight-line basis over 10 years with no estimated scrap value were sold for $4,000.

   (b) During the year, 10,000 shares of common stock with a stated value of $20 a share were issued for $41 a share.

   (c) Uncollectible accounts receivable in the amount of $22,000 were written off against the Allowance for Doubtful Accounts.

   (d) The company sustained a net loss for the year of $50,000. Depreciation amounted to $22,000, and a gain of $9,000 was realized on the sale of available-for-sale securities for $38,000 cash.

17 Classify the following items as (1) operating, (2) investing, (3) financing, or (4) significant noncash investing and financing activities (using the direct method).

   (a) Purchase of equipment.
   (b) Redemption of bonds.
   (c) Sale of building.
   (d) Cash payments to suppliers.
   (e) Exchange of equipment for furniture.
   (f) Issuance of capital stock.
   (g) Cash received from customers.
   (h) Purchase of treasury stock.
   (i) Issuance of bonds for land.
   (j) Payment of dividends.
   (k) Cash payments to employees.
   (l) Cash payments for operating expenses.

18 Clay Walker and David Ball were discussing the presentation format of the statement of cash flows of Martina McBride Co. At the bottom of McBride's statement of cash flows was a separate section entitled "Noncash investing and financing activities." Give three examples of significant noncash transactions that would be reported in this section.

19 During 2002, Bryan Adams Company redeemed $2,000,000 of bonds payable for $1,780,000 cash. Indicate how this transaction would be reported on a statement of cash flows, if at all.

20 What are some of the arguments in favor of using the indirect (reconciliation) method as opposed to the direct method for reporting a statement of cash flows?

21 Why is it desirable to use a work sheet when preparing a statement of cash flows? Is a work sheet required to prepare a statement of cash flows?

BRIEF EXERCISES

BE24-1   American Gladhanders Corporation had the following activities in 2002:

Sale of land, $130,000

Purchase of inventory, $845,000

Purchase of treasury stock, $72,000

Purchase of equipment, $415,000

Issuance of common stock, $320,000

Purchase of available-for-sale securities, $59,000

Compute the amount American Gladhanders should report as net cash provided (used) by investing activities in its statement of cash flows.

BE24-2   Chrono Trigger Corporation had the following activities in 2002:

Payment of accounts payable, $770,000

Issuance of common stock, $250,000

Payment of dividends, $300,000

Collection of note receivable, $100,000

Issuance of bonds payable, $510,000

Purchase of treasury stock, $46,000

Compute the amount Chrono Trigger should report as net cash provided (used) by financing activities in its 2002 statement of cash flows.

BE24-3   Ryker Corporation is preparing its 2002 statement of cash flows, using the indirect method. Presented below is a list of items that may affect the statement. Using the code below, indicate how each item will affect Ryker's 2002 statement of cash flows.

Code Letter	Effect
A	Added to net income in the operating section
D	Deducted from net income in the operating section
R-I	Cash receipt in investing section
P-I	Cash payment in investing section
R-F	Cash receipt in financing section
P-F	Cash payment in financing section
N	Noncash investing and/or financing activity

Items

_____ (a) Increase in accounts receivable.

_____ (b) Decrease in accounts receivable.

_____ (c) Issuance of stock.

_____ (d) Depreciation expense.

_____ (e) Sale of land at book value.

_____ (f) Sale of land at a gain.

_____ (g) Payment of dividends.

_____ (h) Purchase of land and building.

_____ (i) Purchase of available-for-sale investment.

_____ (j) Increase in accounts payable.

_____ (k) Decrease in accounts payable.

_____ (l) Loan from bank by signing note.

_____ (m) Purchase of equipment using a note.

_____ (n) Increase in inventory.

_____ (o) Issuance of bonds.

_____ (p) Retirement of bonds.

_____ (q) Sale of equipment at a loss.

_____ (r) Purchase of treasury stock.

BE24-4   Azure Corporation had the following 2002 income statement:

Sales	$200,000
Cost of goods sold	120,000
Gross profit	80,000

Operating expenses (includes depreciation of $21,000)	50,000
Net income	$ 30,000

The following accounts increased during 2002: accounts receivable, $17,000; inventory, $11,000; accounts payable, $13,000. Prepare the cash flows from operating activities section of Azure's 2002 statement of cash flows using the direct method.

BE24-5 Use the information from BE24-4 for Azure Corporation. Prepare the cash flows from operating activities section of Azure's 2002 statement of cash flows using the indirect method.

BE24-6 At January 1, 2002, Cyberslider Inc. had accounts receivable of $72,000. At December 31, 2002, accounts receivable is $59,000. Sales for 2002 is $420,000. Compute Cyberslider's 2002 cash receipts from customers.

BE24-7 Donkey Kong Corporation had January 1 and December 31 balances as follows:

	1/1/02	12/31/02
Inventory	$90,000	$113,000
Accounts payable	61,000	69,000

For 2002, cost of goods sold was $500,000. Compute Donkey Kong's 2002 cash payments to suppliers.

BE24-8 In 2002, Fieval Corporation had net cash provided by operating activities of $531,000; net cash used by investing activities of $963,000; and net cash provided by financing activities of $585,000. At January 1, 2002, the cash balance was $333,000. Compute December 31, 2002, cash.

BE24-9 Tool Time Corporation had the following 2002 income statement:

Revenues	$100,000
Expenses	60,000
	$ 40,000

In 2002, Tool Time had the following activity in selected accounts:

Accounts Receivable					**Allowance for Doubtful Accounts**			
1/1/02	20,000						1,200	1/1/02
Revenues	100,000	1,000	Writeoffs	Writeoffs	1,000		1,540	Bad debt expense
		90,000	Collections					
12/31/02	29,000						1,740	12/31/02

Prepare Tool Time's cash flows from operating activities section of the statement of cash flows using (a) the direct method and (b) the indirect method.

BE24-10 Red October Corporation reported net income of $50,000 in 2002. Depreciation expense was $17,000. The following working capital accounts changed:

Accounts receivable	$11,000	increase
Available-for-sale securities	16,000	increase
Inventory	7,400	increase
Nontrade note payable	15,000	decrease
Accounts payable	9,300	increase

Compute net cash provided by operating activities.

BE24-11 In 2002, Izzy Corporation reported a net loss of $70,000. Izzy's only net income adjustments were depreciation expense, $84,000, and increase in accounts receivable, $8,100. Compute Izzy's net cash provided (used) by operating activities.

BE24-12 In 2002, Mufosta Inc. issued 1,000 shares of $10 par value common stock for land worth $50,000.

(a) Prepare Mufosta's journal entry to record the transaction.
(b) Indicate the effect the transaction has on cash.
(c) Indicate how the transaction is reported on the statement of cash flows.

BE24-13 Indicate in general journal form how the items below would be entered in a work sheet for the preparation of the statement of cash flows.

(a) Net income is $317,000.
(b) Cash dividends declared and paid totaled $120,000.
(c) Equipment was purchased for $114,000.
(d) Equipment that originally cost $40,000 and had accumulated depreciation of $32,000 was sold for $13,000.

EXERCISES

E24-1 **(Classification of Transactions)** Red Hot Chili Peppers Co. had the following activity in its most recent year of operations:

(a) Purchase of equipment.
(b) Redemption of bonds.
(c) Sale of building.
(d) Depreciation.
(e) Exchange of equipment for furniture.
(f) Issuance of capital stock.
(g) Amortization of intangible assets.
(h) Purchase of treasury stock.
(i) Issuance of bonds for land.
(j) Payment of dividends.
(k) Increase in interest receivable on notes receivable.
(l) Pension expense exceeds amount funded.

Instructions
Classify the items as (1) operating—add to net income; (2) operating—deduct from net income; (3) investing; (4) financing; or (5) significant noncash investing and financing activities (use indirect method).

E24-2 **(Statement Presentation of Transactions—Indirect Method)** Each of the following items must be considered in preparing a statement of cash flows (indirect method) for Turbulent Indigo Inc. for the year ended December 31, 2001.

(a) Plant assets that had cost $20,000 6 years before and were being depreciated on a straight-line basis over 10 years with no estimated scrap value were sold for $5,300.
(b) During the year, 10,000 shares of common stock with a stated value of $10 a share were issued for $43 a share.
(c) Uncollectible accounts receivable in the amount of $27,000 were written off against the Allowance for Doubtful Accounts.
(d) The company sustained a net loss for the year of $50,000. Depreciation amounted to $22,000, and a gain of $9,000 was realized on the sale of land for $39,000 cash.
(e) A 3-month U.S. Treasury bill was purchased for $100,000. The company uses a cash and cash-equivalent basis for its cash flow statement.
(f) Goodwill amortized for the year was $20,000.
(g) The company exchanged common stock for a 70% interest in Tabasco Co. for $900,000.
(h) During the year, treasury stock costing $47,000 was purchased.

Instructions
State where each item is to be shown in the statement of cash flows, if at all.

E24-3 **(Preparation of Operating Activities Section—Indirect Method, Periodic Inventory)** The income statement of Vince Gill Company is shown below:

VINCE GILL COMPANY
Income Statement
For the Year Ended December 31, 2002

Sales		$6,900,000
Cost of goods sold		
Beginning inventory	$1,900,000	
Purchases	4,400,000	
Goods available for sale	6,300,000	
Ending inventory	1,600,000	
Cost of goods sold		4,700,000
Gross profit		2,200,000
Operating expenses		
Selling expenses	450,000	
Administrative expenses	700,000	1,150,000
Net income		$1,050,000

Additional information:

1. Accounts receivable decreased $360,000 during the year.
2. Prepaid expenses increased $170,000 during the year.
3. Accounts payable to suppliers of merchandise decreased $275,000 during the year.
4. Accrued expenses payable decreased $100,000 during the year.
5. Administrative expenses include depreciation expense of $60,000.

Instructions

Prepare the operating activities section of the statement of cash flows for the year ended December 31, 2002, for Vince Gill Company, using the indirect method.

E24-4 (Preparation of Operating Activities Section—Direct Method) Data for the Vince Gill Company are presented in E24-3.

Instructions

Prepare the operating activities section of the statement of cash flows using the direct method.

E24-5 (Preparation of Operating Activities Section—Direct Method) Alison Krauss Company's income statement for the year ended December 31, 2001, contained the following condensed information:

Revenue from fees		$840,000
Operating expenses (excluding depreciation)	$624,000	
Depreciation expense	60,000	
Loss on sale of equipment	26,000	710,000
Income before income taxes		130,000
Income tax expense		40,000
Net income		$ 90,000

Krauss's balance sheet contained the following comparative data at December 31:

	2001	2000
Accounts receivable	$37,000	$54,000
Accounts payable	41,000	31,000
Income taxes payable	4,000	8,500

(Accounts payable pertains to operating expenses.)

Instructions

Prepare the operating activities section of the statement of cash flows using the direct method.

E24-6 (Preparation of Operating Activities Section—Indirect Method) Data for Alison Krauss Company are presented in E24-5.

Instructions

Prepare the operating activities section of the statement of cash flows using the indirect method.

E24-7 (Computation of Operating Activities—Direct Method) Presented below are two independent situations:

Situation A:

Annie Lennox Co. reports revenues of $200,000 and operating expenses of $110,000 in its first year of operations, 2002. Accounts receivable and accounts payable at year-end were $71,000 and $29,000, respectively. Assume that the accounts payable related to operating expenses. Ignore income taxes.

Instructions

Using the direct method, compute net cash provided by operating activities.

Situation B:

The income statement for Blues Traveler Company shows cost of goods sold $310,000 and operating expenses (exclusive of depreciation) $230,000. The comparative balance sheet for the year shows that inventory increased $26,000, prepaid expenses decreased $8,000, accounts payable (related to merchandise) decreased $17,000, and accrued expenses payable increased $11,000.

Instructions

Compute (a) cash payments to suppliers and (b) cash payments for operating expenses.

E24-8 (Schedule of Net Cash Flow from Operating Activities—Indirect Method) Glen Ballard Co. reported $145,000 of net income for 2002. The accountant, in preparing the statement of cash flows, noted several items that might affect cash flows from operating activities. These items are listed below:

1. During 2002, Ballard purchased 100 shares of treasury stock at a cost of $20 per share. These shares were then resold at $25 per share.
2. During 2002, Ballard sold 100 shares of IBM common at $200 per share. The acquisition cost of these shares was $145 per share. This investment was shown on Ballard's December 31, 2001, balance sheet as an available-for-sale security.
3. During 2002, Ballard changed from the straight-line method to the double-declining balance method of depreciation for its machinery. The total cumulative effect was for $14,600.
4. During 2002, Ballard revised its estimate for bad debts. Before 2002, Ballard's bad debt expense was 1% of its net sales. In 2002, this percentage was increased to 2%. Net sales for 2002 were $500,000, and net accounts receivable decreased by $12,000 during 2002.
5. During 2002, Ballard issued 500 shares of its $10 par common stock for a patent. The market value of the shares on the date of the transaction was $23 per share.
6. Depreciation expense for 2002 is $39,000.
7. Ballard Co. holds 40% of the Nirvana Company's common stock as a long-term investment. Nirvana Company reported $27,000 of net income for 2002.
8. Nirvana Company paid a total of $2,000 of cash dividends to all investees in 2002.
9. During 2002, Ballard declared a 10% stock dividend. One thousand shares of $10 par common stock were distributed. The market price at date of issuance was $20 per share.

Instructions

Prepare a schedule that shows the net cash flow from operating activities using the indirect method. Assume no items other than those listed above affected the computation of 2002 net cash flow from operating activities.

E24-9 (SCF—Direct Method) Los Lobos Corp. uses the direct method to prepare its statement of cash flows. Los Lobos's trial balances at December 31, 2001 and 2000, are as follows:

	December 31	
	2001	2000
Debits		
Cash	$ 35,000	$ 32,000
Accounts receivable	33,000	30,000
Inventory	31,000	47,000
Property, plant, & equipment	100,000	95,000
Unamortized bond discount	4,500	5,000
Cost of goods sold	250,000	380,000
Selling expenses	141,500	172,000
General and administrative expenses	137,000	151,300
Interest expense	4,300	2,600
Income tax expense	20,400	61,200
	$756,700	$976,100
Credits		
Allowance for doubtful accounts	$ 1,300	$ 1,100
Accumulated depreciation	16,500	15,000
Trade accounts payable	25,000	15,500
Income taxes payable	21,000	29,100
Deferred income taxes	5,300	4,600
8% callable bonds payable	45,000	20,000
Common stock	50,000	40,000
Additional paid-in capital	9,100	7,500
Retained earnings	44,700	64,600
Sales	538,800	778,700
	$756,700	$976,100

Additional information:

1. Los Lobos purchased $5,000 in equipment during 2001.
2. Los Lobos allocated one-third of its depreciation expense to selling expenses and the remainder to general and administrative expenses.
3. Bad debt expense for 2001 was $5,000, and writeoffs of uncollectible accounts totaled $4,800.

Instructions

Determine what amounts Los Lobos should report in its statement of cash flows for the year ended December 31, 2001, for the following:

1. Cash collected from customers.
2. Cash paid to suppliers.
3. Cash paid for interest.
4. Cash paid for income taxes.
5. Cash paid for selling expenses.

E24-10 **(Classification of Transactions)** Following are selected balance sheet accounts of Allman Bros. Corp. at December 31, 2002 and 2001, and the increases or decreases in each account from 2001 to 2002. Also presented is selected income statement information for the year ended December 31, 2002, and additional information.

Selected balance sheet accounts	2002	2001	Increase (Decrease)
Assets			
Accounts receivable	$ 34,000	$ 24,000	$ 10,000
Property, plant, and equipment	277,000	247,000	30,000
Accumulated depreciation	(178,000)	(167,000)	(11,000)
Liabilities and stockholders' equity			
Bonds payable	49,000	46,000	3,000
Dividends payable	8,000	5,000	3,000
Common stock, $1 par	22,000	19,000	3,000
Additional paid-in capital	9,000	3,000	6,000
Retained earnings	104,000	91,000	13,000

Selected income statement information for the year ended December 31, 2002	
Sales revenue	$155,000
Depreciation	33,000
Gain on sale of equipment	14,500
Net income	31,000

Additional information:

1. During 2002, equipment costing $45,000 was sold for cash.
2. Accounts receivable relate to sales of merchandise.
3. During 2002, $20,000 of bonds payable were issued in exchange for property, plant, and equipment. There was no amortization of bond discount or premium.

Instructions

Determine the category (operating, investing, or financing) and the amount that should be reported in the statement of cash flows for the following items:

1. Payments for purchase of property, plant, and equipment.
2. Proceeds from the sale of equipment.
3. Cash dividends paid.
4. Redemption of bonds payable.

E24-11 **(SCF—Indirect Method)** Condensed financial data of Pat Metheny Company for 2002 and 2001 are presented below.

PAT METHENY COMPANY
Comparative Balance Sheet
As of December 31, 2002 and 2001

	2002	2001
Cash	$1,800	$1,150
Receivables	1,750	1,300
Inventory	1,600	1,900
Plant assets	1,900	1,700
Accumulated depreciation	(1,200)	(1,170)
Long-term investments (Held-to-maturity)	1,300	1,420
	$7,150	$6,300
Accounts payable	$1,200	$ 900
Accrued liabilities	200	250
Bonds payable	1,400	1,550
Capital stock	1,900	1,700
Retained earnings	2,450	1,900
	$7,150	$6,300

PAT METHENY COMPANY
Income Statement
For the Year Ended December 31, 2002

Sales	$6,900
Cost of goods sold	4,700
Gross margin	2,200
Selling and administrative expense	930
Income from operations	1,270
Other revenues and gains	
Gain on sale of investments	80
Income before tax	1,350
Income tax expense	540
Net income	810
Cash dividends	260
Income retained in business	$ 550

Additional information:

During the year, $70 of common stock was issued in exchange for plant assets. No plant assets were sold in 2002.

Instructions
Prepare a statement of cash flows using the indirect method.

E24-12 (SCF—Direct Method) Data for Pat Metheny Company are presented in E24-11.

Instructions
Prepare a statement of cash flows using the direct method. (Do not prepare a reconciliation schedule.)

E24-13 (SCF—Indirect Method) Condensed financial data of McCoy Tyner Company for the years ended December 31, 2002, and December 31, 2001, are presented below.

MCCOY TYNER COMPANY
Comparative Balance Sheet
As of December 31, 2002 and 2001

	2002	2001
Cash	$160,800	$ 38,400
Receivables	123,200	49,000
Inventories	112,500	57,900
Investments (Available-for-sale)	90,000	101,000
Plant assets	240,000	212,500
	$726,500	$458,800
Accounts payable	$100,000	$ 65,200
Mortgage payable	50,000	77,000
Accumulated depreciation	30,000	52,000
Common stock	175,000	131,100
Retained earnings	371,500	133,500
	$726,500	$458,800

MCCOY TYNER COMPANY
Income Statement
For the Year Ended December 31, 2002

Sales	$440,000	
Interest and other revenue	20,000	$460,000
(Includes gain on sale of investments of $5,000)		

Less:		
Cost of goods sold	130,000	
Selling and administrative expenses	10,000	
Depreciation	42,000	
Income taxes	5,000	
Interest charges	3,000	
Loss on sale of plant assets	12,000	202,000
Net income		258,000
Cash dividends		20,000
Income retained in business		$238,000

Additional information:
New plant assets costing $85,000 were purchased during the year. Common stock of $20,000 was issued in exchange for plant assets. Investments were sold during the year. No unrealized gains or losses have occurred in these securities.

Instructions
Prepare a statement of cash flows using the indirect method.

E24-14 (SCF—Direct Method) Data for McCoy Tyner Company are presented in E24-13.

Instructions
Prepare a statement of cash flows using the direct method. (Do not prepare a reconciliation schedule.)

E24-15 (SCF—Direct Method) Brecker Inc., a greeting card company, had the following statements prepared as of December 31, 2002.

BRECKER INC.
Comparative Balance Sheet
As of December 31, 2002 and 2001

	12/31/02	12/31/01
Cash	$ 6,000	$ 7,000
Accounts receivable	62,000	51,000
Short-term investments (Available-for-sale)	35,000	18,000
Inventories	40,000	60,000
Prepaid rent	5,000	4,000
Printing equipment	154,000	130,000
Accumulated depr.—equipment	(35,000)	(25,000)
Goodwill	46,000	50,000
Total assets	$313,000	$295,000
Accounts payable	$ 46,000	$ 40,000
Income taxes payable	4,000	6,000
Wages payable	8,000	4,000
Short-term loans payable	8,000	10,000
Long-term loans payable	60,000	69,000
Common stock, $10 par	100,000	100,000
Contributed capital, common stock	30,000	30,000
Retained earnings	57,000	36,000
Total liabilities & equity	$313,000	$295,000

BRECKER INC.
Income Statement
For the Year Ending December 31, 2002

Sales	$338,150
Cost of goods sold	175,000
Gross margin	163,150
Operating expenses	120,000
Operating income	43,150

Interest expense	$11,400	
Gain on sale of equipment	2,000	9,400
Income before tax		33,750
Income tax expense		6,750
Net income		$ 27,000

Additional information:

1. Dividends in the amount of $6,000 were declared and paid during 2002.
2. Depreciation expense and amortization expense are included in operating expenses.
3. No unrealized gains or losses have occurred on the investments during the year.
4. Equipment that had a cost of $20,000 and was 70% depreciated was sold during 2002.

Instructions

Prepare a statement of cash flows using the direct method. (Do not prepare a reconciliation schedule.)

E24-16   (SCF—Indirect Method)   Data for Brecker Inc. are presented in E24-15.

Instructions

Prepare a statement of cash flows using the indirect method.

E24-17   (SCF—Indirect Method)   Presented below are data taken from the records of Antonio Brasileiro Company.

	December 31, 2002	December 31, 2001
Cash	$ 15,000	$ 8,000
Current assets other than cash	85,000	60,000
Long-term investments	10,000	53,000
Plant assets	335,000	215,000
	$445,000	$336,000
Accumulated depreciation	$ 20,000	$ 40,000
Current liabilities	40,000	22,000
Bonds payable	75,000	–0–
Capital stock	254,000	254,000
Retained earnings	56,000	20,000
	$445,000	$336,000

Additional information:

1. Held-to-maturity securities carried at a cost of $43,000 on December 31, 2001, were sold in 2002 for $34,000. The loss (not extraordinary) was incorrectly charged directly to Retained Earnings.
2. Plant assets that cost $50,000 and were 80% depreciated were sold during 2002 for $8,000. The loss (not extraordinary) was incorrectly charged directly to Retained Earnings.
3. Net income as reported on the income statement for the year was $57,000.
4. Dividends paid amounted to $10,000.
5. Depreciation charged for the year was $20,000.

Instructions

Prepare a statement of cash flows for the year 2002 using the indirect method.

E24-18   (Cash Provided by Operating, Investing, and Financing Activities)   The balance sheet data of Brown Company at the end of 2001 and 2000 follow:

	2001	2000
Cash	$ 30,000	$ 35,000
Accounts receivable (net)	55,000	45,000
Merchandise inventory	65,000	45,000
Prepaid expenses	15,000	25,000
Equipment	90,000	75,000
Accumulated depreciation—equipment	(18,000)	(8,000)
Land	70,000	40,000
Totals	$307,000	$257,000

Accounts payable	$ 65,000	$ 52,000
Accrued expenses	15,000	18,000
Notes payable—bank, long-term	–0–	23,000
Bonds payable	30,000	–0–
Common stock, $10 par	189,000	159,000
Retained earnings	8,000	5,000
	$307,000	$257,000

Land was acquired for $30,000 in exchange for common stock, par $30,000, during the year; all equipment purchased was for cash. Equipment costing $10,000 was sold for $3,000; book value of the equipment was $6,000. Cash dividends of $10,000 were declared and paid during the year.

Instructions

Compute net cash provided (used) by:
- **(a)** operating activities.
- **(b)** investing activities.
- **(c)** financing activities.

E24-19 (SCF—Indirect Method and Balance Sheet)   Jobim Inc., had the following condensed balance sheet at the end of operations for 2001.

JOBIM INC.
Balance Sheet
December 31, 2001

Cash	$ 8,500		Current liabilities	$ 15,000
Current assets other than cash	29,000		Long-term notes payable	25,500
Investments	20,000		Bonds payable	25,000
Plant assets (net)	67,500		Capital stock	75,000
Land	40,000		Retained earnings	24,500
	$165,000			$165,000

During 2002 the following occurred:

1. A tract of land was purchased for $9,000.
2. Bonds payable in the amount of $15,000 were retired at par.
3. An additional $10,000 in capital stock was issued at par.
4. Dividends totaling $9,375 were paid to stockholders.
5. Net income for 2002 was $35,250 after allowing depreciation of $13,500.
6. Land was purchased through the issuance of $22,500 in bonds.
7. Jobim Inc. sold part of its investment portfolio for $12,875. This transaction resulted in a gain of $2,000 for the firm. The company classifies the investments as available-for-sale.
8. Both current assets (other than cash) and current liabilities remained at the same amount.

Instructions

- **(a)** Prepare a statement of cash flows for 2002 using the indirect method.
- **(b)** Prepare the condensed balance sheet for Jobim Inc. as it would appear at December 31, 2002.

E24-20 (Partial SCF—Indirect Method)   The accounts below appear in the ledger of Anita Baker Company.

Retained Earnings		Dr.	Cr.	Bal.
Jan. 1, 2002	Credit Balance			$ 42,000
Aug. 15	Dividends (cash)	$15,000		27,000
Dec. 31	Net Income for 2002		$40,000	67,000

Machinery		Dr.	Cr.	Bal.
Jan. 1, 2002	Debit Balance			$140,000
Aug. 3	Purchase of Machinery	$62,000		202,000
Sept. 10	Cost of Machinery Constructed	48,000		250,000
Nov. 15	Machinery Sold		$56,000	194,000

Accumulated Depreciation—Machinery		Dr.	Cr.	Bal.
Jan. 1, 2002	Credit Balance			$ 84,000
Apr. 8	Extraordinary Repairs	$21,000		63,000
Nov. 15	Accum. Depreciation on Machinery Sold	25,200		37,800
Dec. 31	Depreciation for 2002		$16,800	54,600

Instructions

From the postings in the accounts above, indicate how the information is reported on a statement of cash flows by preparing a partial statement of cash flows using the indirect method. The loss on sale of equipment (November 15) was $5,800.

E24-21 (Work Sheet Analysis of Selected Accounts) Data for Anita Baker Company are presented in E24-20.

Instructions

Prepare entries in journal form for all adjustments that should be made on a work sheet for a statement of cash flows.

E24-22 (Work Sheet Analysis of Selected Transactions) The transactions below took place during the year 2002:

1. Convertible bonds payable with a par value of $300,000 were exchanged for unissued common stock with a par value of $300,000. The market price of both types of securities was par.
2. The net income for the year was $410,000.
3. Depreciation charged on the building was $90,000.
4. The Appropriations for Bond Indebtedness in the amount of $300,000 was returned to Retained Earnings during the year, because the bonds were retired during the year.
5. Some old office equipment was traded in on the purchase of some dissimilar office equipment and the following entry was made:

Office Equipment	50,000	
Accum. Depreciation—Office Equipment	30,000	
Office Equipment		40,000
Cash		34,000
Gain on Disposal of Plant Assets		6,000

   The Gain on Disposal of Plant Assets was credited to current operations as ordinary income.
6. Dividends in the amount of $123,000 were declared. They are payable in January of next year.

Instructions

Show by journal entries the adjustments that would be made on a work sheet for a statement of cash flows.

E24-23 (Work Sheet Preparation) Below is the comparative balance sheet for Stevie Wonder Corporation.

	Dec. 31, 2002	Dec. 31, 2001
Cash	$ 16,500	$ 21,000
Short-term investments	25,000	19,000
Accounts receivable	43,000	45,000
Allowance for doubtful accounts	(1,800)	(2,000)
Prepaid expenses	4,200	2,500
Inventories	81,500	65,000
Land	50,000	50,000
Buildings	125,000	73,500
Accumulated depreciation—buildings	(30,000)	(23,000)
Equipment	53,000	46,000
Accumulated depreciation—equipment	(19,000)	(15,500)
Delivery equipment	39,000	39,000
Accumulated depreciation—delivery equipment	(22,000)	(20,500)
Patents	15,000	-0-
	$379,400	$300,000

Accounts payable	$ 26,000	$ 16,000
Short-term notes payable	4,000	6,000
Accrued payables	3,000	4,600
Mortgage payable	73,000	53,400
Bonds payable	50,000	62,500
Capital stock	140,000	102,000
Additional paid-in capital	10,000	4,000
Retained earnings	73,400	51,500
	$379,400	$300,000

Dividends in the amount of $15,000 were declared and paid in 2002.

Instructions

From this information, prepare a work sheet for a statement of cash flows. Make reasonable assumptions as appropriate. The short-term investments are considered available-for-sale and no unrealized gains or losses have occurred on these securities.

E24-24   (Explain Changes in Cash Flow)   Ellwood House, Inc. had the following condensed balance sheet at the end of operations for 2000.

ELLWOOD HOUSE, INC.
Balance Sheet
December 31, 2000

Cash	$ 10,000	Current liabilities	$ 14,500
Current assets (noncash)	34,000	Long-term notes payable	30,000
Investments (available-for-sale)	40,000	Bonds payable	32,000
Plant assets	57,500	Capital stock	80,000
Land	38,500	Retained earnings	23,500
	$180,000		$180,000

During 2001 the following occurred:

1. Ellwood House, Inc., sold part of its investment portfolio for $15,500, resulting in a gain of $500 for the firm. The company often sells and buys securities of this nature.
2. Dividends totaling $19,000 were paid to stockholders.
3. A parcel of land was purchased for $5,500.
4. $20,000 of capital stock was issued at par.
5. $10,000 of bonds payable were retired at par.
6. Heavy equipment was purchased through the issuance of $32,000 of bonds.
7. Net income for 2001 was $42,000 after allowing depreciation of $13,550.
8. Both current assets (other than cash) and current liabilities remained at the same amount.

Instructions

(a) Prepare a statement of cash flows for 2001 using the indirect method.
(b) Draft a one-page letter to Mr. Gerald Brauer, president of Ellwood House, Inc., briefly explaining the changes within each major cash flow category. Refer to your cash flow statement whenever necessary.

PROBLEMS

P24-1   (SCF—Indirect Method)   The following is Method Man Corp.'s comparative balance sheet accounts worksheet at December 31, 2002 and 2001, with a column showing the increase (decrease) from 2001 to 2002.

Comparative Balance Sheet

	2002	2001	Increase (Decrease)
Cash	$ 807,500	$ 700,000	$107,500
Accounts receivable	1,128,000	1,168,000	(40,000)
Inventories	1,850,000	1,715,000	135,000
Property, plant and equipment	3,307,000	2,967,000	340,000
Accumulated depreciation	(1,165,000)	(1,040,000)	(125,000)
Investment in Blige Co.	305,000	275,000	30,000
Loan receivable	262,500	—	262,500
Total assets	$6,495,000	$5,785,000	$710,000
Accounts payable	$1,015,000	$ 955,000	$ 60,000
Income taxes payable	30,000	50,000	(20,000)
Dividends payable	80,000	100,000	(20,000)
Capital lease obligation	400,000	—	400,000
Capital stock, common, $1 par	500,000	500,000	—
Additional paid-in capital	1,500,000	1,500,000	—
Retained earnings	2,970,000	2,680,000	290,000
Total liabilities and stockholders' equity	$6,495,000	$5,785,000	$710,000

Additional information:

1. On December 31, 2001, Method Man acquired 25% of Blige Co.'s common stock for $275,000. On that date, the carrying value of Blige's assets and liabilities, which approximated their fair values, was $1,100,000. Blige reported income of $120,000 for the year ended December 31, 2002. No dividend was paid on Blige's common stock during the year.
2. During 2002, Method Man loaned $300,000 to TLC Co., an unrelated company. TLC made the first semi-annual principal repayment of $37,500, plus interest at 10%, on December 31, 2002.
3. On January 2, 2002, Method Man sold equipment costing $60,000, with a carrying amount of $35,000, for $40,000 cash.
4. On December 31, 2002, Method Man entered into a capital lease for an office building. The present value of the annual rental payments is $400,000, which equals the fair value of the building. Method Man made the first rental payment of $60,000 when due on January 2, 2003.
5. Net income for 2002 was $370,000.
6. Method Man declared and paid cash dividends for 2002 and 2001 as follows:

	2002	2001
Declared	December 15, 2002	December 15, 2001
Paid	February 28, 2003	February 28, 2002
Amount	$80,000	$100,000

Instructions

Prepare a statement of cash flows for Method Man, Inc. for the year ended December 31, 2002, using the indirect method.

(AICPA adapted)

P24-2 (SCF—Indirect Method) The comparative balance sheets for Shenandoah Corporation show the following information:

	December 31	
	2002	2001
Cash	$ 38,500	$13,000
Accounts receivable	12,250	10,000
Inventory	12,000	9,000
Investments	–0–	3,000
Building	–0–	29,750
Equipment	40,000	20,000
Patent	5,000	6,250
Totals	$107,750	$91,000

Allowance for doubtful accounts	$3,000	$4,500
Accumulated depreciation on equipment	2,000	4,500
Accumulated depreciation on building	–0–	6,000
Accounts payable	5,000	3,000
Dividends payable	–0–	5,000
Notes payable, short-term (nontrade)	3,000	4,000
Long-term notes payable	31,000	25,000
Common stock	43,000	33,000
Retained earnings	20,750	6,000
	$107,750	$91,000

Additional data related to 2002 are as follows:

1. Equipment that had cost $11,000 and was 30% depreciated at time of disposal was sold for $2,500.
2. $10,000 of the long-term note payable was paid by issuing common stock.
3. Cash dividends paid were $5,000.
4. On January 1, 2002, the building was completely destroyed by a flood. Insurance proceeds on the building were $30,000 (net of $2,000 taxes).
5. Investments (available-for-sale) were sold at $3,700 above their cost. The company has made similar sales and investments in the past.
6. Cash of $15,000 was paid for the acquisition of equipment.
7. A long-term note for $16,000 was issued for the acquisition of equipment.
8. Interest of $2,000 and income taxes of $6,500 were paid in cash.

Instructions
Prepare a statement of cash flows using the indirect method. Flood damage is unusual and infrequent in that part of the country.

P24-3 (SCF—Direct Method)   Mardi Gras Company has not yet prepared a formal statement of cash flows for the 2002 fiscal year. Comparative balance sheets as of December 31, 2001 and 2002, and a statement of income and retained earnings for the year ended December 31, 2002, are presented below.

MARDI GRAS COMPANY
Statement of Income and Retained Earnings
Year Ended December 31, 2002
($000 omitted)

Sales		$3,800
Expenses		
Cost of goods sold	$1,200	
Salaries and benefits	725	
Heat, light, and power	75	
Depreciation	80	
Property taxes	19	
Patent amortization	25	
Miscellaneous expenses	10	
Interest	30	2,164
Income before income taxes		1,636
Income taxes		818
Net income		818
Retained earnings—Jan. 1, 2002		310
		1,128
Stock dividend declared and issued		600
Retained earnings—Dec. 31, 2002		$ 528

MARDI GRAS COMPANY
Comparative Balance Sheet
December 31
($000 omitted)

Assets	2002	2001
Current assets		
Cash	$ 383	$ 100
U.S. Treasury notes (Available-for-sale)	–0–	50
Accounts receivable	740	500
Inventory	720	560
Total current assets	1,843	1,210
Long-term assets		
Land	150	70
Buildings and equipment	910	600
Accumulated depreciation	(200)	(120)
Patents (less amortization)	105	130
Total long-term assets	965	680
Total assets	$2,808	$1,890
Liabilities and Stockholders' Equity		
Current liabilities		
Accounts payable	$ 420	$ 340
Income taxes payable	40	20
Notes payable	320	320
Total current liabilities	780	680
Long-term notes payable—due 2004	200	200
Total liabilities	980	880
Stockholders' equity		
Common stock outstanding	1,300	700
Retained earnings	528	310
Total stockholders' equity	1,828	1,010
Total liabilities and stockholders' equity	$2,808	$1,890

Instructions
Prepare a statement of cash flows using the direct method. Changes in accounts receivable and accounts payable relate to sales and cost of sales. Do not prepare a reconciliation schedule.

(CMA adapted)

P24-4 (SCF—Direct Method) Ashley Cleveland Company had the following information available at the end of 2001:

ASHLEY CLEVELAND COMPANY
Comparative Balance Sheet
As of December 31, 2001 and 2000

	2001	2000
Cash	$ 15,000	$ 4,000
Accounts receivable	17,500	12,950
Short-term investments	20,000	30,000
Inventory	42,000	35,000
Prepaid rent	3,000	12,000
Prepaid insurance	2,100	900
Office supplies	1,000	750
Land	125,000	175,000
Building	350,000	350,000
Accumulated depreciation	(105,000)	(87,500)
Equipment	525,000	400,000
Accumulated depreciation	(130,000)	(112,000)
Patent	45,000	50,000
Total assets	$910,600	$871,100

Accounts payable	$ 27,000	$ 32,000
Taxes payable	5,000	4,000
Wages payable	5,000	3,000
Short-term notes payable	10,000	10,000
Long-term notes payable	60,000	70,000
Bonds payable	400,000	400,000
Premium on bonds payable	20,303	25,853
Common stock	240,000	220,000
Paid-in capital in excess of par	20,000	17,500
Retained earnings	123,297	88,747
Total liabilities and equity	$910,600	$871,100

ASHLEY CLEVELAND COMPANY
Income Statement
For the Year Ended December 31, 2001

Sales revenue		$1,160,000
Cost of goods sold		(748,000)
		412,000
Gross margin		
Operating expenses		
Selling expenses	$ 79,200	
Administrative expenses	156,700	
Depreciation/Amortization expense	40,500	
Total operating expenses		(276,400)
Income from operations		135,600
Other revenues/expenses		
Gain on sale of land	8,000	
Gain on sale of short-term investment	4,000	
Dividend revenue	2,400	
Interest expense	(51,750)	(37,350)
Income before taxes		98,250
Income tax expense		(39,400)
Net income		58,850
Dividends to common stockholders		(24,300)
To retained earnings		$ 34,550

Instructions

Prepare a statement of cash flows for Ashley Cleveland Company using the direct method accompanied by a reconciliation schedule. Assume the short-term investments are available-for-sale securities.

P24-5 (SCF—Indirect Method) Michael W. Smith Inc. had the following information available at the end of 2001:

MICHAEL W. SMITH INC.
Comparative Balance Sheet
As of December 31, 2001 and 2000

	2001	2000
Cash	$ 46,000	$ 30,000
Accounts receivable	330,000	296,000
Short-term investments (available-for-sale)	360,000	325,000
Prepaid insurance	16,000	22,000
Merchandise inventory	400,000	350,000
Office supplies	4,000	7,000
Long-term investments (equity)	775,000	700,000
Land	665,000	500,000
Building	1,300,000	1,300,000
Accumulated depreciation—building	(400,000)	(360,000)

Equipment	500,000	550,000
Accumulated depreciation—equipment	(155,000)	(135,000)
Goodwill	63,000	65,000
Total assets	$3,904,000	$3,650,000
Accounts payable	$ 95,000	$ 70,000
Taxes payable	26,000	15,000
Accrued liabilities	47,000	40,000
Dividends payable	–0–	80,000
Long-term notes payable	45,000	50,000
Bonds payable	1,000,000	1,000,000
Discount on bonds payable	(50,750)	(64,630)
Preferred stock	600,000	500,000
Contributed capital, preferred stock	135,000	100,000
Common stock	600,000	600,000
Contributed capital, common stock	550,000	550,000
Retained earnings	876,750	749,630
Treasury stock (common, at cost)	(20,000)	(40,000)
Total liabilities and equity	$3,904,000	$3,650,000

MICHAEL W. SMITH INC.
Income Statement
For the Year Ended December 31, 2001

Sales revenue		$1,007,500
Cost of goods sold		403,000
Gross profit		604,500
Selling/administrative expenses		222,087
Income from operations		382,413
Other revenues/expenses		
Long-term investment revenue	$115,000	
Short-term investment dividend	15,000	
Gain on sale of equipment	15,000	145,000
Interest expense		(98,880)
Income before taxes		428,533
Income tax expense		(171,413)
Net income		257,120
Dividends (current year)		(130,000)
Increase in retained earnings		$ 127,120

Additional information:

1. In early January, equipment with a book value of $45,000 was sold for a gain.
2. Long-term investments are carried under the equity method; Smith's share of investee income totaled $115,000 in 2001. Smith received dividends from its long-term investment totaling $40,000 during 2001.
3. No unrealized gains or losses on available-for-sale securities occurred during the year.

Instructions
Prepare a statement of cash flows using the indirect method.

P24-6 (SCF—Direct Method) Data for Michael W. Smith Inc. are presented in P24-5.

Instructions
Prepare a statement of cash flows using the direct method.

P24-7 (SCF—Indirect Method) You have completed the field work in connection with your audit of Shirley Caesar Corporation for the year ended December 31, 2002. The following schedule shows the balance sheet accounts at the beginning and end of the year.

	Dec. 31, 2002	Dec. 31, 2001	Increase or (Decrease)
Cash	$ 267,900	$ 298,000	($30,100)
Accounts receivable	479,424	353,000	126,424
Inventory	741,700	610,000	131,700
Prepaid expenses	12,000	8,000	4,000
Investment in subsidiary	110,500	–0–	110,500
Cash surrender value of life insurance	2,304	1,800	504
Machinery	207,000	190,000	17,000
Buildings	535,200	407,900	127,300
Land	52,500	52,500	–0–
Patents	69,000	64,000	5,000
Goodwill	40,000	50,000	(10,000)
Bond discount and expense	4,502	–0–	4,502
	$2,522,030	$2,035,200	$486,830
Accrued taxes payable	$ 90,250	$ 79,600	$ 10,650
Accounts payable	299,280	280,000	19,280
Dividends payable	70,000	–0–	70,000
Bonds payable—8%	125,000	–0–	125,000
Bonds payable—12%	–0–	100,000	(100,000)
Allowance for doubtful accounts	35,300	40,000	(4,700)
Accumulated depreciation—buildings	424,000	400,000	24,000
Accumulated depreciation—machinery	173,000	130,000	43,000
Premium on bonds payable	–0–	2,400	(2,400)
Capital stock—no par	1,176,200	1,453,200	(277,000)
Additional paid-in capital	109,000	–0–	109,000
Appropriation for plant expansion	10,000	–0–	10,000
Retained earnings—unappropriated	10,000	(450,000)	460,000
	$2,522,030	$2,035,200	$486,830

Statement of Retained Earnings

January 1, 2002	Balance (deficit)	$(450,000)
March 31, 2002	Net income for first quarter of 2002	25,000
April 1, 2002	Transfer from paid-in capital	425,000
	Balance	–0–
December 31, 2002	Net income for last three quarters of 2002	90,000
	Dividend declared—payable January 21, 2003	(70,000)
	Appropriation for plant expansion	(10,000)
	Balance	$ 10,000

Your working papers contain the following information:

1. On April 1, 2002, the existing deficit was written off against paid-in capital created by reducing the stated value of the no-par stock.
2. On November 1, 2002, 29,600 shares of no-par stock were sold for $257,000. The board of directors voted to regard $5 per share as stated capital.
3. A patent was purchased for $15,000.
4. During the year, machinery that had a cost basis of $16,400 and on which there was accumulated depreciation of $5,200 was sold for $7,000. No other plant assets were sold during the year.
5. The 12%, 20-year bonds were dated and issued on January 2, 1990. Interest was payable on June 30 and December 31. They were sold originally at 106. These bonds were retired at 102 (net of $100 tax) plus accrued interest on March 31, 2002.
6. The 8%, 40-year bonds were dated January 1, 2002, and were sold on March 31 at 97 plus accrued interest. Interest is payable semiannually on June 30 and December 31. Expense of issuance was $839.
7. Shirley Caesar Corporation acquired 70% control in Amarillo Company on January 2, 2002, for $100,000. The income statement of Amarillo Company for 2002 shows a net income of $15,000.
8. Extraordinary repairs to buildings of $7,200 were charged to Accumulated Depreciation—Buildings.
9. Interest paid in 2002 was $10,500 and income taxes paid were $34,000.

Instructions

From the information above prepare a statement of cash flows using the indirect method. A work sheet is not necessary, but the principal computations should be supported by schedules or skeleton ledger accounts.

P24-8 (SCF—Indirect Method)   Presented below are the 2002 financial statements of Carol Cymbala Corporation.

CAROL CYMBALA CORPORATION
Comparative Balance Sheet

	December 31,	
$ in millions	2002	2001
Assets		
Current assets:		
Cash	$ 20.4	$ 7.5
Receivables (net of allowance for doubtful accounts of $5.0 million in 2002 and $4.6 million in 2001)	241.6	213.2
Inventories		
Finished goods	83.7	84.7
Raw materials and supplies	115.7	123.8
Prepaid expenses	6.2	6.7
Total current assets	467.6	435.9
Property, plant, and equipment:		
Plant and equipment	2,361.8	2,217.7
Less: Accumulated depreciation	(993.4)	(890.1)
	1,368.4	1,327.6
Timberland—net	166.3	169.5
Total property, plant, and equipment—net	1,534.7	1,497.1
Other assets	74.7	34.7
Total assets	$2,077.0	$1,967.7
Liabilities and stockholders' investment		
Current liabilities:		
Current maturities of long-term debt	$ 13.2	$ 10.5
Bank overdrafts	25.5	20.2
Accounts payable	102.2	91.3
Accrued liabilities		
Payrolls and employee benefits	73.5	73.9
Interest and other expenses	44.3	29.4
Federal and state income taxes	17.4	12.7
Total current liabilities	276.1	238.0
Long-term liabilities:		
Deferred tax liability	333.6	280.0
4.75% to 11.25% revenue bonds with maturities to 2022	174.6	193.4
Other revenue bonds at variable rates with maturities to 2029	46.3	26.6
7⅞% sinking fund debentures due 2008	19.5	21.0
8.70% sinking fund debentures due 2018	75.0	75.0
9½% convertible subordinated debentures due 2023	–0–	38.9
9¾% notes due 2005	50.0	50.0
Promissory notes	–0–	60.2
Mortgage debt and miscellaneous obligations	25.7	21.7
Other long-term liabilities	21.8	–0–
Total long-term liabilities	746.5	766.8
Stockholders' equity:		
Common stock ($5 par value, 60,000,000 shares authorized, 26,661,770 and 25,265,921 shares outstanding as of December 31, 2002 and 2001)	133.3	126.3
Additional paid-in capital	111.1	70.6
Retained earnings	810.0	766.0
Total stockholders' equity	1,054.4	962.9
Total liabilities and stockholders' equity	$2,077.0	$1,967.7

Statement of Income and Retained Earnings

$ in millions, except per share amounts	2002
Income	
Net sales	$2,044.2
Cost of sales	(1,637.8)
Gross margin	406.4
Selling, general, and administrative expense	(182.6)
Provision for reduced operations	(41.0)
Operating income	182.8
Interest on long-term debt	(33.5)
Other income—net	2.2
Pretax income	151.5
Income taxes	(61.2)
Net income	$ 90.3
Earnings per share	$ 3.39
Retained earnings	
Retained earnings at beginning of year	$ 766.0
Add: Net income	90.3
	856.3
Deduct: Dividends:	
Common stock ($1.76 a share in 2002)	46.3
Retained earnings at end of year	$ 810.0

Additional information:

1. Depreciation and cost of timberland harvested was $114.6 million.
2. The provision for reduced operations included a decrease in cash of $15.9 million.
3. Purchases of plant and equipment were $182.5 million, and purchases of other assets were $40 million.
4. Sales of plant and equipment resulted in cash inflows of $5.2 million. All sales were at book value.
5. The changes in long-term liabilities are summarized below:

Increase in deferred tax liability	$ 53.6
New borrowings	63.2
Debt retired by cash payments	(86.5)
Debt converted into stock	(37.4)
Reclassification of current maturities	(13.2)
Decrease in long-term liabilities	$(20.3)

6. The increase in common stock and additional paid-in capital results from the issuance of stock for debt conversion, $37.4 million, and stock issued for cash, $10.1 million.
7. Interest paid during 2002 was $21.2 and income tax paid was $7.6.

Instructions

Prepare a statement of cash flows for the Carol Cymbala Corporation using the indirect method.

P24-9 **(SCF—Indirect Method, and Net Cash Flow from Operating Activities, Direct Method)** Comparative balance sheet accounts of Jon Secada Inc. are presented below:

JON SECADA INC.
Comparative Balance Sheet Accounts
December 31, 2002 and 2001

	December 31	
Debit Accounts	2002	2001
Cash	$ 45,000	$ 33,750
Accounts Receivable	67,500	60,000
Merchandise Inventory	30,000	24,000

Investments (available-for-sale)	22,250	38,500
Machinery	30,000	18,750
Buildings	67,500	56,250
Land	7,500	7,500
Totals	$269,750	$238,750

Credit Accounts

Allowance for Doubtful Accounts	$ 2,250	$ 1,500
Accumulated Depreciation—Machinery	5,625	2,250
Accumulated Depreciation—Buildings	13,500	9,000
Accounts Payable	30,000	24,750
Accrued Payables	3,375	2,625
Long-Term Note Payable	26,000	31,000
Common Stock, no par	150,000	125,000
Retained Earnings	39,000	42,625
Total	$269,750	$238,750

Additional data: (ignore taxes)

1. Net income for the year was $42,500.
2. Cash dividends declared during the year were $21,125.
3. A 20% stock dividend was declared during the year. $25,000 of retained earnings was capitalized.
4. Investments that cost $20,000 were sold during the year for $23,750.
5. Machinery that cost $3,750, on which $750 of depreciation had accumulated, was sold for $2,200.

Jon Secada's 2002 income statement follows (ignore taxes):

Sales		$540,000
Less cost of goods sold		380,000
Gross margin		160,000
Less: Operating expenses (includes $8,625 depreciation and $5,400 bad debts)		120,450
Income from operations		39,550
Other: Gain on sale of investments	$3,750	
Loss on sale of machinery	(800)	2,950
Net income		$ 42,500

Instructions

(a) Compute net cash flow from operating activities using the direct method.
(b) Prepare a statement of cash flows using the indirect method.

P24-10 (SCF—Direct and Indirect Methods from Comparative Financial Statements) George Winston Company, a major retailer of bicycles and accessories, operates several stores and is a publicly traded company. The comparative Statement of Financial Position and Income Statement for Winston as of May 31, 2002, are shown below and on the next page. The company is preparing its Statement of Cash Flows.

GEORGE WINSTON COMPANY
Comparative Statement of Financial Position
As of May 31, 2002 and May 31, 2001

	2002	2001
Current assets		
Cash	$ 33,250	$ 20,000
Accounts receivable	80,000	58,000
Merchandise inventory	210,000	250,000
Prepaid expenses	9,000	7,000
Total current assets	332,250	335,000
Plant assets		
Plant assets	600,000	502,000
Less: Accumulated depreciation	150,000	125,000
Net plant assets	450,000	377,000
Total assets	$782,250	$712,000

Current liabilities		
Accounts payable	$123,000	$115,000
Salaries payable	47,250	72,000
Interest payable	27,000	25,000
Total current liabilities	197,250	212,000
Long-term debt		
Bonds payable	70,000	100,000
Total liabilities	267,250	312,000
Shareholders' equity		
Common stock, $10 par	370,000	280,000
Retained earnings	145,000	120,000
Total shareholders' equity	515,000	400,000
Total liabilities and shareholders' equity	$782,250	$712,000

GEORGE WINSTON COMPANY
Income Statement
For the Year Ended May 31, 2002

Sales	$1,255,250
Cost of merchandise sold	722,000
Total contribution	533,250
Expenses	
Salary expense	252,100
Interest expense	75,000
Other expenses	8,150
Depreciation expense	25,000
Total expenses	360,250
Operating income	173,000
Income tax expense	43,000
Net income	$ 130,000

The following is additional information concerning Winston's transactions during the year ended May 31, 2002.

1. All sales during the year were made on account.
2. All merchandise was purchased on account, comprising the total accounts payable account.
3. Plant assets costing $98,000 were purchased by paying $48,000 in cash and issuing 5,000 shares of stock.
4. The "other expenses" are related to prepaid items.
5. All income taxes incurred during the year were paid during the year.
6. In order to supplement its cash, Winston issued 4,000 shares of common stock at par value.
7. There were no penalties assessed for the retirement of bonds.
8. Cash dividends of $105,000 were declared and paid at the end of the fiscal year.

Instructions

(a) Compare and contrast the direct method and the indirect method for reporting cash flows from operating activities.
(b) Prepare a statement of cash flows for Winston Company for the year ended May 31, 2002, using the direct method. Be sure to support the statement with appropriate calculations. (A reconciliation of net income to net cash is not required.)
(c) Using the indirect method, calculate only the net cash flow from operating activities for Winston Company for the year ended May 31, 2002.

P24-11 **(SCF—Direct and Indirect Methods)** Comparative balance sheet accounts of Jensen Company are presented below:

JENSEN COMPANY
Comparative Balance Sheet Accounts
December 31, 2001 and 2000

Debit Balances	2001	2000
Cash	$ 80,000	$ 51,000
Accounts Receivable	145,000	130,000
Merchandise Inventory	75,000	61,000
Investments (Available-for-sale)	55,000	85,000
Equipment	70,000	48,000
Buildings	145,000	145,000
Land	40,000	25,000
Totals	$610,000	$545,000

Credit Balances	2001	2000
Allowance for Doubtful Accounts	$ 10,000	$ 8,000
Accumulated Depreciation—Equipment	21,000	14,000
Accumulated Depreciation—Building	37,000	28,000
Accounts Payable	70,000	60,000
Income Taxes Payable	12,000	10,000
Long-Term Notes Payable	62,000	70,000
Common Stock	310,000	260,000
Retained Earnings	88,000	95,000
Totals	$610,000	$545,000

Additional data:

1. Equipment that cost $10,000 and was 40% depreciated was sold in 2001.
2. Cash dividends were declared and paid during the year.
3. Common stock was issued in exchange for land.
4. Investments that cost $35,000 were sold during the year.

Jensen's 2001 income statement is as follows:

Sales		$950,000
Less: Cost of goods sold		600,000
Gross profit		350,000
Less: Operating expenses (includes depreciation and bad debt expense)		250,000
Income from operations		100,000
Other revenues and expenses		
Gain on sale of investments	$15,000	
Loss on sale of equipment	(3,000)	12,000
Income before taxes		112,000
Income taxes		45,000
Net income		$ 67,000

Instructions
(a) Compute net cash provided by operating activities under the direct method.
(b) Prepare a statement of cash flows using the indirect method.

P24-12 (Indirect SCF) Seneca Corporation has contracted with you to prepare a statement of cash flows. The controller has provided the following information:

	December 31	
	2001	2000
Cash	$ 38,500	$13,000
Accounts receivable	12,250	10,000
Inventory	12,000	9,000
Investments	–0–	3,000
Building	–0–	29,750
Equipment	40,000	20,000
Patent	5,000	6,250
Totals	$107,750	$91,000

Allowance for doubtful accounts	$ 3,000	$ 4,500
Accumulated depreciation on equipment	2,000	4,500
Accumulated depreciation on building	–0–	6,000
Accounts payable	5,000	3,000
Dividends payable	–0–	6,000
Notes payable, short-term (nontrade)	3,000	4,000
Long-term notes payable	31,000	25,000
Common stock	43,000	33,000
Retained earnings	20,750	5,000
	$107,750	$91,000

Additional data related to 2001 are as follows:

1. Equipment that had cost $11,000 and was 40% depreciated at time of disposal was sold for $2,500.
2. $10,000 of the long-term note payable was paid by issuing common stock.
3. Cash dividends paid were $6,000.
4. On January 1, 2001, the building was completely destroyed by a flood. Insurance proceeds on the building were $33,000 (net of $4,000 taxes).
5. Investments (available-for-sale) were sold at $2,500 above their cost. The company has made similar sales and investments in the past.
6. Cash of $15,000 was paid for the acquisition of equipment.
7. A long-term note for $16,000 was issued for the acquisition of equipment.
8. Interest of $2,000 and income taxes of $5,000 were paid in cash.

Instructions

(a) Use the indirect method to analyze the above information and prepare a statement of cash flows for Seneca. Flood damage is unusual and infrequent in that part of the country.

(b) What would you expect to observe in the operating, investing, and financing sections of a statement of cash flows of:
  (1) a severely financially troubled firm?
  (2) a recently formed firm which is experiencing rapid growth?

CONCEPTUAL CASES

C24-1 **(Analysis of Improper SCF)** The following statement was prepared by Abriendo Corporation's accountant:

ABRIENDO CORPORATION
Statement of Sources and Application of Cash
For the Year Ended September 30, 2002

Sources of cash	
Net income	$ 95,000
Depreciation and depletion	70,000
Increase in long-term debt	179,000
Common stock issued under employee option plans	16,000
Changes in current receivables and inventories, less current	
liabilities (excluding current maturities of long-term debt)	14,000
	$374,000
Application of cash	
Cash dividends	$ 60,000
Expenditure for property, plant, and equipment	214,000
Investments and other uses	20,000
Change in cash	80,000
	$374,000

The following additional information relating to Abriendo Corporation is available for the year ended September 30, 2002:

1. The corporation received $16,000 in cash from its employees on its employee stock option plans, and wage and salary expense attributable to the option plans was an additional $22,000.

2. Expenditures for property, plant, and equipment $250,000
   Proceeds from retirements of property, plant, and equipment   36,000

   Net expenditures $214,000

3. A stock dividend of 10,000 shares of Abriendo Corporation common stock was distributed to common stockholders on April 1, 2002, when the per-share market price was $7 and par value was $1.
4. On July 1, 2002, when its market price was $6 per share, 16,000 shares of Abriendo Corporation common stock were issued in exchange for 4,000 shares of preferred stock.
5. Depreciation expense $ 65,000
   Depletion expense   5,000

   $ 70,000

6. Increase in long-term debt $620,000
   Retirement of debt   441,000

   Net increase $179,000

Instructions

(a) In general, what are the objectives of a statement of the type shown above for the Abriendo Corporation? Explain.

(b) Identify the weaknesses in the form and format of the Abriendo Corporation's statement of cash flows without reference to the additional information (assume adoption of the indirect method).

(c) For each of the six items of additional information for the statement of cash flows indicate the preferable treatment and explain why the suggested treatment is preferable.

(AICPA adapted)

C24-2 (SCF Theory and Analysis of Improper SCF) Gloria Estefan and Flaco Jimenez are examining the following statement of cash flows for Tropical Clothing Store's first year of operations.

TROPICAL CLOTHING STORE
Statement of Cash Flows
For the Year Ended January 31, 2002

Sources of cash	
From sales of merchandise	$ 362,000
From sale of capital stock	400,000
From sale of investment	120,000
From depreciation	80,000
From issuance of note for truck	30,000
From interest on investments	8,000
Total sources of cash	1,000,000
Uses of cash	
For purchase of fixtures and equipment	340,000
For merchandise purchased for resale	253,000
For operating expenses (including depreciation)	170,000
For purchase of investment	85,000
For purchase of truck by issuance of note	30,000
For purchase of treasury stock	10,000
For interest on note	3,000
Total uses of cash	891,000
Net increase in cash	$ 109,000

Gloria claims that Tropical's statement of cash flows is an excellent portrayal of a superb first year with cash increasing $109,000. Flaco replies that it was not a superb first year, that the year was an operating failure, that the statement was incorrectly presented, and that $109,000 is not the actual increase in cash.

Instructions

(a) With whom do you agree, Gloria or Flaco? Explain your position.

(b) Using the data provided, prepare a statement of cash flows in proper indirect method form. The only noncash items in income are depreciation and the gain from the sale of the investment (purchase and sale are related).

C24-3   (SCF Theory and Analysis of Transactions)   John Lee Hooker Company is a young and growing producer of electronic measuring instruments and technical equipment. You have been retained by Hooker to advise it in the preparation of a statement of cash flows using the indirect method. For the fiscal year ended October 31, 2002, you have obtained the following information concerning certain events and transactions of Hooker.

1. The amount of reported earnings for the fiscal year was $800,000, which included a deduction for an extraordinary loss of $110,000 (see item 5 below).
2. Depreciation expense of $315,000 was included in the earnings statement.
3. Uncollectible accounts receivable of $40,000 were written off against the allowance for doubtful accounts. Also, $51,000 of bad debt expense was included in determining income for the fiscal year, and the same amount was added to the allowance for doubtful accounts.
4. A gain of $9,000 was realized on the sale of a machine; it originally cost $75,000, of which $30,000 was undepreciated on the date of sale.
5. On April 1, 2002, lightning caused an uninsured building loss of $110,000 ($180,000 loss, less reduction in income taxes of $70,000). This extraordinary loss was included in determining income as indicated in 1 above.
6. On July 3, 2002, building and land were purchased for $700,000; Hooker gave in payment $75,000 cash, $200,000 market value of its unissued common stock, and signed a $425,000 mortgage note payable.
7. On August 3, 2002, $800,000 face value of Hooker's 10% convertible debentures were converted into $150,000 par value of its common stock. The bonds were originally issued at face value.

Instructions

Explain whether each of the seven numbered items above is a source or use of cash and explain how it should be disclosed in John Lee Hooker's statement of cash flows for the fiscal year ended October 31, 2002. If any item is neither a source nor a use of cash, explain why it is not and indicate the disclosure, if any, that should be made of the item in John Lee Hooker's statement of cash flows for the fiscal year ended October 31, 2002.

C24-4   (Analysis of Transactions' Effect on SCF)   Each of the following items must be considered in preparing a statement of cash flows for Buddy Guy Fashions Inc. for the year ended December 31, 2002.

1. Fixed assets that had cost $20,000 6½ years before and were being depreciated on a 10-year basis, with no estimated scrap value, were sold for $5,250.
2. During the year, goodwill of $15,000 was completely written off to expense.
3. During the year, 500 shares of common stock with a stated value of $25 a share were issued for $34 a share.
4. The company sustained a net loss for the year of $2,100. Depreciation amounted to $2,000 and patent amortization was $400.
5. An Appropriation for Contingencies in the amount of $80,000 was created by a charge against Retained Earnings.
6. Uncollectible accounts receivable in the amount of $2,000 were written off against the Allowance for Doubtful Accounts.
7. Investments (available-for-sale) that cost $12,000 when purchased 4 years earlier were sold for $10,600. The loss was considered ordinary.
8. Bonds payable with a par value of $24,000 on which there was an unamortized bond premium of $2,000 were redeemed at 103. The gain was credited to income as an extraordinary item. Ignore income taxes.

Instructions

For each item, state where it is to be shown in the statement and then how you would present the necessary information, including the amount. Consider each item to be independent of the others. Assume that correct entries were made for all transactions as they took place.

C24-5   (Purpose and Elements of SCF)   In 1961 the AICPA recognized the importance of the funds statement by publishing *Accounting Research Study No. 2*, "'Cash Flow' Analysis and the Funds Statement." Prior to this time, accountants had prepared funds statements primarily as management reports. The Accounting Principles Board responded by issuing *APB Opinion No. 3*, "The Statement of Source and Application of Funds," which recommended that a statement of source and application of funds be presented on a supplementary basis. Because of the favorable response of the business community to this pronouncement, the APB issued *Opinion No. 19*, "Reporting Changes in Financial Position" in 1971. This opinion required that a statement of changes in financial position be presented as a basic financial statement and be covered by the auditor's report.

In 1981 the Financial Accounting Standards Board reconsidered funds flow issues as part of the conceptual framework project. At this time, the Financial Accounting Standards Board decided that cash flow reporting issues should be considered at the standards level. Subsequent deliberations resulted in *Statement of Financial Accounting Standards (SFAS) No. 95*, "Statement of Cash Flows."

Instructions

(a) Explain the purposes of the statement of cash flows.

(b) List and describe the three categories of activities that must be reported in the statement of cash flows.

(c) Identify and describe the two methods that are allowed for reporting cash flows from operations.

(d) Describe the financial statement presentation of noncash investing and financing transactions. Include in your description an example of a noncash investing and financing transaction.

USING YOUR JUDGMENT

FINANCIAL REPORTING PROBLEM: INTEL CORPORATION

Instructions

Refer to the financial statements and accompanying notes and discussion of Intel Corporation presented in Appendix 5B and answer the following questions.

(a) Which method of computing net cash provided by operating activities does Intel use? What were the amounts of cash provided by operations for the years 1996, 1997, and 1998? Which two items were most responsible for the decrease in cash provided by operating activities in 1998?

(b) What was the most significant item in the cash flows used for the investing activities section in 1998? What was the most significant item in the cash flows used for the financing activities section in 1998?

(c) Where is the "net loss on retirements of property, plant and equipment" reported in Intel's statement of cash flows? How much is the loss in 1998 and why does it appear in that section of the statement of cash flows?

(d) Where is "deferred taxes" reported in Intel's statement of cash flows? Why does it appear in that section of the statement of cash flows?

(e) Where is depreciation reported in Intel's statement of cash flows? Why is depreciation added to net income in the statement of cash flows?

FINANCIAL STATEMENT ANALYSIS CASE

Vermont Teddy Bear Co.

Founded in the early 1980s, the Vermont Teddy Bear Co. designs and manufactures American-made teddy bears and markets them primarily as gifts called Bear-Grams or Teddy Bear-Grams. Bear-Grams are personalized teddy bears delivered directly to the recipient for special occasions such as birthdays and anniversaries. The Shelburne, Vermont, company's primary markets are New York, Boston, and Chicago. Sales have jumped dramatically in recent years. Such dramatic growth has significant implications for cash flows. Provided below are the cash flow statements for the current and prior years for the company.

	Current Year	Prior Year
Cash flows from operating activities:		
Net income	$ 17,523	$ 838,955
Adjustments to reconcile net income to net cash provided by operating activities		
Deferred income taxes	(69,524)	(146,590)
Depreciation and amortization	316,416	181,348
Changes in assets and liabilities:		
Accounts receivable, trade	(38,267)	(25,947)
Inventories	(1,599,014)	(1,289,293)
Prepaid and other current assets	(444,794)	(113,205)
Deposits and other assets	(24,240)	(83,044)
Accounts payable	2,017,059	(284,567)
Accrued expenses	61,321	170,755
Accrued interest payable, debentures	—	(58,219)
Other	—	(8,960)
Income taxes payable	—	117,810
Net cash provided by (used for) operating activities	236,480	(700,957)
Net cash used for investing activities	(2,102,892)	(4,422,953)
Net cash (used for) provided by financing activities	(315,353)	9,685,435
Net change in cash and cash equivalents	(2,181,765)	4,561,525

Other information

	Current Year	Prior Year
Current liabilities	$ 4,055,465	$ 1,995,600
Total liabilities	4,620,085	2,184,386
Net sales	20,560,566	17,025,856

Instructions

(a) Note that net income in the current year was only $17,523 compared to prior year income of $838,955, but cash flow from operations was $236,480 in the current year and a negative $700,957 in the prior year. Explain the causes of this apparent paradox.

(b) Evaluate Vermont Teddy Bear's liquidity, solvency, and profitability for the current year using cash flow-based ratios.

COMPARATIVE ANALYSIS CASE

The Coca-Cola Company versus PepsiCo, Inc.

Instructions

Go to the Digital Tool and, using The Coca-Cola Company and PepsiCo Annual Report information, answer the following questions:

(a) What method of computing net cash provided by operating activities does Coca-Cola use? What method does PepsiCo use? What were the amounts of cash provided by operating activities reported by Coca-Cola and PepsiCo in 1998?

(b) What was the most significant item reported by Coca-Cola and PepsiCo in 1998 in their investing activities sections? What is the most significant item reported by Coca-Cola and PepsiCo in 1998 in their financing activities sections?

(c) Where is "depreciation and amortization" reported by Coca-Cola and PepsiCo in their statement of cash flows? What is the amount and why does it appear in that section of the statement of cash flows?

(d) Based on the information contained in Coca-Cola's and PepsiCo's financial statements, compute the following 1998 ratios for each company. These ratios require the use of statement of cash flows data. (These ratios were covered in Chapter 5.)

   (1) Current cash debt coverage ratio.

   (2) Cash debt coverage ratio.

(e) What conclusions concerning the management of cash can be drawn from the ratios computed in (d)?

RESEARCH CASE

The March 25, 1996, issue of *Barron's* includes an article by Harry B. Ernst and Jeffrey D. Fotta entitled "Weary Bull."

Instructions

Read the article and answer the following questions.

(a) The article describes a cash flow-based model used by investors. Identify the model and briefly describe its purpose.

(b) How does the model classify a firm's cash flows?

(c) Identify one way in which the cash flow classifications described in the article differ from those under GAAP.

(d) How can the model be used to predict stock prices?

ETHICS CASE

Durocher Guitar Company is in the business of manufacturing top-quality, steel-string folk guitars. In recent years the company has experienced working capital problems resulting from the procurement of factory equipment, the unanticipated buildup of receivables and inventories, and the payoff of a balloon mortgage on a new manufacturing facility. The founder and president of the company, Laraine Durocher, has attempted to raise cash from various financial institutions, but to no avail because of the company's poor performance in recent years. In particular, the company's lead bank, First Financial, is especially concerned about Durocher's inability to maintain a positive cash position. The commercial loan officer from First Financial told Laraine, "I can't even consider your request for capital financing unless I see that your company is able to generate positive cash flows from operations."

Thinking about the banker's comment, Laraine came up with what she believes is a good plan: with a more attractive statement of cash flows, the bank might be willing to provide long-term financing. To "window dress" cash flows, the company can sell its accounts receivables to factors and liquidate its raw material inventories. These rather costly transactions would generate lots of cash. As the chief accountant for Durocher Guitar, it is your job to tell Laraine what you think of her plan.

Instructions
Answer the following questions:

(a) What are the ethical issues related to Laraine Durocher's idea?

(b) What would you tell Laraine Durocher?

CHAPTER 25

Full Disclosure in Financial Reporting

What Annual Reports Won't Tell You

Most stockholders receive their corporation's financial statements in the Annual Report, a glossy-covered booklet that sometimes gives a positive spin to even lackluster corporate performance. In addition to comprehending the GAAP-prepared financial statements and notes, you need to know how to translate the glowing nonaccounting phrases that accompany the financials. The following examples may help you make these translations:

Here's what happened: Performance was flat to abysmal for all segments, the company was named in several class-action suits, and the founder's messy divorce was all over the tabloids and TV shows.
Here's how it was described in the annual report: "The past year can be characterized by the words of the immortal Charles Dickens: `It was the best of times, it was the worst of times.'"

Here's what happened: By every measure of corporate performance, the company dropped to or near the bottom of its industry.
Here's how it was described: "We are well positioned for future growth."

Here's what happened: The product launch and/or corporate acquisition that put the company's existence at risk fell flat on its face.
Here's how it was described: "This bold initiative reflects the competitive realities that await all companies in the 21st century."

Here's what happened: The company's stock price has languished for years while the major stock market indexes and competitors' share prices have rocketed to one new high after another.
Here's how it was described: "With perseverance the company's extraordinary performance in generating added value will be recognized in the marketplace."[1]

Clearly, you absolutely need to read and understand the audited financial statements and accompanying notes, in order to be able to read "between the lines" in management's presentation of the year's financial results.

[1]Adapted from David Stauffer, "Manager's Journal," *The Wall Street Journal*, April 7, 1997, p. A14.

LEARNING OBJECTIVES

After studying this chapter, you should be able to:

❶ Review the full disclosure principle and describe problems of implementation.

❷ Explain the use of notes in financial statement preparation.

❸ Describe the disclosure requirements for major segments of a business.

❹ Describe the accounting problems associated with interim reporting.

❺ Identify the major disclosures found in the auditor's report.

❻ Understand management's responsibilities for financials.

❼ Identify issues related to financial forecasts and projections.

❽ Describe the profession's response to fraudulent financial reporting.

As the opening story indicates, you have to be careful when reading the annual report. That is why it is important to read not only the president's letter but also the financial statements and related information. In this chapter, we cover several disclosures that must accompany financial statements so that they are not misleading. The content and organization of this chapter are as follows:

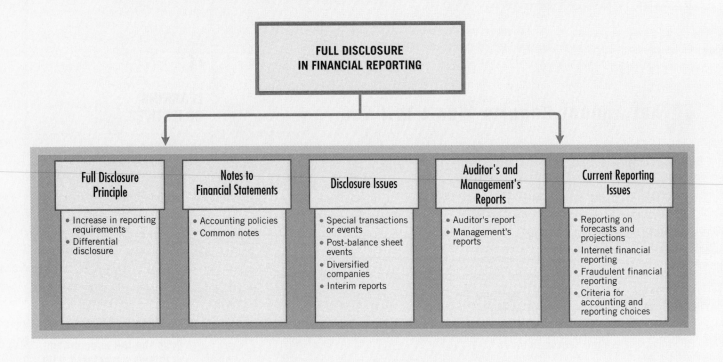

FULL DISCLOSURE PRINCIPLE

FASB Concepts Statement No. 1 notes that some useful information is better provided in the financial statements, and some is better provided by means of financial reporting other than financial statements. For example, earnings and cash flows are readily available in financial statements—but investors might do better to look at comparisons to other companies in the same industry, found in news articles or brokerage house reports.

Financial statements, notes to the financial statements, and supplementary information are areas directly affected by FASB standards. Other types of information found in the annual report, such as management's discussion and analysis, are not subject to FASB standards. Illustration 25-1 indicates the types of financial information presented.

As indicated in Chapter 2, the profession has adopted a **full disclosure principle** that calls for financial reporting of **any financial facts significant enough to influence the judgment of an informed reader**. In some situations, the benefits of disclosure may be apparent but the costs uncertain, whereas in other instances the costs may be certain but the benefits of disclosure not as apparent.

For example, the SEC increased the amount of information financial institutions must disclose about their foreign lending practices. With some foreign countries in economic straits, the benefits of increased disclosure about the risk of uncollectibility are fairly obvious to the investing public. The exact costs of disclosure in these situations cannot be quantified, though they would appear to be relatively small.

On the other hand, the cost of disclosure can be substantial in some cases and the benefits difficult to assess. For example, *The Wall Street Journal* reported that, at one time, if segment reporting were adopted, a company like Fruehauf would have to in-

OBJECTIVE ❶
Review the full
disclosure principle
and describe problems
of implementation.

UNDERLYING CONCEPTS

Here is a good example of the trade-off between the cost/ benefit constraint and the full disclosure principle.

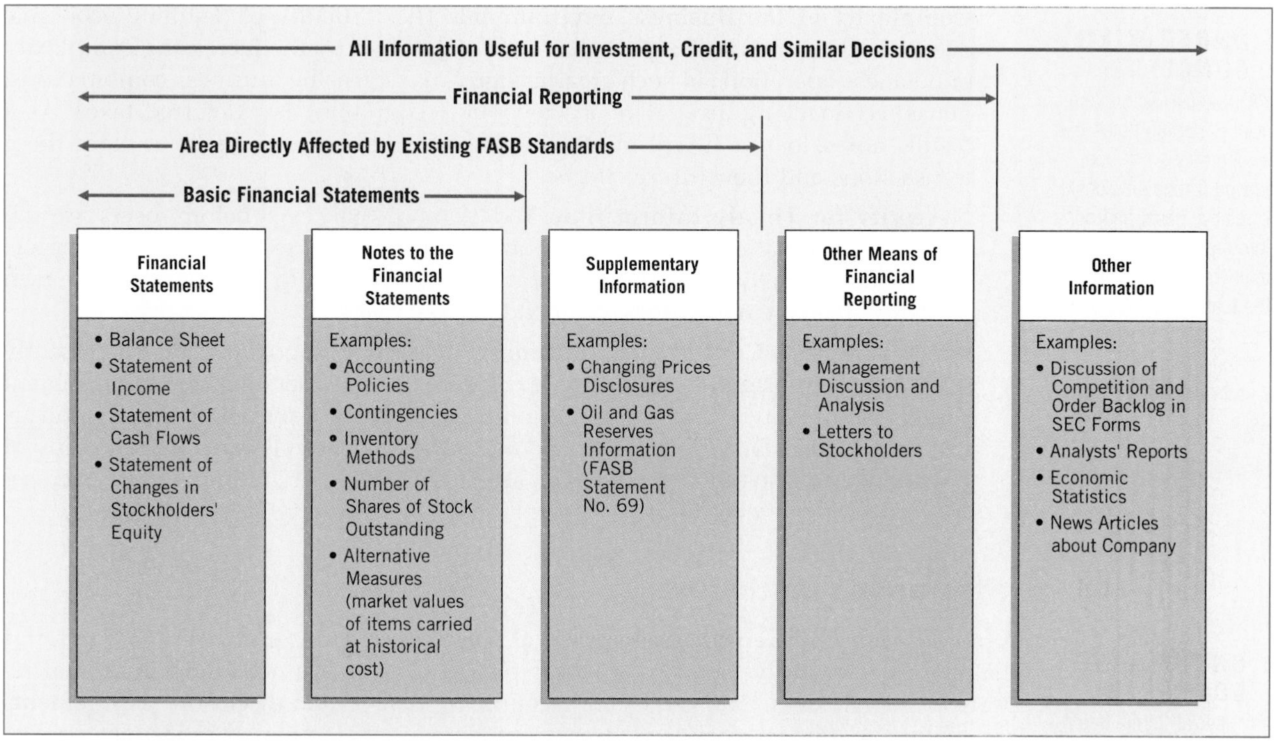

All Information Useful for Investment, Credit, and Similar Decisions
Financial Reporting
Area Directly Affected by Existing FASB Standards
Basic Financial Statements
Financial Statements
• Balance Sheet
• Statement of Income
• Statement of Cash Flows
• Statement of Changes in Stockholders' Equity
Notes to the Financial Statements
Examples:
• Accounting Policies
• Contingencies
• Inventory Methods
• Number of Shares of Stock Outstanding
• Alternative Measures (market values of items carried at historical cost)
Supplementary Information
Examples:
• Changing Prices Disclosures
• Oil and Gas Reserves Information (FASB Statement No. 69)
Other Means of Financial Reporting
Examples:
• Management Discussion and Analysis
• Letters to Stockholders
Other Information
Examples:
• Discussion of Competition and Order Backlog in SEC Forms
• Analysts' Reports
• Economic Statistics
• News Articles about Company

ILLUSTRATION 25-1
Types of Financial Information

crease its accounting staff 50%, from 300 to 450 individuals. In this case, the cost of disclosure is apparent but the benefits are less well defined. Some would even argue that the reporting requirements are so detailed and substantial that users will have a difficult time absorbing the information; they charge the profession with engaging in **information overload**.

The difficulty of implementing the full disclosure principle is highlighted by such financial disasters as **Phar-Mor**, **Miniscribe**, **Lincoln Savings and Loan**, and **BCCI**. Why were investors not aware of potential problems: Was the information presented about these companies not comprehensible? Was it buried? Was it too technical? Was it properly presented and fully disclosed as of the financial statement date—but the situation later deteriorated? Or was it simply not there? No easy answers are forthcoming.

One problem is that the profession is still in the process of developing the guidelines that tell whether a given transaction should be disclosed and what format this disclosure should take. Different users want different information, and it becomes exceedingly difficult to develop disclosure policies that meet their varied objectives.

Increase in Reporting Requirements

Disclosure requirements have increased substantially. One survey showed that in a sample of 25 large, well-known companies, the average number of pages of notes to the financial statements increased from 9 to 17 pages and the average number of pages for management's discussion and analysis from 7 to 12 pages over a recent 10-year period. This result is not surprising because as illustrated throughout this textbook, the FASB has issued many standards in the last 10 years that have substantial disclosure provisions.[2] The reasons for this increase in disclosure requirements are varied. Some of them are:

[2]As one writer has noted, rapid growth in additional financial reporting requirements and rapid changes in existing requirements are likely to be permanent features of the financial reporting environment. For the user, the result is a bewildering increase in financial data to interpret. William H. Beaver, *Financial Reporting: An Accounting Revolution*, 2d ed. (Englewood Cliffs, N.J.: Prentice-Hall, 1989), pp. 1–2. The survey results were taken from Ray J. Groves, "Financial Disclosure: When More Is Not Better," *Financial Executive*, May/June 1994.

UNDERLYING CONCEPTS

The AICPA's Special Committee on Financial Reporting notes that business reporting is not free, and improving it requires considering the relative costs and benefits of information, just as costs and benefits are key to determining the features included in any product. Undisciplined expansion of mandated reporting could result in large and needless costs.

Complexity of the Business Environment. The difficulty of distilling economic events into summarized reports has been magnified by the increasing complexity of business operations in such areas as derivatives, leasing, business combinations, pensions, financing arrangements, revenue recognition, and deferred taxes. As a result, **notes to the financial statements** are used extensively to explain these transactions and their future effects.

Necessity for Timely Information. Today, more than ever before, users are demanding information that is current and predictive. For example, more complete **interim data** are required. And published financial forecasts, long avoided and even feared by management, are recommended by the SEC.

Accounting as a Control and Monitoring Device. The government has recently sought more information and public disclosure of such phenomena as management compensation, environmental pollution, related party transactions, errors and irregularities, and illegal activities. An "S&L crisis" concern is expressed in many of these newer disclosure requirements, and accountants and auditors have been selected as the agents to assist in controlling and monitoring these concerns.

Differential Disclosure

UNDERLYING CONCEPTS

The AICPA Special Committee on Financial Reporting indicated that users differ in their needs for information, and that not all companies should report all elements of information. Rather, companies should report only information that users and preparers agree is needed in the particular circumstances.

A trend toward **differential disclosure** is also occurring. For example, the SEC requires that certain substantive information be reported to it that is not found in annual reports to stockholders. And the FASB, recognizing that certain disclosure requirements are costly and unnecessary for certain companies, has eliminated reporting requirements for nonpublic enterprises in such areas as fair value of financial instruments and segment reporting.[3]

Some still complain that the FASB has not gone far enough. They note that certain types of companies (small or nonpublic) should not have to follow complex GAAP requirements such as deferred income taxes, leases, or pensions. This issue, often referred to as **Big GAAP versus Little GAAP**, continues to be controversial. The FASB takes the position that one set of GAAP should be used, except in unusual situations.

NOTES TO THE FINANCIAL STATEMENTS

OBJECTIVE ②
Explain the use of notes in financial statement preparation.

As you know from your study of this textbook, notes are an integral part of the financial statements of a business enterprise. However, they are often overlooked because they are highly technical and often appear in small print. **Notes are the accountant's means of amplifying or explaining the items presented in the main body of the statements.** Information pertinent to specific financial statement items can be explained in qualitative terms, and supplementary data of a quantitative nature can be provided to expand the information in the financial statements. Restrictions imposed by financial arrangements or basic contractual agreements also can be explained in notes. Although notes may be technical and difficult to understand, they provide meaningful information for the user of the financial statements.

Accounting Policies

Accounting policies of a given entity are the specific accounting principles and methods currently employed and considered most appropriate to present fairly the financial statements of the enterprise. *APB Opinion No. 22,* "Disclosure of Accounting Policies," concluded that information about the accounting policies adopted and followed by a reporting entity is essential for financial statement users in making economic de-

---

[3]Recently, the FASB has embarked on a disclosure effectiveness project. The revised pension and postretirement benefit disclosures discussed in Chapter 21 (*FASB Statement No. 132*) are one example of how disclosures can be streamlined and made more useful.

cisions. It recommended that a **statement identifying the accounting policies adopted and followed by the reporting entity should also be presented as an integral part of the financial statements**. The disclosure should be given as the initial note or in a separate Summary of Significant Accounting Policies section preceding the notes to the financial statements. The Summary of Significant Accounting Policies answers such questions as: What method of depreciation is used on plant assets? What valuation method is employed on inventories? What amortization policy is followed in regard to intangible assets? How are marketing costs handled for financial reporting purposes?

Refer to Appendix 5B, pages 216–242, for an illustration of note disclosure of accounting policies (Note 1) and other notes accompanying the audited financial statements of **Intel Corporation**. An illustration from **Campbell Soup Company** is provided below:

ILLUSTRATION 25-2
Note Disclosure of
Accounting Policies

CAMPBELL SOUP COMPANY

Note 1: Summary of Significant Accounting Policies:

Consolidation

The consolidated financial statements include the accounts of the company and its majority-owned subsidiaries. Significant intercompany transactions are eliminated in consolidation. Investments of 20% or more in affiliates are accounted for by the equity method.

Fiscal Year

The company's fiscal year ends on the Sunday nearest July 31.

Cash and Cash Equivalents

All highly liquid debt instruments purchased with a maturity of three months or less are classified as cash equivalents.

Inventories

Substantially all domestic inventories are priced at the lower of cost or market, with cost determined by the last-in, first-out (LIFO) method. Other inventories are priced at the lower of average cost or market.

Plant Assets

Plant assets are stated at historical cost. Alterations and major overhauls which extend the lives or increase the capacity of plant assets are capitalized. The amounts for property disposals are removed from plant asset and accumulated depreciation accounts and any resultant gain or loss is included in earnings. Ordinary repairs and maintenance are charged to operating costs.

Depreciation

Depreciation provided in costs and expenses is calculated using the straight-line method. Buildings and machinery and equipment are depreciated over periods not exceeding 45 years and 15 years, respectively. Accelerated methods of depreciation are used for income tax purposes in certain jurisdictions.

Intangibles

Intangible assets consist principally of excess purchase price over net assets of businesses acquired and trademarks. Intangibles are amortized on a straight-line basis over periods not exceeding 40 years.

Asset Valuation

The company periodically reviews the recoverability of plant assets and intangibles based principally on an analysis of cash flows.

Pension and Retiree Benefit Plans

Costs are accrued over employees' careers based on plan benefit formulas.

Income Taxes

Deferred taxes are provided in accordance with Statement of Financial Accounting Standards (FAS) No. 109.

Use of Estimates

Generally accepted accounting principles require management to make estimates and assumptions that affect assets and liabilities, contingent assets and liabilities, and revenues and expenses. Actual results could differ from those estimates.

Reclassifications

Certain amounts in the prior years' financial statements and footnotes have been reclassified to conform to the current year presentation.

Analysts examine carefully the summary of accounting policies section to determine whether the company is using conservative or liberal accounting practices. For example, amortizing intangible assets over 40 years (the maximum) or depreciating plant assets over an unusually long period of time is considered liberal. On the other hand, using LIFO inventory valuation in a period of inflation is generally viewed as following a conservative practice.

Common Notes

Many of the notes to the financial statements have been discussed throughout this textbook. Others will be discussed more fully in this chapter. The more common are as follows:

MAJOR DISCLOSURES

INVENTORY. The basis upon which inventory amounts are stated (lower of cost or market) and the method used in determining cost (LIFO, FIFO, average cost, etc.) should also be reported. Manufacturers should report the inventory composition (finished goods, work in process, raw materials) either in the balance sheet or in a separate schedule in the notes. Unusual or significant financing arrangements relating to inventories that may require disclosure include transactions with related parties, product financing arrangements, firm purchase commitments, involuntary liquidation of LIFO inventories, and pledging of inventories as collateral. Chapter 9 (pages 469–470) illustrates these disclosures.

PROPERTY, PLANT, AND EQUIPMENT. The basis of valuation for property, plant, and equipment should be stated: It is usually historical cost. Pledges, liens, and other commitments related to these assets should be disclosed. In the presentation of depreciation, the following disclosures should be made in the financial statements or in the notes: (1) depreciation expense for the period; (2) balances of major classes of depreciable assets, by nature and function, at the balance sheet date; (3) accumulated depreciation, either by major classes of depreciable assets or in total, at the balance sheet date; and (4) a general description of the method or methods used in computing depreciation with respect to major classes of depreciable assets. Chapter 11 (pages 570–571) illustrates these disclosures.

CREDIT CLAIMS. An investor normally finds it extremely useful to determine the nature and cost of creditorship claims. However, the liability section in the balance sheet can provide the major types of liabilities outstanding only in the aggregate. Note schedules regarding such obligations provide additional information about how the company is financing its operations, the costs that will have to be borne in future periods, and the timing of future cash outflows. Financial statements must disclose for each of the 5 years following the date of the financial statements the aggregate amount of maturities and sinking fund requirements for all long-term borrowings. Chapter 14 (pages 734–735) illustrates these disclosures.

EQUITY HOLDERS' CLAIMS. Many companies present in the body of the balance sheet the number of shares authorized, issued, and outstanding and the par value for each type of equity security. Such data may also be presented in a note. Beyond that, the most common type of equity note disclosure relates to contracts and senior securities outstanding that might affect the various claims of the residual equity holders; for example, the existence of outstanding stock options, outstanding convertible debt, redeemable preferred stock, and convertible preferred stock. In addition, it is necessary to disclose to equity claimants certain types of restrictions currently in force. Generally, these types of restrictions involve the amount of earnings available for dividend distribution. Examples of these types of disclosures are illustrated in Chapter 15 (pages 783, 788–790), Chapter 16 (page 827), and Chapter 17 (pages 870–871, 882–883).

CONTINGENCIES AND COMMITMENTS.   An enterprise may have gain or loss contingencies that are not disclosed in the body of the financial statements. These contingencies include litigation, debt and other guarantees, possible tax assessments, renegotiation of government contracts, sales of receivables with recourse, and so on. In addition, commitments that relate to dividend restrictions, purchase agreements (through-put and take-or-pay), hedge contracts, and employment contracts are also disclosed. Disclosures of items of this nature are illustrated in Chapter 7 (pages 360–361), Chapter 9 (page 459), and Chapter 13 (pages 734–735).

DEFERRED TAXES, PENSIONS, AND LEASES.   Extensive disclosure is required in these three areas. Chapter 20 (pages 1077–1081), Chapter 21 (pages 1143–1146), and Chapter 22 (pages 1219–1221) discuss each of these disclosures in detail. It should be emphasized that notes to the financial statements should be given a careful reading for information about off-balance-sheet commitments, future financing needs, and the quality of a company's earnings.

CHANGES IN ACCOUNTING PRINCIPLES.   The profession defines various types of accounting changes and establishes guides for reporting each type. Either in the summary of significant accounting policies or in the other notes, changes in accounting principles (as well as material changes in estimates and corrections of errors) are discussed. See Chapter 23 (pages 1259–1263 and 1266–1267).

Go to the Digital Tool for additional examples of many of these disclosures.

The disclosures listed above have been discussed in earlier chapters. Four additional disclosures of significance—special transactions or events, subsequent events, segment reporting, and interim reporting—are illustrated in the following sections of this chapter.

DISCLOSURE ISSUES

Disclosure of Special Transactions or Events

Related party transactions, errors and irregularities, and illegal acts pose especially sensitive and difficult problems. The accountant/auditor who has responsibility for reporting on these types of transactions has to be extremely careful that the rights of the reporting company and the needs of users of the financial statements are properly balanced.

Related party transactions arise when a business enterprise engages in transactions in which one of the transacting parties has the ability to influence significantly the policies of the other, or in which a nontransacting party has the ability to influence the policies of the two transacting parties.[4] Transactions involving related parties cannot be presumed to be carried out on an "arm's-length" basis because the requisite conditions of competitive, free-market dealings may not exist. Transactions such as borrowing or lending money at abnormally low or high interest rates, real estate sales at amounts that differ significantly from appraised value, exchanges of nonmonetary assets, and transactions involving enterprises that have no economic substance ("shell corporations") suggest that related parties may be involved.

INTERNATIONAL INSIGHT

In Switzerland there are no requirements to disclose related party transactions. In Italy and Germany related parties do not include a company's directors.

---

[4]Examples of related party transactions include transactions between (a) a parent company and its subsidiaries; (b) subsidiaries of a common parent; (c) an enterprise and trusts for the benefit of employees (controlled or managed by the enterprise); and (d) an enterprise and its principal owners, management, or members of immediate families, and affiliates.

The accountant is expected to report the economic substance rather than the legal form of these transactions and to make adequate disclosures. *FASB Statement No. 57* requires the following disclosures of material related party transactions:

❶ The nature of the relationship(s) involved.

❷ A description of the transactions (including transactions to which no amounts or nominal amounts were ascribed) for each of the periods for which income statements are presented.

❸ The dollar amounts of transactions for each of the periods for which income statements are presented.

❹ Amounts due from or to related parties as of the date of each balance sheet presented.

Illustration 25-3 is an example of the disclosure of related party transactions taken from the annual report of General Instrument Corporation.

ILLUSTRATION 25-3
Disclosure of Related
Party Transactions

GENERAL INSTRUMENT CORPORATION

19. Related Party Transactions
In connection with the asset purchase from TCI, which was consummated on July 17, 1998, TCI obtained approximately a 12% ownership interest in the Company, and at December 31, 1998, such ownership interest was 13%. TCI is also a significant customer of the Company. Sales to TCI represented 31% of total Company sales for the year ended December 31, 1998. Management believes the transactions with TCI are at arms length and are under terms no less favorable to the Company than those with other customers. At December 31, 1998 accounts receivable from TCI totaled $81 million.

Errors are defined as unintentional mistakes, whereas **irregularities** are intentional distortions of financial statements.[5] As indicated in this textbook, when errors are discovered, the financial statements should be corrected. The same treatment should be given irregularities. The discovery of irregularities, however, gives rise to a whole different set of suspicions, procedures, and responsibilities on the part of the accountant/auditor.[6]

Illegal acts encompass such items as illegal political contributions, bribes, kickbacks, and other violations of laws and regulations.[7] In these situations, the accountant/auditor must evaluate the adequacy of disclosure in the financial statements. For example, if revenue is derived from an illegal act that is considered material in relation to the financial statements, this information should be disclosed. To deter these illegal acts, Congress enacted the Foreign Corrupt Practices Act of 1977. In addition to affecting business practices, this Act has had a significant impact upon the accounting profession by encouraging increased disclosure and tighter controls.

Many companies are involved in related party transactions; errors and irregularities, and illegal acts, however, are the exception rather than the rule. Disclosure plays a very important role in these areas because the transaction or event is more qualitative than quantitative and involves more subjective than objective evaluation. The users

---

[5]"The Auditor's Responsibility to Detect and Report Errors and Irregularities," *Statement on Auditing Standards No. 53* (New York, AICPA, 1988).

[6]The profession became so concerned with certain management frauds that affect financial statements that it established a National Commission on Fraudulent Financial Reporting. The major purpose of this organization was to determine how fraudulent reporting practices can be constrained. Fraudulent financial reporting is discussed later in this chapter.

[7]"Illegal Acts by Clients," *Statement on Auditing Standards No. 54* (New York, AICPA, 1988).

of the financial statements must be provided with some indication of the existence and nature of these transactions, where material, through disclosures, modifications in the auditor's report, or reports of changes in auditors.

Post-Balance Sheet Events (Subsequent Events)

Notes to the financial statements should explain any significant financial events that took place after the formal balance sheet date, but before it is finally issued. These events are referred to as post-balance sheet events, events subsequent to the balance sheet date, or just plain subsequent events. The subsequent events period is time-diagrammed as shown in Illustration 25-4.

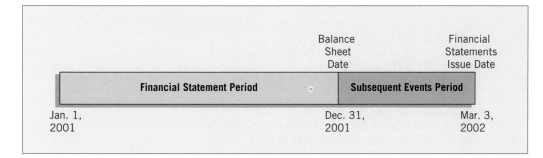

ILLUSTRATION 25-4
Time Periods for
Subsequent Events

A period of several weeks, and sometimes months, may elapse after the end of the year before the financial statements are issued. Taking and pricing the inventory, reconciling subsidiary ledgers with controlling accounts, preparing necessary adjusting entries, assuring that all transactions for the period have been entered, obtaining an audit of the financial statements by independent certified public accountants, and printing the annual report all take time. During the period between the balance sheet date and its distribution to stockholders and creditors, important transactions or other events may occur that materially affect the company's financial position or operating situation.

Many who read a recent balance sheet believe the balance sheet condition is constant and project it into the future. However, readers must be told if the company has sold one of its plants, acquired a subsidiary, suffered extraordinary losses, settled significant litigation, or experienced any other important event in the post-balance sheet period. Without an explanation in a note, the reader might be misled and draw inappropriate conclusions.

Two types of events or transactions occurring after the balance sheet date may have a material effect on the financial statements or may need to be considered to interpret these statements accurately:

1 **Events that provide additional evidence about conditions that existed at the balance sheet date, affect the estimates used in preparing financial statements, and, therefore, result in needed adjustments:** All information available prior to the issuance of the financial statements is used to evaluate estimates previously made. To ignore these subsequent events is to pass up an opportunity to improve the accuracy of the financial statements. This first type encompasses information that would have been recorded in the accounts had it been known at the balance sheet date.

For example, if a loss on an account receivable results from a customer's bankruptcy subsequent to the balance sheet date, the financial statements are adjusted before their issuance. The bankruptcy stems from the customer's poor financial health existing at the balance sheet date.

The same criterion applies to settlements of litigation. The financial statements must be adjusted if the events that gave rise to the litigation, such as personal injury or patent infringement, took place prior to the balance sheet date. If the event

UNDERLYING CONCEPTS

The periodicity or time period assumption implies that economic activities of an enterprise can be divided into artificial time periods for purpose of analysis.

giving rise to the claim took place subsequent to the balance sheet date, no adjustment is necessary but disclosure is. To illustrate, a loss resulting from a customer's fire or flood after the balance sheet date is not indicative of conditions existing at that date. Thus, adjustment of the financial statements is not necessary.

❷ Events that provide evidence about conditions that did not exist at the balance sheet date but arise subsequent to that date and do not require adjustment of the financial statements: Some of these events may have to be disclosed to keep the financial statements from being misleading. These disclosures take the form of notes, supplemental schedules, or even pro forma "as if" financial data prepared as if the event had occurred on the balance sheet date. Below are examples of such events that require disclosure (but do not result in adjustment):

(a) Sale of bonds or capital stock; stock splits or stock dividends.

(b) Business combination pending or effected.

(c) Settlement of litigation when the event giving rise to the claim took place subsequent to the balance sheet date.

(d) Loss of plant or inventories from fire or flood.

(e) Losses on receivables resulting from conditions (such as customer's major casualty) arising subsequent to the balance sheet date.

(f) Gains or losses on certain marketable securities.[8]

An example of subsequent events disclosure, excerpted from Walt Disney Company's Annual Report, is presented in Illustration 25-5.

ILLUSTRATION 25-5
Balance Sheet
Disclosure of
Subsequent Events

WALT DISNEY COMPANY

Note 14: Subsequent Event

In April 1997, the company purchased a significant equity stake in Starwave Corporation ("Starwave"), an internet technology company. On June 18, 1998, the company reached an agreement for the acquisition of Starwave by Infoseek Corporation ("Infoseek"), a publicly held Internet search company, pursuant to a merger. On November 18, 1998, the shareholders of both Infoseek and Starwave approved the merger. As a result of the merger and the company's purchase of additional shares of Infoseek common stock pursuant to the merger agreement, the company owns approximately 43% of Infoseek's outstanding common stock. In addition, pursuant to the merger agreement, the company purchased warrants enabling it, under certain circumstances, to achieve a majority stake in Infoseek. These warrants vest over a three-year period and expire in five years. Effective as of the November 18, 1998 closing date of the transaction, the company will record a significant noncash gain, a write-off for purchased in-process research and development costs and an increase in investments, reflecting the company's share of the fair value of Infoseek's intangible assets. The company is currently performing the necessary valuations to determine the gain, the research and development write-off and the amount of and amortization period for the intangible assets. Thereafter, the company will account for its investment in Infoseek under the equity method. The merger is not expected to have a material effect on the company's financial position.

Many subsequent events or developments are not likely to require either adjustment of or disclosure in the financial statements. Typically, these are nonaccounting events or conditions that managements normally communicate by other means. These events include legislation, product changes, management changes, strikes, unionization, marketing agreements, and loss of important customers.

---

[8]"Subsequent Events," *Statement on Auditing Standards No. 1* (New York: AICPA, 1973), pp. 123–124. *Accounting Trends and Techniques—1999* listed the following types of subsequent events and their frequency of occurrence among the 600 companies surveyed: debt incurred, reduced, or refinanced, 62; business combinations pending or effected, 81; discontinued operations, 46; litigation, 52; capital stock issued or repurchased, 25; employee benefit plans, 15; stock splits or dividends, stock rights, 26.

Reporting for Diversified (Conglomerate) Companies

In the last several decades business enterprises have had, at times, a tendency to diversify their operations. Take the case of conglomerate GenCorp. whose products include tires, Penn tennis balls, parts for the MX missile, and linings for disposable diapers. Its RKO subsidiary owns radio and television stations, makes movies, bottles soda pop, runs hotels, and holds a big stake in an airline. As a result of such diversification efforts, investors and investment analysts have sought more information concerning the details behind conglomerate financial statements. Particularly, they want income statement, balance sheet, and cash flow information on the **individual** segments that compose the **total** business income figure.

An illustration of **segmented** (disaggregated) financial information is presented in the following example of an office equipment and auto parts company.

OBJECTIVE 3
Describe the disclosure requirements for major segments of a business.

OFFICE EQUIPMENT AND AUTO PARTS COMPANY Income Statement Data (in millions)			
	Consolidated	Office Equipment	Auto Parts
Net sales	$78.8	$18.0	$60.8
Manufacturing costs:			
Inventories, beginning	12.3	4.0	8.3
Materials and services	38.9	10.8	28.1
Wages	12.9	3.8	9.1
Inventories, ending	(13.3)	(3.9)	(9.4)
	50.8	14.7	36.1
Selling and administrative expense	12.1	1.6	10.5
Total operating expenses	62.9	16.3	46.6
Income before taxes	15.9	1.7	14.2
Income taxes	(9.3)	(1.0)	(8.3)
Net income	$ 6.6	$ 0.7	$ 5.9

ILLUSTRATION 25-6
Segmented Income Statement

If only the consolidated figures are available to the analyst, much information regarding the composition of these figures is hidden in aggregated totals. There is no way to tell from the consolidated data the extent to which the differing product lines **contribute to the company's profitability, risk, and growth potential**. For example, in Illustration 25-6 above, if the office equipment segment is deemed a risky venture, then segmented reporting provides useful information for purposes of making an informed investment decision regarding the whole company.

A classic situation that demonstrates the need for segmented data involved Caterpillar, Inc. Caterpillar was cited by the SEC because it failed to tell investors that nearly a quarter of its income in 1989 came from a Brazilian unit. This income was nonrecurring in nature. The company knew that different economic policies in the next year would probably greatly affect earnings of the Brazilian unit. But Caterpillar presented its financial results on a consolidated basis, not disclosing the Brazilian's operations. The SEC stated that Caterpillar's failure to include information about Brazil left investors with an incomplete picture of the company's financial results and denied investors the opportunity to see the company "through the eyes of management."

Companies have always been somewhat hesitant to disclose segmented data for the reasons listed below.

① Without a thorough knowledge of the business and an understanding of such important factors as the competitive environment and capital investment requirements, the investor may find the segmented information meaningless or may even draw improper conclusions about the reported earnings of the segments.

2 Additional disclosure may harm reporting firms because it may be helpful to competitors, labor unions, suppliers, and certain government regulatory agencies.

3 Additional disclosure may discourage management from taking intelligent business risks because segments reporting losses or unsatisfactory earnings may cause stockholder dissatisfaction with management.

4 The wide variation among firms in the choice of segments, cost allocation, and other accounting problems limits the usefulness of segmented information.

5 The investor is investing in the company as a whole and not in the particular segments, and it should not matter how any single segment is performing if the overall performance is satisfactory.

6 Certain technical problems, such as classification of segments and allocation of segment revenues and costs (especially "common costs"), are formidable.

On the other hand, the advocates of segmented disclosures offer these reasons in support of the practice:

1 Segmented information is needed by the investor to make an intelligent investment decision regarding a diversified company.
   (a) Sales and earnings of individual segments are needed to forecast consolidated profits because of the differences between segments in growth rate, risk, and profitability.
   (b) Segmented reports disclose the nature of a company's businesses and the relative size of the components as an aid in evaluating the company's investment worth.

2 The absence of segmented reporting by a diversified company may put its unsegmented, single product-line competitors at a competitive disadvantage because the conglomerate may obscure information that its competitors must disclose.

The advocates of segmented disclosures appear to have a much stronger case. Many users indicate that segmented data are the most useful financial information provided, aside from the basic financial statements. As a result, the FASB has issued extensive reporting guidelines in this area.

Professional Pronouncements

The development of accounting standards for segmented financial information has been a continuing process during the past quarter century. Recognizing the need for guidelines in this area of reporting, the FASB in 1976 issued *FASB Statement No. 14*, "Financial Reporting for Segments of a Business Enterprise"; in 1993 it issued *Invitation to Comment*, "Reporting Disaggregated Information by Business Enterprises"; and in 1997 it issued *FASB Statement No. 131*, "Disclosures about Segments of an Enterprise and Related Information."[9] The basic reporting requirements related to the most recent pronouncement are discussed below.

Objective of Reporting Segmented Information

The objective of reporting segmented financial data is to provide information about the **different types of business activities** in which an enterprise engages and the **different economic environments** in which it operates, in order to help users of financial statements:

(a) Better understand the enterprise's performance.

(b) Better assess its prospects for future net cash flows.

(c) Make more informed judgments about the enterprise as a whole.

---

[9]"Disclosures about Segments of an Enterprise and Related Information," *Statement of Financial Accounting Standards No. 131* (Norwalk, Conn.: FASB, 1997).

Basic Principles

A company might meet the segmented reporting objective by providing complete sets of financial statements that are disaggregated in several ways, for example, by products or services, by geography, by legal entity, or by type of customer. However, it is not feasible to provide all of that information in every set of financial statements. *FASB Statement No. 131* requires that general purpose financial statements include selected information on a single basis of segmentation. The method chosen is referred to as the **management approach**. The management approach is based on the way the management segments the company for making operating decisions. Consequently, the segments are evident from the company's organization structure. It focuses on information about components of the business that management uses to make decisions about operating matters. These components are called **operating segments**.

Identifying Operating Segments

An **operating segment** is a component of an enterprise:

(a) That engages in business activities from which it earns revenues and incurs expenses.

(b) Whose operating results are regularly reviewed by the company's chief operating decision maker to assess segment performance and allocate resources to the segment.

(c) For which discrete financial information is available that is generated by or based on the internal financial reporting system.

Information about two or more operating segments may be aggregated only if the segments have the same basic characteristics in each of the following areas:

(a) The nature of the products and services provided.

(b) The nature of the production process.

(c) The type or class of customer.

(d) The methods of product or service distribution.

(e) If applicable, the nature of the regulatory environment.

After the company decides on the segments for possible disclosure, a quantitative materiality test is made to determine whether the segment is significant enough to warrant actual disclosure. An operating segment is regarded as significant and therefore identified as a reportable segment if it satisfies **one or more** of the following quantitative thresholds.

❶ Its **revenue** (including both sales to external customers and intersegment sales or transfers) is 10% or more of the combined revenue of all the enterprise's operating segments.

❷ The absolute amount of its **profit or loss** is 10% or more of the greater, in absolute amount, of
  (a) the combined operating profit of all operating segments that did not incur a loss, or
  (b) the combined loss of all operating segments that did report a loss.

❸ Its **identifiable assets** are 10% or more of the combined assets of all operating segments.

In applying these tests, two additional factors must be considered. First, segment data must explain a significant portion of the company's business. Specifically, the segmented results must equal or exceed 75% of the combined sales to unaffiliated customers for the entire enterprise. This test prevents a company from providing limited information on only a few segments and lumping all the rest into one category.

Second, the profession recognizes that reporting too many segments may overwhelm users with detailed information. The FASB decided that 10 is a reasonable upper limit for the number of segments that a company should be required to disclose.

To illustrate these requirements, assume a company has identified six possible reporting segments (000 omitted):

ILLUSTRATION 25-7
Data for Different
Possible Reporting
Segments

Segments	Total Revenue (Unaffiliated)	Operating Profit (Loss)	Identifiable Assets
A	$ 100	$10	$ 60
B	50	2	30
C	700	40	390
D	300	20	160
E	900	18	280
F	100	(5)	50
	$2,150	$85	$970

The respective tests may be applied as follows:

Revenue test: $10\% \times \$2,150 = \$215$; C, D, and E meet this test.

Operating profit (loss) test: $10\% \times \$90 = \$9$ (note that the $5 loss is ignored); A, C, D, and E meet this test.

Identifiable assets tests: $10\% \times \$970 = \$97$; C, D, and E meet this test.

The segments are therefore A, C, D, and E, assuming that these four segments have enough sales to meet the 75% of combined sales test. The 75% test is computed as follows:

75% of combined sales test: $75\% \times \$2,150 = \$1,612.50$; the sales of A, C, D, and E total $2,000 ($100 + $700 + $300 + $900); therefore, the 75% test is met.

Measurement Principles

The accounting principles to be used for segment disclosure need not be the same as the principles used to prepare the consolidated statements. This flexibility may at first appear inconsistent. But, preparing segment information in accordance with generally accepted accounting principles would be difficult because some principles are not expected to apply at a segment level. Examples are accounting for the cost of company-wide employee benefit plans, accounting for income taxes in a company that files a consolidated tax return, and accounting for inventory on a LIFO basis if the pool includes items in more than one segment.

Allocations of joint, common, or company-wide costs solely for external reporting purposes are not required. **Common costs** are those incurred for the benefit of more than one segment and whose interrelated nature prevents a completely objective division of costs among segments. For example, the company president's salary is difficult to allocate to various segments. Allocations of common costs are inherently arbitrary and may not be meaningful if they are not used for internal management purposes. There is a presumption that allocations to segments are either directly attributable or reasonably allocable.

Segmented Information Reported

The FASB requires that an enterprise report:

❶ *General information about its operating segments.* This includes factors that management considers most significant in determining the company's operating segments, and the types of products and services from which each operating segment derives its revenues.

❷ *Segment profit and loss and related information.* Specifically, the following information about each operating segment must be reported if the amounts are included in the determination of segment profit or loss:
(a) Revenues from transactions with external customers.
(b) Revenues from transactions with other operating segments of the same enterprise.

(c) Interest revenue.

(d) Interest expense.

(e) Depreciation, depletion, and amortization expense.

(f) Unusual items.

(g) Equity in the net income of investees accounted for by the equity method.

(h) Income tax expense or benefit.

(i) Extraordinary items.

(j) Significant noncash items other than depreciation, depletion, and amortization expense.

❸ *Segment assets.* An enterprise must report each operating segment's total assets.

❹ *Reconciliations.* An enterprise must provide a reconciliation of the total of the segments' revenues to total revenues, a reconciliation of the total of the operating segments' profits and losses to its income before income taxes, and a reconciliation of the total of the operating segments' assets to total assets.

❺ *Information about products and services and geographic areas.* For each operating segment that has not been determined based on geography, the enterprise must report (unless it is impracticable) [(a) in the enterprise's country of domicile and (b) in each other country if material]: (1) revenues from external customers, (2) long-lived assets, and (3) expenditures during the period for long-lived assets.

❻ *Major customers.* If 10 percent or more of the revenues is derived from a single customer, the enterprise must disclose the total amount of revenues from each such customer by segment.

Illustration of Disaggregated Information

The segment disclosure for Potlatch Corporation is shown in Illustration 25-8.

ILLUSTRATION 25-8
Segment Disclosure,
Potlatch Corporation

POTLATCH CORPORATION

13. Segment Information (in part)

The company has divided its operations into three reportable segments: wood products, printing papers and pulp and paper, based upon similarities in product lines, manufacturing processes, marketing and management of its businesses.

The reporting segments follow the same accounting policies used for the company's consolidated financial statements and described in the summary of significant accounting policies.

Following is a tabulation of business segment information for each of the past three years. Corporate information is included to reconcile segment data to the consolidated financial statements.

(Dollars in thousands)	1998	1997	1996
Segment sales:			
Wood products:			
Oriented strand board	$ 171,464	$ 106,807	$ 150,545
Lumber	225,668	247,232	201,022
Plywood	54,561	64,511	57,468
Particleboard	14,494	12,875	12,087
Logs, chips, etc.	124,536	119,435	111,118
	590,723	550,860	532,240
Printing papers	406,277	429,217	441,037
Pulp and paper:			
Pulp	12,467	11,183	12,346
Paperboard	390,708	420,054	404,136
Tissue	235,799	218,310	222,169
	638,974	649,547	638,651
	1,635,974	1,629,624	1,611,928
Elimination of intersegment sales	(70,096)	(60,754)	(57,479)
Total consolidated net sales	$1,565,878	$1,568,870	$1,554,449

(Dollars in thousands)	1998	1997	1996
Operating income:			
Wood products	$ 73,811	$ 47,674	$ 68,056
Printing papers	14,204	33,358	48,570
Pulp and paper	53,394	51,043	40,867
	141,409	132,075	157,493
Corporate items:			
Administration expense	(37,247)	(31,385)	(30,752)
Interest expense	(49,744)	(46,124)	(43,869)
Other, net	3,757	69	3,454
Consolidated earnings before taxes on income	$ 58,175	$ 54,635	$ 86,326

(Dollars in thousands)	1998	1997	1996
Depreciation, Amortization, and Cost of Fee Timber Harvested:			
Wood products	$ 54,245	$ 50,586	$ 49,072
Printing papers	41,618	39,436	35,318
Pulp and paper	53,525	58,689	56,092
	149,388	148,711	140,482
Corporate	890	1,074	1,039
Total	$ 150,278	$ 149,785	$ 141,521
Assets:			
Wood products	$ 671,381	$ 690,468	$ 698,151
Printing papers	685,743	644,457	592,228
Pulp and paper	825,547	842,337	850,612
	2,182,671	2,177,262	2,140,991
Corporate	194,635	187,874	124,688
Total consolidated assets	$2,377,306	$2,365,136	$2,265,679

(Dollars in thousands)	1998	1997	1996
Capital Expenditures:			
Wood products	$ 28,404	$ 31,578	$ 43,992
Printing papers	87,147	81,913	103,574
Pulp and paper	30,674	44,054	92,083
	146,225	157,545	239,649
Corporate	802	940	259
Total	$147,027	$158,485	$239,908

All of the company's manufacturing facilities and all other assets are located within the continental United States. However, the company sells and ships products to many foreign countries. Geographic information regarding the company's net sales is summarized as follows:

(Dollars in thousands)	1998	1997	1996
United States	$1,392,223	$1,382,674	$1,357,801
Japan	64,129	69,494	89,355
Australia	23,022	30,869	32,585
Canada	31,234	35,867	25,599
China	25,939	23,061	24,279
Italy	18,631	11,933	8,866
Other foreign countries	10,700	14,972	15,964
Total consolidated net sales	$1,565,878	$1,568,870	$1,554,449

ILLUSTRATION 25-8
Continued

Interim Reports

OBJECTIVE ④
Describe the accounting problems associated with interim reporting.

UNDERLYING CONCEPTS

For information to be relevant, it must be available to decision makers before it loses its capacity to influence their decisions (timeliness). Interim reporting is an excellent example of this concept.

One further source of information for the investor is interim reports. As noted earlier, interim reports are those reports that cover periods of less than one year. At one time, interim reports were referred to as the "forgotten reports"; such is no longer the case. The stock exchanges, the SEC, and the accounting profession have taken an active role in developing guidelines for the presentation of interim information.

The SEC mandates that certain companies file a Form 10Q, which requires a company to disclose quarterly data similar to that disclosed in the annual report. It also requires those companies to disclose selected quarterly information in notes to the annual financial statements. Illustration 25-9 on page 1397 presents the disclosure of selected quarterly data for **Tootsie Roll Industries, Inc.** In addition to this requirement, the APB issued *Opinion No. 28,* which attempted to narrow the reporting alternatives related to interim reports.[10]

Because of the short-term nature of the information in these reports, however, there is considerable controversy as to the general approach that should be employed. One group (which holds the discrete view) believes that each interim period should be treated as a separate accounting period; deferrals and accruals would therefore follow the principles employed for annual reports. Accounting transactions should be reported as they occur, and expense recognition should not change with the period of time covered. Another group (which holds the integral view) believes that the interim report is an integral part of the annual report and that deferrals and accruals should take into consideration what will happen for the entire year. In this approach, estimated expenses are assigned to parts of a year on the basis of sales volume or some other activity base. At present, many companies follow the discrete approach for certain types of expenses and the integral approach for others, because the standards currently employed in practice are vague and lead to differing interpretations.

---

[10]"Interim Financial Reporting," *Opinions of the Accounting Principles Board No. 28* (New York: AICPA, 1973).

TOOTSIE ROLL INDUSTRIES, INC.

For the Year Ended December 31, 1998

ILLUSTRATION 25-9
Disclosure of Selected
Quarterly Data

(Thousands of dollars except per share data)

	First	Second	Third	Fourth
Net sales	$69,701	$85,931	$144,230	$88,797
Gross margin	36,966	45,133	73,251	45,692
Net earnings	11,217	13,910	27,216	15,183
Net earnings per share	.23	.29	.57	.32

Stock Prices

	High	Low	Dividends
1st Qtr	38–13/32	29–27/32	$.0401
2nd Qtr	40–3/4	34–31/32	$.0525
3rd Qtr	47–1/4	33–3/4	$.0525
4th Qtr	42–7/8	34–1/8	$.0525

Interim Reporting Requirements

The profession indicates that the same accounting principles used for annual reports should be employed for interim reports. Revenues should be recognized in interim periods on the same basis as they are for annual periods. For example, if the installment sales method is used as the basis for recognizing revenue on an annual basis, then the installment basis should be applied to interim reports as well. Also, costs directly associated with revenues (product costs), such as materials, labor and related fringe benefits, and manufacturing overhead should be treated in the same manner for interim reports as for annual reports.

Companies generally should use the same inventory pricing methods (FIFO, LIFO, etc.) for interim reports that they use for annual reports. However, the following exceptions are appropriate at interim reporting periods:

❶ Companies may use the gross profit method for interim inventory pricing, but disclosure of the method and adjustments to reconcile with annual inventory are necessary.

❷ When LIFO inventories are liquidated at an interim date and are expected to be replaced by year end, cost of goods sold should include the expected cost of replacing the liquidated LIFO base and not give effect to the interim liquidation.

❸ Inventory market declines should not be deferred beyond the interim period unless they are temporary and no loss is expected for the fiscal year.

❹ Planned variances under a standard cost system which are expected to be absorbed by year end ordinarily should be deferred.

Costs and expenses other than product costs, often referred to as **period costs**, are often charged to the interim period as incurred. But they may be allocated among interim periods on the basis of an estimate of time expired, benefit received, or activity associated with the periods. Considerable latitude is exercised in accounting for these costs in interim periods, and many believe more definitive guidelines are needed.

Regarding disclosure, the following interim data should be reported as a minimum:

❶ Sales or gross revenues, provision for income taxes, extraordinary items, cumulative effect of a change in accounting principles or practices, and net income.

❷ Basic and diluted earnings per share where appropriate.

❸ Seasonal revenue, cost, or expenses.

❹ Significant changes in estimates or provisions for income taxes.

⑤ Disposal of a segment of a business and extraordinary, unusual, or infrequently occurring items.

⑥ Contingent items.

⑦ Changes in accounting principles or estimates.

⑧ Significant changes in financial position.

The profession also encourages, but does not require, companies to publish a balance sheet and a statement of cash flows. When this information is not presented, significant changes in such items as liquid assets, net working capital, long-term liabilities, and stockholders' equity should be disclosed.

Unique Problems of Interim Reporting

In *APB Opinion No. 28,* the Board indicated that it favored the integral approach. However, within this broad guideline, a number of unique reporting problems develop related to the following items.

Advertising and Similar Costs. The general guidelines are that costs such as advertising should be **deferred in an interim period if the benefits extend beyond that period; otherwise they should be expensed as incurred**. But such a determination is difficult, and even if they are deferred, how should they be allocated between quarters? Because of the vague guidelines in this area, accounting for advertising varies widely. Some companies in the food industry, such as RJR Nabisco and Pillsbury, charge advertising costs as a percentage of sales and adjust to actual at year end, whereas General Foods and Kellogg expense these costs as incurred.

The same type of problem relates to such items as social security taxes, research and development costs, and major repairs. For example, should the company expense social security costs (payroll taxes) on highly paid personnel early in the year or allocate and spread them to subsequent quarters? Should a major repair that occurs later in the year be anticipated and allocated proportionately to earlier periods?

Expenses Subject to Year-End Adjustment. Bad debts, executive bonuses, pension costs, and inventory shrinkage are often not known with a great deal of certainty until year end. **These costs should be estimated and allocated in the best possible way to interim periods.** Companies use a variety of allocation techniques to accomplish this objective.

Income Taxes. Not every dollar of corporate taxable income is assessed at the same rate; the tax rate is progressive. This aspect of business income taxes poses a problem in preparing **interim financial statements**. Should the income to date be annualized and the proportionate income tax accrued for the period to date **(annualized approach)**? Or should the first amount of income earned be taxed at the lower rate of tax applicable to such income **(marginal principle approach)**? At one time, companies generally followed the latter approach and accrued the tax applicable to each additional dollar of income.

The marginal principle was especially applicable to businesses having a seasonal or uneven income pattern, because the interim accrual of tax was based on the actual results to date. The profession now, however, uses the annualized approach requiring that "at the end of each interim period the company should make its best estimate of the effective tax rate expected to be applicable for the full fiscal year. The rate so determined should be used in providing for income taxes on income for the quarter."[11]

---

[11]"Interim Financial Reporting," *Opinions of the Accounting Principles Board No. 28* (New York: AICPA, 1973), par. 19. The estimated annual effective tax rate should reflect anticipated tax credits, foreign tax rates, percentage depletion, capital gains rates, and other available tax planning alternatives.

Because businesses did not uniformly apply this guideline in accounting for similar situations, the FASB issued *Interpretation No. 18.* This interpretation requires that the **estimated annual effective tax rate** be applied to the year-to-date "ordinary" income at the end of each interim period to compute the year-to-date tax. Further, the **interim period tax** related to "ordinary" income shall be the difference between the amount so computed and the amounts reported for previous interim periods of the fiscal period.[12]

Extraordinary Items. Extraordinary items consist of unusual and nonrecurring material gains and losses. In the past, they were handled in interim reports in one of three ways: (1) absorbed entirely in the quarter in which they occurred; (2) prorated over the four quarters; or (3) disclosed only by note. **The required approach is to charge or credit the loss or gain in the quarter that it occurs instead of attempting some arbitrary multiple-period allocation.** This approach is consistent with the way in which extraordinary items are currently handled on an annual basis; no attempt is made to prorate the extraordinary items over several years.

Some favor the omission of extraordinary items from the quarterly net income. They believe that inclusion of extraordinary items that may be large in proportion to interim results distorts the predictive value of interim reports. Many accountants, however, consider such an omission inappropriate because it deviates from actual results.

Changes in Accounting. What happens if a company decides to change an accounting principle in the third quarter of a fiscal year? Should the cumulative effect adjustment be charged or credited to that quarter? Presentation of a cumulative effect in the third quarter may be misleading because of the inherent subjectivity associated with the first two quarters' reported income. In addition, a question arises as to whether such a change might not be used to manipulate a given quarter's income. As a result, *FASB Statement No. 3* was issued indicating that **if a cumulative effect change occurs in other than the first quarter, no cumulative effect should be recognized in those quarters.**[13] **Rather, the cumulative effect at the beginning of the year should be computed and the first quarter restated.** Subsequent quarters would not report a cumulative effect adjustment.

Earnings per Share. Interim reporting of earnings per share has all the problems inherent in computing and presenting annual earnings per share, and then some. If shares are issued in the third period, EPS for the first two periods will not be indicative of year-end EPS. If an extraordinary item is present in one period and new equity shares are sold in another period, the EPS figure for the extraordinary item will change for the year. On an annual basis only one EPS figure is associated with an extraordinary item and that figure does not change; the interim figure is subject to change. **For purposes of computing earnings per share and making the required disclosure determinations, each interim period should stand alone. That is, all applicable tests should be made for that single period.**

Seasonality. **Seasonality** occurs when sales are compressed into one short period of the year while certain costs are fairly evenly spread throughout the year. For example, the natural gas industry has its heavy sales in the winter months, as contrasted with the beverage industry, which has its heavy sales in the summer months.

---

[12]"Accounting for Income Taxes in Interim Periods," *FASB Interpretation No. 18* (Stamford, Conn.: FASB, March 1977), par. 9. "Ordinary" income (or loss) refers to "income (or loss) from continuing operations before income taxes (or benefits)" excluding extraordinary items, discontinued operations, and cumulative effects of changes in accounting principles.

[13]"Reporting Accounting Changes in Interim Financial Statements," *Statement of the Financial Accounting Standards Board No. 3* (Stamford, Conn.: FASB, 1974). This standard also provides guidance related to a LIFO change and accounting changes made in the fourth quarter of a fiscal year in which interim data are not presented.

The problem of seasonality is related to the matching concept in accounting. Expenses should be matched against the revenues they create. In a seasonal business, wide fluctuations in profits occur because off-season sales do not absorb the company's fixed costs (for example, manufacturing, selling, and administrative costs that tend to remain fairly constant regardless of sales or production).

To illustrate why seasonality is a problem, assume the following information:

ILLUSTRATION 25-10
Data for Seasonality Example

Selling price per unit	$1
Annual sales for the period (projected and actual)	
100,000 units @ $1.00	$100,000
Manufacturing costs:	
Variable	10¢ per unit
Fixed	20¢ per unit or $20,000 for the year
Nonmanufacturing costs:	
Variable	10¢ per unit
Fixed	30¢ per unit or $30,000 for the year

Sales for four quarters and the year (projected and actual) were:

ILLUSTRATION 25-11
Sales Data for Seasonality Example

		Percent of Sales
1st Quarter	$ 20,000	20%
2nd Quarter	5,000	5
3rd Quarter	10,000	10
4th Quarter	65,000	65
Total for the year	$100,000	100%

Under the present accounting framework, the income statements for the quarters might be presented as follows:

ILLUSTRATION 25-12
Interim Net Income for Seasonal Business— Discrete Approach

	1st Qtr	2nd Qtr	3rd Qtr	4th Qtr	Year
Sales	$20,000	$ 5,000	$10,000	$65,000	$100,000
Manufacturing costs					
Variable	(2,000)	(500)	(1,000)	(6,500)	(10,000)
Fixed[a]	(4,000)	(1,000)	(2,000)	(13,000)	(20,000)
	14,000	3,500	7,000	45,500	70,000
Nonmanufacturing costs					
Variable	(2,000)	(500)	(1,000)	(6,500)	(10,000)
Fixed[b]	(7,500)	(7,500)	(7,500)	(7,500)	(30,000)
Net income	$ 4,500	$ (4,500)	$ (1,500)	$31,500	$ 30,000

[a]The fixed manufacturing costs are inventoried, so that equal amounts of fixed costs do not appear during each quarter.
[b]The fixed nonmanufacturing costs are not inventoried so that equal amounts of fixed costs appear during each quarter.

An investor who uses the first quarter's results can be misled. If the first quarter's earnings are $4,500, should this figure be multiplied by four to predict annual earnings of $18,000? Or, as the analysis suggests, inasmuch as $20,000 in sales is 20% of the predicted sales for the year, net income for the year should be $22,500 ($4,500 × 5). Either figure is obviously wrong, and after the second quarter's results occur, the investor may become even more confused.

The problem with the conventional approach is that the fixed nonmanufacturing costs are not charged in proportion to sales. Some enterprises have adopted a way of avoiding this problem by making all fixed nonmanufacturing costs follow the sales pattern, as shown in Illustration 25-13.

	1st Qtr	2nd Qtr	3rd Qtr	4th Qtr	Year
Sales	$20,000	$ 5,000	$10,000	$65,000	$100,000
Manufacturing costs					
Variable	(2,000)	(500)	(1,000)	(6,500)	(10,000)
Fixed	(4,000)	(1,000)	(2,000)	(13,000)	(20,000)
	14,000	3,500	7,000	45,500	70,000
Nonmanufacturing costs					
Variable	(2,000)	(500)	(1,000)	(6,500)	(10,000)
Fixed	(6,000)	(1,500)	(3,000)	(19,500)	(30,000)
Net income	$ 6,000	$ 1,500	$ 3,000	$19,500	$ 30,000

ILLUSTRATION 25-13
Interim Net Income for Seasonal Business—Integral Approach

This approach solves some of the problems of interim reporting: sales in the first quarter are 20% of total sales for the year, and net income in the first quarter is 20% of total income. In this case, as in the previous example, the investor cannot rely on multiplying any given quarter by four, but can use comparative data or rely on some estimate of sales in relation to income for a given period.

The greater the degree of seasonality experienced by a company, the greater the possibility of distortion. Because no definitive guidelines are available for handling such items as the fixed nonmanufacturing costs, variability in income can be substantial. To alleviate this problem, the profession recommends that companies subject to material seasonal variations disclose the seasonal nature of their business and consider supplementing their interim reports with information for 12-month periods ended at the interim date for the current and preceding years.

The two illustrations above highlight the difference between the **discrete** and **integral** viewpoints. The fixed nonmanufacturing expenses are expensed as incurred under the discrete viewpoint. They are charged to expense on the basis of some measure of activity under the integral method.

Continuing Controversy. The profession has developed some standards for interim reporting; but much still has to be done. As yet, it is unclear whether the discrete, integral, or some combination of these two methods will be settled on.

Discussion also persists concerning the independent auditor's involvement in interim reports. Many auditors are reluctant to express an opinion on interim financial information, arguing that the data are too tentative and subjective. Conversely, an increasing number of individuals advocate some type of examination of interim reports. A compromise may be a limited review of interim reports that provides some assurance that an examination has been conducted by an outside party and that the published information appears to be in accord with generally accepted accounting principles.[14]

Analysts want financial information as soon as possible, before it's old news. We may not be far from a continuous database system in which corporate financial records can be accessed by microcomputer. Investors might be able to access a company's financial records via computer whenever they wish and put the information in the format they need. Thus, they could learn about sales slippage, cost increases, or earnings changes as they happen, rather than waiting until after the quarter has ended.[15]

A steady stream of information from the company to the investor could be very positive because it might alleviate management's continual concern with short-run

UNDERLYING CONCEPTS
The AICPA Special Committee on Financial Reporting indicates that users would benefit from separate fourth-quarter reporting, including management's analysis of fourth-quarter activities and events. Also, quarterly segment reporting was demanded. Under *FASB Statement No. 131*, companies now provide quarterly segment data.

---

[14]The AICPA has been involved in developing guidelines for the review of interim reports. "Limited Review of Interim Financial Statements," *Statement on Auditing Standards No. 24* (New York: AICPA, 1979) sets standards for the review of interim reports.

[15]A step in this direction is the SEC's mandate for companies to file their financial statements electronically with the SEC. The system, called EDGAR (electronic data gathering and retrieval) provides interested parties with computer access to financial information such as periodic filings, corporate prospectuses, and proxy materials.

interim numbers. Today many contend that U.S. management is too short-run oriented. The truth of this statement is echoed by the words of the president of a large company who decided to retire early: "I wanted to look forward to a year made up of four seasons rather than four quarters."

AUDITOR'S AND MANAGEMENT'S REPORTS

Auditor's Report

OBJECTIVE 5
Identify the major disclosures found in the auditor's report.

Another important source of information that is often overlooked is the **auditor's report**. An **auditor** is an accounting professional who conducts an independent examination of the accounting data presented by a business enterprise. If the auditor is satisfied that the financial statements present the financial position, results of operations, and cash flows fairly in accordance with generally accepted accounting principles, an unqualified opinion is expressed as shown in Illustration 25-14.[16]

ILLUSTRATION 25-14
Auditor's Report

INTERNATIONAL INSIGHT

In Germany, auditor's opinions address whether the statements have been prepared in accordance with German law—a statutory audit.

UAL CORPORATION

Report of Independent Public Accountants

To the Stockholders and Board of Directors, UAL Corporation:

We have audited, in accordance with generally accepted auditing standards, the statements of consolidated financial position of UAL Corporation (a Delaware corporation) and subsidiary companies as of December 31, 1998 and 1997, and the related statements of consolidated operations, consolidated cash flows, and consolidated stockholders' equity for each of the three years in the period ended December 31, 1998, appearing in the appendix to the proxy statement for the 1999 Annual Meeting of Stockholders of the Company (not presented herein). In our report dated February 24, 1999, also appearing in that proxy statement, we expressed an unqualified opinion on those consolidated financial statements.

In our opinion, the information set forth in the accompanying consolidated statements of financial position as of December 31, 1998 and 1997, and the related statements of consolidated operations, consolidated cash flows and consolidated stockholders' equity for each of the three years in the period ended December 31, 1998, is fairly stated, in all material respects, in relation to the consolidated financial statements from which it has been derived.

Arthur Andersen LLP

Chicago, Illinois
February 24, 1999

In preparing this report, the auditor follows these reporting standards:

❶ The report shall state whether the financial statements are presented in accordance with generally accepted accounting principles.

❷ The report shall identify those circumstances in which such principles have not been consistently observed in the current period in relation to the preceding period.

❸ Informative disclosures in the financial statements are to be regarded as reasonably adequate unless otherwise stated in the report.

---

[16]This auditor's report is in exact conformance with the specifications contained in "Reports on Audited Financial Statements," *Statement on Auditing Standards No. 58* (New York: AICPA, 1988).

④ The report shall contain either an expression of opinion regarding the financial statements taken as a whole or an assertion to the effect that an opinion cannot be expressed. When an overall opinion cannot be expressed, the reasons why should be stated. In all cases where an auditor's name is associated with financial statements, the report should contain a clear-cut indication of the character of the auditor's examination, if any, and the degree of responsibility being taken.

In most cases, the auditor issues a standard unqualified or clean opinion; that is, the auditor expresses the opinion that the financial statements present fairly, in all material respects, the financial position, results of operations, and cash flows of the entity in conformity with generally accepted accounting principles. Certain circumstances, although they do not affect the auditor's unqualified opinion, may require the auditor to add an explanatory paragraph to the audit report. Some of the more important circumstances are as follows:

❶ *Uncertainties.* A matter involving an **uncertainty** is one that is expected to be resolved at a future date, at which time sufficient evidence concerning its outcome is expected to become available. In deciding whether an explanatory paragraph is needed, the auditor should consider the likelihood of a material loss resulting from the contingency. If, for example, the possibility that a loss will be incurred is remote, then an explanatory paragraph is not warranted. If the loss is probable but not estimable, or is reasonably possible and material, then an explanatory paragraph is warranted.

❷ *Lack of Consistency.* If there has been a change in accounting principles or in the method of their application that has a material effect on the comparability of the company's financial statements, the auditor should refer to the change in an explanatory paragraph of the report. Such an explanatory paragraph should identify the nature of the change and refer the reader to the note in the financial statements that discusses the change in detail. The auditor's concurrence with a change is implicit unless exception to the change is taken in expressing the auditor's opinion as to fair presentation of the financial statements in conformity with generally accepted accounting principles.

❸ *Emphasis of a Matter.* The auditor may wish to emphasize a matter regarding the financial statements, but nevertheless intends to express an unqualified opinion. For example, the auditor may wish to emphasize that the entity is a component of a larger business enterprise or that it has had significant transactions with related parties. Such explanatory information should be presented in a separate paragraph of the auditor's report.

In some situations, however, the auditor is required to (1) express a **qualified** opinion, (2) express an **adverse** opinion, or (3) **disclaim** an opinion. A qualified opinion contains an exception to the standard opinion. Ordinarily the exception is not of sufficient magnitude to invalidate the statements as a whole; if it were, an adverse opinion would be rendered. The usual circumstances in which the auditor may deviate from the standard unqualified short-form report on financial statements are as follows:

❶ The scope of the examination is limited or affected by conditions or restrictions.
❷ The statements do not fairly present financial position or results of operations because of:
   (a) Lack of conformity with generally accepted accounting principles and standards.
   (b) Inadequate disclosure.

If the auditor is confronted with one of the situations noted above, the opinion must be qualified. A qualified opinion states that, except for the effects of the matter to which the qualification relates, the financial statements present fairly, in all material respects, the financial position, results of operations, and cash flows in conformity with generally accepted accounting principles.

An **adverse opinion** is required in any report in which the exceptions to fair presentation are so material that in the independent auditor's judgment a qualified opinion is not justified. In such a case, the financial statements taken as a whole are not presented in accordance with generally accepted accounting principles. Adverse opinions are rare, because most enterprises change their accounting to conform with the auditor's desires.

A **disclaimer of an opinion** is appropriate when the auditor has gathered so little information on the financial statements that no opinion can be expressed.

An example of a report in which the opinion is qualified because of the use of an accounting principle at variance with generally accepted accounting principles is shown in Illustration 25-15 (assuming the effects are such that the auditor has concluded that an adverse opinion is not appropriate).

ILLUSTRATION 25-15
Qualified Auditor's
Report

HELIO COMPANY

Independent Auditor's Report

(Same first paragraph as the standard report)

Helio Company has excluded, from property and debt in the accompanying balance sheets, certain lease obligations that, in our opinion, should be capitalized in order to conform with generally accepted accounting principles. If these lease obligations were capitalized, property would be increased by $1,500,000 and $1,300,000, long-term debt by $1,400,000 and $1,200,000, and retained earnings by $100,000 and $50,000 as of December 31, 1996 and 1995, respectively. Additionally, net income would be decreased by $40,000 and $30,000 and earnings per share would be decreased by $.06 and $.04, respectively, for the years then ended.

In our opinion, except for the effects of not capitalizing certain lease obligations as discussed in the preceding paragraph, the financial statements referred to above present fairly, in all material respects, the financial position of Helio Company as of December 31, 1996 and 1995, and the results of its operations and its cash flows for the years then ended in conformity with generally accepted accounting principles.

The profession also requires the auditor to evaluate whether there is substantial doubt about the entity's **ability to continue as a going concern** for a reasonable period of time (not to exceed one year beyond the date of the financial statements). If the auditor concludes that substantial doubt exists, an explanatory note to the auditor's report would be added describing the potential problem.[17]

The audit report should provide useful information to the investor. One investment banker noted, "Probably the first item to check is the auditor's opinion to see whether or not it is a clean one—'in conformity with generally accepted accounting principles'— or is qualified in regard to differences between the auditor and company management in the accounting treatment of some major item, or in the outcome of some major litigation."

INTERNATIONAL INSIGHT

In 1992, IOSCO agreed to accept international auditing standards for cross-border listings.

Management's Reports

Management's Discussion and Analysis

Management's discussion and analysis (MD&A) section covers three financial aspects of an enterprise's business—liquidity, capital resources, and results of operations. **It requires management to highlight favorable or unfavorable trends and to identify significant events and uncertainties that affect these three factors.** This approach obvi-

---

[17]"The Auditor's Consideration of an Entity's Ability to Continue as a Going Concern," *Statement on Auditing Standards No. 59* (New York: AICPA, 1988).

ously involves a number of subjective estimates, opinions, and soft data. However, the SEC, which has mandated this disclosure, believes the relevance of this information exceeds the potential lack of reliability.

The MD&A section (1999 outlook only) of **Kellogg Company**'s Annual Report is presented in Illustration 25-16.

KELLOGG COMPANY

1999 Outlook

Management is not aware of any adverse trends that would materially affect the Company's strong financial position. Should suitable investment opportunities or working capital needs arise that would require additional financing, management believes that the Company's strong credit rating, balance sheet, and earnings history provide a base for obtaining additional financial resources at competitive rates and terms. Based on the expectation of cereal volume growth, and strong results from product innovation and the continued global roll-out of convenience foods, management believes the Company is well-positioned to deliver sales and earnings growth for the full year 1999. The Company will continue to identify and pursue streamlining and productivity initiatives to optimize its cost structure.

The Company is currently reviewing strategies related to the **Lender's Bagels** business, given its performance since acquisition. The Company has evaluated the recoverability of Lender's long-lived assets as of December 31, 1998, and although this evaluation has not resulted in the recognition of an impairment loss, management expects to update its assessment during 1999.

Additional expectations for 1999 include a gross profit margin of 51–52%, an SGA% of 36–37%, an effective income tax rate of 36–37%, and capital spending of approximately $270 million.

The foregoing projections concerning impact of future borrowing costs, accounting changes, volume growth, profitability, capital spending, and common stock repurchase activity are forward-looking statements that involve risks and uncertainties. Actual results may differ materially due to the impact of competitive conditions, marketing spending and/or incremental pricing actions on actual volumes and product mix; the levels of spending on system initiatives, properties, business opportunities, continued streamlining initiatives, and other general and administrative costs; raw material price and labor cost fluctuations; foreign currency exchange rate fluctuations; changes in statutory tax law; interest rates available on short-term financing; the impact of stock market conditions on common stock repurchase activity; and other items.

ILLUSTRATION 25-16
Management's Discussion and Analysis

UNDERLYING CONCEPTS

FASB Concepts Statement No. 1 notes that management knows more about the enterprise than users and therefore can increase the usefulness of financial information by identifying significant transactions that affect the enterprise and by explaining their financial impact.

The MD&A section also must provide information concerning the effects of inflation and changing prices if material to financial statement trends. No specific numerical computations are specified, and companies have provided little analysis on changing prices.

How this section of the annual report can be made even more effective is the subject of continuing questions such as:

1 Is sufficient forward-looking information being disclosed under current MD&A requirements?

2 Should MD&A disclosures be changed to become more of a risk analysis?

3 Should the MD&A be audited by independent auditors?

Management's Responsibilities for Financial Statements

The SEC has considered requiring companies to include a report on management's responsibilities including its responsibilities for, and assessment of, the internal control system. Some companies already present this type of information, although the SEC requirements would be more detailed about the internal control procedures used and their effectiveness. An example of the type of disclosure that some companies are now making is shown in Illustration 25-17.

Go to the Digital Tool for an expanded discussion of accounting for changing prices.

OBJECTIVE 6
Understand management's responsibilities for financials.

ILLUSTRATION 25-17
Report on
Management's
Responsibilities

UAL CORPORATION

Management Statement on Accounting Controls

The integrity of UAL Corporation's financial records, from which the financial statements are prepared, is largely dependent on the Company's system of internal accounting controls. The purpose of the system is to provide reasonable assurance that transactions are executed in accordance with management's authorization; that transactions are appropriately recorded in order to permit preparation of financial statements which, in all material respects, are presented in conformity with generally accepted accounting principles consistently applied; and that assets are properly accounted for and safeguarded against loss from unauthorized use. Underlying this concept of reasonable assurance is the fact that limitations exist in any system of internal accounting controls based on the premise that the cost of such controls should not exceed the benefits derived therefrom.

To enhance the effective achievement of internal accounting controls, the Company carefully selects and trains its employees, gives due emphasis to appropriate division of clearly defined lines of responsibility and develops and communicates written policies and procedures. Based on a review and monitoring of internal accounting controls, augmented by an internal auditing function and the oversight responsibilities of the outside directors comprising the Audit Committee of the Company's Board of Directors, management believes that the Company's internal accounting control system is adequate and appropriately balances the relationship between the cost of the system and the benefits it provides.

Gerald Greenwald
Chairman and CEO

Douglas A. Hacker
Senior Vice President and CFO

CURRENT REPORTING ISSUES

Reporting on Financial Forecasts and Projections

In recent years, the investing public's demand for more and better information has focused on disclosure of corporate expectations for the future.[18] These disclosures take one of two forms:[19]

> **OBJECTIVE 7**
> Identify issues related to financial forecasts and projections.

Financial Forecast. Prospective financial statements that present, to the best of the responsible party's knowledge and belief, an entity's expected financial position, results of operations, and cash flows. A financial forecast is based on the responsible party's assumptions reflecting conditions it expects to exist and the course of action it expects to take.

Financial Projection. Prospective financial statements that present, to the best of the responsible party's knowledge and belief, given one or more hypothetical assumptions, an entity's expected financial position, results of operations, and cash flows. A financial projection is based on the responsible party's assumptions reflecting conditions it expects would

---

[18]Some areas in which companies are using financial information about the future are equipment lease-versus-buy analysis, analysis of a company's ability to successfully enter new markets, and examining merger and acquisition opportunities. In addition, forecasts and projections are also prepared for use by third parties in public offering documents (requiring financial forecasts), tax-oriented investments, and financial feasibility studies. Use of forward-looking data has been enhanced by the increased capability of the microcomputer to analyze, compare, and manipulate large quantities of data.

[19]"Financial Forecasts and Projections," *Statement of Standards for Accountants' Services on Prospective Financial Information* (New York: AICPA, October 1985), par. 6.

exist and the course of action it expects would be taken, given one or more hypothetical assumptions.

The difference between a financial forecast and a financial projection is that a forecast attempts to provide information on what is expected to happen, whereas a projection may provide information on what is not necessarily expected to happen, but **might** take place.

Financial forecasts are the subject of intensive discussion with journalists, corporate executives, the SEC, financial analysts, accountants, and others. Predictably, there are strong arguments on either side. Listed below are some of the arguments.

Arguments for requiring published forecasts:

❶ Investment decisions are based on future expectations; therefore, information about the future facilitates better decisions.

❷ Forecasts are already circulated informally, but are uncontrolled, frequently misleading, and not available equally to all investors. This confused situation should be brought under control.

❸ Circumstances now change so rapidly that historical information is no longer adequate for prediction.

Arguments against requiring published forecasts:

❶ No one can foretell the future. Therefore forecasts, while conveying an impression of precision about the future, will inevitably be wrong.

❷ Organizations will strive only to meet their published forecasts, not to produce results that are in the stockholders' best interest.

❸ When forecasts are not proved to be accurate, there will be recriminations and probably legal actions.[20]

❹ Disclosure of forecasts will be detrimental to organizations, because it will fully inform not only investors, but also competitors (foreign and domestic).

The AICPA has issued a statement on standards for accountants' services on prospective financial information. This statement established procedures and reporting standards for presenting financial forecasts and projections. It requires accountants to provide (1) a summary of significant assumptions used in the forecast or projection and (2) guidelines for minimum presentation.[21]

To encourage management to disclose this type of information, the SEC has a safe harbor rule. This rule provides protection to an enterprise that presents an erroneous forecast as long as the forecast is prepared on a reasonable basis and is disclosed in good faith.[22] However, many companies note that the safe harbor rule does not work in practice, since it does not cover oral statements, nor has it kept them out of court.

Experience in Great Britain

Great Britain has permitted financial forecasts for years, and the results have been fairly successful. Some significant differences exist between the English and the American business and legal environment,[23] but probably none that could not be overcome if

UNDERLYING CONCEPTS

The AICPA's Special Committee on Financial Reporting indicates that the current legal environment discourages companies from disclosing forward-looking information. Companies should not have to expand reporting of forward-looking information until there are more effective deterrents to unwarranted litigation.

---

[20]The issue is serious. Over a recent 3-year period, 8 percent of the companies on the NYSE have been sued because of an alleged lack of financial disclosure. Companies complain that they are subject to lawsuits whenever the stock price drops. And as one executive noted: You can even be sued if the stock price goes up—because you did not disclose the good news fast enough.

[21]"Financial Forecasts and Projections," op. cit., 44 pages.

[22]"Safe-Harbor Rule for Projections," *Release No. 5993* (Washington: SEC, 1979). The Private Securities Litigation Reform Act of 1995 recognizes that some information that is useful to investors is inherently subject to less certainty or reliability than other information. By providing safe harbor for forward-looking statements, Congress has sought to facilitate access to this information by investors.

[23]The British system, for example, does not permit litigation on forecasted information, and the solicitor (lawyer) is not permitted to work on a contingent fee basis. See "A Case for Forecasting—The British Have Tried It and Find That It Works," *World* (New York: Peat, Marwick, Mitchell & Co., Autumn 1978), pp. 10–13.

influential interests in this country cooperated to produce an atmosphere conducive to quality forecasting. A typical British forecast adapted from a construction company's report to support a public offering of stock is as follows:

ILLUSTRATION 25-18
Financial Forecast of a
British Company

> Profits have grown substantially over the past 10 years and directors are confident of being able to continue this expansion. . . . While the rate of expansion will be dependent on the level of economic activity in Ireland and England, the group is well structured to avail itself of opportunities as they arise, particularly in the field of property development, which is expected to play an increasingly important role in the group's future expansion.
>
> Profits before taxation for the half year ended 30th June 1999 were 402,000 pounds. On the basis of trading experiences since that date and the present level of sales and completions, the directors expect that in the absence of unforeseen circumstances, the group's profits before taxation for the year to 31st December 1999 will be not less than 960,000 pounds.
>
> No dividends will be paid in respect of the year December 31, 1999. In a full financial year, on the basis of above forecasts (not including full year profits) it would be the intention of the board, assuming current rates of tax, to recommend dividends totaling 40% (of after-tax profits), of which 15% payable would be as an interest dividend in November 2000 and 25% as a final dividend in June 2001.

A general narrative-type forecast issued by a U.S. corporation might appear as follows:

ILLUSTRATION 25-19
Financial Forecast for an
American Company

> On the basis of promotions planned by the company for the second half of fiscal 1999, net earnings for that period are expected to be approximately the same as those for the first half of fiscal 1999, with net earnings for the third quarter expected to make the predominant contribution to net earnings for the second half of fiscal 1999.

Questions of Liability

What happens if a company does not meet its forecasts? Are the company and the auditor going to be sued? If a company, for example, projects an earnings increase of 15% and achieves only 5%, should the stockholder be permitted to have some judicial recourse against the company? One court case involving **Monsanto Chemical Corporation** has provided some guidelines. In this case, Monsanto predicted that sales would increase 8 to 9% and that earnings would rise 4 to 5%. In the last part of the year, the demand for Monsanto's products dropped as a result of a business turndown. Therefore, instead of increasing, the company's earnings declined. The company was sued because the projected earnings figure was erroneous, but the judge dismissed the suit because the forecasts were the best estimates of qualified people whose intents were honest.

As indicated earlier, the SEC's safe harbor rules are intended to protect enterprises that provide good-faith projections. However, much concern exists as to how the SEC and the courts will interpret such terms as "good faith" and "reasonable assumptions" when erroneous forecasts mislead users of this information.

Internet Financial Reporting

How can companies improve the usefulness of their financial reporting practices? Many companies are using the power and reach of the Internet to provide more useful information to financial statement readers. Recent surveys indicate that over 80% of large companies have Internet sites, and a large proportion of these companies' Web sites contain links to their financial statements and other disclosures.[24] The increased pop-

---

[24]The FASB has recently issued a report on electronic dissemination of financial reports. This report summarizes current practice and research conducted on Internet financial reporting. Business Reporting Research Project, "Electronic Distribution of Business Reporting Information" (Norwalk, Conn.: FASB, 2000).

ularity of such reporting is not surprising, since the costs of printing and dissemination of paper reports could be reduced with the use of Internet reporting.

How does Internet financial reporting improve the overall usefulness of a company's financial reports? First, dissemination of reports via the Web can allow firms **to communicate with more users** than is possible with traditional paper reports. In addition, **Internet reporting allows users to take advantage of tools** such as search engines and hyperlinks to quickly find information about the firm and, sometimes, to download the information for analysis, perhaps in computer spreadsheets. Finally, **Internet reporting can help make financial reports more relevant** by allowing companies to report expanded disaggregated data and more timely data than is possible through paper-based reporting. For example, some companies voluntarily report weekly sales data and segment operating data on their Web sites.

Given these benefits and ever-improving Internet tools, will it be long before electronic reporting replaces paper-based financial disclosure? The main obstacles to achieving complete electronic reporting are related to equality of access to electronic financial reporting and the reliability of the information distributed via the Internet. Although companies may practice Internet financial reporting, they must still prepare traditional paper reports because some investors may not have access to the Internet. These investors would receive differential (less) information relative to other "wired" investors if companies were to eliminate paper reports. In addition, at present, Internet financial reporting is a voluntary means of reporting. As a result, there are no standards as to the completeness of reports on the Internet, nor is there the requirement that these reports be audited. One concern in this regard is that computer "hackers" could invade a company's Web site and corrupt the financial information contained therein.

Thus, although Internet financial reporting is gaining in popularity, until issues related to differential access to the Internet and the reliability of information disseminated via the Web are addressed, we will continue to see traditional paper-based reporting.

Fraudulent Financial Reporting

The system of financial reporting in the United States is generally considered the finest in the world. The importance of an effective financial reporting system cannot be underestimated, because it provides the financial information that ensures the proper functioning of the capital and credit markets. Unfortunately, the system does not always work as planned. Evidence of the shortcomings of the system includes financial frauds such as E.S.M. Government Securities, Inc., Home-State Savings and Loan of Ohio, American Savings and Loan Association of Florida, Penn Square Bank, Continental Illinois Bank, Beverly Hills Savings and Loan Association, United American Bank, and Drysdale Government Securities as examples.

The case of **E.S.M. Government Securities, Inc. (E.S.M.)** exemplifies the seriousness of these frauds. E.S.M. was a Fort Lauderdale securities dealer entrusted with monies to invest by municipalities from Toledo, Ohio to Beaumont, Texas.[25] The cities provided the cash to E.S.M. which they thought was collateralized with government securities. Examination of E.S.M.'s balance sheet indicated that the company owed about as much as it expected to collect. Unfortunately, the amount it expected to collect was from insolvent affiliates which, in effect, meant that E.S.M. was bankrupt. In fact, E.S.M. had been bankrupt for more than 6 years, and the fraud was discovered only because a customer questioned a note to the balance sheet! More than $300 million of losses had been disguised.

Although frauds such as these are unusual, they do raise questions about the financial reporting process. As indicated in Chapter 1, Congress continues to examine

> **OBJECTIVE 8**
> Describe the profession's response to fraudulent financial reporting.

---

[25]For an expanded discussion of this case, see Robert J. Sack and Robert Tangreti, "ESM: Implications for the Profession," *Journal of Accountancy,* April 1987.

this process to determine whether improvements can be made. As this textbook is being written, for example, Congress is addressing basic issues such as the following:

1. How well are accounting practices and disclosures serving the public?
2. Are auditors meeting their obligations to the investing public?
3. What are the effects of the SEC's disclosure, compliance, and enforcement policies?
4. Could the effect of these regulatory accounting policies have contributed to these failures?
5. What legislative proposals, if any, are necessary to address perceived weaknesses in accounting and auditing standards and regulatory procedures?

Many other groups have been studying the financial reporting environment. One such group, the National Commission on Fraudulent Financial Reporting, chaired by James C. Treadway, Jr.—hereafter referred to as the **Treadway Commission**—identified causal factors that lead to fraudulent financial reporting and provided steps to reduce its incidence.[26]

The Commission defined fraudulent financial reporting as "intentional or reckless conduct, whether act or omission, that results in materially misleading financial statements." It also noted that fraudulent reporting can involve gross and deliberate distortion of corporate records (such as inventory count tags), or misapplication of accounting principles (failure to disclose material transactions).[27]

Causes of Fraudulent Financial Reporting

Fraudulent financial reporting usually occurs because of conditions in the internal or external environment.[28] Influences in the **internal environment** relate to poor systems of internal control, management's poor attitude toward ethics, or perhaps a company's liquidity or profitability. Those in the **external environment** may relate to industry conditions, overall business environment, or legal and regulatory considerations.

General incentives for fraudulent financial reporting are the desire to obtain a higher stock price or debt offering, to avoid default on a loan covenant, or to make a personal gain of some type (additional compensation, promotion). Situational pressures on the company or an individual manager also may lead to fraudulent financial reporting. Examples of these situational pressures include:

1. Sudden decreases in revenue or market share. A single company or an entire industry can experience these decreases.
2. Unrealistic budget pressures, particularly for short-term results. These pressures may occur when headquarters arbitrarily determines profit objectives and budgets without taking actual conditions into account.
3. Financial pressure resulting from bonus plans that depend on short-term economic performance. This pressure is particularly acute when the bonus is a significant component of the individual's total compensation.

Opportunities for fraudulent financial reporting are present in circumstances when the fraud is easy to commit and when detection is difficult. Frequently these opportunities arise from:

1. *The absence of a Board of Directors or audit committee* that vigilantly oversees the financial reporting process.

---

[26]"Report of the National Commission on Fraudulent Financial Reporting" (Washington, D.C., 1987).

[27]Ibid, page 2. Unintentional errors as well as corporate improprieties (such as tax fraud, employee embezzlements, and so on) which do not cause the financial statements to be misleading are excluded from the definition of fraudulent financial reporting.

[28]The discussion in this section is taken from the Report of the National Commission on Fraudulent Financial Reporting, pp. 23–24.

② *Weak or nonexistent internal accounting controls.* This situation can occur, for example, when a company's revenue system is overloaded as a result of a rapid expansion of sales, an acquisition of a new division, or the entry into a new, unfamiliar line of business.

③ *Unusual or complex transactions* such as the consolidation of two companies, the divestiture or closing of a specific operation, and agreements to buy or sell government securities under a repurchase agreement.

④ *Accounting estimates, requiring significant subjective judgment* by company management, such as reserves for loan losses and the yearly provision for warranty expense.

⑤ *Ineffective internal audit staffs* resulting from inadequate staff size and severely limited audit scope.

A weak corporate ethical climate contributes to these situations. Opportunities for fraudulent financial reporting also increase dramatically when the accounting principles followed in reporting transactions are nonexistent, evolving, or subject to varying interpretations.

Response of the Profession

The profession is working to find solutions to the problem of fraudulent financial reporting. For example, the Auditing Standards Board of AICPA has issued numerous auditing standards in response not only to the Treadway Commission report, but also to the public's higher expectation of the auditor.[29] Recently the Board issued a new standard that "raises the bar" on the performance of financial statement audits by explicitly requiring auditors to assess the risk of material financial misstatement due to fraud.[30]

In addition, the SEC requires disclosure of a change in a company's independent auditor. Many observers have expressed concern about so-called "opinion shopping" in which companies attempt to find a more favorable accounting approach by asking various auditing firms how they would report a given transaction. Because a great deal of subjectivity may be involved, an auditing firm may provide a more favorable response to the prospective client and therefore eventually be engaged as the auditor. To increase public awareness of possible opinion-shopping situations, the SEC has adopted new disclosure requirements concerning certain consultations between a company and its newly engaged auditor during the company's two most recent fiscal years.

Criteria for Making Accounting and Reporting Choices

Throughout this textbook, we have stressed the need to provide information that is useful to predict the amounts, timing, and uncertainty of future cash flows. To achieve this objective, judicious choices between alternative accounting concepts, methods, and means of disclosure must be made. You are probably surprised by the large number of choices among acceptable alternatives that accountants are required to make.

You should recognize, however, as indicated in Chapter 1, that accounting is greatly influenced by its environment. Because it does not exist in a vacuum, it seems unrealistic to assume that alternative presentations of certain transactions and events will be eliminated entirely. Nevertheless, we are hopeful that the profession, through the development of a conceptual framework, will be able to focus on the needs of financial

UNDERLYING CONCEPTS

The FASB concept statements on objectives of financial reporting, elements of financial statements, qualitative characteristics of accounting information, and recognition and measurement are important steps in the right direction.

---

[29]Because the profession believes that the role of the auditor is not well understood outside the profession, much attention has been focused on the expectation gap. The **expectation gap** is the gap between (1) the expectation of financial statement users concerning the level of assurance they believe the independent auditor provides and (2) the assurance that the independent auditor actually does provide under generally accepted auditing standards.

[30]"Consideration of Fraud in a Financial Statement Audit," *Statement on Auditing Standards No. 82* (New York: AICPA, 1996).

statement users and eliminate diversity where appropriate. The profession must continue its efforts to develop a sound foundation upon which financial standards and practice can be built. As Aristotle said: "The correct beginning is more than half the whole."

SUMMARY OF LEARNING OBJECTIVES

❶ Review the full disclosure principle and describe problems of implementation. The full disclosure principle calls for financial reporting of any financial facts significant enough to influence the judgment of an informed reader. Implementing the full disclosure principle is difficult, because the cost of disclosure can be substantial and the benefits difficult to assess. Disclosure requirements have increased because of (1) the growing complexity of the business environment, (2) the necessity for timely information, and (3) the use of accounting as a control and monitoring device.

❷ Explain the use of notes in financial statement preparation. Notes are the accountant's means of amplifying or explaining the items presented in the main body of the statements. Information pertinent to specific financial statement items can be explained in qualitative terms, and supplementary data of a quantitative nature can be provided to expand the information in the financial statements. Common note disclosures relate to such items as the following: accounting policies; inventories; property, plant, and equipment; credit claims; contingencies and commitments; and subsequent events.

❸ Describe the disclosure requirements for major segments of a business. If only the consolidated figures are available to the analyst, much information regarding the composition of these figures is hidden in aggregated figures. There is no way to tell from the consolidated data the extent to which the differing product lines contribute to the company's profitability, risk, and growth potential. As a result, segment information is required by the profession in certain situations.

❹ Describe the accounting problems associated with interim reporting. Interim reports cover periods of less than one year. Two viewpoints exist regarding interim reports. One view (discrete view) holds that each interim period should be treated as a separate accounting period. Another view (integral view) is that the interim report is an integral part of the annual report and that deferrals and accruals should take into consideration what will happen for the entire year.

The same accounting principles used for annual reports should be employed for interim reports. A number of unique reporting problems develop related to the following items: (1) advertising and similar costs; (2) expenses subject to year-end adjustment; (3) income taxes; (4) extraordinary items; (5) changes in accounting; (6) earnings per share; and (7) seasonality.

❺ Identify the major disclosures found in the auditor's report. If the auditor is satisfied that the financial statements present the financial position, results of operations, and cash flows fairly in accordance with generally accepted accounting principles, an unqualified opinion is expressed. A qualified opinion contains an exception to the standard opinion; ordinarily the exception is not of sufficient magnitude to invalidate the statements as a whole.

An adverse opinion is required in any report in which the exceptions to fair presentation are so material that a qualified opinion is not justified. A disclaimer of an opinion is appropriate when the auditor has gathered so little information on the financial statements that no opinion can be expressed.

❻ Understand management's responsibilities for financials. Management's discussion and analysis section covers three financial aspects of an enterprise's business: liquidity, capital resources, and results of operations. Management has primary responsibility for the financial statements and this responsibility is often indicated in a letter to stockholders in the annual report.

7 **Identify issues related to financial forecasts and projections.** The SEC has indicated that companies are permitted (not required) to include profit forecasts in reports filed with that agency. To encourage management to disclose this type of information, the SEC has issued a "safe harbor" rule. The safe harbor rule provides protection to an enterprise that presents an erroneous forecast as long as the projection was prepared on a reasonable basis and was disclosed in good faith. However, the safe harbor rule has not worked well in practice.

8 **Describe the profession's response to fraudulent financial reporting.** Fraudulent financial reporting is intentional or reckless conduct, whether act or omission, that results in materially misleading financial statements. Fraudulent financial reporting usually occurs because of poor internal control, management's poor attitude toward ethics, and so on. The profession is working to find solutions, and has issued a number of auditing standards that address part of the problem.

APPENDIX **25A**

Basic Financial Statement Analysis

What would be important to you in studying a company's financial statements? The answer depends on your particular interest—whether you are a creditor, stockholder, potential investor, manager, government agency, or labor leader. For example, **short-term creditors**, such as banks, are primarily interested in the ability of the firm to pay its currently maturing obligations. In that case, you would examine the current assets and their relation to short-term liabilities to evaluate the short-run solvency of the firm. **Bondholders**, on the other hand, look more to long-term indicators, such as the enterprise's capital structure, past and projected earnings, and changes in financial position. **Stockholders**, present or prospective, also are interested in many of the features considered by a long-term creditor. As a stockholder, you would focus on the earnings picture, because changes in it greatly affect the market price of your investment. You also would be concerned with the financial position of the firm, because it affects indirectly the stability of earnings.

The **management** of a company is concerned about the composition of its capital structure and about the changes and trends in earnings. This financial information has a direct influence on the type, amount, and cost of external financing that the company can obtain. In addition, the company finds financial information useful on a day-to-day operating basis in such areas as capital budgeting, breakeven analysis, variance analysis, gross margin analysis, and for internal control purposes.

PERSPECTIVE ON FINANCIAL STATEMENT ANALYSIS

Information from financial statements can be gathered by examining relationships between items on the statements and identifying trends in these relationships. The relationships are expressed numerically in ratios and percentages, and trends are identi-

OBJECTIVE 9
After studying Appendix 25A, you should be able to: Understand the approach to financial statement analysis.

fied through comparative analysis. A problem with learning how to analyze statements is that the means may become an end in itself. There are thousands of possible relationships that could be calculated and trends that could be identified. If one knows only how to calculate ratios and trends without understanding how such information can be used, little is accomplished. Therefore, a logical approach to financial statement analysis is necessary. Such an approach may consist of the following steps:

UNDERLYING CONCEPTS

Because financial statements report on the past, they emphasize the *qualitative characteristic of feedback value*. This feedback value is useful because it can be used to better achieve the *qualitative characteristic of predictive value*.

❶ *Know the questions for which you want to find answers.* As indicated at the beginning of this chapter, various groups have different types of interest in a company.

❷ *Know the questions that particular ratios and comparisons are able to help answer.* These will be discussed in the remainder of this chapter.

❸ *Match 1 and 2 above.* By such a matching, the statement analysis will have a logical direction and purpose.

Several caveats must be mentioned. **Financial statements report on the past.** As such, analysis of these data is an examination of the past. Whenever such information is incorporated into a decision-making (future-oriented) process, a critical assumption is that the past is a reasonable basis for predicting the future. This is usually a reasonable approach, but the limitations associated with it should be recognized. Also, ratio and trend analyses will help identify present strengths and weaknesses of a company. They may serve as "red flags" indicating problem areas. In many cases, however, such analyses will not reveal **why** things are as they are. Finding answers about "why" usually requires an in-depth analysis and an awareness of many factors about a company that are not reported in the financial statements—for instance, the impact of inflation, actions of competitors, technological developments, a strike at a major supplier's or buyers operations, and so on.

INTERNATIONAL INSIGHT

Some firms outside the U.S. provide "convenience" financial statements for U.S. readers. These financial statements have been translated into English, and they may also translate the currency units into U.S. dollars. However, the statements are *not restated* using U.S. accounting principles, and financial statement analysis needs to take this fact into account.

Another point is that a **single ratio by itself is not likely to be very useful.** For example, a current ratio of 2 to 1 (current assets are twice current liabilities) may be viewed as satisfactory. However, if the industry average is 3 to 1, such a conclusion may be questioned. Even given this industry average, one may conclude that the particular company is doing well if the ratio last year was 1.5 to 1. Consequently, to derive meaning from ratios, some standard against which to compare them is needed. Such a standard may come from industry averages, past years' amounts, a particular competitor, or planned levels.

Finally, **awareness of the limitations of accounting numbers used in an analysis** is important. We will discuss some of these limitations and their consequences later in this appendix.

RATIO ANALYSIS

OBJECTIVE ❿
Identify major analytic ratios and describe their calculation.

Various devices are used in the analysis of financial statement data to bring out the comparative and relative significance of the financial information presented. These devices include ratio analysis, comparative analysis, percentage analysis, and examination of related data. No one device is more useful than another. Every situation faced by the investment analyst is different, and the answers needed are often obtained only upon close examination of the interrelationships among all the data provided. Ratio analysis is the starting point in developing the information desired by the analyst.[1]

Ratios can be classified as follows:

---

[1]A fairly comprehensive list and explanation of ratios may be found in the AICPA's *CPA/MAS Technical Consulting Practice Aid No. 3,* "Financial Ratio Analysis," by Joseph E. Palmer (New York: AICPA, 1983), 28 pp.

MAJOR TYPES OF RATIOS

LIQUIDITY RATIOS. Measures of the enterprise's short-run ability to pay its maturing obligations.

ACTIVITY RATIOS. Measures of how effectively the enterprise is using the assets employed.

PROFITABILITY RATIOS. Measures of the degree of success or failure of a given enterprise or division for a given period of time.

COVERAGE RATIOS. Measures of the degree of protection for long-term creditors and investors.[2]

Discussions and illustrations about the computation and use of these financial ratios have been integrated throughout this book. Illustration 25A-1 summarizes all of the ratios presented in the book and identifies the specific chapters in which ratio coverage has been presented.

ILLUSTRATION 25A-1
Summary of Financial Ratios

Summary of Ratios Presented in Earlier Chapters		
Ratio	**Formula for Computation**	**Reference**
I. Liquidity		
1. **Current ratio**	$\dfrac{\text{Current assets}}{\text{Current liabilities}}$	Chapter 13, p. 682
2. **Quick or acid-test ratio**	$\dfrac{\text{Cash, marketable securities, and receivables}}{\text{Current liabilities}}$	Chapter 13, p. 683
3. **Current cash debt ratio**	$\dfrac{\text{Net cash provided by operating activities}}{\text{Average current liabilities}}$	Chapter 5, p. 211
II. Activity		
4. **Receivables turnover**	$\dfrac{\text{Net sales}}{\text{Average trade receivables (net)}}$	Chapter 7, p. 361
5. **Inventory turnover**	$\dfrac{\text{Cost of goods sold}}{\text{Average inventory}}$	Chapter 9, p. 470
6. **Asset turnover**	$\dfrac{\text{Net sales}}{\text{Average total assets}}$	Chapter 11, p. 572
III. Profitability		
7. **Profit margin on sales**	$\dfrac{\text{Net income}}{\text{Net sales}}$	Chapter 11, p. 572
8. **Rate of return on assets**	$\dfrac{\text{Net income}}{\text{Average total assets}}$	Chapter 11, p. 572
9. **Rate of return on common stock equity**	$\dfrac{\text{Net income minus preferred dividends}}{\text{Average common stockholders' equity}}$	Chapter 16, p. 830
10. **Earnings per share**	$\dfrac{\text{Net income minus preferred dividends}}{\text{Weighted shares outstanding}}$	Chapter 17, p. 873
11. **Price earnings ratio**	$\dfrac{\text{Market price of stock}}{\text{Earnings per share}}$	Chapter 16, p. 831
12. **Payout ratio**	$\dfrac{\text{Cash dividends}}{\text{Net income}}$	Chapter 16, p. 831

[2]Other terms may be used to categorize these ratios. For example, liquidity ratios are sometimes referred to as solvency ratios; activity ratios as turnover or efficiency ratios; and coverage ratios as leverage or capital structure ratios.

ILLUSTRATION 25A-1
Continued

IV. Coverage		
13. Debt to total assets ratio	$\dfrac{\text{Debt}}{\text{Total assets or equities}}$	Chapter 14, p. 734
14. Times interest earned	$\dfrac{\text{Income before interest charges and taxes}}{\text{Interest charges}}$	Chapter 14, p. 736
15. Cash debt coverage ratio	$\dfrac{\text{Net cash provided by operating activities}}{\text{Average total liabilities}}$	Chapter 5, p. 211
16. Book value per share	$\dfrac{\text{Common stockholders' equity}}{\text{Outstanding shares}}$	Chapter 16, p. 831

Go to the Digital Tool for an expanded discussion of financial statement analysis techniques.

Supplemental coverage of these ratios, accompanied with assignment material, is contained at our Web site. This supplemental coverage takes the form of a comprehensive case adapted from the annual report of a large international chemical company that we have disguised under the name of Anetek Chemical Corporation.

OBJECTIVE ⑪
Explain the limitations of ratio analysis.

Limitations of Ratio Analysis

The reader of financial statements must understand the basic limitations associated with ratio analysis. As analytical tools, ratios are attractive because they are simple and convenient. But too frequently, decisions are based on only these simple computations. The ratios are only as good as the data upon which they are based and the information with which they are compared.

One important limitation of ratios is that they are **based on historical cost, which can lead to distortions in measuring performance**. By failing to incorporate changing price information, many believe that inaccurate assessments of the enterprise's financial condition and performance result.

Also, investors must remember that **where estimated items (such as depreciation and amortization) are significant, income ratios lose some of their credibility**. Income recognized before the termination of the life of the business is an approximation. In analyzing the income statement, the user should be aware of the uncertainty surrounding the computation of net income. As one writer aptly noted, "The physicist has long since conceded that the location of an electron is best expressed by a probability curve. Surely an abstraction like earnings per share is even more subject to the rules of probability and risk."[3]

Probably the greatest criticism of ratio analysis is the **difficult problem of achieving comparability among firms in a given industry**. Achieving comparability among firms requires that the analyst (1) identify basic differences existing in their accounting principles and procedures and (2) adjust the balances to achieve comparability.

Basic differences in accounting usually involve one of the following areas:

UNDERLYING CONCEPTS

Consistency and comparability are important concepts when financial statement analysis is performed. If the principles and assumptions used to prepare the financial statements are continually changing, it becomes difficult to make accurate assessments of a company's progress.

❶ Inventory valuation (FIFO, LIFO, average cost).

❷ Depreciation methods, particularly the use of straight-line versus accelerated depreciation.

❸ Capitalization versus expense of certain costs, particularly costs involved in developing natural resources.

---

[3]Richard E. Cheney, "How Dependable Is the Bottom Line?" *The Financial Executive,* January 1971, p. 12.

④ Pooling versus purchase in accounting for business combinations.

⑤ Capitalization of leases versus noncapitalization.

⑥ Investments in common stock carried at equity versus fair value.

⑦ Differing treatments of postretirement benefit costs.

⑧ Questionable practices of defining discontinued operations, impairments, and extraordinary items.

The use of these different alternatives can make quite a significant difference in the ratios computed. For example, in the brewing industry, at one time Anheuser-Busch noted that if it had used average cost for inventory valuation instead of LIFO, inventories would have increased approximately $33,000,000. Such an increase would have a substantive impact on the current ratio. Several studies have analyzed the impact of different accounting methods on financial statement analysis. The differences in income that can develop are staggering in some cases.[4] The average investor may find it difficult to grasp all these differences, but investors must be aware of the potential pitfalls if they are to be able to make the proper adjustments.

Finally, it must be recognized that a **substantial amount of important information** is not included in a company's financial statements. Events involving such things as industry changes, management changes, competitors' actions, technological developments, government actions, and union activities are often critical to a company's successful operation. These events occur continuously, and information about them must come from careful analysis of financial reports in the media and other sources. Indeed many argue, under what is known as the **efficient market hypothesis**, that financial statements contain "no surprises" to those engaged in market activities. They contend that the effect of these events is known in the marketplace—and the price of the company's stock adjusts accordingly—well before the issuance of such reports.

COMPARATIVE ANALYSIS

In comparative analysis the same information is presented for two or more different dates or periods so that like items may be compared. Ratio analysis provides only a single snapshot, the analysis being for one given point or period in time. In a comparative analysis, an investment analyst can concentrate on a given item and determine whether it appears to be growing or diminishing year by year and the proportion of such change to related items. Generally, companies present comparative financial statements.[5]

In addition, many companies include in their annual reports 5- or 10-year summaries of pertinent data that permit the reader to examine and analyze trends. *ARB No. 43* concluded that "the presentation of comparative financial statements in annual and other reports enhances the usefulness of such reports and brings out more clearly the nature and trends of current changes affecting the enterprise." An illustration of a 5-year condensed statement with additional supporting data as presented by Anetek Chemical Corporation is presented in Illustration 25A-2.

| OBJECTIVE ⑫ |
| Describe techniques of comparative analysis. |

---

[4]An example of such a descriptive study is: Curtis L. Norton and Ralph E. Smith, "A Comparison of General Price Level and Historical Cost Financial Statements in the Prediction of Bankruptcy," *The Accounting Review*, January 1979, pp. 72–87.

[5]All 600 companies surveyed in *Accounting Trends and Techniques—1999* presented comparative 1997 amounts in their 1998 balance sheets and presented comparative 1996 and 1997 amounts in their 1998 income statements.

ANETEK CHEMICAL CORPORATION
Condensed Comparative Statements
(000,000 omitted)

	2001	2000	1999	1998	1997	10 Years Ago 1991	20 Years Ago 1981
Sales and other revenue:							
Net sales	$1,600.0	$1,350.0	$1,309.7	$1,176.2	$1,077.5	$636.2	$170.7
Other revenue	75.0	50.0	39.4	34.1	24.6	9.0	3.7
Total	1,675.0	1,400.0	1,349.1	1,210.3	1,102.1	645.2	174.4
Costs and other charges:							
Cost of sales	1,000.0	850.0	827.4	737.6	684.2	386.8	111.0
Depreciation and amortization	150.0	150.0	122.6	115.6	98.7	82.4	14.2
Selling and administrative expenses	225.0	150.0	144.2	133.7	126.7	66.7	10.7
Interest expense	50.0	25.0	28.5	20.7	9.4	8.9	1.8
Taxes on income	100.0	75.0	79.5	73.5	68.3	42.4	12.4
Total	1,525.0	1,250.0	1,202.2	1,081.1	987.3	587.2	150.1
Net income for the year	$ 150.0	$ 150.0	$ 146.9	$ 129.2	$ 114.8	$ 58.0	$ 24.3
Other Statistics							
Earnings per share on common stock (in dollars)[a]	$ 5.00	$ 5.00	$ 4.90	$ 3.58	$ 3.11	$ 1.66	$ 1.06
Cash dividends per share on common stock (in dollars)[a]	2.25	2.15	1.95	1.79	1.71	1.11	.25
Cash dividends declared on common stock	67.5	64.5	58.5	64.6	63.1	38.8	5.7
Stock dividend at approximate market value				46.8		27.3	
Taxes (major)	144.5	125.9	116.5	105.6	97.8	59.8	17.0
Wages paid	389.3	325.6	302.1	279.6	263.2	183.2	48.6
Cost of employee benefits	50.8	36.2	32.9	28.7	27.2	18.4	4.4
Number of employees at year end (thousands)	47.4	36.4	35.0	33.8	33.2	26.6	14.6
Additions to property	306.3	192.3	241.5	248.3	166.1	185.0	49.0

[a]Adjusted for stock splits and stock dividends.

ILLUSTRATION 25A-2
Condensed Comparative
Financial Information

PERCENTAGE (COMMON-SIZE) ANALYSIS

OBJECTIVE 13
Describe techniques of
percentage analysis.

Analysts also use percentage analysis to help them evaluate and compare companies. Percentage analysis consists of reducing a series of related amounts to a series of percentages of a given base. All items in an income statement are frequently expressed as a percentage of sales or sometimes as a percentage of cost of goods sold. A balance sheet may be analyzed on the basis of total assets. This analysis facilitates comparison and is helpful in evaluating the relative size of items or the relative change in items. A conversion of absolute dollar amounts to percentages may also facilitate comparison between companies of different size. To illustrate, here is a comparative analysis of the expense section of Anetek for the last 2 years.

ILLUSTRATION 25A-3
Horizontal Percentage
Analysis

ANETEK CHEMICAL

	2001	2000	Difference	% Change Inc. (dec.)
Cost of sales	$1,000.0	$850.0	$150.0	17.6
Depreciation and amortization	150.0	150.0	0	0
Selling and administrative expenses	225.0	150.0	75.0	50.0
Interest expense	50.0	25.0	25.0	100.0
Taxes	100.0	75.0	25.0	33.3

This approach, normally called **horizontal analysis**, indicates the proportionate change over a period of time. It is especially useful in evaluating a trend situation, because absolute changes are often deceiving.

Another approach, called **vertical analysis**, is the proportional expression of each item on a financial statement in a given period to a base figure. For example, Anetek Chemical's income statement using this approach appears below.

ANETEK CHEMICAL Income Statement (000,000 omitted)	Amount	Percentage of Total Revenue
Net sales	$1,600.0	96%
Other revenue	75.0	4
Total revenue	1,675.0	100
Less:		
Cost of goods sold	1,000.0	60
Depreciation and amortization	150.0	9
Selling and administrative expenses	225.0	13
Interest expense	50.0	3
Income tax	100.0	6
Total expenses	1,525.0	91
Net income	$ 150.0	9%

Reducing all the dollar amounts to a percentage of a base amount is frequently called **common-size analysis** because all of the statements and all of the years are reduced to a common size; that is, all of the elements within each statement are expressed in percentages of some common number and always add up to 100 percent. Common-size (percentage) analysis is the analysis of the composition of each of the financial statements.

In the analysis of the balance sheet, common-size analysis answers such questions as: What is the distribution of equities between current liabilities, long-term debt, and owners' equity? What is the mix of assets (percentage-wise) with which the enterprise has chosen to conduct its business? What percentage of current assets are in inventory, receivables, and so forth?

The income statement lends itself to common-size analysis because each item in it is related to a common amount, usually sales. It is instructive to know what proportion of each sales dollar is absorbed by various costs and expenses incurred by the enterprise.

Common-size statements may be used for comparing one company's statements from different years to detect trends not evident from the comparison of absolute amounts. Also, common-size statements provide intercompany comparisons regardless of size because the financial statements can be recast into a comparable common-size format.

SUMMARY OF LEARNING OBJECTIVES FOR APPENDIX 25A

⑨ **Understand the approach to financial statement analysis.** Basic financial statement analysis involves examining relationships between items on the statements (ratio and percentage analysis) and identifying trends in these relationships (comparative analysis). Analysis is used to predict the future, but ratio analysis is limited because the data are from the past. Also, ratio analysis identifies present strengths and weaknesses of a company but it may not reveal why they are as they are. Although single ratios are helpful, they are not conclusive; they must be compared with industry averages, past years, planned amounts, and the like for maximum usefulness.

⑩ Identify major analytic ratios and describe their calculations. Ratios are classified as liquidity ratios, activity ratios, profitability ratios, and coverage ratios: (1) *Liquidity ratio analysis* measures the short-run ability of the enterprise to pay its currently maturing obligations. (2) *Activity ratio analysis* measures how effectively the enterprise is using its assets. (3) *Profitability ratio analysis* measures the degree of success or failure of an enterprise to generate revenues adequate to cover its costs of operation and provide a return to the owners. (4) *Coverage ratio analysis* measures the degree of protection afforded long-term creditors and investors.

⑪ Explain the limitations of ratio analysis. One important limitation of ratios is that they are based on historical cost, which can lead to distortions in measuring performance. Also, where estimated items (such as depreciation and amortization) are significant, income ratios lose some of their credibility. In addition, difficult problems of comparability exist because firms use different accounting principles and procedures. Finally, it must be recognized that a substantial amount of important information is not included in a company's financial statements.

⑫ Describe techniques of comparative analysis. Companies present comparative data, which generally includes two years of balance sheet information and three years of income statement information. In addition, many companies include in their annual reports 5- to 10-year summaries of pertinent data that permit the reader to examine and analyze trends.

⑬ Describe techniques of percentage analysis. Percentage analysis consists of reducing a series of related amounts to a series of percentages of a given base. Two approaches are often used. The first, called horizontal analysis, indicates the proportionate change in financial statement items over a period of time; such analysis is most helpful in evaluating trends. Vertical analysis (common-size analysis) is a proportional expression of each item on the financial statements in a given period to a base amount. It analyzes the composition of each of the financial statements from different years (a) to detect trends not evident from the comparison of absolute amounts and (b) to make intercompany comparisons of different sized enterprises.

Note: All **asterisked** Questions, Brief Exercises, Exercises, Problems, and Conceptual Cases relate to materials contained in the appendix to the chapter.

QUESTIONS

1 What are the major advantages of notes to the financial statements? What types of items are usually reported in notes?

2 What is the full disclosure principle in accounting? Why has disclosure increased substantially in the last 10 years?

3 The FASB requires a reconciliation between the effective tax rate and the federal government's statutory rate. Of what benefit is such a disclosure requirement?

4 At the beginning of 2001, Beausoleil Inc. entered into an 8-year nonrenewable lease agreement. Provisions in the lease require the client to make substantial reconditioning and restoration expenditures at the end of the lease. What type of disclosure do you believe is necessary for this type of situation?

5 What type of disclosure or accounting do you believe is necessary for the following items:

    (a) Because of a general increase in the number of labor disputes and strikes, both within and outside the industry, there is an increased likelihood that a company will suffer a costly strike in the near future.

    (b) A company reports an extraordinary item (net of tax) correctly on the income statement. No other mention is made of this item in the annual report.

    (c) A company expects to recover a substantial amount in connection with a pending refund claim for a prior year's taxes. Although the claim is being contested, counsel for the company has confirmed the client's expectation of recovery.

6 The following information was described in a note of Cebar Packing Co. "During August, A. Belew Products Corporation purchased 311,003 shares of the Company's common stock which constitutes approximately 35% of the stock outstanding. A. Belew has since obtained representation on the Board of Directors.

"An affiliate of A. Belew Products Corporation acts as a food broker for the Company in the greater New York City marketing area. The commissions for such services after August amounted to approximately $20,000." Why is this information disclosed?

7 What are the major types of subsequent events? Indicate how each of the following "subsequent events" would be reported.

(a) Collection of a note written off in a prior period.

(b) Issuance of a large preferred stock offering.

(c) Acquisition of a company in a different industry.

(d) Destruction of a major plant in a flood.

(e) Death of the company's chief executive officer (CEO).

(f) Settlement of a four-week strike at additional wage costs.

(g) Settlement of a federal income tax case at considerably more tax than anticipated at year-end.

(h) Change in the product mix from consumer goods to industrial goods.

8 What are diversified companies? What accounting problems are related to diversified companies?

9 What quantitative materiality test is applied to determine whether a segment is significant enough to warrant separate disclosure?

10 Identify the segment information that is required to be disclosed by *FASB Statement No. 131*.

11 What is an operating segment, and when can information about two operating segments be aggregated?

12 The controller for Fong Sai-Yuk Inc. recently commented: "If I have to disclose our segments individually, the only people who will gain are our competitors and the only people that will lose are our present stockholders." Evaluate this comment.

13 An article in the financial press entitled "Important Information in Annual Reports This Year" noted that annual reports include a discussion and analysis section. What would this section contain?

14 "The financial statements of a company are management's, not the accountant's." Discuss the implications of this statement.

15 Nancy Drew, a financial writer, noted recently: "There are substantial arguments for including earnings projections in annual reports and the like. The most compelling is that it would give anyone interested something now available to only a relatively select few—like large stockholders, creditors, and attentive bartenders." Identify some arguments against providing earnings projections.

16 The following recently appeared in the financial press: "Inadequate financial disclosure, particularly with respect to how management views the future and its role in the marketplace, has always been a stone in the shoe. After all, if you don't know how a company views the future, how can you judge the worth of its corporate strategy?" What are some arguments for reporting earnings forecasts?

17 What are interim reports? Why are balance sheets often not provided with interim data?

18 What are the accounting problems related to the presentation of interim data?

19 Mysteries Inc., a closely held corporation, has decided to go public. The controller, C. Keene, is concerned with presenting interim data when a LIFO inventory valuation is used. What problems are encountered with LIFO inventories when quarterly data are presented?

20 What approaches have been suggested to overcome the seasonal problem related to interim reporting?

21 What is the difference between a CPA's unqualified opinion or "clean" opinion and a qualified one?

22 Mary Beidler and Lee Pannebecker are discussing the recent fraud that occurred at Lowrental Leasing, Inc. The fraud involved the improper reporting of revenue to ensure that the company would have income in excess of $1 million. What is fraudulent financial reporting and how does it differ from an embezzlement of company funds?

*23 "The significance of financial statement data is not in the amount alone." Discuss the meaning of this statement.

*24 A close friend of yours, who is a history major and who has not had any college courses or any experience in business, is receiving the financial statements from companies in which he has minor investments (acquired for him by his now deceased father). He asks you what he needs to know to interpret and to evaluate the financial statement data that he is receiving. What would you tell him?

*25 Distinguish between ratio analysis and percentage analysis relative to the interpretation of financial statements. What is the value of these two types of analysis?

*26 In calculating inventory turnover, why is cost of goods sold used as the numerator? As the inventory turnover increases, what increasing risk does the business assume?

*27 What is the relationship of the asset turnover ratio to the rate of return on assets?

*28 Explain the meaning of the following terms: (a) common-size analysis, (b) vertical analysis, (c) horizontal analysis, (d) percentage analysis.

*29 Presently, the profession requires that earnings per share be disclosed on the face of the income statement. What are some disadvantages of reporting ratios on the financial statements?

BRIEF EXERCISES

BE25-1 An annual report of D. Robillard Industries states: "The company and its subsidiaries have long-term leases expiring on various dates after December 31, 2001. Amounts payable under such commitments, without reduction for related rental income, are expected to average approximately $5,711,000 annually for the next 3 years. Related rental income from certain subleases to others is estimated to average $3,094,000 annually for the next 3 years." What information is provided by this note?

BE25-2 An annual report of Ford Motor Corporation states: "Net income a share is computed based upon the average number of shares of capital stock of all classes outstanding. Additional shares of common stock may be issued or delivered in the future on conversion of outstanding convertible debentures, exercise of outstanding employee stock options, and for payment of defined supplemental compensation. Had such additional shares been outstanding, net income a share would have been reduced by 10¢ in the current year and 3¢ in the previous year.

"As a result of capital stock transactions by the company during the current year (primarily the purchase of Class A Stock from Ford Foundation), net income a share was increased by 6¢." What information is provided by this note?

BE25-3 Linden Corporation is preparing its December 31, 2000, financial statements. Two events that occurred between December 31, 2000, and March 10, 2001, when the statements were issued, are described below.

1. A liability, estimated at $150,000 at December 31, 2000, was settled on February 26, 2001, at $170,000.
2. A flood loss of $80,000 occurred on March 1, 2001.

What effect do these subsequent events have on 2000 net income?

BE25-4 Bess Marvin, a student of Intermediate Accounting, was heard to remark after a class discussion on diversified reporting: "All this is very confusing to me. First we are told that there is merit in presenting the consolidated results and now we are told that it is better to show segmental results. I wish they would make up their minds." Evaluate this comment.

BE25-5 Psuikoden Corporation has seven industry segments with total revenues as follows:

Genso	600	Sergei	225
Konami	650	Takuhi	200
RPG	250	Nippon	700
Red Moon	375		

Based only on the revenues test, which industry segments are reportable?

BE25-6 Operating profits and losses for the seven industry segments of Psuikoden Corporation are:

Genso	90	Sergei	(20)
Konami	(40)	Takuhi	34
RPG	25	Nippon	100
Red Moon	50		

Based only on the operating profit (loss) test, which industry segments are reportable?

BE25-7 Identifiable assets for the seven industry segments of Psuikoden Corporation are:

Genso	500	Sergei	200
Konami	550	Takuhi	150
RPG	400	Nippon	475
Red Moon	400		

Based only on the identifiable assets test, which industry segments are reportable?

*BE25-8 Answer each of the questions in the following unrelated situations:

(a) The current ratio of a company is 5 : 1 and its acid-test ratio is 1 : 1. If the inventories and prepaid items amount to $600,000, what is the amount of current liabilities?

(b) A company had an average inventory last year of $200,000 and its inventory turnover was 5. If sales volume and unit cost remain the same this year as last and inventory turnover is 8 this year, what will average inventory have to be during the current year?

(c) A company has current assets of $90,000 (of which $40,000 is inventory and prepaid items) and current liabilities of $30,000. What is the current ratio? What is the acid-test ratio? If the company borrows $15,000 cash from a bank on a 120-day loan, what will its current ratio be? What will the acid-test ratio be?

(d) A company has current assets of $600,000 and current liabilities of $240,000. The board of directors declares a cash dividend of $180,000. What is the current ratio after the declaration, but before payment? What is the current ratio after the payment of the dividend?

*BE25-9 Aston Martin Company's budgeted sales and budgeted cost of goods sold for the coming year are $144,000,000 and $90,000,000 respectively. Short-term interest rates are expected to average 10%. If Aston Martin can increase inventory turnover from its present level of nine times a year to a level of 12 times per year, compute its expected cost savings for the coming year.

*BE25-10 Ferrari Company's net accounts receivable were $1,000,000 at December 31, 2000, and $1,200,000 at December 31, 2001. Net cash sales for 2001 were $400,000. The accounts receivable turnover for 2001 was 5.0. Determine Ferrari's net sales for 2001.

EXERCISES

E25-1 **(Post-Balance Sheet Events)** Madrasah Corporation issued its financial statements for the year ended December 31, 2002, on March 10, 2003. The following events took place early in 2003.

(a) On January 10, 10,000 shares of $5 par value common stock were issued at $66 per share.
(b) On March 1, Madrasah determined after negotiations with the Internal Revenue Service that income taxes payable for 2002 should be $1,270,000. At December 31, 2002, income taxes payable were recorded at $1,100,000.

Instructions
Discuss how the preceding post-balance sheet events should be reflected in the 2002 financial statements.

E25-2 **(Post-Balance Sheet Events)** For each of the following subsequent (post-balance sheet) events, indicate whether a company should (a) adjust the financial statements, (b) disclose in notes to the financial statements, or (c) neither adjust nor disclose.

_____ **1.** Settlement of federal tax case at a cost considerably in excess of the amount expected at year-end.
_____ **2.** Introduction of a new product line.
_____ **3.** Loss of assembly plant due to fire.
_____ **4.** Sale of a significant portion of the company's assets.
_____ **5.** Retirement of the company president.
_____ **6.** Prolonged employee strike.
_____ **7.** Loss of a significant customer.
_____ **8.** Issuance of a significant number of shares of common stock.
_____ **9.** Material loss on a year-end receivable because of a customer's bankruptcy.
_____**10.** Hiring of a new president.
_____**11.** Settlement of prior year's litigation against the company.
_____**12.** Merger with another company of comparable size.

E25-3 **(Segmented Reporting)** Carlton Company is involved in four separate industries. The following information is available for each of the four industries:

Operating Segment	Total Revenue	Operating Profit (Loss)	Identifiable Assets
W	$ 60,000	$15,000	$167,000
X	10,000	3,000	83,000
Y	23,000	(2,000)	21,000
Z	9,000	1,000	19,000
	$102,000	$17,000	$290,000

Instructions
Determine which of the operating segments are reportable based on the:

(a) Revenue test.
(b) Operating profit (loss) test.
(c) Identifiable assets test.

*E25-4 **(Ratio Computation and Analysis; Liquidity)** As loan analyst for Utrillo Bank, you have been presented the following information:

	Toulouse Co.	Lautrec Co.
Assets		
Cash	$ 120,000	$ 320,000
Receivables	220,000	302,000
Inventories	570,000	518,000
Total current assets	910,000	1,140,000
Other assets	500,000	612,000
Total assets	$1,410,000	$1,752,000
Liabilities and Capital		
Current liabilities	$ 305,000	$ 350,000
Long-term liabilities	400,000	500,000
Capital stock and retained earnings	705,000	902,000
Total liabilities and capital	$1,410,000	$1,752,000
Annual sales	$ 930,000	$1,500,000
Rate of gross profit on sales	30%	40%

Each of these companies has requested a loan of $50,000 for 6 months with no collateral offered. Inasmuch as your bank has reached its quota for loans of this type, only one of these requests is to be granted.

Instructions

Which of the two companies, as judged by the information given above, would you recommend as the better risk and why? Assume that the ending account balances are representative of the entire year.

*E25-5 (Analysis of Given Ratios) Picasso Company is a wholesale distributor of professional equipment and supplies. The company's sales have averaged about $900,000 annually for the 3-year period 2000–2002. The firm's total assets at the end of 2002 amounted to $850,000.

The president of Picasso Company has asked the controller to prepare a report that summarizes the financial aspects of the company's operations for the past 3 years. This report will be presented to the Board of Directors at their next meeting.

In addition to comparative financial statements, the controller has decided to present a number of relevant financial ratios which can assist in the identification and interpretation of trends. At the request of the controller, the accounting staff has calculated the following ratios for the 3-year period 2000–2002:

	2000	2001	2002
Current ratio	1.80	1.89	1.96
Acid-test (quick) ratio	1.04	0.99	0.87
Accounts receivable turnover	8.75	7.71	6.42
Inventory turnover	4.91	4.32	3.42
Percent of total debt to total assets	51	46	41
Percent of long-term debt to total assets	31	27	24
Sales to fixed assets (fixed asset turnover)	1.58	1.69	1.79
Sales as a percent of 2000 sales	1.00	1.03	1.07
Gross margin percentage	36.0	35.1	34.6
Net income to sales	6.9%	7.0%	7.2%
Return on total assets	7.7%	7.7%	7.8%
Return on stockholders' equity	13.6%	13.1%	12.7%

In preparation of the report, the controller has decided first to examine the financial ratios independently of any other data to determine if the ratios themselves reveal any significant trends over the 3-year period.

Instructions

(a) The current ratio is increasing while the acid-test (quick) ratio is decreasing. Using the ratios provided, identify and explain the contributing factor(s) for this apparently divergent trend.

(b) In terms of the ratios provided, what conclusion(s) can be drawn regarding the company's use of financial leverage during the 2000–2002 period?

(c) Using the ratios provided, what conclusion(s) can be drawn regarding the company's net investment in plant and equipment?

*E25-6 (Ratio Analysis) Edna Millay Inc. is a manufacturer of electronic components and accessories with total assets of $20,000,000. Selected financial ratios for Millay and the industry averages for firms of similar size are presented below.

	Edna Millay			2001 Industry Average
	1999	2000	2001	
Current ratio	2.09	2.27	2.51	2.24
Quick ratio	1.15	1.12	1.19	1.22
Inventory turnover	2.40	2.18	2.02	3.50
Net sales to net worth	2.71	2.80	2.99	2.85
Net income to net worth	0.14	0.15	0.17	0.11
Total liabilities to net worth	1.41	1.37	1.44	0.95

Millay is being reviewed by several entities whose interests vary, and the company's financial ratios are a part of the data being considered. Each of the parties listed below must recommend an action based on its evaluation of Millay's financial position.

Archibald MacLeish Bank. The bank is processing Millay's application for a new 5-year term note. Archibald MacLeish has been Millay's banker for several years, but must reevaluate the company's financial position for each major transaction.

Robert Lowell Company. Lowell is a new supplier to Millay, and must decide on the appropriate credit terms to extend to the company.

Robert Penn Warren. A brokerage firm specializing in the stock of electronics firms that are sold over-the-counter, Robert Penn Warren must decide if it will include Millay in a new fund being established for sale to Robert Penn Warren's clients.

Working Capital Management Committee. This is a committee of Millay's management personnel chaired by the chief operating officer. The committee is charged with the responsibility of periodically reviewing the company's working capital position, comparing actual data against budgets, and recommending changes in strategy as needed.

Instructions
(a) Describe the analytical use of each of the six ratios presented above.
(b) For each of the four entities described above, identify two financial ratios, from those ratios presented, that would be most valuable as a basis for its decision regarding Millay.
(c) Discuss what the financial ratios presented in the question reveal about Millay. Support your answer by citing specific ratio levels and trends as well as the interrelationships between these ratios.

(CMA adapted)

PROBLEMS

P25-1 (Subsequent Events) Your firm has been engaged to examine the financial statements of Sabrina Corporation for the year 2002. The bookkeeper who maintains the financial records has prepared all the unaudited financial statements for the corporation since its organization on January 2, 1996. The client provides you with the information below.

SABRINA CORPORATION
Balance Sheet
As of December 31, 2002

Assets		**Liabilities**	
Current assets	$1,881,100	Current liabilities	$ 962,400
Other assets	5,171,400	Long-term liabilities	1,439,500
		Capital	4,650,600
	$7,052,500		$7,052,500

An analysis of current assets discloses the following:

Cash (restricted in the amount of $400,000 for plant expansion)	$ 571,000
Investments in land	185,000
Accounts receivable less allowance of $30,000	480,000
Inventories (LIFO flow assumption)	645,100
	$1,881,100

Other assets include:

Prepaid expenses	$ 47,400
Plant and equipment less accumulated depreciation of $1,430,000	4,130,000
Cash surrender value of life insurance policy	84,000
Unamortized bond discount	49,500
Notes receivable (short-term)	162,300
Goodwill, at cost less amortization of $63,000	252,000
Land	446,200
	$5,171,400

Current liabilities include:

Accounts payable	$ 510,000
Notes payable (due 2004)	157,400
Estimated income taxes payable	145,000
Premium on common stock	150,000
	$ 962,400

Long-term liabilities include:

Unearned revenue	$ 489,500
Dividends payable (cash)	200,000
8% bonds payable (due May 1, 2007)	750,000
	$1,439,500

Capital includes:

Retained earnings	$2,810,600
Capital stock, par value $10; authorized 200,000 shares, 184,000 shares issued	1,840,000
	$4,650,600

The supplementary information below is also provided.

1. On May 1, 2002, the corporation issued at 93.4, $750,000 of bonds to finance plant expansion. The long-term bond agreement provided for the annual payment of interest every May 1. The existing plant was pledged as security for the loan. Use straight-line method for discount amortization.
2. The bookkeeper made the following mistakes:
    (a) In 2000, the ending inventory was overstated by $183,000. The ending inventories for 2001 and 2002 were correctly computed.
    (b) In 2002, accrued wages in the amount of $275,000 were omitted from the balance sheet and these expenses were not charged on the income statement.
    (c) In 2002, a gain of $175,000 (net of tax) on the sale of certain plant assets was credited directly to retained earnings.
3. A major competitor has introduced a line of products that will compete directly with Sabrina's primary line, now being produced in a specially designed new plant. Because of manufacturing innovations, the competitor's line will be of comparable quality but priced 50% below Sabrina's line. The competitor announced its new line on January 14, 2003. Sabrina indicates that the company will meet the lower prices that are high enough to cover variable manufacturing and selling expenses, but permit recovery of only a portion of fixed costs.
4. You learned on January 28, 2003, prior to completion of the audit, of heavy damage because of a recent fire to one of Sabrina's two plants; the loss will not be reimbursed by insurance. The newspapers described the event in detail.

Instructions

Analyze the above information to prepare a corrected balance sheet for Sabrina in accordance with proper accounting and reporting principles. Prepare a description of any notes that might need to be prepared. The books are closed and adjustments to income are to be made through retained earnings.

P25-2 (Segmented Reporting) Friendly Corporation is a diversified company that operates in five different industries: A, B, C, D, and E. The following information relating to each segment is available for 2001.

	A	B	C	D	E
Sales	$40,000	$ 80,000	$580,000	$35,000	$55,000
Cost of goods sold	19,000	50,000	270,000	19,000	30,000
Operating expenses	10,000	40,000	235,000	12,000	18,000
Total expenses	29,000	90,000	505,000	31,000	48,000
Operating profit (loss)	$11,000	$ (10,000)	$ 75,000	$ 4,000	$ 7,000
Identifiable assets	$35,000	$ 60,000	$500,000	$65,000	$50,000

Sales of segments B and C included intersegment sales of $20,000 and $100,000, respectively.

Instructions

(a) Determine which of the segments are reportable based on the:
  (1) Revenue test.
  (2) Operating profit (loss) test.
  (3) Identifiable assets test.
(b) Prepare the necessary disclosures required by *FASB No. 131*.

*P25-3 **(Ratio Computations and Additional Analysis)** Carl Sandburg Corporation was formed 5 years ago through a public subscription of common stock. Robert Frost, who owns 15% of the common stock, was one of the organizers of Sandburg and is its current president. The company has been successful, but currently is experiencing a shortage of funds. On June 10, Robert Frost approached the Spokane National Bank, asking for a 24-month extension on two $35,000 notes, which are due on June 30, 2001, and September 30, 2001. Another note of $6,000 is due on December 31, 2002, but he expects no difficulty in paying this note on its due date. Frost explained that Sandburg's cash flow problems are due primarily to the company's desire to finance a $300,000 plant expansion over the next 2 fiscal years through internally generated funds.

The Commercial Loan Officer of Spokane National Bank requested financial reports for the last 2 fiscal years. These reports are reproduced below.

CARL SANDBURG CORPORATION
Statement of Financial Position
March 31

Assets	2000	2001
Cash	$ 12,500	$ 18,200
Notes receivable	132,000	148,000
Accounts receivable (net)	125,500	131,800
Inventories (at cost)	50,000	95,000
Plant & equipment (net of depreciation)	1,420,500	1,449,000
Total assets	$1,740,500	$1,842,000

Liabilities and Owners' Equity	2000	2001
Accounts payable	$ 91,000	$ 69,000
Notes payable	61,500	76,000
Accrued liabilities	6,000	9,000
Common stock (130,000 shares, $10 par)	1,300,000	1,300,000
Retained earnings[a]	282,000	388,000
Total liabilities and owners' equity	$1,740,500	$1,842,000

[a]Cash dividends were paid at the rate of $1.00 per share in fiscal year 2000 and $2.00 per share in fiscal year 2001.

CARL SANDBURG CORPORATION
Income Statement
For the Fiscal Years Ended March 31

	2000	2001
Sales	$2,700,000	$3,000,000
Cost of goods sold[a]	1,425,000	1,530,000
Gross margin	$1,275,000	$1,470,000
Operating expenses	780,000	860,000
Income before income taxes	$ 495,000	$ 610,000
Income taxes (40%)	198,000	244,000
Net income	$ 297,000	$ 366,000

[a]Depreciation charges on the plant and equipment of $100,000 and $102,500 for fiscal years ended March 31, 2000 and 2001, respectively, are included in cost of goods sold.

Instructions

(a) Compute the following items for Carl Sandburg Corporation:
(1) Current ratio for fiscal years 2000 and 2001.
(2) Acid-test (quick) ratio for fiscal years 2000 and 2001.
(3) Inventory turnover for fiscal year 2001.
(4) Return on assets for fiscal years 2000 and 2001 (assume total assets were $1,688,500 at 3/31/99).
(5) Percentage change in sales, cost of goods sold, gross margin, and net income after taxes from fiscal year 2000 to 2001.

(b) Identify and explain what other financial reports and/or financial analyses might be helpful to the commercial loan officer of Spokane National Bank in evaluating Robert Frost's request for a time extension on Sandburg's notes.

(c) Assume that the percentage changes experienced in fiscal year 2001 as compared with fiscal year 2000 for sales and cost of goods sold will be repeated in each of the next two years. Is Sandburg's desire to finance the planet expansion from internally generated funds realistic? Discuss.

(d) Should Spokane National Bank grant the extension on Sandburg's notes considering Robert Frost's statement about financing the plant expansion through internally generated funds? Discuss.

*P25-4 **(Horizontal and Vertical Analysis)** Presented below are comparative balance sheets for the Eola Yevette Company.

EOLA YEVETTE COMPANY
Comparative Balance Sheet
December 31, 2001 and 2000

	December 31	
	2001	2000
Assets		
Cash	$ 180,000	$ 275,000
Accounts receivable (net)	220,000	155,000
Investments	270,000	150,000
Inventories	960,000	980,000
Prepaid expense	25,000	25,000
Fixed assets	2,685,000	1,950,000
Accumulated depreciation	(1,000,000)	(750,000)
	$3,340,000	$2,785,000
Liabilities and Stockholders' Equity		
Accounts payable	$ 50,000	$ 75,000
Accrued expenses	170,000	200,000
Bonds payable	500,000	190,000
Capital stock	2,100,000	1,770,000
Retained earnings	520,000	550,000
	$3,340,000	$2,785,000

Instructions

(a) Prepare a comparative balance sheet of Yevette Company showing the percent each item is of the total assets or total liabilities and stockholders' equity.

(b) Prepare a comparative balance sheet of Yevette Company showing the dollar change and the percent change for each item.

(c) Of what value is the additional information provided in part (a)?

(d) Of what value is the additional information provided in part (b)?

*P25-5 (Dividend Policy Analysis) Dawna Remmers Inc. went public 3 years ago. The board of directors will be meeting shortly after the end of the year to decide on a dividend policy. In the past, growth has been financed primarily through the retention of earnings. A stock or a cash dividend has never been declared. Presented below is a brief financial summary of Dawna Remmers Inc. operations.

			($000 omitted)		
	2001	2000	1999	1998	1997
Sales	$20,000	$16,000	$14,000	$6,000	$4,000
Net income	$ 2,900	$ 1,600	$ 800	$ 900	$ 250
Average total assets	$22,000	$19,000	$11,500	$4,200	$3,000
Current assets	$ 8,000	$ 6,000	$ 3,000	$1,200	$1,000
Working capital	$ 3,600	$ 3,200	$ 1,200	$ 500	$ 400
Common shares:					
Number of shares					
outstanding (000)	2,000	2,000	2,000	20	20
Average market price	$9	$6	$4	—	—

Instructions

(a) Suggest factors to be considered by the board of directors in establishing a dividend policy.

(b) Compute the rate of return on assets, profit margin on sales, earnings per share, price-earnings ratio, and current ratio for each of the 5 years for Dawna Remmers Inc.

(c) Comment on the appropriateness of declaring a cash dividend at this time, using the ratios computed in part (b) as a major factor in your analysis.

CONCEPTUAL CASES

C25-1 (General Disclosures, Inventories, Property, Plant, and Equipment) Dan D. Lion Corporation is in the process of preparing its annual financial statements for the fiscal year ended April 30, 2001. Because all of Lion's shares are traded intrastate, the company does not have to file any reports with the Securities and Exchange Commission. The company manufactures plastic, glass, and paper containers for sale to food and drink manufacturers and distributors.

Lion Corporation maintains separate control accounts for its raw materials, work-in-process, and finished goods inventories for each of the three types of containers. The inventories are valued at the lower of cost or market.

The company's property, plant, and equipment are classified in the following major categories: land, office buildings, furniture and fixtures, manufacturing facilities, manufacturing equipment, leasehold improvements. All fixed assets are carried at cost. The depreciation methods employed depend upon the type of asset (its classification) and when it was acquired.

Lion Corporation plans to present the inventory and fixed asset amounts in its April 30, 2001, balance sheet as shown below.

Inventories	$4,814,200
Property, plant, and equipment (net of depreciation)	$6,310,000

Instructions

What information regarding inventories and property, plant, and equipment must be disclosed by Dan D. Lion Corporation in the audited financial statements issued to stockholders, either in the body or the notes, for the 2000–2001 fiscal year?

(CMA adapted)

C25-2 (Disclosures Required in Various Situations) Rem Inc. produces electronic components for sale to manufacturers of radios, television sets, and digital sound systems. In connection with her examination of Rem's financial statements for the year ended December 31, 2001, Maggie Zeen, CPA, completed field work 2 weeks ago. Ms. Zeen now is evaluating the significance of the following items prior to preparing her auditor's report. Except as noted, none of these items have been disclosed in the financial statements or notes.

Item 1
A 10-year loan agreement, which the company entered into 3 years ago, provides that dividend payments may not exceed net income earned after taxes subsequent to the date of the agreement. The balance of retained earnings at the date of the loan agreement was $420,000. From that date through December 31, 2001, net income after taxes has totaled $570,000 and cash dividends have totaled $320,000. On the basis of these data the staff auditor assigned to this review concluded that there was no retained earnings restriction at December 31, 2001.

Item 2
Recently Rem interrupted its policy of paying cash dividends quarterly to its stockholders. Dividends were paid regularly through 2000, discontinued for all of 2001 to finance purchase of equipment for the company's new plant, and resumed in the first quarter of 2002. In the annual report dividend policy is to be discussed in the president's letter to stockholders.

Item 3
A major electronics firm has introduced a line of products that will compete directly with Rem's primary line, now being produced in the specially designed new plant. Because of manufacturing innovations, the competitor's line will be of comparable quality but priced 50% below Rem's line. The competitor announced its new line during the week following completion of field work. Ms. Zeen read the announcement in the newspaper and discussed the situation by telephone with Rem executives. Rem will meet the lower prices that are high enough to cover variable manufacturing and selling expenses but will permit recovery of only a portion of fixed costs.

Item 4
The company's new manufacturing plant building, which cost $2,400,000 and has an estimated life of 25 years, is leased from Ancient National Bank at an annual rental of $600,000. The company is obligated to pay property taxes, insurance, and maintenance. At the conclusion of its 10-year noncancellable lease, the company has the option of purchasing the property for $1.00. In Rem's income statement the rental payment is reported on a separate line.

Instructions
For each of the items above discuss any additional disclosures in the financial statements and notes that the auditor should recommend to her client. (The cumulative effect of the four items should not be considered.)

C25-3 **(Disclosures Required in Various Situations)** You have completed your audit of Keesha Inc. and its consolidated subsidiaries for the year ended December 31, 2001, and were satisfied with the results of your examination. You have examined the financial statements of Keesha for the past 3 years. The corporation is now preparing its annual report to stockholders. The report will include the consolidated financial statements of Keesha and its subsidiaries and your short-form auditor's report. During your audit the following matters came to your attention:

1. A vice-president who is also a stockholder resigned on December 31, 2001, after an argument with the president. The vice-president is soliciting proxies from stockholders and expects to obtain sufficient proxies to gain control of the board of directors so that a new president will be appointed. The president plans to have a note prepared that would include information of the pending proxy fight, management's accomplishments over the years, and an appeal by management for the support of stockholders.
2. The corporation decides in 2001 to adopt the straight-line method of depreciation for plant equipment. The straight-line method will be used for new acquisitions as well as for previously acquired plant equipment for which depreciation had been provided on an accelerated basis.
3. The Internal Revenue Service is currently examining the corporation's 1998 federal income tax return and is questioning the amount of a deduction claimed by the corporation's domestic subsidiary for a loss sustained in 1998. The examination is still in process, and any additional tax liability is indeterminable at this time. The corporation's tax counsel believes that there will be no substantial additional tax liability.

Instructions

(a) Prepare the notes, if any, that you would suggest for the items listed above.

(b) State your reasons for not making disclosure by note for each of the listed items for which you did not prepare a note.

(AICPA adapted)

C25-4 (Disclosures, Conditional and Contingent Liabilities) Presented below are three independent situations.

Situation 1

A company offers a one-year warranty for the product that it manufactures. A history of warranty claims has been compiled and the probable amounts of claims related to sales for a given period can be determined.

Situation 2

Subsequent to the date of a set of financial statements, but prior to the issuance of the financial statements, a company enters into a contract that will probably result in a significant loss to the company. The amount of the loss can be reasonably estimated.

Situation 3

A company has adopted a policy of recording self-insurance for any possible losses resulting from injury to others by the company's vehicles. The premium for an insurance policy for the same risk from an independent insurance company would have an annual cost of $4,000. During the period covered by the financial statements, there were no accidents involving the company's vehicles that resulted in injury to others.

Instructions

Discuss the accrual or type of disclosure necessary (if any) and the reason(s) why such disclosure is appropriate for each of the three independent sets of facts above.

(AICPA adapted)

C25-5 (Post-Balance Sheet Events) At December 31, 2001, Joni Brandt Corp. has assets of $10,000,000, liabilities of $6,000,000, common stock of $2,000,000 (representing 2,000,000 shares of $1.00 par common stock), and retained earnings of $2,000,000. Net sales for the year 2001 were $18,000,000, and net income was $800,000. As auditors of this company, you are making a review of subsequent events on February 13, 2002, and you find the following.

1. On February 3, 2002, one of Brandt's customers declared bankruptcy. At December 31, 2001, this company owed Brandt $300,000, of which $40,000 was paid in January, 2002.

2. On January 18, 2002, one of the three major plants of the client burned.

3. On January 23, 2002, a strike was called at one of Brandt's largest plants, which halted 30% of its production. As of today (February 13) the strike has not been settled.

4. A major electronics enterprise has introduced a line of products that would compete directly with Brandt's primary line, now being produced in a specially designed new plant. Because of manufacturing innovations, the competitor has been able to achieve quality similar to that of Brandt's products, but at a price 50% lower. Brandt officials say they will meet the lower prices, which are high enough to cover variable manufacturing and selling costs but which permit recovery of only a portion of fixed costs.

5. Merchandise traded in the open market is recorded in the company's records at $1.40 per unit on December 31, 2001. This price had prevailed for 2 weeks, after release of an official market report that predicted vastly enlarged supplies; however, no purchases were made at $1.40. The price throughout the preceding year had been about $2.00, which was the level experienced over several years. On January 18, 2002, the price returned to $2.00, after public disclosure of an error in the official calculations of the prior December, correction of which destroyed the expectations of excessive supplies. Inventory at December 31, 2001, was on a lower of cost or market basis.

6. On February 1, 2002, the board of directors adopted a resolution accepting the offer of an investment banker to guarantee the marketing of $1,200,000 of preferred stock.

Instructions

State in each case how the 2001 financial statements would be affected, if at all.

C25-6 (Segment Reporting) You are compiling the consolidated financial statements for Vender Corporation International. The corporation's accountant, Vincent Price, has provided you with the following segment information.

Note 7: Major Segments of Business

VCI conducts funeral service and cemetery operations in the United States and Canada. Substantially all revenues of VCI's major segments of business are from unaffiliated customers. Segment information for fiscal 2001, 2000, and 1999 follows:

	Funeral	Floral	Cemetery	(thousands) Corporate	Dried Whey	Limousine	Consolidated
Revenues:							
2001	$302,000	$10,000	$ 83,000	$ —	$7,000	$14,000	$416,000
2000	245,000	6,000	61,000	—	4,000	8,000	324,000
1999	208,000	3,000	42,000	—	1,000	6,000	260,000
Operating Income:							
2001	$ 79,000	$ 1,500	$ 18,000	$(36,000)	$ 500	$ 2,000	$ 65,000
2000	64,000	200	12,000	(28,000)	200	400	48,800
1999	54,000	150	6,000	(21,000)	100	350	39,600
Capital Expenditures[a]:							
2001	$ 26,000	$ 1,000	$ 9,000	$ 400	$ 300	$ 1,000	$ 37,700
2000	28,000	2,000	60,000	1,500	100	700	92,300
1999	14,000	25	8,000	600	25	50	22,700
Depreciation and Amortization:							
2001	$ 13,000	$ 100	$ 2,400	$ 1,400	$ 100	$ 200	$ 17,200
2000	10,000	50	1,400	700	50	100	12,300
1999	8,000	25	1,000	600	25	50	9,700
Identifiable Assets:							
2001	$334,000	$ 1,500	$162,000	$114,000	$ 500	$ 8,000	$620,000
2000	322,000	1,000	144,000	52,000	1,000	6,000	526,000
1999	223,000	500	78,000	34,000	500	3,500	339,500

[a]Includes $4,520,000, $111,480,000, and $1,294,000 for the years ended April 30, 2001, 2000, and 1999, respectively, for purchases of businesses.

Instructions

Determine which of the above segments must be reported separately and which can be combined under the category "Other." Then, write a one-page memo to the company's accountant, Vincent Price, explaining the following:

(a) What segments must be reported separately and what segments can be combined.
(b) What criteria you used to determine reportable segments.
(c) What major items for each must be disclosed.

C25-7 (Segment Reporting—Theory) Presented below is an excerpt from the financial statements of H. J. Heinz Company

Segment and Geographic Data

The company is engaged principally in one line of business—processed food products—which represents over 90% of consolidated sales. Information about the business of the company by geographic area is presented in the table below.

There were no material amounts of sales or transfers between geographic areas or between affiliates, and no material amounts of United States export sales.

(in thousands of U.S. dollars)	Domestic	Foreign United Kingdom	Canada	Western Europe	Other	Total	Worldwide
Sales	$2,381,054	$547,527	$216,726	$383,784	$209,354	$1,357,391	$3,738,445
Operating income	246,780	61,282	34,146	29,146	25,111	149,685	396,465
Identifiable assets	1,362,152	265,218	112,620	294,732	143,971	816,541	2,178,693
Capital expenditures	72,712	12,262	13,790	8,253	4,368	38,673	111,385
Depreciation expense	42,279	8,364	3,592	6,355	3,606	21,917	64,196

Instructions

(a) Why does H. J. Heinz not prepare segment information on its products or services?

(b) What are export sales, and when should they be disclosed?

(c) Why are sales by geographical area important to disclose?

C25-8 (Segment Reporting—Theory) The following article appeared in *The Wall Street Journal*:

WASHINGTON—The Securities and Exchange Commission staff issued guidelines for companies grappling with the problem of dividing up their business into industry segments for their annual reports.

An industry segment is defined by the Financial Accounting Standards Board as a part of an enterprise engaged in providing a product or service or a group of related products or services primarily to unaffiliated customers for a profit.

Although conceding that the process is a "subjective task" that "to a considerable extent, depends on the judgment of management," the SEC staff said companies should consider the nature of the products, the nature of their production and their markets and marketing methods to determine whether products and services should be grouped together or in separate industry segments.

Instructions

(a) What does financial reporting for segments of a business enterprise involve?

(b) Identify the reasons for requiring financial data to be reported by segments.

(c) Identify the possible disadvantages of requiring financial data to be reported by segments.

(d) Identify the accounting difficulties inherent in segment reporting.

C25-9 (Interim Reporting) J. J. Kersee Corporation, a publicly traded company, is preparing the interim financial data which it will issue to its stockholders and the Securities and Exchange Commission (SEC) at the end of the first quarter of the 2000–2001 fiscal year. Kersee's financial accounting department has compiled the following summarized revenue and expense data for the first quarter of the year:

Sales	$60,000,000
Cost of goods sold	36,000,000
Variable selling expenses	2,000,000
Fixed selling expenses	3,000,000

Included in the fixed selling expenses was the single lump sum payment of $2,000,000 for television advertisements for the entire year.

Instructions

(a) J. J. Kersee Corporation must issue its quarterly financial statements in accordance with generally accepted accounting principles regarding interim financial reporting.

   (1) Explain whether Kersee should report its operating results for the quarter as if the quarter were a separate reporting period in and of itself or as if the quarter were an integral part of the annual reporting period.

   (2) State how the sales, cost of goods sold, and fixed selling expenses would be reflected in Kersee Corporation's quarterly report prepared for the first quarter of the 2000–2001 fiscal year. Briefly justify your presentation.

(b) What financial information, as a minimum, must Kersee Corporation disclose to its stockholders in its quarterly reports?

(CMA adapted)

C25-10 (Treatment of Various Interim Reporting Situations) The following statement is an excerpt from Paragraphs 9 and 10 of *Accounting Principles Board (APB) Opinion No. 28*, "Interim Financial Reporting":

Interim financial information is essential to provide investors and others with timely information as to the progress of the enterprise. The usefulness of such information rests on the relationship that it has to the annual results of operations. Accordingly, the Board has concluded that each interim period should be viewed primarily as an integral part of an annual period.

In general, the results for each interim period should be based on the accounting principles and practices used by an enterprise in the preparation of its latest annual financial statements unless a change in an accounting practice or policy has been adopted in the current year. The Board has concluded, however, that certain accounting principles and practices followed for annual reporting purposes may require modification at interim reporting dates so that the reported results for the interim period may better relate to the results of operations for the annual period.

Instructions

Listed below are six independent cases on how accounting facts might be reported on an individual company's interim financial reports. For each of these cases, state whether the method proposed to be used for interim reporting would be acceptable under generally accepted accounting principles applicable to interim financial data. Support each answer with a brief explanation.

   (a)   B. J. King Company takes a physical inventory at year end for annual financial statement purposes. Inventory and cost of sales reported in the interim quarterly statements are based on estimated gross profit rates, because a physical inventory would result in a cessation of operations. King Company does have reliable perpetual inventory records.

   (b)   Florence Chadwick Company is planning to report one-fourth of its pension expense each quarter.

   (c)   N. Lopez Company wrote inventory down to reflect lower of cost or market in the first quarter. At year end the market exceeds the original acquisition cost of this inventory. Consequently, management plans to write the inventory back up to its original cost as a year-end adjustment.

   (d)   K. Witt Company realized a large gain on the sale of investments at the beginning of the second quarter. The company wants to report one-third of the gain in each of the remaining quarters.

   (e)   Alice Marble Company has estimated its annual audit fee. They plan to prorate this expense equally over all four quarters.

   (f)   Lori McNeil Company was reasonably certain it would have an employee strike in the third quarter. As a result, it shipped heavily during the second quarter but plans to defer the recognition of the sales in excess of the normal sales volume. The deferred sales will be recognized as sales in the third quarter when the strike is in progress. McNeil Company management thinks this is more nearly representative of normal second- and third-quarter operations.

C25-11   (Financial Forecasts)   An article in *Barron's* noted:

> Okay. Last fall, someone with a long memory and an even longer arm reached into that bureau drawer and came out with a moldy cheese sandwich and the equally moldy notion of corporate forecasts. We tried to find out what happened to the cheese sandwich—but, rats!, even recourse to the Freedom of Information Act didn't help. However, the forecast proposal was dusted off, polished up and found quite serviceable. The SEC, indeed, lost no time in running it up the old flagpole—but no one was very eager to salute. Even after some of the more objectionable features—compulsory corrections and detailed explanations of why the estimates went awry—were peeled off the original proposal.
>
> Seemingly, despite the Commission's smiles and sweet talk, those craven corporations were still afraid that an honest mistake would lead down the primrose path to consent decrees and class action suits. To lay to rest such qualms, the Commission last week approved a "Safe Harbor" rule that, providing the forecasts were made on a reasonable basis and in good faith, protected corporations from litigation should the projections prove wide of the mark (as only about 99% are apt to do).

Instructions
   (a)   What are the arguments for preparing profit forecasts?
   (b)   What is the purpose of the "safe harbor" rule?
   (c)   Why are corporations concerned about presenting profit forecasts?

*C25-12   (Ratio Analysis and Limitations)   As the CPA for Packard Clipper, Inc., you have been requested to develop some key ratios from the comparative financial statements. This information is to be used to convince creditors that Packard Clipper, Inc. is solvent and to support the use of going-concern valuation procedures in the financial statements.

The data requested and the computations developed from the financial statements follow:

	2001	2000
Current ratio	2.6 times	2.1 times
Acid-test ratio	.8 times	1.3 times
Property, plant, and equipment to stockholders' equity	2.5 times	2.2 times
Sales to stockholders' equity	2.4 times	2.7 times
Net income	Up 32%	Down 9%
Earnings per share	$3.30	$2.50
Book value per share	Up 6%	Up 9%

Instructions
   (a)   Packard Clipper asks you to prepare a list of brief comments stating how each of these items supports the solvency and going concern potential of the business. The company wishes to use these comments to support its presentation of data to its creditors. You are to prepare the comments as requested, giving the implications and the limitations of each item separately, and then the collective inference that may be drawn from them about Packard Clipper's solvency and going-concern potential.

   (b)   Having done as the client requested in part (a), prepare a brief listing of additional ratio-analysis-type data for this client which you think its creditors are going to ask for to supplement the data provided in part (a). Explain why you think the additional data will be helpful to these creditors in evaluating the client's solvency.

(c)   What warnings should you offer these creditors about the limitations of ratio analysis for the purposes stated here?

*C25-13   **(Effect of Transactions on Financial Statements and Ratios)**   The transactions listed below relate to Botticelli Inc. You are to assume that on the date on which each of the transactions occurred the corporation's accounts showed only common stock ($100 par) outstanding, a current ratio of 2.7:1 and a substantial net income for the year to date (before giving effect to the transaction concerned). On that date the book value per share of stock was $151.53.

Each numbered transaction is to be considered completely independent of the others, and its related answer should be based on the effect(s) of that transaction alone. Assume that all numbered transactions occurred during 2001 and that the amount involved in each case is sufficiently material to distort reported net income if improperly included in the determination of net income. Assume further that each transaction was recorded in accordance with generally accepted accounting principles and, where applicable, in conformity with the all-inclusive concept of the income statement.

For each of the numbered transactions you are to decide whether it:

a.   Increased the corporation's 2001 net income.
b.   Decreased the corporation's 2001 net income.
c.   Increased the corporation's total retained earnings directly (i.e., not via net income).
d.   Decreased the corporation's total retained earnings directly.
e.   Increased the corporation's current ratio.
f.   Decreased the corporation's current ratio.
g.   Increased each stockholder's proportionate share of total owner's equity.
h.   Decreased each stockholder's proportionate share of total owner's equity.
i.   Increased each stockholder's equity per share of stock (book value).
j.   Decreased each stockholder's equity per share of stock (book value).
k.   Had none of the foregoing effects.

Instructions

List the numbers 1 through 10. Select as many letters as you deem appropriate to reflect the effect(s) of each transaction as of the date of the transaction by printing beside the transaction number the letter(s) that identifies that transaction's effect(s).

Transactions

_____ 1.   Treasury stock originally repurchased and carried at $127 per share was sold for cash at $153 per share.

_____ 2.   The corporation sold at a profit land and a building that had been idle for some time. Under the terms of the sale, the corporation received a portion of the sales price in cash immediately, the balance maturing at six-month intervals.

_____ 3.   In January the board directed the writeoff of certain patent rights that had suddenly and unexpectedly become worthless.

_____ 4.   The corporation wrote off all of the unamortized discount and issue expense applicable to bonds that it refinanced in 2001.

_____ 5.   The board of directors authorized the writeup of certain fixed assets to values established in a competent appraisal.

_____ 6.   The corporation called in all its outstanding shares of stock and exchanged them for new shares on a 2-for-1 basis, reducing the par value at the same time to $50 per share.

_____ 7.   The corporation paid a cash dividend which had been recorded in the accounts at time of declaration.

_____ 8.   Litigation involving Botticelli Inc. as defendant was settled in the corporation's favor, with the plaintiff paying all court costs and legal fees. The corporation had appropriated retained earnings in 1998 as a special contingency appropriation for this court action, and the board directs abolition of the appropriation. (Indicate the effect of reversing the appropriation only.)

_____ 9.   The corporation received a check for the proceeds of an insurance policy from the company with which it is insured against theft of trucks. No entries concerning the theft had been made previously, and the proceeds reduce but do not cover completely the loss.

_____10.   Treasury stock, which had been repurchased at and carried at $127 per share, was issued as a stock dividend. In connection with this distribution, the board of directors of Botticelli Inc. had authorized a transfer from retained earnings to permanent capital of an amount equal to the aggregate market value ($153 per share) of the shares issued. No entries relating to this dividend had been made previously.

(AICPA adapted)

USING YOUR JUDGMENT

FINANCIAL REPORTING PROBLEM: INTEL CORPORATION

In response to the investing public's demand for greater disclosure of corporate expectations for the future, safe-harbor rules and legislation have been passed to encourage and protect corporations that issue financial forecasts and projections. Review Intel's Management Discussion and Analysis section in Appendix 5B.

Instructions

Refer to Intel's financial statements and accompanying notes to answer the following questions.

(a) What general expectation does Intel have for microprocessors and other semiconductor components in the next year, 1999? How is Intel reacting to this expectation?

(b) Give four examples of hard data forecasts Intel discloses for 1999.

(c) What caveats or other statements that temper its forecasts does Intel make?

(d) What is the difference between a financial forecast and a financial projection?

FINANCIAL STATEMENT ANALYSIS CASE

TRI Inc.

Twin Ricky Inc. (TRI) manufactures a variety of consumer products. The company's founders have run the company for thirty years and are now interested in retiring. Consequently, they are seeking a purchaser who will continue its operations, and a group of investors, Donna Inc., is looking into the acquisition of TRI. To evaluate its financial stability and operating efficiency, TRI was requested to provide the latest financial statements and selected financial ratios. Summary information provided by TRI is presented below.

Go to the Digital Tool for additional financial statement analysis problems.

TRI Statement of Income For the Year Ended November 30, 2001 (in thousands)	
Sales (net)	$30,500
Interest income	500
Total revenue	31,000
Costs and expenses	
Cost of goods sold	17,600
Selling and administrative expense	3,550
Depreciation and amortization expense	1,890
Interest expense	900
Total costs and expenses	23,940
Income before taxes	7,060
Income taxes	2,900
Net income	$ 4,160

TRI
Statement of Financial Position
As of November 30
(in thousands)

	2001	2000
Cash	$ 400	$ 500
Marketable securities (at cost)	500	200
Accounts receivable (net)	3,200	2,900
Inventory	5,800	5,400
Total current assets	9,900	9,000
Property, plant, & equipment (net)	7,100	7,000
Total assets	$17,000	$16,000
Accounts payable	$ 3,700	$ 3,400
Income taxes payable	900	800
Accrued expenses	1,700	1,400
Total current liabilities	6,300	5,600
Long-term debt	2,000	1,800
Total liabilities	8,300	7,400
Common stock ($1 par value)	2,700	2,700
Paid-in capital in excess of par	1,000	1,000
Retained earnings	5,000	4,900
Total shareholders' equity	8,700	8,600
Total liabilities and shareholders' equity	$17,000	$16,000

Selected Financial Ratios

	TRI 1999	TRI 2000	Current Industry Average
Current ratio	1.62	1.61	1.63
Acid-test ratio	.63	.64	.68
Times interest earned	8.50	8.55	8.45
Net profit margin	12.1%	13.2%	13.0%
Total debt to net worth	1.02	.86	1.03
Total asset turnover	1.83	1.84	1.84
Inventory turnover	3.21	3.17	3.18

Instructions

(a) Calculate a new set of ratios for the fiscal year 2001 for TRI based on the financial statements presented.

(b) Explain the analytical use of each of the seven ratios presented, describing what the investors can learn about TRI's financial stability and operating efficiency.

(c) Identify two limitations of ratio analysis.

(CMA adapted)

COMPARATIVE ANALYSIS CASE

The Coca-Cola Company versus PepsiCo, Inc.

Instructions

Go to the Digital Tool and, using The Coca-Cola Company and PepsiCo, Inc. 1998 Annual Report information, answer the following questions.

(a) (1) What specific items does Coca-Cola discuss in its **Note 1—Accounting Policies** (prepare a list of the headings only)?

(2) What specific items does PepsiCo discuss in its **Note 1—Summary of Significant Accounting Policies** (prepare a list of the headings only)? Note the similarities and differences between Coca-Cola's and PepsiCo's lists.

(b) For what lines of business or segments do Coca-Cola and PepsiCo present segmented information?

(c) Note and comment on the similarities and differences between the auditors' reports submitted by the independent auditors of Coca-Cola and PepsiCo for the year 1998.

RESEARCH CASES

Case 1

The May/June 1994 issue of *Financial Executive* includes an article by Ray J. Groves, entitled "Financial Disclosure: When More Is Not Better."

Instructions

Read the article and answer the following questions.

(a) What is the author's professional background?

(b) What does the article assert regarding the quantity of disclosure presently required under GAAP?

(c) What specific disclosure requirements does the author find excessive?

(d) As of 1972, how many pages were devoted to the annual report, the footnotes to the financial statements, and the MD&A? What were these figures as of 1982?

(e) What were the author's two major suggestions?

Case 2

Companies registered with the Securities and Exchange Commission are required to file a quarterly report on Form 10-Q within 45 days of the end of the first three fiscal quarters.

Instructions

Use EDGAR or some other source to examine the most recent 10-Q for the company of your choice and answer the following questions.

(a) What financial information is included in Part I?

(b) Read the notes to the financial statements and identify any departures from the "integral approach."

(c) Does the 10-Q include any information under Part II? Describe the nature of the information.

ETHICS CASES

Case 1

Patty Gamble, the financial vice-president, and Victoria Maher, the controller, of Castle Manufacturing Company are reviewing the financial ratios of the company for the years 2000 and 2001. The financial vice-president notes that the profit margin on sales ratio has increased from 6% to 12%, a hefty gain for the 2-year period. Gamble is in the process of issuing a media release that emphasizes the efficiency of Castle Manufacturing in controlling cost. Victoria Maher knows that the difference in ratios is due primarily to an earlier company decision to reduce the estimates of warranty and bad debt expense for 2001. The controller, not sure of her supervisor's motives, hesitates to suggest to Gamble that the company's improvement is unrelated to efficiency in controlling cost. To complicate matters, the media release is scheduled in a few days.

Instructions

(a) What, if any, is the ethical dilemma in this situation?

(b) Should Maher, the controller, remain silent? Give reasons.

(c) What stakeholders might be affected by Gamble's media release?

(d) Give your opinion on the following statement and cite reasons: "Because Gamble, the vice-president, is most directly responsible for the media release, Maher has no real responsibility in this matter."

Case 2

In June 2001, the board of directors for Holtzman Enterprises Inc. authorized the sale of $10,000,000 of corporate bonds. Michelle Collins, treasurer for Holtzman Enterprises Inc., is concerned about the date when the bonds are issued. The company really needs the cash, but she is worried that if the bonds are issued before the company's year-end (December 31, 2001) the additional liability will have an adverse effect on a number of important ratios. In July, she explains to company president Kenneth Holtzman that if they delay issuing the bonds until after December 31 the bonds will not affect the ratios until December 31, 2002. They will have to report the issuance as a subsequent event which requires only footnote disclosure. Collins expects that with expected improved financial performance in 2002 ratios should be better.

Instructions

Answer the following questions:

(a) What are the ethical issues involved?

(b) Should Holtzman agree to the delay?

Index

OFFICIAL ACCOUNTING PRONOUNCEMENTS

The following list of official accounting pronouncements constitutes the major part of *generally accepted accounting principles* (GAAP) and represents the authoritative source documents for much of the discussion contained in this book.

Accounting Research Bulletins (ARB's), Committee on Accounting Procedures, AICPA (1953–1959)

Date Issued		No.	Title
June	1953	No. 43	Restatement and Revision of Accounting Research Bulletins Nos. 1–42, and Accounting Terminology Bulletin No. 1 (originally issued 1939–1953)
Oct.	1954	No. 44	Declining-Balance Depreciation; Revised July, 1958 (amended)
Oct.	1955	No. 45	Long-term Construction-type Contracts (unchanged)
Feb.	1956	No. 46	Discontinuance of Dating Earned Surplus (unchanged)
Sept.	1956	No. 47	Accounting for Costs of Pension Plans (superseded)
Jan.	1957	No. 48	Business Combinations (superseded)
April	1958	No. 49	Earnings Per Share (superseded)
Oct.	1958	No. 50	Contingencies (superseded)
Aug.	1959	No. 51	Consolidated Financial Statements (amended and partially superseded)

Accounting Terminology Bulletins, Committee on Terminology, AICPA

Aug.	1953	No. 1	Review and Résumé (of the eight original terminology bulletins) (amended)
Mar.	1955	No. 2	Proceeds, Revenue, Income, Profit, and Earnings (amended)
Aug.	1956	No. 3	Book Value (unchanged)
July	1957	No. 4	Cost, Expense, and Loss (amended)

Accounting Principles Board (APB) Opinions, AICPA (1962–1973)

Nov.	1962	No. 1	New Depreciation Guidelines and Rules (amended)
Dec.	1962	No. 2	Accounting for the "Investment Credit" (amended)
Oct.	1963	No. 3	The Statement of Source and Application of Funds (superseded)
Mar.	1964	No. 4	Accounting for the "Investment Credit" (Amending No. 2)
Sept.	1964	No. 5	Reporting of Leases in Financial Statements of Lessee (superseded)
Oct.	1965	No. 6	Status of Accounting Research Bulletins (partially superseded)
May	1966	No. 7	Accounting for Leases in Financial Statements of Lessors (superseded)
Nov.	1966	No. 8	Accounting for the Cost of Pension Plans (superseded)
Dec.	1966	No. 9	Reporting the Results of Operations (amended and partially superseded)
Dec.	1966	No. 10	Omnibus Opinion—1966 (amended and partially superseded)
Dec.	1967	No. 11	Accounting for Income Taxes (superseded)
Dec.	1967	No. 12	Omnibus Opinion—1967 (partially superseded)
Mar.	1969	No. 13	Amending Paragraph 6 of APB Opinion No. 9, Application to Commercial Banks (unchanged)
Mar.	1969	No. 14	Accounting for Convertible Debt and Debt Issued with Stock Purchase Warrants (unchanged)
May	1969	No. 15	Earnings per Share (superseded)
Aug.	1970	No. 16	Business Combinations (amended)
Aug.	1970	No. 17	Intangible Assets (amended)
Mar.	1971	No. 18	The Equity Method of Accounting for Investments in Common Stock (amended)
Mar.	1971	No. 19	Reporting Changes in Financial Position (amended)
July	1971	No. 20	Accounting Changes (amended)
Aug.	1971	No. 21	Interest on Receivables and Payables (amended)
April	1972	No. 22	Disclosure of Accounting Policies (amended)
April	1972	No. 23	Accounting for Income Taxes—Special Areas (superseded)
April	1972	No. 24	Accounting for Income Taxes—Equity Method Investments (unchanged)
Oct.	1972	No. 25	Accounting for Stock Issued to Employees (unchanged)
Oct.	1972	No. 26	Early Extinguishment of Debt (amended)
Nov.	1972	No. 27	Accounting for Lease Transactions by Manufacturer or Dealer Lessors (superseded)
May	1973	No. 28	Interim Financial Reporting (amended and partially superseded)
May	1973	No. 29	Accounting for Nonmonetary Transactions (unchanged)
June	1973	No. 30	Reporting the Results of Operations (amended)
June	1973	No. 31	Disclosure of Lease Commitments by Lessees (superseded)

Financial Accounting Standards Board (FASB), Statements of Financial Accounting Standards (1973–2000)

Dec.	1973	No. 1	Disclosure of Foreign Currency Translation Information (superseded)
Oct.	1974	No. 2	Accounting for Research and Development Costs
Dec.	1974	No. 3	Reporting Accounting Changes in Interim Financial Statements
Mar.	1975	No. 4	Reporting Gains and Losses from Extinguishment of Debt (amended)
Mar.	1975	No. 5	Accounting for Contingencies (amended)
May	1975	No. 6	Classification of Short-term Obligations Expected to be Refinanced
June	1975	No. 7	Accounting and Reporting by Development Stage Enterprises
Oct.	1975	No. 8	Accounting for the Translation of Foreign Currency Transactions and Foreign Financial Statements (superseded)

Date Issued		No.	Title
Oct.	1975	No. 9	Accounting for Income Taxes—Oil and Gas Producing Companies (superseded)
Oct.	1975	No. 10	Extension of "Grandfather" Provisions for Business Combinations
Dec.	1975	No. 11	Accounting for Contingencies—Transition Method
Dec.	1975	No. 12	Accounting for Certain Marketable Securities (superseded)
Nov.	1976	No. 13	Accounting for Leases (amended, interpreted, and partially superseded)
Dec.	1976	No. 14	Financial Reporting for Segments of a Business Enterprise (amended)
June	1977	No. 15	Accounting by Debtors and Creditors for Troubled Debt Restructurings (amended)
June	1977	No. 16	Prior Period Adjustments
Nov.	1977	No. 17	Accounting for Leases—Initial Direct Costs
Nov.	1977	No. 18	Financial Reporting for Segments of a Business Enterprise—Interim Financial Statements
Dec.	1977	No. 19	Financial Accounting and Reporting by Oil and Gas Producing Companies (amended)
Dec.	1977	No. 20	Accounting for Forward Exchange Contracts (superseded)
April	1978	No. 21	Suspension of the Reporting of Earnings per Share and Segment Information by Nonpublic Enterprises (amended)
June	1978	No. 22	Changes in the Provisions of Lease Agreements Resulting from Refundings of Tax-Exempt Debt
Aug.	1978	No. 23	Inception of the Lease
Dec.	1978	No. 24	Reporting Segment Information in Financial Statements That Are Presented in Another Enterprise's Financial Report
Feb.	1979	No. 25	Suspension of Certain Accounting Requirements for Oil and Gas Producing Companies
April	1979	No. 26	Profit Recognition on Sales-Type Leases of Real Estate
May	1979	No. 27	Classification of Renewals or Extensions of Existing Sales-Type or Direct Financing Leases
May	1979	No. 28	Accounting for Sales with Leasebacks
June	1979	No. 29	Determining Contingent Rentals
Aug.	1979	No. 30	Disclosure of Information about Major Customers
Sept.	1979	No. 31	Accounting for Tax Benefits Related to U.K. Tax Legislation Concerning Stock Relief
Sept.	1979	No. 32	Specialized Accounting and Reporting Principles and Practices in AICPA Statements of Position and Guides on Accounting and Auditing Matters (amended and partially superseded)
Sept.	1979	No. 33	Financial Reporting and Changing Prices (amended and partially superseded)
Oct.	1979	No. 34	Capitalization of Interest Cost (amended)
Mar.	1980	No. 35	Accounting and Reporting by Defined Benefit Pension Plans (amended)
May	1980	No. 36	Disclosure of Pension Information (superseded)
July	1980	No. 37	Balance Sheet Classification of Deferred Income Taxes (amended)
Sept.	1980	No. 38	Accounting for Preacquisition Contingencies of Purchased Enterprises
Oct.	1980	No. 39	Financial Reporting and Changing Prices: Specialized Assets—Mining and Oil and Gas
Nov.	1980	No. 40	Financial Reporting and Changing Prices: Specialized Assets—Timberlands and Growing Timber
Nov.	1980	No. 41	Financial Reporting and Changing Prices: Specialized Assets—Income-Producing Real Estate
Nov.	1980	No. 42	Determining Materiality for Capitalization of Interest Cost
Nov.	1980	No. 43	Accounting for Compensated Absences
Dec.	1980	No. 44	Accounting for Intangible Assets of Motor Carriers
Mar.	1981	No. 45	Accounting for Franchise Fee Revenue
Mar.	1981	No. 46	Financial Reporting and Changing Prices: Motion Picture Films
Mar.	1981	No. 47	Disclosure of Long-Term Obligations (amended)
June	1981	No. 48	Revenue Recognition When Right of Return Exists
June	1981	No. 49	Accounting for Product Financing Arrangements
Nov.	1981	No. 50	Financial Reporting in the Record and Music Industry
Nov.	1981	No. 51	Financial Reporting by Cable Television Companies
Dec.	1981	No. 52	Foreign Currency Translation (amended)
Dec.	1981	No. 53	Financial Reporting by Producers and Distributors of Motion Picture Films
Jan.	1982	No. 54	Financial Reporting and Changing Prices: Investment Companies (superseded)
Feb.	1982	No. 55	Determining Whether a Convertible Security is a Common Stock Equivalent (superseded)
Feb.	1982	No. 56	Designation of AICPA Guide and SOP 81-1 on Contractor Accounting and SOP 81-2 on Hospital-Related Organizations as Preferable for Applying APB Opinion 20 (superseded)
Mar.	1982	No. 57	Related Party Disclosures
April	1982	No. 58	Capitalization of Interest Cost in Financial Statements that Include Investments Accounted for by the Equity Method
April	1982	No. 59	Deferral of the Effective Date of Certain Accounting Requirements for Revision Plans of State and Local Governmental Units
June	1982	No. 60	Accounting and Reporting by Insurance Enterprises (amended)
June	1982	No. 61	Accounting for Title Plant
June	1982	No. 62	Capitalization of Interest Cost in Situations Involving Certain Tax-Exempt Borrowings and Certain Gifts and Grants
June	1982	No. 63	Financial Reporting by Broadcasters

Date Issued		No.	Title
Sept.	1982	No. 64	Extinguishment of Debt Made to Satisfy Sinking-Fund Requirements
Sept.	1982	No. 65	Accounting for Certain Mortgage Bank Activities (amended)
Oct.	1982	No. 66	Accounting for Sales of Real Estate
Oct.	1982	No. 67	Accounting for Costs and Initial Rental Operations of Real Estate Projects
Oct.	1982	No. 68	Research and Development Arrangements
Nov.	1982	No. 69	Disclosures about Oil and Gas Producing Activities
Dec.	1982	No. 70	Financial Reporting and Changing Prices: Foreign Currency Translation
Dec.	1982	No. 71	Accounting for the Effects of Certain Types of Regulation
Feb.	1983	No. 72	Accounting for Certain Acquisitions of Banking or Thrift Institutions
Aug.	1983	No. 73	Reporting a Change in Accounting for Railroad Track Structures
Aug.	1983	No. 74	Accounting for Special Termination Benefits Paid to Employees
Nov.	1983	No. 75	Deferral of the Effective Date of Certain Accounting Requirements for Pension Plans of State and Local Governmental Units (superseded)
Nov.	1983	No. 76	Extinguishment of Debt (superseded)
Dec.	1983	No. 77	Reporting by Transferors for Transfers of Receivables with Recourse (superseded)
Dec.	1983	No. 78	Classifications of Obligations that Are Callable by the Creditor
Feb.	1984	No. 79	Elimination of Certain Disclosures for Business Combinations by Nonpublic Enterprises
Aug.	1984	No. 80	Accounting for Futures Contracts (superseded)
Nov.	1984	No. 81	Disclosure of Postretirement Health Care and Life Insurance Benefits
Nov.	1984	No. 82	Financial Reporting and Changing Prices: Elimination of Certain Disclosures
Mar.	1985	No. 83	Designation of AICPA Guides and Statement of Position on Accounting by Brokers and Dealers in Securities, by Employee Benefit Plans, and by Banks as Preferable for Purposes of Applying APB Opinion 20
Mar.	1985	No. 84	Induced Conversions of Convertible Debt
Mar.	1985	No. 85	Yield Test for Determining Whether a Convertible Security Is a Common Stock Equivalent (superseded)
Aug.	1985	No. 86	Accounting for the Costs of Computer Software to be Sold, Leased, or Otherwise Marketed
Dec.	1985	No. 87	Employers' Accounting for Pensions (amended)
Dec.	1985	No. 88	Employers' Accounting for Settlements and Curtailments of Defined Benefit Pension Plans and for Termination Benefits
Dec.	1986	No. 89	Financial Reporting and Changing Prices
Dec.	1986	No. 90	Regulated Enterprises—Accounting for Abandonments and Disallowances of Plant Costs
Dec.	1986	No. 91	Accounting for Nonrefundable Fees and Costs Associated with Originating or Acquiring Loans and Initial Direct Costs of Leases
Aug.	1987	No. 92	Regulated Enterprises—Accounting for Phase-in Plans
Aug.	1987	No. 93	Recognition of Depreciation by Not-for-Profit Organizations
Oct.	1987	No. 94	Consolidation of All Majority-Owned Subsidiaries
Nov.	1987	No. 95	Statement of Cash Flows
Dec.	1987	No. 96	Accounting for Income Taxes (superseded)
Dec.	1987	No. 97	Accounting and Reporting by Insurance Enterprises for Certain Long-Duration Contracts and for Realized Gains and Losses from the Sale of Investments
June	1988	No. 98	Accounting for Leases; Sale-Leaseback Transactions Involving Real Estate; Sales-Type Leases of Real Estate; Definition of the Lease Term; Initial Direct Costs of Direct Financing Leases
Sept.	1988	No. 99	Deferral of the Effective Date of Recognition of Depreciation by Not-for-Profit Organizations
Dec.	1988	No. 100	Accounting for Income Taxes—Deferral of the Effective Date of FASB Statement No. 96
Dec.	1988	No. 101	Regulated Enterprises—Accounting for the Discontinuation of Application of FASB Statement No. 71
Feb.	1989	No. 102	Statement of Cash Flows—Exemption of Certain Enterprises and Classification of Cash Flows from Certain Securities Acquired for Resale
Dec.	1989	No. 103	Accounting for Income Taxes—Deferral of the Effective Date of FASB Statement No. 96
Dec.	1989	No. 104	Statement of Cash Flows—Net Reporting of Certain Cash Receipts and Cash Payments and Classification of Cash Flows from Hedging Transactions
Mar.	1990	No. 105	Disclosure of Information About Financial Instruments with Off-Balance-Sheet Risk and Financial Instruments with Concentrations of Credit Risk (superseded)
Dec.	1990	No. 106	Employers' Accounting for Postretirement Benefits Other Than Pensions (amended)
Dec.	1991	No. 107	Disclosures about Fair Value of Financial Instruments (amended)
Dec.	1991	No. 108	Accounting for Income Taxes—Deferral of the Effective Date of FASB Statement No. 96
Feb.	1992	No. 109	Accounting for Income Taxes
Aug.	1992	No. 110	Reporting by Defined Benefit Pension Plans of Investment Contracts
Nov.	1992	No. 111	Rescission of FASB Statement No. 32 and Technical Corrections
Nov.	1992	No. 112	Employers' Accounting for Postemployment Benefits
Dec.	1992	No. 113	Accounting and Reporting for Reinsurance of Short-Duration and Long-Duration Contracts
May	1993	No. 114	Accounting by Creditors for Impairment of a Loan (amended)
May	1993	No. 115	Accounting for Certain Investments in Debt and Equity Securities (amended)
June	1993	No. 116	Accounting for Contributions Received and Contributions Made

Date Issued		No.	Title
June	1993	No. 117	Financial Statements of Not-for-Profit Organizations
Oct.	1994	No. 118	Accounting by Creditors for Impairments of a Loan—Income Recognition and Disclosures
Oct.	1994	No. 119	Disclosure about Derivative Financial Instruments and Fair Value of Financial Instruments (superseded)
Jan.	1995	No. 120	Accounting and Reporting by Mutual Life Insurance Enterprises
Mar.	1995	No. 121	Accounting for the Impairment of Long-Lived Assets
May	1995	No. 122	Accounting for Mortgage Servicing Rights (superseded)
Oct.	1995	No. 123	Accounting for Stock-Based Compensation
Nov.	1995	No. 124	Accounting for Certain Investments Held by Not-for-Profit Organizations
June	1996	No. 125	Accounting for Transfers and Servicing of Financial Assets and Extinguishment of Liabilities (amended)
Dec.	1996	No. 126	Exemption from Certain Required Disclosures about Financial Instruments for Certain Nonpublic Entities
Dec.	1996	No. 127	Deferral of the Effective Date of Certain Provisions of FASB Statement No. 125
Feb.	1997	No. 128	Earnings per Share
Feb.	1997	No. 129	Disclosure of Information about Capital Structure
June	1997	No. 130	Reporting Comprehensive Income
June	1997	No. 131	Reporting Disaggregated Information about a Business Enterprise
Feb.	1998	No. 132	Employers' Disclosures about Pensions and Other Postretirement Benefits an amendment of FASB Statements No. 87, 88, and 106
June	1998	No. 133	Accounting for Derivative Instruments and Hedging Activities (amended)
Oct.	1998	No. 134	Accounting for Mortgage-Backed Securities Retained after the Securitization of Mortgage Loans Held for Sale by a Mortgage Banking Enterprise (an amendment of FASB Statement No. 65)
Feb.	1999	No. 135	Rescission of FASB Statement No. 75 and Technical Corrections
June	1999	No. 136	Transfers of Assets to a Not-for-Profit Organization or Charitable Trust That Raises or Holds Contributions for Others
June	1999	No. 137	Accounting for Derivative Instruments and Hedging Activities—Deferral of the Effective Date for FASB Statement No. 133 (an amendment of Statement No. 133)

Financial Accounting Standards Board (FASB), Interpretations (1974–2000)

Date Issued		No.	Title
June	1974	No. 1	Accounting Changes Related to the Cost of Inventory (APB Opinion No. 20)
June	1974	No. 2	Imputing Interest on Debt Arrangements Made Under the Federal Bankruptcy Act (APB Opinion No. 21) (superseded)
Dec.	1974	No. 3	Accounting for the Cost of Pension Plans Subject to the Employee Retirement Income Security Act of 1974 (APB Opinion No. 8)
Feb.	1975	No. 4	Applicability of FASB Statement No. 2 to Purchase Business Combinations
Feb.	1975	No. 5	Applicability of FASB St. No. 2 to Development Stage Enterprises (superseded)
Feb.	1975	No. 6	Applicability of FASB Statement No. 2 to Computer Software
Oct.	1975	No. 7	Applying FASB Statement No. 7 in Statements of Established Enterprises
Jan.	1976	No. 8	Classification of a Short-Term Obligation Repaid Prior to Being Replaced by a Long-Term Security (FASB Std. No. 6)
Feb.	1976	No. 9	Applying APB Opinion No. 16 and 17 when a Savings and Loan or Similar Institution is Acquired in a Purchase Business Combination (APB Op. No. 16 & 17)
Sept.	1976	No. 10	Application of FASB Statement No. 12 to Personal Financial Statements (FASB Std. No. 12)
Sept.	1976	No. 11	Changes in Market Value after the Balance Sheet Date (FASB Std. No. 12)
Sept.	1976	No. 12	Accounting for Previously Established Allowance Accounts (FASB Std. No. 12)
Sept.	1976	No. 13	Consolidation of a Parent and Its Subsidiaries Having Different Balance Sheet Dates (FASB Std. No. 12)
Sept.	1976	No. 14	Reasonable Estimation of the Amount of a Loss (FASB Std. No. 5)
Sept.	1976	No. 15	Translation of Unamortized Policy Acquisition Costs by Stock Life Insurance Company (FASB Std. No. 8) (amended and partially superseded)
Feb.	1977	No. 16	Clarification of Definitions and Accounting for Marketable Equity Securities That Become Nonmarketable (FASB Std. No. 12)
Feb.	1977	No. 17	Applying the Lower of Cost or Market Rule in Translated Financial Statements (FASB Std. No. 8) (superseded)
Mar.	1977	No. 18	Accounting for Income Taxes in Interim Periods (APB Op. No. 28)
Oct.	1977	No. 19	Lessee Guarantee of the Residual Value of Leased Property (FASB Std. No. 13)
Nov.	1977	No. 20	Reporting Accounting Changes under AICPA Statements of Position (APB Op. No. 20)
April	1978	No. 21	Accounting for Leases in a Business Combination (FASB Std. No. 13)
April	1978	No. 22	Applicability of Indefinite Reversal Criteria to Timing Differences (APB Op. No. 11 and 23)
Aug.	1978	No. 23	Leases of Certain Property Owned by a Governmental Unit or Authority (FASB Std. No. 13)
Sept.	1978	No. 24	Leases Involving Only Part of a Building (FASB Std. No. 13)
Sept.	1978	No. 25	Accounting for an Unused Investment Tax Credit (APB Op. No. 2, 4, 11, and 16)
Sept.	1978	No. 26	Accounting for Purchase of a Leased Asset by the Lessee During the Term of the Lease (FASB Std. No. 13)
Nov.	1978	No. 27	Accounting for a Loss on a Sublease (FASB Std. No. 13 and APB Op. No. 30)
Dec.	1978	No. 28	Accounting for Stock Appreciation Rights and Other Variable Stock Option or Award Plans (APB Op. No. 15 and 25) (amended)
Feb.	1979	No. 29	Reporting Tax Benefits Realized on Disposition of Investments in Certain Subsidiaries and Other Investees (APB Op. No. 23 and 24)

Date Issued		No.	Title
Sept.	1979	No. 30	Accounting for Involuntary Conversions of Nonmonetary Assets to Monetary Assets (APB Op. No. 29)
Feb.	1980	No. 31	Treatment of Stock Compensation Plans in EPS Computations (APB Op. No. 15 and Interp. 28) (superseded)
Mar.	1980	No. 32	Application of Percentage Limitations in Recognizing Investment Tax Credit (APB Op. No. 2, 4, and 11)
Aug.	1980	No. 33	Applying FASB Statement No. 34 to Oil and Gas Producing Operations (FASB Std. No. 34)
Mar.	1981	No. 34	Disclosure of Indirect Guarantees of Indebtedness of Others (FASB Std. No. 5)
May	1981	No. 35	Criteria for Applying the Equity Method of Accounting for Investments in Common Stock (APB Op. No. 18)
Oct.	1981	No. 36	Accounting for Exploratory Wells in Progress at the End of a Period
July	1983	No. 37	Accounting for Translation Adjustments upon Sale of Part of an Investment in a Foreign Entity (Interprets FASB Statement No. 52)
Aug.	1984	No. 38	Determining the Measurement Date for Stock Option, Purchase, and Award Plans Involving Junior Stock (Interprets APB Opinion No. 25)
Mar.	1992	No. 39	Offsetting of Amounts Related to Certain Contracts (Interprets APB Opinion No. 10 and FASB Statement No. 105)
Apr.	1993	No. 40	Applicability of Generally Accepted Accounting Principles to Mutual Life Insurance and Other Enterprises (Interprets FASB Statements No. 12, 60, 97, and 113)
Dec.	1994	No. 41	Offsetting of Amounts Related to Certain Repurchase and Reverse Repurchase Agreements
Sept.	1996	No. 42	Accounting for Transfers of Assets in Which a Not-for-Profit Organization is Granted Variance Power
June	1999	No. 43	Real Estate Sales (Interprets FASB Statement No. 66)

Financial Accounting Standards Board (FASB), Technical Bulletins (1979–2000)

Date Issued		No.	Title
Dec.	1979	No. 79-1	Purpose and Scope of FASB Technical Bulletins and Procedures for Issuance
Dec.	1979	No. 79-2	Computer Software Costs
Dec.	1979	No. 79-3	Subjective Acceleration Clauses in Long-Term Debt Agreements
Dec.	1979	No. 79-4	Segment Reporting of Puerto Rican Operations
Dec.	1979	No. 79-5	Meaning of the Term 'Customer' as it Applies to Health Care Facilities under FASB Statement No. 14
Dec.	1979	No. 79-6	Valuation Allowances Following Debt Restructuring
Dec.	1979	No. 79-7	Recoveries of a Previous Writedown under a Troubled Debt Restructuring Involving a Modification of Terms
Dec.	1979	No. 79-8	Applicability of FASB Statements 21 and 33 to Certain Brokers and Dealers in Securities
Dec.	1979	No. 79-9	Accounting in Interim Periods for Changes in Income Tax Rates
Dec.	1979	No. 79-10	Fiscal Funding Clauses in Lease Agreements
Dec.	1979	No. 79-11	Effect of a Penalty on the Term of a Lease
Dec.	1979	No. 79-12	Interest Rate Used in Calculating the Present Value of Minimum Lease Payments
Dec.	1979	No. 79-13	Applicability of FASB Statement No. 13 to Current Value Financial Statements
Dec.	1979	No. 79-14	Upward Adjustment of Guaranteed Residual Values
Dec.	1979	No. 79-15	Accounting for Loss on a Sublease Not Involving the Disposal of a Segment
Dec.	1979	No. 79-16	Effect on a Change in Income Tax Rate on the Accounting for Leveraged Leases
Dec.	1979	No. 79-17	Reporting Cumulative Effect Adjustment from Retroactive Application of FASB No. 13
Dec.	1979	No. 79-18	Transition Requirements of Certain FASB Amendments and Interpretations of FASB Statement No. 13
Dec.	1979	No. 79-19	Investor's Accounting for Unrealized Losses on Marketable Securities Owned by an Equity Method Investee
Dec.	1980	No. 80-1	Early Extinguishment of Debt through Exchange for Common or Preferred Stock
Dec.	1980	No. 80-2	Classification of Debt Restructuring by Debtors and Creditors
Feb.	1981	No. 81-1	Disclosure of Interest Rate Futures Contracts and Forward and Standby Contracts
Feb.	1981	No. 81-2	Accounting for Unused Investment Tax Credits Acquired in a Business Combination Accounted for by the Purchase Method
Feb.	1981	No. 81-3	Multiemployer Pension Plan Amendments Act of 1980
Feb.	1981	No. 81-4	Classification as Monetary or Nonmonetary Items
Feb.	1981	No. 81-5	Offsetting Interest Cost to be Capitalized with Interest Income
Nov.	1981	No. 81-6	Applicability of Statement 15 to Debtors in Bankruptcy Situations
Jan.	1982	No. 82-1	Disclosure of the Sale or Purchase of Tax Benefits through Tax Leases
Mar.	1982	No. 82-2	Accounting for the Conversion of Stock Options into Incentive Stock Options as a Result of the Economic Recovery Tax Act of 1981
July	1983	No. 83-1	Accounting for the Reduction in the Tax Basis of an Asset Caused by the Investment Tax Credit (ITC)
Mar.	1984	No. 84-1	Accounting for Stock Issued to Acquire the Results of a Research and Development Arrangement
June	1984	No. 79-1	Purpose and Scope of FASB Technical Bulletins and Procedures for Issuance (Revised)
Sept.	1984	No. 84-2	Accounting for the Effects of the Tax Reform Act of 1984 on Deferred Income Taxes Relating to Domestic International Sales Corporations
Sept.	1984	No. 84-3	Accounting for the Effects of the Tax Reform Act of 1984 on Deferred Income Taxes of Stock Life Insurance Enterprises
Oct.	1984	No. 84-4	In-Substance Defeasance of Debt

Date Issued		No.	Title
Mar.	1985	No. 85-1	Accounting for the Receipt of Federal Home Loan Mortgage Corporation Participating Preferred Stock
Mar.	1985	No. 85-2	Accounting for Collateralized Mortgage Obligations (CMOs)
Nov.	1985	No. 85-3	Accounting for Operating Leases with Scheduled Rent Increases
Nov.	1985	No. 85-4	Accounting for Purchases of Life Insurance
Dec.	1985	No. 85-5	Issues Relating to Accounting for Business Combinations
Dec.	1985	No. 85-6	Accounting for a Purchase of Treasury Shares
Oct.	1986	No. 86-1	Accounting for Certain Effects of the Tax Reform Act of 1986
Dec.	1986	No. 86-2	Accounting for an Interest in the Residual Value of a Leased Asset
April	1987	No. 87-1	Accounting for a Change in Method of Accounting for Certain Postretirement Benefits
Dec.	1987	No. 87-2	Computation of a Loss on an Abandonment
Dec.	1987	No. 87-3	Accounting for Mortgage Servicing Fees and Rights
Dec.	1988	No. 88-1	Issues Relating to Accounting for Leases
Dec.	1988	No. 88-2	Definition of a Right of Setoff
Dec.	1990	No. 90-1	Accounting for Separately Priced Extended Warranty and Product Maintenance Contracts
Apr.	1994	No. 94-1	Application of Statement 115 to Debt Securities Restructured in a Troubled Debt Restructuring
Dec.	1997	No. 97-1	Accounting under Statement 123 for Certain Employee Stock Purchase Plans with a Look-Back Option

**Financial Accounting Standards Board (FASB),
Statements of Financial Accounting Concepts (1978–2000)**

Nov.	1978	No. 1	Objectives of Financial Reporting by Business Enterprises
May	1980	No. 2	Qualitative Characteristics of Accounting Information
Dec.	1980	No. 3	Elements of Financial Statements of Business Enterprises
Dec.	1980	No. 4	Objectives of Financial Reporting by Nonbusiness Organizations
Dec.	1984	No. 5	Recognition and Measurement in Financial Statements of Business Enterprises
Dec.	1985	No. 6	Elements of Financial Statements
Feb.	2000	No. 7	Using Cash Flow Information and Present Value in Accounting Measurements

NATIONAL ACCOUNTING BOARDS AND ORGANIZATIONS

American Accounting Association (AAA)
5717 Bessie Drive
Sarasota, FL 34233
(941) 921-7747
www.aaa-edu.org

American Institute of Certified Public Accountants
(AICPA)
1211 Avenue of The Americas
New York, NY 10036
(212) 596-6200
www.aicpa.org

Association of Government Accountants (AGA)
2200 Mount Vernon Ave.
Alexandria, VA 22301
(703) 684-6931
www.rutgers.edu/accounting/raw/aga/home.htm

Financial Accounting Standards Board (FASB)
401 Merritt 7
P.O. Box 5116
Norwalk, CT 06856
(203) 847-0700
www.fasb.org

Financial Executives Institute (FEI)
10 Madison Ave.
P.O. Box 1938
Morristown, NJ 07962-1938
(201) 898-4609
www.ferf.org

Governmental Accounting Standards Board (GASB)
401 Merritt 7
P.O. Box 5116
Norwalk, CT 06856
(203) 847-0700
www.fasb.org

Institute of Certified Management Accountants
10 Paragon Drive
Montvale, NJ 07645-1760
(201) 573-9000
www.imanet.org

Institute of Internal Auditors (IIA)
249 Maitland Avenue, P.O. Box 1119
Altamonte Springs, FL 32701
(407) 830-7600
www.theiia.org

Institute of Management Accountants (IMA)
10 Paragon Drive
Montvale, NJ 07645-1760
(201) 573-9000
www.imanet.org

Securities and Exchange Commission (SEC)
450 Fifth Street NW
Washington, DC 20549
(202) 942-8088
www.sec.gov